The Encyclopedia of Religion

The Encyclopedia of Religion

Mircea Eliade

EDITOR IN CHIEF

Volume 9

MACMILLAN PUBLISHING COMPANY
New York
Collier Macmillan Publishers
London

MACMILLAN PUBLISHING COMPANY
866 Third Avenue, New York, NY 10022

Collier Macmillan Canada, Inc.

Library of Congress Catalog Card Number: 86-5432

PRINTED IN THE UNITED STATES OF AMERICA

printing number
1 2 3 4 5 6 7 8 9 10

Library of Congress Cataloging-in-Publication Data

The Encyclopedia of religion.

Includes bibliographies and index.
1. Religion—Dictionaries. I. Eliade, Mircea, 1907–1986. II. Adams, Charles J.
BL31.#46 1986 200'.3'21 86-5432
ISBN 0-02-909480-1 (set)
ISBN 0-02-909800-9 (v. 9)

Acknowledgments of sources, copyrights, and permissions to use previously published materials are gratefully made in a special listing in volume 16.

Abbreviations and Symbols Used in This Work

abbr. abbreviated; abbreviation
abr. abridged; abridgment
AD *anno Domini,* in the year of the (our) Lord
Afrik. Afrikaans
AH *anno Hegirae,* in the year of the Hijrah
Akk. Akkadian
Ala. Alabama
Alb. Albanian
Am. *Amos*
AM *ante meridiem,* before noon
amend. amended; amendment
annot. annotated; annotation
Ap. *Apocalypse*
Apn. *Apocryphon*
app. appendix
Arab. Arabic
'Arakh. *'Arakhin*
Aram. Aramaic
Ariz. Arizona
Ark. Arkansas
Arm. Armenian
art. article (pl., arts.)
AS Anglo-Saxon
Asm. Mos. *Assumption of Moses*
Assyr. Assyrian
A.S.S.R. Autonomous Soviet Socialist Republic
Av. Avestan
'A.Z. *'Avodah zarah*
b. born
Bab. Babylonian
Ban. Bantu
1 Bar. *1 Baruch*
2 Bar. *2 Baruch*
3 Bar. *3 Baruch*
4 Bar. *4 Baruch*
B.B. *Bava' batra'*
BBC British Broadcasting Corporation
BC before Christ
BCE before the common era
B.D. Bachelor of Divinity
Beits. *Beitsah*
Bekh. *Bekhorot*
Beng. Bengali
Ber. *Berakhot*
Berb. Berber
Bik. *Bikkurim*
bk. book (pl., bks.)
B.M. *Bava' metsi'a'*
BP before the present
B.Q. *Bava' qamma'*
Brāh. *Brāhmaṇa*
Bret. Breton
B.T. Babylonian Talmud
Bulg. Bulgarian
Burm. Burmese
c. *circa,* about, approximately
Calif. California
Can. Canaanite
Catal. Catalan
CE of the common era
Celt. Celtic
cf. *confer,* compare
Chald. Chaldean
chap. chapter (pl., chaps.)
Chin. Chinese
C.H.M. Community of the Holy Myrrhbearers
1 Chr. *1 Chronicles*
2 Chr. *2 Chronicles*
Ch. Slav. Church Slavic
cm centimeters
col. column (pl., cols.)
Col. *Colossians*
Colo. Colorado
comp. compiler (pl., comps.)
Conn. Connecticut
cont. continued
Copt. Coptic
1 Cor. *1 Corinthians*
2 Cor. *2 Corinthians*
corr. corrected
C.S.P. Congregatio Sancti Pauli, Congregation of Saint Paul (Paulists)
d. died
D Deuteronomic (source of the Pentateuch)
Dan. Danish
D.B. Divinitatis Baccalaureus, Bachelor of Divinity
D.C. District of Columbia
D.D. Divinitatis Doctor, Doctor of Divinity
Del. Delaware
Dem. *Dema'i*
dim. diminutive
diss. dissertation
Dn. *Daniel*
D.Phil. Doctor of Philosophy
Dt. *Deuteronomy*
Du. Dutch
E Elohist (source of the Pentateuch)
Eccl. *Ecclesiastes*
ed. editor (pl., eds.); edition; edited by
'Eduy. *'Eduyyot*
e.g. *exempli gratia,* for example
Egyp. Egyptian
1 En. *1 Enoch*
2 En. *2 Enoch*
3 En. *3 Enoch*
Eng. English
enl. enlarged
Eph. *Ephesians*
'Eruv. *'Eruvin*
1 Esd. *1 Esdras*
2 Esd. *2 Esdras*
3 Esd. *3 Esdras*
4 Esd. *4 Esdras*
esp. especially
Est. Estonian
Est. *Esther*
et al. *et alii,* and others
etc. *et cetera,* and so forth
Eth. Ethiopic
EV English version
Ex. *Exodus*
exp. expanded
Ez. *Ezekiel*
Ezr. *Ezra*
2 Ezr. *2 Ezra*
4 Ezr. *4 Ezra*
f. feminine; and following (pl., ff.)
fasc. fascicle (pl., fascs.)
fig. figure (pl., figs.)
Finn. Finnish
fl. *floruit,* flourished
Fla. Florida
Fr. French
frag. fragment
ft. feet
Ga. Georgia
Gal. *Galatians*
Gaul. Gaulish
Ger. German
Giṭ. *Giṭṭin*
Gn. *Genesis*
Gr. Greek
Ḥag. *Ḥagigah*
Ḥal. *Ḥallah*
Hau. Hausa
Hb. *Habakkuk*
Heb. Hebrew
Heb. *Hebrews*
Hg. *Haggai*
Hitt. Hittite
Hor. *Horayot*
Hos. *Hosea*
Ḥul. *Ḥullin*
Hung. Hungarian
ibid. *ibidem,* in the same place (as the one immediately preceding)
Icel. Icelandic
i.e. *id est,* that is
IE Indo-European
Ill. Illinois
Ind. Indiana
intro. introduction
Ir. Gael. Irish Gaelic
Iran. Iranian
Is. *Isaiah*
Ital. Italian
J Yahvist (source of the Pentateuch)
Jas. *James*
Jav. Javanese
Jb. *Job*
Jdt. *Judith*
Jer. *Jeremiah*
Jgs. *Judges*
Jl. *Joel*
Jn. *John*
1 Jn. *1 John*
2 Jn. *2 John*
3 Jn. *3 John*
Jon. *Jonah*
Jos. *Joshua*
Jpn. Japanese
JPS Jewish Publication Society translation (1985) of the Hebrew Bible
J.T. Jerusalem Talmud
Jub. *Jubilees*
Kans. Kansas
Kel. *Kelim*

Ker. *Keritot*
Ket. *Ketubbot*
1 Kgs. *1 Kings*
2 Kgs. *2 Kings*
Khois. Khoisan
Kil. *Kil'ayim*
km kilometers
Kor. Korean
Ky. Kentucky
l. line (pl., ll.)
La. Louisiana
Lam. *Lamentations*
Lat. Latin
Latv. Latvian
L. en Th. Licencié en Théologie, Licentiate in Theology
L. ès L. Licencié ès Lettres, Licentiate in Literature
Let. Jer. *Letter of Jeremiah*
lit. literally
Lith. Lithuanian
Lk. *Luke*
LL Late Latin
LL.D. Legum Doctor, Doctor of Laws
Lv. *Leviticus*
m meters
m. masculine
M.A. Master of Arts
Ma'as. *Ma'aserot*
Ma'as. Sh. *Ma'aser sheni*
Mak. *Makkot*
Makh. *Makhshirin*
Mal. *Malachi*
Mar. Marathi
Mass. Massachusetts
1 Mc. *1 Maccabees*
2 Mc. *2 Maccabees*
3 Mc. *3 Maccabees*
4 Mc. *4 Maccabees*
Md. Maryland
M.D. Medicinae Doctor, Doctor of Medicine
ME Middle English
Meg. *Megillah*
Me'il. *Me'ilah*
Men. *Menahot*
MHG Middle High German
mi. miles
Mi. *Micah*
Mich. Michigan
Mid. *Middot*
Minn. Minnesota
Miq. *Miqva'ot*
MIran. Middle Iranian
Miss. Mississippi
Mk. *Mark*
Mo. Missouri
Mo'ed Q. *Mo'ed qaṭan*
Mont. Montana
MPers. Middle Persian
MS. *manuscriptum*, manuscript (pl., MSS)
Mt. *Matthew*
MT Masoretic text
n. note
Na. *Nahum*
Nah. Nahuatl
Naz. *Nazir*
N.B. *nota bene*, take careful note
N.C. North Carolina
n.d. no date
N.Dak. North Dakota
NEB New English Bible
Nebr. Nebraska
Ned. *Nedarim*
Neg. *Nega'im*
Neh. *Nehemiah*
Nev. Nevada
N.H. New Hampshire
Nid. *Niddah*
N.J. New Jersey
Nm. *Numbers*
N.Mex. New Mexico
no. number (pl., nos.)
Nor. Norwegian
n.p. no place
n.s. new series
N.Y. New York
Ob. *Obadiah*
O.Cist. Ordo Cisterciencium, Order of Cîteaux (Cistercians)
OCS Old Church Slavonic
OE Old English
O.F.M. Ordo Fratrum Minorum, Order of Friars Minor (Franciscans)
OFr. Old French
Ohal. *Ohalot*
OHG Old High German
OIr. Old Irish
OIran. Old Iranian
Okla. Oklahoma
ON Old Norse
O.P. Ordo Praedicatorum, Order of Preachers (Dominicans)
OPers. Old Persian
op. cit. *opere citato*, in the work cited
OPrus. Old Prussian
Oreg. Oregon
'Orl. *'Orlah*
O.S.B. Ordo Sancti Benedicti, Order of Saint Benedict (Benedictines)
p. page (pl., pp.)
P Priestly (source of the Pentateuch)
Pa. Pennsylvania
Pahl. Pahlavi
Par. *Parah*
para. paragraph (pl., paras.)
Pers. Persian
Pes. *Pesahim*
Ph.D. Philosophiae Doctor, Doctor of Philosophy
Phil. *Philippians*
Phlm. *Philemon*
Phoen. Phoenician
pl. plural; plate (pl., pls.)
PM *post meridiem*, after noon
Pol. Polish
pop. population
Port. Portuguese
Prv. *Proverbs*
Ps. *Psalms*
Ps. 151 *Psalm 151*
Ps. Sol. *Psalms of Solomon*
pt. part (pl., pts.)
1 Pt. *1 Peter*
2 Pt. *2 Peter*
Pth. Parthian
Q hypothetical source of the synoptic Gospels
Qid. *Qiddushin*
Qin. *Qinnim*
r. reigned; ruled
Rab. *Rabbah*
rev. revised
R. ha-Sh. *Ro'sh ha-shanah*
R.I. Rhode Island
Rom. Romanian
Rom. *Romans*
R.S.C.J. Societas Sacratissimi Cordis Jesu, Religious of the Sacred Heart
RSV Revised Standard Version of the Bible
Ru. *Ruth*
Rus. Russian
Rv. *Revelation*
Rv. Ezr. *Revelation of Ezra*
San. *Sanhedrin*
S.C. South Carolina
Scot. Gael. Scottish Gaelic
S.Dak. South Dakota
sec. section (pl., secs.)
Sem. Semitic
ser. series
sg. singular
Sg. *Song of Songs*
Sg. of 3 *Prayer of Azariah and the Song of the Three Young Men*
Shab. *Shabbat*
Shav. *Shavu'ot*
Sheq. *Sheqalim*
Sib. Or. *Sibylline Oracles*
Sind. Sindhi
Sinh. Sinhala
Sir. *Ben Sira*
S.J. Societas Jesu, Society of Jesus (Jesuits)
Skt. Sanskrit
1 Sm. *1 Samuel*
2 Sm. *2 Samuel*
Sogd. Sogdian
Soṭ *Soṭah*
sp. species (pl., spp.)
Span. Spanish
sq. square
S.S.R. Soviet Socialist Republic
st. stanza (pl., ss.)
S.T.M. Sacrae Theologiae Magister, Master of Sacred Theology
Suk. *Sukkah*
Sum. Sumerian
supp. supplement; supplementary
Sus. *Susanna*
s.v. *sub verbo*, under the word (pl., s.v.v.)
Swed. Swedish
Syr. Syriac
Syr. Men. *Syriac Menander*
Ta'an. *Ta'anit*
Tam. Tamil
Tam. *Tamid*
Tb. *Tobit*
T.D. *Taishō shinshū daizōkyō*, edited by Takakusu Junjirō et al. (Tokyo, 1922–1934)
Tem. *Temurah*
Tenn. Tennessee
Ter. *Terumot*
Ṭev. Y. *Ṭevul yom*
Tex. Texas
Th.D. Theologicae Doctor, Doctor of Theology
1 Thes. *1 Thessalonians*
2 Thes. *2 Thessalonians*
Thrac. Thracian
Ti. *Titus*
Tib. Tibetan
1 Tm. *1 Timothy*
2 Tm. *2 Timothy*
T. of 12 *Testaments of the Twelve Patriarchs*
Ṭoh. *Ṭohorot*
Tong. Tongan
trans. translator, translators; translated by; translation
Turk. Turkish
Ukr. Ukrainian
Upan. *Upaniṣad*
U.S. United States
U.S.S.R. Union of Soviet Socialist Republics
Uqts. *Uqtsin*
v. verse (pl., vv.)
Va. Virginia
var. variant; variation
Viet. Vietnamese
viz. *videlicet*, namely
vol. volume (pl., vols.)
Vt. Vermont
Wash. Washington
Wel. Welsh
Wis. Wisconsin
Wis. *Wisdom of Solomon*
W.Va. West Virginia
Wyo. Wyoming
Yad. *Yadayim*
Yev. *Yevamot*
Yi. Yiddish
Yor. Yoruba
Zav. *Zavim*
Zec. *Zechariah*
Zep. *Zephaniah*
Zev. *Zevahim*

* hypothetical
? uncertain; possibly; perhaps
° degrees
\+ plus
− minus
= equals; is equivalent to
× by; multiplied by
→ yields

L

(CONTINUED)

LIU AN (180?–122 BCE), second king of Huai-nan, also known as Huai-nan–tzu; Chinese philosopher, poet, and essayist. Liu An was the grandson of Liu Pang (d. 194 BCE), founder of the Han dynasty. Shortly after the birth of An's father, Liu Ch'ang (b. 199 BCE), the woman who bore him committed suicide when denied formal recognition by the emperor. The seventh of eight sons of the emperor by different women, Liu Ch'ang was twice passed over in the imperial succession, which left him bitter and resentful. In 172 BCE Liu Ch'ang (then king of the vassal state of Huai-nan) was banished to a remote corner of the empire for insulting his half brother, the emperor Wen. He died en route, leaving Liu An and his two younger brothers. In 164 BCE Liu Ch'ang's fief of Huai-nan was divided among his three sons, with the eldest, Liu An, receiving the title of King of Huai-nan. He inherited as well his father's disdain for the imperial line, and twice plotted rebellion.

The biographies of Liu An all speak of him as a youth who eschewed martial pursuits in favor of literature, music, and philosophy. He quickly developed his literary talent, and at the age of twenty-two is said to have written, upon imperial command, a brilliant essay on the famous Ch'u poem the *Li Sao,* in the few hours between dawn and breakfast. In 154 BCE, Liu An almost took part in the unsuccessful rebellion of Liu P'i but changed his mind at the last moment. Some time later he decided to establish his court as a center of learning. He opened his court in Shou-ch'un to philosophers, poets, and masters of esoteric techniques *(fang-shih).* History speaks of a major center developing there, a focal point for the last flourishing of the ancient culture of Ch'u, a region renowned for its mysticism and shamanism. In the great tradition of King Hsüan of Ch'i (c. 310 BCE, the founder of the Chi-hsia Academy at which the *Kuan-tzu* was probably written) and Lü Pu-wei (c. 240 BCE), sponsor of the *Lü-shih ch'un-ch'iu,* Liu An was patron to many of the finest religious and philosophical minds of his time. However, unlike these earlier patrons, An took an active part in philosophical discussions and the writing of essays and poems. He also collected an extensive library that contained all the major pre-Han philosophical texts, including his favorite, the *Chuang-tzu.*

The center of culture and learning founded by Liu An was distinctly oriented toward Taoism and rivaled the largely Confucian center at the imperial court in Ch'ang-an. It lasted for almost three decades. In 122 BCE, imperial representatives were sent to Huai-nan to quell Liu An's incipient rebellion. However, the challenge presented by the rival intellectual center in Huai-nan was undoubtedly a more powerful motivation for the imperial action than Liu An's hopeless plans for rebellion. Whatever the cause for the imperial reaction, Liu An and his family perished, and the vibrant center he established came to a tragic and untimely end.

Today all that remains of this last flourishing of Ch'u culture is one book, the *Huai-nan–tzu,* and an extensive list of others that attest to the vibrancy of the Huai-nan court. Among the writings produced are a number in which Liu An was directly involved. Two essays on the *Chuang-tzu* and a collection of eighty-two poems, all now lost, are credited to him. Also listed under his name are three treatises identified simply as the "Inner Book," which discussed the Tao, the "Outer Book," which discussed miscellaneous doctrines, and the "Middle Book," which dealt with esoteric alchemical techniques. Of the three, only the "Inner Book," which Liu An presented to Emperor Wu in 139 BCE, has survived intact. This is the work that has come down to us under the name of *Huai-nan–tzu.* It stands as his major contribution to Chinese thought.

Of the reportedly several thousand philosophers and adepts at the court of Liu An, eight are named with him in the authorship of the *Huai-nan–tzu.* Liu An probably established the scope and format of the work, wrote some of the essays, and then edited the essays and wrote the final summary and overview. The resulting text consists of twenty-one essays on topics ranging from cosmology, astronomy, and geography, to self-cultivation, human relations, and government. It was clearly intended to be a compendium of knowledge about the nature of the universe and the human role within it. Its extensive use of pre-Han philosophical and religious sources indicates not the mere repetition of earlier ideas, as some have maintained, but rather a bold and innovative attempt at their synthesis and an application to contemporary concerns.

The topics considered and the viewpoints represented in the essays of the *Huai-nan–tzu* occur in the context of a consistent cosmology that is best described as a blend of the Taoism of the *Lao-tzu* and *Chuang-tzu* and the Naturalist philosophy of *yin* and *yang* and the Five Phases *(wu-hsing)* of energy *(ch'i),* first systematized by Tsou Yen (c. 340–270 BCE). This synthesis remains faithful to the earlier Taoist cosmology of an organismic universe of totally interrelated phenomena, which spontaneously tend toward harmony and are interfused by the unifying and creative power of the Tao. However, the *Huai-nan–tzu* provides a more detailed explanation of the actual mechanisms of this universe in terms of *yin* and *yang* and the Five Phases. Because human beings are an integral part of this universe and are thus subject to its laws, all human activity, from politics to warfare to spiritual self-realization, must take these universal forces into account. Whereas the pre-Han social and political thinkers largely ignored cosmology and the Taoists focused primarily upon it, the *Huai-nan–tzu* balances both perspectives in its thorough emphasis on the universal context of human nature and human activity. In so doing, it has made a significant contribution to the evolution of the unique Chinese worldview.

As might be expected in light of the number of religious adepts at the court of Liu An, the *Huai-nan–tzu* has left its mark in the area of spiritual self-cultivation as well. A number of passages stress the importance and provide examples of meditative techniques of "nourishing one's inherent nature" *(yang-hsing)* and "nourishing the higher consciousness" *(yang-shen),* such as controlled breathing and calming the mind. An important contribution of the *Huai-nan–tzu* lies in its explanation of how these techniques function in terms of the Five Phases philosophy of Naturalism. The resulting theory of the physiology of the human body and human consciousness is one of the earliest expressions of Chinese medical knowledge. The techniques comprehended in this theory are among the earliest examples of the physiological alchemy that was later developed and expanded in the Taoist religion. There were undoubtedly adepts who followed these practices at the court of Liu An, perhaps the *fang-shih,* and it was the spiritual descendants of such people who were involved in the early organization of the Taoist church some three centuries later. It is no surprise that the *Huai-nan–tzu* was later included in the comprehensive collection of Taoist canonical works, the *Tao-tsang.* Another contributing factor must be the legend that Liu An did not die, but attained immortality after consuming an elixir given him by the *fang-shih.*

While most of the works written by Liu An and his associates have regrettably been lost, their contribution to the development of Chinese religion and philosophy has survived in the form of the *Huai-nan–tzu.*

[*See also* Yin-yang Wu-hsing; Fang-shih; *and* Taoism, *article on* Taoist Literature.]

BIBLIOGRAPHY

The most complete Western source on the life of Liu An is Benjamin E. Wallacker's "Liu An, Second King of Huai-nan," *Journal of the American Oriental Society* 92 (January-March 1972): 36–49. The article is a thorough examination of the Chinese biographical sources. In addition, the *Shih chi* biographies of Liu An and his father have been translated in Burton Watson's *Records of the Grand Historian of China,* vol. 2 (New York, 1963), pp. 359–381. There is as yet no complete translation of the *Huai-nan–tzu.* However, a number of partial translations do exist. The longest is Evan Morgan's *Tao, the Great Luminant: Essays from Huai-nan tzu* (1935; reprint, New York, 1969). While generally accurate, Morgan's translation of eight of the twenty-one essays in the text suffers from poor scholarly methodology and antiquated renderings of key terms, both of which interfere considerably with the meaning of the text. There are three other published translations of individual essays. The first is Eva Kraft's "Zum Huai-nan-tzu: Einfuhrung, Übersetzung (Kapitel 1 und 2) und Interpretation," *Monumenta Serica* 16 (1957): 191–286; 17 (1958): 128–207. Kraft uses the questionable method of basing her translation on parallel passages in the *Wen-tzu.* The second is Benjamin E. Wallacker's *The Huai-nan Tzu, Book Eleven: Behavior, Culture, and the Cosmos,* "American Oriental Series," vol. 48 (New Haven, 1962). Despite the tendency to translate certain terms too literally, this is a generally excellent translation and sound analysis. The third is Roger T. Ames's *The Art of Rulership: A Study in Ancient Chinese Political Thought* (Honolulu, 1983). This is a solid translation and also contains a long analysis of the position of the essay of this title in the history of Chinese political thought. There are translations of short passages from the *Huai-nan–tzu* in *A Sourcebook in Chinese Philosophy,* translated and compiled by Wing-tsit Chan (Princeton, 1963); Fung Yu-lan's *The Period of the Philosophers,* vol. 1 of *A History of Chinese Philosophy,* 2d ed., translated by Derk Bodde (Princeton, 1952); and *Chinese Philosophy in Classical Times,* edited and translated by E. R. Hughes (New York, 1942). The most thorough textual study of the *Huai-nan–tzu* is my *Textual History of the Huai-nan Tzu* (Ann Arbor, forthcoming).

HAROLD D. ROTH

LIU HAI-CH'AN (fl. tenth century CE), Taoist master under the Liao and Yen states (Five Dynasties period, 907–960). A native of Mount Yen (present-day Hopei Province), Liu's given name was Ts'ao. He was also known as Tsung Ch'eng and Chao Yüan; his Taoist clerical name was Hai-ch'an–tzu. As there is little evidence corroborating the details of his life, we are forced to rely on the anecdotes found in the Taoist hagiographical literature.

Liu is said to have passed the *chin-shih* examination for the civil service at the age of sixteen and to have subsequently distinguished himself by becoming an adviser to the emperor. According to one version of his life, a Taoist master by the name of Cheng-yang–tzu came to him and asked for ten eggs and a coin. He then stacked the eggs on top of the coin. When Liu marveled at this, the master replied, "Your position is even more precarious." After the Taoist master left, Liu abandoned his worldly aspirations and gave a banquet where he acted as though he were drunk, smashing dishes and valuables and angering his wife and children. Although he seemed a madman, he became a Taoist master and took up an ascetic life at the foot of Mount Chung-nan in Shensi Province. In a different version of his life, he is said to have met Lü Ch'un-yang, to have attained the limits of enlightenment, and to have worked many miracles. Neither version can be corroborated.

According to a biography of the Taoist master Wang Che, in 1160 Liu Hai-ch'an appeared before Wang Che in Li-ch'üan Prefecture in Shensi Province. He encouraged Wang Che to become a Taoist master and made him stop his drinking. Consequently, the Ch'üan-shen sect established by Wang Che reveres Liu Hai-ch'an as one of its three founders. Today, Chinese needle merchants revere him as the patron deity who protects their profession. [*See the biography of Wang Che.*]

BIBLIOGRAPHY

Kubo Noritada. *Dōkyō nyūmon.* Tokyo, 1964.
Kubo Noritada. *Chūgoku no shūkyō kaikaku.* Tokyo, 1967.
Kubo Noritada. *Dōkyōshi.* Tokyo, 1977.

KUBO NORITADA
Translated from Japanese by James C. Dobbins

LIU TE-JEN (1122–1180), Taoist master of the Chin period and founder of the Chen-ta sect of Taoism. His Taoist clerical name was Wu-yu–tzu. In 1126, the year the Northern Sung dynasty fell, Liu moved from Lo-ling Prefecture in Shantung Province to the T'ai-p'ing district of Yen-shan Prefecture in Hopei Province, where he studied Confucianism as a youth. It is alleged that early one morning in the eleventh month of 1142, a white-haired old man riding a cart pulled by a blue calf gave Liu the fundamental principles of the *Tao-te ching,* along with a writing brush. The old man declared, "If you can fully understand the essentials of the *Tao-te ching,* your own religious education will be complete and you will be able to enlighten others." Liu followed the old man's advice, deepened his knowledge of Taoism, and attracted an ever greater number of disciples.

In teaching his followers, Liu stressed nine points, including loyalty, filial piety, sincerity, purity, humility, sufficient knowledge, acceptance, and the prohibition of cruelty, lewdness, slander, stealing, gambling, consuming the five pungent substances, drinking intoxicants, and taking life. Chen-ta Taoism represents a syncretization of China's three teachings: Confucianism, Buddhism, and Taoism. But while the influence of Confucianism was pronounced, Taoist magical practices and the use of talismans, incantations, and elixirs of immortality (*chin-tan,* "gold and cinnabar") found little room in his teaching. The Chen-ta sect promoted a rational philosophy centered on practical morality in accordance with the demands of the time.

Liu's teachings were quickly embraced by the people of northern China, who at the time were plagued by social instability. The sect's rapid rise in influence brought Liu's name to the attention of Emperor Shih-tsung of the Chin dynasty. The emperor summoned Liu to the capital and in 1161 established Liu in residence at the T'ien-chang temple, which thereby became the head temple of Chen-ta Taoism. In 1167 the emperor bestowed on Liu the title Tung-yüeh Chen-jen ("perfected one of the eastern peak"). Liu thus developed important ties with the court, thereby paving the way for the expansion of Chen-ta Taoism. He died in 1180.

[*See also* Taoism, *overview article and article on* The Taoist Religious Community.]

BIBLIOGRAPHY

Ch'en Yüan. *Nan Sung ch'u Ho-pei hsin tao-chiao k'ao.* Peking, 1958.
Kubo Noritada. *Chūgoku no shūkyō kaikaku.* Tokyo, 1967.
Kubo Noritada. *Dōkyōshi.* Tokyo, 1977.

KUBO NORITADA
Translated from Japanese by James C. Dobbins

LLULL, RAMÓN. *See* Lull, Ramón.

LOBECK, C. A. (1781–1860), German scholar of classics who contributed much to our understanding of Greek religion, especially of the mysteries. Born at

Naumburg, Christian August Lobeck studied Latin and Greek at the cathedral school where his father was rector. At age sixteen, he entered the University of Jena to study law, but he soon moved to Leipzig and devoted himself to theology. In 1802 he was appointed privatdocent at Wittenberg; in 1807 he became conrector and in 1809 rector of the Wittenberg lyceum. The next year he published an edition of Sophocles' *Ajax* and became professor extraordinarius (and, later, ordinarius).

Driven from Wittenberg by the Napoleonic wars, Lobeck was called in 1814 to a professorship at Königsberg, a chair he was to hold until 1857. He had already made important contributions to the history of Greek religion with *De morte Bacchi* (1810) and his 1810 review of the first volume of G. F. Creuzer's *Symbolik.* In 1829, Lobeck published his most important work, *Aglaophamus, sive de theologiae mysticae Graecorum causis libri tres,* a massive study of the Eleusinian, Orphic, and Samothracian mysteries, based on ancient sources.

Aglaophamus appeared at a time when the Romantic vision of Greek religion held by such figures as Creuzer and Friedrich Schelling dominated scholarly thought. Schelling and Creuzer traced the mysteries to pre-Greek Pelasgians, who in turn had received them from Indian (Creuzer) or Phoenician (Schelling) "missionaries." Others suggested Egyptian sources. Romantic historians also credited the priests and priestesses of the mystery cults with sophisticated, secret, esoteric doctrines, Creuzer seeing evidence there of primitive monotheism, P. Knight of "the knowledge of the God of Nature."

Lobeck argued against this view, maintaining in *Aglaophamus* that the mysteries were not instituted by savants and were not sharply different from the public cults. He rejected notions of foreign origin, as well as the claims of some Christian writers that the mysteries included ritual sexual orgies. His approach combined exhaustive collection of evidence with rationalistic analysis. Although Lobeck's points in *Aglaophamus* were mostly negative, by clearing away scholarly deadwood he made possible the positive results of subsequent scholarship. Lobeck, who also published works on Greek grammar and textual criticism, ranks prominently among the founders of nineteenth-century German *Altertumswissenschaft* (classical scholarship).

BIBLIOGRAPHY

Works by Lobeck

Disputatio de diis veterum adspectu corporum exanimum non prohibitis (1802). Reprint, Königsberg, 1876.

Phrynichi eclogae nominum et verborum atticorum (1802). Reprint, Hildesheim, 1965.

Aglaophamus, sive de theologiae mysticae Graecorum causis libri tres (1829). 2 vols. Reprint, Darmstadt, 1961.

Paralipomena grammaticae graecae (1837). Reprint, Hildesheim, 1967.

Pathologiae Graeci sermonis elementa (1853–1862). 2 vols. Reprint, Hildesheim, 1966.

Work about Lobeck

Friedländer, Ludwig. "Lobeck." In *Allgemeine deutsche Bibliographie.* Leipzig, 1875–1912.

JON-CHRISTIAN BILLIGMEIER

LOCKE, JOHN (1632–1704), English Christian writer on religious toleration, epistemology, political theory, theology, education, and economics. Locke was admitted to Westminster School, London, upon the recommendation of a Puritan family friend and proceeded as a King's Scholar to Christ Church, Oxford, where in 1658 he was chosen as a senior student (fellow) to teach moral philosophy. He studied chemistry and medicine, the practice of which contributed to his friendship with Anthony Ashley Cooper, earl of Shaftesbury and leader of the Whig party. This political association led to Locke's self-imposed exile in Holland and the loss of his Oxford studentship in 1684. With the "Glorious Revolution" of 1689, he returned to England, where he devoted the remainder of his life largely to writing.

Locke's earliest extant writings of substance (not published until the twentieth century) set the course, though not the content, of his later, most influential works. After the restoration of Charles II to the throne in 1660, Locke conformed to the Church of England and wrote two essays defending the right of the civil magistrate to determine and enforce *adiaphora,* indifferent matters of religious worship. He believed that such authoritarianism was the only means to religious and political peace after the conflicts of the interregnum. In 1661 he reiterated this position in an essay on infallibility, which subject perhaps initiated his interest in the relationship between issues of knowledge and religious policy. By 1667, after his association with Shaftesbury, Locke changed his position and defended religious toleration in *An Essay concerning Toleration,* which foreshadowed the liberal views of his *Epistola de tolerantia* (1689), his classic defense of religious liberty. There he argued that religious opinions, even in "matters indifferent," could not and ought not be imposed upon subjects since a government magistrate had no more certain or infallible knowledge than anyone else.

From his consideration of religious toleration, Locke turned his attention to two fundamental attendant issues: the nature of government and the nature of knowledge. His *Two Treatises of Government* (1689) sets forth both a biblical interpretation attacking the basis of traditional patriarchal political theory and a model of human society in which every person has a direct relation to God under natural law. In accord with his views on toleration, Locke's theory of government does not require a uniformity of religion but is instead based on the right and need of individuals to preserve their lives, liberty, and property under natural law, even to the point of revolution.

His *Essay concerning Human Understanding* (1690) addresses issues of epistemology with an eye toward their religious and political implications. He attacks the theory of "innate principles," charging that its proponents (Hobbesians, Enthusiasts, and Roman Catholics) used it to impose their opinions on others as infallible so that they might govern by demanding unquestioning faith in their judgments. He seeks to show how little proper knowledge, that is, certainty, is available and asserts that religion rests primarily upon faith, not on knowledge. By "faith" Locke meant an assent to revelation; such an assent is essentially a judgment of probability, however great an assurance or confidence it carries. Thus, his epistemology supports his claim, with regard to toleration, that the leaders of society have no basis for imposing religion on subjects. However, he firmly believed that each individual could determine what was essential to his or her own salvation and moral life.

In *The Reasonableness of Christianity* (1695), Locke sets forth his own understanding of true religion, which he describes as a simple, intelligible Christianity derived from scripture alone. Drawing on an old tradition, he argues that the fundamental articles of Christian faith had been clearly designated by Jesus and the apostles, and that they are evident to anyone who reads the Bible. Focusing on the Gospels and the *Acts of the Apostles*, he attempts to reconstruct the life and teachings of Jesus and the apostles so as to show that they required for salvation belief only that Jesus was the Messiah, which presupposes belief in the existence of God and carries with it certain "concomitant articles" (such as Jesus' miracles, resurrection, and ascension) that proved him to be the Messiah. He admits that other scriptural doctrines must be believed as one comes to know them and emphasizes that moral obedience must accompany faith. Locke seems to have hoped that such a vision of Christianity, founded on a simple article of faith and clear morality set forth plainly in scripture, could provide a basis for social and political unity in which secondary matters of difference would be tolerated.

Locke's method in *Reasonableness* was also influential in the history of biblical criticism. His attempt to reconstruct the earliest teachings of Christianity led him to write a virtual "life of Jesus," including attention to what would later be called the "messianic secret." He emphasized what he thought were the more historical portions of the New Testament over the more doctrinal letters. His later *Paraphrases and Notes on the Pauline Epistles*, published posthumously (1705–1707), also contributed to the perspective and style of subsequent biblical interpretation.

Locke's views on religion have been labeled as Hobbesian, Socinian or Unitarian, and deistic. The thesis of *Reasonableness* is nearly identical to that of Hobbes, and late twentieth-century Marxist interpreters have revived the charges of Hobbesian inclination made by a few of Locke's contemporaries. However, non-Marxist historians have countered with alternative interpretations of Locke's meaning and broad intentions. Locke's ownership of numerous Socinian books, his several Unitarian friends, and manuscript records of antitrinitarian sentiments have often been cited as evidence of his secret sympathies. Yet such claims depend largely on silence and association, and recent analyses of manuscript sources have revealed that nearly all of Locke's "Unitarian" manuscript writings were not his own opinions but notes taken from his readings. His epistemology became a standard foundation of eighteenth-century Deism, but *Reasonableness* may well have been directed in part against the Deists and was used as a source of anti-Deist polemics. Locke strongly denied that his religious opinions were either the same as or influenced by Hobbes, the Socinians, or the Deists. If he is to be classed with any group or party, he might best be labeled as an independent thinker of the English Latitudinarian tradition.

BIBLIOGRAPHY

Maurice Cranston's *John Locke: A Biography* (London, 1957) is more comprehensive in its biographical detail than compelling in its interpretations of Locke's thought. Peter Laslett's edition of *Two Treatises of Government*, 2d ed. (Cambridge, 1964), provides the best critical text, as well as a revolutionary interpretation that has been widely accepted. Laslett's work is scheduled to be included in "The Clarendon Edition of the Works of John Locke," which will include all of Locke's published works and most of the manuscripts from the Lovelace Collection of the Bodleian Library. This series was initiated by Peter H. Nidditch's critical edition of *An Essay Concerning Human Understanding*, new ed. with corrections (Oxford, 1979). The best work on the religious influence of Locke's epistemology is John W. Yolton's *John Locke and the Way of Ideas* (Oxford, 1956).

JOHN C. HIGGINS-BIDDLE

LOGIC. In the words of Petrus Hispanus, logic is both "ars artium et scientia scientiarum, ad omnium aliarum scientiarum methodorum principia viam habens." Roughly, we may take this to say, in modern terms, that logic concerns itself with the methods of correct statement and inference in all areas of inquiry whatsoever. Traditionally logic has divided into the study of deduction and of induction. The former has had an enormous development in the last hundred years or so, whereas the latter is still lagging behind, awaiting its coming of age.

Deductive logic does not dictate the principles or statements with which a given line of reasoning or inference starts; it takes over after these have been initially decided upon. Such principles or statements are decided upon, in turn, by direct insight, by revelation, by direct experience, by induction from instances, and so on. Deductive logic steps in only in the secondary capacity of directing the course of inferences once the so-called "premises" have been accepted or determined. The principles and rules of correct inference are stated in complete generality and hence are applicable to all kinds of subject matter. They are stated within a limited logical vocabulary—primarily that providing for the notions "not," "and," "or," "for all," "for some," and so on—to which the statements of any discipline must be brought into conformity by the use of suitable non-logical constants providing for the given subject matter. Logic is thus indeed a kind of straitjacket that enforces correct statement and inference, just as moral norms enforce correct behavior and aesthetic norms enforce the beautiful or the artistically acceptable. In logic, however, there is less variation in the norms than in moral or aesthetic matters. Although many varieties of "deviant" logics have been invented, all of these turn out to be mere applications of the one standard logic. This is essentially the logic of Aristotle, brought up to date with the important contributions of DeMorgan, Boole, Peirce, Frege, Schröder, Whitehead and Russell, and Leśniewski.

Principles of logic have played a central role in theology throughout the long history of both, and each has influenced the other in significant ways. To be noted especially is the development, between roughly 1200 and 1500, of the Scholastic logic that aimed at providing the wherewithal for proofs of God's existence, especially those of Anselm, Thomas Aquinas, and Duns Scotus. In recent years, so-called process theology, stemming from the work of Whitehead, owes its origins to Whitehead's early work in logic, and much of the current discussion of the language of theology, especially in England, has been decisively influenced by the contemporary concern with the logic of natural language. In the East, especially in India, logic began to flourish in the first century CE within the confines of the methodology of theological and moral discussion and had a vigorous development that has persisted to the present day.

Logic, especially in its modern form, is a helpful adjunct to theology and should not be viewed with the fear that it will reduce the subject to a long list of sterile formulas. On the contrary, it should be viewed as an instrument that can help theology regain the high cognitive regality it once had as the queen of the sciences.

BIBLIOGRAPHY

Bocheński, Joseph M. *The Logic of Religion.* New York, 1965.

Carnes, John. *Axiomatics and Dogmatics.* Oxford, 1982.

Martin, R. M. *Primordiality, Science and Value.* Albany, N.Y., 1980.

R. M. MARTIN

LOGICAL POSITIVISM. Narrowly defined, logical positivism was an organized, science-oriented movement centered in Vienna during the 1920s and 1930s, a movement severely critical of metaphysics, theology, and traditional philosophy. Also known as logical empiricism, logical positivism may be more broadly defined as a doctrine born of classical empiricism and nineteenth-century positivism and sharpened by an empirical interpretation of the early logical writings of Ludwig Wittgenstein (1889–1951). [*See* Empiricism; Positivism; *and the biography of Wittgenstein.*]

In either case, the distant origins of logical positivism lie in the long history of philosophical empiricism, the tradition holding that all knowledge must be derived from human experience alone. More particularly, the empiricism of John Locke (1632–1704), George Berkeley (1685–1753), and David Hume (1711–1776), with their cumulatively ever more radical elimination of nonempirical sources of knowledge, served as inspiration for the scientific views of the influential Vienna physicist and theorist of science, Ernst Mach (1836–1916). In addition, the positivist movement of the nineteenth century, founded by Auguste Comte (1798–1857), with its intense admiration for natural science, its anticlerical and antimetaphysical commitments, and its self-conscious programs for social and religious reform, lay behind not only Mach but also the small group of mathematical, natural, and social scientists who gathered in Vienna as early as 1907 to discuss Mach's views. In 1922 this group was successful in bringing Moritz Schlick (1882–1936), who was scientifically trained under the great German physicist Max Planck (1858–1947) but also keenly interested in philosophical issues, to the chair once held by Mach at the University of Vienna.

Schlick quickly drew around him a circle of like-minded thinkers, mainly from the sciences, some of whom formed in 1928 the Verein Ernst Mach (the Ernst Mach Society). What soon became known as logical positivism was formulated by this group. The Vienna Circle, as they came to be known, issued a "manifesto" in 1929, organized international meetings, and in 1930 took over a journal, renamed *Erkenntnis,* for the advancement of its increasingly sharp position. [*See the biographies of Locke, Hume, and Comte.*]

The distinctively "logical" character of the radically empiricist Vienna Circle was derived from the careful study (a line-by-line examination from 1924 to 1926) of Wittgenstein's *Tractatus Logico-Philosophicus,* which had been completed by 1918 and first published in 1921 (in German under the title *Logisch-philosophische Abhandlung*), just prior to the formation of the Vienna Circle. Wittgenstein was never a member of the Circle and was not sympathetic either to its party spirit or to the "grandiloquence" of its pronouncements, but from 1927 to 1929 he engaged in conversations with Schlick and other members of the Circle. Wittgenstein's logical doctrine formed the Circle's sharpest weapon against metaphysics and theology: the characterization of them not merely as false or outmoded, as Comte and the classical positivists had claimed, but as strictly "nonsense."

It was from Wittgenstein that the Vienna Circle drew its insistence that all meaningful statements are either analytic (and logically certain merely because they are tautologies) or synthetic (and "truth-functionally" analyzable into basic propositions corresponding to ultimately simple facts). The Circle gave its own characteristic interpretation of what qualified as these "atomic facts": sense-experiences. With this interpretation came support for two of the Circle's three primary positions: (1) the doctrine of the unity of science, Mach's key project, on the ground that all the sciences can be reduced equally to variously complex ("molecular") reports on experience; and (2) the doctrine of the valuelessness of metaphysics, on the ground that metaphysical utterances, by attempting to go "beyond" experience, fail to point to simple sense-experiences and thus are devoid of cognitive content.

Both doctrines were incorporated in and defensible by the third, the single most characteristic doctrine enunciated by the logical positivists: the verification principle of meaning, fashioned in light of Wittgenstein's analysis of the logic of language. The principle itself, "the meaning of a proposition is the method of its verification," though not appearing in the *Tractatus Logico-Philosophicus,* was attributed to a remark by Wittgenstein and was first published in the initial volume of *Erkenntnis* (1930–1931). In all its many later versions, the verification principle was taken to mean that for any nonanalytic (i.e., any would-be informative) statement, the factual meaning of the statement is equivalent to the set of observations (or sense-experiences, or "observation-statements") that would be sufficient to confirm the assertion's truth. Thus a thoroughgoing empiricist interpretation was given to Wittgenstein's more general dictum, and the authority of a powerful theory of meaning was placed behind the old disavowal of metaphysical or theological claims.

Those purported claims, it was said, must (if nontautological) be equivalent to the sensory experiences that might be obtained by an observer ideally positioned to verify the claim. Such confirming experiences, in the end, are alone what the utterances can mean. But if there are (and could be) no such specifiable experiences, as in the case of utterances allegedly "about" nonsensory entities like "God" or the "Absolute," then literally nothing is conveyed by the language, no real claims are made, and no "entity" can be conceived, much less believed in. So ran the fresh, essentially polemical argument of the logical positivists.

This polemic was generally ignored in the German-speaking philosophical world, doubtless because the Vienna Circle was not perceived (and to a large extent did not perceive itself) as engaging in philosophy so much as in a critique, enunciated mainly by professional scientists on behalf of a scientific method and worldview, of philosophy itself. Some English-speaking philosophers, however, long nurtured in the empiricist tradition that had inspired Mach and the Vienna Circle, were quick to notice the logical positivists. Alfred Jules Ayer (b. 1910) and Gilbert Ryle (1900–1976), of Oxford, and John Wisdom (b. 1904) and Susan Stebbing (1885–1943), of Cambridge, were early interpreters of the movement. Ayer, visiting Vienna in 1933, attended the meetings of the Circle, and in 1936 his book *Language, Truth and Logic,* containing a logical positivist critique of theology and ethics, exploded onto the English-speaking scene.

This radical challenge to the logical intelligibility of central theological utterances—those ostensibly about God, the soul, life after death, and the like—provoked a reaction that, though muted by the outbreak of World War II, intensified again in the early 1950s after a renewed challenge was issued by Antony Flew (b. 1923). Flew drew upon a variation of the verification principle for his question: what empirical observations would be incompatible with (would "falsify") theological assertions? If the answer is none, then are not the assertions in fact empty of definite, thinkable content? Theologians in the Catholic tradition (Roman or Anglican) tended to answer in terms of traditional doctrines of analogy. Members of the reformed tradition replied in fideistic terms. Neither group offered direct responses to the logical positivist attack. On the other hand, a third group, mainly liberal Protestants (including some Anglicans), attempted to vindicate the cognitive meaningfulness of theological discourse by satisfying the conditions set by the verification principle, specifying experiences that would be relevant to the verification or falsification of the claims in question. John Hick (b. 1922) proposed that claims about God could be verified, but only by postmortem experiences. Basil Mitchell (b. 1917) suggested that ordinary historical events or personal experiences are relevant to the verification of these claims, though not conclusively (as in many complex or ambiguous situations in life). He further suggested that faith-commitments are shown to be cognitively significant precisely because of the anguish sometimes felt in maintaining them against the evidence. R. M. Hare (b. 1919) and John Wisdom agreed that ordinary cognitive content is missing from theological claims but that these utterances might still have importance otherwise, offering comprehensive interpretations of particular experiences.

This variety of replies, to which many others could be added, underscores the distance that the postwar discussion had come from the rigorous either/or position of the Vienna Circle. But the sharp sword of the verification principle had already been blunted on issues at the very center of logical positivist concern: issues involving the adequate analysis of scientific assertions themselves. Try as they might, the members and allies of the Vienna Circle were not able to make good their program to include with the same criteria all scientifically essential statements but to exclude all metaphysical and theological ones. It soon became clear that the laws of science, being entirely universal in form, are not conclusively verifiable, since finite numbers of observations cannot in principle verify a universal assertion. ("Some" examples, however many they may be, cannot verify claims about "all.") Furthermore, the proffered suggestion that scientific laws are not, after all, assertions, as they seem to be, but disguised "rules" or other logical entities was too paradoxical for most science supporters. Again, the apparently definite meaning of even straightforward, particular factual assertions of science and daily life was found to melt away under verificational analysis into an infinite series of possible observations. Reversing the problem to the criterion of "falsification" did not help, since although a universal proposition can be falsified (in principle) by a single negative observation, no particular assertion can be so falsified; furthermore, universal laws of science are not, either in logic or in historical fact, at once falsified by negative observations. At most a whole network of theories is shown to need revision by a negative observational result (since it is not immediately clear which of the premises ought to be discarded and which retained). Moreover, as argued by such historians of science as Thomas S. Kuhn (b. 1922), science does not actually develop in any such logically neat way.

Other applications, not directly fashioned by the Vienna Circle, of verificationism to science—for instance, the attempt of the Harvard physicist P. W. Bridgman (1882–1962) to reduce all concepts in science to descriptions of specific procedures ("operationalism")—resulted in the unsatisfactory conclusion that entirely different concepts (for example, of "length" or "time") would be fashioned by the various sciences, depending on their subject matter and characteristic methods. Far from supporting the unity of science, which was a central motive in the founding of the logical positivist movement, operationalism tended to make it logically impossible for astronomy, which measures distance by various sorts of procedures, to share a common concept of distance with geology, biology, or microphysics, which rely upon others. Indeed, even within the same science—or within the same laboratory on different occasions—scientifically essential conceptual generality was seen to be forfeited by the particularistic reductionism of operationalism.

Equally alarming to many more realistically-minded scientists and friends of science was the problem of retaining a (non-"metaphysical") concept of the common world studied by science if the meanings of all factual propositions are to be literally equated with those experiences that could verify them. Since experiences are personal and private, the traditional problem of "other minds" (i.e., of how I can escape solipsism if other centers of consciousness are not directly observable by me) was added to the problem of escaping from absolute idealism (i.e., the alarmingly traditional metaphysical view that nothing exists except mentality), even if the egocentric predicament somehow could be avoided.

Finally, the logical status of the verification principle itself could not withstand verificationist analysis. The principle is not just another empirical hypothesis: that is, it certainly does not offer a foothold for confirmation (or falsification) by sense-experiences. Is it then an empty tautology? Most logical positivists took the latter position, holding that the principle was an "important" tautology that had many good reasons for being "recommended" to the intellectual community. This tack, however, allowed others, like Hare and Wisdom, to speak of equally "important" nonverifiable utterances and to make more complex counterrecommendations about the meaning of "meaning."

The disintegration of the organized Vienna Circle can be dated from the murder by a deranged student of Schlick in 1936. Viewed with hostility by the Nazis, the Vienna Circle was formally disbanded in 1938, and in the same year *Erkenntnis* was moved out of Hitler's direct sphere of control, to Holland, where it lasted only another two years. The end of the broader movement is harder to trace, and in some fashion it remains influential as an overtone in the more radically empirical voices of our time. Still, the gradual abandonment by Wittgenstein of his own either/or position on meaning in the *Tractatus Logico-Philosophicus*, in favor of a much more pluralistic approach to the functions of human language, pulled the logical rug out from under logical positivism. Its significance for religion and theology continues to lie in the fact that theologians now have been forced to acknowledge the extent to which their claims cannot be treated as simple empirical hypotheses, open to "crucial experiments," as in the contest between Elijah and the priests of Baal (*1 Kgs.* 18:17–40). Indeed, it may be thought that theology has emerged the better for its cold bath in verificationism, if only because theologians are now required to be aware of the subtlety of their speech and of the many functions it may have both in their technical discourses and in the living religious speech of the faithful.

[*See also* Analytic Philosophy *and* Science and Religion.]

BIBLIOGRAPHY

No single book is more important for the understanding of logical positivism than Ludwig Wittgenstein's difficult but fascinating *Tractatus Logico-Philosophicus* (London, 1922). As a general guide to Wittgenstein's thought and to the *Tractatus* in particular, one might turn to part 1 of George Pitcher's helpful *The Philosophy of Wittgenstein* (Englewood Cliffs, N.J., 1964). The thought of the founder of the Vienna Circle is reflected in Moritz Schlick's posthumously published *Gesammelte Aufsätze 1926–36* (1938; reprint, Hildesheim, 1962). Other representative writings of the Vienna Circle can be found in Rudolf Carnap's *The Logical Structure of the World* (London, 1967) and in *Foundations of the Unity of Science*, vol. 2 of *International Encyclopedia of Unified Science*, edited by Otto Neurath, Rudolf Carnap, and Charles Morris (1938–1962; reprint, Chicago, 1955–1970). The explosive introduction of logical positivism to the English-speaking world was through Alfred Jules Ayer's *Language, Truth and Logic* (London, 1936). After World War II, the key book in focusing the theological aspect of the controversy was *New Essays in Philosophical Theology*, edited by Antony Flew and Alasdair MacIntyre (London, 1955). One of the important sustained efforts to meet the challenge by offering theological verification of a sort, though not in this life, was John Hick's *Faith and Knowledge*, 2d ed. (Ithaca, N.Y., 1966). A detailed analysis of the arguments leading to the verificationist challenge to religious belief, of various attempted replies, and of the transformation of the issues resulting from this debate can be found in the first chapters of my *Language, Logic, and God* (New York, 1961). The best recent survey of the whole phenomenon of logical positivism, readable and authoritative, is Oswald Hanfling's *Logical Positivism* (New York, 1981).

FREDERICK FERRÉ

LOGOS. The noun *logos* is as old as the Greek language itself. It has acquired, over the course of time, a large number of different meanings, which only with difficulty can be drawn into a simple unity. "Reason" is the translation that causes perhaps the least trouble, but "reason" itself is of course far from unambiguous. Perhaps it will help to carve up the vast semantic field covered by the word *logos* if I distinguish three principal meanings, even though this entails considerable simplification. First there is an objective meaning: the rational ground or basis (Ger., *Grund*) for something. This is often of a numerical or logical nature and functions as a principle of explanation. Second, there is a subjective meaning: the power or faculty of reasoning (Ger., *Vernunft*) or thought. Third, there is what I shall call an expressive meaning: thought or reason as expressed in speech or in writing (the "speech" may be either vocalized or purely cerebral).

Stoic Views of Logos. No one of these three meanings is limited specifically to the study of religious thought and experience. One specific use of the word did, however, come to have pride of place in some of the philosophical schools of the ancient world, and especially among the Stoics. In these circles *logos* came to mean the rational order of the universe, an immanent natural law, a life-giving force hidden within things, a power working from above on the sensible world. This use of the word has obvious affinities with the first of the meanings listed above. Clearly we have to do here with the idea of rational ground or basis. There is, however, the obvious difference that we are dealing not with the rational ground of some one particular entity as distinct from some other, but with the cosmos as a whole. It is this extension in the scope of the word, an extension reaching out to embrace the confines of the universe, that gives to this particular use of *logos* a religious dimension. Hence the willingness of the Stoics to call this *logos* "God." Deeply embedded in the matter of the universe, God does not demand our worship, does not cry out for temples built by human hands. He does nonetheless call forth a theology, and he does stir in us a sense of piety; but theology and piety are centered on the cosmos.

The point to appreciate is that, for the Stoics, *logos* is associated with all the functions that are normally attributed to the divine. Logos is destiny and providence. Chrysippus, one of the founders of Stoicism, tells us for example that "it is in conformity with the Logos that what has happened, has happened, that what is happening, is happening, that what will happen, will happen" (*Stoicorum veterum fragmenta* 2.913). The Logos impregnates the world, from within, with its order and rhythm. The Stoic emperor Marcus Aurelius (5.32.2) tells us that wisdom consists in coming to know "the Logos that extends through the whole of matter, and governs the universe for all eternity according to certain fixed periods." For all that, the Logos is not limited to controlling nature. "If there is any common bond between gods and men, it is because both alike share in the Logos, which Logos is the natural law" (*Stoicorum veterum fragmenta* 2.528).

Such were the theses upheld by the oldest of the Stoics, in the third century before the Christian era. Were these Stoics taking over an earlier set of ideas that had been worked out even before their time by Heraclitus of Ephesus toward the end of the sixth century? Heraclitus believed in the existence of a Logos common to all humans, shared by all, over and beyond their private thoughts, a Logos by which all things happen as they do, a Logos clothed with many of the attributes of divinity. There were, besides, many readers in the ancient world who thought that Heraclitus's Logos was close to the Logos of the Stoics and could therefore be taken as the first mapping out of the Stoic conception. On the other hand, one must remember how laconic are the very few quotations from Heraclitus on the nature of his Logos that have come down to us, and how very different are the meanings that can attach to the word. There can therefore be no certainty that the Logos of Heraclitus was really the principle guiding and underlying the universe that the Stoics were going to call by the same name.

It is certain, nevertheless, that of all the theological thinkers of pagan antiquity who made use of the idea of a Logos, the Stoics took the idea furthest and had the greatest influence. Although the great philosophers of the classical period made much use of the word *logos,* they did not attach to it a meaning capable of sustaining the same religious development. Nor can such development be traced in any of the later spiritual movements rooted in the tradition of Greek thought. Contrary to what one might have expected, the Neoplatonists gave only a very limited place to the Logos within the framework of their religious ideas. The Logos does not belong to the hierarchy of hypostases set up by Plotinus. In the *Enneads* there are only two short treatises, both called *On Providence* (3.2.3 [47, 48]), in which Plotinus plays with the idea, perhaps under the influence of gnostic beliefs. Where Jewish and Christian speculative thinkers are to be found giving the word *logos* the full depth of its religious value, they, no less than their pagan counterparts, draw upon ways of thinking that are recognizably Stoic in origin.

Should we then look upon the Stoic philosophers as the fountainhead of the entire subsequent development of a theology of the Logos? Not quite: Stoic influence would hardly have been capable, without reinforcement, of stimulating such a profound development. But as it happened, the Stoic conception was joined by a new way of thinking that probably originated in the Near East and that encouraged people to see as independent and separate personifications what had hitherto been understood as different psychological aspects of a single divine being. What had been simply modes of the divine essence now came to be thought of as substances in their own right, each of which had issued from the divine by a process neatly epitomized in the title of a thesis presented by Helmer Ringgren: *Word and Wisdom: Studies in the Hypostatization of Divine Qualities and Functions in the Ancient Near East* (Lund, 1947). This same shift in thought is brought out by the Christian Tertullian in a treatise against the gnostics (*Against the Valentinians* 4.2), in which he writes of the difference between Valentinus and his disciple Ptolemy. In the thought of Ptolemy, "the Aeons, each distinguished by its own name and by its own number, became personalized substances, characterized independently of God, whereas Valentinus had included them in the divine whole itself, and had taken them as thoughts, feelings and emotions of the divine." Earlier, Irenaeus (*Against Heresies* 1.12.1) had written in a similar vein of the same Ptolemy's belief that there had issued forth from the Father Aeons that had earlier been thought of as mere "dispositions" *(diatheseis)* of the Father. [*See* Hypostasis.]

The Logos should be seen as the chief of these dispositions. As the name itself testifies, it originally designated the divine reason before becoming a reality in its own right, distinct from God, and soon to be personified by taking on the characteristics of the Son of God. A parallel transformation into a hypostasis distinct from God was undergone by another divine faculty, Wisdom (Sophia). [*See* Sophia.] Both developments took place in the first two centuries of the Christian era, in the hellenized Jewish circles of Alexandria, and reached their fullest expression in the works of Philo Judaeus (first century CE). The conceptual effort required by these transformations bears all the marks of Stoicism, but the change has been made on the basis of underlying doctrinal shifts. The personalized Logos, distinct from God insofar as accounted the Son of God, is far removed from the supreme principle immersed in matter that the Stoics called by the same name. A difference in terminology brings out just how far the idea has traveled: the "god Logos" of Stoicism has given way, more often than not, to the "Logos of God," or "divine Logos" (e.g., Philo, *On the Maker of the World* 5.20). This change takes on its full meaning when the Christian Origen contrasts his own belief with that of his adversary Celsus, who on this point can be taken for all intents and purposes as a Stoic. Origen writes as follows (*Against Celsus* 5.24): "The Logos of all things, according to Celsus, is God himself, whereas we believe that the Logos is the Son of God. In our philosophy it is he of whom we say: 'In the beginning was the Logos, and the Logos was with God, and the Logos was God' (*Jn.* 1:1)."

Logos and Wisdom. The theology of Wisdom is inseparable from the theology of the Logos. The theology of Wisdom stems from the Old Testament, where in *Proverbs* (8:22–23) Wisdom speaks: "The Lord created me at the beginning of his work, the first of his acts of old. Ages ago I was set up, at the first, before the beginning of the earth," and so on. Wisdom is plainly presented here as the first of God's creatures and as God's collaborator in the creation of all that was yet to be created. How Wisdom is to be thought of in conjunction with Logos may be gleaned from a Hellenistic Jewish text, the *Wisdom of Solomon* (9:1–9): "God of my fathers and Lord of thy mercy, thou who hast made all things in thy Logos, and who by this Wisdom has called forth man . . . grant me the Wisdom seated by thy throne."

Jews and Christians have devoted much commentary to these two passages. Philo sees the Wisdom of *Proverbs* as the mother of the universe. In accordance with an obviously Stoic train of thought (*Stoicorum veterum fragmenta* 2.1074), she is held to have received from God the seeds *(spermata)* of creation (*On Drunkenness* 8.30–31; *On the Cherubim* 14.49). Elsewhere (*Allegorical Interpretation* 1.19.64; *On Flight and Finding* 20.109; *On Dreams* 2.37.245), she is identified in his eyes with the Logos, and either can be taken as typified by the manna from heaven in *Exodus* 16. These apparent inconsistencies in Philo's thought have a great deal to do with his allegorical exegesis. They also show how ideas of Wisdom and Logos became intertwined in the Judeo-Greek world of Alexandria. Things worked out differently, however, in the purely Jewish tradition, the tradition we speak of as Palestinian. The rabbinical commentators took Wisdom in *Proverbs* 8:22 to mean the preexistent Torah, conceived by them as being the plan according to which God had created the world.

The Christians of the second century exercised their minds on the same pages of the Bible and came up with conclusions that were not dissimilar. This, for example, is how Justin Martyr interprets the text from *Proverbs,* just before quoting liberally from it: "As a principle prior to all his creatures, God has called forth from himself a Power that is like a Logos [*dunamin logikēn*]". He goes on to say that in different contexts, scripture calls this power Son, Wisdom, God, and Logos (*Dialogue with Trypho* 61.1, 129.3–4). But there is a difference, and one with important ramifications, in the way in which Philo and Justin quote from the same verse of *Proverbs.* Philo reads the text in a Greek translation that has Wisdom say: "The Lord, to whom I belong [*ektēsato*], has made me the principle of his ways." But Justin, in common with other Christian writers of his day, follows another Greek translation, the so-called Septuagint, which rightly or wrongly gives the verse as: "The Lord has created me [*ektise*]." One can hardly mistake the significance of the idea of creation that has thus been introduced into the passage.

Justin's aim, an aim that will be shared by the whole of ancient Christianity, is to read this verse from *Proverbs* in the light of the prologue to the gospel according to John, and so to see in Wisdom a prophetical foretelling of the Logos or the preexistent Son of God. But such an aim is not supported by the fact that Wisdom is said to be "created," which obviously could not be applied to the Son of God. This explains why Justin, as we just saw, abandons the idea of creation and adopts instead the idea of generation, an idea altogether more suited to describe the arrival of the Christian Word. Nonetheless, the idea that Wisdom had been "created" was a constant irritant, impeding any attempt at a syncretistic explanation of Wisdom as the Word. It is not until the fourth century that Eusebius of Caesarea (*Ecclesiastical Theology* 3.2.14ff.) resurrects and insists upon the reading *ektēsato* that had been given by Philo of Alexandria, while Jerome, when he comes to translate the same word in his Latin version of the Hebrew scriptures, chooses the meaning of *possessio* and excludes the idea of *creatio* (see his *Letter* 140.6).

Shortly after Justin, the Christian Theophilus of Antioch takes up the association of the Logos and Wisdom and sometimes seems even to identify the two (*To Autolycus* 2.10, 2.22). In other passages, however, he distinguishes them (1.7, 2.8), while once (2.15) he uses a very striking formula to tell us of a triad made up of God, his Logos, and his Wisdom. It is tempting to see at this point a preliminary version of the doctrine of the Trinity, with Wisdom occupying the place of the Holy Ghost. The different ways that Theophilus has of expressing himself on the subject show, however, that the doctrine has not as yet really taken on definite shape in his mind. Not until Irenaeus, who never wavers in his identification of Wisdom with the Holy Ghost, does the idea of the Trinity become a consistent and self-conscious doctrine.

Seminal Logos. We can see here how, from the very beginning, the Christian theology of the Logos, or of the Word, was deeply rooted in the particular way in which theologians read and understood *Proverbs* and the *Wisdom of Solomon* in the cultural circles of Hellenistic Judaism. No less important was the influence that Stoicism exerted on these Jewish speculations, though its importance was of another kind. Stoicism provided the theoretical framework that made it possible for images and ideas drawn from scripture to take on definite doctrinal shape.

Take, for example, the Stoic idea of *logos spermatikos,* seminal or spermatic *logos.* This was an idea that the Stoics had worked out to explain how every being contains within itself a principle of development suitable to itself—an idea that they applied to the individual beings within the cosmos as well as to the cosmos itself in its entirety. When applied to individual beings, the formula is used in the plural. We are told, for example, that God, "in looking to the birth of the world, holds within himself all the seminal *logoi,* according to which each thing is produced, as required by necessity" (*Stoicorum veterum fragmenta* 2.1027). We have already seen how Philo makes use of this way of thinking when he writes of Wisdom receiving from God the seeds of creation.

Justin is no less indebted to the same mode of thought, although the turn of ideas in his case is very different. Justin wonders how pagan philosophers and poets have been able to utter certain truths, despite their having had no access to the truths of revelation. He decides that it is "because of the seed of the Logos that has been implanted in the whole human race," with the difference that the pagans respond to only "a part of the seminal Logos," whereas the Christians' rule of faith is founded on "the knowledge and the contemplation of the whole Logos, that is, of Christ" (*Second Apology* 8.1, 8.3). The same Stoic concept underlies the thought of the gnostic Ptolemy at about the same time (as reported by Irenaeus in *Against Heresies* 1.8.5): Ptolemy claimed that the Father, in the Son, had called forth all things seminally *(spermatikōs).*

Inner Logos and Spoken Logos. Stoic psychology emphasized the lack of coincidence between the reasoning power, which rests within, and language, which gives outward expression to the powers of reason. Since the same word *logos* was used to designate both the power of reasoning and reason as expressed in speech, the difference came to be stated as a difference between two *logoi.* One might no less properly express this as a distinction between two types or states of language. A language within, or an inner language *(logos endiathetos),* is then distinguished from a language that we have in common with talking birds, a language expressed in speech *(logos prophorikos).* We should refrain, however, from giving too much importance to the significance that the Stoics themselves attached to this distinction, for the accounts of it are few and far between. Thus we find in Heraclitus, a commentator on Homer (first century CE?), the claim that if Hermes, god of the *logos,* is given double honors, "this is because language is double. The philosophers call one an 'inner' language and the other a 'spoken' language. The 'spoken' language is the messenger of the thoughts that pass within us, whereas the 'inner' language stays enclosed within the fastness of our heart" (*Homeric Problems* 72.14–16).

From small beginnings, this Stoic way of thinking came to cut deep into the Christian theology of the Logos. No one threw himself with greater abandon into the description of the idea and its transposition into a Christian context than Theophilus of Antioch, at the end of the second century. In his treatise *To Autolycus* (2.2), he gives brilliant proof of the idea outlined earlier, according to which the Jewish and Christian Logos resulted from exteriorizing and personifying what had originally been God's own internal faculty of reflection. At first God is alone, and the Logos is quite simply God's weighing up of things within himself; then, when he wishes to create, God brings forth the Logos to be his instrument and his messenger. By cleverly cutting off the opening of the prologue of John's gospel, Theophilus is able to drum up a scriptural warrant for this Stoic representation of the two *logoi.* The evident weakness in the process lies in introducing into the condition of the Logos a kind of historical development that is ill-suited to the nature of the divine. Because Theophilus has taken over the movement *ad extra* by which the Stoics passed from the *logos endiathetos* to the *logos prophorikos,* the Word of God has to pass through two different and successive states, and it seems clear that his begetting, for all that it is the essential mark of his relation to the Father, belongs only to the second state.

The danger inherent in this view of the Trinity did not escape the eagle eye of Origen, who very neatly seizes upon it in a passage (*De principiis* 1.2.2) written around 230. By means of a subtle philosophical argument, proceeding by dilemma, he establishes that from all eternity God is, and always has been, the Father of his only Son.

Theophilus of Antioch probably best typifies the tendency that we have found in him. Yet he is by no means the only writer able to manipulate such ideas. In the second century and at the beginning of the third, almost all Christian theologians write of the Logos in a way that implies development: starting from a lack of distinction within the innermost being of God, they make the Logos "proceed" from out of God and take upon himself the work of creation. To be sure, only some of these authors deliberately and explicitly draw upon the Stoic model of the two *logoi* and cast their ideas in the technical terms of the theory; but they all have the same model in mind. One may quote Justin (*Dialogue* 61.2) and his disciple Tatian (*Speech to the Greeks* 5), and in the Latin-speaking world Tertullian (*Against Praxeas* 5–7) and finally Hippolytus of Rome (*Against Noëtus* 10; *Refutation* 10.33.1–15). Hippolytus virtually repeats the analyses given by Theophilus, although there are some differences of nuance: for example, Hippolytus splits in two the outward state of the Logos and sees therein a separate stage for the Word incarnate. Yet two noteworthy exceptions should be mentioned: Clement of Alexandria (*Stromateis* 5.1.6.3) and even more so Irenaeus (*Against Heresies* 2.13.8, 2.28.5). His struggle against the gnostics (who in practice shared the views of Theophilus and others) gave Irenaeus an additional reason for forcefully rejecting any assimilation of the generation of the Word with happenings related to the human Logos.

Irenaeus's negative approach won the day. The analogy with Stoic theory of the two *logoi* is heard of no more for a while, then reappears during the fourth century in the theology of the Word expounded by Marcellus of Ancyra and Photinus. Both these writers were condemned and anathematized by synods in 345 and 351. The declaration of faith in 345 ran as follows: "But as for us, we know that Christ is not merely a Logos of God uttered outwardly or resting within [*prophorikos ē endiathetos*]. He is the Logos God, living and subsisting of himself, Son of God, Christ" (*Macrostich Formula* of the third synod of Antioch, pt. 6, in August Hahn, *Bibliothek der Symbole und Glaubensregeln der alten Kirche*, 3d ed., Breslau, 1897, para. 159, p. 194). This conciliar statement had in any case been anticipated by Eusebius of Caesarea (*De ecclesiastica theologia* 1.17; 2.11; 14; 15), and was shortly to receive the approval of Cyril of Jerusalem (*Catechesis* 11.10) and Athanasius (*Speech against the Arians* 2.35). Marcellus of Ancyra and Photinus, then, were fighting rearguard battle. In the dogmatic formula approved in 325 by the ecumenical council of Nicaea (the Nicene Creed), the word *logos*, which Eusebius had suggested, had already disappeared in favor of "Son of God" (Hahn, 1897, pp. 160–161). This substitution obviously brought on the demise of the old Stoic ways of thinking that had been indissolubly linked to the term *logos*. Not until the fifth century, and then only in the Latin-speaking world, does one find, in the great trinitarian synthesis of Augustine, a new way in which the two states of human language *(verbum quod intus lucet, verbum quod foris sonat)* can again be employed to mark out similarities with the divine Word; yet even then the comparison has to be handled with the greatest circumspection. Augustine differs from the theologians of the second century in holding that the spoken human word finds for its analogue not the begotten Logos seen against the background of its participation in creation, but the Word made flesh (*De trinitate* 15.10.19–11.20).

Functions of the Logos. Philo of Alexandria, as well as the early Christians, confers upon the Logos a number of different functions. The chief of these can be described by three words: *creation, revelation, mediation.*

The idea of speech as creative is hardly likely to have arisen in Greece, where men thought instead in terms of an antithesis between the two nouns *logos* and *ergon:* the antithesis of talking and doing, of words and acts, of the lips and the heart. Quite other is the world of the Old Testament, where sentences abound such as those in Psalm 33:9: "For he spoke, and it was done; he commanded, and it stood fast." (See also *Ps.* 148:5, 42:15, et al.) Philo was especially struck by the fact that this temporal coincidence between the divine command and its effect was nowhere to be found in the culture of the Greeks: "At the moment that he speaks, God creates, and there is no gap in time between the two; alternatively one might say, if one wished to improve upon the truth of this opinion, that his Word was act [*logos ergon*]" (*On the Sacrifices of Abel and Cain* 18.65).

This moment in Christian doctrine led naturally to giving the Logos (which is also the divine Word) a part in the creation of the cosmos. Its role was that of an instrument *(organon)*, and Philo takes care to distinguish between the instrument and God himself, who is cause, or *aition* (*On the Cherubim* 35.127). This is the same instrumental causality, a subordinate form of causality, that early Christians normally attributed to the Logos. The idea was nearly always expressed by the preposition *dia* with the genitive, and one should translate it (or at least understand it as meaning) "by means of," starting from *John* 1:3: "All things were made by the Logos."

Philo does, however, take the instrumental role of the Logos in a fairly wide sense and makes room for what the Greek philosophical tradition called the "exemplary cause" (which was distinguished thereby from the idea of instrument; see Basil of Caesarea, *On the Holy Ghost* 3.5). An extract from the *Allegorical Interpretation* (3.31.96) makes clear how the Logos is at one and the same time instrument *(organon)* and model *(archētupos, paradeigma)*. [*See* Archetypes.] And Philo's analyses help us in turn to understand some later texts. Toward the year 177 Athenagoras, no different in this from other Christian writers of the time, writes that "God, by means of the Logos that comes from him, has called the universe into being, has set it in order, and keeps it beneath his governance" (*Legatio* 10). But a little later he adds, and indeed repeats, that "the Son of God is the Logos of the Father in idea and in act [*en ideai kai energeiai*]." These final words would be shrouded in mystery, did we not recall the dual role that Philo assigned to the Logos in creation since, for Philo, the Logos is at one and the same time the ideal model and the agent of creation. At this point, therefore, the influence of Greek philosophy makes itself felt again in the thought of Philo and no less in that of Athenagoras. Thus a pagan contemporary of Athenagoras, the Platonist Albinus, will write of a principle that he calls the first Intellect: "its activity [*energeia*] is itself idea [*idea*]" (*Didascalicos* 10).

In the loose and widespread Platonism with which Jewish and Christian ideas of the time were saturated, the impossibility of an adequate knowledge of God was stressed. In such an intellectual climate the Logos inevitably took on a second function, whereby it became a means of revealing the Father to us. This idea becomes so commonplace that I shall only allude to it. There is, however, one very early noncanonical Christian writer who gives the idea a novel twist. Ignatius of Antioch (d. 107) writes as follows (*Letter to the Magnesians* 8.2): "There is only one God, who makes himself known to us through Jesus Christ his Son, who is his Logos who comes forth from his silence [*logos apo sigēs proelthōn*]." Sigē (Silence) is a figure well known to us from the theogonies current in Simonian and Valentinian gnosticism, where one of the first Aeons—that is, one of the earliest emanations—is called by this name. Are we to conclude that Ignatius has drawn his inspiration on this point from the gnostic theory of divine emanations, as Marcellus of Ancyra later did (according to Eusebius, *Ecclesiastical Theology* 2.9.4)? The possibility cannot be ruled out. But it is more likely that Ignatius made use of this gripping expression to describe how, when the Logos comes forward to reveal the Father, he breaks the silence that God had kept for ages past.

Entrusted from on high with the creation of the cosmos and the revelation of the Father, the Logos is in some ways closer to humanity than is the Father. The Logos stands on the borderline *(methorios stas),* so to speak, between the Father and the human race, and so can play the part of a mediator. To God he offers the prayers and worship of mortal men, while to mortal men he gives the assurance of a divine help that will never fail them. That, at least, is how Philo shapes his ideas, sometimes applying these trains of thought deliberately and explicitly to the Logos (*On Dreams* 2.28.188–189; *On the Special Laws* 1.23.116). But the role of mediator finds its fullest scope only in Christianity, where the incarnate Logos draws together and makes of itself a center for human and divine nature and is thereby in the ideal position to facilitate the communication of one nature with the other. There are some famous passages in Augustine that one could quote as answering exactly to this point (*Confessions* 7.18.24; *City of God* 9.15–17). No less apposite, but less hackneyed, is the following quotation from Clement of Alexandria, where a flavor of baroque archaism results from his quoting Heraclitus: "Heraclitus was quite right to say: 'The gods are men, and men are gods. For the Logos is one and the same.' Light shines through this mystery: God is in man, and man is God, and the Mediator [*mesitēs*] fulfills the will of the Father; for the Mediator is the Logos, which is the same for man and for God, at one and the same time Son of God and savior of men, God's servant and our Teacher" (*Teacher* 1.2.1).

The Christian Logos. With the rise of Christianity, old words and ideas became charged with a new meaning, and new wine was poured into old skins, with all the risks attendant upon such an enterprise, as we have already seen in our study of the Stoic theory of the two *logoi.* Some Christian authors take up with confidence and determination the earlier pagan prehistory of this idea and see therein a providential pattern mirroring sacred history itself: "Those wh lived with the Logos are Christians, even if in their day they passed for atheists: among the Greeks, such are Socrates, Heraclitus, and their like; among the barbarians, Abraham, Ananias, Azarias, Misaél, Elijah, and many others." Such is the claim of Justin Martyr (*First Apology* 46.3), who revels in ferreting out from Greek philosophy and religion ideas that are compatible with the Christian Logos. He draws attention to Mercury, who was called the angelic word of God (22.2), and most of all to the world soul that Plato (*Timaeus* 36b) says is embedded in the universe in the shape of a cross or the Greek letter chi (X), a symbol for the cross of Christ (60.5–7).

This movement toward harmonizing pagan Greek and Christian beliefs, a movement that reflects a grandiose conception of the theology of history, did not keep early Christianity from becoming clearly aware of what, in its conception of the Logos, was most peculiarly its own. Thus the prologue to the *Gospel of John* shows a writer deeply aware of the historical background from which he has sprung (which included the Wisdom of Hellenistic Judaism and the Torah of Palestinian Judaism). But the prologue is also without peer in revealing the overriding importance given to the perfect coincidence between the preexisting Logos and the Jesus of history. Even so, in *John*, the personality of this Logos is taken as the known, and not spelled out, a point to which the early theologians will direct their efforts. Such, for example, is Justin's preoccupation when he writes against those (possibly Jews taking their lead from Philo) who believe that individuality of the Logos is no more distinct from that of the Father than light is distinct from the sun. In his *Dialogue with Trypho* (128.4, 129.3–4), Justin argues instead in favor of a distinction that is not merely nominal but a distinction of number. As proof, he takes his stand on the bringing forth of the Logos: for "what is brought forth is numerically distinct from him who brings forth; anyone must allow us that."

To be perfectly accurate, Justin does not write of the Logos as "numerically distinct," but as "other [*heteros*] in virtue of number." In writing thus, Justin hit upon a word full of pitfalls, a word that could suggest the existence of two gods as well as a debasement of the Logos in relation to the Father. It could even suggest both ideas at once, as seen in another sentence from the same *Dialogue*, a sentence truly staggering in its lack of theological foresight: "There is, as has been said, another [*heteros*] god and lord below the Creator of the universe . . . the Creator of the universe has no other [*allos*] god above him" (56.4). Perhaps Justin's pen has run away with him, forcing his ideas in a direction that he did not really intend. Others, whose thinking was really no different from his, will take much greater care in how they express themselves (e.g., Hippolytus, *Against Noëtus* 11). Origen himself will downgrade the Logos in calling it "second [*deuteros*] god" (*Against Celsus* 5.39, 6.61, etc.) or again in writing "god" *(theos)* without the article, whereas he calls the Father *ho theos*, "the God" (*Commentary of Saint John* 2.2.13–18).

The analyses quoted above may seem oddly archaic in the light of later theology, but they lose a good deal of this quality if we take account of two points. In the first place, the expressions employed by Justin and Origen can already be found in Philo, whose use of them naturally occasions much less surprise. Thus Philo had used the presence or absence of the article to distinguish the "true" God from the Logos god (*On Dreams* 1.39.229–230), and had marked out the Logos as being "the second god" (*Questions and Answers on Genesis* 2.62). Before Justin and Hippolytus, Philo sees in the Logos "another god" (ibid.). The second point to bear in mind is that the Platonist philosophers of the day also contribute to the movement toward giving the Logos only a diminished form of divinity. They refer regularly to a first principle or a first god, obviously implying the existence of a god of second rank. One such Platonist writer, Numenius (later than Philo but known to Origen), uses the term "second god" for the demiurge (fragments 11, 15, 16, 19). It is hard to avoid the conclusion that the Christian theologians of the second and third centuries, even theologians of the caliber of Origen, were simply prisoners of the *Zeitgeist* when they came to see the Logos as a god of second rank. They were as yet unequipped with the conceptual apparatus that their successors were going to need so as to share, without loss of identity, the divine nature between Persons Three.

[*For discussion of related phenomena in Hellenistic Judaism, in Christianity, and in Islam, see* Torah; Jesus; *and* Kalām.]

BIBLIOGRAPHY

Aeby, Gervais. *Les missions divines de saint Justin à Origène.* Fribourg, Switzerland, 1958.

Daniélou, Jean. *Gospel Message and Hellenistic Culture,* vol. 2 of *A History of Early Christian Doctrine before the Council of Nicea.* Translated by John A. Baker. London, 1973.

Harl, Marguerite. *Origène et la fonction révélatrice du verbe incarné.* Paris, 1958.

Hatch, Edwin. *The Influence of Greek Ideas on Christianity* (1888). Reprint, New York, 1957.

Holte, Ragnar. "Logos Spermatikos: Christianity and Ancient Philosophy according to St. Justin's Apologies." *Studia Theologica* 12 (1958): 109–168.

Kretschmar, Georg. *Studien zur frühchristlichen Trinitätstheologie.* Tübingen, 1956.

Kurtz, Ewald. *Interpretation zu den Logos-Fragmenten Heraklits.* Spudasmata, vol. 17. Hildesheim, 1971.

Lebreton, Jules. *Histoire du dogme de la Trinité des origines au Concile de Nicée,* vol. 1, *Les origines,* and vol. 2, *De Saint Clément à Saint Irénée.* 6th ed. Paris, 1927–1928. This is an essential work for the study of the Logos doctrine in early Christianity.

Lebreton, Jules. "La théologie de la Trinité chez Clément d'Alexandrie." *Recherches de science religieuse* 34 (1947): 55–76, 142–179.

Orbe, Antonio. *En los albores de la exegesis iohannea.* Analecta Gregoriana, vol. 65. Rome, 1955.

Orbe, Antonio. *Hacia la primera teología de la procesión del Verbo.* 2 vols. Analecta Gregoriana, vols. 99–100. Rome, 1958. The two works by Orbe are important for the study of the notion of *logos* in gnostic traditions.

Prestige, G. L. *God in Patristic Thought.* London, 1952.

Rendel, Harris J. "Athena, Sophia and the Logos." *Bulletin of the John Rylands Library* 7 (July 1922): 56–72.

Ringgren, Helmer. *Word and Wisdom: Studies in the Hypostatization of Divine Qualities and Functions in the Ancient Near East.* Lund, 1947.

Wolfson, Harry A. "The Trinity, the Logos, and the Platonic Ideas." In his *The Philosophy of the Church Fathers,* vol. 1. Cambridge, Mass., 1964.

JEAN PÉPIN
Translated from French by Denis O'Brien

LOISY, ALFRED (1857–1940), French scholar who held a dual role in the religious history of France: as a Roman Catholic biblical critic who employed the methods pioneered by German Protestant scholars and as the center of the conflict in Catholicism that would come to be known as the modernist controversy.

Alfred Firman Loisy was born in Ambrières (Marne) on 28 February 1857 and died on 1 June 1940 in Paris. While Loisy was a student in a rural seminary, he undertook the study of Hebrew as an antidote to the mediocrity of his theological education. His familiarity with the language gave him a taste for reading biblical texts for their original sense, a taste that developed into a lifelong preference for historical as opposed to theological approaches to biblical questions. In 1878 he was assigned to the fledgling Institut Catholique de Paris to complete his seminary education. There he attracted the attention of the church historian Louis Duchesne, who encouraged Loisy's interest in modern methods of historical research. There, too, he attended classes of Ernest Renan at the Collège de France; Renan embodied the conviction that it was not possible to be both a historian and a Catholic. Loisy's youthful ambition was to prove Renan wrong, to demonstrate in his own life and work that, as he put it, "the great march of history did not pass by Renan's door."

Nevertheless, Loisy's journals for these years indicate that he was deeply distressed by what seemed to be the unwillingness of the church to understand or explain its past in any but the most doctinaire theological categories. However troubled his private thoughts may have been, Loisy exhibited in his studies the clarity of mind, attention to detail, and remarkable discipline that would characterize all his later work. As a result, he was appointed instructor (1882) and then professor of New Testament (1890) at the Institut Catholique. In that position, Loisy began to expose his students to the requirements of a historical study of Christian origins. However, church authorities were wary of scientific studies that would alter or overturn traditional doctrines, and it was inevitable in this environment that a controversy would arise. Loisy soon found himself embroiled in an argument over the nature of biblical inspiration that led first to his demotion and finally to his dismissal.

Loisy's next appointment, to the chaplaincy of a convent school outside Paris, was probably intended to keep him out of higher education. However, unable to do technical research, Loisy began to think about the problem of modern religion in its wider bearings. He developed an entire program for teaching the Catholic faith in a way that would be consistent with the discoveries of modern historical research. When, in 1902, Adolph von Harnack's popular book on the essence of Christianity, *Das Wesen des Christentums* (English title, *What Is Christianity?*), appeared in French translation, Loisy saw an opportunity to demonstrate that Catholics could have the better of an argument with Protestant historians simply on historical grounds; one could show, for example, that Harnack's conclusions were wrong, not because they violated doctrine but because they rested on inadequate research and hasty conclusions. Loisy's book *L'évangile et l'église*, published that same year, created a sensation. However, what proved significant about the book was not so much the success of Loisy's argument with Harnack as his acknowledgment that history allowed for considerably fewer claims about Jesus' divinity and foreknowledge than Catholic theology had traditionally made. When Loisy confirmed this position in a companion volume *(Autour d'un petit livre)* the next year, the issue crystallized into a conflict between historians who would alter doctrine to suit their vision of history and theologians who would refuse historical fact to preserve doctrine. Loisy spent the next several months defending his position while trying to avoid condemnation by the church on whose behalf he understood himself to be speaking. By the end of 1903, he realized that the project to which he had given so much of his life was failing. When, in March 1904, Pius X's accusation that Loisy was not sincere in his wish to remain in the church was conveyed to him, "something inside came apart."

Loisy was excommunicated in 1907. Earlier that year, the encyclical *Providentissimus Deus* was issued by Pius X, describing and condemning "modernist" errors; prominent among them were the principles of biblical research drawn from Loisy's work.

During this controversy, Loisy had begun to teach courses at the Collège de France and to return to the kind of technical research he said he preferred. After his excommunication, he was appointed to the chair of history of religions, where he remained until his retirement in 1931. Loisy continued to publish a remarkable number of books until just before his death at the age of eighty-three. Besides his technical work on aspects of Christian origins, he continued his interest in the nature of religion and its place in the modern world. He understood these latter works as a kind of series that began with *L'évangile et l'église* in 1902 and concluded in 1937 with *La crise morale du temps présent et l'éducation humaine.*

BIBLIOGRAPHY

No full-scale work on Loisy yet exists in English, although several of his works have been translated. *The Gospel and the Church* (1903), Christopher Home's translation of *L'évangile et l'église,* has been reissued (Philadelphia, 1976) with a good introduction by Bernard Scott, and Loisy's autobiography, *Choses passées* (1913), translated by Richard W. Boynton with Loisy's approval and issued as *My Duel with the Vatican* (1924), is still available in a reprint edition (New York, 1968). Loisy's later three-volume *Mémoires pour servir à l'histoire religieuse de notre temps* (Paris, 1930–1931) has not been translated. His last major work on Christian origins, *La naissance du Christianisme* (1933), was translated by L. P. Jacks as *The Birth of the Christian Religion* (London, 1948) but is currently out of print.

RICHARD J. RESCH

LOKI figures prominently in Scandinavian mythology. His position in the Germanic pantheon is unique: while he associates closely with the gods, he is not fully integrated into their circle. He is a frequent companion of Þórr (Thor) on his forays into the land of giants, and he participates in triads with Óðinn (Odin) and Hœnir, but he is excluded from the festive activities and games of the Æsir. He engenders some of their worst enemies, such as the Fenrisúlfr (Fenriswolf), but he also brings forth Sleipnir, Óðinn's horse, and he helps the gods obtain some of their prized possessions, such as Þórr's hammer or Óðinn's spear. Ultimately, he is chased, captured, and submitted to a cruel fettering by the Æsir, from which he will be released only at the end of time, when he will lead the onslaught of the forces of Hel against the gods. He apparently does not play any role in cult and ritual, and no place-name or personal name is recorded that would attest to some worship or reverence paid to him.

As could be expected, an ambivalent figure such as Loki gives rise to very divergent interpretations. Jan de Vries (1933, p. 253) describes him as a trickster, a reading that fits his behavior in many myths in which he plays an ambiguous role, making mischief and ultimately saving those he betrayed. Georges Dumézil (1948, pp. 274–280) contrasts Loki with Hœnir as the incarnation of "impulsive intelligence" as opposed to "careful pondering"—a description that, however, hardly fits the personality of Hœnir, who never thinks by himself but always appears as someone else's mouthpiece (Polomé, "Some Comments on *Vǫluspá,* Stanzas 17–18," in *Old Norse Literature and Mythology,* Austin, 1969, pp. 271–273). Dumézil (1948, pp. 242–254) also compares Loki to the Nart Syrdon (responsible for the killing of the hero Soslan/Sosryko in the Ossetic legends) on account of the responsibility that Snorri Sturluson assigns to Loki for the murder of Baldr. Folke Ström (1956, p. 85) considers Loki as a hypostasis of Óðinn; Loki does indeed share a number of striking features with Alfǫðr, such as his giant parentage and his "double sex" (in *Lokasenna* 23–24, Óðinn and Loki reproach each other for "womanish ways"; cf. Lee M. Hollander, *The Poetic Edda,* 2d rev. ed., Austin, 1962, p. 95), but the "mischievous deceiver" character of Loki does not actually correspond to the sinister side of Óðinn's personality. Anne Birgitta Rooth, in *Loki in Scandinavian Mythology* (Lund, 1961), refers to the use of the word *locke* in Middle Swedish and some Scandinavian dialects to mean "spider" and therefore assigns an arachnoid origin to the deity, a hypothesis that receives only rather tenuous support in the myths about Loki. A major weakness of most of the proposed interpretations (see Turville-Petre, 1964, pp. 144–146) is that each focuses essentially on a single aspect of Loki's personality, assuming it is the basic feature from which all his other characteristic traits derive.

If one examines the dossier on Loki, it appears that his role in the *Poetic Edda* is quite minor compared with the prominent part he plays in Snorri Sturluson's mythical narratives. Leaving aside the *Lokasenna,* only limited information is imparted about Loki in the lays of the *Edda.* He is the son of a giantess called Laufey (see *Hymiskviða* 18). His offspring include the ominous Fenrisúlfr and Miðgarðsormr, the huge serpent that encompasses our world—both resulting from his intercourse with the giantess Angrboða (see *Vǫluspá hin skamma* 13), while he himself brought forth Óðinn's eight-legged steed, Sleipnir, begotten by Svaðilfari, the stallion of the giant master builder of Ásgarðr. Furthermore, a whole race of trolls (ON, *flagð*) is assumed to have sprung from Loki when he became "pregnant" by eating the half-burned heart of a witch (*Vǫluspá hin skamma* 14; *Hyndluljóð* 41).

The *Poetic Edda* also indicates that Loki has a brother called Býleistr (*Hyndluljóð* 40) or Býleiptr (*Vǫluspá* 51), whose name has been associated with sudden gale and thunderstorm (ON, *bylr*). His wife, Sigyn, is a model of loving devotion: when Loki lies fettered with the intestines of his own sons, tortured by the dripping of the poison snake Skaði hung over his face, she patiently sits by him, holding up a bowl to collect the venom before it hurts her beloved spouse (see the prose colophon of the *Lokasenna*).

Loki also goes by the names of Loptr (*Hyndluljóð* 41) and Hveðrungr (*Vǫluspá* 55)—terms that have been related respectively with the Old Norse terms *lopt* ("air") and *hviða* ("gust"), implying that Loki was originally an atmospheric god, which is a rather unwarranted assumption (see Jan de Vries, *Altnordisches etymologisches Wörterbuch,* Leiden, 1961, p. 366).

From a mythological point of view, the role of Loki in the lays of the *Poetic Edda* is limited to three major themes. First, Loki helps Þórr recover his hammer in the *Þrymskviða,* waiting faithfully upon him and cunningly helping him out when the giant starts wondering about the strange behavior of his bride-to-be. Second, in *Hymiskviða* 37 Loki is made responsible for the mutilation of one of Þórr's goats—an action that Snorri Sturluson (*Gylfaginning* 44) ascribes to Þjalfi. Finally, *Reginsmál* 1–5 narrates the story of Loki's capture of the dwarf Andvari and of the ransom in gold Loki exacted from him, including the cursed ring that will play such a prominent role in the saga of the Niflungar (Ger., Nibelungen; see Snorri Sturluson, *Skáldskaparmál* 6.110–117). Whatever Loki does in this context, he accomplishes faithfully at the behest of the gods, to whom he surrenders everything he receives from Andvari. He even honestly warns Hreiðmarr (to whom the gods give the gold as *wergild* for the killing of his son Otr) that there is a curse on this gold that "will work the bane of you both" (i.e., Hreiðmarr and his son Fáfnir; *Reginsmál* 6).

In the lay of Fjǫlsviðr (a late text that many do not consider as part of the original *Poetic Edda*), Loki is said to have forged a sword called Lævateinn (a correction for [MS] Hęvateinn; Gering, *Kommentar zu den Liedern der Edda*, vol. 1, 1927, p. 416), literally "wand of destruction" (st. 26).

It is obvious that none of these passages emphasizes Loki's later prominently devilish nature: his association with the forces of destruction in the *Poetic Edda* postdates his humiliation at Ægir's banquet and the atrocious punishment for his outrageous behavior after he crashes the festive reunion of the gods. After his release from bondage, he avenges himself by taking the lead in the assault against the stronghold of his torturers (*Vǫluspá* 51). The *Lokasenna*, then, appears as the key to his interpretation in the context of the *Poetic Edda*, but this poem may very well be a late medieval satirical description of the divine world in the tradition of the *Assembly of the Gods* of Lucian of Samosata (Franz Rolf Schröder, "Das Symposium der Lokasenna," *Arkiv för nordisk filologi* 67, 1952, pp. 1–29). It appears to have been written about 1200, and notwithstanding the similarity of Loki as a malicious sower of dissension to the Irish figure of Bricriu of the Poison Tongue in the Ulster cycle (Turville-Petre, 1964, p. 145), Loki's destructive and irreverent sarcasm is hardly imaginable in a period when most of the gods he mocks were still the object of deep veneration and respectful devotion, as Jan de Vries rightly points out (1967). Thus, the *Lokasenna* presumably must be regarded as a document informing us of the way Loki was perceived at the beginning of the thirteenth century. In this regard, it is very instructive because it tells us explicitly about his blood-brotherhood with Óðinn, which no other source reports (st. 9; Gering, op. cit., p. 281). It also states that Loki was Óðinn's adopted son (ON, *óskmǫgr*, st. 16; Gering, op. cit., p. 284), emphasizes Loki's sexual inversion (st. 23; cf. Turville-Petre, 1964, p. 131), and implies that, at the time of its composition, Loki was already considered to be *ráðbani Baldrs* ("contriver of Baldr's death"), because he claims responsibility (st. 28) for Baldr's no longer riding to Frigg's hall. He also brags about his sexual bout with Skaði after his participation in the killing of her father, Þjazi (st. 50–52), and about his adulterous relations with Þórr's wife (st. 54). These references, together with the allusions to Þórr's encounter with the giant Skrymir while on his way to the realm of Útgarðaloki (ss. 60, 62), parallel passages in Snorri Sturluson's narratives about Loki.

The role that Snorri Sturluson assigns to Loki in the killing of Baldr represents a tradition different from the older part of the *Poetic Edda* and from the story related by Saxo Grammaticus about the rivalry of Balderus and Hotherus over Nanna (see Polomé, "The Indo-European Component in Germanic Religion," in *Myth and Law among the Indo-Europeans*, ed. Jaan Puhvel, 1970, pp. 63–81). Apart from this role, however, Loki's personality can be further illustrated by three myths narrated by Snorri Sturluson.

The story of Iðunn's capture and release (*Skáldskaparmál* 1) illustrates how Loki is ready to betray the gods—whatever the consequences—to save his own skin (as he did earlier when he promised to deliver Þórr unarmed to Geirroðr) yet is also able to restore the situation once his scheme is found out. He may create problems, but ultimately, if need be, he will find a way all his own to save the day.

In the myth of the master builder of Ásgarðr (*Gylfaginning* 42), Loki's decisive action clearly saves the world of the Æsir from major catastrophe, when the surrender of the sun and the moon would have plunged it into permanent darkness and sterile desolation. A further boon from his metamorphosis is the birth of Sleipnir.

In the story of Sif's hair and the gifts for the gods (*Skáldskaparmál* 5), Loki's perverse trickery again turns ultimately to the advantage of the gods. This interesting tale shows Loki caught at his own game and receiving a well-deserved punishment. Its rather unexpected conclusion indicates that the core of the story must be old; indeed, the Roman historian Florus (early second century CE) relates that the Cherusci inflicted the same treatment upon the Roman soldiers captured after the defeat of Varus's legions (9 CE), after cutting out their tongues "so that the snakes should stop hissing for ever" (de Vries, 1957, p. 258). Another archaic feature in the story is the repartition of the gifts, which follows a characteristic Dumézilian tripartite pattern. Apparently we are dealing here with an Indo-European motif, one for which Dumézil has provided Scythian and Celtic parallels (*Jupiter, Mars, Quirinus,* Paris, 1941, pp. 220–234; *Romans de Scythie et d'alentour,* Paris, 1978, pp. 172–178). The detail of the narrative, however, is presumably due to Snorri's creative imagination.

Summing up, one cannot escape the conclusion that Loki was originally a secondary figure in Germanic mythology whose role expanded considerably during a later period, perhaps because his unscrupulous craftiness made him appear a demonic being largely responsible for the demise of the heroic world of the Æsir. Such a development could have taken place around the time of the conversion to Christianity; this dating would then account for Loki's place in the writings of Snorri Sturluson and his demeaning behavior and slanderous utterances in the *Lokasenna.*

BIBLIOGRAPHY

Dumézil, Georges. *Loki.* Paris, 1948.

Dumézil, Georges. *Gods of the Ancient Northmen.* Edited and translated by Einar Haugen. Berkeley, 1973.

Polomé, Edgar C. "The Indo-European Heritage in Germanic Religion: The Sovereign Gods." In *Athlon: Satura Grammatica in honorem Francisci R. Adrados,* edited by A. Bernabé et al., vol. 1, pp. 401–411. Madrid, 1984.

Rooth, Anna Birgitta. *Loki in Scandinavian Mythology.* Lund, 1961.

Ström, Folke. *Loki: Ein mythologisches Problem.* Göteborg, 1956.

Turville-Petre, E. O. G. *Myth and Religion of the North: The Religion of Ancient Scandinavia.* New York, 1964.

Vries, Jan de. *The Problem of Loki.* Helsinki, 1933.

Vries, Jan de. *Altgermanische Religionsgeschichte,* vol. 2. 2d rev. ed. Berlin, 1957.

EDGAR C. POLOMÉ

LOMBARD, PETER. *See* Peter Lombard.

LONERGAN, BERNARD (1904–1984), Roman Catholic philosopher-theologian and methodologist. Bernard Joseph Francis Lonergan was born on 17 December 1904 at Buckingham, Quebec, not far from Ottawa. Of Irish-English stock, he was the eldest of three sons. His early education took place in the local schools and at Loyola College in Montreal. In 1922 he joined the Jesuits and followed their regular course of study: Greek and Latin classics at Guelph, Ontario, philosophy at Heythrop College in England (with an external bachelor of arts degree from the University of London in 1930), and theology at the Gregorian University in Rome, where he was ordained priest in 1936 and completed his doctoral work in 1940. He taught theology for twenty-five years, thirteen in the Jesuit seminaries at Montreal and Toronto and twelve at the Gregorian University. In 1965 major surgery for lung cancer forced his partial retirement, but he continued writing, first for a decade as research professor at Regis College in Toronto (with a year's leave as Stillman professor at Harvard University, 1971–1972) and then as visiting distinguished professor at Boston College from 1975 to 1983. On taking full retirement in 1983 he returned to his native Canada, where he died at the Jesuit Infirmary in Pickering, Ontario, on 26 November 1984.

Lonergan's first major works were studies of Thomas Aquinas generously laced with references to Aristotle: *Grace and Freedom* (his doctoral dissertation) and *Verbum: Word and Idea in Aquinas.* The latter was a revolutionary study in Thomist cognitional theory and a springboard to the independent *Insight: A Study of Human Understanding* (published in 1957, but completed in 1953), a monumental work that went far beyond Thomas into twentieth-century science, psychology, and social and political theory. Lonergan's second major work, *Method in Theology* (1972), incorporated hermeneutics and history and added personal notions of dialectic and foundations to provide not a theology but an integral framework in which creative theology could be done.

Meanwhile Lonergan was producing theological instruction of considerable importance (though it needs redoing in the light of his own method) for his Latin-language courses, writing articles and reviews, and giving occasional lectures. Toward the end of his life he went back to an early interest in economics and the dialectic of history and had almost completed a work that may turn out to be as revolutionary in those two fields as *Insight* had been in philosophy and *Method* had been in theology.

Although his early focus on questions proper to Roman Catholic theology left religion in general in the margin, Lonergan's relentless drive toward a comprehensive view of things, and his special methodological interest in foundations of thought and conduct, led him eventually to reflection on religion too. His views on this topic are set forth succinctly in chapter four of *Method,* but that account can be enlarged from other writings and set in the context of his general concerns.

Lonergan comes to the question from the two directions of philosophy and theology. First, a thoroughgoing philosophy will raise the question of God's existence and nature. The question is the key step, and Lonergan raises it in his own characteristic way: through inquiry into the possibility of fruitful inquiry, through reflecting on the nature of reflection, and through deliberating on the worthwhileness of deliberation. With the question raised and answered affirmatively, thought may take different routes to arrive at complementary aspects of religion. One route starts with the problem of evil, to work out the anticipated general lines of the solution that a wise, good, and powerful God may be expected to provide: in effect religion as pertaining to the objective order of the universe; this was the approach of chapter twenty of *Insight*. The second is the route of religious experience taken in chapter four of *Method* (though the problem of evil still provides an introduction to the question, p. 288); personal fulfillment is achieved in self-transcendence, love is the crown of self-transcendence, and love of God is the primary religious experience: in effect, religion as a differentiation of human consciousness.

The theological approach starts from the Roman Catholic doctrine that God wills the salvation of the whole human race and so offers everyone the divine transforming grace needed for salvation. On this basis Lonergan proceeds to the love of God flooding our hearts through the Holy Spirit given to us and links this as inner word to the outer word of tradition deriving from the Son. Thus he arrives at a concretely identifiable charismatic and institutional religion to which philosophical inquiry had pointed in a general way.

There remains the question of dialogue, in particular between Christianity and the world religions. Lonergan's starting point is not the institutional church as evangelizing the nations (outer word, Son of God, Christianity), but religious experience (inner word, Holy Spirit, a community enjoying God's love). He does not impose his theological *a priori* on students of religion but leaves it to them to decide whether his model of religious experience is verified in the data, though he finds support in their writings (*Method*, pp. 108–109). Again, the gift from God that he affirms is fundamentally a reality—experienced, but not thematized. It must be thematized and given expression in a process that has its difficulties for the Christian as well as for others (*Method*, p. 290). Further, each religion will have its own categories of expression, so there is then the problem of a common language and communication. He recognizes that his own language (God's love flooding our hearts) is Christian (*Method*, p. 240), but he hopes that the core reality as reality will be a base for cross-cultural discussion (*Method*, pp. 11, 284). That is, the orientation to the otherworldly, the conversion to the transcendent, the being seized by the mystery of love and awe, the fateful call to a dreaded holiness—whatever the language, and all these phrases are culturally conditioned—all this as a reality would bring people together in discussion. But then the first and fundamental need is for self-appropriation (the great thrust of *Insight*), and the further, more specific need is for studies of religious interiority (*Method*, p. 290).

BIBLIOGRAPHY

In addition to the works mentioned above, Lonergan's views on religion can be found in various chapters of *Collection* (New York, 1967), *A Second Collection* (Philadelphia, 1974), *A Third Collection* (New York, 1985), and in *Philosophy of God, and Theology* (Philadelphia, 1973).

The difficulty of drawing up a bibliography of secondary literature stems from the fundamental nature of Lonergan's ideas, which involve study of basic generalities before specific application can be made, and allow ramification into many seemingly disparate areas. But two dissertations can be mentioned: Vernon J. Gregson, Jr.'s "Bernard Lonergan and the Dialogue of Religions: A Foundational Study of Religion as Spirituality" (Ph.D. diss., Marquette University, 1978), somewhat rewritten and published as *Lonergan, Spirituality, and the Meeting of Religions* (Lanham, N. Y., 1985), and Emil J. Piscitelli's "Language and Method in the Philosophy of Religion: A Critical Study of the Development of the Philosophy of Bernard Lonergan" (Ph.D. diss., Georgetown University, 1977). The foundational aspect of Lonergan's work, especially in relation to Jungian psychology, is studied in two works of Robert Doran: *Psychic Conversion and Theological Foundations: Toward a Reorientation of the Human Sciences* (Chico, Calif., 1981) and *Subject and Psyche: Ricoeur, Jung, and the Search for Foundations* (Washington, D.C., 1977). Considerable interest is emerging in the relation of Lonergan's work to mystical theology; see, for example, Harvey D. Egan's *What Are They Saying about Mysticism?* (New York, 1982) and William Johnston's *The Inner Eye of Love: Mysticism and Religion* (San Francisco, 1978). The relation of Lonergan's trinitarian theology to world religions is studied in my own *Son of God, Holy Spirit, and World Religions: Bernard Lonergan's Contribution to the Wider Ecumenism* (Toronto, 1984). A new and important field of application is that of popular religions (Philippines, Africa), but the literature is scattered; for this material and for Lonergan's unpublished works, the Lonergan Research Institute, Toronto, can be consulted.

FREDERICK E. CROWE, S.J.

LÖNNROT, ELIAS (1802–1884), Finnish folklorist and philologist, the compiler of the *Kalevala*, the Finnish national epic. Lönnrot was born in the parish of Sammatti, province of Uusimaa, Finland, as a son of a tailor. In a childhood full of poverty, his schooling was difficult and often interrupted. In 1822 he became a student at the University of Turku, where he supported himself as a private tutor. He received his M.A. degree at Turku in 1827 with his thesis "On Väinämöinen, a Divinity of the Ancient Finns." After the university was destroyed in the fire of Turku, Lönnrot undertook a folklore collecting trip across Finland as far as Finnish Karelia. Part of the material he collected was published under the title *Kantele* (The Harp, 1829–1831).

In 1828, Lönnrot resumed his studies, this time in medicine at Helsinki University. There he came into close contact with a number of young literati who were filled with the national spirit. In 1831, the Finnish Literature Society was founded to further the development of Finnish culture and to collect and study folklore. Lönnrot became its first secretary. This society financed Lönnrot's numerous folklore collection trips. After defending his thesis, "The Magical Medicine of the Finns," he received the M.D. degree in 1832 and was assigned as the district physician in Kajaani, northern Finland.

Lönnrot then got the idea of combining the folk songs of Finland into bigger units. Thus came about the cycles of songs about the major Finnish heroes that constitute the first stage of the Finnish epic. A journey during which he met the greatest folk singers of Karelia yielded a rich harvest that was incorporated into the first version of the *Kalevala,* the so-called *Old Kalevala* (1835–1836), which consisted of thirty-six songs comprising 12,078 lines. From extensive additional folk song material, recorded partly by Lönnrot himself but mostly by others in eastern Karelia and eastern Finland, Lönnrot prepared a greatly expanded and changed version of the *Kalevala.* Published in 1849, it has 22,795 lines and is divided into fifty songs. It is this so-called *New Kalevala* that is considered the Finnish epic.

In the 1830s, Lönnrot published a few popular books on food substitutes and health care and edited some journals. He compiled a large collection of lyrical songs and ballads, entitled *Kanteletar* (The Spirit of the Harp; 1840–1841), which was followed by books of proverbs (1842) and riddles (1844). In 1844 he was granted a leave for five years for the preparation of a comprehensive Finnish-Swedish dictionary.

After defending his inaugural thesis on the Vepse language, Lönnrot was named professor of the Finnish language and literature at Helsinki University in 1853. In this capacity, he had greater significance as a practical linguist than a theoretical scholar. He retired in 1862 and settled down in his native parish of Sammatti, to continue his work. He revised Finnish hymns, completed the Finnish-Swedish dictionary (1866–1880), and published a collection of Finnish charms (1880). His last years were spent in conducting religious services in his community, treating people without charge, and participating actively in numerous charitable enterprises.

The *Kalevala* is not only Lönnrot's greatest accomplishment; it is the most important work in Finnish literature. It is, in its entirety, Lönnrot's compilation, based on the best and most complete variants of about thirty folk songs. Lönnrot made certain changes and modifications in them, adding verses from other variants and even from other songs, increasing the parallelism, and creating linking verses. He had a tendency to reduce the Christian and legendary features while strengthening the heathen and the historical-realistic elements. The songs are, however, not copies of reality, but instead they convey a fictional picture of the ancient Finns' way of life. While the *Kalevala* itself cannot be used as material for folklore study, its heroes and problems have strongly stimulated research into Finnish folklore and mythology.

The *Kalevala* has been called a shamanistic epic, since its great deeds are accomplished by magical means—by the power of words and incantations. All the heroes of the Kaleva group—Väinämöinen, Ilmarinen, and Lemminkäinen—are mythic and/or shamanistic figures and, as a group, are opposed to the people of the North, headed by the witch Louhi. The plot, created by Lönnrot, centers on fights over the possession of a fertility-promoting object, the Sampo, and competition for the Maiden of the North.

The *Kalevala,* according to Martti Haavio, was not only "the symbol of Finnish nationalism, but it was actually its crown symbol." The *Kalevala* gave faith and confidence to the people living under Russian rule. It influenced the development of the Finnish language, literature, and arts, and it played a substantial role in the adoption of Finnish as the language of the country.

BIBLIOGRAPHY

Anttila, Aarne. *Elias Lönnrot: Elämä ja toiminta.* 2 vols. Helsinki, 1931–1935. A detailed and very broad survey of Lönnrot's life and work, presented against the background of his time. An excellent work.

Anttila, Aarne. *Elias Lönnrot.* 2d ed. Helsinki, 1962. An abbreviated version of the preceding work.

Fromm, Hans. "Elias Lönnrot als Schöpfer des finnischen Epos Kalevala." In *Volksepen der uralischen und altaischen Völker,* edited by Wolfgang Veenker, pp. 1–12. Wiesbaden, 1968. A survey of Lönnrot's work on the compilation of *Kalevala.*

Haavio, Martti. "Elias Lönnrot." In *Leading Folklorists of the North,* edited by Dag Strömbäck, pp. 1–10. Oslo, 1971. A splendid essay about Lönnrot.

Honko, Lauri."The *Kalevala* and Myths." *Nordisk Institut for Folkedigtning Newsletter* (Turku, Finland) 12 (1984): 1–11. Turku, 1985. Discusses the interpretations of the *Kalevala* and the authenticity of the epic.

Magoun, Francis P., Jr. "Materials for the Study of the *Kalevala.*" In *The Kalevala, or Poems of the Kaleva District,* compiled by Elias Lönnrot; prose translation with foreword and appendixes by Francis Magoun, Jr., pp. 341–361. Cambridge, Mass., 1963. A concise biography of Lönnrot and discussion of his work on the *Kalevala.*

FELIX J. OINAS

LORD OF THE ANIMALS. The concept of a special type of deity or spirit that reigns over the animal kingdom is common among many Old and New World peoples. The universality of this conception suggests that formerly some form of cultural contact existed that bridged the continents. As a fundamental element in the life of the human as hunter, a lord of the animals is a familiar figure among hunting cultures, but he also occurs, in modified forms, in many agrarian and pastoral societies. In the latter instance the concept is often associated with a spiritual herdsman of wild game, a spirit analogue to human domesticators of animals. But the idea of an animal lord or spirit can be traced even farther back than the development of herding—indeed, as concrete evidence shows, into the Old Stone Age.

The lord of the animals often appears as a lord of the forest, mountain, or sea—natural areas that may possibly have been inhabited by individual spiritual sovereigns that eventually blended together to form a lord of animals. For many cultures, the forest (or tree), the mountain, and the cave are the preferred residence of the animal lord, though for hunters of sea mammals and fish, the sea floor and the deep sea are conceived as his abode. Occasionally the lord is associated with the sun, the moon, a star, or a constellation.

The lord of the animals is often a helper of mankind. He guides the animals to the hunter or helps him discover the trail of his prey. In addition, he often provides a magical weapon or a mystical spell that assures success in finding game. Such assistance, however, often assumes that certain conditions are fulfilled or specific regulations observed: the lord of the animals punishes the malicious, those who wantonly kill more game than is needed and those who are disrespectful of the dead game, especially in handling the bones, which must be meticulously saved, for from the bones, the same type of animal will be re-created (with or without the intervention of the lord of the animals). [*See* Bones.] It is most often assumed that the soul of the dead animal returns to its spiritual master, from whom it will receive another body. Frequently, the lord of the animals is held to be the creator of the game and is therefore often named "Father" or "Mother." At the very least, he gives the animals their names or other distinguishing features. In cases of misbehavior on the part of the hunter, the animal lord either retains the game (which is often believed to reside with him) or strikes the guilty hunter down with sickness, or punishes him by withdrawing his luck in the hunt. To win his favor, the lord of the animals must be called upon before the hunt with a plea to release some of the game, and afterwards must be given thanks. Frequently a small offering is also made before the expedition, some tobacco for example, while after the hunt a portion of the game might be left behind as an offering.

Precise physical descriptions of the lord of the animals vary considerably from culture to culture. He may appear in anthropomorphic as well as zoomorphic form, as a mixture of these or as some other fabulous creature, or as a giant or dwarf. In the majority of instances the lord of the animals is masculine, but we often find a feminine conceptualization and in some instances a bisexual character. [*See* Lady of the Animals.] When envisioned in zoomorphic form, the lord of the animals often combines various parts or markings of different types of animals, thereby emphasizing and enhancing his authority over all game.

In addition to belief in a lord of all animals, a corresponding or supplementary belief may exist in an individual master or lord of each separate kind of animal. Such a being is classified ethnologically as a "species spirit." This spirit, when envisioned theriomorphically, may also represent another animal type besides its own—a relationship that is often alleged to exist naturally. Many scholars maintain that the belief in species spirits is a more recent manifestation of older, more general conceptions of the lord of the animals.

When the lord of the animals is associated with an individual representative of a specific kind of animal, a different situation develops. Such instances occur among hunting groups when a defined game animal plays a predominant role in tribal subsistence patterns. Frequently, the lord of the animals must be propitiated when a member of that particular species is killed. This expression of the idea of an animal lord can be accepted as a more ancient form, especially when it appears concurrently with the conceptualization of this deity as a prototypical or exaggerated version of that animal species. In such cases the spirit is often envisioned as an exceptionally large, and therefore supernatural, member of the species in question. Sometimes he is conceived in human form riding the animal with which he is particularly associated. In general, scholars hold the theriomorphic version of the lord of the animals to be older, in cultural-historical terms, than the anthropomorphic form. In this respect, frequent observation of ceremonies performed for the ritual handling of slain large game (bear, lion, elephant, etc.), and even prehistoric testimony about such ceremonies, have proved to be of great importance. The reverence shown to large game is closely associated with the original form of the lord of the animals and deserves further study.

A distinctive characteristic of the animal lord is the fact that, despite his role as protector of wild game, he makes certain concessions when considering the needs of the hunter. To the extent that this is true, the animal lord functions as a god of the hunt, which in some cases is the predominant role. This aspect has caused many researchers to seek his origin outside a purely zoological sphere. The question remains open, however, whether or not this hunting-god aspect is connected with the anthropomorphic aspect of the lord of the animals. An ethno-religious order can be arranged as follows. In many cases, particularly among hunting peoples, past as well as present, the lord of the animals is clearly a real god, distinctively named and sovereign over his realm. In other cases, however, he is merely a game spirit, who is named solely by his association with a particular animal species. Such a game spirit is sometimes outwitted because of his awkwardness and may be characterized by unpredictability, arbitrariness, and tomfoolery (i.e., he is a trickster); in many conceptions he has the ability to transform himself into many forms and thereby confuse the hunter. [*See* Tricksters.] In still other cases, the lord of the animals may have shrunk to a mere mythological or legendary figure disengaged from the immediate life of the society.

The distinctions between these different categories are, of course, not rigid. The relationship between the lord of the animals and other supernatural beings varies also. He may be incorporated within the character of a tribal father or of the supreme being that creates life and provides subsistence. Many ethnologists of the Vienna school, following Wilhelm Schmidt, viewed the lord of the animals as an offshoot of the supreme being. This theory contradicts an understanding of the lord of the animals as an older, independent god who served as a fundamental element in the construction of the idea of a supreme being. In the opinion of the notable historian of religions, Raffaele Pettazzoni, the supreme being himself was the lord of the animals. [*See* Supreme Beings.]

The primary areas of diffusion for the concept and veneration of a lord of the animals include northern Eurasia, ancient Europe, and Africa, as well as the regions occupied by the indigenous inhabitants of the Americas, from the extreme north to the southernmost tip. Such beliefs are also found elsewhere, but only occasionally.

It is in ancient Greece that one encounters the most familiar animal deity, Artemis, whose double role as goddess of the hunt and mistress of the animals was never fully understood. [*See* Artemis.] In Homer's *Iliad* and other sources from antiquity, she is described in an obviously preexisting formula as *potnia thērōn*, or "mistress of the wild animals." Although she cares for the animals as a mother does her children, she also hunts them with bow and arrow. The deer is her devoted companion, consistently appearing beside her in works of art, and she is sometimes referred to as the "deer huntress" in the Homeric Hymns. She is also mistress over the entire wild animal kingdom, which includes not only land animals but the birds in the sky and fish in the waters.

Artemis herself is depicted as wild and uncanny and is sometimes pictured with a Gorgon's head. The rituals by which she was venerated also took on an archaic character. Reverence was displayed by the hunter's hanging the skin of the animal, including the antlers, on a tree or special pole. Besides the deer, Artemis had other favorite animals, including the lion and, especially, the bear, which has led some researchers to the opinion that, although this was not understood by the Greeks, she originally appeared as a female bear. In keeping with this interpretation, Artemis has been associated with the lord of the animals in the northern hemisphere, where bear rituals were an essential religious element. Even among the ancient Greeks, Artemis was the central figure at the bear feast, and her tradition can be traced to a Cretan or Minoan goddess of animals. Diana was her counterpart among the Roman goddesses. During the period in which the Romans occupied Gaul, the goddess who was interpreted as the indigenous parallel to Diana was known as Artio (from the Celtic *artos*, "bear"; *arta* "female bear"). This information comes down to us in the form of a bronze votive offering with a Latin inscription found in Muri (near Bern, Switzerland), an area occupied by the Helvetii. It depicts a sitting female who is being approached by a bear that has come out of a tree. The veneration displayed in Gaulish ceremonials to the slain bear as a lord of the animals closely resemble the rites dedicated to this animal over an extensive area. According to A. Irving Hallowell (1926), bear ceremonials are widespread among peoples of northern Eurasia, from the Finns, Saami (Lapps), and Mansi (Voguls) in the west, eastward through Siberia to the Yakuts and the Tunguz, further east to the Paleosiberian Nivkhi (Giliaks), the Chuckchi and the Ainu, and across the Bering Sea to the northern regions of North America. Although it cannot be generalized, the most suggestive interpretation of the intent of such ceremonies is that of the Japanese ethnologist Kyosuke Kindaichi concerning the bear feast of the Ainu. Kindaichi suggests that the bear itself is god. All animals are deities that live in human form in another world. [*See also* Animals.] When these deities occasionally come to this world, they appear in the form of animals. The bear is the highest of these gods. Any animal that is not captured, killed, and eaten by the Ainu has the unfortunate fate of wandering aimlessly throughout the world. The killing of an animal is therefore a sacred act, since the god himself has come into their midst. And with his coming he brings presents to mankind: his meat and fur. This divine animal, however, is satisfied, since it will now be able to return to its eternal home ("The Concepts behind the Ainu Bear Festival," *Southwest Journal of Anthropology* 5, 1949).

To ascertain the antiquity of such bear cults, we must return to Europe. [*See* Bears.] Caves in Switzerland, southern Germany, France, Silesia, Hungary, and Yugoslavia, dating from the middle to early Stone Age, have revealed small man-made stone chambers containing the skulls, teeth, and long bones of bears, arranged in orderly fashion. In addition to these bear burial sites, however, particularly important evidence of a bear cult dating from the early Paleolithic period has been obtained from a cave near Montespan in Haute-Garonne, France. In a vault at the end of a tunnel, a clump of molded clay was found that obviously represented a bear. Although headless, the animal figure was distinguishable by its legs and high, rounded withers. In the flat surface at the top of the figure, a hole was bored, apparently to support a forward-projecting pole. Instead of a clay head, which was sought in vain, a bear skull was discovered between the front legs. This led to the conclusion that the figure was a base constructed to support the head and skin of the animal on ceremonial occasions.

This conclusion found substantial support in a similar animal figure reported among the Mande in the western Sudan. A slain lion or leopard, either of which is equivalent to the bear in Europe, was skinned with the head attached. This skin was then laid over a headless clay figure of the animal. Such a figure was placed within a circular hedge of thornbushes especially constructed for ceremonial purposes. The existence of a Eurafrican hunting culture has become an accepted doctrine among many ethnologists, most notably Hermann Baumann (1938). This example, along with many others, fits quite appropriately into a scheme of unifying factors that suggest connections between the two continents.

The conceptual figure of a lord of the animals, appearing among less advanced hunting cultures like the San and the Pygmies in Africa, remains to this day a functional belief; one example should suffice. The creator god Khmwum is the supreme being among the Pygmies of Gabon. He lives in heaven and appears to humans as a rainbow in the eastern sky when he sees that they need his help. A singer raises his bow in the direction of this heavenly "bow" and intones: "Most powerful bow of the hunters that follows a herd of clouds that are like startled elephants, rainbow, give him [Khmwum] our thanks" (R. P. Trilles, *Les pygmées de la forêt équatorial,* Paris, 1931, p. 78). In this way the supreme deity is identified with the lord of the animals. Khmwum also manifests himself to humans in dreams, appearing as a huge elephant who reports the location of an abundance of game. This gigantic elephant is called Gor, and he towers over the tallest tree in the forest. Blue in color, he supports the sky on his shoulders, and since he is immortal, no one can kill him. Gor is the chief of all elephants; he is responsible for giving them life and preserves them from the threat of extinction. He directs the elephants to those paths that the hunters take care to follow. A slain bull elephant is decorated with a bright blue liana, and the chief of the Pygmies dances on the carcass and sings to "father elephant." This song is a solemn incantation in which the chief expresses the conviction that the elephant should not be outraged at being killed but pleased that he is going to the land of the spirits; he also says that the spear that erroneously took the elephant's life was misguided. Such excuses are made to the hunted animal out of fear of revenge and a guilty conscience at having killed the animal; this is a widespread phenomenon, typical of a hunting mentality.

In northern Eurasia we encounter the concept of a lord of the animals who either is anthropomorphic or has affinities with predominant animals other than the bear. Although such a concept occurs among numerous peoples in Eurasia, specific examples need not be mentioned here.

In the New World there exists, among the central and eastern Inuit (Eskimo), an extraordinary deity named Sedna, who is known as the goddess of the sea animals. [*See* Sedna.] She is an old woman who lives on the ocean floor and sends sea animals to the world above as long as humans do not aggravate her. If she does become angry, however, the shaman must venture on a dangerous journey to visit her below. Such an undertaking is made to pacify her so that she will release the animals once again. To accomplish this, the shaman must comb Sedna's hair, which has become soiled by humans—particularly women—whose violation of taboos causes her anger. Through combing, the shaman cleanses her hair of dirt and parasites, an act that Sedna herself cannot perform, since she has no fingers. According to the mythology, Sedna lost her fingers as a young girl because of an undesirable suitor, the storm bird. He appeared as a human and followed Sedna and her father, who fled in a kayak across the water. In his fear Sedna's father threw her into the water, but she held on tightly to the side of the boat. Her father then cut off all her fingers, and as they fell into the water they turned into seals and walruses. Sedna in turn sank to the ocean floor, where she took up her abode and became the mother of sea animals. The souls of these sea animals reside with her for a short period after their deaths; then, when the time has come, she restores them to life once again.

Among the Inuit of western Alaska, a male moon spirit replaces Sedna as lord of the animals. When the shaman is called upon to represent the moon spirit, he wears a mask encircled by miniature figures of reindeer, seals, and salmon, which symbolically depict authority over the animals when the spirit is implored.

The lord of the animals plays an important role among many North American Indians, as for example the Algonquin tribes of the eastern woodlands. According to the Delaware, Misinghalikun ("living solid face"), the "boss" or master of the deer, who himself rides a deer, is the mentor of those placed under his protection. His position was obtained directly from the creator. When a hunter is leaving for the hunt, Misinghalikun will appear to him in person, wearing a bearskin with a large oval mask that is painted red on the right side and black on the left, a form that reflects his name. This masked figure accompanies the hunters a short distance into the woods, during which time a spokesman drops six pinches of tobacco in each of two fires while begging Misinghalikun to seek out deer and help the hunters.

Numerous examples of the conceptual form of the lord of the animals in North America could be mentioned. Josef Haekel (1959) collected all available material source concerning the lord of the animals among the ancient, culturally advanced peoples of Mesoamerica and their descendants. Although the concept arose prior to the full development of these cultures, it becomes apparent that the lord of the animals also possessed qualities of an agrarian deity of the earth and master over cultivated plants. Even among the descendants of the advanced Andean cultures—the Quechua, Aymara, and others—this combined conceptual variation is known to occur. These characteristics are displayed in Pachamama, the Quechua earth mother who is at the same time the maternal progenitor of plants and of humans and animals. She is viewed as the actual owner of all llamas and alpacas, which she lends to mankind; if they are mishandled by humans, she repossesses them. A part of the ritual slaying of the llama involves the interment of the bones of that animal in a burial ground near the area in which the sacrifice took place. Such an act expresses trust that the earth mother will create a new animal from the bones of the old one—a notion typical of hunters.

Sometimes, however, Pachamama also functions as the mistress of the wild animals; thus, creatures like the guanaco, vicuña, and deer are referred to as "animals of the earth." This is reflected in practices like the offering (by burial) of a sacrifice to Pachamama before the start of a vicuña hunt.

Ideas and rites such as these, which either evolve in a hunting culture and are then superimposed on a pastoral one, or vice versa, are also found in the Old World; they have been observed, for instance, among the people of the Hindu Kush, particularly when the animals are conceived as being related. Like the Peruvians, the people of the Hindu Kush associate the wild and domesticated animals—in this instance, goats.

European chroniclers of the sixteenth and seventeenth centuries in the tropical lowlands of the Amazon continually encountered mention of a lord of the animals and a wild game spirit known as Korupira or Kaapora, a familiar figure among the Tupi-Guaraní tribes and comparable to a deity of other agricultural Indians. Among the mixed population of Brazil, belief in Korupira has likewise remained alive. Korupira's characteristic traits were collected and recorded in 1920 by Theodor Koch-Grünberg, a renowned researcher of the Indians of the Amazon whose primary source materials included the sixteenth- and seventeenth-century chronicles.

Among the hunting and planting tribes of eastern Brazil, the Sun is often viewed as the protector of hunted game. The Ge-speaking Indians of this region turn to this male deity with a plea for the maintenance and increased abundance of the various animal species. An appearance of Father Sun to a hunter ensures a successful expedition. Similarly, the hunting and gathering tribes of Tierra del Fuego conceive of a masculine sun (Kran or Lem), who is the "owner" of the animals; he is called upon by the Selk'nam (Ona) and Yaghan peoples to help them acquire subsistence. Watauineiwa of the Yaghan, who is viewed by many researchers as the supreme deity of these people, is in actuality the creator and owner of all animals. He entrusts his animals to humans for food and other essential uses, but only to the extent to which they are needed for survival. He watches out for his animals and assures that they are not killed wantonly, lest the meat be wasted. All these traits can be identified most precisely in describing a lord of the animals, and have also been used by Pettazzoni in describing a supreme being.

BIBLIOGRAPHY

Baumann, Hermann. "Afrikanische Wild- und Buschgeister." *Zeitschrift für Ethnologie* 70 (1938): 208–239. A basic work on the lord of the animals and related deities in Africa.

Dirr, Adolf. "Der kaukasische Wild und Jagdgott." *Anthropos* 20 (1925): 139–147. A specific study, incorporating what was then groundbreaking research, of belief in the lord of the animals in the Caucusus.

Friedrich, Adolf. "Die Forschungen über das frühzeitliche Jägertum. *Paideuma* 2 (1941): 20–43. An exceptionally good overview of the topic, including the lord of the animals in Siberia among ancient hunting cultures.

Haekel, Josef. "Der Herr der Tiere im Glauben der Indianer Mesoamerikas." *Mitteilungen aus dem Museum für Völkerkunde in Hamburg* 25 (1959): 60–69. A study of the relevant concepts of the pre-Columbian peoples of Mesoamerica. Haekel also writes extensively on the basic phenomena of the lord of the animals.

Hallowell, A. Irving. "Bear Ceremonialism in the Northern Hemisphere." *American Anthropologist* 28 (1926): 1–175. The doctoral thesis of this well-known American anthropologist presents a comprehensive investigation of bear ceremonials and is of great importance for the concept of the lord of the animals.

Hultkrantz, Åke, ed. *The Supernatural Owners of Nature.* Stockholm Studies in Comparative Religions, vol. 1. Stockholm, 1961. An article presented at a symposium for Northern studies, about the religious conceptualization of "master spirits" of places and animal types.

Paulson, Ivar. *Schutzgeister und Gottheiten des Wildes (der Jagdtiere und Fische) in Nordeurasien.* Stockholm Studies in Comparative Religions, vol. 2. Stockholm, 1961. A standard work concerned with the lord of the animals and the species spirits of the animals of northern Asia.

Schmidt, Leopold. "Der Herr der Tiere in einigen Sagenlandschaften Europas und Eurasiens." *Anthropos* 47 (1952): 509–538. A study that traces the motif of the restoration of life to slain animals from their bones, in Eurasia.

Zerries, Otto. *Wild und Buschgeister in Südamerika.* Studien zur Kulturkunde, vol. 11. Wiesbaden, 1954. The only work that deals exclusively with the lord of the animals and related manifestations in South America.

OTTO ZERRIES

Translated from German by John Maressa

LORD'S PRAYER. When his disciples asked Jesus to teach them to pray, *Luke* 11:2–4 records the Master's reply in words similar to the teaching in the Sermon on the Mount at *Matthew* 6:9–13. In a slightly simplified tabulation, the two versions of the text may be compared as follows, with the Matthean surplus and variants in brackets and two particularly difficult expressions in parentheses:

[Our] Father [who art in heaven],
Hallowed be thy name,
Thy kingdom come,
[Thy will be done,
On earth as it is in heaven].
Give us [this day] our (daily) bread,
And forgive us our sins [*Mt.*: debts],
For [*Mt.*: As] we [have] forgive[n] our debtor[s],
And lead us not into (temptation)
[But deliver us from evil].

Use in Christian Worship. The church has taken the Lord's Prayer as indicating both the spirit of Christian prayer and a formula to be employed in worship. The Matthean form is at almost all points the more usual in the liturgy. Liturgical use is the probable source of the concluding doxology, "For thine is the kingdom, the power, and the glory for ever," which is found—though not yet with the addition of the word *kingdom*—in a text that is as early as the first- or second-century church manual the *Didache* (8.2). The Lord's Prayer has been used, formally and informally, in daily worship as well as in the eucharistic liturgy. In the latter case, its place has usually been between the great prayer of thanksgiving and the Communion, whither it was doubtlessly attracted by the bread to be consumed.

Classical Commentaries. The early Fathers taught the prayer's meaning to their catechumens, and it has remained a favorite subject of exposition by spiritual writers. Tertullian and, in his wake, Cyprian both wrote pastoral tracts entitled *On (the Lord's) Prayer.* Origen dealt with it in his theological treatise *On Prayer* (chaps. 18–30). Cyril of Jerusalem expounded it to the newly baptized in his *Mystagogical Catechesis* 5.11–18, while Augustine of Hippo preached sermons 56–59 on it to the *competentes* (candidates for baptism) and also treated it as part of his commentary *The Sermon on the Mount* (2.4.15–2.11.39) and elsewhere. John Chrysostom devoted to the Lord's Prayer his *Nineteenth Homily on the Gospel of Matthew.* Gregory of Nyssa discoursed on it in his five *Sermons on the Lord's Prayer.* Conferences on it are ascribed to Thomas Aquinas. Luther explained the prayer in his Large and Small Catechisms and in other writings, such as *A Simple Way to Pray,* written in 1535 for his barber. Calvin presented it in the first edition of his *Institutes of the Christian Religion* (1536; cf. 3.20.34–49 in the final edition of 1559) and commented on it in his *Harmony of the Gospels* (1555). Teresa of Ávila used the Lord's Prayer to instruct her religious communities in *The Way of Perfection* (chaps. 27–42). John Wesley devoted to the prayer one of his Standard Sermons (numbered variously 21 or 26) and versified it in the hymn "Father of All, Whose Powerful Voice." Karl Barth treated it in his 1947–1949 seminar notes entitled *Prayer* and developed the address and the first two petitions in the unfinished part 4.4 of his *Church Dogmatics.* Simone Weil's thoughts on the subject are contained in her *Waiting on God.*

A Contemporary Exegesis. The best contemporary exegesis of the Lord's Prayer is that of Raymond E. Brown, who interprets it as an eschatological prayer. Jesus announced the coming of the kingdom of God. His followers prayed for the definite establishment of God's eternal rule and intimated their own desire to be part of it. They requested a place at the messianic banquet and asked for forgiveness in the divine judgment as well as for deliverance from the mighty struggle with Satan that still stood between the community and the final realization of its prayer. As hopes for the imminent advent of the final kingdom faded, interpreters adapted the prayer to continuing life in the present age with the assurance that God's kingdom had at least begun its entry into this world through the life, death, and resurrection of Jesus.

Recurrent Themes of Analysis. The Lord's Prayer opens with a bold filial salutation. To address almighty God as "Abba, Father" (*Rom.* 8:15, *Gal.* 4:6) is to share by grace a privilege that Jesus enjoyed by nature (*Mk.* 14:36, cf. *Mt.* 11:25–27). Liturgically, believers do in fact proclaim that they "make bold to say" *(audemus dicere)* this prayer. The heavenly Father is near. Moreover, to address the Father as "*our* Father" is to acknowledge that the Christian faith is a communal matter with brothers and sisters who are, at least potentially, as numerous as the human race. After this opening address six petitions follow, which typically attract the kind of comments next summarized.

1. Hallowed be thy name. God is by definition holy, and strictly speaking, only God can hallow the divine name: he does so in history by vindicating his holiness (*Ez.* 36:22–27, *Jn.* 12:28). But humans join in by not despising the Lord's name (*Ex.* 20:7 and, identically, *Dt.* 5:11), by praising the name of the Lord (*1 Chr.* 29:13 and often in *Psalms*), by calling on the name of the Lord for salvation (*Jl.* 2:32, *Acts* 2:21, *Rom.* 10:13), and by living in accord with the name put upon them in baptism (Augustine, sermon 59; cf. *1 Cor.* 6:11).

2. Thy kingdom come. Instead of "Thy kingdom come" a minor variant reads "May thy Holy Spirit come upon us and purify us." Here outcrops the common view that God's rule may at least begin in the present in human lives. Yet the primary agency in establishing the kingdom remains God's.

3. Thy will be done. In the garden of Gethsemane, Jesus accepted the Father's will (*Mk.* 14:36, *Mt.* 26:39, 26:42; cf. *Jn.* 6:38, *Heb.* 10:7–10). Thereby God's eternal will for salvation was implemented (*Eph.* 1:5, 1:9, 1:11). Humans benefit through faithful and obedient participation. The scope of God's plan is no less than heaven and earth.

4. Give us this day our daily bread. The adjective qualifying bread (Gr., *epiousios*) is otherwise practically unknown. Suggested possibilities for its meaning include: food "suited to our spiritual nature" (Origen); the bread "we need" for our "everyday" lives (Syriac and Old Latin traditions—cf. *Mt.* 6:34); an "excellent" bread surpassing all substances (the Vulgate's *supersubstantialis*). The original eschatological tone of the prayer favors the reading "tomorrow's bread," as in some Egyptian versions and in Jerome's report on the "Gospel of the Hebrews" wherein he employs the Latin word *crastinus* ("for tomorrow"); it is an urgent prayer for the feast of the age to come. Whatever their interpretation of *epiousios*, commentators regularly emphasize the graciousness of the divine provision and the human obligation to share the blessings of God, and most of them make a link with the eucharistic Communion.

5. Forgive us our sins. The parable of the unforgiving servant in *Matthew* 18:23–35 suggests that the final execution of God's will to forgive sinners depends on the sinner's readiness to forgive others (cf. *Mt.* 6:14f., *Lk.* 6:37). While humans cannot compel God's gracious forgiveness, they can be prevented from receiving it by their own unforgiving spirit.

6. Lead us not into temptation. Commentators have stressed the indirect character of God's testing of humans (*Jas.* 1:12–14) and insisted that God "will not let you be tempted beyond your strength" (*1 Cor.* 10:13). Some modern liturgical translations have restored the strictly eschatological character of the petition: "Save us from the time of trial" (cf. *Rv.* 3:10). In the present, the devil still "prowls around like a roaring lion, seeking whom he may devour" (*1 Pt.* 5:8; cf. *Eph.* 6:11–13, *1 Jn.* 5:19), but his defeat has already been assured by Christ, and the deliverance of believers is certain (*2 Thes.* 3:3, *Jn.* 17:15).

BIBLIOGRAPHY

Studies on the Jewish background to the Lord's Prayer can be found in Jean Carmignac's *Recherches sur le "Notre Père"* (Paris, 1969) and in *The Lord's Prayer and Jewish Liturgy*, edited by Jakob J. Petuchkowski and Michael Brocke (New York, 1978). Raymond E. Brown's "The *Pater Noster* as an Eschatological Prayer" is contained in his *New Testament Essays*, 3d ed. (New York, 1982), while other contemporary exegesis includes Ernst Lohmeyer's *The Lord's Prayer* (New York, 1965), Joachim Jeremias's *The Prayers of Jesus* (London, 1967), and Heinz Schürmann's *Das Gebet des Herrn*, 4th ed. (Leipzig, 1981). The tightly packed lectures of Thomas Aquinas are accessible in a translation by Lawrence Shapcote under the title *The Three Greatest Prayers: Commentaries on the Our Father, the Hail Mary and the Apostles' Creed by St. Thomas Aquinas* (London, 1956). Modern devotional works include William Barclay's *The Plain Man Looks at the Lord's Prayer* (London, 1964), Gerhard Ebeling's *On Prayer: Nine Sermons* (Philadelphia, 1966), and Romano Guardini's *The Lord's Prayer* (New York, 1958).

GEOFFREY WAINWRIGHT

LOTUS. A poem from a twelfth-century anthology of Sanskrit court poetry, in which the poet visualizes the whole world in the form of a spreading lotus, suggests how comprehensive and intricate a symbol the lotus can be. In it, the lotus encompasses the worlds of gods and humans:

> Its seed is the god Brahmā,
> its nectar are the oceans and its pericarp Mount Meru,
> its bulb the king of serpents
> and the space within its leaf-bud is the spreading sky;
> its petals are the continents, its bees the clouds,
> its pollen are the stars of heaven:
> I pray that he, the lotus of whose navel forms thus our universe,
> may grant you his defense. (Ingalls, 1965, p. 107)

It is especially in Indian art, literature, and religion that the lotus has been a frequent and central symbol. Indeed, lotus symbolism has accompanied Indian cultural influence wherever it has spread, especially in Southeast Asia and East Asia, where it is part of the symbolic language of Buddhism. But the lotus also appears as a symbol in East Asia without any obvious Indian connection, and in ancient Egypt.

The lotuses considered in this article are aquatic plants belonging to the *Nymphaeaceae* (water lily) and *Nelumbonaceae* families. They grow from rhizomes in the mud, and their leaves and blossoms float on the water or rise above its surface. Because the lotus grows out of water, early Indian tradition identified it with the waters (cf. *Śatapatha Brāhmaṇa* 7.4.1.8), with the creative and life-giving potential of the waters, and even with creation itself. So, for example, the *Taittirīya Brāhmaṇa* (1.1.3.5–6), relates that at the beginning of time the creator, Prajāpati, existed alone amid the primordial waters. As he was wondering how to create, he saw a lotus leaf, the sole other existing object. Diving down, he found the mud from which it was growing and brought some to the surface. He then spread the mud on the lotus leaf, and this, supported by the lotus leaf, became the surface of the earth. The later Indian tradition envisioned the world as having the shape of a lotus blossom (cf. *Matsya Purāṇa* 41.86). In either case, the lotus, rising out of the mud and the waters, is a mediating symbol, bridging the amorphous waters and the created earth.

In classical Indian mythology, the lotus as the bridge of creation is preserved in another expression, which forms the basis for the poem quoted above. At the beginning of a new world cycle, the god Viṣṇu lies on a serpent amid the primordial waters. From his navel grows a lotus, which blossoms to reveal Brahmā, the agent of creation. Here, the growth and unfolding of the lotus is both the vehicle for the generation of Brahmā and the image of the emergence of creation from the mind and body of Viṣṇu.

The association of the lotus with the concept of creation appears also in ancient Egypt. According to one tradition from Hermopolis, the highest deity appeared, self-begotten, on a lotus. In the temple at Edgu, built during the Greco-Roman period, an inscription equates the First Primeval One, who "caused the Earth to be when he came into existence," with the Great Lotus. Egyptian mythology connects the lotus especially with the creation of the sun.

The lotus opens not only as the world but also within each person. In both Hindu and Buddhist symbolism, a lotus encloses the center of one's being, which is located in the heart. The lotus is thus not only a bridge between precreation and creation but also a symbol linking the macrocosm and the human microcosm. "For this heart lotus," says the *Maitri Upaniṣad,* "is the same as space. The four regions and the four intermediate regions constitute its leaves. The vital breath and the sun move downward toward its base," (6.2). This symbolism of an inner lotus corresponding to the outer world is elaborated in Tantric yoga. Forms of this yoga identify five or seven lotiform centers in the body; these centers correspond to bodily locations and functions, to particular deities, and to aspects of the macrocosm. Likewise, in the Indo-Tibetan *maṇḍalas*, the opening of the lotus symbolizes the manifestation of divine powers, the world, the mind, and insight. In a typical *maṇḍala,* a principal deity occupies the center. Arranged around this center are four or eight other deities, who are visualized as emerging from it, like petals spreading out from the center of a lotus. Indeed, the fields on which their images or symbols appear are occasionally depicted as lotus petals. The lotus symbolism is also carried to the outer part of the *maṇḍala* which includes at least one circle of lotus petals. These confirm the lotus form of the whole *maṇḍala* and represent, among other possible meanings, the extension of divine power from the center. [*See* Maṇḍalas.]

Because the opening and closing of the lotus follows the rising and setting of the sun, the lotus is also a solar symbol. According to Indian iconographic texts, Sūrya, the Sun, should stand on red lotuses placed in his chariot or on a single lotus, and he may carry a lotus in his hand. Such solar symbolism was developed especially in ancient Egypt. According to one tradition, the newborn sun, identified with the child Horus, arose from the lotus. Corresponding to this conception, Horus was often depicted in the Greco-Roman period as a sunchild on a lotus blossom. In another tradition, the lotus, deified as the god Nefertem, gave life to the sungod Re and, by means of his fragrance, continues to give vitality to Re every day. Therefore, Re is, according to the *Book of Going Forth by Day* 15, the "golden youth, who came forth from the lotus." Elsewhere Nefertem also identified with Re and hence with the sun.

In addition to the Sun, various other Hindu deities have special connections to the lotus. The Moon is symbolized by the night-blooming white lotus. The lotus is also one of the characteristic signs of Viṣṇu. Of all the Indian deities, however, the one most closely associated with the lotus is Śrī, or Lakṣmī, the goddess of prosperity, good fortune, and wealth. The *Śrīsūkta*, which became her principal hymn of praise, surrounds her with lotuses and merges the image of the goddess and the lotus. There, she is called "moist"; she is garlanded and surrounded by lotuses; she is lotus-colored, is perceptible by her scent, and stands within the lotus. Her son is Slime (Kardama), who is asked to dwell with the poet and to make Śrī dwell with him. The widespread image of Gaja-Lakṣmī, the elephant Lakṣmī, also portrays the goddess's close connection with the lotus. Standing on a lotus, she holds two lotuses (or a woodapple and a lotus) and is sprayed with water by two elephants. This image of Lakṣmī is interpreted in the Puranic accounts of her origins. According to the *Viṣṇu Purāṇa* (1.9.100ff.), for example, Śrī emerged from the Ocean of Milk seated on a blossoming lotus and bearing a lotus in her hand. The Ocean himself appeared in human form and presented her with a garland of never-wilting lotuses, and Indra, king of the gods, praised her, saying, "I bow down before Śrī, the mother of all, who resides on the lotus, who has eyes of blossoming lotuses, and who reclines on the heart of Viṣṇu." In all these representations, the lotus blends with the waters and the goddess herself to symbolize fertility, prosperity, and bounty.

The lotus also underscores the beauty of the goddess, for it is a strikingly lovely flower that has become a conventional sign of beauty. According to Indian texts on erotica, the ideal woman is the Padminī, the woman of lotus scent. The hands, feet, and face of a beautiful woman are like lotus blossoms. Her eyes, especially the pupils of her eyes, are like lotuses. The lotus also possessed even more specifically erotic connotations. Iconographically, Kāma, the personification of sexual desire, is ornamented by the conch shell and the lotus, both symbols of the vulva. Lotuses were used in aphrodisiacs, in concoctions to ensure potency and fertility, and in scents to attract a lover. The "lotus position" is not only a yogic posture but a sexual one as well. Such simultaneous religious and erotic connotations were exploited particularly by the Tantric traditions of Buddhism and Hinduism to show the interpenetration of the two realms.

In China, too, the lotus was an erotic symbol. In the following song by Sung Huang-fu, the lotus helps create an erotic atmosphere:

> Water lilies and fragrant lotus across the vast stretch of water,
> A young girl exuberant and playful, picks lotus until late;
> Evening comes, the splashing water dampens her in the boat,
> Making her remove her red skirt and wrap up the ducks.
> The boat glides, the lake shines, overflowing with autumn.
> With desire she watches a young boy letting his boat drift,
> Impetuously across the water she throws lotus seeds,
> As the news spreads and people hear of it, she is bashful for half a day. (Wagner, 1984, p. 146)

The lotus exemplifies the beauty and passion of the young girl. The lotus seeds she throws are love tokens.

The lotus also represents birth as well as beauty and sensuality. In the folk traditions of India and China, the lotus has the power to make a person potent or fertile: both folk traditions have legends of virgin births that occurred after young women bathed in lotus ponds or ate lotus blossoms. A dramatic Indian image of a lotus-headed goddess in a birthing position has been identified by Stella Kramrisch (1983) as the divine Mother, who has given birth to all creatures. In ancient Egypt, too, the lotus was a symbol of birth or, more especially, of rebirth. The god Osiris was reborn from a lotus after he was killed. Such rebirth is the hope of humans as well, and for this reason the lotus appears as a decoration on Egyptian tombs and mummy cases. Because it was a symbol of regeneration, the lotus was a funerary flower also among the Greeks, Romans, and early Christians. One reason for this symbolism may be that the seedpods, open flowers, and buds of a lotus are all visible at the same time. The flower thus contains past, present, and future life.

But if the lotus is a symbol of sensual beauty, it can also be a symbol of transcendence or purity. It grows from the mud, but shows nothing of its origins. Nor are its leaves or petals affected by water, which beads and falls away. Untouched and breaking the surface of the water, the lotus is a natural symbol for rising above the world. It is, in this sense, applied especially to the Buddha in a well-known passage from the Pali texts *Saṃyutta Nikāya* (vol. 3, p. 140) and *Anguttara Nikāya* (vol. 2, pp. 38f.): "Likewise, monks, the blue lotus, the pink lotus, or the white lotus, born in the water and grown in the water, rises beyond the water and remains unsoiled by the water. Thus, monks, the Tathāgata, born in the world, grown up in the world, after having conquered the world, remains unsoiled by the world." This metaphor is usually taken to mean that the Buddha, after his enlightenment, lives within the world but is not affected by it or by the passions that normally govern human life. Within the Buddhist tradition, however, different sects have interpreted the passage in various ways. The "supernaturalist" sects, as Étienne Lamotte calls them (e.g., the Mahāsāṃghikas and the Vibhajyavādins), interpret it to mean that the Buddha's birth is purely apparent. Because his existence is a fiction, his body spiritual, and his human acts and qualities actually foreign to his true nature, the purity of the Buddha is absolute. The lotus as a symbol of purity also occurs in Hinduism. Two passages from the Upaniṣads (*Chāndogya* 4.14.3 and *Maitri* 3.2) reverse the Buddhist metaphor. In them the self is compared to a drop of water on a lotus leaf; it does not cling to the leaf, even while it remains upon it. In China, too, the white lotus is a symbol of purity.

The lotus is associated not only with Gautama Buddha but with other figures in the Buddhist pantheon, especially Prajñāpāramitā, Avalokiteśvara (Chin., Kuan-yin), and Amitābha. In connection with Prajñāpāramitā (Perfection of Wisdom), the lotus signifies purity, transcendence, and beauty. Avalokiteśvara and Amitābha belong to a Buddha "family" whose characteristic mark is the lotus. Here, the lotus functions both as an auspicious sign and as a reminder that these beings act compassionately while remaining unattached.

Like other central symbols of religious traditions, therefore, the lotus has many possible meanings within a cultural sphere; for that reason, it may not have a determinate meaning in a specific context. For example, the lotus is encountered frequently in art as a pedestal or throne for Buddhist and Hindu deities. Those viewing such an image might understand many of the associations outlined above: it could suggest purity, transcendence, the unfolding of a vision of divinity, beauty, the power to create, the centrality of the deity in the world, or the auspiciousness of the image. Moreover, the lotus is a surprisingly complex symbol, which is able to express the contradictory realities of divine and human life. It is both an erotic symbol and a symbol of purity. It signifies the creation of the world as well as the transcendence of it. The same lotus is the world and is within each person. It is the unformed waters and the visible world. And it is much else besides, for having established itself as a central symbol, the lotus gives rise to further interpretation. Blofeld (1978, p. 151), for example, gives a list of the principal emblems of Kuan-yin and their meanings taken from the Chinese edition of the *Heart of the Dhāranī of Great Compassion Sutra*. In this sutra, four lotuses of four different colors serve as the emblems of Kuan-yin: the white lotus signifies the attainment of merit, the blue lotus signifies rebirth in a Pure Land, the purple lotus signifies that one will behold *bodhisattva*s, and the red lotus signifies that one will attain rebirth in a heaven of the gods. Here, the meanings of the lotus pass beyond ideas directly suggested by its colors and parts.

BIBLIOGRAPHY

References in this article to the Nikāyas are to the text edited by the Pali Text Society.

Anthes, Rudolf. "Mythology in Ancient Egypt." In *Mythologies of the Ancient World*, edited by Samuel Noah Kramer, pp. 15–92. Garden City, N.Y., 1961. A useful introduction and overview of Egyptian mythology and symbolism.

Blofeld, John. *Bodhisattva of Compassion: The Mystical Tradition of Kuan Yin*. Boulder, 1978. A study of the Chinese transformation of the *bodhisattva* most closely associated with the lotus.

Bosch, F. D. K. *The Golden Germ: An Introduction to Indian Symbolism*. The Hague, 1960. This work studies the cosmic lotus and the world tree; according to Bosch, Indian and Southeast Asian artists envisioned the genesis and structure of the macrocosm and the human microcosm through these symbols.

Coomaraswamy, Ananda K. *Elements of Buddhist Iconography* (1935). New Delhi, 1972. Part 1 presents the symbolism of the tree of life, the earth-lotus, and the word-wheel; part 2 treats the development of the lotus-throne in Buddhist art.

Ingalls, Daniel H. H., trans. *An Anthology of Sanskrit Court Poetry: Vidyākara's "Subhāṣitaratnakośa."* Cambridge, Mass., 1965. These poems show the mature development of Indian poetry and literary symbolism.

Ions, Veronica. *Egyptian Mythology*. Rev. ed. New York, 1983. This is a splendidly illustrated, easily accessible introduction to Egyptian symbolism.

Kramrisch, Stella. "An Image of Aditi-Uttānapad." In *Exploring India's Sacred Art*, edited by Barbara Stoler Miller, pp. 148–158. Philadelphia, 1983. This article is a study of an image of a goddess who has a lotus blossom in place of her head and who appears to be giving birth.

Lauf, Detlef Ingo. *Tibetan Sacred Art: The Heritage of Tantra*. Berkeley, 1976. This introduction to Tibetan art mentions the lotus frequently, although in passing.

Siegel, Lee. *Sacred and Profane Dimensions of Love in Indian Traditions as Exemplified in the Gītagovinda of Jayadeva*. Oxford, 1978. On pages 195 and following, Siegel offers a short but helpful discussion of the lotus as an erotic and religious symbol.

Wagner, Marsha L. *The Lotus Boat: The Origins of Chinese Tz'u Poetry in T'ang Popular Culture*. New York, 1984. According to Wagner, *tz'u* poetry originated in the popular songs sung by courtesans and other musical entertainers. The lotus appears as a symbol of love and erotic desire.

Zimmer, Heinrich. *Myths and Symbols in Indian Art and Civilization.* Edited by Joseph Campbell. New York, 1946. See pages 90–102 for Zimmer's study of the development of lotus symbolism in connection with goddess figures of Hinduism and Buddhism.

JOEL P. BRERETON

LOVE. The concept of love, in one form or another, has informed the definition and development of almost every human culture in the history of the world—past and present, East and West, primitive and complex.

Broadly conceived, love has been a motivational force in the shaping of culture within both the ideological and behavioral dimensions of life and a substantive theme in the by-products of almost every form of human activity: in religion and the arts, literature and music, dance and drama, philosophy and psychology. It is, perhaps, safe to say that the idea of love has left a wider and more indelible imprint upon the development of human culture in all its aspects than any other single notion.

Indeed, many notable figures (Mo-tzu in China, Nārada in India, Plato in Greece, Augustine and Teilhard de Chardin in Christianity, to name but a few) have argued that love is the single most potent force in the universe, a cosmic impulse that creates, maintains, directs, informs, and brings to its proper end every living thing. In Teilhard's phraseology, "Love alone is capable of uniting living beings in such a way as to complete and fulfill them, for it alone takes them and joins them by what is deepest in themselves" *(The Phenomenon of Man).*

Love has been a universally active potency that has left in its wake an impressively diverse array of artifacts that are signatures of its creative potential. It has been the binding power that has provided the various types of human groupings (family, clan, tribe, state, and nation) with a basis for social coherence and collective experience. Love has motivated the creation of towering religious and cultural edifices, social and religious hierarchies, systems of doctrine and rites, and so on, that constitute the very fabric of the religious life. When viewed in its quintessence, love may even be identified as the invisible power behind the "force that through the green fuse drives the flower" (Dylan Thomas), the "vital impulse" (Henri Bergson) or "the *within* of things . . . [the] internal propensity to unite" (Teilhard) that undergirds and nourishes the entire biosphere.

A survey of religious and secular literature reveals a variety of approaches to the definition of love, based on (1) the nature of the recipient, or object, on which affection is bestowed, whether animate or inanimate, divine or human, male or female, heterosexual or homosexual; (2) the type of feeling, idea, or attitude that motivates the experience; (3) the emotional, aesthetic, or moral quality of the experience itself, ranging from the basest forms of carnal desire through the loftiest forms of human affection and reverence to the purest expression of love as divine grace; and (4) the emotional, moral, and spiritual effects that it exerts upon all parties included in the love relationship.

It is difficult to deal intelligently with the various types of love—affection, reverence, holy awe, and so on—without addressing the question of the relationship between love and desire. Are love and desire synonymous or equivalent experiences? Is desire merely a constitutive element of love? If so, is it an integral or accidental element? [*See* Desire.] And how is the notion of desire to be accommodated to the various images of love, from the carnal to the ethereal? Does God experience desires that demand satisfaction (e.g., a loving acceptance of his grace or the salvation of the entire human family) and, if so, what distinguishes divine wishes from human? [*See also* Transcendence and Immanence.]

Again, is the experience of love solely or primarily emotional or affective in nature? Granted that most, if not all, forms of love include a strong emotional element, are there not also love relationships in which the emotional content is either negligible or subsumed under another experiential factor? One such example might be an experience of mystical union with God in his nondifferentiated mode of being (e.g., Eckhart's experience of the godhead) or with the divine Absolute (the *brahman* in Vedānta), in which all emotional content is either dissolved or transmuted into a higher and purer mode of consciousness. [*See* Mystical Union.]

Viewed within a universal context, the plethora of concepts of love might be reduced to three broad categories that are descriptive of the emotional, moral, and spiritual qualities of the experience: (1) carnal love arising out of the erotic desire to enjoy, possess, or otherwise pursue an object of beauty or virtue for one's own pleasure or gratification, designated by a culturally specific term within each tradition: for example, *eros* (Gr.), *amor* (Lat.), *kāma* (Skt.); (2) friendly love or affection extended to another human being of either gender, motivated by feelings of altruistic generosity and expressed by such terms as *philia* (Gr.), *delictio* (Lat.), *sneha, priyatā* (Skt.); and (3) divine love manifested as self-giving grace and represented as *agapē* (Gr.), *caritas* (Lat.), *karuṇā* (Skt., Buddhism), *prema* (Skt., Hinduism), *raḥmān* (Arab.), and *ḥesed* (Heb.).

Some writers have praised love for its clarifying effects on the mind, its capacity to dissolve the clouds of confusion and give one a direct and undiluted view of reality. Others have decried the power of love to confuse, bedazzle, befuddle, and, in its most debilitating forms, to poison or destroy the human spirit with madness. This potential of love to drive a person insane with passion is especially characteristic of spurned, unrequited, or unfulfilled love.

When viewed panoramically, the materials pertaining to love in its myriad forms appear to make one common distinction between the baser forms of appetite in pursuit of either sensual pleasure or sexual union, on the one hand, and self-emptying or self-sacrificing love, on the other. Some religious and cultural traditions conceive of desire and love as diametrical opposites, while others view them as correlative concepts, each required for the existence of the other, the former fulfilled in the latter.

Ancient Chinese Traditions. Over the ages the Chinese developed a differentiated view of love.

Love as filial piety. According to the *Analects* of Confucius (551–479 BCE), the experience of love begins in the home among one's closest blood relatives. The quality of love is referred to by a variety of terms in Chinese: *hsiao* (filial piety), the cardinal virtue of the Confucian ethic; *ti* (fraternal love); *hao* (goodwill); and *shu* (forgiveness or compassion for others).

Hsiao is the distinguishing mark of the gentleman *(chün-tzu)* and the moral force that binds together members of primary groups such as family, clan, tribe, or phratry. It is to members of one's family or clan that a person is expected to extend acts of affection, patience, and understanding—gestures (*jen,* or human-heartedness), acts that are withheld from foreigners and strangers. In the *Analects,* the presence of *jen* designates a human being as opposed to an animal. *Jen* is an embodiment of goodness, wisdom, and courage in a descending sequence of importance (14.30); in the widest sense, it refers to a person who possesses the virtues of kindness, gentleness, humaneness, and unselfishness (6.28). By virtue of his gentle and affectionate nature, the gentleman draws like-minded persons around himself and through these relationships promotes goodness.

Jen also manifests a mystical dimension that transcends the level of attainment of ordinary humans. In certain passages of the *Analects,* the idea seems to be the Confucian equivalent to the *tao* of the Taoists. Like *tao, jen* is inactive and hence everlasting (6.21). It is unattainable by ordinary human beings and is accessible only to the divine sage *(sheng),* a demigod. For that reason, "the Master rarely discoursed on *jen*" (9.1).

In compliance with this lofty standard, Confucius declared that "it is only the man of *jen* [and *hsiao,* filial piety] who knows how to love and how to hate people" (4.3). His ethic of love is summarized in a principle that is phrased as a negative formulation of the Christian golden rule: "What you do not wish to yourself, do not do to others. Then neither in the country nor in the family will there be resentment against you" (12.2).

The Moist ethics of universal love. Like Confucius, Mo-tzu (sixth century BCE) believed that everyone in society would flourish, live in peace with one another, and find the happiness they desire, to the degree that they lived in conformity to the *t'ien-chih* ("will of Heaven"). In contrast to Confucius, who taught that people should love their family first and foremost and other persons to lesser degrees, according to their distance from the core family, Mo-tzu believed that human love should be modeled on the will of Heaven, which, he held, loves everyone equally. Hence, love should be extended to all persons everywhere without distinction.

Mo-tzu condemned the ethic of family loyalty as the root cause of all social conflict and warfare. In its place he posited the principle of universal love. If everyone in the world practiced universal love (i.e., loved everyone else as oneself), he argued, then the entire world would be pervaded and nourished by a spirit of filial devotion. "If everyone regarded his father, his elder brother, and his ruler just as he does himself, toward whom would he be lacking in devotion? . . . Could there be any thieves or robbers? . . . Would noble clans contend among themselves? Would states attack each other? If everyone in the world practiced universal love, . . . then the whole world would enjoy peace and perfect order" (trans. Y. P. Mei, 1929).

Mo-tzu established his belief in the efficacy of universal love on a utilitarian foundation. His justification for this principle is not only that it is good and righteous in and of itself; it is also the truly authentic and enduring basis of good governmental policy. In defense of this assertion, Mo-tzu argues that a ruler who bases his rule upon the ethic of universal love will himself be loved, appreciated, and trusted by his people, whereas a ruler who fails to practice this ethic will be distrusted, feared, and hated.

A remarkable feature of Mo-tzu's understanding of love *(ai)* is that he distinguished it from emotional experiences of the heart and identified it wholly with the life of the mind. He distrusted the emotions and asserted that all emotions (joy and sorrow, pleasure and pain, love and hate) must be discarded. Unlike Confucius, who believed that music, as the art form that most intimately affects the feelings, was the *sine qua non* to the cultivation of *jen, li,* and all the other gentlemanly virtues, Mo-tzu condemned music as being useless and socially counterproductive.

Love as cosmic force. According to the *Hsiao ching* (Book of Filial Piety), *hsiao* originates within the family but, when allowed to grow according to its natural inclination, will ultimately include the entire human race, as does *jen.* "When love and reverence are thus cherished in the service of one's parents, one's moral influence transforms people and one becomes a model to all within the four seas. This is the filial piety of the Son of Heaven" (chap. 2). [*See* Hsiao.]

As elsewhere in the Confucian tradition, the roots of *jen* and *hsiao* are traced back to the very structure of the universe, that is, cosmic law *(tao)* or the way of Heaven *(t'ien-tao). Hsiao* unites Heaven and earth. It is the ultimate principle of Heaven and the fundamental basis for the operations of the earth. As such, it is the norm for all human conduct. (Related concepts are *dharma* in Hinduism and *dhamma* in Buddhism.)

By adhering to the dictates of Heaven, people will be able to maintain their world in a state of harmony and unity. Elsewhere in the *Li chi* (Book of Rites), *jen* is identified as the cosmic power that brings all living beings into a state of renewed vitality in the springtime and fosters growth throughout the summer.

Love as nonassertive action in Taoism. According to the *Tao-te ching* (sixth century BCE), those persons who truly live in the spirit of the Tao (cosmic law) embody the principle of *wu-wei,* a virtue that is variously translated as nonaction, nonstriving, or nonaggressive action. Commensurate with the universal and eternal Tao, the life of the perfect man *(chih jen)* is governed by and manifests the primary virtues of love, compassion, mercy, patience, meekness, tenderness, and unconditional generosity toward all living beings. The sage "does nothing, yet accomplishes everything," is the classical formulation of the Taoist precept of love.

The Taoist idea of *wu-wei* parallels the Moist concept of love in at least one regard. Both traditions distinguish love from all forms of passion.

> Tao never does; yet through it all things are done. If the barons and kings would but possess themselves of it, the ten thousand creatures would at once be transformed. And, if having been transformed they should desire to act, we must restrain them by the blankness of the Unnamed. The blankness of the Unnamed brings dispassion; to be dispassionate is to be still. And so, of itself, the whole empire will be at rest. (*Tao-te ching,* chap. 37, trans. Arthur Waley)

Love, then, is the culminating fruit of a life of silent meditation and quietude, according to the Taoists.

Hinduism. The Sanskrit language is extremely rich in terms that designate love and its cognate ideas. The most common word for love is *kāma,* meaning "wish, desire, longing," and, by extension, "love or affection." The term *kāma* is frequently used to refer to experiences of pleasure and enjoyment (especially sensuality and sexual love) and is the proper name of the god of love, the Indian counterpart to the Greek Eros and the Roman Cupid. As the god of love, Kama is the divine personification of sensuous attachment, desire, and erotic pleasure and is identified with the basal energy that drives the life force through every living thing.

In the earliest literature of Indian religion, the Vedas, the term *śraddhā* ("faith, trust, desire or reverence") designates the motive force behind the Vedic sacrifice. The primary purpose of the sacrifice was the gratification of the gods in order to obtain certain boons from them in return. In exchange for gifts of praise, food and drink, and other forms of veneration, the gods provided their devotees with a fertile world in which to live, as well as health, longevity, and prosperity for their families and cohorts. The principle on which the entire Vedic sacramental system functioned was, to borrow a phrase from the Latin, *do ut des,* "I give that you may give."

The ethic of devotion in the Bhagavadgītā. It is in the *Bhagavadgītā,* the earliest manifesto of Indian devotionalism, or *bhakti,* that love is given primary spiritual value. The term *bhakti* means, generically, "to eat, partake of, enjoy," and, by extension, "to revere, love." In contrast to the Upaniṣads, which posit a transpersonal spiritual principle *(brahman)* as the object of intuitive knowledge, the *Gītā* identifies the ultimate as a personal deity, under the name of Kṛṣṇa, and points to him as the only legitimate object of devotion.

In the *Gītā,* love or devotion finds its proper and most compelling recipient in the intensely personal nature of Kṛṣṇa. In contrast to the discipline of asceticism, meditation, and self-mortification in yoga, the pathway of devotion is offered to the average devotee as the easier and more accessible route to salvation (8.14). By the cultivation of an unqualified and passionate love of God, a person comes to know God truly and, by knowing him devotedly, to enter his nature and become one with him (18.55). It is by means of this kind of unstinting devotion that Arjuna, the hero of the *Gītā,* persuades Kṛṣṇa to reveal himself in his universal and eternal form.

What, then, is the precise nature of this pathway to God? It is through attaching one's consciousness to God alone and, thereby, knowing, loving, and following him as the only efficacious means to salvation (9.34). The way of *bhakti* demands that one renounce all other religious obligations and spiritual disciplines (18.66). Only then will God return the love of the devotee in the form of divine grace (9.29). Through his grace, God will suspend the law of karmic retribution and bring the person to "that peace that culminates in *nirvāṇa* and that abides in me" (6.15). As Kṛṣṇa himself says, "Whatever you do, or eat, or offer, or give, or mortify, make it an offering to me and I shall undo the bonds of action, both the good and evil fruits" (9.28). But it is the quality of mind and heart with which such gifts are offered to God, and not the size or value of the objects themselves, that is important. Even a modest presentation—of a leaf, a flower, a piece of fruit or a cup of water—if offered in the spirit of true devotion will be an acceptable gift of love (9.27).

The life of the true devotee *(bhakta)* is anchored in a commitment to the achievement of a high degree of self-control, indifference to both pleasure and pain, equal treatment of friend and foe alike, and compassion and friendliness toward all creatures. It is this person, Kṛṣṇa says, "who does my work, who is devoted to me and loves me, who is free from attachment [to worldly values] and from animosity toward any creature who comes to me" (11.55).

The Hindu social ethic. The Indian epics *(Mahābhārata* and *Rāmāyaṇa)* and the law books (*Dharmaśāstras*) distinguish between two widely divergent ethics on which a person may base his life: the way of the worldling *(pravṛtti)* and the way of the ascetic *(nivṛtti)*. The worldly life is established upon the pursuit of objects of desire *(kāma)*, whereas the ascetic life is governed by the restraint and conquest of all desires *(saṃnyāsa)*, including all forms of love. The writings of Manu and Yajñavalkya represent *kāma* as the basis of a value system that aspires to the development of a well-rounded and complete personality. This goal is achieved by pursuing in succession, during the four stages of life, four types of values: pleasure and sensual enjoyment *(kāma)*, wealth and prosperity *(artha)*, righteousness *(dharma)*, and, ultimately, spiritual liberation from ignorance and rebirth *(mokṣa)*. When directed toward the spiritually purer aspirations of the human spirit, the force of *kāma* can foster a desire to live in harmony with the will of God or to be united with God.

The Indian compulsion to organize every major aspect of human life into categorial systems is so pervasive that not even the art of lovemaking escaped analytical treatment. The *Manual of Love (Kāma Sūtra)* by Vatsyāyana (c. 400 CE) laid down canons governing every aspect of love, courtship, and marriage, including effective tactics to win the confidence of a virgin, the proper way to make the first sexual approach to the bride, and the use of tonics, potions, and aphrodisiac compounds that facilitate the increase of sexual performance and sensual pleasure.

The *Kāma Sūtra* enjoins every male member of the three upper castes first to complete his educational training and then to marry, set up a home, and follow the ways of a man of taste and culture. Both men and women are encouraged to study closely and to perfect the methods of love for the enhancement of the aesthetic quality of their lives. In addition, a person should augment his expertise in the sixty-four fine arts. The experience of physical love between two people of either the same or opposite sex is to be engaged in and enjoyed for its own sake as one of these arts.

Love in the Vaiṣṇava tradition. The concept of love that informs the *bhakti* traditions in Hinduism, especially in their Vaiṣṇava or Kṛṣṇaite branches, holds that the path of love and passion is the easiest and most efficacious route to the knowledge of God and, thereby, of the self. The experience of salvation is allegorically depicted by means of the image of the unrestrained ecstasy resulting from complete union.

However, the isolation of love or passion as the surest way to God threw the Vaiṣṇavas into the heart of a troublesome paradox. If every human being is divine by nature (i.e., possesses Kṛṣṇa nature), then to love God unreservedly is to revere one's own self and to elevate oneself to the stature of divinity.

The Vaiṣṇava Sahajiyā cult of Bengal (sixteenth century) attempted to resolve this theological and experiential dilemma by making a clear distinction between ordinary carnal desire or passion *(kāma)* and the completely altruistic and self-abnegating love of God *(prema)*. Whereas *kāma* generates the baser inclinations and instincts, the experience of *prema* disengages one's attachment to the self and transposes feelings of selfishness and greed into total commitment to the pleasure of Kṛṣṇa.

According to the Vaiṣṇavas, generally, *kāma* and *prema* are to be differentiated absolutely. *Kāma* is identified as the root of all the instinctual inclinations toward self-gratification, and *prema* as the selfless love of God that arises in response to his gift of divine grace. The Sahajiyās, on the other hand, "somewhat more alchemically inclined," regard the distinction between the two forms of passion not in terms of essential moral and spiritual qualities, but in terms of the motivation and nature of the recipient. That is, the normal emotions that are concomitants of residency within a human body are mystically transmuted into the purest of affections merely by desiring to know the truth that is God and to be united with or embraced by him.

The Sahajiyā tradition looks back to the *Bhāgavata Purāṇa* for guidelines in defining the route taken by the spiritual pilgrim. The route to salvation progresses along five stages of spiritual development, in which the *bhakta* enjoys an increasingly intimate relationship to God: (1) *śānta*, the feeling of awe, humility, and insignificance experienced by the devotee who views God as the supreme deity; (2) *dāsya,* love in the form of respect or reverence and obedient service, experienced by man as servant or slave toward God as supreme master; (3) *sākhya,* fondness and affection through a personal relationship between man and God as friends; (4) *vātsalya,* parental or fraternal affection; and (5) *mādhurya,* the stage of lover and beloved, the ultimate and purest form of love, epitomized in the love of the cowherd girls for Kṛṣṇa.

This Vaiṣṇava theology of love reached sublime heights of expression in numerous collections of love lyrics that appeared in India between the fourteenth and sixteenth centuries. Most notable are the love songs of Vidyāpati and Chandidās and the *Gītāgovinda* (Love Song of the Dark Lord) by Jayadeva. With great poetic genius and soaring turns of phrase, these singer-saints celebrate a variety of incidents in the relationship between Kṛṣṇa and his beloved cowherdess, Rādhā: the initial stirrings of love at the time of their first encounter, the greening of nature in the springtime, Rādhā's frailty and tenderness contrasted with Kṛṣṇa's strength and robust nature, the inescapable mixture of agony and ecstasy in lovemaking, the emotional torment of being separated from one's beloved, and the excruciating wait for the lover's return.

Most of the lyric poems in the Kṛṣṇa-*bhakti* literature depict the difficulties of maintaining the love relationship during the lengthy period of the lover's absence. Thus, the leitmotifs tend to focus on feelings arising out of the experience of enforced solitude, abandonment, and rejection, rather than experiences of pleasure, playfulness, delight, and joy that normally arise from togetherness.

Viewed theologically, the central message of the Kṛṣṇa cycle is that God appeared in the world at some point in the past. He revealed himself and consorted with humanity, thereby showing his gracious nature and the way to salvation through uncompromising love of him. From the viewpoint of the Kṛṣṇa cult, his devotees (all representing the person of Rādhā) adore him with song and dance, not only to keep alive the memory of Kṛṣṇa's previous appearance, but to furnish those memories with aesthetic and emotional enrichment, such that the devotee's heart will be teeming with intense and unswerving love for the beloved if and when he returns.

Self-abnegating Love in Buddhism. One of the most impressive exemplifications of self-sacrificing love in the entire history of religions is the figure of the *bodhisattva* ("he whose essence is enlightenment"), the perfected being in Mahāyāna Buddhism. Although the *bodhisattva* cannot, by any means, be construed as a god who creates the world and judges the moral qualities of men's actions, he is the nearest equivalent to a savior deity to be developed in this nontheistic tradition.

The *bodhisattva,* by virtue of his decision to decline the rewards of *nirvāṇa,* "until the last blade of grass has been liberated," is revered as an infinite and inexhaustible reservoir of compassion *(karuṇā).* The potency and durability of his commitment to the principle of love is expressed poignantly in the *bodhisattva*'s vow: "However innumerable the beings, I vow to save them. However inexhaustible the defilements, I vow to extinguish them. However immeasurable the teachings, I vow to master them. However incomparable enlightenment, I vow to attain it."

The *bodhisattva* is a celestial embodiment of infinite compassion *(mahākaruṇā)* and the Six Perfections *(pāramitās*: giving, morality, patience, vigor, meditation, and wisdom), as well as other related virtues such as friendliness, goodwill, loving kindness, benevolence, and sympathetic joy. His compassion is expressed by the abandonment of concern for his own salvation out of an inexhaustible concern for the welfare of all other living beings. He refuses the reward of *nirvāṇa* until he has led all beings to that blessed state before him. Instead of passing over into the realm of infinite bliss, which he has earned by myriads of lifetimes of meritorious behavior, he remains within the realm of rebirth, ignorance, suffering, and death to point the way to all other beings still bound by the triple evils of greed, hatred, and delusionment.

He is the perfect personification of unconditional love. His unbounded love of all beings and concern for their salvation manifests itself in acts of compassion, charity, and selflessness. The *bodhisattva* does more than merely present himself to the world as an abstract *model* to be emulated and imitated. He actively shares others' sufferings and takes their pains upon himself in order to relieve them of the burdens that are beyond their capacity to manage. In the words of another formulation of the vow, he declares to the world of suffering humanity: "I myself must grapple with the whole mass of suffering of all beings, to the limit of my endurance I will experience in all the states of woe, found in any world system, all abodes of suffering . . . and so I will help all beings to freedom, in all states of woe that may be found in any world system whatsoever."

He, more than any other creature, deserves the gifts that are bestowed upon him by all beings, because no other being has a mind so full of friendliness *(maitri).* His compassion for the creatures is devoid of all corrupting elements arising out of concern for self. Both concern for self and consciousness of self have been obliterated, for "he does not make either this [his vow of universal compassion] or anything else into a sign with which he becomes intimate." He continues to abide within this realm of tears and death, even after qualifying for entry into *nirvāṇa*, and he does so in order "to point out the path to all beings . . . , to set free from birth-and-death all beings . . . , and to cleanse the organs of visions of all beings" (*Aṣṭasahasrikā* 22.402–404).

The various *bodhisattvas* who populate the Mahāyāna "pantheon" are considered to be embodiments of some aspect of the Buddha himself. Avalokiteśvara ("the lord of the universal survey") represents the compassion of the Buddha for the travails of the creatures. The Buddha is himself the supreme *bodhisattva*. He is capable of canceling the effects of *karman* and bringing a person to salvation. He descends into the various Buddhist hells (*nārakas*) for the purpose of easing the torments of the condemned and encouraging them with a reminder that there is a way that leads to a more felicitous existence. In Buddhist iconography he is customarily pictured with a thousand eyes and arms, all of them aids to seeing and helping with suffering.

No doubt the roots of this notion of universal loving-kindness, which is the cardinal virtue in Mahāyāna, is to be found in the ancient spiritual practice in Theravāda known as "mindfulness of friendliness" (*mettá*). This is the first of the four prime virtues in the latter tradition, the other three being compassion, joy, and equanimity. This first of the "sublime moods" (*brahma-vihāra*), which every monk is enjoined to practice daily, is fostered first, by showering thoughts of friendliness upon oneself, then, by extension, upon one's loved ones and friends, next upon one's adversaries, and finally upon the whole human race. The moral and spiritual flavor of this practice is reflected quintessentially in the middle lines of a *Hymn to Friendliness*, one of the most eloquent poems in the whole of Pāli literature: "May all be happy and safe! May all beings gain inner joy—all living beings whatsoever without exception, weak or strong, whether . . . seen or unseen, dwelling afar or near, born or yet unborn . . . may all beings gain inner joy" (*Sutta Nipāta*).

It should finally be noted that the popular veneration of the *bodhisattva* in his various guises represents the emergence of the *bhakti* religion within Buddhism, a form of religiosity that is pervasive in sectarian Hinduism. Moreover, certain ideational and imagistic elements in the figures of the *bodhisattva* parallel similar traits in the characters and cults of Śiva and Viṣṇu, the most graphic exemplification of this principle being the appearance of the Buddha in some versions of the ten incarnations (*dāśāvatāras*) of Viṣṇu.

Love as the Quest for Immortality in Plato. Plato's discussion of the nature, source, and motivations of the human experience of love is contained in one of the most eloquent and thought-provoking of his dialogues, the *Symposium*. In this most remarkable writing, a succession of speakers rises in the course of a "drinking party" to discourse on the nature of love and its many forms of manifestation in human life. The dialogue is composed of eight addresses that progress from Phaedrus's argument that love is sexual desire stimulated by an experience of beauty and Pausanias's contention that good and bad love must be distinguished according to the degree to which love promotes or inhibits the realization of human happiness. In the end, Socrates, who, as always, serves as the mouthpiece of Plato, declares that love is neither mortal nor immortal, neither pure alteration nor unbroken continuity, but a hybrid combination of the two. Love is the mediator between the divine and human realms, "who bridges the chasm that separates them" and "in whom all things are interconnected." It is through love's agency that the "arts of the prophet and the priest, their sacrifices and mysteries and charms, and all prophecy and incantation find their way."

In broadest terms, love (*eros*) is the passionate struggle to maximize the realization of the potentialities of human life. It is the quest for the maintenance of bodily existence, physical health, worldly goods, aesthetic pleasure, and ultimately, at the termination of the life span, immortality through personal knowledge of the good. In its role as counterpart to the struggle for self-preservation and the acquisition of those goods and values that are an enrichment to life, love is the striving for death, for the dissolution of the life forces and the entrance of the soul into eternity and the state of immortality.

In the *Symposium*, *eros* is epitomized in the figure of Dionysos, who is the patron deity of the symposium, or love feast, itself. It is the *élan vital* that is symbolized in the youth, vigor, and ambition of the young Dionysos, whose life and death are bound up organically with the cycle of life and whose death at the end of the year is transcended by the renewal of that life with the advent of the new year.

Love is declared to be the offspring of *penia*, a feminine principle of need and desire, and *poros*, the male principle of means, way, or design. As such, Eros is both the energy that actualizes all forms of life and the urge toward creative existence (defined by Plato as "the thirst for a knowledge of the good and the beautiful") that surges through all living things.

Later on, in the same speech, Socrates brings his discourse on love to a stirring climax with the declaration that "it is procreation in a beautiful thing—of the body and the soul" (206b). It is the desire of all human beings to give birth to works of beauty, in thought, word, and deed, and thereby to attain the state of immortality, not by "being completely unchanged forever, like the divine, but by what is old and withdrawing leaving behind something else, something new like itself" (208a–b). Love, then, is the quest for the knowledge of the good, the true, and the beautiful that is transformative. It is the veneration of wisdom and, as such, is the treasured possession of the philosopher. Hence, love procreates things immortal within the realm of mortal existence, which arises out of the desire for supreme embodiments of immortality, the good, the true, and the beautiful. Love is the quest for the possession of the good for oneself for eternity. Hence, in a word, "Love is of immortality" (206b).

In the *Phaedrus* (252a), Socrates describes the all-consuming nature of this love when invested in another person who is the recipient of unqualified affection. The lover is willing to sacrifice everything, including allegiance to relatives and friends, property and wealth, even social etiquette, in order to be "as near as he can to his desired one, who is the object of his worship and the physician who can alone assuage the greatness of his pain."

These philosophical considerations on the nature of love in Plato are interwoven with strands of religious narrative from the Hebraic tradition to form the fabric of the concept of divine and human love in the New Testament, and this fabric, in turn, formed the mesh from which the doctrines of love of the church fathers were woven.

The Cardinal Doctrine in Christianity. The concept of love in the Gospels and the letters of Paul shows an unmistakable imprint of both the Hebraic notion of love in the Torah *(ḥesed)* and the various Greek terms *(eros, philia)*, especially those that appear in the dialogues of Plato.

The New Testament writers preferred the use of the term *agapē* to articulate their understanding of the message of Jesus and that of the early church. The probable reason for avoiding the term *eros* was the strong sexual overtones of the word in Greek literature. They may also have felt that *agapē* was closer to the meanings of *ḥesed*, covenantal love, in the Torah.

In its widest semantic sense, the term *agapē* denotes not only the mode of divine action in the world and the proper relationship between God and man, but the essential nature of God himself. *Agapē* designates the self-emptying love of God manifested singularly in his gracious act of sending his only son, Jesus Christ, into the world to take upon himself the consequences of mankind's sins, thereby to absolve them of their guilt and to free them to live eternally in God's love.

The core of the New Testament understanding of love is drawn from the Old Testament (*Dt.* 6:5, *Lv.* 19:18) and is informed by a novel idea that is perhaps unique to Jesus' own message, namely, that God's love is available to all people everywhere. The writers of the Gospels believed that the essence of man's loving response to God's love is summed up in the commandment to love God with mind, heart, and soul, without reservation. The new commandment enjoined all men to love their fellowmen as they love themselves (*Mt.* 22:37–40). The source and inspiration of this love of both God and fellowmen (including one's adversaries) is God's love *(agapē)* unsought by man and freely bestowed by God.

Luke gives voice to another dimension of Christian love by urging people to embrace their enemies, as well as their friends, in a spirit of forgiveness and love. To be authentic, *agapē* must not only be freely offered without any expectation of recompense, but must be bestowed indiscriminately on benefactors and detractors alike, for God is no respecter of persons; he causes the rain to fall upon the unjust and the just. Therefore, the life that is informed and guided by *agapē* will reflect the attitude of the father of the Prodigal Son, who in spite of his son's previous rejection of his love and his thoughtless abandonment of the homestead, approaches the son on his return home with arms extended in the spirit of forgiveness and charity. He does this, not in hopes of deriving some benefit from the son (e.g., productive labor in the fields or care during his own old age), but as an irrepressible expression of love.

The most poetically sublime expression of the New Testament view of Jesus' teachings about love is contained in Paul's letter to the Corinthians (*1 Cor.* 13). Read within the context of his discussion of spiritual gifts (prophecy, divination, the power of healing, etc.), this most beautiful hymn of love should be read as an assertion that, of all the gifts and capabilities that are humanly conceivable, "the greatest of these is love." The essence of *agapē*, according to this text, is manifested in such virtues as patience and kindness, generosity and humility, for "love bears all things, believes all things, hopes all things, endures all things."

The wider theological scope for understanding this selfless form of love is provided in *1 John* 4, where the love of human beings for one another is based upon God's prior love of man, "for love is of God." That is, God manifested his love in a supremely altruistic fashion by sending his only son into the world to die on man's behalf, in order that man might live eternally through knowledge and love of him. So, even as God has loved humanity, so human beings should love one another. For "God is love," and whoever lives in a state of love lives in the presence or being of God and God in him. It is the ethic of selfless love on which "the law and the prophets depend" (*Mt.* 22:40).

In the writings of the most outstanding theologian of the early Christian Middle Ages, Augustine, the *eros* of Neoplatonic mysticism and the *agapē* of the Christian tradition are synthesized. According to Augustine, God became human in order to make man divine, that is, he extended his love toward mankind to enable man to love him in return.

During the early stage of his life, Augustine engaged in a characteristically Platonic pursuit of the good, in the form of a variety of types of worldly possessions and pleasures. In the end, however, he realized that only by embracing God's love for him and abiding securely in that love could he hope to realize the happiness and peace of mind he had sought: "Our heart is restless until it rests in you" (*Confessions* 1.1.1). He compared the frantic search for happiness in sensual and intellectual pleasures to the aimless movements of objects until such time as they find their proper place. He declares, "Love is my weight: wherever I go, my love is what brings me there" (*Confessions* 13.9). The specific gravity of bodies is their love, and the proper place for men to come to rest, to which the force of true love *(caritas)* brings them, is God, "whose eternity is true and whose truth is eternal, whose love is eternal and true" (*City of God* 11.28). Of the two types of love formed by the earthly and heavenly cities, the latter is the only source of truth and happiness, for it alone glories in the love of God, not in men and the works of men (*City of God* 14.28).

Thomas Aquinas, the paramount theologian of the high Middle Ages, makes no attempt to conceal his indebtedness to Aristotle's views of love and friendship in formulating his own doctrine of Christian love. In the *Commentary on the Divine Names,* he declares that "a thing is said to be loved, when the desire of the lover regards it as his good. The attitude of disposing of the appetite to anything so as to make it its good is called love. We love each thing inasmuch as it is our good." He avoids the trap of egocentric love implied in this statement by aligning self-interest with the desire to work toward the benefit of the whole. Hence, every man loves God more than he does any other creature, in recognition of the universality of God's nature, presence, and power. Man is urged, therefore, to love God more than himself, since God "is the common good of all . . . [and] since happiness is in God as in the universal and fountainhead principle of all who are able to have a share of that happiness" (2.2.26.3).

In the writings of Bernard of Clairvaux (1090–1153), there appears a graded discipline that traces the growth of love from the lowest level to the highest. The basest form is the love a person has for himself alone. Next is the love of God, not for God's sake but for one's own sake. Then comes the love of God both for his sake and one's own and, finally, the love of oneself solely because of the love God has for one. Here cupidity and *agapē* arise from a single source, the higher form of love evolving out of the lower by a process of purifying love of all elements of egotism.

One of the most psychologically penetrating accounts of the growth of love is contained in the writings of John of the Cross (1542–1591). In his sublimely lyrical poems, *The Spiritual Canticle, The Dark Night,* and *The Living Flame of Love,* he traces the journey of the human soul from its initial quest for Christ (purgation), through its meeting with Christ (illumination), to mystical union with him. On its way to God, the soul passes through "the dark night of faith to ecstatic union with the Beloved." John declares that the soul seeks equality of love with God, such that it may, in time, be able to love God with the same love that God initially gave to the soul.

Once the soul sees God as he is, God will teach "the soul to love Him purely, with a disinterested love, as He hath loved us," but he will also enable the soul "to love Him with the strength with which He loves the soul . . . so that it may love Him." Thereby, the totally disinterested love that Christians have traditionally referred to as *agapē* (and that closely parallels the Hindu notion of *bhakti* in its highest and purest form) will be brought to full and perfect realization.

This love that arises out of ecstatic union with the divine Beloved denies all canons of reason. It strives to be totally forgetful of self and all its needs, except for the need to love and be loved by God. It is prepared to sacrifice everything, including its own life, for but a moment of blissful union with the Beloved. The soul seeks no reward, for this love is its own end and consummation.

From the Christian point of view, this divine love for man is now fully realized in man. This is the divine love of the New Testament that depicts God as beside himself with love for humanity, suffering ecstasy on our behalf, in order that we might lose ourselves in blissful union with him. "Love slays what we have been, that we may be what we were not" (Augustine).

A Modern Psychological View of Love. The writings of Hegel (1770–1831) on the subject of love may be viewed as a bridge between late medieval and modern and contemporary views in philosophy, psychology, and literature. The idea that the highest form of love is the desire to live on behalf of the welfare of the whole, which lay at the base of Aquinas's view of love, reappears in the writings of Hegel four hundred years later. In his *Philosophy of Right* (Additions, paragraph 158), he contends that love is "consciousness of my unity with another" and of people's unity together with the universal spirit, which is the basis of all ethical feeling. But when love is understood in this fashion, it is found to be at the center of a profound contradiction. This contradiction arises, first, from the realization that each person requires the love and support of other persons; otherwise, his life would be defective and incomplete. Second, love is strengthened in the discovery that "I count for something in the other, while the other in turn comes to count for something in me." Hence, love is at once the deposition and the dissolution of the contradiction between egoistic and altrustic love.

Sigmund Freud (1856–1939) revolutionized the reigning concepts of love in Western culture by making it and its cognate ideas the central core of his system of psychoanalysis. But rather than tracing the sources of love back to some divine model or external historical force, he localized the causes and operations of love within the diverse faculties and functionings of the human psyche. He, his followers, and his successors in the various fields of psychology sought to identify an empirical basis for understanding love and dealing therapeutically with biological and psychological obstacles that inhibit the full realization of human happiness.

Freud identified the motivational center of experience of desire, love, affection, friendship, and all other aspects of the emotional life in the libido. The libido, or channel for the projection into the external world of the forces of eros, is the source and seat of "the energy—regarded as a quantitative magnitude, though not at present mensurable, of those instincts which have to do with all that may be comprised under the word love." The love that theologians, philosophers, poets, and artists throughout history have depicted in such lofty and grandiloquent terms is to be identified singularly with sexual love and with sexual union as its final aim.

As in the case of the Greek *eros* and the Indian *kāma*, so the eros of Freud is to be associated univocally with all manner of objects of love—self-love, love for parents, children, siblings, and humanity as a whole, as well as concrete objects and abstract notions. All the uses to which love is put are traceable to a single instinctual source. When the libidinal energies are directed toward another human being (whether male or female), they press toward sexual union. When projected toward other entities or activities (writing a poem, communing with nature, constructing a bridge), these same forces are sublimated, that is, diverted from the realization of the sexual goal and directed into other forms of creative activity.

As in most of the major religions and cultures the world over, for Freud, love is the focal center for the interplay between the forces of life and death, the drive toward physical survival, the procreation of the species, and the establishment and maintenance of human culture in its all-inclusive sense.

As in the development of the life of the individual, so with the evolution of civilization itself, "love alone acts as a civilizing factor in the sense that it brings a change from egoism to altruism." The energy required to build and preserve civilization exacts an enormous charge against the libidinal life of humanity. Of necessity, the drive for sexual satisfaction has to be compromised with the desire for the preservation of social and cultural values. This is because "when a love-relationship is at its height, no room is left for any interest in the surrounding world. . . . In no other case does Eros so plainly betray the core of his being, his aim of making one out of many" (*Civilization and Its Discontents,* 5).

As a result of the researches and writings of such psychologists as Freud, Karen Horney, C. G. Jung, Erich Fromm, Erik Erikson, and others, our knowledge of the topographical features of the interior human landscape has been greatly extended and enriched, and our understanding of the psychodynamics of love and all the other human emotions has been enhanced. But much work remains to be done to provide a full and accurate account of the impact of modern psychology on our understanding of the premodern views of the world, Eastern and Western, and to assess the proper place for the psychological view of human life in relation to the larger panorama of the religious life of humanity.

In the minds of many psychologists, theologians, and ordinary religious people, Freud committed a serious injustice against the concept of love, on the side of both inflation and deflation. On the one hand, he exaggerated the importance of sexuality in human life by making it central and all-pervasive. On the other hand, he drastically diminished the richness of our understanding of love, when compared with the variegated palette of images of love now available to us from the world over.

From the standpoint of the religious life, Freud and the entire movement of psychology have left behind a valuable legacy of perplexing questions, questions that can now be dealt with honestly and adequately only within the scope of the whole history of humanity. Perhaps the core question on which all other questions depend is this: granted that human beings cannot live without love, is it possible to live a life of love without living it out of an awareness of a transcendent reality, whether that reality be a personal loving God or an all-embracing divine Absolute?

[*See* Devotion *and* Bhakti *for discussions of human love for the divine; for the divine counterpart, see* Grace.]

BIBLIOGRAPHY

General Works

Boyce Gibson, W. R., et al. "Love." In *Encyclopaedia of Religion and Ethics,* edited by James Hastings, vol. 8. Edinburgh, 1915. Numerous articles on the concept of love in various religious traditions.

Hunt, Morton M. *The Natural History of Love.* New York, 1959.

Mohler, James A. *Dimensions of Love: East and West.* Garden City, N.Y., 1975.

Rougemont, Denis de. *Love in the Western World.* Translated by Montgomery Belgion. New York, 1956.

Buddhism

Dayal, Har. *The Bodhisattva Doctrine in Buddhist Sanskrit Literature* (1932). Delhi, 1975.

Hamilton, Clarence Herbert, ed. *Buddhism: A Religion of Infinite Compassion.* New York, 1952.

Wright, Arthur F. *Buddhism in Chinese History.* Stanford, Calif., 1959.

Chinese Religion

Creel, H. G. *Confucius: The Man and the Myth.* New York, 1949.

Waley, Arthur, trans. and ed. *The Analects of Confucius.* London, 1938.

Christianity

D'Arcy, M. C. *The Mind and Heart of Love.* London, 1946.

John of the Cross. *Dark Night of the Soul.* Translated by E. Allison Peers. Garden City, N.Y., 1959.

Nygren, Anders. *Agape and Eros.* Translated by Philip S. Watson. Chicago, 1982.

Williams, Daniel D. *The Spirit and the Forms of Love.* New York, 1968.

Greek Thought

Flacelière, Robert. *Love in Ancient Greece.* Translated by James Cleugh. London, 1962.

Gould, Thomas. *Platonic Love.* New York, 1963.

Hinduism

Buitenen, J. A. B. van, trans. and ed. *The Bhagavadgītā in the Mahābhārata.* Chicago, 1981.

Chakraberty, Candra. *Sex Life in Ancient India.* Calcutta, 1963.

Meyer, Johann Jacob. *Sexual Life in Ancient India.* 2 vols. London, 1930.

O'Flaherty, Wendy Doniger. *Asceticism and Eroticism in the Mythology of Śiva.* London, 1973.

Modern Psychology

Freud, Sigmund. *Civilization and Its Discontents.* Edited and translated by James Strachey. New York, 1962.

Fromm, Eric. *The Art of Loving: An Enquiry into the Nature of Love.* New York, 1956.

Jung, C. G. *Modern Man in Search of a Soul* (1933). Translated by W. S. Dell and Cary F. Baynes. New York, 1964.

May, Rollo. *Love and Will.* New York, 1969.

J. Bruce Long

LOWIE, ROBERT H.

LOWIE, ROBERT H. (1883–1957), American anthropologist. Lowie was born in Vienna and emigrated to New York in 1893. After graduation from City College with honors in classics and an interlude of public-school teaching and additional training in science, he enrolled at Columbia for graduate study in anthropology under Franz Boas. His student cohort included Edward Sapir, Alexander Goldenweiser, Frank Speck, and Paul Radin, all of whom were to exert continuing influence on Lowie's ideas and approach to anthropology. Clark Wissler served as Lowie's principal fieldwork mentor and directed his formative research among the Shoshoni and various Plains tribes. He obtained his doctorate in 1908 with a comparative dissertation, "The Test-Theme in North America Mythology."

While employed by the American Museum of Natural History (1907–1917), Lowie conducted extensive fieldwork among the tribes of the Great Basin, the Southwest, and the Plains, eventually focusing on the Crow Indians of Montana. From this rich and varied data base he produced an impressive corpus of detailed ethnographic writings.

After holding a visiting professorship in 1917–1918, Lowie received a permanent appointment at the University of California, where he remained for the rest of his academic career. At Berkeley he proved a beloved teacher and an able administrator, and he broadened his theoretical horizons and range of ethnological expertise. In the 1930s he developed an interest from afar in the Ge-speaking Indians of eastern Brazil, an interest that was expressed through his promotion and translation of the valuable researches of Curt Nimuendaju. Near the end of his career Lowie studied complex societies and published two books on postfascist Germany.

Lowie's reputation rests primarily on his substantive contributions to ethnography and to theoretical issues in kinship and social organization, but he maintained an abiding interest in problems of religion. Although a freethinker, he came to view religion sympathetically as a vital and perduring force in human culture and society. His approach to religion was essentially psychological. Influenced by the work of the German critical empiricist Ernst Mach (1838–1916), Lowie felt it possible to reach objective analyses of such subjective phenomena as magical thinking, symbolic associations of meaning, and individual religious experience.

Lowie's *Primitive Religion* (1924; rev. ed., 1948) is a loosely integrated composite treatment of the subject. In his autobiography (1959), he comments that the book "met with a cold reception and I doubt whether it has exerted any influence." Nevertheless, *Primitive Religion* repays careful study as an exemplary document of the Boasian approach to religion. After a cautious consideration of the problem of defining religion, Lowie plunges directly into particularistic ethnographic data by offering synthetic sketches of four tribal religions from different regions of the world. Next he offers philosophically informed critiques of major anthropological theories of religion, taking direct aim at E. B. Tylor, James G. Frazer, and Émile Durkheim. The final section of the book comprises an uneven yet suggestive treatment of such diverse topics as individual variability in religious matters, religious movements, the role of women in religion, and relations of religion to art and economics.

Lowie's main legacy to the study of religion consists in his own rich corpus of field materials and his critical assessments of the theories of others. His significance lies in the questions he posed rather than in any synthesis he achieved.

BIBLIOGRAPHY

Details of Lowie's life and work are readily available in his entertaining autobiography, *Robert H. Lowie, Ethnologist: A Personal Record* (Berkeley, 1959). This volume contains his *vita*, outlining his professional career and listing the many honors he received, as well as a nearly complete bibliography of his many publications. A representative collection of Lowie's articles, including some of his more technical essays on myth, ceremonialism, and comparative religious ethnology, can be found in *Lowie's Selected Papers in Anthropology*, edited by Cora DuBois (Berkeley, 1960); DuBois's introductory essay lends valuable perspectives on his work, and the volume contains a fascinatingly detailed syllabus for a graduate seminar that Lowie led on his own work. The biographical picture, along with an acute modern appraisal of his theories, is sensitively filled out in Robert F. Murphy's *Robert H. Lowie* (New York, 1972), which also reprints some of Lowie's articles, including a posthumously published essay entitled "Religion in Human Life." Lowie's major statement on religion, *Primitive Religion*, rev. ed. (New York, 1948), is summarized above. The flavor of Lowie's ethnographic description of religion can be sampled in his classic monograph, *The Crow Indians* (1935; reprint, New York, 1956), and in the chapter on religion in his popular survey *Indians of the Plains* (New York, 1954), reissued, with an introduction by Raymond J. De Mallie, in 1982.

Raymond D. Fogelson

LOYOLA, IGNATIUS. *See* Ignatius Loyola.

LUBA RELIGION. The woodlands south of the African equatorial forest have been the homeland of different Luba tribes and subtribes since the first half of the first millennium, according to the latest archaeological evidence. The area stretches roughly from 5° to 10° south latitude and from 22° to 29° east longitude. Most of the peoples living in this region of central Africa share certain cultural traits and a more or less common language. In terms of political organization, however, there are fundamental differences. Four main groups can be distinguished according to political structure. The political centerpiece of the entire region is the ancient Luba empire, situated west of the Kongo River between the Lomami and Lualuba rivers. Political structure in the area of the Luba empire is based on the sacred authority of a paramount chief, an individual who is crucial to the survival of the people and success of the land. Several minor kingdoms derived their structure from the central empire; sometimes these kingdoms were vassals to the larger Luba state. The second group in terms of political structure is best represented by the matrilineal Hemba-speaking groups east of the Lualuba. The Luba Hemba, the most important of the Hemba-speaking groups, were part of the central Luba empire (at least temporarily) and pretended to derive their political institutions from the central royal court. The third group is composed of the western Luba groups that lack overriding political authority: the Luba Kasai, the Bene Luluwa, and the Bakwa Luntu. In contrast to the central and eastern groups, the western Luba peoples constitute a strict segmentary society. The fourth group, known as the Luba Songye, lives in big, well-organized villages on the southern fringe of the forest, north of the central empire. Although the Songye and the central Luba have clearly influenced each other, when the Songye reached the peak of their power as allies of the Swahili ivory and slave traders coming inland from Zanzibar in the nineteenth century, they liked to entertain a sense of superiority towards the other Luba groups. All of the Luba peoples believe in a more or less common origin, more for the sake of prestige than on historical grounds.

Luba Concepts of Body and Soul. The Luba concept of the human being provides an excellent vantage point for understanding their religious worldview. Basically the Luba believe that each human being *(muntu)* has a single essence. However, this essence has many manifestations. For instance, empirical reality is the manifestation of a deeper level of being that is tied to the Luba concept of "spirit" *(vidye)*. The essential part of each human being is the life shadow *(umvwe wa bumi)*, the soul (that is, the seat of thinking and feeling). The distinction between physical and spiritual reality, or body *(umbidi)* and soul *(muja)*, is also fundamental to the Luba vision of reality as such. According to circumstances and context, a person's inner spiritual reality, which shows through external appearances and constitutes the human being, can be symbolized in various ways: shadow, life breath, blood, voice, and so on. The two elements (body and soul for the sake of simplicity) are interdependent. Whoever destroys the body also destroys the soul—that is, weakens the whole person until finally the soul departs. Anyone who destroys the soul—for example, by casting a spell—at the same time attacks the physical person of the victim. However, there is no special link between body and soul. A slight particle of bodily matter can be sufficient to support and transfer the soul without endangering the life force of the person concerned. If an individual seeks to kill his neighbor and is successful in forcing his neighbor's soul to leave its bodily abode, the neighbor's life is endangered. However, if the same individual performs the same ritual with the intention of protecting his neighbor's life against attacks by evildoers, then the neighbor will feel safe and his life will flourish. The outcome depends upon the intention of the ritual performer. The Luba conception of a human being as a dual entity, coupled with changing modes of interpreting how the body relates to the soul, leads to a wide variety of symbolizations. Hence one hears of "hiding a soul in the bush" for protection or "tying up a soul in the bush" to destroy a person or "transferring the soul of an enemy into the body of an animal" so that this person starts acting like an animal. The soul of a person who dies in a modern city can be buried in ancestral ground by transferring some hair, nail clippings, or some other particle from the dead body to the village.

Unity of Spiritual and Physical Worlds. Anything belonging to the body or having been in contact with it can be used as a reduced and sufficient support for the soul. But conversely, any form of intimate contact with the body impregnates an object, piece of clothing, tool, or utensil with that person's spiritual reality. Getting hold of any such element gives a person power over the owner of the object. Destroying such an object with the intention of harming its owner represents a direct attack against the owner's life. Property, land, crops, dust sticking to a person's body, anything associated with the physical reality of a person is stamped with the owner's personal being. The dirt on a road retains something vital of the people walking over it. A gift is always more than a simple transfer of material objects. This view of reality has a wide range of applications. Principally, it gives rise to sexual taboos and the avoidance of physical contact in certain situations; it also leads to the belief that a blessing can be bestowed by touching a person or that the power of the soul can be depleted by coming into contact with ill-intentioned people.

The unity between humans and their environment manifests itself in a much more complicated way in the patterns of dependence within the human community. The relationship between father and son or mother and daughter seems to be a universal model to express the essence of most relationships (whether the society is matrilineal or patrilineal, the same parent model is used—that of initiator and initiate). Among the Luba, the chief is seen as the father of his subjects. The parents are "spirits" in relation to their children while the husband is the wife's "spirit" as well. The social fabric is rooted in this unified spiritual interdependence. Vital ties between members of the community not only support the essential institution of the social group, that is, the lineage: they are the real substance of group dynamism, group restraint, and group cohesion.

Worlds of the Living and the Dead. The Luba believe that when people die they go to the invisible world of the dead. This world of the shades, located under the earth, is structured according to the world of the living. There the dead live as they did on earth: in family groups, in villages, with forests and gardens and so on. From the world of the dead, the ancestors watch over their children, contacting the living through dreams, in divination sessions, and by making all sorts of strange and unusual things happen. The dead come back to the world of the living, giving their names to newborn children. The Luba Songye are unique in that they believe in the transmigration of the soul. This soul "seems normally to return three times to earth in a human body and the fourth time in the body of an animal before it goes to Efile Mukulu to remain indefinitely" (Merriam, 1961, p. 298).

The dead constantly interact with the living. Their attitude toward their descendants is ambiguous. The living must remember the dead and honor them through the performance of rituals because the survival of the dead depends on the devotion of their relatives. If their descendants neglect to show filial piety, the dead will withhold their favor and show their anger by causing crop failures, disease, bad dreams, and evil omens. Of course, the duty to remember bears most directly upon recently deceased lineage members (deceased parents or grandparents). Those people who have died in the more distant past are referred to as a collectivity under the vague title "ancestors"; among this group, only the most important people and former political leaders are directly named.

Beyond the world of human involvement, the Luba have an almost innate idea of the world as a unified whole; transcending the various Luba representations of human institutions is the idea of a creator god. There is only one creator god and he made this one world, man and woman, and nature and all it contains, including the curative qualities of herbs and roots. He "owns" all the world—"all the countries," as the Luba say. The human species is one and so the human mind is one; it transcends empirical reality. From whatever angle the Luba look at their world, they always end up, from perception to perception, at the concept of a universal. When the Luba declare, time and again, that "vidye udiko" ("spirit does exist"), they mean exactly that: spirit transcends and founds all other reality and, above all, the reality of the ancestors. God is not a sublimation of the idea of the ancestors; on the contrary, the ancestors can exist only because there was first the concept of a creator god. In the old stereotyped prayers God is always the father of all and everything, the one "who carved the fingers in our hands" (or a similar praise-name is used).

Creator God. Human life can only be conceived of as a part of a universal concept of an absolute. The Luba call this absolute Vidye, Mvidie, Efile Mukulu, Maweja, or Mulopo. Usually they use these names in combination with one or more of the praise names that are so abundant in Luba prayers and invocations. Although God is ever present in the back of their minds as the great creator spirit, the Luba do not have shrines where prayers or sacrifices can be offered to him. God is in no place—he is everywhere. Wherever there is power, there is spirit; be it a mighty tree or a thundering waterfall, the Luba will say here is spirit. From consulting the dead in divination to the ancient poison ordeal, from chasing the rain to stopping the sun from setting, there is one vision at work. Mythic language gives this visible world its true dimension.

It is not as if there was a fundamental opposition between ancestors, lineage founders, and political institutions on the one hand and the creator god on the other. Worship of the ancestors or lesser spirits does not mean that the creator god is consigned to oblivion. Indeed, the ancestors, whatever their status and function, are linked to the supreme being; they are "sons of the spirit." Their lives continue to be the existential feeding ground of the living generations. They are heroes, mediators between God and their descendants. At the beginning God worked through agents known as culture heroes who received responsibility for certain domains. These towering figures are the focus of myths and legends. The distinction between culture heroes and ancestors is not always very clear. The Songye developed a well-defined trickster figure in Kafilefile, God's opponent from the beginning. Elsewhere the trickster figure took on less dramatic features.

Medicine, Witchcraft, Sorcery. The Luba believe in a general spiritual force that pervades all nature. Here again, the Songye take an outspoken leading position: "Efile Mukulu is considered to exist in everything, and to be everything, and thus everything is a part of Efile Mukulu" (Merriam, 1961, p. 297). This concept might not be as clearly phrased by other groups, but the idea that a "shadow" or "soul" operates in everything is present in all Luba thought. This hidden force is created by God himself in the works of his own hands. It is as if God left something of his own being in all the things that he created, just as humans communicate something of themselves to the things they create and manipulate. To know the name and the inner life force of things, so as to be able to use them safely for the good of humanity, is to know medicine or witchcraft, that is, power based on knowledge and creative skills. For the central Luba, God is Shamanwa ("the father of skills"). Sorcery—using the forces hidden in things with an evil intention to kill people or destroy things—is bad. Just as people mold their world by the power of their words and through the skills of their hands, so too they try to master the invisible life force behind all material appearances. They try to get on top of this invisible reality, the hidden forces, to mold them into visible material forms. They give them names and animal or human figures to bring them within the reach of the human imagination, vision, and language. They carve them into stone or wooden statues and so doing, give them individuality, so that they may be talked to, aroused, praised, or even cursed. The world of medicine, amulets, and other ritual objects is the link between spiritual realities and the empirical world.

Ritual Life. Ritual activities such as prayers, invocations, and offerings can be performed by individuals or by officials. Officials derive their ability to officiate from their function and position in the group (e.g., head of the household, leading elder of a lineage, headman of a village) or from a special initiation as a diviner and traditional healer. The prophetic type of performer takes over from the official one at particular occasions for a variety of reasons: divination, healing, the cleansing of defiled persons or villages, and so on. These ritual actions take place when the dead interfere with the living by claiming attention or demanding to be consulted; rituals can also be required because the ancestors want to be honored through prayer and sacrifice.

The main characteristic of the duly initiated traditional healer is spirit possession accompanied by prophetic utterances. Diviners and traditional healers constitute a kind of informal guild, one initiating the other, but this guild should not be confused with the secret societies that formerly were abundant in Lubaland. Spirit possession usually occurs at shrines. The shrines themselves consist of tiny huts containing different kinds of receptacles in which simple objects, symbolizing the presence of the spirit during rituals, are placed. Sometimes the shrine is a tree planted to honor an ancestor. Ritual objects, usually receptacles of medicine, can also be placed at the entrance of a village (e.g., hunting spirits) or can be hidden together with special medicine under the roof of the main hut. A man's principal wife will then be entrusted with the keeping of the sacred objects. At certain times standardized rituals take place: first-fruit rituals, fertility rituals at the full moon, rites of passage, burial, and so on. Luba traditional religion forms a well-balanced whole in which the living and the dead can find peace and rest from the anxieties of human existence and through which the Luba find themselves inserted into the universal world of religious quest and spiritual concern.

BIBLIOGRAPHY

Burton, W. F. P. *Luba Religion and Magic in Custom and Belief.* Annales du Musée Royal de l'Afrique Centrale, Sciences Humaines, vol. 8, no. 35. Tervuren, Belgium, 1961. Written by a member of the Congo Garanganze Mission after many years of living and traveling among the central Luba.

Caeneghem, P. R. van. *La notion de Dieu chez les BaLuba du Kasai.* Memoires de l'Académie Royale des Sciences Coloniales, Classe des Sciences Morales et Politques, vol. 9, fasc. 2. Brussels, 1956. The best work of a missionary priest who lived for years among the Luba Kasai.

Colle, R. P. *Les Baluba.* 2 vols. Collection de Monographies Ethnographiques, vol. 10. Brussels, 1913. Also written by a missionary. Still one of the basic sources, especially for the Luba Hemba.

Göhring, Heinz. *BaLuba: Studien zur Selbstzuordnung und Herrschaftsstruktur der baLuba.* Studia Ethnologica, vol. 1. Meisenheim am Glan, 1970. The best synthesis of the available literature; a scholarly work offering, with an extensive bibliography, the indispensable introduction to any further research.

Merriam, Alan P. "Death and the Religious Philosophy of the Basongye." *Antioch Review* 21 (Fall 1961): 293–304. Excellent.

Mukenge, Leonard. "Croyances religieuses et structures sociofamiliales en société luba: 'Buena Muntu,' 'Bakishi,' 'Milambu.' " *Cahiers économiques et sociaux* 5 (March 1967): 6–94. The *thèse de license* of a Luba student at the Lovanium University (now Unaza). Outstanding.

Overbergh, Cyrille van. *Les Basonge.* Collection de Monographies Ethnographiques, no. 3. Brussels, 1908. Based on early reports of travelers and civil service men. Still worthwhile.

Reefe, Thomas Q. *The Rainbow and the Kings: A History of the Luba Empire to 1891.* Berkeley, 1981. Essential to any further study of Luba culture. Outstanding.

Theuws, J. A. (Th.). *De Luba-mens.* Annales du Musée Royal de l'Afrique Centrale, Sciences Humaines, vol. 8, no. 38. Tervuren, Belgium, 1962. Göhring called this work by a missionary an "intuitive synthesis." The information is based on prolonged field research in central Lubaland.

Verhulpen, Edmond. *Baluba et Balubaïsés du Katanga.* Anvers, 1936. A detailed study of Luba groups by a former member of the civil service. As a first orientation, the administrative information is still useful.

J. A. THEUWS

LUBAVITCH. *See* Hasidism, *article on* Habad Hasidism.

LUCK. *See* Chance.

LUDI SAECULARES, the centennial games of ancient Rome, were rites celebrated in fulfillment of a vow pronounced at the beginning of the previous *saeculum.* Because a *saeculum,* in the wider sense of the term, was a period of time longer than the longest human life, no one could attend the games twice. It seems that initially the games went on for three nights; in any case, from the time of Augustus onward they lasted three days and three nights and were held, in principle, every 100 or 110 years, depending on the computation. The functioning and arrangement of this festival changed in the course of time, but its purpose remained the same: to purify the *res publica* at the beginning of a new era, by putting a hopeful end to a given period of time.

We do not know how far back the centennial games go. The ancients, followed by some modern scholars, sometimes claimed an early date: the fifth century BCE; it is certain at any rate that centennial games were celebrated in 249 BCE at the urging of the Sibylline Books; these games included nocturnal sacrifices in honor of Dis Pater (god of the underworld) and Proserpina, to which were added chariot races. It may be, however, that in one or another manner these games replaced a cult of the Valerian gens, which clearly was of greater antiquity but was celebrated on the same site as the centennial games: in the Campus Martius (Field of Mars), near the Tiber River, level with the modern Ponte Vittorio Emmanuele, in that part of the Field of Mars known as the Tarentum (though the connection with the Tarentum is doubtful).

At the beginning of the reign of Augustus, in 17 BCE, centennial games were celebrated with great pomp in order to mark the end of a period of destruction and bloodshed and the beginning of a golden age. It was in the form the games acquired at this time that they were subsequently celebrated in 88 and 204 CE. (A parallel series of festivities was held on 21 April of the years 248, 147, and 47 BCE to commemorate the centenaries of the foundation of Rome; the rites were simpler but also went by the name of centennial games.) The new liturgy comprised a complex series of nocturnal and diurnal rites. The nocturnal rites, which opened each day's festival after midnight and were regarded as a prolongation of the games of antiquity, marked the close of the preceding century with a sacrifice to the Fates (1 June), the Ilithyiae, goddesses of childbirth (2 June), and Mother Earth (3 June). The daytime sacrifices were offered to Jupiter Optimus Maximus (1 June, on the Capitoline), Juno Regina (2 June, on the Capitoline), and Apollo and Diana (3 June, on the Palatine). During the three nights, after the sacrifices, *sellisternia* or religious banquets were celebrated on the Capitoline in honor of Juno and Diana; 110 matrons of senatorial and knightly rank took part, and then plays were presented on the Campus near the Tiber. During the daytime these plays were continued from 1 to 3 June after the sacrifices to Apollo and Diana; other plays were added, known as Latin plays, and there were more banquets in honor of Juno and Diana. The climax of the entire festival came on the third day after the sacrifice to Apollo and Diana: 27 boys and 27 girls of senatorial rank, whose fathers and mothers were still living, recited a *Carmen saeculare* on the Palatine and the Capitoline (the centennial ode for 17 BCE was composed by Horace). After the celebration of the banquets and other rites, the plays ended, and chariot races, held in a temporary arena, brought the liturgy proper to an end.

Along with the festivals of the Arval Brothers, the centennial games of the emperors Augustus and Septimius Severus (193–211) are the Roman religious liturgies best known to us, thanks to the discovery of extensive records in epigraphic form.

BIBLIOGRAPHY

Brind'amour, P. "L'origine des jeux séculaires." In *Aufstieg und Niedergang der römischen Welt*, vol. 2.16.2, pp. 1334–1417. Berlin and New York, 1978.

Gagé, Jean. *Recherches sur les jeux séculaires*. Paris, 1934.

Pighi, Giovanni Battista. *De ludis saecularibus populi Romani Quiritium libri sex*. 2d ed. Amsterdam, 1965.

JOHN SCHEID
Translated from French by Matthew J. O'Connell

LUGBARA RELIGION. The Lugbara are a Sudanic-speaking people of northwestern Uganda and northeastern Zaire, culturally related to the Azande and Mangbetu to the northwest. Numbering about a quarter of a million, the Lugbara are largely peasant farmers who grow grains and keep some cattle and other livestock. Their land is about 4,000 feet above sea level, well watered and fertile, with a population density of over two hundred people to the square mile in the central areas. The Lugbara have a politically uncentralized society in which traditional authority is held by the elders of small patrilineal lineages. Such lineages are the bases of local settlements and are linked into a segmentary lineage system of the classic kind. Above the elders, ritual and political authority is exercised by rainmakers, one to each clan, and occasionally by prophets. Since colonial rule was established by the Belgians in 1900 and the British in 1914, there have been administrative chiefs and headmen, but these stand very much outside the religious system. Catholic Verona Fathers and the Protestant Africa Inland Mission have been active since World War I and have had considerable success in education and conversion; there are relatively few Muslims. In the 1950s, when the main anthropological research was carried out, the mass of the people adhered to the traditional religion. Since then this situation may have changed, due mainly to the political upheavals and population movements under presidents Amin and Obote: the traditional lineage system has been severely weakened, and the cults associated with it have lost their importance.

Myth. The Lugbara have a corpus of myth that tells of the creation of the world and the formation of their society. One myth tells that at the beginning humans dwelt and conversed with the Deity in the sky, coming daily down a rope or tower to farm; a woman who was hoeing cut it down, and since then people have lived on earth, ignorant of divine will and subject to change and death. Another myth states that the Deity (Adroa—the diminutive form of the word *adro*, connotating his distance from mankind, not his lack of power) created a man and a woman far to the north. The woman was created pregnant and gave birth to animals and to a son and a daughter. This sibling pair gave birth to another, and several such generations followed. Each is credited with the invention of processes of transformation of natural products into domestic ones: smithing, potmaking, hunting, and so on. Finally there were born two sons, the culture heroes who formed society as it ideally is today. Each of the two culture heroes hunted with his sons, killing and eating a son each day; this filial cannibalism led to their expulsion, and each hero (accompanied by a sister's son and a bull) was compelled to cross the Nile and to go to the mountains in the middle of the country. There the two heroes hunted and killed buffalo but lacked fire to cook the meat. Each hero then descended to the plains and found there a leper woman with fire. After cooking and eating the meat, each hero cured one of the leper women (thus making her physically complete) and impregnated her. The armed brothers of the leper women forced the heroes to marry the women and provide cattle bridewealth. Each hero eventually did the same with some thirty women, whose sons were the founders of the present sixty or so clans. The heroes then retired to their mountains and died.

The myth explains the existence of social groups and settlements, of marriage and the legitimacy of offspring, and of feuds (the traditional basis for the maintenance of social order). The preheroic period is timeless, asocial, amoral, and marked by lack of order and authority; the postheroic period, structured by the passing of time, is both social and moral, with order maintained by genealogically sanctioned authority. The periods are bridged by the heroic mediators. The same pattern may be seen in spatial terms, with related lineages in a settlement's neighborhood, then a belt of people feared as magicians, and beyond them an amoral wilderness of strange, incestuous, and cannibalistic people. The myths explain the form of society, its relationship with the Deity, and the distinction that runs through Lugbara cosmology between the "inside" of home and settlement and the "outside" of the bushland, where spirits and other manifestations of the extrahuman power of the Deity dwell. Lugbara ritual is concerned essentially with the maintenance of the boundary between these two moral spheres.

Sacrifice to the Dead and Spirits. Sacrifice is not made to the Deity. The central cult is that of the dead, who are considered senior members of their lineages and who bridge the main cosmological boundary. The Lugbara concept of the person is important here. Men are considered "persons of the home" and women "things of the bushland," having the potentially dangerous power of procreation that links them with the Deity. A person is composed of physical elements such as body and blood and the mystical ones of soul, spirit, and influence. Only men have "souls" *(orindi),* the seat of lineage authority, although those women born first of a set of siblings may have souls when they grow old; both men and women have "spirit" *(adro),* the seat of idiosyncratic and antisocial behavior; and both have *tali,* the seat of influence gained over others. At death the soul goes to the deity in the sky and may later be redomesticated by a diviner as a "ghost" *(ori)* as well as an "ancestor" *(a'bi).* Only the heads of lineage segments who leave sons are usually made into ghosts; others join a collectivity of ancestors. The spirit goes to the bushland, where it dwells with the immanent and evil aspect of the Deity (Adro); the *tali* merges with a collectivity of *tali.*

Death is marked by elaborate mortuary rites, which are the only important rites of transition. The corpse is buried and dances are held at which men of lineages related to the deceased dance competitively and aggressively to demonstrate their relative seniority within the total lineage structure. When death occurs, it is said that disorder has entered the community, and clan incest is permitted as a sign of this disorder; after a certain period has elapsed, order is reestablished by more dances and the distribution of food and arrows.

Ghosts are given individual shrines (in the shape of miniature huts) where they may be offered sacrifices; other patrilineal ancestors have collective shrines; and there are shrines for matrilateral ancestors. The ghost shrines for the recently dead are located in the compound, but after a few generations they are moved outside, a sign that their incumbents have merged spiritually with the Deity. The forms, distribution, and details of oblation with regard to these many shrines cannot be given here.

Sacrifice at the ghost shrines is part of the process by which lineage authority is exercised by the elders. Hence, it lies at the heart of the maintenance of social order within the community. Sacrifice follows on the invocation of the ghosts. It is believed that an elder whose authority is flouted by a dependent sits near the shrines in his compound and ponders the offense; the ghosts "hear" him and decide to send sickness to the offender to "show" him the error of his behavior; the offender then falls sick; the elder consults oracles that state which ghost is responsible and what oblation is demanded. In actuality a person falls sick and the process only then begins. If the patient recovers, then a sacrifice is made (if he or she dies, then the Deity is responsible and nothing can be done). The animal (ox, sheep, goat, or fowl) is consecrated and slaughtered. Part of the meat and blood is placed in the shrines; part is cooked and eaten later by the congregation. Some of the cooked meat is divided and taken home by the members of the congregation, who are members of lineages that share the same ghosts. The elder and others concerned discuss the case until a consensus has been reached that the original offense or dispute has been settled and atoned; they bless the patient with their breath and spittle, and the assembled kin, seated by generation and so representing the unity of normally competitive lineages, consume the cooked meat and beer. The stated purpose of this rite is to purify the home, to remove conflict and ensure unity and continuity. Sacrifice is also made, usually on behalf of junior kin, to the collectivity of lineage ancestors and to matrilateral ancestors.

Offerings are also made to many kinds of spirits *(adro),* invisible powers that are of a different order of existence than that of humans. Such spirits are beyond the understanding or control of normal people. Spirits are held to be innumerable. At one time or another, some are attached to prophets; others represent expressions of divine power (e.g., lightning, winds). All have as a central attribute the ability to possess a living person and to make the victim tremble or shake, a condition curable only by a diviner. Initial communication with a spirit is by its possession of a living person; almost all cases are of women, in particular those in an ambiguous moral situation (such as that of a persistently barren wife). The possessed woman consults a diviner to discover the identity of the offended spirit, then places a small shrine for it where she periodically makes offerings of grain and milk. There are no spirit cults as such; offerings are only made by individuals.

Divination. The need for the living to know the identity of the dead and the spirits with whom they come into contact requires divination. There are several kinds of oracles and diviners. Oracles, operated by men in the public space of the open air, consist essentially of material artifacts that "select" names put to them by those consulting them. Diviners are postmenopausal or barren women, who divine under possession in the darkness of their huts with only the client present. They confirm the identity of a spirit or of a witch or sorcerer (which oracles cannot do) and also redomesticate the soul when it has gone outside of the social realm to live with the Deity in the sky. Their power is thought to come directly from the Deity and is feared as being spiritual and dangerous.

Evil. Evil is represented as the work of harmful human beings assumed to be witches and sorcerers. Using the classic distinction made for the Azande by Evans-Pritchard, witches are believed to harm others by an innate mystical power; among the Lugbara they are older men who bewitch their own kin because of envy or anger. Sorcerers use material objects or "medicines," and among the Lugbara they are women and young men who lack the authority that witches have to pervert power for their own ends; because of this lack, sorcerers must turn to material means (including both poisons and nonpoisonous objects). Sorcerers are especially held to be women who are jealous of their co-wives. Both witches and sorcerers are believed to cause sudden and painful sicknesses, and their identities may be discovered by diviners who can also cure the affliction, usually by sucking its essence from the victim's body. Whereas witchcraft is traditional and, although evil, not particularly morally reprehensible (since the witch merely has the innate power and may not always be able to control it), sorcery is seen as a modern phenomenon and an abomination because it is deliberate and malign in its purpose.

Rainmakers and Prophets. Each subclan has one rainmaker, the senior man of the senior descent line. He is believed to be able to control the rainfall by manipulating rain stones kept in a pot buried in his rain grove. In the past he was expected to end interlineage feuds by cursing the antagonists with impotence if they crossed a line drawn by him between their territories. He tells his community the times for planting and harvesting. And he is thought to be able to end epidemics and famines by beseeching the Deity. In brief, he is able to regulate the rain that links sky and earth, to control the fertility of human beings and of crops, to mark territorial and moral space, and to establish the orderly passage of time. He is held to be a repository of some of the secret truth and knowledge of cosmic categories held by the Deity. A rainmaker is symbolically buried at his initiation by other rainmakers, and later, at his actual death, he is buried silently at night in a manner opposite to that of ordinary people.

Prophets have appeared among the Lugbara on rare occasions, as emissaries of the Deity with a message to re-form society in the face of disasters. The most famous was Rembe, a man of the neighboring Kakwa people. In the 1890s the Lugbara approached Rembe requesting that he give them a sacred water. This water was intended to remove the epidemics that were killing both humans and cattle, as well as the Arabs and Europeans who were entering the region at the same time. In 1916 Rembe entered Lugbaraland, called by elders for his help in removing further epidemics and Europeans. He established a cult known as Dede ("grandmother," as it protected people) or Yakan (from the root *ya,* "to make tremble"). Adherents drank water from a sacred pool in which dwelt the power of the Deity; this would drive away the Europeans and bring back ancestors and dead cattle. Members of the cult attempted to establish a new egalitarian community and no longer recognized differences of descent, age, or sex. After the threat of revolt

Rembe was deported by the British colonial authorities and hanged in the Sudan. Today he is still remembered and given mythopoeic attributes of sacredness and inversion, and it is said that he can never die and will one day return.

BIBLIOGRAPHY

The main source is my *Lugbara Religion: Religion and Authority among an East African People* (London, 1960). I have also given a shorter account in *The Lugbara of Uganda* (New York, 1965).

JOHN MIDDLETON

LUGH, a Celtic deity, is the equivalent of Mercury in Julius Caesar's account of the Gaulish divinities (*Gallic Wars* 6.17). The theonym is attested by the latinized toponym *Lugu-dunum* ("fortress of Lug-us"), which was associated with about fifteen localities, principally present-day Lyons (Rhone), Laon (Aisne), Laudun (Gard), Loudun (Vienne), Loudon (Sarthe), and Leiden (Netherlands). The theonym also is attested by the plural *Lugoves* ("the three Lugus") in two Gallo-Roman inscriptions at Avenches and Bonn and by the anthroponym *Lugu-selva* ("that which is the property of Lugh") in an inscription from Périgueux. Finally, it is attested by a small number of suffixed derivatives of the *Lugurix* type in Genouilly (Cher) and of the *Lugius* type in Narbonne.

In Great Britain *Lugh* exists in the hybrid Romano-British toponym *Luguvallium*, the ancient name for Carlisle, near Hadrian's Wall. All other testimonies are from the insular Celts. The god Lugh ("the shining one") is primarily known as the first god of the Irish pantheon and the chief of the Tuatha Dé Danann. The mythological text that relates his adventures is the *Battle of Magh Tuiredh*, of which the oldest version is found in a fifteenth-century manuscript. But the text is very archaic, and there is evidence that Lugh was known prior to the tenth century. Lugh is called Samildanach ("skilled in many arts"), and he bears the surname Lamfada ("of the long arm"). He alone possesses all faculties and assumes all the functions of the other gods: he is at once druid, warrior, and craftsman. It is he who through his magic ensures the victory of the Irish over the demons, the Fomhoire, who oppressed Ireland. The son of the Fomorian Delbaeth ("undifferentiated form") and of Eriu (Ireland), he defeats his grandfather Balar ("flash of lightning") by slaying him with a slingshot. But Lugh is also called the son of Cian ("the remote one"), and Cian is the son of Dian Cécht, the divine leech. Lugh is in turn the father of the great hero of the Ulster saga, Cú Chulainn.

The adventures of the Welsh equivalent, Llew Llaw Gyffes ("of the skillful hand"), are told in the medieval tales of the *Mabinogion*, but the mythology is extremely dull, diluted, and romanticized.

BIBLIOGRAPHY

Guyonvarc'h, Christian-J., and Françoise Le Roux. *Textes mythologiques irlandais*, vol. 1. Rennes, 1980.

Mac Cana, Proinsias. *Celtic Mythology*. Rev. ed. Feltham, England, 1983.

FRANÇOISE LE ROUX and CHRISTIAN-J. GUYONVARC'H
Translated from French by Erica Meltzer

LU HSIANG-SHAN (1139–1193), literary name, Lu Chiu-yüan; important Neo-Confucian thinker, traditionally credited with the founding of the school of Mind *(hsin-hsüeh)* in the Southern Sung dynasty (1127–1279). Lu is noted for his single-minded dedication to the transmission of the Confucian Way as experiential learning (i.e., learning to do good rather than learning about good) and exemplary instruction (i.e., teaching by exemplifying the virtues being taught). Lu was the product of a long family tradition of commitment to scholarship and public service. The Lu clan, with a membership of three thousand and an uninterrupted history of two centuries, is truly exceptional in Chinese history. Lu, however, witnessed the decline of the family fortune. While Lu's success in entering officialdom through the examination system may have helped to enhance the waning prestige of the clan, his governmental positions in the local magistracy do not seem to have benefited the financial status of the family.

Lu spent most of his life teaching and lecturing, and is said to have attracted over a thousand followers to his academy in Hsiang Shan (Elephant Mountain) near his hometown in Fu-chou (Kiangsi Province). Through verbal instructions and direct, individual contact with students he taught that to learn to be human—the continuous, dynamic, and holistic process of self-cultivation that is the ultimate concern of Confucians—one must begin by consciously dedicating oneself to realizing that which is great in one's original mind, in other words, to cultivating the innate goodness in our nature. This distinctively Mencian line of thinking was actively and conscientiously advocated by Lu as the "simple, direct" method, that is, the authentic Confucian way of life. Lu perceived his own intellectual orientation as resulting from an encounter with the thought of Meng-tzu. Since Meng-tzu insists that knowing one's own mind is the main task of education, Lu concluded that the best method of appreciating Meng-tzu is to acquire an understanding of the substance of one's own original mind.

Lu's biography records that as a teenager he was fascinated with the infinite capacity of the human mind to know, to understand, to experience, and indeed to "embody" the world beyond. His famous dictum, "The universe is my mind and my mind is the universe," is said to have been coined when he was merely fourteen years old. It is important to note that in Lu's philosophy of mind *(hsin)* the issue of the primacy of consciousness over existence does not feature prominently. He emphasized that each human being has the potential for full self-realization and that sagehood is attainable through the natural functioning of the original mind. To realize that which is great in us we must follow Meng-tzu's instruction to first develop our "great body" (i.e., our moral nature) before satisfying our "small body" (i.e., our instinctual demands). The task of learning to be human—our ultimate concern—is accomplished by responding to our inner "calling," rather than by acquiring empirical knowledge about the world around us.

Lu's debate with Chu Hsi (1130–1200), commonly described as the conflict between moral self-cultivation and intellectual pursuit, reflects a deep divide within the Confucian tradition on the critical issue of self-cultivation. Lu insisted that a prior ethico-religious commitment is absolutely necessary for initiating the process of moral self-cultivation. The pursuit of knowledge does not lead to self-understanding. Instead, the internal resources of the original mind must be fully explored so that we can gain enough inner strength to encounter the outside world. Fragmented knowledge obtained from the external world cannot help us build moral character. This, however, does not mean that learning involves only introspection. For Lu, learning is based on the concept that the universe is not external to the mind and that the original substance of the mind is the locus of moral creativity.

Understandably, in his critique of Chu Hsi's separation of the mind and principle *(li)* Lu maintained that mind is principle. Lu's thesis, often characterized as a form of subjective idealism, is predicated on the unity of subjective and objective (ontological) reality as a defining characteristic of the original mind. We feel alienated from the world around us only when we privatize our heavenly endowed nature to form a unity with the myriad things. The infinite capacity of the original mind is such that there is nothing that can actually lie outside its sensitivity. The "great body" inherent in our nature is our true self (subjectivity). But far from being our private possession, our true self is universal as well as communal and is shared by all humanity and all things. According to Meng-tzu, the full realization of the feelings of the mind naturally leads to an experiential understanding of our nature. Since our nature is decreed by Heaven, an understanding of our nature brings an understanding of Heaven (ontological reality).

The necessity for experiential learning and exemplary instruction, despite the total self-sufficiency of the original mind, is dictated by two considerations: material desires and private opinions. Lu believed that our failure to return to our original mind is mainly due to the problems of inertia and limitation. Material desires, such as excessive attachment to loved objects, weigh us down. As we become obsessed with our instinctual demands aroused by external forces our original mind is temporarily lost. If we continue to ignore the biddings of our inner calling it is likely that the sensitivity of our original mind will be virtually numbed. Therefore, the greatest sorrow in the human condition is the loss of sensitivity, which signifies a severe case of inertia. While unchanneled material desires numb our senses and, as a result, hamper our moral creativity, private opinions, formed by unreflective acceptance of established conventions, are likely to limit our moral vision and confine our intellectual horizon to a narrow range. To free ourselves from the constraints of material desires and private opinions we need to purify our minds through the art of actively illuminating their original brilliance. The idea of searching for the lost mind, preserving it, nourishing it, and totally identifying with it features saliently in Lu's recorded conversations. Although the influences of "pointing directly to the original mind" in Ch'an (Jpn., Zen) Buddhism and the "fasting of the mind" *(hsin-chai)* in philosophical Taoism are unmistakable, Lu's spiritual and intellectual self-definition as a transmitter of the Confucian way in the Mencian line is fully justified.

Some scholars have falsely contended that Lu's emphasis on experiential learning and exemplary teaching somehow prevented him from taking classical studies seriously. In fact, like his contemporary Confucian masters, Lu taught and lectured from within the perspective of the classics. However, unlike Chu Hsi (the paradigmatic teacher and lecturer of the classical tradition), Lu perceived the classics as the embodiment of a shareable experience that can only be re-experienced through a personal encounter with the sages as exemplary teachers. One encounters the true intentions of the sages by engaging in a dialogue with them through the art of reading. The art of reading, for Lu, involves "refinement" *(ching)* and "thoroughness" *(shu)*. Lu did not advise students to pursue extensive knowledge, as did Chu Hsi in his doctrine of the "investigation of things." Most essential is to acquire a real taste for the sagely message, its subtle meanings and its far-reaching implications. A refined and thorough understanding of three to five chapters, Lu maintained, is far superior to browsing thirty thousand chapters. To him, reading is not simply to extend our information; its primary function is to deepen our self-knowledge. Lu's radical statement that "if one understands the basis of learning, all the six classics are footnotes on oneself [one's true self]" is neither individualist nor subjectivist; it is an articulation of his personal faith in the sharability and commonality of the original mind beyond time and space:

> There is only one mind. My mind, my friend's mind, the mind of sages thousands of years ago, and the mind of the sages thousands of years to come are all the same. The substance of the mind is infinite. If one can completely develop his mind, he will become identified with Heaven. To acquire learning is to appreciate this fact. (Chan, 1969, p. 585)

[*See also* Confucian Thought, *article on* Neo-Confucianism; Hsin; *and the biographies of Meng-tzu and Chu Hsi.*]

BIBLIOGRAPHY

For an edition of Lu Hsiang-shan's collected works, see *Lu Chiu-yüan chi* (Peking, 1980). Useful interpretive literature includes the following.

Cady, Lyman V. "The Philosophy of Lu Hsiang-shan." Ph.D. diss., Union Theological Seminary, 1939.

Chan, Wing-tsit. *A Source Book of Chinese Philosophy.* Princeton, 1969. See pages 572–587.

Fung Yu-lan. *A History of Chinese Philosophy.* 2 vols. Princeton, 1952–1953. See volume 2, chapter 14.

Huang Siu-chi. *Lu Hsiang-shan: A Twelfth-Century Chinese Idealist Philosopher.* New Haven, 1944.

TU WEI-MING

LU HSIU-CHING (406–477), Taoist scholar and liturgical master active during the Liu Sung dynasty (420–479) in China. Regarded as the seventh patriarch of the Celestial Master sect *(T'ien-shih Tao),* founded by Chang Tao-ling in Szechwan Province in the second century, Master Lu was a key figure in the development of the Taoist church during the Six Dynasties period (317–618). He has traditionally been credited with the earliest organization of the Taoist canon *(Tao-tsang)* into its three major sections. Further, by editing and teaching the so-called Ling-pao (Spiritual Treasure) scriptures, upon which he based his instructions for Ling-pao rites, Master Lu laid down basic and enduring patterns for the subsequent development of Taoist liturgical life.

Born in Chekiang Province, Lu is said to have left his family and official career in order to collect and study Taoist scriptures. Although he withdrew to Mount Lu (Lu-shan) in Kiangsi Province, he nonetheless enjoyed close connections with the courts of several Liu Sung emperors, and as a result, both Mount Lu and the Ch'ung-hsü monastery, which was built for him outside the capital (modern Nanking), became renowned centers of Ling-pao Taoism. Traditional accounts of his life include stories of omens surrounding his birth, his healing of Emperor Ming-ti (r. 465–473), and dramatic victories over the learned Buddhists of his day in public debates. His most prominent disciple, Sun Yu-yüeh, was in turn a teacher of the great Taoist scholar T'ao Hung-ching, to whom much of Lu's scriptural collection was passed down. [*See the biography of T'ao Hung-ching.*]

Textual references to the earliest form of the Taoist canon date back to the year 437, when Master Lu signed himself "Disciple of the Three Caverns." These "caverns" *(tung),* evoking traditional beliefs that divine treasures are hidden in caves under the earth, were in fact the collected scriptural revelations of several Taoist groups: the Shang-ch'ing (Supreme Purity) scriptures; the Ling-pao scriptures; and the San-huang (Three Sovereigns) scriptures. *Master Lu's Catalog of the Scriptures of the Three Caverns,* no longer extant but quoted elsewhere, was perhaps the first comprehensive listing of all these texts. Although the notion of three caverns probably did not originate with Master Lu, his early catalog not only served to define what was deemed authentic and Taoist at that time, but may well have established the notion of a single canon common to the various early movements of the emerging tradition.

Master Lu dedicated much of his career to the exposition of the Ling-pao scriptures, which were claimed to have been revealed over a hundred years earlier. In fact, they were composed in the late 390s by Ko Ch'ao-fu, whose remarkable set of "revelations" not only drew upon Shang-ch'ing and Buddhist texts circulating then, but also upon the extensive library of his renowned great-uncle, Ko Hung. [*See the biography of Ko Hung.*] The popularity of these scriptures provoked so many forgeries and imitations that some fifty years after their initial release Master Lu undertook the difficult task of identifying and editing the original corpus. His catalog of the Ling-pao scriptures, of which only the preface *(Ling-pao ching-mu hsü)* remains extant in the Taoist canon, has recently been reconstructed from documents uncovered at Tun-huang.

Actively extolling the ultimate primacy of these particular scriptures and the effectiveness of Ling-pao rites, Master Lu formulated a set of rituals for lay followers, as well as rites for the ordination of Taoist masters and the transmission of sacred scriptures. These liturgical writings helped develop an institutional structure within Taoism by combining Han dynasty (206 BCE–220 CE) court ceremonies with the practices of both the early Celestial Master sect and the old traditions and cults of southern China. Fundamental liturgical practices included the internalization of protective deities within the body of the initiated Taoist (the *tao-shih*) and their projection as messengers in the course of the rite; the use of talismans (especially the five Ling-pao written talismans) to orient and bind the various levels of heaven, earth, and underworld in each of the five directions (four cardinal points and the center); and the proclamation and burning (to effect their transmission heavenward) of official petitions for such ends as the release of ancestors from the sufferings of the underworld and the protection of the state. Basic to Master Lu's liturgies is a macrocosm-microcosm identity of the extended universe and the internal geography of the body, combined with a bureaucratic mediation of proper relations among spiritual realms. These features served to define a distinctive type of religious authority in the centuries of religious innovation after the fall of the Han dynasty, an authority that was not only formally invested, hierarchical, and stable, but also simultaneously holistic and deeply rooted in the practices of local traditions. The Ling-pao liturgies codified by Master Lu were amplified and embellished until the middle of the Sung dynasty (960–1279), when there were major changes and innovations in the ritual tradition as a whole. Even today, however, the rites of ordained Taoist masters in Taiwan still contain sections that faithfully preserve the instructions first penned by Master Lu.

[*See also* Taoism, *article on* Taoist Literature.]

BIBLIOGRAPHY

The sources on Lu Hsiu-ching's life and work are detailed in Ch'en Kuo-fu's *Tao-tsang yüan-liu k'ao* (1949; rev. ed. Peking, 1963), pp. 38–44. Special studies in Western languages include Ōfuchi Ninji's "On *Ku Ling-Pao-Ching,*" *Acta Asiatica* 27 (1974): 33–56, and Max Kaltenmark's "*Ling-pao:* Note sur un terme du taoïsme religieux," *Mélanges publiées par l'Institut des Hautes Études Chinoises* 2 (1960): 559–588. For general background on this period of Taoist history, consult Rolf A. Stein's "Religious Taoism and Popular Religion from the Second to the Seventh Centuries," in *Facets of Taoism,* edited by Holmes Welch and Anna Seidel (New Haven, 1979), pp. 53–81; and Michel Strickmann's "The Mao Shan Revelations: Taoism and the Aristocracy," *T'oung pao* 63 (1977): 1–64.

CATHERINE M. BELL

LUKE THE EVANGELIST, according to Christian tradition the author of both the third canonical gospel and *Acts of the Apostles.* The *Gospel of Luke* and *Acts* are linked by similarities of style and theology, by their dedications to a certain Theophilus, and by reference to a first book, almost certainly the *Gospel of Luke,* in *Acts* 1:1. Unlike the other evangelists, Luke indicates that he was not an eyewitness to the events of Jesus' ministry that he describes (*Lk.* 1:1–3).

Luke is mentioned three times in the New Testament in letters ascribed to Paul (*Col.* 4:14, *2 Tm.* 4:11, *Phlm.* 24). Although a Lucius (a variant of the same name) appears in *Acts* 13:1 and *Romans* 16:21, there is no explicit link between this figure and Luke. In *Colossians* 4:14, Luke, who is with Paul, is called "the beloved physician." In the same context three other disciples seem to be identified as Jewish; apparently Luke was a gentile. Only the reference to Luke in *Philemon* can be certainly ascribed to Paul, inasmuch as *2 Timothy* is probably, and *Colossians* possibly, pseudonymous. In any event, each reference supports a traditional association of Luke with Paul. That association may also be attested to by the so-called "we-passages" of *Acts.* In four separate instances (*Acts* 16:10–17, 20:5–15, 21:1–18, 27:1–28:16) the narration of Paul's travels unaccountably switches from third person to first person plural, creating the impression that the narrator accompanied Paul. Although other explanations are possible, the traditional one, that Luke the physician had joined Paul's party at those points, is a reasonable one. Since Luke is otherwise not a prominent figure in early Christianity, the attribution of two major New Testament books to him becomes understandable if it is, indeed, historically grounded. (A Timothy or Titus would otherwise have been a more obvious choice for such an attribution.) That Luke's understanding and presentation of Pauline theology is in some respects inadequate, scarcely disproves a personal relationship between them.

Irenaeus (c. 180) names Luke as the third evangelist and a companion of Paul and describes Luke as having recorded the gospel as preached by Paul (*Against Heresies* 3.1.1). The Muratorian canon (probably late second century) gives a rather full description of Luke that agrees with Irenaeus and with the slim biblical evidence. (Quite possibly, the earliest tradition is simply based on scripture.) Eusebius (c. 325) reports that Luke was "by race an Antiochian," a physician, and a companion of Paul (*Church History* 3.4.6).

Luke's vocabulary was once thought to reflect his medical training, but comparative studies have shown that his medical terminology does not surpass what might be expected of a Hellenistic author. According to an ancient, anti-Marcionite prologue to the gospel, Luke remained unmarried and lived to a ripe old age. While this is entirely possible, there is no way to confirm such a report. The same goes for the tradition that he was from Antioch, or that his remains, with those of the apostle Andrew, were interred in the Church of the Holy Apostles in Constantinople in 357. Luke's feast is celebrated on 18 October. The evangelist's symbol, the ox, can be traced back to the late second century; it has been thought to mirror the importance of the Jerusalem temple and its sacrifices in Luke's presentation of Christ.

BIBLIOGRAPHY

Aside from the New Testament the most important primary source is Eusebius's *Church History*, which brings together earlier testimony of Christian writers on the origin and authorship of the Gospels. The most convenient edition is the two-volume "Loeb Classical Library" text and translation of Kirsopp Lake, J. E. L. Oulton, and Hugh J. Lawlor (Cambridge, Mass., 1926).

Werner G. Kümmel's *Introduction to the New Testament*, rev. ed. (Nashville, 1975), pp. 147–150, 174–185, finds the difficulties of Lucan authorship insurmountable. On the other hand, *The Gospel According to Luke, I–IX*, translated and edited by Joseph A. Fitzmyer, volume 28 of the Anchor Bible (New York, 1981), pp. 35–53, makes a guarded defense of the Luke tradition, in part because Fitzmyer does not regard the objections to it as entirely cogent.

D. Moody Smith

LULL, RAMÓN (c. 1232–1316), Catalan philosopher, poet, and missionary. Lull was born in Majorca shortly after the Arab occupation of the island had ended. He certainly was acquainted with spoken Arabic, but must have known classical Arabic as well. In his youth he was interested in chivalry and courtly occupations, but the visions of Christ that he experienced around 1265 transformed him into an ardent missionary whose aim was to create an understanding between Christianity, Judaism, and Islam and to resolve their differences. To this end he composed a great number of books in his native Catalan and is said to have traveled to various Islamic countries. Among Lull's works, his *Libre del contemplacio en Deu* (originally written at least partly in Arabic; see *Obres*, vol. 8, p. 645) is a seven-volume encyclopedia in which he sets forth his idea that by contemplation the truth of the Christian religion would be revealed to everyone.

In a vision in 1272 Lull saw the whole universe reflecting the divine attributes, a vision reminiscent of Islamic traditions. There has been much scholarly debate on the extent to which Lull was conversant with Arabic sources. His great novel, *Blanquerna*, best expresses his attitude to and understanding of Islam. Here, as in other early works, he expresses his concern for those who are lost despite many good aspects of their faith and life; he praises the Muslims' faith in the unity of God, which he views as the basis on which the three "Abrahamic" religions could understand one another: he acknowledges the importance of the Ṣūfī practice of *dhikr* ("recollection of God") and describes it as a useful step on the way to God; finally, he expresses the opinion that Muslims are closer to Christians than are other nonbelievers because Muslims accept the virgin birth of Mary. The novel *Blanquerna* closes with the "Book of the Lover and the Beloved," a collection of 365 aphorisms, many of which can be found verbatim in Arabic Ṣūfī sources and may come partly from al-Ghazālī, whose works Lull apparently knew well (he is even said to have translated one of his books) and who may have strengthened Lull's aversion to "philosophy," that is, to Averroism. Again, some of the symbols, his images, letter mysticism, and the use of prose rhyme are reminiscent of Arabic Ṣūfī works, especially of some of Ibn al-ʿArabī's writings.

On the other hand, Lull was very critical of the Muslims in other regards and repeated the traditional medieval accusations against them, such as the sensual image of Paradise, polygamy, and so forth. His attitude hardened over the years, and in the place of his earlier irenic attitude an increasingly militant missionary zeal fills his later works. He requested the church to emphasize the study of Arabic so that disputations with Muslims could be carried out more successfully and he succeeded in persuading James II of Aragon to establish a school of oriental languages in Miramar on Majorca. Later, in 1312, the Council of Vienne decided to found chairs for Arabic in several universities to train missionaries. In 1316, on one of his trips to North Africa, Lull was imprisoned and probably stoned to death. Many years later, in 1376, some of his teachings were condemned by Gregory XI.

Lull was a complex figure, and he himself complained of not being properly understood; this attitude is typically expressed in his *Disputatio clerici et Raymundi phantastici*, in which he portrays himself as the eccentric idealist. Lull's philosophy is based on the mystery of the Trinity: the three powers of the soul reflect the trinitarian principles. He tried to achieve a reduction of all knowledge to first principles so as to establish perfect unity as the underlying structure of the universe. Among his numerous books, the *Ars magna;* the *Arbor scientiae* (The Tree of Knowledge), with its mysterious diagrams; and the *Liber de ascensu et descensu intellectus* (Book of Intellectual Ascent and Decline) best reflect his philosophical ideas and his way of using the various branches of medieval science, from mathematics to alchemy. Some of his ideas were later taken over and elaborated by Nicholas of Cusa.

In each of his writings Lull strove to show that faith and intellect must work together to prove that Christianity is the true religion. His ardent striving to lead to the true faith those who knew it only fragmentarily, and to whom he himself was indebted to a certain degree, is summed up in an aphorism from the "Book of the Lover and the Beloved," which translates an old Ṣūfī saying: "The ways in which the lover seeks his Beloved are long and dangerous; they are populated by meditation, sighs, and tears, and illuminated by love."

BIBLIOGRAPHY

Lull's works have been printed from the sixteenth century onward; the latest edition is *Obres: Edició original,* 20 vols. (Palma de Mallorca, 1906–1936). The best biography is still E. Allison Peers's *Ramon Lull: A Biography* (London, 1929). Peers has also translated *Blanquerna: A Thirteenth Century Romance* (London, 1925), and its last chapter, published separately, *The Book of the Lover and the Beloved* (New York, 1923). Jean Henri Probst's *La mystique de Ramon Lull et l'arte de contemplació* (Münster, 1914) and Otto Keicher's *Raymundus Lullus und seine Stellung zur arabischen Philosophie* (Münster, 1909) are both critical of the extent of Lull's knowledge of classical Arabic. A good selection from Lull's works is *Selected Works of Ramon Llull,* edited and translated by Anthony Bonner (Princeton, 1985), which is well-balanced and readable.

ANNEMARIE SCHIMMEL

LUPERCALIA. The Lupercalia, inscribed in the calendar on 15 February, belongs by virtue of its suffix to the category of Roman feasts that have names ending in *-alia,* such as the Feralia on 21 February. The word is a derivative of *Lupercus* and is semantically related to *Lupercal.* The Luperci were the officiants and were divided into the Luperci Quinctiales (or Quintiliani; Paulus-Festus, ed. Lindsay, 1913, p. 78 L.) and the Luperci Fabiani; the former bound themselves to Romulus, the latter to Remus (Ovid, *Fasti* 2.375–378). For a long time the word was thought to have come from *lupus* ("wolf") and *arceo* ("to keep off") and so to mean "protectors against wolves" (Servius, *Ad Aeneidem* 8.343; Wissowa, 1912, p. 209). But *Luperci* is more a derivative of *lupus* with the ending *-ercus* (analogous to the formation of *noverca,* "mother-in-law") and so means "wolf-men." The Luperci, appearing naked (Servius, *Ad Aeneidem* 8.663), or rather "nude except for a simple loincloth" (Plutarch, *Romulus* 21.7, *Quaestiones Romanae* 68), brought to mind a precivilized state and constituted a "truly savage brotherhood" (*fera quaedam sodalitas;* Cicero, *Pro Caelio* 26).

When the Luperci ran around the Palatine in the midst of a crowd of people, the act had a purifying purpose that Varro (*De lingua Latina* 6.34) sums up thus: "[in February] the people are purified [*februatur*], insofar as the old fortress on the Palatine was circled by nude Luperci for purposes of lustration [*lustratur*]." This ceremony began with a sacrifice in the grotto of Lupercal, located at the southwest corner of the Palatine (Plutarch, *Romulus* 21.5); the offering was a she-goat (Ovid, *Fasti* 2.361; see also Plutarch, *Romulus* 21.6) or a he-goat (Servius, *Ad Aeneidem* 8.343). During their run, they would carry lashes, called *februa,* made from hides of she-goats or of he-goats (Paulus-Festus, op. cit., p. 76 L.). With these lashes they would strike the spectators, especially women, "in order to ensure their fertility" (Servius, *Ad Aeneidem* 8.343). Ovid (*Fasti* 2.441) proposes a strange etiology for this rite: it would be the application (discovered by an "Etruscan augur") of an order from Juno, "Let a sacred he-goat . . . penetrate Italian mothers" ("Italidas matres . . . sacer hircusinito").

Other unusual or unexplained elements enter into the ceremonial. According to Plutarch (*Romulus* 21.8; *Quaestiones Romanae* 68, 111), who seems to be our only source, the Luperci also sacrificed dogs. Stranger still, he tells how "two young people from noble families are led forth: some touch their foreheads with bloody knives while others wipe them with wool soaked in milk. Once they are wiped, they start to laugh" (*Romulus* 21.6–7). Another problem is far from being clarified: what divinity was patron of this feast? Vergil (*Aeneid* 8.344) does not hesitate to designate Pan of Arcadia. Ovid (*Fasti* 2.423–424) interprets *Lupercus* as transposition of the "Arcadian" *Lycaeus:* the cult was supposedly established by the hero Evander on behalf of Pan-Faunus. This late syncretism leaves open the patronage question, for the Latin equivalent of Pan in the third century BCE was not Faunus but Silvanus (Plautus, *Aulularia* 674, 766).

BIBLIOGRAPHY

Dumézil, Georges. *La religion romaine archaïque.* 2d ed. Paris, 1974. See pages 352–356. This work has been translated from the first edition by Philip Krapp as *Archaic Roman Religion,* 2 vols. (Chicago, 1970).

Latte, Kurt. *Römische Religionsgeschichte.* Munich, 1960. See pages 84–87 and especially note 4 on page 84.

Michels, Agnes Kirsopp. "The Topography and Interpretation of the Lupercalia." *Transactions of the American Philological Association* 84 (1953): 35–59.

Wissowa, Georg. *Religion und Kultus der Römer.* 2d ed. Munich, 1912. See pages 209–212.

ROBERT SCHILLING
Translated from French by Paul C. Duggan

LÜ PU-WEI (290?–235 BCE), merchant, patron of letters, and high official at the Ch'in court, known principally for the work that bears his name, the *Lü-shih ch'un-ch'iu* (Spring and Autumn Annals of Mr. Lü).

Lü lived during a period of extreme intellectual and political ferment in China, a time in which conflicting ideologies vied for the attention of powerful princes, each with designs on the conquest of neighboring states. As the state of Ch'in seemed about to prevail over its rivals in this struggle to unify China, Lü, a wealthy and ambitious merchant, attempted to enhance his status by coming to the aid of Tzu-ch'u, a lesser prince of the state of Ch'in who had been sent to the state of Chao as a hostage. (Younger sons of rulers were often sent to the courts of allied states as hostages to guarantee peace.) Lü's principal service to the prince was maneuvering, through skillful manipulation at the Ch'in court, the promotion of Tzu-ch'u to the status of heir apparent. After Prince Tzu-ch'u had wantonly demanded her at a drinking party, Lü also gave him his favorite concubine, who gave birth to a son named Cheng shortly thereafter. As First Emperor of the Ch'in dynasty (Ch'in Shih-huang-ti), Cheng later ruled over the first unifed Chinese empire.

Upon becoming King Chuang-hsiang of Ch'in, Tzu-ch'u made Lü Pu-wei his prime minister, granting him the title "Duke of Wen-hsin." Following the untimely death of Chuang-hsiang, his son Cheng became king. Lü continued as prime minister under Cheng, enjoying ever-increasing wealth and prestige. The king even addressed him as "Second Father," presumably in recognition of both his own and his father's indebtedness to him. But the appellation might not have been far from the truth, for according to the noted historiographer Ssu-ma Ch'ien (149?–90?), the king's mother, Lü's former concubine and now empress dowager, was already pregnant by him at the time he made a gift of her to Chuang-hsiang. Scholars have generally discredited Ssu-ma Ch'ien's assertion, but the strong suspicion of illegitimacy surrounding the birth of Ch'in Shih-huang-ti persists in the popular mind, further discrediting his already blemished reputation as a tyrant.

The fact remains, however, that Lü did not sever his relations with his former concubine even after she became empress dowager, and for this reason the emperor sentenced him to death, commuting the penalty to exile only in consideration of Lü's distinguished service and his general influence. But the humiliation was too much to bear, and thus in 235, after twelve years as one of the most powerful men in the state of Ch'in, Lü committed suicide.

At the height of his career, Lü had three thousand retainers, most of them highly literate gentlemen, who lived and ate at his expense. Eventually he called upon these protégés to repay his generous patronage by contributing essays on various political and philosophical subjects to a massive anthology, which he entitled *Lü-shih ch'un-ch'iu.* When completed, the work comprised twenty-six chapters grouped into three divisions. Lü was so confident of the excellence of the work that he displayed it at the city gates of the capital at Hsien-yang with a thousand ounces of gold suspended over it as a reward offered to anyone capable of improving the text by altering even a single word.

An ambitious, eclectic undertaking, the *Lü-shih ch'un-ch'iu* contains many inconsistencies and repetitions but maintains for the most part a high level of clarity and sophistication. The work purports to offer a plan of government along Confucian and Taoist lines, but also contains many purely theoretical disquisitions that merge Yin-yang cosmological theories with Confucian views of morality and statecraft. Unfortunately, Li Ssu, a strict Legalist, succeeded Lü as prime minister, effectively vitiating his influence, and that of the work, on the Ch'in government. During the Han period (206 BCE–220 CE), however, the work enjoyed a revival in influence. The *Huai-nan-tzu,* itself the product of a literary "symposium" at the court of a powerful prince, took the text as a model, and Tung Chung-shu's (179–104) seminal *Ch'un-ch'iu fan-lu* (Luxuriant Dew of the *Spring and Autumn Annals*), which developed the syncretization of Yin-yang theory and Confucianism into a state ideology, clearly relied on the prior articulation of the notion in *Lü-shih ch'un-ch'iu.*

[*See also* Yin-yang Wu-hsing *and the biographies of Liu An and Tung Chung-shu.*]

BIBLIOGRAPHY

The principal source for the biography of Lü Pu-wei is to be found in Ssu-ma Ch'ien's *Shih-chi.* This biographical essay is translated and discussed in Derk Bodde's *Statesman, Patriot, and General in Ancient China: Shih Chi Biographies of the Ch'in Dynasty* (New Haven, Conn., 1940), pp. 1–22. A more recent translation is Burton Watson's *Records of the Grand Historian of China,* 2 vols. (New York, 1961–1963). There is a German translation of the *Lü-shih ch'un-ch'iu* by Richard Wilhelm, titled *Frühling und Herbst des Lü Bu We* (reprint, Düsseldorf, 1971).

Y. P. MEI

LURIA, ISAAC (1534–1572), known also by the acronym ARiY (ha-Elohi Rabbi Yitsḥaq, "the godly Rabbi Isaac"); Jewish mystic. Isaac Luria was the preeminent qabbalist of Safad, a small town in the Galilee where a remarkable renaissance of Jewish mystical life took place in the sixteenth century. Not only did Luria's original mythological system and innovative ritual practices achieve great popularity in Safad itself; they also exerted profound influence upon virtually all subsequent Jewish mystical creativity. By the middle of the seventeenth century, Lurianic theology and ritual practices had permeated much of the Jewish world. It has been observed that Lurianism was the last premodern theological system to enjoy such widespread acceptance within Judaism.

Luria was born in Jerusalem, where his father had settled after migrating from Germany or Poland. Following his father's death his mother took him to Egypt, where he lived in the home of his uncle, a wealthy tax gatherer. In Egypt, Luria studied with two prominent rabbis, David ibn Abi Zimrah and Betsal'el Ashkenazi, and collaborated with the latter on legal works. During this period Luria apparently immersed himself in the study of the *Zohar* and other qabbalistic texts. In late 1569 or early 1570, Luria traveled to Safad and began studying with Mosheh Cordovero, the principal master of esoteric studies in this community. Luria quickly attracted a circle of students to himself that included Ḥayyim Vital, his chief disciple, as well as Yosef ibn Ṭabūl and Mosheh Yonah.

It appears that Luria possessed the traits of a genuinely inspired and charismatic individual. He became known in Safad as an extraordinarily saintly person who had been privileged to experience personal revelations of qabbalistic knowledge from the Holy Spirit, the prophet Elijah, and departed rabbis. He was regarded as having knowledge of such esoteric arts as metoposcopy and physiognomy and the ability to understand the language of animals. He was able to diagnose the spiritual condition of his disciples and others and provided them with specific acts of atonement for restoring their souls to a state of purity.

To his formal disciples, who numbered about thirty-five, Luria imparted esoteric wisdom, vouchsafing to each one mystical knowledge pertinent to his particular soul, such as its ancestry and the transmigrations through which it had gone. He also gave his disciples detailed instructions on the meditative techniques by which they could raise their souls up to the divine realm, commune with the souls of departed rabbis, and achieve revelatory experiences of their own.

Luria developed an intricate mystical mythology that served to explain, on a cosmic level, the meaning of the exile of the Jewish people, which was felt especially strongly after their expulsion from Spain in 1492. The three elements of this myth correspond to three dramatic events within the life of God. In an attempt to explicate how the world could come into being if God originally filled all space, Luria taught that God had withdrawn into himself, so to speak, thereby creating an "empty space." This divine act of self-withdrawal, known in Hebrew as *tsimtsum,* made possible the existence of something other than God. The second part of the cosmic process, called the "breaking of the vessels" *(shevirat ha-kelim),* concerns the emanation or reemergence of divinity back into the primordial space produced by *tsimtsum.* During this process of emanation, some of the "vessels" containing the light of God were shattered. While most of the light succeeded in reascending to its divine source, the remainder fell and became attached to the now-broken "vessels" below. The result of this chaotic and catastrophic dispersal of divine light was the imprisonment of holy sparks in the lower world, the realm of material reality.

Since these sparks of divine light seek to be liberated and returned to their source, the human task, according to Isaac Luria, is to bring about such liberation through proper devotional means. Known as *tiqqun,* the "mending" or "restitution" of the life of God, this effort is, at its core, a contemplative one. Every religious action requires contemplative concentration in order to "raise up the fallen sparks." The successful struggle on the part of the community will result in the final separation of holiness from materiality, and a return of all divine light to the state of primordial unity that preceded the creation of the world. Lurianic mysticism exercised great influence and had enduring appeal long after Safad itself ceased to be a prominent center of Jewish life. It gave mythic expression to the notion that collective religious action could transform the course of history to redeem both the people of Israel and God.

[*For further discussion of Lurianic mysticism, see* Qabbalah.]

BIBLIOGRAPHY

A general introduction to the teachings of Isaac Luria is found in Gershom Scholem's *Major Trends in Jewish Mysticism* (1941; reprint, New York, 1961), as well as in Scholem's *Kabbalah* (New York, 1974), especially pp. 128–144. An important study of Lurianic rituals is Scholem's essay "Tradition and New Creation in the Ritual of the Kabbalists," in his book *On the Kabbalah and Its Symbolism* (New York, 1965). Those able to read Hebrew will want to consult a lucid study of Lurianic ideas by Isaiah Tishby, *Torat ha-ra' ve-ha-qelippah be-qabbalat ha-Ariy* (Jerusalem, 1942). Special customs and rituals practiced by Isaac Luria are found in my study *Safed Spirituality: Rules of Mystical Piety; The Beginning of Wisdom* (New York, 1984), and for the techniques he taught, see my articles "Maggidic Revelation in the Teachings of Isaac Luria," in *Mystics,*

Philosophers, and Politicians: Essays in Jewish Intellectual History in Honor of Alexander Altmann, edited by Jehuda Reinharz and David Swetschinski (Durham, N.C., 1982), and "The Contemplative Practice of Yiḥudim in Lurianic Kabbalah," in *History of Jewish Spirituality,* edited by Arthur Green (New York, 1986).

LAWRENCE FINE

LURIA, SHELOMOH (c. 1510–1574), known by the acronym MaHaRSHaL (Morenu ha-Rav ["our teacher the rabbi"] Shelomoh Luria); Polish Talmudist and scholar. Luria was born in Poznań to a family that claimed descent from the great medieval Jewish exegete Rashi and that included many of the luminaries of the Ashkenazic rabbinical world. He was trained as a rigorous exponent of the Ashkenazic tradition in Talmudic exegesis, to which he added a distinctive commitment to relentless exactitude in the interpretation of sacred texts. His idiosyncratic method of study caused him to part company with many of the rabbinical authorities of his age and established his reputation as a brilliant, if demanding, Talmud scholar.

Shelomoh Luria appears to have held several rabbinical posts in Lithuania before settling first in the town of Brest-Litovsk, then in the important community of Ostrog, and finally in Lublin, where he died in 1574. In all of these centers Luria established academies that met opposition from the disciplines of his erstwhile teacher and colleague, Shalom Shakhna of Lublin, the primary exponent in Poland of the regnant method of Talmudic hermeneutics known as *pilpul* (dialectic reasoning). Luria fiercely condemned this approach as contrary to the true meaning of the text and argued instead for a "return to the Talmud," a careful explication of the sources, diction, and plain meaning of the Talmud and its later, especially Ashkenazic, interpreters. Particularly irksome to Luria were the corruptions that had recently crept into the Talmudic text through scribal errors and that had become accepted as a result of the new technology of printing; in his *Ḥokhmat Shelomoh* he set about to correct these errors and offered bold emendations and alternate readings that would be celebrated by critical scholars centuries after his death.

In line with this basic stance toward textual criticism, Luria also insisted on a firm command of Hebrew grammar and the Bible and opposed the study of Jewish philosophy. Perhaps most important, he not only rejected the codifications of Jewish law published in his own time, by Yosef Karo of Safad and by Luria's relative and friend Mosheh Isserles of Cracow, but he rejected Maimonides' code, the *Mishneh Torah,* as well. Objecting vehemently to both the form and the goal of these codes, Luria decided to write his own summary of rabbinic law in order to correct their errors. In his *Yam shel Shelomoh,* he cited all relevant authorities, examined the differing interpretations, and then selected the most cogent view, not necessarily the consensus. This ambitious task proved too massive even for Luria, and he was able to complete work on only a few tractates. Nonetheless, his contributions to jurisprudence and Talmudic scholarship marked him as one of the most important rabbis of his age and perhaps the leading eastern European Jewish scholar until the eighteenth century.

BIBLIOGRAPHY

There is no complete critical study of Luria or his works. The most useful analyses are two essays in Hebrew: Simha Assaf's "Mashehu le-toledot ha-Maharshal," in the *Sefer ha-yovel likhvod Levi Ginzberg,* issued by the American Academy for Jewish Research (New York, 1945), pp. 45–63, and Haim Chernowitz's essay on Luria in *Toledot ha-posqim,* vol. 3 (New York, 1947), pp. 74–91. For an English source, parts of Moses A. Shulvass's *Jewish Culture in Eastern Europe: The Classic Period* (New York, 1975) may also be consulted.

MICHAEL STANISLAWSKI

LUSTRATIO. Lustrations, or purifications by sacrifice, played a primordial role in Roman religion, both public and private, inasmuch as they were celebrated every time there was a transition or the likelihood of a transition in the life of an individual or a city, and every time there was need to repel aggressions or at least threats from outside. Lustration rites were celebrated either in a complex liturgy that repeated the act of lustration at length or in a single ritual that effected the desired separation. Whatever the degree of ritual complexity, however, a lustration was always an act of definition. It was a definition, first, in that it distinguished and delimited in time and space two realities that are opposed, such as, for example, living and dead, civilized and savage, good and bad, peaceful and hostile, pure and defiled. A lustration was a definition, second, because this act of disjunction was usually accompanied by a reflection on the reality in question, an inspection, a clear and definite ordering, a verification. This twofold defining that a lustration accomplished may explain why the (still disputed) etymology of *lustrum/lustrare* points in the direction of "inspection, gaze, light shed on" as well as that of "purification."

Lustrations therefore had a central place in the rites of birth and death, whereby the family firmly asserted the separation between what was not yet (or no longer) living and the world of the living, using rituals that enabled it to accompany the deceased or newly born person in his crucial passage without itself being adversely affected. At the community level certain festivals, and even the entire month of February, were given over to the lustration of families; in this way the city established a clear and definite break between its past and its future.

The most typical lustrations were those practiced in regard to fields, territory, city, or citizens. In these cases the lustration took a precise form, that of a procession, a circumambulation by the sacrificial victims around the object to be purified, the integrity of which was verified (i.e., emphasized), as were the threats—human, natural, or supernatural—that impended. The victims were sacrificed at the end of the procession. There were a variety of victims for a variety of divinities, as for instance a sow for Ceres. But in a lustration proper the victims were a boar, a ram, and a bull (or what was called *suovetaurilia*) and they were offered solely to Mars, who was invoked as defender of the city and territory or of an individual's fields (an interpretation denied by some scholars). The most spectacular lustrations, however, were those whose object was a group of citizens either under arms or in civilian dress but ready to form an army. Every five years (but under the empire, only sporadically) one of the censors, after inspecting and setting to rights the affairs of the Roman people, celebrated a solemn *lustrum* in the Campus Martius (Field of Mars) by walking the *suovetaurilia* around the citizens, who were organized in voting units *(centuriae)*. The effect of this lustration was not only to ascertain and assert the perfection of the civic body but also to draw around it a strict boundary that Mars was to defend. The danger threatening the citizens was above all the danger of war; it is not surprising, therefore, that in a critical situation the generals led the sacrificial *suovetaurilia* around their legions or vessels.

[*For a discussion of similar phenomena in cross-cultural context, see* Purification.]

BIBLIOGRAPHY

Volume 13 of the *Real-Encyclopädie der classischen Altertumswissenschaft*, edited by Georg Wissowa (Stuttgart, 1927), includes two articles of particular interest: "Lustrum," by Helmut Berve, and "Lustratio," by Fritz Boehme. Also recommended are W. Warde Fowler's *The Religious Experience of the Roman People from the Earliest Times to the Age of Augustus* (London, 1911), pp. 209–218; Carl Koch's *Gestirnverehrung im alten Italien: Sol Indiges und der Kreis der Di Indigetes* (Frankfurt, 1933); and Georges Dumézil's *Archaic Roman Religion* (Chicago, 1970).

JOHN SCHEID
Translated from French by Matthew J. O'Connell

LUTHER, MARTIN (1483–1546), German theologian and reformer of the Christian church. Luther was born in Eisleben on 10 November, the son of Hans Luder, who was engaged in copper mining. After moving to nearby Mansfeld, the family increasingly acquired modest prosperity. Because Hans Luder appears prominently in Luther's later recollections as a stern and oppressive presence, the question has arisen whether the son's development was significantly affected by intense conflict with his father. No satisfactory answer to this question has been given.

After initial schooling in Mansfeld, Martin Luther attended the cathedral school in Magdeburg from 1497 to 1498, where he came into contact with the Brethren of the Common Life, one of the most spiritual of late medieval religious movements. Between 1498 and 1501 he attended school in Eisenach, and, in 1501, he matriculated at the University of Erfurt to pursue the customary study of the seven liberal arts. Luther was declared ineligible for financial aid, an indirect testimonial to the economic successes of his father. The philosophical climate at the university was that of Ockhamism, which undoubtedly exerted its influence upon the young student. Upon receiving the master's degree in 1505 Luther began the study of law in the summer of that year, in accordance with the wishes of his father. Less than two months later, however, the experience of a terrifying thunderstorm near Stotterheim prompted his vow to Saint Anne to become a monk, resulting in the abandonment of his legal studies.

Undoubtedly, spiritual anxiety and uncertainty about his vocational choice combined to precipitate the determination to carry out the vow. On 17 July 1505 Luther entered the Monastery of the Eremites of Saint Augustine in Erfurt. His choice of this monastic order is explained not only by its strictness but also by its philosophical and theological orientation, to which Luther had been exposed during his earlier studies.

Two years later, on 27 February 1507, Luther was ordained to the priesthood. In his later recollections his first celebration of the Mass stood out as an awesome experience. Afterward, at the behest of his monastic superior, Johann von Staupitz, Luther began graduate studies in theology, first at Erfurt and then, in the fall of 1508, at the recently founded university at Wittenberg, because of his transfer to the Augustinian monastery there. In accordance with custom, he served as philosophical lecturer in the liberal arts curriculum. In 1509 he received his first theological degree, the *baccalaureus biblicus*.

In the fall of 1509 Luther was transferred back to Erfurt, where he continued his theological studies. Sometime thereafter (the exact date is uncertain) he was sent to Rome on monastic business. In his reflections of later years, he attributed great significance to that trip: the Rome that he had presumed to be the epitome of spiritual splendor had turned out to be terribly worldly. Soon after his return from Rome, Luther transferred a second time to Wittenberg, completing his doctorate in theology there in October 1512. He then assumed the *lectura in Biblia,* the professorship in Bible endowed by the Augustinian order.

The first academic courses that Luther taught were on *Psalms* (1513–1515), *Romans* (1515–1516), *Galatians* (1516–1517), *Hebrews* (1517–1518), and another on *Psalms* (1519). His lecture notes, which have been analyzed intensively, chronicle his theological development: his shift from the traditional exegetical method, his increasing concentration on questions of sin, grace, and righteousness, his preoccupation with Augustine of Hippo, and—last but by no means least—his alienation from scholastic theology. At the same time Luther acquired increasing responsibilities in his monastic order. In 1515 he became preacher at the parish church in Wittenberg and was appointed district vicar of his order. The latter position entailed the administrative oversight of the Augustinian monasteries in Saxony.

In his later years Luther spoke of having had a profound spiritual experience or insight (dubbed by scholars his "evangelical discovery"), and intensive scholarly preoccupation has sought to identify its exact date and nature. Two basic views regarding the time have emerged. One dates the experience, which Luther himself related to the proper understanding of the concept of the "righteousness of God" (*Rom.* 1:17), as having occurred about 1514, the other in about 1518. The matter remains inconclusive, partly because nowhere do Luther's writings of the time echo the dramatic notions that the reformer in later years associated with his experience. The import of the issue lies both in the precise understanding of what it was that alienated Luther from the Catholic church, and in understanding the theological frame of mind with which Luther entered the indulgences controversy of 1517. The dating of the experience before or after 1517 is thus important. Placing the experience in 1518 seems to be the most viable interpretation.

The Ninety-five Theses of 31 October 1517 (the traditional notion that Luther nailed them to the door of the Wittenberg castle church has recently been questioned) catapulted Luther into the limelight. These theses pertained to the ecclesiastical practice of indulgences that had not as yet been dogmatically defined by the church. Luther's exploration of the practice was therefore a probing inquiry.

Almost immediately after the appearance of the Ninety-five Theses, a controversy ensued. Undoubtedly it was fanned by the fact that Luther had focused not merely on a theological topic but had also cited a number of the popular grievances against Rome, thus touching upon a political issue. In addition to sending copies of the theses to several friends, Luther sent a copy to Archbishop Albert of Hohenzollern, whom he held responsible for a vulgar sale of indulgences in the vicinity of Wittenberg, together with a fervent plea to stop the sale. Luther was unaware that the sale was part and parcel of a large fiscal scheme by which Albert hoped to finance his recent elevation to the politically important post of archbishop of Mainz. Albert's response was to ask the University of Mainz to assess the theses and, soon thereafter, to request the Curia Romana to commence the *processus inhibitorius,* the proceedings by which Luther's orthodoxy would be ascertained. Thus the theses and Luther became an official matter for the church. The commencement of official proceedings against Luther added far-reaching notoriety to the affair, as did the related accusation of heresy by several theological opponents. The ensuing debate therefore became a public one, eventually allowing for the formation of a popular movement.

In April 1518 Luther presented a summary of his theological thought, which he called the "theology of the cross," at a meeting of the Augustinian order in Heidelberg. In presenting a caricature of scholastic theology, Luther appropriately emphasized its one-sidednesses. Soon afterward he was ordered to appear in Rome in conjunction with the proceedings against him, but the intervention of his territorial ruler, Elector Frederick, caused the interrogation to take place in Augsburg, Germany. With Cardinal Legate Cajetan representing the Curia, the meeting proved unsuccessful, since Luther refused to recant. Luther fled from Augsburg and, upon his return to Wittenberg, issued an appeal to a general council.

Overwhelmed by the unexpected notoriety of the affair, Luther agreed to refrain from further participation in the controversy. All the same, he was inadvertently drawn into a disputation held in Leipzig in July 1519. In the context of a wide-ranging, if tedious, discussion of the fundamental issues in the controversy, Luther's opponent, Johann Eck, professor of theology at Ingolstadt, was intent on branding him a heretic and succeeded in eliciting Luther's acknowledgment that the church's general councils had erred. Luther posited a difference between the authority of the church and that of scripture, a notion that late medieval thinkers had never seen as problematic.

After the election of Charles V as the new emperor, which had preoccupied the Curia for some time, official proceedings against Luther were resumed. In June 1520 the papal bull *Exsurge Domine* (Arise, O Lord) condemned forty-one sentences from Luther's writings as "heretical, offensive, erroneous, scandalous for pious ears, corrupting for simple minds and contradictory to Catholic teaching." Luther was given sixty days to recant. His response was to burn the bull in a public spectacle on 10 December 1520. On 3 January 1521 the bull *Decet Romanum Pontificem* (It Pleases the Roman Pontiff) excommunicated Luther. It was now incumbent upon the political authorities to execute the ecclesiastical condemnation, but Luther was given the opportunity to appear before the German diet at Worms in April 1521.

Several factors converged to bring about the unusual citation. Luther had begun to precipitate a popular movement, in part playing on prevailing anti-Roman and anticlerical sentiment. There was apprehension about popular restlessness. Moreover, Luther claimed persistently that he had not received a fair hearing. To invite Luther to appear at Worms, and, indeed, give him an opportunity to recant, seemed to be to everyone's advantage. When he appeared before the diet, Luther acknowledged that he had been too strident in tone, but he refused to recant anything of theological substance. After several weeks of deliberation, and despite some reluctance, a rump diet promulgated an edict that declared Luther (and all of his followers) political outlaws and called for the suppression of his teachings.

By that time, however, Luther had disappeared from the public scene. At the instigation of his ruler Elector Frederick, he had been taken on his return to Wittenberg to a secluded castle, the Wartburg, where he was to spend almost a full year in hiding. A period of self-doubt, it was also an exceedingly creative time, part of which he spent in translating the New Testament from Greek into German. He returned to Wittenberg in March 1522 to calm the restlessness that had surfaced there over the nature of the reform movement. In a series of sermons he enunciated a conservative notion of ecclesiastical reform, and his stance left its imprint on the subsequent course of the Reformation.

Luther resumed his professorial responsibilities and continued his prolific literary activities, clarifying theological themes and offering guidelines for undertaking ecclesiastical reform. His own theological formation was essentially complete by 1521; his theological work thereafter consisted in amplification and clarification.

The year 1525 proved to be a major theological and personal watershed for Luther: he became embroiled in two major controversies—with Erasmus and Thomas Müntzer—that resulted in a marked division in the reform movement. On 13 June of that same year he married Katharina von Bora, a former nun who had left her convent the previous year. Even though the marriage—coming as it did on the heels of the German Peasants' War—was a subject of notoriety among Luther's enemies, it set the tone for a Protestant definition of Christian marriage for which the term "school for character" was aptly coined.

The next several years were overshadowed by Luther's growing controversy with Ulrich Zwingli over Communion. The controversy reached its culmination in October 1529 with a colloquy held at Marburg at the instigation of Landgrave Philipp of Hesse, who viewed the split of the Reformation movement over this issue as a major political liability. Luther was a reluctant participant in the colloquy, for he saw the theological differences between Zwingli and himself to be so fundamental as to make conciliation impossible. The major issue debated at Marburg was the bodily presence of Christ in the Communion elements. It is unclear whether for Luther the politically more prudent course of action would have been theological conciliation (which would have presented a unified Reformation movement) or intransigence (which by its separation from Zwingli would have underscored the proximity of the Lutheran and the Catholic positions). No agreement was reached at Marburg; as a result, at the diet at Augsburg the following year, the Protestants appeared divided.

As a political outlaw, Luther was unable to be present at Augsburg. He stayed at Coburg (as far south as he was able to travel on Saxon territory), and his close associate Philipp Melanchthon functioned as spokesman for the Lutherans. Several of Luther's most insightful publications appeared during that summer—a tract on translating, an exposition of Psalm 118, and *Exhortation That Children Should Be Sent to School.*

The unsuccessful outcome of the discussions at Augsburg and the subsequent formation of the League of Smalcald (1531) were accompanied by Luther's reconsideration of his views on the right of resistance to the emperor, which he had previousy rejected. The 1530s brought Luther's extensive involvement in the reorganization of the University of Wittenberg (1533–1536). His extensive participation in the academic disputations that were now resumed were evidence of the richness and fullness of his thought.

Luther's final years were overshadowed by his growing antagonism toward the papal church, and the consequences of his well-meant but misunderstood counsel to Landgrave Philipp of Hesse that bigamy was permissible under certain circumstances. In addition, the Lutheran movement was torn by several internal conflicts, and Luther was concerned about the increasing role of the political authorities in ecclesiastical affairs.

Luther's recognition that his norm of authority—scripture—did not preclude disagreement in interpretation and that the papal church was unwilling to accept the primacy of the word of God undoubtedly serve to explain—along with his increasing physical ailments—the vehemence of his last publications, especially those against the papacy and the Jews. He was plagued by insomnia and, from 1525 onward, by kidney stones, which in 1537 almost led to his demise. In February 1546 Luther traveled, together with two of his sons and Philipp Melanchthon, to Luther's birthplace, Eisleben, to mediate in a feud among the counts of Mansfeld. There, having succeeded in that assignment, he died on 16 February.

Not surprisingly, Martin Luther has received considerable scholarly and theological attention throughout the centuries. Assessments of Luther have always been staunchly partisan, with a clear demarcation between Protestant and Catholic evaluations. The former, while uniformly positive, have tended to follow the intellectual or theological currents of their particular time, such as the eighteenth-century Enlightenment or nineteenth-century German nationalism.

In the twentieth century, particularly in the latter part, the biographical and theological evaluation of Martin Luther has focused on a number of specific aspects. There has been a preoccupation with the "young" Luther, that is, Luther between 1512 and 1518, and particularly with Luther's "evangelical discovery," his formulation of a new understanding of the Christian faith. This new understanding has generated much speculation about Luther's relationship to the late Middle Ages, the medieval exegetical tradition, the significance of Augustine, Ockham, and mysticism. The "older" or "mature" Luther, generally defined as Luther after 1526, is only beginning to receive widespread attention; this part of his life has not attracted much scholarly interest because it lacks the excitement of Luther's earlier years. The general question is whether the "older" Luther should be seen in continuity or in discontinuity with the young Luther.

A key theme in Luther's theology is that of the sole authority of scripture, formulated as the notion of *sola scriptura;* this notion, because it implied the possibility of a divergence of tradition from scripture, raised a startling new question. Late medieval theology had formulated the issue of authority in terms of the possible divergency of pope and council. A related theme in Luther's theology was the relationship of law and gospel, which provided the key to the understanding of scripture. God reveals himself as both a demanding and a giving God, two qualities that Luther loosely assigned to the Old and New Testaments respectively; but in truth, so Luther asserted, grace is found in the Old Testament even as law is found in the New.

The notion of justification by faith is traditionally cited as the heart of Luther's thought. It is, in fact, his major legacy to the Protestant tradition. In contradistinction to the medieval notion of a cooperative effort between man and God, between works and grace, Luther only stressed grace and God. Such grace is appropriated by faith, which affirms the reality of the grace of forgiveness, despite the reality of sin. Luther's "theology of the cross" affirmed that God always works contrary to experience.

These themes must be considered in the context of Luther's general affirmation of traditional dogma. His sacramental teaching repudiated the medieval notion of transubstantiation and affirmed a "real presence" of Christ in the bread and wine of Communion. Besides the sacrament of Communion, only that of baptism was affirmed. At least in his early years, Luther advocated a congregationally oriented concept of the church, with the "priesthood of all believers," another key motif, as an important corollary. Luther's teaching of the "two kingdoms" sought to differentiate the Christian principles applicable in society.

[*See also* Reformation.]

BIBLIOGRAPHY

The definitive Weimar edition of Luther's works, *D. Martin Luthers Werke: Kritische Gesammtausgabe,* edited by J. K. F. Knaake and others (Weimar, 1883–1974), in more than a hundred volumes, continues to be the basic tool for Luther research. An exhaustive sampling of Luther in English can be found in his *Works,* 55 vols., edited by Jaroslav Pelikan (Saint Louis, 1955–1976). The *Luther-Jahrbuch* (Munich, 1919–) publishes an annual bibliography, as does, less comprehensively, the Archiv für Reformationsgeschichte (Leipzig and Berlin, 1903–). A useful general introduction to facets and problems of Luther scholarship is found in Bernhard Lohse's *Martin Luther: Eine Einführung* (Munich, 1981). Of the numerous Luther biographies, the following deserve to be mentioned: Roland H. Bainton, *Here I Stand* (Nashville, 1955); Heinrich Bornkamm, *Martin Luther in der Mitte seines Lebens* (Göttingen, 1979); H. G. Haile, *Luther* (Garden City, N.Y., 1980); and Eric H. Erikson, *Young Man Luther* (New York, 1958), a controversial psychoanalytic study. Two useful collections of sources are *Martin Luther,* edited by E. G. Rupp and Benjamin Drewery (New York, 1970), and Walther von Löwenich's *Martin Luther: The Man and His Work* (Minneapolis, 1983).

Important studies on specific aspects of Luther's life and thought are Erwin Iserloh's *The Theses Were Not Posted* (Boston, 1968); Wilhelm Borth's *Die Luthersache (causa Lutheri) 1517–1524* (Lübeck, 1970); and Mark U. Edwards, Jr.'s *Luther and the False Brethren* (Stanford, Calif., 1975) and *Luther's Last*

Battles (Ithaca, N.Y., 1983). A creative statement of Luther's theology is Gerhard Ebeling's *Luther* (Philadelphia, 1970).

HANS J. HILLERBRAND

LUTHERANISM. Martin Luther's Roman Catholic opponents were the first to label the sixteenth-century reform movements "Lutheran." His supporters first called themselves "evangelical" (from the Greek *euaggelion,* "gospel") and then, after 1530, "the churches of the Augsburg Confession." [*See* Reformation.]

Teaching and Worship. Lutheran teachings, which have remained determinative for Lutheranism until today, are preserved in the Book of Concord of 1580. By prefacing this collection of teachings with the three ecumenical creeds (Nicene, Apostles', and Athanasian), Lutherans demonstrate their basic agreement with the ancient trinitarian tradition. The collection includes Luther's Large and Small Catechisms of 1529, his Smalcald Articles of 1537, Philipp Melanchthon's Augsburg Confession of 1530 and its Apology of 1531, and the Formula of Concord, drafted in 1577 by a group of Lutheran church leaders to resolve intra-Lutheran controversies in Germany. [*See the biographies of Luther and Melanchthon.*]

Luther's doctrine of "justification through grace by faith alone, apart from works of law," echoing Paul in his letter to the Romans (3:28), forms the core of Lutheranism. A person is right with God (i.e., "justified") by completely trusting the work of Christ (i.e., "by faith") and not by making any human effort to appease God (i.e., "apart from works of law"). Christ's atonement is communicated both verbally, in preaching and teaching, and visibly, in the celebration of the sacraments. Thus to Luther the doctrine of justification was not one among many doctrines, as medieval theology taught, but was the "chief article of faith" that establishes the norm for Christian faith and life. Consequently the word of God must be seen in its careful distinction between "law" and "gospel." The law, be it divine (especially the First Commandment of the Decalogue) or human (as manifested in the rule of temporal princes), creates necessary order in the face of evil and reveals the human inability to appease God. Through Christ, the gospel, which is communicated in words and sacraments, reveals God's unconditional love for all creatures. Trusting in Christ rather than in one's own efforts restores one's relationship with God. God may indeed reward good and punish evil, but believers no longer need worry about God's justice. Instead, they are free to enjoy God's mercy and thus help the "neighbor" in need. So viewed, all of life is a thanksgiving for what God did in Christ.

In worship, Lutherans have tried to be faithful to the ecumenical tradition of the Mass by regarding its center, the sacrament of Holy Communion, as the means of grace that strengthens and sustains Christians in a world of sin, death, and evil. Luther changed little in the liturgy of the Roman Mass, removing only what he called the "sacrifice of the Mass," namely, the prayers of thanksgiving that surround the act of consecrating bread and wine. He found these prayers too self-righteous, too full of words intended to appease God, rather than offering joyful thanks for what God did in Christ.

Following Luther's careful liturgical reforms in Wittenberg, Lutherans have insisted on the use of the vernacular in the liturgy, introduced congregational singing, and stressed preaching. Worship is thus the basic response to baptism, which discloses God's unconditional promise to be forever with those who trust God in Christ. Lutherans retained the practice of baptizing infants not only because it had been the custom from the beginning of Christianity but also because infant baptism demonstrates that God's grace is not conditioned by human response.

Lutherans recognize only two sacraments, baptism and the Lord's Supper, because Luther could find no clear evidence that Christ instituted any other sacraments. Baptism commissions all believers to a common ministry, but for the sake of enduring witness and good order in the church, there is a divinely instituted, special, ordained ministry. Lutherans have not always agreed on the precise differences between the ministry of all the baptized (the "common priesthood of all believers") and the ministry of the ordained, but they have nevertheless rejected any notion of a divinely instituted structure of hierarchical priesthood. An ordained Lutheran pastor is a baptized Christian who is called to the public ministry of word and sacraments after proper training and examination, and the rite of ordination is the solemn commissioning to be faithful to this call.

The core of Luther's reform movement was the proposal that the church return to the Christocentric stance that he had found in scripture and in the early church fathers. His fundamental insights were neither well understood nor satisfactorily evaluated either by Catholics or by many Lutherans. Nontheological factors seemed to help the spread of Lutheranism more than theological factors.

History. The doctrine of baptism proved to be the most revolutionary aspect of Lutheranism, since it allowed Luther to invite territorial princes to become "emergency bishops" of the new churches. Thus German princes interested in liberating themselves from the domination of Rome established Lutheranism in their own territories and encouraged it to spread, especially to the east into lands now known as Poland, Czechoslovakia, and Hungary. Princes, peasants, patricians, priests, and even bishops joined the Lutheran cause, mainly to break from Rome. Danish and Swedish kings declared Lutheranism the religion of their lands between 1527 and 1593. However, when, in 1525, peasants in Saxony rebelled against their landlords in the name of Luther's call to Christian freedom, Luther sided with the princes, who crushed the rebellion by force; he refused to see his cause identified with liberation from the yoke of feudalism.

The pope and the emperor were forced to soften their implacable opposition to Lutheranism because they needed the support of German princes to meet the threat of Turkish invasion from the south. At the request of Emperor Charles V, the Lutherans submitted a confession of their faith to the Diet of Augsburg in 1530. The signers of the Augsburg Confession included seven princes and two city magistrates, clearly demonstrating the strong political support Lutheranism had achieved. But subsequent negotiations between Lutheran and Catholic theologians failed to produce sufficient agreement to cease hostilities. The Council of Trent (1545–1563) was finally convened a year before Luther's death in 1546, but Lutherans were not invited to attend. In 1547, German Lutherans and Catholics faced each other in military battles; the war ended within a year with the defeat of the Lutheran Smalcald League. But Emperor Charles V was willing to compromise, and the resulting 1555 Peace of Augsburg tolerated "the religion of the Augsburg Confession," although it took almost a century and the Thirty Years' War (1618–1648) before the Peace of Westphalia accepted Lutheranism as a legitimate religion in the empire.

The Formula of Concord used medieval scholastic terminology and Aristotelian philosophical categories to provide a theological system to protect Lutheranism from both Catholic and Calvinist influences and to resolve the dispute between followers of Melanchthon, known as Philippists, and Gnesio-Lutherans (from the Greek *gnesios,* "authentic"). The result was a systematic, rational interpretation of the doctrines of sin, law, and grace, the cornerstones of a Lutheran theology grounded in the forensic notion that God declared humankind righteous by faith in Christ. The Formula rejected both the Catholic notion of cooperation between human nature and divine grace through free will and Calvin's doctrine of Christ's spiritual (not real or bodily) presence in the Lord's Supper. The Formula also insisted that all teachings must be subject to the authority of the prophetic and apostolic writings of scripture, thus opening the door to a biblicism that has at times produced a biblical fundamentalism.

Between 1580 and 1680, German Lutherans favored a uniform religion that fused pure doctrine with Christian laws. The resulting alliance between church and state created seventeenth-century Lutheran orthodoxy. Assisted by orthodox theologians, territorial princes dictated what people should believe and how they should behave, and obedience to political authority became the core of Christian ethics. But Lutheran orthodoxy gave rise to a new reform movement, nicknamed "pietist," which stressed a "religion of the heart" rather than the prevalent "religion of the head." Led by Philipp Jakob Spener, August Hermann Francke, and Nikolaus Zinzendorf, Lutheran Pietism emphasized individual conversion, lay ministry, and a morality distinct from worldly ethics. By the nineteenth century, the pietist impulse had created an "inner mission" movement in Germany that established a female diaconate, built hospitals and orphanages, instituted educational programs, cared for the mentally retarded, and advocated prison reform. The University of Halle trained missionaries for foreign missions, particularly for India and the United States. But social and ecumenical concerns were frequently overshadowed by a narrow-minded moralism. Thus both Lutheran orthodoxy and Lutheran Pietism tended to pervert the original purpose of Lutheranism: to be a reform movement within the church catholic. Both orthodox rationalism and pietist moralism had lost sight of the original Lutheran, ecumenical, holistic vision. [*See* Pietism.]

During the eighteenth-century Enlightenment, Lutheranism again succumbed to rationalist and secularist tendencies. Frederick II of Prussia (1740–1786), for example, initiated an attitude of toleration that valued religion only as it served the general purposes of the state. Lutheran theologians like Johann Semler (1725–1791) considered the doctrine of justification nonessential and supported the general notion of Lutheranism as a moral teaching. In Germany and Scandinavia, however, some Lutheran theological faculties and church leaders reacted against this trend by nurturing a strong historical consciousness and intensive biblical studies, which led to frequent attempts to revive the spirit of Luther and the Lutheran confessions. These "Neo-Lutherans" called for a return to strong biblical and confessional norms to counteract the prevalent cultural Protestantism that had virtually eliminated Lutheranism's distinctive character. By 1817, three hundred years after Luther's posting of the Ninety-five Theses, Neo-Lutherans had produced a significant revival of old Lutheran norms and ideas. German Lutherans founded the Common Lutheran Conference in Prussia in 1868 to provide communication between the various territorial churches. Danish churchman Nikolai F. S. Grundtvig (1783–1872) promoted an ecumenical Lutheranism based on the apostolic tradition and on the creeds; he also revived liturgy and church music.

In the United States, Henry Melchior Mühlenberg (1711–1787), who had come from Halle to Philadelphia, organized the first American Lutheran synod in Pennsylvania in 1748. Synods were organized by regions and were headed by presidents; they met regularly in convention to decide matters of church polity and faith. Lutheran theological seminaries, colleges, and journals were soon founded in regions where Lutherans predominated. Samuel S. Schmucker (1799–1873), president of the oldest Lutheran seminary in the United States (founded in Gettysburg in 1826), envisaged an "American Lutheranism" that would be the leading force to unite all the major Protestant denominations. But he did not receive sufficient support to realize his vision. The country was too vast, and Lutherans were too estranged from one another, especially by ethnic background, to make Lutheran unity a realistic goal. The Lutheran Church–Missouri Synod, consisting of German Lutherans who were disenchanted with Lutheran attempts in Prussia to form a union with the Reformed church, was organized in 1847. Soon there were German, Danish, Norwegian, Swedish, and Finnish groups who cherished their own ethnic traditions more than unity with one another. During the Civil War, the United Lutheran Synod of the South was formed in response to political and cultural pressures. It was not until after World War I that Lutherans in the United States managed to form larger denominations through mergers.

The Nazi tyranny in Germany (1933–1945) strongly affected German Lutherans. A small minority of Lutheran pastors and congregations resisted Hitler, but the great majority of Lutherans either remained silent or actively cooperated with the Nazi regime. The resistance, which called itself the "Confessing church,"was opposed by those who called themselves the "German Christians," who were in basic agreement with the government's desire to link Lutheranism with Nazism. Danish and Norwegian Lutherans refused to cooperate with the German occupation forces, which did not react with persecution. All these groups looked to the Lutheran confessional documents for support of their positions.

After World War II, some 184 delegates representing about 80 million Lutherans from 49 churches in 22 countries organized the Lutheran World Federation in 1947. Headquartered in Geneva (which is also the headquarters of the World Council of Churches) the Lutheran World Federation unites Lutheran churches from around the world in common social-action projects and in regular world assemblies but otherwise has no authority over the churches. The trend toward Lutheran unity has also continued in the United States. The Lutheran Council in the U.S.A. was established in 1967 to facilitate communication and common action among the larger Lutheran denominations and to represent them at the Lutheran World Federation. Although there are almost a dozen different Lutheran groups and denominations in the United States, most Lutherans belong to three large churches: the American Lutheran Church, organized in 1962; the Lutheran Church in America; and the Lutheran Church–Missouri Synod. Almost equal in size, these three churches have a combined membership of about nine million. In 1981 the American Lutheran Church, the Lutheran Church in America, and the Association of Evangelical Lutherans (a dissenting offspring of the Lutheran Church–Missouri Synod with about 150,000 members) agreed to merge within a decade.

Since the 1960s, there have been ongoing official dialogues between Lutherans and other Christian churches. In 1982 the Lutheran Church in America and the American Lutheran Church were able to agree with the Episcopal Church in the United States on an "interim sharing of the eucharist," hoping for total reconciliation between Lutherans and Anglicans in the future. In view of their beginnings, Lutherans have considered their relations with Roman Catholics particularly important. Official Lutheran-Catholic dialogues began in the 1960s and have taken place without interruption in the United States since 1965. There has always been a creative tension between Lutheranism as a movement and the Lutheran denominations. If Lutherans are guided by their confessional convictions, they will remain in this tension.

BIBLIOGRAPHY

The most comprehensive treatment of Lutheranism, albeit from an American perspective, is offered in E. Clifford Nelson's *The Rise of World Lutheranism: An American Perspective* (Philadelphia, 1982). The same author also has written a readable history, *Lutheranism in North America, 1914–1970* (Minneapolis, 1972). In addition, there is a useful historical survey, stressing European and American Lutheranism, by Conrad Bergendoff, *The Church of the Lutheran Reformation* (Saint Louis, 1967). Normative Lutheran teachings, "the Lutheran confessions," are made available in translation in *The Book of Concord*, edited and translated by Theodore G. Tappert (Philadelphia, 1959). The historical roots and theological significance of the Lutheran confessions are described and analyzed by me and Robert W. Jenson in *Lutheranism: The Theological Movement and Its Confessional Writings* (Philadelphia, 1976). The distinctive features of Lutheranism, especially compared with other traditions in the United States, are sketched in Arthur C. Piepkorn's "Lutheran Churches," in volume 2 of *Profiles of Belief* (San Francisco, 1978). The theological center of Lutheranism has been explored, with an eye on ecumenical implications, in Wilhelm Dantine's *The Justification of the Ungodly*, translated by me and Ruth C. Gritsch (Saint Louis, 1968), and in Gerhard O. Forde's *Justification by Faith: A Matter of Death and Life* (Philadelphia, 1982). Detailed information on Lutheran worship is contained in Luther D. Reed's *The Lutheran Liturgy* (Philadelphia, 1947). Basic information on Lutheranism can be quickly obtained in *The Encyclopedia of the Lutheran Church*, 3 vols., edited by Julius Bodensieck (Minneapolis, 1965).

ERIC W. GRITSCH

LYCANTHROPY. *See* Wolves.

M

MABINOGION. The eleven native prose tales extant in Middle Welsh are known collectively as the *Mabinogion*. This convenient modern title, based on a scribal error in a single medieval manuscript, may convey a false impression of the homogeneity of these stories. Found in two related manuscripts of the fourteenth century, the White Book of Rhydderch and the Red Book of Hergest, they are literary compositions ranging in date from the late eleventh century to the mid-thirteenth century. They are derived, as complete tales or their episodes, from traditional oral narratives, and they bear witness, however imperfectly, to a large body of traditional material (Wel., *cyfarwyddyd*), other relics of which are extant in the collections of triads, the *Stanzas of the Graves,* and other allusions. The sources reflected are diverse—mythological, legendary, and international folkloric. The most clearly mythological are those tales known as the "Four Branches" of the *Mabinogion* (c. 1060–1120).

An attempt has been made to associate *mabinogi* with the name of the youth god Maponos (Wel., Mabon), son of Matrona (Wel., Modron), the mother goddess, and to suggest the meaning "Mabonalia," but the word occurs elsewhere in Middle Welsh meaning "childhood" or "beginnings," and there refers to the deeds of the precocious youthful hero which are portents of his future greatness. An extended meaning may be simply a tale of heroes or, perhaps, of ancestors.

The Four Branches are independent stories linked by cross-references and motivating episodes, but accretions and restructuring over a long period have so complicated the narrative that it is difficult to postulate what the original hero-tale may have been. W. J. Gruffydd's attempt to re-create a heroic biography of one major character, Pryderi, is too ambitious and is based on a misinterpretation of the Old Irish tale-types, but the only other convincing explanation of an original, unifying structure for the Four Branches is that offered by Brinley Rees, who follows, after Georges Dumézil, a scheme of three functions.

The First Branch contains the birth-tale of Pryderi, son of Pwyll, lord of Dyfed (in southwestern Wales); Pwyll was known as "head of Annwn" because of his stay in the otherworld in the guise of its king, who had called upon him to help overcome an adversary. Upon his return Pwyll marries Rhiannon and they have a son, but the infant disappears from his crib. The child is subsequently discovered at the court of another nobleman, Teyrnon, some seventy miles distant, when a giant arm is amputated as it attempts to steal a foal on May Eve. There are many inconsistencies and gaps in the narrative, which seems to be a conflation of the motifs of the calumniated wife, the monster hand, and the congenital animals, but presumably it was intended to give an account of the birth of the hero in Annwn or to divine parents. Rhiannon is a Welsh counterpart of *Rigantona, queen-goddess, and is to be compared with Teyrnon, or *Tigernonos, king-god; her name and function are close to those of Matrona, whose son Maponos was taken from his mother's side when three nights old, according to an allusion in the eleventh-century story *Culhwch and Olwen.* She is probably identical with Epona, shown in Gaulish iconography as riding a horse, which recalls Rhiannon's associations with horses. Both Rhiannon and her son Pryderi are abducted in the Third Branch, and his loss is reflected in the wasting of his lordship of Dyfed.

The Third and Fourth Branches are complex narratives, both located in Gwynedd in northwestern Wales. The protagonists of the Fourth Branch are members of the divine family of Dôn (cf. Irish Tuatha Dé Danann)—Gwydion, the magician; Aranrhod, who gave birth to Lleu (cf. Irish Lugh; Gaulish Lugus) and Dylan, who was the son of the Wave and had the nature of a fish; Amaethon, the divine plowman; and Gofannon (cf. Irish Goibhniu), the divine smith. The story relates how Gwydion fashioned a wife from flowers for his nephew Lleu, cursed by his mother never to have a name, arms, or a wife.

The Second Branch describes the tragic result of the marriage of Branwen, daughter of Llŷr, to the Irish king Mathonwy and the devastation caused when her brother Brân, the giant king of Britain, and his brother Manawydan rescue her. *Llŷr* is possibly cognate with the Irish *ler* ("sea"), and there is probably some relationship between the Welsh characters and the Irish Manannán mac Lir and Bran of *The Voyage of Bran*, although the stories in Welsh and Irish do not correspond closely.

The other stories of the *Mabinogion* are briefer and simpler narratives. *Cyfranc Lludd a Llefelys*, first found as an interpolation in a Welsh translation by Geoffrey of Monmouth in his *Historia regum Britanniae* (c. 1200), is an extended triad. It may be a popular version of a mythological account of the winning of Britain by waves of invaders—otherworldly, Roman, and Saxon—or, according to another analysis, its three episodes, about fairy creatures, fighting dragons, and the food thief, reflect the Indo-European tripartite functions of sagacity, warfare, and provision. The *Dream of Maxen* is popular history, an account of the marriage of the Roman emperor Magnus Maximus (r. 383–388) with a British princess and the subsequent foundation of Brittany. *Culhwch and Olwen* (c. 1060) is an extended version of the folk tales *Six Go through the World* and *The Giant's Daughter;* the *Dream of Rhonabwy* (thirteenth century?) is a pastiche of traditions and themes put together as social satire and a parody of literary modes. The three romances, *Geraint, Owain,* and *Peredur,* are related to three romances by the twelfth-century French poet Chrétien de Troyes, although the nature of the interdependence is still problematic. The ultimate sources, however, are Celtic (Welsh or Breton), and they seem to contain examples of the sovereignty myth (better evidenced in Irish) wherein the hero, or king, marries the titular goddess of his land, thereby ensuring its fruitfulness. In the extant versions the significance of the myth has been lost, and little of its primitive value remained for either authors or audiences.

BIBLIOGRAPHY

All these stories are translated into English in Gwyn Jones and Thomas Jones's *The Mabinogion* (London, 1974). Patrick K. Ford translates seven of them and discusses their mythological bases in *The Mabinogi and Other Medieval Welsh Tales* (Berkeley, 1977). W. J. Gruffydd's *Math vab Mathonwy* (Cardiff, 1928) and *Rhiannon* (Cardiff, 1953), pioneer studies of the structure of the Four Branches, should be read with care. Proinsias Mac Cana's *Branwen, Daughter of Llŷr: A Study of the Irish Affinities and of the Composition of the Second Branch of the Mabinogi* (Cardiff, 1958) is a balanced literary study, and his *Celtic Mythology* (London, 1970) is a good introduction to the field.

BRYNLEY F. ROBERTS

MACUMBA. *See* Afro-Brazilian Cults.

MADHHAB. For lack of a better term, "legal school" is the most acceptable translation of *madhhab,* and it is preferable to both "sect" and "rite," terms which have been used in earlier works. A legal school implies a body of doctrine taught by a leader, or imam, and followed by the members of that school. The imam must be a leading *mujtahid,* one who is capable of exercising independent judgment. In his teaching, the imam must apply methods and principles which are peculiar to his own school independent of others. A *madhhab* must also have followers who assist their leader in the elaboration and dissimination of his teachings. A *madhhab* does not imply, however, a definite organization, a formal teaching, or an official status, nor is there a strict uniformity of doctrine within each *madhhab.* The membership of the present-day *madhhab*s is ascertainable on the basis of both individual confession and a loosely defined association of a country or a group to a particular *madhhab.* Legal school is a fitting description of *madhhab* simply because law is the main area in which the schools have widely disagreed. Their differences on the principles of the faith, at least among the Sunnī schools, are negligible. But disagreement on subsidiary matters *(furū')* extends to almost every subject.

The Earliest Schools. The first major split occurred between the Sunnī and the Shī'ī schools of law barely three decades after the death of the Prophet, about 660 CE. The secession of the Shī'ah from the main body of the Muslims, the Sunnīs, took place on political grounds, owing mainly to their differences on the nature and devolution of political authority. The Sunnīs accepted as legitimate the leadership of the four "Rightly Guided" caliphs, the Khulafā' Rāshidūn. But the Shī'ah claimed that 'Alī, the fourth caliph and the cousin and son-in-law of the Prophet, had a superior claim to leadership over any of his three predecessors, hence their name, the Shīʿah ("party") of ʿAlī.

The bitter controversies which arose in the early period of Islam led to the formation of numerous groupings. The range of contested issues must have been extremely diverse: some five hundred schools are said to have disappeared at or about the beginning of the third Muslim century (ninth century CE). But even then the schools had not yet settled down to the number they are now. The real formation of Islamic law starts, at the hands of individual jurists, in the latter part of the first century AH (seventh century CE). This period is followed in the early second/eighth century by the emergence of two geographical centers of juristic activity in the Hejaz and Iraq. Each of these was further divided into two centers: Mecca and Medina in the Hejaz, and Basra and Kufa in Iraq. Of these four centers, usually referred to as the ancient schools of law, Medina and Kufa were the most important. With their further development in the latter half of the second century, geographical schools gave way to personal schools, named after an individual master whom the members of the school followed.

The ancient schools of law adopted two different approaches to jurisprudence. The jurists of Mecca and Medina, cities where the Prophet had lived and Islam had its origin and early development, laid emphasis on tradition as their standard for legal decisions. They thus acquired the name *ahl al-ḥadīth,* or "partisans of tradition." Being away from the Hejaz and culturally more advanced, the Iraqi schools, on the other hand, resorted more readily to personal opinion *(ra'y),* which is why they acquired the name *ahl al-ra'y,* or "partisans of opinion." This group had a tendency to imagine hypothetical cases in order to determine their legal solutions. They had a flair for scholasticism and technical subtlety. The *ahl al-ḥadīth,* on the other hand, were averse to abstract speculation; they were more pragmatic and concerned themselves with concrete cases. Abū Ḥanīfah was the leading figure of the Iraqi school, whereas Mālik, and after him al-Shāfiʿī, led the Hejazi school of legal thought.

The Ḥanafīyah. The founder of the Ḥanafī school, Abū Ḥanīfah Nuʿmān ibn Thābit (d. 767), was born in Kufa, where he studied jurisprudence with Ibrāhīm al-Nakhaʿī and Ḥammād ibn Abī Sulaymān. He delivered lectures to a small circle of students who later compiled and elaborated his teaching. *Qiyās,* or analogical reasoning, which became one of the four sources of law, receives the greatest support from Abū Ḥanīfah. Because of this, and his extensive use of *ra'y,* Abū Ḥanīfah was criticized by the traditionists for emphasizing speculative opinion at the cost of the *ḥadīth.* Abū Ḥanīfah has left no work except a small volume on dogmatics, *Al-fiqh al-akbar* (The Greater Understanding). His teachings were documented and compiled mainly by two of his disciples, Abū Yūsuf and al-Shaybānī. The Ḥanafī school was favored by the ruling Abbasid dynasty. Abū Yūsuf, who became the chief justice of the caliph Hārūn al-Rashīd (r. 786–809), composed, at Hārūn's request, a treatise on fiscal and public law, the *Kitāb al-kharāj.* [*See the biographies of Abū Ḥanīfah and Abū Yūsuf.*]

Muḥammad ibn Ḥasan al-Shaybānī, a disciple of both Abū Ḥanīfah and Abū Yūsuf, compiled the *corpus juris* of the Ḥanafī school. Six of his juristic works, collectively called the *Ẓāhir al-rawāyah,* or works devoted to principal matters, became the basis of many future works on jurisprudence. All of the six works were later compiled in one volume entitled *Al-kāfī* (The Concise), by al-Marwazī, better known as al-Ḥākim al-Shahīd (d. 965). This was subsequently annotated by Shams al-Dīn al-Sarakhsī in thirty volumes, entitled *Al-mabsūṭ* (The Comprehensive). Ḥanafī law is the most humanitarian of all the schools concerning the treatment of non-Muslims and war captives, and its penal law is considered to be more lenient.

The Ḥanafīyah has the largest following of all the schools, owing to its official adoption by the Ottoman Turks in the early sixteenth century. It is now predominant in Turkey, Syria, Jordan, Lebanon, Pakistan, Afghanistan, and among the Muslims of India, and its adherents constitute about one-third of the Muslims of the world.

The Mālikīyah. The Mālikī school was founded by Mālik ibn Anas al-Aṣbaḥī (d. 795), who spent his entire life in Medina except for a brief pilgrimage to Mecca. He served as an official jurisconsult *(muftī),* which may explain why he broke away from the casuistic practices of his predecessors and attempted to formulate the principles underlying the tradition, to which he devoted his famous work, *Al-muwaṭṭa'* (The Leveled Path). Mālik is distinguished by the fact that he added another source of law to those known to other schools, namely the practice of the Medinese *('amal ahl Madīnah).* Since the Medinese followed each generation immediately preceding them, the process would have gone back to the generation that was in contact with the teachings and actions of the Prophet. In Mālik's opinion, the practice of the Medinese thus constitutes basic legal evidence. This pragmatic feature of Mālik's doctrine has been retained to the present in the legal practice *('amal)* of the Maghreb, which takes more notice than other schools of the prevailing conditions and customs. (Islamic law in general does not recognize custom as a source of law although it may validly operate in a subsidiary capacity.) The major reference book of the Mālikī school is *Al-mudawwanah* (The Enactment), compiled by Asad al-Furāt, and later edited and arranged by Saḥnūn, who published it under the name *Al-mudawwanah al-kubrā* (The Greater Enactment). The Mālikī school is currently predominant in Morocco, Algeria, Tunisia, Upper Egypt, the Sudan, Bahrein, and Kuwait. [*See the biography of Mālik ibn Anas.*]

The Shāfiʿīyah. The third major surviving school is called the Shāfiʿīyah, after its founder, Muḥammad ibn Idrīs al-Shāfiʿī (d. 819). A pupil of Mālik, he formulated the classical theory of jurisprudence in the form that it has largely retained ever since. This theory teaches that Islamic law is based on four basic principles, or roots, of jurisprudence *(uṣūl al-fiqh):* the word of God in the Qurʾān, the divinely inspired conduct or *sunnah* of the Prophet, consensus of opinion *(ijmāʿ),* and reasoning by analogy *(qiyās).* [*See* Uṣūl al-Fiqh.] Al-Shāfiʿī studied the works of his predecessors and found that despite the existence of traditions from the Prophet, the early jurists occasionally preferred the opinion of the companions, or ignored traditions when they were contrary to local practice. Insisting on the overriding authority of tradition, al-Shāfiʿī said that authentic traditions must always be accepted. Whereas Abū Ḥanīfah and Mālik felt free to set aside a tradition when it conflicted with the Qurʾān, for al-Shāfiʿī a tradition could not be invalidated on this ground: he took it for granted that the Qurʾān and tradition did not contradict each other.

Al-Shāfiʿī also differed with both Abū Ḥanīfah and Mālik on the meaning of *ijmāʿ*. To al-Shāfiʿī's predecessors *ijmāʿ* meant the consensus of the scholars, but al-Shāfiʿī denied the existence of any such consensus. There could only be one valid consensus—that of the entire Muslim community. He thus restricted the scope of *ijmāʿ* to obligatory duties, such as the daily prayer, on which such a consensus could be said to exist. But the legal theory which prevailed after al-Shāfiʿī returned to the concept of the consensus of the scholars, when it considers infallible in the same way as the general consensus of the Muslims. [*See* Ijmāʿ.]

Al-Shāfiʿī essentially restricted the sources of law to the Qurʾān and the *sunnah.* Should there be no provision in these sources for a particular case, then the solution must be found through the application of analogy, which basically entails extending the logic of the Qurʾān and the *sunnah.* Any expression of opinion which is not related to these sources is arbitrary and excessive. Al-Shāfiʿī thus restricted the scope of *ijtihād* (independent reasoning) by subjecting it to the requirements of strict analogical reasoning; hence he considers *ijtihād* and *qiyās* synonymous. [*See* Ijtihād *and* Qiyās.]

Al-Shāfiʿī has left many works, of which the most important on jurisprudence are the *Risālah* (Letter) and the seven-volume *Kitāb al-umm* (The Book of Essentials). The Shāfiʿī school is now prevalent in Lower Egypt, southern Arabia, East Africa, Indonesia, and Malaysia and has many followers in Palestine, Jordan, and Syria. [*See also the biography of al-Shāfiʿī.*]

The Ḥanābilah. Even al-Shāfiʿī's degree of emphasis on tradition did not satisfy the uncompromising traditionists, who preferred not to use any human reasoning in law and chose, as much as possible, to base their doctrine on the Qurʾān and the *ḥadīth.* This was the avowed purpose of the two new schools which emerged in the third century AH (ninth century CE). The first and the only successful one of these was the Ḥanbalī school, founded by Aḥmad ibn Ḥanbal (d. 855), the orthodox opponent of the rationalists and the *ahl al-raʾy* (the other was the Ẓāhirī school of Dāwūd al-Ẓāhirī which is now extinct). Ibn Ḥanbal's reliance on tradition was so total that for some time he and his adherents were regarded not as real jurists *(fuqahāʾ)* but as mere traditionists. His main work, *Al-musnad* (The Verified), is a collection of some twenty-eight thousand traditions. He uses *qiyās* very little and draws mainly on the sacred texts. Ibn Ḥanbal's teaching was later refined and developed by his disciples and commanded a widespread following, but in spite of a series of brilliant scholars and representatives over the centuries, the numbers suffered a continuous diminution after the fourteenth century CE. In the eighteenth century, the Wahhābīyah, the puritanical movement in the Arabian Peninsula, derived their doctrine and inspiration from the Ḥanābilah as it had been expressed by the celebrated jurist and theologian Ibn Taymīyah (d. 1328).

Ironically, the Ḥanābilah are in some respects more liberal than the other schools. Ḥanbalī law, for example, adopts the doctrine of *ibāḥah* (lit., "permissibility") on matters which are not expressly prohibited by law. It presumes that the validity of acts and transactions is overruled only by the existence of proof to the contrary. For example, only Ḥanbalī law would allow the stipulation of a clause in a marriage contract to prevent the husband from entering into a polygamous contract in the future. While the other schools regard this as interference with the *sharīʿah,* Ḥanbalī law maintains that the basic purpose of the law is fulfilled by monogamy; since polygamy is merely permitted by the law, it may be validly restricted in this manner. Other examples of this nature that may be cited include Ibn Qayyim al-Jawzīyah's validation of one witness of just character as legal proof, and his approval of the acts of a bona fide catalyst *(fuḍūlī),* both of which the other schools have rejected. The Ḥanbalī school is currently predominant in Saudi Arabia, Qatar, and Oman. [*See* Ḥanābilah; Wahhābīyah; *and the biography of Ibn Taymīyah.*]

Shīʿī Schools. In Sunnī law, the head of state, or caliph, is to be elected to office, and his main duty is to supervise the proper implementation of the *sharīʿah,* the divine law of Islam. Shīʿī law, on the other hand, maintains that leadership, the imamate, belongs to the descendants of ʿAlī through hereditary succession. Of the numerous Shīʿī schools, only three have survived to this day: Ithnā ʿAsharī (Twelver), Zaydī, and Ismāʿīlī. The differences among these groups stem from their divergence over the line of succession after the fourth imam. The Twelvers, who are the largest of the three groups, recognize twelve imams, hence their name, Ithnā ʿAsharīyah, or Twelvers, as opposed to the Ismāʿīlīyah, who are also called Sabʿīyah, or Seveners, because they differed with the other Shīʿī groups over the identity of the seventh imam. According to Twelver dogma, the twelfth imam, the imam of the age, who disappeared in 873 CE, will reappear to establish the rule of justice on earth.

For the Sunnīs, divine revelation, manifested in the Qur'ān and the *sunnah,* ceased with the death of the Prophet. For the Shīʿāh, however, divine revelation continued to be transmitted, after the death of the Prophet, to the line of their recognized imams. Accordingly, they maintain that in addition to the Qur'ān and the *sunnah,* the pronouncements of their imams, whom they believe infallible *(maʿṣūm),* constitute divine revelation and therefore binding law. The Shīʿah, moreover, accept only those traditions whose chain of authority *(isnād)* goes back to one of their recognized imams; they also have their own *ḥadīth* collections. Since the imam is divinely inspired, the Shīʿah basically do not recognize *ijmāʿ*. Twelver doctrine, however, permits *ijmāʿ* as interpretation of the command of the imams on a particular question by the jurist *(mujtahid).* The Twelvers are divided into two branches, the Akhbārī and the Uṣūlī. The Akhbarīyah do not recognize *qiyās,* but the Uṣūlīyah do. Shīʿī law, which mainly originates in the teaching of the sixth imam, Jaʿfar al-Ṣādiq (d. 765) bears similarity to Shāfiʿī law but differs with it on many issues. Temporary marriage, or *mutʿah,* for example, is valid only in Shīʿī law. The Shīʿī law of inheritance is also very different from the law of any other school in this field. Twelver doctrine was officially adopted in Persia under the Safavids in 1501; it still commands the largest following in Iran, and it has also followers in Iraq, Lebanon, and Syria.

According to the Ismāʿīlī dogma, the esoteric meaning of the Qur'ān and its allegorical interpretation is known only to the imam, whose knowledge and guidance is indispensible to salvation. The Ismāʿīlīyah are divided into two groups, eastern and western. The former are centered in India, Pakistan, and Central Asia, and their leader is the present Aga Khan, forty-ninth imam in the line of succession. The Western Ismāʿīlīyah followed al-Mustaʿlī, the ninth Fatimid caliph. This line went to the twenty-first imam, al-Ṭayyib, but he became *mastūr* (occult). This group resides in southern Arabia and Syria.

The Zaydīyah follow Zayd ibn ʿAlī, the fifth imam in the order of the Shīʿī imams. They endorse the legitimacy of the caliphs who preceded ʿAlī on the belief that an acceptable leader has a legitimate title notwithstanding the existence of a superior claimant. Their legal doctrine is the nearest of the Shīʿi schools to the Sunnīs, and they mainly reside in the Yemen.

Consensus and Divergence among the Schools. To summarize, disagreement among jurists is basically a consequence of the freedom of *ijtihād* which they enjoyed, particularly in the first three centuries of Islam. They have differed mainly in four areas: interpretation of the Qur'an, acceptance and interpretation of the *ḥadīth,* rationalist doctrines, and subsidiary matters. Concerning the Qur'ān, the jurists have disagreed over the abrogation *(naskh)* of some of the Qur'anic verses by others where two verses provide divergent rulings on the same subject, or when the *ḥadīth* overrules a Qur'anic verse. While al-Shāfiʿī's doctrine of *naskh* is based on the rule that the Qur'ān can only be abrogated by the Qur'ān and *sunnah* only by *sunnah,* the other three schools add that the Qur'ān and the *sunnah* may also abrogate one another.

The words of the Qur'ān are divided into general *(ʿāmm)* and specific *(khāṣṣ).* The jurists have disagreed regarding the meaning and implications of such words. For example, X is unable to pay his debt. His brother Y pays it while acting on his own initiative and out of good will. The question arises as to whether Y, who is called *fuḍūlī,* or catalyst, is entitled to claim his money back from X. Māliki and Ḥanbalī law answer this question in the affirmative on the authority of surah 55:60 of the Qur'ān: "Is the reward of goodness *(iḥsān)* aught but goodness?" But for the Ḥanafīyah and Shāfiʿīyah the words of this verse are too general to be applied to the case in question; hence they deny the *fuḍūlī* the right to a repayment.

The scope of disagreement concerning the *sunnah* is even wider, for in this area differences extend not only to the interpretation of *ḥadīth* but also to its authenticity. Whereas the Ḥanafīyah, and to some extent the Shāfiʿīyah, apply strict rules to verify the authenticity of *ḥadīth,* the Mālikīyah and Ḥanābilah are relatively uncritical. Al-Shāfiʿī and Ibn Ḥanbal, for example, accept a solitary *(aḥād)* tradition, one which is reported by a single narrator, but Abū Ḥanīfah and Mālik accept it only under certain conditions. The jurists have also applied different rules to cases of conflict and abrogation between traditions. Whereas the majority would not, for example, allow the abrogation of a *mutawātir* (a tradition reported by numerous narrators) by an *aḥād*, the Ḥanafīyah permit this in principle. [*See also* Ḥadīth *and* Sunnah.]

Disagreement over rationalist doctrines such as *ra'y*, consensus, analogy, and *ijtihād* has already been discussed. It may be added here that Ḥanafī law applies *istiḥsān*, or juristic preference, as a doctrine of equity where strict implementation of analogy leads to hardships and undesirable results. The Mālikī school, however, adopts *istiṣlāḥ* (regard for the public interest), which is essentially similar to *istiḥsān*, albeit with some difference of detail. Al-Shāfi'ī rejects both *istiḥsān* and *istiṣlāḥ*, which he considers as no more than frivolous and arbitrary interference with the *sharī'ah*. Alternately, the Shāfi'īyah, the Ḥanābilah, and the Twelver Shī'ah adopt *istiṣḥāb*, or deduction by presumption of continuity. *Istiṣḥāb*, for example, assumes freedom from liability to be a natural state until the contrary is proved.

Differences of *ijtihād* concerning subsidiary matters need not be elaborated, as the abundance of legal doctrines and schools within the *sharī'ah* is indicative of such diversity. By the beginning of the fourth century AH there was a consensus established to the effect that all essential issues had been thoroughly discussed and finally settled. With this "closing of the door of *ijtihād*," as it was called, *ijtihād* gave way to *taqlīd*, or "imitation." From then on every Muslim was an imitator *(muqallid)* who had to belong to one of the recognized schools. By consensus also the four schools were accepted, and accepted one another, as equally orthodox. Notwithstanding the emergence of prominent scholars in later centuries (including Ibn Taymīyah and Ibn Qayyim al-Jawzīyah) who objected to *taqlīd*, no one actually provided an independent interpretation of the *sharī'ah*. *Taqlīd* remained a dominant practice for about a thousand years until the reform movements of the late nineteenth century (notably the Salafīyah, whose prominent figure is Muḥammad 'Abduh) and the modernist school of thought in the present century which challenged *taqlīd* and called for a return to *ijtihād*.

A Muslim may join any orthodox school he or she wishes, or change from one school to another, without formalities. Furthermore, Islamic countries have made frequent use of divergent opinions of other schools, including Shī'ī legal doctrines, in modern legislation. In order to achieve desired results, modern reformers have utilized procedural expedients permitted in the *sharī'ah*, such as *takhayyur* and *talfīq*. *Takhayyur*, or "selection," enables the jurist to adopt from the various interpretations of the *sharī'ah* that which is deemed to be most suitable. Reformers in the area of personal status, for example, have frequently adopted a variant doctrine of a recognized school as the basis of reform. Sometimes the view of an early jurist outside the established schools has been so selected. Furthermore, legal rules have been occasionally constructed by combining part of the doctrine of one school or jurist with part of the doctrine of another school or jurist. This variation of *takhayyur* is known as *talfīq*, or "patching," a procedure which has been employed in the modern laws of the Middle East. (For interesting illustrations and details on these procedural devices see Coulson's *A History of Islamic Law*.)

[*For a broader discussion of the legal context, see* Islamic Law.]

BIBLIOGRAPHY

A useful biography of the well-known Sunnī and Shī'ī jurists of early Islam, including the founders of the schools and their doctrines, can be found in Muḥammad al-Khuḍarī's *Ta'rīkh al-tashrī' al-islāmī*, 4th ed. (Cairo, 1934). Subhī Rajab Mahmassani's *Falsafat al-tashrī' fī al-Islām: The Philosophy of Jurisprudence in Islam*, translated by Farhat J. Ziadeh (Leiden, 1961), contains more condensed information on both the Sunnī and Shī'ī *madhhabs*. This book also provides a useful bibliography of Arabic works on the subject. An accurate exposition of the roots of jurisprudence *(uṣūl al-fiqh)* in the Sunnī schools can be found in Muḥammad Ma'rūf al-Dawālibī's *Al-madkhal ilā 'ilm uṣūl al-fiqh*, 5th ed. (Cairo, 1965). Noel J. Coulson's *A History of Islamic Law* (1964; reprint, Edinburgh, 1971) and Joseph Schacht's *An Introduction to Islamic Law* (Oxford, 1964) remain the best English works on the jurisprudence and history of the Sunnī *madhhabs*. There is also much useful information, and a bibliography, on the subject in Nicolas P. Aghnides's *Muhammadan Theories of Finance* (New York, 1916). And finally, Ignácz Goldziher's *Introduction to Islamic Theology and Law*, translated by Andreas Hamori and Ruth Hamori (Princeton, 1981), is comprehensive on the Shī'i *madhhabs* and their theological doctrines.

M. HASHIM KAMALI

MADHVA (1238–1317), also known as Ānandatīrtha or Pūrṇaprajñā; founder of the Dvaita Vedānta school of Indian philosophy. Born in Pajakakṣetra near Udipi in the Tulu country of the Indian state of Karnataka, Madhva attracted attention as a young renunciate by his prodigious abilities in reciting, interpreting, and criticizing scriptural and exegetical texts. Gathering pupils at his classes in Udipi, he made numerous trips throughout India accompanied by his disciples, including at least two visits to Badrinath in the Himalayas. It is believed that he debated a number of prominent scholars during his lifetime.

Madhva established his main temple, consecrated to the god Kṛṣṇa, at Udipi, and installed in it the idol of Bāla Kṛṣṇa secured from Dwarka. The temple has flourished to this day in the charge of a steady line of successors stemming from Madhva and his disciples. Tradition holds that in the year 1317, in the middle of delivering a lecture, Madhva vanished and retired permanently to Badrinath.

Madhva is credited with some thirty-seven works, including commentaries on the *Bhagavadgītā*, the *Brahma Sūtras*, and ten of the older Upaniṣads; ten independent treatises on Dvaita philosophy; short commentaries on the *Bhāgavata Purāṇa*, the *Mahābhārata*, and part of the *Ṛgveda;* and a number of other brief works of a varied nature. Many of these treatises were subsequently commented upon by Jayatīrtha, Vyāsatīrtha, and other famous Dvaitins; the resulting large body of literature forms the basis of Dvaita Vedānta.

Dvaita stands in strong contrast to Śaṅkara's Advaita system in its conception of *brahman* as a personal God, independent of all other things and different from them. Madhva's God, who is Viṣṇu, possesses transcendent attributes of creation, preservation, dissolution, control, enlightenment, obscuration, bondage, and release, and God himself is considered the cause of all causes productive of these results. Each individual self is by nature a reflection of God; however, no one is aware of this until, through study of the scriptures, he comes to understand his real nature, upon which he undertakes fervent devotion to the Lord, who responds by bestowing his grace upon the devotee according to the latter's capacity. The devotee then abides in a state of servitude to God forever, and this state constitutes his liberation.

Dvaita Vedānta is also known for its sophisticated analyses of matters pertaining to logic, epistemology, and metaphysics; many of these investigations were first raised in Madhva's writings.

The influence of Dvaita Vedānta has been felt throughout India, but most profoundly in the South. It has been claimed by some scholars that the direct influence of Madhva's thought played a part in the later development of Bengali Vaiṣṇavism. Certainly, later Dvaita writers were among the most formidable opponents of Advaita Vedānta, and these doctrinal differences led to the famous controversy between Vyāsatīrtha (1478–1539), the Dvaitin author of the *Nyāyāmṛta*, and Madhusūdana Sarasvatī (c. 1540–1600), author of the *Advaitasiddhi*, an extensive response to the *Nyāyāmṛta* and the most celebrated later work of Advaita polemics.

[*For discussion of the tenets of Madhva's Dvaita Vedānta, see* Vedānta.]

BIBLIOGRAPHY

A good overall introduction to the thought of Madhva is B. N. K. Sharma's *A History of the Dvaita School of Vedānta and Its Literature*, 2d rev. ed., 2 vols. (Bombay, 1981).

KARL H. POTTER

MĀDHYAMIKA. The Mādhyamika, or Madhyamaka, school is one of the four great schools of Indian Buddhism, along with the Sarvāstivāda, Sautrāntika, and Yogācāra (Vijñānavāda) traditions. The name Mādhyamika ("one who follows the middle way") is derived from the word *madhyamaka*, found in the title *Madhyamakakārikā*, perhaps the most important work of Nāgārjuna, the founder of the school. The school is referred to as Dbu-ma-pa ("the school of the middle") in Tibet, San-lun-tsung ("the three-treatises school") in China, and Sanronshū ("the three-treatises school") in Japan. Historically, Indian Mādhyamika may be divided into three stages, early, middle, and late.

The Early Period. This period is marked by two great figures, Nāgārjuna and Āryadeva, and a lesser one, Rāhulabhadra. Nāgārjuna (c. 150–250 CE), born in South India, was the author of a number of works variously extant in Sanskrit, Tibetan, and/or Chinese (as subsequently indicated by the parenthetical abbreviations S, T, and C). He was associated with a king of the Śātavāhana dynasty, as is seen from his works, the *Ratnāvalī* (S partially, T) and the *Suhṛllekha* (T), both consisting of admonitions, moral as well as religious, given to the king. His main works comprise five philosophical treatises: the *Madhyamakakārikā* (S, T, C), the *Yuktiṣaṣṭikā* (T), and the *Śūnyatāsaptati* (T), all of which are written in verse and develop the philosophy of *śūnyatā* ("emptiness"); and the *Vigrahavyāvartanī* (S, T, C) and the *Vaidalyasūtra* (T), written in verse and in aphorisms, respectively, both of which are accompanied by autocommentaries in prose. The last two contain Nāgārjuna's criticism of the rules governing traditional Indian logic, especially those of the Naiyāyika. Another genuine work of Nāgārjuna's is, without doubt, the *Pratītyasamutpādahṛdaya* (S partially, T, C), as well as the autocommentary (*Pratītyasamutpādahṛdayavyākhyāna*, S partially, T, C). In this last work, consisting of seven verses and a commentary in prose, the course of transmigration of sentient beings owing to defilements, deeds, and suffering is explained in the light of the theory of twelve-membered dependent co-origination. At the same time, however, the text emphasizes that because everything is devoid of own being or essential nature there is actually no one who moves from this world to another. Many other works are traditionally ascribed to Nāgārjuna; some, for example, the *Mahāprajñāpāramitopadeśa* (Chin., *Ta chih-tu lun,* extant only in Chinese), have influenced the development of Buddhist exegetics, and some, for example, the *Daśabhūmikavibhāṣā* (C), that of Pure Land Buddhism in China and Japan. However, nothing definite can be said as to the authenticity of authorship of these works.

The philosophy of emptiness is found in such early Buddhist *sūtras* as the *Ti-i-i-kung ching* (T.D. 2.92c) and the *Aggi-Vacchagotta Suttanta* (*Majjhima Nikāya,* no. 72) and thus did not originate with Nāgārjuna, who declared that he revived the true teaching of the Buddha. However, Nāgārjuna also relied heavily on the Prajñāpāramitā Sūtras, the *Daśabhūmika Sūtra,* and the *Kāśyapaparivarta* in forming his philosophy. His philosophy of emptiness was a criticism of Indian realism, which was represented by Indian philosophical systems of the Sāṃkhya, the Vaiśeṣika, and the Naiyāyika, and by such Hīnayāna Buddhists as the Sarvāstivādas and other Abhidharma philosophers, who believed that human ideas, insofar as they are rational, have substances that correspond to them in the external world.

In speaking of emptiness Nāgārjuna meant to say not that nothing exists but that everything is empty of *svabhāva* ("own being"), that is, of an independent, eternal, and unchanging substance. All things are, like images in a dream or an illusion, neither substantially existent nor nonexistent absolutely. Nāgārjuna's negation of a self-dependent substance, which he holds to be nothing but a hypostatized concept or word, is derived from the traditional Buddhist idea of dependent origination *(pratītya-samutpāda),* the idea that whatever exists arises and exists dependent on other things. [*See* Pratītya-samutpāda.] Nāgārjuna, however, introduces into that theory the concept of mutual dependency. Just as the terms *long* and *short* take on meaning only in relation to each other and are themselves devoid of independent qualities (longness or shortness), so too do all phenomena (all *dharmas*) lack own being *(svabhāva).* If a thing were to have an independent and unchanging own being, then it would follow that it is neither produced nor existent, because origination and existence presuppose change and transiency. All things, physical as well as mental, can originate and develop only when they are empty of own being. This idea of emptiness necessitates the truth of nonduality. *Saṃsāra* and *nirvāṇa* (defilements and liberation), like any other pair of contradictions, are nondual because both members of the pair are empty of own being. [*See also the biography of Nāgārjuna.*]

Āryadeva (c. 170–270), a direct disciple of Nāgārjuna, was also active in South India. He wrote three works: the *Catuḥśataka,* his main work (S fragment, T, C latter half only); the *Śataśāstra* (C), which has been studied throughout China and Japan; and the *Akṣaraśataka* (T, C), a small work consisting of a hundred words and his autocommentary. Āryadeva inherited Nāgārjuna's philosophy. [*See the biography of Āryadeva.*] Nothing is known about Rāhulabhadra except that he left two hymns, the *Prajñāpāramitāstotra* and the *Saddharmapuṇḍarīkastotra,* and a few fragmentary verses quoted in the Chinese texts.

The Middle Period. Tradition reports that eight Indian scholars wrote commentaries on the *Madhyamakakārikā:* Nāgārjuna himself (*Akutobhayā,* T); Buddhapālita (c. 470–540; *Buddhapālita-Mūlamadhyamakavṛtti,* T); Candrakīrti (c. 600–650; *Prasannapadā,* S, T); Devaśarman (fifth to six centuries; *Dkar-po 'char-ba,* T fragment); Guṇaśrī (fifth to sixth centuries; title unknown); Guṇamati (fifth to sixth centuries; title unknown, T fragment); Sthiramati (c. 510–570; *Ta-sheng chung-kuan shih-lun,* C); and Bhavya (also known as Bhāvaviveka; c. 500–570; *Prajñāpradīpa,* T, C).

The *Akutobhayā* is partially identical with Buddhapālita's commentary, and its authenticity is doubtful. Two fragments from Devaśarman's commentary are cited with appreciation by Bhāvaviveka. A fragment from Guṇamati's commentary is criticized by Bhāvaviveka. The works of Devaśarman and Guṇamati are not extant. Nothing is known about Guṇaśrī or his work. The fact that Guṇamati and Sthiramati, both well-known Yogācārins, commented on the *Madhyamakakārikā* shows that Nāgārjuna was revered not only by Mādhyamikas but also by philosophers of other schools. In addition, there is Ch'ing-mu's commentary extant in Kumārajīva's Chinese translation. The *Shun-chung lun* (C) by Asaṅga (c. 320–400), another Yogācārin, is a general interpretation of Nāgārjuna's verse of salutation found at the very beginning of the *Madhyamakakārikā.*

The middle period is characterized by the split of the Mādhyamika into two subschools, the Prāsaṅgika, represented by Buddhapālita and Candrakīrti, and the Svātantrika, represented by Bhāvaviveka and Avalokitavrata. The names Prāsaṅgika and Svātantrika are not attested to in any Sanskrit texts and thus were probably coined by later Tibetan doxographers. However, the names so appropriately describe the tenets of the two subschools that they are widely used even by modern scholars.

In his arguments Nāgārjuna often used dilemmas and tetralemmas. In *Madhyamakakārikā* 1.1, for instance, he states that things produced from themselves, from others, from both themselves and others, or from no cause at all can be found nowhere. Buddhapālita, the founder of the Prāsaṅgika school, divided this tetralemma into four different *prasaṅga* arguments, or arguments *reductio ad absurdum.* He pointed out that (1) production of a thing from itself would be quite useless because, having own being, the thing would already exist and such production would thus involve the logical fault of overextension *(atiprasaṅga),* for a thing already existing by own being would, under this assumption, never cease being produced; (2) if things are produced from another, all things could be produced from all other things; (3) if things are produced from both themselves and another, the faults attached to the two preceding alternatives would combine in this third one; and (4) if things are produced from no cause, all things would be produced always and from all things.

Nāgārjuna himself used *prasaṅga* as often as dilemmas and tetralemmas, but Buddhapālita, analyzing even dilemmas and tetralemmas into plural *prasaṅgas*, considered the latter to be the main method of Mādhyamika argumentation. As a form of argument, *prasaṅga* had been known among logicians since the time of the *Nyāya Sūtra* (codified in the third century) under the name *tarka.* In the eighth century it was formalized by Buddhist logicians into a syllogistic form under the name *prasaṅga-anumāna* ("inference by *prasaṅga*"). If, for example, seeing smoke on a mountain, we want to prove the existence of fire to someone who objects by denying the existence of fire there, we can argue that if there were no fire on the mountain, there would be no smoke there either. At the same time we would be pointing out the fact that smoke is actually rising on the mountain. This form of argument is known as *prasaṅga,* the essence of which is to indicate that an absurd conclusion would follow, given the opponent's claim. The above example can be put into the following categorical syllogism: wherever there is smoke, there is fire (p); that mountain has smoke (q); therefore, that mountain has fire (r). This syllogism $(pq \supset r)$ can be transformed into the following *prasaṅga-anumāna* $(p \sim r \supset q)$: wherever there is no fire, there is no smoke (the contraposition of p); (if) the mountain has no fire $(\sim r)$, (it would follow that) the mountain has no smoke $(\sim q)$, which is contrary to fact. Likewise, Buddhapālita's *prasaṅga* may be written: production of things from themselves is useless (p); (if) this thing is produced from itself $(\sim r)$, then (it would follow that) its production is useless $(\sim q)$. These examples of *prasaṅga-anumāna* are hypothetical syllogisms because the minor premise $(\sim r)$ is hypothesized by the advocator and only claimed by the opponent and because the conclusion $(\sim q)$, necessarily following from the two premises, is false. [*See also the biography of Buddhapālita.*]

Bhāvaviveka criticized Buddhapālita, saying that his argument was a mere *prasaṅga,* lacking both a true probans (i.e., minor premise) and an example (i.e., major premise). Furthermore, Buddhapālita may be understood to maintain a counterposition to the probans as well as to the example because of the nature of *prasaṅga.* This is to say, Buddhapālita's own opinion would be as follows: a thing is produced from another, et cetera (r), and its production is useful (q). Understood in that way, Buddhapālita's assertion would be contrary to Nāgārjuna, who denied not only production from the thing itself but also production from another, from both, and from no cause. Until some Buddhist logicians came, in the eighth century, to recognize *prasaṅga* as a form of formal inference, it was not regarded as authentic; in fact, although it had been admitted as supplementary to the categorical syllogism, it was classified as erroneous knowledge because its conclusion was false to the arguing party. [*See also the biography of Bhāvaviveka.*]

Bhāvaviveka was strongly influenced by his senior contemporary Dignāga, the reformer of Buddhist logic and epistemology. [*See the biography of Dignāga.*] Accordingly, it was Bhāvaviveka's contention that the Mādhyamikas had to employ categorical syllogisms to prove the truth of their philosophy. In his commentary on the *Madhyamakakārikā* as well as in his other works, Bhāvaviveka formed innumerable categorical syllogisms, the so-called *svatantra-anumāna* ("independent inference"). This is why he came to be called a Svātantrika, in contradistinction to Buddhapālita, who was termed a Prāsaṅgika.

For instance, in commenting on Nāgārjuna's denial of production of things from themselves (*Madhyamakakārikā* 1.1), Bhāvaviveka uses the following syllogistic form, which may be rewritten according to Aristotelian logic thus:

Major Premise: whatever exists is not produced from itself, for example, *caitanya* (an eternal, unchanging spirit in the Sāṃkhya philosophy).

Minor Premise: the cognitive organs (eye, ear, nose, etc.) exist.

Conclusion: therefore, from the standpoint of the highest truth *(paramārthataḥ)* they have not been produced from themselves.

In constituting this kind of syllogism, Bhāvaviveka included three unusual modifications: the word *paramārthataḥ* ("from the standpoint of the highest truth") is added; the negation in this syllogism should be understood as *prasajya-pratiṣedha* ("the negation of a proposition," opposite to *paryudāsa,* "the negation of a term"), in which the negative particle is related to the verb, not to the nominal, so that *not from themselves* may not mean *from another;* and no counterexample is available, that is, no member of the class contradictory to the probandum is available, which means that the contraposition of the major premise (i.e., what is produced from itself is nonexisting) is not supported by actual examples.

Bhāvaviveka's logic, however, had its own difficulties, for which it was criticized by Sthiramati and Candrakīrti as well as by the Naiyāyikas. If the restrictive *from the standpoint of the highest truth* governs not only the conclusion but also the whole syllogism, the minor premise would not be permissible because all things, including the cognitive organs, would be nonexistent from the standpoint of the highest truth according to the Mādhyamika. If, on the contrary, the restriction governed only the conclusion and not the two premises, then the cognitive organs in the minor premise would have to be regarded as existent when seen from the standpoint of truth on the conventional level *(saṃvṛti, vyavahāra),* while the same organs in the conclusion would be nonexistent when seen from the highest truth. Therefore, Bhāvaviveka is to be criticized for using the term *the cognitive organs* on two different levels of discourse. In both cases he commits a logical fallacy.

Candrakīrti says that the negation used by all Mādhyamikas should be regarded as *prasajya-pratiṣedha.* When there is a defect in the counterexample, that is, when the contraposition of the major premise is not attested to in actuality, how can there be certainty with regard to the validity of the original major premise? Candrakīrti, citing one of Nāgārjuna's verses, argued that the Mādhyamikas, having no assertion of their own, should not rely on the syllogistic method and that *prasaṅga* is the only and the best way of argumentation for them.

The commentary on the *Madhyamakakārikā* was Buddhapālita's sole work. Bhāvaviveka, in addition to the *Prajñāpradīpa,* wrote the *Madhyamakahṛdayakārikā* (S, T) with his autocommentary *Tarkajvālā* (T), in which he discussed the truth of the Mādhyamika philosophy in chapters 1, 2, and 3 and the doctrines of Hīnayāna Buddhism, Yogācāra, Sāṃkhya, Vaiśeṣika, Vedānta, and other schools in the following chapters. His *Ta-sheng chang-chen lun* (*Karatalaratna?*) is extant only in Chinese. The authenticity of two other works ascribed to Bhāvaviveka, the *Madhyamakaratnapradīpa* and the *Madhyamakārthasaṃgraha,* is doubtful. In addition to the *Prasannapadā,* Candrakīrti left a great work entitled *Madhyamakāvatāra* (T), consisting of verses and an autocommentary, in which he explicated the essentials of the Mādhyamika philosophy in accordance with the ten perfections *(pāramitā)* of the *bodhisattva.* He was a prolific writer: the *Pañcaskandhaprakaraṇa* and the commentaries on the *Śūnyatāsaptati,* the *Yuktiṣaṣṭikā,* and the *Catuḥśataka,* all extant only in Tibetan, are known to be his works. Avalokitavrata (seventh century), a Svātantrika, wrote a bulky and informative commentary (T) on Bhāvaviveka's *Prajñāpradīpa.* Śāntideva, who tended to be a Prāsaṅgika, wrote the *Śikṣāsamuccaya* (S, T, C), a collection of teachings about learnings and practices of the *bodhisattva,* and the *Bodhicaryāvatāra* (S, T, C), which consisted of more than nine hundred verses and which also taught practices of the *bodhisattva* according to the six *pāramitās.* The *Sūtrasamuccaya,* a collection of passages from Mahāyāna *sūtras,* is ascribed by Tibetans to Nāgārjuna, but it is closely related to the *Śikṣāsamuccaya* and suggests that Śāntideva may have added more *sūtra* passages to Nāgārjuna's original text. [*See also the biographies of Sthiramati, Candrakīrti, and Śāntideva.*]

The Last Period. Philosophers of the middle period of Indian Mādhyamika can be characterized as follows: they wrote their own commentaries on the *Madhyamakakārikā;* they were divided into the Prāsaṅgika and the Svātantrika, according to whether they adopted either *prasaṅga ("reductio ad absurdum")* or *svatantra-anumāna* ("independent syllogism") as a means for establishing the truth of the Mādhyamika philosophy; and they regarded the Yogācāra school as their opponent and criticized its philosophy. In contrast, philosophers of the last period were influenced by Dharmakīrti, the greatest scholar of the Buddhist logico-epistemological school, as much as they were by Nāgārjuna; with a few exceptions, almost all of them belonged to the lineage of the Svātantrika school; and they appreciated the philosophy of the Yogācāra school and even introduced it as part of the Mādhyamika philosophy. [*See the biography of Dharmakīrti.*] Consequently, beginning with Śāntiraksita, they came to be called the Yogācāra-Mādhyamika-Svātantrika by Tibetans. In contrast, the later Tibetan scholars called Bhāvaviveka a Sautrāntika-Mādhyamika-Svātantrika, as he adopted the Sautrāntika theory of the imperceptible but real external world from the standpoint of truth on the conventional level *(saṃvṛti).*

The greatest figure of this last period is Śāntirakṣita (c. 725–784), a disciple of Jñānagarbha (eighth century), of whom very little is known except that he was the author of the *Satyadvayavibhaṅga* (T), his autocommentary the *Satyadvayavibhaṅgavṛtti,* and the *Yogabhāvanāmārga* (T). A scholar at Nālandā Monastery, Śāntirakṣita was invited to Tibet by a Tibetan king. There he established the first Tibetan Buddhist monastery (at Bsam-yas) in cooperation with Padmasambhava, and ordained the first six Tibetan monks. He wrote two works, the *Tattvasaṃgraha* (S, T) and the *Madhyamakālaṃkāra* (T), and a commentary on the *Satyadvayavibhaṅga,* the main work of his master. The *Tattvasaṃgraha,* written in 3,645 verses, introduces the philosophies of various Indian schools, non-Buddhist as well as Buddhist, and also provides a criticism of them. Accompanied by a large commentary by Kamalaśīla, his worthy disciple, this work is extant in Sanskrit and is extremely valuable for the information it imparts on the world of Indian philosophy at that time. In the *Madhyamakālaṃkāra,* to which there exist his autocommentary, the *Madhyamakālaṃkāravṛtti* (T), and Kamalaśīla's subcommentary, the *Madhyamakālaṃkārapañjikā* (T), he criticizes the Buddhist philosophies of the Sarvāstivāda, Sautrāntika, and Yogācāra schools as well as non-Buddhist philosophies, and proclaims the Mādhyamika as the last and highest doctrine of all. The principle underlying his criticism against all other schools that regard specific entities as ultimate metaphysical realities is that they are empty of reality because they are devoid of both singular and plural own beings.

Like the Mīmāṃsā, Vaiśeṣika, Naiyāyika, and other schools, the Sarvāstivāda holds that knowledge, like a clean slate, is pure and is not endowed with the image of an object and that cognition takes place through the contact of mind, a cognitive organ, and an external object, all of which exist at the same moment. Epistemologically, this is a copyist theory of knowledge, called in India *nirākārajñānavāda* ("the theory of knowledge not endowed with the image of the object"). On the other hand, like the Sāṃkhya, Vedānta, and Yogācāra schools, the Sautrāntika contends that what is cognized is not an external object but an image thrown into knowledge by the external reality, which always remains something imperceptible. Knowledge is an effect of an external object that is its cause and that has already disappeared at the moment the knowledge arises. This is the representationalist's theory of knowledge and is called *sākārajñānavāda* ("the theory of knowledge endowed with the image of the object"). But the Sautrāntika, unlike the Yogācāra, does not deny the existence of the external reality. For it, an external reality, though never perceived, must be postulated as existing. According to the Yogācāra, it is unnecessary to postulate the existence of the external reality because what knowledge cognizes is an image that is given not by an external object but by the immediately preceding moment of the knowledge. The mind is a stream of moments containing impressions of experiences accumulated since the beginningless past. The world is nothing but the representations of mind; external objects are in reality nonexistent. Yogācāra holds, as does the Sautrāntika, that knowledge is endowed with an image *(sākārajñāna).* However, the Yogācāras are divided into two groups as regards the nature of that image. One maintains that the image is as real as the self-cognition *(svasaṃvedana)* of knowledge. The other contends that the image is unreal, although self-cognition is real. We often grasp an erroneous image, say of a silver coin that we realize a moment later is nothing but a shell. According to the latter opinion, this means that all images can be unreal, while the illumination *(prakāśa)* itself, which exists with both the silver coin and the shell, is real. This illumination or self-cognition is the only reality. This view is called *alīkākāravāda* ("the theory of the unreal image of cognition"). According to the former opinion, however, the illumination alone is never cognized separately from the image. The image of a silver coin is as real as the illumination because it is not contradicted by the image of a shell. This is because the latter exists not at the same moment as the former but a moment later. What is unreal is not the image but the conception that interprets the image as something other than what it is. This is called *satyākāravāda* ("the theory of the real image").

Śāntirakṣita preferred the Sautrāntika to the Sarvāstivāda and the Yogācāra to the Sautrāntika. As for the Satyākāravādins and Alīkākāravādins, Śāntirakṣita holds that both parties are unable to explain the reason why knowledge, which is unitary, has an image that always appears as a gross or a plural thing. So long as it appears with a dimension, even an image of cognition can be analyzed and broken down into parts or, ultimately, into "atoms of knowledge" *(jñānaparamāṇu)* and therefore is plural. If the image is real, knowledge must be plural; if self-cognition alone is real, why is it not cognized separately? But both cases are not true because, after all, knowledge has neither a single own being nor a plural one and it is empty of own being. Thus the Yogācāra is superseded by the Mādhyamika, which points out that all things, external as well as internal, are empty. [*See the biography of Śāntirakṣita.*]

Kamalaśīla (c. 740–797), a great student of Śāntirakṣita's, wrote the *Tattvasaṃgrahapañjikā* (S, T) and the *Madhyamakālaṃkāravṛttipañjikā* (T), commentaries on two main works of his teacher. Kamalaśīla entered Tibet after his master had passed away there and was victorious at the famous Bsam-yas debate between himself and Mahāyāna Hwa-shaṅ, a Chinese Ch'an monk who had considerable influence on Tibetan Buddhism at that time. In order to introduce Tibetans to Buddhism, he wrote three books, all entitled *Bhāvanākrama* (The Steps of Buddhist Meditative Practice; 1 and 3 in S; 1,

2, and 3 in T; and 1 in C). He also wrote the *Madhyamakāloka* (T), his main work; the *Sarvadharmaniḥsvabhāvasiddhi* (T), a résumé of the *Madhyamakāloka;* and the *Tattvāloka* (T). Because of his victory in the debate at Bsam-yas and his great effort thereafter, Mādhyamika Buddhism became firmly established in Tibet. His three *Bhāvanākramas* were considered by the Tibetans at that time to be the best introductions to the Yogācāra-Mādhyamika form of Indian Buddhism; the same can be said even for modern students of Buddhism. In them, the necessity for the gradual training toward enlightenment is stressed and the sudden enlightenment proclaimed by Chinese Ch'an is denounced. [*See the biography of Kamalaśīla.*]

Vimuktisena (eighth century), the author of the *Abhisamayālaṃkāravṛtti* (S partially, T), and Haribhadra (eighth century), the author of the *Abhisamayālaṃkārālokā* (S, T) and its résumé, the *Abhisamayālaṃkāraśāstravṛtti* (T), claimed a close relationship between the Yogācāra-Mādhyamika philosophy and the *Abhisamayālaṃkāra,* a synopsis of the *Pañcaviṃśatisāhasrikā-prajñāpāramitā Sūtra* ascribed to Maitreyanātha. They developed their philosophies in commenting on the *Abhisamayālaṃkāra.*

Jitāri, Bodhibhadra, Advayavajra (all eleventh to twelfth century), and others were Mādhyamikas whose interest extended to either Tantric Buddhism, logico-epistemology, or both. Jitāri, Bodhibhadra, and Advayavajra are known for having written the compendia of the four great Buddhist schools, the *Sugatamatavibhaṅga* (T), the *Jñānasārassamuccayanibandhana* (T), and the *Tattvaratnāvalī* (S, T), respectively. In these works, the specific doctrines of the four schools are introduced, and in the case of Bodhibhadra, non-Buddhist Indian philosophical schools are included. The schools are arranged in order from lowest to highest, according to their respective estimations. This style of compendium became the model after which later Tibetan Buddhists composed numerous *grubmtha'* (Skt., *siddhānta*) or compendia of doctrinal classification of Buddhist (and non-Buddhist) schools.

Kambala (Lwa-ba-pa or La-ba-pa; date uncertain) wrote the *Prajñāpāramitānavaśloka* and the *Ālokamālā,* and, according to Sahajavajra, belonged to the Alīkākāravāda-Yogācāra-Mādhyamika school. Ratnākaraśānti (eleventh century), an Alīkākāravādin, disputed with Jñānaśrīmitra (eleventh century), a Satyākāravādin. Ratnākaraśānti claimed that the Yogācāra and the Mādhyamika were not different; consequently, he is counted sometimes as a Yogācāra-Mādhyamika and others as a Vijñaptimātra-Mādhyamika. He was a great logician as well, and introduced the theory of *antarvyāpti* (internal determination of universal concomitance) into Buddhist logic.

Tibet. Two or three decades after the debate at Bsam-yas (794), Ye-śes-sde, the first Tibetan Mādhyamika scholar, wrote the *Lta-ba'i khyad-par* (Differences in Doctrines), in which he described the history of Indian Mādhyamika, its divisions into the Yogācāra- and Sautrāntika-Mādhyamikas, and other important Buddhist doctrines. During the ninth and the tenth centuries, Buddhism, as represented by Jñānagarbha, Śāntirakṣita, and Kamalaśīla, flourished in Tibet. After the persecution of Buddhism by King Glaṅ-dar-ma and the fall of the Tibetan dynasty, Atīśa, a great scholar of Vikramaśīla Monastery, entered Tibet in 1041 to reestablish Buddhism there. He revered Candrakīrti and Śāntideva, rather than Bhāvaviveka and Śāntirakṣita, and founded the Bka'gdams-pa school. He also erected the Gsaṅ-phu Temple, which became the center of Tibetan Buddhism under the guidance of Phywa-pa Chos-kyi Seṅ-ge (1109–1169). Ñi-ma-grags (1055–?) translated all Candrakīrti's works. He was probably the first to use the names Prāsaṅgika and Svātantrika. Tsoṅ-kha-pa (1375–1419), the greatest Mādhyamika in Tibet and the first abbot of Dga'-ldan Monastery, founded the Dge-lugs-pa order, wrote many works, including the *Lam rin chen mo* (Great Work on the Gradual Way), and synthesized Mādhyamika philosophy with the Tantras. [*See the biographies of Atīśa and Tsoṅ-kha-pa.*] The so-called *grubmtha'* literature, written by such scholars as Saskya Paṇḍita (1182–1251), Dbus-pa Blo-gsal (fourteenth century), 'Jam-byaṅs Bṣad-pa (1648–1722), and Dkon-mchog 'Jigs-med Dbaṅ-po (1728–1791), in which Buddhist and non-Buddhist schools are arranged as gradual steps culminating in Mādhyamika thought, is unique to Tibetan Buddhism. [*See also* Buddhism, Schools of, *article on* Tibetan Buddhism.]

China and Japan. It was Kumārajīva (350–409) who introduced Nāgārjuna's philosophy into China by translating the *Madhyamakakārikā,* the *Shih-erh-men lun* (Dvādaśamukha?), the *Po lun* (an interpretation of Āryadeva's *Catuḥśataka*), and the *Ta-chih-tu lun* (*Mahāprajñāpāramitopadeśa?*). However, the authenticity of the second and fourth works, ascribed to Nāgārjuna, is doubtful. The third is not a direct translation of Āryadeva's work. [*See the biography of Kumārajīva.*]

Chi-tsang (549–623) of the Sui dynasty, regarding the thoughts of Nāgārjuna and Āryadeva as the core of Buddhist doctrine, founded the San-lun tradition. *San-lun* ("three treatises") refers to the first three of the above-mentioned works. Chi-tsang wrote the *San-lun hsüan-i* (Deep Meaning of the Three Treatises) and also commented on the three treatises. He propagated the

Middle Way and the eight kinds of negation that appear in the salutation verse of Nāgārjuna's *Madhyamakakārikā*. [*See the biography of Chi-tsang.*] The tradition flourished during the early T'ang period but began to decline after Hsüan-tsang's transmission of the works of the Yogācāra school to China. Ekan, a Korean monk, introduced the San-lun doctrine to Japan, where, as the Sanronshū, it enjoyed a brief efflorescence as one of the six schools of the Nara period (seventh century). In China as well as in Japan, the school was short-lived and was overtaken by popular Buddhism as propagated by such traditions as Pure Land, Zen, and others.

[*See also* Śūnyam and Śūnyatā; Yogācāra; Sarvāstivāda; Sautrāntika; *and* Dharma, *article on* Buddhist Dharma and Dharmas.]

BIBLIOGRAPHY

Bhattacharya, Kamaleswar, trans. *The Dialectical Method of Nāgārjuna*. New Delhi, 1978. An English translation of Nāgārjuna's *Vigrahavyāvartanī* with the romanized text.

Iida, Shotarō. *Reason and Emptiness: A Study in Logic and Mysticism*. Tokyo, 1980. A study of Bhāvaviveka's philosophy with partial translations of related documents.

Matics, Marion L., trans. *Entering the Path of Enlightenment*. New York, 1970. An English translation of Śāntideva's *Bodhicaryāvatāra*.

Murti, T. R. V. *The Central Philosophy of Buddhism*. 2d ed. London, 1970. A readable account of the Mādhyamika philosophy based mainly on the *Prasannapadā of Candrakīrti*.

Ruegg, David S. *The Literature of the Madhyamaka School of Philosophy in India*. Wiesbaden, 1981. A valuable conspectus, containing the history, philosophers, doctrines, and documents of the school and a detailed bibliography of studies by modern scholars.

Sopa, Geshe Lhundup, and Jeffrey Hopkins. *Practice and Theory of Tibetan Buddhism*. New York, 1976. An English translation of Dkon-mchog 'Jigs-med Dbaṅ-po's compendium of the four great schools of Indian Buddhism.

KAJIYAMA YŪICHI

MADRASAH. The *madrasah* is an educational institution devoted to advanced studies in the Islamic religious sciences. Its origin has been much debated, but evidence that the term was in use in the eastern Iranian area as early as the late ninth century nullifies the hypothesis that it arose as the Sunnī competitor to the Azhar mosque school in Cairo, founded in 972 for the Ismā'īlī Shī'ī sect. The same evidence likewise casts doubt on the idea that the Sunnīs copied the institution from the then-fledgling Karrāmīyah sect of Muslims, whose founder died in 869. It is also uncertain when the *madrasah* came to be associated with its characteristic architectural form, a rectangular courtyard with a broad arched area (*īwān*) centered on each side and one or two stories of small student cells occupying the remainder of the interior wall space. This form, considered in the light of certain texts, has given rise to the hypothesis that the *madrasah* may ultimately derive from a Buddhist monastic model.

Prior to the mid-eleventh century, *madrasahs* were confined to eastern Iran and played a number of educational roles. Mysticism (Sufism) and the traditions of Muḥammad (*ḥadīth*) were as likely to be studied as Islamic law, which later took pride of place in the *madrasah* curriculum. Consequently, the earliest sense of the word itself is "place of study," a noun of place from the verb meaning "to study." An alternative suggestion that it means "place for studying Islamic law" and that it comes from another form of the verb does not fit the earliest usages.

The early Seljuk period of the mid-eleventh century marks a turning point in the history of the institution. Construction and endowment of *madrasahs* by pious private citizens had earlier been the rule, although pre-Seljuk instances of patronage by rulers or officials are not unknown. From the early Seljuks on, however, the *madrasah* became increasingly linked to official patronage. The first Seljuk sultan, Ṭughril Beg, sponsored a *madrasah* in the northeastern Iranian city of Nishapur, but a far more significant development was the construction of a string of *madrasahs* by Niẓām al-Mulk, the famous vizier of Ṭughril Beg's two successors, Alp Arslān and Malikshāh. [*See* Niẓām al-Mulk.] The earliest and most important Niẓāmīyah *madrasahs*, as they were called, were erected in Nishapur (1058) and Baghdad (1067). Legal science (*fiqh*) of a single interpretive school (*madhhab*) was the primary subject taught, and this subsequently became the dominant pattern, although eventually more than one school of law might be taught in the same *madrasah*.

The significance of the Niẓāmīyahs has been variously explained: they were training centers for Sunnī officials to help the Seljuks supplant Shī'ī functionaries; they provided financial support for staff and students at an unprecedented level; they initiated the process of using patronage to exert government control over the elite of previously independent religious scholars. Yet there is no substantial evidence that bureaucrats attended Niẓāmīyahs; too little is known about earlier institutions to confirm a change in manner or level of funding; and it is apparent that Niẓām al-Mulk and other founding patrons of the period acted more in a private capacity than in a governing capacity.

Possibly the Niẓāmīyah in Baghdad was most influential because it was the first *madrasah* west of Iran; in Baghdad, teaching had previously been practiced in mosques, shrines, shops, and so forth. The Niẓāmīyah *madrasah* became the prototype for the *madrasahs* that spread throughout the western Islamic world from the twelfth century on, and the word *madrasah* became synonymous with Islamic higher education.

In its fully evolved form, the *madrasah* was typically founded by someone who endowed property in perpetuity (*waqf*, "endowment") for the pious purpose of religious education. [*See* Waqf.] The founder, whether a private person or a member of the ruling elite, could maintain a degree of control over the endowment during his or her lifetime and oversee the curriculum and the hiring of faculty, but ultimately, jurisdiction over *madrasahs* and their income reverted to the judge *(qāḍī)* of the Islamic court or to religious authorities designated by the government. The curriculum did not depart from the religious sciences, including jurisprudence, traditions of the Prophet, Arabic grammar, recitation of the Qur'ān. Secular subjects were taught elsewhere until the nineteenth century, when educational reform efforts in various countries forced some expansion of the traditional curriculum. Certification of the completion of specific courses took the place of an overall diploma.

Madrasah attendance seems always to have been quite popular, perhaps in part because of the financial support offered to students. But the *madrasah* education was more a certification of acquisition of religious knowledge than a specific preprofessional training. To be sure, religious judges, jurisconsults, mosque heads, professors, and the like normally had some amount of *madrasah* training, and in the Ottoman empire there evolved a regular *cursus honorum* for such religious officials in certain elite *madrasahs*, which were the most common feeders into the higher ranks. Many students, however, attended simply to improve their knowledge of religion and make manifest their family's piety with no intention of seeking religious employment. Thus the *madrasah* came to serve a general educational function in society as well as a specialized one.

While some of the most important *madrasahs*, such as al-Azhar in Cairo, the Qarawīyīn *madrasah* in Fez, and various Shī'ī institutions in Qom and elsewhere, have survived to the present day as centers of religious education, most have been supplanted or diminished in importance through the growth of secular, government-supported school systems. Those that have survived educationally often have done so under financial and administrative regimes different from those of the premodern period, frequently within a government ministry, and as a consequence have suffered a diminution of their intellectual independence. Today, the *madrasah* is no longer the exclusive institution for advanced study of Islam.

BIBLIOGRAPHY

Discussion of issues surrounding the origin of the *madrasah* can be found in George Makdisi's "Muslim Institutions of Learning in Eleventh-Century Baghdad," *Bulletin of the School of Oriental and African Studies* 24 (1961): 1–56, and his *The Rise of Colleges* (Edinburgh, 1981); in my *The Patricians of Nishapur* (Cambridge, Mass., 1972), appendix 1; and in A. L. Tibawi's "Origin and Character of *al-Madrasah*," *Bulletin of the School of Oriental and African Studies* 25 (1962): 225–238. Representative of the largely uncritical accounts of Islamic educational history is Ahmad Shalaby's *History of Muslim Education* (Beirut, 1954). For studies of recent *madrasah* education in Iran and Morocco, see Michael M. J. Fischer's *Iran: From Religious Dispute to Revolution* (Cambridge, Mass., 1980), chaps. 2–4, and Dale F. Eickelman's "The Art of Memory: Islamic Knowledge and Its Social Reproduction," *Comparative Studies in Society and History* 20 (1978): 485–516.

RICHARD W. BULLIET

MAGEN DAVID. The Magen David (Shield of David, Scutum Davidis), a hexagram or six-pointed star, has been at home in many cultures and civilizations, albeit without any readily identifiable meaning until the present century. In the Middle Ages, the Magen David appeared frequently in the decorations of Hebrew manuscripts from Europe and Islamic lands and even in the decorations of some synagogues, but it seems to have had then no distinct Jewish symbolic connotation. The Magen David, also called the Seal of Solomon (Sigillum Salomonis), was employed in the Middle Ages by Jews, Christians, and Muslims as a symbol with magic or amuletic power. [*See* Amulets and Talismans.]

In the seventeenth century, the followers of the messianic pretender Shabbetai Tsevi adopted the Magen David. Amulets of the movement bore the hexagram with the Hebrew letters *MBD*, standing for *Mashiaḥ ben David*, "Messiah, son of David." Thus the hexagram came to be identified with the shield of the son of David, the hoped-for messiah. [*See* Geometry.]

In the late eighteenth century, the Magen David came into popular use in western Europe, perhaps as a meaningful new sign that could express or symbolize Judaism. As late as the nineteenth century, however, the Magen David was not yet accepted as a symbol by Orthodox Jews. Yitsḥaq Elḥanan Spektor, an influential Orthodox rabbi in Kovno (modern-day Kaunas), Lithuania, warned the local Reform congregations to remove the Magen David that graced their houses of worship.

The twentieth century has seen the use of the Magen

David reinforced by two major happenings. First, in 1897, at Basel, Switzerland, the Magen David was officially adopted as the symbol of the newly formed Zionist Movement at the first Zionist Congress. Since 1948, the Magen David has appeared on the official flag of the state of Israel. Second, in the 1930s and 1940s the Nazis forced all Jews in lands under their control to wear a badge of shame: a yellow Magen David bearing the word *Jude* ("Jew"). Today the Magen David serves to identify most Jewish houses of worship, traditionalist as well as liberal, and it remains a positive symbol of Judaism.

BIBLIOGRAPHY

The best single source on the Magen David is Gershom Scholem's article "Magen David" in the *Encyclopaedia Judaica* (Jerusalem, 1971), which includes an extensive bibliography.

JOSEPH GUTMANN

MAGI. The Old Persian word *magu*, rendered in Greek by *magos*, is of uncertain etymology. It may originally have meant "member of the tribe," as in the Avestan compound *mogu-tbish* ("hostile to a member of the tribe"). This meaning would have been further restricted, among the Medes, to "member of the priestly tribe" and perhaps to "priest" (Benveniste, 1938; Boyce, 1982). The term is probably of Median origin, given that Herodotus mentions the "Magoi" as one of the six tribes of the Medes.

For a variety of reasons we can consider the Magi to have been members of a priestly tribe of Median origin in western Iran. Among the Persians, they were responsible for liturgical functions, as well as for maintaining their knowledge of the holy and of the occult. Most likely, the supremacy of the Median priesthood in western Iran became established during the time of the Median monarchy that dominated the Persians from the end of the eighth century through the first half of the sixth century BCE until the revolt of Cyrus the Great (550 BCE). The Persians were indebted to the Medes for their political and civil institutions as well. Even if hypotheses have been advanced concerning the existence of Magi of Persian origin in the Achaemenid period (Boyce, 1982), we must still maintain that they were of Median origin. This is demonstrated by the episode of the revolt of Gaumāta the Magian, mentioned by Darius I (522–486 BCE) in the inscription at Bīsutūn (Iran), as well as by Greek sources. Indeed, Herodotus insists on the idea of the usurpatory power of the Medes against the Persians through the conspiracy of the Magi.

The fact that the Magi may have been members of a tribe that handed down the sacerdotal arts in a hereditary fashion naturally did not exclude the possibility that some of them undertook secular professions. This seems to be attested by the Elamite tablets at Persepolis.

There is a thesis, put forth by Giuseppe Messina, that denies that the Magi are members of an ethnic group by suggesting that they are simply members of the priesthood—a priesthood of purely Zoroastrian origin. This thesis is untenable; on the other hand, the hypothesis that their name is related to the Avestan term *magavan*, derived from the Gathic *maga* (Vedic, *magha*, "gift"), is not without foundation (Molé, 1963). The meaning of *maga* can probably be found, in conformity with the Pahlavi tradition, within the context of the concept of purity, or separation of the "mixture" of the two opposed principles of spirit and matter. The *maga*, which has been erroneously interpreted as "chorus," from the root *mangh*, which is said to mean "sing the magic song" (Nyberg, 1966) and has been rendered simply by an expression like *unio mystica*, seems to be an ecstatic condition that opens the mind to spiritual vision. In any case, though there may be a relation between the Old Persian term *magu* and the Avestan terms *magavan* and *maga*, we must maintain a clear distinction between the Magi and the Avestan priesthood. The Avesta ignores the Median or Old Persian term, despite a recent hypothesis proposed by H. W. Bailey; Old Persian inscriptions ignore the Avestan term for "priest," *āthravan* (Vedic, *átharvan*), even if this is perhaps present in an Achaemenid setting in the Elamite tablets of Persepolis (Gershevitch, 1964).

The term *magu* has been present in Zoroastrianism throughout its history; the Pahlavi terms *mogh-mard* and *mōbad* represent its continuation. The latter in particular derives from an older form, *magupati* ("head of the Magi"). During the Sasanid period (third to seventh centuries CE), which saw the formation of a hierarchically organized church, the title *mōbadan mōbad* ("the high priest of high priests") came to be used to designate the summit of the ecclesiastical hierarchy.

The Magi practiced consanguineous marriage, or *khvaētvadatha* (Av.; Pahl., *khwēdōdāh*). They also performed a characteristic funeral rite: the exposure of the corpse to animals and vultures to remove the flesh and thereby cleanse it. The corpse was not supposed to decompose, lest it be contaminated by the demons of putrefaction. This practice later became typical of the entire Zoroastrian community and led to the rise of a complex funeral ritual in Iran and among the Parsis in India. Stone towers, known as *dakhmas*, were built especially for this rite. During the time of Herodotus the practice of exposure of the corpse was in vogue only among the Magi; the Persians generally sprinkled the corpse with wax, then buried it. The practice was widespread, however, among the peoples of Central Asia.

The Magi were the technicians of and experts on worship: it was impossible to offer sacrifices without the presence of a Magus. During the performance of a ritual sacrifice, the Magus sang of the theogony (the Magi were possibly the custodians of a tradition of sacred poetry, but we know nothing about the relationship of this tradition to the various parts of the Avesta) and was called upon to interpret dreams and to divine the future. The Magi were also known for the practice of killing harmful, or "Ahrimanical," animals (*khrafstra*) such as snakes and ants. They dressed in the Median style, wearing pants, tunics, and coats with sleeves. They wore a characteristic head covering of felt (Gr., *tiara*) with strips on the sides that could be used to cover the nose and mouth during rituals to avoid contaminating consecrated objects with their breath (Boyce, 1982). The color of these caps, in conformity with a tradition that is probably of Indo-European origin, according to Georges Dumézil, was that of the priesthood: white.

In all likelihood, during the Achaemenid period the Magi were not in possession of a well-defined body of doctrine, and it is probable that they gradually adopted Zoroastrianism; they were most likely a clergy consisting of professional priests who were not tied to a rigid orthodoxy but were naturally inclined to eclecticism and syncretism. Nonetheless, they must have been jealous guardians of the patrimony of Zorastrian traditions. By virtue of this they were the educators of the royal princes. The wisest of them was responsible for teaching the prince the "magic of Zarathushtra, son of Horomazes" and thus the "cult of the gods." Magi who excelled in other virtues were entrusted with the education of the prince so that he would learn to be just, courageous, and master of himself.

During the Achaemenid period the Magi maintained a position of great influence, although they were certainly subordinate to the emperor. Despite several dramatic events such as the massacre they suffered after the death of Gaumāta the Magian—in which, according to Herodotus (who calls him Smerdis), the Persians killed a large number of Magi to avenge the usurpation—the Magi nevertheless managed to maintain their influence at court in Media, in Persia, and in the various regions of the empire where they were stationed as a consequence of the Persian civilian and military administration.

No priesthood of antiquity was more famous than that of the Magi. They were renowned as followers of Zarathushtra (Zoroaster); as the teachers of some of the greatest Greek thinkers (Pythagoras, Democritus, Plato); as the wise men who arrived, guided by a star, at the manger of the newborn savior in Bethlehem; and as the propagators of a cult of the sun in India. But they were also known as the Chaldeans, the priesthood of Babylon, known for its occultism; this was perhaps the reason that the term *magos* had a pejorative sense in Greek, like *goēs*, "expert in the magic arts" (Bidez and Cumont, 1938). Indeed, the Chaldeans were experts in all types of magical arts, especially astrology, and had a reputation for wisdom as well as knowledge.

To understand the reasons for such various and sometimes discordant views, it is necessary to distinguish between the Magi of Iran proper and the so-called western Magi, who were later hellenized. In the Achaemenid period both must have been at least in part Zoroastrian, but the western Magi (those of the Iranian diaspora in Asia Minor, Syria, Mesopotamia, and Armenia), who came in contact with diverse religious traditions, must have, sooner or later and in varying degrees, been influenced by syncretic concepts.

The Greeks were familiar with both kinds of Magi and, depending on their varying concerns, would emphasize one or the other aspect of them. Classical historians and geographers, including Herodotus and Strabo, document their customs, while the philosophers dwell above all on their doctrines: dualism, belief in the hereafter, Magian cosmology and cosmogony, and their theology and eschatology. Those sources most interested in the doctrines of the Magi even speak of Zarathushtra as a Magus. In doing so they are repeating what the Magi themselves said from the Median and Achaemenid periods, when they adopted Zoroastrianism. At that time they embraced Zarathushtra as one of their own and placed themselves under his venerable name.

Zoroastrianism had already undergone several profound transformations in the eastern community by the time of the Achaemenids and was already adapting those elements of the archaic religion that refused to die. It has been said quite often, in an attempt to characterize the precise role of the Magi in the Zoroastrian tradition, that the *Vendidad* (from *vī-daēvo-dāta*, "the law-abjuring *daivas*"), part of the Avesta, should be attributed to them. (This collection of texts from various periods is primarily concerned with purificatory rules and practices.) Nonetheless, the hypothesis is hardly plausible, since the first chapter of the *Vendidad*—a list of sixteen lands created by Ahura Mazdā, the supreme god of Zoroastrianism, but contaminated by an attack by Ahriman (Pahl.; Gathic-Avestan, Angra Mainyu), the other supreme god and the ultimate source of all evil and suffering—does not mention western Iran, Persia, or Media (the land of Ragha mentioned in the text cannot be Median Raghiana). Furthermore, it has been noted (Gershevitch, 1964) that if the authors had been Magi the absence of any reference to western Iranian institutions, including their own priesthood, would be very strange.

The Magi were above all the means by which the Zoroastrian tradition and the corpus of the Avesta have been transmitted to us, from the second half of the first millennium BCE on. This has been their principal merit. We can attribute directly to the Magi the new formulation that Iranian dualism assumed, known to us especially from Greek sources and, in part, from the Pahlavi literature of the ninth and tenth centuries CE. According to this formulation, the two poles of the dualism are no longer, as in the *Gāthās*, Spenta Mainyu ("beneficent spirit") and Angra Mainyu ("hostile spirit") but Ahura Mazdā himself and Angra Mainyu (Gershevitch, 1964). [*See* Ahura Mazdā and Angra Mainyu.] This transformation was of immense consequence for the historical development of Zoroastrianism and was most likely determined by the contact of the Magi with the Mesopotamian religious world. In this new dualism—which was that later known to the Greeks (Aristotle, Eudemus of Rhodes, Theopompus, and others)—we can see the affirmation of a new current of thought within Zoroastrianism, to which we give the name *Zurvanism*. [*See* Zurvanism.]

Thanks to their adherence to Zoroastrianism, the Magi played an enormously important role in the transmission of Zarathushtra's teachings, as well as in the definition of the new forms that these would assume historically. Their natural propensity to eclecticism and syncretism also helped the diffusion of Zoroastrian ideas in the communities of the Iranian diaspora. The Greeks began to study their doctrines and to take an interest in them (Xanthus of Lydia, Hermodorus, Aristotle, Theopompus, Hermippus, Dinon), even writing treatises on the Persian religion, of which only the titles and a few fragments have survived. In the Hellenistic period, the Magi were seen as a secular school of wisdom, and writings on magic, astrology, and alchemy were lent the authority of such prestigious names as Zarathushtra, Ostanes, and Hystaspes, forming an abundant apocryphal literature (Bidez and Cumont, 1938).

Later still, eschatology and apocalyptics were a fertile meeting ground for Iranian and Judeo-Christian religions, as can be seen in the famous *Oracles of Hystaspes*, a work whose Iranian roots are undeniable and which most likely dates from the beginning of the Christian era, probably the second century CE (Widengren, 1968). The Zoroastrian doctrine of the Savior of the Future (Saoshyant) was the basis for the story of the coming of the Magi to Bethlehem in the *Gospel of Matthew* (2:1–12). [*See* Saoshyant.]

The Sasanid period saw the Magi once again play a determining role in the religious history of Iran. Concerned to win back the western Magi (de Menasce, 1956), and eager to consolidate Zoroastrianism as the national religion of Iran, the priests of Iranian sanctuaries in Media and Persia were able to establish a true state church, strongly hierarchical and endowed with an orthodoxy based on the formation of a canon of scriptures. The leading figures in the development of a state religion and of Zoroastrian orthodoxy were Tōsar and Kerdēr, the persecutors of Mani in the third century.

BIBLIOGRAPHY

Benveniste, Émile. *Les Mages dans l'ancien Iran*. Paris, 1938.

Bickerman, Elias J., and H. Tadmor. "Darius I, Pseudo-Smerdis and the Magi." *Athenaeum* 56 (1978): 239-261

Bidez, Joseph, and Franz Cumont. *Les Mages hellénisés: Zoroastre, Ostanès et Hystaspe d'après la tradition grecque* (1938). 2 vols. New York, 1975.

Boyce, Mary. *A History of Zoroastrianism*, vol. 2. Leiden, 1982.

Gershevitch, Ilya. "Zoraster's Own Contribution." *Journal of Near Eastern Studies* 23 (1964): 12–38.

Humbach, Helmut. "Mithra in India and the Hinduized Magi." In *Études mithriaques*, edited by Jacques Duchesne-Guillemin, pp. 229–253. Tehran and Liège, 1978.

Menasce, J. de. "La conquête de l'iranisme et la récupération des Mages occidentaux." *Annuaire de l'École Pratique des Hautes Études* 5 (1956): 3–12.

Messina, Giuseppe. *Der Ursprung der Magier und die zarathuštrische Religion*. Rome, 1930.

Messina, Giuseppe. *I Magi a Betlemme e una predizione di Zoroastro*. Rome, 1933.

Moulton, J. H. *Early Zoroastrianism*. London, 1913.

Nyberg, H. S. *Irans forntida religioner*. Stockholm 1937. Translated as *Die Religionen des alten Iran* (1938; 2d ed., Osnabrück, 1966).

Widengren, Geo. *Die Religionen Irans*. Stuttgart, 1965. Translated as *Les religions de l'Iran* (Paris, 1968).

Gherardo Gnoli
Translated from Italian by Roger DeGaris

MAGIC. [*This entry consists of eight articles that discuss the meanings and applications of the term* magic:

Theories of Magic
Magic in Primitive Societies
Magic in Greco-Roman Antiquity
Magic in Medieval and Renaissance Europe
Magic in Eastern Europe
Magic in Islam
Magic in South Asia
Magic in East Asia

The first article presents the development of scholarly views on magic and its relation to religion. The companion pieces deal with magic in various cultures and traditions in which it has been a salient feature.]

Theories of Magic

Magic is a word with as many definitions as there have been studies of it. In most societies it is an integral part of the sphere of religious thought and behavior; in others, especially in the industrialized West, it is more generally accepted as superstition and even as a form of sleight of hand used for entertainment. [*See* Superstition.] In addition it has almost always been thought to mark a distinction between Western and so-called primitive cultures, or between Christian and non-Christian religions. It is not really feasible to consider "magic" apart from "religion," with which it often has been contrasted, as many of the definitions of magic derive from their opposition to the nonmagical elements of religion.

Magic is usually defined subjectively rather than by any agreed-upon content. But there is a wide consensus as to what this content is. Most peoples in the world perform acts by which they intend to bring about certain events or conditions, whether in nature or among people, that they hold to be the consequences of these acts. If we use Western terms and assumptions, the cause and effect relationship between the act and the consequence is mystical, not scientifically validated. The acts typically comprise behavior such as manipulation of objects and recitation of verbal formulas or spells. In a given society magic may be performed by a specialist.

For example, a man may plant a yam, fertilize it, weed it, and, when the tuber is ripe, harvest it: this is a straightforward technical activity. He may also perform rites, cast spells, or perform other acts that are thought to help the yam grow and ripen. To a Western farmer these are magical acts and any link between them and their intended consequences is a mystical one, existing in the mind of the performer and not in any scientifically verifiable actuality. We therefore distinguish two kinds of performance. Whereas we make this distinction, however, the performers may not do so, regarding both performances as efficacious. In fact, it appears from the available ethnographic evidence that performers of magic may distinguish the two forms of activity but consider both as techniques effective each in their own way in ensuring that the yam ripens.

We must consider the kind of evidence available for the performance and efficacy of magic. Much of it is inaccurate, sensational, and inadmissible, the kind of material found in the many travelers' tales of mysterious powers possessed by exotic practitioners whose behavior they have never actually seen, or the conjuring of devils by accused witches in late medieval Europe. There are, however, other kinds of evidence. One example is the accounts of trained anthropological observers, who can speak the local languages and ask questions of the actual practitioners; another is the writings of scholars of historical societies where there is reliable documentation from original sources. An example of the first kind is the work of Bronislaw Malinowski (1935, 1948), who witnessed and described yam planting and other magical acts in Melanesia. Accounts of this kind have the immense advantage of being placed in the contexts in which the rites are carried out. Examples of the second kind are those of G. E. R. Lloyd (1979) on the ancient Greeks and Keith V. Thomas (1971) on post-seventeenth-century England.

Scholars of many kinds have been writing about magic, its aims, its origins, its methods, and its believed efficacy since before the days of the ancient Greeks. But it seems sensible here not to attempt a historical survey about magic using as sources those who have accepted its validity for themselves but rather to deal with the writers who have tried to understand the practice of magic among other societies whose systems of thought they have not shared at the outset but that they have come to understand during their researches. Little can be gained from the writings of those who could not remain objective observers: for example, the writings of the late medieval inquisitors or of King James I of England are important as data for analysis but in themselves they throw no more light on theories of magic than would the verbal statements of a Melanesian yam magician.

Certain basic questions that have been asked by writers on magic include those of the relationship of magic to science and to religion, its instrumental and technical efficacy, its social and psychological functions, its symbolism, and the nature of its thought. If we omit the once popular concern with magic's evolutionist implications—that it marks an archaic stage of cultural evolution—these questions essentially concern either the functions and efficacy of magic or the nature and processes of the system of thought that lies behind it. It has generally been accepted by those studying magic that magical performances do not "work" in an immediately technical or instrumental sense: Trobriand yams are not affected by magical spells, other than in the indirect sense that a yam farmer might take greater care of magically protected yams and that neighbors might be wary of damaging them. Clearly many cases lie on the borderline: alchemy, which contained much that is generally accepted as magic, did at times stumble onto scientifically correct relations between phenomena and events.

Questions of systems of thought deal with these same problems, but at another level, at which arise questions of symbolism, interpretation, and translation between cultures. Perhaps the most long-standing problem is anthropology (and to a lesser extent in psychology, history, and philosophy) involves the distinction between the notions of "primitive" and "civilized," a distinction that can gather such pejorative implications that the terms are now rarely used, although there are scholars who use the word *primitive* in the sense of "primal." Theories of magic have essentially been concerned with the problem of the relationship between what are usually referred to as "traditional" and "scientific" modes of thought. Other terms that have been used in this context include "prelogical/logical," "prescientific/scientific," "irrational/rational," "preliterate/literate," and "closed/open" beliefs in magic, the performance of magical rites being identified with the first term in each of the above pairs. The discussion of whether these are meaningful distinctions that actually exist between societies begins in the work of Lucien Lévy-Bruhl, discussed below. Much later work has been devoted to refining, refuting, and assessing the worth of his findings, especially once it became clear that if there are indeed two contrasting modes of thought they are normally found together in any particular society, so that references to a dichotomy between "primitive" and "civilized" are misleading.

At the risk of oversimplification it may be said that in the history of theories of magic the battle has been between what have been called the "literalists" and the "symbolists." Briefly, the literalists suggest that performance of magical actions is instrumental, so that the thought behind them (depending on the views of the writer) is either similar or dissimilar to that behind scientific experiments. Therefore the world may be divided into those societies whose magicians try to achieve a cause-and-effect relationship in events, whether technical or psychological, and those where the magician's place is taken by the scientist. The symbolists argue that this distinction misses the point. What is important for them is that magicians and scientists may or may not be trying to achieve the same results but are using different conceptual systems: they speak different "languages," the one symbolic and the other concrete, and translation or interpretation between them is meaningless until this fact is taken into account. The main questions, therefore, are those of the nature of the different modes of thought and how they may be translated into one another.

Magic in Social and Cultural Evolution. The first important writers on magic whose views retain currency are those nineteenth-century evolutionists generally known as the Intellectualists because they based much of their work on their opinions of what prehistoric and archaic peoples would have thought about the world, as imagined from Victorian academic armchairs.

The most influential of these writers were E. B. Tylor (1832–1917) and James G. Frazer (1854–1941). Both distinguish magic from religion as distinct modes of thought and ritual performance. Both claim to base their definitions and analyses on voluminous ethnographic material, although much of it is in fact erroneous and faulty. The method, which they referred to as "comparative," suffers because the data are not placed in their social and cultural contexts; their approaches are essentially psychological in the sense that they depended upon their own assumptions about the behavior of other peoples rather than on categories formulated by those peoples themselves.

Tylor defined magical knowledge and performance as "pseudo-science": the magician and his public (Tylor's "savages") postulated a direct cause and effect link between the magical act and the intended result, whereas the link was not a scientifically valid one but one based on the association of ideas only. Tylor considered magic to be "one of the most pernicious delusions that ever vexed mankind" but nevertheless regarded it as based on a rational process of analogy that he called the "symbolic principle of magic." His predecessors had taken a belief in magic as a sign of the infantile and ignorant thinking of early mankind. To argue that "savages" were capable of rational thought, even in a scientifically unfounded context, was a significant advance. He was also concerned to demonstrate why "savages," capable of rationality, accepted magic even though it was clearly ineffective. His views, which have been accepted by all later anthropologists, were that magical and empirical behavior are often coterminous, in that natural processes often achieve what the magician claims to do; that failure can be attributed to hostile magical forces on the part of rival magicians or to the breaking of taboos; that there is great plasticity of definitions of success and failure; and that the weight of cultural tradition and authority validates the practice of magic. Finally Tylor maintained that "magic" and "religion" are complementary parts of a single cultural institution and are thus not merely stages in the evolutionary development of mankind, although he believed that magical belief and practice decrease in the later stages of human history.

The other great evolutionist of the period, Frazer, held rather different views, which have long persisted in popular thought on the subject. He built up an evolutionary scheme with three main stages of thought, each paramount in turn: magical thought he placed as the most primitive, then religious thought, and finally scientific thought. He contrasted magic with religion and with science, although he discerned certain resemblances between magical and scientific thought. He placed magic at an earlier stage in human development for three reasons: (1) because in his view it is logically simpler; (2) because it persists as superstition even in industrial societies and so forms an underlying and persistent substratum; and (3) because the Australian Aborigines (at that time taken as the extreme case of an archaic remnant people) believe in magic rather than in religion (in this, Frazer's ethnographic facts were simply incorrect). So in his schema magic was the earliest form of thought and behavior involving the supernatural; as people came to realize that magical techniques were ineffective, they postulated the existence of omnipotent gods that controlled nature and needed to be supplicated and propitiated; finally, men began to recognize the existence of empirical natural laws, first by alchemy and later by true science, and religion came to join magic as a superstition. The "evidence" for this development was virtually nonexistent outside Frazer's mind, but he fit a vast amount of data into "proving" his deductive hypothesis.

Frazer defined the magical according to his belief that magical performances are sympathetic rites based upon his Law of Similarity ("like produces like . . . an effect resembles its cause") and the Law of Contact (by which things that have been in physical contact then act upon one another even at a distance). He defined magic based on similarity as Homeopathic Magic and that based on contact as Contagious Magic, and he added taboo as negative magic acting according to the same "laws." Since much of science seemed to him also to be based on the same premises, he linked it with magic by accepting Tylor's earlier view of the existence of a rational link between cause and effect in the magician's mind, magic thus being a "spurious system of natural law." It is easy today to point to the flaws in these "Intellectualist" arguments, citing their authors' projection of their own modes of thought onto other cultures. But at the time these theories were highly influential.

Tylor and Frazer were followed by many less original scholars who refined their predecessors' somewhat crude schemata of evolution. In England were R. R. Marett (1866–1943), Andrew Lang (1844–1912), A. E. Crawley (1869–1924), and others. Marett maintained that in the earliest stages of human evolution religion could not be differentiated from magic, because at that prior preanimistic stage of development religion did not condemn magic as mere superstition. He coined the term *magico-religious*, a blanket term that has muddled the issue of the natures of magic and religion for over half a century. Marett held that magic arises from the recourse to make-believe acts that the magician considers symbolic and different from their realization and as a means of resolving emotional tensions. Magic is a substitute activity that gives courage and confidence, a view later reflected in the work of Malinowski. Crawley, writing less specifically, held that "primitive" peoples' mentalities are totally religious or superstitious, so that magic cannot be differentiated from religion, because both are based on fear in the face of an omnipotent unknown. In the United States, Alexander A. Goldenweiser (1880–1940) made the point against Frazer that magic and science are in fact not similar, in that only the scientist sees order and the working of regularities in nature, whereas the magician is unaware of them; he suggested that in early societies magic was closely linked with religion but that later they grew apart, religion becoming more centrally associated with the formal structure of society and magic assuming a place on the fringes of legality and organized religion.

These were not the only psychologically minded scholars to discuss the nature of magic. An important figure was Wilhelm Wundt (1832–1920), who held that magical thinking, as the earliest phase in the development of religious thought, was based on emotional processes, the principal one being the fear of nature, which appears hostile to human well-being and which is conceptualized as an evil force that can be controlled by magic. In the same line of development came Gerardus van der Leeuw (1890–1950), who maintained that the magician believes that he can control the external world by the use of words and spells, and Sigmund Freud (1856–1939), whose notion of the omnipotence of thought was basic to his argument. Primitive magical rites and words correspond to the obsessional actions and spell-like speech of neurotics, who believe that they can affect reality by their own thoughts and wishes. Freud accepted the gross evolutionist schema of Frazer as a parallel to the psychological development of the individual. It is tension in the face of the sense of impotence that gives rise to magical thought both in the child and in early man: magic is wish fulfillment. Unfortunately this analogy has no basis in the ethnographic data supplied by anthropologists and must be considered a "just-so story" that puts a pattern of coherence into Freud's psychological work but tells us little of the nature of magic and magical thought.

The Sociology of Magic. In the years around 1900 the works of other kinds of thinkers became influential and have continued to be more so than that of the Evolutionists and Intellectualists. The principal theorists among these more sociologically minded scholars were Émile Durkheim (1858–1917), Marcel Mauss (1872–1950), and Lucien Lévy-Bruhl (1857–1939) in France and Max Weber (1864–1920) in Germany.

The three French writers followed Auguste Comte in substituting sociological explanations of social processes for psychological ones. For them religion, including magic, is a social fact, brought into existence by collective action and then possessing an autonomy of its own; it is not merely an illusion (Durkheim realized that the religious and the magical persist in "scientifically" based societies). The "religious" is defined as sacred, a realm set apart by the religion's adherents, whose beliefs and rites unite them into a single moral community or church. Religion is a collective practice, there being no religion without a church in the sense used above. Magic, however, is an individual affair in the sense that although magical rites are also collectively defined as being sacred, the magician has a clientele and not a church. In magic, therefore, the function of ritual to fortify the faith of the group is lacking, and instead the magician attempts to bring about certain consequences by the use of magical or sacred objects and words. Durkheim's study of magic formed an unimportant part of his main study of Australian Aboriginal religion (Durkheim, 1912) and seems to be included there mainly for completeness of his treatment of what had conventionally been included under the "religious." However, in a sense the gap had already been filled by Marcel Mauss's essay of eight years earlier, wherein he set out his general theory of magic (Hubert and Mauss, 1904). Here he preceded Durkheim in defining a magical rite as "any rite which does not play a part in organized cults—it is private, secret, mysterious and approaches the limit of a prohibited rite." Both Mauss and Durkheim thus defined magic not by the structure of its rites but by the circumstances in which these rites occur. Much of Mauss's book is taken up with the relationship of magic to religion and science, the latter being similar to magic by analogy, the former being similar to magic in that both are based on beliefs in *mana* and the sacred.

Lévy-Bruhl (1910) did not present any theories of magic as such, but he was centrally concerned with the mode of thought, which he called prelogical or prescientific, that most later writers have associated with belief in magic. He argued that modern Western societies are scientifically oriented in their thought whereas "primitive" societies are mystically oriented toward using the supernatural to explain unexpected and anomalous events. Prescientific "collective representations" inhibit cognitive activities that would contradict them, so that events attributed to causes that are prescientific are not put to objective verification. "Prescientific" or "prelogical" thought (Lévy-Bruhl was later to withdraw the latter term) contravenes the rules of science and Western logic, but otherwise it is rational and builds up into a single coherent system. Examples are beliefs in the effects of witchcraft or of magical rainmaking. It is important to realize that Lévy-Bruhl stresses the content of thought, which is determined by a society's culture, and not the process of thinking, which is not a social phenomenon but a psychological and physical one (a point on which he has often been misunderstood). A person's perceptions are determined by his culture's notions of the social and ritual value of those elements of experience that are perceived rather than merely being seen: that is to say, "primitives" do not perceive "mystically" because they are some way mentally inferior but perceive phenomena as significant on account of the mystical properties given to them by the culture. Lévy-Bruhl called such thought "mystical" because "primitive" thought, unlike Western scientific thought, does not distinguish between the "natural" and the "supernatural" but considers them to be a single system of experience. There is therefore a "mystical participation" between the "primitive" and what Western science would call the natural, the social, and the supernatural, a participation that composes the "primitive's" total social personality.

In Germany the scholar Max Weber was working on somewhat different yet related problems. He was particularly interested in the problem of rationality and its relationship to economic and political growth and development and based his work mainly on comparisons between precapitalist religions in Europe and in China and India. His main argument was that magic has been the most widespread from of popular religion in pre- and proto-industrial societies and in many parts of the world (especially in Asia, where capitalism might have been expected to develop early but did not) the recourse to magic prevented the rationalization of economic life. Before this rationalization "the whole world is full of magical powers working in an irrational fashion," a generalization that Weber held particularly true of peasant societies. The power of magic might be broken by the appearance of prophets (of whom magicians were the precursors) who introduced new and rational schemes of reward and salvation. As will be mentioned below, much of the significance of Weber's work lies precisely in his views as to the relationship between the decline of magic and advances in technology: for him the former was a necessary forerunner of the latter, a view that has since met with considerable and sustained opposition from more "literalist" writers.

Magic in Its Social and Cultural Setting. The writers just mentioned were the last of the classic anthropologists and sociologists to have written about magic. Their successors based their findings and hypotheses on their own field research, where the importance of what people who believe in magic actually do and say about it and of the social contexts of their actions and statements become evident. The era of armchair scholars, however brilliant, was over. On the other hand, most recent work may be seen at one level to be based largely on proving, disproving, and refining the theories of the classic scholars. The later researches and reports may be usefully divided into the "literalists" and the large and more diverse group of "symbolists," although it must be stressed that these labels are only rough and ready ways of identifying them.

The leading literalist was the Polish-born Bronislaw Malinowski (1884–1942), the first important anthropologist to present a coherent theory of magic based upon his own field research in the Trobriand Islands of Melanesia during the first world war. He recognized that among the Trobriand Islanders what is generally defined as magic is quite different from religion: religion refers to the fundamental issues of human existence while magic always turns round specific, concrete, and detailed problems. For the Trobriand Islanders magic was of several kinds and had several functions. First, its use lessens chance and risk and induces confidence in activities where risk is high and/or linked to techniques that may therefore easily be ineffective. His famous example is that of the use of magic when fishing in the open sea but not when fishing in the shallow lagoon. Besides acting as an extension to the technical, magic extends men's abilities into the realm of the miraculous, as with love magic, by which an ugly man attracts beautiful women, old men become rejuvenated, or a clumsy dancer becomes an agile one. And magic can also extend into the super-material or super-moral, as with the use of black or evil magic, or sorcery, that is thought to kill at a distance: magic is to be expected and generally to be found whenever man comes to an unbridgeable gap, a hiatus in his knowledge or in his powers of practical control, and yet has to continue in his pursuit.

However, he goes further, in an important way: he stresses that the islanders' land is well watered and fertile and their sea rich in fish, so that the use of magic is not merely an extension of technical competence. The production of food provides, in addition to physical nourishment, a means of gift-giving and exchange whereby interpersonal bonds are recognized and prestige made and kept. Magic protects people from failure and enables them to achieve success in which emotional and social involvement are high. Magic raises the psychological self-confidence of its believers, may help them achieve higher stages of technological and moral development, and may enable them better to organize their labor and to control the cooperative work on which the well-being of society's members depends: magic "ritualizes man's optimism." Malinowski stressed also that among the Trobriand Islanders the basis of magic lies in the immaculate saying and transmission of words and spells, which are validated by myth that creates an inviolable tradition as to the magic's efficacy.

Malinowski projected his findings among the Trobriand Islanders onto all mankind, making their particular cultural beliefs, thoughts, motives, and actions into universals, and he has rightly been criticized for so doing. But at the same time he did witness and participate in the magical practices of a "primitive" people: he was not adducing the functions of magic from his own thoughts as to what they might do and think but started from the ethnographic experience itself. It is true that, although he came to know the Trobrianders well, he may be suspected of projecting his own thoughts, emotions, and motives onto them when discussing the psychological functions of magic that he considered so central. Nonetheless, Malinowski revolutionized the study of magic.

Malinowski was essentially a successor to Frazer (who wrote the introduction to his first book on the Trobriand Islanders, [1922]. The first important immediate successor to the writers of the sociological school of Durkheim and Mauss was A. R. Radcliffe-Brown (1881–1955), who carried out research among the Andaman Islanders of the Bay of Bengal ten years before Malinowski's Trobriand work and published *The Andaman Islanders* in 1922, a book that was a landmark in the development of anthropological studies of religion and magic. In his work he does not rigidly differentiate between religion and magic. The Andamanese recognize certain objects and substances as possessing magical qualities in the sense that a magician may use them to cure sickness, control the weather, and the like. The magician acquires magical power and knowledge by coming into contact with spirits that possess a mystical power that is both dangerous and beneficial, for which Radcliffe-Brown uses the Polynesian word *mana*.

He argues that the power of spirits and the substances and objects in which *mana* is manifest, or can be made manifest by a magician, is used to mark the importance of social position when the latter is being changed (e.g., at birth, death, in sickness). When undergoing these transitions people become vulnerable to the dangers inherent in *mana*, and so they must observe taboos and fears of pollution, which are removed by the use of this power in a magical performance. By this means the community is kept aware of the importance of cooperative ties between its members and, thus, of their sense of interdependence. The rites both give confidence to the individual and (more importantly, in Radcliffe-Brown's view) demonstrate the importance of the activities magic marks off in this way—fishing for large animals, for example. These are important precisely because they represent communal activities and dangers and so emphasize the importance of dependence of members on one another. In brief, Radcliffe-Brown introduced to theories of magic the new dimension of ritual and social value and played down its relationship to technical knowledge and science.

The Later "Symbolists." Behind the work of both Malinowski and Radcliffe-Brown lay the problem of Lévy-Bruhl, that of the nature of the "prelogical" or magical mode of thought and worldview, for which the terms "mythopoeic" and "prescientific" have also been used. Since his work there has been continual discussion on the points that he raised. The most important figure in this context has been E. E. Evans-Pritchard (1902–1973), whose *Witchcraft, Oracles, and Magic among the Azande* (1937) has been the most influential of all writings on these topics. Like Radcliffe-Brown and Malinowski, Evans-Pritchard carried out extensive field research, in his case among the Azande people of the southwestern Sudan, largely with the intention of testing Lévy-Bruhl's hypotheses. His book deals with Zande views on mystical causation in the contexts of accusations of witchcraft, of the use and working of oracles and divination to determine the identity of witches, and of the recourse to magic and the performances of magicians. He presents a detailed firsthand account of Zande magical beliefs and practices, setting them in their social contexts and stressing especially the modes of thought and the "collective representations" that lie behind them. Zande magic is based on the use of "medicines," mainly plants and vegetable substances, in which lie magical powers, that are inert until activated by the verbal spells of the "owner," the magician, and which may be used for protection, production, and punishment of evildoers.

Most magical performances are private, carried out by individuals, but there are also public magicians who perform magic that has consequences such as war, rain, and vengeance for death. Magic is in the hands of men, who consider themselves more responsible to use these powers than are women.

In an earlier paper, published in 1929, Evans-Pritchard contrasted Zande magic with that of the Trobriand Islanders described by Malinowski. Among the former there is no concept akin to that of *mana* that provides the power of magical objects for the Trobrianders, and the spell is of less importance and used essentially as a directive to the mystical power of the "medicines." Whereas among the Trobrianders magic is "owned" by clans, as are the myths that validate it, among the Azande it is spread out among the entire community, the distinction being due to differences in social organization, ownership of land and crops, and political authority. Evans-Pritchard emphasized the social context far more than did Malinowski and also stressed that magic cannot be understood as an isolated phenomenon but only as part of a "ritual complex" composed of magic, witchcraft, divination, and oracles; indeed, without belief in witchcraft Zande magic would have little meaning. Making an important point that went back to that made far earlier by Radcliffe-Brown, he concluded that the main objective of the use of magic is not to change nature but rather to combat mystical powers and events caused by other people. It followed that the long-argued link between magic and science falls away: it is the network of social links, tensions, and conflicts that is central.

Evans-Pritchard also discussed the reasons that magic persisted despite what would appear to be its frequent failure: believers in magic have a "closed" system of thought that inhibits verification in a scientific sense. His argument goes back to Lévy-Bruhl and has been taken up by later writers who have contrasted closed and open systems of thought, a dichotomy that has perpetuated the long-standing contrast between magic and science. Lévy-Bruhl had remarked that ignorance is culturally determined, and Evans-Pritchard stressed that what appeared to be failures in magical performances were attributed by the Azande not to their inefficacy in a technical sense but to failure of the magician to perform the magical rites correctly and to the counter-activities of hostile magicians or witches: the system answers its own problems in its own terms.

Later writers, in particular Robin Horton, have enlarged on the contrast between open systems of thought, where efforts are made objectively to prove or disprove hypothesized causal relations between scientific acts and natural consequences, and closed systems of thought, where this kind of verification is not attempted and success and failure are seen in the light of the already culturally accepted worldview. Other writers, especially those in *Modes of Thought,* a collection of essays edited by Horton and Ruth Finnegan in 1973, enlarged on the social and cultural factors, like literacy or division of labor, associated with this basic distinction between closed and open systems.

The discussion was taken further by suggesting that although the causal links in both magic and science are based on analogy, as had been said by Frazer and all later writers on magic (although using such terms as metaphor, metonymy, homeopathy, and the like), the analogies were of different kinds. Stanley J. Tambiah, for example, distinguishes "scientific" analogy from "persuasive," "rationalizing," or "evocative" analogy. He points out that the Azande themselves recognize the analogical or metaphorical basis of magical performances that have as their aim the transferral of a particular property or quality to a recipient person or object: because of the similarity and/or difference between two objects, the magical rite transfers the desirable quality of the one to the other. The performance of the magical rites achieves and marks changes of quality or state through the "activation" of the analogy by the "performative" rite of magic.

The implication of these remarks is that the discussion of magic has widened in recent years from its relationships to religion and science to the mode of culturally determined thought behind it and to the social contexts of magical performances. The discussion has relied largely on the pioneering work of Lévy-Bruhl and Evans-Pritchard, but it has not all taken place among their anthropological followers. Important work has been done by philosophers such as Peter Winch and Martin Hollis, classicists such as G. E. R. Lloyd and E. R. Dodds, and others. A historian whose work merits mention here is Keith V. Thomas; his *Religion and the Decline of Magic* is concerned with the factors that led to the decline of magic in England from the seventeenth century onward. He stresses that, historically, magic cannot be separated from astrology and witchcraft, the relationship between them being both intellectual and practical.

Before the seventeenth century, religion and magic could not easily be distinguished, but with the rise in England of forms of Protestantism there came a separation between the two and the importance of magic declined. Thomas follows Weber in seeing this decline as permitting the "rationalization" of economic life, but he analyzes the historical situation with greater subtlety. He suggests that factors that led to the decline of magic included the growth of popular literacy and education, greater individual mobility, the development of forms of banking and insurance, and the rise of the new disciplines of economics, sociology, and statistics that were to remove much chance and uncertainty from everyday life. He also stresses the importance of optimism and aspirations in science and in medicine: even though available technology had not yet greatly advanced, people considered that it could and would. For the history of English magic, at least, he considers the views of Weber as of more relevance than those of Malinowski: even if the latter are correct for the Trobriand Islanders they are not so for what have become industrial societies. Malinowski's view, put neatly by Godfrey and Monica Wilson as "magic is dominant when control of the environment is weak," can be shown not to hold for "historical" and industrial societies.

Another influential scholar in this context is Claude Lévi-Strauss, who has been concerned for many years with the nature of the magical worldview. He made the point that by his performance the magician is making "additions to the objective order of the universe," filling in links in a chain of causation between events that are distant from each other in space or in time. Magic may therefore be seen as a "naturalization of human actions—the treatment of certain human actions as if they were an integral part of physical determination," whereas in contrast religious rites bring about a "humanization of natural laws." Religion and magic there imply each other and are in that sense complementary and inseparable, neither having priority of any kind over the other.

Lévi-Strauss has suggested that the notion is similar to that of *mana.* Both are subjective notions, used by Westerners to mark off "outside" thought as different from our own "scientific" thought and by the Azande (for example) to distinguish surrounding peoples as more involved with magic and thus inferior to themselves (much as Westerners might call other peoples "superstitious" rather than "religious"). If magic is a subjective notion in that sense then it can have little or no meaning in cross-cultural analysis and understanding. The concept of magic is in itself empty of meaning and thus susceptible to the recognition of any meaning that we care to give to it; following this, Lévi-Strauss has implied that the category of magic must be "dissolved."

Lévi-Strauss's observations notwithstanding, magic remains a category that has been and is used in accounts of systems of belief and ritual and so does merit continued discussion. Rather like the notion of totemism, which has also been "dissolved" by Lévi-Strauss, its shadow remains, and to understand most writings on comparative religion, its history as a concept must be analyzed. This cannot yet be the final word, and arguments about magic indeed continue, but essentially in the wider contexts of differentiation between culturally determined modes of thought and forms of society rather than in the earlier terms of its relationship to religion and science.

[*See also* Witchcraft; Miracle; *and* Spells. *For further discussion of the history of theory, see the biographies of the scholars mentioned herein.*]

BIBLIOGRAPHY

Three important studies of theories of religion in general warrant mention here. E. E. Evans-Pritchard's *Theories of Primitive Religion* (Oxford, 1965) is an excellent summary of anthropological theories of religion and magic, with emphasis on the work of Tylor, Frazer, Durkheim, and Lévy-Bruhl. *Modes of Thought*, edited by Robin Horton and Ruth Finnegan (London, 1973), is a collection of essays on the differences between magical and scientific worldviews, and Claude Lévi-Strauss's *La pensée sauvage* (Paris, 1962), translated as *The Savage Mind* (London, 1966), is a brilliant discussion of the same problem.

Of the numerous works on magic, five are classic. James G. Frazer's *The Golden Bough*, abr. ed. (London, 1922), is a summary of his twelve-volume third edition, a mass of ill-comprehended data that has had enormous influence far beyond its real importance. Henri Hubert and Marcel Mauss's "Esquisse d'une théorie générale de la magie," *Année sociologique* 7 (1904), translated as *A General Theory of Magic* (London, 1972)—the first sociologically oriented discussion of magic—is based on acute analysis of the data then available. Émile Durkheim's *Les formes élémentaires de la vie religieuse* (Paris, 1912), translated as *The Elementary Forms of the Religious Life* (1915; reprint, New York, 1965), is a highly influential study of Australian totemic religion. Lucien Lévy-Bruhl's *Les fonctions mentales dans les societés inferieures* (Paris, 1910), translated as *How Natives Think* (London, 1926), is a seminal work that, although outdated, has led to much fruitful work on the magical worldview. Max Weber's *The Sociology of Religion*, edited and translated by Talcott Parsons (Boston, 1963), contains passages on the problems of rationality from several of Weber's original German works.

Later basic anthropological accounts of magic include Bronislaw Malinowski's *Coral Gardens and Their Magic*, 2 vols. (London, 1935), a detailed ethnographic account of Trobriand magic, and *Magic, Science and Religion* (New York, 1948), a collection of earlier papers on Trobriand religion and magic. A. R. Radcliffe-Brown's *The Andaman Islanders* (1922; 3d ed., Glencoe, Ill., 1948) is an ethnographic account that has had great influence. E. E. Evans-Pritchard's *Witchcraft, Oracles, and Magic among the Azande* (1937; 2d ed., Oxford, 1950), the most important anthropological account yet published on the working of magic, has influenced all later work on the subject. Also noteworthy is his brilliant comparative essay "The Morphology and Function of Magic: A Comparative Study of Trobriand and Zande Ritual and Spell," *American Anthropologist* 31, (1929): 619–641, reprinted in *Myth and Cosmos*, edited by John Middleton (Garden City, N.Y., 1967).

Finally, there are two important historical works that deserve mention: Keith V. Thomas's *Religion and the Decline of Magic* (London, 1971), a historical account of the decline of magic in England since the seventeenth century, and G. E. R. Lloyd's *Magic, Reason, and Experience: Studies in the Origins and Development of Greek Science* (Cambridge, 1979), an innovative study of the relationships between magic and science.

JOHN MIDDLETON

Magic in Primitive Societies

Magic, in the view of many anthropologists and other scholars of small-scale societies—those in which effective political control is restricted to a village or group of villages—is the manipulation of enigmatic forces for practical ends. Magical means are said to be extranatural or supernatural, and the objectives of magical intervention, natural. The magician prepares a variety of special objects or "bundles," "spells," "incantations," or "potions," which are thought to bring about, in some mysterious way, real changes in a person, object, or event.

In the simplest foraging societies everyone knows some magic, and a shaman is usually a part-time specialist in healing and divination who may be called on for public religious ritual. In agrarian and other, more complex societies magicians tend to work for private clients in curing illnesses, in ensuring a positive outcome of an intended act, or in modifying the behavior of a third party. Magic in these societies, where there is greater specialization, tends to be practiced in private and, at times, against the public interest.

Some anthropologists of the late nineteenth and early twentieth centuries believed that so-called primitive peoples confused magical causality and natural causality. Today most anthropologists hold that magicians can distinguish the one from the other. Magic is used to coax nature to do its job, not to replace it; that is, the magician tries to engender a desired natural process as opposed to some other natural process, and this he accomplishes principally through the use of metaphor—the "power of words"—or other magical formulas. The magician may also deceive the client into imagining that some noxious natural substance "removed" from the client's body is the source of his sickness or whatever supernatural harm has befallen him (when, in fact, the magician comes upon the substance through a trick and does not remove it from the client's body). Magic may be used to supplement natural causality so that no chances are taken. When natural causality is not known, use of magic may still be rational: that is, given that many actual or perceived dangers are beyond human control, one must at least try something.

Typically, magic is contrasted with science and religion. It differs from both in that its purposes are practical, not theoretical or cosmic. It shares with science the desire to obtain a utilitarian understanding of everyday events, and with religion the use of extranatural processes. Thus magic is neither primitive science nor the religion of primitive people, contrary to views prevalent among nineteenth-century theorists; rather it supplements each. In small-scale societies magic may be entwined with science and religion to such a degree that their disengagement is arbitrary. Observers of these societies tend to label communal rituals and beliefs "religion" and private uses of mysterious forces for personal gain "magic." In such societies, applied science is craft—the ability to make utilitarian tools and other objects—or the practical knowledge of planting, hunting, or curing. Here again magic is inexorably tied to science in a supplementary way, in that magical procedures give the craftsperson, gardener, or herbalist a measure of confidence in a risky endeavor: magic can protect a newly built canoe against sinking, keep insects out of gardens, and heal the sick. Magic is never an alternative to practical science or technology; rather it is an attempt to tip the odds in the favor of the practitioner in the likely event that scientific knowledge is limited.

In small-scale societies magic may represent the instrumental aspect of religious belief: the same myths—the stories that explain a people's origins or an ultimate cause—validate religion and magic. However, in religion the myths are believed to be universally applicable and are used to support the public good or the established order, whereas in magic the myths are fragmented and used for individual purposes. Thus the conflict between the social good and individual need sometimes finds expression as a conflict between religion and magic. As manifested in Europe, that conflict involved the church and the practice of witchcraft. Anthropologists have applied the term *witchcraft* to practices outside Europe, but the conflict with well-established religion that the use of this term suggests is not necessarily present in simple societies.

The terms *sorcery* and *divination* have also been applied to magical traditions outside Europe. Although there is substantial variation from society to society and among scholars who use these terms to describe indigenous beliefs, witchcraft usually refers to the involuntary practice of magic, and sorcery to the deliberate practice of magic. Witchcraft is thought to be involuntary, since at times the witch may be unaware of the condition. Furthermore, a witch may be possessed against his or her own will. Witchcraft receives greater attention in the literature than does sorcery, possibly because witchcraft appears to be more common and because anthropologists are interested in the social implications of accusations of witchcraft. Witchcraft activities may have good intentions ("white" magic), or they may have evil intentions ("black" magic), although here again field data suggest that such a distinction is not always clear. Divination is not identical to magic, as no manipulation of natural events is sought. Yet it is not entirely separate from magic. Divination is the attempt to reveal hidden information by "reading" the mystical symbolism found in otherwise ordinary objects or action. The oracle exposes the probable result of an intended action. The person who consults the oracle may then choose the action if that result is desired, or he may select some other course of action if it is not. Divination may not necessarily involve foretelling the future. An oracle may reveal the cause of some community problem: someone is a witch and so is the source of harm. Identifying the problem suggests its solution: exorcise the witch. Thus the diviner taps the same mystical forces that the magician employs. But, unlike the magician, the diviner does not attempt to change events; rather he seeks to know what has happened or what will happen.

An early interpretation of magic was set forth by James G. Frazer (1854–1941) in *The Golden Bough*, a massive study of supernatural practices around the world. In common with many social philosophers of the late nineteenth century, Frazer held that use of magic was typical of early societies. Human thought progressed from magic to religion and thence to science. Magic is like science in that both explain the causality of ordinary events by suggesting that cause A has effect B. However, magic is pseudoscience in that it confuses supernatural efficacy with natural results. Today most anthropologists disagree with Frazer on this point and follow the interpretation of Bronislaw Malinowski (1884–1942), who held that the magician is well aware of the distinction between the supernatural and natural realms.

Scholars look more kindly upon Frazer's classification of types of magic, if only for the sake of convenience. According to Frazer, magic follows the "law of sympathy": magical causes may have distinct effects through one or the other of two procedures. The first is homeopathic magic: the magician acts out a procedure on models of the intended victim, and what he does is mysteriously transmitted to the victim himself. "Like produces like" is the principle here. A pin stuck in a doll that represents the victim causes harm to the victim himself. The second type of sympathetic magic is contagious magic: items that have been in contact with the victim, such as his hair or nail clippings, may be magically manipulated to produce harm in the victim.

Malinowski best explicated what is today a commonly held view among scholars: that magic and science supplement each other and are not to be confused. In extensive fieldwork among inhabitants of the Trobriand Islands off northeast New Guinea (1914–1920), Malinowski found that these gardening and seafaring people were highly empirical in their approach to horticulture, canoe building, and sailing. Yet they consistently tempered their pragmatism with magic. In sailing, they ordinarily relied on their craft skills and seamanship, but they understood, too, that native craftsmanship and seamanship were at times insufficient aids in withstanding the unexpected foreboding condition, like a capricious storm on open water. For these possibilities the Trobrianders used magic: it seemed to make the unknown amenable to human action and therefore provided psychological reassurance for a potentially perilous voyage. For Malinowski, then, there is no evolution from magic to religion and ultimately to science; rather these three facets of human behavior must be understood together, as aspects of a cultural system.

In his classic study of a people of Zaire, *Witchcraft, Oracles, and Magic among the Azande* (1937), E. E. Evans-Pritchard (1902–1974) took up Malinowski's argument that magic has its own logic. If one accepts the Zande worldview, then belief in magic follows. "Witchcraft, oracles, and magic are like three sides to a triangle," wrote Evans-Pritchard. "Oracles and magic are two different ways of combatting witchcraft" (p. 387). Consultation of oracles in divination can locate the source of witchcraft, and use of magic can combat it. For example, the Zande hold that all human death is caused by witchcraft. True, if a man walks under a cliff, is struck by a rock, and subsequently dies, the Zande would not deny empirical causality: surely the rock caused the death. Yet they would also claim an attendant causality: what, it could be asked, caused that person to walk under the cliff in the first place? Why did the rock fall just as the person was under the cliff? Surely some witch was responsible. To discover the identity of the witch, the Zande would consult the oracles.

The pioneering work of Malinowski and Evans-Pritchard contributed much to the development of the modern anthropological view of magic: specifically, that it has social, cultural, and psychological functions; that it is a rational activity akin to but separate from science; and that its use is not restricted to the so-called primitive peoples but may also be found in complex societies. These scholars emphasized the practical use of magic, as a private act in a social matrix. But there is a related stream of anthropological thought that concerns magic as an individual's ritual or cognitive act.

In his *Elementary Forms of the Religious Life*, Émile Durkheim (1858–1917) saw magic and religion as embedded in each other. Both contain beliefs and rites, but whereas religious rites are concerned with the sacred, magical rites are directed toward the utilitarian. Religion works toward communal goals while magic deals with private ends. It is this that explains the abhorrence with which organized religions reject magical practices. Religion involves a church operating in public, while magic involves an individual operating in private.

Marcel Mauss (1872–1950), Durkheim's son-in-law and intellectual heir, saw magic as "private, secret, mysterious and tending at the margin towards the forbidden rite" (Lukes, in Sills, 1968, p. 80). Like Durkheim, Mauss emphasized the similarity between magic and religion. In Mauss's view, both involve mystical power. Magic is a "social fact," a fundamental unit of society. Every rite that is not communal involves magic. For peoples of Oceania, the supernatural or mystical force in magic is *mana*, a nonsentient supernatural power. Similar notions are found in many other parts of the world, and anthropologists have labeled them *mana* as well. *Mana* may be located in objects or people. It is the power transmitted through the laying on of hands when one is cured of illness. *Mana* resides in the "ghost shirt," a special garment worn by some nineteenth-century Plains Indians to protect against bullets. And *mana* is to be found in all lucky charms. The transfer of *mana*, or the aura given off by an object or person with *mana*, is at the heart of many magical practices: the transfer is said to ensure supernatural protection.

Central to any discussion of magic are a number of puzzling questions. How can people actually believe that a special garment will protect them against bullets? Why do people let themselves be duped by the hocus-pocus of the magician? Are people so credulous as to believe that placing a photograph of an intended victim in a coffin will actually harm that person?

Lucien Lévi-Bruhl (1857–1939) provided one answer to these questions. Like Frazer, Lévi-Bruhl developed an evolutionary scheme to account for cultural differences. He focused on human thought, however, not social institutions. For most of his career he held to what was essentially an elaboration of the racist notion that so-called primitive peoples are less fully evolved than "civilized" peoples, and that their thinking, which Lévi-Bruhl labeled "prelogical," is fundamentally childlike. Civilized peoples, in his view, think rationally, logically. Prelogical thinking involves a different order of perception: mystic properties are attached to inanimate objects or to living things. Magic is thus part of prelogical thinking, as are many other aspects of so-called primitive culture: language, enumeration, memory. Toward the end of his career, Lévi-Bruhl modified his position on the inherent difference of certain groups of human beings. Humans taken as a whole, he came to believe, have capacities for the various styles of thought: prelogical mentality is to be found everywhere, but it is emphasized more in primitive societies.

This brings us close to Claude Lévi-Strauss's view of the "savage mind." Magical action is, in his view, a subset of analogical thought, the mental activity emphasized in simple societies. Magic involves an assumption that metaphors work according to physical or natural laws. The case of the Zande peripatetic hit by a falling rock might be solved in this fashion: human intent of harm to that individual was paralleled by the natural event of the falling stone.

Lévi-Strauss formulated his own contrast between magic and religion: religion is "a humanization of natural laws," while magic is "a naturalization of human actions—the treatment of certain human actions as if they were an integral part of physical determinism" (1962, p. 221). Lévi-Strauss envisages no evolutionary sequence beginning with magic: magic, religion, and science all shade into one another, and each one has a place in human society.

The contemporary scholar S. J. Tambiah also sees analogy at work in science. Science, however, begins with known causal relationships between phenomena and then, through analogy, discovers the identical causal relations between unknown phenomena. Meaning imbued in the magical act is analogously transferred to the natural activity. This is not, Tambiah argues, faulty science but a normal activity of human thought: magic is a specialized use of analogy and the imputation of meaning from the magical procedure to a natural referent. Thus magic does what science cannot: it helps create a world of meaning. Seemingly bizarre magical behavior is to be understood as an exercise in the exploration of meaning in practical activity, not as a refutation of natural law.

Many anthropologists would argue that magic is part of the normal daily routines of people in modern, complex societies. Clearly magic is involved when a baseball player, in order to get a hit, crosses himself or picks up a bit of dirt before batting. *Mana* is the "charisma" of the persuasive individual; it is also the "prestige" of the person of high social station. Magical protection is afforded the automobile driver who places the statue of a saint on the dashboard. And magic is involved in the daily ritual of personal ablutions and grooming: "I must always wear this tie with that suit," "If my hair is not styled just so, I won't feel right." The doctor says, "Take two pills and call me if you don't feel better in twenty-four hours," and we take his advice, since, like most laymen, we tend to see the science of the expert as a form of magic. And this is necessarily so, as we cannot all be experts in everything, yet we still need to reduce our anxiety and gain a sense of order and meaning in our lives.

BIBLIOGRAPHY

With the publication of *The Golden Bough: A Study in Magic and Religion*, 2 vols. (London, 1890), James Frazer put the study of magic forever on the agenda of anthropologists, folklorists, and all scholars of small-scale societies. Frazer's library study eventually grew to twelve volumes (3d ed., rev. & enl.; London, 1911–1915) plus an *Aftermath* (London, 1936). An abridged, single-volume version, entitled *The New Golden Bough*, edited by Theodor H. Gaster, was published in 1959 (New York).

In a theoretical essay entitled *Magic, Science, and Religion* (New York, 1948) Bronislaw Malinowski criticized Frazer's armchair scholarship, and it is with Malinowski's *Coral Gardens and Their Magic*, 2 vols. (Bloomington, Ind., 1935), that the modern anthropological field study of magic really begins. E. E. Evans-Pritchard's *Witchcraft, Oracles, and Magic among the Azande*, 2d ed. (1937; Oxford, 1950), is a classic field study of magic among a traditional African group. Religion in small-scale societies, especially among the indigenous peoples of Australia, is the subject of Émile Durkheim's *The Elementary Forms of the Religious Life* (1915; New York, 1965). Greater depth is given to the Durkheimian approach to magic in Henri Hubert and Marcel Mauss's "Esquisse d'une théorie générale de la magie," *L'année sociologique* 7 (1904). Subsequently translated as *A General Theory of Magic* (London, 1972), this important essay is quoted by Steven Lukes in his article on Mauss in the *International Encyclopedia of the Social Sciences*, edited by David L. Sills (New York, 1968), vol. 9, pp. 78–82. The racist position that the use of magic is an outcome of "primitive" thought is set forth by Lucien Lévy-Bruhl, especially in his *Primitive Mentality* (New York, 1923).

The nature of magical thought, as a species of normal human thought, is spelled out by Claude Lévi-Strauss in his classic essay *The Savage Mind* (Paris, 1962). Summations of anthropological ideas concerning magic and religion in simple societies can be found in Ruth Benedict's "Magic," in the *Encyclopaedia of the Social Sciences* (New York, 1933), vol. 10, pp. 39–44; Nur Yalman's "Magic," in the *International Encyclopedia of the Social Sciences* (New York, 1968), vol. 9, pp. 521–527; E. E. Evans-Pritchard's *Theories of Primitive Religion* (Oxford, 1965); and the various editions of *The Reader in Comparative Religion: An Anthropological Approach*, edited by William A. Lessa and Evon Z. Vogt. Stanley J. Tambiah's article entitled "The Form and Meaning of Magical Acts: A Point of View" appears in the fourth edition (New York, 1979) of the reader.

DONALD R. HILL

Magic in Greco-Roman Antiquity

From the beginning, magic was an essential part of Greco-Roman culture and religion. Over the course of history, however, it changed in appearance, scope, and importance from being an element of simple rituals to becoming highly complex systems claiming the status of science and philosophy. To the extent that magical ideas were presupposed in early agrarian and sacrificial rites, purifications, and burial customs, magic even preceded the culture of the Greeks. Later, magical beliefs and practices steadily grew in significance and diversity. In the Hellenistic period that followed Alexander the Great (d. 323 BCE), magical material increased considerably. In Classical Greece of the sixth to fifth centuries BCE, Thessaly and Egypt had already been known as the prime sources of magical knowledge; but only Hellenistic syncretism produced the abundance of material now available. Within the Greco-Roman world magic formed to some extent a common tradition, yet at the same time each cultural region put its own stamp on it. The main traditions were those of Greek, Greco-Egyptian, Roman, Jewish, and Christian magic. While clearly distinguishable, these cultural contexts also overlapped to a considerable degree and produced a variety of syncretic forms.

Sources. The material to be considered falls into two categories. First, there is an abundance of primary sources: amulets, magical gems (often with pictorial and verbal inscriptions), curse tablets, spells on papyrus and on strips or sheets of metal, inscriptions, symbols, drawings, paintings, small figurines and larger sculptures, tools, and finally handbooks of magicians that collect the materials they used (especially the Greek Magical Papyri). Second, there is also a vast amount of secondary source material. Almost every ancient author presents literary and artistic descriptions of magical beliefs and practices. There are also many short references to such beliefs and practices as they existed at the time. Philosophers discussed the matter from early on. Scholarly investigations from the Hellenistic and Roman periods are extant (Plutarch's *On Superstition*; Pliny's *Natural History* 30). At that time the distinction between acceptable and unacceptable forms of magic became common, making it possible for even the educated to use magic in some positive way. Legal provisions had to be developed to deal with magic, especially with forms of it that were reputedly used to harm others.

Despite its reputation as illicit, fraudulent, and superstitious, magic was an essential part of daily life at all levels of society. The uses of magic seem to have been unlimited. In any case, they were also connected with legitimate forms of ritual, myth, symbol, and even language in general. Magic was presupposed in all forms of the miraculous, and in medicine, alchemy, astrology, and divination. Even so, magic retained its dubious reputation, and there were always those few who viewed it with total skepticism.

Terminology. The phenomenon of magic is designated by several Greek terms, especially *mageia*, *pharmakeia*, and *goēteia*. The term *mageia* is derived from *magos* (pl., *magoi*), originally a Persian word *(magush)*. Herodotus describes the Magoi (Magians) as a Median tribe. Later they were assumed to be priests and scholars of astrology, divination, and related subjects. Whereas Plato (*Alcibiades* 1.122) still speaks of *mageia* in a positive sense as referring to "the magian lore of Zarathushtra," Aristotle uses the term also in a negative sense as we do today (frag. 36; also Theophrastus, *History of Plants* 9.15.7). This negative meaning, which has little to do with the original meaning, becomes predominant in the Hellenistic period, when new words develop besides *magos* and *mageia*, as for instance *mageuein* and *magikos*. The positive meaning, however, is found in the writings of the magicians themselves, especially in the Greek Magical Papyri.

The negative meaning was taken over by the Romans; in Latin the terms are *magia*, *magicus*, and *magus*, as well as *maleficium* and *maleficus*. Modern English has inherited this negative meaning, with the exception of the Magi of *Matthew* 2:1.

Descriptions of Magic. What constitutes magic was already disputed in antiquity. Roman officials and intellectuals reflect the negative reputation that magic had acquired. Pliny (*Natural History* 30.1–2) points out its fraudulent and dangerous character and has a theory about its origins as a decadent mixture of elements from medicine, astronomy, and religion. Apuleius (*Apology* 26) sums up the view of it as being vulgar and making preposterous claims. By contrast, practitioners of magic provide favorable descriptions of the art (Apuleius, *Apology* 26; Greek Magical Papyri, passim), or they distinguish between lower and higher forms; *goēteia* became the lower, *mageia* the general, and *theourgia* the higher magic. This distinction allowed Neoplatonic philosophers, especially Iamblichus and Proclus, to accept theurgy as a form of philosophical magic. [*See* Theurgy.]

Greek and Roman Magic. For reasons of methodology it is important to distinguish between primary (performative) and secondary (descriptive) material.

Primary sources. Primary sources for ancient magic consist of various kinds of artifacts, images, symbols, and written texts. Collections of such sources are today housed by public museums and libraries or with private collectors. The cataloging and publishing of these widely dispersed materials are still in progress.

Amulets. Greco-Roman antiquity has left us a large number of amulets of different kinds and purposes. The word *amuletum* occurs in Pliny and corresponds to the Greek *phulaktērion.* Amulets were magically potent objects that averted evil or increased a person's or a deity's divine power. [*See* Amulets and Talismans.] They were worn around the neck or on the head, or arm, or were posted in various places in the house (on doors, at thresholds, etc.). Amulets come in many shapes and forms. Best known are the Egyptian scarab, the hand showing the *fica* (the obscene gesture called "the fig"), the phallus, the eye. Other forms are divine symbols and figurines, replicas of other parts of the human body, animals, and plants. Precious and semiprecious gems engraved with images of deities, inscriptions, and magical symbols were very popular. Often amulets were placed in capsules *(bullae).* While Egypt was the classical land of amulets, they were known in all parts of the ancient world. Among Jews the *tefillin* and the *mezuzah* should be mentioned, and among Christians the cross and the fish.

Curse tablets. Curse tablets, or *defixiones* (from Lat. *defixio,* "binding spell"; Gr., *katadesmos*), are known from Greece since the time of Homer. [*See also* Cursing.] A large number of lead lamellae are extant from fifth-century Greece, but curse tablets exist also in the form of ostraca, seashells, and papyri, upon which the curse formulas were inscribed, often with the names of the cursed and the curser. The tablets were deposited in the ground near places where the spirits of the dead were believed to be or in such places as houses, baths, and sports arenas, so as to be communicated to avenging underworld deities (especially Hermes, Hekate, Persephone, and Typhon). Curse tablets were used for a variety of purposes, especially in erotic magic, court trials, political intrigues, and sports (gladiators, horse races). From the earlier and simpler curse developed the later, more elaborate, syncretistic forms of the Hellenistic and Roman eras; besides the magical formulas, inscriptions often included so-called *voces magicae,* characters, or drawings. A special form was the magical letter to the underworld deities.

Curse figurines. Curse figurines, of which several examples and descriptions have survived, were also widely used. To curse someone, one made a wax or clay figurine of the person and then stuck needles or nails into the figurine or mutilated it, while curse formulas were spoken over it. Like curse tablets, the figurines were deposited in the ground. This form of curse was apparently popular in erotic magic.

Drawings. Drawings have magical power in themselves, as extant magical papyri show. The subjects of the drawings can be deities, persons, or animals.

Tools. Magical tools are known to have existed and have in fact been found (nails, disks, etc.). The most important discovery was a set of tools found in Pergamum.

Symbols. A large number of magical signs and symbols appear on amulets, gems, and tablets. Although seemingly in use since Pythagoras (see Lucian, *Pro lapsu* 5), most of them are still unexplained today. The magicians called them *charactēres.* In gnosticism they were also taken over by Christian magic *(Book of Jeu, Pistis Sophia).*

Incantations. Incantations belong to the magic of the word. [*See* Incantations.] They consist of magical formulas, prayers, and chants. The term comes from the Latin *incantamentum,* "incantation, spell" (Gr., *epōidē*). Many examples of *incantamenta* are found in inscriptions, papyri, and literature, where they are quoted or described. They were widely used in medicine (healings, exorcisms), weather magic, cultic invocations of gods and demons, and erotic magic. Their significance for philosophy and rhetoric was recognized by the Sophists and Plato. They also appear as literary motifs in sagas, novels, myths, aretalogies, mystery cults, and collections of oracles.

Hymns. Hymns to the gods are closely related to incantations. In terms of poetry and religion, hymns are more and even highly developed forms. They were composed metrically and sung, with accompanying cithara and dance. Their basic form included the invocation of the gods, the gods' names and epithets (expressed in relative clauses, participles, adjectives, etc.), and the petition. Hymns existed from Archaic times on. Major extant collections include the Homeric Hymns (mainly from the eighth to the sixth centuries BCE), the Orphic Hymns (probably from the second century CE), and the hymn fragments inserted in the Greek Magical Papyri, some of which may be ancient.

Magical handbooks. Magicians collected the material they needed in handbooks, some of which are extant, as for example the great magical papyri of Berlin, Leiden, London, and Paris. Such handbooks include a wide variety of spells to be used by the magicians themselves or to be sold to customers. There are also rituals for acquiring assistant demons *(paredroi daimones),* initiation rituals, deification rituals, invocations for oracular séances with deities, and procedural matters (preparation of ingredients, instructions about when various procedures can be undertaken, etc.). Among the spells, those designed to attract a lover, harm an enemy, or restrain anger are most numerous. Other spells have to do with various illnesses, bedbugs, business problems, catching thieves, and horse races. To find out what the future holds, a host of mantic spells and longer rituals are provided. Outstanding among all these collections are the so-called Mithraic Liturgy, which exhibits yet unexplained relationships to the Mithraic cult, and the "Eighth Book of Moses," which contains three different versions of an initiation ritual. In addition to collecting magical material, the handbooks told magicians how to make and use amulets, curse tablets, figurines, and drawings, and how to use tools.

Secondary sources. Whereas primary sources present magical practices and beliefs directly, secondary sources presuppose, describe, or discuss them. The literature of Greek and Roman antiquity contains innumerable examples of such secondary sources, but careful distinctions must be made: while many authors have real knowledge of popular magic or even access to primary sources of magical literature, there is at the same time a purely literary tradition in which the same themes, motifs, and terms show up again and again. Therefore some authors simply imitate the descriptions of magical acts found in earlier authors or attempt to supersede them. While both kinds of authors may flourish simultaneously, some authors may have received their information from secondary sources exclusively.

Literary texts. Magic is a common literary motif in both Greek and Latin literature. Homer's *Iliad* and *Odyssey* contain many allusions to and descriptions of magical acts. Pliny (*Natural History* 30.1) states that the *Odyssey* in particular was recognized simply as a book of magic. In fact, Homeric verses were used later as magical formulas. Magic plays a role in Odysseus's encounter with the witch Circe (*Odyssey* 10.274ff.) and his descent into Hades and consultation with the seer Teiresias (*Odyssey* 11.14ff.). The Homeric Hymns have numerous references to magic, some of which (depending on whether the hymns actually were used in the cult) may be primary rather than merely secondary sources. The *Hymn to Demeter* 228–230 is especially important because of its reference in the Demophon episode to a ritual baptism of fire. From the beginning, literary interests were focused not only on erotic magic but also on death and the underworld with its deities, especially Hekate and Persephone (e.g., Hesiod's Hekate episode in *Theogony* 411–452). There is also, of course, a close relationship between the literary and the pictorial art. Greek drama took to the subject as well, expressing it either in episodes (e.g., the calling up of the ghost of Darius in Aeschylus's *Persae* 619–842) or in whole tragedies (e.g., Euripides' *Medea,* treating one of the great witches of antiquity). Ancient comedy used magic for its own purposes, as in the description of a *goēs* ("quack") in Aristophanes' *Plutus* (649–747) or Menander's *Deisidaimon* and *Theophoroumene.* Theocritus's second idyll, entitled *Pharmakeutria* (The Witch), became a literary prototype for many later poets.

The superstitious man as a literary and ethical type was described by Theophrastus (*Characters* 16). The hymnic tradition was continued by the third-century BCE poet Callimachus (*Hymn to Demeter* 3–6; *On the Bath of Pallas* 9) and his pupil Apollonius of Rhodes, whose *Argonautica* included several magical sections (3.1ff., invocation to Erato; 744–911, Medea's preparation of magical drugs; 1163–1224, Jason's nocturnal sacrifice to Hekate; 1225–1407, Jason's magical defeat of the giants). Especially popular were descriptions of scenes of necromancy. In the Roman period the second-century Greek satirist Lucian of Samosata provides an almost complete inventory of magical beliefs and practices, as did the Greek novels.

In Roman literature the tradition continues with an increasing interest in the dramatic and the bizarre. Vergil's eighth eclogue (64–110) describes a magical ritual performed by a deserted lover that shows exact knowledge of magical details, although it is based upon Theocritus's second idyll. In the *Aeneid,* dramatic magical scenes are connected with the death of Dido (4.504–676). Horace's fifth epode has a macabre scene of the abduction and murder of a child.

Philosophical and scientific investigations. According to ancient tradition, philosophers have been preoccupied with magic since pre-Socratic times. The names of Heraclitus, Pythagoras, Empedocles, and Democritus appear several times in connection with magic, and spells under the names of Pythagoras and Democritus are found in the Greek Magical Papyri. Although the historical value of these references is doubtful, philosophers seem to have investigated magical phenomena since Pythagoras, who also may have been the first to make a positive use of it.

Greek philosophy in general rejected magic. The Skeptics, Epicureans, and Cynics produced an entire literature combating magic. But the attitude gradually changed with the development of demonology, mantic, and astrology. The Hermetic writings and the Neoplatonic philosophers Iamblichus and Proclus (and probably even Plotinus) accepted forms of magic and integrated them into their systems.

Scientific compendia of magical beliefs and practices are extant from the Roman period. Pliny's *Natural History* contains a history and theory of what he calls the *magicae vanitates* (30.1–18) and a large collection of remedies (see also book 28). Although written as an apology, Apuleius's *Apologia (De magia)* is in fact a compendium of magic. Apuleius's other works are also valuable sources for the magical beliefs of his time (see especially the *Metamorphoses).*

Legal provisions. Ancient law had no provisions for prosecuting magicians for the practice of magic. However, there are numerous accounts of trials in which magic played a role. These were trials not only of magicians and witches but also of philosophers (e.g., Anaxagoras, Socrates, Apollonius of Tyana, and Apuleius of Madaura). According to ancient writers, these persons were accused of murder by poisoning *(pharmakōn)* or of failure to honor the gods properly *(asebeia),* accusations broad enough to add emotional furor to a wide range of charges. If magic as such was not a reason for prosecution, harming a person by means of magic was. Plato included legal provisions against such injury in his *Laws* (11.933.D). The Romans went further and included property damages caused by weather or agricultural magic in the *Tabulae XII.*

Jewish Magic. Magic played a somewhat different role in Judaism as compared with neighboring religions. The Old Testament shows that Israelite religion was well aware of the importance of magic in the religions of Egypt and Babylon, but on the whole it viewed magic negatively. For the Old Testament, magic is either foreign or marginal. Magicians are called in by Pharaoh (*Ex.* 7–10) or Nebuchadrezzar (*Dn.* 2:2); they serve Jezebel (*2 Kgs.* 9:22) and Manasseh (*2 Chr.* 33:6). The prophets warn against magic (*Is.* 47:9–15, *Jer.* 27:9, *Ez.* 13:17–19, *Na.* 3:4, *Mal.* 3:5, *Mi.* 5:11–12). The religion of Israel is believed to be more powerful than all magic, which is excluded by law (*Ex.* 22:18; *Lv.* 19:26, 19:31, 20:6, 20:27; *Dt.* 18:9–22). Especially important is the necromancy in the story of the witch of Endor (*1 Sm.* 28).

This picture, however, is deceptive. Pre-Israelite religions, most of them saturated with magic, have left numerous traces in Israelite religion; furthermore, popular Israelite religion must not be confused with what the Old Testament conveys. In this popular religion, magic has a firm place that was often approved of even by "official" religion (e.g., Moses' and Elijah's magical wands in *Ex.* 4:20, 17:8–13; *2 Kgs.* 4:29, 4:31; Urim and Tummim, ephod and terafim in *1 Sm.* 2:18, 14:3, 14:18; *Jgs.* 17–18; *Dt.* 33:8). More important than amulets and rituals was the magic of the word, especially curses and blessings and above all the name of Yahveh (see especially *Jgs.* 13:6, 13:17–18; *Ex.* 3:14). The name of Yahveh became the most important magical element in Judaism and, beyond it, in Hellenistic syncretism. Therefore the God Iao plays an enormous role in the Greek Magical Papyri, and on the magical gems and amulets of the Hellenistic and Roman period.

These various developments persist on a far broader scale in rabbinic Judaism. The official rejection of magic in rabbinic literature must be seen against the background of popular religion and the whole mystical tradition (Merkavah, Qabbalah), both of which were very open to magical beliefs and practices.

Christian Magic. For early Christianity, magic presented difficulties. On the one hand, Christians had inherited Judaism's negative attitude toward magic (see *Gal.* 5:20, and the typical attitudes expressed in *Acts* 8:9–24, 13:6–12, 19:13–19). On the other hand, the emphasis on miracles and sacraments implied approval of some forms of magic. Jesus' activities as a miracle worker were soon attacked as being the work of a magician possessed by Beelzebub (*Mk.* 3:22–27 and parallels). Beginning with the presynoptic sources of the Gospels, New Testament apologetics was increasingly preoccupied with defending Jesus against classification with the magicians. Since his exorcisms and miracle work could not be ignored, distinctions were introduced to separate miracles from magic. Similarly, miracles worked by Christian healers had to be separated from those of non-Christians. This was accomplished by treating the latter as acts done by magicians.

Problems arose also because of the close affinities between the epiphanies of the crucified and resurrected Christ and the magical concept of the return as demons of persons who had died of violence *(biaiothanatoi)* (see especially *Lk.* 24:36–43, *Jn.* 20:19–23). Moreover, magical presuppositions in the rituals of baptism and the Eucharist led to practices approved by some and disapproved by others (see especially Paul, who tried to correct misuse in *1 Cor.* 1:10–16, 8:1–11:1, 11:17–34, and in *Rom.* 6:3–10). Paul first distinguished between abuse (magical misconceptions) and proper use (sacraments) of these rituals. The fundamental theological problems stated or implied in these early texts continued to assert themselves throughout the history of Christianity and have led to ever new conceptualizations.

From the second century on, popular Christian religion showed greater interest in amulets, relics, symbols, and signs (see the apocryphal gospels and *Acts*). The gnostics also made positive use of magic (see especially the *Book of Jeu,* the *Pistis Sophia,* and the writings found at Nag Hammadi, Egypt). The official church, through its bishops, synods, and the writings of the church fathers, was forced to combat and suppress new Christian forms of magic and superstition. The extant wealth of amulets, spells, relics, holy places, symbols, and images indicates that complete suppression was impossible. Still, Christian theology was able to contain and restrain the lower forms of magic by accepting some forms of christianized magic while eliminating other, unwanted forms. Liturgy and sacramental theology developed special kinds of magic thought to be compatible with the doctrines of the church. By the end of antiquity, the church had become the home of many forms of magic that coexisted in an uneasy and tenuous symbiosis. Some magic was banned, some was tolerated, some was approved, but none achieved domination.

BIBLIOGRAPHY

No complete collection of the vast remains of ancient magic exists, but there are useful editions and translations, indices, and surveys of literature. For new publications, see the annual bibliography in Marouzeau, *L'annee philologique*, section on "Magica."

Texts and Translations

Betz, Hans Dieter, ed. *The Greek Magical Papyri in Translation, Including the Demotic Spells.* 2 vols. Chicago, 1986. Volume 1 contains English translations of the papyri in Preisendanz's work and those published thereafter (until 1983), with introductions, notes, and a glossary. Volume 2 will have an index of Greek words by Edward N. O'Neil and a subject-matter index by Marjorie A. Menaul.

Kropp, Angelicus M. *Ausgewählte koptische Zaubertexte.* 3 vols. Brussels, 1930–1932. Volume 1 has the edition of Coptic texts; volume 2 has their German translation; volume 3 is introductory.

Preisendanz, Karl. *Papyri Graecae Magicae: Die griechischen Zauberpapyri.* 2 vols. Edited by Albert Henrichs. 2d ed. Stuttgart, 1973–1974. Edition of Greek texts, with German translation, notes, and bibliography.

Studies

Abt, Adam. *Die Apologie des Apuleius von Madaura und die antike Zauberei.* Giessen, 1908.

Aune, David E. "Magic in Early Christianity." In *Aufstieg und Niedergang der römischen Welt,* vol. 2.23.2 (Berlin and New York, 1969), pp. 1507–1557. A comprehensive bibliographical report.

Bonner, Campbell. *Studies in Magical Amulets, Chiefly Graeco-Egyptian.* Ann Arbor, 1950.

Burkert, Walter. *Griechische Religion der archaischen und klassischen Epoche.* Stuttgart, 1977. Translated as *Greek Religion* (Cambridge, Mass., 1985). Important and up-to-date comments on various aspects of magic in the archaic and classical periods of Greek religion.

Grant, Robert M. *Miracle and Natural Law in Graeco-Roman and Early Christian Thought.* Amsterdam, 1952.

Herzig, Otto. *Lukian als Quelle für die antike Zauberei.* Würzburg, 1940.

Hopfner, Theodor. *Griechisch-ägyptischer Offenbarungszauber.* 2 vols. Leipzig, 1921–1924. Still the best survey of the entire range of material.

Hopfner, Theodor. "Mageia." In *Real-Encyclopädie der classischen Altertumswissenschaft,* vol. 14 (Stuttgart, 1928), pp. 301–393. Mostly a summary of the former work.

Luck, Georg. *Arcana Mundi. Magic and the Occult in the Greek and Roman Worlds.* Baltimore and London, 1985. A useful collection of sources in translation, with brief introductions and notes.

Nilsson, Martin P. *Geschichte der griechischen Religion.* 3d ed. 2 vols. Munich, 1967–1974. Has important sections on magic at the various stages of development in Greek religion.

Scholem, Gershom. "Der Name Gottes und die Sprachtheorie der Kabbala." *Eranos-Jahrbuch* 39 (1970): 243–297.

Thee, Francis C. R. *Julius Africanus and the Early Christian View of Magic.* Tübingen, 1984. The volume contains the *Kestoi* of Julius Africanus (c. 160–240 CE) in translation, together with commentary, extensive introduction, and a survey of the early Christian views on magic.

Thorndike, Lynn. *A History of Magic and Experimental Science,* vols. 1–2, *The First Thirteen Centuries of Our Era.* New York, 1923. Written from the perspective of the history of science; incomplete series of studies.

Trachtenberg, Joshua. *Jewish Magic and Superstition* (1939). Reprint, New York, 1982.

Trumpf, Jürgen. "Fluchtafel und Rachepuppe." *Mitteilungen des Deutschen Archäologischen Instituts,* Athenische Abteilung, 73 (1958): 94–102.

Widengren, Geo. *Religionsphänomenologie.* Berlin, 1969. References on various aspects of magic can be found in the index, s.v.v. *Magie, Magier.*

HANS DIETER BETZ

Magic in Medieval and Renaissance Europe

A history of magic during the Middle Ages and the Renaissance has yet to be written. New discoveries and, above all, new interpretative viewpoints, have made obsolete the few existing syntheses, like those of Lynn Thorndike, Kurt Seligmann, or Émile Grillot de Givry. Any scholar who still relies on these works—and especially on the first—is by no means better off than would be an anthropologist who relied exclusively on James G. Frazer.

Early Middle Ages. The magic of late antiquity survived into the early Middle Ages along several different lines. The archbishop Synesius of Cyrene (c. 370–413), who before becoming a Christian had been a pupil of the Neoplatonist Hypatia of Alexandria (martyred in 415), laid in his treatise *On Dreams (Peri enhupniōn)* the foundations of a new theory of magic that was to be particularly influential during the Renaissance. Synesius took over the notion of "spirit" *(pneuma)* from the medical and philosophical traditions of antiquity, from

Empedocles to Galen and from Zeno of Citium and Aristotle to Proclus.

The *pneuma* was a vapor of blood, which was supposed not only to give life to all animal organisms but also to form the material substratum upon which the activity of both the five senses and the intellect was based. According to this "subtle physiology," which remained unquestioned down to the eighteenth century, the spirit also forms a sixth or "inner" sense, whose function is to grasp the messages of the five external senses and to codify them so that they become intelligible to reason. The language of the spirit, whose seat as an inner sense, or phantasy, is either the heart or the head, is formed by phantasms *(phantasmata)*, or inner images. According to Aristotle, later recalled by Thomas Aquinas, the human reason is unable to understand anything without the aid of phantasies *(aneu phantasmatos—sine conversione ad phantasmata)*.

For Synesius, the phantasy of man is the very place where the upper and the lower world come together. According to a principle that all of the greatest philosophical schools of antiquity—Platonism, Aristotelianism, and Stoicism—had affirmed on different grounds and stressed with various intensities, man is a compendium of the universe. Synesius's "magic," which is no more than a blending of Platonism, Aristotelianism, and Stoicism, stems from the postulate that there is interaction between man and universe and that this interaction can be practically realized and controlled by means of the *sensus interior*, or phantasy. This represents a continuation of the popular magic of late antiquity, insofar as the latter was equally based on the conceptions of *pneuma* ("spirit") and *pneumata* ("spirits, ghosts"). It also represents a conspicuous improvement over that tradition, insofar as the concept of *pneuma* now becomes a part of a general theory that was labeled as scientific and, accordingly, was endowed with immense prestige.

Synesius's theory, which became known through Marsilio Ficino's 1489 translation of the treatise *On Dreams*, was very influential during the whole of the Renaissance. It also stood in the background of the most outstanding early medieval system of "intellectual" magic, that of the Arab al-Kindī (d. c. 873), whose treatise *On Rays* has been preserved in a twelfth-century Latin translation *(De radiis)*. The work was much appreciated by Roger Bacon and Ficino. In the sixteenth century, al-Kindī's ideas became the center of a debate between defenders and opponents of magic and astrology. According to al-Kindī, all terrestrial and superterrestrial beings send forth rays that are never identical, since there are no identical things in nature. Rays are susceptible to manipulation, and the power to manipulate them can be acquired through will and concentration of the human phantasy *(spiritus ymaginarius)*. This phantasy emits rays that have an impact upon the universal system of rays everywhere. In other words, human desires expressed in phantasies are, under special conditions, transitive; that is, they can have an influence on someone else's phantasy and even on inanimate objects. Magic is actually the knowledge of these special conditions that make possible manipulation by means of the spirit. Such special conditions, and, consequently, special results, can be reached through appropriate sounds, figures, images, and sacrifices.

As far as popular magic is concerned, one could argue that the Jewish *Sefer ha-razim* (Book of Mysteries), compiled in the sixth or seventh century CE and published in 1969, gives room to the hypothesis that early medieval Jewish magic forms the background of such anonymous treatises of practical magic as the *Clavicula Salomonis* (Small Key of Salomo), which circulated from the late Middle Ages to the nineteenth century. This is not actually the case. Whereas the *Clavicula* describes a system of planetary angelology, and, consequently, of astrological magic, the *Sefer ha-razim* is a treatise of *merkavah* mysticism transformed to include the magical conjuration of angels, and it is based on a more rudimentary cosmology. The *Clavicula Salomonis*, otherwise a farraginous text, is a more sophisticated example of magic than the *Sefer ha-razim*.

During the late Middle Ages, a book of practical magic translated from Arabic into Latin that enjoyed much popularity was the *Picatrix*, in Arabic *Ghāyat al-ḥakīm fi-al-siḥr* (The Goal Pursued by the Sages through Magic), ascribed to the philosopher al-Majrītī (d. 1004–1007). The influence of the *Picatrix* on Renaissance magic, which was of a quantitative kind, has been certainly overrated.

Late Middle Ages. Two late medieval personalities connected with magic deserve special mention: Albertus Magnus (c. 1200–1280) and Roger Bacon (c. 1220–1292). Accounts of other magicians, like Michael Scot (c. 1175–1235), are so affected by the traditional and atemporal typology of the "magus" that is is impossible to separate truth from legend. Others still, like Guido Bonatti of Forlì, Peter of Abano, Ramón Lull, or Arnaldus of Villanova were skilled in astrology, alchemy, the art of memory, or, occasionally, geomancy (a form of divination imported from the Moors), but they do not properly belong to the category of actual authors or performers of magic.

The Dominican monk Albertus Magnus was truly well versed in popular magic; a universal man, he could discourse with equal enthusiasm and skill on tin mining or the faculties of the human soul. He was famous through the ages for having discussed at length the properties of stones and plants. His *Book of Minerals* contains the traditional lapidary, with ninety-nine descriptions of precious stones that, among other qualities, are supposed to confer happiness, riches, strength, success in war, and skill in business. They can also stop breathing, protect against theft, prevent storms and hail, provoke or prevent miscarriage, and further cure all sorts of ailments and diseases. The sixth book of Albertus's treatise *On Plants* contains references to the magic and apotropaic properties of plants. Albertus's lapidary and herbary were frequently reprinted during the Renaissance; together with the *Picatrix* they formed one of the principal sources of practical Renaissance magic.

The mere fact of Roger Bacon being a Franciscan may account for the contempt he repeatedly showed toward Albertus. Surprisingly enough, Bacon, like Albertus, was a supporter of natural magic. In his *Experimental Science* he drew a wonderful vision of the new world that was to come about with the application of his "science": he described self-propulsive boats and engines, flying machines, and submarines. Bacon cultivated a form of astrological magic and was also a practitioner of alchemy.

The Renaissance. The father of Renaissance magic was undoubtedly Marsilio Ficino (1433–1499), author of the 1489 *De vita coelitus comparanda,* widely copied or paraphrased by representatives of "spiritual" magic like Heinrich Cornelius Agrippa (1486–1535) and Giordano Bruno (1548–1600). Another kind of magic, of which Ficino himself gives an extensive account, was magic by means of demons; it was a sort of astrologic magic akin to that described in popular books like the *Clavicula Salomonis.* Its greatest representative was the abbot Trithemius of Würzburg (1462–1516). This "demonic" magic left indelible traces in the compilation *Occult Philosophy* of Agrippa and in the magical works of Bruno, who followed both Agrippa and Trithemius.

Another kind of magic, which is neither "spiritual" nor "demonic," is the "natural" magic of the Neapolitan Giambattista della Porta (c. 1535–1615), author of the treatise *Natural Magic,* which grew from four books in its first printing of 1558 to twenty books in the second of 1589 and which has had innumerable reprintings. Like Trithemius in the third book of his *Steganographia,* and unlike Ficino, Bruno, or even the mere compiler Agrippa, della Porta is not much of a theoretician. Although it contains several interesting details, his treatise is a catalogue of curiosities rather than a book of magic in the Renaissance tradition.

Spiritual magic. Like al-Kindī, Marsilio Ficino recognized a universal force radiating into the remotest corners of the universe; but he called this force "love," whereas the Arab philosopher called it "rays." In his treatise *On Love (De amore),* loosely a commentary on Plato's *Symposium,* Ficino resumes the medieval tradition of love as a serious illness of the spirit. Love is a natural form of magic, in which the spell is unconsciously cast by the beauty of the beloved. It is important to recognize that there is no essential difference between the mechanism of love and that of magic. In fact, the latter represents a conscious (as opposed to an unconscious) manipulation of someone (or something) else's spirit by means of one's own spirit. Magic works only under certain conditions, which are governed by the positions of the stars in heaven. Ficino's magic is a more or less complicated astrological magic, consisting of the knowledge and exploitation of the astral influences stored in earthly matter such as those of minerals, plants, and animals. If magic in general is intersubjective, that is, if it works from the spirit of a person (the manipulator) to the spirit of another person (the object of the operation), Ficino's magic, which is also frequently termed "theurgy," represents a particular case of intersubjectivity: it is actually intrasubjective in that it is meant to direct spiritual influence upon the subject himself. By following a diet that is astrologically beneficial and by surrounding himself with objects and persons in which the qualities of the three beneficient planets (the sun, Jupiter, and Venus) inhere, the Ficinian magus could obtain a clean, elastic, and firm spirit, which would open to him the gates of superior contemplation.

This is pure spiritual magic, but it is not free from demonic interferences, since demons, it might be said, are but bodiless spirits. (In fact, demons are also other things, planetary spirits, for instance, of which Ficino speaks at some length in his *De vita coelitus comparanda.*) We may safely state that there is no contradiction between spiritual and demonic magic, since spiritual magic comprehends demonic operations, and demonic magic does not exclude operations by the human or extrahuman spirit. Of course, there are also cases of pure demonic magic.

Demonic magic. Paradoxically enough, the greatest wizard of the sixteenth century, Trithemius of Würzburg, was also a fierce opponent of witchcraft, against which he recommended the most drastic measures, according to the doctrine of the *Malleus maleficarum* (1486). Until he was fifteen, Trithemius was an analphabet, but his desire of learning was so intense that, after an angelic vision, the boy was given the possibility of realizing his dream, which he did with astonishing quickness. He claimed from that time to have constant communication with angels. As a result, he became a Benedictine monk at the age of twenty, and, at twenty-three, he was elected abbot of Sponheim, the poorest convent of the Palatinate. In twenty years, Trithemius transformed the convent into the most famous place of pilgrimage in all humanistic Europe. Its library contained the rarest manuscripts of the time. In 1505, the library possessed almost two thousand volumes, an exceptional number. The Sponheim library probably contained a great many works on practical magic; several are possibly listed in Trithemius's *Antipalus maleficiorum* (1508), which, ironically enough, was a refutation of witchcraft dedicated to the abbot's highest protector, the emperor Maximilian.

Trithemius is the author of two treatises on cryptography: *Steganographia* (posthumously printed) and *Polygraphia* (1508). The former, which was to become one of the most intriguing books of the sixteenth century, was not preserved in its entirety: the extant parts contain the first two books and a fragment of the third. Whereas the first two books really constitute a cryptographic manual, the fragment of the third book presents a bold method of magic that would permit the magus to communicate at great distances by means of planetary demons, properly summoned for this purpose. It is probable that Trithemius thought that through similar methods a magus would be able to know at every moment all things happening in the world. It is likely that the abbot himself destroyed the rest of his *Steganographia*, which logically would have dealt with divination. In the ecclesiastical jurisprudence of the time, demonic invocations were considered to be sacrilegious, whereas divination was heretical. Trithemius would not admit to such a sin.

Heinrich Cornelius Agrippa was Trithemius's disciple. As a matter of fact, his compilation *On the Occult Philosophy*, written from 1509 to 1510 and printed in 1533, is a blending of Ficinian spiritual magic and Trithemian demonic magic; he was also acquainted with treatises in practical magic, and the compilation is a systematic exposition of all these matters.

Erotic magic. Ficino and Trithemius could hardly claim absolute originality in their magic methods, and Agrippa was merely a compiler, but there was one genuinely creative work of Renaissance magic, the two manuscripts by Giordano Bruno entitled *De vinculis in genere* (On Bonds in General). Educated in a Dominican cloister at Naples, Bruno early came into conflict with church authority. Exiled to Protestant countries, he never obtained there the friendly reception he might have expected. For all Christian denominations at that time, Giordano Bruno, a specialist in the mysteries of the art of memory and a magus in the Renaissance tradition, incarnated precisely the archenemy of faith. He was eventually burned at the stake as a witch.

Bruno's work on magic includes a number of compilations *(De magia, Theses de magia,* and *De magia mathematica)* and the two manuscripts entitled *De vinculis in genere.* These manuscripts carry to an extreme end the Ficinian theory of love as a form of natural magic. Thus, if any affection conceived by the spirit of the operator is transitive, then it is enough to produce erotic phantasms loaded with the emotion of passion, in order to be able to influence another person. This person would receive the phantasms through his own spirit and would thus become the prey of the magus. The magus is, however, supposed to be perfectly continent, lest he become himself a prey of his own phantasms. Bruno conceives a world in which everything is manipulable through the same mechanism of phantasmic production. The operator may have three distinct hypostases: he may be a physician, a prophet, or a magus. As a physician, he is responsible for the spiritual healing of his patients; as a prophet, he is able to bind *(vincire)* masses of people and to make new religions; as a magus, he is able to find the appropriate bonds *(vincula)* in order to bind anyone's will through phantasms. As a poet, Bruno described several times the psychic condition of such an operator, who is supposed to be at once burning with desire and completely cold and indifferent toward his own passion.

Phantasms at work. Giordano Bruno's magic is based not only upon the Ficinian tradition but also on techniques relating to the art of memory. This art consisted of a manipulation of phantasms or inner images, whose purpose varied from the mere learning by heart of a text to mystical contemplation. At any rate, the art of memory as a discipline pertained to rhetoric. The first to envisage explicitly the art of memory as a magico-mystical enterprise was the Friulian Giulio Camillo Delminio (c. 1480–1544). Giulio Camillo tried all his life to build up a "theater" of memory organized in seven planetary fields embracing practically all objects and persons. He was followed by the Friulian rhetorician Fabio Paolini, who published his *Hebdomades* at Venice in 1589. Paolini replaced Giulio Camillo's "theater" with a mental scheme of seven series of planetary influences, to be simply filled in with the phantasms of things supposed to reflect the respective planetary characters (for instance, a lion under the sun, etc.). Paolini was convinced that a rhetorician-magus, at any moment during his speech, could call up such a phantasm before his internal sense. The phantasm would not fail subsequently to influence the spirit of the auditors, their emotions, and their decisions.

Giulio Camillo's ideas had an important impact on the aesthetician Giovanni Paolo Lomazzo (1538–1600). Lomazzo is a representative of the magical theory of the subjective value of colors. In his *Idea del tempio della pittura* (1590) he made a sevenfold classification of painting and painters in conformity with the sevenfold classification of Giulio Camillo.

The Modern Debate on Renaissance Magic. The spiritual principle of Renaissance magic and the inner coherence of this discipline have been, for the first time, carefully investigated by Daniel P. Walker (1958). Walker's approach made obsolete the traditional historical approach in search of "origins" and influences. According to the traditional approach, Renaissance magic was a blending of Hermetism and Qabbalah. Further investigations into the figure of the Renaissance magus—John Dee (1527–1608), for instance—have shown that, at a later time, "the Renaissance magus turned into Faust" (Yates). Frances A. Yates seems also to consider—in her last work (1979)—the possibility that the Renaissance magus was turned into a grim and deluded follower of Satan by the ideology of the Reformation. This idea is given particular emphasis in my book *Éros et magie à la Renaissance* (1984).

BIBLIOGRAPHY

The principles of spiritual magic are the foci of Daniel P. Walker's excellent *Spiritual and Demonic Magic: From Ficino to Campanella* (London, 1958). The evolution of erotic magic from Ficino to Bruno has been followed by my *Éros et magie à la Renaissance* (Paris, 1984). Another general work on Renaissance magic, handy but unreliable, is Wayne Shuhmaker's *The Occult Sciences in the Renaissance* (Berkeley, 1972). Magic in the Elizabethan age is the subject of Frances A. Yates's *The Occult Philosophy in the Elizabethan Age* (Boston, 1979). Several works on individual authors are recommended. Excellent articles on the herbary and lapidary of Albertus Magnus by J. Stannard, J. M. Riddle, and J. A. Mulholland are found in *Albertus Magnus and the Sciences*, edited by James A. Weisheipl (Toronto, 1980). The best book to date on Trithemius of Würzburg is Klaus Arnold's *Johannes Trithemius, 1462–1516* (Würzburg, 1971). Two reliable books on Heinrich Cornelius Agrippa are Auguste Prost's excellent biography *Les sciences et les arts occultes au seizième siècle: Corneille Agrippa, sa vie et ses œuvres*, 2 vols. (1881–1882; reprint, Nieuwkoop, Netherlands, 1965), and Charles G. Nauert, Jr.'s reliable *Agrippa and the Crisis of Renaissance Thought* (Urbana, Ill., 1965). Peter J. French has devoted his attention to John Dee in *John Dee: The World of an Elizabethan Magus* (London, 1972). There are a multitude of studies concerning Marsilio Ficino and Giordano Bruno, but none of them is dedicated to their magic. For both these remarkable personalities, the reader should refer to my books, to the books of Daniel P. Walker, and to my article "La Magie de Giordano Bruno," *Studi e materiali di storia delle religioni* 49 (1983): 279–301.

IOAN PETRU CULIANU

Magic in Eastern Europe

Demonology, introduced by Christian religious thought in the fifteenth and sixteenth centuries, profoundly affected western European thought with respect to its conception of magic. The transformation of the witch into an expression of the demon who seeks to ensure his power on earth and prepare for his own advent obscured popular thinking, which possessed its own type of representations and its own system of values inherited from a rather deep-rooted paganism. In eastern Europe, where this intervention did not occur in the same way, the phenomenon of magic continued to evolve in its primary form, as a unified practice anchored in a popular culture of which it represented only one facet.

For so long isolated from the historical and sociological upheavals that affected western Europe, the peoples of eastern Europe still hold to a different worldview and use different means to account for the human condition. As Mircea Eliade states in his *De Zalmoxis à Gengis-Khan* (1970): "As in all other provinces of the Roman Empire, autochthonous religious realities outlived, more or less transformed, both the romanizing and the christianizing processes. There is enough proof of a pagan heritage" (p. 73). The common inherited substratum preserved by the Romanian and Balkan populations is considered by Eliade as "the principal unifying element in the entire Balkan peninsula" (ibid., p. 183). As early as the 1930s, Pierre Bogatyrev, in the introduction to his *Actes magiques, rites et croyances en Russie subcarpatique* (1929), noted a renaissance of paganism among ethnic groups practicing orthodox religions, even though he insists that this renaissance evidently took place "under the aegis of the Revolution and Soviet government." He adds: "Orthodox religion and witchcraft, the rival sisters, . . . form an unexpected ensemble. All of village Russia is divided into witchcraft parishes that do not yield to ecclesiastical parishes."

Given the importance of the pagan heritage (not to mention the circulation of motifs, sociocultural exchanges, and so on), it is not surprising that a rather large body of magical practices is shared by the majority of the traditional societies of southeastern Europe. In fact, there is no domain in which magic is not practiced; magic crosscuts all spheres in which human beings move. But recourse to magic becomes especially obligatory for the different phases of the life cycle; in this way it ensures its principal function, that of integrating individuals into their own collectivity and their own development. Throughout this region, for example, the Fates, those fabulous beings whom the Bulgars call "women or fairies of fate" and whom the Greeks name simply Morai ("fates"), participate in the "programming" of an entire life, from birth to death, including marriage. They are the ones to whom a woman addresses herself (even today, in a hospital setting) on the third day after childbirth:

You, the Saints,
You the Good Ones,
You the Fates
Predestine this child,
This newborn.
Come as sweet as honey,
Come as smooth as water,
And as good as bread,
As gay as wine,
As limpid as water,
And give him intelligence and wisdom.
To this child newborn,
Give him health and good fortune in life.
May he be protected by God.

In Romania, especially in the region known as Little Walachia, the Fates intervene in the principal magical rites dealing with marriage and love through the intermediary of their plant, the mandrake. When, for example, a mandrake is unearthed during rites designed to determine a young woman's mate, the Fates are addressed in the same terms as those used to ask about a child's destiny: "You, the Saints, / You the Good Ones, / You the Pure, / I give you honey, wine, bread, and salt. / Let me know the destiny of [so-and-so]." The Fates are also invoked through their plant in incantations that accompany magical rites aiming to reunite separated couples:

You mandrake,
You the Benefactress,
Herb of the Saints,
Know her lot.
And if her husband had been destined to marry,
If this union be his fate,
Bring him back
And reunite them,
Keep them bound forever. . . .
Give them a second chance. . . .
If God had wanted them to separate,
May they separate.
But if not,
Bring them together, you, Benefactress,
Herb of the saints.
Unite them a second time.
Enliven her home. . . .

At times of death, the Fates through their plant are once again asked to intervene in a sort of ritual magic that is experienced and felt as a form of euthanasia. After the mandrake is unearthed "in order to summon death," an act performed in complete silence and sadness; it is boiled and the ill person is bathed with the decoction; at this time the Fates are invoked and asked to declare the lot they have selected for the sufferer: death or life. If it is death (as is usually the case), they are asked to palliate the victim's suffering: "May his fate be decided. / If it be death may it come quickly. / May he not suffer any longer." This type of magic ritual also appears in the Balkans, at least among the Bulgars, as Christo Vakarelski (1969) demonstrates.

Many other magical practices are shared by these traditional societies. Among them, the most important are the rites aiming to vitiate the contamination associated with childbirth and those aiming to avoid the contamination of death—all intended to ensure the separation of worlds that should not intersect. An extended comparative study, for example, could be undertaken on the magical precautions taken so that the dead remain dead and do not transform themselves into vampires, who are today still dreaded, feared, and fought. Represented as wild or monstrous carnivorous animals, these eternally unsatisfied beings are doomed to seek out earthly pleasures. They refuse to be relegated to the beyond and, instead, assume human form in order to finish on earth what they could not realize in life. In order to make sure the dead do not become vampires, certain preventive measures can be undertaken. One can, for example, deposit nine stones, nine marble chips, and nine millet grains under the person's head and utter the following incantation:

Your mouth, I petrify.
Your lips, I marbleize.
Your teeth, to millet I transform.
So that harm shall you never wreak.

Numerous magical practices (echoing religious rites) are also associated with the cyclical succession of the seasons and with the household. Incantations surrounding the home usually seek to expel malevolent forces and bring good luck:

Just as the waters melt in March,
Just as they are transported by the torrent
And just as they clean and carry
All the rust,
All the trash,

May my home and all those who live in it also be
Cleansed
Of all malfeasance, all bad luck,
All illness, all ill will
That may be in its walls.

These incantations and the rites they accompany are essential, for they situate man in a context of rituals that integrate him with nature and the order of the cosmos. In fact, it is in this domain that, from Romania to Bulgaria to Russia to Greece and Albania, the magical rites most resemble each other in both form and content.

Magical practices are also directed at administrative and legal authorities. For villagers the power of persuasion is the best weapon against these authorities with whom they are usually involved in a "battle of words." Silencing the authorities is seen as the ultimate form of persuasion, and many incantations thus request that they be silenced just like the dead:

Just as the dead have now grown cold,
May all members of the tribunal grow as cold.
May no one be able to proclaim my guilt.
May they stop speaking,
May they lose their voice
Just as the dead have lost theirs.
The arms of the dead are crossed over their chest.
May the case made against me grow as cold as they.
May it go away.

In many regions of eastern Europe one could say that folk culture was not profoundly modified by the more or less important changes that occurred in modes of production. It is, however, not easy to speak of magic and witchcraft as it is currently practiced and experienced in these countries, because both official discourse and research data relegate these practices to an obscure past or consider them forms of charlatanism. A series of field trips conducted in Romania in recent years, however, confirms that folk beliefs remain very much alive and that recourse to magical practices in frequent, especially when it concerns the health of children, the prosperity of the home, the productivity of animals, and so on. In fact, one does not have recourse to magic merely on an occasional basis; it is the imaginary fabric into which all individuals are enveloped. There are few mothers, for example, who do not know one or another incantation to neutralize the effects of the evil eye (belief in the evil eye is found throughout the Mediterranean Basin and elsewhere). The following Romanian example is expressed in extremely violent terms:

May he burst, the envious one.
Evil eye he cast.
May he explode.
If a virgin spellbinds him,
May her braids fall off.
If his wife spellbinds him,
May her milk dry up,
May her breasts wither,
May her child die of hunger.
If a youth spellbinds him,
May he burst completely.

Many practices and incantations form part of any individual's basic knowledge, but one seeks recourse to magic only if one has the gift, the power, the desire, and the daring to do so. The specialists commonly known as witches possess the gift and the daring to practice a distinct form of magic. A witch is frequently described as someone who uses supernatural forces to do evil (although most witches will say they do what they do for the good of mankind). Witches were and still are enormously feared because they are said to "give life or death." Consulting them always means incurring some form of danger, especially since they are thought to collaborate with the Devil (who appears in his diverse forms during the séance). Access to witches is also difficult and troublesome: they live often in faraway places (necessitating a tiresome journey, waiting one's turn among the others who have come for consultations, sleeping in a strange place); one can only see them on specific days and at specific times (at night, for example); one must be recommended to them by someone in whom the witch has confidence. Thus access to specialized magic could be said to presuppose a kind of punitive expiatory path.

People have recourse to witchcraft especially in cases of serious disequilibrium or when a significant disturbance has disrupted the natural order of things. Witches are especially sought out, for example, in cases in which a marriage is endangered by the intervention of a third party (usually the husband's mistress, a rival who wishes to substitute herself for his legitimate wife). Indeed, marital relations and extramarital ties are a source of great conflict and violence, and the greater part of specialized forms of magic is played out in this arena.

To control her husband, who should not waste his energies elsewhere, a woman has recourse to two forms of specialized magic, both of which aim to reunite the legitimate couple. In the first form the wife attempts to kill the intruder (the "rival," the "stranger") or to eliminate her from the protected sphere. In the process, the two women enter into a kind of magical battle using a number of possible weapons: a charmed knife that must symbolically reach the other; dolls made from scraps of the man's or the mistress's clothing: a yellow plant *(dosnica)*, described as "terrifying," which causes the rival to wander to the ends of the earth; the mandrake, which can make people go mad; and an insect or a frog (seen as the mistress's substitute) captured under special conditions and made to suffer the worst treatments.

Specific procedures accompany the use of any of these means. For example, while piercing a symbol representing her rival with the charmed knife, the woman will utter the following incantation:

> You, charmed knife,
> Go into her body.
> Beat her,
> Crush her,
> So that her blood spouts forth.
> If she is alive, pierce her heart.
> If she is dead, seek her out in the Beyond.

While thinking of her rival a woman may prick an insect with a needle or a knife and utter:

> May the one who is breaking my home,
> The one who does not let me live with my man,
> The one who gives me no peace,
> May that one die and disappear.

In the second form—identified as the "magic of filth"—the wife will simply attempt to dissolve the soiled relationship in which her husband is involved in order to reestablish her original tie with him. She will use decoctions made from urine, semen, menstrual blood, fecal matter, sweat, or other secretions of intimate life (which serve as substitutes for the people concerned). These decoctions may be clandestinely fed to the husband. If he eats his own secretions (an act of autocannibalism), he is said to devour himself, thus reintegrating the forces and energies he seeks to dispense elsewhere. If he eats the substitutes of his wife, he is said to become impregnated by her, filled with her person.

Incantations accompany the administration of these decoctions; if, for example, the wife uses menstrual blood, she utters the following words (similar to those used in practices on certain Greek islands today):

> Just as the menses are cyclical,
> Have their hour and time,
> So, to each of my words
> May he likewise return.
> May he return to my body,
> May he return to my desire. . . .
> May my husband cling to me,
> May he explode, may he burst,
> May he not do without me.

The wife may also manipulate these secretions in other ways. She may, for example, take the earth on which her rival has trod and place it on her husband's feces, uttering an incantation all the while.

One could speak at length about these and other forms of magic still practiced in Romania and other east European countries. Indeed, despite all the sociocultural modifications and modernizing trends that have taken place in this part of the world, magic has adapted itself to its new environment. It is not a survival of a bygone era but an integral aspect of popular culture; it provides people with the power and know-how to understand their world and their position within it. Magic is still the arena through which different communities find a common language, a discourse through which they recognize themselves.

[*See also* Incantations.]

BIBLIOGRAPHY

Argenti, Philip P., and H. J. Rose. *The Folk-Lore of Chios*. Cambridge, 1949.

Bîrlea, Ovidiu. "Descîntecul." In his *Folclorul românesc*, vol. 2. Bucharest, 1983.

Bîrlea, Ovidiu, and Ion Muslea. *Tipologia folclorului: Din raspunsurile la chestionarele lui B. P. Hasdeu*. Bucharest, 1970.

Bogatyrev, Pierre. *Actes magiques, rites et croyances en Russie subcarpathique*. Paris, 1929.

Eliade, Mircea. *De Zalmoxis à Gengis-Khan*. Paris, 1970. Translated as *Zalmoxis, the Vanishing God: Comparative Studies in the Religions and Folklore of Dacia and Eastern Europe* (Chicago, 1972).

Eliade, Mircea. *Occultism, Witchcraft, and Cultural Fashions: Essays in Comparative Religions*. Chicago, 1976.

Gorovei, Arthur. *Descîntecele românilor*. Bucharest, 1931.

Kabbadias, Georgios B. *Pasteurs-Nomades méditéranéens: Les Saracatsans de Grèce*. Paris, 1965.

Krauss, Friedrich S. *Slavische Volksforschungen*. Leipzig, 1908.

Lorint, F. E., and Jean Bernabé. *La sorcellerie paysanne*. Brussels, 1977.

Megas, George A. *Greek Calendar Customs*. 2d ed. Athens, 1963.

Stahl, Paul-Henri. "L'organisation magique du territoire villageois roumain." *L'homme* 13 (1973): 150–162.

Vakarelski, Christo. *Bulgarische Volkskunde*. Berlin, 1969.

IOANA ANDREESCO-MIEREANU
Translated from French by Brunhild Biebuyck

Magic in Islam

Magic in Islam forms part of what are called *ʿulūm al-ghayb*, "the occult sciences," which include divination, astrology, oneiromancy, and all fields of learning relating to prophecy. Magic (Arab., *siḥr*) is an important branch, like divination and astrology, with which some forms of magic overlap.

Following the very rich literature of magic in Islam, I shall here treat the various categories of *siḥr* in three sections: black magic (*ʿilm al-siḥr*), theurgy (*ʿilm al-khawāṣṣ wa-al-ṭalāsim*), and white or natural magic (*ʿilm al-ḥiyal wa-al-sha'wadhah).* The first section will deal with divinatory magic, exorcism of demons, spells and the summoning of spirits into bodily forms. The second section will examine the properties of divine names, numbers and certain spells, sympathetic magic or sorcery, amulets, talismans and potions, charms, and the properties of medicinal plants. The third section will consider the mutual connections between effective and efficient forces, the ability to vanish instantly from sight, and prestidigitation.

Black Magic. From the many Qur'anic verses relating to magic (sixty-six, of which only three were revealed in Medina), one might conclude that the phenomenon of *siḥr* occurs in the revelation only in the form of a condemnation of pagan practices. In certain verses, however, magic appears as a fragment of a celestial knowledge that was given to humans by fallen angels such as Hārūt and Mārūt (surah 2:102). These angels revealed to humans secrets "that they ought not to have known" (*Apocalypse of Enoch* 64:10). Thus, "God decided, in his justice, that all the inhabitants of the world would die [by flood], for they knew all the secrets of the angels, and possessed the hateful power of the demons, the power of magic" (ibid., 64:6). Another group of verses, condemning this almost instinctive quest by humans to penetrate the will of God, connects magic with divination.

Divinatory magic. The boundaries between magic and divination remain blurred. In their classification of the sciences, the Muslim encyclopedists, such as al-Afkānī, Tāshköprüzade, and Ḥājjī Khalīfah, call divination a branch of magic. According to Edmond Doutté, the transition from magic to mantic takes place via a phenomenon of "objectivization of the desire" (Doutté, 1909, p. 352). Whether inductive or intuitive, divination partakes of magic in certain of its techniques. One of the sources of knowledge common to the magician and the seer is demonic inspiration. Furthermore, the Arab seer *(kāhin)*, and especially the female seer, practiced magic and divination concurrently (see my book *La divination arabe*, Leiden, 1966, pp. 92ff.), so that in Islamic magical literature, the two run parallel without mingling. Both make use of supernatural means to predict natural elements; both share a practical and nontheoretical character. One searches in vain for a theoretical definition of magic in the Qur'ān or the *ḥadīth* (prophetic traditions).

Exorcism and spells. If divinatory magic has recourse to secrets revealed by fallen angels, the magic of incantations and spells is meant to compel the *jinn* and the demons to accomplish a desired end, by pronouncing the formula "'Azamtu 'alaykum" ("I command you"). The Qur'ān and the *ḥadīth* say nothing of this, but theological consideration led to the following conclusion, formulated by Ḥājjī Khalīfah:

> This thing is possible and lawful, according to reason and the law; whoever denies it is not highly regarded, because he winds up failing to acknowledge the omnipotence of God: to subjugate the spirits, to humble them before him, and to make them subordinate to men, is one of the miracles of [God's] creation. (Ḥājjī Khalīfah, ed. Flügel, 1955–1958, vol. 4, pp. 205–207)

Two kinds of conjuring, however, may be distinguished. One variety consists in directing the mind toward an object other than God, and thus being unfaithful to him. When this unfaithfulness appears as one of the elements making up the magical act through one of the means used to realize it, it becomes forbidden magic. In this case, the magician acts in a manner that is wicked and harmful to others, and, indeed, a controversy arose among medieval jurists concerning the question of knowing "whether they must be killed because of the unbelief which is antecedent to the practice [of sorcery], or because of their corrupting activity and the resulting corruption of created beings" (Ibn Khaldūn, trans. Rosenthal, 1967, vol. 3, p. 159.).

On the other hand, the conjuring of spirits is permissible when it is performed "with perfect piety and the complete absence of all unlawfulness, in solitude and isolation from the world and in surrender to God" (Ḥājjī Khalīfah, op. cit., pp. 205–207). This interpretation is basically consistent with the demonological conception of Islam, which considers the *jinn* servants of God, somewhat in the manner of humans and angels.

The writers differ on how this power derived from God is applied. Fakhr al-Dīn al-Rāzī sums up the opinion of the theologians thus:

> When the conditions are brought together and the incantations pronounced, God makes the latter like a mighty devastating fire, encircling the demons and the *jinn*, until the [four] corners of the world close in around them, and there is no place left for them to hide, nor any other choice than to come out and resign themselves to do as they are commanded. What is more, if the performer is skillful, being of good conduct and praiseworthy morals, God will dispatch powerful, rough, and strong angels to the demons to inspire them and lead them to obey and serve him.
> (quoted in Ḥājjī Khalīfah, loc. cit.)

Summarizing the views of the Muslim theologians, Ḥājjī Khalīfah adds: "The obedience of demons and *jinn* to humans is not something unimaginable, either from the standpoint of reason or from the standpoint of accepted practice." The best illustration of this conception of magical incantation is given by certain exalted mystics, the North African marabouts, or *ṭālib*s, who transform the old pagan magic and subordinate it to the omnipotence of the one God. How, in this case, can obtaining a miracle by divine favor be distinguished from the effects of magic?

For the philosophers, whose views are summed up by Ibn Khaldūn,

> The difference between miracles and magic is this: a miracle is a divine power that arouses in the soul [the ability] to exercise influence. The [worker of miracles] is supported in his activity by the spirit of God. The sorcerer, on the other hand, does his work by himself and with the help of his own psychic power, and, under certain conditions, with the support of devils. The difference between the two concerns the idea, reality, and essence of the matter.
>
> (Ibn Khaldūn, op. cit.)

Ibn Khaldūn himself locates the distinction in external criteria, which he defines as follows;

> Miracles are found [to be wrought] by good persons for good purposes and by souls that are entirely devoted to good deeds. Moreover, [they include] the 'advance challenge' [*taḥaddī*] of the claim to prophecy. Sorcery, on the other hand, is found [practiced] only by evil persons and as a rule is used for evil actions, such as causing discord between husband and wife, doing harm to enemies, and similar things. And it is found [practiced] by souls that are entirely devoted to evil deeds. (ibid.)

He adds that "this is also the view of the metaphysicians," and he concludes that "among the Ṣūfīs some who are favored by acts of divine grace are also able to exercise an influence upon worldly conditions. This, however, is not counted as a kind of sorcery. It is effected with divine support" (ibid.).

One should point out, finally, that wishing does not make a magician; indeed, to be a magician presupposes a disposition and a preparation not required of the worker of miracles. "This art," the Pseudo-Majrīṭī tells us, "can be practiced and applied only by one who has [the power of] it in his nature" (al-Majrīṭī, ed. Ritter, 1933, p. 187), and Ibn Khaldūn says that the philosophers "think that a sorcerer does not acquire his magical ability but has, by nature, the particular disposition needed for exercising that type of influence" (op cit., p. 167). This disposition is called *al-ṭibāʿ al-tāmm*, "the perfect nature"; the person who possesses it attains "knowledge of the secrets of creation, of natural causes, and of the mode of being of things" (al-Majrīṭī, op. cit., p. 187; cf. Fahd, 1966, p. 192, n. 29). Pseudo-Majrīṭī's quotation from the so-called *Book of Hermes the Sage* defines this perfect nature in these terms:

> The microcosm that is man, if he possesses the perfect nature, has a soul like the solar disc, unmoving in the heavens and illuminating every horizon with its rays. It is the same with the perfect nature whose ray is found in the soul; it flashes out, touches the translucent forces of wisdom, and draws them to the soul that is its point [of origin], just as the sun's radiance attracts the forces of the universe and lifts them up into the atmosphere.
>
> (al-Majrīṭī, op. cit., pp. 193–194)

The progressive assimilation of the magician to the forces that he conjures, evokes, or invokes contributes to the effectiveness of his work and the success of his endeavor. The spiritual beings *(rūḥanīyah)* then appear to him as if in person, speaking to him and teaching him all things.

Evocation of spirits. In conjuring and incantation, the magician relies on the service of *jinn* and demons to accomplish his ends; in evocation, he compels the spirits of the dead, the demons, and the planets to carry out his wishes.

Necromancy, which really belongs with divination, is steeped in black magic. Like the summoning of demons, it generally involves two phases: a material phase, consisting of the preparation of a mixture of various products belonging to a special pharmacopoeia and fumigations of every kind, plus an intellectual phase, consisting of the formulation of a prayer naming all the qualities and attributes of the spirit invoked and stating the wishes to be realized.

The evocation of the spirits of the planets is based on the knowledge of the qualities and properties of each of them: its color (red-gray for Saturn, white-gray for Jupiter, the yellow-green-red of red-gold for Mars, red-gold for Venus, a mixture of all colors for Mercury, and green-white for the Moon), its odor, and its flavor (for details, see al-Majrīṭī, op. cit., pp. 140, 150–156). To evoke the spirit of a planet, one must be dressed in its color and perfumed with its scent; further, by means of ingestion, one must assume its essence and flavor. Having done so, one must watch for the moment when the planet reaches the point corresponding to it in the zodiac, on a direct line that does not cross the line of another planet of a different nature. When this is so, the line from the planet to earth will be straight and uninterrupted.

Next, from metals attributed to the planet, one must fashion a cross, hollow from top to bottom and with a hole at the top, resting on two feet. This cross is to be mounted on the image of whatever it is one plans to ask of the spirit invoked: that of a lion, for example, or a serpent, in case one desires to go to war or to overcome an enemy, that of a bird if one wishes to escape danger, of a man seated on a throne if one aspires to fame, power, or respect, and so on. Likewise, to gain control of someone, one carves that person's likeness from a stone characteristic of the planet that presided over his birth, at the proper time and in the position described above. This image then serves as a base for the cross. The choice of a cross has to do with the fact that every body takes this shape; thus it serves to establish a connection between the higher spiritual entity and an image that resembles it. An incense burner made of the same metals as the cross is also used; it must have only one opening at the top of the cover, for the smoke to escape.

To summon a celestial spirit, a proper location must be selected, completely open to the sky. The ground should be strewn with plants of the same properties as the planet whose strength is to be attracted, on the principle that like attracts like; there must be nothing else on the ground or in the area. Incense of the same essence as the planet being evoked must be burned so that the fumes, escaping from the single opening in the burner, will pass through the hollow cross from bottom to top. All this must be done at a propitious time. If all these conditions are met, the upper world will be in harmony with the lower and thus the request will be received favorably. (See al-Majrīṭī, op. cit., pp. 182–186; for a French translation, see Fahd, 1966, pp. 170–171.)

Theurgy. Other techniques aimed at tapping the planetary and stellar virtues lie on the borders between magic and theurgy. The distinction between the two, according to Ibn Khaldūn, lies in the fact that

> the sorcerer does not need any aid, while those who work with talismans seek the aid of the spiritualities of the stars, the secrets of numbers, the particular qualities of existing things, and the positions of the sphere that exercise an influence upon the world of the elements, as the astrologers maintain. The philosophers, therefore, say that sorcery is a union of spirit with spirit, while the talisman is a union of spirit with body. (Ibn Khaldūn, op. cit., p. 166)

"As they understand it," Ibn Khaldūn continues, "that means that the high celestial natures are tied together with the low [terrestrial] natures, the high natures being the spiritualities of the stars. Those who work with [talismans], therefore, as a rule, seek the aid of astrology" (ibid., p. 167).

Such is the theory, but in practice it is rare to find mention in the texts of a magical act carried out without recourse to a material support. While the talismanic art assumes a perfect technique, grounded in astronomical, astrological, and other data, this is not required for the practice of magic, which is performed with the help of prayers, evocations, and attempts to unite spirits, demons, and stars by magical means.

The talisman. According to Ḥājjī Khalīfah, the art of talismanry is intended

> to combine the active celestial forces with the passive earthly forces at moments favorable to the desired action and influence, with the help of vapors [able] to strengthen and attract the spirit of the talisman, with the intent of producing unusual manifestations in the world of generation and decay. In comparison with magic, this science is more accessible, for both its principles and its causes are known. Its usefulness is obvious, but mastery comes only after a great deal of effort. (Ḥājjī Khalīfah, op. cit., pp. 165ff.)

In fact, skill in talismanry can be acquired only by one who understands its principles, which spring from the branches of knowledge making up natural philosophy, in particular mathematics, physics, and metaphysics.

A great many elements come into play in the creation of a talisman. In addition to ease and efficiency, sympathy and antipathy, time and place, there is relativity, a basic principle of the talismanic art, the relationship between the planet and the object of the talisman as well as the similarities and parallels among its various components. To be effective, these connections should be located on the straight line crossing the talisman's field of influence.

Time plays a fundamental role in talismanry. Indeed, the proper moment is a condition *sine qua non* for the success of the undertaking. In order to seize it, one must observe the planet until it arrives at its operative position, the most favorable point in its influence, its conjunction with the other planets and its position with respect to them, the exact instant when the talisman must be set in place, and so forth. Position plays an equally important part, in particular the observer's vantage point, the spot where the talisman is made and set up, and the place of origin of the materials used to fabricate it. Numbers, as the measure of time and moment, are, like speech, necessary for the expression of quantity.

Quality, meanwhile, is equivalent in talismanry to causality. The object on which the talisman acts must bear a perfect resemblance to the quality transferred to it, so that its sphere of activity can spread. This is the basis of the connection between the higher and lower natures. Quality here is none other than inherent nature, the source of causality. Its role is therefore essential, not only in the discovery of the limited properties and influences of the planets but also in the diffusion of these same properties and influences. This leads to an increase in the quality of the material of which the talisman is made, by causing equivalent qualities to act upon it (al-Majrīṭī, op. cit., pp. 99–100).

The properties. In the words of Paul Kraus, the properties of beings are

> the virtues proper to minerals, plants, and animals, their sympathies and antipathies, as well as the use of these virtues in the various arts and in medicine. The miraculous occupies an important place here, and affinities with magic are

undeniable. Men, animals, and plants are no longer considered objects of reasoned inquiry, but are endowed with occult powers, able to heal any malady and to procure happiness and miraculous power of man.

(Kraus, 1942–1943, vol. 2, p. 61)

Among the physical properties, those of stones hold pride of place in talismanic practice, and knowledge of them is one of the essential conditions for a talisman's success, likewise for the properties of animal bodies, where magic comes to the aid of medicine; the latter are considered healthful even for incurable diseases. Plants possess many properties used in the rich magical repertoire of fumigations. A large number of these are found in the geographical compilation known as *Nabatean Agriculture*, and Pseudo-Majrīṭī also collected many of them. Among the plants used in magical operations are laurel, marshmallow, mandrake, elm, pennyroyal, myrtle, olive, horseradish, darnel, rice, beans, chickpeas, watermelon, and chicory.

The magical powers of plants are commonly connected with the natures of the planets. These natures impart their virtues to whatever responds to them. The fact that a plant sprouts in one soil and not in another comes not from the particular nature of the soil but from the marriage of a fixed disposition with given conditions of air and water. "The prime cause of this lies on the line crossing the horizon of this piece of ground and marking the zone of influence of certain planets on certain countries; thus the existence of plants and specific features in a given country to the exlusion of others" (al-Majrīṭī, op. cit., pp. 385ff.).

This learned theurgy, which systematically and "rationally" exploits the virtues of animal, vegetable, and mineral kingdoms, is marked by its Hellenistic origins and by the rich syncretism from which it emanates. [*See* Theurgy.] Popular magic in Islam has preserved this spirit, while opening it to new influences in the various islamized countries, hence the existence of magical practices peculiar to each of the major Muslim regions.

There are innumerable survivals of ancient theurgy in Muslim tradition, where many instances are ascribed to the Prophet himself, and in the abundant magical literature that spread out throughout the Muslim world. A saying attributed to the Prophet reflects an important principle of ancient magic, namely the magical power of the spoken word: "There is," he is supposed to have said, "a kind of utterance that is none other than magic" (quoted in al-Majrīṭī, op. cit., p. 9). By virtue of this principle, onomatomancy became widespread in Muslim lands, and the ninety-nine "most beautiful names" of God, like the most ancient surahs of the Qur'ān, played a very great role in spells, amulets, and potions. Muslim magic was based in large part on the knowledge of the letters that made up the supreme name of God. At the base of these speculations, we find the theory asserting that the letters of the alphabet, being at the root of creation, represent the "materialization" of the divine word.

However, according to Ibn Khaldūn, there is

a real difference between persons who practice talismanry and those who work with the secret virtues of names, regarding the manner in which the soul is made to act on living beings). . . . This soul has inherently the ability to encompass nature and control it, but its effect, among those who operate by means of talismans, is limited to drawing down from above the spirits of the spheres and tying them to certain figures or numerical supports. . . . It is otherwise with those who, to give their souls the ability to act, make use of the secret properties of names; they must be illuminated by the celestial light and sustained by divine help.

(Ibn Khaldūn, op. cit., pp. 175ff.)

These latter avoid giving the name of magic to practices consisting of the use of secret properties of letters, numbers, and names. Nonetheless, in practice, "they fall under the idea of sorcery" (ibid., p. 181), although they tend to locate their activities in the legitimate realm of natural magic.

White or Natural Magic. The branch of magic known in English as white magic, or natural magic, is denoted in Arabic by two terms: one, *simiyā'*, of Greek origin *(sēmeia)*, and the other, *nīrinjāt*, Persian *(neyrang)*. Both are applied generally to illusionism, prestidigitation, fakery, and legerdemain.

According to Ḥājjī Khalīfah (op. cit., pp. 646–647), natural magic involves imaginary phenomena, occurring in space and having no correspondence to anything palpable. Their production and causes remain a secret known only to the practitioners. Often it includes mixtures concocted by the magician out of natural essences, ointments, liquified materials, or even special words with suggestive powers. The range of such practices is very large: aerial illusions, atmospheric vapors, playing with fire, tricks with bottles, cups, and glasses, illusions with eggs, fruits produced out of season, wax figures, animal taming, discovery of hidden objects, preparation of magic ink, and so on.

In the *Ghāyat al-ḥakīm* of Pseudo-Majrīṭī, the term *nīrinjāt* is applied to charms that have an extraordinary power over human beings and natural phenomena alike, such as a magic ring that transfixes anyone who looks at it, amulets that ward off bad weather or neutralize weapons held by enemies, and so on (al-Majrīṭī, op. cit., pp. 242ff.). The making of these *nīrinjāt* requires extreme precision and careful handling of the poisonous materials used in their composition. These are potions that act by mans of absorption or fumigations of various powders and oils. The anticipated effects of these potions vary, and their application depends upon astrological conditions, as in all magical activity, and on the simultaneous utterance of a formulaic spell containing incomprehensible names.

In the same class of magical activity belongs the rainmaker, who commands the stars and who alternates between a demanding, coercive, and occasionally even insulting tone toward the heavens and flattery toward God. The imprecations he pronounces have a clearly magical character: often they include the use of the divine names with the aim of bending the will of heaven. The author of the *Theology of Aristotle*, followed by Ibn Sīnā (Avicenna), affirms that "prayer influences the sun and the stars, by imparting a certain motion to them, because the parts of the world form a single whole, like a 'single animal'" (quoted in A. Goichon, *Directives et remarques*, Paris, 1951, p. 250). For greater effectiveness, the rainmaker stood inside a circle *(mandil)* or a magic square.

In this same category is also included the evil eye. Ibn Sīnā explains it as "an admiring tendency of the soul that exercises, by this property, a weakening influence on the object of its admiration" (ibid., p. 523). For Ibn Khaldūn, the effect is

> natural and innate. It cannot be left alone. It does not depend on the free choice of its possessor. It is not acquired by him. [It is] an influence exercised by the soul of the person who has the evil eye. A thing or situation appears pleasing to the eye of a person, and he likes it very much. This [circumstance] creates in him envy and the desire to take it away from its owner. Therefore he prefers to destroy him.
> (Ibn Khaldūn, op. cit., pp. 170–171)

It may be concluded from the foregoing that Islam, the heir of ancient civilizations, has preserved for us, in its rich cultural and folkloric patrimony, remnants of Semitic and Hellenistic notions that were developed and intermingled in the wide expanse of the ancient and medieval Near East.

BIBLIOGRAPHY

Primary Sources

Būnī, Aḥmad ibn ʿAlī al-. *Shams al-maʿārif wa-laṭāʾif al-ʿawārif.* 4 vols. Cairo, 1905. A most important source for practical and theoretical understanding of Islamic magic. There are three versions of this work: short, medium and long. It exists in several lithographs and numerous manuscripts.

Ḥājjī Khalīfah. *Kashf al-ẓunūn.* 8 vols. Edited by O. Flügel. London, 1955-1958. A large encyclopedia with material arranged in alphabetical order. See especially the articles on *siḥr, sīmiyāʾ, ṭalāsim*, and the keywords given therein.

Ibn Khaldūn. *Al-muqaddimah.* Edited by M. Quatremère. Paris, 1858–. Translated by Franz Rosenthal as *The Muqaddimah: An Introduction to History*, 2d ed., 3 vols. (Princeton, 1967). The emphasis in this work is on the theoretical aspect of magic.

Majrīṭī, Maslamah ibn Aḥmad al-. *Ghāyat al-ḥakim.* Edited by H. Ritter. Leipzig, 1933. Translated by H. Ritter and M. Plessner as *"Picatrix": Das Ziel des Weisen Pseudo-Majrīṭī* (London, 1962). A study of magic and theurgy from the double perspective of theory *(ʿilmī)* and practice *(ʿmalī)*. Completed in AH 395/1004 CE, it is the most important work in this field. On the question of its attribution to Maslamah al-Majrīṭī ("of Madrid"), see H. Ritter's article in *Vorträge der Bibliothek Warburg* 1 (1921–1922): 95–124.

Secondary Sources

Fahd, Toufic. "Le monde du sorcier en Islam." In *Le monde du sorcier*, pp. 157–204. Paris, 1966. Includes an extensive bibliography. The present article owes much to this study.

Doutté, Edmond. *Magie et religion dans l'Afrique du Nord.* Algiers, 1909. An important study on magical practices in North Africa.

Kovalenko, Anatoly. *Magie et Islam.* Geneva, 1981. A 721-page volume containing a detailed description of magical procedures, with an exhaustive bibliography. This is an invaluable reference work.

Kraus, Paul. *Jābir Ibn Ḥayyān.* 2 vols. Cairo, 1942–1943. A valuable tool for the study of the occult sciences in Islam and their relationship to Hellenism.

Mauchamps, Émile. *La sorcellerie au Maroc.* Paris, n.d. A posthumous work preceded by a study on the author and the work by Jules Bris. Mauchamps's investigation into magical practices in Morocco is an exemplary model; every Muslim region needs such an inquiry.

TOUFIC FAHD
Translated from French by David M. Weeks

Magic in South Asia

South Asian religious history offers a unique documentation textually recorded over three thousand years of the manipulation of the powers of the universe in a great variety of methods, aims, and social conditions.

Ideological Position. The oldest preserved corpus of Indian religious tradition, the Veda, is a rich source of magical ideas and devices. In the world view of the Vedic ritualists, all phenomena in the world are interrelated. No fundamental distinction is made between substances or beings and their qualities; powers and processes; symbols and the symbolized, and so forth. Reality is built up from various networks of affinities or connections *(nidāna)*, which can be detected, evoked and activated by man. Many of these similarities are also known from elsewhere. Thus, clear water not only purifies the body but also serves to wash off the impurity caused by untruth *(Śatapatha Brāhmaṇa* 1.1.1.1). In the ritual, the effect-directed interrelations *(bandhu)* between the material and the spiritual, the human and the cosmic levels are employed systematically. Very important as a key to the hidden reality is the realm of sound, which can be manipulated by the power of the sacred, ceremonially uttered word *(mantra)*. [*See* Language, *article on* Sacred Language.]

In Vedic religion, a demarcation between "magical" and "religious" ritual ideologies is difficult to maintain and partly depends on the definition of "magic." One might better, with Hermann Oldenberg, distinguish between unspecified, nonsacerdotal or private magic *(māyā, yātu)* and magical powers manipulated in the cultic sphere *(brahman, tapas)*. The aim of the ritual procedure is to keep the life process of the universe moving, to maintain good relations with the powers of the Unseen, to secure cosmic order on which human welfare depends. Within this decidedly religious context, magical thought patterns and actions find their natural place. If it is true that religion focuses on encounter and magic on manipulation, one can say that both aspects are often present in the intricate religious ceremonies such as the Rājasūya or Aśvamedha described in Vedic texts. Magic predominates, however, when important *mantra*s are applied outside their original context for specified, immediately mundane objectives (e.g., the Ṛgvedic hymns discussed in the Ṛgvidhāna).

In post-Vedic Hindu tradition, supernatural powers are ultimately derived from the Supreme Power, in this connection most commonly Śiva, who in several of his aspects functions as the magician's chosen deity; in popular Buddhism, such powers are subject to Lord Buddha. The spheres of religion and magic continue to overlap, though on a much more restricted scale than in the Vedic period. Although deities are invoked during ceremonies of what we would call magic and magical elements sometimes feature in otherwise purely religious contexts, the distinction between magic and religion is ever present in the popular mind. A distinction is also made between socially approved and disapproved kinds of magic.

Terminology. Of the four branches of Vedic literature, especially the *Atharvaveda* (of sometimes disputed authority) contains a rich collection of spells and magical rites. Later generations distinguished two kinds of Atharvavedic lore: the *ātharvaṇaḥ*, aiming at positive welfare *(puṣṭi)* or pacification *(śānti)* of evil influences, and the *āṅgirasaḥ*, directed against inimical powers or individuals. Vedic and later Sanskrit literature mention different kinds of supernatural power; there is no exact counterpart to our term *magic*. In nontechnical literature, *māyā* perhaps comes closest. The term denotes a creative faculty originally in the possession of superhuman beings and applicable to good as well as evil purposes. [*See* Māyā.]

A prominent feature of *māyā* is the creation by its possessor *(māyāvin)* of deceptive phenomena (e.g., a wild animal or one's own double, or even the phenomena of existence) by which the victim is beguiled or subjugated. In younger texts (especially the *Mahābhārata)*, divine *māyā* is associated with the subjugation of creatures by the tricks of fate or supernatural agency. This divine faculty can be appropriated by human performers who emulate or associate themselves with divine prototypes renowned for their powers of *māyā* (Indra, Viṣṇu). *Māyā* has also epistemological and metaphysical connotations that dominate its semantic field; in recent Sanskrit literature, the term is seldom used in a purely magical context.

Other Sanskrit terms cover related meanings, partly overlapping each other but never entirely synonymous. To mention a few: *brahman* is wielded by the specialist of the sacred word for the weal of the Aryan community. *Tapas* (internal heat) is a special possession of yogins and ascetics. *Yātu* is the dreaded power of the inimical sorcerer *(yātudhāna)* or sorceress; the term survives in the Hindi *jādū*. The most encompassing term for rites of magic in Sanskrit is simply *karman* ("deed, act"); indeed, all human activity is felt automatically to create its consequence. From the same root is derived *kṛtyā* ("creation"), known since the *Atharvaveda* as a female evil spirit dispatched by a sorcerer. Also yoga ("method, practice") is used in a magical sense; among the people, a yogin often functioned as a miracle worker.

Specialists developed a voluminous literature in Sanskrit and vernaculars on magically applied ritualism, most often called *mantravāda* ("doctrine of *mantra*"). They continued to distinguish rites of protection *(śānti)* and aggression *(abhicāra)*, while realizing the relative value of this criterion: the protection of A might imply the downfall of B. Widely known is a series of "six acts" *(ṣaṭ karmāṇi)*: subjugation *(vaśīkaraṇa)*, immobilization *(stambhana)*, eradication *(uccāṭana)*, causing dissension *(vidveṣaṇa)*, liquidation *(māraṇa)*, and pacification *(śānti)*. There are varieties to this standard list. This theoretical framework was devised to cover a multitude of sophisticated and popular devices actually practiced by unscrupulous brahmans and others. The subject is treated in Tantras, religious books of the non-Vedic esoteric tradition (Hindu and Buddhist) or in monographs derived from these. Influence of this sanskritized tradition of magic is also traceable in Jainism, in Buddhist countries, in tribal cultures of South Asia, and in Indonesia (especially Bali).

Practices and Conditions. The Veda-oriented theorists distinguished three contexts for ritual action: regular, motivated (i.e., performed on special occasions such as festivals), and desire-oriented (*kāmya;* e.g., curing of disease, prolongation of life, elimination of rivals, softening of a beloved's heart, exorcism). A performer's ritual activity is again held to comprise three spheres: thought, word, and action, the latter subdivided into the rites proper, the preparation and handling of paraphernalia, and corporeal particulars such as symbolic gestures or a powerful glance. The *mantra,* although changing its outward form after the Vedic period, maintains its predominant position. [*See* Mantra.] Very often, elements from Sanskrit *mantra*s persist in the spells uttered by tribal or low-caste magicians. Usually, such spells contain invocations of deities who are ordered to execute the performer's command. In *mantravāda,* initiation into a *mantra,* which is phonic manifestation of the world-sustaining power, can only be obtained under the guidance of a guru and implies several preparatory procedures such as astrological computation, protracted recitation, and regulation of breath. The *mantrin* should always carefully concentrate his thoughts and will upon the desired effect.

Descriptions of the rites proper tend to contain gaps while the social context is often altogether omitted. Actual practice includes prognostication, divination, witch-finding, manipulation of spirits or deities, exorcism (e.g., by striking with a broom over the patient's body while muttering spells) application of herbs or potions, innumerable small protective rites and customs (e.g., burying the placenta of a newborn child within the house's precincts) and aggressive rites of many kinds, such as piercing a small image representing the enemy. Besides, we find ample reference in literature to the art of *indrajāla,* which enabled clever performers to make a living by fascinating the public with hypnotism or juggling. Many magical practices have entered folklore as convention or customs that may persist for a considerable period along with alternatives such as medical aid; charms or amulets continue to be worn as "ornaments."

Magic is of course most prominent in exceptional circumstances when human life or welfare are at stake and psychic stress is intensified: sickness of children or other members of the family, or of cattle; attacks by poisonous snakes or other dangerous animals; pollution ("poisoning") of food or water; barrenness; tensions between families. The community needs protection in case of epidemics or plagues, drought, and so forth. In the past, magic was a necessary complement to military operations.

Those who cherish private desires or grudges (envy, fear) may also have recourse to magic. Antisocial rites of sorcery are proscribed by common opinion; countermagic, however, is desirable against malevolent ghosts such as *churel*s (women who died in childbirth) or deceased first wives who appear envious of their husband's second partner. Aggressive rites of countermagic are also well known from Sri Lanka *(kodivina)* and elsewhere. Witchcraft is still widely believed in and women in certain positions (e.g., daughters-in-law) are often suspected of it. Persecution of witches is occasionally reported.

Magicians and Their Position. In South Asian religious tradition (Buddhist as well as Hindu) the common opinion has always been that the endeavor to manipulate superhuman powers, even if possible, is inferior (because motivated by immediate worldly ends) and therefore detracts man from his ultimate purpose: release from mundane existence. But practice and theory are widely divergent. Ironically, creative and influential religious leaders who were guides on the road to release have often been credited by the popular imagination with powers of miracle working. Thus, for instance, the Buddha is said to have miraculously crossed the Ganges only a moment before his death *(Mahāparinibbāna Sutta).* Of his disciples, especially Moggallāna (Skt., Maudgalyāyana) is known to have possessed an enormous store of supernatural power (Pali, *iddhi, Aṅguttara Nikāya* 1.23, etc.), which he used for such ends as the humiliation of conceited supernatural beings. In later Indian Buddhist as well as Hindu tradition, Siddha Nāgārjuna (eighth century CE?, often confused with the philosopher Nāgārjuna) has earned fame as an alchemist, inventor of elixirs, and author of magical books. [*See also* Alchemy, *article on* Indian Alchemy.]

In practice, magic is most often entrusted to a recognized specialist. As religious functionaries, the brahman, the village priest, and the diviner or exorcist can act on complementary levels. The latter might be characterized by his knowledge of *mantra*s (probably corruptions from some Tantric written source), his familiarity with and supremacy over relevant lesser deities and spirits, his ability for the diagnosis and cure of disease, and his strength of character, which inspires confidence in his clients. After thorough training, he settles as an independent practitioner who is remunerated by his clientele; his status depends on his personal qualities, not on ascription or heredity. In different regions, he bears different titles, for instance *ojha, gunia, baiga,* or *bhagat.* These titles can also overlap and be in vogue in the same place for different functions; thus, the *bhagat* may work through possession by his favorite deity, while the *ojha* claims mastery over the spirit world by means of his mantric expertise. In hinduized regions, the *ojha* can be a degraded brahman; in Buddhist countries, magic is sometimes practiced by monks. Also in tribal communities, the functions of village priest and healer-magician tend to be separated, although the village priest can help people through possession by or invocation of his deity. The functionary who sincerely and successfully works for the common weal is highly respected; but unscrupulous people who lend themselves to antisocial activities are disliked and feared.

Magic in South Asia is rooted in both high-status religion (where it has been relegated to a marginal position) and popular (or tribal) tradition. Although it is usually associated with the latter, there has been constant interaction between the two spheres. But respectable people, even if not denying the possibility that "things are done," have a definite conviction that they are done in circles of low repute.

BIBLIOGRAPHY

A comprehensive historical or phenomenological study of Indian magic has not yet been written. Data must be gathered from extremely dispersed sources. Vedic magic is covered in Hermann Oldenberg's *Die Religion des Veda*, 2d ed. (Stuttgart, 1917), pp. 465–522, and in Jan Gonda's *Vedic Literature (Saṃhitās and Brāhmaṇas)*, vol. 1, fasc. 1, or *A History of Indian Literature* (Wiesbaden, 1975). Studies on Vedic magic most often concentrate on the *Atharvaveda;* see Maurice Bloomfield's *The Atharvaveda and the Gopathabrāhmaṇa* (Strassburg, 1899), N.J. Shende's *The Religion and Philosophy of the Atharvaveda* (Poona, 1952), and Margaret Stutley's *Ancient Indian Magic and Folklore: An Introduction* (Boulder, 1980). Many particulars on "sanskritized" magic can be found in my book *Māyā Divine and Human* (Delhi, 1978). Two of the many books and articles concerning the role of magic in tribal communities of South Asia by dedicated workers in the field are *Tribal Religion* (Delhi, 1978), by Joseph Troisi (see especially pages 199–237), and *Maria Murder and Suicide*, 2d ed. (Oxford, 1950), by Verrier Elwin (see pages 61–81). Although much of the data in William Crooke's *The Popular Religion and Folk-lore of Northern India* (1894), 2 vols., 2d ed., rev. (Delhi, 1968), is antiquated, there is much of interest to recommend it. Beni Gupta's *Magical Beliefs and Superstitions* (Delhi, 1979), although substandard, is also recommended for its interesting data on popular Hinduism. Gupta concentrates on Rajasthan. A recent historical study of witchcraft and sorcery is Rajaram N. Saletore's *Indian Witchcraft: A Study in Indian Occultism* (New Delhi, 1981). For an interesting article on witchcraft, see Scarlett Epstein's "A Sociological Analysis of Witch Beliefs in a Mysore Village," in *Magic, Witchcraft and Curing*, edited by John Middleton (Garden City, N.Y., 1967), pp. 135–154. Data from Sri Lanka can be found in Paul Wirz's *Exorcism and the Art of Healing in Ceylon* (Leiden, 1954) and in a more recent study by Gananath Obeyesekere, "Sorcery, Premeditated Murder and the Canalization of Aggression in Sri Lanka," *Ethnology* 14 (1975): 1–23.

TEUN GOUDRIAAN

Magic in East Asia

Magic and mantic arts are endemic in Chinese life and prominent in the religions of China, both in popular religion and in Buddhism and Taoism. The same is true of Korea and Japan, where indigenous beliefs have been overlaid by the cultural influence of China. The magical practices of China found ready acceptance in Korea and Japan. Although many of the practices traveled on their own, religion—chiefly Buddhism, which had already absorbed elements of Chinese popular beliefs and of Taoism—was an important vehicle for the transfer of Chinese magic. The result was an amalgam of magical lore in East Asia, with Chinese knowledge often providing a frame to which specifically Korean or Japanese practices and permutations were affixed.

China. In general, we should distinguish between magic, which provides a means to accomplish specific ends (through spells, gestures, amulets, talismans, and the like), and various occult sciences (such as yarrow-stalk divination with the *Book of Changes*, astrology, hemerology, geomancy, and alchemy), even though this distinction was not strongly maintained in the traditional Chinese schema of magic and the occult. There was in fact a fluid boundary between magic (where there was no cause for rationalization) and occult sciences, which were elaborated in terms of a theory of symbolic correspondence based on the concepts of *yin-yang* dualism and of Five Actions (*wu-hsing:* water, fire, wood, metal, and earth). Not only was this theory the product of prior conceptions of the magical power of fire, water, and other primary forces in nature (e.g., wind), but even after its full elaboration the symbolic correspondences did not negate the validity of magical practices. Not infrequently, occult theory supplied a *modus operandi* for magic and religious worship. For example, an astrological instrument designed to calculate the position of the Big Dipper (Chinese archaeology has recently brought to light a second-century BCE specimen of the device) was used by the usurper Wang Mang to direct the power of the Dipper against his enemies in 23 CE. From the beginning, this astrological instrument served as one means for conjuring the god of the Dipper and polestar (talismanic replicas of the constellation cast in metal were also used). The same instrument was influential in Taoist star magic, and it was the model for an astrological *maṇḍala* in the esoteric Buddhism of the T'ang period (618–907 CE). Similarly, the hemerological symbols of the calendrical cycle were not simply neutral signs marking the passage of time; they constituted a succession of spirits whose magical powers could be summoned through spells and talismans.

The Warring States (403–221 BCE), Ch'in (221–207 BCE), and Han (206 BCE–220 CE) periods were the formative age for Chinese magic. Earlier, magic was employed in dealings with the spirits and was important in the royal ancestral religion of the Shang and early Chou (c. sixteenth–eighth centuries BCE). But the proliferation of magical arts, and an increasing differentiation between magic as employed in archaic religion and magic for its own sake, began during the Warring States and continued to develop in Ch'in-Han times. The history of Chinese magic in later centuries followed from the developments of this period. It was during the same period that the theory of symbolic correspondence was formulated, and developments in occult sciences paralleled significantly those in magic.

Before the Warring States the principal practitioners of magic were the *wu*, a class of female (and in lesser numbers, male) shamans who mediated between the human and spirit worlds. Their methods included trances in which spirits might descend into their bodies or in which the shaman might journey into the spirit world, invocations and maledictions, and the utilization of magical materials to either attract or repel the spirits. Their functions overlapped those of incantators *(chu)* and other ritual officiants; however, the latter did not engage in ecstatic trances. The Warring States and Ch'in-Han periods witnessed the decline in prestige of these shamans, who came to be increasingly associated with witchcraft; the rise of occult specialists *(fang-shih,* literally "masters of recipes"), whose skills extended to magical operations; and the formation of a Taoist clergy, who adapted magic to fill the needs of the newly emergent religion (organized Taoist religious communities made their first appearance in the second century CE). The general populace also practiced forms of superstitious magic in the course of daily life.

Historical records of Han rulers who favored shamans and masters of recipes provide an important source of information about ancient Chinese magic. Liu Ch'e (posthumously titled Wu Ti; r. 140–87 BCE), for example, established cults for shamans and made his court a gathering place for masters of recipes who claimed to possess magical powers and the secrets of immortality. One master of recipes, Li Shao-weng, was a psychopomp who gained Liu Ch'e's favor by conjuring the ghost of the ruler's recently deceased concubine; he was executed after he was exposed for fabricating portents. Near the end of Liu Ch'e's reign the court was paralyzed by an outbreak of a type of shamanic witchcraft known as *ku*. The word *ku* referred to a demonic affliction that attacked its victim as the result of witchcraft. According to some accounts, *ku* was a poison produced by sealing certain creatures in a vessel until only one remained, which became the *ku*. The tradition that the *ku* is a magical potion cultivated by women and passed down through generations is still alive today. Men who ingested the *ku* were believed to die and become the demon-slaves of the *ku* and its keeper. In two of the witchcraft incidents at Liu Ch'e's court the *ku* agent was discovered to be a wooden effigy buried in the ground, where it was intended to bring harm to the ruler. There were other cases of witchcraft during the Han period in which shamans were hired to work black magic.

Accusations of charlatanism against masters of recipes and fear of shamanic witchcraft were widespread during the Han period. A negative perception of magical practices crystallized around the government's concern for its own political and spiritual authority. All magic and occultism were potentially subversive. They incited social unrest and infringed upon the holiness of the monarch, whose position as the Son of Heaven made him the only legitimate authority to oversee dealings with the spirit world. Popular religious cults not under the direct control of the government were branded "abusive worship" *(yin-ssu),* and ordinary citizens could be executed if caught illicitly performing magic or uttering imprecations. Such practices were identified as the "way of the left" *(tso-tao).* The word *left* did not connote the sinister aspects Western cultures associate with the left. Rather, in cosmo-ritual symbolism the left was the ruler's position of honor, and those who practiced the way of the left were abusing powers belonging properly to the ruler.

The Taoist sects that arose in the second century CE inveighed against those who placed their faith in shamans, worshiped demons, and believed the occultists' shams. These practices were an offense to the true deities of the Tao. Taoist liturgy incorporated many elements of popular worship, however, and the clergy engaged in many of the magical practices that they condemned in others. Indeed, in the eyes of the Han government the Taoist sects were rebel organizations whose religion represented simply another outbreak of "abusive worship." For the Taoist sects the fundamental issue was heterodoxy—the use of magic not sanctioned by religious authority. But in the continual process of syncretization that occurred over the centuries as Taoism interacted with popular religion and with Buddhism, the standard of orthodoxy fluctuated.

The Buddhist attitude toward magic was similar. Illicit magical practices fell under the category of the "arts of Māra" *(mo-shu),* Māra being the tempter and chief of malevolent demons. *Mo-shu* parallels other Chinese terms such as "shamanic arts" *(wu-shu)* and "way of the left" in referring to the forms of magic prohibited by the orthodox church (and the government).

However, as early as the fifth century CE there was a tradition of Buddhist spell-casting in China rivaling the Taoist practices. Buddhist magic was most prominent in the esoteric practices of Tantrism. The Tantric literature contained magical formulas to be used to gain prosperity or harm adversaries; Tantric *mantras*, *mudrās*, and *maṇḍalas* were utilized as instruments for working magic. Tantric magic incorporated elements of native Chinese magic and occultism, while at the same time enriching Taoist and popular practices.

Most of our knowledge of actual magical procedures in premodern times comes from Taoist and Buddhist writing, which naturally reflect the practices of Taoism and Buddhism. Recently, Chinese archaeologists have discovered manuscripts from the third and second centuries BCE that describe magic as it was practiced in the ancient popular religion and occult tradition. Two of the manuscripts are almanacs that are strikingly similar to Chinese almanacs in use today and attest to a continuity in magic and occult practice. The Chinese almanacs combine information on portents to watch for during the year with material on spells, talismans, and other magical devices.

Many of the common forms of magic described in premodern sources are still practiced. There are spells to summon deities and to drive off demons (versions of popular, Taoist, and Buddhist spells are preserved). Spitting and spouting water over which a spell has first been uttered is another common device (sometimes Taoist or Buddhist priests will spout ignited alcohol). Substances believed to have magical properties are often identified in traditional materia medica. Amber, for example, wards off nightmare demons and is used in making headrests. Amulets to be hung in the open or worn on the body exist in many forms. Peachwood amulets are perhaps the most ancient. Talismans *(fu)* made from strips of silk and inscribed with undecipherable writing have been discovered in a second century BCE tomb. A medical manuscript discovered in the same tomb includes a recipe for curing *ku* witchcraft by burning a talisman, scattering its ashes over sheep broth, and bathing the victim with the brew. Water over which the ashes of talismans have been scattered has been used in Taoism to cure sickness since the time of the earliest Taoist sects. Taoism talismans inscribed with symbols and magic writing have many uses. The deities are summoned with talismans, which may be used in conjunction with spells. And, in addition to using the ashes, Taoists may wear talismans as phylacteries or swallow them in order for them to take effect. Love magic is represented in a second century BCE manuscript that provides recipes for two philters with which a person can "obtain the object of desire." Another example in the same manuscript is a recipe that instructs a person engaged in a lawsuit to write the opponent's name on a slip and insert it in a shoe, magically trampling the opponent.

Korea and Japan. In Korea, cults formed around female shamans were a source of native Korean magic. This popular religion is known as Mu-sok ("shamanic customs"). Contacts between Korea and China began well before the T'ang, but increased markedly during that period. Knowledge of Chinese magic and occultism was part of the general flow of Chinese culture into Korea. And the initial impact of Chinese religion—before, for example, there was a more sophisticated understanding of Buddhist theology—was an admiration for its great magical power as compared with native practices. Chinese political institutions and ethics were also influential in the formation of the early Korean kingdoms. In general, the antagonism between government and practitioners of magic, and between Buddhism and popular religion, followed along lines similar to the situation in China.

In the native religion of Japan, which came to be known as Shintō ("way of the spirits") after Buddhism took hold, there were two categories of religious personnel. The *miko* (female shaman) was a medium into whose body a spirit might descend, sharing essential characteristics with shamans throughout East Asia. The *kannushi* (spirit controller) was more in the nature of a priest who oversaw the worship of the spirits. As with the shamans in China, the *miko* were increasingly associated with witchcraft, whereas the *kannushi* came to function as officiants in the state cult. Esoteric tantric Buddhism had a strong influence in Japan, leading to a syncretism of Shintō and Chinese-Buddhist magic. Buddhist ascetics called *hijiri* (sage) and *yamabushi* (mountain recluse) traced their origins to the eighth century CE and were renowned for their magical powers. As in Korea, in Japan other forms of Chinese magic and occultism were absorbed into the culture.

BIBLIOGRAPHY

Blacker, Carmen. *The Catalpa Bow.* London, 1975. A well-documented and groundbreaking study of shamanistic traditions in Japan, both from a historical and contemporary perspective.

Chang Chu-keun. "Mu-sok: The Shaman Culture of Korea." In *Folk Culture in Korea,* edited by Chun Shin-yong, pp. 59–88. Seoul, 1982. A more popular account of Korean shamanism.

Groot, J. J. M. de. *The Religious System of China* (1892–1910). 6 vols. Reprint, Taipei, 1967. A comprehensive description of religion in China, valuable for its copious translations of primary sources.

Haguenauer, Charles M. "Sorciers et sorcières de Corée." *Bulletin de la Maison Franco-Japonaise* (Tokyo) 2 (1929): 47–65. A scholarly examination of shamanism and magic in Korea.

Ngo Van Xuyet. *Divination, magie et politique dans la Chine ancienne.* Paris, 1976. An excellent study of magic and occultism in the formative Ch'in-Han period, including a translation of the chapter of biographies of occult specialists in the *Hou Han shu* (Documents of the Later Han).

Sieffert, René. "Le monde du sorcier au Japon." In *Le monde du sorcier,* "Sources orientales," vol. 7, pp. 355–389. Paris, 1966. An excellent survey of the practice of magic in Japan, with a detailed discussion of magic in Buddhism and Shintō.

DONALD HARPER

MAGICO-RELIGIOUS POWERS. The term *power* here refers to the energy or ability that enables an individual to cause a desired effect. The essence of magic is that it utilizes techniques that are mysterious to its beholders and commonplace to its masters. [*See* Magic.] Religious powers are magical in the above sense but are equally mysterious to master and beholder. Those who wield religious powers may operate as mediums for some higher divine being, who is presumed to be the master of the power and who knows how the effects are caused.

Belief in the existence of magical powers has existed in many cultures. One of the most elaborate formulations of various kinds of magico-religious powers is found in the Buddhist Abhidharma Piṭaka, the multivolumed philosophical commentary on the teachings of the Buddha. In the "inner sciences" *(adhyātmavidyā)* section of the Abhidharma Piṭaka, magical powers are classified according to a basic scheme of six "superknowledges" *(abhijña),* as follows: (1) magical power, or *ṛddhi,* which derives from the concentration of the will—it makes possible teleportation, thought transference, and the ability to see things from a great distance, (2) clairaudience, (3) telepathy, (4) memory of former lives, (5) knowledge of future lives, and (6) liberation, or cessation of mental defilements. The first five powers can be attained by both ordinary people and saints, but the sixth can be attained only by saints. All six are wisdoms *(prajñā)* derived from ectatic releases attained in the four contemplative realms of the heavens of form.

In this Abhidharma scheme are also magical creations, or *nirmāṇa,* which belong either to the desire realm (the realm of bodies that consist of matter, odor, taste, and texture) or the form heavens (the heavens where bodies consist only of matter and texture). These two categories are further subdivided into those creations formed when a magician either transforms only himself or creates another being entirely. Only a Buddha can emanate limitless creations. Magical powers can be innate among nonhuman beings; for humans, they can be generated by meditation, spells, *mantras*, medicines, or past karmic actions.

Such typologies of superknowledges and powers are connected with Buddhist categories of beings, of which there are six types: gods, titans, humans, animals, hungry ghosts, and hell-beings. In addition, there are selfless beings, saints, *bodhisattvas*, and Buddhas. Some of the superknowledges are possessed naturally by gods. Even hell-beings are naturally telepathic and can remember previous lives. Humans can achieve superknowledges by entering into the contemplative states of the realm-form abodes of the gods, which can be done by systematic trance, the use of drugs, incantations, or by a powerful evolutionary imprint derived from an act in a former life.

A Hindu classification of magical powers is found in the *Yoga Sūtras* of Patañjali, an Indian scholar of the second century BCE. The *Yoga Sūtras* discuss those powers attainable through the withdrawal of subtle energies from their habitual investment in the gross physical body of the yogin. A modern scholar of yoga, H. Chaudhuri, has divided these powers as follows: (1) extrasensory perceptions and mental powers, (2) physical powers, (3) wisdom powers and transcendent powers, and (4) ecstatic powers. Under the first category are included the first five superknowledges of the Buddhist classification, with the addition of heightened senses, knowledge of the cosmos, knowledge of the interior aspects of the body, knowledge of all words, and comprehension of the sounds of animals. Under the second category of physical powers are included the eight great powers of the body: the ability to (1) shrink into the microworld, (2) expand into the macroworld, (3) levitate, (4) increase in weight, (5) travel through the cosmos, (6) manifest instant wish-fulfillment, (7) create objects, minds, souls, and societies and transform oneself and others, and (8) control one's own physiology and emotions and the thoughts and actions of others. In addition, the powers of the body include the powers to transmit psychic energy, heal, feed on air, generate inner bliss, raise the dead, create mass illusions, shine radiantly, and so on. Under the category of wisdom powers and transcendent powers are included knowledge of reality, the absolute, the subtle and causal realms, the essence of forms, oneness, law, bliss, and so on. Finally, the category of ecstatic powers consists of ecstasies that arise from union with the divine, which is seen as the creative energy at the root of all life in its playful restoration of the world.

Mircea Eliade (1969), seeking to develop a typology that would incorporate religious phenomena from all cultures, discerned three main types of powers: (1) shamanic or "ecstatic" powers; (2) yogic or "enstatic" powers; and (3) the powers of a *jīvanmukta,* one who has attained liberation while still living. Ecstatic practices are externally directed experiences in which the practitioner attempts to leave his physical body; enstatic practices are internally directed experiences in which the practitioner attempts to withdraw himself from the physical world. Among shamanic phenomena, he has discerned as essential four types: (1) an initiatory experience involving dismemberment and descent and ascent within a multilevel cosmos, (2) the ability to the soul to travel, (3) the mastery of fire, and (4) the ability to change shape and assume animal forms.

The Hindu and Buddhist Tantras provide the most complete explanation of magical powers and the psychophysical causality underlying their manifestations. Key to Tantric analyses of powers are notions of the subtle body and mind. Tantric theories are concerned with both the physical and the mental in their metaphysical assumptions. They tend to repudiate the relevance of body-mind dualism, yet they consider analyses of the relationship of the body and mind to be philosophically useful.

Buddhist Tantric theoreticians refer to the final nature of reality as "emptiness" *(śūnyatā);* Hindu Tantric theoreticians refer to it as the Absolute *(brahman).* They consider that the cosmos follows a coherent patterning that is beyond final characterization as matter or mind. It is pure energy that can be reached and controlled most effectively by the human nervous system while focused on precise and subtle imagery. According to the Tantras, no machine can be as sensitive and finely tuned as the mind. Every being has unconscious contact with this subtlest energy of life. In dreams, it is this energy that constructs the experiential facsimile of self and environment. In death, it is this energy that gradually withdraws from the senses and body and then constructs a "between state" *(bar do)* form that seeks a new rebirth.

The shaman or yogin who seeks to transcend the ordinary gross world of birth and death employs ecstatic and contemplative techniques to withdraw this energy from its habitual investment in the activities of the senses and the gross body. Once the identification with the gross body/mind complex is abandoned, a subtle form emerges that can identify directly with the subtle energy on the subatomic level. This level is beyond the three normal states of waking, dreaming, and sleeping/unconsciousness. Using a building code of "seed mantras," the yogin then builds a new gross reality where the sleep/unconsciousness is fused with absolute reality and the dream consciousness is fused with a beatific, heavenly reality. In this reality, the yogin is no longer subject to the rigid "laws" of a material objective world but is in a dreamlike world that can be shaped at will. If the yogin is still egotistical, then his ability to influence the world is very limited, but if, in the process of disidentification with the gross material self, he has transcended habitual ego drives, then his will is directed only by compassion for others, and his ability to reshape the world is enormous.

In the case of the shaman, the same processes are involved, but there is no technical description of the coarse and subtle body/mind complex. The wisdom the shaman desires to attain is available in culturally developed archetypes: in the nature spirits and deities that emerge from the subtle reality to shape the world. Thus, the initiatory experiences of the shaman involve images of dissolution and dismemberment and correspond to the yogic process of withdrawal from the gross physical body. For the shaman, the subtle energy is dismembered from the gross senses and body. The shaman's ecstatic journeys to heavens and hells correspond to the yogin's experimentation with the simulated "between state" or "dream state"; it is in this state that the subtle energy, in the form of a subtle body/mind, explores the inner universe and learns to wield the seed patterns of world-construction. The shaman's mastery of fire (and of the other gross elements, especially wind, the subtlest) corresponds to the yogin's mastery of the process of reconstruction of gross reality. And the feats of soul catching, shape changing, and so on are all part of the repertoire of healing and world-mending techniques through which the fully adept shaman serves his or her community.

This general Tantric explanatory framework makes it possible to understand the ecstatic and enstatic tendencies observed by Eliade, not as exclusive techniques of contradictory disciplines, but as phases or aspects of a universal process, the development of magico-religious powers. Thus the enstatic preoccupations of the Hindu yogin or Buddhist monk *(bhikṣu),* while clearly concerned with liberation from the world, correspond to the initiatory dissolution stage for the shaman or adept. Here the term *world* refers to the entrapment of the subtle body/mind energies in the gross body and senses. The individual must first enstatically withdraw from the world; once freedom from it has been attained, true ecstatic experiences can ensue, as the subtle body/mind journeys in the dream state or between state beyond the realm of the gross body/mind. The next stage, that of the "liberated person" *(jīvanmukta)* or "great adept" *(mahāsiddha),* is a stage where the subtle form is voluntarily (according to Buddhist Tantra) or playfully (according to Hindu Tantra) engaged with the world of social reality, and where the enstatic/ecstatic dichotomy has been reconciled in balance. In this stage, the yogin as *bodhisattva-siddha* or *jīvanmukta* creates manifestations, self-transformations, transmutations of others, and so on, in order to help others overcome their delusions and passions, just as the shaman works to heal his community.

The above framework for understanding magico-religious powers in general helps to organize the variety of such religious phenomena that occur in all cultures. In most cultures, such powers are routinely attributed to superhuman or subhuman species, such as gods, angels, fairies, dragons, underworld serpent-spirits, demons, and sometimes malevolent ancestors or ghosts who have somehow been stuck in a between state from which they discontentedly molest the world. Some cultures, such as the Tibetan or the Amerindian, have hundreds of species of such nonhuman beings.

According to the Tantras, magical powers can be inborn or can be obtained through drugs, spells, ascetic energy, or contemplation *(samādhi)*. Any of these methods can be combined with the propitiation of a deity or spirit who possesses such powers and who can be cajoled or coerced into sharing them. In shamanic cultures, a person might have an innate calling to be a shaman or might be inducted into shamanic practices by means of ceremonies using drugs. He also might receive shamanic powers as the gift of a deity or spirit or might develop them by generating ascetic energy through an ordeal or vision quest. Spells and contemplations are widely used, but they are not systematically employed in shamanic cultures as they are in the magical traditions of the East.

In general, it seems that humans who come to possess magical powers may do so in three main ways: as mediums, by way of possession by a deity or spirit; as instruments, by way of election or commission by a spirit or deity; and as free agents, by way of their own attainment of mastery of the subtle body/mind.

In the Buddhist Tantras, powers are first divided into extraordinary and ordinary. The extraordinary power is that of Buddhahood. The general power of Buddhahood is considered to be total freedom from all faults as well as possession of all excellences, including a virtual omniscience. With Buddhahood comes an enormous number of specific powers. A Buddha's powers are thought to be greater than those of a god (neither a Buddha nor a god possesses the power to create a universe, which is an evolutionary or karmic development in one respect and is beginningless in another). A Buddha is defined as one who is able to transform himself into anything, including inanimate objects (as many at a time as he wishes), out of his interest in helping beings. A Buddha can travel anywhere (even many places at once) at the speed of thought and can temporarily transform any other person into another form. The supreme miracle he works is the education of others, thereby providing them with the means of achieving their own freedom. A Buddha's powers are believed to be inconceivable in scope.

The Buddhist Tantras divide the ordinary powers into categories of inferior, mediocre, and superior. The inferior ones are attained through ritual and contemplative magic and are said to consist of pacifying (diseases, evil forces, or obstacles), increasing (life, harvests, wealth, or happiness), controlling (enemies, demons, or oppressors), and destroying (evil). The mediocre powers include the ability to levitate, become invisible, control zombies, and so on. They are organized into the "eight great powers," whose vehicles are (1) eye ointment, (2) foot ointment, (3) mouth-sword (enabling one to fly), (4) magic pill of invisibility and transformation, (5) alchemy of life and body, and (6) alchemy of fortune. They also include (7) the power to find underworld treasure and (8) mastery of women and female spirits. The superior powers include sky walking (the ability to visit different universes), *mantra* holding (similar to the control of the subtle patterning force discussed earlier), and universal sovereignty (enabling one to pacify the world).

The world of magical powers bears a striking resemblance to the world of scientific technology in that it is an expression of the age-old human desire to understand, control, and even to transform nature. This goal is clearly expressed in the desire to attain magical powers, in the systems of knowledge and means of practice designed to attain them, and in the mythic vistas of how they should be employed to better human life. The difference in the nonmodern systems is that the emphasis is on *inner* understanding, control, and transformation. The "outer sciences" of material technologies *(śilpa)*, medicine *(vicikitsā)*, reason and communication *(pramāṇa)*, and linguistics *(śabda)* all deal with the natural and social environments. But the supreme science for the ancients of India was the "inner science" *(adhyātmavidyā)*, the philosophies, psychologies, and interior technologies of understanding, controlling and transforming the subjective self. This was considered the most practical method of mastery of the world.

[*See also* Shamanism; Yoga; *and* Tantrism.]

BIBLIOGRAPHY

Bengali Baba, ed. and trans. *Yogasūtra of Patañjali, with the Commentary of Vyāsa.* Delhi, 1976.

Beyer, Stephan. *The Cult of Tārā: Magic and Ritual in Tibet.* Berkeley, 1973.

Bhattacharyya, Benoytosh. *Introduction to Buddhist Esotericism.* London, 1932.

Eliade, Mircea. *Yoga: Immortality and Freedom.* 2d ed. Princeton, 1969.

La Vallée Poussin, Louis de, trans. *L'Abhidharmakośa de Vasubandhu* (1923–1931). 6 vols. Brussels, 1971.

ROBERT A. F. THURMAN

MAGNA MATER. *See* Cybele.

MAGYAR RELIGION. *See* Hungarian Religion.

MAHĀBHĀRATA. Hindu India's national epic takes its name from Bharata, an ancestor of the central family of heroes. It is the story of his descendants, the Bhāratas or Kurus. The *Mahābhārata* (Great Story of the Bhāratas) is a massive encyclopedic text. In one famous verse it claims to contain everything. It is said to consist of 100,000 verses, although no known recension comes to quite that number. The text is also known as *Jaya* (Victory), a reference to its concern with the victory of *dharma* over *adharma* as assured by Kṛṣṇa, who as the incarnation of Viṣṇu guides the main action of the story. The text is further called the *Kārṣṇaveda* (Veda of Kṛṣṇa), a reference whose ambiguity may be intended since the text not only is concerned with this Kṛṣṇa but is alleged to have been written by Kṛṣṇa Dvaipāyana, the "island-born Kṛṣṇa," whose more familiar name is Vyāsa. Finally, it is called the "fifth Veda," indicating the importance that the epic's brahman poets attached to its prolongation of the Vedic heritage. The epic is a *smṛti* ("traditional") rather than *śruti* ("revealed") text, but its reputed author, Vyāsa, is the very person whom epic and classical mythology credits with the "division" of the Vedas into four.

The actual composition of the epic seems to have been carried out between about 500 BCE to 400 CE. The authors, however, probably drew on older bardic traditions with roots in Aryan lore of much greater antiquity. The central story is set in the area of the Ganges-Yamunā doab, and recalls tribal kingdoms that had settled in and around that area, after earlier residence in the Punjab, from about 1000–500 BCE. It is sometimes assumed that the Painted Gray Ware culture of this period provided the historical setting for a real war, of which the text of the *Mahābhārata* is but an embellished account. More likely, if the Painted Gray Ware peoples transmitted an early version of the story, it was as part of their mythology, for the epic has an Indo-European mythological structure.

Scholarly work since the 1940s, initiated by Stig Wikander and Georges Dumézil, has shown that the text is essentially mythological, though not denying that it integrates much "didactic" material, particularly in its postwar books. It prolongs the Vedic heritage by correlating the epic story and its leading characters with Vedic, and in some cases para-Vedic and Indo-European, mythological figures and narrative (particularly eschatological) themes. More recent work has focused on the epic's treatment of the war as a "sacrifice of battle," relating the narrative to Indian sacrificial traditions, particularly from the Brāhmaṇas. Most notably, Madeleine Biardeau has shown that the treatment of Vedic mythology and Brahmanic sacrifice in the epic forms part of a *bhakti* rereading of the Vedic revelation *(śruti)*. From this perspective the epic is the first and grandest monument of *bhakti*, focused on Kṛṣṇa as the *avatāra* (incarnation) of Viṣṇu.

The main story begins when Viṣṇu and other gods descend or in some way assume human forms to relieve the burden of the goddess Earth, who is oppressed by demons. Following a succession crisis in the Lunar (i.e., Bhārata) dynasty, which rules India's "middle region," demons (*asuras*) infiltrate the royal lineages of the other kingdoms. In this situation two groups of cousins are born into the central lineage, each with its own succession claims: the five sons of King Pāṇḍu (the Pāṇḍavas) and the hundred sons (the Kauravas) of Pāṇḍu's older brother, Dhṛtarāṣṭra, who is prevented by blindness from ruling. The Pāṇḍavas are actually sons of gods, and their birth is part of the divine plan to rescue Earth. By means of a *mantra* their mothers (Kuntī, the senior wife of Pāṇḍu, and Mādrī, the junior wife) had invoked deities to sire them, thus circumventing a curse that would have caused Pāṇḍu's death had he had sexual relations with his wives. Thus, with Kuntī, the god Dharma sired Yudhiṣṭhira, Vāyu sired Bhīma, and Indra sired Arjuna; with Mādrī, the twin Aśvins sired the twins Nakula and Sahadeva.

Following the interpretation of Wikander and Dumézil, these groups of gods and heroes may be seen to represent a hierarchical axis within the Vedic (and Indo-European) pantheon that further evokes the order of the upper three Aryan classes (*varṇas*) and, more archaically, what Dumézil has called the three functions: (1) religious sovereignty and law (Dharma and Yudhiṣṭhira), (2) warfare (Vāyu and Bhīma, Indra and Arjuna), and (3) economic welfare and service (the Aśvins and the twins). While the Pāṇḍavas thus represent the nucleus of social and divine hierarchy and the principle of *dharma*, their hundred cousins—incarnations of *rākṣasas* (disruptive goblins), except for the eldest, Duryodhana, who is an incarnation of the *asura* Kali (Discord), the demon of the *kaliyuga*—represent undifferentiated chaos and *adharma*.

During their youth the two groups of cousins vie with each other and form alliances that continue into the war. Thus Karṇa, son of Kuntī and the sun god Sūrya (Kuntī had first tried out her *mantra* with Sūrya before marriage, and then abandoned the son), allies with Duryodhana. At the Pāṇḍavas' polyandric wedding with Draupadī (incarnation of Śrī, goddess of prosperity), they ally themselves with Draupadī's brother Dhṛṣṭadyumna, the incarnation of Agni (Fire), who will lead their army. It is also at the marriage of Draupadī that the Pāṇḍavas first meet their cousin Kṛṣṇa (who is Kuntī's brother's son) and consolidate their relation with him.

For a brief period the two parties divide the kingdom; the Kauravas retain the ancestral throne at Hāstinapura, while the Pāṇḍavas build a new palace at Indraprastha. But when Yudhiṣṭhira performs a Rājasūya sacrifice to lay claim to universal sovereignty, Duryodhana is inconsolable until his friends suggest he invite the Pāṇḍavas to a dice match and win their wealth at gambling. At the dice match Yudhiṣṭhira gambles away everything; the last stakes are his brothers, himself, and finally Draupadī. Duryodhana then orders his vilest brother, Duḥśāsana, to drag Draupadī into the assembly hall, and when she protests, Karṇa commands Duḥśāsana to disrobe her. But Duḥśāsana is unsuccessful, for new saris keep descending upon Draupadī—according to most versions, thanks to her prayer to Kṛṣṇa—to keep her covered. When Draupadī is thus miraculously saved, Dhṛtarāṣṭra grants her husbands their freedom and returns their weapons, which the Pāṇḍavas will use in the war to fulfill their vows to destroy Draupadī's offenders.

In a second gambling match the Pāṇḍavas lose again, and together with Draupadī they are exiled for thirteen years. The last year must be spent incognito if they are to get back their kingdom. They adopt disguises and escape detection, yet when the thirteen years are over Duryodhana refuses to return the Pāṇḍavas' half of the kingdom. But the brothers have spent their exile in pilgrimage and penance (Arjuna in particular has done *tapas* to get weapons from Śiva). Their last year in exile has the character of a *dīkṣā* (consecration preparatory to a sacrifice), and they have thus prepared themselves for the sacrifice of battle.

As the war looms, Kṛṣṇa's role becomes increasingly central. Although he serves as the Pāṇḍavas' peace ambassador and is himself sworn to noncombatancy, he actually prepares both sides for war. Then, just before the first day's battle, as Arjuna's charioteer he "sings" the *Bhagavadgītā*, thus convincing Arjuna of his duty to fight. The eighteen-day war on the plain of Kurukṣetra (an ancient sacrificial terrain) then follows, in which all the divine and demonic forces converge in a vast holocaust that has been variously interpreted as a sacrifice or as the end of the universe (*pralaya*). By leading the Pāṇḍavas to victory, Kṛṣṇa as *avatāra* achieves his task of relieving Earth's burden and renovating the *dharma* at the juncture between the *dvāpara* and *kaliyugas*, the latter of which is our present age.

[*See also* Kṛṣṇa; Bhagavadgītā; Arjuna; Kurukṣetra; *and* Epics. *For a general discussion of the structure of Indo-European mythology and social organization reflected in the text, see* Indo-European Religions, *overview article.*]

BIBLIOGRAPHY

The most accessible full translation is that by P. C. Roy and K. M. Ganguli, *The Mahabharata of Krishna-Dwaipayana Vyasa*, 12 vols. (1884–1896), 2d ed. (Calcutta, 1970). A partial translation by J. A. B. van Buitenen, *The Mahābhārata*, 3 vols. (Chicago, 1973–1978), covers five of the epic's eighteen books and is now being continued by several translators. C. V. Narasimhan's *The Mahābhārata* (New York, 1965) is the best abridgment.

Early work on the *Mahābhārata* culminates and is best summarized in E. Washburn Hopkins's *The Great Epic of India* (1901; reprint, Calcutta, 1969) and *Epic Mythology* (1915; reprint, New York, 1969). Stig Wikander's "Pāṇḍava-sagan och Mahābhāratas mytiska forutsattningar," *Religion och Bibel* 6 (1947): 27–39, can also be read in French in Georges Dumézil's *Jupiter Mars Quirinus*, vol. 4, *Explication de textes indiens et latins* (Paris, 1948). Dumézil's own most comprehensive treatment of the *Mahābhārata* can be found in his *Mythe et épopée*, vol. 1, *L'idéologie des trois fonctions dans les épopées des peuples indo-européens* (Paris, 1968).

Other works that develop various views in connection with Indo-European and Indian myth and ritual include Madeleine Biardeau's "Études de mythologie hindoue, Chap. II, Bhakti et avatāra," *Bulletin de l'École Française d'Extrême Orient* 63 (1976): 111–263 and 65 (1978): 87–238; Alf Hiltebeitel's *The Ritual of Battle: Krishna in the "Mahābhārata"* (Ithaca, N.Y., 1976); Heino Gehrts's *Mahābhārata: Das Geschehen und seine Bedeutung* (Bonn, 1975); and Jacques Scheuer's *Śiva dans le Mahābhārata* (Paris, 1982). See also Vishnu S. Sukthankar's *On the Meaning of the Mahābhārata* (Bombay, 1957), which emphasizes the epic's reliance upon Upaniṣadic formulations, and B. B. Lal's "Excavation at Hastināpura and Other Explorations in the Upper Gangā and Sutlej Basins, 1950–52," *Ancient India* 10/11 (1954/55): 5–151, which discusses epic place names in relation to Painted Gray Ware.

ALF HILTEBEITEL

MAHARAL OF PRAGUE. *See* Yehudah Löw ben Betsal'el.

MAHĀSĀṂGHIKA. One of the earliest of the non-Mahāyāna Buddhist "sects" (the so-called Eighteen Schools of Hīnayāna Buddhism), the Mahāsāṃghika has been generally considered the precursor of Mahāyāna. However, although the Mahāsāṃghika and its subschools espoused many of the most radical views later attributed to the "Great Vehicle," other factors and early schools also contributed to the development of this movement.

Early Development. Traditional accounts differ on the occasion and reason for the schism that gave rise to the Mahāsāṃghika. Some accounts claim that the Mahāsāṃghika separated from the Sthavira at the time of the Second Buddhist Council (Vaiśālī, c. 340 BCE), others, that it occurred during a third council (sometimes confused with *the* Third Council held at Pāṭaliputra under King Aśoka, 244 BCE). The reasons for the schism have also been much debated. It is agreed that the split was motivated by matters of monastic discipline, but scholars disagree on the precise issues at stake. Most Western scholars are inclined to accept that the Mahāsāṃghika represented the more lax position in matters of discipline. Less common is the position of those who would claim the opposite, pointing to the fact that the Mahāsāṃghika had a very conservative Vinaya and that its Prātimokṣa was as strict as that of other Hīnayāna schools. It seems therefore unlikely that laxness in monastic regulations was the motive for the split.

Moreover, recent scholarship tends to distinguish the dispute that provoked the Second Council, which ended in reconciliation in the order, from a dispute that probably occurred shortly thereafter (anywhere between sixteen and sixty years later). It was this latter dispute that produced the schism that divided the Hīnayāna schools into its two major camps, the Sthaviras and the Mahāsāṃghikas. Be that as it may, it seems obvious that the Mahāsāṃghika criticized the *arhat* ideal and exalted the image of the Buddha, turning the historical life of the founder into an event of secondary importance and the *arhat* ideal into an inferior goal. In this sense they were making an argument against tradition, and whatever the significance of their Vinaya may be, their doctrinal positions were clearly innovative.

Literature. The Mahāsāṃghika tendency to innovate can be seen also in the content and structure of their Tripiṭaka. Although in its early stages it is believed to have been comprised of only three parts (Sūtra, Vinaya, and Abhidharma), the Sūtra Piṭaka was later expanded so that the *Kṣudraka Āgama* became a separate Piṭaka called Saṃyukta Piṭaka. According to some sources this section came to include *"vaipulya sūtras,"* an expression that could refer to Mahāyāna texts. The last addition to the Mahāsāṃghika Tripiṭaka was a fifth section, the Dhāraṇī Piṭaka, a collection of spells and incantations. Some accounts, however, say that the fifth Piṭaka was a Bodhisattva Piṭaka, which presumably refers to a collection of Mahāyāna texts.

Unfortunately, little remains of this canon and it is now impossible to confirm or even clarify such general statements. The Prātimokṣa of the Mahāsāṃghika survives in its original Sanskrit, and part of the Vinaya survives in the Sanskrit work *Mahāvastu,* which claims in its colophon to be a work of the Lokottaravādin Mahāsāṃghika of Central India. Apart from these and a few fragments of the Vinaya and the Sūtra section of their canon found at Bāmiyān, the rest of the Indian texts of the school are lost. Even in translation only a few texts survive. There is a Chinese translation of their Vinaya by Fa-hsien, and what seems to be part of their Sūtra Piṭaka *(Ekottarāgama).* The latter text appears to be a translation from a prakritic language. There is also a distinct Mahāsāṃghika influence on a Dharmaguptaka text, the *Śāriputrābhidharma Śāstra.*

The *Mahāvastu*—the Buddhist Hybrid Sanskrit text of which was preserved in Nepal as a Mahāyāna Sūtra—represents only that section of the Vinaya that establishes the "historical" basis for monastic institutions, that is, the life and early ministry of the Buddha. It is primarily a biography of the Buddha from his meeting with Dīpaṃkara to his first sermon and the conversion of the first disciples. It also contains a number of *avadānas.* But it contains no material on matters of monastic discipline and its main narrative is interpolated with numerous digressions, mostly stories of the *jātaka* or *avadāna* genre. Although the oldest portions of this work must go back to the early stages of the formation of canonical Buddhism, it contains numerous late interpolations that place the extant recension in the fifth century CE.

Although the *Mahāvastu* is regarded as a transitional work, for the most part it does not show doctrinal leanings radically distinct from those of most Vinayas. There are, however, a few clear signs of those elements of doctrine and language that have been traditionally considered characteristics of Mahāsāṃghika, some of which also define Mahāyāna. The text speaks of the Buddha's *lokottara* ("supramundane") status, of his presence in the world only by dint of an illusion created in order to conform to the aspirations and perceptions of living beings. The fact that the *Mahāvastu* is written in Hybrid Sanskrit would seem to confirm the tradition according to which the Mahāsāṃghika used some form of Prakrit in their religious literature.

Doctrinal Developments. The most characteristic doctrine of the Mahāsāṃghika group are the famous "Five Points of Mahādeva" (sometimes attributed to a certain Bhadra), an attack on the *arhat* that has been the object of at least two interpretations: it can be regarded as an argument for more lax moral standards or it can be seen as an indirect way of arguing for the value of the *bodhisattva* ideal. These five points are (1) that an *arhat* can be seduced by another (*para-upahṛta*—meaning that he can have nocturnal emissions accompanied by an erotic dream); (2) that ignorance *(ajñāna)* is not totally absent in an *arhat* (his spiritual insight does not give him knowledge of profane matters); (3) that an *arhat* can have doubts *(kaṃkṣā);* (4) that an *arhat* can be surpassed by another *(para-vitīrṇa*—a term of obscure meaning); and (5) that an *arhat* can enter the higher stages of the path by uttering a phrase *(vacibheda)* such as "Oh, sorrow!" The exact meaning of these doctrines is far from obvious. Even the general intent is not transparent; one may ask if the Five Points imply that the *arhat* is more human than he was thought to be in other schools, or that he is weaker than others believe. Or is the implication that the *bodhisattva* path is superior? [*See also* Arhat.]

Other doctrines attributed to the Mahāsāṃghika are equally tantalizing. For instance, it is said that they held that only *prajñā* liberates, a thesis that may reflect an early emphasis on *prajñā* such as would have led to the eventual centrality of the Perfection of Wisdom (Prajñāpāramitā) literature in Mahāyāna. The Mahāsāṃghika seem also to have claimed that all word of the Buddha are *nītārtha;* that is, they are in no need of interpretation. But this may mean not so much that the canon needs no exegesis as that the Buddha when he preaches has no hidden intent except for what living beings may find in his words, according to their capacities. At least this would be the only way this doctrine could accord with other statements attributed to the Mahāsāṃghikas, for they held that the Buddha preaches all *dharmas* with one word, that he preaches even when he does not speak, and that there is no conventional truth *(saṃvṛtti-satya)* in his Dharma. [*See also* Language, *article on* Buddhist Views of Language.]

Buddhology. Also characteristic of the Mahāsāṃghika is the belief that there are many Buddhas in all of the ten directions and at all times in the past, the present, and the future. In this they differ from more conservative Buddhists who believe that a Buddha is a rare phenomenon. But the Mahāsāṃghika claim may be another side of the doctrine that has been called "Buddhist docetism," that is, the belief that Buddhas do not lead a human life, even when they seem to be appearing in history. Perhaps related to this doctrine is the notion that *bodhisattvas* make a vow *(praṇidhāna)* to remain in the cycle of transmigration for the sake of sentient beings. They prolong their stay voluntarily; in fact, *bodhisattvas* may choose a life in hell for the sake of living beings. [*See also* Bodhisattva Path.]

Sectarian Outgrowths. Of the various sects that issued from the Mahāsāṃghika, the most important are the Lokottaravādins and the Prajñaptivādins. It has been suggested that these two branches represent two major doctrinal departures as well as two geographical centers of activity. Although both branches and their derivatives were active in more than one part of India, the Lokottaravādin group centered in the North (Mathurā), the Prajñaptivādin groups in the southeast of India. It also seems that the northern groups preferred Sanskrit as their canonical language, whereas the groups in the South used Prakrit. Doctrinally, however, the distinction is difficult to maintain, since the traditional sources are often contradictory.

Lokottaravāda. The Lokottaravādins seem to have emphasized the general docetic tendencies of the Mahāsāṃghika more than did the other subschools. Unfortunately, as the sources seem to conflate all doctrines of the Mahāsāṃghika splinter groups into their general description of the Mahāsāṃghika, it is difficult to distinguish one from the other or from the parent school. The tenet from which the Lokottaravāda derives its name, the belief that the "career," or sequence of lives leading to and including the complete enlightenment of Buddhas, is only a series of apparitional events, is also attributed to the main school. According to this doctrine, Buddhas are supramundane; that is, they are not human beings but perfectly pure spiritual beings, free from the limitations of a physical body. This doctrine can be recognized in at least one key passage in the *Mahāvastu,* but it is far from being the dominant theme in that work. This does not necessarily prove that the belief was not as central to the school as claimed by the doxographers. It may be that much of the Mahāsāṃghika doctrinal speculation took place in the Abhidharma and the commentarial literature of the school—all of which is now lost. The monastic, meditational, and liturgical life of the communities probably did not reflect the doctrinal rifts that defined the schools.

Prajñaptivāda. In contrast to the general Mahāsāṃghika view, this subschool held that all statements of doctrine are merely of provisional or purely conventional meaning. Still, the Prajñaptivadins appear to have preserved some distinction between absolute and relative truths. In spite of the obscurity of this notion, one can see the connection between it and certain ideas of the Bahuśrutīyas. This may be due to a common origin from the Gokulika branch of the Mahāsāṃghika.

From the Prajñaptivāda arose other groups, the most important being the Aparaśailas and the Pūrvaśailas, whose main center of activity was in Dhānyakaṭaka (modern Andhra Pradesh). They seem to have counted in their literature some works of Mahāyāna tendency, perhaps even Prajñāpāramitā texts in Prakrit.

If the Bahuśrutīya school is also an offshoot of the parent Mahāsāṃghika line then we would have to count among Mahāsāṃghika literature Harivarman's scholastic treatise, the *Satyasiddhiśāstra* (third century CE). This work clearly occupies an intermediate position between the Abhidharma of the Hīnayāna schools and the philosophical treatises of Mahāyāna.

Influence. Direct Mahāsāṃghika influence did not extend beyond the Indian subcontinent. But through its influence in the formation of Mahāyāna the school left its mark in the history of Buddhism in East Asia and Tibet. Its key doctrines—the centrality of *prajñā,* the *bodhisattva* vows, the apparitional life of the Buddha, the distinction between conventional and absolute truth—even today continue to affect Buddhist Mahāyāna perception of the world and of the Buddhist tradition.

[*For an overview of the relationship of the Mahāsāṃghikas to the other schools of early Buddhism, see* Buddhism, Schools of, *article on* Hīnayāna Buddhism. *For further discussion of Buddhist docetism, see* Buddha.]

BIBLIOGRAPHY

Aung, Shwe Zan, and C. A. F. Rhys Davids, trans. *Points of Controversy.* London, 1915. Classical Theravāda polemics against the doctrines of the Eighteen Schools.

Bareau, André. "Les sectes bouddhiques du Petit Véhicule et leurs Abhidharmapiṭaka." *Bulletin de l'École Française d'Extrême-Orient* 50 (1952): 1–11. Bareau is the leading scholar on the early history of the Hīnayāna schools. See also his "Trois traités sur les sectes bouddhiques attribués à Vasumitra, Bhavya et Vinītadeva," *Journal asiatique* 242 (1954): 229–266; 244 (1956): 167–200; *Les premiers conciles bouddhiques* (Paris, 1955); *Les sectes bouddhiques du petit véhicule* (Saigon, 1955); and "Les controverses rélatives à la nature de l'arhant dans le bouddhisme ancien," *Indo-Iranian Journal* 1 (1957): 241–250.

Bareau, André and H. G. A. van Zeyst. "Andhakas." In the *Encyclopaedia of Buddhism,* vol. 1, edited by G. P. Malalasekera. Colombo, 1965. Analysis of a representative group of "southern" Mahāsāṃghikas.

Bechert, Heinz. "Zur Frühgeschichte des Mahāyāna-Buddhismus." *Zeitschrift der Deutschen Morgenländischen Gesellschaft* 113 (1963): 530–535. Summarizes contemporary understanding of the breadth and complexity of Hīnayāna sources for Mahāyāna.

Demiéville, Paul. "L'origine des sectes bouddhiques d'après Paramārtha." In *Mélanges chinois et bouddhiques,* vol. 1, pp. 15–62. Brussels, 1931–1932. See also his "À propos du concile de Vaiśālī," *T'oung pao* 40 (1951): 239–296.

Dutt, Nalinaksha. *Early History of the Spread of Buddhism and the Buddhist Schools* (1925). Reprint, New Delhi, 1980. See also Dutt's *Aspects of Mahāyāna Buddhism and Its Relation to Hīnayāna* (London, 1930), and "The Second Buddhist Council," *Indian Historical Quarterly* 35 (March 1959): 45–56. Most of Dutt's earlier work on the sects, found hidden in various journals, was compiled in *Buddhist Sects in India* (Calcutta, 1970).

Jones, J. J., trans. *The Mahāvastu.* 3 vols. London, 1949–1956. This is the English translation of one of the few surviving Mahāsāṃghika texts.

La Vallée Poussin, Louis de. "Mahāvastu." In *Encyclopaedia of Religion and Ethics,* edited by James Hastings, vol. 8. Edinburgh, 1915. This article and the one by Rhys Davids listed below are dated, but they contain valuable information and historical hypotheses still defended by some scholars.

Lamotte, Étienne. "Buddhist Controversy over the Five Propositions." *Indian Historical Quarterly* 32 (1966): 148–162. The material collected in this article is also found, slightly augmented, in Lamotte's great *Histoire du bouddhisme indien: Des origines à l'ère Śaka* (Louvain, 1958), pp. 300–319, 542–543, 575–606, and 690–695. This erudite work is still the standard reference on the history of early Indian Buddhism.

Masuda Jiryō. "Origins and Doctrines of Early Indian Buddhist Schools." *Asia Major* 2 (1925): 1–78.

Prebish, Charles S. "A Review of Scholarship on the Buddhist Councils." *Journal of Asian Studies* 33 (February 1974): 239–254. Prebish has dedicated serious reflection to the problem of the early schools, especially to the history and significance of their Vinaya. See also "The Prātimokṣa Puzzle: Facts versus Fantasy," *Journal of the American Oriental Society* 94 (April–June 1974): 168–176, and *Buddhist Monastic Discipline: The Sanskrit Prātimokṣa Sūtras of the Mahāsāṃghikas and Mūlasarvāstivādins* (University Park, Pa., 1975).

Prebish, Charles S., and Janice J. Nattier. "Mahāsāṃghika Origins: The Beginnings of Buddhist Sectarianism." *History of Religions* 16 (February 1977): 237–272. A well-argued challenge to the perception of Mahāsāṃghikas as "Liberals."

Rhys Davids, T. W. "Sects (Buddhist)." In *Encyclopaedia of Religion and Ethics,* edited by James Hastings, vol. 11. Edinburgh, 1920.

Wayman, Alex. "The Mahāsāṅghika and the Tathāgatagarbha." *Journal of the International Association of Buddhist Studies* 1 (1978): 35–50. Discusses possible connections between the Mahāsāṃghika subsects of Andhra and the development of Mahāyāna.

LUIS O. GÓMEZ

MAHĀSIDDHAS. The Buddhist *mahāsiddha* ("fully perfected one"), or simply *siddha* ("perfected one"), is the central enlightened ideal of Tantric or Vajrayāna Buddhism, the last major developmental phase of Indian Buddhism and particularly prominent on the subcontinent between the eighth and twelfth centuries CE. Best known are the list of eighty four of the greatest Buddhist *siddhas* (as enumerated by the twelfth-century Indian author Abhayadatta) and the grouping of *siddhas* into seven lineages (by the Tibetan author Tāranātha). Like the Buddha for earliest Buddhism, the *arhat* for the pre-Mahāyāna tradition, and the *bodhisattva* for the Mahāyāna, the *siddha* stands as the preeminent model of an accomplished person for the Vajrayāna tradition. And like those earlier ideals for their traditions, the *siddha* embodies in his person the particular character and ideals of the Vajrayāna, with its emphasis on meditation, personal realization, the master-disciple relationship, and the nonmonastic ways of life of the householder and the wandering yogin.

Sources. Our knowledge of the Buddhist *siddhas* comes from a considerable amount of biographical material that survives chiefly in Tibetan texts, which are either translations of, or are based directly or indirectly on, Indian written and oral tradition. These biographies of the *siddhas*, which vary in length from a few lines to hundreds of pages, tell the "liberation story" *(rnam thar)* of their subjects, recounting their individual journeys from the ordinary human state to one of full awakening.

The biographies of the *siddhas* are especially characterized by strong mythological, symbolic, and magical overtones. As in the case of the Buddha Śākyamuni in his biographies, but to a much greater degree, the *siddhas* are depicted as beings whose lives are charged with the transcendent and supernatural. At the same time, the *siddhas* are shown as real men and women with specific connections to the everyday, historical world. Their stories depict them as coming from particular places, belonging to certain castes, and following this or that occupation. Their teachers, Tantric practices, and lineages are carefully noted. The greatest among them figure as great teachers, lineage founders, monastic officials, and prolific authors of extant Tantric texts. Many *siddhas* are known historically to have played important roles in the transmission of the Vajrayāna from India to Tibet, China, and Southeast Asia, and are part of the social and political history of those countries. This confluence of the mythological and transcendent on the one hand, and the historically tangible and specific on the other, is one of the particular marks of the *siddhas* and of the Vajrayāna in general.

Structure of the Siddha Ideal. The *siddhas* are depicted in their biographies both as particular individuals and as members of a common type: their lives share a certain general structure or pattern, resumed here, that marks them as Buddhist *siddhas*.

Before enlightenment. The *siddha's* life story generally begins with his birth, sometimes in the great Tantric areas of Kāmarūpa (northeast India), Uḍḍiyāna (northwest India), or Nāgārjunikoṇḍa (southeast India), sometimes in some other region. There typically follow details of caste status. In contrast to earlier Buddhism, where the higher castes are implicitly regarded as preferable, the *siddhas* come not only from the high castes *(brāhmaṇa* and *kṣatriya)* but as often from the low; some of the greatest *siddhas* were originally hunters, fishers, herdsmen, weavers, cobblers, blacksmiths, prostitutes, and even thieves. This diversity of social origins gives particularly vivid expression to the classical Buddhist insistence that caste and social distinctions are not spiritually rooted or inherent in reality, and that enlightenment can occur equally in any conditioned situation, whatever its conventionally stated social value.

The *siddhas* are typically depicted at the beginning of their careers as ordinary people who possess some often unspecified longing. They are men and women, monks and laypeople, privileged and destitute, but they all share a sense of unavoidable dissatisfaction and circularity in their lives. They reach a critical point in their religious career when they encounter a Tantric teacher who presents them with the possibility of a spiritual path—of meditation, of the shedding of habitual patterns, and of awakening. Their response is often a mixture of attraction and fear, but they share a feeling of connection with the teacher and with the message he articulates. Following this encounter, the future *siddhas* begin a demanding course of training under their *gurus*. The importance of the teacher-disciple relationship in each *siddha's* biography reflects the Vajrayāna emphasis on the primacy of individual awakening and of the necessity of a realized, personal teacher to that process.

There follows in each *siddha's* life a period of study with a teacher, whom the pupil sometimes attends for many years, and sometimes meets only periodically for new instructions. Formless meditation and liturgical Tantric practice *(sādhana)* are unremitting parts of the student's training, but so is activity "in the world"; many of these later-to-be-*siddhas* are instructed to carry out caste occupations and to marry. Some are instructed to perform tasks that are anathema to their former identities, such as the *brahmans* Bhadrapa and Lūyipa, who are told to make their living cleaning latrines and serving a prostitute, respectively. In general, hard tasks and humiliation of previous ego ideals marks the testing and training of the *siddhas* during their student days and their journey toward classic Buddhist realization of egolessness.

Siddhas as enlightened figures. After many years of arduous training, the *siddhas* emerge as fully enlightened people. In contrast to the Buddha, who was regarded as one of a kind thus far in our world age, to the *arhat*, whose enlightenment was seen as less than the Buddha's, and to the *bodhisattva*, who is enjoined to postpone his full awakening, the *siddhas* are depicted as having attained full awakening, thus fulfilling the Vajrayāna intention to make possible "enlightenment in this very lifetime."

As enlightened figures, the *siddhas* manifest a lively individuality as householders, yogins, or monks. Although the *siddhas* represent a basically nonmonastic ideal, they not infrequently turn up as followers of monastic discipline outwardly, but realized *siddhas* within.

The classical Vajrayāna understands itself as a development of the Mahāyāna; the *siddhas* are depicted as *bodhisattvas* whose primary motivation is to work for the benefit of others. Thus, the realized *siddhas* are all primarily teachers of others. Later Tibetan tradition explains the great diversity of origins, training, and teaching methodologies of the *siddhas* as a fulfillment of the Mahāyāna *bodhisattva* vow to help sentient beings in all stations and conditions by adopting their way of life.

This compassionate motivation is also given in explanation of the *siddhas'* undeniable unconventionality. As I have already noted, teachers sometimes send their students into situations conventionally forbidden to their caste. The *siddhas* themselves often break social and religious taboos as part of their teaching. The depiction of such unconventional activity is intended to reinforce the Tantric insistence that genuine spirituality cannot be identified with any particular external social form. Here, the *siddhas* give characteristic expression to the ancient dictum of the Buddha: awakening is a matter of seeing the conditioned structure of the world as such, not of slavishly identifying with a particular way of life or religious norm.

Magical elements. Magic also plays an important role in the lives of the realized *siddhas*. On one level, the *siddha* biographies articulate the traditional Buddhist (and pan-Indian) belief that spiritual awakening puts one in possession of miraculous powers. In this sense, the *siddha* carries on a motif present in the depiction of the Buddha, of some of the *arhats*, and of the *bodhisattvas* of higher attainment. But in the *siddhas'* lives, magic plays a more prominent role than it does in the earlier hagiographical traditions. This greater prominence is probably due to a combination of (1) the great emphasis in the Vajrayāna on practice and realization; (2) its alignment with nonmonastic, and thus yogic and lay, life; and (3) its bent toward breaking what it sees as the conservatism and stolid fixations of earlier Buddhism.

Some accounts of magic appear to be metaphorical, such as when *siddhas* turn others into stone, "petrifying" them with their unconventional teaching. Other feats, such as the production of jewels from a worthless substance, are perhaps psychological, indicating the way in which the *siddhas* can, through their insight, transform apparently worthless passions of the personality into the highest prize of enlightenment. Other examples of magic, such as Saraha's walking on water, may illustrate the *siddhas'* freedom from cause and effect. In all these examples the *siddhas'* use of magic points to the basic Vajrayāna (and classical Buddhist) teaching that the commonsense world is not as definite and fixed as it appears, but in fact contains unlimited freedom, power, and sacredness.

A final characteristic of the realized *siddha* is his passing away, which is understood not as a death in the ordinary sense but as a passing into a state that is invisible, but nevertheless real and potentially available. The *siddhas*, we are told, do not die, but rather go to a celestial realm from which they may appear at any time.

Historicity and the Siddha Biographies. The historical concreteness of the *siddha* biographies, the existence of texts, songs, and lineages they created, their social and political impact, and the existence of the Vajrayāna itself leave little doubt that the *siddhas* were historical individuals. But to what extent are their stories simple historical accounts and to what extent do they represent a gathering of originally disparate elements around a particular figure?

Study of the Vajrayāna biographies themselves shows that it would be a mistake to take them simply as accounts of single individuals, at least in the ordinary sense. Many sometimes different, sometimes apparently contradictory accounts are given in the same and different texts about a single *siddha*. In addition, one finds the same motifs and even entire stories appearing in the lives of several different *siddhas*. In light of these factors, one perhaps best understands the *siddhas'* lives as sacred biographies, some elements of which undoubtedly emerged originally in the lives of those individuals, and others of which originated from elsewhere. These became the general property of the tradition, to be used and reused to clarify the nature of the *siddha* ideal itself through the medium of specific biographies.

Does this rather flexible approach to writing history reflect a lack of historical awareness on the part of Vajrayāna biographers? The temptation to answer this question in the affirmative must be resisted, at least until the particular Vajrayāna attitude toward history is clearly understood. The lives of the *siddhas* do not restrict themselves to what we in the West have typically understood as the legitimate domain of a person's "life," beginning with birth and ending with death. The "life" of a *siddha* may include "events" that precede birth and postdate death, and may also include dreams, visions, and supranormal experiences other respected persons may have had of those *siddhas* before, during, and after their human lives. This more inclusive attitude taken by the Vajrayāna toward a *siddha*'s life is due not so much to its lack of historical awareness, but rather to the particular understanding of history that it possesses. The *siddhas* are real people who are significant precisely because they embody cosmic, timeless, and universal dimensions of human reality. They may express themselves equally from their ordinary human as well as their transhuman aspects. For the tradition itself, contradictory stories about a *siddha* may simply indicate multiple manifestations of that person, while the repetition of the same stories in several lives may just mean a later *siddha* is teaching according to an earlier, typical pattern. Such elements are considered in the Vajrayāna not only a legitimate but a necessary part of proper historical writing about the *siddhas*.

Finally, it is necessary to mention the important impact of liturgy and of certain later Tibetan Tantric masters' lives on the understanding of the *siddhas*' biographies. What is understood as the universal and timeless essence of the *siddhas* makes it possible to invoke the living and tangible presence of the *siddhas* through liturgy. Moreover, many of the most famous *siddhas* are understood to be present, in later incarnations, in the persons of Tibetan *tulkus* (incarnate lamas). The living example of the *tulkus* and the invocation of the presence of the *siddhas* in ritual contribute significantly to the making present and interpreting of the *siddhas* whose lives and teachings can be read in the texts.

Historical Role of the Siddhas. The major historical legacy of the *siddhas* is the tradition they represented and the Vajrayāna lineages they helped build, many of which are alive today. On a more restricted front, the *siddhas* were the authors of a great many Tantric works, hundreds of which survive in Tibetan translation. The most characteristic compositions of the *siddhas* are perhaps their *dohās* ("enlightenment songs"), which survive in independent collections, in biographies, and in the Tantras themselves. These songs are supposed usually to have been composed in liturgical situations to express the individuality and sacredness of that moment of awakened experience. The *siddhas* also composed other varieties of texts, including commentaries on the *tantras*, biographies of great masters, liturgical texts, and so on. A list of some six hundred works by Indian *siddhas* is given in the Tantric section of the Tibetan Bstan-'gyur (Tanjur); works of the *siddhas* are also included in other parts of the Tanjur and in Tibetan collections of Indian Buddhist texts.

The *siddhas* also played an important part in the history of Indian and Asian Buddhism. In India, the *siddhas* were the prime carriers of the Vajrayāna for a millenium, in its early formative period (pre-eighth century CE), during the time of its prominence (eighth to twelfth century CE), in the several centuries following the Islamic decimation of monastic Buddhism at the end of the twelfth century, through the sixteenth century, when contemporary Tibetan accounts give a first hand picture of a strong and vital Vajrayāna tradition in India. In the history of Tibetan Buddhism, it was the *siddhas* who carried the Vajrayāna to that land. All four of the major surviving schools, and many that did not survive, ultimately derive from Indian *siddhas*: the Bka'-brgyud-pa from Ti-lo-pa (988–1069) and Nā-ro-pa (1016–1100); the Rñiṅ-ma-pa from Padmasambhava and Vimalamitra (both eighth century); the Sa-skya-pa from 'Brog-mi (922–1022); and the Dge-lugs-pa from Atīśa (982–1054), who, while not himself a *siddha*, inherited some of their traditions). [*See* Dge-lugs-pa.]

Siddhas such as Śubhākarasiṃha, Vajrabodhi, and Amoghavajra, all of whom journeyed to T'ang China in the eighth century, were responsible for bringing the Vajrayāna to that land. [*See* Chen-yen.] Although their unconventional and wonderworking activity proved ultimately discordant with the Chinese outlook, and although the Vajrayāna they brought did not long survive in China, their activity provided the foundation for the transmission of the Vajrayāna to Japan by Kūkai (774–835), who founded the Shingon school there. [*See* Shingonshū.] The *siddha* ideal played an indirect role in the religious history of the Mongols as well, following Mongol appropriation of Tibetan Buddhism in the thirteenth century.

Finally, the *siddhas* carried the Vajrayāna to Southeast Asia, where there is evidence of their activity in Java, Sumatra and Kamboja from the early ninth century onward. The Vajrayāna continued there until the sixteenth century at least, when the Indian Vajrayānist Buddhaguptanātha visited that area and gave firsthand accounts of the Tantric tradition there.

[*For further discussion of soteriological paths in Buddhism, see* Soteriology, *article on* Buddhist Soteriology; Arhat; *and* Bodhisattva Path. *See also the biographies of Padmasambhava, Ti-lo-pa, Nā-ro-pa, Mar-pa, Mi-la-ras-pa, Tsoṅ-kha-pa, Śubhākarasiṃha, Vajrabodhi, Amoghavajra, and Atīśa.*]

BIBLIOGRAPHY

Abhayadatta's *Caturśīti-siddha-pravṛtti* (History of the Eighty-four Siddhas), the most important extant Indian text on the *siddhas*, has been translated from the Tibetan by James B. Robinson as *Buddha's Lions* (Berkeley, 1979). The extended Tibetan biographies of two of the most important Indian *siddhas*, Padmasambhava and Nā-ro-pa, are given respectively in W. Y. Evans-Wentz's *The Tibetan Book of the Great Liberation* (Oxford, 1954) and *The Life and Teachings of Naropa*, translated by Herbert Guenther (Oxford, 1963). Per Kvaerne's *An Anthology of Buddhist Tantric Songs* (Oslo and New York, 1977) analyzes an important collection of the Indian *siddhas'* songs. Shashibhusan Dasgupta's *Obscure Religious Cults*, 3d ed. (Calcutta, 1969), attempts to see the Indian *siddhas* in their larger religious context; my "Accomplished Women in Tantric Buddhism of Medieval India and Tibet," in *Unspoken Worlds*, edited by Nancy A. Falk and Rita M. Gross (New York, 1980), pp. 227-242, discusses Indian women *siddhas*. Several works provide useful summaries of the role of the Indian *siddhas* and of the Vajrayāna outside of India. For Tibet, see David L. Snellgrove and Hugh Richardson's *A Cultural History of Tibet*, (New York, 1968; reprint, Boulder, 1980), pp. 95–110 and 118ff.; for China, see Kenneth Ch'en's *Buddhism in China* (1964; reprint, Princeton, 1972), pp. 325–337; for Japan, see Daigan and Alicia Matsunaga's *Foundation of Japanese Buddhism* (Los Angeles, 1974), vol. 1, pp. 171–200; and for Southeast Asia, see Nihar-Ranjan Ray's *Sanskrit Buddhism in Burma*, (Calcutta, 1936), pp. 12–14 and 62–99.

REGINALD RAY

MAHATMA GANDHI. *See* Gandhi, Mohandas.

MAHĀVAIROCANA (lit., "the great illuminator"), the Great Sun Buddha, is the transcendent and cosmocratic apotheosis of the historical Buddha, Śākyamuni. Under the earlier designation *Vairocana* ("the luminous one"), he represents Buddhism's most profound speculation on the emptiness and interpenetration of all elements in the universe *(dharmadhātu)*. As Mahāvairocana he is concretely envisaged as the all-encompassing lord of the cosmos and is the object of worship for a form of Tantric Buddhism that spread from India to Sumatra, China, Japan, and Tibet.

In India, the name *Virocana* appears in the *Ṛgveda* in connection with celestial phenomena and the luminous residence of Varuṇa. Other Vedic contexts link Virocana variously with Sūrya, the solar deity; Candra, the lunar deity; and Agni, god of fire. In the *Chandogya Upaniṣad*, Virocana, king of the *asuras* (anti-gods), loses a competition for true knowledge of the Self to his counterpart Indra, king of the *devas* (gods). Pali Buddhist literature identifies the deity Verocana with the demon Bali, and in the *Saṃyutta Nikāya* he again opposes his nemesis Sakka (Indra), this time in seeking knowledge from the Buddha.

Vairocana is mentioned in other Buddhist texts such as the *Mahāvastu* and the *Lalitavistara*, but his role as a symbol of ultimate reality is developed only in Mahāyāna scriptures such as the *Daśabhūmikā Sūtra* and the *Gaṇḍavyūha Sūtra*, both found in the huge collection known as the *Avataṃsaka Sūtra*. According to the Chinese Hua-yen and the Japanese Kegon traditions, both of which are grounded in the *Avataṃsaka Sūtra*, Śākyamuni, the Buddha who preached the *Avataṃsaka*, had like all Buddhas before him spent aeons as a *bodhisattva* striving toward enlightenment. On the night of his final enlightenment, he ascended to the palace of the Akaniṣṭha Heaven—the summit of the cosmos—where *abhiṣeka* ("initiation, consecretion") was conferred upon him by the Buddhas of the Ten Quarters. He thus attained the "body of enjoyment" *(saṃbhogakāya)* and came to reign from the Akaniṣṭha Heaven as the celestial sovereign who preaches to highly advanced *bodhisattvas*. Simultaneously with this attainment, Śākyamuni realized his identity with the *dharmakāya* (reality as total, transcendent, and ineffable). The earthly body of Śākyamuni took up his preaching, but that body, as well as the "body of enjoyment," were now recognized as manifestations of the transcendent *dharmakāya*. Thus, Vairocana represents ultimate reality and at the same time permeates all levels of the manifest cosmos and the beings in it. The universe is his infinite body. All things are in him, and his presence shines in all things.

This notion of interpenetration—of the part in the whole and the whole in every part—is closely linked with images of light and illumination in the mythology of Vairocana/Mahāvairocana. The *Gaṇḍhavyūha Sūtra* describes reality as a universe of infinitely reflected light. As the solar deity, Vairocana is the center of the cosmos, its ruler and sovereign. He is above the cosmos, yet all its variations are reflections of him. A frequently used image is that of Indra's net. The net constitutes the universe, and at each knot there is a jewel that reflects all the other jewels in the net.

Mahāvairocana and Tantra. The name Vairocana points to an ultimate perspective to be realized through insight. Mahāvairocana, in contrast, is realized concretely in ritual practice. Mahāvairocana, the chief deity in much of the Buddhist Tantric tradition, rose to prominence sometime between the fifth and seventh century CE. While sharing Vairocana's symbolism, Mahāvairocana's distinctiveness in iconography, doctrine, and ritual is signaled by the Sanskrit prefix *mahā* ("great"). The principal scriptures that extol Mahāvairocana and describe his cult, the *Mahāvairocana Sūtra* and the *Tattvasaṃgraha*, are no longer fully extant in Sanskrit, but their Chinese translations are the basis of the Chinese Chen-yen and Japanese Shingon *(mantra)* schools of Buddhism. Tibetan translations of these scriptures are regarded as the root texts of two of the four classes of Tantra in that country, Caryā Tantras and Yoga Tantras. Although Mahāvairocana was important in Tibetan Buddhism, his cult was overshadowed by deities of the Anuttarayoga Tantras. For the Tibetans the Buddha Akṣobhya, the "primordial Buddha" (Ādibuddha), and the dialectical symbolism of cosmic sexuality represented by *yab-yum*, or "father-mother," images found in the *Guhyasamaja Tantra* and *Hevajra Tantra*, were more compelling.

Mahāvairocana in East Asia. The *Mahāvairocana Sūtra* and the *Tattvasaṃgraha* were brought to China by two Indian *ācāryas* ("teachers") from the North Indian monastic university at Nālandā, which in the seventh century CE had become a center for Tantric studies. Śubhākarasiṃha (637–735) and Vajrabodhi (671–741) arrived to missionize the T'ang court in 716 and 720 respectively. [*See the biographies of Subhākarasiṃha and Vajrabodhi.*] Through their efforts and those of their disciples, the major texts and commentaries concerning Mahāvairocana were translated. A small but stable cult was established under the cautious patronage of the pro-Taoist Emperor Hsüan-tsung (r. 712–756). Mahāvairocana as he is revealed in what became known as Esoteric Buddhism (Chin., Mi-chiao; Jpn., Mikkyō) assumes the symbolism of Vairocana. Mahāvairocana is described as the lord of the vast palace of the *vajradharmadhātu* that has been created by his wondrous power of transformation *(adhiṣṭhāna)*. This palace is identified both as the Akaniṣṭha Heaven and as the entire cosmos. Like Vairocana, Mahāvairocana has received initiations (*abhiṣekas*) from all the Buddhas, and the Akaniṣṭha Heaven is the scene of these initiations as well as of the revelation of the new Tantric scriptures. In the *Mahāvairocana Sūtra*, Mahāvairocana is portrayed as the light and sustenance of the manifest cosmos and as its supreme sovereign. He is at once the cosmocrat and the active participant in all manifestation; his presence is felt not only in the salvific action of *bodhisattvas* but also in weather, constellations, and all other phenomena. The *Tattvasaṃgraha* tends to emphasize the cosmos as it is reflected in Mahāvairocana. He is the Lord of Light, and the universe is an endless series of reflections of him.

Iconography and Worship. Mahāvairocana's distinctiveness is apparent in his texts, which are almost entirely devoted to ritual. While Vairocana represents absolute reality, to be realized through insight developed over long aeons, Mahāvairocana is realized through an active and immediate ritual participation in his very being. Practice is a ritual drama based upon iconographic conventions detailed in *maṇḍalas*, or cosmograms, drawn from the two major texts, and it consists of two intertwined acts. The disciple first attempts to realize his identity with the deity through imitating the iconographic conventions, or "marks," of the deity as revealed in the texts, and through oral instruction. His body and hand posture *(mudrā)*, ritual incantation *(mantra)*, and meditative vision *(samādhi)* seek to duplicate the very consciousness of the divinity he worships. Success in this *imitatio* is termed *siddhi* ("accomplishment"). The disciple undergoes a series of initiations *(abhiṣeka)* identifying him with deities at various levels of the *maṇḍala*. Should he be deemed fit, he may attain final realization of his identity with Mahāvairocana, reenacting the Buddha's quest and final ascent to the Akaniṣṭha Heaven to become an *ācārya*. Having realized his identity with the deity, he may now exercise that deity's powers for the good of others. This second act is also called *siddhi*.

Under the aegis of Vajrabodhi's disciple Amoghavajra (d. 774), under his Chinese successors, and under Kūkai (774–835), the Japanese founder of Shingon, the iconography of Esoteric Buddhism took a definitive form. [*See the biographies of Amoghavajra and Kūkai.*] Certain *maṇḍalas* were drawn from the *Mahāvairocana Sūtra* and the *Tattvasaṃgraha* to produce the Womb Maṇḍala (Garbhakośadhātu Maṇḍala) and the Diamond Maṇḍala (Vajradhātu Maṇḍala). Mahāvairocana of the Womb Maṇḍala is usually golden, seated in meditative posture on a lunar disc that rests on a red lotus blossom. He is regally adorned as the master of the cosmos and represents the final achievement of Buddhahood. Other divinities depicted in the *maṇḍala* represent his compassionate activity *(karuṇā)* in all phenomena and the possibility of illumination. The Diamond Maṇḍala is composed of nine *maṇḍalas* selected from the *Tattvasaṃgraha*. They represent Mahāvairocana's consciousness or wisdom *(prajñā)*. The central image of Mahāvairocana is usually white or blue, seated upon a lotus blossom resting on a lunar disc. He is adorned and crowned and his hands are clasped in the Gesture of All-Embracing Wisdom (Jñānamuṣṭi Mudrā). Shingon tradition describes the *maṇḍala* as representative of the cosmos as Mahāvairocana sees it, the timeless universe of the interpenetrating light of wisdom. These two *maṇḍalas*, which like conditional reality and ultimate reality are said to be nondual, provide a framework for classifying all phenomena. Initiation and ritual practice were organized around the new scheme, and therefore an *ācārya* must be initiated into both *maṇḍalas*. Kūkai introduced several refinements, the most important of which is the identification of the first five material elements of the cosmos with the Womb Maṇḍala and the sixth element, mind, with the Diamond Maṇḍala. Thus, for Kūkai, the material cosmos was the body of the transcendent *dharmakāya,* not an ontologically secondary manifestation as might be surmised from Hua-yen doctrine.

The Religious Meaning of Mahāvairocana. The Great Sun Buddha Mahāvairocana represents one of the world's most profound religious conceptions. Like the physical sun, Mahāvairocana Buddha is the pivot of the manifest cosmos, the source of light and life. Yet this is far from pantheism, since Mahāvairocana transcends the universe just as he *is* the universe. Nor is this docetism. Indeed, no better term may be found than that coined by Masaharu Anesaki (1915), who speaks of Shingon's "cosmotheism." The full meaning of Mahāvairocana is apprehended in Tantric practice, for there Mahāvairocana functions as an icon, as both the embodiment of the divine and as a symbol pointing to divine transcendence. Thus, in the ritual drama of Tantra the practitioner realizes his own iconic nature. He is both the worshiper and the object of worship; he experiences the paradox of divinity that is the world and yet transcends the world. He is Mahāvairocana in this very body.

[*See also* Celestial Buddhas and Bodhisattvas; Buddhism, Schools of, *article on* Esoteric Buddhism; Maṇḍalas, *article on* Buddhist Maṇḍalas; *and* Shingonshū. *For a general discussion of associated solar deities, see* Sun.]

BIBLIOGRAPHY

The best introduction to the cult of Mahāvairocana in the context of Tibetan Tantric practice is David L. Snellgrove's *Buddhist Himalaya* (Oxford, 1957). On Vairocana and his symbolism in the Hua-yen and Kegon traditions see Francis D. Cook's *Hua-yen Buddhism: The Jewel Net of Indra* (University Park, Pa., 1977) and Thomas Cleary's *Entry into the Inconceivable: An Introduction to Hua-yen Buddhism* (Honolulu, 1983). The only study of the Chen-yen school in China is Chou I-liang's excellent annotated translation (with introductions) of the lives of Śubhākarasiṃha, Vajrabodhi, and Amoghavajra, "Tantrism in China," *Harvard Journal of Asiatic Studies* 8 (1945): 241–332. Studies of Esoteric Buddhism and thus of Mahāvairocana from the doctrinal perspective of Japanese Shingon are Minoru Kiyota's *Shingon Buddhism* (Los Angeles, 1978), which includes an explanation of the two *maṇḍalas*, and a hard-to-find but excellent work in French by the Shingon priest Tajima Ryūjun, *Étude sur le Mahāvairocana-sūtra* (Paris, 1936). Tajima's study includes a translation of the first chapter of this important text. Yoshito S. Hakeda has provided a fine introduction to Kūkai's life and thought and translations of some of his works in his *Kūkai: Major Works* (New York, 1972). The best study of the Shingon *maṇḍalas* is also by Tajima Ryūjun but again his *Les deux grands maṇḍalas et la doctrine de l'ésotérisme Shingon*, "Bulletin de la maison franco-japonaise," n.s. vol. 6 (Tokyo, 1959), is in French and hard to obtain. Somewhat easier to find is Beatrice Lane Suzuki's article on the Womb Maṇḍala, "The Shingon School of Mahayana Buddhism," part 2, "The Mandara," *Eastern Buddhist* 7 (May 1936): 1–38. Finally, a brief but excellent understanding of the two *maṇḍalas* may be found in Masaharu Anesaki's "Buddhist Cosmotheism and the Symbolism of Its Art" in his *Buddhist Art in Its Relation to Buddhist Ideals* (1915; reprint, New York, 1978).

CHARLES D. ORZECH

MAHĀVĪRA. Among the numerous philosophers and religious teachers who preached in eastern India during the sixth century BCE was the Jina ("conqueror"), considered to be the founder and systematizer of Jainism. The name given to him by his parents was Vardhamāna ("prospering"), for soon after his conception, it is said, things began to flourish and prosper for him and for those around him. The gods called him Mahāvīra ("great hero"), because, they claimed, "he stands fast in the midst of dangers and fears" (*Jinacaritra* 108). He is regarded as the twenty-fourth *tīrthaṃkara* ("fordmaker") or prophet, and the reformer of Jainism. Mahāvīra's symbol is the lion; like other *tīrthaṃkaras*, he is sometimes represented with his two guardian deities.

Hagiography. The main episodes of Mahāvīra's life and religious career are often described in Jain literature and are prominent in the Śvetāmbara canon. The five principal "auspicious moments" of his life—his conception, birth, renunciation, enlightenment, and passing into *nirvāṇa*—are celebrated by his followers to this day.

According to the Jains, Mahāvīra was born seventy-five years and eight and a half months before the end of the fourth descending period of the current *avasarpiṇī* era (or 599 BCE); by the calculations of Western scholars, the event probably took place at least some fifty years later. He was born in Kuṇḍagrāma, apparently a village near Vaiśālī, to the north of modern-day Patna in northern Bihar—where a Mahāvīra memorial has been erected and where the Research Institute of Prakrit, Ahiṃsā, and Jainology was founded by the government of Bihar in 1956.

Like all *tīrthaṃkaras*, Vardhamāna was alleged to have come from a princely family; the Jains hold that he had a *kṣatriya* lineage and that his mother, Triśalā, was closely related to the Vaiśālī ruler. The Śvetāmbara scriptures and miniatures even show the transplantation of his embryo, following Indra's orders, from the womb of a brahman mother, Devānandā, into that of Triśalā. This episode, which is reminiscent of the Kṛṣṇa legend, is rejected by the Digambaras. As will be seen, the two churches disagree on certain points in the biography of the twenty-fourth *tīrthaṃkara.* Both agree, however, that his conception was foretold to his mother in a series of fourteen (or sixteen) auspicious dreams by a white elephant, a white bull, a lion, the goddess Śrī, the full moon, the rising sun, an ocean of milk, and so forth. These dreams are frequently described in the literature and represented in manuscripts and in temples.

While still in the womb Vardhamāna began to practice *ahiṃsā:* he was careful not to cause his mother any pain, and even vowed not to renounce the world before his parents' death. His birth was the occasion of universal rejoicing and liberality. As a boy he received a princely education and his family appears to have followed the doctrine of the twenty-third *tīrthaṃkara,* Pārśva, whose teachings Mahāvīra was to reconsider and complete, but not, apparently, to oppose. According to the Śvetāmbaras he married the princess Yaśodā, who gave birth to a daughter; their daughter's husband was later to start the first schism of Jainism. The Digambaras, however, consider that Vardhamāna had no such worldly ties. They emphasize that Mahāvīra was one of an unending succession of *tīrthaṃkaras*: his earlier births are linked with Ṛṣabha (through one of the latter's grandsons), while one of his disciples, King Śreṇika Bimbisāra, will be reborn as the first *tīrthaṃkara* of the next *utsarpiṇī* age.

By the time Vardhamāna was thirty years old his parents had died. Having gained the consent of his elder brother he distributed his property, plucked out his hair, and renounced the world; this is an event commonly depicted in Jain iconography, with Indra devotedly receiving the saint's hair in his hands. Thereafter, Mahāvīra led the hard, solitary life of a wandering ascetic *(śramaṇa),* begging for food and shelter, moving from place to place (except during the four months of the rainy season) in the eastern region of the Ganges Valley. According to the Digambaras, Mahāvīra immediately abandoned clothing as well as ornaments, whereas the Śvetāmbaras hold that this occurred only after thirteen months of renunciation. Such discussions again reflect a difference of opinion, in this case concerning the importance of nakedness in the holy life.

Both sects do agree that the prophet shunned all violence to living beings, took nothing that was not explicitly given to him, spoke no lies, strictly avoided unchaste behavior in thought, word, and deed, and had no possessions—in short, he followed what were to become the five major vows of the Jain monk. Moreover, he endured severe hardships (due to nature, animal, and man) and practiced systematic penances that involved many kinds of prolonged and complicated fasts, "exerting himself," according to the *Jinacaritra* (119), "for the suppression of the defilement of *karman.*" He gained disciples, with whom he conversed in a Prakrit language. In this way he spent twelve years, six months, and fifteen days on the mendicant's path. Finally, on a summer night, near a sal tree on the bank of the river Ṛjupālikā, he attained omniscience *(kevala-jñāna),* "which is infinite, supreme, unobstructed, unimpeded, and full. . . . He knew and saw all conditions of all living beings in the world—what they thought, spoke, or did at any moment" (*Jinacaritra* 120–121). He had in fact acquired full knowledge of the world (and the nonworld), and of the past, present, and future of its inhabitants, whether divine, infernal, animal, or human. Concerning the state of enlightenment there are again differences between the Śvetāmbaras, who consider that even a *kevalin* eats and complies with constraints of the body without any defilement, and the Digambaras, who believe that following enlightenment one is free from all human imperfections (such as hunger) and only sits in perfect omniscience while a divine sound emanates from his person and instructs his hearers, directly or otherwise.

After attaining omniscience Mahāvīra preached the truth to immense assemblies of listeners and successfully organized the fourfold Jain community of monks, nuns, male laity, and female laity. He was assisted in this task by eleven *gaṇadharas* (chiefs of religious communities): the first chief was Indrabhūti Gautama, who is responsible for having retained and handed down Mahāvīra's teachings. One of Mahāvīra's earlier disciples was Gośāla, who turned against him to become head of the Ājīvika sect. [*See also* Ājīvikas *and the biography of Gośāla.*]

Finally, at the age of seventy-two, sitting "single and alone . . . , reciting the fifty-five lectures that detail the results of *karman,*" Mahāvīra passed into *nirvāṇa.* According to tradition, this occurred in the town of Pāpā, near Patna, toward the end of the monsoon in the year 527 BCE. This year was to become the starting point of the era known as the Vīra Saṃvat; nevertheless, Western scholars tend to place Mahāvīra's death in 467 or 477–476 BCE, or even later. Be that as it may, at that time (which was a fast-day) the neighboring kings "instituted an illumination. . . . For they said: 'Since the spiritual light is gone, let us make a material illumination' " (*Jinacaritra* 128). As it happened, this homage coincided with the Hindu festival of Dīvālī, so that Hindus and Jains simultaneously conduct these two different celebrations.

Mahāvīra's Teachings. Although the various discrepancies between the Digambara and Śvetāmbara accounts of Mahāvīra's career naturally imply doctrinal differences, the fundamental tenets upheld by the two churches are, nonetheless, basically similar, and can be regarded as deriving from Mahāvīra. Mahāvīra defined a pluralist substantialism that, typical of Jainism, is characterized by seven (or nine) *tattvas* (principles).

The first *tattva* is the soul or "life" *(jīva);* it is immaterial, eternal, characterized by consciousness, and capable of cognition. The *tattva*s serve to explain the mechanism of transmigration, the innumerable reincarnations of the soul, and the soul's final liberation. In this context Mahāvīra explained *jīva* and its opposite, *ajīva;* the influx of karmic matter into the soul; bondage; stoppage of karmic influx; expulsion of previously accumulated karmic matter; and the final accomplishment of "perfection" *(siddhi),* when karmic matter has been exhausted and the *jīva* has regained its pure spiritual nature. [*See also* Mokṣa.]

This ultimate goal cannot be attained except by those who tread "the ford" that Mahāvīra built to the other shore of *saṃsāra.* They must train themselves to follow the ideal pattern of life, which has been set by the Jina, and they must master the "three jewels" of right (Jain) faith, right knowledge, and right conduct; "right conduct" necessitates performing the difficult and constant ascetic exercises that were undertaken by the Jina himself. As a consequence, from the beginning great importance has been attached to religious life and to the organization of the community, in which the female devotees seem to have been particularly active and numerous. According to the *Jinacaritra* (134–137), "the Venerable Ascetic Mahāvīra had an excellent community of 14,000 *śramaṇa*s with Indrabhūti at their head: 36,000 nuns with Candanā at their head; 159,000 lay votaries with Śaṅkhaśataka at their head; 318,000 female lay votaries with Sulasā and Revatī at their head. . . ."

Mahāvīra's Significance in the Indian Tradition. It cannot be denied that in the traditional biography of Mahāvīra some episodes are stereotypes that systematically serve elsewhere to describe the career of other "great men" (*mahāpuruṣa*s). Additionally, there are many discrepancies concerning the date and place of his birth, his *nirvāṇa,* and so forth. Nevertheless, there is no reason to doubt the historicity of this vigorous original thinker and extremely capable organizer. While naturally accepting many of the basic assumptions of his society and his era, he was one of the first to oppose the Brahmanic ritualistic orthodoxy and to suceed in building a coherent system aimed at explaining the laws of the universe and the place of mankind therein, thus clearly linking metaphysics with ethics and speculation with social organization.

It has been justly emphasized that Jainism (like early Buddhism) integrated many older beliefs and practices that had previously been nurtured only by isolated Brahmanic ascetics. With Mahāvīra, these ideas appear to have gained in influence. Jainism has thus been equated with some of the most typically Indian tendencies and ideals; indeed, Jainism did much to enrich Indian ideals of spirituality. Among its contributions are the belief in the powers of asceticism, in the spiritual benefit to be derived from fasting (even unto death), and in the absolute necessity of avoiding injury to life *(ahiṃsā),* whether in thought, word, or deed. This last ideal constitutes the first vow of the Jains, which is a dedication to tolerance, unabated benevolence, and vegetarianism. [*See also* Ahiṃsā.]

The Jain movement probably owes much of its influence to the missionary zeal and gifts of Mahāvīra, and to his ability to organize a coherent society of religious and lay believers. The well-structured Jain community of monks and nuns was, together with the Buddhist *saṃgha,* one of the first to exist in India. In the course of time it proved to be remarkably dynamic, capable of continuing Mahāvīra's action, and even, as he himself is alleged to have done, of gaining the sympathy and support of many rulers. Following his path and the example he had set, Jain *nirgrantha*s (religious mendicants) as well as laymen have achieved the material as well as the spiritual glory of Jainism.

[*See also* Jainism *and* Tīrthaṃkaras.]

BIBLIOGRAPHY

All standard books on Jainism discuss the life of Mahāvīra. The Digambara views are clearly presented in Padmanabh S. Jaini's *The Jaina Path of Purification* (Berkeley, 1979). Two valuable books are Bimala Churn Law's *Mahāvīra: His Life and Teachings* (London, 1937) and Hiralal Jain and A. N. Upadhye's *Mahāvīra: His Times and His Philosophy of Life* (New Delhi, 1974).

Two important Śvetāmbara canonical texts tell the story of Mahāvīra's life: one text is included in the first book of the canon *(Ācārāṅga Sūtra* 1.8); the other forms a major part of the *Jinacaritra* (Lives of the Jinas), edited in 1882 and 1879 respectively by Hermann Jacobi, and translated from Prakrit into English by Jacobi in volume 1 of *Jaina Sûtras,* "Sacred Books of the East," vol. 22 (1884; reprint, Delhi, 1964). The teachings of Mahāvīra are somewhat discursively presented in other canonical books, among them the *Sūtrakṛtāṅga* and *Uttarādhyayana,* also translated by Hermann Jacobi, in volume 2 of *Jaina Sūtras,* "Sacred Books of the East," vol. 45 (1895; reprint Delhi, 1964).

Comparisons between the Buddha and the Jina have been attempted by Ernst Leumann in *Buddha und Mahāvīra, die beiden indischen Religionsstifter* (Munich, 1921). Mahāvīra's career is the subject of a number of Jain quasi-epic poems from both the Digambara and Śvetāmbara traditions, and an important chapter in the *Triṣaṣṭiśalākāpuruṣacaritra,* translated by Helen M. Johnson as *Triṣaṣṭiśalākāpuruṣacaritra, or The Lives of Sixty-three Illustrious Persons by Hemacandra*, "Gaekwad's Oriental Series," vols. 51, 77, 108, 125, 139, and 140 (Baroda, 1931–1962).

COLETTE CAILLAT

MAHĀYĀNA BUDDHISM. *See under* Buddhism, Schools of.

MAHDISM. *See* Messianism, *article on* Islamic Messianism.

MAḤZOR. *See* Siddur and Maḥzor.

MAIMONIDES, MOSES (c. 1135/8–1204), hellenized name of Mosheh ben Maimon; also known by the acronym RaMBaM (Rabbi Mosheh ben Maimon); distinguished Talmudist, philosopher, and physician, and one of the most illustrious figures of Jewish history. He had a profound and pervasive impact on Jewish life and thought, and his commanding influence has been widely recognized by non-Jews as well as Jews. His epoch-making works in the central areas of Jewish law *(halakhah)* and religious philosophy are considered to be unique by virtue of their unprecedented comprehensiveness, massive erudition, and remarkable originality and profundity. Their extraordinary conjunction of halakhic authority and philosophic prestige has been widely acknowledged. While the generations before the age of Maimonides produced philosophically trained Talmudists—scholars well versed in both Greek science and rabbinic lore—the extent to which Maimonides thoroughly and creatively amalgamated these disciplines and commitments is most striking. Many people of differing ideological inclinations throughout successive generations tend to find in or elicit from his great oeuvre a kind of *philosophia perennis*.

Early Life and Works. Maimonides was born in Córdoba, Spain, to a family of scholars. In 1148 Córdoba was conquered by the Almohads, a fanatical Islamic confederation. To escape religious persecution, the family fled the city; they wandered through southern Spain and North Africa from 1148 to 1158 and settled in Fez for several years. In 1165 Maimonides resumed his wanderings, going from Morocco to the Land of Israel, which was then the scene of the Crusades, turbulent and inhospitable. He was unable to take root there, and after making his way southward from the Crusaders' port city of Acre through Jerusalem to Hebron, stopping for prayer in the holy sites, he settled in Fusṭāṭ (Old Cairo). He began to practice medicine and became the house physician of Saladin's vizier. In a candid letter to his favorite disciple, Maimonides comments revealingly about his medical practice:

> I inform you that I have acquired in medicine a very great reputation among the great, such as the chief *qāḍī*, the princes . . . and other grandees. . . . This obliges me continually to waste my day in Cairo visiting the [noble] sick. When I return to Fusṭāṭ, the most I am able to do . . . is to study medical books, which are so necessary for me. For you know how long and difficult this art is for a conscientious and exact man who does not want to state anything which he cannot support by argument and without knowing where it has been said and how it can be demonstrated.

Simultaneously, Maimonides emerged as the untitled leader of the Jewish community, combining the duties of rabbi, local judge, appellate judge, administrative chief responsible for appointing and supervising community officials, and overseer of philanthropic foundations. He refused all remuneration for these services, a practice that reflected his religious and philosophical principles. His only son, Avraham, who was to become the official head *(nagid)* of the Jewish community and the author of important exegetical and philosophical works, was born in 1187; his writings are a significant source of Maimonidean doctrine.

Maimonides' biography underscores a noteworthy paradox. A philosopher by temperament and ideology, a zealous devotee of the contemplative life who eloquently portrayed and yearned for the serenity of solitude, he nevertheless led a relentlessly active life that regularly brought him to the brink of exhaustion. He was a harassed physician, subject to the pressures and whims of court service, and a conscientious leader of his community, sensitive to the physical and spiritual needs of its members. Yet he combined this arduous routine with constant scholarship and literary productivity in a way that reflected his conviction that superior leaders should combine intellectual perfection with practical and moral virtue (*Guide of the Perplexed* 3.54).

His determination to preserve his economic independence is completely consonant with his belief that scholars or religious functionaries should not seek or receive communal support. Some of his most passionate and animated prose (e.g., *Mishneh Torah*, Study of the Torah 3.10, Sanhedrin 23.5; *Commentary on the Mishnah, Avot* 4.7) was elicited by his distaste for this practice and his unyielding opposition to the existence of an institutionalized and salaried rabbinate dependent upon the largesse of patrons or charitable collections. But history did not favor the Maimonidean view, and such a rabbinate did emerge.

The natural integration of traditional Torah study and philosophy, which was a pivot of his massive literary achievement and an axiom of his understanding of Judaism, is emphasized even in existential contexts. In a plaintive letter written in 1184, after the completion of his fourteen-volume code of law, the *Mishneh Torah,* and while he was working on the *Guide of the Perplexed,* he underscored his devotion to these two disciplines: "Were not the study of the Torah my delight, and did not the study of wisdom divert me from my grief, I should then have perished in mine affliction." This is related, of course, to his intellectual open-mindedness and his conviction that one should "accept the truth from whatever source it proceeds." Hence he affirms concerning a certain work "that the ideas presented . . . are not of my own invention . . . but I have gleaned them from the words of the wise occurring in the *midrashim,* in the Talmud, and in other of their works as well as from the words of the philosophers, ancient and recent." Torah and philosophy are consistently juxtaposed as sources of his teaching and as natural companions.

Finally, Maimonides' creativity reflects a strong pedagogic drive. His youthful works (*Millot ha-higgayon,* on logic, and *Ma'amar ha-'ibbur,* on the astronomical principles of the Jewish calendar) were composed in response to specific requests. Throughout his life he wrote hundreds of *responsa (teshuvot)*—decisions concerning the interpretation or application of the law—and letters of advice, comfort, or arbitration to all parts of the world, including Yemen, Baghdad, Aleppo, Damascus, Jerusalem, Alexandria, Marseilles, and Lunel. *Iggeret ha-shemad* (Epistle on Conversion) and *Iggeret Teiman* (Epistle to Yemen) are especially noteworthy. His code of law was intended for "small and great"; indeed, law for him was an educative force leading to ethical and intellectual perfection, and his code was intended to be not only a manual of commands but an instrument of education and instruction. His multifaceted erudition and constructive expository skills were widely appreciated, and he freely shared their fruits with inquirers and readers. Failure to share one's knowledge with others would be tantamount to "robbing one who deserves the truth of the truth, or begrudging an heir his inheritance" (*Guide,* intro. to part 3).

Maimonides' major works are the *Perush ha-Mishnah* (Commentary on the Mishnah), *Sefer ha-mitsvot* (Book of the Commandments), *Mishneh Torah* (Review of the Torah; also known as *Yad ha-ḥazaqah*), and *Moreh nevukhim* (Guide of the Perplexed). He also wrote some ten medical treatises that illustrate his vast erudition and the high ethical standards he brought to medicine. They are based to a large extent on Arabic medical literature. One of them deals with Galen and contains a rejoinder to Galen's criticisms of the Mosaic Torah.

Commentary on the Mishnah and Book of the Commandments. The pioneering, comprehensive *Commentary on the Mishnah,* which engaged the attention of Maimonides for about ten years (1158–1168), was intended as both an introduction to and a review of the Talmud. Because it was composed in Arabic and translated into Hebrew in installments over the next two centuries, it did not have as great or immediate an impact as his other works. It combines minute textual study, even lexicographical annotation, with conceptual analysis. Maimonides often digresses to elaborate a theological principle or elucidate a philosophic or scientific issue, for, as he confesses, "expounding a single principle of religion is dearer to me than anything else that I might teach." The book includes noteworthy discussions of many problems: prophecy; the reconciliation of physics with the traditional understanding of the biblical account of creation *(ma'aseh bere'shit)* and of metaphysics with traditional interpretations of Ezekiel's vision of the divine chariot *(ma'aseh merkavah);* the reconciliation of belief in free will with belief in predestination; reward and punishment; the history of religion; magic, medicine, and miracles; immortality and the world to come; and the proper methodological use of allegory.

In the *Commentary* Maimonides was already preoccupied with a problem that was to engage him intermittently for the rest of his life and that was also becoming a staple theme of Jewish religious thought: the metaphorical interpretation of the *aggadah,* the sections of the Talmud that deal with lore rather than law. Maimonides had planned to write a special commentary that would classify, explain, and rationalize the *aggadah,* but abandoned the idea; the *Guide of the Perplexed,* which was devoted in great part to matters of exegesis and allegory, was, by his own account, intended as a partial replacement for this work. The interest shown by Maimonides in *aggadic* interpretation gives that subject more prestige and also suggests that the *Guide* is part of the aggadic as well as the philosophic tradition.

Embedded in the *Commentary* are three separate monographs. The general introduction is a comprehensive inquiry into the theoretical, historical, and doctrinal foundations of the oral law—its origin in the act of revelation at Sinai and, in particular, the ongoing process of its transmission and interpretation. Maimonides emphasizes that the oral law is a completely rational enterprise, subject to its own canons of interpretation and brooking no suprarational interference. Even prophecy is of little relevance to the juridical process.

Only the prophecy of Moses was legislative; all subsequent prophecy was merely exhortatory and could not produce new laws (see also *Guide* 2.39).

Chapter Ten *(pereq ḥeleq)* of the Talmudic tractate *Sanhedrin,* beginning "All Israelites have a share in the world to come," provides an occasion for Maimonides to include a lengthy excursus on Jewish belief. After criticizing crude, materialistic conceptions of the world to come and identifying the religious concept of the world to come with the philosophical notion of the immortality of the soul, Maimonides defines the term "Israelites" by formulating the famous thirteen principles, or articles of faith, that every Israelite is expected to endorse. The thirteen principles may be reduced to three basic groups: God—his existence, unity, incorporeality, and eternity, and the prohibition of idolatry; the law—prophecy, the uniqueness of Mosaic prophecy, the divine origin of the written and oral law, and the eternity and immutability of the law; beliefs relating to reward and punishment—God's omniscience, divine compensation for good and evil, the coming of the Messiah, and resurrection. All subsequent discussion of dogma by Jewish thinkers relates to this Maimonidean formulation.

Maimonides' introduction to *Pirqei avot* (Ethics of the Fathers), entitled "Eight Chapters," is a psychological-ethical treatise: its basis is an analysis of the soul and its powers, while its goal is a full presentation of Maimonides' theory of the golden mean. Maimonides defines virtues as psychological dispositions situated between extremes of excess and deficiency; a good deed is one that maintains the mean between these two bad extremes. This theory is the basis for a forceful repudiation by Maimonides of asceticism and all forms of extremism. Maimonides criticizes Jews who imitate "the followers of other religions" (probably Sufism) by adopting self-mortification and renunciation of "every joy." The last chapter contains an unequivocal affirmation of human freedom and, concomitantly, the rejection of all views (e.g., astrology and divine predestination) that would undermine free will. These introductions or excursuses, with their philosophical, psychological, and ethical disquisitions, enable the reader to take a rather accurate measure of the Maimonidean temper. Some scholars suggest that the *Guide* contradicts these earlier writings of Maimonides on many points (including, for example, free will).

In preparation for his great code of law, Maimonides wrote the *Book of the Commandments,* which provides a complete list of the 613 commandments thereby helping him to guard against forgetfulness and omissions and ensuring the comprehensiveness of the code. A major achievement of this work is the introduction, which defines fourteen guiding principles that determine which laws should be included in the enumeration of the 613. The ninth principle introduces an interesting classification of laws: (1) beliefs and opinions (e.g., to acknowledge the unity of God); (2) actions (e.g., to offer sacrifices); (3) virtues and traits of character (e.g., to love one's neighbor); (4) speech (e.g., to pray). This fourfold classification is significant for its all-inclusiveness and its repudiation—intentional or incidental—of narrow "legalism," in the pejorative sense that is often attached to the term as a description of Judaism.

Mishneh Torah. Completed around the year 1178, the *Mishneh Torah* is a presentation of Jewish law without precedent or sequel in rabbinic literature. It is distinguished by five major characteristics: its codificatory form, its scope, its system of classification, its language and style, and its fusion of *halakhah* and philosophy.

1. *Codificatory form.* Maimonides presented the massive material in crisp, concise form, eliminating indeterminate debate and conflicting interpretations and formulating unilateral, undocumented decisions. He occasionally cites sources, mentions names of authorities, presents more than one view, includes exegetical and explanatory material, and describes personal views and practices.

2. *Scope.* One of the most revolutionary aspects of the code is its all-inclusive scope, which obliterates accidental distinctions between the practical and the theoretical. Maimonides opposed the pervasive tendency to study only those parts of the Talmud that were practical and relevant. He insisted that the abstruse, "antiquated" sections of the Talmud were not inferior to the popular, practical sections and should receive equal time and consideration. Laws concerning sacrifices or the messianic period were codified by him as precisely and comprehensively as laws concerning prayer and marital relations.

3. *Classification.* Maimonides abandoned the sequence of the Mishnah and created a new topical and pedagogical arrangement. Classification is, of course, a prerequisite for codification and necessitates interpretation, sustained conceptualization, a large measure of abstraction, and a synoptic view of the entire body of material. Legal classification concerns itself not only with the sum total of individual laws but with the concept of law per se. The ruling passion of Maimonides' life was order, system, conceptualization, and generalization, and this received its finest expression in *Mishneh Torah.*

4. *Language and style.* Maimonides chose the Hebrew of the Mishnah rather than the Hebrew of the Bible or the Aramaic of the Talmud and developed a rich, flexible style characterized by precision, brevity, and elegance. As a result, the *Mishneh Torah* contains substantial portions of the Talmud translated into fluent, felicitous Hebrew.

5. *Fusion of halakhah and philosophy.* Maimonides sought to bring about the unity of practice and concept, external observance and inner meaning, visible action and invisible experience, law and philosophy. This unification of the practical, theoretical, and theological components is underscored by Maimonides in a letter in which he describes the twofold objective of the *Mishneh Torah* as the provision of an authoritative compilation both of laws and of "true beliefs."

Book 1 of the *Mishneh Torah* (*Sefer ha-madda'*, Book of Knowledge) is a summary of the essential beliefs and guiding concepts that constitute the ideological and experiential substructure of Judaism. Maimonides explains that he could not compose a comprehensive work on the details of practical precepts while ignoring the fundamentals of essential beliefs, those commandments that are the "root" *('iqqar)* of Mosaic religion and that should be known before anything else. The systematic treatment of metaphysics and ethics; the use of separate sections for laws of study *(talmud torah)* and laws of repentance *(teshuvah);* the devotion of a section to idolatry, including a history of religion and a review of superstitions and magical practices that must be uncompromisingly rejected—all these are combined in book 1, which serves as an introduction to, as well as an integral part of, the entire code.

Philosophic comments, rationalistic directives, ethical insights, and theological principles are also incorporated in other parts of the *Mishneh Torah.* Maimonides' systematization of the *halakhah* includes a good measure of ethical interpretation, spiritualization, and rationalization—the whole system of *ṭa'amei ha-mitsvot,* the reasons for the commandments. While not too many laws are actually rationalized, the mandate to engage in rationalization, to penetrate to the essence and the real motive powers of the commandments, is clearly issued in the *Mishneh Torah.* It is thus most significant that this code reveals Maimonides as jurist and philosopher simultaneously.

The *Mishneh Torah,* all the criticism of it notwithstanding, exercises a decisive, extensive, nearly constant influence on the study and practice of *halakhah.* This tightly structured work has become a prism through which passes practically all reflection on and analysis of Talmudic study. There is hardly a major literary development in the broad field of rabbinic literature—not only in the field of codification—that does not relate in some way to the *Mishneh Torah,* a work that remains *sui generis,* unprecedented and unrivaled.

Guide of the Perplexed. Maimonides' philosophic testament *par excellence,* his *Guide of the Perplexed,* was composed in Arabic sometime between 1185 and 1190 and was translated into Hebrew just prior to Maimonides' death by Shemu'el ibn Tibbon (c. 1150–c. 1230). It is divided into three parts and covers a wide spectrum of philosophic problems. Maimonides deals with the basic problems that engaged all medieval religious philosophers: faith and reason, or the relation of philosophy to scripture; the existence, unity, incorporeality, and freedom of God; God's relation to the world in terms of its origin and government; communication between God and man through revelation; and the issues of ethics, free will, and human destiny, including immortality and doctrines of eschatology. The *Guide* was used extensively by Jewish thinkers and also by Christian scholastics, most notably Thomas Aquinas.

Why and for whom was the *Guide* written? Specifically, Maimonides composed it for his student Yosef ben Yehudah Sham'un; generally, he addresses himself to the "perplexed," who is characterized as "a religious man for whom the validity of our law has become established in his soul and has become actual in his belief—such a man being perfect in his religion and character, and having studied the sciences of the philosophers and come to know what they signify." Maimonides is not concerned to teach "the vulgar or beginners in speculation nor those who have not engaged in any study other than the science of the law, I mean the legalistic study of the law. For the purpose of this treatise . . . is the science of law in its true sense." His reader is a religious intellectual, well versed in Jewish law and classical philosophy, who is perplexed because he wants to preserve the integrity of both and is unwilling to renounce either. Maimonides undertakes to achieve this objective by explaining metaphysics, revealing the mistakes of the philosophers, and interpreting the esoteric meaning of the Hebrew Bible and Talmud.

Maimonides emphasizes his insistence upon intellectual rigor and proper method in achieving these goals; hence his determination to expose the mistakes of certain "philosophers, particularly the followers of the *kalām,*" who frequently "violate that which is perceived by the senses." He gives primacy to purity of method. The esoteric meaning of the Bible is elicited by proper use of the method of allegory—that is, the identification of the supraliteral sense of the religious texts. This is one way of affirming that the religious tradition contains the basic truths of philosophy. Moreover, there is essential harmony between faith and reason. In common with other medieval religious philosophers, Maimonides adds revelation to reason and sense perception as sources of knowledge. It is this epistemological assumption that alters classical epistemology and that accounts for Maimonides' axiom of the compatibility of religious tradition and philosophic reasoning. While there is no contradiction between them, Maimonides believed that demonstrated belief is superior to faith—he held what the historian of religion Harry A. Wolfson called a "single-faith theory of the rationalist type."

Maimonides' ideal was a blending of "the science of law, i.e., the legalistic study of the law" with "the science of the law in its true sense." The phrase "legalistic study of the law" is not a tautology. Maimonides here establishes in one bold stroke that law is two-dimensional: legal (in the restricted, positive sense) and metalegal or philosophical. Both, in Maimonides' view, are components of the oral law. According to his history of philosophy (*Guide* 1.71), which was shared by many Jewish, Christian, and Muslim writers down to the beginning of the modern era, the Jews in antiquity cultivated the sciences of physics and metaphysics, which they later neglected for a variety of historical and theological reasons; they did not borrow from Greek thought because philosophy was an integral part of their religious tradition. This dovetails perfectly with Maimonides' halakhic formulation (*Mishneh Torah,* Study of the Torah 1.11, 1.12), which grafts philosophy onto the substance of the oral law and makes its study mandatory. This is Maimonides' intellectual conviction and philosophic position: the essential relationship and constant intersection of philosophy and *halakhah.* For him, the issue is not the legitimacy of philosophy in religion, but the legitimacy of religion without philosophy. Just as Yehudah ha-Levi considered philosophy an unwelcome intrusion, Maimonides considered its absence undesirable and intolerable.

A third issue in Maimonides' treatment of philosophy—in addition to the epistemological issue (reason and revelation as twin sources of knowledge) and the historical issue (the existence of philosophy as a part of traditional Jewish lore)—is cultural: philosophy implies a measure of universality. Hence Maimonides assumes the identity of the lost classical philosophic tradition of Judaism with the study of philosophy that was in his own day being restored under foreign influence. He does not need to be uncomfortable when in his reconstruction of the history of philosophy he acknowledges the non-Jewish, primarily Muslim, stimulus for the medieval revival of Jewish philosophy. "We have already explained that all these views do not contradict anything said by our prophets and the sustainers of our law. . . . When in consequence of all this [exile and loss of wisdom] we grew up accustomed to the opinions of the ignorant, these philosophic views appeared to be, as it were, foreign to our law, just as they are foreign to the opinions of the ignorant. However, matters are not like this" (*Guide* 2.11). In a letter to his translator, Shemu'el ibn Tibbon, he mentions his main philosophic sources: Aristotle, whose books are "the roots and foundations of all works in the sciences"; al-Fārābī, whose "writings are faultlessly excellent—one ought to study and understand them"; and the important commentaries on Aristotle by Alexander of Aphrodisias, Themistius, and Ibn Rushd (Averroës).

Maimonidean philosophy is full of problems and dialectical pressures. In order to enlighten some readers without disconcerting others, Maimonides abandoned his fastidious organization, separated a unified presentation of views into unrelated sections, and even introduced premeditated, carefully wrought contradictions. Reading the *Guide* is thus a major challenge. To this day this dialectic continues to befuddle students of the *Guide,* who disagree concerning Maimonides' true intention and actual religious-philosophic stance.

There is, of course, a basic tension in the very attempt to combine Aristotelian philosophy with Judaism, and it is not certain that the two sides of Maimonides—the sovereign master of *halakhah* and the zealous disciple of Aristotle—could be completely at ease together. Given the supremacy of the contemplative life for Maimonides, what significance did the practical religious life have for him? Is there a genuine incompatibility between the meaningful observance of *mitsvot* and the serious study and appreciation of physics and metaphysics?

All difficulties notwithstanding—and he himself (*Guide* 1.33) mentions the view of those who contend that philosophic inquiry "undermines the foundations of law"—Maimonides remained unswervingly committed to his brand of rationalism. Indeed, he believed that there is a religious obligation to apply one's intellect to the study of God and the world. "One only loves God with the knowledge with which one knows him; according to the knowledge will be the love. If the former be little or much, so will the latter be little or much. A person ought therefore to devote himself to the understanding and comprehension of those sciences and studies which will inform him concerning his master, as far as it lies in human faculties to understand and comprehend."

Achievement and Legacy. Maimonides' lifework—the fastidious interpretation and thoughtful reformulation of Jewish belief and practice—seems to have been clear in his mind from an early age. There is a conscious unity and progressive continuity in his literary career. It is striking how early his ideas, ideals, and aspirations were formed, how logically they hang together, and how consistently and creatively they were applied. As his work moves from textual explication to independent exposition, and from one level of exposition to another, the reader, moving with it, feels that Maimonides had from the very beginning a master plan to achieve one overarching objective: to bring *halakhah* and philosophy, two apparently incongruous attitudes of mind, into fruitful harmony.

Maimonides consistently espoused a sensitized view of religion and morality, demanding an uncompromising observance of the law, openly disdaining the perfunctory view of the masses, searching for the ultimate religious significance of every human action, and urging a commitment to, and quest for, wisdom and perfection. He pursued a vision of a meaningful observance of *mitsvot* combined with a genuine appreciation of philosophy. Routine piety and unreflective behavior he denigrated; Talmudism divorced from spiritual animation he found wanting. He emphasized the nobility of philosophic religion, in which rationalism and piety are natural companions and through which human perfection is advanced. As a religious rationalist, he was convinced of the interrelatedness and complementarity of divine and human wisdom and strove doggedly for their integration.

Maimonides knew that this could not be done easily or indiscriminately, but he was convinced that the very attempt, full of tension and problems, was indispensable for the achievement of true religious perfection. It may be said that Maimonides allowed religious rationalism, which had led a sort of subliminal existence in earlier rabbinic writing, to claim and obtain legitimacy and dignity. Maimonides picked up the various strands of rationalism and, by criticizing, refining, and extending them, emerged as the symbol of the religious rationalist mentality and the harbinger of a new direction in religious thought. To a great extent, subsequent Jewish religious-intellectual history may be seen as a debate concerning the wisdom and effectiveness of the Maimonidean position.

BIBLIOGRAPHY

Altmann, Alexander. "Maimonides' 'Four Perfections.'" *Israel Oriental Studies* 2 (1972): 15–24.

Bacher, Wilhelm, Marcus Brann, and David Jacob Simonsen, eds. *Moses ben Maimon.* 2 vols. Leipzig, 1908–1914; reprint, Hildesheim, 1971.

Baron, Salo W., ed. *Essays on Maimonides.* New York, 1941.

Berman, Lawrence. "Maimonides, the Disciple of Alfārābī." *Israel Oriental Studies* 4 (1974): 154–178.

Epstein, Isidore, ed. *Moses Maimonides.* London, 1935.

Halkin, Abraham, and David Hartman. *Crisis and Leadership: Epistles of Maimonides.* Philadelphia, 1985.

Hartman, David. *Maimonides: Torah and Philosophic Quest.* Philadelphia, 1976.

Lerner, Ralph. "Maimonides' Letter on Astrology." *History of Religions* 8 (November 1968): 143–158.

Maimonides, Moses. *The Book of Divine Commandments.* Translated and edited by Charles B. Chavel, London, 1940.

Maimonides, Moses. *The Code of Maimonides.* 15 vols. to date. Yale Judaica Series. New Haven, 1949–.

Maimonides, Moses. *Guide of the Perplexed.* Translated by Shlomo Pines with introductory essay by Leo Strauss. Chicago, 1963.

Twersky, Isadore, ed. *A Maimonides Reader.* New York, 1972.

Twersky, Isadore. *Introduction to the Code of Maimonides (Mishneh Torah).* New Haven, 1980.

Wolfson, Harry A. *Studies in the History of Philosophy and Religion,* vol. 2. Cambridge, Mass., 1977.

ISADORE TWERSKY

MAITREYA. Among the pantheon of Buddhist personages none offers such a complex array of incarnations as does Maitreya. His first and most important role is that of successor to Śākyamuni as a Buddha who achieves the ultimate state of enlightenment after having been born as a human. The notion of Maitreya as the future Buddha is found within the traditions of all Buddhists, although there is no universal agreement about his life history or about the way in which he will realize the destiny set forth by his position as the next Buddha.

Textual Accounts. A survey of the literature provides us with some indication of the ways the Maitreya story has developed and increased in importance. The Pali canon, the source of much of our information on the early teaching, does not give Maitreya much significance, mentioning his name in only one of the early texts, the *Cakkavattisīhanāda Sutta.* In the noncanonic literature, two works are devoted primarily to Maitreya, the *Anagatavaṃsa* and the *Maitreyavyākaraṇa,* but the origin of these works and their precise dating are not known. An expanded version of the Maitreya story can be found in the *Divyāvadāna* of the Mūlasarvāstivādin school. Among this collection of tales is a story of a *bodhisattva* who wishes to perform an extreme act of ascetic practice and donate his head to a brahman teacher as a sign of his sincerity to pursue truth. But a deity, watching over the garden in which this scene occurs, attempts to save the *bodhisattva*'s life by keeping the brahman at a distance. The *bodhisattva* pleads with the deity to allow him to proceed because it was in this very garden that Maitreya had previously turned away from his desire to sacrifice his life for his teacher, thus failing to fulfill his highest aspirations, a flaw that should not be repeated.

The *Mahāvastu,* a text from the Mahāsāṃghika sect, provides a list of future Buddhas, placing Maitreya's name at the top. In this early account we find the name Ajita used to refer to Maitreya in his past lives. Later, Theravādins became quite interested in Ajita, and the story of his life was the focus of much attention by the fifth and sixth centuries. Ajita's identification as the son of King Ajātasattu of Magadha allowed the *saṃgha* to determine exactly where and how the *bodhisattva* will make his appearance when he achieves Buddhahood. According to a section on Maitreya's life in the *Mahāvaṃsa,* a well-known history of Sri Lanka, Maitreya will reside in Tuṣita Heaven before descending to his earthly birth and maturation. The timing of this event is noted clearly. After Śākyamuni's *parinirvāṇa,* the world will enter a period of social and cosmological decline; five thousand years after the last Buddha, the teaching will have fallen to a low ebb, and the human lifespan will have been reduced to ten years. At this time the cycle will be reversed: life will improve until the length of an average lifespan on earth will be eighty-thousand years. In this world of long life and an environment that will be conducive to the teaching of the Buddha, there will be a ruler, a *cakravartin,* who will provide for the welfare of the people and promote the teachings of the Buddha. [*See* Cakravartin.] When this paradise is ready, Maitreya will descend from Tuṣita Heaven, realize his full potential as a Buddha, and teach the Dharma to advanced beings. Mahākāśyapa, one of the major disciples of Śākyamuni, will arise from the trance state he entered after the *parinirvāṇa* of his former teacher to once again serve a Buddha and hear the teaching of the enlightened one.

This millenarian view of Maitreya is still held in the Buddhist areas of South and Southeast Asia, and in northern Burma there is a belief that a contemporary teacher known as Bodaw was a universal king as well as the future Buddha Maitreya. The identification of Maitreya with leaders and founders is found consistently throughout Buddhist Asia.

Scholars have suggested that the idea of the future Buddha may be derived from the Iranian concept of the savior Saoshyant. [*See* Saoshyant.] In this light, Maitreya would represent the establishment of a world in which there is peace and abundance and where the Dharma will be taught and fully understood. Others, however, take the position that these ideas were already present in India at the time of Śākyamuni. The Buddhists, as well as the Ājīvikas and Jains, taught that there would be new *tīrthaṃkaras, jinas,* and Buddhas in the future. P. S. Jaini suggests that the source for the Maitreya development was within the Mahāsāṃghika school. Whereas the Theravāda paid little attention to Maitreya, giving only one canonic reference, the *Mahāvastu* of the Mahāsāṃghikas devotes a number of paragraphs to Maitreya, noting his name as Ajita, detailing events from his past lives, and telling of Śākyamuni's prediction of Buddhahood for him. Thus, there is ample material to justify the study of Maitreya as a part of the Indian cultural and religious domain, without having to rely on a diffusionist theory of external influences to account for the notion of the future Buddha.

The Mahāyāna tradition has given much attention to Maitreya, and we find in the literature many references to his life and activities. Since the Mahāyāna has emphasized the career and development of the *bodhisattva,* it is understandable that it would place Maitreya in this honored group. As with the earlier tradition, all Mahāyāna groups believe that Maitreya will follow in the footsteps of Śākyamuni. In the pantheon of *bodhisattvas*, Maitreya is not always given the highest place; he shares with such *bodhisattvas* as Mañjuśrī and Avalokiteśvara the esteem of the community of believers. In the Prajñāpāramitā texts, Maitreya is involved in dialogue with the Buddha and a group of disciples made up of *bodhisattvas* and *arhats*. The *arhats*, even the famous followers of Śākyamuni, are ranked far below the *bodhisattvas* in terms of their level of understanding. Thus the Prajñāpāramitā literature depicts Maitreya as ranking above an *arhat* such as Śāriputra. But Maitreya is not always portrayed so flatteringly in Mahāyāna literature. For example, in an account from the *Saddharmapuṇḍarīka Sūtra,* Mañjuśri tells Maitreya that in the past, when he had taught the Dharma to Maitreya, Maitreya was a slothful student more interested in fame than understanding. Thus, in this meeting with his old teacher, Maitreya still needs answers to his questions. [*See* Mañjuśrī.] The question of whether Maitreya and Śākyamuni had ever met in any of their former lives also arises in Mahāyāna literature. The *Mahākarmavibhaṅga* states that the Buddha had indeed met Maitreya and praised him for his desire to live as a *bodhisattva.*

The Tantric tradition of later Mahāyāna seems to have had little interest in Maitreya. This tradition's dismissal of Maitreya may be seen in the *Guhyasamāja Tantra,* in which Maitreya is described as afraid and upset when he hears the Vajrayāna teaching. Because he is of limited learning, he is not able to comprehend this advanced instruction. The same questioning of Maitreya's level of comprehension is found in the *Vimalakīrtinirdeśa,* in which Maitreya is unable to give a proper response to the layman Vimalakīrti, who challenges the prediction of Buddhahood by questioning whether the three times (past, present, and future) can be accepted as real. If they are not real, asks Vimalakīrti, in what sense can one say that a past prediction will result in future events? Unable to respond, Maitreya is reduced to silence. Thus the Mahāyāna texts present a varied view of this *bodhisattva,* showing him as destined for a great position in the future but still lacking the training necessary for a full understanding of the highest teaching within the tradition.

A much more glorified depiction of Maitreya occurs in the *Gaṇḍhavyūha Sūtra.* Here, Maitreya appears as a teacher of the young Sudhana, who travels about searching for answers from more than fifty teachers. Upon entering Maitreya's palace, Sudhana experiences, through the power of Maitreya, a trance in which he has visions of important places in the life of the future Buddha, including the place where Maitreya achieved the trance called *maitra* ("kind, amicable") that is the basis for his name. Sudhana then witnesses a long line of incarnations of Maitreya, including the life in which the *bodhisattva* was a king and another in which he was the king of the gods. Finally, Sudhana sees the Tuṣita Heaven, where Maitreya's rebirth will occur just prior to Buddhahood. Maitreya tells Sudhana that they will meet again when the final birth has been accomplished. Even the texts that teach the superiority of the Pure Land of Amitābha and are usually considered affiliated with a school that was in competition with the Maitreya cult indicate that Sudhana is one of the privileged ones who have the ability to see the realm of Amitābha. [*See* Amitābha.]

Cult. The practice that has grown up around the figure of Maitreya goes far beyond the aspects that have been noted in the canonical and popular literature.

China. When Buddhism arrived in China (c. first century CE), there was considerable interest in Maitreya, in part because of the Taoist belief in the ever-possible appearance of a sage capable of giving salvation to an elite band of devotees. As early as the Eastern Chin dynasty (317–420), Buddhist cultic life was directed toward Maitreya. Indeed, one of China's most famous monks, Tao-an, took a vow to be reborn in Tuṣita Heaven in order to be near Maitreya and with him when he descends to earth. [*See the biography of Tao-an.*] In the succeeding centuries, the Northern Wei (386–535) carved two great cave complexes, the first at Yün-kang and the other at Lung-men. At Yün-kang, the earlier of the two sites, the Maitreya figures are prominent, and even today visitors can see him depicted in a number of poses. The caves at Lung-men also contain many Maitreya figures, most dating to the first part of the sixth century. Tsukamoto Zenryū, who charted the number of images made in Lung-men, has shown that although Śākyamuni and Maitreya were the chief models in the early days, by the seventh century attention was centered instead on Amitābha and Avalokiteśvara. (See his *Shina bukkyōshi kenkyū: Hokugi-hen,* Tokyo, 1942, pp. 355ff.)

Interest in the Pure Land teaching reached a high level during the seventh century and continued to have support throughout the T'ang period (618–907); consequently, Maitreya's image was hardly ever depicted. But while Maitreya was no longer a popular subject for cave paintings or court-sponsored projects, he was not forgotten. At this time the Chinese people transformed him into a folk deity of great importance. Although majestic images of Maitreya carved in the caves disappeared from the repetoire of artists, a new form of Maitreya—as a fat, laughing, pot-bellied person—emerged in the Sung dynasty. There is evidence that this vision of Maitreya was based on a popular historical figure, a tenth-century wandering sage. He is said to have been a native of Chekiang and to have carried a hemp bag wherever he went. Children were especially attracted to him, and he is often depicted surrounded by them. Many stories arose about his miraculous abilities, including one that tells of the discovery of a third eye on his back. Because of the eye people called him a Buddha, even though he begged them not to spread the word about his characteristics. Such stories led to the belief that this wanderer was none other than Maitreya himself, who had come down to earth and taken this unlikely form, attracting people through his wisdom and loving patience. Today, the figure of Maitreya in this guise is placed at the main entrance of Chinese monasteries, where he is revered by all laymen who wish for good fortune and prosperity.

Because he was conceived as a future Buddha who will come at a time when a great king rules, Maitreya was often used by those who wanted to secure political power or give themselves a legitimate basis for ruling. As early as the seventh century, Chinese rulers and would-be leaders were declaring themselves his incarnation or claiming they were destined to prepare the nation for the advent of the new Buddha. In 613, for example, Sung Tzu-hsien, calling himself Maitreya, planned a revolt against the dynasty; later, during the T'ang, Empress Wu made the same claim when she came to power. The Sung dynasty (960–1279) saw the emergence of secret societies oriented to the notion that Maitreya was already in the world or that the world needed to be changed to accommodate him. The political use of Maitreya by those who challenged established authority may be one reason for the decline of royal patronage of artworks using this *bodhisattva* as a theme.

In Chinese cultic life Maitreya came to be associated with the three stages of cosmic time; he is the herald of the last age. In *pao-chüan* ("precious scroll") literature, which reflects the attitudes and beliefs of folk religion, we find the notion that he is a messenger who comes to earth during the last age as an ambassador of the Great Mother in order to save the sinful. A seventeenth-century *pao-chüan* text describes Maitreya as the controller of the heavens during the third age, which is symbolized by the color white. He sits on his throne, a nine-petaled lotus blossom, and waits for the time when he will rule for 108,000 years.

Maitreya was an important part of Chinese Buddhist development, in part because many millenarian movements could make full use of him without considering that he was anything but a Chinese deity; his foreign origin was forgotton. An example of the way in which motifs can spread from one culture to another is the case of Doan Minh Huyen, the charismatic Vietnamese leader who preached in regions devastated by the cholera epidemics of the nineteenth century. Doan advocated the founding of communities of believers who would teach followers and lead them to a state of spiritual perfection, thus ensuring that they would be protected from the upcoming holocaust. According to Doan, Maitreya would descend from Tuṣita Heaven to the mountains near Cambodia to preside over the Dragon Flower Assembly and bring about a new era.

The more orthodox Buddhists among the monastic and lay community were interested in Maitreya because they faced the uncertainity of living in a time when the "true teaching" was thought to be disappearing. In Maitreya, the Chinese found a deity that met their needs at many levels, and they did not hesitate to invest him with a variety of costumes, abilities, and cultic functions. [See also Millenarianism, *article on* Chinese Millenarian Movements.]

Korea. Another East Asian nation, Korea, has also paid much attention to Maitreya, in part because Buddhism was introduced on the peninsula at a time when the Maitreya cult was at the pinnacle of its importance in China. Since Maitreya practice was one of the first to be introduced, Korea held it in high esteem and continued to do so long after Chinese interest in the traditional aspects of Maitreya had died. The belief in Maitreya came to Korea from the Northern Wei and the kingdoms that followed it, and we can see him depicted in triad compositions from both the Paekche and Koguryŏ periods. Some scholars maintain that Maitreya practice in Korea was divided into two distinct approaches. Under Paekche rule, believers assumed that the nation had to prepare a proper environment for Maitreya before he would descend. During the Silla kingdom, on the other hand, it was thought that Maitreya would descend to the world and operate within it even if the times were troubled.

During the Three Kingdoms period (late fourth century–668), a semimilitary organization of young men, known as Hwarang, came to have a special relationship to Maitreya. Their association with Maitreya may be rooted in a sixth-century story about a monk who wished to have Maitreya reborn in the world so that he could pay homage to him. During a dream he discovered that Maitreya had already come into the world and had taken the form of a *hwarang* ("flower boy"). Identification of the *hwarang* with Maitreya was widespread, and it may be that the images of the *bodhisattva* that depict him as a pensive prince with one leg crossed over the knee of the other are visual representations of this association. During the Koryŏ period, there was much interest in the three periods of the teaching, and many believed that the final period, in which the true teaching would disappear to be replaced with a misunderstood one, had approached. Since the *sūtras* taught that this era would be reached fifteen hundred years after the *parinirvāṇa* of the Buddha, the Koreans assumed that the evil age was to start in the year 1052. There was much in subsequent centuries to justify the notion that an evil time had indeed come, and during these times of social disorder many understandably longed for the appearance of Maitreya in his role of protector. Even in the present, believers look to Maitreya for protection and assistance. Local people in Korea still approach statues of Maitreya to pray for good fortune, the birth of a son, the cure to an illness, and for protection in times of trouble.

The most distinctive images of Maitreya in Korea show a large platform secured to the top of his head, with either a tiered or a rounded form placed upon it. This headpiece may represent the stupa that Maitreya characteristically wears on the head.

The role of Maitreya in fertility cults is most easily seen in the practice now found in Korea's Cheju Island, in the northern East China Sea. At one site on the island an image of Maitreya has been placed next to a phallic stone; women come to the spot to touch the stone in the hope that this act will result in the birth of a son. When one takes an inventory of the objects toward which prayers for sons are directed, Maitreya is found alongside the Dragon King, the Mountain Spirit, and the Seven Stars. Of all the figures in the Buddhist pantheon, Maitreya was the one thought to be most able to answer particular prayers for children. This may explain the fat belly and surrounding children found in the Chinese form.

Maitreya also appears as a major element in the messianic groups that have arisen in Korea. One of these is a new religion founded in the late nineteenth century known as Chungsan-gyo, whose followers believe that a disease is present in the Kunsan area that, if not controlled, could spread throughout the world and bring destruction to the human race. Chungsan, the founder of this sect, taught that he alone had the magical spell necessary to control the disease. His followers believe that he was an incarnation of Maitreya and that he had descended to earth and for thirty years lived within an image of Maitreya. A more recent group, which has grown up around Yi Yu-song, teaches that Hananim, the primordial deity of Korean epics, the ruler of Heaven, will descend to Korea in the form of Maitreya Buddha.

In the twentieth century, Korean Buddhists continue to recognize Maitreya; twenty-seven major images of him in his majestic standing position have been constructed. Although the Chogye order of monks and nuns pays little attention to this *bodhisattva*, the laypeople of Korea, like those of China, refuse to let Maitreya fade from their religious practice. [*See also* Buddhism, *article on* Buddhism in Korea, *and* Korean Religion.]

Japan. The Japanese received the first information about Maitreya from Korea, a transmission that included images of the *bodhisattva*. Most of the monasteries said to have been founded by Shōtoku Taishi (574–622) contain statues of Maitreya in the pose of the pensive prince. It is probable that the Japanese viewed Maitreya as a *kami*, able to bring long life and prosperity, and thus rituals directed toward him were similar to those performed for indigenous spirits. During the later Heian period (794–1185), many felt that the time of the false teaching had been reached and found solace in the thought that Maitreya would soon descend to the earth and preach three sermons under the Dragon Flower Tree. Among those who hoped to see Maitreya was Kūkai (774–835), the founder of the Shingon sect, who proclaimed on his deathbed that he would be born into Tuṣita Heaven, where he would spend thousands of years in the presence of the future Buddha before descending with him to the world.

Later developments of the Maitreya cult can still be seen in Japan. In Kashima, for example, it is believed that the rice-laden Ship of Maitreya will one day come from a paradise out in the sea. During the Edo period (1600–1868) the Kashima area was the site of Maitreya dances in which the priestess of the shrine gave an oracle that foretold the coming year's fortune. In this capacity she reached out to the world of Maitreya, a paradise of abundance.

Some groups expect that Maitreya's future appearance will take place in Japan, on top of Kimpusan, where the Golden Land will be established and Maitreya will teach his three sermons. Followers in each of the major Buddhist areas in Asia have put forth the belief that Maitreya will be born within their own region and thus can be considered as one of their own rather than a foreigner.

Many of those who, by virtue of their membership in a Maitreya group, consider themselves an elite hope to remain on earth until Maitreya descends. In other cases, devotees believe that he has already appeared. For example, in 1773 a group known as Fujikō claimed that Maitreya had manifested himself on top of Mount Fuji. The leader, a priest named Kakugyō, announced the advent of the World of Maitreya. Later, Kakugyō sealed himself in a cell, drinking only water until his death, which his followers believe is but a stage of waiting for the new age with the future Buddha. The Fujikō articulated the hopes and aspirations of agrarian communities of the time. During the peasant rebellions of the Edo, large numbers of the group went on a pilgrimage called *eejanaika*, making the Ise Shrine the focus of their attention. Dancing themselves into ecstatic states, the pilgrims proclaimed that Maitreya would bring abundant harvests.

The twentieth century has been a time of great interest in the "new religions" *(shinkō shūkyō)*, and within them we see the continuing thread of belief in the future Buddha and his appearance in the world. The Ōmotokyō, for example, have close ties with Maitreya. In 1928, Deguchi Onisaburō declared himself an incarnation of Maitreya. This proclamation was made during the year of the dragon, which the oracle had described as the year when great changes would take place. Another new group, the Reiyūkai, was founded by Kubo Kakutarō and his sister-in-law Kotani Kimi, who was renowned as a faith healer and called a living Buddha by her followers. After her death the sect established a mountain training center in which her teachings are the center of attention. The identification of Kotani with Maitreya can be seen in the name of the retreat, Mirokusan, or Maitreya's Mountain. [*See* Ōmotokyō *and* Reiyūkai Kyōdan.]

Concluding Remarks. Maitreya has been a significant figure in Buddhist thought wherever the religion has found support. For lay followers, the Maitreya cult was one method of creating good karma (Skt., *karman*) for themselves and of assuring that the future would be one of bliss. The element of hope for the future is a crucial part of the idea that Maitreya will or has appeared to lead mankind toward a better time. Since the story of Maitreya has yet to be completed, he can play a part in an infinite variety of scenarios, each established to meet the requirements of a specific time and place.

[*See also* Celestial Buddhas and Bodhisattvas.]

BIBLIOGRAPHY

Primary Sources

"The *Anagata-vaṃsa.*" Edited by J. Minayeff. *Journal of the Pali Text Society* (1886): 33–53.

Aṣṭasāhasrikāprajñāpāramitāsūtra. Edited by Wogihara Unrai. Tokyo, 1932–1935.

Dīgha Nikāya. 3 vols. Edited by T. W. Rhys-Davids and J. Estlin Carpenter. Pali Text Society Series. London, 1890–1911. Translated by T. W. Rhys-Davids and C. A. F. Rhys-Davids as *Dialogues of the Buddha,* "Sacred Books of the Buddhists," vols. 2–4 (London, 1889–1921).

Divyāvadāna. Edited by E. B. Cowell and R. A. Neill. Cambridge, 1886.

Gaṇḍhavyūha Sūtra. Edited by D. T. Suzuki and Idzumi Hokei. Kyoto, 1934–1936.

Guhyasamāja Tantra. Edited by Benoytosh Bhattacharyya. Gaekwad's Oriental Series, no. 53. Baroda, 1931.

Le Mahāvastu. 3 vols. Edited by Émile Senart. Paris, 1882–1897. Translated by J. J. Jones as *The Mahāvastu,* "Sacred Books of the Buddhists," vols. 16, 18, 19 (London, 1949–1956).

Maitreyavyākaraṇa. Edited by Sylvain Lévi. Paris, 1932.

Saddharmapuṇḍarīkasūtra. Edited by Hendrik Kern and Bunyiu Nanjio. Bibliotheca Buddhica. Saint Petersburg, 1914. Translated by Hendrik Kern as *Saddharma-Puṇḍarīka; or, The Lotus of the Good Law,* "Sacred Books of the Buddhists," vol. 21 (1884; reprint, New York, 1963). Kumārajīva's fifth-century Chinese translation of the *Lotus* has been translated by Leon N. Hurvitz as *Scripture of the Lotus Blossom of the Fine Dharma* (New York, 1976).

Sukhāvativyūhasūtra. Edited by F. Max Müller and Bunyiu Nanjio. Anecdota Oxonensia Aryan Series. Oxford, 1883. Translated into English by F. Max Müller in *Buddhist Mahāyāna Texts,* edited by E. B. Cowell et al., "Sacred Books of the East," vol. 49 (1894; reprint, New York, 1969).

Vimalakīrtinirdeśa. Translated from Tibetan by Robert A. F. Thurman as *The Holy Teaching of Vimalakīrti: A Mahāyāna Scripture* (University Park, Penn., 1976).

Secondary Sources

Hayami Tasuku. *Miroku shinkō-mō hitotsu no jōdō shinkō.* Nihonjin no kōdō to shisō, vol. 12. Tokyo, 1971.

Miyata Noboru. *Miroku shinkō no kenkyū.* Tokyo, 1975.

Murakami Shigeyoshi. *Japanese Religion in Modern Century.* Translated by H. Byron Earhart. Tokyo, 1980.

Sponberg, Alan, and Helen Hardacre, eds. *Maitreya.* Princeton, 1986.

Tsuruoka Shizuo. "Nihon ni okeru Miroku geshō shinkō ni tsuite." *Shūkyō kenkyū* 144 (1955): 22–35.

LEWIS R. LANCASTER

MAJLISĪ, AL- (AH 1037–1110/11, 1627–1699/1700 CE), Muḥammad Bāqir ibn Muḥammad Taqī, preeminent Persian Shīʿī theologian in the late Safavid period. Born to a family of renowned scholars, he was made leader of the Friday prayers in Isfahan sometime after the death of his father in 1659. Shah Sulaymān appointed him as *shaykh al-Islām,* the highest religious official in the land, in 1687, and he reached the zenith of his power under Shah Sulṭān Ḥusayn, the last Safavid ruler (1694–1722). He died and was buried in Isfahan.

Al-Majlisī's career epitomizes the increasing predominance of the Shīʿī religious hierarchy. He used his influence in court circles to propagate his brand of Shiism, to persecute Ṣūfīs and non-Muslims, and to encourage the often forcible conversion of Sunnīs to Twelver Shiism. In order to reach beyond the learned circles in which Arabic was used as a means of expression he produced a large number of works in Persian, of which the best known are *Ḥayāt al-qulūb* (Life of the Hearts), a work of biographies of the prophets and imams, and *Ḥaqq al-yaqīn* (Certain Truth), his last completed work, which sets out the main tenets of Twelver Shiism.

In his Arabic works, al-Majlisī dealt with a variety of doctrinal issues; he also composed commentaries on some of the classical Shīʿī legal texts. Yet he is best known for his *Biḥār al-anwār* (Oceans of Light), a voluminous encyclopedia containing a vast number of Shīʿī traditions from various sources. As such, it spans virtually all major aspects of Twelver Shīʿī religious thought: the unity of God and the divine attributes; the concepts of knowledge, belief and unbelief, and free will and predestination; the lives of the prophets and imams and the pilgrimages to their graves; the position of the Qurʾān; and positive law.

Thanks to the *Biḥār,* much of the corpus of Shīʿī tradition was saved from oblivion and returned to center stage. In preparing the work, al-Majlisī relied heavily on the help of pupils and enlisted the financial backing of the Safavid court to obtain manuscripts of rare or inaccessible works. The first volume of the *Biḥār* appeared in 1666, and by the time of al-Majlisī's death seventeen of the twenty-six projected volumes had been finished. The rest were completed by his pupil ʿAbd Allāh Efendī. A lithograph edition of the entire work was first published between 1885 and 1897, and a new edition containing 110 volumes has been published in Tehran. Various volumes of the *Biḥār* have been translated into Persian, and the many excerpts, abridgements, and supplements in existence attest to the continuing influence of the work.

BIBLIOGRAPHY

The fullest account to date of al-Majlisī's life and works, with special emphasis on his *magnum opus,* is Karl-Heinz Pampus's *Die theologische Enzyklopädie Biḥār al-Anwār des Muḥammad Bāqir al-Mağlisī, 1037–1110 A.H. = 1627–1699 A.D.* (Bonn, 1970). There is a useful analysis of some aspects of al-Majlisī's theology on pages 93–95 of Said Amir Arjomand's "Religion, Political Action and Legitimate Domination in Shi'ite Iran: Fourteenth to Eighteenth Centuries A.D.," *European Journal of Sociology* 20 (1979): 59–109. Al-Majlisī's influence on Safavid policies is discussed in Laurence Lockhart's *The Fall of the Ṣafavī Dynasty and the Afghan Occupation of Persia* (Cambridge, 1958). Abdul-Hadi Hairi's "Madjlisī" in *The Encyclopaedia of Islam,* new ed. (Leiden, 1960–), contains a good bibliography. A highly competent rendition of selected passages from the *Biḥār* is included in *A Shī'ite Anthology,* edited and translated by William C. Chittick (Albany, N.Y., 1981).

ETAN KOHLBERG

MAKARIOS OF EGYPT (300–390), also known as the Presbyter and Makarios the Great; Christian ascetic and monastic leader. Known from childhood for his prudence and virtue, Makarios was characterized as a "child–old man," that is, a child in age and an old man in conduct. At the age of thirty he renounced the worldly life and went to the desert to become a monk. He repeatedly visited Antony of Egypt and was influenced both by his way of thinking and by his manner of life, which stressed flight from the world, austere asceticism, and constant struggle against Satan. In order to avoid the esteem and praise of others, Makarios went to Scete, in the remote part of the desert, south of Nitria. Because the inhospitality of the place made the ascetic life there difficult, only the most disciplined were able to endure it.

The reputation of Makarios as a saintly man, and his deeds, attracted many ascetics to Scete. In a short time, under his spiritual direction, the monastic center of Scete was enlarged and reorganized. The monks' work, their *ergocheiron* as it is called in monastic language, consisted of the preparation of baskets woven with straw cut from the marsh. They prayed at appointed hours of the day, and on Saturdays and Sundays they all gathered from the huts scattered around the church for the Divine Liturgy, which was usually celebrated by Makarios himself. Makarios had been ordained a priest at the age of forty, at which time he received the title of Mark the Presbyter. Once a day the monks ate a meal consisting of bread and vegetables, without oil, which was used only on Saturdays and Sundays. During the periods of the great fasts, their diet was more severe. Silence was regarded as one of the greater virtues.

During the more than sixty years that Makarios remained in the desert, he acquired the reputation of a great saint and wonder-worker. He was exiled for a short time to a small island in the Nile by the Arian bishop Lucius and died at the age of ninety. In the Orthodox church his feast day is 10 January; in the Western church it is 15 January.

The main works that come from the mouth, if not the hand, of Makarios are his *Forty-six Sayings,* included in *Gerontica* (narratives on the ascetical accomplishments of the Gerontes, or elders, of Scete). Gennadius of Marseilles mentions a letter of Makarios's that probably is the same as the first letter, *Ad filios Dei,* of the Latin collection. There is another short ascetical text of about two hundred lines, preserved in the Codex Jerusalemitus 113.

Some collections of homilies, discourses, and letters attributed to Makarios probably do not belong to him. Current research regards Asia Minor or Syria as their place of origin and the ascetic Symeon of Mesopotamia as their author. Preeminent among these is the collection of fifty homilies known as the *Spiritual Homilies.* However, the question of authorship of the *Spiritual Homilies* still remains open. Also attributed to Makarios are three other collections of various numbers of homilies; four letters (among which is the *Great Epistle*); seven treatises, or ascetical discourses; and two prayers, still used in the Greek Orthodox church.

In his writings Makarios presents the struggle of the faithful against evil, the world, and the passions. The believer can, with the help of divine grace, keep the senses of the soul clean so that they may be inundated by the divine light and become entirely light and spirit. Denial of the desires of the world, of material cares, and of earthly bonds is carried out so that one can receive the Holy Spirit and through the Spirit be enlightened and deified. Because of their mystical and ascetical character, Makarios's writings are highly esteemed, especially in the East. They exerted a great influence on the mystical theology of the Orthodox church, for example in the work of Gregory Palamas. Makarios's influence is also evident through the monastic figure and spiritual writer Evagrios of Pontus, his disciple.

BIBLIOGRAPHY

Davids, E. A. *Das Bild vom neuen Menschen.* Salzburg, 1968.

Desprez, V. *Pseudo-Macarie: Œuvres spirituelles,* vol. 1. *Sources chrétiennes,* vol. 275. Paris, 1980.

Dörries, Hermann. *Symeon von Mesopotamien: Die Überlieferung der messalianischen "Makarios" Schriften*. Leipzig, 1941.

Jaeger, Werner. *Two Rediscovered Works of Ancient Christian Literature: Gregory of Nyssa and Macarius*. Leiden, 1954. See pages 233–301. Includes the *Great Epistle*.

Makarios. *Patrologia Graeca*, edited by J.-P. Migne, vol. 34. Paris, 1860. Includes his letter *Ad filios Dei*.

Makarios. *Die 50 geistlichen Homilien des Makarios*. Edited by Hermann Dörries, Erich Klostermann, and Matthias Kroeger. Berlin, 1964.

THEODORE ZISSIS
Translated from Greek by Philip M. McGhee

MALALASEKERA, G. P. (1899–1973), Buddhist scholar, founder of the World Fellowship of Buddhists, and a dominant figure in the cultural life of Ceylon (now Sri Lanka). Born in Panadura, the son of a prosperous family, Gunapala Piyasena Malalasekera grew up in a scholarly atmosphere. As a schoolboy he was tutored in the Sinhala, Sanskrit, and Pali classics by his father, an Ayurvedic physician. During his formative years, Malalasekera was also deeply influenced by learned monks whom he came to know through his father, and he was inspired by men like Anagārika Dharmapāla (1864–1933), a leader in the Buddhist revivalist movement that had arisen in the age of British colonial repression of nationalistic aims and aspirations.

Preparing to follow in his father's footsteps, Malalasekera entered the Medical College in Colombo in 1917, but he had to abandon his medical studies the following year, upon his father's untimely death. Via external registration at the University of London, he then turned to the study of Western classics, graduating with first-class honors in 1919. In 1921 he joined the premier Buddhist school in Colombo, Ānanda College, as a teacher, and in ensuing years he became first its vice-principal and then its acting principal.

Upon the return of Ānanda's principal, Patrick de Silva Kularatne (1893–1976), Malalasekera was profoundly influenced by him in matters both educational and nationalistic. He went abroad for postgraduate studies at the University of London and obtained both the M.A. and the Ph.D. degrees in 1925. On his return home in 1926 he was appointed principal of Nālandā Vidyālaya, the new sister school of Ānanda, and within a year developed it to some stature. He was then appointed lecturer in Sinhala, Sanskrit, and Pali at University College, Colombo, and for most of the next three decades he pursued a brilliant academic career. He held the chair of Pali and Buddhist studies from the establishment of the University of Ceylon in 1942 until his resignation in 1959. As professor and dean for the greater part of this period, which saw the rapid expansion of the Faculty of Oriental Studies, he was a highly respected member of the academic community.

In 1957 Malalasekera was appointed ambassador to the Soviet Union, and he represented Ceylon at the ambassadorial level in Canada, the United Nations, and the United Kingdom until 1967, when he was called home to chair the National Council of Higher Education, a post in which he served with distinction for five years. Despite the demands of diplomatic assignments and administrative responsibilities, his scholarly activities were undiminished.

Malalasekera's major works include *The Pali Literature of Ceylon* (London, 1928); *Vaṃsatthappakāsinī* (London, 1935), a critical edition of the exegesis on the *Mahāvaṃsa* (Great Chronicle of Sri Lanka); the *Extended Mahāvaṃsa* (Colombo, 1937); *The Dictionary of Pali Proper Names* (London, 1937); and *An English-Sinhalese Dictionary* (Colombo, 1948). He wrote a large number of other scholarly books and articles, and he contributed extensively to popular journals both in Ceylon and abroad. His highest intellectual achievement, however, was the work he did on the *Encyclopaedia of Buddhism*, whose completion he, as editor in chief, did not live to see. This undertaking, sponsored by the government of Ceylon in commemoration of twenty-five hundred years of Buddhism, was commenced in 1956 and is still in progress. As a contribution to Buddhist learning, it will stand as a monument to Malalasekera's love of scholarship and great perseverance as a student of the divers aspects of Buddhist thought, culture, and civilization.

Throughout his life, Malalasekera participated in various spheres of interest in Ceylon, religious and social, cultural and intellectual. At government level his advice was sought in many fields and was acceptable to people of all shades of political opinion, for he discreetly steered clear of party politics. He stood for equity and social justice, always taking up the cause of the underprivileged. As a social worker, he traveled the country at his own expense and addressed gatherings large and small. He was frequently heard over Radio Ceylon. His was a receptive mind, and he was noted for his ability to expound with precision and clarity on topics from fine arts and humanities to social sciences and current affairs. As a religious leader, for twenty-five years Malalasekera was president of the All-Ceylon Buddhist Congress (ACBC), an important platform for shaping public opinion, and he was principally responsible for the founding, in May 1950, of the World Fellowship of Buddhists, modeled largely after the ACBC.

Until that time, the voice of the Buddhist population, which forms more than a fifth of the human race, had not been heard, nor its views adequately expressed, nor its aspirations respected in world assemblies. Communication among Buddhists of various lands had been limited, and Buddhists the world over had had no forum to air their grievances or to redress injustices. The differences between the Mahāyāna and Theravāda schools had led to disunity. It was Malalasekera's indefatigable efforts that brought them together. As a sequel to a resolution passed at the twenty-eighth session of the ACBC in 1947, a resolution was passed at a conference of world Buddhist leaders held in 1950 in the historic Temple of the Tooth, in Kandy, to establish the World Fellowship of Buddhists. Malalasekera was founder-president from 1950 to 1958. During his lifetime it grew into a dynamic organization, expressing Buddhist opinion and unifying Buddhists under the six-hued flag bearing the emblem of the *dharmacakra,* the Wheel of the Law, as a symbol of peace.

BIBLIOGRAPHY

Dharmabandhu, T. S. *Siṃhala vīrayō.* Colombo, 1949. In Sinhala.

Guruge, Ananda, ed. *Return to Righteousness: A Collection of Speeches, Essays and Letters of the Anagarika Dharmapala.* Colombo, 1965.

Hewage, L. G., et al., eds. *All Ceylon Buddhist Congress: Malalasēkara anusmaraṇa saṅgrahaya.* Colombo, 1973. In Sinhala.

Wijesekera, O. H. de A., ed. *Malalasekera Commemoration Volume.* Colombo, 1976.

Wijewardena, Don Charles. *The Revolt in the Temple.* Colombo, 1953.

N. A. JAYAWICKRAMA

MALBIM, acronym (MaLBIM) of Me'ir Loeb ben Yeḥi'el Mikha'el (1809–1879), European rabbi and exegete. Born in Volhynia, Russia, Malbim was chief rabbi of Romania from 1858 to 1864, having earlier served as rabbi to a number of communities in eastern Europe.

Malbim's life coincided with the struggle of European Jewry to achieve political rights. Some Jews, considering that the Judaism of the ghetto impeded their acceptance by their Christian neighbors, drifted away from Judaism. Others, who called themselves reformers, questioned the binding authority of the oral law, much of which seemed to them incompatible with the spirit of their age and therefore an impediment to emancipation. Malbim, a passionate and unyielding exponent of traditional Judaism, challenged the new Reform movement in his sermons and in his major work, a multivolume commentary on the entire Hebrew Bible. *Ha-Torah ve-ha-mitsvah,* his commentary on the Pentateuch, and *Miqra'ei qodesh,* his commentary on the Prophets and Hagiographa, were published between 1845 and 1876. In them, Malbim undertook to demonstrate that both the written law and the oral law form a unity, each component of which can be understood only through the other, and that, since the entire corpus of law and lore contained in the Talmud and Midrash had been revealed at Sinai together with the written law, no provision of either could be abrogated or amended. His stern refusal to compromise his convictions brought him into repeated conflict with the leaders of the communities he served, and his rabbinate was not a happy one.

Malbim introduces his commentary to *Leviticus* with a detailed analysis of 613 features of Hebrew lexicography, grammar, and biblical style that he insists had been forgotten by the medieval Jewish exegetes. He denies, for example, that true synonyms are to be found in the Hebrew Bible. Instead, an apparent synonym really introduces a new thought that demands its own exposition. Every word in scripture is the only word that could have been used in that particular context, and every verse conveys its own sublime meaning, though often that lofty message can be fathomed only by reference to Talmud, Midrash, and the literature of the Jewish mystics.

Because of his vigorous advocacy of traditional Judaism, Malbim remains a revered figure in Orthodox Jewish circles. Unfortunately, he is little known to the world of biblical scholarship because few of his writings have been published in English.

BIBLIOGRAPHY

Malbim's commentary on the Hebrew Bible has been republished in four volumes in the series "Otsar ha-perushim" (Jerusalem, 1956–1957). Volume 1, on *Genesis,* has been translated into English by Zvi Faier in two volumes (Jerusalem, 1978–1979). M. M. Yoshor has written a biography in Hebrew entitled *Ha-ga'on Malbim* (Jerusalem, 1976). Yehoshua Horowitz's brief article on Malbim in the *Encyclopaedia Judaica* (Jerusalem, 1971) is the best source of information on Malbim in English.

A. STANLEY DREYFUS

MALCOLM X (1925–1965), American Black Muslim leader, born Malcolm Little on 19 May 1925 in Omaha, Nebraska. His father, the Reverend Earl Little, a follower of Marcus Garvey and a Baptist minister, died when Malcolm was six years old, and his mother, the sole support of nine children, was later committed to an insane asylum. Malcolm attended school in East Lansing, Michigan, dropped out at the eighth grade, and then moved to live with an older sister in the Roxbury section of Boston. There he became involved in petty criminal activities. As an unemployed street hustler and the leader of an interracial gang of thieves in Roxbury, and later in Harlem, he was known as "Detroit Red" for the reddish tinge of his hair. During his prison years (1946–1952), he underwent the first of his two conversion experiences when he converted to the Nation of Islam led by Elijah Muhammad. Following the tradition of the Nation of Islam, he replaced his surname with an *X*, symbolizing what he had been and what he had become: "Ex-smoker. Ex-drinker. Ex-Christian. Ex-slave."

An articulate public speaker, charismatic personality, and indefatigable organizer, Malcolm X expressed the rage and anger of the black masses during the major phase of the civil rights movement from 1956 to 1965. He organized Muslim temples throughout the country and founded the newspaper *Muhammad Speaks* in the basement of his home. He articulated the Nation of Islam's beliefs in racial separation and rose rapidly through the ranks to become minister of Boston Temple No. 11 and was later rewarded with the post of minister of Temple No. 7 in Harlem, the largest and most prestigious temple of the Nation of Islam after the Chicago headquarters. Recognizing Malcolm's talents and abilities, Elijah Muhammad also named him "national representative" of the Nation of Islam, second in rank to Elijah Muhammad himself.

In 1963, after his public comments on President John F. Kennedy's assassination, Malcolm X was ordered by Elijah Muhammad to undergo a period of silence, an order that reflected the deep tensions and disputes among Black Muslim leaders. In March 1964, Malcolm left the Nation of Islam and founded his own Muslim Mosque, Inc. During his pilgrimage to Mecca that same year, he experienced a second conversion, embraced the orthodox universal brotherhood of Sunnī Islam, and adopted the Muslim name el-Hajj Malik el-Shabazz. He then renounced the separatist beliefs of the Nation of Islam. In 1965, he founded the Organization for Afro-American Unity as a political vehicle to internationalize the plight of black Americans, to make common cause with Third World nations, and to move from civil rights to human rights. On 21 February 1965, Malcolm X was assassinated while delivering a lecture at the Audubon Ballroom in Harlem. His martyrdom, ideas, and speeches contributed to the development of black nationalist ideology and the black power movement in the late 1960s in the United States.

[*See also the biography of Elijah Muhammad.*]

BIBLIOGRAPHY

Breitman, George, ed. *Malcolm X Speaks*. New York, 1965. A collection of Malcolm X's speeches.

Goldman, Peter. *The Death and Life of Malcolm X*. New York, 1973. Focuses on the last year of Malcolm X's life and on the events, personalities, and controversies surrounding his assassination.

Lincoln, C. Eric. *The Black Muslims in America*. Boston, 1961. Remains the best historical overview of the development of the Nation of Islam under the leadership of Elijah Muhammad and Malcolm X.

Malcolm X and Alex Haley. *The Autobiography of Malcolm X*. Still the best source of insights regarding Malcolm X's life and the development of his views, including his conversion experiences and the reasons for his dispute with other Black Muslim leaders.

Mamiya, Lawrence H. "From Black Muslim to Bilalian: The Evolution of a Movement." *Journal for the Scientific Study of Religion* 21 (June 1982): 138–152. Examines Malcolm X's influence on the leaders of the major schismatic groups in the Black Muslim movement—Warith D. Muhammad and Louis Farrakhan—and their divergent directions.

LAWRENCE H. MAMIYA

MĀLIK IBN ANAS (d. AH 179/795 CE), renowned Muslim jurist and eponymous founder of the Mālikī school. Mālik was born sometime between 90 and 97 AH (708 and 715 CE) in Medina, where he spent most of his life and where he died. Biographical tradition records that he was, for a while, a professional singer, but because he was ugly, his mother advised him to give up that career. Instead, he became, like an uncle and a grandfather before him, a religious scholar. Mālik studied with a number of well-known scholars of Medina and then, as his fame spread, acquired many pupils of his own.

In 762 he lent the weight of his reputation to a revolt against the Abbasid caliph al-Manṣūr. When that failed, he was punished by the governor of Medina, but his prestige did not suffer, and he regained royal favor. The next three caliphs, al-Mahdī, al-Hādī, and Hārūn al-Rashīd, were personally interested in his work, and Hārūn, while on a pilgrimage in the last year of Mālik's life, even attended one of his lectures.

Mālik's intellectual activity belongs to the period of Islamic jurisprudence when the explicit legislative legacy provided by the Qur'ān and the prophet Muḥammad was proving insufficiently complete for the needs of the rulers of the expanding empire, and they were turning for further guidance to religious specialists such as Mālik. These were the early legal scholars of Islam, and it became their task to ensure the Islamic character of public administration, as well as to suggest ways in which individual Muslims could lead more pious lives. The work of these scholars had an important influence on the development of Islam. Before Mālik's time, legal literature consisted of compendiums of *ḥadīth* (traditions)—biographical reports of the actions and statements of the Prophet and his contemporaries that were considered authoritative guidelines for behavior—and compendia of the decisions of authoritative scholars on various theoretical and practical issues. Mālik's achievement was to combine these two sources of authority. In his major work, *Kitāb al-muwaṭṭa'* (Book of the Smoothed Path), which is the earliest surviving law book of Islam, Mālik set forth, within the context of the *ḥadīth,* the legal practices that had evolved in Medina. Despite the inconsistencies of his own procedure, the use of *ḥadīth* to support existing legal opinion came to play a vital role in the subsequent systematization of Islamic legal thinking and in the codification of Islamic law.

The *Muwaṭṭa'* is arranged in chapters that deal with the ritual and legal concerns of the Muslim community, and it represents the accepted legal practice of Medina as it was taught by Mālik and his contemporaries. The enduring and widespread influence of the *Muwaṭṭa'* may in part be due to the middle-of-the-road quality of the Medinese doctrine it presents, but should be attributed even more to the activities and geographical distribution of successive generations of Mālik's pupils, who gradually came to think of themselves as followers of a distinctive school. The Mālikī school predominates in North Africa and in the other Muslim communities of Africa; it is also the dominant school in Upper Egypt.

BIBLIOGRAPHY

Abbott, Nabia. *Studies in Arabic Literary Papyri,* vol. 2, *Qur'anic Commentary and Tradition.* Chicago, 1967. A valuable study of early Muslim scholarly activity.

Goldziher, Ignácz. *Muslim Studies,* vol. 2. Edited by S. M. Stern and translated by Stern and C. R. Barber. Chicago, 1973. The fundamental work on the development of *ḥadīth* in Islamic thought.

Schacht, Joseph. *An Introduction to Islamic Law.* Oxford, 1964. The authoritative general introduction, with valuable bibliography.

SUSAN A. SPECTORSKY

MALINOWSKI, BRONISLAW (1884–1942), Polish-English social anthropologist. Born into an educated and aristocratic family, Bronisław Kasper Malinowski received his Ph.D. in physics and mathematics from the Jagiellonian University of his native Cracow in 1908. Switching from the natural sciences to the human sciences, he entered the London School of Economics in 1910 and received a D.Sc. in 1916. He later traced his decision to study anthropology to his reading of James G. Frazer's *The Golden Bough.* The tribute was apt, for Malinowski became the leading British anthropologist of the generation following Frazer's, but also ironic, for no one did more to repudiate Frazer's method.

Malinowski's first contact with primitive society came during five months among the Mailu of Toulon Island off the southern coast of New Guinea in 1914–1915. In June 1915 he began the first of two extended periods of observation on the Trobriand Islands, to the east of New Guinea. Although colored by personal stress and ambivalence toward the natives, his twenty-one months in the Trobriands shaped his entire career. He became the apostle and exemplar of a new standard of anthropological fieldwork: ethnography must rely, he believed, on the participation of the ethnographer in the society under observation, rather than on the reports of travelers, missionaries, and hasty surveys. His fieldwork completed, Malinowski married Elsie Masson, daughter of a Melbourne chemistry professor. He began teaching at the London School of Economics after completing the manuscript of *Argonauts of the Western Pacific* (1922), the first of his many books on the Trobriands. In 1927 he became the first professor of anthropology at the University of London.

Malinowski's approach to anthropology was psychological, but not psychoanalytic. His most celebrated work among nonspecialists was probably *Sex and Repression in Savage Society* (1927), in which he denies Sigmund Freud's claim that the Oedipus complex is universal. In this book Malinowski argues that among the Trobriand Islanders matrilineal descent (reinforced by ignorance of physiological paternity) diverted a boy's hostility from his father to the distant authority figure of his maternal uncle. Trobriand men repressed sexual desire for their sisters, not their mothers. Malinowski rejects Freud's claim in *Totem and Taboo* (1913) that an original Oedipal "crime" had established human culture: Freud's Lamarckian group psychology is simply wrong, Malinowski argues, and any other means of perpetuating the memory of the act requires the preexistence of culture.

Malinowski's attack on Freud reflected no personal reluctance to generalize; he had none of the methodological caution of his American contemporary Franz Boas. Malinowski's generalizations were rarely the product of systematic cross-cultural comparison: having rejected the Victorians' reliance on written sources, he went to the other extreme and generalized from his own intensive but necessarily limited fieldwork. His theory—"functionalism"—stressed the role of human culture in satisfying a hierarchy of human needs, consisting of those that are basic (i.e., biological), derived (i.e., cultural or social), and integrative (i.e., normative). He attacked the evolutionists' concept of "survivals" and the diffusionists' concept of "culture complexes," with their implications that cultures are heterogeneous accumulations of sometimes useless objects and institutions. While his American contemporaries, notably Ruth Benedict, saw cultural unity in terms of a culture's dominant style or personality, he saw it in the fulfillment of individual and group needs. In part because of Malinowski's own work, evolutionism and diffusionism were both in retreat by the 1930s. As they receded from view, functionalism lost much of its original force, and after his death Malinowski the ethnographer was praised above Malinowski the theorist.

Malinowski never wrote an account of Trobriand culture as a whole; he studied individual institutions in their social settings. The attention he paid to Trobriand economics and sex was in line with the premises of functional theory. His book *Argonauts of the Western Pacific* describes the complex and highly ritualized inter-island trade known as *kula; The Sexual Life of Savages* (1929) deals with sex and the family; and *Coral Gardens and their Magic* (1935) discusses Trobriand agriculture. In all these works Malinowski de-emphasizes the "primitive" nature of Trobriand life by stressing the rational organization of economic life and focusing on the nuclear family rather than on the segmentary kinship system.

Malinowski also applied functional analysis to less obviously useful activities. In *Myth in Primitive Psychology* (1926), he argues that myths are neither explanations of natural phenomena nor poetry; instead, they are validations of the social order. The mythic "charter" strengthens tradition by appealing to the design and experience of a supernatural past. Myths of origin, for example, explain the relative superiority and inferiority of different Trobriand clans. Malinowski's explanation of magic denies both Lucien Lévy-Bruhl's claim that primitive thought is "prelogical" and Frazer's theory of an evolutionary progression from magic to religion to science. In "Magic, Science and Religion," an essay in *Science, Religion and Reality,* edited by Joseph Needham (London, 1925), Malinowski argues that magic provides psychological encouragement and a rationale for group cooperation in those activities where primitives lack the knowledge or technical ability to ensure success. Magic is a supplement to, not a substitute for, practical activity.

Malinowski's analysis of religion was not only less original but also less successful than his treatments of myth and magic. He denied Émile Durkheim's claim that the object of worship is society itself, although conceding that religion is socially organized. Religion is man's consolation in the face of tragedy and uncertainty, not a means of social cohesion. It can be distinguished from magic by the absence of an external goal, in that worship is an end in itself. Malinowski never resolved the tension between his individualistic analysis of religious motivation and his sociological analysis of religious practice. The absence of worship on the Trobriand Islands may have denied him the stimulus necessary for a more sustained inquiry.

Elsie Malinowski died in 1935, after a long illness. At the end of 1938, Malinowski left London for an American sabbatical; rather than return to Europe during World War II, he was for three years a visiting professor at Yale University. In 1940 he married Valetta Swann, an artist. During the summers of 1940 and 1941 he went into the field again to study Mexican peasant markets in conjunction with a young Mexican ethnologist, Julio de la Fuente. In early 1942 he accepted Yale's offer of a permanent professorship effective that October. He never took up the appointment; his death of a heart attack on 16 May 1942 caught him in the midst of new beginnings. Doubly an émigré, he lost the chance to play in America the commanding role he had held in British social science between the wars.

BIBLIOGRAPHY

A full list of Malinowski's works appears in the essential secondary work, *Man and Culture; An Evaluation of the Work of Bronislaw Malinowski,* edited by Raymond Firth (London, 1957). Malinowski's *A Diary in the Strict Sense of the Term* (New York, 1967) covers his Mailu research and his second stay in the Trobriands. Malinowski's and Julio de la Fuente's *Malinowski in Mexico: The Economics of a Mexican Market System,* edited by Susan Drucker-Brown (London, 1982), is the result of his last fieldwork. *The Ethnography of Malinowski: The Trobriand Islands, 1915–18,* edited by Michael W. Young (London, 1979) is a convenient reader, and its editorial notes cite recent work on both Malinowski and the Trobriands. The first comprehensive challenge to *Sex and Repression* is Melford E. Spiro's *Oedipus in the Trobriands* (Chicago, 1982).

MICHAEL A. BAENEN

MAMI WATA is a spirit worshiped by Africans in more than fifty cultures from Senegal to Tanzania. Her name, Pidgin English for "water mother/woman," reflects the fact that Africans regard her as a foreigner, and yet she is distinctly African. She is thought to bring wealth and good fortune to those she favors but misfortune to those who anger her.

In their worship of Mami Wata, Africans study, interpret, and re-present data from European and Indian imagery, literature, trade goods, and actions. Using these sources as models for behavior and then processing them further in dreams and visions, devotees recreate Mami Wata's attire, construct her watery world, and impersonate her during rituals that frequently include possession trances. By these means they project themselves in their interpretations of divinity.

The early history of Mami Wata worship remains conjectural. Some have suggested an origin among Africans in the New World; however, it seems more likely that its beginnings coincide with the arrival of Europeans along African shores in the late fifteenth century. According to early travelers' accounts, Africans associated Europeans with the water and water spirits. More importantly, they associated European icons, especially ships' figureheads, with representations of those spirits. Thus marine sculptures have been documented in widely dispersed African water spirit shrines. One European icon in particular, the mermaid, became Mami Wata's primary image. As familiarity with European ways and lore increased, Africans transformed the concept of the mermaid, evolving an elaborate belief system that has been filtered through many cultural lenses to make Mami Wata a significant transcultural religious phenomenon.

Between 1885 and 1900, Mami Wata's mermaid representation was joined by another exotic image—a popular German chromolithograph of a female snake charmer—that combined elements of the mermaid with allusions to indigenous African water serpent deities. Printed in Hamburg about 1885, the chromolithograph had already inspired an African water spirit headdress in the Niger River delta of Nigeria by 1901. Its influence spread to other areas and in many cases supplanted the earlier image of Mami Wata as a mermaid. In 1955 large numbers of the chromolithograph were reprinted in India for sale in Africa. This and other more recent editions have become Mami Wata icons, inspiring altarpieces in at least forty-one cultures.

The 1950s signaled a new phase in Mami Wata worship. The popularity of the snake charmer lithograph and the presence of Indian merchants in West Africa led to a growing African interest in Indian prints of Hindu deities, which Africans interpreted as representations of a host of Mami Wata spirits associated with specific bodies and levels of water. Using these prints as guides for rituals and for the preparation of altars known as Mami Wata tables, Africans expanded the pantheon of spirits, fostering a growing complexity in Mami Wata worship that includes elements of Christian, Hindu, Buddhist, astrological, and occult beliefs and practices.

As they shape their devotions, Mami Wata followers select fragments from their study of foreign cultures and invest them with new meanings. Creating sacred symbols and performing rites for a foreign, yet accessible, spirit, they exploit a force that promises wealth and well-being in an Africa where external social and economic factors continue to play a considerable role.

BIBLIOGRAPHY

Drewal, Henry John. "Interpretation, Invention, and Re-presentation in the Worship of Mami Wata." In *Performance in Contemporary African Arts*, edited by Ruth Stone, John Johnson, and Patrick McNaughton. Bloomington, Ind., forthcoming. An examination of the process by which Ewe, Mina, and Igbo devotees use dreams, imported images and documents, and observations of the actions of foreigners from overseas to shape their Mami Wata beliefs, religious icons, and rites.

Salmons, Jill. "Mammy Wata." *African Arts* 10 (April 1977): 8–15, 87–88. A general and readable description of Mami Wata worship and the development of her imagery in the work of several sculptors among the Ibibio of southeastern Nigeria.

Szombati-Fabian, Ilona, and Johannes Fabian. "Art, History, and Society: Popular Art in Shaba, Zaire." *Studies in the Anthropology of Visual Communication* 3 (1976): 1–22. A provocative semiological study of the social significance of popular painting in the urban centers of Shaba, Zaire, that includes a consideration of the mermaid genre associated with Mami Wata.

Wintrob, Ronald M. "Mammy Water: Folk Beliefs and Psychotic Elaborations in Liberia." *Canadian Psychiatric Association Journal* 15 (1970): 143–157. A general account by a clinical psychiatrist of beliefs about and possessions by Mami Wata among various peoples in Liberia; offers tentative hypotheses on the origins, status symbolism, and psychodynamic significance of Mami Wata beliefs.

HENRY JOHN DREWAL

MAN. *See* Masculine Sacrality.

MANA. *See* Polynesian Religions; Power; *and* Taboo.

MANANNÁN MAC LIR is a deity of the Irish pantheon whose importance is masked by a geographically specific name (related to the name of the Isle of Man) and a hidden mythological tradition. He does play a fundamental role in several narratives. In the christianized but archaic version of *The House of the Two Goblets (Altrom Tige Da Medar)* in the cycle of Édaín, he is the supreme god of Ireland, in unequal competition with Christ. In two variants of the legend of Mongan, Manannán comes from the otherworld to the queen of Ulster in order to engender Mongan in the place and likeness of Fiachra, king of Ulster. In recompense, he saves Fiachra's life during a battle against a mortal enemy. In a third account, *The Adventures of Cormac in the Land of Promise (Echtra Cormaic i Tir Tairngiri)*, Manannán is the god who makes the great king Cormac come to the otherworld to give him the cup of sovereignty and of truth, which becomes the principal talisman of the king's exemplary reign.

Manannán was considered by the medieval Irish to be a god of the sea. His patronymic, *mac Lir*, means "son of the waves," but he is a sea god only in the sense that the sea is the usual path to the underworld, of which he is the uncontested master. Indirect evidence suggests that he is a major god of the pantheon. *Manannán* would then be the surname of either Lugh or Daghdha. He appears in the Welsh *Mabinogion* under the almost identical name *Manawydan*. It is not known whether this common name is the result of a borrowing or of a community of origins.

BIBLIOGRAPHY

Guyonvarc'h, Christian-J., and Françoise Le Roux. *Textes mythologiques irlandais,* vol. 1. Rennes, 1980.

Vendryes, Joseph. "Manannan Mac Lir." *Études celtiques* 6 (1953–1954): 239–254.

FRANÇOISE LE ROUX and CHRISTIAN-J. GUYONVARC'H
Translated from French by Erica Meltzer

MANCO CAPAC (probably thirteenth century), first Inca ruler, demigod ancestor of succeeding Inca rulers, and the founder, possibly legendary, of the Inca capital city of Cuzco, in the southern highlands of Peru. Early Spanish chroniclers reported various Inca creation myths. In one version, the Sun, taking pity on the miserable world, sent down his own son—presumably Manco Capac—and daughter to govern the people. According to another version, after the creation of the world the Sun summoned Manco Capac and, "speaking like an older brother," told him that the Inca would rule the world and that they must proudly regard the Sun as their father and worship him appropriately. In the most frequent variation, four brothers and four sisters emerged from a "window," or cave, in a rock at Pacaritambo ("inn of origin"), not far from Cuzco. After a period of wandering, one brother, Ayar Manco (later Manco Capac), having sent word that his father was the Sun, went to a hill above what is now Cuzco. The people of the valley looked up to see him dressed in gold ornaments that reflected dazzling sunlight. He founded Cuzco with a simple shrine on what would be the site of the great Temple of the Sun. He is said to have taught the people not only social and religious structure and ritual but also irrigation, planting, and harvesting.

When he was about to die, Manco Capac told his people that he must return to the sky, for his father had summoned him. His body was adored as a *huaca*, a sacred object. The Spaniards, seeking to destroy idolatry, removed the mummified bodies of other Inca rulers, but they could not find that of Manco Capac, which was kept in a village outside Cuzco. It was said to have turned into a stone (stone was particularly sacred to the Inca). This stone, elaborately dressed and adorned, was one of the most holy Inca objects, and ceremonies and sacrifices were held before it.

[*See also* Atahuallpa.]

BIBLIOGRAPHY

Bernabé Cobo's mid-seventeenth-century *History of the Inca Empire* (Austin, 1979) is a rich source of lore about Manco Capac. Harold Osborne's *South American Mythology* (London, 1968) contains a number of Inca origin myths. J. H. Rowe's "Inca Culture at the Time of the Spanish Conquest," in the *Handbook of South American Indians,* edited by Julian H. Steward, vol. 2 (Washington, D.C., 1946), presents the legends in their general cultural context.

ELIZABETH P. BENSON

MANDA D-HIIA ("knowledge of life") is the primary savior, messenger, and instructor in Mandaeism, a still-surviving gnostic religion in Iraq and Iran. Dispatched from the world above, the Lightworld, to the lower realms, Manda d-Hiia brings saving knowledge, warnings, and consolation to human beings and to deficient Lightworld beings stranded between the earth and the Lightworld. His descents and ascents parallel the route of the soul, which, having come from the Lightworld, returns to its home at the body's death. The "life" of which Manda d-Hiia is "knowledge" is the upper, ultimate Lightworld principle, in some texts called the King of Light and other names. The names *Manda d-Hiia* and *Life* are pronounced over Mandaeans at baptism, and Manda d-Hiia's name occurs frequently in prayer formulas.

The savior appears most often in the two main collections of Mandaean mythological speculation, *Ginza,* separated into *Right Ginza* and *Left Ginza,* and the Mandaean *Book of John.* The *Right Ginza,* the larger part of *Ginza,* contains cosmologies and mythologies dealing mainly with the earthly world, while the smaller *Left Ginza* centers primarily on the ascent of the soul toward the Lightworld. In *Right Ginza* 3, Manda d-Hiia descends to the underworld, vanquishing the evil powers there. His devastating effect on the evil ones on earth is described in *Right Ginza* 5.2. This tractate makes use of the Old Testament's Psalm 114 in portraying the frenzied reaction of mountains and ocean to the savior's appearance. In *Right Ginza* 11, as in 15.17, Manda d-Hiia battles with Ruha, the personified female spirit, and with the planets, the wicked world-rulers who ensnare human beings.

According to *Left Ginza* 1.3, Manda d-Hiia released Hawwa, Adam's wife, from the world, and warned against mourning for the dead, a behavior repudiated by Mandaeism. *Right Ginza* 5.4 tells of the death of John the Baptist, the Mandaean prophet. Manda d-Hiia appears to John in the guise of a small boy who wishes to be baptized. When John takes the boy to the river, it floods, owing to the presence of the savior. John nearly drowns, but Manda d-Hiia makes the water recede. As birds and fishes praise Manda d-Hiia, John realizes that his baptism candidate is the very Lightbeing in whose name John performs his baptisms. This baptism turns out to be John's last: Manda d-Hiia has come to take him away from the world. The baptist's body is left on the riverbank, the savior covering it with sand, and the two ascend together to the Lightworld.

Occasionally, Manda d-Hiia is portrayed unflatteringly. The *Book of John* 2 informs us that the savior has caused strife in the Lightworld by revealing the secrets of salvation to Ruha, his adversary. In the eighth tractate of the same book, a messenger pleads for Yushamin, a rebellious, jailed Lightbeing. The King of Light is favorably inclined toward Yushamin, but Manda d-Hiia thinks that Yushamin deserves no forgiveness. To this the King of Light responds that Manda d-Hiia harbors a long-standing jealousy toward Yushamin: Manda d-Hiia hates Yushamin because the latter once refused him a wife.

In general, though, Manda d-Hiia is a positive figure. He was the guardian of Adam's epoch, the first of the four ages of the world. Today we live in the fourth age, an evil age, which will end when no Mandaeans are left on earth.

[*See also* Mandaean Religion *and* Ginza.]

BIBLIOGRAPHY

The two main Mandaean sources that present Manda d-Hiia have been published in German under the editorship of Mark Lidzbarski as *Ginza: Der Schatz; oder, Das grosse Buch der Mandäer* (Göttingen, 1925; new edition in preparation by Kurt Rudolph) and *Das Johannesbuch der Mandäer* (1915; reprint, Berlin, 1966). Excerpts from myths found in these texts appear in *Gnosis: A Selection of Gnostic Texts*, vol. 2, *Coptic and Mandean Sources* (Oxford, 1974), edited by Werner Foerster. Kurt Rudolph's *Theogonie, Kosmogonie und Anthropogonie in den mandäischen Schriften* (Göttingen, 1965) devotes considerable space to myths in which Manda d-Hiia appears.

JORUNN JACOBSEN BUCKLEY

MANDAEAN RELIGION. The religion of the Mandaeans (from *manda,* "knowledge") is a self-contained, unique system belonging in the general stratum of the gnosticism of late antiquity. Thus, Mandaeism shows affinities with Judaism and Christianity. For geographical reasons, it also exhibits certain early influences from the Iranian religious milieu. The Mandaeans of today live, as their ancestors did, along the rivers and waterways of southern Iraq and Khuzistan, Iran. Known by their neighbors as Subbi ("baptizers"), they form a gnostic baptist community.

The Mandaeans can be traced to the second or third century of the common era. Evidence from their language and literature indicates that they emigrated, during the first centuries of the common era, from the Jordan Valley area eastward to the environs of Haran, on the border between present-day Turkey and Syria, and finally to southern Babylonia. According to their text *Haran Gawaita* (Inner Haran), they fled persecution and came east under the protection of one of the three Parthian kings named Ardban who ruled from the early first century to 227 CE.

An East Aramaic dialect, the Mandaean language nevertheless contains West Syrian linguistic elements that point to the probability of a migration from west to east. Examples of these are *yardna* ("running water"; also designates the river Jordan), *sba* ("baptize"), *kushta* ("truth; ritual handshake"), *manda* ("knowledge"), and *nasuraiia* ("observant ones"). The last term (in English, "Nasoraeans"), also used by early Christians, refers primarily to the Mandaean priests. According to Rudolf Macuch, the date 271–272 may be argued as that appearing, in the hand of a Mandaean copyist, in the colophon of a hymnal *(qulasta),* published in *The Canonical Prayerbook of the Mandaeans* (Leiden, 1959). This colophon may well be the oldest extant Mandaean text. Macuch also dates Mandaean script on coins from what is now Luristan and Khuzistan as of the second and third centuries CE. Inscriptions on leather and lead strips, on clay tablets, and on magical bowls (labeled "magical" because they are used on a "folk religion" level) belong largely to the younger sources.

The Mandaean codex and scroll literature is found in the voluminous book *Ginza,* which is divided into *Right Ginza* and *Left Ginza.* It is a collection of mythological, revelatory, hortatory, and hymnic material. [*See* Ginza.] The *Right Ginza* contains generally cosmological, "thisworldly" prose material, while the left part, much of it in verse, centers on the "otherworldly" fate of the soul. Symbolism of "right" and "left" is pervasive in Mandaeism, but in the case of the *Ginza* titles these terms are puzzling, for the right is usually connected to the beyond, and the left to the earthly world. The Mandaean *Book of John* contains a variety of myths and legends. *The Canonical Prayerbook* includes hymns, liturgies, and instructions for priests. Central mythical and ritual material in this work and in *Ginza* dates from the third and fourth centuries. Comments, exegeses, and instructions for rituals attested in *The Canonical Prayerbook* are found in the texts *The Thousand and Twelve Questions, The Original Great World, The Original Small World,* and *The Coronation of the Great Shishlam.* The Mandaeans also have illustrated scrolls, such as *The Scroll of Abatur* and *The Scroll of the Rivers,* and a book on astrology, *The Book of the Zodiac.* Much of this literature was probably collected and edited after the seventh century, although most of the material is older.

Traditionally hostile to both Judaism and Christianity, the Mandaeans were confronted with the Islamic conquest in the seventh century. In reponse, the Mandaean leaders declared *Ginza* to be their holy scripture and proclaimed John the Baptist as the Mandaean prophet, since a holy book and a prophet were the Islamic requirements for recognition as a "people of the book" (i.e., Jews, Christians, and Sabaeans), exempt from forcible conversion. The Mandaeans endured hardships under Islamic rule, but they were generally left in peace. Never aspiring to secular power or political expansion, the traditionally endogamous Mandaeans survived. The group was threatened by an outbreak of cholera in 1831 that eliminated the priestly class, but new priests were drawn from the ranks of literate laymen. Again, as secularization set in during the twentieth century, scholars have considered Mandaean culture to be in danger of extinction; however, a recent cultural, if not traditionally religious, revival seems to be taking hold. In Iraq, two new baptismal pools and a new *mandi* (a clay and reed hut used by priests) were constructed in the 1970s. Mandaeans recently translated into Arabic Ethel S. Drower's *The Mandaeans of Iraq and Iran,* first published in 1937. In 1972, these translators compiled a Mandaean catechism for the benefit of the laity, who formerly were not allowed even to touch Mandaean books.

In bulk, the Mandaean corpus exceeds anything transmitted from other gnostic traditions, except perhaps that of Manichaeism. Relationships to other forms of gnosticism are difficult to trace, but in 1949 Torgny Säve-Söderbergh demonstrated that the Manichaean *Psalms of Thomas,* dating from 250 to 275, depend on a Mandaean original. In addition, the long-held view that Mani had his roots in Mandaeism has recently been refuted by the discovery of the Cologne Mani-Codex. However, the Syrian *Odes of Solomon* and a number of the Nag Hammadi tractates do show correspondences with Mandaean ideas.

In the sixteenth and seventeenth centuries Portuguese missionaries were among the first to bring Mandaean manuscripts out of the Orient. Thinking that they had found the "Christians of Saint John," a misnomer for the Mandaeans, the missionaries were eager to trace the Mandaeans back to their putative origins. The possibilities of such a Christian connection contributed to the heyday of studies in Mandaeism in the first half of the twentieth century. Debates on Mandaeism's relationship to early Christianity have continued in recent decades, although the question of a pre-Christian Mandaeism no longer holds the fascination it once did. Comparative issues are still central, but Mandaeism is also studied today for its own sake. The relationship between the mythological and the cultic components remains a crucial issue, for in Mandaeism one faces a gnosis closely aligned with cultic practices. Kurt Rudolph, in particular, has sought to unravel the historical development of Mandaean mythology and cult and to reconstruct the sequence of the variegated segments in the sources.

Mythology. Mandaeism testifies to a basic framework of dualism in which diametrically opposed entities clash but also intertwine and to some extent recognize one another's claims. Good and evil, light and darkness, soul and matter vie for control from the very inception of the world. Mandaean mythological speculations center on the preexistent Lightworld (the upper, "heavenly" realm), on the creation of the earth and of human beings, and on the soul's journey back to its Lightworld origin. The primary Lightworld entity is "the Great Life" (also called by various other names), who resides with his consort, "Treasure of Life," and numerous Lightbeings *(utria),* the prototypes of earthly priests. The *utria* gradually become involved in the creation, an entanglement causing their degradation and accrual of their sins. One of them, Ptahil, the pathetically unsuccessful creator of the earthly world and of man, fails to make Adam stand upright, for the creature is wholly material. A soul is brought—sometimes reluctantly—from the Lightworld, making Adam complete. The soul not only causes erect posture but functions as a revealer, instructing Adam and his wife, Hawwa, in *nasiruta,* the totality of Mandaean gnosis and cult.

Adam is taught to free his soul and spirit to return to the Lightworld, leaving the body behind. Of the three human constituents, *ruha* ("spirit") is the middle, ambiguous component torn between body and soul. There is also a personified *ruha,* at times called Ruha d-Qudsha ("holy spirit"), who was originally fetched from the underworld prior to the creation of earth and human beings. By necessity, Ptahil enters into fateful cooperation with this personified spirit, who has a stake in the human being. Ruha also enlists the planets and the zodiac spirits, her children, to help her. Together, they demonize time and space. Arranging a noisy party in order to blot out the soul's revelatory voice in Adam, Ruha and her cohorts merely manage to frighten him, reawakening his quest for salvation beyond the earth (*Right Ginza* 3).

In addition to the *utria* Yushamin, Abatur, and Ptahil, there are others less stained by involvement in the lower realms. Manda d-Hiia ("knowledge of life") and his son/brother Hibil are Lightworld envoys, revealers, and saviors, busily shuttling between the Lightworld and the earth. [*See* Manda d-Hiia.] Anosh-Utra, who imitates and competes with Jesus, and Shitil (the biblical Seth) are two less central messengers. Shitil appears both as one of the *utria* and as the first son of Adam. In the latter capacity, Shitil dies vicariously for his father, who, at the ripe age of one thousand years, refuses to die. As a reward for his sacrifice, Shitil ascends and becomes the pure soul against which all human souls are weighed in the scales of Abatur on the threshold of the Lightworld.

Between earth and the Lightworld the *matarata,* or purgatories, provide tests and tribulations for ascending souls and spirits. The *matarata*—depicted in *The Scroll of Abatur*—present an inverted parallel to the underworlds mapped by Hibil before the creation of the earth. Demons, including some of the degraded *utria,* serve as purgatory keepers, performing the thankless task of testing and punishing. Depending on the realm in which they appear, *utria* and other divine beings may show themselves as good or evil. Abatur himself has been demoted from *rama* ("elevated") to "man of the scales." He must carry out his task until the end of time, though complaining bitterly (*Book of John* 70–72).

Nonbelievers do not escape the *matarata.* Jesus, an apostate Mandaean, is doomed—unlike his mother, Mirjai, who converted from Judaism to Mandaeism, thus serving as the prototype of the west-to-east migrating Mandaean. In the *Book of John* 30, Jesus seeks baptism from John the Baptist, who at first hesitates, knowing Jesus' wicked intentions. John relents owing to a command from Abatur, but at the moment of baptism Ruha makes the sign of the cross over the Jordan, which immediately loses its luster, taking on many colors—a bad omen.

Rituals. Among the Mandaeans, repeated baptism *(masbuta)* takes place on Sundays and special festival days. Two small rites of ablution, *rishama* and *tamasha,* are performed by the individual Mandaean and, unlike the *masbuta,* require no priest. At baptism, the white-clad male candidates (women wear a black cloak over the white garment) line up on the riverbank. One at a time each descends into the water and immerses himself three times, whereupon the priest, in full ritual garb, submerges him thrice again. As the candidates crouch in the water, each receives a triple sign on the forehead with water and drinks three handfuls of water. Investiture with a tiny myrtle wreath—a symbol of spirit and of life—follows. Baptisms completed, the candidates sit on the riverbank. Now each is anointed on the forehead with sesame oil and partakes in a meal of bread *(pihta)* and water *(mambuha).* Finally each baptized person exchanges a ritual handshake *(kushta)* with the priest. The entire ceremony is accompanied throughout by set prayers, formulas, and hymns uttered by the priest.

The laity undergo baptism as often as they wish. Moreover, baptism is required on specific occasions: at marriage, after childbirth (for a woman), and as close to the moment of death as possible. Water not only cleanses sins and other impurities; it also represents the Lightworld as reflected in the earthly world. *Masbuta* anticipates and in some sense parallels the deathmass, the *masiqta* ("raising up"), a complicated, lengthy, and essentially secret ritual celebrated for the dead and shielded from the view of the laity. Because baptismal river water symbolizes the Lightworld, the *masbuta* can be said to constitute a "horizontal" *masiqta:* immersion in water here on earth prepares for ascension at life's end.

The *masiqta* conveys spirit and soul from the dead body into the Lightworld. Three days after burial the "seals" put on the grave are broken, for spirit and soul are now ascending on their perilous journey through the *matarata* to the Lightworld. On this third day, several priests celebrate the *masiqta.* In handling objects that symbolize the ascending spirit and soul, the priests' aim is threefold: to join spirit and soul, to create a new, Lightworld body for this joined entity, and to incorporate the new body into the community of deceased Mandaeans living in the Lightworld.

The majority of the symbolic objects in the *masiqta* are foodstuffs that feed the departed and act as creation material. Food links the living to the dead, maintaining the *laufa,* the connection between earth and the Lightworld. The priests personify the ascending spirit and soul, act as parents for the new body, and impersonate Lightbeings. As mediators, priests are Lightbeings on earth, carrying out on earth rituals that have their models in the Lightworld. *Ganzibra* ("treasurer") and *tarmida* (from *talmid,* "disciple") are the two surviving priestly ranks, each of which requires special initiation ceremonies; the supreme office of the *rishama* ("head of the people") has been extinct since the mid-nineteenth century. Constituting the "Right," the Lightworld, the priests are complemented by the laity, who belong to the "Left," the material world. Neither can do without the other; the laity are required as witnesses for public rituals carried out by priests. This arrangement furnishes one among many examples of the carefully tempered dualism prevalent in the religion. The dualism and the relationship between myth and ritual remain among the most urgent issues confronting scholarship on Mandaeism, as do the editing and translating of still-unpublished Mandaean manuscripts. [*See also* Gnosticism.]

BIBLIOGRAPHY

The two main Mandaean collections have been published in German under the editorship of Mark Lidzbarski as *Das Johannesbuch der Mandäer* (1915; reprint, Berlin, 1966) and *Ginza: Der Schatz; oder, Das grosse Buch der Mandäer* (Göttingen, 1925; new edition in preparation by Kurt Rudolph). *The Canonical Prayerbook of the Mandaeans,* translated by Ethel S. Drower (Leiden, 1959), contains a great number of Mandaean hymns and prayers. Representative excerpts from these three main texts (as well as from other Mandaean sources) can be found in *Gnosis: A Selection of Gnostic Texts,* vol. 2, *Coptic and Mandean Sources* (Oxford, 1974), edited by Werner Foerster, which contains an introduction by Kurt Rudolph. The classical eyewitness account of Mandaean religious life remains Ethel S. Drower's *The Mandaeans of Iraq and Iran* (1937; reprint, Leiden, 1962). Kurt Rudolph's *Die Mandäer,* vol. 1, *Prolegomena: Das Mandäerproblem,* and vol. 2, *Der Kult* (Göttingen, 1960, 1961), is the most comprehensive treatment of Mandaeism to date. The bibliography in this work should be supplemented by that in Rudolf Macuch's *Handbook of Classical and Modern Mandaic* (Berlin, 1965). A list of works on Mandaeism after 1965 appears in *Zur Sprache und Literatur der Mandäer: Studia Mandaica I* (Berlin, 1976), edited by Rudolf Macuch.

JORUNN JACOBSEN BUCKLEY

MAṆḌALAS. [*This entry consists of two articles.* Hindu Maṇḍalas *discusses the role of the* maṇḍala *in Hindu ritual.* Buddhist Maṇḍalas *treats the forms and associated practices of the* maṇḍala *in the Tantric traditions of Buddhism.*]

Hindu Maṇḍalas

The *maṇḍala,* a complex geometric design, is used in Hindu rituals in order to involve the whole cosmos in the ritual act. *Maṇḍalas* were first described in Tantric texts, but they already appear there in such detail and in such highly evolved forms that an earlier, unrecorded tradition of *maṇḍala* construction must be assumed.

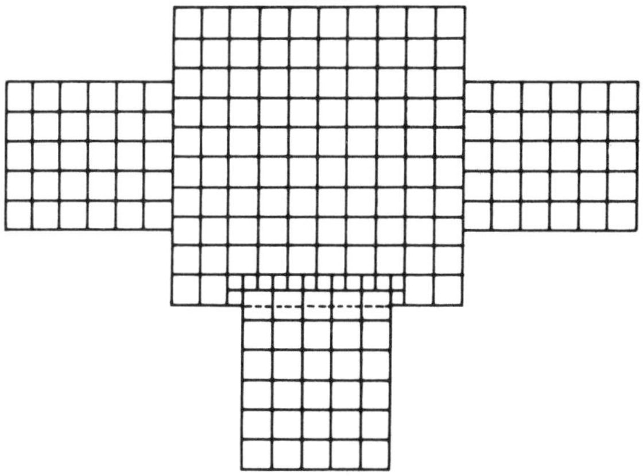

FIGURE 1. *Caturaśraśyenacit Altar Design*

The interest of the early Hindus in geometric designs with cosmological implications is attested by the careful construction of Vedic altars mentioned in the *Taittirīya Saṃhitā* (5.4.11) and in the *Baudhāyana Śulvaśāstra* and the *Āpasthamba Śulvaśastra.* The best-known design is the falcon-shaped altar for the Agnicayana ritual. In this design, well-defined places are demarcated as seats for the gods during the ritual. Other geometrically shaped altars were in the forms of triangles, wheels, and so forth. They all developed out of a basic design, called *caturaśraśyenacit,* a fire altar "resembling a falcon [constructed] from squares" (see figure 1). The shape of a particular *maṇḍala* depends on the special purpose of the sacrifice.

Another description of the geometrical designs for ritualistic purposes is found in the Vastuśāstras, the handbooks on architecture. Instead of an outline in reduced

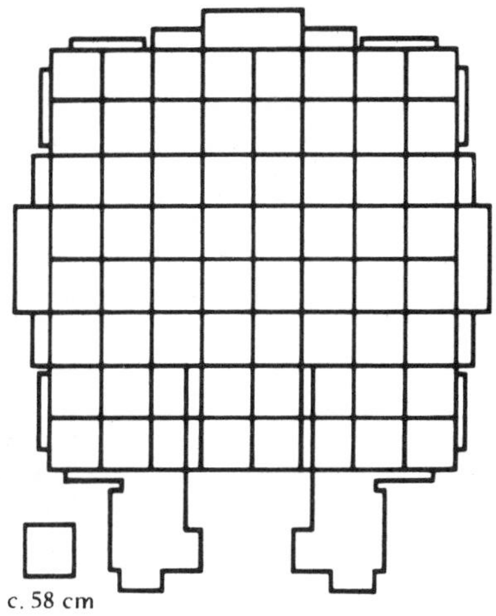

FIGURE 2. *Vastumaṇḍala as Part of Temple Design*

scale, the Indian architect used a square *(vastumaṇḍala)* consisting of a grid of 64, 81, or more small squares as the starting point of a temple construction. Such a *vastumaṇḍala* was regarded as the body of the cosmic being *(vastupuruṣa)* in whose various parts the main deity, auxiliary deities, and temple guardians resided. The *vastumaṇḍala* is often closely connected with the actual design of the building (see figure 2) and assures the builder of the presence of the gods.

Square forms, in contrast to the circular plans of Hindu and Jain cosmology, are also the basis for Hindu *maṇḍala*s used in Pāñcarātra (Vaiṣṇava Tantra) as well as Śaiva and Śākta Tantric rituals. The most elaborate designs to appear in the Pāñcarātra ritual are described in the *Lakṣmī Tantra* (c. tenth century CE), which contains a whole chapter on *maṇḍala* construction, and in the earlier *Jayākhya Saṃhitā.*

These texts prescribe at the beginning of the worship the construction of a square, which is divided into 256 small squares. The 16 small squares at the center and 8 squares of identical size at the margins are filled with one lotus each. The great square has gates and is surrounded by *śobhā*s (ramparts; literally, "ornaments") and *koṇa*s ("corners"). This *maṇḍala* is called Navapadma Maṇḍala ("*maṇḍala* of nine lotuses"; see figure 3). The texts state that no matter whether the deity is worshiped in an image, in a pitcher, or under any other circumstances, the worshiper should always "recall to his mind the nine lotuses" of the *maṇḍala*, "which contains the whole world and is the exalted home of all gods, which encompasses all [other] loci and is the paramount abode" (*Lakṣmī Tantra* 37.22, 37.25). The Pāñcarātrins also used a Cakrābja Maṇḍala ("*maṇḍala* having a lotus circle"), in which a large lotus fills the entire great square (see figure 4). A third form, the Navanābha Maṇḍala ("*maṇḍala* of the nine navels") has the great square divided into nine smaller squares, in each of which is a seat *(bimba)* for one of the nine manifestations of Lakṣmī (i.e., Vāsudeva, Saṃkarṣaṇa, Pradyumna, Aniruddha, Nārāyaṇa, Virāṭ, Viṣṇu, Narasiṃha, and Varāha; see figure 5).

In several North Indian Tantric Śaiva and Śākta texts, *maṇḍala* worship is mentioned along with the *dīkṣā* ("initiation") ceremony, (e.g., *Prapañcasāra Tantra* 5.36–70). The similarities in preparation and designs with those of the Pāñcarātrins is striking: in both traditions a pavilion must be erected over the prepared ground on which the *maṇḍala* is to be constructed. Of four *maṇḍala*s, mentioned in Tantric texts, the first, called Sarvatobhadra Maṇḍala ("*maṇḍala* that is auspicious on every side"), is identical with the Navapadma Maṇḍala; the second is only its smaller variant. The third, the Navanābha Maṇḍala, is identical in form with the *maṇḍala* of the same name of the Pāñcarātrins, but instead of the nine seats for deities it has five lotuses and four *svāstika*s. The fourth *maṇḍala* is identical with the third but has only five lotuses and no *svāstika*s. Therefore, it is called Pañcābja Maṇḍala ("*maṇḍala* of five lotuses"). During the initiation ceremony among the Fāñcaratrins and among Tantrics, the blindfolded

FIGURE 3. *Navapadma Maṇḍala*

FIGURE 4. *Cakrābja Maṇḍala*

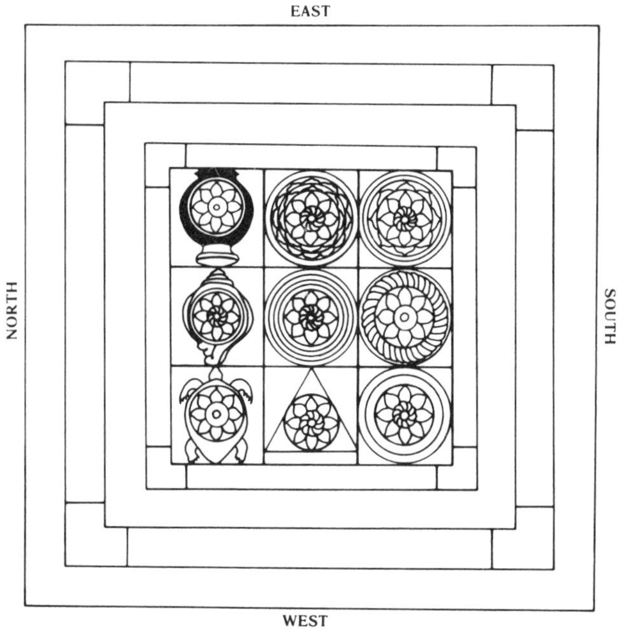

FIGURE 5. *Navanābhā Maṇḍala*

adept is led to the *maṇḍala* and throws flowers upon it. The deity on whose seat the flowers fall will provide him with a name or will become his special object of worship.

In their daily and thus more private rituals, Tantrics of all denominations start the ritual with the drawing of geometrical designs in vermilion or red sandalwood paste on a purified surface. For the devotee, these diagrams are a source of cosmic power and the place on which the deity dwells during the ritual. Although such diagrams are also often called *maṇḍalas* and their function of providing a proper abode for the deity is the same as in the *dīkṣā* rituals, it has become customary to call the simpler designs for daily worship *yantras*, and to reserve the term *maṇḍala* for the larger ones in public ceremonies where the whole cosmos has to be present. [*See also* Yantra.]

Hindu *maṇḍalas* have attracted the curiosity of modern symbolists and psychoanalysts such as Mircea Eliade and C. G. Jung. However, as their interpretations are not always based on the evidence of the available texts, the explanatory value of these studies is limited. A definitive history of the geometric designs used in Hindu rituals has yet to be written.

[*See also* Tantrism *and* Temple, *article on* Hindu Temples.]

BIBLIOGRAPHY

Bürk, Albert. "Das Āpastamba-Śulva Sūtra." *Zeitschrift der Deutschen Morgenländischen Gesellschaft* 56 (1902): 327–391.

Gupta, Sanjukta, trans. and ed. *Lakṣmī Tantra: A Pāñcarātra Text.* Leiden, 1972.

Gupta, Sanjukta, and Teun Goudriaan. "Hindu Tantric and Śākta Literature." In *History of Indian Literature,* edited by Jan Gonda, vol. 2, fasc. 2. Wiesbaden, 1981.

Gupta, Sanjukta, Dirk Jan Hoens, and Teun Goudriaan. *Hindu Tantrism.* Leiden, 1979.

Kramrisch, Stella. *The Hindu Temple.* 2 vols. Calcutta, 1946.

Meister, Michael W. "Maṇḍala and Practice in Nāgara Architecture in North India." *Journal of the American Oriental Society* 99 (1979): 204–219.

Pott, P. H. *Yoga and Tantra: Their Interrelation and Their Significance for Indian Archeology* (1946). Translated from Dutch by Rodney Needham. The Hague, 1966.

PETER GAEFFKE

Buddhist Maṇḍalas

Maṇḍala is a Sanskrit word that literally means "circle" (Tib., *dkyil 'khor;* Jpn., *mandara*). As a graphic symbol, the *maṇḍala* appears throughout ancient Indian texts and plays a mystical and ritual role in Indian religions, especially Hinduism, Buddhism, and Tibetan Lamaism, as well as in Japanese Esoteric Buddhism. *Maṇḍalas* share certain common points in their plastic representations, whether they take the form of architectural monuments, and are thus "permanent," or whether they are drawn on the ground, on silk, or on paper, or rendered in sculpture in the round, and are hence "temporary." The main characteristic common to all *maṇḍalas* is their layout, which takes the form of a geometric diagram with numerous variants. The *maṇḍala* has a center and possesses an axis and directional headings. It may be aptly called a cosmogram (Tucci, 1969), for it depicts a divine cosmos.

The *maṇḍala* can be traced to very old notions of cosmology, especially in countries that come under the influence of ancient Indian culture. Some scholars find evidence for *maṇḍala*-like diagrams in pre-Buddhist China as well. The idea of a cosmogram can probably be traced back to the Mesopotamian ziggurat, the ancient Babylonian temple-tower, pyramidal in shape with outside stairs and a shrine at the summit, but there is no direct evidence linking these structures with Indian forms. The relation of macrocosm and microcosm and, in the practice of the *maṇḍala,* between the human body and the cosmos, derives from yogic doctrines; the practitioner makes a *maṇḍala* in his own body and in that sense identifies with the cosmos. The *maṇḍala* form doubtless reflects the layout of the house or, more precisely, the royal palace, inhabited by the universal sovereign *(cakravartin).*

In India the *maṇḍala* may perhaps be traced as far back as the Vedic period (1500–500 BCE). The Vedic sacrifice was performed on a *maṇḍala*-like altar, which symbolized the cosmos and cosmic time. This was placed in the center of a consecrated space, a sort of magic circle. The *maṇḍala* developed in India, Tibet, and China, and was later transmitted to Japan during the evolution of the Vajrayāna ("the thunderbolt vehicle"), which was imprinted with a strong esoteric element, and it was further expanded by Indian and Buddhist Tantrism.

In a general way, the *maṇḍala* is the central piece in a rite of liberation and is endowed with diverse functions: it is used in initiation rites and is also a means of magical coercion. As a projection of the cosmos (i.e., as a cosmogram), it consists of an assemblage of deities arranged in hierarchic order around a central divinity. Layouts differ according to the text on which the *maṇḍala* is based. The assembly of deities and the forces they represent are realized and made efficacious through the meditation of the officiant.

The *maṇḍala* is a kind of labyrinth that the initiate penetrates, accompanied by the master officiant (*sādhaka*). [*See* Labyrinth.] The initiate's goal is to arrive at the center and there unite with the central deity. This act of identification is one of supreme deliverance. But in order to succeed, it is necessary to observe the correct astrological moment as well as to choose the propitious site for the *maṇḍala,* which in turn is consecrated by rites and set off by cords, sand, or colored powder. The various sections have portals located in the four directions. At the end of the initiation rite, the whole apparatus is destroyed and the colored elements are disposed of in a river.

The voyage of the novice through the *maṇḍala* is comparable to rites of pilgrimage that regularly followed certain prescribed routes, some lasting for several months. The layouts of certain Buddhist and Brahmanic monuments, some of which are of considerable size, correspond to *maṇḍala*s. The Bsam-yas temple (Tibet, eighth century), for example, in fact constitutes a *maṇḍala;* it was constructed for the purpose of exorcizing local underground demons who opposed the installation of Buddhism in Tibet. Borobudur (Java, ninth century) is a veritable temple-mountain in elevation, a *maṇḍala* in layout. The various divisions ("courts") of this temple-*maṇḍala* take the form of the successive planes of a pyramid, at the top of which is located the primordial Buddha. Through meditation, the symbolic step from court to court, from microcosm to macrocosm, becomes possible. This symbolic mental passage is possible either before an architectural *maṇḍala* or before one depicted on plastic material. In both cases, the *maṇḍala* plays the important role of support for meditation. Through his intense meditation, the officiant realizes the universe being represented, animates the deities and their forces, and unites himself with the central divinity. [*See also* Pilgrimage, *articles on Hindu and Buddhist traditions and* Temple, *article on* Buddhist Temple Compounds.]

A great variety of painted *maṇḍala*s exist, especially in Nepal and Tibet, their details determined by canonical texts. In Tibet, common elements predominate, each having a set symbolic value. The *maṇḍala* itself is surrounded by three or four concentric circles. The first is of fire (representing knowledge); the second is of cemeteries (representing the world of the senses); the third is of *vajra* (representing stability); and the fourth is of the lotus (representing the spiritual world). Within these circles appear several different partitions (or "courts"), each side having an entryway surmounted by a portal in the form of a *T*. In the center, an eight-petaled lotus houses the supreme deity.

Gods are usually represented by images, but in the Samaya Maṇḍala, especially in Japanese Esoteric Buddhism, these images are replaced by conventional symbols. The symbol may be an article associated with the deity or by a magic syllable that represents the essence or "seed" *(bīja)* of the divinity in question. The latter form is known as a "seed" *maṇḍala (bījamaṇḍala).*

Other forms of ritual connected with the *maṇḍala,* especially in India, include the offering of the universe to the deity, that is, of all cosmic worlds in the form of a *maṇḍala* object. Frequently, the offering is represented by a little mound of dough, rice, or ghee marked with circular ridges, but in Tibet there exist complex examples in sculpted bronze, such as the design on a cylindrical drum depicting waves at whose center rises the cosmic mountain Meru, at once the cosmic axis and the home of the deity Indra. This mountain is surrounded at the four cardinal points by the cosmic continents peopled by gods and symbols.

The Two Maṇḍalas. The observances of the Shingon tradition of Japanese Esoteric Buddhism center around two *maṇḍala*s, the Womb World Maṇḍala (Skt., Garbhakośadhātu; Jpn., Taizōkai) and the Diamond World Maṇḍala (Skt., Vajradhātu; Jpn., Kongōkai). These two, known in Japanese as *genzu,* or "iconographic" *maṇḍala*s, were allegedly transmitted from India to China in the eighth century. Traditions vary widely as to their provenance, but one legendary account maintains that the Indian Tantric master Śubhākarasiṃha, who arrived in China in 716, painted them himself after witnessing their miraculous manifestation in the skies over a monastery in Gandhāra. Another account credits Vajrabhodhi, who arrived in China in 720, with the transmission of the Kongōkai *maṇḍala*. However obscure the origins and initial appearance of these *maṇḍala*s, their present form is probably based on a rendition by the Chinese Tantric master Hui-kuo (746–805), who is credited with passing this tradition of the "two *maṇḍalas*" to Kūkai (774–835), the founder of the Shingon school in Japan. [*See also* Shingonshū *and the biographies of Śubhākarasiṃha, Vajrabodhi, and Kūkai.*]

The Womb Maṇḍala, the composition of which is based on the *Mahāvairocana Sūtra,* consists of twelve "courts," containing in all 414 deities. (See figures 1 and 2.) The central divinity is the cosmic Vairocana, whose key quality here is "knowledge (Jpn., *chi*). The various other deities represent the fragmentation of this central unity. [*See also* Mahāvairocana.]

The Diamond Maṇḍala, with 1,461 deities, is based on the *Tattvasaṃgraha* and represents "principle" (Jpn., *ri*); it consists of a group of nine individual *maṇḍalas*, of which the central "Karma Assembly" represents the Buddha's function *(karman)* to enlighten. (See figure 3.) The central divinity is the cosmic Vairocana, who in this *maṇḍala* represents principle *(ri)*.

The *maṇḍalas* represent the essence of the secret esoteric teaching. In graphic form they present the esoteric concept of Buddhahood and explain the nature of Vairocana and the relationship that exists between this Buddha and men. They "actualize" Vairocana in man and prove that the Buddha essence *(dharmakāya)* of this deity can communicate the Law, an important Shingon tenet.

Although the Womb World and Diamond World *maṇḍalas* are fundamental, there are numerous other arrangements featuring a variety of deities. Some *maṇḍalas* have divinities other than Vairocana, such as Śākyamuni or Amitābha. The so-called Lotus Maṇḍala

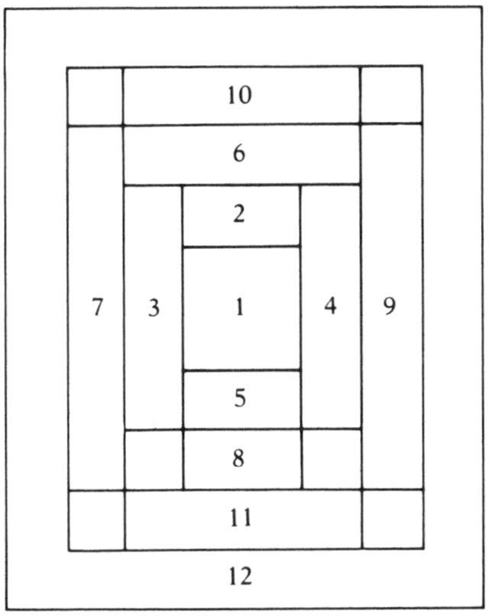

FIGURE 1. *The Twelve Courts of the Garbhakośadhātu (Womb World) Maṇḍala*

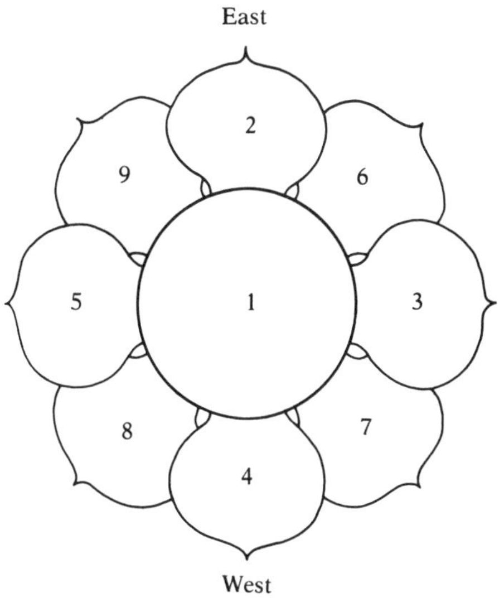

FIGURE 2. *The Central Court of the Garbhakośadhātu Maṇḍala.* Buddhas and *bodhisattvas* are placed in an eight-petaled lotus configuration as follows: (1) Mahāvairocana (center); (2) Ratnaketu (east); (3) Saṃkusumitarāja (south); (4) Amitābha (west); (5) Divyadun-dubhimega-nirghosa (north); (6) Samantabhadra; (7) Mañjuśri; (8) Avalokiteśvara; (9) Maitreya.

(Hoke Mandara), for example, is the main object of worship in the *Lotus Sutra* rite. A jeweled pagoda is located in the center; in it, side by side, are seated Śākyamuni and Prabhūtaratna. Eight *bodhisattvas* surround them in an arrangement that recalls the eight-petaled lotus of the Womb Maṇḍala. *Maṇḍalas* may feature other deities as central divinities: *bodhisattvas*, wisdom kings, *devas*. There is even a *maṇḍala* for invoking rain for use in the "altar ceremony for praying for rain according to the *Great Cloud Sutra.*" Śākyamuni, his hands held in the Gesture of Preaching the Law, is seated in the sea dragon's palace while Avalokiteśvara and Vajrapāṇi appear on his left and right.

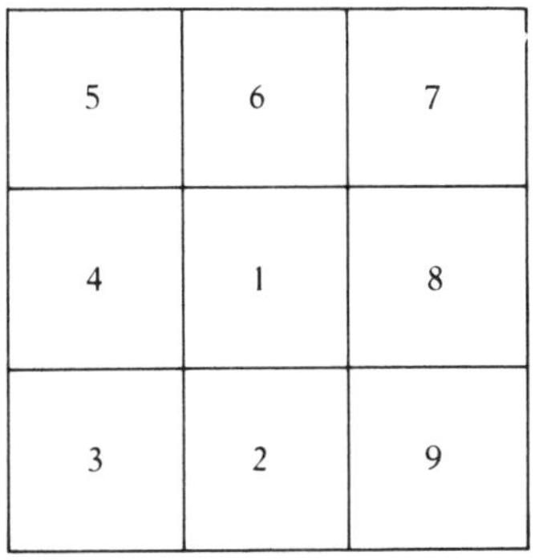

FIGURE 3. *The Nine Assemblies of the Vajradhātu (Diamond World) Maṇḍala*

The historically close relationship in Japan between Buddhism and Shintō favored the appearance there of *maṇḍalas* that feature Shintō deities and shrines. Shintō deities were considered to be "manifestations" *(suijaku)* of certain Buddhas and *bodhisattvas* who were their fundamental substance *(honji)*. First appearing in the twelfth century, such *maṇḍalas (suijaku mandara)* became popular in the thirteenth and fourteenth centuries. [*See* Honjisuijaku.] They feature views of shrines and shrine scenery with images in round, golden mirrors above the shrine or sometimes on the back of a deer. "Palace" *maṇḍalas* show the natural scenery of shrine precincts from a bird's-eye perspective. Sometimes Buddhist deities and their Shintō manifestations appear in parallel rows. In some *suijaku maṇḍaras* Buddhas are arranged in the style of Esoteric *maṇḍalas* to which shrine scenery is added.

[*See also* Tantrism; Buddhism, Schools of, *article on* Esoteric Buddhism; *and* Celestial Buddhas and Bodhisattvas.]

BIBLIOGRAPHY

Probably the best basic book on *maṇḍalas* is Giuseppe Tucci's *The Theory and Practice of the Maṇḍala*, translated by Alan Houghton Brodrick (London, 1969), in which the author explains just how *maṇḍalas* work, particularly in Tibet. A more recent work is José Arguelles and Miriam Arguelles's *Maṇḍala* (Berkeley, 1972). For the *maṇḍala* in India, there is an excellent treatment of one dedicated to Mañjuśrī by Ariane MacDonald, *Le maṇḍala du Mañjuśrîmûlakalpa* (Paris, 1962). This work is complemented by Marie-Thérèse de Mallmann's excellent iconographic study *Étude iconographique sur Mañjuśrî* (Paris, 1964). See also Raoul Birnbaum's *Studies on the Mystery of Mañjuśrī*, Society for the Study of Chinese Religions Monograph No. 2 (Boulder, 1983). A general work on Buddhist symbolism that includes *maṇḍalas* is Gustav Mensching's *Buddhistische Symbolik* (Gotha, Germany, 1929). Paul Mus has written a definitive description and discussion of the temple-monument of Borobudur in the *Bulletin de l'École Française d'Extrême-Orient* (Hanoi) 32 (1932): 269–439; 33 (1933): 577–980; 34 (1934): 175–400. Tajima Ryūjun's *Les deux grands maṇḍalas et la doctrine de l'ésotérisme Shingon* (Tokyo, 1959) is a thorough discussion of the two *maṇḍalas* and the textual basis for their composition. Probably the best general work on Esoteric Japanese art is Ishida Hisatoyo's *Mikkyōga*, in "Nihon bijutsu," no. 33 (Tokyo, 1969), my translation of which will soon appear under the title *Esoteric Buddhist Painting*. For a general treatment of Japanese Esotericism, including a discussion of the two *maṇḍalas*, one will find a clearly written treatment in Minoru Kiyota's *Shingon Buddhism: Theory and Practice* (Los Angeles, 1978). By far the best and most detailed treatment of the two *maṇḍalas* is Toganoo Shoun's *Mandara no kenkyū* (Kyoto, 1927). For painted Tibetan *maṇḍalas*, see Odette Monod-Bruhl's *Peintures tibétaines* (Paris, 1954).

E. DALE SAUNDERS

MANI, prophet and founder of Manichaeism, a gnostic religion influenced by Christianity, Judaism, Zoroastrianism, and Buddhism. Mani was born in the year 527 of the Seleucid era, which corresponds to 216 CE (according to sources and calculations based on the Babylonian, Iranian, Chinese, and Egyptian calendars), on the eighth day of the month of Nisan in the Babylonian calendar. This is equivalent to 14 April or to the eighth day of the month of Pharmuti in the Egyptian calendar.

Mani was born to the southeast of Ctesiphon, a city on the eastern bank of the Tigris in the Parthian province of Asōristān in Mesopotamia. Though he was given the epithet *al-Bābilīyu* (Arab., "the Babylonian") and proclaimed himself "the messenger of God come to Babylon" and "the physician coming from the land of Babel," he was not of Babylonian origin, for his parents were Iranian. His father, Patīk (Pattikios in the hellenized form in the Manichaean Codex of Cologne), was a native of the Hamadān, and his mother, Maryam (?), was a member of the princely family related to the ruling Arsacid dynasty. The name *Mānī* is perhaps of Semitic origin, and the form *Manichaios* is a hellenization of the Aramaic *Mānī Ḥayyā'*, "Mani the Living" (Schaeder, 1927). In Manichaean texts this epithet is often given to transcendental and benevolent things or beings. Mani is also called *mar* (Aram., "lord") or *mārī* (Syr., "my lord"). His Chinese name, *Mo-mo-ni*, is a version of *Mār Mānī*, "Lord Mani."

The environment in which Mani spent his youth accounts for the strong elements of eclecticism and syncretism that marked the religion he founded. A great number of diverse religions were present in third-century Mesopotamia—gnostic sects, esoteric communities, and philosophical and religious schools that combined Greek thought and Chaldean astrology. Moreover, from a sociocultural point of view, Babylonia and its neighboring provinces, part of the Parthian empire, were characterized (especially in contrast to the Iranian plateau) by a highly developed urban civilization. In addition, strong commercial ties bound Babylonia and its surrounding areas both to the Roman West and to the East (Central Asia, China, and India).

The spread of gnosticism, typical of the era's spiritual atmosphere, also affected the atmosphere of Mani's family. His father, a religious seeker, searched for salvation through the purification of his own being and through liberating knowledge. Having first joined a community that, according to the Arab encyclopedist Ibn al-Nadīm in the *Fihrist al-'ulūm* (Index of the Sciences; 988 CE), gathered around an idolatrous temple, Patīk soon moved on to a Mughtasilite community (Arab., *al-mughtasilah*, "they who cleanse themselves," parallel to Greek *baptistai*) that practiced sexual abstinence and followed rigid dietary laws prohibiting meat and wine. According to tradition Patīk's conversion occurred when Mani's mother was already pregnant with her only son. Today we are in a position to identify this religious community as Elkesaite Mughtasilism, a Judeo-Christian sect of baptists whose beliefs, beginning in the second century CE, spread significantly throughout Transjordan and then Syria, Palestine, and Mesopotamia. According to Ibn al-Nadīm, the sect's founder, al-Khasayh, is the same person called Elkesai by Christian heresiologists and identified as Alkhasaios in the Manichaean Codex of Cologne.

These facts should be kept in mind when we attempt to reconstruct the spiritual environment in which the young Mani grew up, but it would be a serious error to consider the Judeo-Christian component the determining factor in the shaping of the future "apostle of Babylonia." We must not exclude other equally essential components, for example, the extremely diverse religious and cultural ambience of Mesopotamia during this period, which, as we know, gave birth to such religious movements as Mandaeism. The Judaic origins of Mandaeism, which has survived to the present in southern Iran, are interwoven with beliefs that were strongly influenced by Iranian gnosticism. Nor should we underestimate the fact that at Edessa, in the northern part of Syria, two great gnostic teachers, Marcion of Pontus (d. around 160 CE) and Bardesanes (Bardaisan) of Edessa (154–222 CE), both of whom were strongly influenced by Iranian dualism (Widengren, 1983, pp. 965–972), had already established schools.

At the age of four Mani joined the religion of the baptists. At twelve—more precisely, on the eighth of Nisan of the Seleucid period, corresponding to 1 April 228 CE, two years after the end of the Parthian dynasty of the Arsacids and the beginning of the reign of Ardashīr, the founder of the Persian dynasty of the Sasanids—he received his first revelation through the angel al-Tawm ("the twin"), who ordered him to forsake the community but to delay doing so until he was older. At twenty-four—on 8 Nisan 551 of the Seleucid era, corresponding to 19 April 240, seven days after the coronation of Ardashīr's son Shāpūr I as co-ruler—Mani received an angelic command to appear in public and preach the true doctrine. He did not achieve success in his own circle: after disputes with influential persons in his community, he left it, together with his father and just two disciples. But by now he had become the "apostle of light" in whom the Paraclete was incarnated, with the task of fulfilling a universal mission to provide salvation and hope for the whole of suffering humanity. Because of its legalistic and ritualistic doctrine, Mani's community had been unable to comprehend the ecumenical and antiritualistic spirit of the new message: purity came not from baptism, baths, or ablutions, he declared, but from the separation of light from darkness, of life from death, of living water from dead water.

The fundamental inspiration of the new religion took shape, based on a radical dualism obviously of Iranian origin. Mani conceived the grand plan of creating a church founded on a universalistic and prophetic doctrine, in conscious and irreducible contrast to the particularistic traditions dominant to the west and east of the ecumene of the Sasanid empire. In Mani's view, these particularistic traditions were the result of aberrant interpretations of the original messages of the great prophets of the past—the Buddha, Zarathushtra (Zoroaster), Jesus—all of whom proclaimed the truth, each in a single part of the world and in one language, while he, Mani, the Seal of the Prophets, had proclaimed it for the whole world, and the voice of his preaching would be understood in all languages. This would demonstrate the superiority of his church.

Indeed, the life of the prophet was dedicated to missionary work, which he performed with extraordinary fervor, utilizing the means of communication most suited to the diffusion of the apostolic message: the writing and illustration of the work he was carrying out. The pictorial arts, graphics, and calligraphy were held in high regard by him personally—his reputation as a great painter endured for centuries—and by his disciples and successors. It was imperative that the good news of the religion of light be entrusted to writing and be translated into the greatest possible number of languages, in order to facilitate its rapid and correct diffusion. The Buddha, Zarathushtra, and Jesus had not done as much; others had written their gospels for them, which caused misunderstandings, deviations, and errors. In his use of linguistic tools, Mani was also an innovator insofar as the Iranian languages—Middle Persian and Parthian—were concerned. In fact, he reformed the difficult writing systems of these languages, which had an insufficient number of symbols and used numerous Aramaic ideograms. Mani enormously reduced the distance between writing and phonetics and made it easier to comprehend the living written language, abandoning ideographic writing and replacing it with the Eastern Syriac alphabet.

Mani wrote the greater part of his works not in Iranian but in Eastern Aramaic, although the *Shābuhragān (Nībēg;* Book Dedicated to Shāpūr), addressed to the great Sasanid monarch, was written in Middle Persian. The canon of his works includes the *Living Gospel,* the *Treasure of Life,* the *Mysteries,* the *Treatise,* the *Book of Giants,* the *Epistles,* the *Psalms,* and the *Prayers.* Outside the canon were the *Images,* an album of painted images intended to illustrate the principles and fundamental themes of his doctrine, and the *Shāhbuhragān*, perhaps remaining outside the canon because of the tragic events affecting the relations between the prophet and the reigning dynasty. Of all these works we have only fragments, passages quoted by other authors, and lists of the arguments that they treated.

What we know of these writings and what we can deduce from the same doctrinal constructions in Manichaeism lead us to see Mani as a man of broad culture who certainly knew the four synoptic Gospels and the epistles of Paul; the apocalypses of Adam, Seth, Enoch, and Noah; and, most likely, the "acts" of John, Peter, Paul, Andrew, and above all of Thomas, the apostle of India, who in a certain sense must have served as an apostolic model. He was probably also familiar with the philosophical and poetical writings of Bardesanes, of whom he speaks in the *Mysteries*, and with the *Oracles of Hystaspes*. In addition, he certainly knew the Zoroastrian tradition, despite the fact that very little of it was written down at the time and despite the altered form it took among the Magi. Later, during his apostolic travels, he came in contact with many other living traditions, and there is no doubt that he had the opportunity to study Mahāyāna Buddhism.

It is therefore significant that Mani's first apostolic mission was to "India," that is, he traveled along the coasts of Fārs and Makran and in Baluchistan and Sind (240–242). It was then that he converted the Buddhist king of Tūrān and the great dignitaries of the kingdom to his beliefs. This first mission served to penetrate the Buddhist environment and probably to win over to the new religion the Christian community founded there by the apostle Thomas. The Coptic *Kephalaia* speaks of Mani's return to Persia and Babylonia during the year in which Ardashīr's son Shāpūr I became king. During the return voyage, Mani converted numerous people in Persia (242–244), Susiana, and Mesene (245–250).

Through two brothers of the king, Mihrshāh and Pērōz, both converts, Mani obtained an audience with Shāpūr. It was crowned with success: he entered the monarch's retinue and was granted the power to preach freely throughout the empire (250–255). It was then that he wrote the *Shābuhragān* and that he accompanied Shāpūr in the campaign against the Roman emperor Valerian (255–256). Between 258 and 260 Mani traveled in northeastern Iran, Parthia, and Khorasan. In the following years, settling down at Wēh-Ardakhshīr, on the west bank of the Tigris, he dedicated himself to the organization of his church, his scriptures, and his missions. Until 270 he continued to travel, reaching even the Roman border in the northwestern provinces of the Sasanid domains.

Until that point the success of the religion of light had been extraordinary, in part because of Shāpūr's favor. Mani had dedicated a book to Shāpūr, perhaps in the hope that the monarch would be led to adopt the new doctrine as the official religion of the empire, as part of his universalistic political program. The death of Shāpūr in around 272, however, signaled the beginning of the prophet's fall from favor. Shāpūr's successors Hormīzd I (r. 273) and Bahrām I (r. 273–277) not only remained Zoroastrian but also fell increasingly under the influence of the Zoroastrian clergy of the Magi, led by a conniving and influential priest, Kerdēr, the author of important inscriptions that have been preserved.

The reactions of the Magi, who were worried by Mani's growing success, became increasingly strong and negative and succeeded in winning over Bahrām. Mani was unable to complete his final apostolic program or to travel to the eastern lands of the Kushan empire: overtaken by a police order he was forced to turn back to Gundeshahbur in Susiana, where the king was staying. After being subjected to a dramatic interrogation at the instigation of Kerdēr, in which he was accused of having converted a prince named Bat, Mani was condemned to death by Bahrām. According to tradition, the interrogation and passion of the prophet lasted a month (four days and twenty-six days, respectively). Mani died, probably in chains, most likely in 277, at approximately sixty years of age.

The *damnatio memoriae* of Mani was especially striking: he was considered, by Zoroastrians, Christians, and Muslims alike, the heretic *par excellence*, and he remained the target, for centuries, of implacable hatred.

[*For further discussion of Mani, see* Manichaeism.]

BIBLIOGRAPHY

Christensen, Arthur. *L'Iran sous les Sassanides.* 2d ed. Copenhagen, 1944.

Cumont, Franz. "Mânî et les origines de la miniature persane." *Revue archéologique* 22 (1913): 82–86.

Decret, François. *Mani et la tradition manichéenne.* Paris, 1974.

Ernst, J. W. *Die Erzählung von Sterben des Mani aus dem Koptischen übertragen und rekonstruiert.* Basel, 1941.

Haloun, Gustav, and W. B. Henning. "The Compendium of the Doctrines and Styles of the Teaching of Mani, the Buddha of Light." *Asia Major,* n.s. 3 (1952): 184–212.

Henrichs, A., and Ludwig Koenen. "Ein griechischer Mani-Codex." *Zeitschrift für Papyrologie und Epigraphik* 5 (1970): 97–216.

Henning, W. B. "Mani's Last Journey." *Bulletin of the School of Oriental and African Studies* 10 (1942): 941–953.

Jackson, A. V. W. "The personality of Mānī, the Founder of Manichaeism." *Journal of the American Oriental Society* 58 (1938): 235–240.

Klíma, Otakar. *Manis Zeit und Leben.* Prague, 1962.

Klimkeit, Hans-Joachim. *Manichaean Art and Calligraphy*. Iconography of Religions, sec. 20, fascs. 4–8. Leiden, 1982.

Lidzbarski, Mark. "Warum schrieb Mānī aramäisch?" *Orientalistische Literaturzeitung* 30 (1927): 913–917.

Maricq, André. "Les débuts de la prédication de Mani et l'avènement de Šāhpuhr Ier." In *Mélanges Henri Grégoire*, pp. 245–268. Brussels, 1951.

Ort, L. J. R. *Mani: A Religio-Historical Description of His Personality*. Leiden, 1967.

Pestalozza, U. "Appunti sulla vita di Mani." *Rendiconti, Reale Istituto Lombardo di Scienze e Lettere*, 2d series, 81 (1938): 3–52.

Puech, Henri-Charles. *Le manichéisme: Son fondateur, sa doctrine*. Paris, 1949.

Sundermann, W. "Zur frühen missionarischen Wirksamkeit Manis." *Acta Orientalia* 24 (1971): 79–125.

Taqizadeh, S. H. *Mānī va dīn-i ū*. Tehran, 1955.

Taqizadeh, S. H. "The Dates of Mani's Life." *Asia Major*, n.s. 6 (1957): 106–121.

Widengren, Geo. *Mani and Manichaeism*. New York, 1965.

GHERARDO GNOLI
Translated from Italian by Roger DeGaris

MANICHAEISM. [*This entry comprises two articles. The first,* An Overview, *discusses the origins, development, and doctrines of Manichaeism and the survival of Manichaean thought in religions from China to Europe. The second article,* Manichaeism and Christianity, *concentrates on the influence of Manichaeism in the West.*]

An Overview

The doctrine professed by Mani and the path to salvation that he revealed constitute a form of gnosis. It originated during the first half of the third century in Mesopotamia, a region of the Parthian empire in which a number of different religious and philosophical schools were actively present, notably Christianity, Judaism, and Zoroastrianism. The sects and communities of the region reflected the influence of one or the other of these cults to varying degrees and were often characterized by an evident gnostic orientation. Hellenism was well rooted and widespread in Mesopotamia (as in neighboring Syria), especially in the urban centers of Seleucid origin. Open to commercial and cultural exchanges, Mesopotamia was the region within the vast Parthian empire that was most likely to absorb syncretic and eclectic cultural and spiritual trends. Manichaeism, however, was not only a gnosis in the narrow sense; it was primarily a universal gnostic religion—the only great universal religion to arise from the Near Eastern gnostic tradition. No other gnostic school was as successful as Manichaeism, and no other aimed, as it did, to establish itself as a truly universal religion, founded and nurtured by an enterprising missionary spirit.

As with all gnostic movements, Manichaeism holds that knowledge leads to salvation and that this is achieved through the victory of the good light over evil darkness. As with all gnosticism, Manichaeism is permeated by a deep and radical pessimism about the world, which is seen as dominated by evil powers, and by a strong desire to break the chains holding the divine and luminous principle inside the prison of matter and of the body. Knowledge leads to salvation through an anamnesis, in which the initiate recognizes that his soul is a particle of light, consubstantial with the transcendental God.

Manichaean Literature and Sources. Very little remains of the rich and varied Manichaean literature. We know the canon of its scriptures mainly through the titles of individual works, of which seven were attributed to Mani himself, and through fragments preserved in quotations by authors who were hostile to Manichaeism. Sometimes we do have most of the text, as, for example, in the *Living Gospel*, which was translated from Syriac to Greek (Oxyrhynchus Codex). So too was the *Treasure of Life*, some passages of which were quoted by Augustine and by al-Bīrūnī; the *Mysteries*, of which we know the subtitles quoted by Ibn al-Nadīm and a few passages preserved by al-Bīrūnī; the *Treatise*, the *Book of Giants*, and the *Epistles*, of which Ibn al-Nadīm gives a list; and the *Psalms* and *Prayers*. All of these works were attributed to the founder of the faith, and rare and scattered fragments of them have been preserved in Manichaean texts from Central Asia (Turfan) and Egypt (Fayum). Two more works were attributed to Mani but are outside of the canon: the *Image* and the *Shābuhragān*, the book dedicated to the Sasanid king Shāpūr I. The purpose of the *Image* was to illustrate the main themes of the doctrine in a way that would be clear even to those not able to read. The *Shābuhragān*, the only work written in Middle Persian—Mani usually wrote in Syriac or Eastern Aramaic—discussed cosmology, anthropogony, and eschatology and is known to us through fragments preserved in the Turfan manuscripts and through an essential quotation by al-Bīrūnī concerning the Seal of the Prophecy.

Manichaean patrology is relatively better known to us than Mani's writings, mainly through the texts discovered at Turfan around the beginning of this century and those found at Fayum in 1930. Among the hagiographic works, we should mention the Manichaean Codex of Cologne, a Greek translation of a Syriac original, found in Oxyrhynchus and dating from the fifth century, and the Coptic *Homilies;* among the doctrinal ones, the Coptic *Kephalaia* and the *Chinese Treatise* of Tun-huang; among the hymns, the Coptic *Psaltery* and the Iranian hymn books, in Middle Persian and in Parthian, found in Turfan, as well as those in Chinese from Tun-huang; among the practical and liturgical writings, the *Compendium of Doctrines and Rules of the Buddha of Light, Mani,* a treatise dating from 731, found in Tun-huang, that was translated from Parthian into Chinese for use in the administration of the cult. To the last category also belonged the *Khwāstwānēft,* a handbook of formulas for the confession of sins, which has come down to us in a Uighur text from Central Asia.

Thus the discoveries of the twentieth century have brought to light, albeit only partially and in a fragmented fashion, a literature that in many cases, especially in the psalms and hymns, is distinguished by its considerable litarary value and by its strong and delicate poetic sensibility. These writings substantially modified the picture of Manichaeism that had been reconstructed through indirect sources before the end of the nineteenth century.

These sources, however, are still valuable, and they contribute now in a more balanced way to a reconstruction of Manichaean doctrine and history. They are numerous, and all by hostile authors, Neoplatonic, Christian, Zoroastrian, Muslim. There are Greek sources, from Alexander of Nicopolis to the *Acta Archelai;* Latin sources, from the Pseudo-Marius Victorinus to Augustine; Syrian sources, from Aphraates and Ephraem of Syria in the fourth century to Theodoros bar Kōnaī in the eighth; Middle Persian and Pahlavi sources, from passages in the *Dēnkard* (The Acts of Religion) to a chapter of the *Shkand-gumānīg Wizār* (The Definitive Solution to Doubts), a Zoroastrian apologetic work (ninth and tenth centuries); Arabic and Persian Muslim sources, from al-Ya'qūbī (ninth century), al-Ṭabarī, al-Mas'ūdī, and Ibn al-Nadīm (tenth century) to al-Bīrūnī, Ṭa'ālibī (eleventh century), al-Sharastānī (twelfth century), Abūal-Fidā, and Mirkhwānd (fourteenth and fifteenth centuries).

Until Manichaean literature was rediscovered, the works of Augustine, al-Bīrūnī, Ibn al-Nadīm, and the *Acta Archelai* were the cornerstones of Manichaean studies. Although the situation has undoubtedly changed considerably thanks to the more recent discoveries, the accounts of some anti-Manichaean authors remain extremely important, especially when viewed alongside those passages in Manichaean literature that discuss similar or identical subjects. It is now easier to distinguish between that which was written in polemic and apologetic ardor and that which resulted from accurate and intelligent information concerning Manichaean doctrines. Some of the sources are particularly relevant since they provide likely and precious data: for example, the *Letter of Foundation* by Augustine, the Manichaean cosmogony of Theodoros bar Kōnaī, and a few quotations and excerpts by al-Bīrūnī and Ibn al-Nadīm.

The Fundamental Doctrines. Manichaean doctrine places great importance on the concept of dualism, which is deeply rooted in Iranian religious thought.

Dualism. Like Zoroastrian cosmology, which we know through relatively late texts (ninth century CE), Manichaean dualism is based on the doctrine of the two roots, or principles, of light and darkness and the three stages of cosmic history: Gumēzishn (MPers.), the golden age before the two principles mixed together; the middle, or mixed, period, the present age, in which the powers of light and darkness battle for ultimate control of the cosmos; and the last age, when the separation of that which had become mixed, and between followers of good and evil, occurs. This is the time of *frashgird* (MPers., "rehabilitation"; Av., *frashōkereti*) in which the two poles of good and evil will once again be distinguished. [*See* Frashōkereti.] The holy books that he himself has revealed are those of the two principles and three stages. The two principles are light and darkness; the three stages are the past, the present, and the future; this information comes to us from a fragment of a Chinese text. This is the doctrine to which Augustine makes reference—*initium, medium, et finis*—in his anti-Manichaean treatises *Against Felix* and *Against Faustus.* It is more fully expressed in another Chinese text:

> First of all, we must distinguish between the two principles. He who wishes to join this religion must know that the two principles of light and darkness have absolutely distinct natures; if he cannot distinguish this, how can he practice the doctrine? Also, it is necessary to understand the three stages, that is, the prior stage, the middle stage, the posterior stage. In the prior stage, heaven and earth do not yet exist: there are only light and darkness, and they are separate from each other. The nature of light is wisdom, the nature of darkness is ignorance. In all motion and in all repose, these two are opposed to each other. At the middle stage, darkness has invaded light. The latter lunges forward to drive it back and thus itself enters the darkness and attempts at all costs to drive it out. Through the great calamity we acquire disgust, which, in turn, drives us to separate our selves from our bodies; in the burning abode the vow is made to attempt an escape. (Chavannes and Pelliot, 1913)

The "great calamity" is a metaphor for the body, and the "burning abode" stands for the world, seen as a burning house from which one is saved by escaping. The text continues: "At the later stage, instruction and conversion are accomplished, truth and falsehood have returned each to its roots: light has returned to the great light, and darkness has returned to the mass of darkness. The two principles are reconstituted" (Chavannes and Pelliot, 1913).

The two roots are not generated and have nothing in common: they are irreducible opposites in every way. Light is good, equated with God; darkness is evil, equated with matter. Because good and evil are coeval, the problem of the origin of evil (a central dilemma of Christian doctrine) is resolved, in the most radical and extreme way. Its existence cannot be denied; it is everywhere, it is eternal and can only be defeated by knowledge (gnosis), which leads to salvation through the separation of light and darkness.

The way in which the two principles are represented is reminiscent of the two spirits, or *mainyus*, in the original Zoroastrian concept. Spenta Mainyu and Angra Mainyu are opposites in all things (*Yasna* 30.3–6), and their choice between good and evil, between *asha* ("truth") and *druj* ("falsehood"), is also prototypical of the choice that must be made by man. The ethical value of Manichaean dualism is no less strong, although its answer to the problem of evil is, of course, more typically gnostic. The Manichaeans refused to consider Ōhrmazd and Ahriman, the Pahlavi equivalents of the two *mainyus*, as two brothers who are opposed one to the other. The Uighur text *Khwāstwānēft* states: "If we once asserted that Khormuzta [Ōhrmazd] and Shīmnu [Ahriman] are brothers, one the cadet, one the firstborn . . . I repent of it . . . and I beg to be forgiven for that sin" (1c.3–4). Thus they were not so much addressing the dualism of the *Gāthās*, as opposing the later dualism of Zurvanism, which had demoted Ahura Mazdā to the role of a symmetrical opposite of Angra Mainyu and placed Zurwān, who personified infinite time, above the dualistic formula. In fact, it is interesting to observe how the Manichaeans restored Ōhrmazd to a central role in the drama of salvation and in the very gnostic approach to the *prōtos anthrōpos*, while considering *Zurwān* as one of the names. The other Iranian name was *Srōshaw*—for the Father of Greatness, "sovereign god of the heaven of light," "god of truth," that is, one of the two terms of the dualistic formula. Terms for the opposite pole are *Devil, Satan, Ahriman, Shīmnu, Hulē, Matter, Evil,* the *Great Archon,* and the *Prince of Darkness.*

Rather than metaphysical speculation, we find at the root of Manichaean dualism a merciless analysis of the human condition, a pessimism largely common to all forms of gnosis and to Buddhism. By the mere fact of being incarnate, man suffers; he is prey to evil, forgetful of his luminous nature as long as he remains asleep and dimmed by ignorance in the prison of matter. While the two principles remain mixed, all is waste, torture, death, darkness: "Liberate me from this deep nothingness, from this dark abyss of waste, which is naught but torture, wounds unto death, and where there is no rescuer, no friend. There can be no salvation here, ever! All is darkness . . . all is prisons, and there is no exit" (Parthian fragment T2d.178).

This pessimistic attitude toward the world and toward life, which perpetuates itself in the snares of matter, accompanied Manichaeism throughout its history, increasingly strengthened by the bitter and often violent confrontations between its followers and the other established religions of the eastern and western empires. It was probably also at the root of an antinomic tendency of these "subversives," who could see nothing good in a world full of horror, evil, and injustice. This was probably also an important reason for the fierce persecutions they suffered—as is evident from the testimony of Zoroastrian sources (*Dēnkard,* Madan edition, pp. 216–218)—as well as for their refusal to conform to traditional customs and practices. It also helped to bring about that *damnatio memoriae* to which Mani and Manichaeism were universally subjected.

Knowledge as the path to salvation. An essential and specific characteristic of Manichaeism is its gnosticism, that is, its mixture of religion and science in a sort of theosophy. Manichaeism was attempting to give a universal explanation of the world, and it did not believe that mere faith and dogma were effective instruments in the search for redemption. On the contrary, Manichaean soteriology was based on knowledge. So it is understandable that Augustine should confess that he had most been attracted by precisely this aspect of Manichaeism during the years of his adherence to it (377–382), that is, to the promise that man could be freed of the authority of faith and tradition and led back to God simply by the strength of reason.

Manichaeans did not accept tradition, be it that of the New Testament or that of the Zoroastrian scriptures (*Kephalaia* 7), without first making a distinction between what they recognized as true and authentic in them and what, in their view, was simply the result of deceitful manipulations and interpolations by ignorant or insincere disciples. Only Mani's authority was worthy of trust, as it was based on reason and drawn from revelation. It was also set down in writing by him with extreme care and with the precise intent of not letting his teachings be misrepresented. Manichaeans, therefore, prided themselves on not asserting any truth without a logical and rational demonstration thereof, and without first opening the doors of knowledge.

Such knowledge was, ultimately, an anamnesis, an awakening; that is, gnosis was an *epignosis,* a recognition, a memory of self, knowledge of one's true ego and, at the same time, knowledge of God, the former being consubstantial with the latter, a particle of light fallen into matter's obfuscating mix. Thus God is a "savior saved," or one to be saved: a transcendental, luminous principle, spirit, or intelligence *(nous)*. It is the superior portion of man's ego, exiled in the body, and is the subject of the act of knowledge, thanks to which we will know where we are, where we come from, and where we are going. Man has forgotten his nature, a blend of light and darkness, spirit and matter. The enlightening power of knowledge makes him understand his own nature, that of the universe, and their destiny. It is, therefore, a universal science, blending theology, cosmology, anthropology, and eschatology. It includes everything: physical nature as well as history. Reason can penetrate anything: "Man must not believe until he has seen the object with his own eyes" (*Kephalaia* 142).

The cosmogonic and anthropogonic myths. It may appear paradoxical to find that the doctrine of Manichaeism, founded in reason, whose ability and dignity it praised, was expressed in a language of myth, one that was crowded with figures and images and painted in strong, often dark colors. In fact, its mythology, which was invented by Mani himself, is intellectualistic and reflexive, almost metaphorical in character: Manichaean myths serve the purpose of illustrating the truth about the drama of existence, both macrocosmic and microcosmic. They achieve their objective with the aid of powerful images, most of which are derived from the mythological heritage of previous traditions—a fact that lent them greater weight and authority—and by the use of divine figures, both angelic and demoniacal, familiar, at least in part, to the popular imagination. Because Mani's teachings were directed to all the world's peoples, the actors in the great play could, to be more easily understood, adopt different names in different countries, drawing from local pantheons. Thus, Manichaean mythology is like a great album of pictures arranged in a sequence aimed at awakening in the adept reminiscences and intuitions that will lead him to knowledge. Small wonder, then, that Mani, who was famous for his paintings, should also use a book of illustrations, the *Image* (Gr., *Eikon;* MPers., and Pth., *Ārdahang*), to convey his doctrine, or that his disciples later continued to do the same in their missionary activities.

Such a mythology must, of necessity, have keys to its interpretation. The first of these is the omnipresent dominant theme: that of the soul which has fallen into matter and is freed by its *nous*. Next, in order to understand what are often described as the aberrations of Manichaean myths—those repugnant acts of cannibalism and sexual practices with which they are studded, as well as the self-destructiveness and autophagia of matter—one must keep in mind two basic concepts: the Indo-Iranian idea of the equivalence of spirit, light, and seed (Eliade, 1971, pp. 1–30) and that of the distillation of light through the "gastric machine" of the chosen, an act that corresponds to the great purification of the luminous elements (Syr., *zīwānē*), which was carried out by the demiurge and his children at the beginning of time (Tardieu, 1981). The premise of the first concept is that light resides in the seed and through procreation is decanted from one body into another, undergoing the painful cycles of births and deaths (Skt., *saṃsāra*). This follows the related doctrine of metempsychosis (Syr., *tashpīkā;* Lat., *revolutio;* Gr., *metangismos*), an idea that originally came from India and that Mani adopted as pivotal to his system. The premise of the second is that just as the universe is the place in which all luminous bodies are healed, so the stomach is like a great alchemist's alembic, in which the chosen, thanks to the high degree of purification he has attained, is able to separate the light present in food from all impurities, through a double cycle of filtering and return. This cycle is a microcosm, whose corresponding macrocosm is the distillation of the *zīwānē* into the moon and the sun (Tardieu, 1981).

The Manichaean origin myth is based on the doctrine of two principles (light and darkness) and three stages of creation. During the first stage of existence, the two principles, personified as the Father of Greatness and the Prince of Darkness, are separate, residing, respectively, in the north and in the south, kept apart by a border between their two kingdoms. The Prince of Darkness—that is, agitated and disorderly matter—wishes to penetrate the kingdom of the Father of Greatness. Thus begins the second stage, in which the Father of Greatness, not wishing to compromise his five "dwellings" (Intelligence, Science, Thought, Reflection, and Conscience), decides to battle the Prince of Darkness and engenders an avatar, the Mother of the Living, who, in turn, produces Primordial Man. But the Prince of Darkness defeats Primordial Man and devours his five children. The avidity and greed of the Prince of Darkness, however, bring about his downfall; the five children of Primordial Man are like a poison within his stomach.

The Father of Greatness responds by creating a second being: the Living Spirit (who corresponds to the Persian god Mithra). The Living Spirit, who is also the father of five children, and Primordial Man confront the demons of the powers of darkness, and so the demiurgic action begins: from the bodies of the demons arise the skies, the mountains, the soil, and, finally, from a first bit of liberated light, the sun, moon, and stars. The Father of Greatness then creates a third being, called the Messenger, who incarnates *nous;* he is also called the Great Wahman, the god of thought (Av., Vohu Manah). The Messenger calls forth twelve Virgins of Light, and they show themselves nude to the demons, both male and female, so that they will all ejaculate at the sight of such beauty and thus free the elements of light that they had ingested and imprisoned. The seed spilled on the dry earth gives life to five trees: thus is accomplished the creation of the world.

The creation of the human race then occurs as follows. The she-demons, thus impregnated, thanks to the Messenger's ruse, give birth to monsters, who swallow plants in order to absorb the light contained within them. Then Matter (darkness), in the guise of Az, the personification of concupiscence, in order to imprison the elements of light in a more secure fashion, causes the demons Ashaglun and Namrael, male and female, to devour all the monsters, and then to mate. They then generate the first human couple, Adam and Eve. At this point, the work of salvation begins: Adam, kept wild and ignorant by the snares of darkness, is awakened from this state by the savior, the son of God, sent by the powers above. The savior is identified with Primordial Man, Ōhrmizd, or, later, with the transcendental Jesus, or the god of *nous.* The savior awakens Adam from his slumber, opens his eyes, shows him his soul, which is suffering in the material world, and reveals to him the infernal origins of his body and the heavenly origins of his spirit. Thus Adam acquires knowledge of himself, and his soul, thanks to gnosis, is resuscitated.

The third stage is the Great War between the forces of good and evil, characterized on the one hand by the desperate attempt of the Prince of Darkness to spread evil throughout the world by means of procreation—that is, by the creation of more and more corporeal prisons to entrap the elements of light—and on the other hand by the the efforts of the Father of Greatness to spread good. Through the practice of the laws of the religion and, in particular, by interrupting the cycle of reincarnation, light is liberated; that is, the soul is freed by knowledge. When the church of justice triumphs, the souls will be judged, and those of the chosen will rise to Heaven. The world will then be purified and destroyed by a fire lasting 1,468 years. All, or most, of the light particles, will be saved; Matter, in all its manifestations, and with its victims (the damned), will be forever imprisoned in a globe inside a gigantic pit covered with a stone. The separation of the two principles will thus be accomplished for all eternity.

Origins. We now know something more about the origins of the Manichaean religion, by comparing the Manichaean Codex of Cologne to other available sources, mainly the Arabic ones. Mani was raised in the environment of a Judeo-Christian gnostic and baptist sect, which had been founded by a figure, almost more mythical than historical, by the name of Elkesai (Gr., Alkhasaios; Arab., al-Khasayh). Elkesaism was a particularly widespread movement during the third and fourth centuries in Syria, Palestine, Mesopotamia, Transjordan, and northern Arabia. It survived for many centuries and is mentioned by the Arabic encyclopedist Ibn al-Nadīm as still existing during the fourth century AH in what is today southeastern Iraq.

It would, however, be a mistake to view the origins of Manichaeism only, or even mainly, in the light of such information, for one might erroneously conclude that the principal inspiration for the Manichaean doctrine was Judeo-Christian gnosticism. The origins of Manichaeism are still open to question (as are, in fact, those of gnosticism). The most likely interpretation would recognize the dominating imprint of Iranian dualism since without a doubt the dualistic doctrine is central and pivotal to Mani's thought and to the teachings and practices of his church. We must, however, consider the presence of three different forms of religious doctrine: the Iranian, which is basically Zoroastrian; the Christian or Judeo-Christian; and the Mahāyāna Buddhist. Of these, the Iranian form held the key to the Manichaean system and provided the essence of the new universalistic religious concept that developed from the main themes and aspirations of gnosticism. If we were to separate the Manichaean system from its Christian and Buddhist elements, it would not suffer irreparably.

Manichaeism was long thought of as a Christian heresy, but this interpretation was already being abandoned during the last century and has now been entirely rejected. We must also reject the approach that perceives the Judeo-Christian components, more or less affected by Hellenism, as dominant (Burkitt, 1925; Schaeder, 1927). There is a widespread tendency today to give equal emphasis to what we have called the three forms of Manichaeism and to consider it a great and independent universal religion, although such an approach is sometimes still weighted in favor of the relationship between Manicheaism and Christianity (Tardieu, 1981). Nevertheless, if we discount certain obvious differences, we can assert that Manichaeism has its roots in the Iranian religious tradition and that its relationship to Mazdaism, or Zoroastrianism, is more or less like that of Christianity to Judaism (Bausani, 1959, p. 103).

History. We can trace the beginnings of the religion to the second revelation received by the prophet at the age of twenty-four, that is, on the first of Nisan of 551 of the Seleucid era, which corresponds to 12 April 240

CE (his first occurred at the age of twelve while he was living in the baptist community). It was then that there appeared to him an angel, his "twin" (Gr., *suzugon;* Arab., *al-Tawm*), described as the "beautiful and sublime mirror" of his being, and it was then that Mani began his prophetic and apostolic ministry, breaking off from Elkesaism and its strict legalistic ritualism. He presented himself as the Seal of the Prophets and preached a new doctrine aimed at all peoples—Buddhists, Zoroastrians, and Christians.

A number of factors lead us to believe that, at the beginning of his ministry, Mani saw the universalistic religion he was founding as one that could be adapted to the new political reality of the Persian empire of the Sasanids, founded by Ardashīr I. To the emperor Shāpūr he dedicated a work, written in Middle Persian, that opened with a declaration of the universalistic idea of the Seal of the Prophecy. Any ambitions that great Sasanid ruler might have harbored for a universal empire would have found congenial a religious doctrine that presented itself as the sum and perfection of all the great prior religious traditions.

A missionary spirit moved Manichaeism from its very inception. Mani traveled first in the direction of the "country of the Indians" (perhaps in the footsteps of the apostle Thomas), with the hope of converting the small Christian communities scattered along the coast of Fārs and Baluchistan (Tardieu, 1981) and perhaps, also, in order to penetrate lands in which Buddhism was already widespread. Manichaean tradition remembers this first apostolic mission by its conversion of Tūrānshāh, that is, the Buddhist ruler of Tūrān, a kingdom in southeastern Iran. That mission was a relatively brief one owing to the turn of events in the Sasanid empire. The death of Ardashīr and the accession to the throne of Shāpūr, the "king of kings of Ērānshahr," recalled Mani to Persia. Manichaeism began at that time to spread to Iran, where it acquired a prominent position, thanks also to the conversion of high court officials and even members of the royal family, and encouraged, to a certain degree, by the king's support. In fact, the image of Shāpūr in Manichaean tradition is a positive one: Manichaeism almost became the official religion of the Persian empire. Mani himself, after obtaining a successful audience with Shāpūr, joined the ruler's court and obtained his permission to preach the new creed throughout the empire, under the protection of local authorities. During this fortunate period for Manichaean propaganda in Iran, in the 250s, Mani wrote the *Shābuhragān*, a work he dedicated to his royal protector and which has reached us only in a fragmented form.

Once the work of its founder had established it as a real church, Manichaeism soon spread beyond the borders of Persia, both in the Roman empire and in the east, southeast, and south. Mani wrote: "My hope [that is, the Manichaean church] has reached the east of the world and all inhabited regions of the earth, both to the north and to the south. . . . None of the [previous] apostles has ever done anything like this" (*Kephalaia* 1).

The political good fortune of Manichaeism in the Persian empire lasted only a few years. The official state religion, Zoroastrianism, grew increasingly hostile as the Magian clergy, guided by influential figures such as the high priest Kerdēr, organized it into a real national church, with its own strict orthodoxy and a strong nationalistic spirit. The reasons for the conflict between the Zoroastrianism of the Magi and Manichaeism during the third century are numerous: a hereditary clerical caste within a hierarchical social structure based on caste tended to be conservative and traditionalist; the eastern empire's cultural and spiritual horizons were narrow, typical of an agrarian and aristocratic society such as that of the Iranian plateau and very different from the ethnically and culturally diverse and composite one in the westernmost regions of the empire, where there had arisen a flourishing and cosmopolitan urban civilization. The alliance between the throne and the Magi, which remained strong despite some internal contrasts for the entire duration of the Sasanid empire, did not allow Manichaeism to take over and, by subjecting it to periodical and fierce persecutions, finally weakened its drive and confined it to a minority position.

On the one hand, Manichaeism accurately reflected the most widespread anxieties and aspirations of that period's religious preoccupations, through its soteriology, the idea of knowledge as freedom, and the value it placed on personal experience of the divine; on the other hand, the restored Zoroastrianism of the Magi reflected a tendency, widespread during the third century in both the Persian and Roman empires, toward the formation of a national culture. From this standpoint, we can view Manichaeism more as heir to Parthian eclecticism and syncretism—"one of the last manifestations of Arsacid thought" (Bivar, 1983, p. 97)—than as an interpreter of the vast cultural and political changes witnessed in Iran upon the ascent to power of the Sasanid dynasty.

The first anti-Manichaean persecution in the Iranian state began, after the death of Shāpūr and of his successor, Hormīzd I, with the killing of Mani himself, ordered by Bahrām I, probably around the beginning of the year 277. Many other episodes followed, affecting Manichaean communities in all regions of the empire, from Khorasan to Mesopotamian Seleucia (Ctesiphon), the seat of the Manichaean papacy. Manichaeism, however, was not completely eradicated from the Iranian world; in fact, it survived for centuries. Under the caliphate of the Umayyads it remained alive in those territories that had been Sasanid, despite internal schisms and disciplinary controversy.

During the third and fourth centuries Manichaeism moved west, into the Roman empire. It spread through Egypt, North Africa, Palestine, Syria, Asia Minor, Dalmatia, and Rome and as far north as southern Gaul and Spain. Its adherents were the subjects of persecution by both central and peripheral imperial authorities, meeting everywhere with the strong hostility of the political and religious establishment. The Manichaeans were seen by Rome as a dangerous subversive element and were often thought to be agents of the rival Persian power. Despite persecutions and imperial edicts, such as that of Diocletian in 297, the faith for the most part persisted, except in some western areas of the Roman empire. Manichaeism was perceived as a threat well into the Christian era. Repressive measures were repeatedly taken by Roman imperial and church authorities (notably Pope Leo the Great, in 445); nevertheless, in 527 the emperors Justin and Justinian still felt the need to promulgate a law inflicting capital punishment on the followers of Mani's teachings.

Like Zoroastrianism and Christianity, Islam had at first been tolerant of Manichaeism but in the end acted with equal violence against it. The advent of the Abbasid caliphate marked a renewal of bloody repressive measures, which succeeded in pushing the Manichaeans east, in the direction of Transoxiana, during the tenth century. It was in Khorasan, Chorasmia, and Sogdiana that the Manichaean faith expanded and gained strength, and there it became an outpost for the dissemination of Mani's gospel to China and Central Asia. In the last decades of the sixth century, the religion suffered a schism with the so-called Dēnāwars ("observers of *dēn*," i.e., of the true religion), a rigorist and puritan sect. Samarkand became the new see of the Manicaean papacy.

Toward the end of the seventh century, Manichaeism reached the Far East. As the great caravan route from Kashgar to Kucha to Karashahr was reopened following the Chinese conquest of eastern Turkistan, Manichaeism made its appearance in China, mainly through Sogdian missionaries. In 732, an imperial edict allowed Manichaeans the freedom to practice their cult there. The religion also spread to Central Asia and Mongolia, to the vast empire of the Uighurs, who adopted Manichaeism as their official religion in 763. But political and military events following the fall, in 840, of the Uighur empire caused Manichaeism's supremacy in Central Asia to be short lived, although it probably survived there until the thirteenth century. In China, where the Manichaeans were persecuted during the ninth century and banned by edict in 843, just after the collapse of the Uighurs, Manichaeism nonetheless survived until the fourteenth century, protected by secret societies, alongside Taoism and Buddhism.

The Manichaean Church. At the core of the ecclesiastical structure was a marked distinction among classes of clergy, which were subdivided into four. The first included teachers or apostles, never more than 12; the second, minister deacons, never more than 72; the third, stewards, never more than 360; and the fourth were the chosen (that is, the chosen in general). The laity made up a fifth class. Only men could belong to the first three classes, that is, the true clergy, and above these stood the leader of the faithful, the Manichaean pope. The clergy lived in monasteries in the cities and supported itself through the gifts and foundations of the laity, according to a system clearly derived from Buddhist, rather than Christian, monasticism (Baur, 1831; Widengren, 1965).

Different moral codes governed the clergy and the lay population. The former was required to observe the five commandments: truth, nonviolence, sexual abstinence, abstinence from meat and from food and drink that were considered impure, poverty. The laity was required (1) to observe the ten laws of good behavior, which, among other things, prescribed a strictly monogamous marriage and abstinence from all forms of violence, both against men and against animals; (2) to pray four times a day (at dawn, midday, sunset, and night), after observing particular rituals of purification; (3) to contribute the tenth, or the seventh, part of their worldly goods to support the clergy; (4) to fast weekly (on Sundays) and yearly for the thirty days preceding the celebration of the festival of the Bēma; and (5) to confess their sins weekly (on Mondays), as well as during a great yearly collective confession at the end of the fasting period.

The liturgy was simple: it recalled episodes of the life of Mani, his martyrdom, and that of the first apostles. The principal festivity was the Bēma (Gr.; MPers., *gāh;* "pulpit, throne, tribunal"), which, on the vernal equinox, celebrated Mani's passion through gospel worship; the collective confession of sins; the recitation of three hymns to Mani; the reading of the apostle's spiritual testament, the *Letter of the Seal;* chants glorifying the triumphant church; and a sacred banquet offered to the elect by the listeners. In Manichaean holy places the *bēma,* a throne on five steps, was left empty in memory of the one who, having left the world, nonetheless remained as an invisible guide and judge of his church. The empty throne was probably originally a Buddhist symbol.

Heritage and Surviving Elements. The survival of Manichaeism as a source of inspiration for a number of medieval heresies in the West poses complex questions. Manichaean dualism has been adduced as an explanation for the origin of those heretical movements that were based on dualism, on moral asceticism, and on a more or less pronounced antinomism. Accusations of Manichaeism—the most widely despised of Christian heresies—were pronounced by adversaries against heretics to show their relation to the doctrines of Mani, although such a connection has been generally hard to prove beyond doubt.

Priscillianism, which arose in Spain at the end of the fourth century, was probably not related to Manichaeism, although Paulicianism, in seventh-century Armenia, probably was, as was Bogomilism. The latter arose in Bulgaria during the tenth century and spread along the Balkan Peninsula to the coastline of Asia Minor, along with the Cathari in southern France and northern Italy during the twelfth and thirteenth centuries; together they were considered links in the same chain, which might be called "medieval Manichaeism" or "Neo-Manichaeism." A connection among these movements is probable, and in fact such a link is certain between the Bogomils and the Cathari. However, it is not possible to prove their derivation from Manichaeism. Their popular character, the social environment in which they developed, and the typically gnostic nature of Manichaeism all suggest a generalized influence rather than a direct derivation, that is, a background inspiration from the great dualistic religion of late antiquity. It now appears certain that in some instances Manichaeism itself did survive in the West in clandestine groups and secret forms, especially in Roman Africa, despite the proscriptions and persecutions of the sixth century.

The problem is analogous in the East, except in China, where we know that Manichaeism did survive, camouflaged in Taoist or Buddhist guise, until the fourteenth century. A Manichaean origin has been ascribed to Mazdakism, a religious and social movement of Sasanid Iran between the fifth and sixth centuries (Christensen, 1925), and some degree of Manichaean influence upon it is undeniable, although a more accurate perception would probably see the movement as a heretical form of Zoroastrianism. There has been an occasional attempt to consider Manichaean any Muslim *zindīq* (Arab., "heretic, free thinker"). The word derives from the Middle Persian *zandīg,* used by Zoroastrians to describe those who used the *Zand,* the Middle Persian translation of and commentary on the Avesta, in a heterodox manner. Although it is true that *zindīq* is often used to mean "Manichaean," its sense is actually broader; *zandaqah* cannot, therefore, be strictly identified with Manichaeism.

In any case, Manichaeism survived in the Islamic world, even through the persecutions of the Abbasid caliphate, and exercised some degree of influence on gnostic currents in this world. Finally, there is a great likelihood of a direct connection between Manichaeism and some Tibetan cosmological concepts, presumably transmitted through the Hindu Kush (Tucci, 1970).

[*For further discussion of Manichaeism, see* Mazdakism. *See also the biography of Mani.*]

BIBLIOGRAPHY

A work that by now belongs to the prehistory of Manichaean studies is Isaac de Beausobre's *Histoire critique de Manichée et du manichéisme,* 2 vols. (Amsterdam, 1735–1739), which presented Manichaeism as a reformed Christianity. A hundred years later, Manichaean studies reached a turning point with F. C. Baur's *Das manichäische Religionssystem nach den Quellen neu untersucht und entwickelt* (Tübingen, 1831), which gave particular consideration to the Indo-Iranian, Zoroastrian, and Buddhist backgrounds.

In the years following, a number of general studies were published that still remain important—G. Flügel's *Mani, seine Lehre und seine Schriften* (Leipzig, 1862); K. Kessler's *Mani: Forschungen über die manichäische Religion,* vol. 1 (Berlin, 1889); F. C. Burkitt's *The Religion of the Manichees* (Cambridge, 1925); and H. H. Schaeder's *Urform und Fortbildungen des manichäischen Systems* (Leipzig, 1927)—even though more recent studies and discoveries have, by now, gone beyond them. Also useful are A. V. W. Jackson's *Researches on Manichaeism, with Special Reference to the Turfan Fragments* (New York, 1932) and H.-J. Polotsky's *Abriss des manichäischen Systems* (Stuttgart, 1934).

A quarter of a century apart, two important status reports concerning the question of Manichaean studies were published: H. S. Nyberg's "Forschungen über den Manichäismus," *Zeitschrift für die neutestamentliche Wissenschaft und die Kunde der älteren Kirche* 34 (1935): 70–91, and Julien Ries's "Introduction aux études manichéennes," *Ephemerides Theologicae Lovanienses* 33 (1957): 453–482 and 35 (1959): 362–409.

General works that remain valuable, although they give a partially different picture of Manichaeism, are Henri-Charles Puech's *Le manichéisme: Son fondateur, sa doctrine* (Paris, 1949) and Geo Widengren's *Mani and Manichaeism* (London, 1965). We are also indebted to Puech for a very useful collection of essays, *Sur le manichéisme et autres essais* (Paris, 1979), and to Widengren for another, with an important introduction, *Der Manichäismus* (Darmstadt, 1977), pp. ix–xxxii, as well as for a more recent essay, "Manichaeism and Its Iranian Background," in *The Cambridge History of Iran*, vol. 3, edited by Ehsan Yarshater (Cambridge, 1983), pp. 965–990.

The volume *Der Manichäismus* contains some of the most important contributions to Manichaean studies, reprinted entirely or partially (all in German), by H. S. Nyberg, F. C. Burkitt, H. H. Schaeder, Richard Reitzenstein, H.-J. Polotsky, Henri-Charles Puech, V. Stegemann, Alexander Böhlig, Mark Lidzbarski, Franz Rosenthal, W. Bang-Kaup, A. Baumstark, Charles R. C. Allberry, Prosper Alfaric, W. Seston, J. A. L. Vergote, W. B. Henning, Georges Vajda, Carsten Colpe, and A. V. W. Jackson. Two noteworthy syntheses of Manichaeism in French are François Decret's *Mani et la tradition manichéenne* (Paris, 1974) and M. Tardieu's *Le manichéisme* (Paris, 1981); the latter is particularly full of original suggestions.

Two works from the 1960s are dedicated more to Mani himself than to Manichaeism, one concerning mainly the social and cultural background from which Manichaeism emerged and the other mainly dedicated to the religious personality of the founder: Otakar Klíma's *Manis Zeit und Leben* (Prague, 1962) and L. J. R. Ort's *Mani: A Religio-Historical Description of His Personality* (Leiden, 1967).

Although the once-classic work on Manichaean literature, Prosper Alfaric's *Les écritures manichéennes*, 2 vols. (Paris, 1918), is now quite dated, there is a wealth of more recent works to which we can turn. A whole inventory of Iranian documents from Central Asia can be found in Mary Boyce's *A Catalogue of the Iranian Manuscripts in Manichaean Script in the German Turfan Collection* (Berlin, 1960). Excellent editions of Iranian and Turkic texts are due to F. W. K. Müller, A. von Le Coq, Ernst Waldschmidt and Wolfgang Lentz, W. Bang, and Annemarie von Gabain, F. C. Andreas, and W. B. Henning, published in the *Abhandlungen* and in the *Sitzungsberichte* of the Prussian Academy of Sciences between 1904 and 1936. W. B. Henning's pupil, Mary Boyce, has also published, in addition to the above-mentioned catalog, two other important contributions to Manichaean studies, *The Manichaean Hymn Cycles in Parthian* (Oxford, 1954) and *A Reader in Manichaean Middle-Persian and Parthian*, "Acta Iranica," no. 9 (Tehran and Liège, 1975). Editions of Iranian texts, as well as a number of extremely careful philological studies, can be found in W. B. Henning's *Selected Papers*, 2 vols., "Acta Iranica," nos. 14–15 (Tehran and Liège, 1977), where are reprinted also Henning's fundamental *Mitteliranische Manichaica aus Chinesisch-Turkestan*, written in collaboration with F. C. Andreas between 1932 and 1934.

W. Sundermann and P. Zieme, two scholars from the Academy of Sciences of the German Democratic Republic, are currently responsible for continuing research in the Iranian and Turkish texts from Turfan, which are preserved in Berlin. We owe to them, among other things, Sundermann's *Mittelpersische und parthische kosmogonische und Parabeltexte der Manichäer* (Berlin, 1973) and Zieme's *Manichäisch-türkische Texte* (Berlin, 1975). On the state of research into Iranian texts, see also Sundermann's "Lo studio dei testi iranici di Turfan," in *Iranian Studies*, edited by me (Rome, 1983), pp. 119–134. Recent research on Sogdian Manichaean texts has been done by N. Sims-Williams (London) and E. Morano (Turin), following the lead of Ilya Gershevitch (Cambridge). Again in the context of Central Asian texts, the handbook for the confession of sins has been carefully edited, after the work of W. Bang and W. B. Henning, and with an ample commentary, by Jes P. Asmussen in *X̌āstvānīft: Studies in Manichaeism* (Copenhagen, 1965); the *Shābuhragān* is the subject of an extremely useful work by D. N. MacKenzie, "Mani's *Šābuhragān*," *Bulletin of the School of Oriental and African Studies* 42 (1979): 500–534 and 43 (1980): 288–310.

Concerning the Chinese texts, the following are useful works. On the *Treatise*, see Édouard Chavannes and Paul Pelliot's "Un traité manichéen retrouvé en Chine," *Journal asiatique* (1911): 499–617 and (1913): 99–392. On the *Compendium*, see Chavannes and Pelliot's "Compendium de la religion du Buddha de Lumière, Mani," *Journal asiatique* (1913): 105–116 (Pelliot fragment), and Gustav Haloun and W. B. Henning's "The Compendium of the Doctrines and Styles of the Teaching of Mani, the Buddha of Light," *Asia Major*, n.s. 3 (1952): 184–212 (Stein fragment). On the London Chinese hymn book, see, in addition to the work of Ernst Waldschmidt and Wolfgang Lentz, Tsui Chi's "Mo-ni-chiao hsia-pu tsan," *Bulletin of the School of Oriental and African Studies* 11 (1943): 174–219.

On the Coptic texts of Fayum, a survey of the state of research can be found in Alexander Böhlig's "Die Arbeit an den koptischen Manichaica," in *Mysterion und Wahrheit* (Leiden, 1968), pp. 177–187. Among editions of the texts are *Manichäische Homilien*, by H.-J. Polotsky (Stuttgart, 1934), *Kephalaia*, by C. Schmidt, H.-J. Polotsky, and Alexander Böhlig (Stuttgart, 1935–1940; Berlin, 1966), and Charles R. C. Allberry's *A Manichaean Psalm-Book*, vol. 2 (Stuttgart, 1938). On the Manichaean Codex of Cologne, see Albert Henrichs and Ludwig Koenen's "Ein griechischer Mani-Codex," *Zeitschrift für Papyrologie und Epigraphik* 5 (1970): 97–216, 19 (1975): 1–85, and 32 (1979): 87–200.

Of indirect sources, I shall mention here only the following few. On Augustine, see R. Jolivet and M. Jourion's *Six traités anti-manichéens*, in *Oeuvres de Saint Augustin*, vol. 17 (Paris, 1961); on Theodoros bar Kōnaī, see Franz Cumont's *Recherches sur le manichéisme*, vol. 1 (Brussels, 1908); on Zoroastrian sources, see J.-P. de Menasce's *Une apologétique mazdéenne du neuvième siècle 'Škand-gumānīk vicār'* (Fribourg, 1945); and on Islamic sources, see Carsten Colpe's "Der Manichäismus in der arabischen Überlieferung" (Ph.D. diss., University of Göttingen, 1954).

Three valuable anthologies of Manichaean texts are A. Adams's *Texte zum Manichäismus*, 2d ed. (Berlin, 1962), Jes P. Asmussen's *Manichaean Literature* (Delmar, N.Y., 1975), and Alexander Böhlig and Jes P. Asmussen's *Die gnosis*, vol. 3 (Zurich, 1980).

Concerning the spread of Manichaeism in Asia, in North Africa, and in the Roman empire, there are numerous works. The old text by E. de Stoop, *Essai sur la diffusion du manichéisme dans l'Empire romain* (Ghent, 1909), heads the list, followed by Paul Pelliot's "Les traditions manichéennes au Fou-kien," *T'oung pao* 22 (1923): 193–208; M. Guidi's *La lotta tra l'Islam e il manicheismo* (Rome, 1927); Uberto Pestalozza's "Il manicheismo presso i Turchi occidentali ed orientali," *Rendiconti del Reale Istituto Lombardo di Scienze e Lettere,* 2d series, 67 (1934): 417–497; Georges Vajda's "Les Zindiqs en pays d'Islam au debout de la période abbaside," *Revista degli Studi Orientali* 17 (1937): 173–229; Giuseppe Messina's *Cristianesimo, buddhismo, manicheismo nell'Asia antica* (Rome, 1947); H. H. Schaeder's "Der Manichäismus und sein Weg nach Osten," in *Glaube und Geschichte: Festschrift für Friedrich Gogarten* (Giessen, 1948), pp. 236–254; O. Maenchen-Helfen's "Manichaeans in Siberia," in *Semitic and Oriental Studies Presented to William Popper* (Berkeley, 1951), pp. 161–165; Francesco Gabrieli's "La *zandaqa* au premier siècle abbasside," in *L'élaboration de l'Islam* (Paris, 1961), pp. 23–28; Peter Brown's "The Diffusion of Manichaeism in the Roman Empire," *Journal of Roman Studies* 59 (1969): 92–103; François Decret's *Aspects du manichéisme dans l'Afrique romaine* (Paris, 1970); and S. N. C. Lieu's *The Religion of Light: An Introduction to the History of Manichaeism in China* (Hong Kong, 1979) and *Manichaeism in the Later Roman Empire and Medieval China* (Manchester, 1985).

Among studies devoted to special topics, note should be taken of Charles R. C. Allberry's "Das manichäische Bema-Fest," *Zeitschrift für die neutestamentliche Wissenschaft und die Kunde der älteren Kirche* 37 (1938): 2–10; Geo Widengren's *The Great Vohu Manah and the Apostle of God* (Uppsala, 1945) and *Mesopotamian Elements in Manichaeism* (Uppsala, 1946); Henri-Charles Puech's "Musique et hymnologie manichéennes," in *Encyclopédie des musiques sacrées,* vol. 1 (Paris, 1968), pp. 353–386; and Mircea Eliade's "Spirit, Light, and Seed," *History of Religions* 11 (1971): 1–30. Of my own works, I may mention "Un particolare aspetta del simbolismo della luce nel Mazdeismo e nel Manicheismo," *Annali dell'Istituto Universitario Orientale di Napoli* n.s. 12 (1962): 95–128, and "Universalismo e nazionalismo nell'Iran del III secolo," in *Incontro di religioni in Asia tra il III e il X secolo,* edited by L. Lanciotti (Florence, 1984), pp. 31–54.

In the most exhaustive treatment of Manichaeism to have appeared in an encyclopedic work, Henri-Charles Puech's "Le manichéisme," in *Histoire des religions,* vol. 2, edited by Puech (Paris, 1972), pp. 523–645, we also find a full exposition of the problem concerning the heritage and survival of Manichaeism, with a bibliography to which one should add Raoul Manselli's *L'eresia del male* (Naples, 1963).

Despite the length of the present bibliography, there are some works cited in the text of my article that have not yet been mentioned here. On the relationship between Manichaeism and Zoroastrianism, see Alessandro Bausani's *Persia religiosa* (Milan, 1959); on the Parthian heritage in Manichaeism, see A. D. H. Bivar's "The Political History of Iran under the Arsacids," in *The Cambridge History of Iran,* vol. 3, edited by Ehsan Yarshater (Cambridge, 1983), pp. 21–97; and on the influence of Manichaeism in Tibet, see Giuseppe Tucci's *Die Religionen Tibets* (Stuttgart, 1970), translated as *The Religions of Tibet* (Berkeley, 1980).

GHERARDO GNOLI
Translated from Italian by Ughetta Fitzgerald Lubin

Manichaeism and Christianity

The teaching of Mani (216–277) was essentially gnostic, its constituent elements deriving from Iranian religion, especially Zoroastrianism in its Zurvanist form. It incorporated features from Marcion of Pontus (d. around AD 160) and from Judeo-Christian gnosticism typified by Bardesanes (Bardaisan) of Edessa (AD 154–222). Despite this latter ancestry, it is doubtful whether Manichaeism can be regarded as a Christian heresy. In favor of calling it a heresy, it can be said that Mani declared himself to be an apostle of Jesus Christ and the recipient of the Paraclete, and that within the Roman empire the Manichaeans regarded themselves as the true believers and all other members of the church as semi-Christians. According to his opponent Augustine of Hippo, writing around the year 400, Faustus, the Manichaean bishop of Milevis, claimed to accept the preaching of Jesus and to believe in the Trinity.

Mani himself, however, believed he was promulgating a new universal religion that would supersede all others. In this sense, unlike his followers in the West, he could not have regarded himself as a Christian. Moreover, when Manichaeism moved East, its claims became different. In southern China, Mani was presented as a reincarnation of Lao-tzu, the founder of Taoism. To some, Mani was the "Buddha of Light." In other words, eastern and western Manichaeism were not identical. The Coptic psalms, for example, that reveal the spread of the religion in Egypt in the fourth century, are all but indistinguishable from their entirely orthodox counterparts, but the Parthian hymn cycle, which has frequent references to a savior, does not identify that savior by name. This lack of direct reference may be simply the result of the chance survival of documents, but it is more likely that the omission was deliberate, so that "savior" could refer to all redeemers, whether Zarathushtra, Christ, Buddha, Lao-tzu, or Mani. Mani's syncretistic system could give prominence now to Christ, now to Buddha, in a deliberate adaptation to fit the religion into whatever situation it found itself.

Manichaeism was essentially dualistic. It held that there are two eternal principles: light (i.e., spirit) and darkness (i.e., matter). The present world is constituted by an interplay between these two and is the outcome of an attack by the latter on the former, which resulted in a scattering of particles of light. This fragmentation of spiritual substance and its enclosure in matter led to the existence of the soul in human beings and life in plants. All this is quite evidently gnostic teaching with its central concept of "gold in mud" (i.e., spirit imprisoned in the material), the precious element being in need of release to return to its source. In "Christian" Manichaeism this release is in part assisted through Jesus, who is regarded as a transcendent being, a manifestation of *nous* (intelligence). It is he who has brought saving gnosis to Palestine. But this Jesus is a docetic figure; he only seemed (Gr., *dokeō*) to be a man of flesh and blood. He did not undergo the processes of birth; he was not truly crucified and therefore did not need to rise from the dead. Insofar as the Manichaeans preserved any concept of Jesus' passion, it was related to his supposed suffering in every fruit on every tree. Jesus is in agony until the end of the world, when he will come as judge; then light and darkness will once again be separated.

Far removed from Christian orthodoxy, this teaching was supported by the Manichaean scriptures, that is, the writings of Mani, and by a special edition of the New Testament. The latter consisted of a revised version of the gospels (possibly using the harmony drawn up by Tatian, c. 160), together with some New Testament books drastically altered, in the manner of Marcion, to exclude what were held to be interpolations with other books entirely rejected as compilations by false apostles.

Western Manichaeism owed something to orthodox Christianity in its organization, in that it had bishops, priests, and deacons, as well as twelve apostles. There were, possibly under the influence of Buddhism, two grades—the elect and the hearers. The latter served the former, who were under the rule of the three seals: *signaculum oris*, not to partake of flesh or wine; *signaculum manus*, not to be occupied in external things (e.g., tilling the ground); and *signaculum sinus*, not to have sexual intercourse or to engage in marriage.

In the final decades of the fourth century, Manichaeism made great strides in Egypt and North Africa, but in 439 many of its adherents became refugees with the onslaught of the Vandals. Hence, in Rome, Leo the Great (r. 440–461) actively sought out Manichaean refugees in order to suppress them. In 527 there were lawsuits against them in Constantinople. Nevertheless, some Manichaeans survived in North Africa until at least the eighth century. In the East, on the other hand, especially in Chinese Turkistan, there is evidence that Manichaeans were still active in the thirteenth century.

Statements by Christian writers in the Middle Ages suggest that Manichaeism persisted in the West. The Paulicians, the Bogomils, and the Cathari, as well as those who followed Priscillian, were all charged with being Manichaeans. In fact, all these authorities were using "Manichaean" as a synonym for "dualist," and any teaching that manifested a tendency toward dualism was accordingly called Manichaean. The teaching of Priscillian (c. 370) and his followers is by no means easy to define, but it is doubtful that the epithet *Manichaean* is applicable. The Paulicians, first noted in Armenia in the seventh century, seem to have been straightforward gnostics; they had a direct influence on the Bogomils, who emerged in Bulgaria in the tenth century. In the eleventh century the Cathari began to achieve notoriety in Italy, Germany, and France—being called Albigensians in France—but it is unlikely that there was a historical connection between any of these and the ancient Manichaeans.

[*See also* Cathari.]

BIBLIOGRAPHY

The most comprehensive survey of Manichaeism is Geo Widengren's *Mani and Manichaeism*, translated by Charles Kessler (London, 1961), which also contains an excellent bibliography. For "Christian" Manichaeism, especially as related to Augustine, see chapters 4 and 5 of Gerald Bonner's *St. Augustine of Hippo: Life and Controversies* (London, 1963) and chapter 5 of Peter Brown's *Augustine of Hippo: A Biography* (London, 1967). Augustine's writings expounding the views of Faustus are translated in the fifth volume of *A Select Library of Nicene and Post-Nicene Fathers of the Christian Church* (1956; reprint, Grand Rapids, Mich., 1979). The title of Steven Runciman's *The Medieval Manichee* (1947; reprint, Cambridge, 1955) is slightly misleading, and its subtitle more accurately describes the contents, *A Study of the Christian Dualist Heresy*; it covers the Paulicians, Bogomils, and Cathari.

J. G. DAVIES

MĀṆIKKAVĀCAKAR (ninth century CE), Tamil poet-saint devoted to the god Śiva. Māṇikkavācakar ("he whose speech is like rubies") is generally acknowledged to have been the greatest poet of Tamil Śaivism. For at least the past thousand years he has also enjoyed the status of a saint in South Indian temples consecrated to Śiva, where one frequently sees his image and hears his hymns sung by professional reciters (*ōtuvār*s) as part of the regular temple ritual.

Māṇikkavācakar probably flourished about the middle of the ninth century. He was born in the brahman settlement at Tiruvātavūr, a village near Madurai. According to the *Tiruvātavūrar Purāṇam*, a fifteenth-century hagiography, he was a precocious child and at an early age entered the service of the Pandya king at Madurai; there he soon became prime minister. His high position notwithstanding, Māṇikkavācakar harbored religious longings that remained unfulfilled until, while on a trip to Perunturai (modern-day Avadayarkoyil in Pudukkottai District), he unexpectedly met and was initiated by a guru who was none other than Śiva himself. This abrupt change led to a series of bizarre and amusing incidents revolving around the interactions of Māṇikkavācakar, the Pandya king, and Śiva in various guises—all counted among Śiva's "sacred sports" as narrated in the *Tiruviḷaiyāṭal Purāṇam,* the sacred history of the great Mīnākṣī-Sundareśvara temple in Madurai.

After gaining release from the king's service, Māṇikkavācakar is reputed to have visited several shrines of Śiva in the Tamil country, composing hymns as he went. He eventually settled in Chidambaram, site of the Naṭarāja temple. Here he composed more poems, defeated Buddhists from Lanka in a debate, and finally, according to the hagiography, disappeared into the inner sanctum of the temple, having merged with the god.

Two works are ascribed to Māṇikkavācakar. His premier poem is the *Tiruvācakam* (Sacred Speech), a collection of fifty-one hymns addressed to Śiva. The *Tiruvācakam* displays a rich variety of poetic forms skillfully utilized. Some of the poems are based on women's folk songs that accompany certain domestic activities or village games. In these instances, form and theology coincide, for in the *Tiruvācakam* Māṇikkavācakar typically casts himself as a female who is in love with Śiva. The hymns of the *Tiruvācakam* have long been venerated by Tamil speakers not just for their musicality but also for their paradigmatic expression of devotion. These hymns frequently give voice to the intense emotions of longing for, separation from, and union with the deity. They celebrate a god who overwhelms his devotee, resulting in an experience of melting and surrender. Viewed historically, the *Tiruvācakam* forms a bridge between early Tamil devotional poetry with its inheritance of forms and images drawn from the Caṅkam period, and the later systematic treatises of the Tamil Śaiva Siddhānta school of philosophy.

Māṇikkavācakar's other work, the *Tirukkōvaiyār,* is a poem of four hundred quatrains modeled on Caṅkam *akam* ("inner," i.e., love) poetry. Ostensibly an erotic poem, the *Tirukkōvaiyār* has traditionally been interpreted as an allegory on the relationship between Śiva and the soul. Along with the far more popular *Tiruvācakam,* it comprises the eighth section of the twelve-part *Tirumuṟai,* the canonical poetry of Tamil Śaivism.

In addition to the deep reverence many Tamils have for the *Tiruvācakam,* the cult of the saint is still prominent at several locations in modern Tamil Nadu. Especially noteworthy is the Śrī Ātmanātacuvāmi temple in Avadayarkoil, marking the site of Māṇikkavācakar's initiation. Here the saint is ritually identified with the god, for only the saint's image, decorated to look like various forms of Śiva, is carried in procession at festivals. Also, both major annual festivals of this temple conclude with a dramatic ritual reenactment of Māṇikkavācakar's initiation by Śiva.

[*For a discussion of Tamil Śaiva saints, see* Śaivism, *article on* Nāyaṉārs. *The religious tradition to which Māṇikkavācakar belongs is treated generally in* Tamil Religions *and more specifically in* Śaivism, *article on* Śaiva Siddhānta.]

BIBLIOGRAPHY

Besides numerous Tamil editions of the *Tiruvācakam,* there have been several translations of the text into English and German. The first English translation was that of G. U. Pope, *The Tiruvāçagam or 'Sacred Utterances' of the Tamil Poet, Saint and Sage Māṇikkavāçakar* (1900; reprint, Madras, 1970). While Pope's translation is in a late Victorian style of English poetry that is now outdated, his work contains the Tamil text and a lengthy introductory "appendix" that is still useful. A translation into more modern English by a Tamil devotee of Śiva is *Pathway to God through Tamil Literature,* vol. 1, *Through the Thiruvaachakam,* translated and edited by G. Vanmikanathan (New Delhi, 1971). The translator's 100-page introduction interprets the *Tiruvācakam* as a "handbook of mystical theology." A recent study that discusses Māṇikkavācakar and the religio-historical context of his major work is my own *Hymns to the Dancing Śiva: A Study of Māṇikkavācakar's Tiruvācakam* (Columbia, Mo., 1982).

GLENN E. YOCUM

MANISM (from Lat. *manes,* "departed spirit, ghost") was a theory of the origin of religion briefly advocated in the late nineteenth century by the popular British philosopher Herbert Spencer (1820–1904) and by one of his disciples, the Canadian-born Grant Allen (1848–1899). It bears no relation to, and should not be confused with, theories based on the concept of *mana.* [*See* Preanimism.]

That the spirits of the dead occupy an important place in the history of religion is verifiable simply by observation. [*See* Ancestors.] All primal and many later cultures have regarded the dead—and particularly the newly dead—as continuing to be active and concerned members of their respective families. Having passed beyond the limitations of earthly life, they are in possession of power greater than that of mortals. This power may be turned to the advantage of the living if the memory of the dead is respected and offerings continue to be made at the graveside or elsewhere. The unburied or uncremated dead, who have not been sent into the afterlife with the proper rituals, or those neglected by their families, are, on the other hand, liable to be dangerous. Always, however, they are believed to occupy a relatively lowly position in the supernatural hierarchy.

They have power, but their power is limited as a rule to the circles within which they moved while still alive. Naturally, those who possessed greater power and influence during their lifetimes (chieftains and kings, for instance) were held to wield greater, though still limited, power after death.

The first attempt to link belief in the power of departed spirits with the world of religion was made in the early third century BCE, by the Greek writer Euhemeros (c. 330–260 BCE), in his *Hiera anagraphē* (Sacred History). Euhemeros claimed that all the gods had been prominent men and women of their own day, revered when alive and worshiped after death. In fact, of course, examples abound in societies past and present of human beings accorded divine honors after death, and similar theories have often been put forward to account for the otherwise obscure origins of several deities. Snorri Sturluson in his *Prose Edda,* for example, traced the ancestry of Þórr (Thor) and Óðinn (Odin) back to the heroes of the Trojan War. This type of explanation is generally called "euhemerism," after its first advocate.

But euhemerism seeks not to account for the origins of religion as such but only for the worship of particular deities. The theory is certainly sound, if kept within appropriate limits, since the deification process is well attested historically. Manism, on the other hand, sought to explain—or to explain away—the whole of religion on this one principle.

Herbert Spencer's essay "Manners and Fashion" was first published in *The Westminster Review* in April 1854, thus antedating E. B. Tylor's *Primitive Culture* (London, 1871) by seventeen years. In it, Spencer claimed to have established a close relation between "Law, Religion, and Manners," in the sense that those who presided over these three areas of human activity ("Deity, Chief, and Master of the Ceremonies") were identical. Reflecting further on the role of chiefs and medicine men in primitive belief, Spencer came to the conclusion that "the aboriginal god is the dead chief: the chief not dead in our sense, but gone away, carrying with him food and weapons to some rumoured region of plenty, some promised land, whither he had long intended to lead his followers, and whence he will presently return to fetch them. This hypothesis, once entertained, is seen to harmonize with all primitive ideas and practices" (Spencer, *Essays,* vol. 3, London, 1891, p. 7). Thus mankind's earliest deity had been a deified "big man," a deceased chief, whose power had been sufficiently great to have become a tradition and whose power was believed still to be operative from the other side of the gulf between life and death.

In 1862 Spencer published the first volume of his massive composite work of "sociology," appropriately called *First Principles* (these principles were, however, greatly revised in subsequent editions). There he stated:

> As all ancient records and traditions prove, the earliest rulers are regarded as divine personages. The maxims and commands they uttered during their lives are held sacred after their deaths, and are enforced by their divinely-descended successors; who in their turn are promoted to the pantheon of the race, there to be worshipped and propitiated along with their predecessors; the most ancient of whom is the supreme god, and the rest subordinate gods.
>
> (Spencer, *First Principles,* London, 1862, pp. 158–159)

This was, in essence, Spencer's theory of what subsequently came to be called "manism," also known as the "ghost theory" of the origin of religion.

Following the publication in 1876 of the first volume of Spencer's *Principles of Sociology,* in which the theory was again stated, E. B. Tylor made perhaps his only entry into the field of public controversy. He reviewed Spencer's book in the journal *Mind* (2, no. 6, April 1877, pp. 141–156); Spencer replied in the same journal (pp. 415–419), with a further rejoinder by Tylor (pp. 419–423), by Spencer again (pp. 423–429), and a final short contribution by Tylor (p. 429). Tylor's contention was that "Mr. Spencer seems to stretch the principle of deities being actual ancestors deified somewhat far," that his contentions often could not be tested, and that when they could, his cases "hardly look encouraging." His theory, Tylor concluded, was "in conflict not merely with the speculations of mythologists, but with the canons of sober historical criticism." Spencer, who did not like to be criticized and seldom ventured into public controversy, nevertheless penned a reply, suggesting that Tylor actually was in agreement with him "in regarding the ghost-theory as primary and other forms of superstitions as derived . . . [although] it appears that he does not hold this view in the unqualified form given to it by me." Tylor answered, virtually accusing Spencer of plagiarism on some points, but stating that although Spencer had the right to hold his "ghost theory" (which closely resembled the theory put forth by Euhemeros), "I look on this theory as only partly true, and venture to consider Mr. Spencer's attempt to carry it through unreservedly as one of the least satisfactory parts of his system."

The trouble was that it was so hard to envisage any process by which ghosts could become the other inhabitants of the spiritual world. Andrew Lang sketched the broad outlines of this hypothetical process: "The conception of ghosts of the dead is more or less consciously extended, so that spirits who never were incarnate as men become credible beings. They may inform inanimate objects, trees, rivers, fire, clouds, earth, sky, the great natural departments, and thence polytheism results" (*Cock Lane and Common Sense,* London, 1894, p. 339). This Lang did not accept. He was moving steadily in the direction of his theory of the existence of "high gods" and was disposed to question not only Spencer's "ghost theory" but also Tylor's theory of animism (which resembled Spencer's theory on certain points) as being inadequate explanations of the origin of the concept of deity. Lang appears actually to have believed in ghosts—which neither Spencer nor Tylor did—and was a keen psychical researcher (or at least a theorist about the researches of others). He was unable to discern any connection between ghosts and the higher gods, though "a few genuine wraiths, or ghosts . . . would be enough to start the animistic hypothesis, or to confirm it notably, if it was already started" (ibid., p. 346).

Although Herbert Spencer was enormously widely read in the late nineteenth and early twentieth centuries, his popularity was due to the completeness of his system of "synthetic philosophy" rather than to his theory of manism, which won very few adherents. But in 1897 Grant Allen produced his book *The Evolution of the Idea of God* (abr. ed., London, 1903; reprint, London, 1931), which accepted the manism theory with very few modifications. Allen maintained that "in its simplest surviving savage type, religion consists wholely and solely in certain acts of deference paid by the living to the persons of the dead" (1931 ed., p. 18). But religion is not mythology; indeed, Allen, following Spencer, insisted that mythology, cosmogony, ontology, and ethics were all "extraneous developments," which sprang from different roots and had "nothing necessarily in common with religion proper" (ibid., p. 25). Religion, then, had developed from corpse worship to ghost worship and then to shade worship. All else had developed later and need not be considered as an essential part of religion.

Writing to Allen in 1892, James G. Frazer had stated his agreement with the manism thesis: "so far as I believe ancestor-worship, or the fear of ghosts, to have been on the whole the most important factor in the evolution of religious belief" (quoted in Edward Clodd, *Grant Allen: A Memoir,* London, 1900, p. 145). Others at the time certainly concurred, wholly or in part, though they preferred the more comprehensive term *animism* to describe the same set of phenomena and recognized that the theory of manism could accommodate other spirit phenomena only with the greatest difficulty.

Manism in the form proposed by Spencer and Allen was too narrow to account for the genesis of more than a certain selection of religious phenomena. It therefore appealed to very few scholars. Exceptions included, however, Julius Lippert (1839–1909) of Berlin, who applied it to the biblical material in *Der Seelenkult in seinen Beziehungen zur althebräischen Religion* (Berlin, 1881) and other works produced during the 1880s. It might also be argued that the manism theory exercised a certain indirect influence on the Myth and Ritual school. In his book *Kingship* (London, 1927), Arthur M. Hocart (1883–1939) stated categorically that "the earliest known religion is a belief in the divinity of kings . . . in the earliest records known, man appears to us worshiping gods and their earthly representatives, namely kings" (p. 7). But this connection was at best oblique.

Summing up, we may say that what binds together Euhemerus and Herbert Spencer (for manism might well also be called neo-euhemerism) marks a genuinely important aspect of the history of religion. It cannot, however, be seriously put forward as the origin of religion per se without very serious distortion. This was true even in the high period of evolutionary theory; today, Spencer's manism remains no more than a historical curiosity.

[*See also the autobiography of Spencer.*]

BIBLIOGRAPHY

The fullest expression of Herbert Spencer's theory is in his *Principles of Sociology,* vol. 1 (London, 1876), pp. 304–440. For a good short account of Spencer's system of thought, see J. W. Burrow's *Evolution and Society: A Study in Victorian Social Theory* (Cambridge, 1970), pp. 179–227. On Grant Allen, see Edward Clodd's *Grant Allen: A Memoir* (London, 1900), pp. 142–147, and Allen's own *The Evolution of the Idea of God,* new ed. (London, 1931). See also Henri Pinard de la Boullaye's *L'étude comparée des religions,* 3d ed., vol. 1, *Son histoire dans le monde occidental* (Paris, 1919), pp. 381–382. Reference may also be made to the series of articles "Ancestor-Worship and Cult of the Dead," by William Crooke and others, in the *Encyclopaedia of Religion and Ethics,* edited by James Hastings, vol. 1 (Edinburgh, 1908), pp. 425–467; in discussing Spencer's theory, Crooke comments, "Needless to say, these views have not met with general acceptance" (p. 427).

ERIC J. SHARPE

MANITOU. *See* Power; *see also* North American Indians, *article on* Indians of the Northeast Woodlands.

MAÑJUŚRĪ, an important figure in the Mahāyāna Buddhist pantheon, is a *bodhisattva,* one of a number of celestial heroes whose compassion has led them to postpone the bliss of final enlightenment until all other beings are freed of suffering. Especially associated with wisdom, Mañjuśrī is a key figure in numerous Mahāyana scriptures, and he has been the focus of significant cultic activity throughout Mahāyāna Buddhist countries. His name means "gentle glory." Many of his alternate names and epithets refer to his relation to speech (Vāgīśvara, "lord of speech") and to his youth (Kumārabhūta, "in the form of a youth" or "having become the crown prince"). Because he is destined soon to become a Buddha, Mañjuśrī is often called "prince of the teachings"; for his role as master of the wisdom teachings *(prajñāpāramitā)* he is frequently described as "progenitor of the Buddhas."

Mañjuśrī's role in Mahāyāna scriptures is often that of interlocutor; as a senior *bodhisattva* at teaching assemblies, he frequently questions Śākyamuni Buddha and requests teachings of him. Although he is not highlighted in the early Mahāyāna texts on the perfection of insight, Mañjuśrī came to be known for his profound wisdom, and is associated with this textual tradition as its patron lord. The most common artistic representations and literary descriptions of Mañjuśrī (including scriptures, ritual texts, and meditation manuals) depict him as a golden-complexioned sixteen-year-old prince wearing a five-peaked crown. In his right hand he wields the sword of discriminating insight, which cuts through all ignorance and illusion, penetrating to the truth. In his left hand he grasps a book, the *Prajñāpāramitā Sūtra* (Scripture on the Perfection of Insight), whose teachings he has mastered and upholds. He sits upon a lion, which represents the roar of sovereign truth.

Mañjuśrī has been the focus of significant cultic activity. Perhaps the most extraordinary site for this has been a mountain complex in northern China named Wu-t'ai Shan, Five Terrace Mountain, where—until the mid-twentieth century—pilgrims from all over Asia have traveled in quests for visions of the *bodhisattva*. Beginning as a local mountain cult, the numinous precincts of this region eventually were identified as the special earthly domain of Mañjuśrī, and by the mid-eighth century it had become a thriving international Buddhist center, with seventy-two notable monasteries and temples, as well as numerous retreat huts.

Mañjuśrī traditionally is believed to be a celestial *bodhisattva* of the tenth stage *(bhūmi)*, the highest level prior to attaining buddhahood. He dwells continually in a meditative trance known as "heroic valor" *(śūraṃgamasamādhi)*, and is thus able to manifest himself at will throughout the universe, including Mount Wu-t'ai, in order to aid all beings. Wu-t'ai Shan was identified as Mañjuśrī's principal seat of manifestation through two means: time and again notable persons had visions of the *bodhisattva* there; and these visions received scriptural legitimation in the form of prophecies in a series of texts. The most significant of these texts is the *Avataṃsaka Sūtra* (Flower Garland Scripture), in which Śākyamuni declared that in a future age Mañjuśrī would dwell on a five-peaked mountain in northern China. According to pilgrims' accounts of these visions, the *bodhisattva* manifests himself on the mountain in several forms, most typically as a sphere of glowing light, as a five-colored cloud, as a lion-riding youth, or as an old man. Further mountain sites in the Himalayas and Central Asia, including Mount Gośṛṅga in Khotan, were identified as sacred to the *bodhisattva*, but, unlike Mount Wu-t'ai, they never gained international recognition and acceptance. As a further element in the mountain theme, Mañjuśrī popularly plays a role in the founding tales of Nepal: with his sword, he cut an opening in the mountains to drain a great lake, thus creating the Katmandu Valley.

Mañjuśrī has been especially venerated in the Ch'an and Zen traditions of East Asia for his uncompromising quest for insight. He is also linked closely to the teachings of the Tantric schools, both as lord of profound knowledge and as a potent protector and guide of those on this path. While Mañjuśrī's special role within the Buddhist pantheon is to protect and uphold the wisdom teachings and to inspire students of these teachings, a wide range of scriptures, ritual texts, and popular traditions makes clear the multifaceted nature of his cult, which was extended far beyond Buddhist scholastic circles.

[*See also* Celestial Buddhas and Bodhisattvas. *For further discussion of the mountain as sacred dwelling place, see* Mountains.]

BIBLIOGRAPHY

The standard cross-cultural monograph on Mañjuśrī, containing much information organized in a systematic way, is Étienne Lamotte's "Mañjuśrī" (in French), *T'oung pao* 48 (1960): 1–96. Intensive analysis of a group of East Asian paintings of Mañjuśrī, emphasizing religious dimensions and including a chapter on the Wu-t'ai Shan cult in T'ang China, may be found in my *Studies on the Mysteries of Mañjuśrī*, Society for the Study of Chinese Religions Monograph No. 2 (Boulder, 1983). The translation of an important Tantric text in praise of Mañjuśrī, the *Mañjuśrī-nāma-saṅgīti Sūtra*, has been made by Alex Wayman, *Chanting the Names of Mañjuśrī* (Boston, 1985).

RAOUL BIRNBAUM

MANNHARDT, WILHELM (1831–1880), pioneer of scientific folklore in Germany. He was born on 26 March 1831 in Schleswig, the son of a Mennonite pastor; five years later the family moved to Danzig. Mannhardt was always in very poor health, having been afflicted with curvature of the spine at about the age of seven. Unsuited to active life, he read assiduously and showed an early interest in both Germanic mythology and folklore. The shape of his early thinking was established by 1848, when he read Jakob Grimm's *Deutsche Mythologie* (Göttingen, 1835). While still at school he began his inquiries into the oral traditions of northern Germany, and was on one occasion suspected by one of his informants of being one of the dwarfs about which he was asking—he was at the time only one and a half meters tall.

Mannhardt studied German language and literature at the universities of Tübingen and Berlin, receiving his doctorate at Tübingen in 1854 and his habilitation at Berlin three years later. In 1855 he assumed the editorship of the *Zeitschrift für deutsche Mythologie und Sittenkunde,* a journal which survived only four years. In autumn 1855 he came into contact with the brothers Grimm, whose work he admired greatly, and in 1858 he published his first book, *Germanische Mythen,* extending his inquiries to cover not only European but also Indian material. He was perhaps the first scholar to compare the Germanic Þórr (Thor) with the Vedic Indra as two deities associated with thunder. In the early 1860s Mannhardt was forced by ill health to return to Danzig; there he obtained a librarian's post, which he held until 1873.

It was in Danzig that Mannhardt began the research work for which he was to become famous. He planned a comprehensive work to be called *Monumenta mythica Germaniae,* to be based not only on written sources but on firsthand information from the rural community (which was, however, even then beginning to change under the impact of scientific farming). The great work was never completed, but in its preparation Mannhardt circulated a questionnaire, and in so doing created a technique. The original questionnaire contained twenty-five questions (later expanded to thirty-five) concerning popular beliefs and practices connected with the harvest *(Erntesitten).* His methodology was in general that of the emerging sciences of geology and archaeology, and was aimed at uncovering lower "layers" of belief, which might finally contribute to a "mythology of Demeter." Mannhardt also traveled widely in search of material in northern Europe, and interviewed prisoners of war in and near Danzig. After writing two preliminary studies, *Roggenwolf und Roggenhund* (1865) and *Die Korndämonen* (1867), he published in 1875 and 1876 the work for which he is chiefly known today, the two volumes of *Wald- und Feldkulte.* But his health was unequal to the sustained effort which his program required, and on Christmas Day 1880, at the age of forty-nine, he died, leaving behind a vast collection of material that has been little used during the past century.

Perhaps intimidated by the thoroughness of Mannhardt's methods, scholars for many years tended to accept his results virtually unaltered. His work provided most of the European material for James G. Frazer's *The Golden Bough,* and in general was used more by scholars of comparative religion than by folklorists. And certainly his studies marked an epoch in comparative study. In recent years scholars have begun to examine Mannhardt's material afresh. The emphasis is in process of shifting from beliefs in "spirits of the corn" to the function of harvest rituals in preindustrial, agrarian societies, but the irreplaceable material that Mannhardt collected remains a lasting memorial to his pioneering effort.

BIBLIOGRAPHY

Schmidt, Arno. *Wilhelm Mannhardts Lebenswerk.* Danzig, 1932.

Sydow, C. W. von. *Selected Papers on Folklore.* Copenhagen, 1948. See the papers on pages 89–105 and 146–165.

Weber-Kellermann, Ingeborg. *Erntebrauch in der ländlichen Arbeitswelt des 19. Jahrhunderts auf Grund der Mannhardtbefragung in Deutschland von 1865.* Marburg, 1965. Includes a biographical sketch on pages 9–24.

ERIC J. SHARPE

MANSI RELIGION. *See* Khanty and Mansi Religion.

MANTRA.

[*This entry discusses* mantra *in the Hindu tradition. For the role played by* mantra *in the Buddhist Tantras and in the Vajrayāna tradition, see* Buddhism, Schools of, *article on* Esoteric Buddhism.]

Mantra is the Sanskrit term for "sacred utterance." The word is derived from the root *man,* "think," and thus means "a vehicle of thought"; hence, by implication, a *mantra* is not considered efficacious unless the utterer concentrates on it. All Hindu rituals are accompanied by *mantras,* whether or not they are uttered aloud. The length of a *mantra* can be anything from a single syllable to a whole hymn. The words of a *mantra* may or may not convey meaning in ordinary language. A *mantra* may be used for secular, magical purposes or for religious, soteriological purposes; in the latter case it may be an object of meditation or means of addressing a deity. In Hindu theology a *mantra* incorporates the divine and its correct use necessarily involves the manipulation of divine power.

Vedic Mantra. The original *mantras* of Hinduism are the four Vedas or any parts thereof. All orthodox Hindu schools (by definition) consider the Vedas to be of transcendent, impersonal origin, though transmitted to us by inspired seers. The Vedic *mantras* thus put us in touch with eternal reality; in fact, they emanate from the ground of reality. Their words are unchanging and so have a higher ontological status than the things to which they refer. Each Vedic hymn is considered to be addressed to or to refer to a god; many end with a prayer to that god. Eternal and uncreated, the *mantras* in theory admit of no variation whatever: not only is their phonetic form minutely prescribed—a fact that led to the remarkable flowering of linguistics in ancient India—but they must be uttered with correct gestures and attitudes, both physical and mental.

Theoretical Primacy. While Brahmanic theory holds that Vedic *mantra* is impersonal, extracted from the essence of the universe, the relation of the *mantra* invoking a particular god to that god has in fact always been complex, even ambiguous. If language is ontologically prior to empirical reality, the name of a god can appear to be more fundamental than the god himself. On the other hand, the worshiper invoking a god imagines that god as person, perhaps as accessible to the senses. The Hindu worshiper may thus identify a deity with his or her invocatory *mantra,* which can be just a name *(nāma-mantra).*

Ritual Use. A similar rationale lies behind the fact that the performer of a rite has to state what he is doing or about to do; these statements, too, are *mantras* and are integral to the rite. For example, all rites for special purposes, whether obligatory *(naimittika)* or optional *(kāmya),* must begin with a statement called *saṃkalpa-mantra:* who is performing the ritual, when, and why. Objects used in the ritual, like the deities invoked, must first be addressed; these salutations, referred to as the *mantras* of the objects, divinize the objects, that is, render them ritually effective.

Mantras form part of rituals of every category. The principal feature of the twice-daily worship of the sun obligatory on every brahman is the recitation of the Gāyatrī *mantra,* a three-line verse from the *Ṛgveda* (3.62.10), addressed to the sun; the ideal manner in which to recite this and many other ritual *mantras* is *japa,* that is, *sotto voce.* The Gāyatrī is preceded by the syllable *oṃ* and the three "utterances" *(vyāhṛti),* the words *bhūr bhuvaḥ svaḥ,* which must originally have signified the tripartite cosmos (earth, atmosphere, heaven) but which later were no longer felt to be meaningful. The syllable *oṃ,* to be pronounced at the beginning and end of every Vedic recitation, came to be regarded in early monistic thought as the symbol of the one reality (*Chāndogya Upaniṣad* 1.1.1–4).

No one can perform an orthodox Hindu ritual unless qualified by initiation *(dīkṣā);* and the core of every initiation is the imparting of a *mantra,* which renders its knower ritually efficacious and is subsequently used in his or her ritual performances. A member of one of the *dvija* ("twice-born") classes becomes entitled to perform the daily obligatory *(nitya)* rituals by receiving the Gāyatrī at his initiation (Upanayana), described as his second birth. All *saṃskāras* (rites of passage) contain *mantras;* and if he undertakes a wholly religious life, whether temporarily *(vrata)* or permanently *(saṃnyāsa),* he has to accompany every deliberate act with a *mantra.* Moreover, anyone entitled by initiation to a *mantra* can use it to sacralize an ordinary act such as bathing, and so render it more efficacious. For example, a man who wants to beget a son should sanctify his sexual act by uttering a *mantra* at each stage.

In Tantrism. The theory of the *mantra* was elaborated and its use further intensified—but neither theory nor use radically changed—in the religious movement generically known as Tantrism. Hindu Tantrics are monotheists: innumerable gods exist, but they, like the rest of the world, are only aspects of the supreme deity and are generated by his *śakti,* his power and potency. Tantrics are admitted by initiation to sects in which each individual strives for salvation and for the acquisition of occult powers by an indissoluble combination of ritual and meditation, in both of which *mantras* are central. *Mantras* are inscribed in ritual diagrams (*yantras*, *maṇḍalas*), and the meditator in imagination places them in various parts of his body to divinize himself. His aim is to realize his identity with his god, an identity that he attempts to enact literally.

Each deity has two forms, that which can be visualized and the sonic form, or *mantra;* the latter form is the closer to ultimate reality and is thus the more potent. Indeed, the supreme God himself has a sonic form, *nāda,* which is the transcendent matrix of all language and of all reality. From the soteriological point of view, *mantras* are manifestations of God's divine grace, which he has provided out of compassion to enable individuals to free themselves from the cycle of rebirth and suffering, for to know a *mantra* is to acquire gnosis. For magical purposes, *mantras* embody the essence of what they designate, and when used with appropriate concentration, gestures, and so on, enable the user to gain power over objects and other beings.

[*See also* Oṃ.]

BIBLIOGRAPHY

Gonda, Jan. "The Indian Mantra." *Oriens* 16 (1963): 244–297. Still the best work on the Indian *mantra,* this book deals with both the Vedic and the classical-medieval development of the concept.

Hoens, Dirk Jan. "Mantra and Other Constituents of Tantric Practice." In *Hindu Tantrism,* edited by Sanjukta Gupta, Dirk Jan Hoens, and Teun Goudriaan. Leiden, 1979.

Padoux, André. *Recherches sur la symbolique et l'énergie de la parole dans certains textes tantriques.* Paris, 1963. Contains a comprehensive study on *mantra* in the Tantric tradition.

SANJUKTA GUPTA

MANU. There is no general agreement on the origin and etymology of the Sanskrit name *Manu.* It obviously is related to the verbal root *man-,* "think," and to various words meaning "human being, man," including *manuṣa, manuṣya,* and so on.

As early as the *Ṛgveda* (c. 1200 BCE), expressions such as "Father Manu [or Manuṣ]" seem to indicate that Manu was already conceived at that time as the progenitor of the human race. As such, he has often been compared with Mannus, the "origo gentis" in Tacitus's *Germania* (2.3). Manu most definitely is characterized as the father of mankind in a well-known story from the *Śatapatha Brāhmaṇa* (1.8.1), dating to around 900 BCE. Following the advice of a fish, Manu builds a ship and, with the fish's help, survives the great flood alone among men. After the water recedes, he worships and performs penance. As a result, a woman, Iḍā (also Iḷā or Ilā), is produced, by whom "he begets this offspring of Manu."

Manu was not only the first man but also the first king. All royal lineages, in some way or other, descend from him. His principal son, Ikṣvāku, reigned at Ayodhyā. One of Ikṣvāku's sons, Vikukṣi, carried on the Aikṣvāku dynasty, also known as the solar race, at Ayodhyā, whereas his other son, Nimi, established the dynasty of Videha. Manu's second son, Nābhānediṣṭha, founded the kingdom of Vaiśāli; his third son, Śaryāti, the kingdom of Ānanta; and his fourth son, Nābhāga, the dynasty of the Rathītaras. Manu's "daughter," Iḍā, also had a son, Purūravas, who became the founder of the Aila, or lunar race, at Pratiṣṭhāna. Purūravas's romance with the *apsara* Urvaśī became one of the most popular stories in Sanskrit literature.

Certain texts refer to Manu as being the first to have kindled the sacrificial fire. According to the *Śatapatha Brāhmaṇa* (1.5.1.7), "Manu, indeed, worshiped with sacrifices in the beginning; imitating that, this offspring of his performs sacrifices." More particularly, Manu's name is connected with the origin of the Śrāddha, the ritual for the dead (*Āpastamba Dharmasūtra* 2.7.16.1).

In addition, Manu is considered to have been the originator of social and moral order. Many texts quote maxims relating to various aspects of *dharma,* and attribute them to Manu. In this connection he also became the *ṛṣi* who revealed the most authoritative of the Dharmaśāstras.

In later literature Manu—or rather a succession of Manus—can be seen to play a role in the Hindu cyclical view of time. Each *kalpa,* or "day," of Brahmā, corresponding to one thousand *caturyuga*s or *mahāyuga*s, is divided into fourteen *manvantara*s, "periods of Manu." In the most sophisticated system a *manvantara* consists of seventy-one *caturyuga*s, or 306,720,000 human years. The *manvantara*s are separated by fifteen transitional periods (Skt., *saṃdhi*s) of four-tenths of a *caturyuga.* Each *manvantara* is presided over by a different Manu. In the present *Śvatavārāhakalpa,* six *manvantara*s have by now elapsed (presided over by Svāyambhuva, Svārociṣa, Auttami, Tāmasa, Raivata, and Cākṣuṣa, respectively). The present, seventh Manu is Manu Vaivasvata, who will be succeeded by Sāvarṇi, Dakṣasāvarṇi, Brahmasāvarṇi, Dharmasāvarṇi, Rudrasāvarṇi, Raucya or Devasāvarṇi, and Bhautya or Indrasāvarṇi.

[*For discussion of the Mānava Dharmaśāstra, a central Hindu text attributed to Manu, see* Śāstra Literature.]

BIBLIOGRAPHY

Many Sanskrit passages dealing with Manu have been collected and translated in John Muir's *Original Sanskrit Texts,* vol. 1 (1872; reprint, Amsterdam, 1967). See also Georg Bühler's introduction to *The Laws of Manu* (1886), "Sacred Books of the East," vol. 25 (reprint, Delhi, 1964).

LUDO ROCHER

MAORI RELIGION. New Zealand is the southernmost island group in Polynesia and was one of the last places in the world to be settled. Its native inhabitants, a Polynesian people who call themselves Maori, reached New Zealand not much more than six hundred years before the Dutch explorer Abel Tasman became the first European to lay eyes on the country, in 1642. No other European arrived until James Cook's visit in 1769, which inaugurated regular and steadily increasing outside contact. At that time, the Maori numbered about one hundred thousand, the great majority of them residing on the North Island.

Gods and Their Influence. In common with other Polynesians, the Maori conceived of reality as divided into two realms: the world of physical existence (*te ao marama,* "the world of light") and the world of supernatural beings (comprising both *rangi,* "the heavens," and *po,* "the underworld"). Communication between the two realms was frequent. Birth, for example, was regarded as the passage of a human spirit from the spiritual realm into this one, and death marked the return of the spirit to its point of origin.

Gods or spirits, termed *atua*s, were frequent visitors to the physical world, where they were extremely active. Indeed, any event for which no physical cause was immediately apparent was attributed to the gods. This included winds, thunder and lightning, the growth of plants, physical or mental illness, menstruation, involuntary twitches in the muscles, the fear that gripped a normally brave warrior before battle, the skill of an artist, even—after the arrival of Europeans—the operation of windmills. As the naturalist Ernest Dieffenbach summarized the Maori view, "*atua*s are the secret powers of the universe" (Dieffenbach, 1843, vol. 2, p. 118).

Another critical concept in traditional Maori religion is *tapu* (a term widespread in the Pacific, often rendered in English as "taboo"). Numerous definitions of the Maori *tapu* have been advanced, some identifying it as a set of rules regarding proper and forbidden conduct, others as a condition diverse enough to cover both the "sacred" and the "polluted." Perhaps the most useful view is that of the nineteenth-century magistrate and physician Edward Shortland, who defined *tapu* simply as the state of being under the influence of some *atua*. Because the influencing *atua* might be of any nature, from a protecting and strengthening god to an unwelcome, disease-dealing demon, the condition of a *tapu* person or thing could be anything from sacred to uncommonly powerful or brave; from dangerous to sick, deranged, or dead.

In the last analysis, Maori religion was concerned with the exercise of human control over the movements and activities of *atua*s in the physical world. It attempted to direct the influence of the gods into areas where their influence was deemed beneficial and to expel it where it was not, or where it was no longer desired.

Establishing tapu. Directing the influence of the gods was primarily pursued by means of ritual. One common way of instilling *tapu* (that is, inviting the gods to extend their influence over someone or something) was through ritual incantations called *karakia*. Many of these are long and difficult to translate, but one brief and simple example is a *karakia* recorded by the nineteenth-century missionary Richard Taylor, which might be chanted for a war party setting out on a campaign:

> E te rangi, ho mai he riri!
> E te atua, ho mai he riri!
>
> O heaven, give us fury!
> O god, give us fury!

Maori gods did not look into the hearts of their devotees; impeccable delivery was sufficient for a *karakia* to work its power. One man, in fact, was within the bounds of orthodoxy when he had the incantation necessary for planting sweet potatoes and other crops recited by a talking bird.

Another means of attracting *atua*s and disposing them to lend their influence to human affairs was to give them gifts. Many Maori rituals included the preparation of several ovens; the food cooked in one of them was reserved for the gods. When an important new canoe was launched, the heart of a human sacrifice might be offered to the gods for protection of the craft.

The influence of *atua*s was considered to be highly contagious, readily spreading from things that were *tapu* to things that were not. One common pathway was physical contact. Death was highly *tapu*, and anything that came in contact with a corpse—the tree on which it was exposed during decomposition, the people who scraped the bones a year after death, the place where the bones were finally deposited—became *tapu* as well. The supreme conductor of *tapu* was cooked food, which drew the *atua* influence from whatever it contacted and transferred this influence to anything it subsequently touched. One young woman, for example, died within forty-eight hours of being informed that a sweet potato she was eating had grown on a spot where an important chief was buried. The *tapu* of death, particularly stemming from someone of such high rank, was more than she could sustain.

Another avenue for the passage of *tapu* was resemblance. In the early 1840s, the artist George French Angas encountered stiff resistance in the Lake Taupo region whenever he wished to sketch *tapu* persons or things. The loss or contamination of *tapu* was thought to be detrimental, and the Maori reasoned that godly influence would pass from someone or something to its representation, and thus to anything with which the representation might come in contact. The Maori also feared that desecration would occur if sketches of *tapu* persons or objects were stored in the same portfolio—or were executed with the same pencil—as sketches of lowly or defiling objects.

The principles of *tapu* contagion were used ritually to introduce godly influence into places or situations where it was desired. One means of doing this was to put rudely carved stone images in sweet potato fields during the growing season. These *taumata atua*s were resting-places that attracted the gods, whose influence would then permeate the field and stimulate the growth of the crop. Similar reasoning underpinned the notion that certain rocks or trees, which virile gods were thought to frequent, had the power to impregnate barren women who embraced them. Another rite designed to enlist the aid of a deceased ancestor in easing a difficult childbirth called for music to be played on a flute made from one of his bones.

Dispelling tapu. *Tapu* was by no means an invariably desirable state. Disease, as I have already noted, was thought to be the work of certain gods or demons noted for their maliciousness. *Atua kahu*, for example, were a special class of supernatural beings that originated in human stillbirths. Nasty by nature, to be *tapu* from their influence was to succumb to illness, anxiety, or confusion. Well-known mischief workers in the Rotorua area were Te Makawe, an *atua* who caused people to be scalded by geysers or hot pools, and the *atua* Tatariki, who rejoiced in swelling people's toes and ankles.

Even the *tapu* so necessary for the achievement of desired ends had its drawbacks. A fine house or canoe was *tapu* while under construction, because *atuas* animated the creative work of the craftsmen. That same *tapu*, however, precluded ordinary use of the house, or canoe, once completed. Likewise, the craftsmen themselves were *tapu* during construction, as were priests performing rituals or warriors on campaign. Being in a state of *tapu*, while essential for the successful accomplishment of their goals, placed a number of restrictions on one's activities. Given the propensity of *tapu* to spread, such persons exercised great caution regarding contact with other persons or things; one of the more irksome constraints was that they might not use their hands while eating.

The disadvantages associated with undesirable *tapu*—as also with desirable *tapu*, once its benefits had been realized—meant that quite often it was important for persons and things to be released from this state, to be rendered *noa*, free from the influence of *atuas*. The Maori had a number of means for terminating the *tapu* state. One was simply to leave the area. Many *atuas* were limited in their activities to a certain locale; thus one cure for disease was to take a long trip and thereby escape the afflicting *atua*'s sphere of influence. The most common procedure, however, was to perform a ritual of the type known as *whakanoa* ("to make *noa*"). Most of these rituals involved the use of one of the following agents: water, the latrine, a female, or cooked food.

Whakanoa rituals, designed to dispel *tapu*, were as important in Maori religion as those used to instill it. The study of *whakanoa* rituals is fascinating, largely because of the initial implausibility in Western eyes of some of the agents used (such as the latrine), and the challenge of working out the rationale peculiar to each one. Scholarly consensus has yet to be reached in this area; the following are some contemporary theories under consideration.

The property of cooked food as supreme conductor of *atua* influence has already been mentioned; this apparently has to do with growth. In Maori eyes, growth was an unmistakable sign of *atua* activity. Hence a sweet potato field during the growing season was extremely *tapu*, and the head—as the site of the most vigorous growth of hair—was the most *tapu* part of the body. By exposure to fire or intense heat, cooking destroys the capacity of food for growth. Thus a proverb that may be applied to someone who has not yet accomplished much, but from whom great things are expected, runs *iti noa ana, he pito mata* ("only a little morsel, but it has not been cooked"). It still has, that is, the capacity for growth. If, upon removing food from an earthen oven, a morsel was found that had not been cooked, it was suspected that an *atua* was lurking in it. Cooking, then, was thought to rout *atua* influence, leaving the food a veritable vacuum for *tapu*. Therefore, a cooked sweet potato or piece of fern root might be passed ritually over the hands of someone who had engaged in a *tapu* activity, such as tattooing or cutting the hair of a chief. The *atua* influence would be drawn into the food, leaving the hands *noa*, and the now-*tapu* food might then be thrown into a stream, deposited at the latrine, or eaten, often by a woman.

Water was thought to remove *atua* influence by washing it away. Those who had handled a corpse or who had been involved in the *tapu* activity of teaching or learning sacred lore might return to the *noa* state by immersing themselves in water, preferably the flowing water of a stream.

Women frequently played important roles in *whakanoa* rituals. A war party might be released from *tapu* by a rite in which a woman would eat the ear of the first enemy they had killed. A newly constructed house could be rendered *noa* by a ceremony in which a woman stepped over the threshold. Women had to be careful of their movements because they might inadvertently dispel beneficial *tapu*. The arrival of a woman at the site could spoil the construction of a house or canoe, drive cockles from a beach or birds from the forest, blight sweet potatoes in a garden, even stop the black mud that was used to dye flax from "growing." These female powers were intensified during menstruation.

Opinions vary as to the basis of the female's capacity to dispel *tapu*. Some scholars hold that women were repulsive to the gods; thus at the approach of a female the gods would withdraw, leaving a *noa* state behind them. Given this interpretation, however, it is difficult to explain the fact that women were able to instill *tapu* ritually as well as to dispel it. Students might be rendered *tapu* prior to training in sacred lore, for example, by eating a piece of food that had been passed under the thigh of a woman.

Another view is that women could make *tapu* things *noa* because they were thought to attract *atuas*, not repel them. According to this theory, the female—specifically her genitalia—represented a passageway between the two realms of existence. When brought in proximity with a woman, an *atua* would be drawn into and through her, and thereby repatriated to the spiritual realm. This would leave the person or thing that had been *tapu*, by merit of that *atua*'s influence, in a *noa* state.

As I have pointed out, the Maori viewed birth as the transit of a human spirit from the world of the gods to the physical world. That transit, of course, occurred via female genitalia. The female was also significant at death, when the spirit would leave this world and return to the realm of the *atuas*. This point is expressed mythologically in the story of the death of the culture hero Māui. He resolved to give humankind eternal life by killing Hine-nui-te-po, the personification of death. Māui intended to kill the huge woman by entering her vagina as she slept, passing through her body and emerging at the mouth. But she awoke as Māui was entering her, clenched her thighs, and crushed him to death. And it is the common fate of all of us, claimed a Maori who recounted this story, to be drawn at death into the genitals of Hine-nui-te-po. As with human spirits, other *atuas* might enter and leave the physical world by means of the female. This theory might account for the capacity of women to instill and to dispel *tapu*.

The remaining *whakanoa* agent to be discussed is the latrine. Built on the edge of a cliff or brow of a hill, the Maori latrine was made with a low horizontal beam supported by two upright, often carved, posts. The user placed his feet on the beam while squatting, preserving his balance by grasping hand grips planted in the ground in front of the beam. A person could be ritually released from a *tapu* state by biting the latrine's horizontal beam. This might be done instead of, or in addition to, immersion in water by students following a teaching session. Maori mythology provides a further example: the pedigree of humankind begins with the union of the god Tane with Hine-hau-one, a female being who was formed from the earth to be Tane's mate. The formation, vivification, and impregnation of Hine-hau-one were *tapu* procedures, at the conclusion of which she became *noa* by biting a latrine beam.

The latrine beam marked a sharp line of separation: before it was the village, humming with life; behind it was a silent, shunned area where excrement fell and where people ventured only for murderous purposes, such as to learn witchcraft. In Maori culture the latrine beam became a metaphor for the notion of separation in general and, most specifically, for the separation between life and death. Since the dead belong to *po*, part of the realm of the *atuas*, the latrine beam can further be understood to represent the threshold between the two realms of existence. From this perspective, *whakanoa* rituals utilizing the latrine are susceptible to the same sort of interpretation suggested above for those involving women. *Tapu* persons or things were taken to a portal between the two worlds, where the godly influence was ritually repatriated to the spiritual realm.

Also in common with the female, the latrine sometimes constituted a point of entry into, or departure from, the physical world for *atuas* and their influence. For instance, at the beginning of the construction of an important house or canoe, a chip from the carving work would be placed at the latrine. This can be interpreted as contributing to the *tapu* quality of the project by imbuing the chip (and therefore, by extension, the undertaking as a whole) with the influence of the gods. The clearest example, however, is the consecration of the Takitumu canoe. According to traditional history, Takitumu was one of the canoes that brought the Maori ancestors from their original homeland of Hawaiki to New Zealand. Before setting sail, Takitumu was rendered *tapu* so as to be under the gods' protection during the long voyage. This was accomplished by literally hauling the canoe up to a latrine. There, certain images that had been stored in a burial cave were placed on board, and the gods themselves—particularly Kahukura, a rainbow god—were ritually invited to embark.

Modern Maori Religion. Christianity was introduced to New Zealand in 1814, when Samuel Marsden, chaplain of the penal colony at New South Wales in Australia, preached a sermon at the Bay of Islands on Christmas Day. Conversion proceeded rapidly after 1825, and by midcentury nearly the entire North Island was covered by Anglican, Roman Catholic, and Wesleyan missions. Today, the Maori belong to a variety of Christian denominations, the largest of which are the Anglican, Roman Catholic, Methodist, and Mormon churches. Also important are two Christian sects unique to New Zealand: Ringatu ("upraised hand") was founded in the 1860s by the Maori warrior and preacher Te Kooti; Ratana, a larger sect, was established in the 1920s by the reformed alcoholic and visionary Tahupotiki Wiremu Ratana. The Ratana church, which stresses faith healing, has been a major force in Maori politics.

BIBLIOGRAPHY

Among the many fascinating accounts of Maori life written by early visitors to New Zealand, two are George French Angas's *Savage Life and Scenes in Australia and New Zealand*, 2d ed., 2 vols. (London, 1847), and Ernest Dieffenbach's *Travels in New Zealand*, 2 vols. (London, 1843). Two other nineteenth-century works with considerable information on religion are the missionary Richard Taylor's *Te Ika a Maui, or, New Zealand and Its Inhabitants* (London, 1855) and the magistrate Edward Shortland's *Traditions and Superstitions of the New Zealanders*, 2d ed. (London, 1856). An important collection of exclusively Maori myths (despite its title) is George Grey's *Polynesian Mythology* (1855), edited by W. W. Bird (New York, 1970). The anthropologist Elsdon Best has written many works on Maori religion (as on all aspects of Maori culture), among them *Some Aspects of Maori Myth and Religion* (1922; reprint, Wellington, 1954), *Spiritual and Mental Concepts of the Maori* (1922; reprint, Wellington, 1954), *Maori Religion and Mythology* (Wellington,

1924), and *Tuhoe: The Children of the Mist* (Wellington, 1925). Important monographs by the historian of religion J. Prytz Johansen are *The Maori and His Religion in Its Non-Ritualistic Aspects* (Copenhagen, 1954) and *Studies in Maori Rites and Myths* (Copenhagen, 1958). Two recent anthropological studies are Jean Smith's *Tapu Removal in Maori Religion* (Wellington, 1974) and *Counterpoint in Maori Culture* (London, 1983) by F. Allan Hanson and Louise Hanson.

F. Allan Hanson

MAPONOS, a Celtic deity associated with youth, but of otherwise uncertain attributes, was identified by the conquering Romans with Apollo. The name is attested by several Romano-British and Gallo-Roman inscriptions in insular Britain and Gaul. It has also been found in an inscription in Gaulish at Chamalières (Puy-de-Dôme). In insular Britain, an inscription found in Ribchester, County Durham, reads "Deo sancto Apollini Mapono(o)," and another found in Hexham, County Northumberland, reads "Apollini Mapono" (*Corpus inscriptionum Latinarum,* Berlin, 1863, vol. 7, nos. 218, 1345). These indicate with exactitude the *interpretatio Romana:* Maponos is Apollo in his aspect of youth, an interpretation that takes into account the meaning "young man" associated with the stem *map-* ("son") and the theonymic suffix *-ono-s.*

Although no accounts of Gaulish theology survive, the name is enough to prove that the two aspects of the Celtic Apollo that are attested in Ireland—god of youth and leech god—also existed in Gaul and in insular Britain. The Irish equivalent is Mac ind Óg ("young son"), whose other name is Oenghus ("only choice"), son of Daghdha and of Boann, wife of Elcmhaire. Mapono's conception is recounted in the first version of the cycle of Édaín: Daghdha has sent Elcmhaire away and has magically suspended the course of the sun—and consequently the march of time—for nine months. The child is thus born on the evening of the day he was conceived. For this reason he is both the symbol of youth and the god of time, in opposition and complementarity to his father, the god of eternity.

Under the name of Mac ind Óg he is the hero of the adventure known as *The Taking of the Sid,* and, under the name of Oenghus, he is one of the principal personages of the cycle of Édaín. To him befalls the adventure of *The Dream of Oenghus,* a tale of a quest for sovereignty disguised as an amorous anecdote. And it is he who, at the end of the cycle, will vainly fight with Patrick over Eithne (Édaín), a personification of Ireland.

The Welsh form *Mabon mab Modron* ("Mabon son of Modron": *Modron* from **matrona,* "mother") is attested on several occasions, for example in the story *Culhwch and Olwen.* But this account gives only very brief indications as to his character: it is said only that he is kept prisoner from birth and that King Arthur ends up releasing him during the quest for marvelous objects needed for the marriage of Culhwch and Olwen.

BIBLIOGRAPHY

Guyonvarc'h, Christian-J., and Françoise Le Roux. *Textes mythologiques irlandais,* vol. 1. Rennes, 1980.

Le Roux, Françoise. "Notes d'histoire des religions, V. 9: Introduction à une étude de l' 'Apollon celtique'." *Ogam* 12 (1960): 59–72.

Mac Cana, Proinsias. *Celtic Mythology.* Rev. ed. Feltham, England, 1983.

Françoise Le Roux and Christian-J. Guyonvarc'h
Translated from French by Erica Meltzer

MAPPŌ. The Japanese term *mappō* (Chin., *mo-fa*) denotes the third and eschatologically decisive period in the history of the Buddha's Dharma as revealed in certain texts that were to have a significant impact on the evolution of East Asian Buddhism, particularly the Pure Land tradition. The three-stage periodization of which it is a part includes the period of the True Dharma *(shōbō),* when the Buddha's teachings were correctly practiced and people thereby attained enlightenment; the period of the Counterfeit Dharma *(zōbō),* when the teachings existed but very few upheld the practices and none attained enlightenment; and the period of Final Dharma (*mappō,* often translated as the "Latter Days of the Law"), when only the teachings remained, the practices were no longer pursued, and enlightenment was a mere word. In the view of those who espoused this eschatology, such a declining view of history, which was ascribed to the growing spiritual deficiencies of the *saṃgha,* spelled doom for the traditional schools of Buddhism. As many Buddhists came to believe that the traditional teachings had lost their relevance to the times and to the religious needs of the people, the Pure Land path emerged on the stage of history, claiming to have been especially prepared by the Buddha for the age of *mappō.*

The concept of the three stages of Dharma culminating in *mo-fa* appeared in the form we know it today in China during the second half of the sixth century, where it is first mentioned in the *Li-shih yüan-wen* (Vows) of the T'ien-t'ai master Hui-ssu (515–577), composed in the year 558. A few years later, a Mahāyāna *sūtra,* the *Ta-chi yüeh-tsang ching,* was translated into Chinese, introducing a variety of similar eschatological views concerning the period of Final Dharma. The Japanese scholar Yamada Ryūjō has shown that this *sūtra* was the product of four major strands of scriptures woven together, each containing various forebodings on the destiny of the Buddhist *saṃgha.* One of the earliest mentions of the three stages of Dharma is found in another text of the period, the *Ta-sh'eng t'ung-hsing ching;* however, the precise source of Hui-ssu's formulation remains unclear.

The notion of three stages of Dharma evolved gradually through the centuries in the historical experience of Buddhism, incorporating the multiple and variegated factors that contributed to the progressive decline of the church. These factors, some of which had existed since the time of Śākyamuni Buddha himself, became exacerbated with the passage of time: the violation of monastic precepts, debates surrounding the ordination of women, sectarian rivalries, a tendency to adhere to the letter, rather than the spirit, of the teachings, corruption in the monastic centers, the emergence of anti-Buddhist despots in India and Central Asia, social and political unrest throughout Buddhist Asia, and finally, the devastation of Buddhist communities in Gandhāra by the Ephthalites in the sixth century, an event that convinced many of the impending destruction of the *saṃgha.*

Prior to the mid-sixth century, various texts had made reference to the eras of True and Counterfeit Dharma, but none to the period of Final Dharma. However, the appearance of the *Ta-chi yüeh-tsang ching,* coinciding with the wholesale devastation of institutional Buddhism during the Northern Chou persecution of 574–577, confirmed the arrival of the age of Final Dharma foretold in that and other texts. In response to this historical crisis two powerful movements emerged, both proclaiming their teachings as eminently suited for the times: the Three Stages (San-chieh) school of Hsin-hsing (540–595) and the Pure Land path of Tao-ch'o (562–645).

Ultimately, four basic chronologies emerged, each reckoned on the basis of the Buddha's decease, universally accepted in China as having occurred in 949 BCE:

1. True Dharma, 500 years; Counterfeit Dharma, 1,000 years
2. True Dharma, 1,000 years; Counterfeit Dharma, 500 years
3. True Dharma, 500 years; Counterfeit Dharma, 500 years
4. True Dharma, 1,000 years; Counterfeit Dharma, 1,000 years

Calculated on the basis of the first of these chronologies, the prevailing belief was that the period of Final Dharma, which was to last for ten thousand years, had begun in 552 CE. Although this belief was inherited by Japanese Buddhists, the year 1052 was also widely embraced in medieval Japan as the beginning of the age of Final Dharma, based on the fourth of the above-mentioned chronologies.

Belief in the three stages was combined with another popular view concerning the destiny of the *saṃgha,* one that divided Buddhist history into five five-hundred-year periods. This notion too had a complex history, but in its final form characterized the gradual eclipse of the Dharma as follows; an age in which enlightenment was the dominant feature of the religious life, an age in which meditative practices were firmly established, an age in which the study of scripture was firmly established, an age in which the building of stupas and temples was firmly established, and an age in which fighting and bickering and the decline and disappearance of the Dharma were the dominant features of the religious life. The period of Final Dharma was identified with the last of these ages. Another prevalent view, intimately connected with that of *mappō,* characterized our time as one of Five Defilements, in which the age itself, all religious views, all desires, all sentient beings, and all human life are defiled.

Mo-fa is mentioned by almost all of the eminent Buddhist writers of the Sui and T'ang dynasties, but it was Hsin-hsing and Tao-ch'o who refused to regard it as merely descriptive of external historical events and actually incorporated it into the very foundation of their teachings. That is, both thinkers affirmed the reality of the end time in their own religious awakening and realized the extent to which the fundamental ignorance *(avidyā)* of all beings precluded the mastery of traditional practices leading to supreme enlightenment. Such an admission of contemporary deficiencies, both inner and outer, justified in their view a new path to salvation.

In the case of Hsin-hsing, this new path called for the universal recognition of the Buddha nature in all beings and the consequent practice of selfless acts of compassion toward everyone, regardless of status, as an antidote to the blind ignorance and profound egocentricity of the age. For Tao-ch'o it meant entrusting the ego-self to the saving vows of the Buddha Amitābha (Chin., O-mi-t'o-fo; Jpn., Amida) as the only viable means of deliverance from the ocean of *saṃsāra.* Hsin-hsing's Three Stages school experienced a turbulent history and eventually disappeared during the Hui-ch'ang persecution of Buddhism in 845, but the Pure Land lineage of Tao-ch'o gained wide acceptance and became a major force in East Asian Buddhism. [*See the biographies of Hsin-hsing and Tao-ch'o.*]

In China, the implications of the concept of *mo-fa* were mitigated by the continuing vigor of mainstream

Mahāyāna Buddhism, which insisted on the observance of precepts, adherence to meditative practices, and cultivation of wisdom as essential for supreme enlightenment. Tao-ch'o and the subsequent Pure Land masters, while proclaiming a new path suited for the age of *mo-fa,* were not entirely free from the weight of this great tradition and continued to advocate a variety of more traditional Buddhist practices. By contrast, in Japan a forboding sense of doom permeated the whole of medieval society, involving all of the Buddhist schools. Recognition of the advent of *mappō* was thus a decisive factor in the formation of the major schools of Japanese Buddhism in the thirteenth century—Jōdo, Jōdo Shin, Nichiren, and Zen—and even affected the earlier schools founded during the Nara (710–794) and Heian (794–1185) periods.

The first nonscriptural citation of the term in Japan appears in the *Nihon ryōiki* (Miraculous Stories from the Japanese Buddhist Tradition), compiled in the ninth century. A lament in this text states, "We are already in the age of Degenerate Dharma. How can we live without doing good? My heart aches for all beings. How can we be saved from calamity in the age of Degenerate Dharma?" The nature of *mappō* is also the topic of the *Mappō tōmyōki* (The Lamp to Illuminate the Age of Final Dharma), attributed to Saichō (767–823), the founder of the Japanese Tendai school. According to Saichō, each of the three stages of history is characterized by practices relevant to that particular age. The practices suited to the period of True Dharma include observance of the precepts and the practice of meditative disciplines. Those practices endemic to the period of Counterfeit Dharma are the violation of the precepts and the accumulation of property by monks. In the period of Final Dharma all monks must be honored, even though they violate or disregard the precepts, since the very nature of the times precludes the very existence and validity of the precepts. [*See the biography of Saichō.*]

Such a view of the end time, widely held by both clerics and laity, meant not only the bankruptcy of the Buddhist *saṃgha* but appeared also to herald the end of the world itself through the operation of inexorable historical forces. In the twelfth and thirteenth centuries a variety of events seemed to confirm the reality of *mappō:* the impotence of imperial rule, the decline of the aristocracy, social upheaval, local uprisings, internecine warfare, natural calamities and pestilence, and conflagrations that destroyed the capital.

This sense of impending collapse generated a variety of responses among the Buddhist clergy. These were of two basic types. One vigorously rejected this pessimistic view of history and reaffirmed the power of traditional paths to enlightenment. The other accepted the fact of *mappō* as the manifestation of the basic human condition—weak, imperfect, vulnerable, and subject to temptations—and saw the working of Dharma in the very midst of such karmic limitations, whether through the Nembutsu, containing the saving vows of Amida Buddha, or in the Daimoku, manifesting the miraculous salvific powers of the *Lotus Sutra.*

It was Hōnen (1133–1212), one of the pioneering figures of the Kamakura period (1185–1333), who incorporated the implications of the doctrine of *mappō* into a virtual revolution in Japanese Buddhism. For him, the end time of history did not signal the decline and destruction of the Buddhist *saṃgha* but rather the opening up of the true *saṃgha* to both men and women, upper and lower classes, clergy and laity alike. For Hōnen, *mappō* did not mean the rampant violation of precepts but the disintegration of the sacrosanct authority of precepts that discriminated against certain groups of people. Since the age of *mappō* meant the nonexistence of precepts, the path of enlightenment was now open to people considered evil in the eyes of traditional Buddhism: those who made a living by taking life (hunters, fishermen, peasants, and warriors) and those who were outcasts from society (traders and merchants, prostitutes, monks and nuns who had violated the precepts, and others). Such people he proclaimed to be the primary concern of Amida Buddha's Primal Vow *(hongan),* the ultimate manifestation of true compassion. On the basis of this conviction Hōnen proclaimed the founding of an independent Jōdo (Pure Land) school in 1175. [*See the biography of Hōnen.*]

Thus, while *mappō* spelled doom and despair for the established sects, it was an age of boundless hope and optimism for the disenfranchised. More fundamentally, in this view history became witness to the truth and relevance of the Pure Land path to enlightenment, as had been prophesied by Śākyamuni in the Pure Land *sūtras.* The end time of history was here and now, but it was in the here and now that Amida's compassionate vow had become fully operative.

Shinran (1175–1262) pushed this acute sense of historical crises even more radically into an existential realization of the human condition. [*See the biography of Shinran.*] He saw the particular evils of the age of *mappō* as revealing the very ground of self-existence. For Shinran, evil, though particularized in the individual, forms the essence of humanity in *saṃsāra.* But this realization of profound karmic evil is not final, for deeper and wider still is the working of Amida's compassionate vow, operating through samsaric existence to deliver the self, as well as all suffering beings, into the Pure Land.

For Shinran, then, *mappō* was no longer a particular period of history but the fundamental reality of life itself, embracing all ages, past, present, and future. The Primal Vow of Amida is working not only in the end time but has always been responding to the deepest yearnings of humanity, whether in the period of True Dharma, Counterfeit Dharma, or Final Dharma, whenever and wherever man is steeped in brutish egoism. It took the radical breakdown of history, however, for this truth to surface within human consciousness. As Shinran wrote in the *Shōzōmatsu wasan* (Hymns on the Last Age):

> Throughout the three periods of True, Counterfeit,
> and Final Dharma
> Amida's Primal Vow has been spread.
> In this world at the end of the Counterfeit Dharma
> and in the Final Dharma age
> All good acts have entered the Palace of the Dragon.

[*For further discussion of the influence of the notion of mappō in Pure Land Buddhism, see* Amitābha; Ching-t'u; Jōdoshū; *and* Jōdo Shinshū.]

BIBLIOGRAPHY

The groundwork for the study of the origin of *mappō* is found in Yamada Ryūjō's *Daijō bukkyō seiritsuron josetsu* (Kyoto, 1959), pp. 567–592. A discussion of Hsin-hsing's Three Stages sect can be found in Kenneth Ch'en's *Buddhism in China: A Historical Survey* (Princeton, 1964), pp. 297–300. Readers of Japanese will want to consult Yabuki Keiki's monumental study of the sect, *Sangaikyō no kenkyū* (Tokyo, 1927). There is no adequate study of the *mappō* concept in Western languages, but Shinran's view may be seen in the English translation of his *Shōzōmatsu wasan* (Hymns on the Last Age), "Ryūkoku Translation Series," vol. 7 (Kyoto, 1981). An attempt to relate the three stages of history to the dialectical evolution of Shinran's faith and thought is found in *The Heart of Buddhism* by Takeuchi Yoshinori (New York, 1983), pp. 48–60.

TAITETSU UNNO

MAPUCHE RELIGION. The Mapuche currently live in Chile and Argentina. In Chile, they have settled between the Bio-Bio River to the north and the Channel of Chacao to the south, a territory that encompasses the provinces of Arauco, Bio-Bio, Malleco, Cautin, Valdivia, Osorno, and Llanquihue (approximately between 37° and 41° south latitude). In Argentina, they are found at similar latitudes in the northern Patagonian province of Neuquén and, to a lesser extent, in the Río Negro and Chubut provinces; to the north there are scattered and isolated groups in the Pampas region. The most optimistic calculations estimate that there are five hundred thousand Mapuche in Chile and fifty thousand in Argentina.

The Mapuche belong to the Araucana-chon linguistic family. Most of the Mapuche live in small settlements in a pattern of scattered encampments. The basic economic activity among the Chilean Mapuche is agriculture; the Argentinians rely on sheep and goat herding, as dictated by varying ecological settings. Patrilineal descent, patrilocal residence, and matrilateral marriage are the most noteworthy traits of contemporary Mapuche society. Patrilineage or, in many cases, a subdivision thereof, as well as the residential family, increasingly constitute the minimal units of the settlement in economic, social, and religious terms.

The structural changes undergone by the Mapuche in the past hundred years—a product of their adaptation to a new natural and social environment—have transformed Mapuche economy and, to a lesser degree, Mapuche society. Nonetheless, despite insistent missionary activity by Roman Catholics and Protestants (particularly fundamentalists), the foundation of their system of religious beliefs and practices remains practically intact in many regions.

To describe their mythico-religious beliefs even briefly, to characterize the numerous major deities, both regional and local, and to elucidate the symbolic content and meanings of each of the many rites of this people are tasks far beyond the scope of this work. I have therefore chosen to summarize them, making use of two cognitive structures common to them all, which will allow me to piece together the complex Mapuche belief system of religious practices and images and to outline their internal logic.

The first structure—apparently the most widespread—is dualism, which orders and defines two polar elements according to their relationships of opposition and complementarity. The second is the tetradic division generated as a result of a first bipartition that brings two opposed couples face to face and a second bipartition of degree that defines in each couple a climax and its attenuation.

The vast Mapuche pantheon is divided into two great antithetical and complementary spheres. The first is made up of beneficent deities, organized into a tetradic family based on a combination of sex and age (old man and old woman, young boy and young girl). These deities are the agents of good, health, and prosperity, and their tetradic nature symbolizes perfection. Cosmologically and vertically, they are found in the celestial sphere, or *wenú mapú*, which is the summit of the positive aspect of the four vertical components of the universe. Horizontally, some of them are ranked, with varying degrees of positivity, with the four regions of the world (the east, south, north, and west cardinal points). Temporally, they are associated with clarity.

Given that the tetradic division is also the ordering principle of the day, they have their most exact manifestations in *epewún* ("dawn"), a superlative concretion of *antí* ("clarity"), whose sign is positive, and in *kɨrinɨf* ("dusk"), the attenuation of *pún* ("darkness"), whose sign is negative. Finally, they are associated with positive colors—blue (the most important) and white-yellow (denoting attenuation).

The second sphere of this theophanic dualism is made up of the malefic beings, of *wekufɨ*, who appear isolated, in odd numbers, and of indeterminate age and sex. They are agents of evil, illness, and chaos, and they symbolize imperfection. Their place in the cosmos is ambiguous; some groups place them in the *anká wenú*, or middle heaven, but generally they are considered to belong to the *pu mapú*, or netherworld—the climax of the negative aspect in the vertical conception of the universe. The temporal acts of the *wekufɨ* are most evident during *rangɨn púñ* ("midnight"), the most negative moment, and, to a lesser extent, during *rangíñ ánti* ("midday"), the attenuation of the positive pole. *Wekufɨ* that are associated with red and black, the malefic hues, play an even greater role in determining the qualities attributed to them.

The implied symbolic network arises from various levels of discourse, such as the *ngetrán* (accounts of mythical or historical events characterized by truthfulness) and the decoding of dreams and signs—present events that anticipate the qualities of future occurrences. The social correlative of this theophanic dualism is incarnated in the figures of the *máchi* ("shaman") and *kalkú* ("witch"), who manipulate the forces of good and evil, respectively. The paraphernalia of the *máchi* include, among other things, the *kultrún* (a kettledrum), which serves as a symbolic microcosm; the *wáda* (a rattle); and the *kaskawílla* (a girdle with small bells). The *máchi* are assisted by benevolent deities and are responsible for staving off illnesses caused by the *kalkú*, who are assisted by the *wekufɨ* beings.

Shamanic rites include Machiluwún, an initiatory rite carried out after the *máchi* has undergone a period of revelation through illness or dreams and after he has received instruction from an initiated shaman, and the Ngejkurrewén, a postinitiatory rite of power renewal. The Pewutún is a diagnostic ritual. There are two therapeutic rites: the Datwún, for serious illnesses, and the Ulutún, for minor ailments. All these rites and their associated artifacts and actions—including the *réwe*, a wood carving representing the cosmic stages; branches from sacred trees; ritual displacements of objects from the right (positive) to the left (negative), facing east and counting in twos, fours, or multiples thereof; songs and dances beseeching the benevolent gods to act; blue and white flags; and the moments (dawn and dusk) when the rites are performed—are symbolic expressions denoting supplication to the forces of good and the restoration of health.

In contrast, the witch directly or indirectly causes *kalkutún* ("harm") by throwing objects with malefic powers around the victim's house or by working magic on the victim's nails, hair, clothing, sweat, or footprints. The witch may poison the victim, or may enlist the help of a *wekufɨ*—such as a *witranálwe*, the soul of a dead man that has been captured by the *kalkú*. The nocturnal appearance of the *witranálwe* in the form of a great, resplendent, cadaverous horseman causes illness and death.

Community members take part in numerous rituals outside of the specialized orbit of shamanism and witchcraft. The funerary rites, or Aẃn, are still practiced in the Chilean settlements. Their object is twofold: to ensure that the soul of the dead can cross into the world where the ancestors live (a site that some scholars say is very close to, or is associated with, the domain of the benevolent deities) and to prevent the spirit of the dead person from being captured by a witch and transformed into his aide during his nocturnal ambushes.

The term *ngillatún* alludes to the act of prayer and connotes diverse practices on individual, family, and group levels. Strictly speaking, on the group level it designates a "ritual complex" that varies in several respects according to the traditions of the community performing it. These variations include the number and affiliation of the participants, the extent of group cohesion, the ritual's duration, its association with agrarian or pastoral economic cycles, and its occasional or periodic nature, that is, whether it is carried out to counteract natural phenomena or to observe crucial dates of the annual cycle. Despite this great diversity, what finally defines the *ngillatún* is its strongly propitiatory nature, its characters—varying with the time it is performed—as restorer of the cosmic order, and its enrichment of coherence and meaning within communal life through the ritual congregation.

Within this cultural domain, the symbolic network also impregnates with meaning each of the ritual episodes—for example, the forms of spoken and sung prayer, ritual sprinkling, ritual painting, women's songs, men's dances and mixed dances, sacrifices, libations, and horseback rides. It is this network that determines the temporal bounds of the episodes, the meaning of the displacements, and the colors used, as well as the number of times (twice, four times, or a multiple thereof) that each action must be repeated.

This summary, centered around the ideological principles that serve to organize and define a large part of the symbolic beliefs, rites, and images of the Mapuche, should not lead the reader to suppose that this is a closed system lacking flexibility. The history of the Mapuche people indicates exactly the opposite. They have adapted to new conditions while preserving their traditional knowledge and beliefs, even if these have sometimes been modified or given new meanings.

BIBLIOGRAPHY

Among the classic studies of the subject, the most noteworthy for the Chilean region include Ricardo E. Latcham's *La organización social y las creencias religiosas de los antiguos araucanos* (Santiago, 1924) and Tomas Guevara's *Folklore araucano* (Santiago, 1911) and *Historia de Chile: Chile prehispánico*, 2 vols. in 1 (Santiago, 1925–1927). The North American anthropologist Louis C. Faron, who spent several years living in Chilean settlements, offers an excellent analysis of Mapuche society and its connections with religious practices in *Mapuche Social Structure: Institutional Reintegration in a Patrilineal Society of Central Chile* (Urbana, Ill., 1961); one of his many articles on this ethnic group, "Symbolic Values and the Integration of Society among the Mapuche of Chile," *American Anthropologist* 64 (1962): 1151–1163, deals with the dualism of the Mapuche worldview and offers valuable contributions. Other articles that should be cited, both because of the wealth of their data and the new outlooks they bring to the subject, are Maria E. Grebe's "Mitos, creencias y concepto de enfermedad en la cultura mapuche," *Acta psiquiatrica y psicologica de America Latina* (Buenos Aires) 17 (1971): 180–193, and "Cosmovision mapuche," *Cuadernos de la realidad nacional* (Santiago, Chile) 14 (1972): 46–73.

One of the most extensive monographs on the religion of the Argentinian Mapuche is Rodolfo M. Casamiquela's *Estudio del nillatún y la religión araucana* (Bahía Blanca, 1964). The compilations and observations of Bertha Koessler-Ilg in *Tradiciones araucanas* (La Plata, 1962) are a good addition. Other books worthy of mention are Else Marta Waag's *Tres entidades 'wekufü' en la cultura mapuche* (Buenos Aires, 1982), which is outstanding for its wealth of information, and the anthology of essays *Congreso del Area Araucana Argentina* (Buenos Aires, 1963). The theoretical and methodological bases as well as the development and exemplification within different cultural domains of the two cognitive structures summarized in this article can be found in two essays by C. Briones de Lanata and me:"Che Kimín: Un aborde a la cosmologica Mapuche," *Runa: Archivo para las ciencias del hombre* (Buenos Aires) 15 (1985) and "Estructuras cognitivas e interacción social: El caso de la brujeria entre los Mapuche argentinos," in *Actas del 45° Congreso Internacional de Americanistas* (Bogotá, 1985).

MIGUEL ANGEL OLIVERA
Translated from Spanish by Erica Meltzer

MĀRA ("death-causer") is a god identified in Buddhist legend and cosmology as Lord of the Kāmadhātu ("realm of sense-desire") and principal antagonist of the Buddha and his followers. Māra is also called Maccu ("death"), Antaka ("the end"), Pāpimā ("evil one"), and sometimes Kaṇha ("dark one") or Namuci ("not loosing"). His mount is an elephant; his chief attribute is the snare of worldly thoughts and pleasures that binds his captives to repeated death and suffering.

Māra is best known for his attempts to prevent the Buddha's enlightenment (as described especially in the *Padhāna Sutta* of the *Sutta Nipāta* and in the Enlightenment accounts of the *Mahāvastu, Lalitavistara, Nidāna-kathā,* and *Buddhacarita*). As the Buddha-to-be seats himself under the Bodhi Tree and prepares for his final breakthrough, Māra first tries to dissuade him verbally and then attacks, albeit futilely, with the full might of his demonic hosts. In later accounts, this attack culminates with the "earth-touching" incident whose characteristic gesture identified representations of the Enlightenment in Buddhist iconography. Here the Buddha-to-be, with a touch of his finger, summons the earth to witness his claim to preeminence. Several accounts append a return attempt by Māra's daughters, who try to seduce the great being who has conquered their father.

Māra's second most noteworthy deed, described in accounts of the Buddha's last months (for example, *Mahāparinibbāna Sutta* 3.1–10), was to ensure the Buddha's final departure from the human realm. When the Master drops broad hints about a Buddha's ability to remain on earth until the end of an aeon, Māra clouds the disciple Ānanda's understanding; hence Ānanda does not beg his master to linger. Māra himself then urges the Buddha to leave, citing an old promise that the Buddha will depart once his teaching and community are well established. The Buddha then rejects his remaining life span, ensuring that the final *nirvāṇa* will occur three months later.

Māra further harasses both Buddha and disciples in a host of lesser incidents. In the collection of Pali *sutta*s called *Mārasaṃyutta* (*Saṃyutta Nikāya* 1.4), Māra strives to distract or frighten the Buddha, and to tempt him to self-doubt or worldly enjoyment. In the collection called *Bhikkunīsaṃyutta,* he tries unsuccessfully to seduce, confuse, or demoralize ten meditating nuns (*Saṃyutta Nikāya* 1.5). At times he works within, appearing as an unruly thought or as fear or pain. Or he inspires others to oppose or abuse the monastic community.

Māra's most famous post-Enlightenment target is the monk Upagupta, said to be a contemporary of the emperor Aśoka. When Upagupta preaches, Māra distracts his audiences, first by causing a shower of gold and pearls to rain down, and then by staging a competing performance with heavenly musicians and dancers. Upagupta finally traps Māra by garlanding him with corpses, converts him, and persuades the shape-shifter to duplicate for Upagupta the Buddha's own image (retold in a number of sources, especially *Aśokāvadāna*).

Although Māra appears in such legends as a concrete personage, he is also recognized as a figurative summation of the passions, fears, doubts, and delusions that impede a practitioner of the Buddhist path. Thus anger and false views are called his snares; fetters and defilements are his armies; his daughters are craving, discontent, and passion; and his sons are confusion, gaiety, and pride. Māra himself is variously identified with the *kleśas* ("impurities"), *āsravas* ("depravities"), *avidyā* ("ignorance"), and *skandhas* ("personality aggregates") that precipitate craving and hence rebirth and redeath.

BIBLIOGRAPHY

The best sources in English are T. O. Ling's *Buddhism and the Mythology of Evil* (London, 1962) and James W. Boyd's *Satan and Māra: Christian and Buddhist Symbols of Evil* (Leiden, 1975). Ling is based on Pali sources only; Boyd draws on early texts of both the Pali and Sanskrit traditions. See also Ernst W. O. Windisch's *Māra und Buddha* (Leipzig, 1895), the classic study of the textual history of the Māra legend.

NANCY E. AUER FALK

MARANKE, JOHN (1912–1963), African religious prophet and founder of the Apostolic Church of John Maranke. John (or Johane) Maranke was born Muchabaya Ngomberume in 1912. His birthplace is believed to be near Bondwe Mountain in the Maranke Tribal Trust Land of Southern Rhodesia. His father, Momberume, was part of the royal Sithole lineage, and his mother was the daughter of the Shona chief Maranke.

Church records indicate that Maranke was baptized a Methodist under the name of Roston at the local mission. Some of his instructors thought that he would eventually enter the Methodist ministry. In July of 1932, however, John, as he is referred to by his followers, received a spiritual calling to start the Apostolic church. An account of the visionary experiences leading to his calling is presented in the *Humbowo Hutswa we Vapostori* (The New Revelation of the Apostles) a book composed in the Shona language by Maranke and viewed by the movement as a major ecclesiastical text.

When John was five years old, he began to hear strange voices and see visions. After a year of Methodist primary school, he claimed that he had been visited by the Holy Spirit. He prayed continually and stood on top of anthills preaching to the trees. During this time, John was plagued by a mysterious childhood illness that could not be diagnosed. Following this illness, he lived for a short period of time in the mountains and was thought by his relatives and friends to be dead.

On the evening of 17 July 1932, near Mount Nyengwe in Umtali District, John allegedly witnessed a bright light and heard a heavenly voice that said: "You are John the Baptist, an Apostle. Now go and do my work. Go to every country and preach and convert people." John regarded this vision as a divine calling from the Holy Spirit to found the Apostolic church.

Between 1932 and 1934, John's church grew rapidly. After the initial spiritual revelation, John, his brothers Conorio and Anrod, and his uncle Peter Mupako went to spread the news to the neighboring settlements. Ruka (Luke) Mataruka, John's brother-in-law, became the first convert and evidenced signs of his spiritual calling immediately. John himself was baptized by Ruka. As the news of John's revelation spread beyond his extended family, people from all parts of the district flocked to him to receive spiritual healing.

On Saturday, 20 July 1932, the first Apostolic Sabbath was held near the Murozi, or "Jordan," River, in which the new converts were baptized. It is estimated that approximately 150 new members were baptized on that day. Ruka was made the first evangelist of the church. Two of John's cousins, Simon (Mushati) and Gwati, were designated respectively as the first prophet and first secretary of the church; his brother Conorio became the first healer. Momberume, John's father, was also baptized then and was made the elder judge *(mutongi)* of the church, charged with resolving disputes.

On 24 August 1934, the Passover (*Paseka* or *Pendi*) of the Apostolic church was held. This celebration was a combined reenactment of the Last Supper and a eucharist. It was also intended to commemorate the moment at which John Maranke received his initial calling from the Holy Spirit and, hence, was also known as the Pendi, or Pentecost. After John's death, the date of the celebration was changed to 17 July, in honor of the date of John's first calling. During the Passover, Apostles from all regions gather to confess sins of the preceding year and to celebrate spiritual renewal. As the church has grown, the importance of this celebration has increased.

Eventually, a leadership hierarchy consisting of four spiritual gifts *(bipedi)* and three ranks *(mianza)* was established for each Apostolic congregation. The spiritual gifts are designated as works of healing, evangelism, prophecy, and baptism. Members are ordained within each spiritual gift. The ranks within each gift are derived from the sacred word *Lieb-Umah* that John Maranke received in a prophetic revelation. The Apostles assert that this word means "he who speaks with God." John specified that each Apostolic congregation should contain three Lieb-Umahs, or priests, for each of the four gifts. Together, all of the men holding degrees of the Lieb-Umah rank within a single congregation constitute the Committee of Twelve Elders charged with its governance.

John and his relatives controlled the church from its center in Bocha, Zimbabwe (then Southern Rhodesia), until his death (allegedly by poisoning) in 1963. In the late 1940s, however, Ruka Mataruka gained a considerable following of his own and broke away from the parent church. John challenged Ruka's bid for power and was ultimately able to regain many of the dissident followers. After John's death, a schism again divided the Zimbabwean branch of the church when Simon Mushati formed another rival group. Simon argued that he had always been second to John in the leadership structure of the church and challenged the right of John's eldest son, Abel, to succeed his father. Invoking Shona customary law, John's brother Anrod performed a christianized version of the traditional inheritance ceremony and passed on the leadership to John's eldest sons, Abel and Makebo. By this time, the church was so large that it was necessary to travel to outlying districts and to other countries to perform the Passover. Abel, as John's legitimate successor, was given the power to perform the Passover and to lead the church. He divided these responsibilities with his younger brother Makebo, who traveled north to Nyasaland (now Malawi) and east to Mozambique on his behalf. By the 1960s, there were an estimated fifty thousand Maranke Apostles in Zimbabwe alone.

The Apostolic Movement on an International Scale. The Apostolic church entered Zambia (then Northern Rhodesia) and Malawi (then Nyasaland) by 1948. Initially, the Shona evangelist Kasimil visited these areas and baptized many new converts who subsequently spread the word among their relatives and in neighboring villages. The early congregations also contained many Shona members who had migrated north in search of work.

In 1952, Nawezi Petro, a Zairian of Lunda origin, encountered the Shona Apostles on a visit to Southern Rhodesia. He claimed that they healed his wife of tuberculosis after a series of European doctors had failed to do so. Nawezi and his wife immediately converted and returned home to introduce the church to Katanga Province (now Shaba). Meanwhile, the church spread northward to the Kasai Province of Zaire and to the capital, Kinshasa (then Léopoldville). Kasanda Vincent and Mujanaie Marcel, the first spokesmen for the group in the Kasai area, quickly acquired a large following. Over the years, several schisms developed in the Zairian branch of the Apostolic church. The major rift took place when Nawezi's brother-in-law Musumbu Pierre broke away from the Katanga congregation and acquired a large local following in the Kasai region. This struggle between Musumbu and Nawezi was finally resolved in 1974 when the church center acknowledged Musumbu's status as the first leader of the Zairian branch and the official representative of the Zairian congregations.

A similar pattern of growth took place in Angola and Mozambique, where the Apostolic church went through the characteristic pattern of rapid growth and subsequent schism. By the early 1980s, there were an estimated three hundred thousand members of the Maranke Apostolic church in six central and southern African nations: Zimbabwe, Zaire, Angola, Mozambique, Malawi, and Zambia. The largest membership is concentrated in eastern Zimbabwe and southwestern Zaire.

The Impact of the Apostolic Church in Central and Southern Africa. Apostolic theology is highly moralistic, emphasizing the keeping of commandments, observation of food and other taboos, and the regular confession of sins. The Apostles accept the Old and New Testaments of the Bible equally as the foundation for their belief. Saturday is kept as the sabbath day. Biblical teachings are supplemented by John's prophetic book *New Witness of the Apostles,* which is considered to provide spiritual and moral directives for a better life. Emphasis is placed on Holy Spirit inspiration and faith healing.

Apostolic doctrine involves a clear reaction to the mission churches. Voluntary polygamy is condoned, and church members are encouraged to avoid Western medical treatment. At the same time, Apostles eschew many aspects of traditional religion, including the veneration of the ancestors and the use of herbal medicines and charms. The role of women as ceremonial leaders is emphasized in the church, and they hold the positions of prophetesses and healers. Although marriage is not considered a sacrament among the Apostles, the customary dowry is de-emphasized and the importance of the family unit is stressed.

Ceremonies are conducted in multiple languages, and church liturgy varies somewhat from one congregation to another, although the basic format of worship remains consistent. While the influence of John Maranke as a prophet and founder is acknowledged by all congregations, there has been no attempt to elevate him to divine or messianic status. He is considered to be a messenger of God and a reformer whose interpretation of Christianity has made it relevant to large segments of the African population. The movement contains an innovative combination of African customs and Christianity. The charismatic appeal of the church and an ability to absorb cultural variations have accounted for its spread and popularity across several African nations.

BIBLIOGRAPHY

Aquina, Mary, O.P. "The People of the Spirit: An Independent Church in Rhodesia." *Africa* 37 (1967): 203–219. Contains a brief account of the Apostolic movement in the Karanga area of Southern Rhodesia during the 1950s with an explanation of its doctrine and rituals. Emphasis is placed on the role of confession for church members.

Daneel, M. L. *Old and New in Southern Shona Independent Churches*, vol.1, *Background and Rise of the Major Movements.* The Hague, 1971. A detailed historical account of the background and rise of several Shona traditional cults and independent churches, including a discussion of the early years of the Apostolic Church of John Maranke in eastern Zimbabwe.

Jules-Rosette, Bennetta. *African Apostles: Ritual and Conversion in the Church of John Maranke.* Ithaca, N.Y., 1975. A study of the Apostolic Church of John Maranke in Zaire, Zambia, and Zimbabwe, containing a detailed account of the Zairian branch and discussion of ritual and the conversion process in the church based on firsthand ethnographic materials.

Jules-Rosette, Bennetta, ed. *The New Religions of Africa.* Norwood, N.J., 1979. An edited collection of eleven essays on new African religious movements containing an article on the role of women as leaders in the Maranke Apostolic church and an introductory comparison of the Maranke Apostles with related movements in the same region.

Maranke, John. *The New Witness of the Apostles.* Translated by J. S. Kusotera. Bocha, Rhodesia, 1953. A mimeographed pamphlet, giving an autobiographical account of the spiritual visions of John Maranke and the history of the founding of the church from his perspective; outlines the commandments and moral directives governing church membership.

Murphree, Marshall W. *Christianity and the Shona.* New York, 1969. A study of Christianity among the Shona of the Budja area of Mtoko District in Zimbabwe, containing an account of the relationships among the Methodists, the Roman Catholics, and the Maranke Apostles in the area. A description of Apostolic doctrine and ritual is included.

BENNETTA JULES-ROSETTE

MARATHI RELIGIONS. The Marathi language, which has demarcated the area in western India called Maharashtra for almost a thousand years, is an Indo-European language of North India that includes elements from the Dravidian languages of South India as well. Other elements of Maharashtrian culture—food, marriage customs, the patterns of caste groupings, and many aspects of religion—also reflect the fact that the Marathi-speaking area is a bridge between North and South. To the mix of Indo-European and Dravidian is added a mix of Vaiṣṇava and Śaiva traditions, and the whole is contained by a remarkable sense of the area's unity and integrity.

The major persistent natural and cultural subregions of Maharashtra are the coastal strip between the Arabian Sea and the Sahyādrī Mountains (Western Ghāṭs), called the Koṅkaṇ; the fertile northeastern region of Vidarbha, in central India; and, between these, the Deś, the Marathi-speaking part of the Deccan plateau, including the upper parts of the Godāvarī and Kṛṣṇā river systems.

The Development of Marathi and Maharashtrian Religion. The earliest examples of the Marathi language are found in inscriptions from the eleventh century. By the late thirteenth century, when the Yādava kingdom governed most of the area known as Maharashtra and Marathi literature began to appear, the language was already well developed. Three sorts of writings came into being at about the same time, setting in motion three very different religious movements.

In Vidarbha, a court-supported philosopher, Mukuṇḍarājā, wrote the *Vivekasindhu*, a philosophical treatise in the Advaita Vedānta tradition of Śaṅkara. Mukuṇḍarājā created no cult or school, but his influence is reflected in later work, particularly that of the seventeenth-century Rāmdās, a religio-political saint contemporaneous with the birth of the Marāṭhā nation under Śivājī.

The Deś saw the beginnings of two movements, each tracing its origin to a religious thinker of the thirteenth century and continuing today. The Vārkarī sect, which is the most popular devotional religious movement with an important literature in the area, understands itself to have begun with Jñāneśvar. Jñāneśvar was the author of an approximately nine-thousand-verse commentary on the *Bhagavadgītā* called the *Jñāneśvarī*, another work strongly influenced by the Advaita of Śaṅkara. A number of devotional poems (*abhaṅgas*) addressed to the deity Viṭhobā of Paṇḍharpūr are also ascribed to Jñāneśvar; it is on the basis of these that he is considered the first of a line of poet-saints who composed songs in honor of Viṭhobā, whom Vārkarīs take to be a form of Kṛṣṇa. These poet-saints include Nāmdev, a contemporary of Jñāneśvar to whom Hindi as well as Marathi poems are ascribed; Cokhāmeḷā, an untouchable; Eknāth, a sixteenth-century brahman from Paiṭhaṇ on the Godāvarī River; and Tukārām, the most popular Maharashtrian poet-saint, a seventeenth-century *śūdra* grocer who lived in Dehu, near Pune (Poona). Members of the Vārkarī sect, virtually all Maharashtrians, still sing the songs of these poet-saints and carry images of their feet in an annual pilgrimage to Paṇḍharpūr. [*See also* Poetry, *article on* Indian Religious Poetry.]

The Mahānubhāv sect is not so widely popular today as the Vārkarī sect, but it has an important place in the religious history of Maharashtra. Founded by the thirteenth-century Cakradhar, the Mahānubhāv sect produced a large body of prose hagiographies and poetry. The sect spread primarily in the valley of the Godāvarī River and in Vidarbha. Like the Vārkarīs, Mahānubhāvs are devotees of Kṛṣṇa; but they exceed the Vārkarīs in their rejection of brahmanic caste and pollution rules, and in their espousal of an ascetic way of life.

A third sect important in medieval Maharashtra was that of the Nāths. The Nāths' literature has not survived, but their influence can be discerned in the early history and literature of the Vārkarīs and Mahānubhāvs. The Nāths were a sect of ascetics and yogins who specialized in various kinds of occult knowledge and who were devoted to the god Śiva. Aside from legends concerning the Navanāth, or Nine Nāths, the strongest Nāth influence today is probably in the figure of Dattātreya, to be discussed below.

Maharashtrian Deities. Although the two surviving *bhakti* (devotional) sects of Maharashtra are more pronouncedly Vaiṣṇava (Kṛṣṇaite) than Śaiva, there is evidence of a Śaiva background against which they spread. And in the village and pastoral cults of Maharashtra, goddesses and Śaiva gods are far more prominent than Viṣṇu or Kṛṣṇa.

Pilgrimage deities. The most important pilgrimage deity of Maharashtra is Viṭhobā of Paṇḍharpūr, whose primary mythological indentification is with Kṛṣṇa, but who also has strong connections with Śiva and who may have originated in a pastoral hero cult. Besides Viṭhobā, most other major Maharashtrian pilgrimage deities are goddesses and Śaiva gods. Of the many Śiva temples in Maharashtra, the two most important to Indian pilgrimage traditions may be Bhīmaśaṅkar in Pune District and Tryaṃbakeśvar in Nasik District. Both temples are basic to the Maharashtrian landscape, since they are at the sources of the important Bhīmā and Godāvarī rivers, respectively. Along with several other Maharashtrian Śiva temples, these two claim to be among the most important Śiva temples of all of India, the twelve *jyotirliṅgas*. And Tryaṃbakeśvar, together with the nearby city of Nasik, is one of the four sites of the twelve-year cycle of Kumbha Melās.

Several other important pilgrimage deities, more or less closely identified with Śiva, appear to be deities of pastoralists and warriors, eventually adopted by settled agriculturalists as well. Perhaps the most prominent of these is Khaṇḍobā, whose temples at Jejurī, near Pune, and at Māḷegāv (Nanded District) attract large numbers of pilgrims from a wide range of castes. Other extremely popular pilgrimage deities of this sort are Śambhu Mahādev at Śiṅgṇāpūr (Satara District) and Jyotibā at Vāḍī Ratnāgiri (Kolhapur District).

Four goddess temples that ring the Marathi-speaking area are also among the principal Maharashtrian pilgrimage places: the temple of Mahālakṣmī at Kolhāpūr, that of Bhavānī at Tuḷjāpūr (Usmanabad District), that of Reṇukā at Māhūr (Nanded District), and that of Saptaśṛṅgī, at Vaṇī near Nasik. These temples are linked to the religious geography of all of India as three and a half of the one-hundred-eight *satī pīṭhas*, places where parts of Śiva's wife Satī were scattered throughout India; Saptaśṛṅgī is said to be the one-half *pīṭha* and thus is somewhat less important than the other three. Although they are all identified as *satī pīṭhas*, each goddess has her own history and individuality as well. Bhavānī, for example, is something of a warrior goddess. She was worshiped by the seventeenth-century Marāṭhā king Śivājī in the form of his sword. [*See also* Pilgrimage, *article on* Hindu Pilgrimage.]

Distinct from temple priests, who in Śaiva and goddess temples often belong to the *gurav* caste, there are special types of mendicant devotee-performers attached to several of the major pilgrimage deities of Maharashtra. *Vāghyā*s and *muraḷī*s, for instance, are such devotees of Khaṇḍobā: *muraḷīs* are a type of dancing girl attached to his temples, and *vāghyās* are male devotees whose devotional performances sometimes involve acting like dogs. The most popular of such folk-religious figures are *gondhaḷī*s, who are devotees of goddesses, particularly of Reṇukā of Māhūr. Their performance, the *gondhaḷ*, combines music and storytelling, usually at a wedding or other family occasion, but the *gondhaḷī* also serves as bard, singing the heroic *pavāḍā*s which celebrate Maharashtrian bravery from the time of Śivājī on. [*See also* Indian Religions, *article on* Rural Traditions.]

Other deities. The figure of Dattātreya illustrates a Maharashtrian reworking of religious influences from both North and South, and the synthesizing of Śaiva and Vaiṣṇava motifs as well. A *ṛṣi* ("seer") in Sanskrit epic and Puranic literature, Datta first appears in Marathi literature as one of the five Mahānubhāv incarnations of the supreme God, Parameśvara. By the sixteenth century, however, Datta is clearly in the mainstream Hindu tradition, and has begun to be represented as the Brahma-Viṣṇu-Śiva triad, in one body with three heads. Shortly before that time, incarnations of the god began to appear on Maharashtrian soil, and many believe that Datta as Sāī Bābā, as the Svāmī of Akkalkoṭ, or as some other *avatāra* has appeared in modern times. Datta's chief and very popular pilgrimage center is at Gaṇgāpūr, located to the south of Maharashtra in northern Karnataka state. As in the northern tradition, Datta is seen as the patron deity of ascetics. Another element in Maharashtrian Datta worship is that while he is seen as a brahman, and his temples are chiefly centers for brahman worshipers, he has also become *guru* for people in all walks of life, even, it is said, for prostitutes, and his three-headed image or an image of one of his *avatāras* is found at all levels of society.

The elephant-headed god Gaṇeś or Gaṇapati is also particularly important in Maharashtra. There is a formal pilgrimage route of eight centers, all fairly near Pune, where *svayaṃbhū* ("self-formed") elephant-headed stones bestow blessings as images of Gaṇeś, but much more frequently worshiped are the representations of Gaṇeś fixed over the doors of homes, brilliant with red coloring, among the stone sculptures on temple walls, and appearing here and there in the open countryside or in small shrines on city streets. Gaṇeś was the family deity of the Peśvās, the Citpāvan brahmans who ruled from Pune after the time of Śivājī, and the numerically weak but nevertheless influential Citpāvans are still among Gaṇapati's principal worshipers. The annual Gaṇeś festival has become a widely popular public event since 1893, when the nationalist leader Bal Gangadhar Tilak organized it as a way to celebrate patriotism through religious means. [*See also the biography of Tilak.*]

The god Rām is found in temples throughout Maharashtra, but seems not to carry the cultural importance found in great public events like the Rāmlīlā in the Hindi-speaking area. Rām's devotee, the monkey god Māruti (Hanumān), is tightly woven into Maharashtrian rural life, as a Māruti temple is found inside almost every Maharashtrian village or on its outskirts. Other deities prominent as village protectors are goddesses with names ending in *āī* ("mother"), *bāī* ("lady") or *devī* ("goddess").

Rituals. The ritual life of Maharashtrian Hindus includes festivals regulated by the calendar, celebrations of events in the human life cycle, and rituals performed in response to individual or collective crises.

Calendrical rites. Rituals occurring annually include pilgrimage festivals (*jatrās*) to particular places at particular times, and festivals celebrated locally or domestically in an annual cycle. Maharashtra follows the Hindu luni-solar calendar, ending months with the no-moon day (the *amānta* system), as in South India, rather than with the full moon day (the *pūrṇimānta* system), as in North India. The greatest concentration of pilgrimage festivals occurs during the month of Caitra (March–April), the first month of the Hindu calendar, but such festivals take place throughout the year. The pilgrimage deities mentioned above account for only a fraction of the thousands of *jatrās* occurring every year in Maharashtra.

Of local and domestic festivals, some of the most popular in Maharashtra are the following.

- Divāḷī: a complex of several festival days occurring at the end of the month of Āśvin and the beginning of the month of Kārtik (generally in October), celebrated domestically, most prominently by the decorating of homes with lighted lamps.
- Navarātra: a festival in honor of goddesses celebrated for the first nine days of the month of Āśvin (September–October); Navarātra culminates on the tenth day with Dasarā or Vijayadaśamī, a festival of triumph that is traditionally considered an auspicious day for inaugurating military campaigns or other enterprises.
- The Gaṇeś festival: a ten-day festival ending on the fourth day of the month of Bhādrapad (August–September), in which temporary images of the elephant-headed deity Gaṇeś are worshiped in home shrines (and, following Tilak's innovations, in elaborate neighborhood shrines in cities and towns as well); in some homes, women set up temporary shrines in honor of the goddess Gaurī (Pārvatī) for three days during the Gaṇeś festival.
- Vaṭasāvitrī: a *vrata* (a fast and ritual) performed by married women on the full moon day of the month of Jyeṣṭha (May–June) for their husbands' welfare.
- Nāg Pañcamī: one of the many days of fasting and worship during the month of Śrāvaṇ (July–August), this festival is held on the fifth day of the month and is characterized by the worship of snakes and by women's songs and games.
- Poḷā: a festival usually celebrated on the no-moon day at the end of the month of Śrāvaṇ, a day on which the bullocks used in agricultural work are decorated, worshiped, and led in procession around the village.

In addition to such annual festivals, there are certain days of each fortnight and of each week that are especially dedicated to particular gods and that are observed by special worship of those gods and/or by fasting in their honor. For example, Monday is for Śiva, Tuesday and Friday for goddesses, Thursday for Dattātreya, Saturday for Śani (Saturn), Sunday for Khaṇḍobā, the fourth day of each fortnight for Gaṇeś, the eleventh day of the fortnight for Viṭhobā, the thirteenth day for Śiva, and so on. [*See also* Hindu Religious Year.]

Life-cycle rites. Besides marriage and funeral rituals, those of the classical Hindu life cycle rites (*saṃskāras*) most commonly celebrated in Maharashtra today are the ceremony of naming a child (this is performed on or near the twelfth *(bārāvā)* day after the child's birth and is hence called Bārseṃ), and the ceremony, primarily among brahmans, of initiating young boys and investing them with the sacred thread *(muñja)*. In addition, there are several rituals celebrating the early married life and pregnancy of young women. These rituals are generally performed by women and are not included in the classical list of *saṃskāras*. Such, for example, are Maṅgaḷā Gaurī, the worship of the goddess Gaurī and playing of women's games on a Tuesday of the month of Śrāvaṇ, for the first five years of a woman's married life, and Ḍohāḷejevaṇ, a celebration in honor of a pregnant woman, named for the cravings of pregnancy *(ḍohāḷā)*. [*See also* Rites of Passage, *article on* Hindu Rites.]

Crisis rites. Rituals of crisis in Maharashtra most commonly take the form of a *navas:* one promises a deity that one will do a particular fast or pilgrimage in his honor, or make some particular offering to him, if one gets a certain desired object—most typically, the birth of a son. If that object is attained, one must keep, or "pay off," one's promise *(navas pheḍaṇeṃ)*. With the notable exception of Viṭhobā of Paṇḍharpūr, many of the chief pilgrimage deities of Maharashtra are said to answer such prayers *(navas pāvaṇeṃ);* and many Maharashtrian pilgrimages, whether at special festival times or otherwise, are made in fulfillment of a *navas*.

In addition, there are village deities, such as Marīāī, the cholera goddess, and Śītalā, the smallpox goddess, who are especially propitiated for curing individuals of disease and for averting or bringing to an end such disasters as epidemics and droughts which affect an entire village. Marīāī is served by a *potrāj*—always, until the contemporary conversion to Buddhism, an untouchable *mahār*—who carries a whip and a burning rope, wears a skirt made of women's blouse pieces, and acts as priest for the goddess.

A popular but elaborate ritual called the Satyanārāyaṇ Pūjā is most common in modern, urban environments. It is performed in fulfillment of a *navas*, for thanksgiving, or for prosperity or success of some sort.

Religion in Modern Maharashtra. Modern changes in Maharashtrian religion are many and varied, ranging from the training of women as ritual priests to a large-scale Buddhist conversion. Two streams of change in the nineteenth century affected the intellectual history of Hinduism, but seem not to have influenced common practice. Gopal Hari Deshmukh (1823–1892), writing as Lokahitavāḍī ("he who is concerned for the people's welfare"), set in motion a reform and liberalization of Hindu practice which was later organized as the Prārthanā Samāj, the "prayer society." This was the Maharashtrian counterpart of the Bengali Brāhmo Samāj, but was not as separated from mainstream Hindu life as the latter. [*See also* Brāhmo Samāj.] The "non-brahman movement" begun by Jyotibā Phule (1828–1890) was also liberalizing and rationalizing, but carried the additional message that brahman dominance was socially, politically, and, indeed, religiously destructive to the welfare of the lower classes. The chief carryover of Phule's movement in the twentieth century was political rather than religious.

The institutional changes of the modern period that do affect life in Maharashtra today include the Gaṇapati festival as reorganized by Tilak; the formation of the Rāṣṭrīya Svayaṃsevak Saṅgh, a paramilitary service organization for young men; and, most unusual of all, a mass conversion to Buddhism, chiefly among *mahār* untouchables. While the Rāṣṭrīya Svayaṃsevak Saṅgh (R.S.S.) has spread over much of India, it originated in the city of Nagpur in Vidarbha, and is still of great importance all over Maharashtra, particularly among brahmans. Begun by Dr. K. B. Hedgewar (1889–1940), the R.S.S. was both a Hindu revival organization that combined Sanskrit prayer with military drill, and a nationalistic service organization. Its leadership is celibate and promises lifelong dedication to the organization, but the majority of its members become associated with the youth groups of the R.S.S., and maintain their affiliation only as long as they are students. The R.S.S. is linked to the conservative Jan Sangh political party, but retains its separate existence as a nonpolitical body. It traces its intellectual heritage to the Hindu revivalistic thought of Bal Gangadhar Tilak and Vīr Savarkar, both also ardent nationalists.

The initial Buddhist conversion also took place in the city of Nagpur and has spread all over Maharashtra (and to many urban areas of India), but is of a completely different origin and purpose than any of the Hindu revival movements. After a series of frustrated attempts on the part of untouchables to enter temples, B. R. Ambedkar (1891–1956), an untouchable *mahār* educator, reformer, and statesman, declared in 1935 that he "would not die a Hindu." The conversion was postponed for twenty years while political activities took precedence, but just before his death, Ambedkar publically became a Buddhist and called for conversion to that once-important Indian religion. Four million adherents, chiefly in Maharashtra, now list themselves as Buddhist, and a Buddhist literature in Marathi, a growing order of Buddhist monks, and a program of building Buddhist *vihāras* (temples) now mark the Maharashtrian scene. Many of the converts draw inspiration from the presence of an astonishing series of ancient Buddhist cave-temples in Maharashtra, the most famous at Ajanta and Ellora. [*See also the biography of Ambedkar.*]

Women have been of consequence in Maharashtrian religion at least from the days of Cakradhar and Jñāneśvar. A pattern of prominent women devotees of even more prominent male saints was repeated in the twentieth century as Godāvarī Mātā succeeded Upāsanī Bābā at the important ashram at Sakori in Ahmadnagar District. Here the Kanyā Kumārī Sthān, a young women's religious training institute, was established, enabling women to become full-fledged ascetics. The most recent development is a program in Pune that trains women as Vedic ritual priests.

Religious Minorities. Of the non-Hindu religions in Maharashtra, Buddhism, Islam, and Christianity account for roughly 7, 8, and 1.5 percent of the population, respectively. There is little writing on either contemporary Islam or Christianity in the Maharashtrian context, but the past would indicate a considerable mixture of Hinduism and Islam: Shaykh Muḥammad was an honored saint-poet within the *bhakti* tradition in the fifteenth century; the god Dattātreya often appeared as a *faqīr,* or Muslim holy man, to his disciples; Hindus participated in great numbers in the Muslim Muḥarram festival, and visited the shrines of Ṣūfī saints. Christian conversion in the area, outside of the Portuguese presence in Goa, began in the nineteenth century, with the American Marathi Mission being the most important of the foreign groups. Justin Abbott and others of this mission did much to translate the Vārkarī poets into English, and one famous convert of the mission, Narayan Vaman Tilak, wrote Christian *bhakti* hymns in Marathi. The small but culturally and economically important group of Parsis, eighth-century Zoroastrian immigrants from Persia, is primarily based in Bombay and other large cities of Maharashtra. [*See* Parsis.] There is also a small group of Marathi-speaking Jews, the Bene Israeli, many of whom have migrated to Israel in recent years.

[*For further discussion of some of the important deities of Maharashtra, see* Gaṇeśa; Hanuman; Kṛṣṇaism; *and* Gāṇapatyas.]

BIBLIOGRAPHY

The most thorough and prolific writer on the religious traditions of Maharashtra, including folk traditions, is R. C. Dhere, who writes in Marathi. His *Viṭṭhala, Eka Mahāsamanvaya* (Poona, 1984) is the most comprehensive work on the Viṭhobā cult to date. The best work on this subject in English is G. A. Deleury's *The Cult of Viṭhobā* (Poona, 1960). Shankar Gopal Tulpule's *Classical Marāṭhī Literature from the Beginning to* AD 1818 in *A History of Indian Literature,* vol. 9, fasc. 4, edited by Jan Gonda (Wiesbaden, 1979), gives a thorough survey of Vārkarī and Mahānubhāv literature, as well as of other premodern religious literature in Marathi; this work includes generous bibliographical footnotes. An earlier work, R. D. Ranade's *Indian Mysticism: The Poet-Saints of Maharashtra* (1933; reprint, Albany, N.Y., 1983) provides extensive summaries of the thought of Rāmdās and most of the Vārkarī poet saints.

Madhukar Shripad Mate's *Temples and Legends of Maharashtra* (Bombay, 1962) describes several of the most important pilgrimage temples of Maharashtra; and thousands of pilgrimage festivals are listed in *Fairs and Festivals in Maharashtra,* vol. 10 of *Census of India, 1961,* part 7B (Bombay, 1969). Günther-Dietz Sontheimer's *Birobā, Mhaskobā und Khaṇḍobā: Ursprung, Geschichte und Umwelt von pastoralen Gottheiten in Mahārāṣṭra* (Wiesbaden, 1976) is a richly detailed study of the religious traditions of Maharashtrian pastoralists, including numerous oral myths in German translation. John M. Stanley analyzes the meaning of a Khaṇḍobā festival in "Special Time, Special Power," *Journal of Asian Studies* 37 (1977): 37–48. Two older works containing a wealth of information on Maharashtrian folklore are R. E. Enthoven's *The Folklore of Bombay* (London, 1924) and John Abbott's *The Keys of Power: A Study of Indian Ritual and Belief* (1932; reprint, Secaucus, N.J., 1974).

For the modern period, Matthew Lederle's *Philosophical Trends in Modern Mahārāṣṭra* (Bombay, 1976) provides a good survey of the major religious-philosophical thinkers. "Tradition and Innovation in Contemporary Indian Buddhism" by Eleanor Zelliot and Joanna R. Macy, in *Studies in the History of Buddhism,* edited by A. K. Narain (Delhi, 1980), pp. 133–153, is a study of the recent movement of conversion to Buddhism.

ELEANOR ZELLIOT and ANNE FELDHAUS

MARCION (d. 160?), founder of an independent Christian church in the second century and influential exponent of the idea that God's sole attribute is goodness. Marcion was born toward the end of the first century in Sinope, a city in Pontus, on the southern coast of the Black Sea. A shipowner by profession and a man of wealth, he was a member of the Christian church in his home city (where, according to some sources, his father was bishop), but he left there after being ejected by the church. He lived for a time in western Asia Minor but again left because his ideas found little acceptance. In Rome he became a member of that city's more cosmopolitan congregation, presenting it with the large gift of 200,000 sesterces, and came under the influence of Cerdo, a Christian teacher from Asia. As his ideas became more clearly defined, he ran into conflict with the leaders of the church in Rome, and in 144 he founded his own church (his money was returned), which spread rapidly throughout the Roman empire and came to rival the catholic church. By the end of the century, there were Marcionite congregations in cities throughout the Roman world, and writers in Greek (Justin Martyr), Latin (Tertullian), and Syriac (Bardesanes, or Bardaisan) were refuting his views.

Both because of his success in establishing an organization parallel to the "great" church, with its own bishops, elders, catechumens, liturgy, and canon of holy scripture, and his radical conception of God as love,

Marcion is a significant figure in early Christian history. He taught that Christianity has no relation to the Judaism from which it sprang, he rejected the Hebrew scriptures in their entirety, and he abbreviated the New Testament to conform to his teaching. He believed that the God of Jesus Christ has nothing to do with, and is superior to, the God of the Hebrew scriptures who created the world, and he believed that Jesus came to reveal an utterly new and strange God, who is of pure goodness and mercy and without wrath or judgment. Marcion claimed to have learned this message from the apostle Paul, who, he believed, was alone among the early Christian leaders in understanding the revelation in Christ. While most Christians saw continuity between the covenant with Israel and the new covenant initiated under Jesus, Marcion saw only contradiction and opposition, and by a selective reading of the scriptures he sought to restore and repristinate the original and authentic faith that had been obscured by Christian teachers. He did not, however, make any claims for himself, either as a prophet or as a holy man. He saw himself as a teacher and a man of learning who pointed beyond himself to the teachings of Jesus and Paul.

Like other Christian thinkers from this period whose views were not accepted by the growing consensus, Marcion has gone down in history as a "heretic," but this epithet should not obscure his importance. At a time when questions such as the relation of Christianity to Judaism, the place of the Hebrew scriptures (Christian Old Testament) in Christian life and thinking, the proper method for interpreting scripture (especially passages that describe God as capricious, despotic, or vindictive), and indeed the very terms in which the Christian faith would be expressed, were matters of intense dispute, Marcion provided clear and unequivocal answers. He also emphasized a central element in Christianity, the boundless grace of God, a point that was lost on his critics. Marcion repudiated all attempts to see Christ as the fulfillment of ancient prophecy. Christ is wholly unique and must be set apart from everything, that is, from Judaism, the created world, and the God who made the world.

His critics classified him among the gnostics, but he does not fit easily into this classification. On certain points—his contrast between the creator God and the high God who is the father of Jesus, his depreciation of the world, his dualism, his docetic Christology (his view that Christ did not have a real human body), and his rejection of the Old Testament—there were affinities with gnosticism, perhaps through the influence of Cerdo and others he met at Rome. But Marcion had little sympathy for the speculative systems of the gnostic teachers: he did not think that salvation comes through *gnōsis* ("knowledge"), and he had a different anthropology (there is no "spark of light" in human beings; they are wholly the work of the creator God) and a different view of redemption.

Marcion was the first Christian to put together a collection of books (a canon) as a standard for Christian life and teaching. His canon of the New Testament, in contrast to the generally accepted Christian collection of twenty-seven books, comprised an edited version of the gospel of Luke (omitting such parts as the infancy narratives, genealogy, baptism, and temptation) and ten epistles of Paul (not including *1 Timothy*, *2 Timothy*, and *Titus*) with the references to God as judge and passages dealing with punishment or the fulfillment of Jewish prophecy edited out. His effort to provide an original and authentic witness to the gospel was a powerful impetus toward the adoption of an approved list of books by the catholic church. Marcion also figures in the history of textual criticism of the New Testament, although recent scholarship has tended to see his work less as that of an independent witness and more as a testimony to one branch of the textual tradition.

Marcion wrote one book, *Antitheses*, which is known only through fragments and allusions in the writings of his critics. It consisted of a series of contradictory statements setting forth opposition between the creator God of the Old Testament and the good and benevolent God of Jesus, between the Jewish law and the Christian gospel. Though designed as a polemical and theological work, it assumed a creedlike status as a confession of faith within the Marcionite congregations and served as a key for interpreting the scriptures.

Besides taking an active part in the formation of the biblical canon, Marcion indirectly forced Christian thinkers of the second and third centuries to clarify their ideas on the relation between the Old Testament and the New Testament and led them to affirm that the Hebrew scriptures were not to be discarded by the church. In modern times, largely through the historical and theological interpretation of the nineteenth-century German church historian Adolf von Harnack, there has been renewed interest in Marcion as an original Christian thinker with an alternative vision of the Christian faith. In the twentieth century Marcion continues to have admirers as diverse as the Marxist Ernst Bloch and the historian Arnold Toynbee.

BIBLIOGRAPHY

Aland, Barbara. "Marcion: Versuch einer neuen Interpretation," *Zeitschrift für Theologie und Kirche* 70 (1973): 420–447.

Blackman, Edwin C. *Marcion and His Influence*. London, 1948.

Harnack, Adolf von. *Marcion: Das Evangelium vom fremden Gott; Eine Monographie zur Geschichte der Grundlegung der*

katholischen Kirche. Leipzig, 1921. A fundamental study, with a collection of the most important texts.
Hoffman, R. Joseph. *Marcion and the Restitution of Christianity.* Chico, Calif., 1984.

ROBERT L. WILKEN

MARCIONISM. The movement known as Marcionism was founded in the second century by Marcion, an early Christian teacher from Sinope in Asia Minor. Of the many early Christian sects the Marcionites were among the most successful, creating a parallel organization to the catholic church. The Marcionite church existed in recognizable form for over three hundred years, until the middle of the fifth century. The oldest inscription from any Christian church building is from a Marcionite church in a small village south of Damascus. The inscription, in Greek, identifies the building as the "gathering place [*synagoge*] of the Marcionites of the village of Lebabon of the Lord and Savior Jesus Christ under the leadership of Paul the presbyter" and is dated 318–319. This inscription is evidence not only of the continuation of the Marcionite movement into the fourth century, but of the benefit it received from the toleration extended to the catholic church. The use of the word *Marcionite,* a term of opprobrium to other Christians, shows the veneration in which the founder was held.

Marcion broke with the catholic church in Rome in 144. By the end of the second century, Marcionite churches could be found in cities throughout the Roman empire. The central elements of Marcionism are rejection of the Old Testament (the Hebrew scriptures) and the creator God portrayed there; belief in a strange God who has nothing to do with the world and who is revealed in Jesus Christ; acceptance of Marcion's Bible, a pared-down version of the New Testament comprising an edited text of the gospel of Luke and ten epistles of Paul; and acceptance of Marcion's own work, *Antitheses,* used as a key to the interpretation of the scriptures. The Marcionites followed a strict ascetic life that forbade marriage and encouraged the avoidance of wine and meat (but allowed fish). Perforce the movement spread through the winning of new converts, not by birth, and yet was extraordinarily successful.

Marcionism developed its own brand of orthodoxy, but under Apelles, a disciple who eventually broke with his master, there was an effort to modify Marcion's dualism and to trace all things back to a single principle. Apelles also taught that Christ had a real body though he did not undergo a human birth. Over the centuries, however, the main ideas of the group remained remarkably durable.

Evidence of the survival of Marcionism can be found from the third, fourth, and fifth centuries in all parts of the Roman world: Asia Minor, Crete, western and eastern Syria, Palestine, Alexandria, Carthage, and Rome. To untutored Christians its churches could hardly be distinguished from the catholic church, so similar were they in organization and ritual. To bishops and theologians, however, Marcionism was a deadly foe, and a series of key thinkers opposed it vigorously. It is mentioned by such diverse writers as Irenaeus, Tertullian, Origen, Cyril of Jerusalem, Basil of Caesarea, Epiphanius of Cyrus, Adamantius, Bardesanes (Bardaisan), Theodore of Mopsuestia, and Theodoret of Cyrus. A fourth-century creed from Laodicea, a city on the Syrian coast, confesses "one God, ruler, God of the law and the gospel," suggesting that the framers thought it necessary to separate catholic Christianity from Marcionism. As late as the fifth century some villages in Syria were predominantly Marcionite. After that time little is known about the movement.

BIBLIOGRAPHY

Blackman, Edwin C. *Marcion and His Influence.* London, 1948.
Harnack, Adolf von. *Marcion: Das Evangelium vom fremden Gott; Eine Monographie zur Geschichte der Grundlegung der katholischen Kirche.* Leipzig, 1921.

ROBERT L. WILKEN

MARDUDJARA RELIGION. I have coined the name *Mardudjara* to refer collectively to Aborigines belonging to the Gardudjara, Budidjara, Guradjara, Manjildjara, and Giyadjara linguistic groups. Their homelands surround Lake Disappointment, a huge salt lake on the western side of the Gibson Desert in Western Australia, between 22° to 25° south latitude and 122° to 126° east longitude. It is impossible to estimate accurately the population of these groups prior to contact with Europeans, but in 1985 they numbered about eight hundred. Most of them, members of the now-dominant Manjildjara and Gardudjara groups, live at the Aboriginal settlement of Jigalong. All Mardudjara speak mutually intelligible dialects of the Western Desert language, which is spoken over a wider area than any other Aboriginal language in Australia.

There are no longer any Mardudjara living a nomadic hunter-gatherer life beyond the range of white Australian cultural influences. A steady outmigration took place during the half century preceding the mid-1960s. They have abandoned their former local organization, which was based on small, scattered bands exploiting large overlapping tracts in their homelands. Despite major changes that resulted from their involvement with whites, the Mardudjara have retained strong continuities with their past in major cultural elements such as kinship, marriage, religion, and values. Although this account refers to the era before contact, it is based on direct observation as well as interviews, for much of the religious life has continued since the Mardudjara became sedentary. Because religion was so fundamental to their lives in the desert, it has been tenaciously maintained in the settlement milieu and retains its vital importance to the Mardudjara.

The Spiritual Imperative. Australian Aboriginal cultures are notable for the great contrast they exhibit between material technologies that are relatively unelaborated and social and religious forms that reveal great richness and complexity. The adaptational skills of the Aborigines are evidenced by their success in colonizing a predominantly arid land; yet to appreciate fully their cultural accomplishments, one must understand how completely religion pervades their lives. The Aborigines base their existence firmly in the belief that spiritual beings are the sources and controllers of all power. Spiritual power flows freely into the human realm as long as the Aborigines act out their lives in accordance with the design laid out by their spiritual forefathers in the world-creating era. Aborigines learn obedience to the dictates of a heritage that, while transmitted by their ancestors, is nonetheless believed to have its origins in spiritual, not human, actions. Since all knowledge and power are said to derive from the spiritual realm, the Aborigines in effect deny the human innovatory component in their culture. They understand history in cosmic rather than chronological terms, and primacy is accorded to spiritual conceptions of cause, being, and purpose. This does not mean that people are denied their individuality, but simply that creativity is not admissible as part of the measure of a person's social worth. In the Aboriginal view, human worth is based on conformity to the founding design and on its perpetuation, which ensures that power will continue to flow from the spiritual realm and thus maintain the fertility of all life forms.

At the heart of Aboriginal religion is the Dreaming, a complex concept that embodies the creative era long past, as well as the present and the future. During the Dreaming powerful ancestral beings, singly or in groups, transformed the face of Australia in the course of their wanderings and creative activities. They hunted and gathered in much the same way as their human descendants, but much of their behavior was on a grander scale and with a level of unpredictability, perversity, and amorality not permitted the humans they left behind as pioneers of human society. Aborigines point to a host of topographical features as undeniable proof of the Dreaming's reality. The eternal verities of the Dreaming are also encoded in mythology, rituals, songs, and objects, but all relate back to the land, the bedrock of metaphysical conceptions that formulate an indivisible unity of spirit and substance. [*See* Dreaming, The.]

When at the conclusion of their earthly wanderings the creative beings "died," they metamorphosed into landforms or celestial bodies, where their spiritual essence remains, withdrawn from, but watchful of, human affairs. The creative beings release enabling power into the human realm in response not to prayer or sacrifice, which have no place in Aboriginal religion, but to ritual performance. Individuals who are able to transcend their human consciousness for brief periods (during dreams, dances, visions, or heightened emotional states) may also bring about a release of power. The withdrawn creative ancestors use spirit beings as intermediaries for direct intervention in human affairs, most often while people are sleeping, and such encounters result in the transference of new knowledge and power from the spiritual realm. To maintain the unity they perceive in their cosmic order, the Mardudjara must, as their spiritual imperative demands of them, perform rituals regularly and in the proper manner, and they must also obey the dictates of the life design that is the creators' legacy.

The Totemic Connection. The Mardudjara see themselves as quite distinct from the natural world because of their culture and their ritual control over all fertility, yet they acknowledge their intimate relationship with it. Totemic beliefs express and affirm this link, by positing a unity between individuals or groups and elements of the natural world. To the Mardudjara, the animals, birds, plants, or minerals that are identified as totems are signs or exemplifiers of the link between humans and nature, so their religious significance lies not in the particular identity of the totem, but in the linkage it represents. Totemic connections between groups and natural species are not of great importance to the Mardudjara, for whom the major significance of totemism lies in its role of connecting individuals to their spiritual origins. These ascribed affiliations are experienced as enduring and unbreakable bonds uniting every Aborigine to the great powers of the Dreaming. The two most important forms of individual totemism among the Mardudjara I term "ancestral" and "conception"; they are closely related. Wherever creative beings traveled during the Dreaming, they left behind inexhaustible supplies of life essence or power from which tiny spirit-children emanate. Thus a person's ancestral totem derives from whichever creative being or group of beings "left him or her behind." The totem is identified by linking the area or site at which an individual was conceived with knowledge regarding which creative beings are known to have traveled there during the Dreaming. Before entering its human mother, the spirit-child disguises itself in some plant, animal, or mineral form, which, when recognized by the parents, becomes the child's conception totem. Although people may share the same object or species as a totem, no two individuals share the same set of circumstances or events that mark their "coming into being."

The combination of these two forms of totemic affiliation not only enables everyone to establish his or her descent from the marvels of the Dreaming epoch, but also provides each individual with a unique facet of social identity. The medium of the totem itself is less important culturally than the message of a personalized link between the individual and the associated spirit-child and Dreaming event.

Life Cycle and Male Initiation. The Mardudjara do not possess reincarnation beliefs, but they view life as cyclical in that it begins and ends with a spirit or soul that is indestructible. The life crises of birth, menarche, and marriage are not ritualized. A young woman's change of status to wife and mother is unheralded, and involves an essential continuity in activities, for she is already an accomplished food provider. Males, by comparison, undergo a protracted and richly detailed initiation into social adulthood and are not permitted to marry until they have passed through a long series of named initiatory stages. They learn to endure physical operations, to obey their elders, to observe strict taboos, to hunt meat for the older men in payment for ritual knowledge, and to assist in the supervision and care of younger novices.

At about age sixteen, after they have undergone minor rites involving tooth evulsion and the piercing of the nasal septum, youths are circumcised amid a great deal of ceremonial that is modeled symbolically on death and rebirth. The large ceremonies that conclude several months of preparation focus the energy and attention of the community on the several novices who are circumcised together. Within a year full manhood will be attained via subincision, an operation in which the ventral surface of the penis is slit open. Of the initiatory stages that follow, the most important is the Mirdayidi, a ceremonial feast held at the site of a group's secret cache of sacred objects, which are then revealed to the novice for the first time. After his introduction to the spiritual roots of his own being, a young man must subsequently go through the same ritual in neighboring territories and thus gain formal admission to the natural resources and ritual activities in those areas. The final initiatory stages entail the cutting and carving of sacred objects symbolizing the novice's links to his home territory, its creative beings, and the Dreaming. This stage completed, a man is entitled to claim his betrothed in marriage. Throughout the rest of his life he continues to acquire more knowledge through participation in rituals, and by middle age he is referred to as a *nindibuga* ("knowledgeable one"). With old age comes increased wisdom, respect, and a less physically active role in ritual life.

Women's Role in the Religious Life. Men control the secret and sacred core of the religion and the major rituals whose performance is considered by all Mardudjara to be essential to the future of their society. Women do not dispute men's dominance of the religious life. They, too, are actively involved in many aspects of it, and have their own secret-sacred rituals and associated objects, but they devote much less time to religious activities than men do and must arrange their activities to fit in with the plans of the men, not vice versa. Women collect the bulk of the food supply and maintain the life of the camp while men are engaged in religious activity, but they are also active participants in many rituals that are held in the camping area. In a passive sense, too, women and children provide a vital baseline or antithesis for men's division of life into dangerous-exclusive and mundane-inclusive dimensions. The conviction of mature men that only they have the knowledge to control powerful and dangerous spiritual forces invests their religious life with much of its tension and excitement. [*For further discussion of the religious life of Aboriginal women, see* Australian Religions, *overview article.*]

Mythology and Song Sequence. Mardudjara learn much about their spiritual heritage and about the Dreaming from a rich mythology, which relates how things came to be as they are and outlines the memorable events of the Dreaming era. Long narrative myths chronicle the travels of the creative beings, following the paths they took and dwelling on the naming of places, but details of their secret-sacred doings are known only to initiated men. Together with song sequences and, in many cases, rituals, these narratives broaden people's horizons by providing vivid mental and "historical" maps of areas that may as yet be unseen, so that when people do visit such places for the first time they already "know" them in a religious sense. There are times and situations that are conducive to the telling of myths, even when this is an informal affair: for example, when children have the spiritual significance of landforms explained to them, or when initiates view secret-sacred objects for the first time and have extra details added to the version of the myth they already know.

All major rituals have an associated sequence of

songs, which follows the movement of the creative beings concerned and highlights in cryptic fashion the more notable events of the Dreaming. Rote learning of the hundreds of songs in a given sequence is made easier by the brevity of each song, which consists only of a few words, and by repetition (each is sung several times). There is great variation in pitch, tempo, and loudness, and the singing often generates great excitement among performers and audience alike. In some public rituals women and children join in the singing and sometimes dance. The song sequence and myth associated with a given ritual are often very similar in theme, but the song sequence is not a mnemonic for the myth such that it would be possible to reconstruct the myth from the songs.

Ritual. Mardudjara group rituals are culturally more important than individual rites, but both have the same aim: to induce the flow of power from the spiritual realm for human benefit. The manipulative aspects of ritual as communication are most evident in individual rites, most of which are publicly performed and socially approved. However, some individuals and groups are believed to practice sorcery, which is invoked at times as an explanation for serious illness or sudden death. Most individual ritual acts are spontaneous, as when magic is used to make a strong wind abate or to beckon a rain-bearing cloud. Although any adult with the requisite knowledge can perform such acts, they are most often the task of diviner-curers *(mabarn)*, who are said to possess stronger psychic and magical powers than others. These part-time specialists use their diagnostic and curative skills for the benefit of sick individuals and the community at large.

One vitally important ritual that involves relatively few actors is the "increase" rite. This generally simple and brief rite is performed annually at particular sites, scattered throughout the Western Desert, that are the spirit homes of many different plants and animals. The purpose of the increase rite is to summon the spirits concerned to emerge, scatter, and be plentiful. There is at least one such site within the home area of every local group, so the Mardudjara and their neighbors are mutually dependent in ensuring through ritual the continued supply of food resources.

The major focus of group rituals is the Gabudur ("big meeting"), a large assembly of bands from a wide area, who meet perhaps once or twice a year at a prearranged site when food and water resources permit. These gatherings mark the high points of the Mardudjara social calendar, when much activity is crammed into a short space of time in an atmosphere of excitement and intensified sociality. Besides their centrally important religious functions, the Big Meetings provide an occasion for settling major disputes, arranging marriages, gift exchanges, and disseminating a large amount of information and gossip. Initiatory rituals usually form the major focus of religious activity, but many other ceremonies are held as well, and the exchange of religious lore is a major item of business. Initially there is an important division between hosts and visitors, but this soon dissolves in favor of kinship considerations in the conduct of the affairs at hand. The timing and coordination of large numbers of people and a complex division of labor demand planning and direction. An informal gathering of mature men directs the meeting, and the host group is most active in master-of-ceremonies roles. There is much discussion and consultation between the sexes and among the groups present. Ritual leadership is situational and changes as the rituals performed change. Ritual activities usually alternate between the camp area and secret bush grounds that are tabooed to women and children. Singing and dancing sometimes continue day and night.

Both men and women attain senior ritual status by repeated participation in the religious life over a period of many years and by diligent performance of their allotted tasks. The men with the highest status are generally older; they prepare food for ceremonial feasts, advise and direct rituals, dance the major secret-sacred dances, and caretake the caches of sacred objects. Next in the hierarchy are the active middle-aged men, who manage the ritual activity, transmit directives from those above them, and perform many important dances. Below them are the legmen, who play major roles as hunters and as supervisors of novices. At the lowest level are the partly initiated young male novices, who must obey all instructions, look on in silence, and learn.

Group rituals may be organized, too, when enough bands are assembled to provide the needed personnel. The death of anyone older than an infant is an occasion for ritual, which is performed by members of bands that are in the vicinity at the time.

The Mardudjara have two major ritual categories: *mangunydjanu*, said to have been passed down from the Dreaming; and *bardundjaridjanu* ("from the dream spirit"), which have been revealed to humans during their dreams. The Dreaming rituals predominate, but it is highly likely that they were originally of the second type, wherein spirit-being intermediaries of the creative beings encounter humans during dreams and reveal ritual information. Men share these revelations with others, who then have similar dream experiences and add details concerning the necessary body decorations, song lyrics and tunes, and dances. When a new ritual comes into being, the old one is passed on to other groups and, with the passage of time and over great distances, becomes identified as a Dreaming ritual. The great appeal of the dream-spirit ritual is that it requires no special ground and can be staged with a minimum of preparation by small groups. Women and children join in the singing and a little of the dancing, and are excluded from only a small part of the proceedings. Although its secret-sacred element is not large, dream-spirit ritual is taken just as seriously by the men as are the important Dreaming rituals.

The Mardudjara identify some of their rituals in terms of a specific, primary purpose, such as rainmaking or increase of species, but all their rituals fulfill very important functions in the culture. As acts of communication and commemoration, rituals maintain the relevance of the Dreaming in the present. They are educational because novices are invariably involved, and they are beneficial because participants acquire strength and protection against malevolent powers through contact with the spiritual realm. To be effective, rituals require the harmonious unity of participants and the complete absence of conflict. In the Western Desert, group rituals override many other kinds of allegiances and thus serve to dilute rather than reinforce any tendencies toward local parochialism. The widely shared major rituals, in particular, force people's attention outward to regional concerns and wider bonds of interdependence, in which survival in this extremely harsh land is ultimately grounded.

Sites and Portable Objects. Particular landforms and a variety of portable objects provide tangible reminders of the reality and power of the Dreaming. The sites created in the epoch of the Dreaming elicit powerful emotions of belonging that anchor a people to their home territory. Portable objects derive sacredness and power from their believed origins in, or close association with, the Dreaming. The most sacred are stones said to be the metamorphosed parts of the bodies of ancestral beings and wooden boards that men carve in representation of similar power-laden objects that were carried by the creative beings. In addition to these highly valued group-owned objects are those that are individually owned. Each man has a bundle of secret and nonsecret paraphernalia; these are often items of gift exchange and are frequently displayed and discussed when groups of men meet informally.

Conclusion. The genius in Mardudjara religion resides in its successful accommodation of two strongly contradictory elements: the reality of an inherently dynamic culture and a dominant ideology of changelessness. This ideology is founded in the concept of the Dreaming, which ordained a life design that is held to be fixed and immutable, so as to assure (prior to the coming of Europeans, that is) the continuity of present and future with the founding past. Throughout the desert there is a continual diffusion and circulation of religious lore, and Aborigines are regularly engaged in the creation, acquisition, performance, and transmission of their religion. How, then, can the Mardudjara accommodate the undeniable facts of change in an ideological framework that entertains no notion of progress or evolution?

A close examination of the structure of their rituals provides an important clue. Each "new" ritual is in fact a unique recombination of already existing constituent elements rather than a structure fabricated from hitherto unknown components. The assimilation of incoming rituals is made easy because they contain so much that is already familiar. In their long history of isolation from the rest of the world, Aborigines were spared the trauma of confronting radically different or alien cultural forms. Thus the kinds of change and innovation they have encountered are those which "fit the forms of permanence," as W. E. H. Stanner so aptly put it in his seminal work *On Aboriginal Religion* (1968, p. 168).

Not all the knowledge derivable from the Dreaming is embodied in the life-design legacy that the Mardudjara faithfully perpetuate. Further knowledge and power are available to the living through the mediating activities of spirit beings, which link the spiritual and human realms. But how, then, can newly acquired knowledge undergo transformation from peripheral, individually experienced phenomena into communally shared and supposedly timeless structures of the religious life? One example of this process was provided above, in the brief description of the creation of dream-spirit rituals from what initially are highly individual experiences. But once in existence, both ritual structures and song sequences become highly circumscribed in performance, and the necessity for faithful reproduction precludes them from becoming common avenues for the incorporation of new religious knowledge that is individually acquired. Mythology, on the other hand, has an inherent flexibility that makes it an ideal vehicle for incorporative purposes. In the easy and informal atmosphere of myth telling, people are free to indulge in elaboration and character development while leaving intact the main story line and theme. But myths also lend themselves readily to expansion to accommodate new information flowing from dream revelations and the discovery of hitherto unlocated sacred objects. Once new knowledge is embedded within existing myths, the Aborigines may examine the associated song sequence, if one exists, and reinterpret the meaning of the cryptic references therein, so as to accord with the truths of the expanded myth. In this way, and in the absence of the written word, changing political, social, and religious realities are validated and absorbed effortlessly into the ahistorical, cosmological flow of time. Thus is the "is-now" transformed into the "ever-was" of the Dreaming.

BIBLIOGRAPHY

Two monographs that deal with the past and present of Mardudjara religion are my own *The Jigalong Mob: Aboriginal Victors of the Desert Crusade* (Menlo Park, Calif., 1974) and *The Mardudjara Aborigines: Living the Dream in Australia's Desert* (New York, 1978). Aspects of Western Desert religion are discussed in Ronald M. Berndt's *Australian Aboriginal Religion*, 4 vols. (Leiden, 1974), in Ronald M. Berndt and Catherine H. Berndt's *The World of the First Australians*, 2d ed. (Sydney, 1977), and in an early monograph by the same authors, *A Preliminary Account of Field Work in the Ooldea Region, Western South Australia* (Sydney, 1945). A book by Richard A. Gould, *Yiwara: Foragers of the Australian Desert* (New York, 1969), contains details concerning desert ritual and belief.

ROBERT TONKINSON

MARDUK (also known as Bel, "lord") was a god of the city of Babylon who rose from being an obscure god of the Sumerian pantheon to become head of the Babylonian pantheon by the first millennium BCE. The name was probably pronounced *Marutuk,* which possibly had the short form *Marduk.* Etymologically it is probably derived from *amar-Utu* ("bull calf of the sun god Utu"). This name may not be genealogically accurate, since Marduk was normally considered to be the son of Enki, the god of underground fresh waters. It may reflect an earlier genealogy, or may have had a political origin, in which case it would indicate that the city of Babylon was in the cultural orbit of the more important city of Sippar (whose god was Utu, the sun god) in the Early Dynastic times (early third millennium BCE). Marduk was probably already the god of Babylon in this early period, but he first became a great god with the rise of Babylon as capital of the Old Babylonian kingdom under Hammurabi in the eighteenth century BCE. The kings of the Old Babylonian dynasty owed special allegiance to Marduk as god of Babylon, and he became in effect the royal god.

Marduk continued to rise in popularity after the decline of the Old Babylonian period. When his (captured) cult statue was returned to Babylon during the reign of Nebuchadrezzar I in the twelfth century BCE, Marduk was officially recognized as head of the Babylonian pantheon. His rise was effected in theological terms through his identification with Asarluhi, the god of the minor southern city of Kuaru, who was closely associated with Enki and was considered his firstborn son. The process of identifying Marduk and Asarluhi began before the establishment of the Old Babylonian kingdom, for it is attested in a letter-prayer of King Siniddinam of Larsa in which Asarluhi is called "god of Babylon." Marduk became known as the firstborn of Enki, and he took Asarluhi's place as Enki's assistant/partner in the magical literature. The identification of Marduk with Asarluhi was eventually so thorough that Asarluhi ceased to be remembered as an originally distinct god, and the name "Asarluhi" was simply used as the name for Marduk, both in Akkadian literature and in the Sumerian portion of bilingual Sumerian-Akkadian literature (where Marduk appears in the parallel Akkadian line).

The ultimate rise of Marduk to become king of the Babylonian pantheon is described in *Enuma elish,* the most important mythological work in which Marduk appears. This lengthy myth was written in the second half of the second millennium, probably circa 1200 BCE. It declares its main purpose to be the exaltation of the god Marduk. *Enuma elish* was a state myth, and it was read aloud to the assembled populace as part of the Akitu festival, the spring New Year celebration, in the first millennium BCE. [*See* Enuma Elish *and* Akitu.]

Marduk's political fortunes are also mythologized in an esoteric text called the *Tribulations of Marduk* or the *Ordeal of Marduk.* Although it was originally understood to be a tale of a dying and resurrected god, there is no basis for this interpretation and no evidence at all that Marduk was a vegetation-type dying god. The text is cast in the form of an esoteric cultic commentary, possibly of events of the New Year ritual. Unlike other extant esoteric commentaries, this one was written for wide distribution. It relates cultic elements of the ritual to the misfortunes of Marduk, who has been captured, sentenced, and imprisoned by other gods; at the time of the text someone is interceding on behalf of Marduk, and there is a hint in the text that Marduk is or is about to be freed. The text is manifestly political, with the enmity between Ashur and Marduk alluding to that between Assyria and Babylonia. There may also be an allusion to the return of the statue of Marduk in 669 BCE from the "Assyrian captivity" it had remained in since Sennacherib's destruction of the temple of Marduk twenty years earlier. The celebration of the statue's return as a vindication of Marduk may be analogous to the composition of *Enuma elish* on the occasion of an earlier return of the god's statue.

Marduk is prominent in the magical literature, particularly in the Marduk-Ea (originally, Asarluhi-Enki) type of incantation. In these texts, a problem situation (such as illness) is described. Asarluhi (Marduk) relates the problem to Enki (Ea), who responds with a formulaic "My son, what do I know that you do not know, to your knowledge what can I add?" Enki then spells out a ritual to be followed to alleviate the problem. Here Asarluhi-Marduk is seen as almost the overseer of humanity. This involvement with humanity is also underscored in *Shurpu,* a ritual text used to relieve the distress of someone suffering for a sin of which he has no knowledge; in it Marduk is addressed as the god who is able to preserve and restore his worshipers. Marduk was considered a powerful and fierce god who punished sinners but who at the same time could be merciful and pardon his followers. In this judgmental role he is the subject of several literary prayers and of *Ludlul bel nemeqi* ("I will praise the wise lord"), sometimes called "the Babylonian *Job,*" a wisdom work about a righteous sufferer whose fortunes declined abysmally but who was ultimately restored by Marduk.

[*See also* Dying and Rising Gods *and* Mesopotamian Religions, *overview article.*]

BIBLIOGRAPHY

Frymer-Kensky, Tikva. "The Tribulations of Marduk: The So-called 'Marduk Ordeal Text.'" *Journal of the American Oriental Society* 103 (January–March 1983): 131–141.

Lambert, W. G. "Three Literary Prayers of the Babylonians." *Archiv für Orientforschung* 19 (1959–1960): 47–66.

Lambert, W. G. *Babylonian Wisdom Literature.* Oxford, 1960. See pages 21–62.

Lambert, W. G. "The Reign of Nebuchadnezzar I." In *The Seed of Wisdom: Essays in Honor of Theophile James Meek,* edited by W. S. McCullough, pp. 3–13. Toronto, 1964.

Lambert, W. G. "Studies in Marduk." *Bulletin of the School of Oriental and African Studies* 47 (1984): 1–9.

Soden, Wolfram von. "Gibt es ein Zeugnis defür, dass die Babylonier an die Wiederauferstehung Marduks geglaubt haben?" *Zeitschrift für Assyriologie* 51 (May 1955): 130–166.

Sommerfeld, Walter. *Der Aufstieg Marduks: Die Stellung Marduks in der babylonischen Religion des zweiten Jahrtausends v. Chr.* "Alter Orient und Altes Testament," vol. 213. Neukirchen-Vluyn, 1982.

TIKVA FRYMER-KENSKY

MARETT, R. R. (1866–1943), British philosopher and anthropologist, who introduced the theory of preanimism and the term *animatism* into the scholarly debate. Robert Ranulph Marett was born on the Channel Island of Jersey on 13 June 1866. He was educated at Balliol College, Oxford, specializing in the classics, philosophy, and ethics, and in 1891 he was elected fellow of Exeter College, Oxford, where he remained for the whole of his academic career. His anthropological interests were fired by reading his fellow-Oxonian Andrew Lang's book *Custom and Myth* (1884) and after 1893 by association with E. B. Tylor (1832–1917), whose friend and disciple he became. In 1893 he submitted a prize essay entitled "The Ethics of Savage Races" which was examined by Tylor. Despite the difference in their ages, a close friendship began, and as Tylor's powers began to wane, Marett became his assistant. Marett later wrote a bibliographical memoir, *Tylor* (1936).

On Tylor's retirement, Marett was appointed in 1910 reader in social anthropology at Oxford, a post which he held until 1936, when he was succeeded by A. R. Radcliffe-Brown. For some years he was also rector (i.e., president) of Exeter College. He traveled widely in Europe, visited Australia once, in 1914, and in 1930 delivered the Lowell Lectures in Boston. He was Gifford Lecturer at the University of Saint Andrews twice, in 1931–1932 and 1932–1933, and the two published volumes of these lectures, *Faith, Hope and Charity in Primitive Religion* (1932) and *Sacraments of Simple Folk* (1933), Marett believed to embody his best work. He also had an interest in prehistoric archaeology, and he conducted and supervised excavations at the Mousterian site of La Cotte de Saint Brelade on his native island of Jersey. He died on 18 February 1943.

As an anthropological theorist, Marett's reputation was made virtually overnight, by the publication in 1900 of his paper "Preanimistic Religion" (*Folklore,* June 1900), in which he called into question Tylor's theory of "animism" and introduced the terms *preanimism* and *animatism* (which are not synonyms). During the next few years he wrote extensively on this theme, suggesting that *tabu* is best understood as "negative magic" and emphasizing the importance of the Melanesian—actually common Pacific—word *mana* as its positive counterpart. *Mana* he explained most fully in a paper, "The Conception of *Mana,*" delivered at the Oxford Science of Religion Congress in 1908, and in an article, "Mana," in Hastings's *Encyclopaedia of Religion and Ethics,* vol. 8 (1915).

Where Marett differed most strikingly from other late Victorian anthropologists in Britain was in his degree of fellow-feeling with and indebtedness to the French sociologists of the *Année sociologique* school. This made him, in effect, the first of the British social anthropologists and gave his later work especially a dimension largely absent from the writings of his predecessors.

Marett's style was always admirably lucid, often being further illuminated by wit and a certain irony. Today he tends to be evaluated chiefly for work done between 1899 and 1910, to the neglect of his more mature writings. He will, however, always have an important place in the history of both anthropology and comparative religion, and he was also highly significant as an advocate of academic anthropology and as a trainer of anthropologists.

[*See also* Animism and Animatism; Preanimism; *and the biography of Tylor.*]

BIBLIOGRAPHY

Works by Marett. In addition to works cited in the text, Marett's *Anthropology* (London, 1911) should be consulted, as should *The Threshold of Religion*, 3d ed. (London, 1915), a collection of his important early papers. Included in this collection are "Preanimistic Religion" (1900) and "The Conception of *Mana*" (1908). *A Jerseyman at Oxford* (Oxford, 1941) is Marett's highly informative and entertaining autobiography.

Works about Marett. There is no biography or full critical study, but see *Custom Is King: Essays Presented to R. R. Marett on His Seventieth Birthday*, edited by Leonard Halford Dudley Buxton (London, 1936). This work contains a personal appreciation by the editor and a full bibliography. See also the entry on Marett by John N. Mavrogordato in the *Dictionary of National Biography, 1941–1950* (Oxford, 1959), and the discussion in my book *Comparative Religion: A History* (London, 1975), pp. 65–71.

ERIC J. SHARPE

MARI AND MORDVIN RELIGION. The Mari and Mordvin languages together form the so-called Volga group within the Finno-Ugric linguistic family. In international literature, the Mari people are better known as the Cheremis (from the Old Russian name *Chermisy*). Recently, the self-designation *Mari* also has become accepted into administrative use. In the mid-1980s most of the Mari were living on the left bank of the big curve of the Volga River in the Mari A.S.S.R. Their population in 1980 was 599,000, or 91.2 percent of the total population of this republic. The Mari may be divided into three groups based on their differing environments: the Mountain Mari, the smallest group; the Meadow Mari, the largest group; and the so-called Eastern Mari, which is the youngest group, having developed only in the seventeenth century.

The Mordvins (from the Old Russian name *Mordva*) consist of two related groups, speaking the Erzä and Mokša dialects of the Mordvin language. They differ from each other to such an extent that the speakers of Erzä and Mokša do not understand one another. Two separate literary languages have been formed accordingly. The total number of the Mordvin population, living between the Volga and Oka rivers in the Mordovian A.S.S.R., is 1,263,000, 77.8 percent of the total population of the republic. In addition, there are some separated settlements in the Tatar and Bashkir republics. The population of the Erzä is approximately twice that of the Mokša. The Erzä could also be called Western Mordvins, living on the banks of the Sura River, and the Mokša of the Mokša River could be called Eastern Mordvins.

The Mari and Mordvin languages, with the Balto-Finnic and Saami (Lapp) languages, are believed to stem from a common Volga Finnic protolanguage, spoken from 1500 to 500 BCE. Around the beginning of the common era, Mari and Mordvin started to develop into separate languages. Although they possess a common linguistic background, the Mari and Mordvin cultures have, in the course of centuries, undergone diverse developments under the influence of Tatar and, later, Russian domination. For this reason, the Mari and Mordvins are culturally quite different from each other, particularly in their religious views and activities. There are very few common features in Mari and Mordvin religion, and many differences become manifest in the comparison of their specific cultural groups as well.

Sources. The first mention of the Mordvins is in the chronicle of the historian Jordanes (551 CE). He relates that in the fourth century, Ermanarik, the king of the East Goths, subjugated a people called Mordens. Nestor, on the other hand, tells in his eleventh-century chronicle of three peoples living at the Oka River where it meets the Volga: the Cheremis, the Mordvins, and the Muromans, a distinct third group. Giovanni da Pian del Carpini, the papal emissary, wrote in his report of 1245 that the Tatars occupied the domain of the Mordui people, living between Russians and Bulgars. Marco Polo, on the other hand, mentions Mordui as one of the groups under Mongolian power.

The influence of the foreign cultures, beginning with the Tatar hegemony of the medieval period, is evident in Mari and Mordvin religion. The conversion to Christianity began in the middle of the sixteenth century, when the Russians finally overthrew the Tatar khanate of Kazan. The often quite violent mission was strengthened in the seventeenth century, with the result that many features of pre-Christian Mari and Mordvin religion gradually disappeared. Many fieldworkers of the nineteenth and twentieth centuries have, however, been able to report religious beliefs and practices that clearly belong to the autochthonous elements of the Mari and Mordvin cultures.

Our earliest information on Mordvin religion comes from an earlier Italian explorer, G. Barbaro, who visited the district now called Eastern Russia in 1446. He gives an account of the horse sacrifices of the Mokša. In regard to the Mari, some valuable information can be found in the report published by an envoy from Holstein, Adam Olearius (1663), on Mari offering rituals. The sources of the eighteenth century include the accounts by N. Witzen, P. J. Strahlenberg, G. F. Müller, I. Lepeshchin, J. P. Georgi, N. Rytshkov, and P. S. Pallas.

A valuable study on Mordvin religion is the Russian manuscript written by a surveyor named Mil'kovich in 1783. In addition to Russian scholars, several Finnish ethnographers, including Albert Hämäläinen, Heikki Paasonen, and Uno Holmberg Harva, have done fieldwork among the Mari and Mordvins in the late nineteenth and early twentieth centuries. Their collections have been published by the Finno-Ugric Society in Helsinki. Uno Holmberg Harva edited the monographs on the religion of the Mari (1914) and Mordvin (1942). Holmberg's study of Finno-Ugric mythology published in volume 4 (1927) of *The Mythology of All Races* is still a classic in its field, a comparative survey of Finno-Ugric worldviews. More recent publications include N. F. Mokshin's work on Mordvin religion (1968) and Thomas A. Sebeok and Frances J. Ingemann's work on Mari religion (1956).

Mari and Mordvin ethnic religions are described here mainly on the basis of the folklore sources of the nineteenth and twentieth centuries. As a result of the Russian socialist revolution, Mari and Mordvin cultures have undergone rapid changes that have had great influence on their religious views (secularization and acculturation).

Life and Death. Both the Mari and the Mordvins employ a complex system of soul concepts. The Mordvins describe physical death with such expressions as "ojm'eze l'iśś" ("his spirit left") or "ojm'enze noldaś" ("he overthrew his spirit"). Various terms for soul denote the life-keeping elements, breathing, or simply "up"; in Mokša languages, *ojm'e* or *vajm'ä*, in Erzä, *arńe*, in Mari, *šüloš*. The life of this kind of soul is related to the length of the life of the individual whose body it inhabits, beginning with the first symptoms of physical life and ending with body's last breath. The soul then leaves the body like warm air or smoke. This kind of soul is linear, living only once with its personal character. The cyclical soul concept, in which the soul lives on after the physical death, in manifest in such words as *tšopatša* (Erzä), *šopatša* (Mokša), and *ört* (Mari). These souls are described as living with the body both in its lifetime in this world and after death in the place where the corpse has been buried. The *ört* may leave the body during a trance or dream or when a person is senseless. After death, the *ört* may appear as a ghost who disturbs relatives or wanders through the home. It is the *ört* that is moved to the land of the dead. The *tšopatša* is conceived of as a kind of personal guardian spirit that is embodied in the shadow or a picture of its carrier. It also lives after the physical death of its corporeal carrier and often takes the form of a soul bird.

Family cult rites associated with death are organized by the dead person's relatives. Life after death was regarded as a direct continuation of earthly life. The departed were believed to live in much the same way as they had upon earth, in log cabins within fenced groves that were called *šugarla* (Mari), *kalmazur* (Erzä), or *kalma-kuža* (Mokša). The articles used by them in life were carefully carried to the cemetery and placed beside their bodies in the grave. In death as in life family and kin remain together, so that the graveyard is simply the counterpart of the village. In this view, there is no realm of the dead in the universal sense. It was thus natural to construct the cabin of the dead in such a way that a window faced home; there also was a hole to allow the *ört* or *tšopatša* to revisit the living members of the family.

Each family worships its own dead. Festivals in honor of a departed individual were celebrated during the first year after death: immediately after burial, six weeks (or the fortieth day) after death, and one year after death. After this last ritual, the deceased was no longer honored as an individual but rather as a member of the collective group of the family dead in ceremonies celebrated annually in accordance with the economic and religious calendar.

Twice a year the Mordvins hold a festival called Pokštšat Babat or At'at Babat ("grandfathers and grandmothers") for all departed ancestors. The ancestors are then requested to participate in a banquet shared between the living and dead members of the family. Formerly, animal sacrifices, often horses, were offered to the departed. Heikki Paasonen points out that this practice may derive from an earlier practice of human sacrifice. He also believes that the worship of some gods *(pas)* is related to the ancestor cult. The Erzä annually worship Staka, a god resembling a Turkic ruler or prince; in addition, the Erzä and Mokša worship a god called Keremet, who is given the title *soltan* ("sultan"), which seems to be a manifestation of a former local hero cult.

Universe and Nature. According to a Mordvin myth recorded by the Russian clergyman Fedor Saverskii in 1853, there were a pair of creators in the beginning of time. God was sitting on a rock in the midst of the huge proto-ocean contemplating the creation of the universe. A devil *(šaitan)* appeared and promised to help him in the act of creation. God asked him to dive into the depth of the ocean and to bring sand from the bottom. After having succeeded in his third attempt, the devil brought the material but hid some of it in his mouth, planning to create his own world. God threw the sand he had been given on the surface of the proto-ocean and it started to grow both there as well as in the devil's mouth, forcing him to empty it. Because of this dualistic conflict, there is evil as well as good in the universe.

The creator god is called Niške-pas or Niške in Mordvin languages, literally meaning "the great procreator." According to Erzä and Mokša folklore, he created heaven and earth, the rising sun, the wandering moon, black forests, and green grass. He also created the world sea and placed in it three mythical fish who support the universe on their backs. According to Mordvin incantations, the fish are white beings, probably whales; their movements cause earthquakes. According to this same myth, the Erzä were created as the first human beings to cut the forest and harvest the grass. The Erzä man is put to plow and sow; his position is superior to that of his wife, whose duty it is to cook.

In international literature, there are scholarly accounts of complex hierarchical systems of deities of the universe in Mari and Mordvin religions. However, they follow the well-known theoretical patterns of the supreme being, lord of the earth, and the Olympic idea of a system of twelve gods to such an extent that it is more probable that the theory has arranged the cultural material than vice versa. In spite of this, we may refer to the interesting account by Strahlenberg, who states that the highest deity of the Mordvins (meaning the Erzä) is Jumishipas, the sky god. The first part of the name is the same as the Mari *Jumo* and Finnish *Jumala*, meaning "God"; the latter part is equivalent to *Škipas*, the name of the sun god. There probably was some kind of sun worship in both Mari and Mordvin cultures.

Nature and culture were divided among the various supernatural beings, each of whom had control over a certain building or an area in nature. It was believed that these guardian spirits existed in order to aid the people in their struggles with neighboring tribes, competitive outgroups, and unknown supernatural powers. They also controlled the affairs and actions that took place in the area in their charge, warned for danger, and punished for wrong, immoral, or improper behavior. In Mari and Mordvin folklore, there are plenty of narratives about personal encounters with the supernatural in the natural and cultural realms. In family and clan festivals held during certain seasons of the economic year, sacrifices, for example, food offerings, were offered to them as a part of family or regional cult practice.

The Erzä and Mokša had a guardian spirit called Mastor-ava, an earth mother who was thought to grant good harvests and good health upon the tillers of the fields. Each tilled field was thought to have its own particular spirits. The guardian spirits of forests, water, and fire were often conceived of as female supernatural beings, as evidenced by their feminine names. Among the Mordvins, there were such spirits as Vir-ava ("forest mother"), Vedmastor-ava ("water mother"), and Tol-ava ("fire mother"). The first person buried in a graveyard was considered to be the guardian spirit of that particular cemetery. The important economy of the beehives was also guarded by a guardian spirit, P'erna-azor-ava, the hostess or keeper of the bees. She was given the first taste of the annual harvest of honey.

The guardian spirits of the cultural realm watched over their own buildings and controlled behavior there. The dwelling place as a whole, that is, the courtyard, the house, and its adjoining buildings, were later called *jurt (yurt)*, a word borrowed from the Tatar language. The spirit of this area was called Jurt-ava ("mother of the dwelling place"). This concept, particularly among the Erzä, replaced such former Finno-Ugrian concepts as Kudon'-tšin ("house god") or the Mokša Kud-ava ("house mother"). The word *kud* is similar to the Finnish *koti* or Saami *kota*, meaning "home."

Christianity, accepted by the Mari and Mordvins in its Russian Orthodox form, replaced the guardian spirits of the former autochthonous religion with the names of the saints and patrons of the Orthodox church. The functions of the spirits were easily mixed with the attributes and patronages of the Christian saints. The cult was transferred from the *keremet* (sacred groves) and so on to the cemeteries and neighborhood of the church. Some syncretic religious movements also appeared as a result of the encounter between the old and new religions, as, for example, the Kugu Sorta ("big candle") movement among the Mari at the end of the nineteenth century, combining monastic asceticism with pre-Christian blood sacrifices in the old sacred groves and the worship of pre-Christian deities.

[*See also* Finno-Ugric Religions, *overview article, and* Finnic Religions.]

BIBLIOGRAPHY

Beke, Ödön, comp. *Tscheremissische Texte zur Religion und Volkskunde*. Oslo, 1931.

Hämäläinen, A. *Tseremissien uhritapoja*. Helsinki, 1908.

Harva (Holmberg), Uno. *Die religiosen Vorstellungen der Mordwinen*. Helsinki, 1952.

Holmberg, Uno. *Die Religion der Tscheremissen*. Helsinki, 1926.

Holmberg, Uno. *The Mythology of All Races*, vol. 4, *Finno-Ugric, Siberian*. Boston, 1927; reprint, New York, 1964.

Mokshin, N. F. "Proiskhozhdenie i sushchnost' mordovskikh dokhristianskikh religioznykh prazdnikov (ozks'ov)." In *Uchenye zapiski Mordovskogo gosudarstvennogo universiteta (seriia istorischeskikh nauk)*. Saransk, 1965.

Mokshin, N. F. *Religioznye verovaniia Mordvy*. Saransk, 1968.

Paasonen, Heikki. "Mordvins." In *Encyclopaedia of Religion and Ethics*, edited by James Hastings, vol. 8. Edinburgh, 1915.
Paasonen, Heikki, and Paavo Ravila. *Mordwinische Volksdichtung*. 4 vols. Helsinki, 1938–1947.
Shakhmatov, A. A. *Mordovskii etnograficheskii sbornik*. Saint Petersburg, 1910.

Juha Pentikäinen

MARITAIN, JACQUES (1882–1973), French Neo-Thomist philosopher. Born in Paris, he was baptized in the French Reformed church and received religious instruction from the liberal Protestant theologian Jean Réville. During his youth, Maritain considered himself an unbeliever. He studied at the Sorbonne (1901–1906) but found the dominant positivism and rationalism—epitomized in the influence of the philosopher Auguste Comte and the historian and writer Ernest Renan—spiritually barren. At the Sorbonne, Maritain joined a circle of friends that included the writer Charles Péguy and a young Russian Jew, Raïssa Oumansoff. He also attended the lectures of the philosopher Henri Bergson at the Collège de France. Bergson's vitalistic philosophy liberated Maritain from positivism and made possible for him the rehabilitation of metaphysical thinking.

In 1904 Maritain married Raïssa Oumansoff, and soon they came under the influence of the fiery, uncompromising Catholic writer Léon Bloy. Primarily through Bloy's tutorship and personal example, they were baptized in the Roman Catholic church in 1906. Maritain spent the next two years in Heidelberg studying with the distinguished biologist and neovitalist Hans Dreisch. On returning to France he began reading the *Summa theologiae* of Thomas Aquinas. Thomas's philosophical realism became for Maritain a second and more decisive intellectual deliverance. For the rest of his long life, he revered Thomas as his master and saw as his own vocation the application of the perennial wisdom of Thomism to contemporary philosophy, art, politics, and education. "Woe unto me," he wrote, "should I not thomistize!"

Maritain served as professor of philosophy at the Institut Catholique de Paris (1914–1933), the Institute of Medieval Studies in Toronto (1933–1945), and Princeton University (1948–1952), as well as at other North American universities. At the invitation of Charles de Gaulle, he served as French ambassador to the Vatican from 1945 to 1948. During his years in North America, Maritain's influence on Catholic thought, as well as on arts and letters, was enormous.

Raïssa Maritain died in 1960, and the following year Maritain returned to France and retired to Toulouse to live with the Little Brothers of Jesus, a Dominican monastic order. In 1969 he entered the order. In 1966 Maritain published *The Peasant of the Garonne,* a sharp warning to the post–Vatican II reformers in the Roman church. Because Maritain had championed some liberal influences in the church, especially in the field of politics, the book surprised many and provoked widespread discussion. However, the work reflects a long-standing tension in Maritain between adherence to tradition and openness to new ideas, as well as his disdain of any modern ways that deviate from Thomas.

Maritain's literary output was prodigious, including about forty books published over a span of some sixty years. He ranged over almost every aspect of philosophy, and all his works—from *La philosophie bergsonienne* (1914) to his penultimate book, *On the Church of Christ* (1970)—are informed by the thought of Thomas Aquinas. Maritain traces what he perceives to be a cultural breakdown in the West to a disease of the mind. That disease has its beginnings in the early modern repudiation of Thomistic philosophy, first in William of Ockham's nominalism and rejection of Aristotelian metaphysics; then in Luther's severing of faith from reason; in Descartes's rationalism, in which reason is divorced from sensory experience and existing things; and, finally, in Rousseau's sentimental appeal to the inner feelings of the heart. Maritain sees metaphysical thinking brought to a close with Kant, and the future turned over to scientism and positivism on the one hand and subjectivism and relativism on the other.

Maritain's genius lay not only in his skill in demonstrating the inadequacies of a good deal of modern philosophy but also in exhibiting how the authentic truths of modern thought are consistent with, and conceptually more adequate when understood in terms of, Thomistic realism. Existentialism is a case in point. Its emphasis on action, and on what Maritain calls its "imprecatory posture," isolates the idea of existence from a genuine knowledge of being, since it involves philosophizing in a posture of dramatic singularity. Maritain argues that one can never know pure subjective existence. Objective philosophic knowledge necessarily involves a distinction between essence and existence, for the essence of a thing is what makes it intelligible as a being, what defines its nature. Essence and existence are correlative and inseparable. Maritain therefore insists that an "authentic" existentialism must go beyond the cry and agony of the subject to a genuine analysis of being.

Such an analysis will lead reflection beyond finite existence to that being whose essence is to exist, who exists necessarily (God). In works such as *Approaches to God* (1954), Maritain attempts to show that the Thomistic cosmological proofs of the existence of God are the development of a primordial, prephilosophical intuition of being. Furthermore, he seeks to demonstrate that Kant's widely approved critique of the Thomistic cosmological proofs—which holds that they imply the ontological argument—is in error. Maritain reconceives the five Thomistic proofs by appropriating ideas from modern physics and the philosophy of science. However, the philosophical critics of natural theology remain largely unconvinced.

Among modern religious philosophers, Maritain stands preeminent in his reflections on aesthetics, for example, in works such as *Art and Scholasticism* (1920; Eng. ed., 1962) and *Creative Intuition in Art and Poetry* (1953). Maritain's discussion of poetic intuition and knowledge and of the relationship between art and morality are profound and have influenced numerous writers and critics.

In *Scholasticism and Politics* (1940), *True Humanism* (1936; Eng. ed., 1938), and *Man and the State* (1951), Maritain argues eloquently for the dignity of the person, for human rights and liberty, and for what is essentially an American model of church-state relations. Maritain's writings on the person and on society and politics have had wide influence and are reflected in the documents of Vatican II.

Maritain represents, perhaps better than any other thinker, the intellectual confidence, indeed the aggressiveness, of Roman Catholicism in the 1940s and 1950s. Like the Protestant theologian Reinhold Niebuhr, Maritain was a brilliant critic of secular culture and a superb apologist for the Christian life. He was also, like Niebuhr, a "relative" pessimist who nevertheless held out hope for the recovery of an integral, Christian humanism—a humanism permeated by works of genuine sanctity.

Many Catholic intellectuals consider Maritain's Thomism as no longer an adequate guide and call instead for a philosophical pluralism in the church. The form of Thomism that does continue to have a wide following, the "transcendental" Thomism associated with Joseph Maréchal (1878–1944) and, more recently, with Karl Rahner, was repudiated by Maritain. While his work is presently in eclipse and his future influence is uncertain, Maritain will be remembered as one of the intellectual giants in the period between the two world wars.

BIBLIOGRAPHY

Maritain's greatest work on metaphysics and the theory of knowledge is *Distinguish to Unite, or the Degrees of Knowledge*, translated under the supervision of Gerald B. Phelen (New York, 1959). In *Approaches to God*, translated by Peter O'Reilly (New York, 1954), Maritain restates the five ways of Thomas Aquinas to demonstrate the existence of God and proposes a "sixth way." *True Humanism*, translated by Margot Adamson (New York, 1938), is Maritain's most important work in social philosophy, and *Man and the State* (Chicago, 1951) is his most comprehensive examination of political philosophy. *Creative Intuition in Art and Poetry* (New York, 1953) is Maritain's masterpiece in the philosophy of art. *Challenges and Renewals*, edited by Joseph W. Evans and Leo R. Ward (Notre Dame, Ind., 1966), is a useful selection of writings by Maritain covering all aspects of his philosophy.

No definitive critical study of Maritain has been written. Joseph W. Evans's *Jacques Maritain: The Man and His Achievement* (New York, 1963) includes a variety of essays on aspects of Maritain's work. Julie Kernan's *Our Friend, Jacques Maritain: A Personal Memoir* (Garden City, N.Y., 1975) is a rather full biographical account. The definitive bibliography of works by and about Maritain up to 1961 is Donald Gallagher and Idella Gallagher's *The Achievement of Jacques and Raïssa Maritain: A Bibliography, 1906–1961* (New York, 1962).

JAMES C. LIVINGSTON

MARK OF EPHESUS (1392–1444), a leader of the Greek Orthodox resistance against the unionist movement with the Western church. A native of Constantinople, Mark studied under prominent teachers and then opened a private higher school. He was elected metropolitan of Ephesus and participated in the Council of Ferrara-Florence as a representative of the patriarchate of Antioch at the expressed wish of the emperor John VIII Palaeologus. However, he became the strongest adversary of union with the Roman church. Mark abstained from the sessions of the council and was the only Eastern bishop to refuse to sign the decisions of the council in 1439. When Pope Eugenius IV—for whom unanimity and the support of Mark were determinant factors for union—learned of his refusal, he said, "Therefore, we have accomplished nothing."

After his return to Constantinople, Mark was offered the patriarchal see by the emperor and bishops in the hope that his zeal against union would decrease under the burden of the great responsibilities of office. Mark refused the offer. Attempting to go to Mount Athos, probably with the aim of mobilizing the monks against union, he was seized on the island of Lemnos by the imperial police and was not allowed to leave the island for two years. After his liberation, he directed the struggle in Constantinople. Shortly before his death he persuaded Gennadios Scholarios, the future patriarch of Constantinople, to succeed him in his function as head of the antiunionists.

Mark's theology is basically hesychastic with occasional use of Aristotelian categories to support his arguments. His work *Syllogistic Chapters on the Divine Es-*

sence and Energy reveals his spiritual and intellectual origins. His polemics against the Roman church are included in various writings, of which the most important is *Syllogistic Chapters against the Latins.* By an encyclical letter, *To Christians All Over the Earth,* he directed the attention of Orthodox believers to the danger from those who were wavering and finding themselves in agreement with both Easterners and Westerners; he called these people "Greco-Latins."

Mark believed that differences with the Westerners over such matters as the procession of the Holy Spirit, purgatory, and the use of unleavened bread for the Eucharist were dogmatic differences; therefore, he considered the Latins heretics. A summary of his position may be found in his statement regarding a patriarch who favored union: "The further I stay from this man and others like him the nearer I come to God and to the faithful and holy fathers."

BIBLIOGRAPHY

A lengthy sketch of Mark's person and work may be found in Louis Petit's article "Marc Eugénicos," in *Dictionnaire de théologie catholique,* vol. 9 (Paris, 1927), and a shorter sketch in Hans Georg Beck's *Kirche und theologische Literatur im byzantinischen Reich* (Munich, 1959), pp. 755–758. The most complete study is Katerina Mamoni's *Marcos Eugenicos* (Athens, 1954). Mark's ecclesiastical policy from the Roman Catholic point of view is treated by Joseph Gill in *Personalities of the Council of Florence* (Oxford, 1964). Constantine N. Tsirpanlis provides the Greek Orthodox point of view in *Mark Eugenicus and the Council of Florence: A Historical Re-evaluation of His Personality* (New York, 1979).

PANAGIOTIS C. CHRISTOU

MARK THE EVANGELIST, traditionally the author of the second canonical gospel, who wrote in Rome during the emperor Nero's persecution of Christians (early to mid-60s). Mark was not one of the twelve disciples of Jesus. Whether the evangelist is mentioned in the New Testament depends on the accuracy of the commonly accepted identification of him with the John Mark of Jerusalem mentioned in *Acts* and Paul's letters.

John Mark first appears in *Acts* 12:12: Peter is said to go "to the house of Mary, the mother of John, whose other name was Mark." (John would have been Mark's Semitic, Jewish name; Marcus is a common Latin, Roman name.) He is referred to in a similar way again in *Acts* 12:25 and 15:37, but in 15:39 he is called simply Mark. Elsewhere he is called only Mark (*Col.* 4:10, *2 Tm.* 4:11, *Phlm.* 24, *1 Pt.* 5:13). In *Colossians,* we read that Mark was the cousin of Barnabas, with whom he continued missionary labors after the break with Paul (*Acts* 15:38–39). Significantly, he is there grouped with the Jewish members of Paul's company (*Col.* 4:11), which fits the identification with John Mark. Since *2 Timothy* was almost certainly not written by Paul and the Pauline authorship of *Colossians* is questionable, *Philemon* 24 is the only unimpeachable Pauline reference to Mark as one of Paul's fellow workers. Yet all these references are significant because they show the traditional association of Mark with Paul. The same is true for *1 Peter* 5:13, which suggests Mark's association also with Peter in Rome (i.e., "Babylon").

The earliest statements about Mark the evangelist by Christian writers, beginning with those of Bishop Papias of Hierapolis in the first half of the second century, do not identify him explicitly with John Mark, but almost unanimously associate him with Peter as Peter's interpreter (cf. Eusebius's *Church History* 3.39.15). Frequently it is said that Mark and Peter worked together in Rome, and this, of course, accords with ancient church tradition about Peter's final place of abode, as well as with *1 Peter* 5:13. A somewhat later tradition recounts that Mark was the first to preach and to found churches in Egypt (*Church History* 2.16.1), and that he became the first bishop of Alexandria. A recently discovered letter of Clement of Alexandria, which, if genuine, dates from the end of the second century, relates how Mark came to Alexandria with the early canonical gospel and there augmented it for the sake of a special spiritual elite.

That the *Gospel of Mark* is actually the work of someone of that name is probable; that he was associated with Peter in Rome is possible, although that association would not entirely explain the character and content of the gospel; that he was actually John Mark cannot be said with certainty, nor can it be denied categorically. If Mark the evangelist was John Mark of Jerusalem it is at least striking that in his gospel Jesus' ministry is centered in Galilee (in contrast to the *Gospel of John,* which centers the ministry in Jerusalem) and that the disciples are encouraged to look to Galilee for the fulfillment of their hopes and plans whether by their own mission or by Jesus' return (*Mk.* 14:28, 16:7). Moreover, the gospel seems to assume a gentile-Christian rather than a Jewish-Christian readership (cf. *Mk.* 7:3–4).

Legend has it that Mark was martyred in Alexandria during Nero's reign and that his remains eventually were moved to Venice. The evangelist's symbol, the lion, became the emblem of that city. The symbolism, as old as the second century, is probably drawn from *Revelation* 4:7 and ultimately from *Ezekiel* 1:10. Mark's feast is celebrated on 25 April.

BIBLIOGRAPHY

Aside from the New Testament the most important primary source is Eusebius's *Church History*, which brings together earlier testimony of Christian writers on the origin and authorship of the Gospels. The most convenient edition is the two-volume "Loeb Classical Library" text and translation of Kirsopp Lake, J. E. L. Oulton, and Hugh J. Lawlor (Cambridge, Mass., 1926).

Vincent Taylor's *The Gospel According to St. Mark* (London, 1952), pp. 1–8, cites fully and discusses the patristic evidence on Mark, taking the position that the evangelist was, in fact, John Mark. Werner G. Kümmel's *Introduction to the New Testament*, rev. ed. (Nashville, 1975), pp. 95–98, states a more skeptical critical consensus. Old and new evidence of Mark's relation to Alexandria is given and discussed in Morton Smith's *Clement of Alexandria and a Secret Gospel of Mark* (Cambridge, Mass., 1973), pp. 19–44, 446.

D. MOODY SMITH

MAROON RELIGIONS. *See* Afro-Surinamese Religions *and* Caribbean Religions, *article on* Afro-Caribbean Religions.

MAR-PA (1012–1096), also known as Mar-pa of Lho-brag (the region of his birth) and Dvags-po Lha-rje ("physician of Dvags-po"); a key figure in the "second spreading" of Buddhism in Tibet (begun in the tenth century). Mar-pa was a renowned translator of Indian Vajrayāna texts into Tibetan and the first Tibetan member of the Bka'-brgyud lineage. This lineage begins with the primordial, celestial Buddha Vajradhāra and includes the Indian *mahāsiddha*s Ti-lo-pa (988–1069) and Nā-ro-pa (Mar-pa's teacher, 1016–1100), Mar-pa himself, and his student, the yogin Mi-la-ras-pa (1040–1123), with whom the Bka'-brgyud tradition, one of the four major Tibetan schools, properly begins.

Mar-pa was born at the beginning of, and played a major role in, the so-called second spreading of Buddhism in Tibet. Although Buddhism had enjoyed royal support in Tibet since the seventh century, its power base remained unstable, depending largely on the shifting political fortunes of its patrons. In the mid-ninth century, with the assassination of the last of three "Buddhist kings" (*dharmarājā*s) and the disintegration of royal authority, Buddhism suffered a setback sufficiently severe that later tradition marks this as the end of the "first spreading" of Buddhism in Tibet. After a hundred years of disorganization and centripetal tendencies within Buddhism, the Tibetans began to make a concerted, well-organized effort to reestablish Buddhism on a more consistent and stable footing. Crucial to this process was the willingness of Tibetans to undertake the long and dangerous journey to India to master Indian languages, study with Indian Buddhist teachers, and translate Buddhist texts. The greatest of these men were given the honorific title of *lo tsā ba*, translator; among these, Mar-pa was one of the most renowned.

The most famous and best-loved Tibetan biography of Mar-pa, summarized here, was written by the fourteenth-century "Mad Yogin of Tsang." This author has a lively, colloquial, and earthy style, in common with the best Vajrayāna hagiographers; he sees Mar-pa as an ordinary human being on a long and difficult, but always unmistakably real, spiritual journey, a journey that also has its equally real breakthroughs and fulfillments.

According to our biography, Mar-pa was born in southern Tibet of relatively prosperous parents. Owing to a violent temper and stubbornness, he was sent off by his parents to study Buddhism, first in a Tibetan monastery nearby, then in one much farther away. The parents' expediency became the child's inspiration, and Mar-pa was soon on his way to India to pursue his study of Buddhism; after two years of acclimatization in Nepal he descended to the Indian plains. He had heard the name of Nā-ro-pa, experienced a strong, if not understood, connection to him, and thus felt unaccountably drawn to study with him. Having found Nā-ro-pa, Mar-pa spent the next ten years as his student, imbibing Vajrayāna teachings from him and from others to whom his teacher sent him, and translating texts. [*See the biography of Nā-ro-pa.*] After this he returned to Tibet, where he married, began teaching, and established himself as a wealthy farmer. After a second trip to India for six years of further study with Nā-ro-pa, Mar-pa again returned to Tibet and gathered about him a number of close disciples, including Mi-la-ras-pa, to whom he would eventually entrust full transmission of his knowledge. Finally, although well into middle age, Mar-pa made a third journey to India.

In his previous journeys his relationship with his *guru* had gone relatively smoothly, but now Mar-pa experienced the agonies, the searching, and the aloneness that are so often characteristic of Tantric students in their relation to their teachers. After abandoning all hope of ever seeing Nā-ro-pa again, Mar-pa succeeded in finding him, and they communicated without the barriers that had previously existed between them. Mar-pa returned to Tibet for the last time three years later, at which time tragedy befell him, whose life had heretofore been so successful. Mar-pa's only son, on whom he had placed great hope and whom he had planned to make his *dharma* heir, was mortally injured after being thrown from his horse. The biography describes in intimate and moving detail the last hours together of the son and parents. Mar-pa spent the ensuing years passing his teachings to four chief disciples, and died at the age of eighty-four.

Mar-pa was instrumental in the beginnings of the second spreading of Buddhism to Tibet through his journeys to India, his thorough study under Nā-ro-pa, his translations—sixteen of which are in the Tibetan Bka'-'gyur (Kanjur) and Bstan-'gyur (Tanjur)—and his fresh implantation of Buddhism into eleventh-century Tibet. The most important outcome of this work was his role as forefather of the Tibetan Bka'-brgyud school, and his training of Mi-la-ras-pa, from whom the school directly flowed. In addition, Mar-pa articulated in his life the classical Indian Vajrayāna ideal of the householder-yogin, one who is not a monk but a layman, whose ordinary family and occupational life become vehicles for, and expressions of, his full realization. Although this Tantric ideal was generally not prominent in the Tibetan Vajrayāna, with Mar-pa and some later figures it reasserted itself at particularly creative periods in Tibetan Buddhist history. Mar-pa was also instrumental in introducing into Tibet a new kind of religious poetry, based on the Indian Tantric tradition of the *dohā*s, or mystical songs, and expressive of personal insight and experience on the Tantric path. This latter inheritance he passed on to his student Mi-la-ras-pa, who explored this idiom in a particularly rich and creative way that had a great impact on subsequent Tibetan literature.

[*See also* Buddhism, *article on* Buddhism in Tibet; Buddhism, Schools of, *article on* Tibetan Buddhism; Mahāsiddhas; *and the biography of Mi-la-ras-pa.*]

BIBLIOGRAPHY

The most celebrated Tibetan biography of Mar-pa, by the fourteenth-century "Mad Yogin of Tsang" (Tsang Nyon Heruka) has been translated into English by the Nālandā Translation Committee under the direction of Chogyam Trungpa as *The Life of Marpa the Translator* (Boulder, 1982). This work supersedes a good but dated and abridged translation of the same work by Jacques Bacot, *La vie de Marpa le "traducteur,"* (Paris, 1937). The new English translation contains a readable and clear introduction summarizing what is known about Mar-pa's life and times.

REGINALD RAY

MARRANOS, a term of opprobrium designating Jews (and, occasionally, Muslims) converted to Christianity and their descendants, was used in the Iberian world in late medieval and early modern times. The Castilian word *marrano* (deriving from an Arabic word for "prohibited, illicit") means "swine, pork" and either expressed the same abhorrence toward converts as the converts had previously felt toward the ritually unclean animal or insinuated suspicions regarding the converts' continued loyalties to Judaism. Usage of the term appears to have been limited to common parlance and satirical literature. In modern times, Jewish historians revived the term to underscore the uniqueness of the "Marrano" phenomenon in Iberian and Jewish history.

More commonly and more neutrally, the converts and their descendants are designated *conversos,* "converts," and *cristianos nuevos* (Span.) or *cristãos novos* (Port.), "New Christians." Referring specifically to *conversos* suspected or found guilty of practicing or adhering to some form of Judaism, Inquisitorial documents employ the term *judaizante,* "judaizer" (or, in modern variations, "secret" or "crypto-Jew"). In premodern and modern Hebrew sources, the *conversos* are designated as *anusim,* "forced [converts]." To avoid the confusions of earlier historiography, present historians use *converso* and *New Christian* synonymously to refer strictly to the social group of converts and descendants, and reserve *judaizer* and *Marrano* as synonyms for those *conversos* whose retention of some form of Judaism may be demonstrated or suspected.

The "Converso Problem." The large and problematical *converso* population and the concomitant Marrano phenomenon were the outcome of unprecedented, large-scale conversions of Spanish and Portuguese Jews between 1391 and 1497. In 1391 and 1392, social resentment of prospering urban Jewish minorities and religious militancy nurtured by a pugnacious Spanish tradition of spiritual warfare provoked a nationwide chain of pogroms, in the course of which large numbers of Jews fell victim to forced, legally irreversible baptism. The unrelenting persistence of anti-Jewish pressures resulted, in subsequent decades, in a second wave of more or less voluntary conversions, creating an initial population of tens of thousands of *conversos* of questionable religious sincerity.

Envy of the *conversos'* social and economic gains, made possible by their liberation from anti-Jewish restrictions, and lingering suspicions of their secret and private loyalty to Judaism, rekindled popular anger and violence against them and gave birth to a social and religious "*converso* problem" that was politically threatening in that it potentially harbored antiroyalist sentiment. In 1478, a Castilian Inquisition, whose appointments were controlled by the crown, was established to deal with the problem's religious dimension; that is, to prosecute and punish insincere judaizing individuals and thus protect the purity of Catholic orthodoxy and, at the same time, lay to rest the popular suspicions and the indiscriminate, anti-*converso* scapegoating that were viewed as a political danger. Addressing the social dimension, "purity of blood" (Span., *limpieza de sangre;* Port., *limpeza de sangue*) statutes—the earliest was adopted (but nullified) in 1449 (in Toledo)—sought, whenever the circumstances proved opportune, to exclude the New Christians as a group from upper-echelon ecclesiastical, civil, and military positions by virtue of their Jewish or Muslim descent. The statutes became a more widely adopted mode of anti-*converso* social discrimination after 1555–1556, when the archbishop of Toledo, Juan Martínez Silíceo (1486–1557), obtained papal and royal ratification, in the midst of a vociferous debate, of a *limpieza* statute excluding New Christians from positions in the cathedral chapter of Toledo.

The remaining Jews of Spain, meanwhile, were implicated in fostering the persistence of Jewish loyalties among the *conversos* and in subverting the new state-church-city alliance. They were expelled by the Catholic rulers, Isabella of Castile (r. 1474–1504) and Ferdinand of Aragon (r. 1479–1516), from Andalusia, the scene of the first Inquisitorial discoveries of widespread judaizing, in 1483 and from the rest of Castile and Aragon in 1492. Seeking to avoid exile, many Spanish Jews hastily converted or returned converted after a temporary exile and joined the ranks of a not insignificant *converso* minority of approximately 2–3 percent of the total Spanish population. An estimated 150,000 Jews fled—about 120,000 to neighboring Portugal, where they raised the Jewish population to about 10 percent of the total population, and the rest to North Africa, Italy, and the Ottoman empire. During 1496 and 1497, Manuel I, king of Portugal (1495–1521), forcibly converted the vast majority of these now Portuguese Jews in a move meant to both rid his kingdom of the Jews, in compliance with a condition set forth by the Catholic king whose daughter he was to marry, and retain their services, which were deemed important for the country's and its colonies' economic development.

In Portugal, too, the "unsatisfactory" (i.e., forced) conversions as well as the social and economic advances of the *conversos* created a proportionally more substantial "*converso* problem," notwithstanding royal promises not to investigate the *conversos'* religious life made in the expectation of their eventual total assimilation. Despite vigorous New Christian efforts to stave off its institution, a Portuguese Inquisition on the Spanish model was established in 1536. And, in ensuing years, Portuguese institutions adopted "purity of blood" statutes to turn the tide of upwardly mobile New Christians tainted by suspicions of judaizing (willfully retaining Jewish loyalties and practices) that were seemingly confirmed by Inquisitorial proceedings. As the Spanish and Portuguese colonies attracted larger populations, Inquisitorial tribunals were established in Goa (1560), Lima (1570), Mexico (1571), and in Cartagena, Colombia (1610). Only Brazil was treated differently and remained under the jurisdiction of the Lisbon tribunal, which sent periodic "visitors" (that is, small and occasional commissions of inquiry) to the colony.

Historical Sources. The records of the Inquisition, preserved in great abundance, are our primary and often exclusive source of information about the extent and nature of the Marrano phenomenon, that is, the secret and heretical (by definition of the church) retention of Jewish doctrines, rites, and customs by groups and individuals within the larger *converso* populations. The reliability of these documents is the subject of continual debate. Some historians deny them all validity because they originated from an entirely self-contained and secret organization whose stated aims of religious orthodoxy they dismiss. Most historians accept them as a faithful record of the Inquisitorial proceedings: some without further questioning, others with more or less serious reservations about Inquisitorial (as opposed to accusatorial) procedure. For the Inquisition operated without external checks and balances and, as accuser, judge, and jury, controlled every aspect of the trial, in complete secrecy. Its decisions to prosecute (whom and when), imprison (and for how long), torture (and how often), and sentence (and how harshly) were, wittingly or unwittingly, exposed to—and generally unprotected from—internal infusions of malice, prejudice, bias, error, or misunderstanding. Only a complete statistical and comparative profile of all the Inquisition's tribunals, as is now being assembled, will reveal where and when any such infusion must be suspected and taken into consideration. Inquisitorial procedure may also have influenced the accusations, testimonies, and confessions of witnesses and defendants. Inasmuch as witnesses as well as defendants communicated with the inquisitors, they often had to bridge a social and cultural gap and speak in a voice not quite their own and might therefore intentionally or unintentionally misconstrue the realities under discussion. Only a complete reexamination of accusation, testimony, and confession can measure the manner in which "translation" and misconstruction may have affected the reliability of any given Inquisitorial record.

The Nature of the Marrano Phenomenon. Inquisitorial documents (such as manuals, edicts of faith, testimonies, and confessions) and statistics about the numbers of judaizers are helpful in charting the extent of the phenomenon, but do not afford a rounded picture of its nature. The Inquisition's definition of heresy, moreover, inspired a preoccupation with the external manifestations but rarely with the spiritual content of judaizing and thus deprives us of a significant dimension of the phenomenon. Within these limitations, little more than a catalogue of judaizing practices—constituting a maximum of observance rarely, if ever, attained by any individual Marrano—can be offered. The following summary focuses on the "full-fledged" Marranism of the later sixteenth and seventeenth centuries. When Jews were still present and memories yet alive, the earliest transitional generations of Marranos no doubt practiced a wider range of observances and traditions.

Loyalty to Judaism. Echoing Inquisitorial parlance, the Marranos defined themselves as those who believed salvation could be achieved only through the Law of Moses (by which they meant Judaism). This thoroughly un-Jewish formula clearly reveals the two elements in Marrano religion: a rejection of salvation through Jesus and a loyalty to the Law of Moses. As either one constituted in itself sufficient proof of heresy, the Inquisition never queried deeper to establish which of the two elements weighed heavier.

The Marranos' loyalty to Judaism, encumbered by the need for secrecy, expressed itself in an ever more restricted variety of Jewish observances and traditions, a restriction that was due to the loss of knowledge about Jewish law and, especially, Jewish doctrines, and the virtual absence of sources of Jewish education. Fairly rapid to disappear were circumcision, ritual slaughtering, the covering of the head during prayer, the use of phylacteries, and such festivals as Ro'sh ha-Shanah, Shavu'ot, and Ḥanukkah. Passover and Sukkot survived here and there but were celebrated in attenuated forms.

The Sabbath, fasts, prayers, and certain domestic traditions formed the main staples of Marrano Judaism. These observances and customs not only lend themselves well to concealment but have also been central to the home-based daily rhythm of traditional Judaism. The cleaning of the house, the changing of linen and clothes, the taking of baths, the preparation of food, including the so-called *adafina* (a stew prepared before the onset of the Sabbath), and the kindling of lights are mentioned in connection with the Marrano observance of the Sabbath. On the Sabbath itself, Marranos abstained from work as often as the opportunity presented itself and whenever the spirit moved them, that is to say, with a definite measure of irregularity. Some Marranos contented themselves with an abstention from work "in intention" only.

Fasting occupied a particularly prominent place in Marrano religious life. Not only was it easy to conceal, it also mirrored and opposed, to some extent, Christian practice. Yom Kippur (Day of Atonement) and the Fast of Esther were the holiest days of the Marrano calendar. As the Marranos had lost count of the Jewish lunar calendar, the dates of these fasts were computed on the basis of a mixed lunar-solar calendar: Yom Kippur on the tenth day after the New Moon in September (or, sometimes, on the tenth of September) and the Fast of Esther on the full moon of February. On Yom Kippur, Marranos customarily extended mutual forgiveness to each other, but only rarely does one encounter a Marrano who went barefoot on that day, as did Jews. Either on the eve of Yom Kippur or on that of the Sabbath, Marrano fathers often blessed their children, even when the children had as yet no knowledge of the Jewish origin of this custom. The Fast of Esther, on the eve of Purim, has minor importance in traditional Judaism. As Purim itself fell into oblivion, Marranos retained and expanded the fast, undoubtedly because of the similarity between their situation and that of Queen Esther, who had also been forced to hide her ancestral religion in order to survive in an alien environment.

On the Sabbath and Yom Kippur and other festive or special occasions, Marranos recited—rather than chanted, as in traditional fashion—Jewish prayers. As the original Hebrew prayers were lost and memory of their content dimmed, Marranos resorted to readings of the Psalms of David and vernacular creations of their own to replace the Qiddush, grace after meals, and other prayers. These vernacular prayers—some transcribed verbatim in the Inquisitorial documents—stress the unity, omnipotence, and mercy of Adonai ("my Lord," one of the few Hebrew words to survive among the Marranos), the God of the heavens, creator and ruler of the universe, in conscious opposition to Christian trinitarianism. Several prayers beseech God to deliver the Marranos from their tribulations. A great many of these locally or familially transmitted prayers were still current among the Marranos of twentieth-century Portugal.

Among the domestic traditions recorded, some may be termed culinary or dietary, while others are associated with rites of passage. Whereas ritual slaughtering other than that of an occasional fowl fell into desuetude, the kosher preparation of meat—the draining of blood, the removal of nerves, and the salting of meat—did not. This is, perhaps, the reason that Marranos, not having a chance to prepare meat properly, preferred meals of fish and vegetables when breaking a fast. As much as possible and as desired, again irregularly, Marranos avoided eating meats and seafoods traditionally declared nonkosher: pork, rabbit, shrimp, and lobster, in particular. And when baking bread, Marrano women had a habit of throwing three small balls of dough into the fire, in imitation of a *ḥallah*-baking custom. In rites-of-passage traditions, there was a great deal of local variety. Jewish names were generally lost, except in a few particularly "noble" Jewish families that retained a memory of their ancestral family name. Otherwise Marranos adopted Christian first names and surnames. In many places, a festive ceremony called Hadas ("fate"?) took place on the eighth night after a child's birth. The origin and the meaning of this custom are uncertain. Death and burial rites associated with traditional Judaism were quite common. The washing and dressing in shrouds of the corpse and the meals taken during the period of mourning as well as sundry superstitious acts are mentioned with relative frequency. [*For comparison to traditional Jewish practices, see* Domestic Observances, *article on* Jewish Practices, *and* Rites of Passage, *article on* Jewish Rites.]

Rejection of Christianity. The Marranos' rejection of Christianity consisted not only of a denial of salvation through the law of Jesus, of their opposition to the Trinity, and of their appropriation of the Paternoster for Marrano purposes. In early years, it sometimes included a ceremony intended to undo baptism. Later, Marranos more commonly were lax in their attendance at the Mass, which, however, was also not infrequently neglected by Christians. Some Marranos used to recite a deprecatory formula denying the efficacy of the sacraments or the veneration of images before entering a church. Others remained silent or mumbled through christological parts of the liturgy or bent rather than kneeled at the requisite times. Evidence of Marranos' spewing out the Host after Communion is sparse, and accusations of Marranos' desecrating the Host may reflect the preconception of malevolent witnesses more than actual practice.

Messianic inclinations. One final aspect of Marrano religion remains largely in the dark: messianism. Many Marrano prayers reflect a commitment to traditional Jewish messianism, but the degree to which this commitment explains New Christian participation in specific, often Christian messianic movements remains a matter for speculation. In the early years following the expulsion of the Jews, several reports from various parts of Spain speak of visionary experiences by *conversos* with more or less explicitly messianic overtones. Later the Jewish adventurer David Reubeni's visit to Portugal and reception by the king from 1525 to 1527 stirred *converso* emotions, perhaps so deeply as to have provoked messianic expectations. And toward the end of the sixteenth century, messianic beliefs surrounding the deceased King Sebastian of Portugal, who had fallen in battle in 1578, again attracted *converso* attention and may even have been inspired by *conversos*. The participation of Spanish and Portuguese *conversos* in messianically inclined popular movements appears undisputed. On the basis of our meager sources, however, it is difficult to gauge whether they responded so eagerly as Marranos who rejected Jesus and retained Jewish messianic hopes or as New Christians prompted by a radical desire to alter the contemporary situation of Inquisitorial repression and socioreligious discrimination, or whether they were swept up by a general enthusiasm that also drew Old Christians *(cristianos viejos,* or *cristãos velhos)* into these movements.

The Transmission of Marranism. Originally the transmission of Marranism was confined to the *converso* population. After the first generation, as more and more New Christians intermarried with Old Christians, their "partially" New Christian descendants often proved as susceptible to judaizing as did the "pure" New Christians. For reasons that smack of racialist prejudice, the Portuguese Inquisition made a point of carefully noting the exact degree of *converso*-parentage of its suspects. Only rarely does one encounter a "pure" Old Christian among the Inquisition's judaizer victims.

Most commonly Marranism was transmitted through the family. In Inquisitorial documents, parents, grandparents, and close relatives figure most prominently as the teachers of the Marrano heresy. In fact, the Inquisition generally dismissed as incomplete any confessions that failed to reveal this familial link. Neither in "pure" nor in "partial" New Christian families was judaizing always continual: sometimes the Marrano tradition skipped a generation and was revived only among the grandchildren. Within the family, women played an important role in fostering the continuity of Marrano traditions. Less exposed to the assimilatory pressures of public life than men were, wives, mothers, grandmothers, and aunts perpetuated the essentially domestic rites and customs of Marranism. Thus they maintained a Marrano home within which the male members of the family, exposed to public denigration and suspicion of *conversos*, found solace, approval, and peace of mind. In the Marrano communities of twentieth-century Portugal, spiritual leadership rests, more often than not, on the shoulders of highly venerated older women. In general, children were not informed of the judaizing meaning of family ceremonies until they were between the ages of ten and fifteen, to protect the family against slips of the juvenile tongue or inopportune revelations before ever vigilant Inquisitorial authorities.

Another channel of transmission ran through professional associations. In the earliest days, a Marrano refused to do business with another until the latter had sworn a Jewish oath. Later, such formal arrangements disappeared, yet informally shared and avowed Marranism appears to have infused subsequent commercial associations with highly prized trust and stability. In turn and up to a point, this trust, based on a common loyalty and kept secret, contributed significantly to the socially created momentum of Marranism. Universities, too, with their colleges and student organizations, their relatively large concentrations of New Christians, and their pervasive preoccupation with purity of blood, proved important centers of judaizing. Especially in medicine, a profession traditionally associated with Jews and generally mistrusted by the religious establishment, Marranos reinforced each other's ancestral loyalties and, where opportune, drew wavering *conversos* into their orbit, by the attraction of New Christian solidarity or in reaction to Old Christian antagonism.

The religious education of the Marranos was extremely limited. For the most part, judaizers had to rely on family traditions of Jewish practices and prayers. Those who wished to deepen their intellectual understanding of Judaism culled information from the Vulgate translation of the Hebrew Bible, including the Apocrypha and Pseudepigrapha, which are not part of the rabbinic canon, and the abundant vernacular literature on biblical themes. Marranos also turned anti-Jewish texts to their advantage, for polemic literature and Inquisitorial edicts of faith never tired of denouncing innumerable Jewish practices and ideas and, thus, publicized forbidden traditions. [*See* Polemics, *article on* Jewish-Christian Polemics.] Genuinely Jewish literature was occasionally smuggled in from the vernacular Spanish and Portuguese presses established by former *conversos* in Italy and Holland.

The Inquisition. In Spain, the initial Inquisitorial hunt for judaizers was begun by district, in stages between 1480 and 1495, depending on the tribunal. Its duration varied widely from jurisdiction to jurisdiction: until about 1510 in most of Old Castile, into the 1520s in Valencia, and into the 1560s in Cuenca. In most of Spain, judging from Inquisitorial documentation, judaizing would appear to have been eradicated within one or two generations after the expulsion and the final wave of conversion, except where it appeared sporadically in isolated regions and in Majorca, where there were dramatic proceedings against several hundred "Xuetas" (probably, "little Jews") from 1675 to 1691. In Portugal, prosecution of judaizers started in 1536 and lasted without major interruptions until the 1760s, that is, across almost ten generations.

The activity of the Portuguese Inquisition is particularly uneven when viewed over time. Dramatic increases in Inquisitorial vigilance occurred between the years 1618 and 1640, between 1660 and 1674, and during the 1720s and 1730s. During the same period, Portuguese judaizers also made their appearance outside of Portugal. Under the union of the Spanish and Portuguese crowns (1580–1640), large numbers of Portuguese New Christians sought economic opportunities or respite from the Portuguese Inquisition, or both, in Spain and its American colonies. The Portuguese rebellion of 1640 rendered these somewhat suspect and increasingly more prosperous immigrants political enemies and provoked retaliation in Spain and its territories in America that lasted into the 1660s. Some Portuguese New Christians nonetheless remained in Spain, and their descendants became the final object of antijudaizing activity in Spanish Inquisitorial history, between 1720 and 1731. Ultimately, the Portuguese Marrano phenomenon survived Inquisitorial repression, and distinct vestiges of judaizing were discovered in Beira Alta and Trás-os-Montes provinces in the twentieth century and have persisted until today.

Some evidence suggests that women were as numerous as men among the judaizer victims of the Inquisitions. During certain periods, such as the first century of the Portuguese Inquisition, women may even have outnumbered men. Two groups stand out as constant and ubiquitous targets of Inquisitorial vigilance: professionals (especially physicians) and merchants of various ilk and size. Almost as numerous are the artisans and public servants, but their incidence varied more, presumably in accordance with local conditions. An occasional cleric is encountered, more apparently before the widespread introduction of *limpieza* statutes. In the earliest days of the Spanish Inquisition, the Jeronymite order, among others, was discovered to harbor a relatively large number of judaizers who had found in the monastery the perfect shelter for their secret activities.

A number of historical circumstances may account for the greater persistence and larger extension of the Marrano phenomenon in Portugal than in Spain. The coexistence of *conversos* and Jews in Spain from 1391 until 1492 forged a clear and permanent distinction between sincere and judaizing *conversos* and undermined *converso* solidarity. In Portugal, where the entire Jewish community was converted at once, ancestral loyalties remained latent, and so acted as a catalyst of group solidarity. Conversion there was even harder for these Spanish exiles, who by their act of emigration had already expressed a strong attachment to Judaism. The forty years that elapsed between the conversion and the institution of the Portuguese Inquisition, moreover, gave judaizers an opportunity to adjust themselves to the exigencies of secrecy. Finally, as former Spanish exiles, the vast majority of Portuguese New Christians (only a very small minority of whom were the descendants of native Portuguese Jews) constituted a distinct ethnic group whose primordial ties reinforced ancestral religious commitments.

Some of the geographic, chronological, and professional variations in Inquisitorial repression are undoubtedly a reflection of differences in the persistence and preponderance of judaizers. The 1618 Oporto arrests (and others of the same sort), the periodic increases in Portuguese Inquisitorial vigilance, and the anti-Portuguese campaign of the Spanish and American Inquisitions smack of arbitrariness and extrareligious inspiration. In these instances, victimization occurred in an atmosphere of commercial rivalry, xenophobia, political discontent, or economic decline. It is difficult, however, to pinpoint exactly how political or economic tension engenders a widening or deepening of Inquisitorial repression. Historians who accept the reality of the Marrano phenomenon and the reliability of Inquisitorial recording seek—but have not yet found, by reason of the sheer magnitude of such a project—reverberations of extrareligious considerations in the trial records themselves: in increases in spontaneous accusations and extorted denunciations, in a greater readiness (on flimsier evidence) to prosecute, or in a slackening of procedural rigor.

The Marrano phenomenon also extended beyond the Iberian world. Most New Christians who emigrated to non-Iberian Europe or to America returned to Judaism; some immediately, others after several generations, depending on the climate of toleration in the land of settlement. These ex-*conversos* founded Jewish communities during the sixteenth century in North Africa, Italy, and Ottoman Greece and Turkey and, during the seventeenth century, in southwestern France, Amsterdam, Hamburg, London, the Caribbean, and North America. The reasons behind their emigration are the subject of an interminable scholarly debate. Some *conversos* migrated in search of economic opportunities, others to reembrace their ancestral Judaism. Most, however, appear to have fled the threat or experience of Inquisitorial persecution. At first, immediately following the institution of the Portuguese Inquisition, this threat gave rise to a general fear prompting many *conversos*, including those not directly threatened, to flee the country. Later the Inquisitorial threat became particularized and was feared primarily by those families one of whose relatives or close associates had been incarcerated and might be forced, by Inquisitorial pressure or torture, to denounce his or her judaizing associates.

Interpretations of the Marrano Phenomenon. Theories about the Marranos are almost as numerous as the scholars who have studied the subject. Difficulty arises from the nearly total lack of sources in the Marrano voice and our need, therefore, to rely almost entirely on the documentation of the Inquisition, a not disinterested adversary, for our information. Some have seen the Inquisition as an instrument of the seignorial class designed to combat, through incarceration and expropriation, the economic, social, and political advances of a rising and largely *converso* middle class. Others have viewed the Inquisitorial persecution of the *conversos* as a continuation of the age-old anti-Jewish struggle of the church inspired by ecclesiastical paranoia. Both views considered the reality of Marranism an Inquisitorial myth and dismissed Inquisitorial documentation as a malicious or misguided fabrication. The *conversos*, they opined, had completely assimilated into Christian society, give or take an occasional atavistic Jewish custom.

At the other extreme, historians have been convinced that many *conversos* consciously attempted to remain Jews to the degree that their enforced clandestinity permitted. The Inquisitorial efforts to stamp out all remaining traces of Judaism were therefore a response to a reality that an intolerant church defined as heretical, and Inquisitorial documentation reveals more or less substantial snippets of a vibrant and tenacious crypto-Judaism. The subsequent resettlement of many Marranos in Jewish communities in more tolerant parts of Europe and America confirms, according to these historians, their unwavering loyalty to Judaism.

Most historians today probably reject both interpretations. No matter what motivation one imputes to the inquisitors, the once secret and immensely detailed archives of the Inquisition are there now for everyone to see, examine, and compare, and the stories they tell are clearly beyond the powers of even the most devious imagination. On the other hand, a simple loyalty to Judaism is inadequate to account for the regional and chronological differences in the manifestations of Marranism; to explain why some and not other Jewish traditions were retained; or to justify the protracted and voluntary lingering of most Marranos in Portugal, Spain, and the colonies.

Historians now generally acknowledge the variety of *converso* religious commitments spanning a spectrum from the sincere Christian via the indifferent or wavering *converso* to the sincere judaizer. They accept that the social experiences of the New Christians, such as "purity of blood" discrimination and pressures to assimilate, influenced the *converso*'s religious commitment so that every New Christian was a potential Marrano who by any one of a number of social accidents or personal idiosyncracies could become an active judaizer. With Israel S. Révah (1959–1960), they define Marranism as "a potential Judaism, which entry into a Jewish community transformed most often into a real Judaism."

Another avenue of approach recognizes Marranism as a popular tradition, that is, the continuation of a popular Jewish tradition that, even when Judaism was a licit religion in Spain and Portugal, had always differed from the Judaism of the rabbinically educated elite. The domestic centrality of popular religion lodges it primordially in a network of familial and ethnic ties at the same time that its private nature renders it less susceptible to public dynamics. The fortunes of popular religion and of Marranism, therefore, fluctuate with the individual's or the Marrano's relation to his or her family, extended group of families, or ethnic community. This relation, in turn, is shaped by the family's or ethnic community's place in society at large. Under the conditions of social discrimination prevailing in Portugal and Spain, the New Christian family or ethnic community experienced differing and intermittent forms of social rejection. At this point, Marranism became the focus of a counterculture, a rejection of the religious principles under which the New Christians were refused their equal place as Christians in Iberian society. The variety of *converso* commitments to Marranism, therefore, spans a spectrum from a more or less witting retention of popular Jewish traditions to a more or less willful embrace of New Christian counterculture.

Aftermath and Impact. The impact of the *converso* problem and the Marrano phenomenon on Iberian and Jewish history cannot be denied, however difficult it may be to gauge its profundity precisely. Scholarly estimations, therefore, vary widely, but the following observations have found a certain general acceptance.

Originally founded to inquire into the religious orthodoxy of the *conversos*, the Spanish and Portuguese Inquisitions usurped the supervision of many other religious affairs, set the strictest limits on religious dissension and innovation, and, in the end, encouraged Iberian Catholicism's drift toward conformism and ritualism. On the other side, the *conversos'* forced induction into Christianity, their rejection by Iberian society, and their involuntary marginality could not but have complicated New Christian attitudes toward Christianity in particular and toward religion in general. Some espoused the complication and vented their misgivings at contemporary Iberian Catholicism or sought satisfaction in more profound religious experiences than were available through the official church. New Christians (e.g., Luis de León, 1527–1591, a poet and writer) were particularly numerous among the anticlerical, antiritualistic Erasmian humanists and pietists, some of whom (e.g., the Sevillian cleric Constantino Ponce de la Fuente) were confusedly accused of Lutheranism. Other New Christians were attracted to the urbane, reformist, heterodox mysticism of the *alumbrados*, who claimed direct, unmediated divine illumination (e.g., the brothers Ortiz), or to the enlightened and militant spirituality of the Jesuits (e.g., Laínez and Polanco, generals of the Jesuit order; possibly Juan de Mariana, a historian; and Baltasar Gracián y Morales, a writer). A few exceptional individuals (e.g., the cleric and reformer John of Ávila, Teresa of Ávila, and, possibly, the priest Miguel de Molinos) formulated their personal, mystical "innovations" in such orthodox terms that they passed even the rigorous examinations of the Inquisition. Other New Christians evaded the complication and retreated into religious indifference or a more or less radical rejection of any and all religions, with or without a public facade of piety and devotion. All in all, the criticism and spiritual quest as well as the contrasting indifference of many sincerely Christian *conversos* left an indelible mark on the Christianity of sixteenth-century Spain and Portugal.

Various significant religious developments in seventeenth-century Jewish history, too, have been explained as reverberations of the Marrano phenomenon. Not surprisingly, among several first-generation Marrano refugees who reconverted to Judaism one encounters an apologetic need to defend Jews and Judaism, as well as a polemic urge to counter the claims of Christianity, that is more common and more strong than that found among traditional Jews. Several of the apologetic works (e.g., those by Menasseh ben Israel, Isaac Cardoso, and Isaac Orobio de Castro) were published in the vernacular, became classics, and have influenced modern perceptions of Jews and Judaism. For reasons of law and self-censorship, the polemic treatises (e.g., by Eliau Montalto, Saul Levi Morteira, Orobio de Castro, and Abraham Gomes Silveyra) circulated in manuscript, in Spanish and Portuguese, among Jews only and have been brought to public attention only recently.

Scholars have also pointed to an unmistakable note of disillusionment with revealed and institutional religion among another group of ex-Marranos. They argue —differing in the weight they give this argument—that some Marranos carried their forceful rejection of Christianity over into a critique of parts or all of the Jewish tradition. Having lost faith in both the Christian and the Jewish traditions, these ex-Marranos joined the growing European community of skeptics; each in a personal way thus projected a distinctly modern alternative to traditional revealed religion. Uriel da Costa (1585–1640) embraced Epicureanism; Barukh Spinoza pursued and reworked Cartesian philosophy to the point of *amor Dei (sive Naturae) intellectualis* ("an intellectual love of God [or Nature]"); and Isaac La Peyrère, according to one theory, envisioned a meta-Judeo-Christian messianism according to the manner in which the Marranos had combined and transcended both the Jewish and the Christian traditions.

Finally, ex-Marrano Jews played a leading role in the most important new Jewish movement of the seventeenth century, that of the pseudomessiah Shabbetai Tsevi. They were among the first and most ardent followers as soon as news of Shabbetai's messianic mission reached the European Jewish communities, and some (e.g., Abraham Cardoso) became prominent advocates of the heretical Shabbatean movement, which retained faith in Shabbetai's messiahship even after his apostasy. In the early days of the movement, ex-Marranos saw in Shabbetai Tsevi a confirmation of the Jewish messianic expectations many of them, as Marranos, had nurtured for several generations in the face of insistent Christian denunciations. Shabbetai's claims that he had apostatized for a messianic purpose reminded a few ex-Marranos of their former double life, and their acceptance of these claims helped put their guilt-laden memories in a new and positive light. Distinct echoes of the Marrano experience, therefore, resound in the two most novel Jewish movements of the seventeenth century: skepticism and mystical messianism. [*See* Messianism, *article on* Jewish Messianism; *see also the biographies of Spinoza and Shabbetai Tsevi.*]

Non-Iberian Parallels to Marranism. Jewish loyalties among converted Jews survived elsewhere and at other times in Jewish history. A certain degree of Marranism attended every instance of a forced conversion of Jews. In most cases, the forcibly converted Jews either fled and returned to Judaism, were eventually assimilated completely into the native population, or were permitted, by a subsequent decree, to return to Judaism. In a few cases, however, the forcibly converted Jews remained a group apart. Thus, in Italy in the early 1290s, the Jews of Apulia were forcibly converted. Throughout the fourteenth and much of the fifteenth centuries, sources continue to speak of the *neofiti* ("neophytes") or *mercanti* ("merchants"), the descendants of these converted Jews, as a group that had not completely abandoned its ancestral Jewish practices.

The other documented cases of Marranism occurred in Persia. In the middle of the seventeenth century, first the Jews of Isfahan and later those of the rest of Persia were forcibly converted. The converts and their descendants were known as *Jadīd al-Islam* ("New Muslim"). In 1839, the Jews of Mashhad were forcibly converted and also called *Jadīd al-Islam.* In both cases the Jedidim successfully resisted pressures to intermarry with the rest of the Muslim population. The ultimate fate of the earlier Jedidim is not known. The Mashhad Jedidim, however, maintained themselves as a community through endogamy, religious leadership, and communal observances and instruction. Some settled elsewhere either as Jedidim or as Jews (as in Jerusalem in the 1890s) and so gave rise to an economically important Jadīd diaspora; others remained in Persia, where they still formed a distinct Judeo-Muslim group as late as the 1940s.

In sum, Marrano-like survivals of Jewish loyalties among converted Jews appeared where the converted Jews chose to stay in their native land, where the religious and social intolerance that had given rise to the forced conversion persisted unabatedly for many subsequent generations, and where the Jewish, neophyte, or Jadīd community constituted a more or less distinct and cohesive socioeconomic group. The extent to which variations in the intensity of Jewish commitments prior to conversion played a role in emergent Marrinism cannot be precisely assessed.

[*For related discussions, see* Inquisition, The, *and* Heresy, *article on* Christian Concepts. *See also* Judaism, *article on* Judaism in Southern Europe.]

BIBLIOGRAPHY

General Studies. The only comprehensive book-length study of the Marranos remains Cecil Roth's outdated and not always reliable *A History of the Marranos* (Philadelphia, 1932). Roth summarized the then limited state of knowledge almost entirely on the basis of far from satisfactory secondary literature. Shorter, updated, better informed, and fully annotated is Israel S. Révah's "Les Marranos," *Revue des études juives* 108 (1959–1960) 2–77.

Marranism in Spain and Portugal. For Spain we possess two substantial overviews: Julio Caro Baroja's *Los Judíos en la España moderna y contemporánea*, 3 vols. (Madrid, 1962), an uneven, but, when used with discrimination, extremely informative history by a well-known anthropologist; and Antonio Dominguez Ortiz's *Los Judeoconversos en España y América* (Madrid, 1971), a sober and judicious account by one of Spain's most eminent historians. The early history of the Marranos of Ciudad Real is covered on the basis of all available Inquisitorial documentation in Haim Beinart's *Conversos on Trial* (Jerusalem, 1981); a more exhaustive and surefooted treatment especially of the Jewish element in Marranism than the previous overviews. On the basis of contemporary Hebrew sources, Benzion Netanyahu's *The Marranos of Spain from the Late Fourteenth to the Early Sixteenth Century* (New York, 1966) argues against the theory of a persistent and vibrant judaizing among the forced converts. For Portugal, the classic account of João Lucio d'Azevedo, *História dos cristãos novos portugueses* Lisbon, 1921), focuses more on the political history of the New Christian problem than on the evolution of the Marrano phenomenon. Although primarily a history of the fierce political struggle surrounding the establishment of the Portugese Inquisition, Alexandre Herculano's *History of the Origin and Establishment of the Inquisition in Portugal,* translated by J. C.

Branner (Stanford, Calif., 1926), contains much invaluable information on the early sixteenth-century history of the Portuguese Marranos. António José Saraiva's *Inquisição e cristãos-novos* (Oporto, Portugal, 1969) interprets the Inquisition's prosecution of the Portuguese New Christians in terms of a class struggle. The best study of the Marranos in the Spanish and Portuguese colonies is Anita Novinsky's *Cristãos novos na Bahia* (São Paulo, 1972), which stresses the anti-Catholic, defensive nature of the Marrano phenomenon.

Marranos in a Non-Iberian Context. Surveying the Marranos in a non-Iberian context, Brian Pullan's *The Jews of Europe and the Inquisition of Venice, 1550–1670* (Oxford, 1983) offers a new and promising perspective on Marranism in general.

Biographic Sources. Marranism has been studied successfully in a number of excellent biographies. Yosef Hayim Yerushalmi's *From Spanish Court to Italian Ghetto: Isaac Cardoso; A Study in Seventeenth-Century Marranism and Jewish Apologetics* (New York, 1971) delivers far more than the title indicates and probes deeply into the intellectual world of a Marrano who returned to Judaism. In Hebrew, Yosef Kaplan's *From Christianity to Judaism: The Life and Work of Isaac Orobio de Castro* (Jerusalem, 1982) meticulously reconstructs the life of another ex-Marrano. Martin A. Cohen's *The Martyr: The Story of a Secret Jew and the Mexican Inquisition in the Sixteenth Century* (Philadelphia, 1973) beautifully tells the story of the famous adventurer, Luis Carvajal the Younger.

Works of Related Interest. Edward Glaser's "Invitation to Intolerance: A Study of the Portuguese Sermons Preached at Autos-da-fé," *Hebrew Union College Annual* 27 (1956): 327–385, offers keen insights into the anti-*converso* mentality of the inquisitors. Albert A. Sicroff's *Les controverses des statuts de "pureté de sang" en Espagne du quinzième au dix-septième siècle* (Paris, 1960) gives a detailed outline of the intellectual debate surrounding the "purity of blood" statutes.

Daniel M. Swetschinski

MARRIAGE. Every culture of the world recognizes some form of the institution of marriage. In most cultures and religions neither man nor woman is considered complete, after reaching maturity, without a spouse. Many religions consider marriage as a sacred act that originates from a god or as the union of souls or spirits with the sacred realm.

Jewish beliefs trace the origin of marriage to Adam and Eve and view their union as a part of the fabric of creation. The nuptial blessings emphasize marriage in the scheme of creation and speak of the state of marriage as paradise regained. As a blessing from God, Jewish marriage should not only perpetuate humankind but should also enhance and complete the partners' personal growth.

Christian marriage is also identified with the sacred union of Adam and Eve and is regarded as a vocation. The ceremony joins the bride and groom into one spirit in union with Christ and God. In Christianity, marriage is also a metaphor for the marriage of the church to Christ. In this sense the bride and groom become the "bride" of Christ and are heirs together of the grace of life through the spirit of Christ.

For the Hindu, marriage is also a sacred institution whereby man and woman become one in spirit. Hindu marriage is also a social duty, and in the Vedic period it was a moral and religious obligation as well. Marriage and the siring of male children was the only possible way in which a man could repay his debt to his ancestors.

Marriage among the Zinacantecos, a Maya Indian group in central Mexico, is a mixture of native Indian religion and sixteenth-century Catholicism, as it is in most Latin American cultures. In these societies the celebration of a Christian marriage was urged on the native Indians by the Spanish conquerors as the only means to attain heaven at death. Marriage here takes place on two levels. It is not simply the relationship between two individuals and their families, but it is also a bond between the souls of the bride and groom.

Among the Hopi Indians of the American Southwest, a woman initiates a marriage and brings a husband to her father's house. The marriage is necessary for the girl's life after death. The wedding clothes that are provided by her husband's male relatives will become her shroud upon her death and will transport her spirit into the afterworld. And so, without entering into marriage, one cannot truly die.

Purpose of Marriage. The purpose of marriage and the beliefs that surround this institution must be viewed differently for every culture. Marriage in industrialized societies is very different from that in societies where kinship relations and the alliances created through those relations will be the most important part of an individual's life. Here, the marriage arrangements may not take individual choice into account. There are three major categories of belief about the purposes of marriage: marriage may be viewed as existing primarily for the continuation of the family and society through procreation; it may be considered most importantly as an alliance, that is, the means to bring about the integration of society by setting up kinship ties and kinship terminology; and finally, the union of bride and groom may be perceived as a complex system of exchanges between groups and/or individuals. These categories will be validated through the religious beliefs of the society.

Continuation of society. The institution of marriage perpetuates society by socially recognizing the union of man and woman and incorporating their offspring into the fabric of social life. There are variants of marriage forms that exist in many cultures to allow for the continuation of the family and of society in the event that one of the marriage partners dies. The two best known forms are the levirate and the sororate. In the levirate, when the husband of a marriage dies, an approved male relative of his may live with the widow and the children. This replacement husband will conceive more children for the deceased as if he were the deceased. In the sororate, the place of a deceased wife is taken by her sister.

The Nuer and Zulu societies of Africa practice another variant of the more traditional marriage in order that the family of the deceased may continue. There are two types of this "ghost marriage." If a man is engaged and dies before the marriage, his fiancée should marry one of his kinsmen and conceive children for the dead man, in much the same way as in the levirate. A man may also "waken" a dead relative who was never married by marrying a wife to his name and conceiving children for him. Also among these two groups, women may "become" men to carry on the male line. A rich, important woman, or the eldest daughter in a family with no sons, can marry another woman and become the father of her wife's children who are conceived by some male relative of the female husband. The importance of all these forms of marriage is that they allow for the perpetuation of the family line, and indirectly the entire society, through the existing structure of social relations.

While these forms of marriage perpetuate society through those who have died, many societies ensure their continuation into the future by marrying off those individuals not yet born. Among the Tiwi of Australia, a young girl is contracted for her future marriage before her birth, at her mother's wedding ceremony. When the girl enters puberty her wedding ceremony is held. This ceremony is attended by the girl, her father, and her husband, as well as her future sons-in-law. For in the same way that she has been married since her mother's wedding, here at her wedding she also marries her daughters to their future husbands.

Alliance. The importance placed upon marriage in many societies is in its role in integrating society. Marriage is the starting point for the kinship ties that run across and between different and independent kinship or descent groups. A marriage will be used to create an alliance between two lines of descent with very little focus upon the relationship between the bride and groom. In many cases these will be arranged marriages, often making use of go-betweens to reach an agreement between the two families. Love is not a requirement here, but the affection that exists after many years of successful marriage is a product of the marriage. Among Georgian Jews, when dowry is unavailable, a love marriage may be effected by elopement, the legitimacy of which is later recognized if the match appears to be successful.

System of exchange. In the final category of marriage beliefs, marriage represents the gift or exchange of women between two descent groups. The position of giving or receiving wives sets up a constantly changing mechanism by which status is expressed and validated between the two kinship groups. The ideal exchange is for both descent groups to exchange sisters, thereby maintaining the status of each group as equal. Marrying a woman in compensation for the death of a man is also an exchange recognized as equivalent in many cultures for the settlement of quarrels.

When women are not exchanged equally, then the balance between the two groups remains unequal and must be achieved through other means. This balancing may take the form of payments made on behalf of the husband to the man or the family who has given up the wife. These payments are viewed as equivalent to the reproductive powers of the woman who is being given to another group as well as a return on the labor and usefulness the bride's family will lose upon her marriage. These payments are known as "bride-price" or "bride-wealth."

Postmarital residence or marriage service may be used in a similar way as bride-price or may even be combined with bride-wealth payments. To repay the bride's family for the loss of a daughter, the groom will serve his in-laws for an agreed-upon time. In the Hebrew scriptures, for example, this type of service is described in *Genesis* 29, which tells of Jacob's serving his father-in-law for seven years for each of his wives, Leah and Rachel.

Dowry is not the opposite of bride-price; rather, it is an endowment of property upon the bride from her own family and is generally viewed as her share of the family inheritance. In some instances, however, dowry may closely resemble the practice of paying bride-price, as in marriages between castes in India and Sri Lanka. Most Hindu marriages are traditionally made between members of the same caste, and no dowry will be given. However, when a girl marries into a higher caste she will be accompanied by a substantial dowry in symbolic payment for her movement to a higher status. This practice is known as hypergamy.

Exchange relationships at marriage may be expressed primarily through the flow of gifts between families, and frequently these expenses will be about equal on both sides. The power of the gift is not only in the object as gift but in the relationships that lie behind the gifts. It is the exchange itself that is essential to the completion and success of the marriage. This exchange of gifts is often an important part of the religious ceremony of marriage.

Forms of Marriage. There are two basic forms of marriage: monogamy, the union of one man with one woman, and polygamy, the union of a man or a woman with multiple marriage partners. Polygamy can also be divided into two types: polyandry, in which a woman has more than one husband, and, conversely, polygyny, in which a man has more than one wife. Polygyny is the most common form of multiple marriage, and the plurality of wives is mainly the privilege of older men and their wealth. Polygyny augments the power of a man by increasing his alliances and following. But it may cause conflict among co-wives, as among the Ndembu of Zambia. Conflict between wives is very common in Islamic lands. The Tiv of Nigeria manage the problem differently: the first wife becomes the "husband" of the "little wives," and grows very attached to them.

The classic case of polyandry is in Tibet, where a group of brothers may jointly marry a wife. The wedding takes place when the eldest brother has reached the appropriate age, and on formal occasions it is he who will perform the role of father, although all brothers are viewed as the father to the children of the marriage. One effect of polyandry is to keep down the population, an important goal where arable land is a scarce resource. There is, however, an alternative to polyandrous marriage open to younger brothers: they may become monks and commit themselves to a life of celibacy. Such a "marriage" to religion or to God is an avenue available to both sexes in most societies.

Societies regulate not only how many spouses one can have but from what general categories these individuals should be selected. Exogamy, marriage outside a defined kinship group, is primarily concerned with incest prohibitions. Brother-sister and parent-child unions are forbidden in nearly every culture; cousin marriage is forbidden in the third degree of the collateral line among Roman Catholics, while it is recommended among many peoples of Africa. Endogamy is marriage within a defined group as required by custom or law. This group may be defined by culturally recognized kinship ties or by a religious tradition. Pious Roman Catholics and Jews obey the rule of endogamy and take a spouse from within their own religion. Good Hindus will keep marriage within their own caste, except when practicing hypergamy.

Marriage as a Rite of Passage. A rite of passage is a vehicle for moving an individual or a group of individuals from one way of being to another through a series of culturally recognized stages. A marriage ceremony moves the bride and groom from being unmarried to being husband and wife. Just as the definition of what marriage is will vary cross-culturally, so will the manner in which the union of marriage is created and recognized. The rite of passage may extend over a long period of time and include great finery and complex symbolism, or there may be no traditional ceremony at all, simply an action conducted in public view. [*See* Rites of Passage.]

Marriage Ritual. The ceremonials of marriage may be entirely of a religious nature, include both religious and secular elements, or be entirely within the secular and legal realm. Two elements are used to mark a marriage, whether there is a ceremony or not: the sharing of food between the bride and groom (or some passage of food or other substance between them) and the necessity of a public statement or the requirement of witnesses to the marriage event, which may even include proof of virginity and consummation, as among Arabs.

Among the Mundurucu of South America, a marriage is marked only when the man brings the day's kill to his bride instead of to one of his close female relatives. The Ndembu of Africa, like the Tiwi of Australia, combine the puberty rites for a young girl with her marriage ceremony. Here the emphasis is upon fertility. The rites take place where the groom has planted his arrow by the "milk tree," a tree that represents the matrilineage. Among Trobriand Islanders, a man and a woman may have been sleeping together for a long while, but their marriage is not acknowledged until they eat yams together in public. The Burmese wedding ceremony does not create marriage but is, rather, the public statement that a couple intend to live together as husband and wife. The symbol of marriage here is the sharing of food from the same bowl by the bride and groom after the ceremony.

The Jewish marriage ceremony must have witnesses for the signing of the marriage contract and for the symbolic consummation, the *yiḥud,* or time of privacy. It is during this time of privacy that the couple break their fast and eat together for the first time. When they emerge from their seclusion, they are husband and wife and will then share a meal with their guests.

The wedding ceremony in Burma is not attended by Buddhist monks. This ceremony is a secular affair contained within religious rites. The Buddhist monks are fed a special meal in the bride's home the morning before the wedding. This feast acquires merit for the couple to be married and for the parents of the bride. A religious ceremony is held the evening after the wedding at the village shrine and offerings are made by the bride, her mother, and the mother of the groom to the guardian spirits of the village and to the spirits of the ancestors. During the secular wedding ceremony the couple are instructed to worship their parents and the Buddha. Their hands are held together and immersed in a bowl of water so that "their union should be as indivisible as water."

Christian marriage may be regarded as a sacrament, one of the outward signs of inward grace, and may include the Eucharist within the ceremony, the sacred sharing of the mystical body of Christ that unites all participants with God. [*See* Sacrament, *article on* Christian Sacraments.] In most Christian churches this is an optional rite, but a wedding will usually be followed by a sharing of food and drink with guests. This part of the ceremony is not sacred. One can also be a Christian and include few if any religious elements in the marriage ceremony—which may be performed entirely within the secular domain by various officers of law. Or a couple may become married simply by living together for a set period of years, thus forming a marriage in "common law." These options to the traditional marriage ceremony are available in other religions as well.

The necessity for consummation to occur in order for a marriage to be legally binding is not universal but is culturally and religiously specific. Although the Virgin Mary bore Christ without intercourse with her husband, any Christian marriage can be annulled or canceled if the couple do not consummate the marriage. In Hinduism, however, the most important rite for validation of a marriage is the ceremony called Sāptapadī, the "taking of seven steps" by the couple before the sacred nuptial fire. Legally the marriage is complete with the seventh step, for according to the Hindu Marriage Act of 1955 consummation is not necessary to make marriage complete and binding.

The marriage ceremony of Java is a syncretism of Hinduism, Islam, and folk religion from the villages. The evening before the ceremony, a feast called the Slametan is held. Then the bride must sit by herself for five hours until midnight. At midnight an angel enters her and will remain in her until five days after the wedding. The actual wedding begins the next day when the groom makes a trip to the office of the government religious official to register and legalize the marriage. For Javanese Muslims, this is the important part of the marriage ceremony, for it is here that the marriage is made official in the eyes of God and the government. However, according to the folk religion the couple is not married until they exchange their *kembang majang* ("blossoming flowers"), which stand for their virginity. And then they must eat from one another's dish but they must not finish their food. Consummation of the marriage is believed to have occurred when this food begins to smell in five days, or when the angel has left the bride.

Creation Myths and the Institution of Marriage. Many origin myths that explain the creation of the world and of humankind also explain marriage. In Samoa the marriage of the creator god Tangaloa with a woman he has created begins the world and, through their union, all of mankind. The Makasar of Indonesia believe that the son of the sky deity was sent to earth on a rainbow to prepare the world for humans. This god married six female deities and their offspring became the peoples of the world. The union of the Japanese gods Izanagi and Izanami consolidates and fertilizes the moving earth. Through their union, they produced the islands of Japan. The marriage of Osiris, one of the greatest of ancient Egyptian deities, with his sister Isis accounts for the continuation of the pharaohs and their practice of marrying their sisters. And, for Jews, Christians, and Muslims alike, the marriage of Adam and Eve, two beings created by God, generates all of humankind.

[*See also* Hieros Gamos *and* Mystical Union.]

BIBLIOGRAPHY

One of the first scholars to concern himself with marriage practices was Lewis Henry Morgan in *Ancient Society* (New York, 1877). Following this evolutionary approach, Edward A. Westermarck compiled his classic *The History of Human Marriage* (1891), 3 vols., 5th ed. (1921; reprint, New York, 1971). This three-volume set treats everything believed to be related to marriage in that time, including marriage rites, customs, and kinship organizations. One of the classic studies of the constitution of social groups and their unity was written by W. Robertson Smith following the precedents set by Morgan and Westermarck. Smith's *Kinship and Marriage in Early Arabia,* edited by Stanley A. Cook (1903; Oosterhuit, 1966), goes beyond these first works and is particularly concerned with the laws of marriage and how this institution functioned within the tribal organization in Arabia at the time of Muḥammad. The theories of primitive promiscuity and group marriage as the earliest forms of marriage in human history that are put forth by all of these books have never been substantiated, but these works provide valuable insights into human society.

For a contemporary view of love and marriage in the Jewish religion and its place in society, see Maurice Lamm's *The Jewish Way in Love and Marriage* (San Francisco, 1980). This book also includes a thorough description of a contemporary Jewish wedding ceremony. The best review of marriage and kinship beliefs for cultures of Africa is *African Systems of Kinship and Marriage,* edited by A. R. Radcliffe-Brown and Daryll Forde (Oxford, 1962). This book considers marriage in relation to other aspects of culture including economic, political, and religious beliefs. Melford E. Spiro's *Kinship and Marriage in Burma: A Cultural and Psychodynamic Analysis* (Berkeley, 1977) is an excellent presentation of kinship beliefs in Burma and includes a full account of Burmese Buddhist views on marriage. Clifford Geertz's seminal work *The Religion of Java*

(Glencoe, Ill., 1960) describes the syncretism of Hindu, Islamic, and folk beliefs that comprise Javanese religion. This book focuses on the five major occupations of the population and their religious beliefs that shape the moral organization of the culture of Java. The mixture of Catholic and Maya Indian beliefs is explored in Evon Z. Vogt's *Zinacantan: A Maya Community in the Highlands of Chiapas* (Cambridge, Mass., 1969). An extensive study of the Tzotzil-speaking Indians of Guatemala, it includes a full account of their religious beliefs and marriage practices, especially the relationships created between families and *compadres*, or ritual godparents. For an excellent view of marriage as a life process, begun before the birth of the bride and occurring in gradual stages as she matures, see Jane C. Goodale's *Tiwi Wives: A Study of the Women of Melville Island, North Australia* (Seattle, 1971).

EDITH TURNER and PAMELA R. FRESE

MARS. The Latin name *Mars*, found throughout Italy, lacks any Indo-European etymology. It appears in both a simple form and in doubled form. The Latin *Mars* coexists with an ancient form, *Mavors* (kept in use by poets), as well as a contracted form, *Maurs* (see *Corpus inscriptiorum Latinarum*, Berlin, 1863, vol. 1, no. 49). As for the doubled form, *Marmar*, it very likely stems from **Mar-mart-s;* it is found in the *Carmen Arvale* along with *Marmor*, which seems an odd form. The dative *Marmartei*, found in an inscription at Satricum dating from the sixth century BCE, implies the existence of a nominative, **Mamars. Mamers*, which the ancients identified as an Oscan term (Paulus-Festus, ed. Lindsay, 1913, p. 150 L.), derived from **Mamars* by apophony of the second vowel.

Mars is the Roman god of power, particularly of war. He held the second position in the archaic triad Jupiter-Mars-Quirinus. He received the second share of the *spolia opima* in the threefold distribution of that highest of military spoils established by the law of Numa (Festus, op. cit., p. 204 L.). He had not only a particular priest, the *flamen Martialis*, but also a specific kind of offering: the *suovetaurilia*, a set of three victims (boar, ram, and bull).

The liturgy concerning Mars consisted of two sets of feasts corresponding to the opening and closing of the military season. The first, in the spring, comprised the following feasts: the horse races on 27 February and 14 March for the Equirria on the Field of Mars; the Agonium Martiale on 17 March; and the lustration of arms at the Quinquatrus on 19 March and that of battle trumpets at the Tubilustrium on 23 March. The second set, in autumn, included the rite of purification at the Tigillum Sororium on 1 October; the sacrifice of a war horse during the rites of the Equus October, on 15 October; and the lustration of arms, Armilustrium, on 19 October.

In spring as in autumn, the priestly brotherhood of the Salii displayed themselves at these feasts dancing while brandishing lances *(hastae)* and shields *(ancilia)*. (One of the shields was said to have dropped from the sky; see Ovid, *Fasti* 3.369ff.) In ordinary times these arms were kept in the *sacrarium* of Mars within the Regia ("king's house"). The Salii, divided into two twelve-member groups called the Salii Palatini and the Salii Collini, were under the protection of Jupiter, Mars, and Quirinus (Servius, *Ad Aeneidem* 8.663). It is probable that the opening service for the military season in spring was handled by the Salii Palatini, with Mars as their patron, and the closing service by the Salii Collini with Quirinus as their patron.

The god's military character was well established. While some scholars (e.g., Hermansen, 1940) have imagined an agrarian Mars as well, it would seem that this opinion is based on a confusion between the god's intrinsic nature and the range of applications for his intervention. His power could be employed not only in warfare but also in agriculture. In the *Carmen Arvale*, the Arval Brothers prayed to the "fierce Mars" *(fere Mars)* to protect Roman territory by "leaping to the border" *(limen sali)*. Likewise, Cato the Elder's peasant invoked Mars "to halt, rebuff, and cast away visible and invisible maladies" (*De agricultura* 141).

The god's most ancient place of worship was situated on the Field of Mars at the *ara Martis*, the altar near which D. Junius Brutus Callaicus erected a temple in 138 BCE. The most important sanctuary was the temple of Mars outside the Porta Collina, near the Via Appia. It was dedicated on 1 June 338 BCE and served as the starting point for the annual cavalry parade (Dionysius of Halicarnassus, 6.13.4).

On the occasion of the *lectisternium* of 217 BCE, Mars was associated with Venus after the pattern of Ares and Aphrodite, but with the aim of exalting the connection between the father of the city (Romulus, son of Mars) and the mother of the nation (Venus, ancestor of the Aeneades). Later Augustus created the cult of Mars the avenger (Mars Vltor). The basis for this was twofold: he was avenger of the Roman disaster suffered by M. Licinius Crassus at Carrhae in 53 BCE (negotiations with the Parthians, resulting in the restitution of Roman insignia, had been presented as a victory), and also avenger of the assassination of Julius Caesar (the victory at Philippi in 42 BCE). Later, Augustus in 20 BCE had a round temple erected upon the Capitoline in honor of Mars Vltor (Dio Cassius, 54.8.3). Still later, in 2 BCE, he built the great temple situated in its own forum (ibid., 60.5.3). Thus Mars enjoyed new prestige.

BIBLIOGRAPHY

Dumézil, Georges. *Archaic Roman Religion.* 2 vols. Translated by Philip Krapp. Chicago, 1970. Discusses the theory of the agrarian Mars.

Dumézil, Georges. *Fêtes romaines d'été et d'automne.* Paris, 1975. Pages 139–156 and 177–219 treat the Equus October.

Hermansen, Gustav. *Studien über den italischen und den römischen Mars.* Copenhagen, 1940. Supports the theory of the agrarian Mars.

Ramat, A. G. "Studi intorno ai nomi del dio Marte." *Archeologia e glottologia italiano* 47 (1962): 112ff.

Schilling, Robert. *La religion romaine de Vénus.* 2d ed. Paris, 1982. Pages 107ff. treat the association between Mars and Venus in the *lectisternium* of 217 BCE.

Stibbe, C. M., et al. *Lapis Satricanus: Archaeological, Epigraphical, Linguistic and Historical Aspects of the New Inscription from Satricum.* The Hague, 1980.

Wissowa, Georg. *Religion und Kultus der Römer.* 2d ed. Munich, 1912. See pages 141ff.

ROBERT SCHILLING

Translated from French by Paul C. Duggan

MARSILIUS OF PADUA (c. 1275–1342), originally Marsilio dei Mainardini; Italian political theorist. Marsilius probably studied medicine at the University of Padua. In 1313 he was rector of the University of Paris, where he met such leading Averroists as Peter of Abano and John of Jandun. He is famous chiefly for his antipapalist treatise *Defensor pacis* (Defender of Peace; 1324), a landmark in the history of political philosophy. When his authorship of this work became known in 1326, he was forced to flee to the court of Louis of Bavaria in Nuremberg; Pope John XXII thereupon branded him a heretic. Marsilius subsequently assisted Louis in various imperial ventures in Italy.

The primary purpose of the *Defensor pacis* was to refute the papalist claims to "plenitude of power" as advanced by Pope Innocent IV, Egidius of Rome, and others in the thirteenth and fourteenth centuries. The papal position had held that secular rulers must be subject to the papacy even in "temporal" affairs, so that they must be established, judged, and, if necessary, deposed by the pope. Marsilius, in contrast, undertook to demonstrate that the papacy and the priesthood in general must be subject not only in temporal but even in "spiritual" affairs to the whole people, with the powers of the priesthood reduced to the administration of the sacraments and the teaching of divine law.

Marsilius's doctrine overthrew the attempt to base human society on religious values under priestly control; instead, the way was opened for a purely secular society under the control of a popularly elected government. Hence, it is understandable that Marsilius has been hailed as a prophet of the modern world. His treatise exerted a marked influence on the conciliar movement and during the period of the Reformation.

Equally as important as these revolutionary conclusions are the three premises from which Marsilius derived them. These premises are found in his general theory of the state. The first is the Aristotelian teleological view of the state as subserving the good life. The various parts of the state, including government, are defined by the contribution they make to the rational "fulfillment" of man's natural desire for the highest ends of a "sufficient life," which include the common benefit and justice.

The second theme, in contrast, is a negative and minimal utilitarianism. It emphasizes the inevitability of conflicts among persons and the consequent need for the formal instrumentalities of coercive law and government in order to regulate these conflicts and avert the destruction of human society. In developing this theme, Marsilius presents a positivistic concept of law, which stands in contrast to his nonpositivistic conception of justice (a distinction often overlooked in discussions of his ideas). Marsilius, unlike most medieval political philosophers, holds that justice is not a necessary condition of law. What is necessary is that the legal rules have coercive force. These rules and the government that enforces them must be unitary in the sense that, if a society is to survive, it cannot have two or more rival coercive bodies of law and government.

The third theme of Marsilius's political theory is that the people are the only legitimate source of all political authority. It is the people, the whole body of citizens or its "weightier part," who must make the laws either by themselves or through elected representatives, and it is also the people who must elect, "correct," and, if necessary, depose the government.

Although all three themes of Marsilius's general political theory were found in earlier medieval political philosophers, no other philosopher had given the second and third themes as central a position as did Marsilius. The full consequence of these emphases emerges in the applications he makes of his general political theory to the problems of ecclesiastical politics.

In keeping with his first theme, Marsilius views the Christian priesthood as one of the parts of the state dedicated to achieving the "sufficient life" for all believers. Unlike the other parts of the state, however, the priesthood subserves the "sufficient life" to be attained primarily "in the future world" rather than the present one. Marsilius manifests skepticism about the rational demonstrability of such a future life; nevertheless, he officially accepts the Christian doctrine that the future life is superior to the present life. He also holds, however, that secular and religious values are in basic opposition. Here he seems to be applying in the realm of the practical the Averroist doctrine of the contrariety of reason and faith in theoretical philosophy.

At this point, however, Marsilius's second and third themes have their effect. Since the essence of political authority is the coerciveness required for the minimal end of preserving society, it follows that the higher end subserved by the priesthood does not entitle it to superior political authority. The question of the order of political superiority and inferiority is thus separated from the question of the order of moral and religious values. According to Marsilius's second theme, the secular government, as bearer of coercive authority, must be politically superior to the priesthood. If the priests refuse to obey the government and its laws, then they must be compelled to do so, because such disobedience threatens that unity of coercive authority without which society cannot survive.

In addition to this political argument against diverse centers of coercive power in any society, Marsilius also stresses, from within the religious tradition itself, that religious belief, in order to be meritorious, must be purely voluntary. Hence, in order to fulfill its mission, divine law and the priesthood that teaches and administers it cannot be coercive in this world.

Marsilius's third theme, republicanism, also plays an important role in the political subordination of the priesthood and papacy. The only rules and persons entitled to the status of being coercive laws and government officials are those ultimately chosen by the people; hence, there can be no crediting the claims of divine law and the priesthood to a separate derivation of coercive political authority from God. Because the whole people is superior in virtue to any of its parts and because freedom requires popular consent or election, the priesthood itself must be elected by the people of each community rather than being appointed by an oligarchically chosen pope. Also, the pope himself must be elected by the whole of Christendom. Similarly, the whole people must elect general councils to provide authoritative interpretations of the meaning of divine law. In these ways Marsilius's general political theory leads to a republican structure for the church as opposed to its traditional monarchical structure.

BIBLIOGRAPHY

There are two critical editions of *Defensor pacis*, one edited by C. W. Previté-Orton (Cambridge, 1928), the other edited by Richard Scholz in *Fontes juris Germanici antiqui* of the *Monumenta Germaniae Historica* (Hanover, 1932). I have translated it in volume 2 of my *Marsilius of Padua, the Defender of Peace* (New York, 1956). This translation has been reprinted in several later editions.

For studies of Marsilius's doctrines, see my *Marsilius of Padua and Medieval Political Philosophy* (1951; reprint, New York, 1979); Georges de Lagarde's *La naissance de l'esprit laïque au déclin du moyen age*, vol. 3, *Le defensor pacis* (Louvain, 1970); and Jeannine Quillet's *La philosophie politique de Marsile de Padoue* (Paris, 1970). Two volumes of essays from the Convegno Internazionale su Marsilio da Padova, held at the University of Padua in 1980, are in the historical journal *Medioevo: Rivista di storia della filosofia medievale* 5–6 (1979–1980).

ALAN GEWIRTH

MARTIAL ARTS.

[*This entry consists of two articles that focus on the martial arts as spiritual disciplines.* An Overview *presents the religious and meditative dimensions of the martial traditions of India, China, Japan, and Indonesia.* Buddhist Martial Arts *treats the role of martial traditions in Japanese Buddhism.*]

An Overview

The role of the warrior has been a position of importance to many cultures historically, with the efficacy of combat strategies and warrior skills often determining the course of history and the continued existence of groups of people. In the cultures of South Asia, Southeast Asia, and the Far East, religious beliefs and teachings often interpenetrated the martial traditions. Just as the physical forms of these arts have varied from one country to the next, so too have their religious and meditative components. For some martial traditions, these spiritual elements constitute the highest levels of practice. This article will introduce the varied religious and meditative dimensions of martial traditions as found in India, China, Japan, and Indonesia—an orientation often overlooked by practitioners of such disciplines, who prefer to concentrate upon the physical dimensions of practice. Regrettably, most of what is known about many martial arts is limited to information transmitted by oral tradition. Hence, even theories about the origins of the martial arts remain speculative and nebulous. However, most historians agree that some of the earliest traceable roots lead either to India or China.

India. The origins of the martial traditions of India are difficult to trace and verify, but vestiges of fighting techniques used in ancient India do remain. Early references to combative situations can be found in such classic epics as the *Ṛgveda*, the *Rāmāyaṇa*, and the *Mahābhārata*. Contemporary writings generally emphasize wrestling forms *(kuṣṭhi, varja-muṣṭi, binoṭ, masti)* and weaponry (e.g., *bāṇa, pharī-gatkā, lāṭhī, paṭā, cilampam).* Wrestling flourished in India before the beginnings of the Aryan invasions (c. 1500 BCE).

Aside from wrestling and weaponry, there exists surprisingly little information concerning any organized martial disciplines. Some systems are mentioned sporadically in the literature, including *aṭitaṭa, cilampam, kuttu varicai* (Tamil), and *mukkebazi,* though no reference to religious practices is to be found. However, recent Western investigations of the Indian martial system known as *kaḷarippayaṯṯu* have begun to uncover the association between religious and physical aspects of practice in Indian culture today.

Kaḷarippayaṯṯu (*kaḷari,* "fencing school"; *payaṯṯu,* "fencing exercise"; *kaḷarippayaṯṯu,* "place where martial exercises are taught") is a system of martial training found in Kerala which, in its present form, dates back to at least the twelfth century CE. It was developed primarily to prepare Kerala's martial caste (Nairs) for combat, although higher-caste Yatra brahmans, lower-caste Tiyyas, and many Muslims and Christians were also proficient in the form. This system rests upon preliminary physical culture training (physical exercise and body massage) that is later followed by practice in unarmed combat as well as a variety of weapons.

In *kaḷarippayaṯṯu,* in-depth knowledge of the *marma*—vulnerable points of the human body—is required in order to know where to attack one's opponent, how to protect one's own body, and how to treat injuries to these vital spots during training or battle. Further, the use of breathing exercises, repetition of *mantra*s, visual concentration, and performance of special rituals (paying respects to deities and teachers) all aid in achieving proper mind-body coordination and may lead to the development of power *(śakti).* The lower abdominal region referred to as the *nabhi* or *nabhi mūla(m),* as well as the three lower *cakra*s of *kuṇḍalinīyoga,* may also be stressed in *kaḷarippayaṯṯu.* The *nahbi mūla(m)* corresponds to the second yogic *cakra, svādhiṣṭhāna,* and is recognized as the source of *prāṇa-vāyu* ("energy").

Attempting to articulate the spiritual dimensions of an Indian martial system is difficult in a culture that possesses such an indigenous spiritual tradition as yoga. It is evident that some of the techniques and practices employed in *kaḷarippayaṯṯu* overlap with yoga. However, within most schools, the process of spiritual emancipation *(mokṣa)* is overtly reserved for the discipline of yoga. These *kaḷarippayaṯṯu* masters familiar with yoga acknowledge that both disciplines develop the ability to focus at will on one point (i.e., the ability to "concentrate") but beyond this similarity the practices diverge, with yoga continuing as a self-conscious path of meditation. Among the Ṣūfī *kaḷarippayaṯṯu* practitioners of the Cannanore area of northern Kerala, however, great emphasis is placed upon spiritual training and development. Advanced training in meditation involves progressing through a series of rituals known as *dhikr*s (Arab., lit., "remembrance, recollection" of God), which are performed silently or aloud. Such practices can lead to experiences of ecstasy, realization of the internal white light, and union with God. As the connection between Indian martial traditions and religious practices is evident historically, it is safe to assume that additional investigations will provide more information on the practices and aims associated with the overlap of these martial traditions with meditative techniques and philosophies. [*See* Attention.]

China. Though lacking in strong documentation, historical reviews generally credit Bodhidharma (c. 448–527 CE) with playing a central role in the development of a systematized martial discipline in China. Bodhidharma is an obscure figure. However, he is generally acknowledged to be the first patriarch of the Ch'an (Jpn., Zen) school in China. Although no Indian records of his life are known to exist, Chinese sources indicate that he was trained in Buddhist meditation in Kāñcīpuram, a province south of Madras. Upon the death of his master Prajñātara, he reportedly left India for China, in part due to the decline of Buddhism in those areas outside of India proper. After visiting with the emperor at Nanking, Bodhidharma proceeded north to the Shao-lin Temple in Honan Province. In his teaching there he reportedly became disturbed by the inability of monks to stay awake during meditation. To eliminate this tendency as well as to improve their health, Bodhidharma allegedly introduced a systematized set of exercises to strengthen the body and mind—exercises that purportedly marked the beginning of the *shao-lin* style of temple boxing. These exercise forms were transmitted orally and transcribed by later monks in the *I-chin ching* and *Hsi-shui ching.* [*But see the biography of Bodhidharma.*]

In addition to his contributions in the area of physical training, Bodhidharma was also said to have been centrally involved in transmitting the *Laṅkāvatāra Sūtra* to his disciple Hui-k'o, insisting that it represented the key to Buddhahood. The teaching of the *Laṅkāvatāra Sūtra* focuses upon enlightenment, with specific reference to such doctrines as "mind-only" *(vijñāptimātra)* and "all-conserving consciousness" *(ālaya-vijñāna).* It essentially records the Buddha's own inner experience *(pratyātmagata)* concerning the religious teachings of Mahāyāna Buddhism. A central theme of the *Laṅkāvatāra Sūtra* is the importance of transmission of doctrine from mind to mind without reliance upon written texts. In keeping with the Ch'an tradition, it appeals directly to the enlightened mind as its source of authority, rather than depending upon words to convey its message.

Many of these teachings were later incorporated into Chinese philosophy, interspersed with the already prevailing Taoist precepts of the *tao, yin-yang,* and the principle of dualism and change, the importance given to deep breathing *(lien-ch'i)* and its relationship to the goal of longevity or immortality, and the doctrines of "nonaction" *(wu-wei)* and "natural spontaneity" *(tzu-jan).* The interpretation of Buddhist and Taoist precepts transformed martial and nonmartial teachings into a new form, the early search for *tao* being later replaced by the goal of *chien-hsing* ("illumination"), because of the Ch'an Buddhist influences noted above.

Contemporary Chinese martial arts are said to be derived from the original *shao-lin* techniques introduced by Bodhidharma. These forms of *kung-fu* are generally divided into two groups—"internal" *(nei-chia ch'uan-fa),* or "soft" *(jou),* and "external" *(wai-chia ch'uan-fa),* or "hard" *(kang).* In addition to stressing the importance of the Taoist and Buddhist philosophical-experiential principles described above, the "internal" system also concentrates on the will *(i),* vital energy *(ch'i),* and internal strength. Further, Taoist deep breathing techniques of *ch'i-kung* are practiced to cultivate *ch'i* in the *tan-t'ien* ("cinnabar fields"), where it is collected and stored. Styles falling within the "internal" category include *t'ai-chi, pa-kua,* and *hsing-i,* while *shao-lin* boxing is classified as "external." Principles of Taoist philosophy and cosmogony are reflected in the three primary internal styles. Ironically, while the internal styles clearly draw upon the principles of Taoist and Ch'an teachings in the employment of specific self-defense techniques, strategies, and forms, few of the internal schools today emphasize the transformative religious goals stressed by the classical meditative systems and by some of the earlier practitioners of these martial disciplines.

Japan. From roughly the eighth century to the end of the sixteenth century CE, Japan was beset by numerous domestic wars. This sociopolitical climate provided the classical professional warriors *(bushi)* with not only a prominent role in molding the natural character of Japan, but also an opportunity to further develop and refine the combative techniques of the *bujutsu* (martial arts). During these centuries martial traditions *(ryū)* were founded with the specific purpose of formalizing and perpetuating practical combat systems. It was during the Kamakura period (1185–1333 CE) that Zen Buddhism was introduced to Japan from China, largely through the work of the Japanese Buddhist priests Eisai (1141–1215) and Dōgen (1200–1253), who had studied Ch'an in China. Through the efforts of their followers Tokiyori (1227–1263) and Tokimune (1251–1284), Ch'an, as Zen, was introduced into Japanese life, having a distinct impact upon the life of the samurai. The successful cooperation of the martial and spiritual disciplines led to the creation of Bushidō, the warrior code, which idealized such virtues as loyalty and courage and espoused the goal of achieving that state of mind in which the warrior's thoughts would transcend life and death *(seishi o chōetsu).* [*See* Bushidō.]

In 1603, the Tokugawa military government *(bakufu)* was founded by Tokugawa Ieyasu, an event that marked the end of war as a pervasive aspect of the Japanese culture and the beginning of the Edo period (1603–1868 CE). In this era of peace, maintained by strict tyrannical rules, governmental influences stressed the redirection of the people's attention to the ideals of the past. This marked a notable shift in social awareness for *bushi* and commoner alike, leading to the development of the classical *budō* forms. Influenced by the Confucian interpretation of the Tao, the Japanese culture took the principle of *tao—dō* in Japanese—and modified it in such a way as to be compatible with Japanese feudal society and applicable to man in his social relationships. The shift from *bujutsu* (*bu,* "military [martial] affairs"; *jutsu,* "art") to *budō* (*dō,* "way") signified a change in emphasis from combat training to cultivation of man's awareness of his spiritual nature. The primary goal of classical *budō* was enlightenment as outlined in Zen teachings—a shift again from simply external perfection of (martial) techniques to self-mastery via "spiritual forging" *(seishin tanren).* The distinction between *bujutsu* ("martial arts") and *budō* ("martial ways") still holds true today.

The formation of specific *budō* systems began during the early seventeenth century. *Kenjutsu* ("sword art") was transformed into *kendō* ("sword way"); and the essence of *iaidō* ("sword drawing technique") as a spiritual discipline appeared at this time in contrast to *iaijutsu.* Weaponless *budō* systems, such as *jikishinryū,* also appeared. The classical *budō* forms continued to evolve until the latter part of the nineteenth century when, with the rise of ultranationalism among the Japanese people, both the aims of classical *budō* and classical *bujutsu* disciplines were redirected to support this effort.

Modern *bujutsu* and modern *budō* are generally viewed as beginning in 1868, after the overthrow of the Tokugawa government. However, there are significant differences between these modern martial traditions and their classical counterparts. Collectively speaking, the modern disciplines are generally characterized as methods of self-defense or as tactics for sparring or grappling with an opponent. Modern *bujutsu* consists of hand-to-hand combat systems that are used as methods of self-defense and spiritual training. Modern *budō* consists of various systems of physical exercise or sport seen as methods of self-defense or as spiritual training aimed at bringing man into harmony with a peace-seeking international society. Examples of modern *budō* include modern *kendō*, modern *jūdō, karatedō, aikidō, (nippon) shōrinji kenpō,* and *kyūdō.*

In many cases, a comparison of the modern *budō* to their classical counterparts (which are still practiced today in Japan) reveals major differences in purpose. While the proclaimed concern for discipline, morals, and the importance of "spirit" carries over from the classical traditions, the concept of *dō* is largely distorted in the modern disciplines. Modern exponents have been accused of re-interpreting the *dō* to fit their own subjective interpretation of their personal role and needs in the world, rather than focusing upon classical martial-meditative goals. However, to dismiss all of the modern *budō* systems as poor imitations of once-thriving, authentic spiritual disciplines may be premature. For example, select schools of modern *kendō* and *kyūdō* do stress goals associated with the classical *(budō)* disciplines. It may be that the individual practitioners within a particular discipline remain the best measure of the degree to which the classical *budō* aims are stressed, realized, and exemplified.

Indonesia. Throughout its history, Indonesia has been subject to the cultural and combative influences of other countries, including India, China, and Indochina. Furthermore, Java, its cultural and political core, has always been a center of magical and mystical beliefs and practices, which have become even more widespread since independence from the Dutch in 1949. With ongoing migrations of peoples of the many Indonesian islands and the combative and mystical elements continuing to evolve over time, highly sophisticated martial arts have developed, which are currently referred to as *pukulan.*

While several major combative forms are presently found in Indonesia, the martial art known as *pencak-silat* is the dominant self-defense discipline and the one with the strongest spiritual roots. It reportedly first developed on the Riouw archipelago in the eleventh century CE. By the 1300s it had become a highly sophisticated technical art that was open solely to members of nobility and the ruling classes. Indian, Chinese, Arabic and, later, Japanese influences permeated in varying degrees a number of the styles. These developments as well as travel between the different islands further modified its combative form (which was no longer limited exclusively to select social classes) leading to rapid diversification. There are now hundreds of different styles.

Though varying definitions exist, *pencak* usually connotes skillful body movements in variation, while *silat* refers to the fighting application of *pencak. Pencak-silat* is known to have been influenced by Hindu religious elements and to have evolved further through contact with a rich Islamic spiritual tradition. The emphasis placed on the spiritual aspects of the art will vary from one style to another, but most systems start with physical training aimed at learning and applying various techniques for avoiding physical harm at the hands of an assailant. Upon successful acquisition of these motor skills, the practitioner may develop his inner power, which can be expressed in varying forms. For example, the practitioner of the Joduk style of Bali is able to engage in mystic, trancelike states—an ability that distinguishes the individual as a guru ("teacher"). Further internal development in the various styles of *pencak-silat* leads to the title of *maha guru* ("master teacher") while those who have attained the summit of technique are given the title of *pendekar* ("fighter"; also connotes "spiritualist" and leader or champion who has obtained an understanding of true—inner—knowledge).

The final stage of training in *pencak-silat* is referred to as *kebatinan.* Importance is placed on inner emotional experience and personal revelation as derived from the practice of the mystical discipline, although the practices and methods employed as one advances on the mystical path vary noticeably from one sect to another. The path of *kebatinan* stresses intuitive feeling *(rasa)* and surrender *(sujud);* man rids himself of impulses and bodily desires by emptying himself so as to be filled with the divine presence of God—the revelation of the divine residing within the heart *(batin).* The path of *kebatinan* is no easy understanding. Overcoming one's attachment to the outward aspects of existence *(lahir)* may involve ascetic practices *(tapa):* fasting, prayer, meditation (particularly visual concentrative techniques), sexual abstinence, remaining awake throughout the night, or retreating to the mountains and into caves. It should be pointed out, however, as noted earlier with other martial systems, that the degree to which the mystical practices are pursued and realized will vary from one practitioner to another. For example, some *pendekar* avoid all involvement with mysticism and *kebatinan,* while others practice also the noncorporeal, mystical aspects of their discipline.

Conclusions. While the spiritual dimensions of several martial systems of India, China, Japan, and Indonesia have been briefly outlined, the meditative-religious dimensions of martial arts and martial traditions of other countries still need to be critically and comprehensively assessed. Today, the spiritual dimensions of practice are often overlooked, although increased interest in the concept of the "spiritual warrior" has begun to appear. Inclusion of this important component will serve to broaden our understanding of the interrelationship between the physical and spiritual sides of human existence.

[*See further* Spiritual Discipline *and* War and Warriors.]

BIBLIOGRAPHY

A scholarly overview of martial arts in general can be found in Donn F. Draeger and Robert W. Smith's *Comprehensive Asian Fighting Arts* (New York, 1980), originally published as *Asian Fighting Arts* (Tokyo and Palo Alto, Calif., 1969); discussions of religious dimensions are limited, as are references supporting textual material. A less critical discussion of Indian martial arts can be found in the *Encyclopedia of Indian Physical Culture*, edited by Dattatraya C. Mujumdar (Baroda, India, 1950). An excellent discussion of *kaḷarippayaṯṯu* appears in Phillip B. Zarrilli's "'*Kalarippayatt*' and the Performing Artist East and West, Past, Present, Future" (Ph.D. diss., University of Minnesota, 1978). Perhaps the best historical review of the Chinese martial arts can be found in *A Source Book in the Chinese Martial Arts*, 2 vols., edited by James I. Wong (Stockton, Calif., 1978). Donn F. Draeger's three volumes on the martial arts and martial ways of Japan—*Classical Bujutsu* (New York, 1973), *Classical Budo* (New York, 1973), and *Modern Bujutsu and Budo* (New York, 1974)—are among the best writings on the topic. For the Indonesian martial arts, Draeger's *Weapons and Fighting Arts of the Indonesian Archipelago* (Rutland, Vt., 1972) remains the definitive source. Finally, an in-depth discussion of the spiritual dimensions of the martial arts appears in my forthcoming *Meditative-Religious Traditions of Martial Arts and Martial Ways*.

MICHAEL MALISZEWSKI

Buddhist Martial Arts

The Japanese Buddhist martial arts are the traditional combat skills of medieval warriors that were transformed through Zen Buddhist thought and practice into both a way of life and a vehicle for mental training and religious concentration. This process of religious acculturation occurred particularly in those martial arts involving swordsmanship *(kenjutsu)*, archery *(kyūjutsu)*, and wrestling *(jūjutsu)*. Only Zen, of all the schools of Mahāyāna Buddhism, was able to have an effect on these forms.

This remarkable development was set in motion during the Kamakura period (1185–1333). At that time the Buddhist reformation movements were carrying the message directly to the mass population. Zen, which had been recently introduced from China, was adopted by the rising warrior *(bushi)* class as it took over the political leadership of Japan under the military government. The Hōjō (1213–1333) and Ashikaga (1336–1573) military regimes found in Zen a new basis for its religious and cultural authority. Innumerable changes also occurred during these and subsequent centuries, both in the political arena and in the nature of warfare itself, as the disorder of the Ashikaga period gave way to the gradual appearance of peace and prosperity. This helped to create a highly individualized cultural environment allowing those who excelled in each branch of the martial arts to establish schools for professional instruction and the propagation of their art.

These schools developed as early as the fourteenth century, first with archery and then with the five remaining traditional divisions: horsemanship (fourteenth to fifteenth century), swordsmanship (mid-fifteenth century), spearsmanship (mid-sixteenth century), wrestling (mid-sixteenth century), and riflery (seventeenth century).

Principles and Specific Practices. The founders of these schools invariably advocated a philosophy of life and attached religious meaning to their martial arts practice through an emphasis on the concept of *dō* (Chin., *tao*), or "way, path," rather than on *jutsu*, or "technique." Conceptually, *dō* was complex. In Confucianism, it meant an ideal way of life for the individual and the state, as well as a universal moral law pervading human society. In Taoism, the same term signified a state of transcendence, completely spontaneous action that was effortless and inexhaustible, and the ontological basis of the universe. In the native Japanese conception, *dō* implied a harmonious existence with nature, since in Shintō nature itself was the focal point of religion and assisting the progress of life and avoiding its obstruction was the goal. In Zen, *dō* referred to insight and practice as well as to the Dharma, as may be seen in the following examples: "the way of the Buddha and patriarchs," "the way one realizes through meditation," "the way that permeates the universe," "one who sees the way practices it," and so on.

While the conception of *dō* adopted by the founders of the various martial art schools was, in general, eclectic, their organization and instruction were patterned after the forms of Zen institutions. As models of secularization, they featured (a) the practice of meditative concentration, (b) the maintenance of rigorous disciplines and an austere lifestyle, and (c) nonverbal communication through direct interaction between teacher and disciples.

The martial arts schools shared three practical features in common:

1. *The Way as conformity with nature.* Each art is a "way" in that its principles correspond to those that pervade nature. The principles of movement in *kendō* should coincide precisely with those in nature even though, unlike nature, man's actions involve thought and judgment. Indeed, the way an expert shoots an arrow at a target while galloping on horseback must conform to perfectly natural movement if it is to be successful.

2. *The Way as spontaneous action.* Although freedom generally means freedom of choice, the freedom cultivated by these arts consists of a translucent mind, free from preoccupation, or spontaneous action derived from a pure state of mind. Only by cultivating this mental state can the well-trained *jūdō* player maintain his center of gravity in the midst of dynamic movement. Similarly, an expert in *kendō* can anticipate an opponent's oncoming strike as if it were his own. In both cases, one is aware of one's center of gravity with each move, not before or after.

3. *The Way as its own system.* Because the forms of each art are different, each art has its own body of practical rules and disciplines. Actions that are appropriate in *kendō* cannot be applied to *kyūdō*, as those of *jūdō* cannot properly be substituted for those of *kendō*. Although the systems vary for the different branches of the martial arts, the masters of each claim that the forms themselves are tools and that the ultimate goal is to transcend these and achieve the state of no-sword, no-archery, and so forth.

Contemporary Significance. The martial arts as practiced today in Japan are neither a pseudoreligion nor, strictly speaking, methods of combat. The schools, which were once numerous, have been reduced to a small number—the remaining legacy of a rich past—and reorganized for modern practicality. On the most popular level, they serve the purposes of recreation, self-defense, and physical fitness programs. On the next level, each respective art is studied with great interest as a training for technical skill and character formation. Last, at the highest level, they are practiced by experts for their inherent value and beauty and in order to pass them on to future generations. The structure of the martial arts is presently dependent on the continuation of this hierarchy.

[*See also* Bushidō.]

BIBLIOGRAPHY

Two essays treating the ethos of the Japanese martial arts are the *Fudōchi shinmyō roku* of the Zen master Hakuin (1685–1768) and the *Gorinjo* of the sword master Miyamoto Musashi (1584–1645). Both are included in the seven volume compendium of original sources *Nihon budō zenshū*, edited by Imamura Yoshio (Tokyo, 1967), vols. 7 and 1, respectively. For a general introduction, see D. T. Suzuki's excellent *Zen and Japanese Culture*, 2d ed., rev. & enl. (1959; reprint, Princeton, 1970). Suzuki's discussion of Hakuin's essay is especially recommended. Eugen Herrigel's *Zen and the Art of Archery*, translated from German by R. F. C. Hull (1953; reprint, New York, 1971), is also commendable for its insightful introduction.

Ichimura Shōhei

MARTINEAU, JAMES

MARTINEAU, JAMES (1805–1900), English Unitarian. Born in Norwich, England, and educated at Manchester College, Martineau served as a minister, principally in Liverpool (1831–1857), and as a professor, and later principal, of Manchester College (1840–1885).

An early devotee of the materialistic philosophical determinism that Joseph Priestley (1733–1804) had absorbed from David Hartley (1705–1757) and transmitted to the English Unitarians, Martineau turned away from that position in the mid-1830s, in part under the influence of William Ellery Channing (1780–1842). He gave up external proof for intuition, metaphysics for ethics, and determinism for conscience and free will, and gradually abandoned his early belief in the historical validity of the scriptural miracles. Study in Germany in 1848–1849 reinforced the biblical skepticism that had led him to give up his belief in the evidential value of miracles. In his struggle to break the Priestleyan hold on his denomination, the passing of time and changing sensibilities gave Martineau a victory of sorts by the 1860s, but he had made many enemies in the older school, and he watched younger colleagues turn away from the theism to which he remained loyal to preach antisupernaturalism, humanism, and a variety of enthusiasms. In his later works, the impact of Darwinism and other scientific developments led him to a vast expansion of the argument from design, while the centrality he assigned to divine will bears some resemblance to his former determinism.

For most of his career, Martineau was highly controversial. A brilliant critic, he could be deliberately provocative, sometimes unscrupulous, and often wounding. He was denied the chair in philosophy at University College, London, after agitation by leading anticlerical intellectuals, among them his sister Harriet Martineau (1802–1876), whose book celebrating her conversion to free thought he had gratuitously and savagely reviewed in 1851. From the 1830s on, he rejected the Unitarian name, seeing it as sectarian and preferring the older Presbyterian or newer Free Christian labels, but few of his co-religionists followed him in this, and his plan in 1888 for sweeping denominational reform was a failure.

But his prolonged and more irenic old age brought him almost universal admiration, and his stature in Unitarian history ranks with that of Priestley.

Martineau's subtle, complex, and self-consciously lyrical preaching was highly influential, as were his collections of hymns and liturgical services. His principal works are *The Rationale of Religious Enquiry* (1836), *A Study of Spinoza* (1882), *Types of Ethical Theory* (1885), *A Study of Religion* (1888), and *The Seat of Authority in Religion* (1890).

BIBLIOGRAPHY

The principal collection of Martineau's papers is in Manchester College, Oxford, but there are other major collections in many places. His most important sermons, reviews, and occasional papers are collected in *Essays, Reviews, and Addresses*, 4 vols. (London, 1890–1891). The two biographies are by students and close associates. The best is J. Estlin Carpenter's *James Martineau, Theologian and Teacher: A Study of His Life and Thought* (London, 1905), but James Drummond and C. B. Upton's *The Life and Letters of James Martineau*, 2 vols. (London, 1902), contains much valuable material. As yet there is no satisfactory extended study of English Unitarianism, but there is an excellent brief sketch: H. L. Short's "Presbyterians under a New Name," in *The English Presbyterians: From Elizabethan Puritanism to Modern Unitarianism*, by C. Gordon Bolam and others (Boston, 1968).

R. K. WEBB

MARTYRDOM. [*This entry deals with religious witness that involves loss of life. For discussion of ritual death in a cross-cultural context, see* Suicide. *For death suffered because of religious identity, see* Persecution.]

The badge of martyrdom is awarded by the leadership of a community to men and women who offer their lives voluntarily in solidarity with their group in conflict with another, ideologically contrasting, group. The martyr and his or her slayer are delegates, champions, or defenders of their societies. A few martyrs are suicides, but most are slain by judicial, military, police, religious, or other functionaries. These functionaries execute the martyr as a terrorist, a criminal, or a heretic who threatens fundamental social values or the physical safety of members of the society. The societies of the slayer and the slain struggle to control the meaning of the slaying: is it to be understood by the world as martyrdom or as judicial retribution?

Martyrs may be "witnesses," the literal meaning of the Greek term, of politically disestablished groups claiming self-determination or heroes of the expansionist wars of established groups. Contemporary images race before our eyes—a self-immolating Buddhist monk in Vietnam, an Irish Republican Army soldier dying of starvation in a British jail, a Japanese kamikaze diving his bomb-plane into an American warship. Martyrdom is an attempt to break through the ideological and social boundaries between the conflicting groups with hierocratic, religiously based power. A minority's religious power invokes a higher, purifying vengeance (Jacoby, 1983) upon a dominant adversary, who in turn vengefully slays the martyr.

The confrontation may unite the martyr's people, strengthening their opposition as they, under charismatic leadership, inch toward their own organizational power. The exemplary act of a martyr strengthens people's courage to bear their daily tribulations and directs their anger to the cruel, murderous adversary, the source of these tribulations. The martyrdom may also strengthen the adversary's will to repress the martyr's society. Martyrdom politicizes the relationship between the groups.

Martyrdom seems not to have appeared until rather late in history, perhaps the fourth century BCE. The identification of ideology as an independent cultural reality has been a prerequisite for martyrdom. The ideologies at issue serve as symbols of mobilization, principles around which the societies rally, reinforcing, even radicalizing, more mundane economic or political conflicts.

The religions of Egypt and Mesopotamia and Greek philosophy treat ideologies as distinct cultural realities already hosting the seeds of the ideas of active good and evil and heroism. Zoroastrian dualism proposed an independent evil force, and Judaism of the Maccabean age adapted this view of a struggle with evil for monotheism. Hellenism brought a personalistic element to the ideologies in the image of the ascetic philosopher. Oriental Christianity synthesized the dualistic idea with that of the individual hero and so previewed Islamic ideas of martyrdom, including the pledge of eternal life to martyrs, forgiveness of sins, exemption from the Last Judgment, and the intercessory ability of the souls of martyrs.

Martyrdom imbues economic and political conflict with sacred meaning, subjecting it to what Max Weber called "the ethic of absolute ends," the pursuit of goals with little attention to the cost. In fact, action guided by an "ethic of responsibility," the value of the goal weighed against the cost of the means, discourages martyrdom.

Martyrdom is a free voluntary act. It is also an altruistic act. The martyr may avoid death by conceding to the adversary, but nevertheless accepts, affirms or even seeks death. A soldier, even a gladiator, strives to defeat the adversary without being hurt or killed. If death occurs, it is an accident of the situation. Only when that situation is sacralized, as in the case of the Muslim *jihād,* is the slain soldier a martyr. [*See* Jihād.]

This article develops some elements of a social theory of martyrdom. The basic queries are: under what conditions does a society generate martyrs; what are the types of martyrs; and what special social circumstances give rise to each type?

How Martyrdom Fits into Social Life. Martyrdom infuses a mundane event with divine grace. The symbolism parallels that of a sacrificial animal attaining a sacred quality. The animal victim disappears, either eaten by the worshipers, delivering its sanctity to their fellowship, or, as a burnt offering, rising as a sweet savor to the Lord. The martyr, a human sacrifice, attains an indelible sanctity. The sanctity may take the form of a redemptory promise, softening the pain or enabling the martyr to persist despite pain. Early Christians imprisoned and awaiting martyrdom were believed to have the power to forgive sins. Those released might retain this power, perhaps becoming presbyters of the church.

The martyr dies convinced of his or her legitimate authority, an authority challenging that of the executioners. A religious martyr may believe himself or herself to be an incarnation of the Holy Ghost, as did Montanus (Frend, 1972); the Spirit of God, al-Ḥaqq, as did al-Ḥallāj (Massignon, 1982); or a receiver of the Torah, as did 'Aqiva' ben Yosef.

The martyr, deceased, is a sacred symbol of an authority around which the society rallies. The authority created is charismatic, untethered by tradition. Such charismatic authority discards an older order in a breakthrough to a new social and cultural order, often conceived as a spiritual order.

Martyrdom is exemplary. A martyr is often a model for lesser forms of martyrdom. In Islam the idea of a martyr's death "in the way of Allāh" is applied metaphorically to the giving of *ṣadaqah,* or alms.

While suicide, being self-inflicted, is rarely accepted as martyrdom, asceticism, also self-inflicted, is a minor martyrdom. The adversary of the ascetic is bodily desire. The conquest of desire is a propaedeutic for the conquest of the social adversary.

The martyr demonstrates the human possibility of the act. That a person of flesh and blood succeeds in dying, sometimes painfully, facilitates the recruitment of future martyrs. Such a death is also a message deterring future deviance. That a member of a despised minority can show such commitment challenges the courage of members of the dominant group. The adversary may attempt to obscure the event. To be exemplary, martyrdom must be public and publicized. A private act, meaningful only to the martyr and the executioner, fails in this exemplary function. The martyr's group may be denied the benefits of its champion as witness. Undoubtedly, unrecorded martyrs died in dungeons with their ashes cast into the sea. However, martyrologies reveal no martyrs who sought social concealment.

In Jewish tradition, death for *qiddush ha-shem,* sanctifying of the name—or better, the reputation—of God, is intended to impress the gentiles. This norm derives from a reading of the phrase in *Ezekiel,* "in the sight of the nations." Publicity for the Islamic *shahīd* ("martyr") is implicit in the idea of the *jihād* as a collective, rather than a personal obligation. Ibn Rushd (Averroës) wrote in his twelfth-century work on the *jihād, Bidāyat al-mujtahid,* that for *shahīds* to cancel the obligation for others, these others must know and recognize the volunteer's martyrdom. (Averroës, in Peters, 1977).

Martyrdom is political. Martyrdom is a political act affecting the allocation of power between two societies, or between a subgroup and the larger society. The Maccabean Revolt, which offered early and paradigmatic martyrs, was the action of a small community seeking a measure of local cultural independence. The Christian communities of Asia Minor, in the first and second centuries, offered martyrs to the Roman authorities in their struggle to limit the power of Rome to coerce particular expressions of loyalty. Certain religious martyrs may refuse to inflict physical violence on an adversary, but, as a political act, martyrdom is never a passive submission. The nonviolent martyr strikes the enemy psychologically.

The martyr's cry for vengeance mobilizes action against the adversary. The martyrdom of Mary Stuart followed a religious struggle over the crown of England. Elizabeth Tudor feared a bitter religious war were Mary to come to the throne. Mattingly (1959) writes of Catholic kings beyond the seas more eager to avenge the Queen of Scots dead than to keep her alive. Her shed blood cried out for vengeance on her enemies more unmistakably than her living voice could ever have done.

Where hierocratic power appears, political power may not be far behind. Sometimes one is transformed into the other. In this sense, the pope commands battalions. The Irish Republican Army tapped the church's hierocratic power to support its struggle for Irish independence from Great Britain.

Martyrdom aims to reduce political authority to ineffectiveness by challenging the sacred basis of the legitimacy of the adversary's authority. The potential martyr is a rival claimant to authority and this political claim may be religiously legitimated.

The political struggle may be internal: an established society and a schismatic minority may share a faith and a political system. The Maccabees, Arnold of Brescia, Jan Hus, and Savonarola, for example, accused the leaders of their established groups of treason. The minority attack was treated as heretical, endangering the faith.

The eleventh-century Persian-born Ṣūfī ʿAyn al-Quḍāt al-Hamadhānī challenged Islamic authorities. The authorities' claim to power rested on Qur'anic revelation and the *sunnah,* the traditions deriving from it. He claimed that divine grace poured down on him with all manner of esoteric knowledge and precious revelations, and he was thus an independent source of law.

Jan Hus (1373–1415) was directly political. Hus challenged the legitimacy of the papacy, the see of Peter, by preaching that Peter is not the head of the church, that ultimate appeal must be made directly to Christ. Condemned at the Council of Constance in 1414 and imprisoned, he wrote a characteristic martyr's message to a friend in Prague: "In prison and in chains expecting tomorrow to receive sentence of death, full of hope in God that I shall not swerve from the truth nor abjure errors imputed to me by false witnesses." He was urged to recant after being tied to the stake but replied, as is the custom of martyrs, "God is my witness that I have never taught nor preached that which false witnesses have testified against me. . . . I now joyfully die."

The fire was kindled and Hus repeated the Kyrie Eleison until stifled by the smoke. His ashes were scattered in the river, a final device to control the meaning of the event, discouraging a sepulchral shrine. After his death, Hussites fought in Prague and established the ecclesiastical organization of Tábor, recognizing only two sacraments, baptism and communion, and rejecting most of the ceremonial of the Roman Catholic church.

The minority may organize as a secret society, a sect practicing an uncommon cult. The twelfth-century Tanchelm in the Low Countries and Edus de l'Étoile in Brittany both declared themselves sons of God. Their sectarian followers were repressed, and they were imprisoned and martyred (Cohn, 1961). Ecstatics and ascetics, critical of the established church, gather around such claimants and perpetuate the movements.

Martyr Types: Political Independence and Action Orientation. The relative political power of the conflicting communities determines the task of martyrdom and the characteristics of the martyrs selected to carry out that task. Crescive, self-determining, and decaying societies all generate a peculiar form of martyrdom.

Christian communities within the Roman empire were a politically crescive minority. The martyrs of this minority suffered passively, inviting violence but inflicting only moral or psychological pressure on the adversary. An expansive Islam in its early centuries exemplifies the self-determining society. Its martyrs were active and belligerent. The post-Enlightenment Jewish community of western Europe was a politically decaying society. Jews who died at the hand of their adversaries were not, by and large, martyrs but mere victims of pogroms and, lately, of the Holocaust.

The attitude of the society toward worldly action is a second influence on the type of martyrdom. Orientation to action may be primarily "otherworldly" or primarily "innerworldly," to borrow Max Weber's terms. These two orientations are related dialectically. The active political innerworldly understanding of life is a minor motif for crescive and decaying societies, but a major motif for a self-determining society. Segments of the society animated by innerworldly orientations tend not to be at peace with otherworldly segments. Heterodoxy is the case in which internal schismatics, themselves in a crescive stage, offer a religious otherworldly counterpoint to the political orientation of a ruling self-determining society.

The discussion will be organized in terms of the degrees of political independence of the societies. References to inner- or otherworldly attitudes are subsumed within the social type. Figure 1, illustrated by concrete examples, may aid the reader in keeping the typology in mind.

Martyrdom in crescive societies. A crescive society is one that is politically powerless but beginning to stir, perhaps renascent. The resistance of Jews to hellenization under the Seleucid ruler Antiochus Epiphanes in the second century BCE is an early model. The elderly Eleazar, according to the apocryphal *2 Maccabees,* is the martyr type, choosing to give his life rather than eat pork in an already desecrated Temple in Jerusalem. That image is reconstituted in the second-century Ju-

FIGURE 1. *Types of Martyrs according to the Level of Societal Independence and Orientation to Action*

PREDOMINANT ORIENTATIONS	LEVEL OF SOCIETAL INDEPENDENCE *Crescive*	*Self-Determining*	*Decaying*
Otherworldly	Early Christian Martyrs	Missionary Martyrs	Pogrom Victims
Innerworldly	Irish Republican Army Soldiers	Islamic *shahīd*	Anti-Martyrs

dean rebellion against Hadrianic Rome in which the scholar and political leader ʿAqiva' ben Yosef joined with Bar Kokhba, the leader of the revolt. Tradition has it that ʿAqiva' was burned, wrapped in a Torah scroll, in a Roman arena.

The exemplar of Christian martyrdom is the trial and the crucifixion on Golgotha as that event is related in the Gospels. Later martyrs strive to imitate Christ. The sacrificed Lamb of God survives, not in this world, but in the world beyond. Anomalously the divinely designated executioners were pagans. Ordinarily, only a priest could perform a valid sacrifice. This point was not lost on the eleventh-century Jews of Mainz, who, facing impending slaughter by Crusaders, slew their children and then themselves. They sanctified the sacrifice by their "priestly" hands, symbolically reviving the temple rite in Mainz. (Gentile slaughterers would have polluted the offering.) The adversary is made impotent by delivering to him dead bodies, the ultimate in noncooperation, and the spiritual strength and authority of the martyr's society is affirmed.

Martyrdom in crescive societies creates authority, escalates the struggle, unifies the minority, and legitimates the new culture by demonstrating its priority over nature. Furthermore, martyrs propel a politically crescive society toward self-determination, toward social and cultural freedom. The establishment of new authority is a step in this process, the martyr's group, for instance, becoming infused with the Holy Spirit (Klawitzer, 1980). The death of the martyr makes the ideological choice a matter of life and death. This escalates the struggle, perhaps expediting the resolution in favor of the minority. As the society moves toward increased responsibility, the culture itself changes. Ironically, the values for which the early martyrs surrendered their lives may not be significant to members of a succeeding and successful self-determining society.

Radicalizing and escalating the conflict unifies the two parties internally. The grievous injustice of the slaying of the defenseless martyr and the gruesome inhuman circumstances under which the slaying occurs leave few individuals on the sidelines. Martyrdom further unifies and strengthens the group in its struggle. If social solidarity is a prerequisite for martyrdom, how does the precrescive, perhaps fractured, group find its initial martyrs? Part of the answer to this question is that the martyrs constitute a small group within the minority. Intense primary relations in this group enable it to stand against the powerful larger group.

The unity of the minority community may be thwarted by a defection of some of its members to the majority. During the Christian conquest of Spain, from the thirteenth to the fifteenth century, for example, a number of Muslims and Jews manifestly accepted Christianity, while surreptitiously continuing to practice their previous faiths. Both Muslim and Jewish societies were decaying. The Inquisition struck at these New Christians and, at the same time, urged the state to expel those who had remained Jews and Muslims. Some unification was achieved by the Jewish émigrés in their diaspora.

A crystallizing around a self-assertive core of a divided minority is necessary before serious manifest resistance is thinkable. The tragedy of unification amidst disunity is dramatized in the apocalypse in the *Gospel of Mark* (13:9–13), where it is written that brother shall betray brother, and father his child, and the children shall rise up against their parents and have them put to death.

With martyrdom, the culture of the minority, its ideology and law, is sanctified, a covenant established, stamped with blood. It is written in *Mekhilta'*, a Jewish interpretative work, that every commandment that the Israelites have not died for is not really established, and every commandment that they have died for will be established among them (Herr, 1967).

Martyrdom, by placing ideology ahead of physical survival, affirms the priority of culture over nature and the group's life, law, and civilization over biological self-interest. A crescive society that values individual life above group survival and above its cultural survival is not ready to become self-determining.

The self-determining society: heroic martyrs. The self-determining society has achieved political control of its life. Examples are fourth-century Christians in Asia Minor following the victory of Constantine, Islam of the Umayyad caliphate in eighth-century Damascus, and the *Yishuv*, the Jewish community of Palestine during the 1920s led by the Vaʿad Le'umi, the National Council. Martyrs in such a society are active, aiding the society in its expansion, openly propagandizing, sending missionaries to the unconverted, and warring against adversaries. In Islam the *jihād* is a religious obligation and the martyr, the *shahīd*, one who dies in this sacred battle. The European Christian society that sent an armed pilgrimage to Jerusalem under Pope Gregory VII, in the words of Cohn (1961), raced toward a mass sacrifice, a mass apotheosis in Jerusalem. Defending against external enemies is the major problem; the achievement of internal unity is a minor social problem. Nevertheless, the self-determining society suffers its internal schisms. Islamic historians say little about Muslim martyrs executed by Arab pagans, the early opposition group, beyond the early oppression in Yathrib. The record is clear on Islamic martyrs of internecine conflict, Muslim martyrs killed by Muslims during the crescive and during the self-determining periods are remembered by their sects. The historic example is Muḥammad's grandson, Ḥusayn, the son of ʿAlī, slain by the soldiers of Yazid, the son of the caliph Muʿāwiyah, to prevent Ḥusayn's accession to the caliphate. This martyrdom is commemorated yearly with flagellation, imitative suffering, in Shīʿī circles. The ideological conflict was between Shīʿī insistence on blood succession from the Prophet and an elective basis of caliphal legitimacy.

The politically decaying society: victims and anti-martyrs. The politically decaying society is losing its ability to be self-determining. Roman provincial societies were decaying as they were co-opted by a victorious Christianity. Zoroastrian society became a weak minority in Persia, with a diaspora in India, shortly after the Islamic conquest. The world's smaller societies, such as those of the North American Indian civilization and of the Polynesian islands, were submerged by modern imperial powers.

The cause and the characteristic of this decay is loss of political autonomy. The society's symbols fail to command the loyalty of its members. Western European Jewish society, by the late eighteenth century, fits this mold. Local Jewish community control, supported by charters, was weakened as new concepts of statehood and citizenship took hold in Europe. Christian or secular frames of reference and values began to control the interpretations of Jewish tradition itself. The Jewish Haskalah, or Enlightenment, was built on the back of such intellectual symbols. Major civilizational contributions of Jews were made, not to Jewish society, as such, but to the environing societies. Heine, Mahler, Freud, and Einstein contributed to their German and Austrian cultures.

Martyrdom is latent in a decaying society. The adversary claims mere victims who affirm no ideology by their deaths. Jewish leaders tend to remember the victims of the Holocaust as martyrs for the sanctification of God's name. Breslauer (1981), in a dissent, writes that they were on the whole not sacred witnesses but passive victims, not proud martyrs for a cause but political pawns.

Leaders of a decaying society may dismiss resistance and martyrdom in favor of negotiation with the adversary. Rubenstein (1975) charges the Hungarian Jewish community leaders during World War II with near complicity in their own destruction. Though they knew about Auschwitz, one meeting with Eichmann convinced them that they had nothing to fear if they cooperated with the Schutzstaffel (SS) in enforced ghettoization, confiscation of real and personal property, and deportation for "labor service" in Poland.

Jewish resistance, independent and in cooperation with local partisans, produced genuine martyrs but was rarely supported by the officials of the *Judenrat*, the Jewish councils of the ghetto. The Warsaw ghetto uprising, authorized by ghetto leaders, was a final suicidal thrust, Samson at the temple of Dagon. Self-immolation requires a residue of moral strength, a will to protect the group's honor. Slaves may commit suicide, like concentration camp inmates throwing their bodies against the electrified wire, in order to relieve their suffering. [*See* Holocaust, The.]

The negotiating victims may become collaborators or even converts. They may even become anti-martyrs. An anti-martyr may be a convert to the dominant ideology, remaining a leader of the minority and seeking to manage the conflict by collaborating with the dominant group. This effort may cost them their own lives. Anti-martyrs may strive to suppress martyrs whom they consider wrong-headed. They are not opportunistic turncoats, moved by personal avarice, but quislings, deeply committed to an enemy ideology, believing it best for their group. If they lose, they die unrelenting. The anti-martyr may meet his death at the hands of his new associates after they lose faith in him. Some new Christians, accused by the Spanish Inquisition of reverting to Judaism, went to the stake holding a cross. Leaders who suppress martyrdom out of a survivalist instinct without accepting the adversary are not anti-martyrs in the sense used here.

A martyr is delegated by the community and apotheosized by it. Anti-martyrs act individually or as members of a small separatist cadre. The minority condemns them as traitors and their apotheosis as evil.

How a Group Produces Martyrs. Martyr candidates may not always be found when needed. How does a community recruit and prepare individuals to sacrifice themselves? Ignatius of Antioch, seeking martyrdom, pleaded with his co-religionists in Rome not to try to rescue him but to allow him to die. At the same time, some bishops of the church denied their faith and fled to avoid court proceedings (Riddle, 1931). Not all sectors of the minority society are equally productive of martyrs. The level of devotion of most members of the community is insufficient to sustain martyrs. Zealots form cells within the wider community of devotees. These cells become a foundry for martyrs, supporting them throughout their ordeal.

The martyrs of politically crescive minorities, being leaders, tend to be recruited from its nobility. By and large these martyrs are males, not because females resist martyrdom, but because martyrs are drawn from the religio-political leadership. Female martyrs die affirming family principles. Barbara, one of a group of

Catholic virgin martyrs, said to have been a follower of Origen in the third century, was immured in a tower, and ultimately beheaded by her father when he learned of her conversion to Christianity. Cecilia reportedly died as a martyr during the reign of Marcus Aurelius, along with her husband and friends whom she had converted.

What are the psychological characteristics, the motives of those who seek suffering and are willing to die? Although some writers tend to cite self-enhancing motives, such as a promise of redemption, or, as in Augustine's view, a way of avoiding a sin, one can safely say that altruism is the central motive. The basic commitment to moral action transcends the martyr's immediate interest in his personal fate. Sustaining such commitment requires ego integrity and the ability to overcome instinctive drives to escape.

Doubtless, some individuals throw themselves into martyrdom out of a mental derangement. But psychotics must be rare among martyrs, since they cannot usually establish and maintain the human bonds required in martyr cells. Many a stable mind, however, must become deranged during the tortures that can precede execution.

A martyr is prepared through life in a cell, that is, by social support. There he or she finds succor. The act is clothed ideologically and the potential martyr rehearsed. A martyr's ideology centers on the meaning of life in relation to death. It does not aim simply to attenuate the pain of martyrdom through a fantasy of a future life but provides a meaning for dying continuous with the meaning of the martyr's life. The martyr goes forward despite the pain.

Martyrologies, narrative or cultic, praise martyrs and expose evil. They prepare martyrs by example and encourage popular minor martyrdoms. A Christian cult of the martyr, in place by the end of the second century, exhibited relics—a bone, a lock of hair or some drops of blood—upon the anniversary of a martyrdom (Riddle, 1931). The more contemporary training of the kamikaze included worship at a special shrine for those who had died in training or in combat. There the trainees sought spiritual "intoxication" (Warner and Warner, 1982).

Exemplary martyrs need not be from one's own group. Invidiousness and pride can be as important as anger in strengthening the resolve to endure physical pain and degradation. The early Christians, not yet distinctively non-Jewish, identified with Maccabean martyrs. Gandhi, while struggling against the Boers in the Transvaal, praised the stalwart Boer women who survived an abominable incarceration by the English during the Boer War.

Ideology for preparing the martyr argues for the sanctity of the mission and the satanic quality of the adversary. It evokes earlier exemplary martyrs, including some from other groups. The lifelong preparation for the confrontation is materialized in a rehearsal for martyrdom. The rehearsal begins with the study of martyrologies, a vicarious experience, and follows with exercise of the minor martyrdoms—giving charity, fasting, and receiving the sacraments.

The early Christians offered organized rehearsals for the ordeal. The Roman process, being judicial, was predictable. Its stages included arrest, examination, threatening and persuasion, acquittal for recantation, and, as a test of loyalty, the performance by the recanter of pagan rites. Persons likely to be examined were trained in prepared responses for each stage.

How Society Controls Its Own Martyrs. A practical danger to a politically crescive minority is that some members will initiate open political action, perhaps open rebellion, before the community is ready to support such an act and, therefore, to succeed. Martyrdom, a harbinger of an uprising, is also a temporary alternative to it. A community must control its martyrs as it does its military zealots.

The community sets rules governing the occasions for martyrdom. Which principles are worth dying for? Who should die? When should one not die? The loss of such control among the Judean provincials during the latter part of the first century BCE was fatal for Jewish autonomy and nearly fatal for Jewry as a whole.

The thoroughness of the Jewish defeat in the Judean rebellion of 70 CE, which led to the destruction of the Temple, was symbolized in the redesignation of the Temple mount as Aeolia Capitolina. The subsequent Bar Kokhba Revolt (c. 132–135) was severely suppressed. The community, not prepared for these acts of desperation, had not widely supported Bar Kokhba. These catastrophes shifted the center of Jewish life to the diaspora. The evidence is that the edicts of Hadrian, such as the edict forbidding circumcision, which were cited as giving the Jews no choice but to rebel, actually followed the rebellion as martial law.

Control is also a matter of ruling when martyrdom is not expected. A Muslim is forbidden to wish for death or for an encounter with the enemy. The *ṭalab al-shahādah*, the seeking of martyrdom, even on the battlefield, is too close to suicide for Islamic jurists. Mahmud Shaltiut, a recent Shaykh al-Azhar, allows the community but three reasons for declaring *jihād:* to repel aggression, to protect the mission of Islam, and to defend religious freedom, that is, the freedom of Muslims to practice their faith in non-Muslim lands (Shaltiut, in Peters, 1977).

The Talmudic laws of martyrdom were formulated at

the Council of Lydda in the second century. These laws governed a minority in a province of pagan Rome. By the Middle Ages, Jews were a minority in powerful Islamic states from Arabia to Spain and in equally powerful European Christian states. From time to time the pressure on the Jews to convert increased to the point where martyrdom became an issue. Group, not simply individual, survival was also a sacred obligation. Moses Maimonides (Mosheh ben Maimon), writing his *Epistle on Apostasy* in 1162–1163, warned that the death of the martyr condemns all of his potential descendants to nonbeing (Maimonides, 1979). For this and other reasons, Maimonides sought to restrict the occasions for obligatory martyrdom.

The rabbis of the Talmud had restricted martyrdom to avoiding public worship of strange gods, incest or adultery, and murder. Under pressure it is permissible, writes Maimonides, to utter the Shahādah, the Muslim declaration of the unity of God and the prophetic mission of Muḥammad. The coerced Jew could think whatever he wished. If a Jew is coerced to violate publicly commands of the Torah other than the three specificed above, Maimonides advises submission, a position not repeated in his *Epistle to Yemen*, nor in his *Mishneh Torah*, his major work. It is not unlike Muslim dissimulation—acting when under pressure as if one has abandoned Islam. The person is culpable, however, if the violations are of his own free will. Maimonides recommends migration to more friendly shores, rather than awaiting the Messiah in the land of oppression.

Rules control the candidacy for martyrdom. Candidates who might not stand up to the adversary, who cannot assure that their action is voluntary, are to be discouraged. The rules given by Ibn Rushd (Averroës) for recruiting for a *jihād* recall the biblical rules limiting military service according to age, marital status, and attitude to danger. The *shahīd* should not recoil from fighting if the number of enemies is but twice the number of his own troops, an estimate based on a Qur'anic verse (surah 8:66), but should flee before a greater disproportion (Shaltiut, 1977).

The Suppression of Martyrdom by the Dominant Group. A dominant group may strive to prevent martyrdom when it cannot exploit the public meaning of the event. Potential martyrs may be co-opted or suppressed.

The adversary group may, for instance, assimilate a sympathetic sector of the minority. The new "converts," given positions in the dominant society, may become a showcase for attenuating minority resistance. (This approach misfires when it polarizes the minority, inciting the resisters to attack the assimilationists, as in the case of the Maccabean assault on the hellenizing Jews.) Since martyrdom depends on charismatic authority, any move toward rationalizing the social order gives the minority a sense of justice and order and undermines martyrdom.

Repressive measures may parallel co-optive measures in a kind of carrot-and-stick process. The martyr-producing cells may be attacked, for instance, by an infiltrating agent provocateur. Resistance cells may be made illegal and their members executed as part of a "witchhunt." Government-sponsored terror against the primary community may deprive the resisting cells of support.

Other ways of raising the penalty for martyrdom include inflicting more painful deaths or executing more martyrs, thus overtaxing the minority's supply of martyrs. Such increased viciousness may be an act of desperation. Its very horror may further radicalize the minority in its thrust against the dominant society.

Persecutions involve centrally sponsored repressions of the minority, not unique or local actions against potential martyrs. Christian tradition speaks of ten persecutions, including those under the emperors Decius, Valerian, and Diocletian. Under Valerian, for instance, an edict was issued in 257 CE compelling acts of submission in conformity with the Roman religion. Christians refusing them were condemned to the mines, beaten with whips and rods, branded on their foreheads, and shaven on one side so that if they escaped they could be recognized as runaway slaves or criminals. This extreme persecution occurred but two generations before Constantine's victory.

If martyrs must be taken, the impact of the martyrdom on the adversary's society may be limited by isolating the killing from view. Assigning the killing to specialists is one way to accomplish this. As there is preparation of martyrs, so there is preparation of their specialized slayers. The SS in Nazi Germany conceived of itself as a sacred order, an elite trusted to guard the messianic Führer. The concentration camps were a training ground toughening them for the task. Prisoners were thought of as belonging to inferior races, shiftless and asocial; subjected to starvation and unsanitary conditions, they came to resemble the walking dead. Any SS officer who showed compassion could be eliminated from the group. Those who made common cause with the prisoners were stripped of their rank, given twenty-five lashes, and consigned to the company of the "subhuman" (Kogon, 1973).

Precisely the opposite approach is to encourage wide public participation in the repression of the minority community as a whole. The goal is to eliminate or demoralize it to the extent that it cannot function as a hinterland for martyrs. Elements putatively out of the control of the authorities may carry out the establishment's justice, and so mask its intent. Operating with two faces, the dominant community may pretend to provide legal and police protection, diverting the minority from a planned defense. The same objective situation may occur, without duplicity, when more than one authority exists in society. In medieval Germany and in Poland, for instance, Jews resided under charter from the local bishop or nobility. This guarantee of safety was ineffective when Jews were attacked by soldiers and mobs during the Crusades and in the early Polish pogroms. The lynching of blacks in the post–Civil War American South has the same character of mob action, sometimes disapproved of, sometimes condoned by the authorities.

A society may deprive martyrs of an exemplary function by declaring them criminals. Justice is done by removing them from the society. By the second century the Romans had developed a literature justifying the suppression of the Christians and defining their martyrdom as insane. The works of Marcus Cornelius Fronto and Lucian, for instance, attacked Christians as public enemies, atheists, a fanatical species enamored of death, who ran to the cruelest tortures as to a feast. To discredit the ideology, these works ridiculed Christians who claimed that Jesus was born of a virgin into a poor family in a small town in Judaea, when, in reality, his mother had been cast off by her husband for committing adultery with a soldier named Panthera.

The meaning of the event is controlled in subsequent time by myths about the meanings of the event. The martyr views the battle as a prelude to the subjugation of his executioner and then as taking vengeance on the executioner and his society. The dominant society, seeing the event as punishment or vengeance, hopes that it will have no sequel, that the cycle is complete, the criminal punished, justice achieved.

Destruction of records is aimed to control later historical reconstruction. Allard (1971) reports that during the Diocletian persecutions (285–323 CE), churches were burned along with their manuscripts, which included passions of the ancient martyrs. Books were burned at public book burnings. The persecutors, having failed to stop the apostasies, attempted to abolish their memories.

Perhaps the greatest weapon of the state, particularly the modern state, is its ability to make martyrdom appear obsolete and meaningless. Bureaucratizing the killing accomplishes this end. Rubenstein (1975) says that the Holocaust could only have been carried out by an advanced political community with a highly trained, tightly disciplined police and civil service bureaucracy. The moral barrier to the riddance of a surplus population was overcome by taking the project out of the hands of bullies and hoodlums and delegating it to the bureaucrats.

BIBLIOGRAPHY

Allard, Paul. *La persecution de Dioclétian et le triomphe de l'église.* 3d rev. ed. 2 vols. Rome, 1971.

Ben Sasson, H. H. "Kiddush Hashem: Historical Aspects." In *Encyclopaedia Judaica.* Jerusalem, 1971.

Bickerman, Elias J. *The God of the Maccabees.* Leiden, 1979.

Breslauer, S. Daniel. "Martyrdom and Charisma: Leo Baeck and a New Jewish Theology." *Encounter* 42 (Spring 1981): 133–142.

Cohn, Norman R. C. *The Pursuit of the Millenium.* 3d ed. New York, 1970.

Coogan, Tim Pat. *On the Blanket: The H Block Story.* Dublin, 1980.

Frend, W. H. C. *Martyrdom and Persecution in the Early Church.* Oxford, 1965.

Gandhi, M. K. *Satyagraha in South Africa.* Translated by Yalji Govindji Desair. Madras, 1928.

Hazrat, Ahmad. *Ahmadiyyat or the True Islam.* New Delhi, 1980.

Historical Society of Israel. *Milḥemet qodesh u-marṭirologyah.* Jerusalem, 1967.

Jacobs, I. "Eleazar ben Yair's Sanction for Marytrdom." *Journal for the Study of Judaism in the Persian, Hellenistic, and Roman Period* 13 (December 1982): 183–186.

Jacoby, Susan. *Wild Justice: The Evolution of Revenge.* New York, 1983.

Klawitzer, Frederick C. "The Role of Martyrdom and Persecution in Developing the Priestly Authority of Women in Early Christianity: A Case Study of Montanism." *Church History* 49 (September 1980): 251–261.

Kogon, Eugen. *The Theory and Practice of Hell.* New York, 1973.

Lamm, Norman. "Kiddush Ha-shem and Hillul Ha-shem." In *Encyclopaedia Judaica.* Jerusalem, 1971.

Maimonides, Moses. *Epistle to Yemen.* New York, 1952.

Maimonides, Moses. *Iggeret ha-shemad.* In *Iggrot ha-Rambam,* pp. 13–68. Jerusalem, 1979.

Massignon, Louis. *The Passion of al-Hallaj: Mystic and Martyr of Islam.* Princeton, 1982.

Mattingly, Garrett. *The Armada.* Boston, 1959.

Peters, Rudolph, trans. *Jihad in Medieval and Modern Islam.* Leiden, 1977.

Poliakov, Leon. *La causalité diabolique: Essai sur l'origine des persécutions.* Paris, 1980.

Rahner, Karl. *On the Theology of Death.* New York, 1961.

Riddle, Donald W. *The Martyrs: A Study in Social Control.* Chicago, 1931.

Rosenberg, Bruce A. *Custer and the Epic of Defeat.* University Park, Pa., 1974.

Rubenstein, Richard L. *The Cunning of History: The Holocaust and the American Future.* New York, 1975.

Sachedina, Abdulaziz Abdulhussein. *Islamic Messianism: The Idea of Mahdi in Twelver Shi'ism.* Albany, N.Y., 1981.

Szaluta, Jacques. "Apotheosis to Ignominy: The Martyrdom of Marshall Petain." *Journal of Psychohistory* 7 (Spring 1980): 415–453.

Vööbus, Arthur. *History of Asceticism in the Syrian Orient.* Corpus Scriptorum Christianorum Orientalium, vol. 189. Louvain, 1958.

Warner, Dennis, and Peggy Warner. *The Sacred Warriors: Japan's Suicide Legions.* New York, 1982.

Wensinck, A. J. "The Oriental Doctrine of the Martyrs." In *Semietische Studien uit de Nalatenschap.* Leiden, 1941.

Zerubavel, Yael. "The Last Stand: On the Transformation of Symbols in Modern Israeli Culture." Ph.D. diss., University of Pennsylvania, 1980.

SAMUEL Z. KLAUSNER

MARX, KARL (1818–1883), German social and economic theorist. Marx was born in Trier on 5 May 1818. Both his grandfather and his uncle had been rabbis in the city and so had several of his paternal grandmother's ancestors. His mother also descended from a long line of rabbis in Holland. His father, Heinrich, had in 1817 converted to Protestantism in order to retain his position as a lawyer at the High Court of Appeals in Trier when the Rhineland, formerly French, became, through annexation, subject to the discriminatory laws of Prussia. Marx was baptized in 1824. During his high school years he enjoyed the literary tutelage of his father's friend, Baron Ludwig von Westphalen, whose daughter Jenny he would later marry.

In 1835 Marx registered in the faculty of law at the University of Bonn. A year later he transferred to the University of Berlin, but there he soon became ill through overwork. The following months of convalescence in the country completely changed his intellectual outlook. At first a romantic, vaguely religious idealist, he now converted to Hegel's philosophy. He joined a discussion group of "Young Hegelians," consisting of instructors and advanced students in a variety of disciplines, mostly of radical political and religious leanings. For them Hegel's dialectical method, separated from its conservative content, provided a powerful weapon for the critique of established religion and politics. The leading voices in the *Doktorklub,* as the group was called, were those of the theologians David Friedrich Strauss and Bruno Bauer. In his *Life of Jesus* Strauss had interpreted the gospel narratives as mythologizing the aspirations of the early Christian community. After some initial criticism, Bauer went even further: those narratives contained no truth at all, while the faith based on them had become the main obstacle on the road to political and cultural progress.

The young Marx extended these critical conclusions to all religion. His doctoral dissertation, *On the Difference between the Philosophies of Nature in Democritus and Epicurus,* which he submitted in 1841 to the Jena faculty of philosophy, was prefaced by a motto taken from Aeschylus's *Prometheus:* "In one word, I hate all the gods."

In 1843 Marx married Jenny von Westphalen. After his wedding and a prolonged vacation near Trier, he returned to Bonn, where he started writing for the radical Cologne paper *Die Rheinische Zeitung.* His first contribution consisted of a series of critical articles on the proceedings of the Rhineland parliament dealing with freedom of the press and the debates concerning the punishment of wood thefts. Other reports, on religious disputes, were censored and never appeared. In October 1842 Marx, having been appointed editor-in-chief, moved to Cologne. Six months later the paper folded under the pressure of Prussian censorship. In October 1843 Marx left the Rhineland for Paris, where he expected to find more freedom as well as make direct contact with French revolutionary workers' movements.

During his final year in Germany Marx's political position had developed from radically democratic to communist. At the same time he had increasingly come under the influence of that other critical interpreter of Hegel's philosophy, Ludwig Feuerbach. In *The Essence of Christianity* (1841) Feuerbach had applied Hegel's concept of alienation to all divine reality: in religion man projects his own nature into a supernatural realm and thus "alienates" from himself what rightly belongs to him. Marx instantly embraced the theory of religion as alienation, but he found Feuerbach's interpretation of the origin of the religious attitude inadequate. Religion, Marx asserted, mythically justifies a fundamental social frustration. Far from constituting the essence of human alienation, the need for religion implies a tacit protest against the existing, dehumanizing conditions of society. In that sense Marx called it "the opium of the people" in his essay "Introduction to a Critique of Hegel's Philosophy of Right" (1844), published in the Paris-based *Deutsch-Französische Jahrbücher.* "The abolition of religion as the illusory happiness of men is a demand for real happiness. The call to abandon their illusions about this condition is the *call to abandon a condition which requires illusions.*" Full emancipation demands that the social structures that create the need for religion be changed.

The secondary character of religious beliefs with respect to social-economic conditions appears in another essay Marx published in the same issue of the *Jahrbücher,* "On the Jewish Question." Bauer had proposed the thesis that the Jewish problem could be solved instantly if Jews would cease to claim religious privileges from the state. By so doing, they maintained the religious state and prevented their own as well as other people's emancipation. Bauer held that emancipation of man required a secular state that recognizes neither Christians nor Jews. Marx agreed that the existence of religion always indicates an incomplete emancipation, but he denied that religion is the cause of the problem or, for that matter, that political rights are the solution. Bauer had simply identified religion with alienation and political equality with emancipation. But political emancipation is by no means human emancipation. "To be *politically* emancipated from religion is not to be finally and completely emancipated from religion, because political emancipation is not the final and absolute form of human emancipation." Even if the state should suppress religion, its own existence would remain a profane expression of an alienation that in time would irresistibly produce its religious form. So instead of being a remedy for religious alienation, the secular state is the purest symptom of its presence. Even more than religion, the state keeps alive the inhuman conditions that separate the individual from his fellow human beings and thereby prevent mankind from realizing its full potential. If religion means deception, the state is more religious than the church.

Henceforth Marx devoted his critical efforts entirely to the critique of the state. But under the influence of an essay by Friedrich Engels on political economy, published in the same issue of the *Jahrbücher* that had featured Marx's own two essays, he saw that political attitudes are rooted in economic conditions. This "genial" insight inspired the so-called *Economic Philosophical Manuscripts* of 1844, which would remain unpublished until 1927. Here, for the first time, Marx aims his attacks exclusively at the capitalist economy itself, a system that alienates the worker from the very activity through which he should achieve his humanization as well as from the kind of social cooperation required by genuine humanization.

In 1845 the French government (under Prussian pressure) forbade Marx all political activity and threatened him with imprisonment. Once again Marx emigrated, this time to Brussels, where he would remain until March 1848. This second stage of his mature life was to be a very productive one, even though little of his literary activity ever reached print.

Foremost among his unpublished writings from this period is *The German Ideology* (1845–1846). In it Marx developed the crucial concept of ideology and, with it, the basic principles of a powerful theory of history. Not what human beings think or imagine, not conscious decisions or theoretical schemes, but social-economic relations are the primary determining factors of history. Ideas, shaped by language, emerge from social-economic structures. The division between mental and physical labor, severing thinking from its vital, social roots, has given birth to an independent realm of abstract speculation. In fact, the theories accepted in a particular society express the interests and aspirations of the ruling class. As soon as one class acquires control over the process of material production, it falls heir to the "means of mental production" and begins to impose such ideas as best serve its dominion. Detached from its social-economic basis, theory turns into ideology. The term *ideology* refers to any theory that ignores the social conditioning of ideas and presents itself with a semblance of intellectual autonomy.

Engels later qualified Marx's position by suggesting that conscious processes, developed through the impact of social relations, in turn influence these relations. Unfortunately, Marx's later metaphorical reformulation of the relation (in the preface to his *Critique of Political Economy*) as one between base and superstructure confirmed the "derived" character of ideas rather than eliminating it. Clearly, religion considered as a "superstructure" can hardly do more than "reflect" its social origins.

In Brussels, Marx and Engels, who had met in Paris in 1844 and by now had become constant, though often distant, collaborators, intensified their revolutionary activity. For the newly founded Communist League they wrote their famous *Manifesto* (1848), an entirely new vision of history. Since his early Paris days, the social-economic category of class had, for Marx, come to dominate all others. In the *Manifesto*'s scenario, the class of the bourgeoisie, created by the capitalist system, would function as the revolutionary lever toward the communist society of the future. An unprecedented social and cultural mover in its own development, the bourgeoisie is now destined to terminate the class structure of society itself. It does so by creating an underclass, the proletariat, that will increase in numbers and in misery until its members, for the sake of sheer survival, will be forced to rise throughout the entire industrialized world. "What the bourgeoisie, therefore, produces above all else, is its own gravediggers."

In the same year, 1848, revolutions started all over the European continent. But when the Belgian authorities learned of an imminent republican putsch, they expelled Marx from the country for illegal political agitation. The exile barely interrupted Marx's revolutionary activity. Returning to Paris on 5 March with the papers of the Communist League, which a few days earlier had had its headquarters transferred from London to Brussels, Marx was, on 10 March, elected as its president. In his French headquarters his attention remained fixed on Germany, where he still expected a "total" revolution to take place. Through his speeches to the German Working Men's Club (based in Paris) and his articles in the new communist paper of Cologne, the *Neue Rheinische Zeitung,* Marx continuously bombarded the German community with his revolutionary messages.

The June revolution in Paris confirmed at least part of Marx's theories, for in it social issues clearly prevailed over political ones. Meanwhile, Marx again had moved to Cologne to direct the *Neue Reinische,* which, not surprisingly, was gradually censored into extinction. Its editor was expelled from Prussian territory for having instigated open rebellion. During that same summer of 1848 Marx definitively settled down in London.

Here, amidst extreme poverty, domestic tragedy (several of his children died, possibly due to their living conditions), occasional family turmoil (his young servant bore him a child), and constant polemics, Marx completed the third stage of his career. Apart from revolutionary activity (mainly through the reorganized Communist League), he devoted himself entirely to his lifetime theoretical project: a definitive social critique of the capitalist economy. Only two parts of his voluminous theoretical writing during this period reached completion before his death: the *Contribution to the Critique of Political Economy* (1859) and the first volume of what by then had already become a reduced project, *Capital* (1867).

In all his later writings Marx criticizes capitalist theories in categories often borrowed from the classical economists, especially Adam Smith and David Ricardo. Even his central concept of surplus value, the value generated by labor beyond the cost of wages and tools, appears in Ricardo. But the perspective differs substantially. For Marx shows how capitalist theory merely expresses the practice of a society at a particular historical stage of its development. Indeed, capitalism is now approaching the point where its internal "contradictions" (in fact, mostly social conflicts) must openly erupt and destroy the system itself. Throughout his development Marx never wavered in his confidence that bourgeois society would break down in a social revolution that would result in a socialist state and, in due time, generate a stateless communist society.

Yet during this same period Marx also produced an enormous output of noneconomic writings, most important among them, two historical studies on the French revolution of 1848 and the subsequent events leading to the Second Empire of Napoleon III: *The Class Struggles in France* (1850) and *The Eighteenth Brumaire of Louis Napoleon* (1852). In addition, he wrote hundreds of newspaper articles for the *New York Daily Tribune* and for the *Neue Oder-Zeitung,* his main source of support (beside the gifts of the ever-generous Engels) during that period.

From 1870 on Marx's health steadily declined. He increasingly suffered from respiratory problems, which, after 1880, forced him for prolonged periods to seek refuge from the damp, polluted London air in Margate, the Isle of Wight, Karlsbad (where he took the baths), Nice, and even North Africa. Yet despite his poor health his literary activity continued unabatedly, and his travels provided him with opportunities for establishing new revolutionary contacts as far away as Algiers. Still, it became gradually obvious that he would never complete his lifework, and during his final years he felt increasingly reluctant even to attempt bringing some order to his papers. Thus when he died on 14 March 1883, he left an enormous estate of unpublished manuscripts. Out of the more than a thousand pages of notes Marx had accumulated for the sequel of *Capital,* Engels published *Capital II* (1885) and *Capital III* (1894). In addition, in 1927 Karl Kautsky published the historical notes, *Theories of Surplus Value,* under the title *Capital IV.* In 1953 Marx's earlier preparatory notes for *Capital* appeared under the title *Grundrisse der Kritik der politischen Ökonomie* (in English, simply *Grundrisse*).

BIBLIOGRAPHY

Dupré, Louis. *The Philosophical Foundations of Marxism.* New York, 1966.

Kolakowski, Leszek. *Main Currents of Marxism: Its Rise, Growth, and Dissolution,* vol. 1, *The Founders.* Oxford, 1978.

Marx, Karl, and Friedrich Engels. *On Religion.* New York, 1964.

Marx, Karl, and Friedrich Engels. *Collected Works.* 50 vols. Translated by Richard Dixon et al. New York, 1975–.

McLellan, David. *Karl Marx: His Life and Thought.* London, 1973.

Rubel, Maximilien, and Margaret Manale. *Marx without Myth: A Chronological Study of His Life and Work.* Oxford, 1975.

Louis Dupré

MARXISM. The Judeo-Christian tradition is both the spiritual ancestor of the Marxist movement and the view of reality that Marxism first repudiated in proclaiming its own message of judgment and hope. The story of the complex relation between the two may be divided conveniently into five sections: (1) Judeo-Christian influences on the origin of Marxism itself and its attitude toward religion; (2) the interaction between Christian socialism and Marxist socialism before 1917 and in social-democratic movements since 1917; (3) religion under Soviet communism from 1917 to 1945; (4) religion in Marxist-Leninist societies since World War II; and (5) Marxist-Christian interaction and dialogue since Stalin.

Judeo-Christian Influences. Neither Karl Marx (1818–1883) nor Friedrich Engels (1820–1895) had a profound grasp of the Christian faith or the Jewish tradition. Though Marx was the grandson and the nephew of rabbis, his father turned to liberal Protestant Christianity, and Marx was confirmed in the state Church of the Old Prussian Union. Engels was educated in the Reformed piety of Prussian Westphalia but broke with it early in his life. Nevertheless, the Marxism they formulated shared in and interacted with the Judeo-Christian heritage in two fundamental ways: (1) Marxism continually confronted, and drew on, the heritage of radical Christianity, and (2) Marxism was a result of a process, rooted in the Enlightenment and developed by G. W. F. Hegel and the left-wing Hegelians, that transposed the structure of Christian faith and hope into a humanist key.

Marx and Engels were surrounded, in the revolutionary movements of their times, by socialists claiming Christian bases for their radical convictions. Claude-Henri de Rouvroy, Comte de Saint-Simon, the most influential mind of the French utopian socialist movement, expounded his conception of a society rationally organized for the benefit of all workers, especially the poor, in his book *Nouveau christianisme* (1825). Charles Fourier appealed to the Gospels in *Le nouveau monde* (1848) to support his proposal for ideal cooperative communities, which he called "the expression of the true Christianity of Jesus." Marx and Engels ignored this Christian dimension, which was admittedly unorthodox, and attacked these men and their followers as aristocratic planners for the poor, rather than as participants in the revolutionary action of the poor to overthrow the existing system. Yet they acknowledged the educative value of their goals for human society. More difficult to refute was Wilhelm Weitling. Founder of the League of the Just (which was the predecessor to the First International), a labor organizer, a revolutionary agitator, and also a passionately evangelical Christian, Weitling advocated a class war of the poor against the rich. He maintained that Jesus was the first socialist, whose "repudiation of power and riches, self-abasement and self-sacrifice" had been betrayed by the established church since Constantine. The worker's violent struggle for a new "socialism of love" was, in his view, also a modern renewal of original Christianity.

Marx attacked this point of view from the left and the right in the name of "scientific socialism." He scorned Weitling's faith as sentimentalism, and fought Weitling's demand for direct mass action as unplanned and premature. It was, however, precisely in this heritage of radical Christianity that Marxism found its own antecedents. Building on the critical New Testament studies of Bruno Bauer, Engels discovered a mass movement of "the laboring and the burdened," that is, of slaves, debt-laden peasants, and poor freedmen of the Roman empire, which expressed its revolt in early Christianity (*Bruno Bauer and Early Christianity*, 1852). This revolt had to be religious, given the hopeless social situation; but it was informed, he wrote in *On the History of Early Christianity* (1895), by an urgent this-worldly eschatology, the vehicle of which was the New Testament book of *Revelation*, which Engels, following Bauer, took to be the earliest Christian document. Only later, according to Engels, did this faith become a sacramental, trinitarian, escapist, and conformist religion. Christianity, in Engels's view, has therefore a dual character. On the one hand, in breaking with rituals and ceremonies designed to symbolize a particular culture's relation to the divine, it became the first genuinely universal religion, and hence a vehicle for the protest and revolt of all humanity against oppression. On the other hand, its doctrines of sin and sacrificial atonement turned people inward for salvation and undermined this protest. In *The Peasant War in Germany* (1874) and other writings, he applied this analysis to conflicts in the history of the church.

Engels's theme of duality was also used by the German Social Democrats, notably Karl Kautsky and Rosa Luxemburg. Its more sophisticated development, however, comes from Ernst Bloch, whose *Das Prinzip Hoffnung* (1959), *Atheism in Christianity* (1972), and other writings have influenced Jürgen Moltmann and other modern theologians. For Bloch the Judeo-Christian tradition is unique despite analogies in other traditions (e.g., Prometheus). The Judeo-Christian God is the spirit of the exodus from Egypt and a projection of human utopian hope that cannot be defined and known beforehand, but realized only in the struggle against existing order. The Bible is the early story of this struggle. Jesus was, with his projection of the kingdom of God, one of its prophets. Throughout the history of Christianity, there has been an underground of revolutionary, heretical theology which has carried this struggle forward. Bloch mentions Marcion, Joachim of Fiore, and Thomas Müntzer especially. The goal of this history, Bloch maintained, is the emergence of atheist humanity projecting its own utopias forward, guided by the science of Marxism, no longer needing the symbols of theology. But for Bloch, Marxism is the heir of the unique Judeo-Christian tradition, which for centuries has expressed human hope and energized human revolt by means of these symbols.

Marxism's indebtedness to the Enlightenment and to Hegel and the left-wing Hegelians is revealed in three principal stages. The first is the Enlightenment's confidence in the continuity between the human and the divine, between human reason and conscience and divine order, and therefore in the unbounded human capacity for progress. Educated in the Enlightenment tradition, Marx in his youth shared this confidence. The second stage is Hegel's conversion of that continuity into a divine-human dialectical struggle for self-realization in history through alienation (expressed in human oppression and suffering but supremely in the crucifixion of Christ) and reconciliation (the work of the Holy Spirit through human power to establish the supremacy and moral order of a human society). The third stage is embodied in the view of the left-wing Hegelians, given definitive expression in Ludwig Feuerbach's *Essence of Christianity* (1841) that the divine dimension of this struggle is itself alienating, that God is essentially a projection of the ideal human essence onto the heavens, and that the whole doctrine and ceremony of the Christian church can be enjoyed as a celebration of the true quality of the human species, realizing itself in love between person and person.

Marx adopted Feuerbach's humanistic inversion of Christianity but radicalized it. Religion is, for him, the projection in fantasy of a humanity that finds no fulfillment in this world. It is "the sigh of the oppressed creature," at once a protest against oppression and an adaptation to it. It is the opium the people take to dull their pain and give them dreams. But it is not enough, he criticizes Feuerbach, to expose this fact; one must go on to analyze the contradictions in human society that produce religious illusions, and one must revolutionize them in practice. In doing this, Marx radicalized left-wing Hegelian humanism into an antitheology that cut all remaining links with spirituality. First, he redefined Feuerbach's concept of "species humanity" not in terms of human relationships, but as "free, conscious activity" of the species expressed in each individual *(Economic Philosophical Manuscripts of 1844,* first published 1927). The human being is a self-creator through labor, the agent who molds nature and history. Second, he rooted Hegel's concept of alienation in the expropriation of the fruits of a person's labor by others who employ or use him. The dehumanization that this produces amounts, in Marx's view, to total depravity. It divides humanity into classes between which there is no shared consciousness or conscience. It condemns society to ever-intensified class conflict, which no divine or human law can relativize. Third, Marx found the savior in this conflict to be the class most completely deprived and exploited, lacking all stake in existing order or power. In the utter negation of proletarian existence the image of true species humanity is formed, in solidarity free from all personal ambition, and in revolutionary determination. Fourth, what for Hegel is the cunning of the Spirit realizing its goals in history through the human struggle becomes for Marx the dialectical operation of the "material" laws of history, expressed in the forces of production overturning the relations of production, by means of the strategy and tactics of the revolutionary struggle. Fifth, communism for Marx, like the kingdom of God for Christians, is genuinely eschatological. Hope in its coming is not dimmed by its delayed arrival. It is always at hand. It will bring a transformation of human nature by new social conditions that, Marx believed, will be prepared in the struggle itself and in transitional socialist societies.

At all these points, the structural analogy—and therefore the challenge—of Marxism to Christianity is clear. The stage was set for later interaction.

Christian and Marxist Socialism before 1917. Before the death of Marx, the lines of conflict were drawn between the Christian church and Marxist socialism. Karl Kautsky, in *Foundations of Christianity* (1908), recognized Jesus as an early socialist, but was more severe than Engels in his condemnation of the other-worldliness of the Christian religion. Lenin made the propagation of atheism a subordinate but critically important task of the Communist party, before and after it seized power. On the Christian side, Pope Leo XIII, in the first year of his reign, condemned socialism as "a deadly plague" that undermines religion, the state, family, and private property *(Quod apostolici numeris,* 1878). Protestant church responses were no more friendly. The Marxist challenge, however, also stimulated some churches with a strong precapitalist tradition in ethics to elaborate their own social teachings. In 1891, Leo XIII recognized that in capitalist industrial development, "a small number of very rich men have been able to lay upon the masses of the poor a yoke little better than slavery itself" *(De rerum novarum).* Still rejecting socialism, he set forth the state's responsibility to intervene in the economic order to promote justice, the employers' duty to use wealth and power for the welfare of their workers and the public, and the workers' right to organize Catholic trade unions to assure their rights in the context of seeking harmony between classes. This encyclical laid the foundation of a Roman Catholic social reform movement, redefined forty years later in the *Quadragesimo anno* of Pius XI. A similar response arose among the Protestants with the formation of the Anti-Revolutionary party by Dutch Calvinists, who were led by Abraham Kuyper. Kuyper and his party opposed "organic spheres of creation" to the individualism of the capitalists and the collectivism of the socialists. They held that the state is indeed the guardian of justice, defending the weak and curbing the abuse of power in the social realm, but also that its power, like that of a factory, is mechanical and therefore external. Justice is secured only when the communities of family, neighborhood, learning, and production are strengthened at their base.

This hardening of the front was, however, only part of the story. Revisionism, which for the most part held that evolutionary progress toward socialism is achieved by democratic means, and which barely mentioned religion, came more and more to dominate the policy of socialist parties. It also broke decisively with the idea of the economic determinism of human consciousness. "The materialist conception of history does not preclude an idealist interpretation of it," said the French Socialist leader Jean Jaurès (*Idealism in History*, 1905). Justice and right, whatever the philosophical or religious form they take, are driving principles in the history of human development alongside a realistic analysis of the powers of economic exploitation. In Britain, the democratic evolutionary socialism of the Fabians provided a context that absorbed outspoken Marxists (Henry Hyndman and the Social Democratic Federation) and active Christians of various kinds (Keir Hardie, the Church Socialist League) into the ideological mixture that became the Labour party. In the United States, the Socialist party was a turbulent mixture of Marxist, utopian socialist, and Christian ideas. A clergyman, George D. Herron, was, with Eugene V. Debs, a founder. After the death of Debs, it was led by a former Presbyterian minister, Norman Thomas, who described the party's philosophy as Marxist in "a very loose sense of the word" mixed with broader humanist ideals and psychological insights (*A Socialist's Faith*, 1951).

Christian socialists pursued their goals in various relationships to Marxist movements. In Germany Friedrich Naumann organized a Christian socialist group in the 1890s, which, however, had little influence and gradually moved to a left-liberal position. His countryman Christoph Blumhardt declared his conversion, on the grounds of his biblical Christian faith, to the Social Democratic party. In Switzerland Hermann Kutter and Leonhard Ragaz, inspired in part by Blumhardt, founded a religious socialist movement. The young Karl Barth was also pastorally engaged with the labor union in his working-class parish of Safenwil and imbued the first edition of his *Epistle to the Romans* (1919) with a Christian socialist perspective. In the United States the Society of Christian Socialists was formed in 1889; its publication *The Dawn* published contributions by Marxists but basically promoted socialism as "the application to society of the way of Christ." In 1906 the Christian Socialist Fellowship supported the Socialist party, published parts of Marx's *Capital*, and advocated participation in the international socialist movement as a way of realizing what was variously called the Christian revolution, the economic expression of the religious life, or anticipation of God's redemption in the social sphere.

These movements did not engage Marxism with any depth of analysis. Walter Rauschenbusch, for example, used Marxism as a tool to expose the moral evils and injustices of capitalism: the spirit of competition, irresponsible power, exploitation, and the selfish profit motive. Rauschenbusch proposed economic equality, public ownership of the basic means of production, and industrial as well as political democracy imbued with a spirit of social fraternity in place of the capitalist system (*Christianizing the Social Order*, 1912). Kutter understood the socialist movement, despite its materialist atheism and emphasis on class war, to be the judgment of God on the capitalist system and on the church for its self-centered comfort therein, and, through its socialist program, to be the only effective force moving toward a more Christian social order (*They Must*, 1908). Ragaz found the Marxist socialist movement to be at heart an idealism demanding justice and prayed that this would prevail over the violence and dictatorship of Bolshevism (*Signs of the Kingdom*, 1984). Only in Russia were the ideological lines drawn so sharply that choices had to be made. There, a remarkable group of converts from revolutionary Marxism (three Orthodox Christians—historian Piotr Struwe, theologian Sergei Bulgakov, and philosopher Nikolai Berdiaev—and the Jewish philosopher S. L. Frank) formed a group that took basic issue with the dogmatic utopianism and the utter submission of means to ends that characterized Russian Marxism, both Menshevik and Bolshevik. The group was dispersed in the revolution of 1917, but its influence continued. Berdiaev, who, in *The Origin of Russian Communism* (1937), wrote one of the most penetrating studies of that movement, continued throughout his life to expound a form of Christian communal philosophy in dialogue with the Marxist alternative.

The Russian Revolution and the Great Depression brought a new depth to Christian social reflection on Marxism and to Christian-Marxist relations. Jacques Maritain in his *Integral Humanism* (1936) contrasted the incarnation of Christ with the "absolute realist immanentism" of Marx. He called for a "secular Christian" pluralist society inspired, but not dominated, by the church toward a practical vision of the common good and composed of a structure of communities gathered around personal (family, neighborhood, cultural affinity) or functional (economic or social) foci, of which the state is the highest and most general. The struggle to realize this ideal by Christian groups within the various secular communities must be motivated by evangelical love and respect for human personhood. This philosophy inspired Christian Democratic alternatives to

Marxist socialism not only in Europe between the world wars, but in Latin America as late as the 1970s, where it has been the principal opponent of liberation theology.

The most comprehensive Protestant effort to provide an alternative Christian vision, that of the Religious Socialists, was inspired by Paul Tillich. Tillich understood Marxism as "prophecy on the grounds of an autonomous self-contained world" (*The Socialist Decision,* 1933) and saw a structural analogy between Marx's thought and prophetic theology in its view of history, its analysis of human alienation in present society, and its unity of theory and practice in social involvement. According to Tillich, a socialism integrated with religion would enable society to understand its roots in the original powers of creation and its destiny in confrontation with the demand of the unconditioned (God) and could thus lead it from a bourgeois autonomy to a new theonomy that would be open to the grace of God, which informs and transforms human culture. The mission of religious socialists is to lead Marxist socialism into the depth of its historical being, lest it miss its *kairos.* This means imbuing Marxism with an understanding of the human as spiritual and material, society as communal prebourgeois and class-divided, power as "realized social unity" and political force, and reality as rooted in "a harmony of religious and profane symbolism." [*See the biography of Tillich.*]

Tillich's conception had very little influence in Germany on either Social Democrats or Communists. It did, however, contribute to the thought of the Fellowship of Social Christians in America, whose leader was Reinhold Niebuhr. Niebuhr found in Marxism a tool of analysis that exposes liberal illusions about social power and the depth of social conflict. He saw the proletarian revolution as an instrument of God's judgment and of the hope for greater justice in society, despite its utopian illusions of a society without classes. The task of Christian socialists, in his view, was to work within both the church and the revolutionary movement (for Niebuhr, the Socialist party) so that the change to socialism would be marked by as little violence as possible, so that the conscience of the church would accept it, and so that the victorious proletarians would not in self-righteous vindictiveness turn justice into a new tyranny. German religious socialist principles went into defining the form of the socialist society for which the Fellowship of Socialist Christians hoped.

This was, however, a transitional position. From it Niebuhr and the Fellowship moved, together with British Christians, notably Stafford Cripps and William Temple, toward advocacy of a mixed economy that would curb private economic power and direct it toward the common good, but not at the price of creating political tyranny in a socialist society. In 1947, the word *socialist* was dropped and the group became the Frontier Fellowship. The definition of a "responsible society" by the British ecumenist J. H. Oldham and its adoption by the first assembly of the World Council of Churches in 1948 as a guide for Christian social ethics between the rejected extremes of communism and laissez-faire capitalism was the next movement in this trend. For two decades after World War II this moderate spirit reigned among social democrats, Marxists, and Christians. Socialist parties of Marxist background welcomed Christian members and leaders emerged in both Europe and Africa who were socialist and Christian.

Soviet Communism from 1917 to 1945. Vladimir Il'ich Lenin (1870–1924) had no personal tolerance for religion in any form. Even humanist, "god-creating" religious imagery in the style of Feuerbach or Maxim Gorky violated, in his view, the integrity of the "science" of dialectical materialism, just as utopian visions of stateless freedom in a communist society undermined social construction of the conditions for communism (*State and Revolution,* 1917). Nevertheless, Lenin was a revolutionary statesman. He regarded atheist propaganda as an essential but subordinate part of socialist education and action. The primary task was the proletarian conquest of power and the building of socialism. Religious opposition to tsarist or capitalist oppression should therefore be supported. As Lenin wrote in 1909, "If a priest comes to cooperate with us in our work—if he conscientiously performs party work and does not oppose the party program—we can accept him into the ranks of Social Democracy, for the contradictions between the spirit and principles of our program and the religious convictions of the priest could, in those circumstances, be regarded as a matter in which he contradicts himself, as one which concerns him alone." Of course, were he to "propagate religious views" in the party, he would have to be expelled. The state should treat religion as a private matter and separate it totally from education, from influence on public policy, and from participation in public life, while respecting the religious prejudices and practices of people who otherwise behave as good socialist citizens. The party should be an agent, first of the strategy and tactics, second of the dialectical materialist worldview, of the socialist revolution. To the latter, atheism belongs.

Soviet policy, since the Revolution of 1917, has followed these guidelines. The 1917 laws nationalized property, including that of the church, prohibited religious education in any school, and granted freedom of worship and belief insofar as these did not interfere with public order, civic duty, or the rights of citizens.

In 1929 further restrictions were spelled out; the conduct of worship became the sole legal activity of the church. Religious instruction was allowed only above the age of eighteen, and then only in private. The formula of the Soviet constitution of 1936—"Freedom for religious profession and antireligious propaganda"—has been used to silence all public defense of religion and all public evangelism. Under these laws the state and the party have over the years conducted a two-pronged attack on religion. First, beginning in 1926 with the League of the Militant Godless and continuing after World War II with the Scientific-Atheist Section of the Society for the Dissemination of Scientific and Political Knowledge, state and party have kept up a constant propaganda pressure against religion in communities, schools, youth organizations, and labor groups, down to the present. The approach varies: attacks on the hypocrisy, the immorality, and the superstition of the church, the synagogue, and the mosque; expositions of dialectical materialism and evolutionary theory as refutations of God, creation, and providence; charges of reactionary, antisocialist political influences in organized religion; studies of the evil psychological effect of the religious home on growing children, and of conversions to scientific atheism by children and adults—all are tactics that have been used. In recent years more sophisticated analyses of Western theology and ethics have also been produced, but not for a broad market. Of course, no religious response to all of this is allowed. The second part of the attack has been administrative harassment and control of churches and other religious organizations, varying in intensity and style, throughout the history of the Soviet Union. The attack against the Orthodox church (which resisted strongly) and the small Roman Catholic church in the Ukraine began immediately after the revolution. Between 1917 and 1927, bloody clashes occurred between believers and government over interference with church activities and confiscation of church property. Thousands of priests and believers suffered execution, imprisonment, or exile. A schismatic "living church" was promoted by the government. In 1927 the patriarchal administration was officially registered, but the pressure did not change. By 1941 Orthodox churches and priests had been reduced to one-tenth of their number in 1917.

On other religious groups the blow fell not as soon but just as heavily. Baptist and evangelical Christians—poor, without property, and persecuted by the tsars—were at first viewed favorably and allowed to organize youth groups and Christian collective farms. After 1929, however, the laws against religious activity were strictly enforced against them, and a repressive campaign led to imprisonments and some executions. During the 1920s procommunist reform movements appeared in both Islam and Buddhism, claiming roots in the Qur'ān for government policies and even, in the case of Buddhism, an ideological congruence between Marxist and Buddhist atheism. This, however, offended not only the traditional leaders of both communities, but also the antireligious ideology of Communism itself. In 1928 the government engaged the Muslim community in a bitter struggle over the status of women, which broadened into a suppression of Islam more severe than that visited on Christianity. The next year a similar campaign began in Buddhist areas and was extended in 1937 to Mongolia. By 1941 no Buddhist monasteries and only a few mosques were still functioning. The pattern was similar for other religious communities: the Orthodox Old Believers, the Georgian Orthodox church, the Armenian church, the Roman Catholic church, and the Jews.

World War II produced a relaxation of restrictions that lasted roughly until the ascendancy of Nikita Khrushchev in 1957. The Russian Orthodox church was allowed to enthrone a new patriarch, replenish its episcopate and clergy, reopen many churches and monasteries, and establish seminaries and academies for the training of clergy for the first time since the revolution. The All-Union Council of Evangelical Christians/Baptists was allowed to form and to spread its evangelistic and unifying efforts throughout the Soviet Union, though not, so far, to establish a theological seminary. Lutheran churches in Estonia and Latvia, a Reformed church in the Carpathian Ukraine, and Roman Catholic churches in Lithuania and eastern Poland came into the Soviet Union through territorial annexations and were recognized. Pressure was eased on Islam, and the number of registered mosques more than doubled in the country. A similar relaxation occurred for other communions, with, however, certain exceptions: (1) the Uniate churches of Belorussia and the Ukraine were completely suppressed and forced, for survival, to join the Russian Orthodox church; (2) sectarian congregations that, for reasons of conscience and faith, refused to register with the government were and still are ruthlessly persecuted; (3) the government-established Muslim leadership is not well respected, and more than half of Muslim clergy and mosques are unregistered (the same is true among Buddhists, despite the reopening of two monasteries); and (4) the relaxation policy has never applied to the Jewish religious community, which was denied the right to publish any literature, refused facilities for training rabbis, and often the registration of synagogues, save for a few concessions made after the death of Joseph Stalin in 1953.

The present situation is the result of these trends,

curbed by new repression under Khrushchev, and somewhat stabilized since then. Churches, synagogues, and mosques do function, though few new ones have been registered and some have been closed in the past generation. They are closely controlled by the Ministry of Religious Affairs, to which the leadership must be acceptable, and they are infiltrated by government agents. Religious leaders have been allowed increasing ecumenical contacts abroad, which are also monitored. Dissenters have been harshly dealt with among Christians and Jews, less harshly among Muslims.

The responses of believers to all of this are varied, but four elements stand out. First, the patient persistence of religious faith and practice is passed on from one generation to the next, despite all obstacles. Only for Buddhism can a case be made that religion is dying out. Second, the officially recognized leadership of the Russian Orthodox church, the Baptist Union, the other churches, and the Jewish, Muslim, and Buddhist communities pursues an extremely delicate vocation, shepherding and nourishing the church or community on the one hand and bargaining with or accommodating itself to the government so as to win maximum space for the life of faith on the other. Third, religious life in the Soviet Union is continually goaded and challenged by dissenters in the name of a purer faith and practice. The Baptist Union faces the sharpest challenge from the *initsiativniki*, a group almost as large in number as that composed of registered Baptists; the *initsiativniki* reject the state control involved in registration and practice an uncompromising commitment to evangelism and personal discipline. Fourth, there is among dissident intellectuals a revival of interest in Christianity, expressed in the *samizdat*, or privately circulated literature, and in the published works of Boris Pasternak and Aleksandr Solzhenitsyn. The focus, however, is not on the encounter of Marxist and Christian worldviews, but rather on the recovery of an authentic Russian heritage with its spiritual foundations in the Orthodox church, and on providing that church with a philosophy and ethic for the twenty-first century.

Postwar Marxist-Leninist Societies. Following World War II, Marxist-Leninist control expanded from the Soviet Union to all of eastern Europe and North Korea by conquest, and to China, Vietnam, Albania, and Yugoslavia by internal revolution. The variations in government policy and in the responses of churches and other religious groups in all these lands cannot be detailed here. Two books cover the eastern European scene in detail: Trevor Beeson's *Discretion and Valor* (1982) and Paul Mojzes's *Christian-Marxist Dialogue in Eastern Europe* (1981). Some basic characteristics and trends can, however, be delineated.

First, in all countries except Albania, which has ruthlessly suppressed all religion and imprisoned Christian and Muslim clergy, North Korea, about which little is known, and the People's Republic of China during the Cultural Revolution of 1966–1972, religious groups have been allowed to function legally for worship on the local level and with some national organization. Only in Bulgaria have the restrictions been as severe as in the Soviet Union. In Poland a Catholic university at Lublin still functions. In Czechoslovakia, Yugoslavia, and the German Democratic Republic (East Germany) religious instruction may be given to school children on church premises. In principle all activities outside church premises require special permission, but in most countries priests and ministers extend their ministries to the homes of parishioners and, in the church, conduct religious instruction as well as baptisms, weddings, funerals, and regular worship. In East Germany an unofficial Youth Congregation functions nationally, with occasional retreats and conferences. In Poland three Christian lay organizations are active, with representation in the parliament. Social service by religious organizations has been generally prohibited, but the Roman Catholic church in Croatia (Yugoslavia) and Protestant churches in Hungary and East Germany have been allowed to continue or resume some of this work. Most churches in eastern Europe and in the People's Republic of China are allowed to publish religious education and worship materials and some journals, all subject, of course, to censorship.

Second, everywhere in these lands, religious believers live under the limits, controls, and pressures imposed by the government's antireligious ideology, which dominates all aspects of public life. With rare exceptions, the communist parties do not accept religious believers as members. They are usually excluded from certain key vocations, such as teaching or government service, and have difficulty advancing to responsible positions in other fields. Access to higher education, except in theology, is often difficult for them. Antireligious propaganda is usually part of public education. Churches, mosques, and synagogues face continual restrictions, controls, and interference in program planning, in fundraising, in the education of clergy and lay leadership, in church building and development, in publication, and in preaching, worship, and community life, which are likely to be monitored by government agents.

However, the picture changes radically according to time and place. In Poland, with its formidable Roman Catholic tradition, these pressures are the constant subject of dispute, resistance, and compromise. In China, in the decade after the death of Mao Tse-tung in 1976, the government began to return churches, temples, and mosques to the control of believers and even paid back rent for the use of the property. In East Germany the authorities have accepted the fact that the conformist line of their minority party, the Christian Democratic Union, is not that of the Evangelical (Protestant) majority church or that of the Roman Catholics, and they therefore work with both sides. Christians in the most Eastern European countries and even in China often, despite descrimination, rise to play a significant role in scholarship, in public service, or in mass organizations under Communist domination, knowing that tomorrow policy may tighten to exclude them or loosen to give them new opportunity.

Third, the response of religious communities to the challenge of Marxist-Leninist domination has been more varied than the religious policies of these governments. Generally, from central Europe to Vietnam, a groundswell of piety among the people sustains churches, mosques, and temples in the face of government opposition and restrictions. This piety has little to do with Marxism pro or con. The fact of a socialist society run by the Communist party is largely accepted, though in Poland and Yugoslavia struggles continue over its form. It is simply witness to a reality in the life and tradition of the people, strongest where religious national identity has continued unbroken through the centuries, that Marxist-Leninist ideology cannot comprehend.

Another level of response, however, is present in many countries, most strongly represented by the Evangelical church in East Germany. This church has steadfastly resisted all government attempts to control or set conditions for its internal life. At the same time, on the basis of an independent Christian social ethic, it has affirmed "critical solidarity" with the government's intention to build a just socialist society in the country and to establish world peace. In practice this means that the church has been in constant critical encounter with the state through the years on basic political and social issues. But the church has cultivated basic loyalty to the government against the pan-German longings of many of its members and affirms a Christian role within a socialist world.

Marxist-Christian Dialogue and Interaction since Stalin. This dialogue began with soul-searching among communists. The discrediting of Stalin and the continuation of so many Stalinist policies led to profound reflection in the East and West about the whole range of Marxist theory and practice, including its relation to the claims of Christian faith and the practice of religion. Christian theologians responded with eager enthusiasm to the challenge. The result was that a vigorous Marxist-Christian dialogue erupted in Europe during the 1960s wherever political conditions permitted. In Yugoslavia, where an open, flexible philosophical approach to Marxist thought had been established over the previous decade, this dialogue, primarily with the Roman Catholic theologians of Croatia and Slovenia, was especially rich in the variety of its themes and points of view (Mojzes, 1981). In Poland a quiet conversation between Catholic and Marxist intellectuals, which began in 1962 and continues to the present, was enlivened by two unorthodox Marxist contributions: Adam Schaff with his concern for the form of individual human life in a socialist society (*Marxismus und das menschliche Individuum*, 1965) and Leszek Kolakowski with his efforts to understand Marxism—and by extension Christianity—not as universal systems of truth but as "living philosophical inspiration within a general way of perceiving the world" (*Toward a Marxist Humanism*, 1968). The encounter in Czechoslovakia was especially dramatic and for a time influenced government policy. Its chief spokesmen were J. L. Hromadka, dean of Czech Protestant theologians and friend of many Communists, whose *Gospel for Atheists* (1965) set the Christian tone, and Milan Machovec, a Marxist philosopher, whose *Sinn des menschlichen Lebens* (1965) and *A Marxist Looks at Jesus* (1976) provided an eloquent defense of dialogue as a way of human living, and a practical example of it. The interaction proceeded on two levels. Through Machovec, other Marxists were drawn into the conversation, notably Vitezslav Gardavsky, whose *God Is Not Quite Dead* (1972) drew a parallel between the calling and risk of a faith commitment in Marxist atheism and in Christianity. Meanwhile, under the program of "socialism with a human face" promoted by the government under Alexander Dubcek, most restrictions on churches were removed, religion was welcomed as a constructive part of socialist society, and the Bureau of Religious Affairs was turned from a regulative bureaucracy into an agency to further cooperation and dialogue.

The high point of this development was the only Christian-Marxist congress ever to be held in Eastern Europe, in Marianske Lazne, Czechoslovakia, in 1967. The Paulusgesellschaft, which published the proceedings as *Schöpfertum und Freiheit* (1968), brought to this meeting a history of several conferences and published reports involving Western European Catholic theologians (Karl Rahner, J. B. Metz, Giulio Girardi, et al.) and Marxist scholars from France (Roger Garaudy), Italy (Lucio Lombardo-Radice), Austria, and West Germany with Eastern European Marxists from Poland, Yugoslavia, and Hungary. It was a moment of revision and new direction for all involved, a triumph of Machovec's belief that dialogue, in which each risks deepest convictions in openness to the other, is indeed basic to the meaning of life.

The triumph was short-lived. In August 1968 the Soviet army snuffed out the Czech socialist experiment. Restrictions more severe than before were imposed on churches. The Marxists who had taken part in the dialogue lost their positions and were silenced. In Poland Schaff was expelled from the party and Kolakowski went into exile. In December 1971, Tito cracked down on liberalization in the Yugoslav Communist party; Marxist scholars came under heavy pressure to be more orthodox and more circumspect. Throughout Eastern Europe during the years that followed, open critical interaction was replaced by "carefully managed dialogue," devoted to particular purposes and conducted by authorized party or government representatives, in which basic ideological questions were not raised. The Soviet-sponsored International Institute for Peace and the Roman Catholic Institute for Peace Research in Vienna, joined later by the Institute for Peace and Understanding (an American Christian group), have held a series of low-profile international symposia starting in 1971 with semiofficial participation from the East. In Poland, Hungary, and East Germany conversations initiated by the government with the churches to persuade them to support its policies often serve to reveal the churches' agenda as well. Such conversations are limited but often frank and useful. They may provide channels for that day when Marxist-Leninist dogma relaxes.

Meanwhile the dialogical relation was also attacked from another angle. The desideratum is "not a Christian-Marxist dialogue," writes José Miguez-Bonino, expressing a perspective common to Latin American liberation theology, "but a growing and overt common participation in a revolutionary project, the basic lines of which are undoubtedly based on a Marxist analysis" (*Christians and Marxists*, 1976). Marxism is the "language" by which the Christian understands how his obedience to God must be expressed in the inhuman conditions of society. Christians and Marxists find themselves together in a common struggle. This solidarity in "praxis" is basic in their view, not their opposing ideas of religion.

The question of the relation between Christianity and Marxism arises therefore, in this view, within the common enterprise. However, with this relation comes the beginning of an encounter on two levels, despite the failure of many liberation theologians to notice the fact. The first level is that of political power. Gustavo Gutierrez authorized revolutionary struggle theologically by describing political liberation as "the self-creation of man" rooted in divine creation and fulfilled by re-creation in Christ (*A Theology of Liberation*, 1973). Basic Christian communities, founded alongside parishes throughout Latin America, have become schools of social activism against oppressing powers. But in violent revolutionary movements themselves and in the governments they form, Christians have tended to be junior partners to Marxist-Leninists, who are not tolerant of deviations from their military, economic, or political policies. Camillo Torres wrestled with this problem before joining the Colombian guerilla movement with which he met his death (*Revolutionary Writings*, 1969). The second level is the interpretation of Marxism itself. A few have taken it seriously. In *Marx against the Marxists* (1980), José Miranda has attempted a bold reinterpretation of Marx and Engels as humanists rather than determinists, as moralists rather than just scientists, and as at least open to the possibility of God. Miguez-Bonino recognizes that dialectical materialism devalues humanity and turns Marx's criticism of religion into absolute atheism. But he claims for Christians who are Marxists an equal right to interpret the movement and to prove by participation that biblical faith can lead to revolutionary action. This is the stuff of dialogue yet to come.

In western Europe and North America, on the other hand, Marxist-Christian dialogue has continued to develop, because in these areas Marxism has been allowed to unfold in its creative variety. The Italian Communist party has been most open, making clear that religious consciousness, far from dying out in a socialist society, will contribute constructively to its development, and accepting practicing Christians into membership and positions of influence. On the Christian side, Giulio Girardi developed a careful theory of the conditions for convergence between Christian and Marxist beliefs as a program for future conversations (*Marxism and Christianity*, 1968).

In 1965, the French Marxist Roger Garaudy called for "a dialogue without prejudice or hindrance. We do not ask anyone to stop being what he is. What we ask, on the contrary, is that he be it more and that he be it better. We hope that those who engage in dialogue with us will demand the same of us" (*From Anathema to Dialogue*, 1965). Christians have continued to examine Marxism as a call to Christian repentance and renewal and a different worldview to be challenged (Thomas Ogletree's *Openings for Marxist Christian Dialogue*, 1968; J. M. Lochman's *Encountering Marx*, 1975; A. F. McGovern's *Marxism: An American Christian Perspective*, 1980). Marxists have responded with their own self-analysis and challenge (Herbert Aptheker's *The Urgency of Marxist-Christian Dialogue*, 1970). In 1979 a series of biennial dialogues with American Marxists of various stripes was instituted in the United States under the sponsorship of the Christian-Marxist Relations Task Force of Christians Associated for Relations with Eastern Europe.

The dialogue therefore continues. Dogmatists—whether communist or Christian—to whom it is a threat can hinder it, but they tend thereby, as the experience of the Soviet and eastern European governments illustrates, to weaken the integrity and power of their own worldview. Enthusiasts may override it for a time, but the mutual challenge of opposing beliefs about God, humanity, history, and hope is so deep and so practical that it cannot be avoided for long. There is no synthesis; there can be no separation.

BIBLIOGRAPHY

Beeson, Trevor. *Discretion and Valour: Religious Conditions In Russia and Eastern Europe*. Rev. ed. Philadelphia, 1982. This work, by a team of scholars acquainted directly with religious conditions in various eastern European countries, was assembled by the British Council of Churches under Mr. Beeson's direction. It is the most sensitive and informed guide available.

Berdiaev, Nikolai. *The Origin of Russian Communism*. Translated by R. M. French. London, 1937. A classic study of Russia's leading Christian philosopher of the twentieth century.

Fried, Albert, and Ronald Sanders, eds. *Socialist Thought: A Documentary History*. Chicago, 1964. Excerpts and brief expositions of socialist writers from pre-Marxist France to the present, including the social-democratic and communist streams of Marxism.

Gollwitzer, Helmut. *The Christian Faith and the Marxist Criticism of Religion*. Translated by David Cairns. New York, 1970. The most complete study of this subject available in English.

Hopkins, Charles Howard. *The Rise of the Social Gospel in American Protestantism, 1865–1915*. New Haven, 1940. A classic study that traces also Marxist interaction with Christian socialism.

Jones, Peter d'A. *The Christian Socialist Revival, 1877–1914: Religion, Class and Social Conscience in Late-Victorian England*. Princeton, 1968.

Kolarz, Walter. *Religion in the Soviet Union*. New York, 1961. The most thorough study of this field, including the variety of Christian and non-Christian religious communities, up to the time of its publication.

Lenin, V. I. *Religion*. New York, 1933. A Soviet publication containing in a brief pamphlet most of the writings from Lenin on this subject that are usually quoted.

Marx, Karl, and Friedrich Engels. *On Religion*. New York, 1964. A reprint of a compilation by Soviet scholars of the most important statements of the two authors on religion. Includes an introduction by Reinhold Niebuhr.

Mojzes, Paul. *Christian-Marxist Dialogue in Eastern Europe*. Minneapolis, 1981. A complete study of this activity in Communist Europe. Especially informative on Yugoslavia, the author's land of origin, Czechslovakia, and Poland, but comprehensive both geographically and in subject matter.

Thomas, Madathilparampil M. *The Secular Ideologies of India and the Secular Meaning of Christ*. Bangalore, 1976. Examines Marxism-Leninism in its various expressions, socialist humanism with its Marxist component, liberal rationalism, and several forms of post-Hindu humanism as they relate to Christian and Hindu theology and practice.

Tucker, Robert C., ed. *The Marx-Engels Reader*. 2d ed. New York, 1978. See especially part 1, "The Early Marx." This volume shows the scope of Marx's own humanism.

CHARLES C. WEST

MARY, the mother of Jesus. The New Testament description of Maria, or Mariam, includes her virginal conception of Jesus. [*See* Jesus.] Preeminent among the saints, the Virgin Mary later became the object of piety and cult and, especially in the Roman Catholic church, of dogmas such as the Immaculate Conception and the Assumption. Protestant treatment of her as a biblical saint varies. She is honored in the Qur'ān (surahs 3 and 19).

Traditionally, Mary has been presented by combining all the references to her in the Gospels and *Acts of the Apostles* and viewing them in the light of the infancy narratives (*Mt.* 1–2, *Lk.* 1–2), which have been taken as her memoirs revealed years later to an evangelist. These accounts have then been psychologized and interpreted in light of later Marian thought. Further, *Revelation* 12, which speaks about "a woman clothed with the sun, with the moon under her feet, and on her head a crown of twelve stars," who gives birth to a male child who in turn is caught up to God after escaping a dragon on earth, has been regarded as a reference to Mary. Similarly, passages in the Hebrew scriptures have been said to refer to Mary; in *Genesis* 3:15 she (as the Vulgate reads) "shall bruise" the serpent's head; in *Isaiah* 7:14 (*Mt.* 1:23) a young girl (Septuagint, "virgin") shall give birth to a son; in *Proverbs* 8 and other passages about Wisdom (personified as a woman); and in the female figure of the daughter of Zion (e.g., *Zep.* 3:14–20).

Modern scholarship finds differing pictures of Mary in each gospel. Earlier accounts can be ascertained from sources used by the gospel writers, and a "historical Mary" can be sought behind such sources. The concatenation of biblical images, together with evolving Marian piety and influences from other religions, led to post–New Testament developments that were initially connected with Christology, then with ecclesiology, but by the Middle Ages and certainly since the seventeenth century, Roman Catholic dogmatics were treated separately as Mariology.

Mary in the New Testament. The *Gospel of Mark* (written about AD 70) describes Jesus' mother and brothers on the edge of a crowd listening to him teach (*Mk.* 3:31–35). "His own" (3:20), likely "his family" (RSV), have come to take him away because Jesus was, they thought, "beside himself"; they are like the hostile scribes who claim that he is "possessed by Beelzebub" (3:22). In *Mark* 3:34–35, Jesus designates as "my mother and my brothers" those who do the will of God, thus contrasting his natural family, including Mary, with his "eschatological family" of disciples. The passage in *Mark* 6:1–6a, about the rejection of Jesus in his home synagogue, does nothing to change this picture of Mary and Jesus' brothers as sharing the unbelief of those of the surrounding countryside. References to another Mary, in addition to Mary Magdalene, in 15:40, 15:47, and 16:1 do not denote Jesus' mother. Hence the overall picture of Mary in *Mark* is a negative one. (For details, see Brown et al., 1978, pp. 51–72, 286–287.)

In the *Gospel of Matthew* (perhaps before AD 90), a more positive view of Mary results, especially from the first two chapters about the birth and infancy of Jesus, the fruit of meditation upon the Hebrew scriptures within the Matthean community. The genealogy (*Mt.* 1:1–17), from Abraham through David to "Jesus who is called Christ," mentions five women, including "Mary, of whom [fem.] Jesus was born" (1:16). This genealogy was probably designed to emphasize how God carried out his plan to save his people through Jesus the Messiah (1:21) in spite of "marital irregularities" in each of the cases of the five women. With Mary, the irregularity is that Joseph learns she is "with child from the Holy Spirit." But this is in accord with God's plan (*Mt.* 1:21–22). The evangelist cites *Isaiah* 7:14 (Septuagint) to verify that a virgin has conceived and that the child will be "God with us" (*Mt.* 1:23).

Matthew's portrait of Mary during the ministry of Jesus is also ameliorated by other details. In the scene of Jesus' eschatological family (*Mt.* 12:46–50) no reference is made to Jesus' natural family coming to take custody of him. In the synagogue scene at Nazareth (*Mt.* 13:53–58), Matthew drops out the Marcan reference to "his own relatives" in what Jesus says (12:57; cf. *Mk.* 6:4).

The most positive synoptic portrayal of Mary comes in the *Gospel of Luke* plus *Acts* (perhaps after AD 90). In *Acts* 1:14, Mary is a member of the Jerusalem church. In *Luke* 1–2, Mary is described as Joseph's "betrothed" (*Luke* 2:1–20, where, however, a virgin birth is not mentioned). More striking are (1) the scene where the angel Gabriel tells Mary that she will bear "the Son of the Most High" and "The Holy Spirit will come upon you, and the power of the Most High will overshadow you," and Mary responds, "Be it to me according to your word" (*Lk.* 1:26–38); (2) the story of Mary's visit to Elizabeth (*Lk.* 1:39–56) and Mary's song, the Magnificat (1:46–55), in particular, the words about her blessedness (esp. 1:42 and 1:48); (3) the account of Mary in the Jerusalem Temple where she comes for purification after childbirth and where Jesus is presented to the Lord (*Lk.* 2:21–40); and (4) the story of Jesus in the Temple as a twelve-year-old (*Lk.* 2:41–52). These accounts show Mary's faith in God (*Lk.* 1:38, 1:45); tell of the virginal conception (*Lk.* 1:31–34, cf. 3:23) and of Mary's status as a "favored one" (*Lk.* 1:28; Vulgate, *gratia plena*), employing the term *hail (ave)*; and relate Simeon's prophecy to Mary: "A sword will pierce through your own soul also" (*Luke* 2:35, probably meaning that Mary, too, must transcend the natural bonds of family and come to faith in Jesus). This she does, for Jesus declares blessed not the womb that bore him but those who hear and keep God's word (*Lk.* 11:27–28). The rejection scene at Nazareth (*Lk.* 4:16–30) is presented very differently, and the saying about Jesus' eschatological family (*Lk.* 8:19–21) lacks any contrast with his natural family. In *Luke* 2:19 and 2:51, Mary ponders over Jesus' birth and thus grows in faith and discipleship.

The *Gospel of John* (c. 90) contains no reference to the virgin birth, in part because the preexistence and incarnation of the Word are emphasized (*Jn.* 1:1–18). The scenes involving "the mother of Jesus" (never "Mary") during Jesus' ministry are totally different from those in the synoptic Gospels. In the story about a wedding feast at Cana (*Jn.* 2:1–11), his mother does not yet seem to have grasped that his "hour" does not parallel the wishes of his natural family. Although she accompanied Jesus to Capernaum (*Jn.* 2:12), perhaps this was because she was seeking to bring him home (cf. *Mk.* 3:20–35). The mother of Jesus appears in one other Johannine scene (*Jn.* 19:25–27), standing at the foot of the cross with the Beloved Disciple. This *stabat mater* reference occurs only in *John*, among all the Gospels.

Earlier New Testament writings, like Paul's letters (c. 50–60), make no reference to Mary, nor does the Q source, a reconstructed collection of Jesus' sayings, presumed to have been used by Matthew and Luke. A pregospel tradition could be behind *John* 2:1–11, or a common source could be the basis of the Matthean-Lucan stories of Mary's conceiving and the genealogy. More likely these are deductions of post-Easter Christology, theologoumena, dramatizing the divine origins of Jesus.

Regardless of the backgrounds and symbolism of the scene in *Revelation* 12 that are suggested by scholarship in the history of religions, the passage is intended to assert God's triumph in Christ over Satan's attacks. The woman who gives birth to the Messiah is Israel and the church, Christ's suffering people. Marian applications to the passage developed only in the fourth century.

Marian Piety and Mariology. In the second century, references to Mary are rare, found chiefly in the letters of Ignatius of Antioch about the "mystery" of Jesus' birth (e.g., *Ephesians* 19.1) and in Justin Martyr (*Dialogue with Trypho* 100). Justin typologically compares Eve and Mary, a theme developed by Irenaeus (*Against Heresies* 3.21.10). The New Testament Apocrypha and gnostic documents from Nag Hammadi expand references to Mary. The *Protevangelium of James* (an infancy gospel and life of Mary, written mid-second century), with its hagiographic details, was to have great influence. It said that Mary remained a virgin while delivering her son *(in partu)* as well as after Jesus' birth *(virginitas post partum)*. Growing Christian emphasis on asceticism, with Mary as virgin model, and contacts with "mother goddesses" in other religions, especially in Asia Minor, encouraged Marian themes. But even in the third century there is no trace of belief in Mary's assumption into heaven (Brown et al., 1978, pp. 241–282). [*See also* Virgin Goddess; Virgin Birth; *and* Goddess Worship.]

Popular piety concerning Mary usually developed first in the East, often in a liturgical context, sometimes involving groups deemed heretical. The prayer in the Byzantine liturgy *Sub tuum praesidium confugimus* ("Under your mercy we take refuge, O Theotokos . . .") has been traced back to perhaps the fourth century (for details, see O'Carroll, 1983). In the *Refutation of All Heresies* 78–79 (c. 375), Epiphanius, bishop of Cyprus, refers both to "opponents of Mary" who denied that she was perpetually a virgin (Gr., *aeiparthenos;* Lat., *semper virgo*), and to the Collyridians, women who offered cakes *(kollyrides)* to the Virgin as a goddess (cf. *Jer.* 7:18, 44:15–28). At the Second Council of Nicaea (787) clear distinctions were made: *latr(e)ia* ("worship") is for God alone; *d(o)ul(e)ia* ("reverence"), for the saints; and *huperdouleia* ("more than reverence"), for Mary. [*See* Cult of Saints.]

In the christological controversies of the fifth century, Mary took on more and more of the status of her Son. While Nestorius (d. 451) was willing to call Mary *christotokos* ("the one who bore Christ"), he boggled at the term *theotokos*, "God-bearer." This term became the rallying cry of Cyril of Alexandria (d. 444) and was proclaimed as a title for Mary at the councils of Ephesus (431) and Chalcedon (451). The intent was to assert that he whom Mary bore was, while "truly man," also "truly God." Use of the term *theotokos* also led to emphasis on Mary not simply as *Dei genitrix* ("she who gives birth to God") but also as *mater Dei*, the "mother of God." [*See* Councils, *article on* Christian Councils.]

Marian festivals generally developed in the East; they rapidly spread elsewhere and multiplied in number. Some had biblical roots, for example, the Annunciation on 25 March (*Lk.* 1:26–38) and the Purification on 2 February (*Lk.* 2:21–39, cf. *Lv.* 12). Others, like the Nativity of the Blessed Virgin Mary (8 September) and her Presentation in the Temple (21 November), have their roots in the *Protevangelium of James.* The fifteenth of August became the date for the Dormition, or "falling asleep" of the Virgin. Later there arose accounts of Mary's bodily assumption into heaven, paralleling Jesus' exaltation. Mary was regarded as now reigning with her Son, and thus she could be intercessor, or mediatrix, with Christ and God. A legend about Theophilus, who made a pact with the devil but obtained forgiveness through Mary, was an indication of her power to intervene. The Feast of the Immaculate Conception of Mary (8 or 9 December) arose around the theme of her sinlessness from the time of her birth (cf. *Protevangelium of James* 4). However, in the West there was a long debate over Mary's sinlessness in light of the Augustinian doctrine of original sin; the Dominicans (including Thomas Aquinas) opposed the feast, while the Franciscans promoted it.

Celebration of Mary had now moved from the realm of Christology to that of ecclesiology. Mary was Mater Ecclesiae ("mother of the church"), for she had brought forth Christ, the head of the church. One principle at work was *"potuit, decuit, fecit":* God *could* do a thing, it *was fitting* that God should, and therefore God *did* it—for example, God saw to it that Mary was born or exalted much like her Son. Other principles were exhibited by Bernard of Clairvaux's dictum "Everything through Mary" and the widespread medieval belief that one can never say too much about Mary. Reflections of this cascading piety can be seen in the Akathistos, a Greek hymn of the fifth or sixth century that has elaborate epithets for Mary, or in Western antiphons like *Alma redemptoris mater* (Sweet Mother of the Redeemer), or in the Ave Maria prayer ("Hail, Mary," *Luke* 1:28 and 1:48, with the later addition of "Pray for us sinners . . .").

Some of the Protestant reformers grew up with Marian piety of this sort. Luther seems at times to have affirmed Mary's immaculate conception and even her bodily assumption and retained some Marian festivals, but with a christological emphasis. More revealing is Luther's 1521 exposition of the Magnificat (*Works*, Saint

Louis, 1956, vol. 21, pp. 297–358), where Mary is "the foremost example" of God's grace and of proper humility. The Lutheran confessions simply assume the virgin birth of Jesus Christ and even use stock phrases like *semper virgo.* Calvin praised Mary as "holy virgin," though he expressed misgivings about calling her "mother of God." But Protestant reaction to the post-Tridentine emphases in Roman Catholicism gave Mary less and less place.

Eastern Orthodox regard for Mary has continued as living piety, but without the emphasis on dogmatic articulation found in Roman Catholicism (see Nikos Nissiotis, in *Concilium* 168, 1983, pp. 25–39, with bibliography). For Roman Catholic theology, the seventeenth and eighteenth centuries brought new developments in spirituality having to do with Mary (for example, the devotion to the Immaculate Heart of Mary promoted by Jean Eudes, 1601–1680). In Italy, Alfonso Liguori (1696–1787) gathered stories about the Virgin in his book *The Glories of Mary.* In the nineteenth century, widespread emphasis on Mary was encouraged by reported visions and appearances of Mary, for example, at Lourdes in 1858, with the announcement, "I am the Immaculate Conception," or at Fatima, Portugal, in 1917; by international Marian congresses; by Marian years proclaimed by the pope; and by pilgrimages (for example to Częstochowa in Poland).

Reflective of such popular piety was Pius IX's 1854 definition of the Immaculate Conception as dogma for Roman Catholics in *Ineffabilis Deus:* "The most blessed Virgin Mary . . . was preserved free from all stain of original sin." In 1950, Pius XII defined the Assumption of the Blessed Virgin Mary as a dogma in the apostolic constitution *Munificentissimus Deus:* "The Immaculate Mother of God, the ever Virgin Mary . . . was assumed body and soul to heavenly glory." Protestant reaction was negative. The Orthodox reacted against the 1854 dogma because of their belief that everyone, Mary included, is afflicted with sin in the sense of human infirmity, but in 1950 they reacted only against papal claims of authority inherent in the proclamation.

Although some Catholic "maximalists" on Mary hoped that the Second Vatican Council would declare her coredemptrix with Christ, the council did not make such a statement. In fact, it voted in 1963 to include the material on Mary as chapter 8 of the Constitution on the Church, *Lumen gentium,* rather than to treat it as a separate schema. The dogmatic constitution treats her role in the economy of salvation, as Mother of God and of the Redeemer, as a model for the church, and as a sign of hope and solace for God's people in pilgrimage. There are also paragraphs on devotion to the Blessed Virgin, warning against exaggeration. However, the speech by Paul VI in 1964, promulgating *Lumen gentium,* proclaimed Mary as Mater Ecclesiae, and his apostolic exhortation in 1974, *Marialis cultus,* sought for renewal in devotion to Mary and called her "our sister." John Paul II has often spoken in more traditional Marian terms of piety. The net effect since Vatican II has generally been a greater restraint and balance in Roman Catholic Mariology and in Catholic devotional life. Some statements have suggested that Mary provides "the model of all real feminine freedom" (U.S. Catholic Bishops, *Behold Your Mother,* 1974). But for many feminists, Mariology, certainly in the church writers of the early centuries, has been all too androcentric (cf. Borrensen, Halkes, and Moltmann-Wendel, in *Concilium,* 168, 1983).

BIBLIOGRAPHY

Walter Delius's *Geschichte der Marienverehrung* (Munich, 1963) provides a standard treatment, supplemented by his *Texte zur Geschichte der Marienverehrung und Marienverkündigung in der alten Kirche,* 2d rev. ed. (Berlin, 1973). Somewhat more popular in tone are Hilda Graef's *Mary: A History of Doctrine and Devotion,* 2 vols. (New York, 1963–1965); Marina Warner's *Alone of All Her Sex: The Myth and Cult of the Virgin Mary* (New York, 1976); and Christa Mulack's *Maria: Die geheime Göttin im Christentum* (Stuttgart, 1985). Sympathetic articles on persons, terms, and themes, with bibliography, will be found in Michael O'Carroll's *Theotokos: A Theological Encyclopedia of the Blessed Virgin Mary,* rev. ed. with supplement (Wilmington, Del., 1983). For biblical materials, see *Mary in the New Testament: A Collaborative Assessment by Protestant and Roman Catholic Scholars,* edited by Raymond E. Brown, Karl P. Donfried, Joseph A. Fitzmyer, and John Reumann (Philadelphia, 1978). *Mary in the Churches,* edited by Hans Küng and Jürgen Moltmann, *Concilium* 168 (New York, 1983), surveys biblical origins and confessional attitudes today as well as trends in feminist and liberation theology and depth psychology and literature. *Mary's Place in Christian Dialogue,* edited by Alberic Stacpoole (Wilton, Conn., 1982), reflects over a decade of work by the Ecumenical Society of the Blessed Virgin Mary. Stephen Benko's *Protestants, Catholics, and Mary* (Valley Forge, Pa., 1978) deals also with Josephology.

JOHN REUMANN

MASCULINE SACRALITY is the designation of some domain of the supernatural universe as masculine. It is a feature of numerous religious systems in human societies around the world. A comparison of such systems reveals three levels of expression for the masculine valuation of the sacred.

At one level, certain natural symbols recur in religious systems in the form of hierophanies or sacred manifestations of masculine higher being. These natural symbols include sky, peaks and mountains, thunder, rain, and certain horned beasts, as well as such creatures of flight as eagles. At a second level of expression, religious systems often attribute certain cosmic functions to masculine metaphysical entities and/or specifically male supernatural beings. Thus gods as opposed to goddesses tend to be credited with such cosmic functions as creation of the mundane universe, establishment of the moral code, invention of the elements of mortal subsistence, and the like. Finally, in many religious systems there is a belief in the masculine orientation of certain sacred values. These commonly include order, stability, permanence, and essentiality. This level of religious expression may be basic to the social ethic and organization of a community, and may furnish it with a model and sanction for the pursuit of distinctive life patterns on the part of men and women.

A masculine being or entity of a particular system may have reality at more than one of these levels of expression and possibly at all three simultaneously. A brief illustration may be furnished by Indra, one of the highest gods in the Vedic religion of ancient India. An atmospheric divinity, he is credited with the unleashing of rain and storms, expressive of the masculine fecundating force. In general, Indra personifies cosmic vitality: he fertilizes the earth and makes rivers, sap, and blood alike to circulate; his retinue is the winds. He is also sagacious and deceptive, given to fooling his adversaries by changing his form. Finally, the power of Indra is sovereign: he is the chief of the heavenly council of gods, and in iconography he usually wears a crown.

As a figure of the Vedic religious universe, Indra exemplifies a particular set of conceptions about the masculine nature of the sacred. These are realized at the three levels of expression discussed above. At the level of natural symbols Indra is represented by lightning, his cosmic projectiles, and by the rainbow, whereby he dispatches those projectiles. At the level of cosmic functions, Indra is associated with fecundation and life-giving force. Finally, at the level of religious values, Indra has the meaning of sovereignty: he is the prototype of the ruler. He exemplifies the values pertaining to the proper relationship of ruler and ruled, for he is lauded and invoked more than any other deity in the oldest of Indian sacred texts, the *Ṛgveda*. As a secondary value, Indra represents a force of mystery and delusion, since he is a cosmic magician, able to generate new aspects and shapes at will.

From Indra's example it should be apparent that the levels at which masculine sacrality is expressed in religious systems frequently interrelate. It is difficult to discuss natural symbols, cosmic functions, and religious values of the masculine in isolation from one another. Nevertheless, these levels of expression should be borne in mind in the following discussion of the basic attributes of masculine sacred being.

Primordiality. In religious systems, a form of higher being anterior to and/or prerequisite to other varieties of being tends to be masculine. Thus if differentiated forms of being are said to arise from some primordial undifferentiated entity, the latter is frequently masculine. The Arapaho of North America, for instance, believe in a supreme god out of whom the entire manifest world originated. Their name for him is Spider, presumably because the spider weaves his web out of himself.

Alternatively, the being that first dwells in or emerges from the undifferentiated cosmic mass tends to be masculine. In world mythologies, masculine first beings are abundant. The supreme god of the Flathead of North America is Amotken ("the old one"). Similarly, the supreme god of the Yahgan of Tierra del Fuego is Watauniewa ("the old, eternal, unchangeable one"). Among the Hawaiians, the supreme male divinity is the god who dwells primordially, at the dawn of sacred time, in Pō, the world of obscurity or darkness. Again, for the inhabitants of the Gilbert Islands, the earliest being in the primordial void is a male divinity, Na Areau the Elder. In Australian religions, during the primordial time called the Dreaming, over the earth roamed the first beings called Great Men, who are fathers to the creatures of the present world.

In mythology, feminine being tends to be secondary to masculine being. Thus, in the Navajo creation myth, First Man is paired with First Woman; both of them emerged from the union of primordial mists, but the emergence of First Woman follows that of First Man. In general, where there occur masculine and feminine forms of primordial being, the former tends to provide precedent for the latter: Eve emerges out of the body of Adam, not Adam out of Eve.

Height. Religious systems widely associate with masculine sacrality the attribute of height, as well as the corollaries of ascendancy and transcendence. Mircea Eliade points out in *Patterns in Comparative Religion* (1958) that belief in the celestiality of the divine being is nearly universal in religious systems. To this it may be no less validly appended that the highest entities and beings of religion and mythology overwhelmingly tend to be masculine. Moreover, the sky is the most fundamental of all natural symbols of masculine sacrality.

In cosmology, sky beings are preponderantly male as opposed to female. Io, meaning "raised up" or "on high," is the supreme god of the Maori, while the Yoruba of Africa call upon a god named Ọlọrun, "owner of the sky." In mythology, masculine first beings not infrequently represent sky divinities: Amotken, the previously mentioned first being of the Flathead, is also a celestial god, living in the crown of the cosmic tree.

In some mythologies, high gods originate elsewhere than in heaven, but journey there before the onset of profane time. This theme is particularly well attested in Australia. Bunjil, the god of the Wotjobaluk, for instance, lived on earth as a Great Man but later went to the sky. Among the Aranda, some earthborn first beings fell slumbering to the ground and reemerged into it, while others climbed sacred passages to the sky. The former are identified with totemic ancestors, the latter with high divinity—the sun, moon, and stars.

Because the nearly universal attribute of masculine sacrality is height—often expressed symbolically in terms of celestiality—the idea of access to godhood tends to be expressed through the imagery of ascent or, occasionally, of descent. In the Tantric tradition of southern Asia (India, Nepal, Tibet), the sublime is taken to be masculine; integration with it demands a technique of focusing and directing upward the feminine energies of the physiological microcosmos. In popular Hinduism, on the other hand, humans are said to approach the sublime at the god's instance, by his willful descent to the mundane world on a series of occasions called *avatāra.* Thus a popular myth cycle portrays the high god Viṣṇu mercifully descending upon earth to be born in a series of mortal forms: as a fish, as a boar, as King Rāma, as the rambunctious cowherd Kṛṣṇa, and so on. By contrast, while a mother goddess occurs in popular Hinduism and at times manifests herself on earth, she is not specifically credited with the capacity of *avatāra,* or divine descent.

As an attribute of masculine sacrality, height is fundamentally but not exclusively symbolized by sky and atmosphere. Height may also find expression in the symbolism of entities associated with loftiness. Sacred mountains are often the dwelling places of gods: the mythical Mount Meru of India and the Greek Olympus are well-known examples, as are certain peaks in Japan and other parts of the world. In some religious systems, height as an attribute of masculine sacrality finds expression in the natural symbolism of sky-dwelling creatures. Fabulous birds, especially eagles, tend to be associated with godhood. The Bella Coola of the northwestern coast of America, for instance, believe in an *axis mundi,* or sacred pole connecting heaven and earth, that was erected by the highest god; it is topped by a seated eagle. Elsewhere in the religions of North America, and in parts of Siberia as well, an important position is held by a mythical creature of eaglelike appearance, the Thunderbird. The Thunderbird's association with the awesome and fecundating masculine force of the sky is underscored by the fact that he is said to cause wind and thunder by flapping his wings, and lightning by opening and closing his eyes. [*See* Sky; Transcendence and Immanence; *and* Supreme Beings.]

Effulgence. Along with loftiness and sublimity, effulgence is a common attribute of masculine sacrality suggested by the natural symbolism of the sky. Various religious systems characterize the supreme god as white or shining. The Khanty and the Mansi of the Asian Arctic, for instance, describe their supreme god Num-Tūrem as luminous, golden, and white. One of the most powerful gods of Hinduism—dwelling, incidentally, on mountains—is Śiva, the "shining one." Devotional literature sometimes refers to him as "the lord white as jasmine." In Hawaiian mythology, at the dawn of sacred time the first light in the universe was that of the original being and high god. Navajo mythology has it that First Man and First Woman arose in unparalleled radiance from the primordial mists of the sky, the former in the place of sunrise and the latter in the place of sunset. While each burned a fire to light the firmament, the light of First Man's fire was stronger.

In cultic practices, sacred objects associated with masculine divinities tend to be chosen for whiteness or luminosity. This is true, for instance, of the crystal stones used in some Australian rituals. (The supreme god Baiame of certain southeastern Australian tribes sits on a crystal throne.) Similarly, the First Man of Navajo legend burned crystal for his fire and was accompanied at his birth by white corn.

Fire, of course, is a common accompaniment to religious ritual. In Vedic India, not only was fire itself a god, but it served as the purifier and sacred conveyance of sacrificial oblations to the high gods in heaven. [*See* Light and Darkness *and* Fire.]

Pervasiveness. The attribute of being immanent in the universe is widely associated with masculine sacred being. It is not without significance that the name of the Hindu god associated with *avatāra* or divine descent, Viṣṇu, means "pervader." However, in relation to the concept of supreme godhood, the attribute of pervasiveness should be carefully qualified because sky gods, those quintessential exemplifications of masculine sacrality, are typically characterized as distant, remote, and inactive.

Accordingly, in many religious systems no special cult centers on the high being of the heavens. He may be left out of ritual and worship altogether, or be called upon only in times of extraordinary crisis. Many mythologies speak of the sky god as having once been actively engaged in cosmic business, but as having withdrawn from direct intervention in the universe for all time.

As *deus otiosus,* or retired divinity, the sky god nevertheless often remains in touch with mundane affairs and manifests his presence indirectly. A particularly widely held belief is that thunder is a manifestation of such a god. For instance, people of the Andaman Islands believe that thunder is the voice of their supreme god Pulaga, and the Kansa Indians similarly maintain that thunder is the voice of their high god Wakantanka, whom they have never seen. Conceived of as a masculine epiphany, the growling sound of thunder may be imitated in ritual to invoke the presence of the sublime. In Australian ritual one of the most sacred objects is the bull-roarer, a piece of wood with a string tied through a hole in one end. When swung around, this object makes a growling sound suggestive of a bull's bellowing or of thunder; it is particularly used in boys' initiation rites. Similarly, in religious rituals, particularly male initiation ceremonies, of the North American Southwest, an instrument called a bull-roarer or whiner is used to invoke and evoke the presence of the high god. [*See* Bull-Roarers *and* Tjurunga.]

As a variant on the treatment of thunder as a masculine epiphany, the growling force of volcanoes is occasionally regarded as a sign of the immanence of sacred masculine being. In South America, for instance, the Puruhá tribesmen of La Montaña occasionally sacrificed humans to a volcanic mountain inhabited by a god who made his presence felt from time to time.

Another way in which the high god, as *deus otiosus*, maintains an immanent presence in the affairs of the universe is by delegating authority to lesser supernaturals. The high god is often credited with initiating creation, but not always with completing it. In many mythologies the completion of the work is delegated to other figures of the high god's designation. For instance, the supreme god Gicelamu'kaong of the Delaware delegates creation to the sun, the moon, the thunder gods, the four winds, the earth mother, and the master of animals. It is common in mythology for the *deus otiosus* to withdraw, leaving his own son behind to carry on his cosmic activities. One of the many instances of this is found in the creation myth of the Gilbert Islands, where the divine protagonist Na Areau the Younger inherits the task of creation from his progenitor, Na Areau the Elder, the primordial being.

As son and successor to the high god, a secondary celestial may acquire considerable preeminence over the original high divinity. This preeminence is graphically symbolized in some belief systems by treating the high god's offspring and successor as a solar deity. Thus among the Tiv of Africa, the sun is the male child of the supreme being Awondo. Similarly, among the Wiradjuri and the Kamilaroi of southeastern Australia, the sun is the creator god's son.

In many mythologies, a type of supernatural who mediates between a withdrawn cosmic father figure and the mundane sphere is called the culture hero. A culture hero is usually portrayed as being with the high god in primordial times, and his sacred activities are sometimes performed at the high god's instance. As a stand-in for higher divinity, the culture hero may play a role in mythology that is more important than that of the high god. Culture heroes are sometimes represented anthropomorphically, but just as frequently the culture hero has a theriomorphic representation: as a coyote among some southwestern North American peoples, and as a great hare on the eastern North American coast; as a wolf or a raven in eastern Siberia; as a bat among the Paresí of Bolivia; and as a tapir in the Amazon Basin. Whatever his representation, the culture hero invariably serves to keep terrestrial society in touch with godhood, and almost without exception is portrayed as a male.

The activities of the culture hero are varied. In some mythologies he assists in the work of creation. This holds of the earth diver, a culture hero widely revered in North America who, at the instance of the high god, brings up the first land from the primal waters. Another typical task of the culture hero is to provide the elements of culture and/or the basic tools of subsistence to the ancestors of modern men. Among the Northwest Coast people and in eastern Siberia, for instance, the culture hero Raven brings light and various elements of culture to the mundane world in primordial time.

Acting as he does as a kind of rival to the ethically sublime high god, the culture hero is often portrayed as a schemer or trickster. He may assist men at the expense of higher being, as, for example, by stealing water, sun, or subsistence materials from the other world or by releasing game enclosed in a cave or other place inaccessible to humans. This aspect of the culture hero's character is exemplified by the fire-giver Prometheus of Greek mythology. [*See* Culture Heroes.]

Culture heroes are also frequently portrayed as sacred ancestors of human descent groups. In the case of theriomorphic culture heroes, such beliefs may find expression through totemistic cults like those common in Australia and North America. More generally, religious systems commonly embody a belief that sacred substance, as an immanent component and inheritance of human individuals, is masculine—that is, it is derived from a high god, is transmitted by supernatural males acting in sacred time as ancestors of men, and is passed along in profane time through the male descent line. Thus, according to Hindu social theory and law, men alone pass the sacred substance of their lineage to their descendants, whereas the sacred substance inherited by a woman is not immutable, being transformed to correspond to that of her husband at the time of marriage. According to Hindu doctrine, then, women transmit to their offspring no sacred substance of their own but only that of their husbands.

Finally, regarding pervasiveness, it should be mentioned that the natural symbolism of the sky overlaying and embracing the supine earth powerfully suggests the immanence of the masculine sacred principle. A sexual dichotomy is commonly featured in religious systems, the sky being associated with the masculine and the earth with the feminine. Earth goddesses are not infrequently paired with sky gods. Moreover, earth and sky together constitute the prototype of the cosmic pair. A common theme in world mythologies is that of the primordial separation of the mutually embracing sky and earth. The creatures responsible for forcing sky and earth apart are variously represented as culture heroes, ancestors of the present earth dwellers, and/or the divine offspring of sky and earth themselves.

Contact between the separated celestial and terrestrial realms is frequently achieved in sacred time (and, by that precedent, is renewable in present, profane time) by means of certain sacred paraphernalia or entities of a fairly obvious sexual symbolism. [*See* Hieros Gamos.] Apertures in rocks or clouds are commonly portrayed as sacred means of passage, as are fabulous pillars, trees, ladders, mountains, and the like. In other words, Sky the father and Earth the mother are mediated by sacred holes and poles. These devices, moreover, contrast somewhat in their orientation: the sacred holes tend to be earth-directed, and the sacred poles sky-directed. Thus in the creation myth of the Gilbert Islanders the culture hero Na Areau the Younger walks in sacred time upon the rocklike upper surface of the sky, then pokes a hole down through it to apprehend the earth. From the bowels of the earth Na Areau then enlists an eel that braces himself against the earth with his tail in order to lift the sky upward by his snout. Thus the once direct contact between earth and sky comes to be mediated by the phallic force of that cosmic uplifter, the divine eel.

The performance of rituals for reestablishing primordial contact between the mundane world and the sublime is fairly common in religious systems. Such rituals tend to embody the symbolism of ascent, and the implements used in them are often of a phallic appearance. Thus to symbolize the *axis mundi*—the sacred connector of heaven and earth—a pole, ladder, or tree is often used; it may be ascended by a ritual specialist, who thereby symbolically journeys to heaven on behalf of his community. Such ascent rituals are typically performed in Siberia and other areas of the world by shamans, ritual specialists in techniques of healing and ecstasy. [*See* Ascension; Axis Mundi; *and* Shamanism.]

Fecundity. Masculine sacred being is widely associated with generative and fecundating powers. This association seems to be based on the natural functioning of the sky, which fecundates the receptive earth by precipitation. One ritual of ancient India gives explicit expression to the association: the *Bṛhadāraṇyaka Upaniṣad* enjoins the husband to unite with the wife after uttering the formula, "I am the heavens, thou, the earth."

High gods and important male supernaturals tend to be credited with extraordinary potency and sexual capacity. These capabilities may be seen as independent of and additional to any role played by a given divinity in the creation of the cosmos. In popular Hinduism, for instance, the high god Śiva shakes the cosmos by the force of his copulation. A symbol of Śiva is the lingam, a stylized phallus usually given concrete realization in black stone.

In natural symbology, the masculine attribute of fecundity is often expressed by animals of high fertility. Bulls are a particularly common symbol. Śiva's cosmic vehicle is a fabulous bull, and the bull is also the form assumed by Zeus in the early Greek myth of Europa's ravishment.

As a symbol of the masculine, the bull tends to be cross-linked with the symbolism of thunderbolts. The latter are sometimes represented in the shape of stylized horns. Also, the bull's bellowing, like thunder, is an epiphany of godhood. Thus in the ancient Near East, the god Min had the epithet Great Bull, lightning was one of his attributes, and he was responsible for rain and for giving life. In Papua New Guinea, the culture hero Sosom is aurally evoked by the bull-roarer, which is his voice; his body is of stone, and he has an exaggerated penis, suggesting his sexual and fertile powers. Indeed, Sosom is credited with fertilizing man as well as soil. [*See* Phallus.]

Acculturation. Man's conception of order as a sacred force plausibly derives from observation of the events and entities of the heavens. Within the sky, which is itself unchanging and stable, celestial bodies move about according to a placid and unvarying rhythm. Because the sky is associated with the masculine, masculine sacrality comes to be seen more or less universally as the principle of permanence and order.

Thus, in mythology, the establishment of things that give permanence and stability to existence—rule, law, and the structured bases of things and institutions—tends to be treated as a masculine function. High gods and culture heroes delineate the features of the primordial landscape. They separate land from water and establish landmarks in the cosmos: sacred mountains, boulders, trees, rivers, and the like. Moreover, male supernaturals furnish society with the permanent institutions of culture, including law, moral code, and the forms of religious practice itself. At the same time, high culture tends to be perceived in religious communities as a domain proper to men. This is particularly true in regard to religion. Virtually without exception, human societies exclude women from the most sacred religious rites, as well as from manipulation of the most sacred objects of cult.

Where sacred values are associated with a dichotomy of gender, the usual tendency is for the masculine to be associated with stability and essentiality, and the feminine with change and materiality. The masculine may be identified with being's inner form—thought or structure—while the feminine is identified with being's outer forms—word or substance. The masculine may be associated with the potential, inactive form of being; the feminine, with kinetic, active being. The masculine is one and/or integrated; the feminine is plural and/or diffuse.

Thus in the Yoga and Sāṃkhya religious philosophies of India, the universe is said to be based on a polarity of two metaphysical principles. The masculine principle, *puruṣa* (which itself means "male" or "man"), is that of immanent and essential being, whose nature is immutable. By contrast, the feminine principle is associated with *śakti,* the energy that activates the ever-changing material universe. In the philosophical writings of the tradition, the masculine deprived of its *śakti* is compared to a lifeless god, while the feminine principle out of balance with the masculine is said to be rampant, capricious, and dangerous.

Navajo religion likewise associates dichotomies of cosmic function and religious value with the sacred masculine and feminine. In mythology the primordial being, First Man, creates a son and a daughter who are respectively Thought and Speech. The latter is called the outer form of Thought, and the former, the inner form of Speech; both are necessary for the creation of the inner forms of the present universe. As first boy and first girl, these entities are also said to have produced a daughter, a feminine deity identified with the earth. Her name, not insignificantly, is Changing Woman.

Gender dichotomies expressed in Navajo mythology are reflected with great consistency in the cultural and social patterns of the community. In *Language and Art in the Navajo Universe* (Ann Arbor, 1977), Gary Witherspoon points out that the Navajo associate the ritual and ceremonial domain with thought and the masculine. Thus most ceremonial practitioners are men. The ceremonies they conduct, moreover, are rigidly structured and must be performed without mistakes or modifications. Usually, Navajo ceremonies are concerned with restoring prior states of being. The fact that such ceremonies are the domain of men bespeaks a religious view that masculinity has to do with the origins of things and their culmination.

On the other hand, Navajo women are active in productive and domestic matters. They head most domestic groups and control land and sheep on behalf of those groups. This life pattern is consistent with the religious view of the feminine as the domain of growth, process, and change. For the Navajo, social and economic life concerns the generation of new conditions and new beings; it is characterized by movement, change, activity, and productivity. Here, then, it is appropriate that women dominate.

Summary. Belief in a masculine domain of the sacred universe is common in religious systems and tends to be associated with recurrent natural symbols, cosmic functions, and religious values. Based on the patterns discussed above, the following can be enumerated as more or less universal tendencies. (1) Primordial first beings of cult and/or mythology are most often male or masculine. (2) Cosmic functions pertaining to creation and fecundation are usually associated with masculine—as opposed to feminine—entities, principles, and beings. (3) Elements of culture tend to be associated with or attributed to masculine—as opposed to feminine—principles and/or supernaturals. (4) In community life, important differences in life patterns between the sexes have sanction and justification in beliefs about gender sacrality. In particular, manipulation of sacred objects and ceremonies tends to be seen as the appropriate domain of men. (5) The most exalted beings and entities of the masculine sacred universe are almost always associated with the natural symbolism of the sky and derive their attributes accordingly.

[*See also* Feminine Sacrality. *Further symbolism associated with masculine sacrality is discussed in* War and Warriors and Kingship.]

BIBLIOGRAPHY

There is no single reference work devoted to the topic of masculine sacrality, though many pertinent sources are available. Concerning male supernaturals, a worthwhile and concise, if dated, treatment is Wilhelm Schmidt's "The Nature, Attributes and Worship of the Primitive High God." It appears in a volume edited by William Lessa and Evon Vogt, *Reader in Comparative Religion,* 4th ed. (New York, 1979). The standard reference work on comparative religions by Mircea Eliade, *Pat-*

terns in Comparative Religion (London, 1958), contains much useful material on masculine sacrality.

Also worth citing are a number of studies on religious systems in particular world areas. For material on Australian systems, see Eliade's *Australian Religions* (Ithaca, N.Y., 1973). Some pertinent material on Papua New Guinea is found in Roy Wagner's *Habu* (Chicago, 1972). For a wealth of material on religious systems of the Western Hemisphere (and some references to northeastern Asia), see the valuable survey by Åke Hultkrantz, *The Religions of the American Indians* (Los Angeles, 1979). For Hawaiian and related Polynesian religions a standard source is Martha Warren Beckwith's *Hawaiian Mythology* (1940; Honolulu, 1970). A legend of the Gilbert Islanders that speaks for itself in the richness of its gender symbolism is reproduced by Arther Grimble in "A Gilbertese Creation Myth," included in the Lessa and Vogt collection mentioned above.

On religious traditions of India and southern Asia there is a profusion of material related to masculine sacrality, among which several studies may be particularly recommended. Heinrich Zimmer provides a very accessible treatment on Indian sacrality in general, including much information on masculine sacrality, in *Myths and Symbols in Indian Art and Civilization*, edited by Joseph Campbell (1946; Princeton, 1972). Zimmer's *Philosophies of India*, also edited by Campbell (1951; Princeton, 1969), offers in its chapter "Sāṅkhya and Yoga" a penetrating discussion of the relationship of gender sacrality to the philosophical traditions of India. As a detailed account of sexual technique and symbolism in relation to metaphysics and philosophy within a single religious tradition, no study supersedes Mircea Eliade's classic *Yoga: Immortality and Freedom*, 2d ed. (Princeton, 1969). A stimulating treatment of masculinity and the sacred in Nepalese and Tibetan religious traditions is furnished by Robert A. Paul in *The Tibetan Symbolic World: Psychoanalytic Explorations* (Chicago, 1982). The joint monograph *Women in India: Two Perspectives* by Susan S. Wadley and Doranne Jacobson (Columbia, Mo., 1977) contains in Wadley's essay one of the best concise treatments available of *śakti* and its relationship to the Indian conception of the masculine and feminine sacred worlds.

Lastly, for a general anthropological perspective on the relationship of gender sacrality to social ethic and male/female life patterns, consult Sherry Ortner's "Is Female to Male as Nature Is to Culture?" in the collection *Woman, Culture, and Society*, edited by Michelle Rosaldo and Louise Lamphere (Stanford, Calif., 1974).

M. H. Klaiman

MASHTOTS', MESROP (c. 345–440), inventor of the Armenian alphabet and saint of the Armenian church. The major source for his biography is the *Life of Mashtots'* written by his pupil and associate, Koriwn. The name *Mesrop*, the etymology of which is still unknown, does not appear in the works of Armenian writers until after the fifth century.

Mashtots' was born to a peasant named Vardan in the village of Hats'ekats', in the district of Tarōn (present-day Muş, Turkey). He was educated in Greek letters as a youth. As a young man he entered military service, becoming a clerk in the royal army stationed at Vagarshapat (present-day Echmiadzin). Led to solitary life by his interest in the scriptures, Mashtots' became an anchorite. He evidently headed a *kellion* (a small group of anchorites) in the 390s. While proselytizing the people of the district of Goght'n (in present-day Nakhichevan A.S.S.R.), he conceived the idea of inventing an alphabet for the Armenian language and making the scriptures available to the common people. After deliberating with Bishop Sahak of Armenia and King Vṛamshapuh of Persarmenia, he learned that a certain Syriac bishop by the name of Daniel had in his possession an alphabet for Armenian, which was immediately solicited. Finding Daniel's alphabet unsuited to the phonetic structure of Armenian, Mashtots' and his pupils set out for Edessa to do research, and there in 404 Mashtots' himself invented an alphabet consisting of thirty-six letters.

Returning to Armenia, Mashtots' founded schools and continued the task of translating the scriptures that he had begun in Edessa. He devoted the rest of his life to literary, educational, and missionary works. At first his activities were concentrated in the southeastern and eastern parts of historical Armenia (i.e., Armenia Magna). He preached in Goght'n and then in Siwnik', where he founded schools and established an episcopal see. Subsequently, he went to Georgia, where he invented a script for Georgian and preached the teachings of the Christian church. His concern for the Armenians on the Byzantine side of the border led him in the 420s to Constantinople, where he met the emperor Theodosius and the patriarch Atticus. Having received from them the necessary permission for carrying out cultural work, he returned to Byzantine Armenia, where he established schools and introduced the new script. During his stay there he persecuted an obscure sect known as the Barbarianos and invented a script for Albanian.

After his return to Persarmenia, Mashtots' went to preach in Caucasian Albania (corresponding to parts of present-day Azerbaijan and Dagestan). He then visited those districts of historical Armenia that had been annexed to Georgia and Albania in 363. An important contribution of Mashtots' was to unify the Armenians of these districts through linguistic bonds.

Mashtots' spent the final two decades of his life in Armenia devoting himself to writing homilies and letters, none of which has survived. Some scholars identify Mashtots' with the chorepiscopus Mastoubios of Armenia. Mashtots' died on 17 February 440 and was buried in the village of Oshakan. A martyrium was built over his grave and he was venerated as a saint. The Armenian people consider him the father of the Armenian literary tradition and the creator of the Armenian national identity. His grave is still a major site of pilgrimage in Soviet Armenia.

BIBLIOGRAPHY

Akinian, Nerses. *Der hl. Maschtotz Wardapet: Sein Leben und sein Wirken, nebst einer Biographie des hl. Sahak, mit einer deutschen Zusammenfassung.* Vienna, 1949.

Koriwn. *Vark' Mashtots'i.* Yerevan, 1941. Translated into English by Bedros Norehad as *Koriun: The Life of Mashtots* (New York, 1964).

Marquart, Josef. *Über den Ursprung des armenischen Alphabets, in Verbindung mit der Biographie des heil. Mašt'oc'.* Vienna, 1917.

Peeters, Paulus. "Pour l'histoire des origines de l'alphabet arménien." In *Recherches d'histoire et de philologie orientales,* vol. 1, pp. 171–207. Brussels, 1951.

KRIKOR H. MAKSOUDIAN

MASKS. [*This entry, treating the role of masks in religious life, consists of three articles:*

Theoretical Perspectives
Ritual Masks in Nonliterate Cultures
Ritual Masks in European Cultures

The first article surveys scholarly definitions and theories about the nature and function of masks. The companion pieces examine ritual masks in cultural contexts where the applicability of these ideas has been particularly fruitful for religious studies.]

Theoretical Perspectives

In this article I shall not attempt to establish a comprehensive inventory of masks and their various ritual uses, since even larger works have been able to accomplish this task only imperfectly. Rather, I shall limit myself to a survey of some of the most general ideas and theories that have arisen from the study of masks. I shall also outline some of the larger principles in the light of which—with all the caution that dealing with such generalities requires—the study of ritual masks must be placed.

Historical Overview. Although the importance of descriptions by travelers, missionaries, and topographers from at least as early as the sixteenth century should not be overlooked, it can be argued that effective study of ritual masks began only in the nineteenth century. At this time the first interpretations and general theories about European folk traditions emerged, among others following the work of the Grimm brothers (Jakob, 1785–1863; Wilhelm, 1786–1859), for whom folk tales revealed traces of beliefs and myths connected with ancient pagan gods. Later, the German folklorist Wilhelm Mannhardt (1831–1880) took an interest in the folk religion of his time, in particular that of the rural communities. Collecting vast amounts of data, Mannhardt underscored the predominance of beliefs in fertility spirits and in the existence of a connection between vegetal and human life. Under his influence, a number of mask rituals came to be understood as incorporating ancient beliefs dealing with fertility, the masks used being thus interpreted as representing demons of the vegetal world.

At the same time, E. B. Tylor (1832–1917) began to establish anthropology as a science of human beings and their culture. I shall not focus on his theory of "animism" here, but rather on the fact that he described the evolution of civilization from the first humans, who in his eyes were in large part represented by contemporary "primitive" peoples, up to the civilized man of his days. To this end he used a comparative method to organize an impressive number of facts and documents in support of his evolutionary perspective. He also analyzed the process whereby elements belonging to an older stage of evolution survive into later stages in which they do not function adequately.

As early as the last quarter of the nineteenth century, therefore, one finds the different elements that formed the core of the study of masks by folklorists as well as anthropologists up to World War II. (1) First of all, the evolutionist perspective, following which the history of Western society can be reconstructed by classifying all known societies according to the degree of civilization they have reached. From this point of view, the "nonliterate" peoples studied by ethnology enabled modern man to relive, as it were, stages experienced by the Western world thousands of years ago. (2) Second, the notion of "survival," used to describe those remnants of ancient customs that resisted evolution and survived outside the period in which they are truly meaningful. (3) Finally, intensive use of the comparative method: on the basis of what ethnology reported on primitive people, it was thought possible to recover the original meaning of a particular custom and to reconstruct the earlier stages in the evolution of the society under study.

By the end of the nineteenth century, scholars were in possession of an ever-increasing amount of comparative data on masks. In 1883, Adolf Bastian wrote a general study on the role of masks. In 1886, Richard Andree published an overview and summary of far-ranging documents from various periods. He thus made a large data base available while organizing it into categories that have been constantly taken up again. Finally, in 1898, Leo Frobenius (1873–1938) linked masks, seen as representing spirits of the dead, to secret societies. From his perspective, this relationship originated as a male reaction to matriarchy and provided an explanation for the exclusion of women from practically all mask rituals. These early theories of ritual masks marked the anthropological and folkloric study of masks for several decades.

In a well-known article, Karl Meuli (1933) formulated a general theory of primitive masks that he then applied to European traditions. According to him, there is a close connection between masks and so-called matriarchal societies. Furthermore, the majority of primitive masks represent spirits, and the majority of spirits represented in such a way are spirits of the dead. Indeed, the strange appearance of masked figures indicates that they do not belong to the human realm. Their behavior reinforces this interpretation: the masks beg while threatening, reprimand, and punish, after which they distribute gifts and grant wishes of prosperity, and then disappear. Meuli explained this behavior as the result of a primitive belief that no death is natural, every death being the result of the malevolence of a living person. At particular times, during the transition from an end to a beginning (the passage from one year to the next, for example), the underworld opens up, allowing the dead to return among the living. The masked figures represent these dead, who first seek revenge. By letting them pilfer and chastise as they please, one gives them the opportunity to calm down, after which they bestow benevolence again.

Applicable equally to the masks of nonliterate peoples and to European folk masks, this interpretation is a synthesis of the theories founded on evolutionism, the notion of survival, and the comparative method, to which it adds psychoanalysis. Influential both within and outside scholarly circles, it played an important role in the history of the study of masks. It appeared, however, at a time when anthropology itself was gradually turning away from the ambitious theories developed at the beginning of the century to focus instead on elaborate and detailed localized research, employing a more demanding method. A similar trend was to emerge somewhat later, in the 1940s, in the study of folk traditions.

In both cases, this evolution in ideas raised serious questions both about the attitude of researchers toward the traditions they studied and the interpretations they accepted. Because of the survival theory, a given culture was not studied as a coherent contemporary phenomenon but rather as a patchwork of various elements that could be analyzed somewhat independently of each other. Critics noted, however, that a custom could not be considered as a mere relic: it survived because it still had a role to play in the society in which it was observed. From then on, studies tended increasingly to consider each custom as part of a contemporary system, analysis of which would illuminate the function of each of its components. Similarly, comparison was no longer applied to isolated elements; rather, scholars compared systems of relationships. Finally, the problem of the continuity of culture and cultural traits was tackled on a new basis: the historic dimension was reintroduced into the analysis and replaced the notion of survival, which, in effect, canceled out history.

The populations studied by ethnologists were again placed in the historical framework that general theories concerning the primitive had somewhat obscured. In folkloric studies, consideration of the historic dimension tended to lead to a reassessment of traditions that had been considered very ancient and now appeared younger. For example, certain Swiss masks that had been regarded as archaic because of their snarling expressions and monstrous faces are now thought to date back only to the nineteenth century. They might have appeared as the result of the exotic current that marked this century and of the awareness of primitive customs that was spread by missionary publications, among other factors (see Chappaz-Wirthner, 1974). This does not mean that these traditions can no longer be seen as extensions of ancient customs. However, scholars now feel compelled to take into account the action of the numerous and continuous influences and changes that have affected them in the course of history. Thus ethnologists as well as folklorists have come to carry on their research within concrete historical frameworks.

Problems of Definition. Although everybody seems certain of what a mask is, the definition of this term in the history of religions poses important problems. In the narrow and usual sense of the word, a mask is a false face behind which one hides one's own face for purposes of disguise. In ethnology *mask* also refers to headpieces that do not cover the face, as well as elements of costumes that are worn over the face (such as veils, fringes) and other full or partial adornments of the body or face. The term *mask* is also used to refer to any representation of a face, whether or not it is worn on the face of a dancer. Consequently this includes mannequins, effigies, faces painted, molded, or carved on buildings and boats, pendant masks as well as finger or pocket masks, and so on. Finally, the definition is sometimes widened to include face or body paintings as well as tattoos. [*See* Bodily Marks.] Since scholars do not agree on the denotation of the term, confusion permeates the literature on the subject. This has led some specialists to conclude that the word *mask* identifies no coherent class of institutions of any use to social anthropology (see Jedrej, 1980).

It is very important to keep in mind this problem of definition when trying to understand some of the ideas frequently advanced on the subject of masks, such as, for example, the claim for universality of the mask: it is only when makeup, paintings, and tattoos are included in the definition of *mask* that one can say that masks can be found in virtually all cultures. But is such a broad definition justified? No one can say, for this question has not yet been systematically investigated.

It is important to note as well that the focus on the face that museums, art galleries, and books on masks often maintain gives a distorted view of the ritual mask. This interest in the face has encouraged relegating to the background the many masks that, lacking a face, are simple hoods or fringes of fibers falling in front of the face of the wearer, and so on. Fascination with the face has also tended to minimize interest in the costume of the mask, which has often been hastily dismissed either as fundamentally designed to conceal the wearer or as merely accompanying the mask. The mask must, however, be considered from a larger perspective, so as to include the costume, the headdress, the possible accessories, as well as immaterial factors such as the behavior, the dance steps, and the songs or texts pertaining to the mask. Among the Dan of Liberia and the Ivory Coast, it is the headdress that immediately signals what type of mask one is dealing with. Consequently, the first step in the transformation of a mask from one category to another is the alteration of the headdress. The Dan also have "night masks," which comprise no tangible face masks but may include feathered headdresses (see Fischer, 1980). In this connection, let us recall that in Egypt the priests' masks were adorned only with animal heads. The priests playing the roles of anthropomorphic deities did not require masks: the headdresses and the specific emblems of the gods were enough to identify them.

The face, therefore, is not necessarily the place where the meaning of the mask is concentrated. Granted this and the premise that the primary function of a mask is to represent rather than to dissimulate, it is easy to understand that when faced with an ensemble that includes all the elements of a mask (costume, headdress, dance, and so on), it is rather difficult to decide that there is no mask simply because the face of the dancer is painted rather than covered with a hood or false face. In any case, some scholars see a continuity between paintings and masks, because of the similarities between the two phenomena: both are temporary adornments, both appear on special occasions (initiation, marriage, death, or the lifting of a prohibition), and both seem to have comparable functions. This relationship between masks and paintings is seen from two main points of views. Some scholars see a chronological relation: in this case, the painting is viewed either as a primitive form of the mask, or as a relic, a derivative of or substitute for the mask. Others, without claiming any genetic link between the two, merely see a functional relationship between masks and facial paintings.

The inclusion of tattoos in the definition of masks poses a much more delicate problem. It is difficult to see how masks and paintings, which are temporary, could simply be classified with tattoos, which are permanent. In any case, the inclusion of tattoos in the category of masks seems to create more problems than it resolves.

The Geography of Ritual Masks. A narrower definition of masks, that is, one that takes as a criterion the existence of one element of costume (false face, hood, and so on) to be worn in front of the face, forces us to realize that even in regions that are traditionally considered to be the privileged domains of masks, there exist important zones in which masks are not used. In Africa, for instance, masks are found mostly along a strip that cuts across the center of the continent from west to east and curves toward the south. In the Americas the intensive use of masks is most frequent in the western heights of both North and South America. Finally, in Oceania, the mask is practically absent from Polynesia. It is extremely widespread in Melanesia, although it is not used among most of the highland peoples of New Guinea, in the main part of Irian Jaya and in eastern Papua New Guinea, in parts of the Bismark archipelago, in the central and southeast Solomons and the Santa Cruz group, and in the Fiji group.

Several hypotheses have been put forward to explain the gaps in the distribution of masks. According to one of them, peoples without masks simply lack the wish to express themselves plastically and use other means to formulate and express their beliefs. Besides being an example of circular reasoning, this theory runs against a number of exceptions that it cannot explain, particularly among peoples that have a statuary but no masks. The absence of masks in certain regions of Africa has also been attributed to the influence of Islam. However, anthropologists have demonstrated that the islamization of a given region did not necessarily lead to the elimination of the art of masks. On the contrary, certain African tribes created new masks after the advent of Islam in order to represent the *jinn,* for instance (see Bravmann, 1977). Masks have also been said to be more characteristic of agricultural peoples. This hypothesis, however, accounts only imperfectly for the presence of masks among hunters in Asia and the Americas. The general theory that has been most successful has been that of the historical cultural school, which explained the distribution of masks by arguing for their relationship with so-called matriarchal societies. An examination of the available data has, however, discredited this hypothesis as well. To date, no global model is available to help us understand the geographic distribution of masks.

As a matter of fact, ever since they have had to give up the broad theories of the nineteenth and beginning of the twentieth centuries, scholars have no longer shown much interest for the study of questions of this amplitude. Most of them have focused instead on the in-depth analysis of a particular society, avoiding any far-reaching comparative evaluation that they consider responsible for part of past mistakes. Others have merely argued that ritual masks are too widespread to allow anybody to pinpoint a center of diffusion. Some have even contended that this widespread distribution eliminated the need to look for the origin of the institution of masks in the particular society that they were studying, arguing either that such research was irrelevant to an understanding of the contemporary society being considered or that the fundamental concepts at the root of the use of masks were probably present in embryo in all human beings and consequently may have developed independently in different places. Needless to say that such a hypothesis, which is far from being verified, by no means explains why certain populations utilize masks and others do not.

Nevertheless, some interesting localized studies have attempted to specify the status of masks within certain populations. Some try to elucidate the relationship that may exist in particular societies between the mask and other religious and sociopolitical structures. Others look for the provenance of the masks of particular tribes, or even attempt to reconstruct its history. For instance, in certain parts of New Caledonia, the development of the art of masks seems to have been linked to the development of chieftainships in the same region (see Guiart, 1966). In West Africa the use or nonuse of masks to manifest spiritual forces seems directly related to the dominant features of social organization in particular areas and especially to the role of lineages and political structures (see Siegmann, 1980). But we still lack a general model that would enable us to explain the distribution of ritual masks and to understand, by the same token, an extremely important element of this institution.

The Dating of Masks. How far back can we trace the appearance of the ritual mask? Many scholars do not hesitate to go as far back as the early Stone Age but this raises a number of problems. The documents on which they base their conclusions are far from clear and admit of various interpretations. Let us look at the example of the well-known "Sorcerer" of Les Trois Frères cave (Ariège, France, middle Magdalenian age; c. 12,000 BCE). It is often considered by folklorists and ethnologists as the oldest representation of a masked man, whereas many paleontologists now prefer to see in it the portrayal of a mythical mixed man (half man and half beast). Such a figure may or may not be linked to the existence of masks; it may or may not constitute the inception or consequence of mask use. In any case, one cannot be categorical about it. This is true as well for an important number of the documents that have been interpreted as representing masked beings because they showed anthropomorphic figures with stylized or animal heads. [*See* Paleolithic Religion.]

At an early Mesolithic site at Seamer near Scarborough, Yorkshire, some worked stag frontlets were discovered, which might have been worn as some kind of mask or headdress. But it is impossible to determine with certitude if these frontlets were used as a hunting disguise or for a ritual dance.

In a cave at Nahal Hemar in the Judean Desert, archaeologists have discovered fragments of several stone masks dating back to the pre-pottery Neolithic B period (seventh millennium BCE). It seems unlikely that these stone masks were affixed to the face of a wearer during ceremonies. They might be funerary masks or the facial part of effigies or even masks that are hung from poles. In the present state of our knowledge, nothing allows us to decide in favor of one or the other of these hypotheses. Nevertheless, these stone artifacts are the oldest reliable dated documents testifying to the existence of masks in the seventh millennium BCE. One cannot conclude from this find that there existed, at the same time, masks worn by living human beings during ceremonies. The oldest document from this point of view seems to belong to Egypt, where the representation of a masked figure appears on a fragment of a wall of the funerary temple of King Sahoure (fifth dynasty, c. 2500 BCE). It is however certain that with the late Stone Age the plausibility of the existence of ritual masks increases, particularly in parts of the Middle East, Africa, and Europe.

BIBLIOGRAPHY

Bar-Yosef, Ofer. *A Cave in the Desert: Nahal Hemar, Nine-Thousand-Year-Old Finds.* Jerusalem, 1985.

Bastian, Adolf. "Masken und Maskereien." *Zeitschrift für Völkerpsychologie* 14 (1883): 335–358.

Bravmann, René A. "Gyinna-Gyinna: Making the Djinn Manifest." *African Arts* 10 (April 1977): 46–52, 87.

Chappaz-Wirthner, Suzanne. "Les masques du Lötschental." *Annales valaisannes* 49 (1974): 3–95.

Fischer, Eberhard. "Masks in a Non-Poro Area: The Dan." *Ethnologische Zeitschrift Zürich* 1 (1980): 81–88.

Frobenius, Leo. "Die Masken und Geheimbünde Afrikas." *Nova Acta* 74 (1899): 1–128.
Guiart, Jean. *Mythologie du masque en Nouvelle-Caledonie.* Paris, 1966.
Jedrej, M. C. "A Comparison of Some Masks from North America, Africa, and Melanesia." *Journal of Anthropological Research* 36 (1980): 220–230.
Le masque. Paris, 1960. Catalog of an exhibition held at the Musée Guimet, Paris.

HENRY PERNET
Translated from French by Michele P. Cros

Ritual Masks in Nonliterate Cultures

Throughout the principal regions in which ritual masks are found—Africa, Melanesia, and the Americas—the majority of the figures depicted in masks are primordial beings, mythical ancestors, culture heroes, and gods. The past misconception that most masks represent "spirits of the dead" was due to a large extent to confusion between "the dead" and "the ancestors" and to lack of precision in the definition of "spirit." In fact, in most cases the mask does not simply represent a particular figure; it contextualizes it as well. That is, it evokes the paradigmatic events in which the figure in question has played a role. These events are not necessarily enacted as on a theatrical stage; they can be recalled by a dance, by a song or chant, by a piece of costume, or by the recital of a text that accompanies the performance of the mask. They can even be implicit: the mask intervenes in certain circumstances, because the figure it represents was implicated in similar circumstances at the time of origins—a fact known to the initiates at least.

Among the Senufo of the Ivory Coast, for instance, the *kponiougo,* "head" or "face" of the Poro, the men's secret society, recalls the original state of the world as it is described in mythological narratives. Among the Dan the mask of the toucan recalls the events that led God to create the earth. Although we have only a fragmentary knowledge of Melanesian myths, many masks of that part of the world seem to strive to recall paradigmatic events. For instance, the performance of the Mai masks of the middle Sepik of New Guinea is accompanied by the recital of totemic names and mythical texts through a bamboo megaphone. Another mask represents a feminine spirit, who, along with a masculine being often represented in the form of a crocodile, is the protagonist of events that accompanied the creation of the present world.

On the northwest coast of North America "the great majority of Kwakiutl masks are worn in representations, in stylized dance form, of incidents from hereditary family myths. In some cases, the dance dramatizes the mythical adventure of the ancestor, while in others it recreates a dance given to the ancestor by a mythical being with whom he came in contact" (Bill Holm, *Crooked Beak of Heaven,* Seattle, 1972, p. 10).

Among the Iroquois, at the beginning of each reunion of the False Faces, their chief recalls the confrontation between the original False Face and the Great Spirit, in memory of which the False Faces wear masks with crooked noses. Before entering the home of a sick person in order to minister to him or her, the False Faces produce weird noises. These nasal sounds are said to be in imitation of the utterances that the original False Face made during one episode of his challenge of the Great Spirit (Frank G. Speck, *Midwinter Rites of the Cayuga Long House,* Philadelphia, 1949, pp. 86–87).

In the Southwest of the United States, the masked dances of the Zuni represent various episodes of their mythology. In the Shalako ceremony, for instance, some dances consist of a mimetic representation of the actions of the *kachinas* when they want to send rain to the Zuni.

In South America the rituals and the symbolism often have an elementary character. However, a careful analysis of the ceremonies nevertheless reveals that many commemorate the principal episodes of the tribal mythology. The Carajá, who live along the middle course of the Araguaia River, have masks that portray a pair of supernatural parrots whose descent to mankind is related in myth. The Aruanã, a dance performed in the same region, bears the name of a fish whose form the Carajá bore before they became human beings.

It is important to note that the use of masks can be derived as much from the will to enact certain events as from the desire to portray certain figures. The masks, at times, represent no particular character but only events. For instance, among the Mali-Baining of the Gazelle Peninsula of New Britain the main purpose of the Mandas festival is to represent the events that took place in the primordial mythic time. While a choir of women chants the story of creation, eighty masks enact its various phases: the birth of the sea, the appearance of the earth, the primordial forest, the flora, the winds, the animals and the birds, and, when the stage has thus been set, the appearance of the first human couple and their sons. In this festival some masks depict events rather than characters: the ngoaremchi masks portray whirlpools and explain thereby the birth of the sea, which swirled forth in all directions; the ngavoucha masks show how the earth was separated from the waters; and so on (Carl Laufer, "Die Mandas-Maskenfeier der Mali-Baining," *Jahrbuch des Museums für Völkerkunde zu Leipzig* 27, 1970).

The Dogon of Mali have a mask called *sirige*, a term that can be translated literally as a "two-storied house." This mask consists of a rectangular face surmounted by a very high sculpted mast sometimes measuring more than five meters. At first, anthropologists were told that the *sirige* was recent and profane, a mere sculpture inspired by the view of a "two-storied house," and that the wide movements traced by its mast served only to allow the wearer to show off the power of his jaw and neck (Marcel Griaule, *Masques Dogons*, Paris, 1938, p. 587). Later, they were given a more complex idea of Dogon cosmology and another interpretation of the mask, with four variants: (1) The first recalls the work of the supreme god (Amma); the whirling of the wearer of the mask, with mast being maintained horizontally, recalled the twirling of the god Amma while creating the world. (2) The second variant recalls the adventures of Ogo, a very important figure who is known as the "pale fox." (3–4) The third and fourth variants represent aspects of the descent and impact of the ark that plays a very significant part in Dogon mythology. In light of the second level of interpretation, consisting of these four variants, it appears that the mask does not represent the two-storied house, but that both the mask and the house recall the same series of mythical events.

Similar analyses can be made of other masks (Marcel Griaule and Germaine Dieterlen, *Le renard pâle*, Paris, 1965). Therefore, when the masks are shown in the main square of a Dogon village, the rich ensemble of things, of animal and human figures, is a reproduction of the world, a catalog of both the live and extinct fauna of the cliffs and the plains. This display recalls all of the public functions, the trades, the ages; it presents a host of strangers, friends, or enemies; it mimics a wide variety of essential activities, all in a specified order, at least theoretically. It is truly a cosmos. When the mask society gets under way in the public square, it dances the march of the world; it dances the system of the world.

Depending on the degree of knowledge reached by the onlookers and participants, they understand this dance differently. At a first level the masks are seen as representing elements of the Dogon cosmos, that is, as describing what this world is and how it functions; here the masks are understood mainly on the basis of their appearance (storied house, hare, stranger). On another level, however, the same masks may also refer to primordial events that explain how and why the world came to be as the Dogon now experience it. The two levels do not contradict each other but correspond to different points of view, to different degrees of sophistication in the understanding of the masked performance.

Those diverse and complementary meanings, so well documented among the Dogon, a population whose cosmology and masks could be studied in detail, merely confirms what was said above, that is, that masks are not necessarily limited to representing a particular person but can be used to represent an event or a more or less abstract quality or trait of character.

In some cases, the system within which a population lives may be represented not only by the ensemble of masks but by one particular mask that summarizes the entire system. For instance, among the Northern Igbo of eastern Nigeria the mask *ijele* is a lofty tableau of figures with trappings hanging from its bottom edge to conceal the performer, who carries the whole structure on his head. The theme of the tableau that occupies the upper section of the *ijele* is the life of a typical Igbo community (John S. Boston, "Some Northern Ibo Masquerades," *Journal of the Royal Anthropological Institute of Great Britain and Ireland* 90, 1960).

Among the Bantsaya group of the western Teke the mask of the Kidumu dancer is a true summary of the culture of the group (M.-C. Dupré, "A propos d'un masque des Téké de l'ouest (Congo-Brazzaville)," *Objets et Mondes* 8/4, 1968). The mask is thus closely linked to the founding events of the society and its institutions, as well as to its values. It is, therefore, easy to understand why among many peoples the mask is linked to conservative forces and plays an important role in so cial control, assuming even a quasi-police function.

Sometimes the masks lose their ritual value at the end of the ceremonies of which they have been a part. This widespread phenomenon often surprised observers. For instance Francis E. Williams, in his *Drama of Orokolo* (Oxford, 1940, pp. 373–376), asked why the *hevehe* of the Elema of New Guinea had to be killed and destroyed at the end of the ritual cycle, only to be recreated in the next cycle, when they might pass from one into the other as if living throughout. He was puzzled to see the products of years of industry and art so readily consigned to the flames. This surprise in the face of the abandonment or destruction of the masks once they have been used reveals two preconceived notions. First, our interest in the mask as an artifact makes us highlight the finished product and underestimate the ritual value involved in its making. Further, we tend to consider the masked ceremonies as theatrical performances and to think that all the preparations that precede them find their meaning in the representation itself. This is a distorted view of those ritual cycles; often the making of the mask is in itself a ritual, which reproduces the various phases of the creation of the archetypal mask. Therefore, it is vitally important that the following cycle start anew at the beginning, that is, with the making of the mask. This is probably the reason why masks can be destroyed or left to rot without regret at the end of a cycle.

The Mask and Its Wearer. The notion of the "primitive mentality" was prevalent among writers at the beginning of the twentieth century. Even after Lucien Lévy-Bruhl had given up the notion of the prelogical character of this so-called primitive mentality and had renounced his concept of mystical participation, the idea that primitive man had a different mentality persisted. One of the principal characteristics of this mentality, or of "archaic consciousness," would be the inability to truly differentiate between the being and its appearance, the thing and its image, "le signifiant et le signifié." Influenced by this view, most of the books on ritual masks have spread the theory according to which the wearer of the mask does not only represent a certain figure (ancestor, culture hero, god, etc.) but actually becomes, *is* this figure. For these authors, to put a mask on was, therefore, akin to undergoing a real transformation. Some scholars took this theory even further and claimed that it provided an explanation for the phenomenon of the mask itself. According to them, the mask stems from the possibility it gives man to liberate himself, to repudiate his current personality, to undergo metamorphosis.

The conditions of ethnographic fieldwork do not always lend themselves to evaluate at which precise level of reality the presence of a mythical being in a given ritual is located. But in light of our present knowledge, the range in which the various hypotheses mentioned above may apply is becoming narrower and narrower. In fact, the best studies show that cultures that utilize masks are perfectly capable of distinguishing between the thing and its image.

For instance, in 1938, Marcel Griaule *(Masques dogons)* wrote that the Dogon did not fit the prevalent assumption made about the attitude of Africans toward the images that they create. Far from being fooled by the appearances or the material effects of the ritual, they were definitely aware of the difference between the thing represented and its image. They even have a word *bibile,* or *belay,* to express the terms of reproduction, image, resemblance, and double. A photograph is the *bibile* of the person it represents. The shadow of a living being is considered a *bibile* because it reproduces the silhouette, the posture, and the movements of that person. A masked dancer is called *imina bibile,* appearance or reproduction of the mask. Similar findings have been made among numerous other nonliterate peoples of Africa, Oceania, and the Americas.

Other factors also seem to reduce the range of the metamorphosis thesis. One notes the fact, for example, that masks are rarely associated with possession of the wearer, although that would be in the logic of the hypothesis. Finally, the initiates in those communities in which masks are found constantly stress the fact that only the noninitiates believe that they are actually in the presence of a spirit or a god. These statements are difficult to reconcile with the metamorphosis thesis. They have from the very first forced the proponents of that thesis to embark on often complicated explanations in order to bring their theory into harmony with the ethnographic data.

Similarly, attempts to explain the ritual mask phenomenon by a desire, a need, even an instinct of the wearer, were probably influenced by theories geared to explain the persistence of the Carnival masks in the Western world. In one example of what Evans-Pritchard called the "if I were a horse" type of guesswork, the feeling of liberation experienced by the Western mask wearer has been transferred to the so-called primitive populations. Without denying that such a feeling may exist among nonliterate people, I am forced to admit that it cannot be used as a general explanation of the masked ritual phenomenon.

Wearing a mask falls under the head of service rather than liberation. This service is often compulsory: reprobation, a fine, or worse await those who try to sidestep it. One particular person or a more or less large group of people is compelled to perform this task: one or several members of the family of the deceased, all the members of a brotherhood, all circumcised males, and so forth. Although the wearing of a mask can bring honor and prestige, it also burdens the wearer with various duties, such as the payment of a tax in cowries or in kind to purchase the right to wear a particular mask, or several months of preparation during which the mask wearers learn the dance steps, intensively rehearse combined movements, and may have to memorize complicated texts sometimes in a secret language.

Among the Asmat of Irian Jaya, for example, it takes four to five months to prepare the masks for the ritual called Jipae. During all of that time, the mask wearers have to support the mask makers. The relatives of the deceased for whom the Jipae is celebrated must, in turn, give daily supplies of food to the mask wearers. Furthermore, the mask wearers act as the surrogate for the dead and adopt the children of the deceased (H. C. Van Renselaar and R. L. Mellema, *Asmat,* Amsterdam, 1956).

The Mask and the Dead. One mask has been constantly associated with the representation of the dead: the skull mask. Some experts have considered it the most primitive form of mask (e.g., Hans Nevermann in *Die Religionen der Südsee und Australiens,* Stuttgart, 1968). Those partial or complete skulls, worn on the top of the head or in front of the face, decorated, remodeled, or covered with tight skin, have provoked a number of speculations. Leo Frobenius, the German ethnologist and explorer (1873–1938), considered them as part of a logical continuum that began with the use of a complete skull and moved to the use of a skull mask to conclude with the mask carved out of wood. Skull masks are found in three main regions. In Africa, such masks are sometimes tightly covered with skin in a manner peculiar to the Cross River region, where this same technique is used also to cover the wooden supports of the masks (e.g., Keith Nicklin, "Nigerian Skin-Covered Masks," *African Arts* 7/3, 1974). In Mesoamerica, the Aztec often combined the techniques of remodeling and decorating the skulls (e.g., with turquoise). However, it is the Melanesian masks that have given rise to the most speculation (Hans Damm, "Bermerkungen zu den Schädelmasken aus Neubritannien," *Jahrbuch des Museums für Völkerkunde zu Leipzig* 26, 1969). In Melanesia the skull is partially or entirely remodeled or molded over with a kind of wax; it is then painted and often adorned with human hair that has been glued on to it. These techniques are not however limited to the making of masks. They are also used in the making of funerary effigies (for example the *rambaramp* of Malekula) and in the making of remodeled heads that are preserved in cult houses and in dwellings.

The same techniques are also used to mold human heads on wooden supports. The early observers of these societies paid little attention to the function and the meaning of these masks. Because of the radical changes that these traditions have undergone to date, many of the assumptions made and questions raised about them may never be checked or resolved. However, an examination of some other Melanesian masks portraying deceased historical persons (as opposed to those that portray the dead as a class) will help us to define a general context in which the skull mask can most probably be placed.

In the Jipae ceremony of the Asmat, for example, masked men represent the dangerous dead, especially children, great warriors, and the victims of headhunters. Beginning at dusk the masqueraders dance, imitating the waddle of the cassowary. At sunrise the dancers move toward the men's house followed by the women. Suddenly, the men of the village attack the masks with sticks, forcing them to enter the men's house and thus ending the ritual. In the Jipae, the mask represents a specific dead person but several solar characteristics are also ascribed to it. This ritual begins at nightfall, when, according to the Asmat, the sun puts on its mask to descend into the land of the dead. The dancers imitate the cassowary, which the Asmat associate with the sun. Finally, the ritual ends at sunrise, that is, when the sun leaves the land of the dead and removes its mask.

To understand the meaning of a ceremony of this type one must keep in mind that for a large number of societies, in Melanesia as well as in other parts of the world, it is not death itself but ritual that opens the way toward the next life. This ritual fulfills several functions linked together: it prevents the spirit of the dead from wandering among the living; it allows the deceased to enjoy the status due to his rank in the hereafter; it removes the risk that—in despair about his unresolved fate—the deceased might act against the living to force them to celebrate the appropriate ritual. This ritual can also mark the end of mourning, be the occasion of the redistribution of the land, or serve as a framework or a background for initiations.

The organization of these ceremonies is often costly. In addition to financing the making of the masks and other ritualistic objects, the family may have to provide for the persons who make them, supplying abundant food and drink for all of the ritual's participants, sometimes even providing them with gifts. Perhaps this costliness explains why in some societies only the deceased of a certain socioeconomic level are entitled to this type of ritual. This distinction, along socioeconomic lines, has also been explained as the remnant of an ancient tradition in which only the chief or the king was honored by this type of ritual.

It is mostly during this kind of ritual that masks representing deceased individuals intervene. Understandably, it is out of the question for some individual or other to decide, just because he so fancies, to organize a ceremony in which he would represent a dead person chosen at random. The mask wearer must be related or allied to the deceased in a precise way (e.g., all husbands of sisters and daughters of the deceased must act as impersonators in turn) or must belong to a clan or a village that, because of a complex network of relations based on exchange and reciprocity, is entitled to represent the deceased. This reinforces the notion that wearing the mask is a service rather than a search for liberation or metamorphosis.

Early twentieth-century scholars were so preoccupied with the idea that the mask wearer was adopting a new personality that they overlooked one of the mask's main purposes—which may have been to identify the dead with his paradigm (the first dead human, a culture hero, etc.), and not just to associate the mask wearer with the spirit of the dead. This is, nevertheless, one of the important elements of such rituals as the Melanggan of New Ireland, the Ne-leng of Malekula, the Horiomu of the Kiwai, the Jipae of the Asmat, the Mbii-kawane of Mimika (New Guinea), and so on (Henry Pernet, "Le mort et son modèle," *Numen* 29, 1982).

This identification can take various forms that fall between two extreme poles. In some cases nothing is done to bring the appearance of the masked figure, as it is defined by tradition, closer to that of the deceased. In those cases, it is mainly the attitude of kin that express this identification; they act toward the masked figure as they would toward the departed they are mourning. The ceremony called Mbii-kawane is close to this type (J. Pouwer, "A Masquerade in Mimika," *Antiquity and Survival* 5, 1956). In other cases, a considerable effort is made so that the masked person will resemble the deceased as closely as possible. In this case the identification with the paradigmatic figure is made through the text, which is sung or recited, through the dance steps, and so on. This seems to be the case with the Horiomu of the Kiwai. During the burial of the deceased, his height is measured with a stick, and throughout the ritual he is impersonated by a man of equal height wearing his ornaments. Afterward, these ornaments are sent out to be inspected by the women, and they are never worn by any other dancers except the supposed owner (Gunnar Landtman, *The Kiwai Papuans of British New Guinea*, London, 1927, p. 335).

The above remarks also pertain to a number of funerary masks. Since the last century, the term *funerary mask* has been used to categorize various types of masks that were found on mortal remains, on mummies, on funerary urns, or among the funerary furnishings found in certain tombs. Some of these masks are realistic, seem like portraits, and have on occasion been molded directly onto the dead person's face. Others, sometimes called "idealistic," reveal traits that obviously did not belong to the deceased. In between those two categories, variations such as idealized or stylized portraits are found. Others, finally, do not have a real face. In some cases the mask could have been worn by somebody during a burial ritual, while in other cases there is no evidence to support that interpretation.

The traditions that manifest funerary masks are extremely scattered both historically and geographically; however, some authors do not despair of finding their common origin and retracing their history in ancient Egypt, Mycenae, Etruria, ancient Rome, ancient China, Siberia, Tibet, pre-Columbian America, and the America of the eighteenth and nineteenth centuries, and so on.

The funerary mask category, therefore, does not correspond to a well-defined class of masks; not surprisingly, this has led to a wide range of interpretations. However, taking into account the extensive variations that can be found from one tradition to the next, the funerary masks seem to operate on two basic principles. The first principle is to prevent the spirits of the dead from wandering among the living (by offering them a new support, by luring or forcing them away from the living, and so on). The second principle is to insure that the deceased will reach safely the resting place that must be his in the hereafter.

The identification with a paradigm in the achievement of this goal should not be overlooked. That identification can be expressed in the features of the masks, or in the very fact of the wearing of a mask, or through other elements of the funerary ritual. Among the Egyptians, for example, Osiris was represented as a mummified king. The mummification of the deceased along with the use of a coffin in the shape of a mummy then reinforced the identification of the deceased with Osiris.

Masks, Women, and Secret Societies. At the end of the nineteenth century, a whole school of thought developed around the concept of a close connection between the institution of the masks and so-called matriarchal societies. As defined by the Swiss jurist and classical scholar J. J. Bachofen (1815–1887), the concept of matriarchy encompassed a legal and political system in which power belonged to the women in societies with matrilineal descent. Frobenius took over and slightly altered this notion and launched the basis for the *Kulturkreiselehre* ("culture circles theory") that would be developed and popularized by his followers. [*See* Kulturkreiselehre.]

According to the proponents of this theory, the division of the social macrounit into two halves was linked to matrilineal descent and to the practice of agriculture. This dualistic organization was accompanied by men's secret societies whose members wore masks in order to incarnate and honor the dead. Conforming to evolutionist presuppositions, the "matriarchy" was assigned a place in the history of civilization. It was believed that at a certain period women played a leading role in society and that, as an attempt to escape from their domination, men created secret societies. Their masks were then the aggressive means by which they regained power over women. This quasi-organic link between secret societies and masks can be expressed in the following theoretical framework: (a) the goal of secret societies is to terrorize the noninitiates, in particular women; (b) this is achieved through the use of masks representing spirits; (c) for the masks to represent spirits the wearer must not be recognizable; (d) from this it follows that originally the mask must have disguised the wearer's entire body (Felix Speiser, *Ethnographische*

Materialien aus den Neuen Hebriden und den Banks-Inseln, Berlin, 1923).

This theory, which offered a logical and unique framework for an array of puzzling facts, was immensely popular. However, along the road taken by anthropology since the 1930s all of its elements have been gradually disputed. For instance, it has been impossible to find, in history or among the populations studied by ethnology, a single society living in matriarchy as defined by Bachofen. The concept of matriarchy was shown to have arisen out of a confusion between the rule of power, on the one hand, and matrilineal descent on the other. As for the position given to the concept of matriarchy in the history of civilization, it was found to have been a purely arbitrary result of the evolutionist mentality.

As far as the secret societies are concerned, the apparent simplicity of this explanation stemmed from the fact that at the beginning of this century the authors regrouped a significant number of very different institutions under the term *secret society*. A lot of them were secret only in name, such as brotherhoods of men, age-group organizations, initiation societies, societies based on social rank, and more or less restricted cultic societies. Furthermore, later studies showed that masks could very well exist independently of secret societies, and that many secret societies did not have masks, while others had only recently adopted the mask, which had been known in other contexts. The concept of a primary and original link between masks and secret societies can, therefore, no longer be taken uncritically; in the same way, scholars can no longer indiscriminately gather under the heading "secret societies" all the heterogenous institutions that the early authors were wont to amalgamate.

The theory contended that the masks were meant to terrorize women. This was possible only if the wearers were able to deceive the women into believing themselves to be in the presence of spirits rather than of men in disguise, which in turn presupposed the use of a costume hiding the mask wearer completely. According to this hypothesis, masks that were not accompanied by an entire disguise had, therefore, lost their original character and were thought to be more recent. However, this aspect of the theory also crumbles under close examination. The best documented ethnographic accounts from Africa, Melanesia, and the Americas show that women are aware of the true nature of the masks: they are not fooled by a ritual, the purpose of which would be to deceive them. Yet they display emotions, sometimes violent ones, during the performance of certain masks. If they are not fooled by appearances, then how can those feelings be explained?

In many cases it seems to be a "compulsory expression of feelings." For instance, when women express fear when confronted with the masks, or when they recognize in them the deceased of their own families and implore them with cries and tears, one is forced to wonder if such a display of emotions is not an essential and mandatory part of the ritual itself. There is no doubt that women are frightened in many societies. But they are afraid of the consequences that would follow if they did not behave as tradition requires or if they breached the prohibitions surrounding the masks. Depending on the situation and the society, a fine would be levied, a sacrifice would have to be made, the woman would become sick, sterile, or even die, the men might kill her, the mask wearer would die, the entire community would disappear, and so on. This does not mean that women act merely out of fright and that their emotions (for instance, their grief) are not genuine. But their sincerity addresses itself to the cultural significance of the mask and the ritual and can be understood only if we accept the idea that all those who take part in the ritual are doing so at the level of its meaning in their tradition, and that they remain aware of the means deployed for the representation. Present studies lead us to consider that the deep meaning of a masked ritual can only be perceived if one admits that all of the behaviors observed are meaningful, those of women as well as those of men, both contributions being necessary to the ritual and constituent of it (Henry Pernet, "Masks and Women: Toward a Reappraisal," *History of Religions* 22, 1982).

Rejecting the elegant "culture circles" hypothesis does not solve all of the problems, however, for a lot of the facts on which it was based remain. The fact that women are, as a general rule, excluded from wearing masks, cannot be denied. Even if one takes into consideration the numerous exceptions to this rule (exceptions that in the past were considered to be relics of a matriarchal stage), a simple statistical study would be enough to show that in most cases, masks are worn by men. Therefore, if the masked ritual must be viewed in the context of a symbolism shared by men and women, the dialictic between the two sexes that the ritual reveals must not be neglected. It brings us back to the sacredness peculiar to each sex and to the ambivalent attitude of men toward the power of women: particularly with regard to women's ability to conceive and to self-regulate their uncleanness through their menstrual cycles. (The symbolism of the menstrual cycle is of considerable importance for Dogon and Yoruba masks, for example.) If this male/female dialectic cannot be simply reduced to the opposition "deceiver-dominator/deceived-dominated," it nevertheless continues to exist (see, for example, Annette Leleur's "Sexes or Chaos?" *Folk* 21/22, 1979–1980), as do the numerous myths that tell that masks were discovered or first owned by women, and that women ruled the society at the time. These tales are no longer considered to be historic reminiscences. They are instead interpreted from a synchronic perspective, that is, as having meaning in their present context: the contemporary society in which they are found. Depending on the case, they delimit the domain peculiar to each sex, justify the hierarchy of the sexes, legitimize the exclusion of women by stating its origin, that is, usually by recalling that the women themselves are responsible for this transfer to the men: out of stupidity or ignorance, they did not know what to do with their discovery and had to turn to the men; they tyrannized the men, who were forced to react; an enemy attacked and the women, unable to conduct the war, had to abandon the power to the men; the spirit of the ritual object refused to enter into contact with the women once he saw them menstruating; or, simply, the women of the early days, of their own account, gave the object to the men.

Nevertheless, the problem remains of the presence in Africa, Melanesia, and the Americas of similar traditions including the ritual mask; the myth of its discovery by a woman and of its subsequent loss to men; the bull-roarer as the voice of the spirits of the masks; sterility or death as the consequence of any contact between a woman and a mask; and various other elements more or less clearly attested. Many hypotheses and speculations can and have been made in order to explain this fact. What is certain is that, whatever approach one takes to it, and whatever reticence one may have for researches covering such a wide field, only a comparative study of the three main regions in which masks are used will be able to bring us closer to an understanding of this question. It is not available yet and will have to be undertaken on the basis provided by the new archaeological, historical, and anthropological findings available on these areas.

[*See also* Culture Heroes *and* Ancestors, *article on* Mythic Ancestors.]

BIBLIOGRAPHY

The bibliography on masks is too extensive to give here in full. My "'Primitive' Ritual Masks in the History of Religions: A Methodological Assessment" (Ph.D. diss., University of Chicago, 1979) lists more than twelve hundred references, including books on masks in general as well as masks from particular regions or from particular societies, booklets from exhibitions, various articles published in specialized journals (anthropology, art history, the history of religions, etc.), and chapters in various ethnographies.

There is an urgent need to review the subject from the point of view of the history of religions and on the basis of the data currently being collected by historians, anthropologists, and folklorists, since contemporary research has contested many of the theses that underly the available literature. The list below simply refers to a number of possible departure points for anyone interested in the study of masks. The books cited adopt a variety of theoretical positions and must be read with due caution, while keeping in mind the various points made in this article.

Bastin, Marie-Louise. *Introduction aux arts d'Afrique noire.* Arnouville, 1984.

Bédouin, Jean-Louis. *Les masques.* Paris, 1967.

Bühler, Alfred. *Kunst der Südsee / Art of Oceania.* Zurich, 1969.

Cole, Herbert M., ed. *I Am Not Myself: The Art of African Masquerade.* Los Angeles, 1985.

Crumrine, N. Ross, and Marjorie Halpin, eds. *The Power of Symbols: Masks and Masquerade in the Americas.* Vancouver, 1983.

Ebeling, Ingelore. *Masken und Maskierung: Kult, Kunst and Kosmetik; Von den Naturvölkern bis zur Gegenwart.* Cologne, 1984.

Guiart, Jean. *The Arts of the South Pacific.* New York, 1963.

Hartmann, Günther. *Masken südamerikanischer Naturvölker.* Berlin, 1967.

Holý, Ladislav, and Dominique Darbois. *Masks and Figures from Eastern and Southern Africa.* London, 1967.

Huet, Michel. *Danses d'Afrique.* Paris, 1978.

Lévi-Strauss, Claude. *The Way of the Masks.* Translated by Sylvia Modelski. Seattle, 1982.

Lommel, Andreas. *Masks: Their Meaning and Function.* Translated by Nadia Fowler. New York, 1981.

Lupu, François, ed. *Océanie: Le masque au long cours.* Rennes, 1983.

Malin, Edward. *A World of Faces: Masks of the Northwest Coast Indians.* Portland, Oreg., 1978.

Mathews, Zena Pearlstone. *The Relation of Seneca False Face Masks to Seneca and Ontario Archeology.* New York, 1978.

Mead, Sidney M., ed. *Exploring the Visual Art of Oceania: Australia, Melanesia, Micronesia, and Polynesia.* Honolulu, 1979.

Palavecino, Enrique. *La máscara y la cultura.* Buenos Aires, 1954.

Pernet, Henry. *Mirages du masque.* Forthcoming.

Ray, Dorothy Jean. *Eskimo Masks: Art and Ceremony.* Vancouver, 1975.

Segy, Ladislas. *Masks of Black Africa.* New York, 1976.

Tischner, Herbert. *Südseemasken in der geistigen Kultur der Melanesier.* Hamburg, 1976.

Washburn, Dorothy K., ed. *Hopi Kachina: Spirit of Life.* Seattle, 1980.

Wherry, Joseph H. *Indian Masks and Myths of the West.* New York, 1974.

HENRY PERNET

Translated from French by Michele P. Cros

Ritual Masks in European Cultures

In Europe, as elsewhere, the use of masks is connected with a variety of purposes. In small ethnic communities, they may provide camouflage in the face of real or imagined enemies. As disguises, masks alter a person's physical aspect to create the illusion of his being someone else. In the context of a masquerade, masks may be used to create psychological or social confusion or to alter one's personality. Masks may also fulfill a religious function, transforming the wearer into a priest, a demigod, or a demon, whether in the context of a myth or ritual or in connection with various acts of consecration. As is the case throughout the world, masks in Europe have been used as magical instruments that transform human beings, enabling them to communicate with or control supernatural powers or divine beings. Similarly, masks may represent the metamorphoses of the divinities themselves; thus human beings can engage in miraculous and strange adventures. In addition, certain popular European masks are reminiscent of the ancient hierophanies that introduced order into the world.

In prehistoric times, during the Neolithic, Bronze, and Iron ages, when masks were used for camouflage, for disguise, or in masquerades, in the context of public ritual and ceremony, they had a purely formal function. By contrast, when used as instruments of magical transformation, masks brought about actual spiritual changes in the wearer. Such changes included the alteration of identity, the loss of personality, the creation of a double personality, the inducement of a dreamlike trance. Masks could also bring about a metamorphosis or a hierophany. It was especially the prehistoric priest, and through him the faithful, who underwent such transformations.

When serving as camouflage, as disguise, or in masquerades, masks were used both individually by magicians and collectively by the participants in various rites and ceremonies connected with seasonal festivals. The community participated in masked processions called prosopophories (from Greek *prosōpon*, "face," and *phoros*, "wearer of"). These prosopophories were in general solemn affairs, stern and orderly, consisting of maskers who paraded in silence or hummed melodies to the accompaniment of flutes, zithers, drums, cymbals, or small bells.

Ethnologists view the mask as a cultural instrument that human beings employ in order to rise above mere animal existence. Thus as important means for the representation of ideals and the construction of culture, masks reveal a fundamental dimension of human creativity. As Mircea Eliade has remarked, "A mask makes [man] what he has decided to be, *homo religiosus* ["religious man"] and even *zōion politikon* ["political animal"]" (Eliade, 1964).

Our knowledge of masks in prehistoric Europe is based upon various accounts given by ancient Greek and Roman authors and upon the examination of various archaeological and paleontological remains made in the light of what we know about the popular use of masks in medieval and modern Europe.

Ancient writers from Homer to Julius Caesar mention the magical or practical use by the earliest Europeans of tattoos and powders made of humus. Their reports have been confirmed by archaeological discoveries of statuettes decorated with tattooed masks. Such tattooing with magical and mythical emblems was undoubtedly intended to provide a magical disguise for the wearer.

Evidence can also be found for the more developed use of masks. These masks often depict various exaggerations or complete transgressions of normal human physiognomy. For instance, a mask may depict a face half sad and half happy, or indeed half human and half beast. Such masks were intended to set the wearer apart from the common run of humanity and to evoke the presence of various mythical beings or recall sacred events. They were most probably used in the context of rituals and initiation ceremonies and no doubt elicited the fervor of devotion or even unearthly terror. In our own day, such masks are evidence of the transformation of instruments of belief into mere instruments of amusement.

The manufacture of masks reveals other aspects of their magical and mythological significance. The selection of materials is based both on the mask's symbolism and on its functional structure. Integral masks (masks that cover the entire body of the wearer) of animals require the whole hides of stags, wild bears, wolves, or other animals. Smaller masks require only part of a skin. Wood may be used for head masks; pumpkins, melons, foliage, flax, hemp, berries, and metals may also be used. What is interesting is the extent to which the selection of materials is dictated by the desired symbolic effects, which range from the hideous to the burlesque, from the grotesque to the comic, from the naive to the hieratic, and from the demonic to the angelic.

In western Europe, masks are made in serial production, while in eastern Europe they are made by the wearers themselves and bear a definite individual mark derived from tradition. Those taking part in prosopophories are obliged to make their masks in accordance with proper ritual and must also be in a state of perfect physical and spiritual purity.

The final adorning of the masks is done in the context

of a ritual or ceremonial dance held prior to the prosopophory. During this rehearsal the masks are seen in all their brillance, their ornaments sparkling with the movement of the dance, which is performed to the sound of percussion or wind instruments.

Integral masks are the most primitive type and the most significant in regard to magical and religious ritual. They mark the nomadic period of the prehistoric era, when the hunter and his family wandered in quest of game and when those who cultivated land traveled in search of fertile lands. This nomadic condition explains why the earliest paleo-ethnological documents consist of drawings, engravings, and cave paintings depicting the ritual use of masks. As depicted on the walls of the Trois Frères cave in France, the hunter-wizard figure, dressed in a stag's hide, sometimes also called the Sorcerer, practices a ritual designed to give him better access to game. In the same cave we see a dancing hunter-wizard figure dressed in a bison's hide chasing what is probably an antelope running in fear behind a stag. [*See* Paleolithic Religion.] It is possible that these representations mimed the spirit of the hunted animals. Such prehistoric rituals for approaching game are analogous to hunting rituals found as late as the eighteenth and nineteenth centuries among various non-European peoples.

From the use of stag and bovine masks in prehistoric hunting rituals, the peoples of Europe passed to the festive and ceremonial prosopophories of the historical period. Integral masks of stags and bulls continued to be used in early historical times, though by sedentary populations and for different reasons. Of particular importance in this development was the role of certain cultural elements spread by the Indo-European migrations, especially through the intermediary of the Celts and the Greeks, who promoted the cults of the stag, bull, horse, and wild bear. The Celts, who considered the stag a sacred animal, used it as a cult emblem and prosopophoric instrument. The god wearing stag horns, Cernunnos, the "prince of savage animals," was the focus of Celtic religiosity in the Bronze Age in western Europe. A mask of a horned goddess (now in the Museum of Kent) and a votive mask of a cervine goddess have also been discovered in the ethnocultural area of the Celts. The iconography and sacred bestiary of the Celts also featured the masks of the horse, wild bear, and stag. All these have been preserved by popular tradition down to the present day. This popularity explains the existence of a wide range of integral masks of stags and horses among almost all the peoples of Europe, accompanied by the corresponding legends of stags, bulls, and miraculous horses.

In the Neolithic Age, war masks developed, made from the hides of fierce carnivorous animals. They were worn on the head and pulled down over the face like a visor during battle. Masking in battle was accompanied by wild cries, animal-like leaping, and the clanging of arms. These war masks caused a warlike fury within their wearers and spread the terror of death among their foes. The Celts preferred stags' heads as masks; the Dacians, the heads of wolves and bears.

During the Bronze Age, the Etruscans and Thracians created metal helmets with visor masks as well as magical masquettes superimposed on the foreheads of the helmets. The masquettes featured protuberant eyes and eyebrows made of snakes, suggesting the magical power of the warriors wearing them.

The magicians and priests of the Celts and Dacians wore white hoods with masks when they paraded in ceremonial processions at consecrated places in the woods or in mountains or when they performed rites of passage or consecration. At the same time, funeral masks began to be used, some integral and some only for the face. They were intended to protect the corpse against the baneful action of evil spirits. Until the beginning of the twentieth century, Romanians in the province of Oltenia buried their dead dressed only in a funeral shirt and mask. Today certain zoomorphic and anthropomorphic masks traditionally used only in prosopophories have been introduced into shows, festivities, and even the popular theater.

From the thematic, structural, and functional points of view, the archaic and traditional masks of the various peoples of Europe reflect a mythological outlook that derives from their ethnic background, an outlook expressed by a variety of rituals, ceremonial activities, and festivities. To this common mythological foundation, different cultural elements have been added gradually, owing to a variety of historical influences. Of major importance were the great migrations prior to our era, in particular the Indo-European migrations and also the Indo-Asian. From as early as the second century CE, there was also the impact of the christianization of Europe. The missionaries of the new religion had to struggle against the persistence of ancient European cults and mythologies, some of which have continued down to the present day as "pagan survivals" in the artifacts and folklore connected with village carnivals and masquerades. Between the tenth and sixteenth centuries, the Roman and Orthodox churches fought these vestiges of the ancient cults with every means at their disposal. In particular, the church forbade prosopophories and masquerades.

In the modern period, unable to suppress such activities completely, both churches have tolerated a few ceremonies and popular festivities that do not offend

Christian sensibilities. Among these have been a few prosopophories connected with the popular celebrations of the solstices and equinoxes. In general, the churches have adopted a policy of accepting, adopting, and transforming the practices that have been preserved by the people. In some cases, parishioners have attempted to convert the prosopophories into carnivals.

In their new Christian guise, the ancient prosopophories are now celebrated at Christmas and the New Year and especially at Lent and Shrovetide. Although Christian in character, these carnivals take over themes from the earlier mythology, which celebrates the joy and exuberance of life and the rebirth of nature. Ethnologists view these carnivals as "cathartic" festivals, since they purge the souls of the participants in a kind of popular liturgy outside the church. The rites and ceremonies can remind people of the ancestor worship of their ancient predecessors. Each carnival adapts the ancient prosopophoric structure of metamorphosis and hierophany to suit the new conditions.

In this way, practices that were not tolerated and yet escaped the control of the church were preserved through carnival masques. These were especially disliked by the church because of the disrespect they showed for the new social and religious order.

As they have survived in the carnivals, the archaic masks preserve many of their original characteristics. They remain connected with mythological themes, their use displays a ritual structure (which may be both individual and collective), and they exhibit archetypal features. They are still made of the same traditional materials. Furthermore, their themes have remained more or less unchanged. Thus, through the continued use of these traditional masks, age-old rituals and family ceremonies have passed over into the rituals and ceremonies of Christian communities.

On the whole, the prosopophories that have been preserved in the social and cultural practices of the majority of European peoples commemorate the spiritual events that lie at the foundation of their religiosity. These practices may include devotion to and glorification of certain mythical sacred beings (gods, demigods) or sanctified human beings (eponymous ancestors, heroes, saviors, civilizers, and popular saints). The exact nature of many of these masked processions can no longer be determined because of the changes they have undergone over the centuries. Some have been changed into masquerades, while others have lost their social character altogether. Still, one can occasionally detect the survival of rituals that are no longer considered sacred (former fertility, birth, and death rituals, for instance) as well as a faint glimmer of the ancient hierophanies and metamorphoses of mythical beings that have long since disappeared from popular memory.

The carnival traditions of the European peoples prolong such archaic beliefs and traditions primarily through the use of theriomorphic and anthropomorphic masks. In Roman Catholic countries, anthropomorphic masks formerly employed in ancient rites such as the Saturnalia or the Calends of January have been adopted for use in lay carnivals with a religious background at the time of the equinoxes and solstices. In Eastern Orthodox countries, archaic masks have been maintained in their traditional forms, often contributing to less elaborated rituals and religious ceremonies. Examples are the bridal and funeral masks still worn by Romanians at weddings and funerals. This transformation of archaic prosopophoric rituals into the form of modern carnivals and religious ceremonies is a general cultural process found in many parts of Europe. In those countries most influenced by the Enlightenment and modern secularization, however, these rituals have often become no more than popular amusements endowed with certain ethnic overtones.

Integral masks of horses have been maintained in the funerary rituals of southeastern Europe, chiefly among the Romanians. These masks are made of a kind of wooden skeleton in the form of a horse that is carried by two young men on their shoulders and sometimes ridden by a third, unmasked youth. The integral masks of funerary horses remind one of the motifs of the Thracian Rider found in southeastern Europe. Parallel to these integral masks one also finds the so-called skirt horses, elaborate masks in the shape of horses that were fastened to the wearer at the waist and covered him from the waist down. This type of mask is sometimes used in large daytime processions of white-horse masks at the winter and summer solstices. Such masks are found in various countries and are known as Koni (Polish), Pferdritter (German), Cheval-jupon (French, Belgian, and Swiss), Căiuții (Romanian), and Hobbyhorse (English). They were also used in the masked processions of ancient Greece. Two such skirt horses are depicted confronting each other on an early Corinthian vase that also features images representing two centaurs squaring off before a fight.

At the summer solstice, the Romanians organize processions of Călușari, maskers with stick horses. During the Middle Ages, they wore white masks. The Călușari call to mind sun cults, earth rites, and various healing practices. Opposed to the processions employing white horses are those that use black horses, symbols of the infernal forces unleashed on the earth in winter or spring. These more somber processions, which take place at dusk or dawn rather than during the day, remind one of the cult of the centaurs in ancient Greece.

Modern-day Greeks stage Kallikantzari (horse mask) processions between New Year's Day and Epiphany, corresponding to the Tudorovitzi of the Bulgarians, the Saint George's Horses of the Slovenians, the Zeleni Jurj of the Serbians, and the Caii Sfîntului Toader (Saint Tudor's Horses) of the Romanians. Despite variations in detail, all the processions mentioned above employ integral or partial masks representing horses. In the case of partial masks, the maskers often wear only horse heads, with horse's tails hanging from their belts behind them.

At opposite ends of Europe, in England and Romania, animal masks played a part in the caroling held at the New Year. In England, shepherds or hunters went caroling accompanied by a wild bear mask (which was in fact the wild bear's head itself) carried on a serving tray. In Romania, the wild bear mask was replaced by the mask of a domestic bear, also carried on a serving tray. The carolers sang of a wild bear that had come down from the mountains only to be killed by hunters.

In western, central, and eastern Europe one finds a variety of masked processions, masquerades, and carnivals, varying in detail from one place to another. In Roman Catholic countries, the most significant are the New Year festivals and the spring carnivals, organized by societies of parishioners under the sponsorship of the church. In eastern Europe, they are initiated and organized by groups of young people, in the spirit of the local community's traditions. In western Europe, they involve the participation of the entire local community. Some of these carnivals are world famous, drawing the devout and the curious alike and competing with one another for the tourist trade.

In Portugal we find the Festa des los Rapazos, the Festa de Santo Estevao, the Festa de Natal, Ano Nuovo, and Rais, each of which involves masked processions. In Spain, the masquerades and carnivals of Valencia and Lanz (Navarra) are well known, with their Janus-faced masks that pass judgment on the year's events and on people's misdeeds. At Varin and Laza (Oronse), almost everyone participates in the local carnival, wearing grotesque masks, paying visits to neighbors and asking the hosts if they can recognize them. The carnival of the village of Alberca (Salamanca) involves a bullfight-procession centering around a bull made of straw; the carnival of Navamoral de la Mata (Estremadura) traditionally culminated in the beheading of a cock by a rider on horseback. In Herencia, the carnival ends with a procession headed by a priest who leads the souls returning from Purgatory, and in Catalonia a procession is held for the dead King of Carnival.

In France there is similar variety. Here carnival festivities used to take place in the context of the so-called Carnaval-Carême cycle. In Paris, a carnival that rivaled that of Nice in size and pomp concluded with the parade of a fat ox driven by youths carrying bludgeons. The carnival of Saint-Claude (in Jura) is dominated by the Soufflacules, or wind instrumentalists, who play in the streets. One also finds a variety of masquerades and allegorical festivities in France, although masquerades have been outlawed because of the commotion they cause. The masquerade called Charivari is particularly impressive, with its *tintamares* ("loud noises, confusions"), which are intended to punish misdeeds. One of the most important allegorical festivities, the Fête-Dieu of Aix-en-Provence, has a religious character. The festivities consist of the Guet, or nocturnal parade, and, on the next day, a processional pageantry that takes place after the Mass and includes priests, tradesmen, and bearers of standards and ecclesiastical and guild emblems.

Carnivals in Belgium vary according to their location. Among the Walloons they resemble those of France, whereas in the Flemish areas they resemble German carnivals. Belgian carnivals make use of some original masks and disguises. At La Fasses-la-Ville, for instance, in the Chinele pageant (whose main character is a Punch-like figure) the participants wear velvet costumes, hairdos decorated with plumage, and wax masks and carry wooden swords. Other well-known carnivals are the Masquerade of the Long Arms (Le Long Bras) at Malmédy and the dissolute Women's Hours Masquerade at Eben-Basel. At Stavelot, the Blanc-Moussis masquerade satirizes priests who take part in carnivals. The carnival pageantry of Binche on Mardi Gras at Gille consists of two parts. In the morning a pageant is held featuring people wearing cloth masks, green glasses, mustaches and Vandyke beards, and fanciful costumes stamped with the heraldic lion, the emblem of Belgium. The participants wear belts covered with small bells and carry a kind of fasces, the emblem of justice. In the afternoon, they take walks without their masks, dressed up in tall hats and plumes of ostrich feathers. As they walk, they throw fruits at passersby as a gesture of reproach and punishment.

In Germany the carnival and the masquerade blend into Fastnacht, which was tolerated by the Reformation although it was viewed as a kind of christianized Bacchanalia. Originally organized by societies and guilds, its form differs from province to province according to the individual local incorporation of archaic prosopophoric elements: wooden masks, rich costumes, wooden swords, belts laden with small bells, whips, and bladders filled with air, ashes, or flour. At Fastnacht one also finds original masks that were invented after World War II, the so-called fool's masks: the Narre ("fools"), figures wearing brightly colored rococo costumes, the Weissnarre ("white fools"), and the Klaperdasche, figures that personify the notion of madness. The eve of Fastnacht begins with the pageantry of Hansels, figures wearing fringed costumes and masks featuring huge pointed noses. At the height of the carnival, the Putzesel, figures wearing asses' masks made of leaves, are also introduced, followed by the Brieler Rössel, figures in skirt-horse masks.

Austrian carnivals are somewhat different from German ones. There Fasching is dominated by masks that are generally ugly (such as those worn by the Perchten) and that vary from region to region. The most spectacular are found in the carnivals of Styria, Carinthia, and Tyrol. Certain Perchten masks are considered beautiful, however. They have very high hairdos, are decorated with beads and mirrors, and are worn with rococo costumes. Other Perchten masks represent dragon's heads, unicorns, wild bears, horned devils, ghosts, and witches.

In Denmark carnival festivities generally resemble those in Germany. Masquerades with an ancestral background are predominant. These employ justiciary masks, which represent the moral sanction of the local rural society. The most representative masquerade is the one dedicated to Twelfth Night, which ends with feasts in every household that are shared with the maskers.

In Switzerland the influence of the French, German, and Italian populations can be felt in the carnivals found in the various cantons. The Fasnacht pageantry in Basel is remarkable for its Rumpel groups, bands of masked pipers and drummers who "rattle around" through the city's streets. But the Basel Fasnacht is principally notable for floats featuring Waggis, a satirical figure mocking the Alsatians, and for the groups of Old Aunts, who wear masks of the heads of birds of prey. Also remarkable are the pageants of Saint Nicholas and of the Klausjagen, the wearers of bishops' mitres. Finally, there are the impressive pageants of the Savage Men, wearing masks of tree moss on their faces and fir tree branches on their heads, held at Gersau, and the pageant of the Schellenkläuse (good spirits) and Wüstenkläuse (bringers of misfortune), held at Urmensch.

In Great Britain the majority of ancient prosopophories were forbidden as early as the Middle Ages. Some relics of the cult of the Celtic horse have survived, however, in rituals of fertility employing the skirt horses: the Hobbyhorses at Padstow and the dance of the White Mare and the Gray Mare in Wales. Relics of the agrarian cult have survived in the New Year's pageantry of the Skeklers in Scotland and in the groups of mummers who go caroling at Christmas, improvising sketches with a religious or legendary medieval background.

In Ireland ancient prosopophories have survived as reminders of agrarian rituals. One finds the straw masks of the Strawboys, the maskless pageantry of the Wrenboys, and the Brideoga (wearers of wedding wreaths). At Christmas, groups wearing masks perform mummers' plays, popular dramas with heroic themes.

In Italy the Christmas carnival maintains an ancient tradition that celebrated the rebirth of nature. The carnival takes place between Christmas and the beginning of Lent and symbolizes a reversal of the normal social order, serving as a kind of safety valve for social tensions. The carnival has two distinct variants, one rural, the other urban. Rural carnivals are the more authentic, owing to their structure and ancient symbolism. Most famous are the carnivals of Campania. Despite their Christian transformation, one can still perceive traces of the Calends, Saturnalia, Brumalia, and the like.

Italian carnivals move through three stages. They begin on Saint Anthony's Day when a youth carries a flame, accompanied by a fiendish animal from the medieval bestiary. During this same period, pyres of useless household objects are lit in the streets. The second stage features a pageant of maskers riding asses and symbolizing the months of the year. The third stage is marked by the pageant of the Death of Carnival, represented by a masked youth carried through the village in a coffin. All three stages symbolize the struggle between the moral and the immoral, joy and sadness, life and death. The other rural carnivals are burlesque processions based on local legendary themes. On the whole, they derive from agrarian rituals intended to ensure prosperity.

The most beautiful of the urban carnivals are found at Venice, including a pageant of gondolas on the Grand Canal, and at Rome, where floats fill the large squares of the capital. Both carnivals symbolize the sheer joy of life freed from the encumbrances of modern urban living.

Carnival games in central Europe, especially in Hungary, developed under the influence of both the Eastern and Western churches. The Roman Catholic carnival at Carême (Lent) has never reached the size or the diversity of its Western counterparts, although it was patronized by both the royal court and the church. Carnival performances in the villages, although imbued with Christian elements, are more often representative of the native traditions of Hungary. Of the many carnival performances, the most significant are the dance of the Cszoban, in which masked shepherds sing carols at

Christmas; the performance of Csömör, involving wooden masks *(buso)* and deafening noises for driving away evil spirits that cause sensual passions; the spectacle of the Matraalmas, a ceremony involving the drowning of a large doll as the symbolic destruction of illness and death; and the impressive pageantry of the masks at Easter at Calgamacsa.

In eastern Europe carnivals take a rather different form. Communities do not celebrate single, unified festivals, nor are the carnivals the product of a single group of maskers. Instead, one finds several different carnival groups, each acting in its own way. Nevertheless, there remains an underlying unity of purpose. Particularly interesting are the winter and spring carnivals held in villages and the smaller carnival performances at Whitsuntide and Midsummer Day. From Poland and Romania to as far as Greece, virtually identical prosopophories, masquerades, and carnival performances take place at the solstices and equinoxes. Although Poland is Roman Catholic, many Eastern Orthodox rituals, ceremonies, and traditions are found among its prosopophories and masquerades. The various performances can be seen to vary slightly in form as one moves from province to province.

At Opole (Silesia) in Poland, the carnival begins with the drowning of Marzamma, a life-size doll, which symbolizes the drowning of winter and the coming of spring. Around Cracow, groups of maskers disguised as old men and old women, Dziady and Baba, wearing straw costumes, enter the courtyards of the peasants, perform various antics, and receive gifts from the onlookers.

In European Russia, the situation was different. At Christmas and the New Year, one traditionally found processions of masked carolers that were striking by virtue of the central role played by an integral mask of a bear, made of pea pods or occasionally of bear's skin. The bear was led about, accompanied by an old man, an old woman, and a person wearing a mask of a she-goat, he-goat, or horse. The old man was hunchbacked and wore a mask made of birch tree rind. From the various forms of the carol, which was dedicated to the she-goat or he-goat, one can see the magical role that these masks played in an agricultural community. (The he-goat symbolized virility and the she-goat fertility. In the case of the Russians, as also with the Poles and Romanians, the magical roles of the she-goat and he-goat were taken up by the folk theater at the beginning of the twentieth century.) These carols in Belorussia, accompanied by he-goat masks, resemble the masked pantomimes of demonic he-goats found in Scandinavia, which survived until the eighteenth century, undoubtedly because they were combined with rituals celebrating the cult of mythical ancestors.

The New Year's procession found in Belorussia and Polesia is similar to that in Bulgaria, Serbia, and Romania. In Belorussia, the European Russians traditionally held masquerades at the winter solstice that in most cases ended with theatrical sketches. At Shrovetide, they, like the Ukrainians, organized village troika races in which the competitors were sometimes masked in order to avoid favoritism in selecting the winner. At one time, the carnival at Shrovetide in Romania, Yugoslavia, Bulgaria, and Greece was an elaborate affair. Groups of young people wearing fanciful zoomorphic and anthropomorphic masks walked around the villages and took all sorts of liberties with their fellow villagers and with the local authorities.

The summer carnivals show a remarkable ethnic consistency across southeastern Europe. The carnival performances of the Horsemen (Călușarii) at Whitsuntide among the Romanians, as well as the ritual of Sancta Diana (Rom., Sânziana), represent an archaic complex of magical rituals associated with cults of the sun and moon, earth, and fertility. The procession of the Brezaia, a fantastic Romanian mask that resembles the Perchten of Austria and the Habergeis of Germany, takes place around Epiphany and symbolizes the rebirth of nature. This mask is probably of Indo-European origin.

A little less complex, but just as archaic, are the carnival performances of the Bulgarian Kukkers, the Serbian Korentis, and the Greek Kalogeros. These three carnivals, the remnants of ancient prosopophories, upset the peace of the villages of southeastern Europe for a week at a time with their music, dances, and hubbub. Autumnal carnival performances took place until the end of the nineteenth century or the beginning of the twentieth century, especially at harvest and at village rituals performed to protect the domestic animals against demonic spirits.

The most beautiful carnivals are often the winter carnivals. Among the southeastern Europeans, the beginning of the winter festivities is marked by Christmas carols for Father Christmas or Santa Claus, which are followed by carols for Jack Frost at the New Year. Coming in between are various spectacles and the carols of individual carolers, who may or may not wear masks. The winter festivities also include popular observances on Saint Demeter's Day (or Saint Martin's Summer); on Saint Mina's Day (the shepherd's holiday in Greece); on Saint Andrew's Day, with its antidemonic rituals against wraiths and witches; and on Saint Nicholas's Day, when gifts are given to children and masked parties are held. The most impressive ceremonial and ritual manifestations, however, take place at Christmas and the New Year. At Christmas, children go from house to house wearing masks and carrying a big star fixed on a stick or performing a folk drama depicting Herod (Rom., Irozii) and caroling. The winter carnival culminates in the New Year's procession of the she-goat, found throughout southeastern Europe. Especially in Romania, this procession can be most ostentatious and entertaining. In Moldavia, for instance, the train of the procession traditionally contains about two hundred different masks, each associated with its own dance and dramatic sketch. The winter carnival is dominated by the rural theater pageants with their tragicomic plays. Most common are sketches involving outlaws or, in modern times, a satellite (in a science-fiction sketch introduced after the first successful launch into space). While these pageants are being held, children go caroling and confer New Year's blessings on their neighbors, accompanied by a figure in a bear's mask (Vasilca). The winter carnival in Bulgaria is dominated by the Sirvaskari and the children carolers as well as by figures of an old man and an old woman. In Yugoslavia, groups of carolers armed with staves go about wearing masks made of animal hides. They go caroling with masked figures portraying camels (Gambelas) and goats (Klocalica) with the Zvoncari (figures wearing an assortment of bells), and with the Gaffer and the Gammer ("old man," "old woman"). Here, as elsewhere in southeastern Europe, some of these masked figures are considered attractive, others ugly.

In Greece, during the twelve days between Christmas and Epiphany, there are masquerades of mummers and the Rhoghatsaria and Kallikantzaroi. The latter are masks of evil spirits that come out of the earth at Christmas and return to it at Epiphany. They belong to neo-Hellenic Christian mythology and represent either centaurs who come out of the ground to punish the wicked, unjust, and avaricious, or souls of the dead who inhabit Hades and visit the earth in order to torture the living. The steps taken by the Greeks to protect themselves from the Kallikantzaroi are somewhat similar to those taken by others on Saint Andrew's Day.

[*See also* Carnival.]

BIBLIOGRAPHY

Campbell, Joseph. *The Masks of God*, vol. 3, *Occidental Mythology*. New York, 1964. Presents the theoretical aspects of the so-called masks of God and their leading role in early Western cultures (Hellenism and Byzantium) and points out the spiritual dialogue between Europe and the Levant.

Eliade, Mircea. "Masks: Mythical and Ritual Origins." In *Encyclopedia of World Art*, vol. 9, pp. 521–525. London, 1964. A synthesis of the mythical and ritual genesis of masks in ancient times, folk medieval traditions, and modern and contemporary periods. The most significant masks are those that reflect all the levels of cosmic life represented in the rites, ceremonies, and festivities in which they are used.

Gaignebet, Claude, and Marie-Claude Florentin. "Le carnaval: Essai de mythologie populaire." In *Le regard de l'histoire*, edited by Claude Mettra. Paris, 1974. Refers to the folk calendar of winter and spring carnivals in Europe, of the time, place, structure, and magico-mythical function of the carnivalesque bestiary and folk liturgy.

Megas, George A. *Greek Calendar Customs*. 2d ed. Athens, 1963. A general abstract concerning contemporary Greek customs and traditions, presented in relation to their Hellenistic substratum.

Moszynski, Kazimierz. *Kultura ludowa slowian*. 2 vols. Cracow, 1929–1930. Dedicated to Slavic religious culture, these general comparative historical surveys make reference to the folk masks of the festival calendar that are found in processions and masquerades.

Pereira, Benjamin. *Mascaras portuguesas*. Lisbon, 1973. A study of Portuguese masks describing the popular festivities in which they are found.

Schmidt, Leopold, ed. *Masken in Mitteleuropa: Volkskundliche Beiträge zur europäischen Maskenforschung*. Vienna, 1955. The first anthology on the folk masks of central Europe. Each contributor offers a micromonograph concerning his country (Austria, Bavaria, Switzerland, Poland, Slovenia, and Hungary).

Vulcanescu, Romulus. *Măștile populare*. Bucharest, 1970. An extensive monograph of Romanian folk masks as magico-mythological instruments for camouflaging, masquerading, and transfiguring folk religiosity, from the Neolithic period to the modern age. Romanian folk masks are examined within the context of the evolution of Romanian folk culture and are compared with the history of masks in eastern and southeastern Europe. Discusses the magical significance of the prophylactic and funerary use of masks and the conditions and forms resulting from reciprocal influences between Romania and its neighbors.

ROMULUS VULCANESCU

MAṢLAḤAH is the Arabic term for the Islamic concept of public interest or general welfare of the community of Muslims. Consideration for the public interest (*istiṣlāḥ*) is held by Muslim legal scholars to be ancillary to the four canonical sources of Islamic law, namely the Qur'ān; the *sunnah*, or normative behavior of the Prophet; *ijmā'*, or the historical consensus of the community; and *qiyās*, analogical extension of accepted law or judgment. Although these sources are meant to provide guidelines for all eventualities, there have always been instances that seem to require abandoning either the specific ordinances of the Qur'ān and *sunnah* or the results of analogical reasoning, because of the overriding nature of the public interest.

In positive or applied law, considerations of *maṣlaḥah* in social and economic matters have usually led to the inclusion of pre-Islamic or non-Islamic local laws and customs in regional legal practice. Historically, the concept of *maṣlaḥah* has been associated more often with the Mālikī school than with the other Sunnī schools of law. This is largely due to the attention the Mālikī scholars of Morocco have given it in their recognition of the validity of local practice (*'amal*), even though they thereby allow institutions that strict Mālikī theory would reject. But the association of *maṣlaḥah* with the Mālikīyah should not be overemphasized; all Sunnī schools of law have contributed to its development and utilization.

The early and medieval Muslim scholars who wrote on *maṣlaḥah* defined it in various ways. Some approached it purely from a practical point of view; others considered it a problem of the philosophy of law and discussed its moral and ethical aspects. They all indicated, however, that the investigation of *maṣlaḥah* involved concern for the spirit rather than the letter of the law. Focusing on this feature of *maṣlaḥah*, a few twentieth-century Muslim reformers have put forward the idea of redefining *maṣlaḥah* in terms of the needs of contemporary society and then using *istiṣlāḥ* as a vehicle for modernizing and revitalizing Islamic law. Thus far, at least, their efforts have not been successful.

BIBLIOGRAPHY

Aghnides, Nicolas P. *Muhammadan Theories of Finance*. New York, 1916. Very useful and detailed introduction to the sources of Islamic law.

Kerr, Malcolm H. *Islamic Reform: The Political and Legal Theories of Muhammed Abduh and Rashid Rida*. Berkeley, 1966. Discusses the history of *maṣlaḥah* and some modern attempts to utilize it for Islamic reform.

Schacht, Joseph. *An Introduction to Islamic Law*. Oxford, 1964. The authoritative general introduction, with a very valuable bibliography.

SUSAN A. SPECTORSKY

MASORAH. *See* Biblical Literature, *article on* Hebrew Scriptures.

MASPERO, HENRI (1883–1945), French Sinologist and pioneer of Taoist studies. Son of the Egyptologist Gaston Maspero, Henri Maspero did his first research in 1904 in Cairo on the financial system of ancient Egypt. In 1907 he obtained his *licence en droit* and his diploma in Chinese. From 1908 to 1920, he was a member of the École Française d'Extrême-Orient (EFEO) and was stationed in Hanoi, whence he traveled extensively throughout Southeast Asia and China. He was in Peking during the winter of 1908–1909, at the time of the death of Emperor Te-tsung and the Dowager Empress Ts'u-hsi, and he witnessed some of the ensuing revolutionary agitation. His research and publications covered an amazing range of subjects: the administrative geography of ancient Indochina, the beginnings of Buddhism in China, Chinese epigraphy, history of law, architecture, art, and astronomy, as well as linguistics. His articles on the Thai languages and on the phonetics of Annamese were the first serious studies of Southeast Asian languages. The Chinese elements in Annamese led him, before Bernhard Karlgren, to the study of ancient Chinese phonology.

In 1914, on a study mission to China, Maspero began an investigation of contemporary Chinese religious life, which he continued among Chinese expatriates in France during World War I. This fieldwork enabled him later to describe the modern Chinese folk religion in a remarkably lively fashion.

Maspero initiated and supervised, until 1920, the vast EFEO collection of Indochinese documents, a unique repository of the history of this region. Some of this material served him for comparative studies on modern Thai and ancient Chinese religion, studies that confirmed the results of Marcel Granet's epoch-making work (1919) on the *Book of Odes*. [*See the biography of Granet*.]

In 1920 Maspero was recalled to Paris and appointed the successor of Édouard Chavannes at the Collège de France. The only book he published in his lifetime, *La Chine antique* (1927), is a history of China from the beginnings to the third century BCE. The remaining years of his life were devoted to a thorough preparation of a second volume dealing with Chinese history up to the T'ang dynasty.

The summaries of Maspero's courses at the Collège de France (1921–1944) show that, among many other aspects of Sinology that he treated in numerous articles, he was most interested during this period in the emergence of the Taoist religion. This was virgin territory, uncharted not only by Western scholars but also by Chinese scholars, who traditionally had despised everything Taoist except the philosophers Lao-tzu and Chuang-tzu. In 1926 the sole remaining complete set of the Taoist canon was published in 1,120 Chinese-style volumes. Maspero was the first to start extracting from this huge store of documents (dating from the fourth century BCE, in the case of the early Taoist mystical writings, to the sixteenth century CE) a chronology of texts and a coherent history of the origins and the first five centuries of the Taoist religion. He discovered that this religion, far from being the popular hodgepodge of superstitions described by missionaries, or the illiterate and seditious demon-worship denounced by the Chinese scholarly elite, was in fact the native high religion of all classes of Chinese society, with a literate tradition going back to the second century CE. Realizing the importance in Taoism of physiological longevity techniques and of mystical techniques for gaining union with the Tao (and participating in its immortality), Maspero devoted a detailed study to them.

On 27 July 1944, Maspero was expected in vain at a session of the Académie des Inscriptions et Belle-Lettres, of which he was president at the time. He had been arrested by the German occupation forces because of his son's activities in the French Resistance. On 15 August 1944, he was aboard the last prisoner transport to Germany before the liberation of Paris. He succumbed to disease amid the horrors of Buchenwald on 17 March 1945, less than one month before the liberation of this concentration camp by American troops.

BIBLIOGRAPHY

Maspero's *La Chine antique* (Paris, 1924) has been translated as *China in Antiquity* (Amherst, Mass., 1979), and the majority of Maspero's studies on Taoism have been collected in *Le taoïsme et les religions chinoises* (Paris, 1971), translated as *Taoism and Chinese Religion* (Amherst, Mass., 1981). Among Maspero's writings on Buddhism are "Le songe et l'ambassade de l'empereur Ming" and "Communautés et moines bouddhistes chinois au deuxième et troisième siècles," both of which appear in the *Bulletin de l'École Française d'Extrême-Orient* (Hanoi) 10 (1910): 95–130 and 222–232, respectively, and "Les origines de la communauté bouddhiste de Lo-yang," *Journal asiatique* 225 (1934): 88–107. On mythology and popular religion, see "Légendes mythologiques dans le *Chou king*," *Journal asiatique* 204 (1924): 1–100; "The Mythology of Modern China," in *Asiatic Mythology*, edited by Joseph Hackin and others (New York, 1932); and "Les ivoires chinois et l'iconographie populaire," in *Les ivoires religieux et médicaux chinois d'après la collection Lucien Lion*, edited by Maspero, René Grousset, and Lucien Lion (Paris, 1939).

An obituary by Paul Demiéville, including a useful bibliography, appears in *Journal asiatique* 234 (1943–1945): 245–280, and Demiéville's summary of Maspero's contribution to Chinese studies, "Henri Maspero et l'avenir des études chinoises," can be found in *T'oung pao* 38 (1947): 16–42.

ANNA SEIDEL

MASS. *See* Eucharist.

MASSIGNON, LOUIS (1883–1962), French Islamicist. Louis-Fernand-Jules Massignon grew up in Paris, where he enrolled at the university and pursued various disciplines, including Arabic. He spent most of the period 1906–1910 studying in Cairo and carrying out research in Iraq and Istanbul, and in 1912–1913 he was visiting professor at the Egyptian (later Cairo) University. In 1922 he submitted his two requisite doctoral theses on al-Ḥallāj and early Islamic mysticism to the University of Paris; published in two volumes as *La passion d'al-Hosayn-ibn-Mansour al'Hallâj, martyr mystique de l'Islam exécuté à Bagdad le 26 mars 922* (1922), his *thèse principale* has since become a classic. A second, greatly enlarged edition appeared posthumously (1975). In 1926 Massignon was elected professor of sociology and sociography of Islam at the Collège de France in Paris, and in 1933 he was appointed director of studies for Islam at the École Pratique des Hautes Études, also in Paris, in the section of *sciences religeuses*. In the same year he was elected a member of the new Academy of the Arabic Language in Cairo, where he spent several weeks working each winter.

Born and raised a Roman Catholic, Massignon underwent a particular inner experience in 1908, which he spoke of as his "conversion." As a result he became once more a loyal member of the Roman Catholic church, increasingly with a spiritual vocation with regard to Islam. In 1931 he became a third-order Franciscan, and in 1934 he founded the Badaliya sodality, the members of which were inspired by compassion and devoted themselves to "substitution" for their Muslim brethren. (The idea of substitution involves one person's taking another's suffering upon himself.) After joining the Greek Catholic (Uniate) church in 1949, Massignon was ordained a priest on 28 January 1950 in Cairo. Even though ordination in this church is possible for a married man, as Massignon was, the Vatican imposed the condition that Massignon's priesthood, which turned out to be an essential element in his spiritual life and vocation, should remain secret. Even after his retirement in 1954 Massignon continued to take an active part in defending victims of violence (e.g., Palestinians and Algerians) until his death on 31 October 1962 in Paris.

Massignon's work is the accomplishment and creation of a mind of remarkable stature, illuminated by flashes of genius but capable of being carried away, to the verge of aberration, by ideas. A reader is confronted with the difficult task of recognizing the particular perspectives in which Massignon interpreted his subject matter and correcting them according to the scholarly criteria of factual interpretation and validity. If Massignon's unique spiritual commitments made his oeuvre one of the richest in the whole field of Islamic studies, one must recognize that it drew its strength from an existential position unrelated to scholarship. While its originality deserves respect and admiration, the lack of scholarly standards must also be recognized.

Massignon's monumental study of al-Ḥallāj will probably remain his lasting contribution to the study of Islam and religion generally. It is more than a careful historical reconstruction of facts and bygone spiritual worlds. It is the record of a spiritual encounter in which a scholar fascinated by a religious truth meets a mystic of the past in whom this truth is recognized. Were it not for Massignon, such spiritual dimensions might not have been revealed in al-Ḥallāj, but to what extent the spiritual al-Ḥallāj discovered by Massignon is the result of valid hermeneutics of the texts and not a spiritual creation born of the religious needs and passions of Massignon as a person is a question that haunts the reader. Massignon's inner experiences of May and June 1908, as a result of which he received a "new life" of adoration and witnessing, welded together for him the figures of al-Ḥallāj and Christ, the existence of God and the experience of divine grace. Thereafter, al-Ḥallāj, Christ, and their witness Louis Massignon could no longer be separated either by Massignon himself or by those studying his reconstruction of the Hallajian drama.

Massignon's second contribution is his precise technical investigation of the religious, particularly the mystical, vocabulary in Islam. Apart from his claim that the spiritual realities to which these words allude can be rediscovered through the study of the words themselves—and that the researcher at a certain moment finds himself confronted precisely with that reality to which the mystic testifies—his technical achievements were enormous and have inspired such scholars as Paul Nwyia to proceed with their researches on religious vocabulary along the same line.

Massignon's third major contribution is to have succeeded, in a period of ever-growing specialization, in retaining a global view of what may be called the world of Islam in its various material and spiritual dimensions. He could see it all as forming a meaningful whole under the sign of Islam, just as he could see Islam as meaningful in the perspective of al-Ḥallāj. Thus his "minor works," collected in *Opera minora* (1963), include articles on widely varying subjects. Throughout these articles we find a complex hermeneutics of texts, personalities, and ideas directed to revealing not only their literary, historical, and semantic meanings but also their spiritual intentions. In his hermeneutical research, Massignon showed both an immense erudition and an extraordinary sensitivity, particularly to religious and devotional realities. His sensitivity extended to those realities that exist partly in the realm of dreams and partly in that of fact, realities to which the religious mind and what was once commonly called the "Oriental mind" are so attuned.

BIBLIOGRAPHY

Massignon's principal work is his monumental study of al-Ḥallāj, the second, greatly expanded version of which appeared posthumously in four volumes (Paris, 1975), and has been translated by Herbert Mason as *The Passion of al-Hallāj: Mystic and Martyr of Islam*, 4 vols. (Princeton, 1982). Another classic study is his *Essai sur les origines du lexique technique de la mystique musulmane*, 3d ed. (Paris, 1968), which deals with the development of mystical vocabulary during the first centuries of Islam. A number of mystical texts were edited by Massignon in his *Recueil de textes inédits concernant l'histoire de la mystique en pays d'Islam* (Paris, 1929). A translation of al-Ḥallāj's poems, the *Dîwân* (1955; reprint, Paris, 1981), was also published by Massignon. Of Massignon's other books, mention should be made of *Mission en Mésopotamie, 1907–1908*, 2 vols. (Cairo, 1910–1912), and of the various editions of the important *Annuaire du monde musulman* that were compiled by Massignon (1st ed., Paris, 1922–1923; 2d ed., Paris, 1926; 3d ed., Paris, 1929; 4th ed., Paris, 1954). (The last of these volumes was accomplished with the collaboration of Vincent Monteil.) A collection, edited by Youakim Moubarac, of 205 of Massignon's articles has been published under the title *Opera minora*, 3 vols. (1963; reprint, Paris, 1969); two more volumes have been announced.

Bibliographies of works by and about Massignon appear in Youakim Moubarac's *L'œuvre de Louis Massignon* (Beirut, 1972), pp. 7–107; the book is, however, difficult both to find and to use, and is incomplete. A definitive bibliography with complete references has yet to be compiled. Most accessible at present is the succinct bibliography given in my *L'Islam dans le miroir de l'Occident*, 3d ed. (The Hague, 1970), pp. 351–358. These bibliographies may be supplemented by that contained in Guy Harpigny's penetrating study of Massignon's work and spirituality, *Islam et christianisme selon Louis Massignon* (Louvain-la-Neuve, 1981), pp. 295–301. To celebrate the one hundredth anniversary of Massignon's birth, UNESCO issued a useful brochure entitled *Centenaire de la naissance de Louis Massignon, 1883–1962* (Paris, 1983).

JACQUES WAARDENBURG

MATERIALISM. As a philosophical doctrine, materialism can be given a deceptively simple definition: the view that matter is all there is. The simplicity is deceptive because, of course, the term *matter* can itself be understood in so many different ways. It is more illuminating, perhaps, to define materialism in terms of what it denies. It excludes the existence of entities that are radically different in kind from, and in some sense superior to, the matter of our ordinary experience. It rejects, therefore, a God or gods on whom the universe would depend for its existence or mode of operation; it denies the existence of angels or spirits that can affect the material order while ultimately escaping its limitations; it questions the notion of a soul, if taken to be an immaterial entity separable in principle from the human body it informs. Its two main targets are, therefore, theism and dualistic views of human nature.

Materialism has, in the past, usually derived from one or the other of two sources. The first is the conviction that the world can be understood in terms of a single set of categories derived from our everyday physical experience, without having to introduce a second set of "immaterial" entities of an altogether different kind. The second is the criticism of organized religion on the grounds of its superstitious or politically oppressive character and a linking of religion with belief in gods, angels, souls, miracles. The former allies materialism with naturalism. The stress in both is on "natural" modes of explanation; "supernatural" forms of action are rejected as unnecessary or even incoherent. Materialism also resembles reductionism, since both seek to reduce the diversity of the explanations offered for events in the world to a single category, or at least to a minimal number of categories. There are, for the same reasons, overtones in it of positivism, at least to the extent that both lay stress on science as the only legitimate source of knowledge about the causalities of the world. Where classic materialism would differ from these other philosophic emphases would be mainly in the specificity of its objections to the category of "spirit" on which religious belief is taken to rely.

Beginnings. It is to Aristotle (384–322 BCE) that we owe the first explicit articulation of a concept of "matter," that is, an underlying substratum to which reference must be made in explaining physical change. Aristotle criticizes the Ionian physicists, his predecessors of two centuries earlier, because of their supposedly exclusive reliance on a common underlying "stuff" (water, air, fire) in explaining change in nature. Such a stuff would retain its own identity throughout all change; substantial change would, therefore, be excluded and the apparently fundamental differences between different kinds (different species of animal, for instance) would be reduced to mere differences in arrangement of the fundamental "stuff." Aristotle rejected this "materialist" doctrine. But he did not believe the Ionians to be materialists. He notes that Thales thought all things to be "full of gods" and to be in some sense "ensouled"; similar views are attributed to the other major figures in the early Ionian tradition. Though these men made the first known attempt to explain physical changes in a systematic way, they did not question the traditional explanatory roles of the gods and of soul.

A century later, the founders of atomism, Leucippus and Democritus, came much closer to a clear-cut materialist doctrine. Their view that all things consist of "atoms," imperceptibly small, indivisible, eternal, and unchanging entities, derived from the metaphysical arguments of Parmenides regarding the One, not from an empirical starting-point in observation. Change is nothing more than the movement and redistribution of atoms in the void. The planets, the stars, and even the earth itself have come to be by the aggregating of vortices of atoms. Since space is infinite, there will be infinitely many worlds produced in this way. Sensation is to be understood in purely physical terms; the soul itself consists of atoms, admittedly smaller and finer than even the particles of fire, but still of the same general kind as other atoms. All interaction is thus mechanical and explanation in terms of final causes is prohibited. Yet the atomists do not appear to have excluded the gods. Though Democritus is critical of those who would base ethical behavior on religious sanctions, he does seem to allow that the gods may visit men. This may, of course, have been no more than a concession to the orthodoxy of the day. Yet it would seem more likely that he had not yet reduced the gods, as he had done soul, to matter.

Epicurus (341–270 BCE) took this further step. The gods are situated in the intervals between the innumerable universes; they too must be composed of atoms, and they live in a state of bliss undisturbed by the affairs of mortals. Lucretius (99–55 BCE) popularized the teachings of Epicurus in the Roman world through his great poem, *De rerum natura,* which was the most complete expression of materialist doctrine in ancient times. The gods here seem to be dismissed entirely; insofar as there is a deity it is nature itself. Lucretius views the state religion of Rome as a primarily political institution and sees no reason for any exception to the atomist claim that all there is, is atoms and void.

The Renaissance. With the growth of Christianity, the attraction of Epicurean materialism diminished. During the Middle Ages, atomism was sometimes discussed by philosophers, but the Aristotelian arguments against it seemed overwhelming. There could be no serious defense of materialism in an age when the influence of spirit, in all its forms, seemed so palpable and when no plausible argument had been found for the claim that all change can be explained in atomic or material terms only. It was only when the "new science" of mechanics made its appearance in the seventeenth century that the outlines of an argument became faintly visible. Galileo and Descartes took for granted that matter is composed of a multitude of tiny corpuscles whose properties ("primary qualities") are precisely those required to make them subject to, and entirely predictable by, mechanical law. There was no real evidence for this, but it seemed plausible to extend the realm of the new mathematicized mechanics to the very small and thus make all types of physical change explicable, perhaps, in mechanical terms.

Pierre Gassendi (1592–1655) could now revive the ancient Epicurean atomism and present it as the best available (though admittedly hypothetical) scientific explanation of the sensory qualities of things. However, he did not carry his Epicureanism all the way to materialism; though an opponent of the claims to demonstrative knowledge made by scholastics and Cartesians alike, he was not disaffected with religion and saw no reason to extend atomism to the soul or to use it to deny the need for a creator God. His friend Thomas Hobbes (1588–1679) had no such scruples. A severe critic of institutional religion, he argued that mechanical modes of explanation must be extended not only to sensation but to thought, which is no more than the motion of material particles in the brain. Nothing other than body can exist, so that God, if he exists (and Hobbes's real views on this issue are very difficult to discover), must be corporeal.

Reductive Materialism. If all material things are to be understood by a single set of laws, the general laws of mechanics, it would follow that human action, too, can be reduced to mechanical law. This is the conclusion Hobbes reached; Descartes avoided it only by placing within man an immaterial mind. Reductive materialism or sharp dualism—these seemed to be the only options, if one decided to bring the entire domain of physical interaction under one science. Most philosophers of the seventeenth and eighteenth centuries found the alternatives unappealing, but it was not at all evident where a stable solution might be found. In France, where reaction against royal as well as ecclesiastical authority continued to mount, reductive materialism found favor with a number of writers, of whom the most original was Denis Diderot (1713–1784), editor of the great *Encyclopedia*. Influenced by George-Louis Buffon's *Natural History* (1749), he speculated about the sort of developmental laws that might have brought about the organic world we know from an initial chaos of material particles. A number of medical writers, of whom the most notable was Julien de La Mettrie (1709–1751), were at the same time developing a materialist physiology in which human action is reduced to simple mechanical causes. Paul d'Holbach (1723–1789), on the other hand, was much more metaphysical in his approach. His *Système de la nature* (1770) was the most thoroughgoing materialist statement of the century; in it, the two sources of classic materialism are especially evident: a conviction that because matter is one, only one sort of explanation is permissible, and a strong hostility to religion.

But the weaknesses of this kind of material monism were still evident. The claims to explain in mechanical terms the operations of the human body, to reduce sensation and thought to mechanical action between molecules, and to derive the profusion of organic species from an original undifferentiated matter were still almost entirely promissory. Materialism was still, at best, a program, not an achieved philosophy. To become something more, a genuine materialist science would have to be available to serve as support. And one of the fundamental premises of classic materialism, its reductionist principle, might have to be abandoned.

Major philosophers of the day were struck by the crudity, as they saw it, of the materialist doctrine. Hegel, in particular, attacked the mechanistic presuppositions of Newtonian science, its assumption that all motion can be explained by the single science of mechanics. In its stead, he attempted to construct a philosophy of nature and a theory of history in which spirit is the moving force. Motion involves contradiction, since for it to occur, a body has to be "both here and not here at the same time." Thus, contradiction pervades both nature and society; it is out of the consequent struggle and opposition that advance comes.

Dialectical Materialism. The most influential form of nonreductive materialism is undoubtedly that of Marx and Engels. Marx took over much of the structure of Hegel's account of society and of social change, retaining the discontinuities of the Hegelian "dialectical" method, but inverting the order of matter and mind. Mind originates from matter (as the reductive materialists had held), but in a discontinuous way that makes it irreducible to the categories of matter (which they had denied). Beliefs in God or in an immortal soul are no more than the projections of those who would rationalize an unjust social order instead of trying to change it. All knowledge of the world and of society must be based on sense experience and ultimately on science.

Marx's "historical materialism" is restricted to human history; by taking economic and industrial factors as the fundamental agencies of change, Marx believed that he could give a thoroughly "materialist" (i.e., empirical, naturalistic, scientific) account of history. Engels went on to a broader focus on nature. His "dialectical materialism" (as Plekhanov later called it) is first and foremost a philosophy of nature in the Hegelian tradition. He rejects Ludwig Büchner's claim that the sciences alone suffice; in Engels's view (and this has become a central tenet of Marxist-Leninist thought), positivism is inadequate because the sciences have to be supplemented by a unified and guiding philosophy. This philosophy is "dialectical" because it recognizes the presence of contradictions and of discontinuous change in nature and is unified insofar as it proposes a scheme that can grasp things in their totality. Engels characterizes as "idealist" any philosophical view that would deny that mind and spirit must originate from matter. Thus, anyone who believes in a transcendent God or in the dualism of soul (mind) and body would automatically qualify as "idealist" in this new sense.

The attempt on the part of Marx and Engels to "materialize Hegel" led to notable internal strain (many have argued, incoherence) within the materialism they proposed. On the one hand, there is the stress on the primacy of sense-experience (which is said to "reflect" the world) and consequently of science. On the other, the dialectical element (which is crucial to Marx's political theory) is difficult to sustain by science alone, unless it be almost emptied of content. This tension is even more evident in Lenin's version of dialectical materialism, which tries to mediate between positivism and Hegelian idealism, utilizing a rather naive realist epistemology.

Christianity and Materialism. The progress of science since the mid-nineteenth century has undercut the older reductive materialism by showing that the categories of mechanics at any one time are never definitive and that there are, besides, different levels of explanation that are probably not reducible to one another, not in the sense in which reduction was supposed to be possible, at least. On the other hand, the progress of science has also demonstrated the strength of the naturalistic program of explanation. More and more, it seems possible to explain the entire order of nature in a single interlinked set of categories that leave no gaps "of principle" into which a different order of causality has to be interposed in order to render a coherent account of world process. It is hard *not* to be a "naturalist" in that sense.

Nonetheless, there are unsolved philosophical problems about the relation of mind and body, about the reality of human freedom in a world scientifically fully explicable, that have led to the formulation of alternatives besides that of a sophisticated nonreductive materialism, alternatives that would still maintain a broadly naturalist orientation. These would differ from materialism in the degree of stress they would lay on causal categories that derive from the domain of mind and freedom rather than from that of mechanical action even if the term *mechanical* be construed as broadly as it could plausibly be.

When naturalism/materialism is carried to the point of denying the possibility of a creator God or an afterlife for man, a conflict with religious, and specifically with Christian, belief is unavoidable. Christian theologians, however, have gone to some lengths to try to show that the notions of the natural order as sufficient in its own right, or of resurrection as independent of a strong dualism of soul and body, are perfectly compatible with—indeed entirely faithful to—the Christian tradition. The grounds for the materialist exclusion in principle of God or of a personal afterlife are thus brought into question.

Some have gone further to argue the propriety of a "Christian materialism" that would draw on the positive insights of the materialist tradition, particularly in its Marxist form. Such a view would suggest that all that happens in nature and in history is in principle explicable at its own level without directly invoking the intervening agency of God. "Christian materialism" would note and deplore the manner in which Christianity, like other religions, has often allowed itself to become the ideological legitimation of structures of social domination. It would oppose the "idealism" that would make Christianity a set of doctrines to be believed rather than a doctrine of redemption that finds its reality first in action and transformation.

The limits of such a view are set by the Christian doctrines of the dependence of nature and history on divine grace and of the entrance of the Word of God, as man, into the human story. There would be the reality to acknowledge of a God whose action entirely transcends the categories of nature. And that is something that materialism cannot do without ceasing (it would seem) to be materialism.

[*See also* Empiricism; Idealism; Naturalism; Positivism; Skeptics and Skepticism; *and the biographies of Aristotle, Descartes, Hegel, Marx, and Newton. For discussion of religious beliefs and practices concerning the sacredness of matter, see* Earth.]

BIBLIOGRAPHY

The most detailed general history of materialism is still Friedrich Lange's *Geschichte des Materialismus* (Marburg, 1865), translated by E. C. Thomas as *The History of Materialism* (London, 1925). Many helpful essays will be found in *The Encyclopedia of Philosophy,* edited by Paul Edwards (New York, 1967); see, in particular, Keith Campbell's "Materialism"; H. B. Acton's "Dialectical Materialism" and "Historical Materialism"; G. E. R. Lloyd's "Leucippus and Democritus"; R. S. Peters's "Hobbes, Thomas"; and Norman L. Torrey's "Diderot, Denis." For a survey of the varied roles played by the concept of matter in the history of philosophy and of science, see *The Concept of Matter,* edited by me (Notre Dame, Ind., 1963), especially the essay by Nicholas Lobkowicz, "Materialism and

Matter in Marxism-Leninism," pp. 430–464. For further reading on Marxist versions of materialism, see Gustav A. Wetter's *Der dialecktische Materialismus* (Vienna, 1952), translated by Peter Heath as *Dialectical Materialism* (London, 1958). For a useful historical study of the strains within the Soviet development of materialism, see David Joravsky's *Soviet Marxism and Natural Science, 1917–1932* (London, 1961). In his *A Matter of Hope: A Theologian's Reflections on the Thought of Karl Marx* (Notre Dame, Ind., 1982), Nicholas Lash defends the view that "it is the 'materialist' rather than the 'idealist' forms of Christianity which conform most closely to the demands of obedience to the gospel" (p. 148).

ERNAN MCMULLIN

MATERIALISTS, HINDU. *See* Cārvāka.

MATHER FAMILY. Members of three successive generations of the Mather family were Puritan ministers in the Massachusetts Bay Colony in New England: Richard (1596–1669), Increase (1629–1723), and Cotton (1663–1728). Each achieved fame as a preacher and writer, and collectively they exerted a formative influence on the religious life of colonial America.

Richard Mather, who was born in Lowton, near Liverpool, matriculated at Brasenose College, Oxford, in 1618 but studied there for only a few months. He was preaching at Toxteth Park when, late in 1633, he was removed from the pulpit. His offenses are not known, although they were doubtless ecclesiastical; he did not conform to the practices of the Church of England in all ways. He and his family then immigrated to Massachusetts Bay, arriving in mid-August 1635. The people of Dorchester, Massachusetts, after failing to organize a church in April 1636, succeeded in August of that year, and Mather was immediately called to the church as its teacher.

In the pulpit in Dorchester, Mather served quietly and faithfully. Although in most ways he probably resembled most Puritan ministers of his time in Massachusetts Bay Colony, in several notable accomplishments he differed. He published defenses of the "New England Way," as the church polity of the Bay Colony was called; he helped to write the Cambridge Platform (1648) defining ecclesiastical polity; he contributed to the definition of Puritan baptismal practice in the so-called Halfway Covenant (1662); and he served as an overseer of Harvard College.

Increase Mather, sixth son of Richard, was the outstanding minister of his generation. Born in Dorchester, he entered Harvard College when he was twelve years of age; after graduation he went to Ireland, where he took an M.A. at Trinity College, Dublin. Preaching followed at Torrington in Devonshire, to the garrison on Guernsey, and in Gloucester. However, his heterodox opinions made life in England dangerous for him after the Restoration, so in 1661 he returned to New England. There he was soon asked by the Second Church in Boston (Boston North Church) to fill its pulpit.

Increase Mather spent his life expounding the "New England Way." He was not an innovator in religion; like his father he defended nonseparating Congregationalism. But Increase Mather was a much more imaginative man than his father and a more passionate one. The Puritan vision of New England as a redemptive society was one of the passions of his life. He saw his American homeland as the one place on earth where true church polity might be established and the Protestant Reformation completed. The defense of New England carried him to England a second time shortly after the Glorious Revolution. He returned with a charter that protected much of the colony's—and its Congregational churches'—autonomy. Increase Mather's other achievements were varied: he acted as president of Harvard College; he wrote about science, especially astronomy; he advised governors; he helped to halt the persecution of those accused in the Salem witchcraft episode; and he preached and published on New England Christianity.

Cotton Mather was the first of Increase Mather's nine children. Although he never left New England, his visible achievements outnumbered those of his father. After a brilliant performance at Harvard College (A.B., 1678), Cotton Mather was ordained a minister in his father's church in 1685; the two served there together until Increase Mather's death almost forty years later. In 1689, while his father was in England securing a new charter for the colony, Cotton Mather played an important role in the expulsion of Sir Edmund Andros, governor of Massachusetts and head of the Dominion of New England. He also supported the witchcraft trials in Salem in 1692, although he was uneasy and had reservations about the proceedings.

Most of Cotton Mather's life was not spent in public affairs. He was a scholar of great learning and power and an immensely successful preacher. His learning extended to almost all fields of knowledge, although theology was the subject he knew most profoundly. Cotton Mather wrote histories, the greatest being his *Magnalia Christi Americana* (London, 1702), biographies (many first appearing in sermon form), scientific treatises, practical guides to medicine, prophetical works, and guides to conduct for the young, for sailors, and for almost every other order of society; most of his works, however, were sermons. He preached a "practical divinity," filled with exhortation and advice on the Christian life. Many of his sermons were intended to convert his listeners; others provided solace and nourishment to believers. Much of his work remains in manuscript, including "The Biblia Americana," his massive commentary on the scriptures.

Like his father, Cotton Mather was obsessed with the history and the future of New England. His great hope was that the second coming of Christ would take place in his lifetime and that New England would in reality prove to be the site of the New Jerusalem. He never surrendered his faith in the Congregationalism of his country, but he did come to preach an ecumenism embodied in his conception of a Christian Union, a worldwide league of believers. Cotton Mather earned a reputation in his day as a splendid preacher and scholar, but he was also widely disliked for the excesses of his style and expression. Despite his pride in his family and his attainments, he died feeling unappreciated and, to some extent, unfulfilled.

BIBLIOGRAPHY

The standard bibliographies of the works of the Mathers are those edited by Thomas J. Holmes: *The Minor Mathers: A List of Their Works* (Cambridge, Mass., 1940), for Richard Mather; *Increase Mather: A Bibliography of His Works,* 2 vols. (Cleveland, 1931); and *Cotton Mather: A Bibliography of His Works,* 3 vols. (Cambridge, Mass., 1940). Useful studies of the Mathers include Kenneth Murlock's *Increase Mather: The Foremost American Puritan* (Cambridge, Mass., 1926), my own *The Mathers: Three Generations of Puritan Intellectuals, 1596–1728* (New York, 1971), and Kenneth Silverman's *The Life and Times of Cotton Mather* (New York, 1984).

ROBERT MIDDLEKAUFF

MATRES.

MATRES. The *matres* or *matrae* ("mothers"), Celtic feminine divinities, are attested throughout the ancient continental and insular Celtic domain (with the exception of non-romanized Ireland) by abundant Romano-British and Gallo-Roman epigraphic and iconographic testimony. The word is Latin, but it can only be the translation or adaptation of a Celtic word, as the Gaulish inscription at Nimes consecrated to the *matrevo namausikavo* ("Nimesian mothers") witnesses. On the evidence, the *matres* as a group are very diverse, and it would be difficult to propose a single explanation for them. A *matre* may be conceived in terms of a particular locale, a certain function, or a principle and sphere of sovereignty. Specific instances are frequently multiple: the Suleviae, solar goddesses who have been unduly transformed into psychopomps; the Iunones, who are multiple forms of the Latin goddess Juno; the simple Triviae or Quadruviae, who watch over crossroads (but may not be truly Celtic).

Thus the term *matres* has come to designate several types of feminine divinities who are in some instances anything but mother goddesses or protectors of fecundity. At first, prior to the identifications and multiplications, there was certainly a single feminine divinity. Described briefly by Caesar under the name of Minerva in his account of Gaulish religion, she is at once mother, spouse, sister, and daughter of the gods.

This unique goddess in multiple form may be identified, in the context of Irish myth, with a range of feminine deities. There is Brighid, daughter of Daghdha, but also mother of the gods and protector of leeches, poets, and smiths. There is Boann, who is wife to Elcmhaire but bears a son to Daghdha. Also, and preeminently, there is Édaín, sovereign and ancestor of a long line of Irish kings. Further, there is Morríghan ("the great queen"), goddess of war and wife of Daghdha, she who washes the bloody remains of heroes who have died in combat. There is Macha ("plain" or "level land"), eponym of Emhain Mhacha, capital of Ulster. There is the gentle Fann ("swallow"), wife of the god Manannán, who loves and tempts Cú Chulainn, and there is Tailtiu ("earth"), foster mother of Lugh. Finally, there are the allegorical personifications of Ireland and queens of the Tuatha Dé Danann: Ériu, Banbha, and Fódla.

BIBLIOGRAPHY

Guyonvarc'h, Christian-J., and Françoise Le Roux. *Textes mythologiques irlandais,* vol. 1. Rennes, 1980.

Mac Cana, Proinsias. *Celtic Mythology.* Rev. ed. Feltham, England, 1983.

FRANÇOISE LE ROUX and CHRISTIAN-J. GUYONVARC'H
Translated from French by Erica Meltzer

MATTHEW THE EVANGELIST,

MATTHEW THE EVANGELIST, traditionally the author of the first canonical gospel, which bears his name. His exact dates are unknown, but the gospel was probably written in the last quarter of the first century, possibly in Syrian Antioch.

The name *Matthew* appears in every list of the twelve disciples of Jesus (*Mt.* 10:3, *Mk.* 3:18, *Lk.* 6:15, *Acts* 1:13). In the *Gospel of Matthew* Jesus calls him from his toll booth and his role as a despised tax collector to be a disciple (9:9–10), and in that gospel's list of the Twelve he is called Matthew the tax collector. Otherwise, Matthew does not appear in the gospel narratives or in the rest of the New Testament.

Mark 2:13–14 and *Luke* 5:27–28 relate the calling of a tax collector whose name is Levi, rather than Matthew (in *Mark* 2:14 he is called the son of Alphaeus; cf. "James the son of Alphaeus" in all the lists of the Twelve). Otherwise, the stories are quite similar, and in each case the call is followed by Jesus' eating at table with tax collectors and sinners and saying that he has come to call not righteous people, but sinners. (Tax collectors were regarded as egregious sinners, because the government sold the right to collect taxes to private entrepreneurs, who then realized as large a profit as possible at the expense of the public.)

The tradition of Matthean authorship of the first gospel has been questioned by critical scholarship for significant reasons. Matthew the tax collector turned disciple would have been an eyewitness of the events he narrates. Yet the close relationship between the narrative attributed to Matthew and that of Mark, which is generally accounted to be earlier, suggests that *Mark* was the principal narrative source. The fact that *Mark* was written in Greek (not Jesus and Matthew's native Aramaic) by someone who was not one of the Twelve makes it unlikely that the apostle Matthew would have relied upon it. Moreover, the gospel attributed to Matthew seems to have been written after the destruction of Jerusalem in the Roman War (AD 70; cf. *Mt.* 22:7), rather late for an apostolic writing. Quite possibly the name Matthew has been substituted for Levi in the call story of the first gospel, in which he is also singled out as the tax collector in the apostolic list.

Ancient church tradition, nevertheless, unanimously ascribes the gospel to the apostle Matthew. The fourth-century church historian Eusebius cites Papias (bishop of Hierapolis in Asia Minor during the first half of the second century) who wrote that "Matthew collected the sayings of the Lord in the Hebrew language, and each one interpreted them as he was able" (*Church History* 3.39.16). Later church authorities attribute a gospel to Matthew, agreeing that it was written in Hebrew. Matthew is frequently said to have preached among Hebrews. Interestingly, modern gospel criticism continues to see a pervasive Jewish or Jewish-Christian dimension in Matthew's gospel, whether in its tradition or intended audience. The statement of Papias concerning Matthew's collection of Jesus' sayings has sometimes been taken to refer to an earlier source (which can be discerned in *Matthew* and *Luke* and is usually called Q by biblical scholars) rather than to the present gospel. This interpretation avoids the difficulties of attributing the gospel to the apostle directly and helps to explain why the name of a relatively obscure figure became attached to the most prominent gospel, but it remains at best a plausible conjecture.

Legends about Matthew grew in time. He is said to have worked among gentiles in remote lands toward the end of his career. He came to be revered as a martyr (although tradition is not unanimous on this point), and he is commemorated in the Western church on 21 September. However, we know nothing for certain of his career or fate. Since the second century Matthew has been represented in Christian symbolism as a winged man, said by Irenaeus to represent the humanity of Christ.

BIBLIOGRAPHY

Aside from the New Testament the most important primary source is Eusebius's *Church History*, which brings together earlier testimony of Christian writers on the origin and authorship of the Gospels. The most convenient edition is the two-volume "Loeb Classical Library" text and translation of Kirsopp Lake, J. E. L. Oulton, and Hugh J. Lawlor (Cambridge, Mass., 1926).

The most important testimonies of patristic authors are collected in *The Gospel According to St. Matthew*, edited by A. H. McNeile (London, 1915), pp. xxx–xxxii. For a concise statement of the modern, critical view of Matthean authorship, see Werner G. Kümmel's *Introduction to the New Testament*, rev. ed. (Nashville, 1975), pp. 119–121. A more conservative, maximal statement of what can be known or conjectured about Matthew is Ronald Brownrigg's *The Twelve Apostles* (New York, 1974), pp. 141–159; although fascinating, it must be used with caution.

D. MOODY SMITH

MĀTURĪDĪ, AL- (d. AH 333/944 CE), more fully Abū Manṣūr al-Māturīdī; Islamic theologian and eponym of a school of theology that represented an intermediate position between that of the traditionalists and that of the Muʿtazilah, or advocates of rational investigation. He was born in Māturīd, apparently a locality in or near the Central Asian city of Samarkand. Under the Persian Samanid rulers (874–999) al-Māturīdī lived in a setting of intense cultural and intellectual activity. He was trained by scholars of the Ḥanafī school of Islamic law. Nothing else is known of his life except that he wrote thirteen books on theology, Qurʾān interpretation, jurisprudence, and heresiology. He died in Samarkand. Subsequent generations remembered him by the honorific title Imām al-Hudā ("leader of the right guidance").

Al-Māturīdī is a somewhat enigmatic figure in the history of Islamic theology because of the gaps in the information presently available. No source earlier than the fourteenth century mentions a school of theology carrying his name. The manuals speak of the Māturīdīyah together with the Ashʿarīyah, or followers of al-Ashʿarī (d. 935), as the theological spokesmen of the *ahl al-sunnah wa-al-jamāʿah* ("people of the prophetic norms and the community"), the majority group in the Muslim world, commonly known as the Sunnīs. Al-Ashʿarī lived in Baghdad and was a contemporary of al-Māturīdī, but there is no indication that they were aware of each other's efforts. Many similarities in their theological formulations have been noted. Al-Ash'arī is much better known than his Ḥanafī counterpart, but recent studies have shown that the latter came nearer to providing a bridge between traditionalism and philosophical theology than did the Baghdad scholar. Substantial differences between the two are few, but they are sufficient to have created some rivalry between their respective schools.

Al-Māturīdī, like al-Ash'arī, was firmly grounded in the Qur'anic revelation, but he also developed a rational epistemology, giving a high place to human capacity. He was much concerned with proofs for the existence of God and with the doctrine of creation, questions that probably reflect the intellectual climate of Samarkand and the terms of his encounter with other currents of religious thought. Al-Māturīdī accepted the reality of human freedom, as against the determinism of al-Ash'arī, but he also opposed the Mu'tazilī view of human beings as creators of their own deeds. He maintained that every act of humankind is at the same time the result of human capacity and a divine creation. Using somewhat the same language as al-Ash'arī and as his opponents, the Mu'tazilah, he nevertheless described a balance between divine omnipotence and human freedom that was distinctive.

On the question of the divine attributes, al-Māturīdī went no further than an essentially negative formulation: that the attributes are neither identical with the divine essence nor distinct from it. Against al-Ash'arī he held that faith, as the act that makes a person a member of the Muslim community, is immutable, incapable of either decrease or increase. This tenet was a part of the Ḥanafī doctrinal heritage.

As Sunnī theology matured after the tenth century, scholars freely appropriated elements of thought from al-Māturīdī and al-Ash'arī alike. No clear-cut lines of distinction between the Ash'arīyah and the Māturīdīyah can be discerned in the later history of Muslim thought.

BIBLIOGRAPHY

No monograph on al-Māturīdī exists, and only one of his books has been edited. Fathalla Kholeif prepared a critical edition of *Kitāb al-tawḥīd* (Beirut, 1969), thus making available for the first time the printed Arabic text of al-Māturīdī's most important existing theological work. The editor has provided a forty-three-page introduction in English, describing in an incomplete and somewhat unsystematic way the contents of *Kitāb al-tawḥīd.* W. Montgomery Watt furnishes a brief but helpful introduction to the Ḥanafī theologian in *The Formative Period of Islamic Thought* (Edinburgh, 1973), pp. 312–314 et al.

A. K. M. Ayyub Ali is the author of the most detailed general treatment of the life, thought, and influence of al-Māturīdī. It is found in *A History of Muslim Philosophy,* vol. 1 (Wiesbaden, 1963), edited by M. M. Sharif. Ali bases his discussion on an examination of *Kitāb al-tawḥīd,* existing only in manuscript at the time, and *Ta'wīlāt al-Qur'ān,* al-Māturīdī's book on Qur'ān exegesis. The latter, existing in several manuscript copies, was described for the first time by Manfred Götz in an article, "Māturīdī und sein Kitāb Ta'wīlāt al-Qur'ān," *Der Islam* 41 (1965): 27–70. This article also contains a helpful discussion of some aspects of al-Māturīdī's thought. Finally, a section of Daniel Gimaret's *Théories de l'acte humain en théologie musulmane* (Paris, 1980), pp. 175–190, deals in a perceptive and detailed way with the discussion in *Kitāb al-tawḥīd* concerning the relationship between human acts and divine sovereignty.

R. Marston Speight

MĀUI is the most versatile, popular, and widely known supernatural hero in South Pacific mythology. Islanders as far west as the Micronesian island of Yap narrate how Māui, with his enchanted fishhook, pulled up a big "fish": an island complete with people, villages, and gardens of new food plants. Māui is, however, primarily a Polynesian hero; inhabitants of every island from Hawaii to New Zealand and from Mangareva to Tonga and Samoa narrate versions of his exploits in separate myths or unified myth cycles. In the traditional culture, islanders recited his spells for success in their mundane lives; priests converted secular, humorous myths about Māui to their own serious purposes.

Māui is not only the earth-fisher but also the Polynesian sun-snarer, sky-raiser, fire-stealer, monster-slayer, seeker of immortality, and, in fact, the hero of so many mischievous exploits that Tuamotuans nicknamed him Maui-of-a-Thousand-Tricks and Tupuatupua ("super-superman"). To Hawaiians he was *aīwaīwa* ("wonderful") because he was marvelously skilled, yet weird, bad, and notorious. His best-known cognomen, Maui-tikitiki-a-Taranga (or cognates), originated, the New Zealand Maori claimed, when his mother, Taranga, wrapped him—her last born and a miscarriage—in a topknot *(tikitiki)* of hair and cast him with a prayer into the ocean. Ocean and sky gods rescued and reared him until, as a boy, he rejoined his family. His tricks finally ended when he entered the womb of the sleeping goddess Hine-nui-te-po ("great Hine of the underworld") in order to gain immortality. He intended to depart through her mouth, but when his bird companion laughed at the sight, the goddess awoke and crushed Māui to death.

Māui was a shape-shifting trickster and, usually unintentionally, a culture hero. He was also the quintessential demigod, neither wholly god nor wholly man, a misfit, who continually tested his magic and *mana* against the cosmogonic gods and against his father and elder brothers in his attempts to usurp their privileges, to humiliate them, and to demonstrate his superiority. He was also a bridge in time between the ending of the era of creation and the beginning of the era of human migrations.

Polynesians believed that by using his incantations and referring to his deeds they would sanctify their work and, at its conclusion, lift taboos on the workers. New Zealand provides the clearest examples of this. A priest of bird-catching rituals regarded the sun as a great bird and would chant Māui's sun-snaring spell to ensure a good catch. To kindle sacred new fire he would recite the incantation by which Māui had overpowered the fire deity and learned to make fire. A priestly expert on the ceremonies accompanying the planting and harvesting of *kumara* (sweet potato) would chant Māui's "song of plenty" over a feather-ornamented, crescent-topped digging stick. The song recalled how Māui, in the guise of a pigeon, had perched on his father's stick after having sneaked after him to his underworld sweet potato garden. Using Māui's charm, fishermen would weaken a large fish's reluctance to leave the ocean, and hostile invaders would recite it to unnerve people and force them to leave their homes. High priests who had been influenced by Western religion rejected the common version of the earth-fishing story and divulged its esoteric, "real" meaning. The high god Io, they explained, gave Māui, his brothers, and their descendants—the Maori—possession of the earth (i.e., New Zealand).

Wherever Māui was known he was claimed as an ancestor. In the Hawaiian Islands the claim received royal recognition in the genealogical prayer chant, the *Kumulipo* ("source in deepest darkness"), which belonged to the family of King Kalakaua (1836–1891) and his sister Queen Lili'uokalani (1838–1917), and which described the family's descent from the time of primary gods to that of deified chiefs. Eighteen lines of the fifteenth of the sixteen chants comprising the *Kumulipo* cryptically list the principal events in Māui's life. The sixteenth chant opens with the names of Māui and his wife and ends with that of Lono-i-ka-makahiki. High chiefs once intoned this two-thousand-line prayer to consecrate an infant sacred chief; they gave him the revered name of Lono-i-ka-makahiki and activated his *mana* by naming his ancestors (who included spiritualized natural phenomena, cosmogonic gods, demigods like Māui, and deified chiefs). In 1778, high chiefs chanted the *Kumulipo* over Captain James Cook, welcoming him as a returned god whose name, like the sacred child's, was Lono-i-ka-makahiki.

Priests exploited Māui for several reasons. To Society Islands priests, Māui was a submissive helper who raised the low-lying sky and regulated the time of the sun's journey to enable his eldest brother, a priest, to build temples. In Rarotonga in the Cook Islands, high priests interpreted Māui as a giant who, the first time he stood up, pushed up the sky with his head; later Māui became the weary avenger of insults made by other gods against Tangaroa, his foster father.

References to worship of Māui are obscure, rare, and based on unsupported hearsay. Tongans, it is said, formerly had a shrine and priest of Māui. One Hawaiian priest declared that Hawaii had long ago had a Māui cult and priests; another informant stated that Kamehameha I had built a temple to honor Māui. Most Polynesians usually respected Māui as an ancestor, despite his tricks, and they appreciated the benefits derived from his craftiness. But rather than to worship him, it seems that they preferred simply to enjoy the stories of how he humiliated many senior gods and earthly elders.

BIBLIOGRAPHY

Lessa, William A. *Tales from Ulithi Atoll: A Comparative Study in Oceanic Folklore.* Berkeley, 1961. Included are previously unrecorded versions of the earth-fishing myth, a description of its distribution in the Pacific, and a detailed comparative analysis of the versions.

Luomala, Katharine. *Oceanic, American Indian, and African Myths of Snaring the Sun.* Honolulu, 1940. A detailed study of the distribution and versions of sun-snaring myths in three parts of the world.

Luomala, Katharine. *Māui-of-a-Thousand-Tricks: His Oceanic and European Biographers.* Honolulu, 1949. The most comprehensive general survey to date on Māui in Oceanic culture, the major myth cycles that interpret his character and exploits, and the many theories of European scholars about him.

Luomala, Katharine. *Voices on the Wind: Polynesian Myths and Chants.* Honolulu, 1955. Includes a chapter on Māui and, with chapters on other heroes and on Polynesian narrative art, puts him in a broad setting.

KATHARINE LUOMALA

MAURICE, FREDERICK DENISON

MAURICE, FREDERICK DENISON (1805–1872), Anglican theologian, founder of Christian Socialism. John Frederick Denison Maurice was born near Lowestoft, Suffolk, England, the only son of a Unitarian minister, Michael Maurice, and Priscilla Hurry Maurice. Childhood memories of bitter family religious dissension (his mother and three older sisters abandoned Unitarianism for a form of Calvinism) left the young Frederick with a thirst for unity that was to motivate him all his life.

At Cambridge from 1823 to 1826, Maurice was influenced by Coleridge. During his intense conversion experience beginning in 1828, Maurice was deeply affected by the Scottish theologians Edward Irving (1792–1834) and Thomas Erskine (1788–1870). He decided to read for holy orders as an undergraduate, this time at Oxford, and was rebaptized and ordained in the Church of England in 1834.

At the core of this experience was Maurice's desire to know God directly as an actual, living person, in contrast to the abstract God of the Unitarians. This was not merely a romantic reaction to Western rationalism, but the discovery of a biblical, Christocentric, Pauline worldview, the great paradox of Christian faith, in which the holy and invisible God was at the same time in the person of a man. For Maurice, the fundamental, unchanging relationship at the heart of reality was that between God as revealer and man, the creature formed to know God. Man as the receiving image possesses no nature or life of his own. Man's sin is his assertion of independence, his striving hard not to be a receiver. Christ, the perfect image of the Father, is the image after which man was created. Christ is in every man, but the condemnation of every man is that he will not believe or act as if this were true. Maurice found the objective structure of this subjective faith in the articles, creeds, and liturgy of the English church. These formed a permanent witness to the fact that God had established a spiritual and universal kingdom on earth.

Maurice applied this worldview consistently to what he perceived as the basic need of his time: the rediscovery of revelation as the ground of faith. A divine-human struggle has marked all human history through man's distortion or denial of God's revelation. Instead of receiving and living within the given, divine order or constitution of the universe, man has been busily creating theories, systems, and opinions of his own as substitutes. These have resulted in the fragmentations of religious and political sects, parties, and factions and in philosophical attempts to bring heaven and earth within the terms of the intellect, Hegel being the latest offender. Maurice's method was the reverse: to be a digger, uncovering the original purpose and intent of all institutions, in order to show they were meant to be signs to the world of something invisible and permanent, the lineaments of an actual, existing kingdom of Christ.

In his writings, Maurice deliberately took the offensive, impelled by an urgent sense that a serious crisis of faith was growing among the young and that what passed for religion was a perversion of the Judeo-Christian faith that could not win their allegiance. His experience with young men was considerable: with medical students as chaplain of Guy's Hospital, London (1836–1845); as professor of English literature and history and then of theology (1840–1853) at King's College, London; with law students as chaplain of Lincoln's Inn, London (1846–1860). His luminous personal qualities and passionate devotion to truth attracted a growing circle of young men who were deeply influenced by him. These close contacts increased his concern about their questionings and doubts. They were being dosed with religion about God rather than with the living God himself: "Religion against God: this is the heresy of our age."

The revolutions of 1848 and the potentially explosive social situation in England found Maurice as spiritual leader of the short-lived but significant Christian Socialist movement (1848–1854), together with John Malcolm Ludlow (1821–1911) and Charles Kingsley (1819–1875). Convinced that cooperation, not competition, was the true foundation of a Christian society, their practical focus became that of cooperative associations for tailors and other trades. For Maurice the kingdom of Christ was the actual constitution of the universe, the "great practical existing reality which is to renew the earth." Society was not to be made anew but regenerated through uncovering its true functions and purpose, a view opposed to Ludlow's aim for reorganizing society on a socialist base. Maurice's interest in the education of the young was extended through his experience with workers, resulting in the founding in London of the Working Men's College (1854) to express his conviction that the true ground of human culture was not utilitarian but theological, the original purpose for which the ancient universities had been founded. His concern to set high standards for the education of governesses led to the founding of Queen's College, London, early in 1848.

Negative reactions to Maurice's theological and social views and to his growing influence reached a climax with the publication of his *Theological Essays* in 1853. These essays were written with the doubts and questions of the young in mind, as an alternative to the prevailing evangelical orthodoxy, which presented only theories and systems about God, Judgment Day, the verbal inspiration of the Bible, and everlasting punishment. This last Maurice viewed as a cosmic struggle between two eternal opposites: eternal life, which God presents to man, and eternal death, which man chooses for himself. But Christ's gospel reveals an abyss of love below that of death. This view was interpreted by the religious press as a denial of everlasting punishment and led finally to Maurice's expulsion from King's College in 1853 for unsettling the minds of the young.

Despite such controversies, increasing recognition and acceptance came to Maurice in his lifetime and he is viewed today as one of the most original thinkers of the Church of England. His permanent influence remains that of a prophet whose writings formed a sustained, passionate critique of the religious world of his time, comparable in depth to that of Søren Kierkegaard in the nineteenth century and of Karl Barth in the twentieth.

BIBLIOGRAPHY

Works by Frederick Denison Maurice. *The Life of Frederick Denison Maurice Chiefly Told in His Own Letters*, edited by his son, Frederick Maurice (London, 1884), is a major source for understanding Maurice's thought. For a selection of the letters, see *Toward the Recovery of Unity*, edited by John F. Porter and William J. Wolf (New York, 1964). Characteristic themes appear in his early work *The Kingdom of Christ, or, Hints on the Principles, Ordinances, and Constitution of the Catholic Church in Letters to a Member of the Society of Friends* (1838; revised, London, 1842). A new edition by Alec Vidler, based on the 1842 edition, has been published in two volumes (London, 1958). The post-Reformation religious bodies—Protestant, Roman Catholic, and Anglican—have turned their true principles into separate systems and theories, thereby losing sight of that church universal that existed before these systems and whose signs are indicated in the book's title. A variation of this theme is applied to the history of philosophy in *Moral and Metaphysical Philosophy: Philosophy of the First Six Centuries*, 2 vols., 2d ed., rev. (1854; reprint, London, 1872), begun in 1835, which contrasts man's independent search for wisdom with that Wisdom that first sought him. A lengthy controversy over Henry L. Mansel's Bampton Lectures of 1858 resulted in an important statement of the actual revelation of God to man presented in two works: *What Is Revelation? A Series of Sermons on the Epiphany* (Cambridge, 1859) and *A Sequel to the Inquiry, What Is Revelation?* (Cambridge, 1860). Some of the flavor of Maurice's views on Christian Socialism may be gleaned from *Politics for the People*, weekly papers from May through August 1848 (London), and *Tracts on Christian Socialism* (London, 1850).

Works on Frederick Denison Maurice. Among the works by the many distinguished twentieth-century Anglicans interested in Maurice, Alec Vidler's pioneering study *Witness to the Light: F. D. Maurice's Message for Today* (New York, 1948), his later *F. D. Maurice and Company* (London, 1966), and Arthur M. Ramsey's *F. D. Maurice and the Conflicts of Modern Theology* (Cambridge, 1951) are outstanding. Frank M. McClain's *Maurice: Man and Moralist* (London, 1972) is a perceptive account of how Maurice's personal relationships shaped his outlook on those givens of the Kingdom: the self, the family, the nation, and the church as universal society. My own *Frederick Denison Maurice: Rebellious Conformist* (Athens, Ohio, 1971) is a historical study emphasizing the centrality of Maurice's conversion from Unitarianism to Anglicanism and assessing his stature as a major Victorian figure. The Danish scholar Torben Christensen's *The Divine Order: A Study of F. D. Maurice's Theology* (Leiden, 1973) is a detailed analysis of Maurice's thought as a fusion of the message of the Bible and the Platonic idea of reality, in which Christianity is adjusted to Platonism. See also his excellent critical work *Origin and History of Christian Socialism, 1848–1854* (Aarhus, 1962).

OLIVE J. BROSE

MAUSS, MARCEL (1872–1950), French sociologist and ethnologist, was born in Épinal of devout Orthodox Jewish parents. Émile Durkheim was Mauss's uncle, and a bond developed early between the two that was to be lifelong and richly productive in scholarship. Like Durkheim, Mauss broke with personal religion of any kind, but, also like Durkheim, he devoted much of his career to the study of religion, chiefly primitive and pre-Buddhist Indian. Mauss studied philosophy under his uncle at Bordeaux, then went on to advanced study at the École Pratique des Hautes Études, where he specialized in Sanskrit and early Indian religious writings. In 1901 he was given the chair in comparative religion at the École Pratique, where he remained all of his life, although he took on extra teaching at the famous Collège de France during the 1930s. In 1925 Mauss participated in the founding of the Institut d'Éthnologie de l'Université de Paris, in time becoming codirector.

Mauss's scholarly work began in 1898, when he was chosen as one of a number of brilliant young social scientists invited to join Durkheim in founding the journal *Année sociologique*. Twelve rich volumes of sociological and ethnological research appeared during the ensuing years until the journal was obliged to suspend publication on the eve of World War I. Mauss was one of the contributing editors of the journal, specializing in religion, and his work appeared in every one of the twelve volumes of *Année*, alongside that of such illustrious minds as Gaston Richard, Paul Fauconnet, Célestin Bouglé, Emmanuel Lévy, and Henri Hubert. After Durkheim's death, in the 1920s and again in the 1930s, Mauss led a group of followers of Durkheim in efforts to revive the famous journal. In politics Mauss was an ardent socialist, and he had been a Dreyfusard under Zola's influence. He was one of the regular contributors to the socialist journal *L'humanité*.

Mauss's influence upon the sociological study of religion was, and continues to be, rich and diverse. Claude Lévi-Strauss has called Mauss "genius-like," referring to his "bold imagination" and "unlimited knowledge," and Mauss clearly had a crucial influence upon the development of the ideas contained in Lévi-Strauss's notable study *The Elementary Structures of Kinship* (1949). Most of Mauss's own studies were in the area of religion, focusing upon recurrent symbols and rites in the world's religions; and, by Lévi-Strauss's own testimony, it was in large degree the methods developed by Mauss in his inquiries into religion that Lévi-Strauss applied to the world of kinship.

Without question, the most famous of Mauss's works is his "Essai sur le don" (1925), published in English as *The Gift: Forms and Functions of Exchange in Archaic Societies* (1954; reprint, New York, 1967). The book is a comparative study of rituals of exchange found among certain ancient European peoples and also in Polynesia, Melanesia, and the Northwest Coast cultures of North America. *The Gift* admirably fuses perspectives Mauss had acquired from Durkheim—chiefly those pertaining to the objective character of social facts and to the functional interdependences among social facts—with Mauss's own insights in psychology. In its attention to the integrative and stabilizing effects upon a social order of ritual exchange of gifts among its members, *The Gift* is Durkheimian; but in the further attention that Mauss gives to the emotional lives of the individuals participating in the gift ritual, Mauss goes well beyond his illustrious uncle. Mauss thought the ritualized gift exchange to be as reinforcing to individual personality as to the social order as a whole. It is entirely characteristic of Mauss that he should have added to the purely scholarly objectives cited in the book the hope that his research might serve to regenerate such gift exchange as continues to exist in modern civilization.

BIBLIOGRAPHY

The best account of Mauss and his work is in the long introduction that Lévi-Strauss wrote for Mauss's *Sociologie et anthropologie*, 2d ed. (Paris, 1960). In English, Steven Lukes's treatments of Mauss in his definitive *Émile Durkheim* (New York, 1972) and in his detailed article in the *International Encyclopedia of the Social Sciences* (New York, 1968) are the most valuable. See also Rodney Needham's perceptive assessments in his preface to Durkheim and Mauss's joint study, *Primitive Classification* (Chicago, 1963). Marvin Harris, in *The Rise of Anthropological Theory* (New York, 1968), treats in some detail the influence of Mauss upon Lévi-Strauss.

ROBERT NISBET

MĀWARDĪ, AL- (AH 364–450/974–1058 CE), more fully Abū al-Ḥasan ʿAlī ibn Muḥammad ibn Ḥabīb; Muslim jurist and political theorist. Al-Māwardī was born in Basra but spent most of his life in Baghdad. He studied Islamic law in both cities with eminent legists of the Shāfiʿī school of jurisprudence. Because of his reputation as a scholar, he was appointed judge in several towns, including Ustuwā in Iran and Baghdad in Iraq. In Baghdad the caliph al-Qādir (991–1031) chose him to write a resumé of Shāfiʿī jurisprudence; al-Qādir's successor, al-Qā'im (1031–1074), used al-Māwardī for diplomatic missions to the Buyid and Seljuk rulers of Iran.

Although al-Māwardī is remembered primarily as the author of *Kitāb al-aḥkām al-sulṭānīyah* (Book of Governmental Ordinances), he wrote other books on jurisprudence and government, as well as treatises on such varied topics as Qur'anic exegesis, the prophethood of Muḥammad, the conduct of judges, proverbs and traditions, and Islamic ethics. The report that he did not permit circulation of his books until after his death is regarded as apocryphal. While his book on ethics, entitled *Kitāb adab al-dunyā wa-al-dīn* (Book of Manners in Worldly and Religious Affairs), is still read by Muslims, it is seldom taken into account in discussions of al-Māwardī's importance in the development of Islamic thought; surprisingly enough, the same holds true even for his works closely related in subject matter to *Al-aḥkām*. Accordingly, in the absence of any comprehensive study of al-Māwardī's complete works, estimates of his significance must be regarded as tentative despite the fact that the place assigned him in political thought by Western scholars is firmly fixed and widely accepted.

The date of composition of *Al-aḥkām* is not known, nor is the nature of the relationship of this book to a similar, in many respects identical, book of the same title written by al-Māwardī's contemporary, the Ḥanbalī jurist Abū Yaʿlā ibn al-Farrā'. However, scholars assume, without documentation, that since al-Māwardī's *Al-aḥkām* seems to be a mature work, it must have been written toward the end of his life; since, moreover, al-Māwardī was sixteen years older than Ibn al-Farrā', it is believed that the latter must have borrowed, without acknowledgment, from the former. Clearly these are problems that need to be solved before al-Māwardī's originality and development as a thinker can be understood. In the meantime, an indication of the content of *Al-aḥkām* and its possible connection with the author's milieu must suffice.

According to al-Māwardī he wrote *Al-aḥkām* at the behest of a ruler, perhaps a caliph, as a convenient compendium of ordinances relating to government, culled from manuals of jurisprudence. This work, and Abū Yaʿlā's, are rightly regarded as the first books of jurisprudence to be devoted exclusively to the principles and practice of Islamic government. The parts of *Al-aḥkām* that have attracted most attention discuss the three highest offices of the medieval Islamic state: the caliphate, the vizierate, and the emirate by usurpation, even though at least two-thirds of the work is devoted to lesser administrative and judicial offices, taxation, and land policy. Scholars are divided as to whether the book, either as a whole or in parts, reflects actual political conditions prevailing in al-Māwardī's time or constitutes a program for establishing an ideal state or for reasserting the power of the caliphate in the face of threats posed by secular, military rulers. The prevailing view is that al-Māwardī was a supporter of al-Qā'im and al-Qādir in their struggle against the Buyids and the Seljuks. His support, never explicitly expressed as such, came in the form of arguments derived from the Qur'ān, tradition *(ḥadīth)*, and jurisprudence *(fiqh)* for the necessity of maintaining the caliph as executor of Islamic law and for the duty of the Muslim community to obey him. Admittedly, this dual principle seems remote from the realities of al-Māwardī's day, when generals exercised political power in Islamic states. But al-Māwardī tried to come to terms with this reality and to accommodate it within the scope of Islamic law in his chapter on the emirate by usurpation. There he argued that rule by emirs based on force was to be sanctioned as long as they acknowledged the authority of the caliphs and implemented Islamic law. In effect, such an admission constituted a first step toward concession to political expediency, which was characteristic of the subsequent development of medieval Islamic political thought. Be that as it may, al-Māwardī's formulation of the character of the Islamic state has been regarded as authoritative by many Muslim thinkers and Western scholars alike.

BIBLIOGRAPHY

The fullest published study of al-Māwardī is the long article by Henri Laoust, "La penseé et l'action politiques d'al-Māwardī," *Revue des études islamiques* 36 (1968): 11–92. I discuss problems that Laoust does not treat in my article "A New Look at *al-Aḥkām al-Sulṭāniyya*," *Muslim World* 64 (January 1974): 1–15. *Al-aḥkām al-sulṭānīyah* has been translated into French by Edmond Fagnan as *Les statuts gouvernementaux* (Algiers, 1915).

DONALD P. LITTLE

MAWDŪDĪ, SAYYID ABŪ AL-AʿLĀ (1903–1979), popularly known as Mawlānā Mawdūdī; Indian (later Pakistani) writer, religious thinker, political figure, and founder and leader of an Islamic revivalist movement. Mawdūdī was born into a religious family in Aurangabad, British India. With the exception of a short period in a Hyderabad *madrasah*, his education was gained at home or through his own efforts. His earliest occupation was journalism, and in 1920 he became editor of the highly influential newspaper of the Jamʿīyat-i ʿUlamāʾ (the organization of Indian *ʿulamaʾ*), where he remained for seven years. As one of the Indian Muslim leaders outraged by Gandhi's abandonment of the Swarāj movement for independence, he began to argue that Muslim interests could not be reconciled with those of Hindus. Although Mawdūdī had participated in the religio-political Khilāfat movement, he and his brother criticized the Khilāfat leaders for the fiasco of the *hijrah* ("emigration") movement from India to Afghanistan.

In the mid-1920s, in response to Hindu attacks on Islam resulting from the murder of a Hindu leader by a Muslim fanatic, Mawdūdī wrote a series of articles in defense of Islamic beliefs, subsequently published as *Al-jihād fī al-Islām* (Religious War in Islam). He later said that this volume, his first serious work on Islam, represented his true intellectual and spiritual conversion to the religion.

Mawdūdī left journalism in 1927 for literary and historical pursuits. In the following years he wrote a history of the Seljuks and an unfinished history of the Asafi dynasty of Hyderabad. From 1932 he was associated with a Hyderabad religious journal, *Tarjumān al-Qur'ān*, which he edited from 1933 until his death; this publication has been the principal instrument for the propagation of his views. Criticizing the westernized class of Indian Muslims, Mawdūdī began to call for the mobilization of Muslims in the cause of Islam. In the political debates of the late 1930s he rejected both the Indian nationalism of the Congress and the Muslim nationalism of the Muslim League, calling instead for an Islamic order in India. His views from the period are collected in three volumes called *Musalmān awr mawjūdah siyāsī kashmakash* (The Muslim and the Present Political Struggle).

In 1941 Mawdūdī founded the Jamāʿat-i Islāmī, an organization for the promotion of Islamic principles, and was elected its chief, or *amīr*, which he remained until 1972. From 1941 until the partition of India he devoted his time to building the organization and to writing. In 1947, despite his unhappiness with the Muslim League, Mawdūdī moved to Pakistan, where he and his group became the leading spokesmen for an Islamic state. The Jamāʿat-i Islāmī sought political power, and its activities attracted the disapproval of government. Mawdūdī and his principal followers were imprisoned on several occasions; he himself was condemned to death by a military court after the anti-Aḥmadīyah disturbances of 1953, but the sentence was never carried out. His ideas and activities brought criticism from both modernist and conservative Muslims as well as from secularists.

Mawdūdī's teachings are set out in a large number of writings that include a six-volume commentary on the Qur'ān, *Tafhīm al-Qur'ān.* These writings have been translated into numerous languages, and he is at present one of the most widely read authors in the Islamic world. He believed Islam to be an ideology that offers complete guidance for human life, laid down by God in his holy book, the Qur'ān, and through his prophet, Muḥammad. The task of Muslims is to follow the eternal divine law by building an Islamic state, by creating an Islamic society as well as an individual Islamic life. The paramount feature of his teaching is the demand for an Islamic state, which he intended to be realized in the form of the Jamā'at-i Islāmī. His vision of society was rigorous, puritanical, authoritarian, antisecular, and antidemocratic but was based upon a deeply held conviction that people must live according to the law of God.

BIBLIOGRAPHY

A sympathetic discussion of the import of Mawdūdī's perspective for many aspects of life is *Islamic Perspectives: Studies in Honor of Mawlana Sayyid Abul A'lā Mawdudi*, edited by Khurshid Ahmad and Zafar Ishaq Ansari (Leicester, 1979). Kalim Bahadur's *The Jamā'at-i-Islāmī of Pakistan* (New Delhi, 1980) is informative as to the history of that organization. Leonard Binder's *Religion and Politics in Pakistan* (Berkeley, 1963) gives the Pakistani background. Charles J. Adams's "The Ideology of Mawlana Mawdudi," in *South Asian Politics and Religion*, edited by Donald Smith (Princeton, 1966), pp. 371–397, is a balanced account; see also his "Mawdudi and the Islamic State," in *Voices of Resurgent Islam*, edited by John Esposito (New York, 1983), pp. 99–133.

SHEILA MCDONOUGH

MAWLID is an Arabic word that literally means the time and place of a birth, but the word is used in particular for the birth of the prophet Muḥammad *(mawlid al-nabī)*. In some Islamic countries it also refers to the festival days of local saints (*walīs*). The actual birth date of the prophet Muḥammad is unknown, but the anniversary of his birth is celebrated on 12 Rabī'ah al-Awwal of the Islamic lunar calendar, a day prior to the anniversary of his death (in 632 CE).

Muḥammad is portrayed in the Qur'ān as a messenger of God who was an ordinary mortal in other respects. Only in later centuries did many Muslims begin to assert a higher sanctity for his person. The first recorded celebrations of his birth occurred during the latter part of Fatimid rule in Egypt (909–1171). As Shī'ī Muslims who held descendants of the Prophet in particularly high esteem, the Fatimid elite similarly observed the *mawlids* of Muḥammad's son-in-law 'Alī, his daughter Fāṭimah, and the reigning caliph. Palace dignitaries and religious notables held daylight processions and delivered sermons, a practice briefly prohibited but later revived. The Sunnī majority in Egypt took no part in these ceremonies.

The first popular *mawlid* occurred in 1207. Muẓaffar al-Dīn Kökbürü, brother-in-law of the famed Ṣalāḥ al-Dīn (Saladin), arranged for a festival in Arbalā', a town near Mosul in present-day northern Iraq. As described by the historian Ibn Khallikān (d. 1282), a native of the town, the *mawlid* became an elaborate annual event, attracting scholars, notables, preachers, and poets from throughout the region. The deeds and person of Muḥammad were celebrated in religious poetry and songs and culminated on the eve of the *mawlid* in a torchlight procession led by the prince. Followers of Ṣūfī orders were also prominent in the celebrations, and gifts were lavishly distributed to participants.

Some aspects of early *mawlids* appear to have been influenced by Middle Eastern Christian traditions of the period, such as lavish entertainments and nighttime processions in honor of saints. Even as *mawlids* also developed for saints and other holy persons, especially in Egypt, the Prophet's *mawlid* continued to be the most elaborate. *Mawlids* quickly became highly popular occasions associated with mysticism, during which Ṣūfī orders congregated in public, reciting rhythmical chants in praise of God and in some cases entering into trance. [*See* Dhikr.] From Egypt, *mawlids* spread to many other parts of the Islamic world.

The popularity of *mawlids* met initial resistance from some theologians. Ibn Taymīyah (d. 1328) and others condemned the Prophet's *mawlid* as a harmful innovation *(bid'ah)*. After considerable discussion, most theologians, except those precursors of the later Wahhābī movement, who espoused Islam in its most idealized and fundamental form, tolerated the *mawlid* as a praiseworthy innovation *(bid'ah ḥasanah)*, since it inspired reverence for the Prophet. The central activity of *mawlids* is the recital of long panegyrical poems and legends commemorating Muḥammad and his deeds, recitations so popular that they are repeated on festive occasions throughout the year.

The acceptance of popular practice by theologians shows the Islamic principle of consensus *(ijmā')* at work. A key doctrinal tenet in Islam is that the community of believers cannot agree upon error. The legal opinions of religious jurists appear to have had minimal influence in reducing the popularity of *mawlids*, so that most jurists were encouraged to accommodate theological doctrine to social realities.

As with other Islamic celebrations and rites of passage, *mawlids* show considerable differences throughout the Islamic world. In some contexts, the *mawlid* is minimally distinguished from other festive occasions; elsewhere, it is one of the most important annual religious events. In nineteenth-century Cairo, *mawlid* celebrations started on the first day of Rabī'ah al-Awwal. Large tents were pitched in one of Cairo's quarters and decorated with lamps and Qur'anic inscriptions. Each night Ṣūfī orders carried their banners in procession to their tents, where they chanted the name of God, recited poems in praise of Muḥammad, and provided refreshments to guests. In the daytime, dancers, clowns, and storytellers entertained the audience in a carnival atmosphere. Festivities climaxed on the eleventh and twelfth evenings of the month, with elaborate poems and songs in praise of Muḥammad that continued until morning. In recent times government restrictions against large public gatherings sought to curtail these events. Nonetheless, the Prophet's *mawlid* and to a lesser extent those for local saints continue to be large communal festivals attracting hundreds of thousands of people in Egypt's larger towns.

Elsewhere in the Islamic world, religious orders play a less central role in *mawlid* festivities. In Morocco, the month in which the Prophet's birthday occurs is popularly known as *mulūd*, the local pronunciation of *mawlid*. Children born during this month are considered especially fortunate and are often named after it, and it is a good time to circumcise boys. Celebrations last a week, culminating with recitations of panegyrics of Muḥammad in decorated and illuminated community mosques. On the final night, recitations continue until daybreak. Some families offer a feast and distribute food to the poor; women decorate their hands and feet with henna and visit cemeteries. In Java, a feast is offered for the *mawlid*, which is one of the two most important calendrical ceremonies in a region given over to elaborate festival cycles. A popular Javanese belief is that the giving of feasts for the Prophet's birthday and the end of Ramaḍān distinguishes Muslims from non-Muslims and humans from animals; this view of the importance of the occasion is not necessarily shared by those Javanese who have a more elaborate understanding of Islamic doctrine and ritual.

The symbolism of the *mawlid* is especially highly developed among Swahili-speaking East African Muslims. In the town and island of Lamu, located off the northern coast of Kenya, most Muslims hold that the prophet Muḥammad, created of dust, like all other persons, carried "light" to the earth in this month. The discipline of fasting during the month of Ramaḍān emphasizes the separation of nature and culture and the distance between actual human society and the Islamic ideal. Likewise, the month of Muḥammad's birth is regarded as a joyous occasion that emphasizes life as lived here and now, combined with belief in the Prophet's willingness to intervene on behalf of his people and to accept them in full recognition of their individual shortcomings. It is said that during this month the Prophet lives on the earth like a human being and loves and hates just as they do. The first twelve days of the month are marked by processions, singing, and the music of tambourines and flutes. Intense competitions are held on successive evenings in the mosques and religious associations of the various quarters in Lamu. Each quarter vies in enthusiasm to praise Muḥammad's life and deeds in song and prose and to show its love for the Prophet. *Sharīfs*, descendants of Muḥammad, are especially honored in Lamu during this period.

Sharīfs are invited to recite poems in praise of Muḥammad in most of the nineteen mosques of Lamu town. In beautiful performances on successive evenings, assemblies of young boys from mosque schools and musicians perform songs and poems that have been rehearsed for months. Brightly colored tunics, donated by wealthy Muslims, are worn for the ceremonies. The freeborn and the ex-slaves, members of two important local social categories, compete with one another during these celebrations to express a willingness to use earthly wealth—the offer of food and refreshments to guests—and talent to show their love for the Prophet. If not enough effort is put into the preparations for quarter festivities, the *sharīfs* are said to participate with less enthusiasm and to attract fewer blessings for the quarter. Love of the Prophet is said to join together the world of nature and the world of culture. Ceremonies include the sacrifice of cows, highly valued on the island, visits to cemeteries, and the distribution of rose water by *sharīfs* to symbolize Muḥammad's ability to cleanse his followers of their sins. Until the 1970s distinctions between freeborn and ex-slave and *sharīf* and commoner remained significant for many East African Muslims, although in recent years such distinctions have been eroded under pressure from reformist Muslims.

BIBLIOGRAPHY

In his *Muhammadan Festivals* (New York, 1951) G. E. Von Grunebaum discusses the early history of the *mawlid* and includes translations from original source materials. For the *mawlid* in more recent times, see Edward W. Lane's *An Account of the Manners and Customs of the Modern Egyptians*, 3d ed. (1846; reprint, New York, 1973), which includes a description of the celebrations as he saw them in Cairo in 1834. Michael Gilsenan's *Saint and Sufi in Modern Egypt* (Oxford, 1973) provides a brief commentary on contemporary Egyptian practices. For Morocco, Edward A. Westermarck's *Ritual and Belief in Morocco*, vol. 2 (1926; reprint, New Hyde Park, N.Y., 1968), remains the best-documented ethnographic account, while Pessah Shinar's "Traditional and Reformist Mawlid Celebrations in the Maghrib," in *Studies in Memory of Gaston Wiet*, edited by Myriam Rosen-Ayalon (Jerusalem, 1977), pp. 371–413, provides a richly analytic account of how *mawlid* practices have changed over time throughout North Africa. In *The Religion of Java* (Glencoe, Ill., 1960) Clifford Geertz mentions the *mawlid* only briefly but fully situates it in a highly elaborate ritual context. By far the most extensive discussion of the symbolism of occasion as elaborated in one local context is Abdul Hamid M. el-Zein's *The Sacred Meadows: A Structural Analysis of Religious Symbolism in an East African Town* (Evanston, Ill., 1974).

DALE F. EICKELMAN

MAWU-LISA is a complex deity found among several coastal West African peoples, including the Fon and most of the Ewe. Occasionally Mawu and Lisa are considered as separate deities; sometimes they are seen together as a complementary sexual pair. The issue is complicated because the Ewe peoples use the term *mawu* both to refer to God in a general way or to a specific deity.

As a specific deity, Mawu is seen as a creator, but she rarely has shrines, priests, or rituals dedicated to her. Among peoples such as the Fon, Mawu is conceived of as a female deity associated with the moon, and it is in this manifestation that she is most often paired with Lisa. Among the Fon, the cult of Mawu-Lisa was centered in Abomey, the capital of the old kingdom of Dahomey. Mawu is depicted as an elder female figure in conjunction with Lisa, a younger male consort. Other complementary qualities are seen in them. For example, whereas Mawu is associated with the moon (night) and is cool (gentle and forgiving), Lisa is associated with the sun (day) and is hot (fierce and punitive). Sometimes even their actions are complementary. In one mythic tradition, Mawu created the earth and then retired to the heavens. When she saw that things were not going well with men, she sent Lisa to make tools and clear the forests so that men could farm and live a civilized life.

The name *Lisa* among the Fon appears to be derived from the nearby Yoruba people, who use the word *orișa* to refer to lesser deities. Lisa is an analogue for the Yoruba *orișa* Ọbatala and is variously described as the twin brother, husband, or son of Mawu. This paired complementarity is not all that unusual in West Africa. Other pairs of spiritual beings include Nana-Buku of central Benin and Togo, Dada-Sogbo of the Ewe, and Eṣu-Legba of the Yoruba. Their pairing need not refer to sexuality but merely to the unity of duality, however that may be defined.

Mawu also creates human souls and rules their destinies. The soul is called *mawuse* ("the Mawu within a person"). At first, Mawu made people out of clay, but after running short, she began to make them out of reused bodies (hence we can see resemblances in people). Mawu upholds moral law and also metes out rewards and punishments after death.

The priests of Mawu wear white, and at Abomey there is a rare statue of Mawu. The figure, painted red, has large breasts and holds a crescent moon. The cult of Mawu is not limited to West Africa. There are scattered instances of Mawu's cult in the New World. For example, in Yoruba houses in São Luiz, Brazil, there is said to be an *encantado* ("spirit") of Mawu. There, as in West Africa, Mawu connotes a generalized notion of divinity.

BIBLIOGRAPHY

Herskovits, Melville J. *Dahomey: An Ancient West African Kingdom.* 2 vols. New York, 1938. An excellent description by one of the great ethnographers of Africa.

Pelton, Robert D. *The Trickster in West Africa.* Berkeley, 1980. Includes a good discussion of the Mawu-Lisa cult and the role played by Legba, the Fon trickster figure.

JAMES S. THAYER

MAXIMOS THE CONFESSOR (c. 580–662), Byzantine theologian, Eastern Orthodox saint, ascetic writer, and opponent of monothelitism. What is known about Maximos's life largely derives from an anonymous biography.

Born in Constantinople, Maximos received a good education, which was rare for his time. Indicative of his abilities was his appointment as first secretary to the emperor Heraclius (r. 610–641), but Maximos soon recognized his ecclesiastical calling. He entered the Monastery of Philipikos, in Chrysopolis (present-day Üsküdar, Turkey), probably in 614, where he eventually became abbot. Because of attacks by the Persians, Maximos and the other monks were forced to flee to the Monastery of Saint George, at Cyzicus (present-day Kapıdağı, Turkey). Two years later Maximos was again obliged to flee because of Persian expansionism. His path likely took him through Crete, and probably Cyprus, to North Africa (626). It is well known that he was in Carthage on Pentecost of 632. At the Eucratas Monastery he became acquainted with Sophronios, another refugee, who later became patriarch of Jerusalem (634–638). Maximos was greatly influenced by Sophronios and later called him his forerunner, father, and teacher.

The two monks journeyed to Alexandria in an effort to overturn an agreement of union with the monophysites but were unable to persuade the former patriarch, Cyrus of Alexandria (d. 641), to their cause. Because such concessions to monophysitism were likely to terminate in the heresy of monoenergism, Sophronios had turned against the agreement; Maximos continued in the struggle against the union but acted in a reserved way. After Heraclius published his *Ecthesis* (638), and a monothelite direction was given to the heresy, Maximos cut off relations with the patriarch Pyrrhus and began his own antimonothelite activities.

Important stages of Maximos's struggle against monothelitism are his dialogue with the deposed Pyrrhus in Carthage; the convocation in North Africa of three antimonothelite synods, where he explained his position; and the continuation of his endeavors in Rome (646), which had become the new center of antimonothelitism. Maximos's efforts were now carried out with unmitigated zeal. He composed treatises and letters to the emperor, the pope, and the patriarch of Constantinople. His antiheretical struggle prompted the convocation of a synod in Rome (649) where he condemned monothelitism.

Maximos's initiatives were regarded by the imperial authorities as hostile to its policy of union and reconciliation. Therefore, Maximos and his companions, one of whom was the papal legate, were taken to Constantinople for questioning. (This was in 655, not, as is commonly reported, during the reign of Pope Martin I.) Although the charge that he had betrayed the interests of the empire was not proved, Maximos was exiled (along with his two disciples) to Byzia in Thrace for refusing to sign the new conciliatory declaration, the *Typus* of Constans II, under Patriarch Peter (655–666). Maximos was called back to Constantinople in 656 for another investigation, but after refusing once again to sign, he was exiled and imprisoned at Perbera. Although his opponents were determined, Maximos's intransigence in matters of faith prevented him from giving in to them. Six years later, Maximos, Pope Martin, and Sophronios were anathemized. There followed exchanges of messages, rumors of torture (some say Maximos was beaten, his tongue cut out, and his right hand lopped off), and further exiling. Maximos was finally imprisoned in the fortress of Schimaris, where after two months he died, on 13 August 662.

Maximos composed numerous works on the interpretation of scripture and on the teachings of the fathers. His doctrinal writings consist largely of short treatises against monophysitism, a more important series against monothelitism, and numerous other ascetical writings. He wrote commentaries on mystical theology and on the work of Dionysius the Areopagite (Pseudo-Dionysius). Also extant are many letters by Maximos, including the letters and disputation that he wrote to Pyrrhus. Some other writings exist only in manuscript.

The teachings of Maximos developed in two directions: on the one hand, in a theoretical direction, with strong metaphysical emphasis; and on the other, in an existential direction, which elaborated a spiritual way of life. In his theology of the unity and trinity of God, Maximos follows the ontological method and the teachings of the Greek fathers. The interpretation by some Western theologians that Maximos agrees with the view that the Holy Spirit proceeds from the Father and the Son cannot be demonstrated definitively. For example, Maximos sees in the Trinity the relation of three persons who participate jointly in one essence and jointly express a common divine energy: the Father, "by grace"; the Son, "by self-operation"; the Holy Spirit, "by synergy."

Maximos believed that the world was created by God so that beings could participate in his goodness. Accordingly, man holds the dominant place in creation and is the natural link between God and creation; further, all will is united to God through man. The first man, Maximos thought, was created with an orientation toward God and was meant to bridge the distance between "image" and "likeness." For Maximos, disobedience to the divine will constitutes deliberate sin, in which man's will is distorted and his nature corrupted; thus, man loses the grace of *apatheia*. Also, corruptibility in human nature is inherited; therefore, there is no human possibility of self-regeneration or of exemption from death. However, what man has done out of negligence, the man Christ has corrected.

Maximos's Christology is devoted to his struggle against monophysitism and monothelitism. For Maximos, in Christ, human nature, which had no previous existence as such, became substantial and received existence in the preexisting substance of God the Word (the Logos). As one being, Christ has the same humanity as man but he also has divinity. However, as in the Trinity, in Christ's being one essence is confessed without confusing the two natures.

The resolution of the question of whether there are one or two energies (or one or two wills) in Christ lies in the determination of their origin, that is, whether in the nature or in the person of Christ. For the monoenergists, Christ has only one energy because he has only one active element. For the monothelites, he has only one will because nature, according to doctrines of natural philosophy, is governed by the rule of necessity.

In order to oppose monophysitism, Maximos attempts to define the operational autonomy of the person on the basis of the dynamism of nature. He argues that nature, which is both noetic and created, "has no necessity" (*Patrologia Graeca* 91.293). Will, as a reasonable desire, presupposes the habit of nature, which is movement and energy, not stasis. The will governs this nature within the functions of the person. For example, sight and speech are capacities inherent in nature, but "how" one sees is dependent upon the person. In this way, Maximos distinguishes between the natural origin of the will and its personal (that is, "gnomic") orientation. As such, will does not violate the order of nature but diverts its movement and, in this case, expresses the ethical responsibility of the person.

According to Maximos, Christ is recognized as God and man from his divine and human qualities. Christ willed, or acted, as God and man. Maximos sees a "divine-human will" and a "divine-human energy" in Christ's very nature. In distinction from his opponents, Maximos argues that if will is identical with persons (and not nature), then the Trinity, which is a trinity of persons, and not of natures, would have to comprise three wills. Further, if the energy were to flow from persons, there would be three energies in the Trinity, and Christ would be cut off from the energy of the Father and that of the Holy Spirit.

The human will of Christ is, by the logic of nature, the same as ours, but its manifestation in Christ is directed by the person of God the Word. Hence, Christ's will experienced everything human except sin. The famous phrase "My Father, if it is possible, let this cup pass from me; nevertheless, not as I will, but as thou wilt" (*Mt.* 26:39) expresses the will of the human nature in Christ, that is, his resistance to death as well as his acceptance of it. This is an indication that salvation is completed by the human will. Thus Maximos's intention is to defend the human will of Christ, which also constitutes a defense of the freedom of man in relation to God. Under such presuppositions, Christ healed and divinized corruptible human nature. Christ also formulated a new way of existence for man, free from sin and death. Furthermore, it is through the work of the church, Maximos believed, that familiarization with these gifts of Christ can occur. Likewise, in his dogmatic teaching, Maximos describes the spiritual life as a pedagogical way to salvation and divinization.

The three factors, according to Maximos, that mold man are God, human nature, and the world. It is man's will that moves him in relation to these factors. *Being* refers to the essence of man, *well-being* to the call of God to pass from the "image" to the "likeness" of God; *eternal being* is granted to those worthy of the grace of God. The development of the inner life cultivates the gift of baptism, through which human nature is renewed by Christ's existence. The discovery of freedom and the acquisition of virtues, especially of love, promote the social life of the person and union with God. Spiritual formation, which is carried out through natural and theological vision, follows. In the principles of creation and in the principles of human nature, God is discovered. In the divine Word we possess the unity of the Creator and creation, as the revelation of his person and work to the world.

Spiritual formation is fulfilled in the work of the Holy Spirit, which enlightens man, enabling him to understand beings, the meaning of the scriptures, and the mysteries of worship. At the very center of their existence Christians participate in the divine energy and receive awareness of the spiritual presence of God. Such a process—internal, moral, and spiritual—makes the person capable of *theōsis* (deification), that is, exemption from the corruption of creation and acquisition of union with God. Finally, full communion and union in the second coming of Christ is awaited as a consummation of our own personal lives, just as resurrection was the consummation of Christ's life.

Maximos's contribution to the intellectual support of orthodox views, his ecclesiastical conduct, and his witness as a confessor were recognized by the Third Council of Constantinople (680–681). The basic themes of his teaching, such as the distinction between nature and divine energy, the principles of nature and human will, the communion and synergy of God and man as persons, the participation of man in God, and *theōsis*—all of these influenced the spirituality and later direction of orthodox theology. For example, Maximos's authority was invoked during the hesychast dispute of the fourteenth century. The successful application of Aristotelian dialectic in theology was inaugurated by Maximos, and his teaching has provoked interest in modern theological circles.

BIBLIOGRAPHY

Works by Maximos. Maximos's collected works are available in *Patrologia Graeca*, edited by J.-P. Migne, vol. 4 (Paris, 1857) and vols. 90–91 (Paris, 1860). *Questions to Thalassius* is available in *Corpus Christianorum, Series Graeca*, vol. 7 (Turnhout, 1980). *The Ascetic Life* has been translated by Polycarp Sherwood in "Ancient Christian Writers," edited by Johannes Quasten et al., vol. 21 (Westminster, Md., 1955).

Works on Maximos

Balthasar, Hans Urs von. *Kosmische Liturgie: Das Weltbild Maximus', des Bekenners.* 2d ed. Einsiedeln, 1961.

Garrigues, Juan Miguel. *Maxime le confesseur: La charité, avenir de l'homme.* Paris, 1976. Includes a complete bibliography.

Karazafiris, Nicholas. *Hē peri prosōpou didascalia Maximou tou Homologētou.* Thessaloniki, 1985.

Léthel, François-Marie. *Théologie de l'agonie du Christ.* Paris, 1979.

Matsouka, Nikos. *Kosmos, anthrōpos, koinōnia kata ton Maximon ton homologētēn.* Athens, 1980.

Piret, Pierre. *Le Christ et la Trinité selon Maxime le confesseur.* Paris, 1983.

Radosavljevic, A. *To mustērion tēs sōtērias kata ton hagion Maximon ton homologētēn.* Athens, 1975.

Riou, Alain. *Le monde et l'église selon Maxime le confesseur.* Paris, 1973.

Sherwood, Polycarp. *An Annotated Date-List of the Works of Maximus the Confessor.* Rome, 1952.

Thunberg, Lars. *Microcosm and Mediator: The Theological Anthropology of Maximus the Confessor.* Lund, 1965.

Volker, Walther. *Maximus Confessor als Meister des geistlichen Lebens.* Wiesbaden, 1965.

NICHOLAS KARAZAFIRIS

MĀYĀ is one of the key terms in Indian religious tradition. Its original meaning may be "creation" or "construction" (from the Sanskrit *mā*, "measure" or "mete out"), but the term can be used in several connotations, implying a power, a process, and the result of that process.

Development of the Concept. In the history of Indian thought the term *māyā* is used with remarkable consistency, to express, define, and explain the enigma of life and the material world. The viewpoint expressed by Śaṅkara, admittedly pivotal, is often stressed too much, at the cost of other opinions conceived by intelligent minds from the time of the Vedas to the modern period. For the Vedic authors, *māyā* denoted the faculty that transforms an original concept of creative mind into concrete form, a faculty of immense proficiency and shrewdness such as is suggested by the English word *craft*.

In the Vedas, performances of *māyā* are mainly ascribed to divine beings, *devas* ("gods") or *asuras* ("countergods"). Each god works *māyā* in his own way and for his own ends. Thus, through *māyā* Varuṇa metes out the earth and creates order in nature (*Ṛgveda* 5.85.5 et al.), and Indra employs it to defeat the demon Vṛtra or to transform himself into another shape (*Ṛgveda* 6.47.18: "By his powers of *māyā*, Indra goes around in many forms," an oft-quoted phrase). The reality of all these mayic creations, however incomprehensible to common man, is never questioned. The Upaniṣads develop a metaphysical notion of *māyā* as the emanation of the phenomenal world by *brahman*, the cosmic Self. In post-Vedic Hinduism, the term can be used to convey a metaphysical, epistemological, mythological, or magical sense, depending on the immediate context.

Metaphysical Aspect. In Indian thought, *māyā* is the metaphysical principle that must be assumed in order to account for the transformation of the eternal and indivisible into the temporal and differentiated. Beginning with the Upaniṣads (*Chāndogya Upaniṣad* 6.1.4–6), empirical reality is most often conceived as a polymorphous modification or transformation of the Absolute, and thus maintains a "derived reality." Mahāyāna Buddhism, however, developed a concept of the world as a "substitution" or "delusion" conjured up by *māyā* as by an act of illusionism. The world process and our experience of it are devices to hide the inexpressible total void (Nāgārjuna, second century CE?), or cosmic consciousness. Even the Buddha's teaching is said to belong to this sphere of secondary reality. An attitude of nihilism is avoided by the concept of two levels of reality developed by Nāgārjuna: *pāramārthika* ("ultimate") and *vyāvahārika* ("practical"). It is therefore not correct to state that for these thinkers the world of *māyā* is a mere illusion.

In Hindu philosophy (especially the Vedānta school), the concept of *māyā* follows the Vedic tradition of a mysterious power of self-transformation. The Buddhist doctrine of an ultimate void is emphatically denied: the nonexistent cannot be the source of creation, just as a barren woman can never have a son, says Gauḍapāda (sixth century CE?). After him, Śaṅkara (c. eighth century CE) and later scions of the Advaita ("Nondualist") school also deny ultimate reality to the phenomenal world. But creation is not totally unreal either, since it cannot be separated from the truth that is *brahman* (what else could be its cause?), and also because it retains a pragmatic validity for the individual as long as the liberating experience of all-oneness has not been reached. "Illusion" thus implies the mysteriously different, not the *nihil*.

Other Vedānta theorists tend to emphasize the reality of the mayic transformation. According to Rāmānuja (eleventh century CE), the world is a mode of existence of *brahman*, related to it as the body is to the soul. The Śaiva and Śākta schools of thought also held a realistic view of *māyā*. In the recent period, Vivekananda, Aurobindo, and others have endeavored to restate the doctrine of *māyā* in reaction to objections by other philosophical systems without deviating in essentials from the tradition.

Epistemological Aspect. *Māyā* deludes cosmic consciousness into associating itself with individuality, sense perception, and the sensory objects of phenomenal reality. Gauḍapāda interprets this process as a misconception *(vikalpa)* of the pure and undivided self-consciousness of the *ātman*, just as in darkness a rope is mistakenly perceived as a snake. To dispel false perception is to attain true insight into the undivided Absolute. Śaṅkara prefers the term *avidyā* ("nescience") or *ajñāna* ("ignorance"). This is not just the absence of insight but a positive entity, the cause of superimposition of external experience on the undefiled self-consciousness. Besides, there is a metaphysical *avidyā* assumed by Śaṅkara as a necessary cause for cosmic evolution in order to vindicate the doctrine of the static unity of *brahman*. Śaṅkara rejects the equation of ordinary waking experience with dream experience held by the Mahāyāna theorists and Gauḍapāda. In modern Hindu philosophy, the epistemological aspect of *māyā* is emphasized: *māyā* does not imply the denial of the reality of the world, but refers only to the relative validity of our experience.

Other Aspects. The speculative concept described above has often been clothed in religious myth and popular legend. In the popular mind, the power of *māyā* often amounted to feats of magic or illusionism *(indrajāla)*. In the epic *Mahābhārata* (and elsewhere), this power is said to be wielded by God to beguile and delude mankind. "The Lord plays with his subjects as a child with its toys" (*Mahābhārata* 3.31.19f.). In other contexts, the phenomenal world is likened to a bubble on the water, a drop trickling from a lotus leaf, evanescent autumnal clouds, a colorful patch, or a circle of fire created by a torch. Several legends express the same view in allegorical form. Such religious imagery remains very important in later Hinduism. In religious poetry, *māyā* is sometimes embodied as a tempting or fear-inspiring woman; she can be the consort of the male supreme being (Śrī for Viṣṇu, Rādhā for Kṛṣṇa, Devī for Śiva) or, in Śāktism, a manifestation of the Cosmic Mother in her own right as Māyādevī or Bhuvaneśvarī (Goddess of the World).

[*For further discussions of* māyā *in Indian philosophy, see* Vedānta *and* Avidyā.]

BIBLIOGRAPHY

Discussions of *māyā* and its place in Indian religious and philosophical thought are dealt with in several books of more general scope. A very scholarly, thoughtful, and dependable survey by a classical Indologist can be found in Jan Gonda's *Change and Continuity in Indian Religion* (The Hague, 1965), pp. 164–197. Gonda's discussion of *māyā* in this work is a summary and restatement of two of his earlier studies. Also very readable as an introduction is Paul D. Devanandan's *The Concept of Māyā: An Essay in Historical Survey of the Hindu Theory of the World, with Special Reference to the Vedānta* (London, 1950; Calcutta, 1954). The author's Christian viewpoint is not stressed. Anil K. Ray Chaudhuri's *The Doctrine of Māyā*, 2d rev. & enl. ed. (Calcutta, 1950), is a philosophical study with special emphasis on the epistemological doctrine of nescience in the Vedānta. A concise book that focuses mainly on *māyā* in twentieth-century Hindu philosophy is Ruth Reyna's *The Concept of Māyā from the Vedas to the Twentieth Century* (London and Bombay, 1962). My own book, *Māyā Divine and Human* (Delhi, 1978), is a study of Indian and Balinese sources in Sanskrit concentrating on the magical side of the *māyā* concept. Predating all of these works is Heinrich Zimmer's *Maya, der indische Mythos* (Stuttgart, 1936), which contains a wealth of legends and personal interpretations.

TEUN GOUDRIAAN

MAYA RELIGION. The religion of Classic Maya civilization (300–900 CE) flourished in the Petén lowlands of northern Guatemala, producing a distinctive cosmology and worldview that still persist among contemporary Maya Indians despite four and a half centuries of Hispanic domination and Christian missionization. In Classic times, the Maya were organized into city-states centered on "ceremonial centers" that were dominated by pyramids and other monumental architecture. They practiced both swidden and intensive maize agriculture, sustaining a population that may have reached two million by 800 CE. Today, more than three million descendants of the Classic Maya occupy the area stretching from the Yucatán Peninsula in the north to the highlands of Guatemala and Chiapas, Mexico, in the south (roughly 14°20′–21°30′ north latitude, 87°30′–93° west longitude). They speak nearly thirty distinct but related languages of the Maya family and are primarily subsistence maize agriculturalists dwelling in dispersed rural hamlets composed of patrilineal, patrilocal extended families.

Classic Maya Religion. Ironically, the hieroglyphic inscriptions preserved on Classic Maya monuments provide deeper insight into Maya religious thought than into Maya ritual. Maya religion sanctified a conception of time that identified recurring calendrical cycles with particular and inescapable destinies. The Maya, however, did not passively await their fate, but endeavored to know it through precise and absolute reckoning of the passage of time, through accurate recording of events during each calendrical period, and through careful prophecy based on the juxtaposition of their calendar and history.

This concern with the passage of time led the Maya to chart the motion and phases of the sun, moon, Venus, and various constellations. By calculating the duration of different celestial cycles in terms of whole-day units (e.g., 149 lunations = 4,400 days), Classic Maya astronomers were able to compute lunar periods, the length of the solar year, and the revolutions of Venus, all to within minutes of their modern values. These calculations were greatly facilitated by the invention of a system of place-value arithmetic, an achievement that the Maya share only with the ancient Mesopotamians. Using a vigesimal (base 20) system, any number of days could be represented as a sum of *kin*s (days), *uinal*s ("months" of 20 days), *tun*s ("years" of 18 *uinal*s, or 360 days—the closest multiple of 20 to the length of the solar year), *katun*s (20 *tun*s, or 7,200 days), and *baktun*s (20 *katun*s, or 144,000 days). Some scholars suggest that such place notation—read in double columns from left to right, top to bottom in descending order from *baktun* to *kin*—provided the framework on which the Maya developed their entire system of hieroglyphic writing. The coalescence in Maya thought of time, astronomy, mathematics, and writing finds expression in Itzamná, the principal deity of the Classic Maya: he was alternately the creator god, the sun, and the first priest who invented writing and books.

For the Maya, time (and thus creation) began with movement—most concretely the motion of the sun. Indeed, space and time coalesced in the single dimension of the sun's passage across the sky. The eastern and western horizons constituted the principal cosmological directions because of the sun's movement between them. Lacking a clear view of the polestar, the Maya conceptualized those arcs of the horizon where the sun never rose or set as simply the intervals—both in time and space—between east and west. East was associated with the color red, west with black; intervals between east and west—sometimes identified with north but more accurately conceptualized as the sun's zenith—were associated with white, whereas intervals between west and east—representing the sun's nadir and possibly south—were associated with yellow. At the center of the world stood the *yaxche,* "first tree" or "green tree," marking a fifth direction, possibly up-and-down, associated with blue-green. Seven layers of the heavens extended above the earth, ruled by thirteen Lords of the Heavens: six marked the sun's ascent into the sky, six its descent, and one the sun's position at noon. Similarly, below the earth lay the five layers of Xibalba, the realm of the dead, ruled by nine Lords of the Underworld. Each night, the sun passed through the underworld in the guise of a jaguar, descending four layers to reach the nadir at midnight and then ascending four more to rise again in the east. Here again, the primordial importance of the sun and of the ecliptic in Maya cosmology can be seen in representations of Itzamná as a two-headed reptilian "celestial monster" whose serpentlike body encircled the plane of the earth's surface. The name *Itzamná* ("lizard house," or "iguana house") is itself suggestive: *Itzam* refers to the reptilian monster who represented the earth's surface in Maya iconography, and *na* alludes to the cosmic "house" of Itzam circumscribed by the diurnal and annual movements of the sun.

Maya calendrics developed from the pan-Mesoamerican 260-day calendar, which consisted of a permutating cycle of twenty named days intermeshed with the numbers 1 to 13, much as the days of the week in the Gregorian calender mesh continuously with the coefficients of the days of the months. Because 13 is a prime number, a day name occurred with the same coefficient once every 260 days (20 × 13 = 260) as the cycle endlessly repeated itself. Alongside this ritual calendar ran a second cycle covering the vague year of 365 days and consisting of eighteen named months of twenty days each and a final "unnamed" month of five days (365/18 = 20 + 5). Since these two calenders ran concurrently and continuously, a day with the same position in both the 260-day round and the vague year would occur only once every 52 years (or more precisely, once every 18,980 days, the least common multiple of 260 and 365). For most Mesoamerican cultures, this 52-year Calendar Round was the longest time period recognized. The Maya, however, refined this system into an absolute reckoning of time called the Long Count. Apparently lacking a geometry that allowed them accurate measurement of diurnal time, the Maya made the day their fundamental calendrical unit and calculated time's passage from a base date in the year 3114 BCE. By counting day units rather than annual cycles, the Maya measured astronomical time more accurately, but, ironically, their calendar came to have less and less seasonal relevance. Although they precisely calculated the slippage of the vague year against the tropical year by counting lunar cycles, the Maya evidently refused to adjust their sacred count to mere agricultural or seasonal concerns.

The twenty day names of the calendar also represented deities who ruled over the cosmos, successively exerting their influence on human fate and destiny. Because the twenty day names did not divide evenly into the 365 days of the vague year, every fifth day name in the sequence of twenty alternately began a new year, yielding four "yearbearers." These four days represented the most powerful calendrical deities, each of which initiated, and thus influenced, every fourth year. Years were grouped into longer cycles called *katuns*, periods of roughly twenty years, each named by its final day. Although *katuns* always ended with the day name *Ahau,* they were distinguished by the coefficients from 1 to 13 that accompanied the day name. Thus after an arithmetically complex permutation containing *katuns* 1 Ahau to 13 Ahau, the *katun* round began again, repeating itself every thirteen *katuns*, or once about every 256 years. Within this cycle, often called the Short Count, the Maya expected history to repeat itself according to the esoteric nature, as well as the past events, of each *katun.* This belief was so strong that at times it may have actually influenced the course of Maya history.

Classic Maya religion, however, involved more than time and astronomy. Figures in Classic inscriptions once thought to depict deities are now known to represent actual Maya rulers, and the dynastic histories of such sites as Yaxchilan, Tikal, and Palenque have been reconstructed. Ancestor worship and the apotheosis of deceased rulers were essential aspects of Classic Maya religion. Some archaeologists further suggest that the impressive temples and pyramids that dominate Maya sites were funerary monuments to these deified rulers. The magnificent tomb of Lord Pacal (603–683 CE) found beneath the Temple of Inscriptions at Palenque clearly supports this theory, but insufficient excavation of the interiors of other Maya pyramids leaves the issue unresolved.

The intervals between the birth, accession, and death dates of rulers depicted in historical inscriptions often coincide with important Maya calendrical periods, suggesting that Maya priests may well have manipulated the life histories of their lords to conform to celestial cycles of the sun, moon, and other heavenly bodies. Ultimately, however, both human and celestial cycles were grounded in the internal logic and permutations of Maya arithmetic and numerology. Indeed, the Maya calculated dates millions of years into the past and thousands of years into the future, testimony to their mathematically abstract conception of time.

Postclassic Maya Religion. Despite the rapid decline of Classic Maya civilization after 900 CE, Maya religion survived in the Postclassic states of Yucatán and highland Guatemala (900–1530 CE). The Long Count was abandoned after 908 CE, but at least in Yucatán the *katun* prophecies of the Short Count continued to order Maya life well into the eighteenth century. Old agricultural deities such as the *chac*s (rain gods), the *balam*s (guardians of field and hearth), Kauil (the maize god), and Ixchel (the moon goddess and patroness of weaving, medicine, and childbirth) undoubtedly also survived intact. Although human sacrifice by decapitation had been practiced throughout Maya history, central Mexican influence between the tenth and thirteenth centuries introduced heart sacrifice to the Maya and prompted calendrical and cosmological reforms, including the importation of Kukulkan, the Maya version of Quetzalcoatl, the feathered serpent god of the Toltecs. The Spanish conquest of the Maya area (1524–1540 CE) came as only another in a series of foreign incursions that never quite obliterated the distinctiveness of Maya culture and religion.

Contemporary Maya Religion. Contemporary Maya religion has been transformed by Roman Catholicism, but strong continuities with the pre-Hispanic past persist. Such links can be found in colonial-era documents written both by Spanish chroniclers and by Indians who learned to write their own languages in Roman script. Among the latter, the *Books of Chilam Balam* of Yucatán and the *Popol Vuh* and *The Annals of the Cakchiquels* from highland Guatemala provide rich information on Maya mythology, cosmology, and history. Although obviously influenced by Christianity, these writings show that the Maya neither passively nor naively accepted the new religion; indeed, a passage in the *Book of Chilam Balam of Chumayel* uses Maya concepts of the beginning of time to criticize biblical creation. Nonetheless, by the eighteenth century Maya religion had become syncretized with Christianity, producing the fusion of the two religions found among the Maya today.

The motion of the sun still defines Maya cosmology, making the eastern and western horizons the primary cardinal directions. The circular paths of the sun and moon unite the various layers of the cosmos above and below the earth's surface. The preeminence of the sun as "Our Father" or "Our Grandfather" is reflected in its identification with God or, more frequently, Christ. Similarly, the moon is often associated with the Virgin Mary and called "Our Mother" or "Our Grandmother." In quotidian affairs, Catholic saints have become the supernatural guardians of field, hearth, and health, although in Yucatán the old *balam*s still persist, and in some highland communities autochthonous ancestral deities remain important. The earth and its products are controlled by earth lords who must be propitiated before any planting, harvesting, building, or hunting can be done. Although both saints and earth lords can send sickness or death, the saints usually do so as punishment for transgressing social norms; the earth lords do so out of anger at ritual neglect or to recruit souls to labor inside their mountains. Because Indians often identify their local saints as Indians and conceptualize earth lords as avaricious mestizos, these deities clearly embody the ethnic conflict between Indians and non-Indians that still smolders in Mesoamerica.

Both the 260-day and 365-day calendars have survived, although the Maya of the Chiapas highlands use only the names of the eighteen months of the vague year, while in the highlands of Guatemala the twenty day names are most frequently retained; the lowland Maya of Yucatán have lost the pre-Hispanic calendar entirely. Where they are remembered, the day lords associated with the twenty day names still rule over human existence through divinations performed by "daykeepers" in scores of highland Indian communities. Although techniques vary widely, divination often involves reciting the names of the days in their proper order while counting out random handfuls of dried *tzite (Erythrina corallodendrum)* seeds, rock crystals, or even corn kernels. The day name reached at the end of the count determines the daykeeper's prognostication. Although each day may carry a particular set of associations, the daykeeper also uses paronomasia—metaphoric play on the sound rather than the meaning of the day name—to arrive at specific interpretations of the day name's significance for any given divination. Divinations are performed to ascertain the cause of illness or death, to determine propitious days to undertake important or risky enterprises, and to choose local religious and political leaders.

Human destiny also involves the welfare of the soul.

Unlike the eternal Christian soul, Maya souls are largely involved with the here and now, since the soul represents the seat of reason, most concretely expressed in articulate speech and proper social behavior. In their very essence, individuals are enmeshed in their community and the social morality that it presupposes. Individuals can lose all or part of their soul through illness, through experiencing strong emotions such as anger or fright, or through other forms of culturally inappropriate behavior. Saving one's soul requires the constant attention to one's relations with fellow community members rather than merely purity of action and intent. Consequently, the Christian doctrines of original sin and divine salvation are of little concern to Maya religion. The dependency of the "inner" soul on external conditions can also be seen in the Maya concept of animal spirit-companions. These mythical beasts share with their human counterparts the same life history and destiny, and tales abound of the Maya hunter who inadvertently shoots his animal double, thus killing himself.

The formal institutions of the contemporary Maya religion focus on the saints and the Roman Catholic religious calendar. The fiesta of the local patron saint is usually the largest community celebration of the year. In highland Chiapas, Carnival is the most important nonpatronal fiesta, whereas in Guatemala Holy Week receives more attention. The highland Maya also practice saint exchange, in which images of local saints "visit" the images of patron saints of neighboring communities on their feast days.

Individuals serve the saints by joining *cofradías* ("brotherhoods"), where for one year they care for the saint's image and perform the proper rituals, often at considerable personal expense. In return, individuals gain social prestige and access to higher political and religious offices. Political offices also traditionally require heavy ritual responsibilities and expenditures, especially during change-of-office ceremonies when incoming officeholders must seek approval—and thus legitimation—from God, the saints, and the earth lords alike. Outside the *cofradías,* traditional Maya religion recognizes no formal institutions. Daykeepers, curers, and midwives depend on personal reputation rather than public office for their legitimacy. The eloquence of their prayers determines the efficacy of their rituals. They kneel before church altar and mountain shrine alike, wrapped in clouds of copal incense as they appeal to Christian God and Maya deity, guardian saint and capricious earth lord. Like their ancestors before them, they continue to measure the count of time, discerning a meaning for the present out of the infinite pattern of the past.

BIBLIOGRAPHY

The best general introduction to Maya religion is J. Eric S. Thompson's *Maya History and Religion* (Norman, Okla., 1970), although his views on Classic Maya social structure and the nature of Maya hieroglyphic writing have been challenged. David H. Kelley's *Deciphering the Maya Script* (Austin, 1976) presents a broad view of different approaches to Maya writing, especially in regard to the phonetic nature of the script. The proceedings from four recent conferences concerning Maya epigraphy, religion, and society have been published in six volumes, the latest of which is *Fourth Palenque Round Table 1980* (Austin, 1984), edited by Merle Greene Robertson and Elizabeth Benson. Technical but highly stimulating articles can be found in a volume edited by Norman Hammond and Gordon R. Willey, *Maya Archaeology and Ethnohistory* (Austin, 1979); papers therein by Clemency Coggins, Dennis Puleston, and Gordon Brotherston are extremely valuable. Anthony F. Aveni's *Skywatchers of Ancient Mexico* (Austin, 1980) is an indispensable guide to the "ethnoastronomy" of Mesoamerican civilizations. Of the colonial sources on Maya religion, *Landa's Relación de las cosas de Yucatán* (Cambridge, Mass., 1941), translated and edited by A. M. Tozzer, is the most thoroughly annotated edition of the work of the famous chronicler Diego de Landa, although the pagination in the index and syllabus is occasionally frustratingly faulty. Munro S. Edmonson's translation of *The Book of Counsel: The Popol Vuh of the Quiche Maya of Guatemala* (New Orleans, 1971) was the first to demonstrate the parallel couplet verse form of this epic of Maya mythology and history. Among the many ethnographies of modern Maya religions, Evon Z. Vogt's *Tortillas for the Gods: A Symbolic Analysis of Zinacanteco Rituals* (Cambridge, Mass., 1976) stands out as one of the most extensive and detailed studies to date. Barbara Tedlock's *Time and the Highland Maya* (Albuquerque, 1982) is an excellent study of contemporary Maya divination and calendrics. Finally, Eva Hunt's *The Transformation of the Hummingbird: Cultural Roots of a Zinacantecan Mythical Poem* (Ithaca, N.Y., 1977) provides a masterful structuralist analysis of both contemporary and pre-Hispanic Maya religion.

JOHN M. WATANABE

MAY DAY is the only major festival of pre-Christian Europe that was not adapted by the Christian church for its own purposes. Part of a yearly cycle that includes midwinter and harvest celebrations, it stands midway between the long, cold nights of winter and the days of plenty at summer's end, with symbolism and ceremony that reflect its pivotal position.

Across Europe the key symbol of the day is fresh spring growth, and the general hope is for fecundity. Traditionally, youths spent the eve of May Day in neighboring woods and awoke the villagers the next morning by visiting each house, singing a traditional carol and bearing garlands of fresh leaves and flowers. Or they might disguise one of their number as Jack-in-the-Green by enshrouding him with a portable bower of fresh greenery. Jack and his followers danced around the town collecting money from passersby for later feasting. In many villages these young people also cut down trees, which they then erected as maypoles in the village centers. Each pole served as a gathering place for community dances and activities.

Traditional dramas enacted on May Day in many European countries commemorated the triumph of summer over winter, while in England the focus was on dancing and pageantry. Youths elected a king and queen of the May to preside over the day's proceedings; sometimes they were dressed as Robin Hood and Maid Marian, with members of their entourage representing Friar Tuck, Little John, and Robin's other merry men.

Although the origins of May Day are unknown, what is known of its history is suggestive. The festival is not based on a magical ritual to secure the fertility of the crops, as once thought, but instead is a community expression of hope and joy. The emphasis has always been social solidarity, and not the supernatural or the metaphysical.

BIBLIOGRAPHY

Forrest, John. *Morris and Matachin: A Study in Comparative Choreography.* Sheffield, England, 1984.

Judge, Roy. *The Jack-in-the-Green: A May Day Custom.* Ipswich, England, 1978.

JOHN FORREST

MAZDAKISM. Also known as the *khurram* ("happy, cheerful") or *drist* ("right") religion, Mazdakism flourished under the reign of Kawād (488–531) in Sasanid Iran. The name of the religion is derived from that of its founder, Mazdak. The social implications of Mazdakism are important, particularly because it is often considered to have been an archaic and Oriental form of socialism or communism (Nöldeke, 1879; Christensen, 1925; and others), but it would be an exaggeration to reduce it to an essentially social movement (Klíma, 1957).

Sources of knowledge about Mazdakism (Byzantine and Syriac, Pahlavi, Arab, and Persian) are few, and almost all are hostile to the religion. For example, the *Mazdak-nāmag* (Book of Mazdak), a short work written in Pahlavi and translated into Arabic by Ibn al-Muqaffaʿ, condemns the misdeeds and deceitfulness of the heresiarch. Several fragments of the text were quoted in the works of Muslim writers, from Abū Rayḥān al-Bīrūnī to Niẓām al-Mulk, Ibn al-Balkhī, and Ibn al-Athīr. Firdawsī also hands down a version of the story of Mazdak that is derived from an aristocratic source from the Sasanid period, the lost *Khwadāy-nāmag* (Book of the Kings) in Pahlavi. The heresiographer al-Sharistānī (eleventh to twelfth century) gives us a particularly important note on Mazdak's doctrine since it is probably derived from a Mazdakean source. No less valuable, however, are the other Muslim authors who have provided information, such as al-Ṭabarī, al-Thaʿālibī, and Ibn al-Nadīm.

Mazdakism has been interpreted as a religious movement with a predominantly Manichaean heritage or as a Zoroastrian heresy (Molé, 1960–1961, pp. 1–28; Yarshater, 1983). It has a number of elements in common with Manichaeism, especially the gnostic traits present in the little we know of Mazdak's teachings, but there is no doubt that the religion presented itself as a reinterpretation of Zoroastrianism.

The background of Mazdakism is linked to two persons, of whom we know little other than their names: Bundos, a Manichaean who lived for a time in Rome under the emperor Diocletian (245–313), and Zarādusht (son of Khurragān), a Zoroastrian priest, a *mōbad* of Fasā in Fārs (fifth century). These two men were probably the predecessors of Mazdak (son of Bāmdād) himself, who preached his religious and social doctrine at the end of the fifth century. This was a period of profound crisis in the Sasanid state, which was conquered by the Ephthalites in 484 and shaken by a grave disturbance of its aristocratic, feudal, and clerical structure. Social innovations are certainly not incompatible with a gnostic outlook; one has only to think of the egalitarian spirit and love for social justice expressed by the Carpocratians, the followers of Zarathushtra (Zoroaster), Pythagoras, and Plato. There are thus good reasons for the attempt on the part of scholars to find links between the movement of Carpocrates and that of Mazdak (Klíma, 1957, 1977; Yarshater, 1983).

Mazdak, the heretic *par excellence (zandīg,* "he who relies on interpretations"), taught that the supreme deity was not a supreme providence and that the whole of being is due to the mixture or separation, absolutely fortuitous, of light and darkness. He spoke of three elements—water, fire, earth—and of four powers—discernment, understanding, preservation, joy—which act through seven viziers who circulate in twelve spiritual entities. He taught that there was a system of correspondences between the spiritual macrocosm, the mesocosm (earth), and the human microcosm. Mazdak proclaimed that a person arrived at a liberating knowledge through an understanding of the symbolic powers of letters, words, and numbers and that the individual who had realized in himself the four, the seven, and the twelve no longer had need of exterior religious obligations.

Mazdakism's moral philosophy was inspired by the principles of equality, solidarity, and pacifism. Since it found the origin of all spiritual, moral, and social evils in property, it preached that both goods and women should be shared.

After having embraced Mazdakism, Kawād temporarily lost the throne, owing to the reaction of the aristocracy and the clergy. He then abandoned Mazdak and his numerous followers, among them his firstborn son, Kāūs, to their fate. His favorite son, the future Khosrow I (531–579), had the Mazdakists massacred and restored the old social order.

Mazdakism survived as an underground movement, however. It exercised a powerful influence on various Muslim heresies, especially on the Khurrāmīyah and the Qarāmiṭah (Yarshater, 1983).

BIBLIOGRAPHY

Altheim, Franz. "Mazdak and Porphyrios." *History of Religions* 3 (1963): 1–20.

Bausani, Alessandro. *Persia religiosa da Zaratustra a Bahâ'u'llâh.* Milan, 1959.

Christensen, Arthur. *Le règne du roi Kawādh I et le communisme mazdakite.* Copenhagen, 1925.

Christensen, Arthur. *L'Iran sous les Sassanides.* 2d ed. Copenhagen, 1944.

Gaube, H. "Mazdak: Historical Reality or Invention?" *Studia Iranica* II (1982): 111–122.

Klíma, Otakar. *Mazdak: Geschichte einer sozialen Bewegung im sassanidischen Persien.* Prague, 1957.

Klíma, Otakar. *Beiträge zur Geschichte des Mazdakismus.* Prague, 1977.

Molé, Marijan. "Le problème des sectes zoroastriennes dans les livres phelevis." *Oriens* 13–14 (1960–1961): 1–28.

Nöldeke, Theodor. "Orientalischer Socialismus." *Deutsche Rundschau* 18 (1879): 284–291.

Pigulevskaia, Nina V. *Les villes de l'État iranien aux époques parthe et sassanide.* Paris, 1963.

Widengren, Geo. *Die Religionen Irans.* Stuttgart, 1965. Translated as *Les religions de l'Iran* (Paris, 1968).

Yarshater, Ehsan. "Mazdakism." In *The Cambridge History of Iran,* vol. 3, edited by Ehsan Yarshater, pp. 991–1024. Cambridge, 1983.

GHERARDO GNOLI
Translated from Italian by Roger DeGaris

MAZE. *See* Labyrinth.

MBONA (sometimes also spelled M'Bona or M'bona) is the name of the patronal deity of a famous shrine near the township of Nsanje in the Republic of Malawi (southeastern Africa). Although he is usually referred to as a rain god, Mbona is also invoked on the occasion of locust plagues, floods, epidemic diseases, and other acute threats to the productive and reproductive capacities of the land and its population.

Mbona's is a territorial cult, which may be defined as a cult whose constituency is a territorial group identified by common occupation of a land area, so that membership, in the final instance, is a consequence of residence and not kinship or ethnic designation. The cult is supervised by local chiefs and headmen under the chairmanship of a high priest and a chief administrator. In addition to these officials, there is also a spirit medium, a man or woman who on occasion claims to be possessed by Mbona and who comments on a variety of urgent political issues while possessed. Formerly, the cult also maintained a spirit wife, a woman consecrated for life to Mbona's service, who was supposed to receive revelations from the deity in her dreams and was regularly consulted by chiefs and other important people. There no longer is a permanent spirit wife, but on ceremonial occasions her place is taken temporarily by a local woman. Although the oldest known written documents on the cult date only from the middle of the nineteenth century, it is much older, predating even the Portuguese penetration of the southeast African interior in the first half of the sixteenth century.

According to oral tradition, Mbona was a celebrated rainmaker who, on account of his great popularity, came into conflict with the secular and religious authorities of the day, who in the end had him killed. Following his death, the local populace is said to have erected a shrine to his name and thus to have initiated the cult. The story of Mbona's life and death is known in many versions, but all follow a common structure and can be reduced to three streams or clusters depending on whether the events of the narrative take place in a stateless setting, an emergent state, or a highly centralized kingdom. The mightier the state, the more Mbona is portrayed as a marginal person. Mbona's diminishing status therefore seems to symbolize the increasing subjection of the commonalty to the aristocracy at successive stages of state formation.

As stated before, we do not know of any written documents on the cult prior to the middle of the nineteenth century; nevertheless, certain names and events referred to in the Mbona legends are also found in Portuguese documents pertaining to the sixteenth and seventeenth centuries. From a comparison between the legends and the historical texts it can be inferred, among other things, that the cult underwent major organizational and theological changes about 1600 and that, probably under Portuguese missionary influence, Mbona was attributed certain Christ-like traits. After this radical transformation, the cult gained its widest geographical acceptance and became one of the most influential religious organizations on the north bank of the Zambezi. Over the past century, however, its importance has diminished to the extent that as of 1985 the cult has little more than local significance.

BIBLIOGRAPHY

Discussions of various aspects of the Mbona cult can be found in essays I have contributed to several special collections. Among them are "The History and Political Role of the M'Bona Cult among the Mang'anja," in *The Historical Study of African Religion*, edited by T. O. Ranger and Isaria N. Kimambo (Berkeley, 1972); "The Interaction of the M'Bona Cult and Christianity, 1859–1963," in *Themes in the Christian History of Central Africa*, edited by T. O. Ranger and John Weller (Berkeley, 1975); "Cult Idioms and the Dialectics of a Region," in *Regional Cults*, edited by R. P. Werbner (New York, 1977); "The Chisumphi and Mbona Cults in Malawi: A Comparative History," in *Guardians of the Land*, edited by J. Matthew Schoffeleers (Gwelo, 1978); and "Oral History and the Retrieval of the Distant Past: On the Use of Legendary Chronicles as Sources of Historical Information," in *Theoretical Explorations in African Religion*, edited by Wim van Binsbergen and J. Matthew Schoffeleers (London, 1984).

J. MATTHEW SCHOFFELEERS

MCPHERSON, AIMEE SEMPLE (1890–1944), American Pentecostal evangelist and divine healer. McPherson was born Aimee Elizabeth Kennedy on a farm near Ingersoll, Ontario, Canada. Raised in the Salvation Army, she was converted to Pentecostalism through the preaching of Robert James Semple, whom she married in 1908 and accompanied to China, where they served as missionaries until Semple's death in 1910. Two subsequent marriages ended in divorce.

In 1917, McPherson embarked upon an evangelistic and divine healing career in the United States that quickly brought her national and international fame. In 1923, she settled in Los Angeles and built the five-thousand-seat Angelus Temple, a center of welfare services, and in 1927, she incorporated her large network of churches as the International Church of the Foursquare Gospel. She also founded a ministerial institute, later named the Lighthouse of International Foursquare Evangelism (LIFE) Bible College.

McPherson's turbulent personal life, involving her alleged kidnapping, rumors of romantic liaisons, dozens of lawsuits, conflicts with her mother and daughter, and divorce from her third husband, brought her much notoriety. Nevertheless, she retained the unswerving loyalty of her followers. Her denomination grew to four hundred congregations in the United States, two hundred mission stations abroad, and a worldwide total of twenty-two thousand members at the time of her death.

McPherson's Foursquare Gospel was a restatement of standard Pentecostal doctrine focusing on Jesus Christ as savior, baptizer in the Holy Spirit, healer, and coming king. She wrote several autobiographical books, published numerous pamphlets and articles, edited two periodicals, and composed some eighty hymns and five sacred operas. In her preaching she avoided condemnation and appeals to fear, emphasizing instead the love and joy that religion provides.

McPherson was unique in her evangelistic style. Her mastery at promoting herself and her work through the media made "Sister Aimee," or simply "Aimee," a household name. She was a pioneer in religious broadcasting, establishing the first church-owned radio station (KFSG) in the United States in 1924. She adapted the techniques of vaudeville and the theater to evangelism, using costumes, lighting, scenery and props, orchestras and brass bands, huge choirs, and dramatizations to achieve an unforgettable emotional impact on her audiences. Endowed with enormous energy and optimism, a powerful, melodious voice, rare acting ability, and a physical attractiveness heightened by an aura of sexuality, she was acclaimed a spellbinding platform personality by the millions to whom she preached.

BIBLIOGRAPHY

Bahr, Robert. *Least of All Saints: The Story of Aimee Semple McPherson*. Englewood Cliffs, N.J., 1979. A popular, fictionalized account that captures much of the whirlwind spirit of McPherson's career and temperament.

McLoughlin, William G. "Aimee Semple McPherson: Your Sister in the King's Glad Service." *Journal of Popular Culture* 1 (Winter 1968): 193–217. An analysis and evaluation that places McPherson's life and career in their cultural context, by an eminent historian of American religion.

McPherson, Aimee Semple. *This Is That: Personal Experiences, Sermons, and Writings*. Los Angeles, 1923. A reconstruction of McPherson's early years as she wanted others to see them, and a collection of sermons and tracts that reveal her public message.

McWilliams, Carey. "Aimee Semple McPherson: 'Sunlight in My Soul.' " In *The Aspirin Age, 1919–1941*, edited by Isabel Leighton, pp. 50–80. Los Angeles, 1949. A sympathetic interpretation of McPherson's life that reveals the tragic element behind the radiant facade.

ROBERT MAPES ANDERSON

MECCA. *See* Pilgrimage, *article on* Muslim Pilgrimage.

MEDIATORS. *See* Angels; Atonement, *article on* Christian Concepts; Demons; Logos; Priesthood; Prophecy; Shamanism; *and* Spiritual Guide.

MEDICINE. [*This entry consists of three articles:*

Medicine and Religion in Tribal Cultures
Medicine and Religion in Eastern Traditions
Medicine and Religion in Western Traditions

The first article explores the relation between religious belief and practices of healing and curing in the traditions of tribal peoples. The second article examines these issues in the context of the great religious traditions of the East, paying particular attention to the religious traditions of China and Japan. The last article discusses the roots and development of modern Western medical science and its historical interaction with Western religious traditions.]

Medicine and Religion in Tribal Cultures

In traditional societies, the field of medicine—that is, the way illness is conceived of and treated—is inextricably linked to the area of social relationships and to the magico-religious world. Physical diseases, psychic disorders, and even death itself are all, for the most part, thought of as the results of ethicosocial or personal situations, and as having been effected through the intervention of spirits, ghosts, gods, or other forces belonging to collective belief. Only a few types of illnesses, disturbances, and deaths are, as a rule, viewed as being independent of human responsibility or supernatural agency. Even in the interpretation of endemic and relatively common diseases, an attempt is made to assign a cause to what otherwise seems a purely chance occurrence of the type that easily prompts men to ask "Why me? Why now?"

Causation and Treatment of Illness. The presupposition of a human and/or spiritual agent is fundamental to the entire process of medical treatment in traditional societies. Diviners, magicians, shamans, and priests make use of their special relationship with the spirit world to diagnose illness and to prescribe preliminary therapeutic procedures aimed at securing the effectiveness of subsequent physical treatment. The preliminary therapeutic procedures may, depending on the context, entail: (1) confession of personal responsibility by the patient or his kin; (2) appropriate reparation for any wrong or infringement committed; (3) the identification of an external evil-maker and prescription of control or retaliation techniques; (4) the readjustment of interpersonal relationships; or (5) the offering of expiatory and cleansing sacrifices. Subsequent physical treatment may include the use of plants and other medicines and the manipulation of the patient's body.

Many of these elements are found in the traditional therapeutic system of the Akan peoples of Ghana (Appiah-Kubi, 1981; Twumasi, 1975). The Nzema tribe of the Akan, which also has been studied by Vinigi Grottanelli and myself, provides an instructive example. Among the Nzema, some light and temporary ailments such as headaches, diarrhea, and aches of the joints are accepted as natural and chance occurrences. All serious and obscure afflictions, however, are explained in terms of "rational" causation and supernatural interference. Serious illness or death is never ascribed to the workings of chance, but rather to some cause of a mystical nature involving the workings of supernatural beings or forces. Ethical and social relationships are also involved in the causation of illness, inasmuch as someone is supposed to have infringed, deliberately or inadvertently, some rule. "Health is not an isolated phenomenon, but part of the magico-religious fabric of existence," and of the social, ethical, and cosmic equilibrium. "Disease is considered as a disequilibrium in the body as well as in society" (Appiah-Kubi, 1981, pp. 2, 14). It is also a disruption of the cosmic order, which is thought of as dependent on the relationship between men and spirits or gods.

Among the Nzema, it is the responsibility of magico-religious experts to diagnose the real source of sickness and death, and to prescribe ritual, behavioral, and medicinal remedies. The experts are supposed to "have eyes" to see the spirits and to know the truth unknown to others. The native doctor or medicine man *(ninsinli)* is a specialist whose knowledge of divination, exorcism, witch-hunting, and herbalism is acquired in an apprenticeship under personal deities. His activities as a healer and diviner are carried out in private, at home, with the simple participation of the client.

The *kōmenle,* or priest, receives his or her power from a spirit-god who calls the priest through dreams or charismatic visions, often following some sickness or misfortune. After having studied with an older practitioner, a *kōmenle* becomes a full-time priest in the cult of his or her god and periodically carries out village ceremonies such as public dances. During his dance, the *kōmenle* is possessed by a single god or a series of gods in succession. The possessing spirit speaks through the priest in a language incomprehensible to all except a "linguist" assistant who interprets the utterances for patients. The community as a whole benefits from the ceremonies as they provide an opportunity for social gatherings and for communion with deities.

Another type of diviner-healer is the *ēsofo*, a priest of one of the new cults that blend native beliefs with elements derived from contacts with Christianity. The *ēsofo* employs traditional techniques to diagnose illness but does not receive inspiration from ancestral gods. The healer's first task is to divine where responsibility for the disease lies—whether it was induced by a malevolent person using sorcery, or by the patient's kin, or whether the patient himself is responsible. Through negligent or disrespectful behavior toward a god, it is possible to create the state of tension between humans and gods known as *sipe*. The offender may also have breached social or ethical rules, or he may have violated a sexual or food taboo. The inadvertent omission of a libation to the *asongu* (the gods who protect children), or to the *awosonle* (the deities who preside over the general welfare), or any infringement of ritual law, may result in angered gods or ghosts sending all types of calamities, sickness, or death.

Once the *ninsinli, kōmenle,* or *ēsofo* has been summoned by the patient or his relatives, he inquires into the moral, social, and ritual behavior of the entire clan and about possible enemies. In performing his inquiry, the Nzema priest-healer may make use of cowrie-shell or string divination. In both procedures, lots are drawn and the results are interpreted according to a traditional and esoteric code. In general, the healer relies upon the sanction of the gods, who observe human behavior and guard the social and ritual order, to help him determine who is responsible for an illness. The person who committed a breach or who perpetrated witchcraft is urged to confess his guilt. Anyone who refuses to confess exposes himself to the risk of sickness or death.

The healing practices of the Akan entail magico-religious beliefs and rituals—divination, propitiatory rites, possession—that are typical of systems of healing in many traditional societies. These systems imply a meaning, namely that humans are dependent on the power of divine beings; they also express a fundamental value, that is, the desire to reach an equilibrium in human relationships. Finally, they fulfill an important cognitive function by offering an explanation for sickness and death, which, if left unexplained, would engender ever-increasing levels of anxiety. The society has thus discovered a logically consistent and psychologically reassuring means of combating evil.

Witchcraft, Sorcery, Medicine, and Magic. Witchcraft and sorcery are considered to be two of the main causes of sickness and death in the traditional societies of sub-Saharan Africa, Oceania, and the Americas. E. E. Evans-Pritchard, when studying the Azande of the Sudan, defined witchcraft as an ability to perpetrate evil that derives from an intrinsic quality of the evildoer that is not deliberately acquired. It is, he points out, purely a psychic act.

Sorcery, on the other hand, is evil deliberately effected by experts in harmful magic who have the power to send the so-called juju (evil) against their own enemies or those of their clients. The phenomenon of the evil eye, which is found in many cultures, and the evil worked by the so-called gallbladder men (found by Evans-Pritchard among the Azande) can be placed in an intermediate position between witchcraft and sorcery. All of these phenomena imply a rational cause for evil, inasmuch as the evil is thought to be due to human agency. On the other hand, the agent is thought to receive his power from supernatural forces.

The activities of witches, sorcerers, users of the evil eye, and gallbladder men in working evil are an offense against the supernatural forces that are in charge of protecting or restoring the equilibrium of human relationships. Those who work such evil thus destroy confidence among members of the community and harm social cohesion in general. For this reason, societies develop various defenses against witchcraft and sorcery. Those suspected of such practices are avoided or bribed; oracles are used to identify culprits; and medicines and charms, and sometimes retaliatory threats, are used against workers of harmful magic.

An important figure in counteracting witchcraft and sorcery is the magician. The magician's task is to restore the equilibrium of ethical and social conventions that have been handed down from the sacred world of the ancestors. In this way, he restores the balance of interpersonal relationships in the community. We have seen that, in a parallel way, among the Akan and especially among the Nzema, a restoration of social equilibrium is made possible by the belief that the curse of an offended man is also endowed with intrinsic magical power that can induce the gods to send illness against the offender.

It is generally recognized that witchcraft and sorcery are expressions of tension within a society. The practices themselves arise from an antisocial feeling and a desire to transgress rules on the part of the practitioner, while they engender fear, hatred, and aggression among the members of the community. The society indeed derives some satisfaction from the identification of a witch or sorcerer in that a cause is discovered for otherwise inexplicable illnesses or deaths. But once accusations of witchcraft have been made, they tend to lead to greater apprehension within the community and may result in great social upheavals. The witch-hunts that occurred in sub-Saharan Africa and Melanesia, usually during times of heavy social stress (e.g., after a clash with white men), exemplify this pattern. Witchcraft and sorcery are, in fact, a constant threat to the delicate balance between personal interest and sociocultural order.

The magician is supposed to have the power to undo the evil caused by witches and sorcerers or to take vengeance by inflicting sickness or death upon them. In this way the magician serves as an antiwitch operator and attempts to heal the witch's or sorcerer's victim by means of his own esoteric techniques, although his ability to defeat his opponent is uncertain. For this reason, witchcraft and good magic stand in ambivalent relationship with regard to the field of medicine.

Among the Aborigines of Australia, a distinction is drawn between witchcraft and sorcery on the one hand and good magic on the other. This aspect of Aboriginal culture was first described by A. P. Elkin and has since been restudied by Catherine Berndt. Among the Aborigines, only illness and the death of infants and the very old are considered natural occurrences. All other instances of disease, and indeed all kinds of misfortunes, are attributed to the work of witches or sorcerers. It is noteworthy that the Aboriginal doctor unites, in his person, the worker of harmful magic and the purveyor of healing magic. In other cultures, these roles are usually held by separate persons.

Magic and witchcraft dominate both the overall sociocultural system and the everyday life of Australian Aborigines. Accordingly, they rely heavily on the healer to help combat adversaries who might send misfortune, sickness, and death. The Aboriginal doctor receives his power for both good and evil from spirits who are believed to have created the world of humans and to have founded the rules and customs of tribal life during the time of mythical origins (the Dreaming). His status is formally sanctioned in an initiation rite or by particular occurrences in which he experiences visions or dreams of spiritual beings. Among the Aborigines of Arnhem Land, for example, the healer receives his power directly from Rainbow Snake, a highly important mythical being who lives in water holes and at times stretches his neck up to the sky. The initiate is thought "to be swallowed by the rainbow serpent and to be vomited out as a newborn infant and ritually restored to adult stature as a medicine man" (Berndt, in Kiev, 1964, p. 269).

Some Aboriginal doctors claim to have received their power from a spirit or ghost that appeared to them. "The spirit-ghost inserted into the man's head a thin bamboo stick, sometimes identified with a spirit-snake, and he blew into the man's ear giving him 'breath,' equivalent to the spirit or power" (Berndt, in Kiev, 1964, p. 269). Among the peoples of southeastern Australia, those who aspired to be healers would, in former times, climb to the sky in a trance and receive a quartz stone or pearl shell from the supreme being as tokens of their power. These objects would be used in healing, rainmaking, and other magical rituals.

Indeed, the Australian Aboriginal doctor has multiple roles, functioning as healer, rainmaker, and diviner. He also controls ghosts and malignant spirits, identifies sorcerers and murderers, interprets dreams, and discovers what breaches of taboo are at the root of particular misfortunes. As a sorcerer he performs protective magic by using the bone-pointing technique, or by the taking of kidney fat. The bone-pointing is a magical projective rite. While chanting a powerful song, the performer points an animal or human bone toward his victim, who is killed both by the power of the song and by the ritual action. The fat extraction is a symbolic revivification. It is employed not only to heal persons by means of incisions in his body but also to mummify the corpse of the deceased in order to admit him to the sky and to initiate a healer by an analogous revivifying procedure. As the stealer of souls, the Aboriginal doctor causes death. As a healer, he makes use of plants and medicines and often pretends to have extracted from the patient's body such objects as stones or bones, which he exhibits to the patient as the material source of the illness. This procedure is used particularly in cases where the illness is thought to have been provoked by a sorcerer who has employed the bone-pointing technique.

The Aboriginal doctor's relation to the supernatural gives him the status of a religious figure. In his activities, however, he does not concern himself with ensuring that socioreligious values be upheld. He merely offers emotional help in times of anxiety, sickness, or death, and he protects individuals from evils that threaten and avenges injuries already suffered.

The evidence presented thus far indicates that among traditional societies there are basically two conceptions of the origin of misfortune, sickness, and death; concomitantly, there are two approaches to alleviating evil. According to the first conception, evil is divine punishment for bad behavior on the part of the patient or one of his relatives. Once restitution is made for wrongs committed, the way is open for the patient's successful recovery. The path is also then clear for reestablishment of the equilibrium guaranteed by social values. African possession cults typify the kind of religious system in which beliefs about illness are closely intertwined with social and ethical values. Likewise, emphasis is placed on the maintaining of traditional social values in the system of tribal medicine found among the Indians of North and South America. Among these peoples the confession of sin is a preliminary step in the process of treatment, and in all of these systems divine beings or ancestral spirits are present throughout the entire healing procedure. According to the second conception, evil and sickness are attributable to the actions of malevolent humans, namely witches and sorcerers. Divine beings do not intervene, and only human agents can counteract the evil by means of magical procedures. In such a system, no effort is made to restore the social and ethical balance, and the only point at issue is the respective effectiveness of the sorcerer and magician. Often, both of these conceptions coexist within the same culture.

Healers and Healing Practices. Traditional societies generally make no distinction between mental and physical illness with regard to beliefs concerning their respective origins, methods of treatment, or social attitudes toward them. The view that the mind and body are, for medical purposes, a single entity arises from the fact that all pain or deprivation (e.g., sterility, death) is seen as affecting the whole person. The experience of illness threatens areas of fundamental concern, such as the ability to converse and the capacity to act. As Gilbert Lewis observes in regard to the Gnaw people of New Guinea: "In fact what shows the illness, is the withdrawn, inert and wretched behaviour which follows: a behaviour which resembles a *rite de passage* and constitutes an appeal for help" (Lewis, in Loudon, 1976, p. 54). The Gnaw's basic belief is that "once critically ill, whatever are the causes which produce illness, such as spirits, destructive magic, and sorcery, you are more vulnerable and in danger of further and cumulative attacks from the spirits" (p. 62).

In other cultures, the condition of illness is actually treated as if it were a rite of passage. Among the Acawai (Akawaio) Indians of Guyana, resting and fasting or dieting are essential parts of the treatment of disease. Their shaman is reported to have remarked, "People should eat very little when ill." These same rituals of resting and fasting are observed by the Acawai on other occasions: by both parents when a baby is born; by both parents and especially the mother when a baby is ill; by a girl undergoing initiation after her first menstruation; by persons in mourning for deceased relatives; by an apprentice shaman preparing for his first public séance (A. Butt Colson, in Loudon, 1976, pp. 429–437). As we shall see in the Ndoep cult of the Wolof of Senegal, psychic disturbance is likewise treated as a rite of passage. The disturbance is thought to be provoked by possessing spirits, which are exorcised or controlled by means of passage ritual.

The essential similarity of mental and physical disorders is that both are provoked by the same kinds of agents: supernatural beings, witches, and sorcerers. Among the Mandari, a pastoral nomadic people of the Sudan, both acute instances of mental disturbance and physical illnesses affecting the head or upper body (headache, eye infection, cold, cough, sore throat) are thought to come from the Celestial Spirit, or Spirit of the Above. The explanation that the Mandari consistently give for these diseases is "the logical consequence of their observation of properties of natural phenomena. Swift mental illness is a 'falling down' of a celestial agent on the victim. Where the symptoms are revealed in physical form, it is the head, the upper part pointing to the sky, and the chest . . . that are most typically affected" (Buxton, 1973, p. 46). Treating such diseases involves an appeal to the spirit, and the preliminary treatment of all these sicknesses is analogous. When a "doctor," using the rattle divination, has ascertained the origin of the illness from the Above, a sacrifice of an ox or sheep is carried out to the Celestial Spirit. Each family dedicates a shrine to this spirit, but other shrines may be dedicated also to different spirits or powers and ghosts. Sacrifices are performed to conciliate their protection. Exorcism and sacrifice are common features in the relationship between men and supernatural forces in view of illness and evils.

The Mandari explain the origin of disease according to set principles. All diseases affecting men or even cattle are believed to result from the relations of men either to spirits or other men. A predominant role is assigned to spirits or powers operating along lines that are totally inscrutable. A secondary role is played by phenomena such as the rainbow, the moon, witchcraft, sorcery, the evil eye, the action of ghosts, or breaches of prohibitions and other sins. For example, chronic mental illness is supposed to be provoked by contact "with certain celestial phenomena in association with witchcraft" (Buxton, 1973, pp. 36–37). Uncontrolled and violent convulsions are associated with spirit possession *(molja)*. This condition is thought to be a sign of special election, and from it a person may derive healing power through which he becomes a physician-priest.

In fact, only a special set of experiences can qualify a Mandari as a doctor. First, one must have suffered a mental or physical illness of the celestial type. Second, one must have received a "call," which typically consists of a psychic crisis involving visions, withdrawal to the bush, and a refusal to eat or speak. The power to heal comes ultimately from the creator and, more directly, from celestial spirits or powers. Some doctors may, however, employ their power to do evil, and thus take on the character of sorcerers or witches. It is noteworthy that the Mandari doctor's profession does not make him influential socially. Mandari society shows a marked concern with speculative inquiry for its own sake; attempts are made to understand the nature of disease without emphasizing its ethicosocial implications.

The Maguzawa subgroup of the Hausa people in West Africa is similar to the Mandari, in that its ritual treatment is also essentially preventative. The treatment itself, as Murray Last has noted, is carried out "through initiation into a spirit possession cult for adults who are not ill, but who want to safeguard against anything wrong. . . . Loss or lack of children is the commonest cause for seeking treatment for spirit possession. The cure consists of getting oneself in harmony with the disease spirits" (Last, in Loudon, 1976, pp. 128–129).

As we have seen in the examples of the Akan and Mandari, in many societies illness itself is a passport to a new status, particularly that of priest-healer. In the Ndembu cults of Zimbabwe, certain roles are open only to those who have passed through illness and its treatment. Any illness that is interpreted as spirit possession can lead to the sufferer's assuming the role of shaman (Lewis, in Loudon, 1976, p. 74). Among the spiritualist churches of Ghana, founded by prophet-healers who blend traditional beliefs with elements of Christianity, the prophet himself and various church members will often have received their call from a supernatural power after they have been healed of some illness. Claude Lévi-Strauss has emphasized the parallel between the Cuna shamans of Panama, who undergo an initial crisis that confers upon them their formal status, and the psychoanalyst who undergoes analysis to obtain professional status.

A typical example of a genuine psychotherapy effected through a spirit-possession ritual is found in the Ndoep cult. A person suffering from disease, hallucinations, prophetic dreams, and pathological possession by an unknown spirit (called a *rab*) is subjected to ritual treatment known as *ndoep,* in which the spirits are invited to participate. The patient undergoes a symbolic death and rebirth; by recognizing the particular possessing *rab* and calling it by name, the initiate-patient recovers his power of speech. He is transformed completely, going from the status of psychiatric patient to that of ritual therapist. The Ndoep cult enables him to heal ritually the illness of others and to ward off the attacks of witches *(dömm)* or ambivalent spirits (called *jinn,* because of the Islamic influence in Senegal). The new healer is now permanently allied to his personal *rab,* to whom libations and sacrifices will be dutifully and forever performed. "Ndoep, in the whole context, reveals the structure and meaning of an initiation rite" (Zampleni, 1968; Lospinoso, 1978).

Ronald Frankenberg and Joyce Leeson's analysis of healing procedures among practitioners in Lusaka, Zambia, provides an example of how there may be a great variety of personal attitudes and behaviors among healers within the same community. Among healing practitioners in Lusaka, a wide range of treatment is found, from the herbalist's simple remedies to the elaborate rituals necessary to placate angry spirits.

> Many *ngangas* (practitioners) have mystical powers which enable them to diagnose and treat or even prevent illness and death. These powers are derived from spirits or gods who visit them in dreams or in trances, or guide them by other signs [in diagnosing the patient's trouble]. . . . Spirits are speaking through the *nganga* whilst he is in a trance, and an assistant listens, interprets where necessary, and relays the information to those consulting him. Some *ngangas* have no need to ask the trouble or to examine, nor to see the patient at all. (Frankenburg and Leeson, in Loudon, 1976, p. 240)

Some other practitioners combine questioning the patient with magical and herbal treatment. Some, in order "to supplement the supernatural guidance have been apprenticed to other healers. Becoming possessed by spirits is a result of a particular routine, as dancing, listening to singing or donning appropriate dress" (pp. 241–242).

Thus, herbal, magical, and religious practices coexist in the same environment. This multiplicity of practice is not due solely to the fact that the population of Lusaka is drawn from several different cultures. Generally speaking, the methods used by healers in traditional societies vary according to a variety of factors. These include the patient's—or patient's family's—preconception of the nature of the trouble, the traditional classification of the symptoms and causes of illness, and the type of healers available locally. The spiritual or religious component of treatment will also vary during the various stages of the treatment: there is the initial summoning of the healer and his first inspiration, the attempt to determine the cause of the illness, and the ritual treatment itself.

The attribution of the disease to one or another agent also depends upon a variety of factors, such as the results of divination, the nature of the illness and its symptoms, and the healer's personal specialization. A useful example of the variety of causes that may be ascribed to different illnesses is recorded by Eva Gillies with reference to the Ogori people's interpretation of diseases within a Yoruba-style culture in Nigeria. Different causes are assigned to different types of illness among the Ogori. For instance, "the immediate cause of leprosy is believed always to be the Earth. This goddess may afflict a man either because he has offended her in some way causing a titleman [political-ritual leader] to fall to the ground; or because someone has invoked his anger against him by a curse, or by magical means through the assistance of a medicine man" (Gillies, in Loudon, 1976, p. 369). In this instance, ethical, social, and religious origins of illness coexist with sorcery and cursing. The goddess Earth stands as a theoretical and supernatural cause above the practical and natural human cause. In many cases, the variety of symptoms accompanying a given disease will lead a sick person to appeal to several different specialized practitioners and treatments. In Ghana, I met a priest whose inability to cure his own child's serious illness had led him to appeal to a European doctor. In Brazil, native peoples, mostly in suburban areas, used to appeal to different types of healers—fetish priests, exorcists, faith healers, or priests of Afro-Brazilian cults such as Umbanda—depending on the nature of the individual case.

Similarly, a range of specialized practitioners is found among the Indian peoples of Mesoamerica. In Mexico, for example, the most common types of healers are the *curandero* and the *brujo*. The *curandero* employs the traditional pharmacopoeia but is also supposed to be able to discover the causes of illnesses. The *brujo* is endowed with mystical and ambiguous powers. In fact, he may help to combat another, malevolent *brujo* by healing his victim; but he can also cause illness by throwing the evil eye or by nagualism—that is, by transforming himself into an animal in order to attack and destroy his victim.

Interpretations of Illness. It is noteworthy that the validity of medical interpretations and procedures prevalent among traditional societies is not subject to empirical verification. Within the context of these societies themselves, however, such proof is not required. In cultures that are basically dependent upon the natural environment and that lack a coherent body of scientific theory, explanation of diseases lies outside the realm of the natural and the observable. Doctors and priests formulate interpretations and courses of action in terms of supernatural agents. The ever-impending presence of disease, more than any other factor, determines the degree to which the experience of sickness is founded in a theoretical or cognitive context based on the activity of a supernatural world. Traditional societies are indeed characterized by high infant mortality and general morbidity. Anxiety and stress could not be overcome in such societies without reference to invisible forces nor without recourse to forms of healing whose efficacy cannot be proven objectively. In such an environment, the potential for psychosomatic illness is great, as is the possibility of treating the patient successfully with mystical or traditional physical cures, especially given the influence of a commonly shared system of thought.

Exorcism is a widespread practice among traditional societies. Some diseases are attributed to the entrance into the body of evil spirits or impersonal forces, and these must be exorcised by the healer in order for the patient to regain his health. An Aboriginal doctor of Australia, as we have seen, will often "extract" stones or bones from a patient's body, claiming they are the embodiment of the evil forces causing the affliction. In a very different cultural context, that of the islamized northern Somali, certain illnesses *(wadaado)* characterized by coughing, sneezing, vomiting, trance, and similar symptoms are thought to be due to spirit possession. The job of exorcising these spirits belongs to the "man of religion" *(wadaad)*. His exorcism techniques are a mixture of traditional and Islamic practices, a syncretism based on the belief that the spirits represent both ancestors and the *jinn*. One such technique consists of the sprinkling of perfume and the reading of verses from the Qur'ān. Among other peoples, such as the Trobriand Islanders of Melanesia, the Maori of New Zealand, and the Azande of the Sudan, malignant spirits are expelled by the use of occult spells that may or may not be uttered over a mixture of magical ingredients.

The system of beliefs peculiar to shamanism gives rise to a special set of exorcism techniques. Such practices are found particularly among the traditional societies of the Arctic region, in both North America and Eurasia, and in Inner Asia. Asen Balikci (1963) noted that among the Netsilik Inuit (Eskimo) of northern Canada the shamanistic séance is a social phenomenon involving at least two persons. The community as a whole, however, expresses its belief in the shaman's acts. In this culture, sicknesses of all kinds are blamed on spirits and ghosts of several classes. These usually attack the sufferer because they have been angered by some breach of taboo. A powerful shaman is supposed to be in control of a class of spirits known as *tunraq*s, which he unleashes against the spirits that have entered the patient's body. In a typical séance, the shaman—equipped with his paraphernalia and drum—crouches before the audience assembled in utter darkness inside an igloo. He calls out to one or more of his protective spirits. While the shaman is in a trance the *tunraq* who is to aid him enters his body and begins to speak very rapidly in the shaman's secret language. At this point the malicious spirits leave the patient's body and fly out of the igloo, but the shaman's protective spirit, aided by benevolent ghosts, is dispatched by the shaman to seize them and bring them back into the igloo. Once the evil spirits have been retrieved the shaman kills them with his snow knife. The shaman's success in this fight is evidenced by the evil spirits' blood on his hands. If the patient dies, it is said that the attacking spirits were too numerous, or that a second attack was carried out after the séance.

In order to become a shaman qualified to perform such a ceremony, a person must receive special training under an older shaman. An apprenticeship of this kind must, however, be preceded by the candidate's receiving a call. On the other hand, the shaman rarely has full control over the spirits. They may, in fact, be very independent and have quite an ambiguous connection with their master, the shaman. It is for this reason that the shaman may fail to chase the hostile spirits out of a patient's body, and thereafter the shaman himself, or one of his relatives, may be attacked by the *tunraq,* who is now totally out of control. This aspect of shamanism reflects the inherent belief that crisis situations represent a structural and existential maladjustment of the natural order of things. Shamanism attempts to make rational the obscurities underlying the relationship between health and illness, but, on a deeper level, it leaves space open for permanent and continual ambiguity in the human condition.

Another concept widely used by the Inuit and other Arctic peoples, as well as by North American Indians, to explain the causes of illness is the theory of "soul loss." According to this theory, sickness is provoked not by the intrusion of spirits into the body, but by the theft of the soul from the body by malevolent spirits, ghosts, shaman-sorcerers, or—among the Inuit—by a hostile bear or by Sedna, goddess of the sea animals. In some cases, the soul is thought to have flown away of its own accord. It is the task of the shaman to determine whether an illness is due to spirit intrusion or soul loss.

Among certain North American Indian tribes, illness is thought to be due to the insertion of a material object into the patient's body by an evil spirit; it is up to the medicine man to extract the object. The medicine man will indeed pretend to suck an object from the affected area of the body and will then exhibit an insect or feather as the item removed.

A case of soul loss must be rectified by a shaman. The shaman employs certain techniques, learned in his apprenticeship, to enter a trance state. He then sends forth his tutelary spirit, or even detaches his own soul from his body, sending it into the sky or another realm where the spirits dwell. There he struggles mightily to break the resistance of the evil spirits. During the battle, his behavior takes on the aspect of an ecstatic performance that may attain moments of great drama. The shaman may in fact lose the battle with the forces of evil and actually die. From a medical standpoint, it is noteworthy that physical disorders are usually diagnosed as being due to spirit intrusion, while the theory of soul loss is applied to psychic disturbances (see Åke Hultkranz and Ivar Paulson, in Puech, 1970).

Current Syncretic Trends. A new area of interest in the field of ethnomedicine has been opened by the encounter of traditional medical customs with modern scientific practices and with Christianity. The introduction of scientific methods into native societies by Western doctors and hospitals has given rise to a dualistic attitude among peoples of traditional cultures. Their general tendency is to choose either the traditional or modern approach, depending on the nature of the illness. Traditional healers are, with increasing frequency, advising their patients to seek the aid of modern physicians for certain types of afflictions. For their part, westernized medical professionals and institutions sometimes accept the cooperation of traditional healers in curing psychic illness, as in the case of Dr. Henri Collomb and his psychiatric hospital in Dakar.

The worldwide activity of Christian missionaries has caused the appearance and expansion of numerous native sects and churches, the leaders of which employ healing practices that are a blend of traditional and Christian elements. Pentecostalism in particular has deeply influenced these new syncretic churches because of its strong emphasis on charismatic experiences. Especially attractive is its appeal to the Holy Spirit for manifestations of glossolalia, prophecy, and healing. The prophet-founders of these new churches are continuing and further developing the ancient practices of their predecessors, the traditional priest-healers, who were (and in many cases still are) possessed by spirits and who received inspiration in dreams and visions. The prophets of these new churches have merely substituted the Holy Spirit for traditional deities as the source of such dreams.

The new prophetic cults, like the traditional possession cults, place special emphasis on healing as a fundamental feature of religion. The new cults have, however, brought about some changes in the patterns of healing procedures, as they have introduced new ideological themes and ritual actions and have applied new methods of treatment. Emphasis is generally given to healing by prayer and faith. The Harrist, Neo-Harrist, and Aladura churches in Ghana, Nigeria, and the Ivory Coast, respectively, are examples of sects that employ such practices. Doctrines of baptism by immersion and of the "rescuing" power of the Bible are generally adopted from these modern and syncretic churches. Healing methods differ from one prophet to another and entail traditional customs blended with Christian procedures and meanings. Some prophets use ordinary water or florida water; others use consecrated holy water. Some elicit confession of sins or touch their prophet's staff to the patient's head. Adherents of the new cults seek help for all types of bodily pain, psychosomatic disturbance, and psychic crisis. The prophet's charismatic powers offer a new source of confidence to believers. The intensely emotional nature of worship services, which involve a high degree of communal participation, provides an additional basis for believers' faith that they may attain total well-being and salvation (see Appiah-Kubi, 1981; Lanternari, 1983).

[*For related discussion, see* Diseases and Cures; Healing; Magic, *article on* Magic in Primitive Societies; Shamanism, *overview article;* Spirit Possession; *and* Witchcraft, *article on* African Witchcraft.]

BIBLIOGRAPHY

Appiah-Kubi, Kofi. *Man Cures, God Heals: Religion and Medical Practice among the Akans of Ghana.* Totowa, N.J., 1981.

Balikci, Asen. "Shamanistic Behavior among the Netsilik Eskimos." *Southwestern Journal of Anthropology* 19 (Winter 1963): 380–396.

Buxton, Jean. *Religion and Healing in Mandari.* Oxford, 1973.

Elkin, A. P. *The Australian Aborigines: How to Understand Them.* 3d ed. Sydney, 1954.

Evans-Pritchard, E. E. *Witchcraft, Oracles, and Magic among the Azande.* 2d ed. Oxford, 1950.

Grottanelli, Vinigi. *Una società guineana: Gli Nzema.* 2 vols. Turin, 1977–1978.

Kiev, Ari, ed. *Magic, Faith and Healing.* New York, 1964.

Landy, David, ed. *Culture, Disease and Healing.* New York, 1977.

Lanternari, Vittorio. *Incontro con una cultura africana.* Naples, 1976.

Lanternari, Vittorio. "Carismatici in Africa. Le chiese spirituali nel Ghana." In *Festa, carisma, apocalisse.* Palermo, 1983.

Lospinoso, Mariannita. *Maghi e medici di un paese africano.* Genoa, 1978.

Loudon, J. B., ed. *Social Anthropology and Medicine.* London, 1976.

Middleton, John, ed. *Magic, Witchcraft and Curing.* Garden City, N.Y., 1967.

Morley, Peter, and Roy Wallis, eds. *Culture and Curing: Anthropological Perspectives on Traditional Beliefs and Practices.* London, 1978.

Murdock, George P. *Theories of Illness: A World Survey.* Pittsburgh, 1980.

Petri, Helmut. "Der australische Medizinmann." *Annali Lateranensi* 16 (1952): 159–317 and 17 (1953): 157–225.

Puech, Henri-Charles, ed. *Histoire des religions,* vol. 1, *Les religions antiques.* Paris, 1970.

Twumasi, P. A. *Medical Systems in Ghana: A Study in Medical Sociology.* Accra, Ghana, 1975.

Zempleni, Andras. *L'interprétation et la thérapie traditionnelle du désordre mental chez les Wolof et les Lebou (Senegal).* Paris, 1968.

Zempleni, Andras, et al. "Guérisons et faits religieux." *Archives de sciences sociales des religions* 54 (1982): 5–76.

VITTORIO LANTERNARI

Medicine and Religion in Eastern Traditions

Although the practice of medicine varies greatly in the Eastern and Western worlds, Eastern traditions of medicine have much in common with those of the West. All medical systems have similar beginnings, related to religious beliefs, and medical practitioners have always been highly esteemed. So great is the admiration for the healing profession, in fact, that in practically every culture known to us the first physician was believed to have been a god or a divine personality. The attribution of divinity to the earliest healer in each society indicates above all the great respect that has been universally extended to the art of healing. Healers have been able at times to cure severely ill patients; they have been able to stay the process of dying and keep fatally ill patients alive; and they have been able to return to sanity those patients who seemed demented by the delirium of fever. No wonder that persons so gifted were thought to have been touched by divine powers.

Medicine in Ancient Japan. In ancient Japan, the first healer was believed to have been Amaterasu Ōmikami, the sun goddess and founding ancestor of the imperial house. She transferred her healing skills to her two offspring, Izanagi and Izanami, who first discovered their power of healing when they cured a dying hare in the open fields. From that modest medical beginning sprang the Japanese tradition of healing. In the next generation Onamuchi no Mikoto and Sukunahikuna no Mikoto, Amaterasu's grandsons, were credited with a number of experiments, the most important of which resulted in the discovery of the benefit of bathing in hot springs. Onamuchi, it is reported, experienced the healing effect of a hot spring on his own body when it cured him of a severely painful, though historically unidentifiable, illness. Having confirmed this discovery by the successful cure of an eye disease contracted by his daughter, Onamuchi, together with Sukunahikuna, then tested and gave his seal of approval to a number of spas throughout Japan.

These two physicians inspired their disciples and descendants with their own experimental spirit, and sent them out into the various provinces of Japan. The *Shindaiki* (Records of the Divine Age) report that at the time of Jimmu Tennō (the divine emperor who was said to have founded the empire of Japan in 660 BCE and thus defined the "Divine Age"), blind and dumb people were apprenticed to physicians in order to learn from them the art of massage. This art, however, they were not allowed to administer independently until they had reached the age of thirty.

Neither the *Shindaiki* nor other ancient chronicles indicate in any way when the concept of the divine ancestry of the early physicians came into being. It is possible that this concept arose early and spontaneously. But it is more likely that it was a later development, artificially created so as to strengthen the theory of the divine origin of the rulers of the Yamato dynasty. For they, basing their ancestral line upon Amaterasu, the sun goddess, considered their clan directly related to the two earliest physicians. This fact may also account for the reports contained in the *Shindaiki* that the sixteenth Yamato emperor appointed twenty of his fifty-two sons to be instructed in the medical teachings of his distinguished ancestors Onamuchi and Sukunahikuna, that several of the sons of the twentieth emperor desired to become medical officers, and that two of the three sons of Jimmu Tennō chose medicine as their profession and were granted permission to practice it.

If these legends are not historical fact, they are, nevertheless, strongly indicative of the high social rank from which physicians were recruited in ancient Japan up to the eighth century CE. The chronicles, questionable as they are for historical accuracy, would not contain such numerous and explicit reports on princes of the divine imperial dynasty who elected to be physicians had the social status of the medical profession not been high.

Early Chinese Medicine. Like the Japanese, the ancient Chinese also attributed the art of medicine to divine personalities, namely, to three god-emperors, Huang-ti, Shen Nung, and Fu Hsi, who were said to have lived from about 3000 to 2852 BCE. The eldest of the three, Huang-ti, also known as the Yellow Emperor, is said to have written the first textbook of medicine. This text, aptly entitled *Huang-ti nei ching su-wen* (Yellow Emperor's Classic of Internal Medicine) is a superb introduction to the art and philosophy of healing. It is written in the style of a dialogue, carried on by the divine emperor with his prime minister Chi Po, in which the prime minister, well versed in the supernatural aspects of medical practice, responds to questions posed by the emperor.

The second of the three legendary divine emperors, Shen Nung, also known as the Divine Husbandman, was not only the god of agriculture but also the deity of pharmacology, as well as of the healing substances of nature. To him is attributed the authorship of the *Pen ts'ao* (Great Herbal). The oldest and richest book in the Chinese *materia medica,* it includes descriptions of healing substances from the animal, vegetable, and mineral kingdoms. Shen Nung is traditionally pictured with a sheaf of ripe grain, a symbol of nutrition and plant life, in his folded hands and, as another symbol of his connection with nutrition and animal life, with two horns on his head. (The similarity of the traditional portrait of Emperor Shen Nung with Michelangelo's statue of Moses is extraordinary; the horns on the head of *Moses* are, however, the result of a biblical mistranslation [*see* Horns].)

The third of the Chinese divine healing emperors, Fu Hsi, was not so much endowed with a human persona and tasks as were his two imperial colleagues. This was due in large part to the fact that his name did not have an easily understood nonclerical meaning, nor was his function practical enough to be comprehensible to common folk, or even to those priests who performed the function of physicians. To this third emperor is attributed the development of the philosophical framework of Chinese medicine.

None of these three medical deities ever became a cult figure; no formal religious rituals were performed in their names or at their temples. Nevertheless, among the vast numbers of temples in ancient China, which were generally crowded with believers sunk in prayer to a variety of holy figures, were several devoted to the deities of medicine. At the far end of these temples, opposite the entrance, there usually were statues of Huang-ti, Shen Nung, and Fu Hsi, whose healing powers were sought by pious suppliants.

If there was any religious element in the art of healing in ancient Chinese thought, it was the remnant of early animistic religious beliefs, which saw good or evil spirits in every facet of nature. Every tree, every cave, every mountain, and every canyon was believed to be inhabited by its own specific spirit, which could cause disease and perhaps even cure it. Respect for the powers of nature is threaded throughout both medicine and religion in China. Among other religious healers in ancient China were, for example, a great many mendicant Taoist priests, who carried with them secret remedies, or prescriptions for them, whose ingredients were always natural substances. The use of such remedies is closely related to the Taoist concept of *wu-wei,* which can be literally translated as "doing nothing" but which should, according to Joseph Needham, be interpreted as "doing nothing contrary to nature." That transgressions of the natural order bring about corresponding internal disequilibria (i.e., illness) is one of the fundamental tenets of Chinese medicine.

Derived from the early Chinese system of nature religion was the shamanic method of medical treatment, in which a shaman chastised himself severely for the transgressions that had caused his patient's illness. Using whips, bamboo canes, and various other instruments of torture, a shaman inflicted upon himself punishment for the transgressions that his patients had amassed in their previous and present lives and that had caused their illnesses. This practice hints at a belief in transmigration of souls and at the Indian notion of *karman*, introduced into China at the beginning of the common era.

In the philosophy of ancient India all events of life were likely to be attributed to the "law of *karman*." Illness, suffering, and death were seen as part of everyone's *karman*. Illness, especially, was believed to be caused by sins and moral infractions committed in one's previous and present lives. In India, however, in contrast to China, some physicians sought the origin of disease not necessarily in religious terms but in terms of the natural order, viewing disease as the result of causes innately present in man. In China, belief in reincarnation has never been so strong as in India, although there has been a certain acknowledgment of the amassing of sins and their deleterious influence.

The Indian belief that illness was caused by accumulated transgressions was, however, an important part of the relationship between medicine and religion in ancient China. By the second century CE, devotees of the Celestial Master sect (T'ien-shih Tao) were made to retire to quiet rooms and there to meditate upon their past mistakes and possible offenses in former lives. It has been said that many such penitents found recovery through their meditative actions. As in many healing shrines, recovery was hastened by bringing presents to the altars of the gods of healing or by making donations to worthy causes. As is reported by Joseph Needham, "The patient went into retreat to reflect on his wrongdoings, while at the same time prayers were made on his behalf, with his name and history on papers despatched to the gods; then he paid money to the public funds and so gained cure and release."

It is impossible to simplify a description of the relationship of Asian religious traditions with medicine because of the variety of religions that have been practiced in Asia, few of which have been so formalized as, for example, Christianity. The outstanding feature of traditional Chinese and Japanese religion is a deep veneration of ancestors, a veneration that necessitated a multitude of offspring, preferably of the male sex, so as to guarantee continuance of the family and further generations of worshipers at the ancestral graves. Because ancestors were so highly venerated, great care was given to the burial of deceased family members, and great emphasis was placed upon the inviolate condition in which corpses were to be delivered to their graves. Any disfiguring operation had to be avoided, even if it was essential to save the life of a dying person. Even if gangrene had set in and the patient was doomed to lose a leg or an arm, it was preferable to leave such a disfigurement to natural developments rather than to attempt a cure by amputation.

Ritual Defilement in Asian Traditions. In the Taoist religion, as in the Japanese Shintō, any contact with wounds, pus, blood, or death was considered ritually defiling. The Japanese word *kega* stood for "wound" as well as for "uncleanness." For this reason priests of the Shintō or even the Buddhist faith did not actively participate in the care and treatment of a wounded or dying person. That Taoist and Buddhist priests fulfilled the roles of itinerant physicians is evident from the belletristic literature of both China and Japan. But these itinerant priest-physicians restricted their ministrations to prescribing medications and occasionally dispensing samples of secret medicines.

An important task of Taoist priests in China was the search for a substance that would confer long or even everlasting life and permanent youthfulness and beauty. Like the European alchemists of the Middle Ages, these priests searched everywhere for such an elixir of life. This search for eternal health and beauty reached its height during the T'ang dynasty. Not only the people at large but also the emperors of the dynasty participated in experimenting with these questionable elixirs, many of which were composed in part of poisonous plants and mushrooms. It thus happened that of the twenty-two rulers of the T'ang dynasty seven experimented in this presumably health-giving research, and several of them fell victim to their curiosity.

Among the endless variety of herbs that were believed to possess the power of conferring immortality were the cyprus and the pine. Their seeds and resins, used in tonics, are still today treasured for their potency. In addition to these there were many other plants whose leaves or flowers were to be dried, ground into fine powder, and then combined with a precious liquid such as mountain well water, so that a thick paste ensued. From such paste large pills were rolled and dried and taken over a period of many weeks. In addition to plant substances, various minerals were believed to have beneficial qualities. Other substances, such as powder of freshly ground deer horns, which was believed to restore and maintain male potency, had a symbolic and suggestive value rather than an actual physical effect. This last-mentioned medication is still being widely used in the Far East as well as in the various "Chinatowns" of Western cities.

Anatomical Knowledge. The system of religious beliefs that associated surgery, wounds, inflammation, and death with ritual impurity and that considered surgical invasion of the body a disfigurement also militated against any attempt to undertake anatomical studies on corpses, for the dismemberment of an adult body was considered an infringement of that person's normal afterlife. For this reason anatomical knowledge was practically nonexistent in Japan, China, or Tibet until the sixteenth century, when Western teachings began to filter through to the Far East. The few early anatomical drawings that stem from an earlier period are so incorrect that they betray a total lack of serious study and observation.

However, because there did exist a certain curiosity about the structure and function of the body and its internal organs, cursory observations were made on some criminals who had been condemned to death and who had, by their very crime and harsh judgment, forfeited their roles as ancestors worthy of veneration. Occasional chance observations were also made on the bodies of victims of deadly accidents or wild animals. Since these bodies were often lacerated and in the process of decay, they did not furnish any reliable insight into the actual anatomical structure of the human body.

Because clerical physicians were forbidden to touch these accidentally found bodies, so as to divest them of flesh and intestines long-handled brooms were used to move the bodies into streams of fast-running water, where they were left for several weeks. After that time, the bodies were taken out with the help of wooden rods; the bones were scraped free of soft tissue with whiskbrooms; and the inner organs were removed. As a result of this rather rough procedure, the inner organs were likely to be misshapen, and early drawings made from them are thus often quite inaccurate. Oddly enough, depictions of the liver, which was generally shown as a five-lobed viscus, closely resemble the earliest European representations, made by doctors or investigators laboring under religious interdictions similar to those that restricted their Asian colleagues.

Like the East Asian physicians and priest-physicians, European and Near Eastern doctors were prevented by religious proscriptions from performing autopsy and anatomical dissections. The religious maxim that was most influential upon the European medical scene was "Ecclesia abhorret a sanguine," that is, "The church abhors [the sight of] blood." This principle, which had of course been originally based upon Christian participation in wars and the infliction of battle wounds, was so persistently applied to the practice of medicine that it led to the complete avoidance of surgical procedures. Instead, the physicians of the Western world resorted to cautery whenever an incision would have been necessary.

Since the tradition of cautery and absolute avoidance of bloodshed also found its way into the medical thought of Islam, we find a persistent and careful avoidance of actual surgery in Arabic medical literature. A prime example of the use of cautery for surgical operations was Abū al-Qāsim, the most prominent of the Arab surgeons, whose important treatise is richly illustrated with representations of cautery instruments. In the course of time it can be observed that such instruments were not only copied by other Near or Middle Eastern surgeons but that they eventually reached distant Tibet, probably via the famous Silk Route that led from Asia Minor by way of India to China and back. While there is no literary documentation of the Arab provenance of such quasi-surgical instruments, we see it confirmed in the rich illustrations of Tibetan surgical texts, which show cautery instruments engraved with typically Islamic patterns of decoration.

So far as Tibetan medicine is concerned, it is important to mention that this was a purely religious matter. Medicine was practiced and taught solely in Buddhist monasteries, the predominant one of which was in Lhasa, the repository of the thirteen scrolls that represent the totality of Tibetan medical concepts and practice. These scrolls, like the old Chinese anatomical illustrations, reveal somewhat fantastic concepts of the structure of the human body and the formation and shapes of the internal organs. These were, of course, due to a similar prohibition of dissection and to the haphazard study of human anatomy. In addition to the chance observations that were occasionally made on the corpses of victims of accidents or wild animals, careful examination could be made only upon the corpses of infants who had died before the age of two. Thus, most anatomical scrolls from the monastery of Lhasa picture bodies with disproportionately large heads and with the seams of the skull bones marked very prominently, as though the posterior fontanelles had not been completely closed. Why the bodies of infants under two years of age were permitted to be dissected has never been satisfactorily explained and is open to various surmises, such as that a child that young was thought not yet capable of expiating the sins of its former existence; an infant, furthermore, is far removed from its role as a family ancestor.

If religious elements can be traced through the healing systems of most civilizations, they are nowhere so explicit and easy to follow as they are in the history of Japanese medicine. Both pharmacology and early Japanese medicine in general were based upon an empirical approach. As mentioned above, the grandsons of the sun goddess Amaterasu, Onamuchi and Sukunahikuna, were credited with a number of experiments, one of which resulted in recognizing the value of bathing in the waters of hot springs. Health as well as cleanliness ensued. Similarly, it may be assumed that the custom of washing one's hands prior to a religious service or to eating is not only a gesture of ritual purification but also the result of recognizing that frequent cleansing of hands, especially before meals, preserves good health.

Like nearly all primitive peoples, the preliterate Japanese—as we know from the records of early Chinese observers—considered religion and medicine to be closely related: health, illness, and death were parts of the religious pattern in which illness and death were elements of evil. These made people unclean and required elaborate rites of purification. Ritual purity was the prime requisite for the performance as well as for the attendance of religious services.

Medicine in Later Japan. The early Shintō priest was thoroughly restricted to his office; he could not take care of bodily illness or the resulting psychological needs of the people. The situation changed abruptly as soon as Japan made contact with other civilizations who brought their own gods and religious practices to the island empire. The first such formal contact with a foreign culture was made with the Chinese civilization during the sixth and seventh centuries CE.

Although Japanese intercourse with China dates back to the beginning of the common era, the formal introduction of Chinese civilization is of a much later date. Japanese chronicles contain a number of legendary reports that attempt to account for the occasional fragments of Chinese medical knowledge that found their way into Japan between 200 BCE and 500 CE. But these legends seem to be an artificial explanation for a natural phenomenon, for it is self-evident that the Chinese of the Han dynasty, even though they were simple men, left notions of their intellectual achievements, like those of medicine and philosophy, as well as of their crafts, such as the making of mirrors and bronzes. At the time when Chinese medicine was formally introduced to Japan, Japanese medicine had for centuries already been tinged with Chinese medical concepts, and although these concepts had been diffuse and scattered, they nevertheless helped in the understanding and integration of Chinese medicine when it was introduced as a complete system during the sixth and seventh centuries CE.

Chinese learning found its way to Japan not from China directly but by way of Korea. Nor were Chinese script, literature, and philosophy introduced independently, but as by-products of Buddhism. Since Korean Buddhism decisively influenced Japanese medical thought and history and since the adoption of Buddhism in Japan was affected by medical considerations, it is necessary to devote some space to the political circumstances that led to the importation of a new religion into Japan.

Contrary to their later practice of seclusion, the Japanese in their earlier history strove to establish concrete links with the Asian mainland. For this purpose they brought under their sway the smallest and southernmost of the four kingdoms into which ancient Korea was divided. From this colony, Mimana, the Japanese were able to use their influence to maintain a balance of power among the other three independent kingdoms of Korea, named Paekche (also known as Kudara), Silla (also known as Shiragi), and Koguryŏ. This balance was, however, precarious, because the warlike attitude of the men of Silla tended to threaten Paekche, which had become more peace-loving with the adoption of Chinese culture and civilization. To ensure military protection, Paekche submitted to a voluntary dependency upon Japan, which was expressed by means of regular embassies, bearing gifts and tributes. Paekche had adopted Buddhism at the end of the fourth century, and several embassies of the fifth and sixth centuries were composed of Buddhist scholars, carrying volumes of the *sūtra*s and even an image of the Buddha.

This image was accompanied by a recommendation of the king of Paekche that the emperor of Japan accept the new god. The emperor, a great admirer of Chinese civilization, but indifferent to the question of religion, left the decision as to the acceptance of Buddhism to his ministers; only the chancellor of the empire, Soga no Iname, adopted it. He thereupon received the statue of the Buddha and propagated the new religion. However, two severe epidemics of a disease accompanied by skin eruptions (now generally believed to have been measles) followed in quick succession and proved to be a retarding factor in the general acceptance of Buddhism, for the statue of the Buddha was believed to be responsible for this new disease.

Clans that were opposed to Soga no Iname and that were also the hereditary custodians of the ancient Japanese religion advised the emperor and the people that the importation of the foreign deity had incurred the wrath of the ancient native gods, who had therefore sent the pestilence as an expression of their displeasure. The emperor, unwilling to share the responsibility for the plague, ordered the destruction of the image of the Buddha and the new temples, and also the proscription of the new religion. Yet his successor, Emperor Yomei, when taken seriously ill, sought and found healing by joining the Buddhist faith. He thus permanently bestowed upon Buddhism the imperial favor, without, however, giving up Shintō; and his example of adhering to both religions became a lasting practice throughout the nation.

The sudden change from the belief that Buddhism was the cause of disease to the assumption that it healed disease was the result of the efforts of the first Buddhist priests who came to Japan from Korea. Many of these priests did not actually practice medicine, but, knowing the value attached to health, healing, and recovery from illness, they also knew how to convince the Japanese that the *sūtras* were effective in warding off and combating illness. It is clear that the Buddhist *sūtras* were not read for their philosophical content; the early Korean priests, themselves only recently converted to Buddhism, were not trained to interpret the *sūtras*, nor were many Japanese at the beginning of the sixth century ready to search for philosophical meanings in the Chinese religious texts, which they had been given by the Korean priests; nor were they able to read the Chinese ideograms. However, the emphasis on the healing powers of the *sūtras* could be appreciated by all. After the emperor Yomei had been converted to Buddhism, elaborate rites were held whenever an emperor was ill, and soon afterward, temples devoted to the worship of Yakushi (Skt., Kṣitigarbha), the Buddha of healing, were erected in many places.

While Shintō prescribed that its priests must keep themselves rigidly aloof from the sick and dying, Buddhist priests, almost from their start in Japan, performed the dual function of priest and physician. They paved the way for the Buddhist scholars who in the latter part of the sixth century introduced and explained Chinese medical texts to the Japanese.

These Buddhist priests had succeeded in stimulating interest in foreign medical knowledge to such an extent that the Japanese were no longer content to depend on the mere chance that an embassy from Paekche might bring them scholars learned in the art of medicine. Instead, when Japan was threatened in 553 by a recurrence of the earlier epidemics, the emperor Kimmei requested the king of Paekche to send a physician and several kinds of medicines to Japan to help avert the dread disease. In compliance with the request, the king of Paekche dispatched one of his best physicians and teachers of medicine, Nasotsu Nurioda (Oyu-Ryoda), and two herbalists who were to search for medical plants in Japan. These men were later followed by other Korean physicians who taught their art to the Japanese.

As Buddhism spread in Japan, the inability to read Buddhist scriptures became intolerable to Japanese scholars who wished to obtain a deeper insight than the Korean priests were able to provide. The necessity for Chinese studies was further emphasized when the Koreans brought Chinese medical books to Japan. Therefore, in 607, Japan sent an envoy to China, her first official ambassador to that country. Having established official relations between the two countries, the ambassador returned to Japan; the following year he was accompanied by two Chinese envoys. In 608 he traveled once again to China, this time followed by a group of young Japanese scholars and physicians who had been selected by the government to study the Chinese language and Chinese working methods in their respective fields of interest. After spending many years in China, the Japanese physicians returned to their homeland fully equipped to teach the Chinese system of medicine. It is therefore clear that Chinese medicine, which was so much more sophisticated than the medical system of ancient Japan, found its way to Japan only by way of the introduction of Buddhism from Korea to Japan.

Since there were now in Japan a sizable number of Japanese who had received their training in China directly, it was no longer necessary to depend upon Korean scholars for the interpretation of Chinese medical texts. To make this new learning effective in Japan, it was imperative to make medical studies possible for a wider circle of Japanese than could be sent to China. For this purpose medical schools were opened to implement definite courses of medical study, as they had been laid down in the *Taihō-ryo* (Code of Laws of the Taihō Era) in 702.

It is interesting to note that admission to one of these Japanese medical schools depended partly upon knowledge of the Chinese language, which was not only a *sine qua non* for the study of all texts to be used but was also one of the rigid social prerequisites for a well-trained physician. The curricula of the newly founded medical schools were based entirely on the Chinese examples, and like the Chinese, the Japanese maintained two different types of medical schools, the *daigaku*, or university school, and the *kokugaku*, or provincial school.

The training of the medical students in the university and the provincial medical schools was long and arduous. The average time spent in the university was seven years, after which the graduates were taken into the imperial service. The curriculum was based entirely upon Chinese precepts, even as to the study of such works on general conduct and ethics as the Confucian classics *Hsiao ching* (Book of Filial Piety), *Lun-yü* (the Confucian Analects), and the *Ch'ien-tzu wen* (Classic of a Thousand Characters). In addition to these works, which were closer to religion, philosophy, and the study of ethics than to the actual practice of medicine, the Japanese medical curriculum contained numerous Chinese medical works that had been adapted to the Japanese language. The list of required medical reading increased rapidly and soon included nearly the entire Chinese medical literature.

Since court and provincial physicians were recruited

from the ranks of the young men who had received their training at the university or at one or the other of the provincial schools, it is perhaps surprising that Buddhist priests were still called upon for medical assistance. This was the result of their clever adjustment to changing times. While many of the early Korean Buddhist priests were actual practioners of medicine, dispensers of medicaments, and scholars in medical science, their successors were no longer learned in the art of medicine. Their methods of combating and preventing disease were based upon their alleged possession of magic powers. With their practices of incantation and exorcism—familiar to the Japanese from their ancient Shintō rites—the Buddhist priests appealed to a great part of the population. Even a number of emperors fell under their sway and participated in Buddhist ceremonies performed in order to avert pestilences.

Buddhism and the practice of Chinese medicine suffered a temporary setback, early in the ninth century, when Japan was struck by several epidemic waves of the plague. Chinese medicine was incapable of coping with that disease, and the emperor Heizei (r. 806–809) decided that only the return to the old Japanese religion could save the youth of the country from the dreaded return of the disease. He therefore commissioned two physicians to gather material on the methods of pure Japanese medicine, so that it might again be practiced. These reforms were enforced for a short time only; with the passing of the plague they fell into disregard without having caused any serious disruption of medical education or the practice of Buddhism, which was then about as widespread in the empire of Japan as it was in China and Korea.

While the Chinese way of medicine furnished the Japanese with an outline for medical practice and instruction, a number of outstanding Japanese medical scholars filled in this outline and molded Japanese theory and Japanese practice into an organic entity that was essentially derived from the teachings of the earliest Buddhist monks who had come to Japan.

For several centuries Japan had been virtually free from internal and external conflict, and the pursuit of arts and sciences, honorific in itself, had been considered a highly desirable occupation, for proficiency in these fields was rewarded with the highest honors and influential positions at the imperial court. In the eleventh and twelfth centuries, however, new developments unsettled the existing social systems and depreciated the value of imperial honors. Individual clans had grown in strength and fought each other in an effort to acquire supremacy over land and men. The victorious chieftain of feuding clans received the title *shōgun,* which was conferred by the imperial court upon military dictators. With the growing might of the shogun, the power of the emperor waned rapidly, since for all practical purposes the shogun was the actual ruler of the country. Until 1600 the shogunate rarely remained the prerogative of one clan for any length of time, and the successive accession to power of the various clans was accompanied by numerous and ferocious civil wars. The interest of the upper classes was thus deflected from intellectual pursuits, which had become unrewarding, and they turned to occupations connected with political and armed conquest.

The destruction caused by the numerous civil wars was followed by poverty and disease, and the dearth of properly trained physicians forced the people once again to seek help and healing from Buddhist priests. These priests were even called to the imperial court when the office of court physician became vacant.

Under these conditions medical knowledge declined rapidly; it disappeared almost entirely when Kyoto, then the center of learning, was ruined during the War of Ōnin (1467–1477). Wars and the resulting social upheaval brought about a deterioration of the medical profession, but the result was not entirely detrimental, for the period of unsettlement eradicated completely the imported and native prejudices against a development of surgery in Japan. With the decay of the medical schools the Confucian stigma attached to the practice of surgery, which had been adopted by the Japanese together with the Chinese medical system, fell into oblivion. Similarly the Shintō interdictions against inflicting, receiving, and touching wounds were greatly modified with the growth of a socially prominent warrior class.

Japanese medicine so far had been molded by the Shintō and Buddhist religions and by Confucian ethics. Surgery, especially battle surgery, became increasingly important during the centuries of internal strife.

The next and final religious influence upon Japanese medicine arrived by way of Christianity and the distinguished Jesuit missionary Francis Xavier, who arrived in Kagoshima in 1549 together with two other Portuguese Jesuits. They were received most cordially and given permission to carry out their missionary duties. Conversion progressed rapidly, and even Buddhist priests, far from hampering the efforts of a competing religion, attended many of Francis Xavier's sermons.

The encouragement given to Francis Xavier and his fellow missionaries by the lords of the various fiefs was not so much the result of their interest in Christianity itself as of their desire to attract Portuguese traders and obtain medical help from missionaries trained in the practice of medicine. Like the Buddhist missionaries of a thousand years earlier, the Jesuits saw that medical services rendered to people in general helped to increase the number of converts. So successful were the Portuguese priests in their role as physicians that in 1568 the shogun confirmed his approval of the medical missionaries by an astonishing act: he presented to the Jesuits a temple that had formerly belonged to Buddhist monks. The Buddhist name of the temple was changed to Nambanji, or Church of the Southern Barbarians; with priests as well as physicians, it served as a church as well as a dispensary and hospital.

From then on, and as long as the Portuguese missionaries were tolerated in Japan, exponents of Christianity were the last religious transmitters of medical practice and innovations in Japan. With the expulsion of the Portuguese from Japan, and during the centuries of rigid isolation of the island empire, all religions—indigenous Shintō as well as Buddhism and Christianity—were severed from the practice of medicine.

[*For related discussions, see* Alchemy, *article on* Chinese Alchemy; Āyurveda; Korean Religion; Onmyōdō; Shintō; Taoism; *and* Yin-yang Wu-hsing.]

BIBLIOGRAPHY

Clifford, Terry. *Tibetan Buddhist Medicine and Psychiatry: The Diamond Healing.* York Beach, Maine, 1984.

de Bary, Wm. Theodore, et al., comps. *Sources of Chinese Tradition.* New York, 1960.

Fitzgerald, Charles P. *China: A Short Cultural History* (1935). 3d rev. ed. London, 1961.

Rémy, Charles. "Des Japonais." *Bulletins de la Société d'Anthropologie de Paris,* 3d series, 6 (1883): 908–914.

Sansom, George B. *Japan: A Short Cultural History* (1931). Rev. ed., New York, 1962.

Ts'ao, Hsueh-chin. *Dream of the Red Chamber.* With a continuation by Kao Ou. Translated by Chi-chen Wang. New York, 1958.

Veith, Ilza, trans. *Huang-ti nei ching su wên: The Yellow Emperor's Classic of Internal Medicine.* Baltimore, 1949.

Veith, Ilza. "Medicine in Japan." *Ciba Symposia* 11 (1950): 1190–1220.

Veith, Ilza. *Medizin in Tibet.* Berlin, 1961.

ILZA VEITH

Medicine and Religion in Western Traditions

Religion attempts to enable people to coexist with superior powers or beings by winning the favor or averting the disfavor of these superior entities, or by responding positively to benevolent revelation offered by the deity. Thus religion is concerned in great part with well-being in the broadest sense. Medicine has a similar but much more limited goal: to restore to wellness, through natural means, those who are afflicted by disease, dysfunction, or injury; to alleviate, in some cultures, the sufferings of those whom it cannot restore to wellness; and to preserve wellness by preventing, or by protecting people from, disease or dysfunction. Since religion is concerned with well-being in a broad and sometimes all-encompassing sense, medicine, in focusing on the wellness of the body, deals with a subset of interests and values that may be compatible with religion when religion's conception of well-being includes wellness of the body. This compatibility depends on the comparative priority of wellness of the body in religion's economy of goods, and on the propriety of the mechanisms employed by medicine to achieve its ends. Medicine is incompatible and in a state of tension with religion in those relatively rare instances where religion's conception of wellness does not include wellness of the body, or where religion regards as licit for maintaining or restoring physical wellness only those means that are themselves religious.

Relations through History. In most cultures another phenomenon may overlap with both religion and medicine: magic, which through practices and substances regarded as possessing supernatural power seeks to manipulate and control nature and destiny. In traditional and archaic cultures there are often no strict distinctions between religion, magic, and medicine.

Egypt and Mesopotamia. In ancient Egyptian and Mesopotamian religions, the entire cosmos was divine. Well-being consisted of harmony between the individual and deified nature. Illness was understood as disharmony between the individual and his total environment. Egyptians and Mesopotamians viewed disease etiologically rather than symptomatically. Spirit intrusion was both the cause and the disease, and the identification of the condition involved discerning the motive of the causal agent. The causal agent could be the dead, an enemy using malevolent magic, or the gods. To whom one had recourse when ill depended upon the sufferer's perception of cause.

Both cultures had distinct but complementary healing professions. In Mesopotamia the *ashipu,* a priest and exorcist, was concerned with diagnosis and prognosis. Relying on prayer, libations, and incantations, he would withdraw from cases if the prognosis was unfavorable. The *asu,* who was not a priest, used a wide variety of empirical methods in treating acute symptoms. He was a craftsman employing techniques whose efficacy was thought to be enhanced by a limited use of incantations or prayers. These two healers were not competitors; sometimes they even worked together with the same patient.

In Egypt there were three categories of practitioners. The *swnw* was nearly identical to the Mesopotamian *asu;* a craftsman and not a priest, he used empirical therapy supplemented by prayers and incantations. The *sau,* a sorcerer or exorcist, used techniques similar to those of the Mesopotamian *ashipu,* but would occasionally employ drugs. The third category was the *wabw,* the priest of Sekhmet, a goddess of healing. The role of the *wabw* seems originally to have been to mediate between the patient and the goddess, but over time this mediation was supplemented by empirical methods, including drugs and minor surgery. There was no rivalry between these three healers; indeed, two or all three roles were at times combined in one person.

Greece. A similar condition prevailed in the early stages of Greek civilization. Specific deities or vague spiritual powers *(daimones, kēres,* and *alastores)* were popularly viewed as agents of disease, sending pandemic disease in response to pollution, or individual sickness as divine punishment. For the latter, the afflicted might have recourse to prayer and sacrifice. Pestiferous pollution called for the intervention of itinerant *iatromanteis,* physician-seers who were common during the Archaic period (c. 800–500 BCE). The *iatromanteis* disappeared for the most part by the end of this period, but various healing cults came into existence, the most significant being that of Asklepios, which combined a form of faith healing with empirical therapy.

As early as the period of the Homeric epics there were craftsmen who dealt with injuries and illnesses empirically, employing techniques probably similar in many ways to those used by their Mesopotamian and Egyptian counterparts, although generally without the magico-religious additions typical of the latter. Their lack of reliance on any supernatural power inherent in their therapeutic processes or drugs reflects a climate conducive to the development of a medical science. A body of reasonably efficacious medical techniques is not properly a body of knowledge. To be such, a body of techniques must be placed within, and made subordinate to, a theoretical framework. Pre-Socratic philosophy's effort to explain the world in terms of natural processes rather than mythological categories was the catalyst for the development of a medical science in the late fifth century BCE, particularly as evidenced in the Hippocratic corpus. [*See the biography of Hippocrates.*] This development, however, does not mark a rejection of traditional Greek religion. Medicine was viewed as a divinely bestowed art; the Hippocratic physician's theology was rational, but he was no atheist. Greek polytheism accommodated without tensions a medical rationalism that explained illness in natural terms.

The Hebrews. Contemporary with the Greeks and with later stages of Egyptian and Mesopotamian civilizations were the Jews. As reflected in the Hebrew scriptures (Old Testament), they differed considerably from other people of their time, holding that there is only one God, the creator of all things, who exists above and outside nature, which draws its existence from him. In the Old Testament all material evil is seen as a result of the Fall. Suffering and disease, as physical evils, are moral evils; further, they are under God's control. Disease, on a national and individual level, is a consequence of sin, sent by God to punish and correct (*Gn.* 38:7; *Nm.* 12:1–16; *2 Sm.* 12:15–18, 24:10–25; *2 Kgs.* 5:25–27; *2 Chr.* 21:11–18, 26:16–21). It is especially within the context of the covenant of God with the children of Israel, given through Moses, that a fixed cause-and-effect relationship is enunciated: prosperity, health, and happiness will follow obedience and faithfulness; sword, famine, and pestilence will be inflicted for disobedience and unfaithfulness (*Ex.* 23:25–26, *Lv.* 26, *Dt.* 8, 28). The prophets frequently emphasize that apostasy will bring these dire consequences upon the people (*Jer.* 24:10, *Ez.* 14:21).

In the Old Testament, illness is not seen in its physical nature but rather in its spiritual and moral dimensions. While this was also true to an extent in Egypt and Mesopotamia, where a sacerdotal medical practice prevailed, among the Jews the only involvement of priests in any medical function was in enforcing a code of personal and social hygiene and in diagnosing a variety of dermatological conditions loosely called leprosy.

Rarely, prophets healed, raised the dead, or made prognoses. An instance of the last is involved in the condemnation of Ahaziah, king of Israel, who inquired of Baal-Zebab, god of Ekron, whether he would recover from an injury (*2 Kgs.* 1:2–4). The reasons for the condemnation of Ahaziah for consulting a foreign god are probably similar to those governing the judgment upon Asa, king of Judah. When seriously ill, Asa sought help from physicians, rather than turning to the Lord; for this, he was to die (*2 Chr.* 16:12–13). While some scholars have taken this as a condemnation of secular medicine, it is likely that the only physicians whom Asa could have consulted were pagans whose medicine was a mixture of empirical and magico-religious procedures. Magic—including soothsaying, augury, sorcery, and necromancy—was strictly prohibited in the Mosaic code (*Ex.* 22:18, *Dt.* 18:10). And calling upon foreign gods was of course apostasy, even if done by physicians for one's healing.

Hellenistic Judaism and afterward. Although there is ample evidence of knowledge of folk remedies and the setting of broken bones (and so forth) in ancient Israel, there appears to have been no systematized therapeutics, much less a distinct medical profession. It was during the Hellenistic period that a Jewish medical profession developed. Contact with Greek civilization provided Jews with a scientific or rational medicine that in its theoretical framework was religiously neutral when disengaged from the philosophical cosmology that had made its theoretical development possible. As expressed in Ben Sira (early second century BCE), God created both medicines and physicians; therefore, a sensible person will not despise them. One should not, however, rely upon them: all healing comes from God. Thus when sick, one should both pray to God and heed the doctor who also relies upon God (*Sir.* 28:1–14).

The ethos of Egyptian and Mesopotamian cultures, being starkly magico-religious, was uncongenial to a naturalistic view of disease and health, but Greek polytheism was sufficiently flexible to accommodate easily a natural etiology. Similarly, late Hellenistic Judaism embraced a naturalistic medicine whose religious neutrality allowed for divine explanations of ultimate causality, but provided for natural processes of proximate causality within God's created order. Since the Hellenistic period, Judaism's emphasis upon the moral neutrality of natural processes has fostered such a positive attitude toward secular medicine that Talmudic tradition even forbids Jews to live in any city where there is no physician.

A similarly favorable attitude has prevailed in Islam. The *ḥadīths*—early postprophetic opinions of the ninth to tenth centuries CE—express a very high regard for the art of medicine. Islamic society soon adopted Greek medicine and established centers for medical education where Jewish and Christian physicians taught and practiced alongside Islamic physicians.

Christianity. The attitudes toward medicine expressed in Christian literature of the first several centuries are for the most part as congenial as those that arose in contemporary Judaism and were later to characterize Islam nearly from its inception. Fundamental principles that the church fathers shared with Judaism were that the material world was created by God for man's use and that the medical art was one of God's gifts for the succoring of his creatures' ills. The charitable use of medicine was clearly seen as a means of extending Christ's love by applying his categorical imperative of loving one's neighbor as oneself. The visitation, care, and comfort of the sick was a duty incumbent upon all believers. Physicians were especially lauded when they conceived their medical efforts as complementing their care for the spiritual needs of the sick. By late antiquity many physicians were also priests. The practice of medicine by the clergy found its primary vehicle, however, in cenobitic monasticism. Certain monks, designated as physicians, extended medical care to the needy as an act of Christian charity, sometimes tending the ill in institutions that, with considerable qualification, could be called hospitals.

Throughout the Middle Ages the clergy, especially monks, practiced medicine. Their efforts were not always for charity, however, and concern was expressed in canon law about the practice of medicine by clergy for financial gain, the propriety of their treating females, and the dangers attending surgical practice. The charitable practice of medicine increased with the inception of the mendicant orders and remained a feature of Roman Catholicism, particularly in remote areas, until modern times. In missionary endeavors, Catholics have effectively combined medical activities and proselytizing; in the sixteenth century, for example, they established over one hundred fifty hospitals in Mexico alone.

The attitude of the reformers to medicine was equally favorable, as seen in efforts by many Protestant pastors at different times to tend the physical ills of their flocks because of a shortage of physicians or the high cost of professional care. Puritans were prominent in this combination of spiritual and physical care, which the American Puritan divine Cotton Mather (1663–1728) called the "angelical conjunction." The Methodist John Wesley (1703–1791) was especially sensitive to the desperate need of the poor for simple remedies. He sought to provide assistance directly by ministering to their ills in uncomplicated cases, referring more difficult ones to physicians, and by compiling a book of remedies, *Primitive Physick* (1747), which was reprinted in numerous editions.

While some early Protestant missionaries engaged in limited medical activity, it was only from around the middle of the nineteenth century that trained physicians were welcomed with any enthusiasm by mission organizations. The favorable posture centered on the hope that caring for the ills of the heathen would soften their hearts for the gospel. By the last quarter of the century, the good inherent in succoring the ills of the heathen as a form of Christian philanthropy was becoming more and more the focus of medical activities. This emphasis continued to rise with the growth of Christian liberalism and the Social Gospel movement and was bolstered by the increasing doubt of many Christians that Christianity held a monopoly on eternal verities. The wonders of modern medicine seemed the greatest gift the West could bestow on less-developed peoples. Ironically, this gift was greeted with an enduring receptivity primarily in those places where religion and healing could be easily separated conceptually. Where traditional worldviews encompass a magico-religious medicine, much of the white man's desacralized medicine has met resistance.

Secular Medicine. The desacralization of medicine, which had begun in Classical Greece and had rendered the three monotheistic religions of the West congenial to the medical art, was essentially completed in the mid- to late nineteenth century. It was then that an enduring alliance was fostered between theological orthodoxy and medical orthodoxy. This resulted from two developments: first, there was a reaction, especially by mainstream Christianity, against the attraction that a variety of sects in both Great Britain and America felt for medical heterodoxies such as botanical medicine, homeopathy, hydrotherapy, mind cure, and many others; and second, the scientific revolutions that established anatomy, physiology, biochemistry, pathology, and bacteriology as the foundational sciences for medicine made its practitioners, in the ultimate sense, "objective neutrals" in the theological arena.

The hospital. The institution that most typifies this "objective neutrality" of modern desacralized medicine is the modern hospital. Institutions specifically for the care of the sick were first created in late antiquity as instruments of Christian charity. These spread to the East and later appeared in Islamic form. In the West hospices for the care of the destitute, including the ill, continued throughout the Middle Ages. These were religious institutions for charity and continued as such until a subtle change occurred in the eighteenth century, when physicians began to view them as possible centers for the study of clinical medicine. Disagreements frequently arose between Roman Catholic nursing sisters and secular physicians over the very purpose of these institutions, which by then could be called hospitals in the modern sense of the word. Protestant denominations also were active in founding hospitals, especially in the nineteenth century. The religious aspect of these ostensibly religious-clinical institutions has gradually diminished in the highly pluralistic twentieth century. They are, for the most part, indistinguishable from secular hospitals.

Causality of disease. Before the advent of modern medicine, there had been discordant encounters between medicine and Christian doctrine regarding the proximate causality of certain diseases, especially pandemic scourges such as the plagues that ravaged Europe for several centuries beginning in 1348. When both prevention and treatment were viewed by some as calling for natural methods and by others as requiring strictly religious exercise, disagreements frequently occurred. This was also the case with smallpox and cholera. But when inoculation proved prophylactic for the former, and the latter was shown to be caused by poor sanitation rather than by sin, God's proximate involvement vanished in the minds of many. Since then, God's ultimate causality has been significantly deemphasized, particularly in those Christian denominations that have become theologically liberal.

There have also been significant disagreements between orthodox medicine and the three Western monotheisms, especially Christianity, on the very nature of some conditions. Conditions variously called "possession," "madness," or "insanity" became mental illness and lost their perceived spiritual nature when, in early modern times, both medical and religious authorities began to regard them as medical problems resulting from such causes as lesions or chemical imbalance. Mental illness, however, is not always viewed with the same neutral objectivity as is, for instance, cholera. Explanation for mental illness is sometimes regarded by religious conservatives as being at least partially in the realm of religious understanding if a strictly natural explanation is found wanting and secular medicine offers only psychotherapeutic treatment.

Attitudes toward death. The desacralization of disease, accompanied by the depersonalization of death in the sterilized atmosphere of the modern hospital, is graphically illustrated by the iconography of the death chamber. In the *ars moriendi* (treatises on the art of dying well) of the late Middle Ages through the early modern period, illustrations of the death chamber depict the scene in the dying person's bedroom, where spiritual forces quarrel over his soul. At the head of the bed a variety of clergy stand prominently, giving comfort and advice. Off to the side physicians linger helplessly and inconspicuously. As we approach the present, however, pictorial or verbal descriptions of the death scene begin to change: the location is still the dying person's bedroom, but physicians and nurses are now the dominant figures, with the clergy receding or, in some instances, vanishing entirely. Finally, this scene gives way to the hospital terminal ward, in whose antiseptic confines the dying person's primary companions are medical apparatus. A sometimes religiously stimulated response to this dehumanization of death has been the hospice movement, which has attempted to restore dignity, religious meaning, and spiritual solace to the dying process.

Tensions between medicine and religion. Uneasiness between the three Western monotheisms and desacralized medicine involves more than the conditions surrounding the process of dying. Several other areas of tension are readily identifiable. (1) A recognition of God's hand in all healing can easily be obfuscated by naturalistic explanations of disease and natural models of care. (2) The medicalizing of particular acts or conditions into illnesses requiring medical intervention sometimes conflicts with religious definitions, as in the case of alcoholism. (3) Medical enhancement of conditions viewed as natural by some physicians but as sinful by some religious bodies, as for instance homosexuality, gives rise to disagreements. (4) There is religious concern that the practice of medicine may be abused by negligence or incompetence or be used evilly, as in grossly immoral experimentation. (5) Medicine sometimes obtrudes into areas of scruple peculiar to a religion or to some sect within it, as when it uses or recommends therapeutic techniques or substances prohibited by the religion or sect. (6) Age-old problems such as birth control, abortion, and euthanasia remain the common terrain of medicine and religion. (7) Recent medical advances, such as life-support systems, organ transplants, genetic engineering, and *in vitro* fertilization, have created new areas of moral perplexity that are currently being examined by religious bodies. A rising concern with the moral and religious implications of modern technological medicine is causing religious bodies to address the questions raised at a level far deeper than that of cost-benefit analysis and econometrics.

Distinct from these tensions, although often confused with them, is a strong prejudice against orthodox medicine or, more often than not, against physicians. Expressed sometimes even by prominent religious figures, this prejudice generally stems from reasons that have essentially nothing to do with any religious beliefs. A hearty distrust, indeed hatred, of medical practitioners and the medical orthodoxy of the moment knows no religio-cultural boundaries, usually represents a small minority opinion at any time, and is sometimes couched in religious or quasi-religious terms. This negative attitude toward physicians has arisen in part from an uneasiness toward their natural explanations of disease and their reliance upon natural processes in conjunction with their supposed disregard of religious undertakings and values. The medieval adage *tres medici, duo athei,* "Where there are three physicians, two will be atheists," well illustrates the hostility of some religious people to medical practitioners. In such a case the suspicions, though based on religious concerns, are not justifiable by strictly theological reasoning.

Christian belief versus medical practice. Somewhat similar, but more specifically subordinate to broader theological positions, is a latent or sometimes open hostility toward medicine on the part of certain Christian groups or individuals that arises from two different factors that have had little place in Judaism and Islam: a fundamental flesh-spirit dichotomy, and a strong tradition of miraculous healing.

The New Testament, particularly the Pauline epistles, stresses the conflict between the flesh and the spirit. While this is never presented in starkly dualistic terms in scripture, it seemed close enough to both Platonic and gnostic dualism to provoke some early Christians to imitate the more bizarre features of these two movements, particularly a severe asceticism. The early church condemned various extremes of asceticism but condoned and even encouraged some forms of mortification of the flesh and self-imposed suffering that were rendered meritorious by a theology of redemptive suffering. Such execration of the body has sometimes fostered a self-imposed denial of medical alleviation of suffering or care of treatable conditions. Although this has arisen intermittently throughout the history of Christianity, it is seldom encountered now.

A more common cause of tension between medicine and Christianity is the tradition of miraculous healing. Beginning with Christ's healing miracles and continuing down to the present, a belief in and practice of miraculous healing has existed in various forms and among various Christian groups. A belief in divine healing does not always create strong tensions with secular medicine, however. Even though accounts of healings have often stressed the failures of physicians' efforts, it is nevertheless demonstrable that many who have recounted such miracles, rejoicing in miraculous healings where physicians have failed or simply been absent, were entirely supportive of secular medicine. Likewise, some eminent Christian authors have maintained that while the average Christian does no wrong in seeking medical care, the more spiritual Christian should rely on divine healing alone. Quite rarely has a carte blanche condemnation of secular medicine for Christians been precipitated by an emphasis on miraculous healing. The use of medicine has been unequivocally condemned primarily by those late nineteenth- and early twentieth-century sects (for example, some Pentecostal groups) whose theology of the atonement includes a promise of complete physical health for all "spirit-filled" believers. Such a condemnation of medicine is sometimes enhanced by a perceived demonic causality of disease. Secular courts now typically intervene in spectacular cases in which parents of this persuasion refuse to allow their critically ill children to receive medical treatment.

Possibilities for Rapprochement. Although some tensions exist between modern desacralized medical orthodoxy and mainstream Judaism, Christianity, and Islam in the West, a theological capacity to compartmentalize the functions of religion and medicine has kept these tensions at a minimum. But new problems and challenges to this relationship are now on the horizon. A burgeoning interest in the occult, Eastern metaphysics, the "new consciousness," psychic healing, and inner healing, or in various amalgams of these, has cut through religious distinctions and socioeconomic barriers. This interest often focuses on holistic health, healing, and medicine. An increasing willingness in some fields of orthodox medicine to reexamine and reconstruct some of the basic premises of health and healing has precipitated a (usually cautious) flirtation with mysticism by some medical practitioners and researchers. This still tentative and occasional tendency, demonstrated by such explorations as, for example, courses at some medical schools with titles like "A Taoist View of Health Care" or "Psychic Healing," evokes alarm among conservative groups, especially within Christianity.

The same climate that has caused some physicians to explore the relations of medicine and mysticism has also encouraged the exploration of the connections between traditional Western religions and health care. This is a marked change from the usual attitudes of secular physicians toward religion, especially those that have prevailed over the last century. While many physicians have been deeply religious, many more have been suspicious of and hostile toward any encroachment by representatives of religion on the ostensibly neutral terrain of medicine. Even deeply religious physicians have been quite uneasy when religion claims to contribute to the therapeutic process other than through encouragement and solace. The possible benefits of a close relationship between the medicine of the soul and the medicine of the body—for an understanding of wellness and sickness, for efficacy in the preservation of health and the curing and alleviation of afflictions, for a wide variety of concerns within the ever-broadening spectrum of health care—these are only beginning to be explored. Such efforts are greeted with very mixed reactions by both religious and medical organizations. Tensions that remain latent while religion and desacralized medicine are tidily separated will inevitably come to the fore in any attempt to involve religion meaningfully in health and healing.

BIBLIOGRAPHY

There is a vast literature on the relationship of religion and medicine. A useful starting point is *Health/Medicine and the Faith Traditions: An Inquiry into Religion and Medicine,* edited by Martin E. Marty and Kenneth L. Vaux (Philadelphia, 1982). This volume contains a variety of essays: two on sociocultural context, three on historical setting, a philosophical perspective, and two theological, two medical, and two pastoral perspectives. The volume ends with a comprehensive bibliography.

While numerous articles deal with specialized features of the history of medicine and religion, there are few books devoted exclusively to the topic. A volume of essays by historians treating the relationships of twenty-three religious traditions, mostly Judeo-Christian, with health and medicine is *Caring and Curing: Health and Medicine in Western Religious Traditions,* edited by Ronald L. Numbers and myself (New York, 1986). *The Church and Healing,* edited by W. J. Sheils and Derek Baker (Oxford, 1982), contains many useful essays. For specialized studies of the relationship of religious and medical authorities in the face of pandemic diseases, two useful works are Carlo M. Cipolla's *Faith, Reason, and the Plague in Seventeenth-Century Tuscany* (Ithaca, N.Y., 1979) and Charles E. Rosenberg's *The Cholera Years: The United States in 1832, 1849, and 1866* (Chicago, 1962). There is no satisfactory, comprehensive study of the interaction of religion and mental health. An excellent starting point is the case study by Michael MacDonald, "Religion, Social Change and Psychological Healing in England, 1600–1800," in *The Church and Healing,* cited above.

Individual religions and denominations are increasingly addressing the wide range of issues that arise from the meeting of medicine and religion. This has resulted in a vast literature typically published by denominational organs or publishing houses. Crossing religious and denominational lines, the Park Ridge Center, a division of the Lutheran General Health Care System (Park Ridge, Ill.), is commissioning the publication of volumes dealing with health and medicine in individual religions and denominations. The series includes Martin E. Marty's *Health and Medicine in the Lutheran Tradition: Being Well* (New York, 1983); Kenneth L. Vaux's *Health and Medicine in the Reformed Tradition: Promise, Providence and Care* (New York, 1984); Richard A. McCormick's *Health and Medicine in the Roman Catholic Tradition: Tradition in Transition* (New York, 1984); David M. Feldman's *Health and Medicine in the Jewish Tradition: L'Hayyim—To Life* (New York, 1985); and David H. Smith's *Health and Medicine in the Anglican Tradition: Conscience, Community, and Compromise* (New York, 1986).

DARREL W. AMUNDSEN

MEDICINE MAN. *See* Shamanism.

MEDITATION. [*This entry consists of two articles: an overview of theories and practices of meditation and contemplation in Western and Eastern traditions, followed by a discussion of meditation in the Buddhist tradition.*]

An Overview

The terms *meditation* and *contemplation* are applied to a variety of manifestations throughout the historical and cultural geography of world religions. *Meditation* and *contemplation* are used in English to translate a number of specialized terms in several different languages. Attention will be paid here to the etymologies of these terms in English, so that the reader may determine the suitability of their application to foreign terms. Some general categories through which meditative and contemplative systems can be described will be introduced.

Confusion sometimes arises when the words *meditation* and *contemplation* are used interchangeably. However, a working distinction between the two terms can be suggested. Meditation is considered preparatory and contributory to the achievement of contemplation. Meditation involves concentration, the narrowing of the focus of consciousness to a single theme, symbol, catechism, or doctrine, yet it remains cognitive and intellectual. Meditation is usually rumination on a particular religious subject, while contemplation is a direct intuitive seeing, using spiritual faculties beyond discursive thought and ratiocination. In the felicitous phrase of Richard of Saint-Victor, a Christian theologian of the twelfth century, "Meditation investigates, contemplation wonders."

The English word *meditate* comes from the Latin *meditari. Meditari* connotes deep, continued reflection, a concentrated dwelling in thought. Contemplation is derived from the Latin *cum* ("with") and *templum* ("a consecrated place"). Frequently, contemplation is itself a spiritual state and serves as the end of an ascetic quest. Particularly in the monotheistic traditions of Judaism, Christianity, and Islam, this state is sometimes considered tantamount to the beatific vision bestowed upon the individual through the grace of God. This distinction between *meditation* and *contemplation* will serve for an examination of the following materials, but the reader should bear in mind the difficulty of translating these concepts from one language and culture to another.

As for the morphology of the theories and practices indicated by the terms *meditation* and *contemplation*, it may be useful to mention some categories of spiritual discipline. Meditation leading to contemplation can be apophatic. Involved here is an emptying procedure, in which the individual systematically removes from consciousness any content that is not the object of his quest. In Christian mysticism, this type of path is referred to as the *via negativa;* it is also an important technique in Buddhism. [*See* Via Negativa.]

Other forms of meditation and contemplation may be termed cataphatic. In this type of practice, a specific image, idea, role, or deity is held in the mind's eye. The object of the individual is to assimilate, or to participate in some way with, the chosen object. Apophatic forms of meditation tend to be more speculative, cognitive, and intellectual, at least in their early stages. They tend to be centered in the mind. Cataphatic forms of meditation and contemplation, on the other hand, tend to be more emotional and devotional. They tend to be centered in the heart. In what follows, meditation and contemplation represent a continuum, with different systems and traditions illustrating shifting perspectives within a descriptive framework that opposes the apophatic and speculative to the cataphatic and affective.

Western Traditions

The practice of prayer has always held a central place in the Western traditions of Judaism, Christianity, and Islam. Although prayer may devolve into meditation and even into contemplation, these are more directly the concerns of the mystical and, in many instances, the monastic dimensions of these traditions.

Judaism. Meditation and contemplation in the Jewish tradition acknowledge the centrality and authority of the Hebrew scriptures. Reading and interpreting the Torah require concentration and discursive meditation. This meditation led to the development of commentary, such as the Mishnah and the Talmud, and schools came into being that fostered an experiential approach. Heavily influenced by gnosticism and Hellenism, this movement is referred to as *heikhalot* mysticism. Ascetical practices culminated in a contemplative ascent of the soul through seven heavens to reach its final home in a state of beatitude. The final state is viewed as one in which the mystic stands before the throne of God and sees and hears directly. There is no experience of mystical union, and God remains "wholly other." This tradition remained essentially cataphatic and nonaffective, although the symbolism of the ascent and the attainment of ecstatic consciousness is characteristic of Jewish contemplation.

A more immanentist approach to the contemplation of God developed within the Hasidic tradition. One can trace here the influence of Philo Judaeus, a Jewish philosopher of the first century CE who later was to have an important influence on Christianity. In Hasidic contemplation, the transcendent majesty of God is preserved by making the object of contemplation the *shekhinah,* or the spirit of the living God. God can be contemplated directly only at the end of the world, or the Day of Yahveh. The Jewish contemplative almost always retains a sense of the distance between himself and God. The quest ends not with mystical union but with a sense of adhesion (or being joined) to God, which is short of an actual union.

The qabbalistic school from the thirteenth century onward produced some major developments in the Jewish meditative and contemplative tradition. A major exponent of this school was the Spaniard Avraham ben Shemu'el Abulafia. He developed a meditative technique designed to release the individual from bondage to the sensible forms and images that one must deal with in everyday life and that delimit the soul. Meditation is an avenue through which the soul can come to apprehend more than the forms of nature. Abulafia looks for a means to deautomatize the human faculties from the normal preoccupation with daily events. He seizes upon a system of meditation based on the Hebrew alphabet. The letters of the alphabet are sufficiently abstract so as not to preoccupy the mind with any specific meaning, but concrete enough to supply an object of intense focus and concentration. The letters of the alphabet are regarded by the meditator as constituents of the holy name of God. The meditator is instructed to combine and recombine the letters of the alphabet without any attempt to form words, thereby constructing a kind of nonrepresentational mystical logic. [*See* Alphabets.] Such exercise produces interior freedom and detachment from natural objects and prepares the adept for the final achievement: the pure contemplation of the divine name.

Christianity. Meditation and contemplation, particularly within monastic circles, reached a high degree of differentiation and sophistication in the Christian tradition. The practices of the early church took form in an atmosphere influenced by Hermetic literature and the philosophy of Neoplatonism. Syncretic in nature, the Hermetic books present the theme of a mystical ascent to the knowledge of God. This important image (found also in Jewish mysticism) becomes central to the mysticism of Christianity. The idea of an ascent from the many to the One is taken over from the thought of the Neoplatonist Plotinus. Plotinus describes four movements in the ascent to divine knowledge: (1) purgation in the practice of virtue; (2) the development of thought beyond sense perception; (3) the transcendence of thought in the achievement of union; and (4) the final absorption in the One. In the Christian circles of third-century Alexandria, these non-Christian ideas came to be absorbed into the tradition and to exert an important influence. Two important figures of this development were Clement and Origen.

For Clement, meditation led to the apprehension of the intelligible realities and then, through *gnosis* as a gift of Christ, to hidden spiritual realities. Reflective reading of, and meditation on, the scriptures in order to discern this hidden meaning was important. Within this metaphorical framework, Origen introduces the symbol of a contemplative marriage between the soul and the Logos (Christ).

Anchoritism, or withdrawal into the desert, was a form of spirituality in the early church that gave full rein to ascetic and meditative practices. Disengagement from the concerns of ordinary life provided a favorable atmosphere for the awakening of the spirit to the word of God. The austere life of the desert could produce a deep, inner quiet and was conducive to a life of continual meditation on the scriptures in an attempt to hear the word of God and to ascend the ladder of perfection through grace. [*See* Eremitism.]

Within this context, as early as the third century, a life of constant prayer developed as an ideal for the anchorite. The beginnings of the prayer of the heart, or the Jesus Prayer, are found here. The Jesus Prayer is an apothegm translated as "Lord Jesus Christ, Son of God, have mercy on me." The first reference to this prayer comes from the seventh century. The practice of the Jesus Prayer became important in Eastern Orthodox spirituality and in the development of the movement known as hesychasm. Meditation came to be seen, in a movement away from Neoplatonism, as more properly centered in the heart rather than in the mind. Control of breathing and the fixation of the gaze were important ancillaries to the constant repetition of the apothegm. This tradition has survived down to the present day in its major center on Mount Athos, in Greece.

The sixteenth and seventeenth centuries in the Roman Catholic church were a period of rationalization and the systematization of meditative and contemplative processes. This movement looked back to a medieval interest in the methodology of meditation developed among the Franciscans. A major figure in this movement was Bonaventure (1217–1274). In his *De triplici via,* he gives an exemplary statement for Western Christianity on the three processes of meditation: purgation, illumination, and union.

Ignatius Loyola (1495–1556), the founder of the Jesuits, wrote a treatise entitled *Spiritual Exercises,* in which he outlines a progression in meditative practice. His notions of meditation may not be so exalted as others, but his methods are of interest insofar as they involve cataphatic visualization techniques that bear some resemblance to Hindu and Buddhist practices. For example, Ignatius's fourth method requires that the practitioner choose a specific image, such as the passion or the resurrection of Jesus, and apply each of the five senses to that image. Thus, through seeing, hearing, smelling, tasting, and touching, the image is vivified in the consciousness of the meditator.

Teresa of Ávila (1515–1582) was a member of the Carmelite order. In her *Autobiography,* she narrates her meditative experiences and describes a period of spiritual desiccation followed by a series of ecstatic experiences. Teresa describes the latter in sexual images and draws upon the symbolism of the bride and the bridegroom, a symbolism that dates back at least to the time of Origen. In the *Autobiography* she catalogs degrees of meditation, using the symbolism of the husbandry of plants. She compares discursive meditation to watering the garden, bucket by bucket; recollection is analogous to the use of a water wheel, and quiet, to springs of water. Union is compared to a drenching rain.

Teresa's contemporary and fellow Carmelite, John of the Cross (1542–1591), modified the three ways of meditation developed by Bonaventure. Purgation is retained but illumination is replaced, using the bridal imagery, with betrothal, and union with spiritual marriage. Both Teresa of Ávila and John of the Cross describe a stage in contemplation referred to as the "dark night of the soul," an experience of alienation and isolation preparatory to illumination through the grace of God. This theme continues a long-standing tradition of a vision of God that includes the perception of darkness.

A major figure of the French church involved a codifying meditation was Francis of Sales (1567–1622). In his *Introduction to the Devout Life,* he teaches a five-step meditation. The preparatory stage of meditation involves three steps: (1) placing one's self in the presence of God, (2) praying for divine assistance, and (3) imagining a scene from the life of Jesus. The second step builds on the first through identification with those images that most affect the practitioner. In the third step feelings generated in the second are converted into acts of understanding and will. The fourth step involves thanksgiving and offering up the results of the meditation as a sacrifice, and petition for the putting into practice of the insights gained. The fifth step is the development of the "spiritual nosegay" or the preparation of some content of the meditation to sustain one in daily affairs.

Islam. The prophet Muḥammad (b. 570) considered his prophecy to be a continuation and reaffirmation of the Judeo-Christian tradition. The word *islām* means "submission" in Arabic; thus a Muslim is one who submits. Islamic theology emphasizes the transcendent majesty and unity of God. Man is considered to exist face to face with this transcendent majesty without intercessors. Man is not expected to try to share the secrets of God.

In the more orthodox forms of Islam, daily prayer *(ṣalāt)* is one of the obligatory observances. Usually this prayer is conducted communally. Although it is also recommended that a Muslim perform *dhikr,* or remembrance of God, these practices are external formalities and not necessarily related to contemplation and meditation in the present sense. [*See* Dhikr.]

By the eighth century, strict Muslim orthodoxy began to be challenged by Sufism, the generic term for Islamic mysticism. The Ṣūfī movement favored an interiorization and esotericization of the basic institutions of Islam. The orthodox religious attitudes of fear and obedience before the transcendence of God changed in Sufism to an attitude of ecstatic love of God and hope of union with him through a transcendence of the phenomenal self. Meditative and contemplative practices became an important part of this quest, and *dhikr* became a constant practice of the presence of God.

Ecstasy is the goal of the Ṣūfī path, and *dhikr,* in an expanded and intensified form, becomes a means to the goal. Techniques familiar in other traditions such as control of the breath, visualization of sacred words, and repetition of sacred phrases were adopted as important means to this end. The goal is termed *fanā',* or annihilation of the lower self, which enables God through his grace to bestow on the mystic the rapture of union with him.

The Ṣūfīs developed sacred dance as a technique for the induction of ecstasy. The turning and whirling movements of the dance accompanied by hypnotic music and chanting of poetry bypassed the intellectual faculties and created a trancelike state of centeredness and concentration. The Mevlevī order of Ṣūfīs founded by Jalāl al-Dīn Rūmī institutionalized this practice as the foundation of its worship.

Eastern Traditions

Sophisticated psychologies and techniques of contemplation and meditation were developed within the spiritual traditions of India and China. These traditions, which antedate the beginning of the common era, developed independently until the introduction of Buddhism into China in the first century CE. Thereafter, India's techniques of meditation strongly influenced Chinese religious thought.

India. A concern for meditative asceticism, which runs through Indian religious history, can be traced as far back as the Indus Valley civilization of the third millennium BCE. Artifacts recovered from this civilization can be interpreted as representing individuals or deities in meditative attitudes.

Yoga. An early systematization of meditative technique is found in the *Yoga Sūtra* of Patañjali, dating from the third century BCE. Patañjali defines *yoga* as "the cessation of the modifications of the mind." This statement forms the basis of much of pan-Indian spirituality. The Yoga system is one of the classical *darśanas*, or "viewpoints," of Indian philosophy. The object of meditation and other ascetic practices is to still the mind and the emotions with which the individual usually identifies. When this is accomplished, consciousness can reflect the pure absolute spirit (or *puruṣa*), which is the principle of consciousness itself. Realization of the *puruṣa* as one's true and ultimate identity brings with it release *(mokṣa)* from the tendency to identify with temporal experience.

The mind *(citta)* in Yoga philosophy is considered to be the repository of *saṃskāra* (the root impressions of past deeds). These impressions are stored from present and past lives in unconscious layers of the psyche and, in turn, produce binding proclivities, good and bad habits, and all forms of limited vision and false identification, which modify and determine a man's life in the unenlightened state. The unenlightened mind is modified by its past ignorant experience and in turn perpetuates such modifications into the indefinite future. (This is the pan-Indian doctrine of *karman,* which becomes axiomatic for much of Indian spirituality.) Hence the importance of causing the modifications of the mind to cease so that the pure unconditioned spirit may become manifest in meditation.

A primary object of Yoga discipline is to bring the mind into a state of one-pointedness or intense concentration. Moral and ethical abstinences and observances form the first two limbs of an eightfold prescription for attaining this state. A comfortable posture *(āsana)* is recommended, especially one that enables the practitioner to keep the spine correctly aligned and one that can be comfortably held for protracted periods of time as the mind becomes abstracted from the body. Breath control *(prāṇāyāma)* is then recommended, since states of breathing and states of consciousness correspond closely to each other. A calming and quieting of the breath produces a corresponding calming and quieting of the mind. [*See* Breath and Breathing.]

As concentration deepens, the next limb of Yoga, *pratyāhāra* (withdrawal of the senses from their objects), contributes to a further interiority. The next step is *dharaṇa,* or the concentration of the mind on a single object. This is followed by *dhyāna,* or the achievement of an uninterrupted nonverbal current of consciousness focused on the meditative object. The eighth and last limb of this meditative program is *samādhi,* in which the goal of complete cessation of the modifications of the mind is achieved, and a transcendent awareness of one's ultimate identity as *puruṣa,* or unconditional spirit, is attained. In this state of ecstasy, the normal ego sense and the experience of a dichotomy between subject and object is overcome. Yoga discipline in a variety of forms becomes an important ingredient in several Indian spiritual traditions and religions, including Jainism, various forms of Hinduism, and Buddhism. [*See* Samādhi *and* Yoga.]

Hinduism. *Hinduism* is a generic term used to refer to a variety of religious manifestations within the Indian subcontinent and other areas subject to Indian influence. In the early history of Hinduism, a stage referred to as Brahmanism, there was a movement away from the practice of exoteric ritual and toward meditative interiority and realization. As the tradition developed, Hindus came to be divided into three main sects: the Vaiṣṇava, the Śaiva, and the Śākta.

Vaiṣṇavism. The Vaiṣṇavas, worshipers of the god Viṣṇu and his many incarnations, developed a form of active, affective, and cataphatic meditation in which chanting, singing, and dancing used to induce transic absorption into the deity. Perhaps the most popular incarnation of Viṣṇu is the deity Kṛṣṇa, whose worship is *bhakti* ("devotion"). In addition to performances of chanting and dance, a devotee was expected to remain ever mindful of his object of devotion. In turn, the deity extends his grace and love to the devotee. In both Vaiṣṇava and Śaiva forms of theistic meditation, the emotions are given a much freer rein than in the more abstract classical Yoga system. Transmutation of the emotions through devotion to Viṣṇu, Śiva, and their *avatāra*s became popular and had a far-reaching effect on Indian art and literature.

Devotional theism borrowed some of its elements from Sanskrit poetics. The term *bhāva,* which refers to an intense personal emotion in poetic theory, was adapted by the Vaiṣṇavas to refer to the meditative attitude that a devotee assumes toward Kṛṣṇa. There are four types of contemplative mood, determined by the form of relationship with the deity. These range from a relationship to Kṛṣṇa as supreme deity, as friend, as brother, and, perhaps most importantly, as lover. A devotee's chosen *bhāva* was to be cultivated through meditation, chanting, and dance until he experienced himself as the friend or lover of Kṛṣṇa. Continual absorption into these various roles enabled the adherent to experience the love and the personality of the deity.

Śaivism and Śaktism. The devotees of Śiva developed their own forms of contemplative worship. One is the growth of a cult dedicated to Śakti, the female consort of Śiva. Śakti is the active female energy of the universe in contradistinction to the passive contemplative energy of Śiva himself. Śāktism became an important part of the Tantric manifestations of Hinduism. Tantric Hinduism developed several techniques of meditation, including the use of the *yantra.* A *yantra* is a geometric diagram that represents an abstract form or manifestation of a deity. Deities are essentially formless in their own nature but are thought to manifest themselves in a movement from the subtle to the gross, in the forms of sound, the geometric forms of the *yantra,* and the *mūrti* (or sculpted) image. A *yantra* is a series of triangles, squares, and circles emanating from a central point, which serves to focus the mind of the meditating yogin. [*See* Yantra.]

Visualization of a sculpted or painted form of the deity became important in Tantric meditation. The object was to achieve a high degree of absorption in the outward form so that it could be reproduced in complex detail within the mind of the meditator. When this stage was reached the outward form could be dispensed with. The general goal of Tantric meditation is the complete unification of the body, speech, and mind of the Tantric yogin with the body, speech, and mind of his chosen divinity. *Mantra*s, symbolic sounds or phrases for the sound form of the divinity, were used in this practice. *Mudrā*s were used in meditation also as symbolic gestures of the hands and body representing various stages of the unification process. [*See* Postures and Gestures; Mantra; *and* Mudrā.]

In *kuṇḍalinīyoga,* the macrocosmic Śakti is further identified, within the microcosm of the human body, as *kuṇḍalinī. Kuṇḍalinī* literally means "coiled" and refers to the visualization of Śakti as an energy within the body in the form of a sleeping serpent. This energy is associated with a meditative physiology of the subtle body of man. The meditator visualizes six vital centers called *cakra*s placed along the spine from its base to the crown of the head. The *cakra*s are connected to each other by a central vein with two lesser veins, or channels, on either side. The object of the meditation and physical exercises of this form of Tantric yoga is to wake the latent energy of Śakti coiled at the base of the spine and to cause it to enter the central vein. As *kuṇḍalinī* ascends and is drawn upward through meditation, it energizes the six *cakra*s until it reaches the topmost *cakra,* where it is reunited with Śiva. At this point the body of the yogin and the body of the cosmos are resolved into the primal unity.

Buddhism. Buddhism is a tradition that seeks to penetrate the veil of appearances and social conditioning and, through meditative insight, to achieve a vision of the truth of reality. This vision leads to liberation from the round of karmic cycles and the achievement of ultimate freedom in *nirvāṇa. Nirvāṇa* is the goal of Buddhist ascesis subsumed under the term *bhāvana,* or meditation. *Bhāvana* has two secondary objectives: the first is the achievement of *śamatha,* or calm; the second is *vipaśyanā,* insight or higher vision.

As a foundation for other Buddhist meditation practices, a monk starts with the practice of mindfulness (Pali, *sati*). This practice is basic to both *śamatha* (Pali, *samatha*) and *vipaśyanā* (Pali, *vipassanā*) and can be used for both calming and higher vision. The practice of mindfulness, or total awareness, takes place in four main areas: the body itself, the sensations, thought, and mental objects. Mindfulness of the body begins with the observation of breathing. Strict attention is paid to inhalation and exhalation, note being taken of the duration of each as the practitioner becomes aware of this usually unconscious activity. Such concentration involves narrowing of the mind's focus. The effects of mindfulness of breathing include a refined awareness of the entire body and a sense of tranquillity.

Mindfulness of the body is next applied to a monk's postures and movements. Every bodily action is performed with complete awareness and consciousness. This discipline brings into awareness bodily activity, which normally goes on beyond the conscious level. As activities are performed, mindfulness tranquilizes, calms, and controls the body; mindfulness can then proceed with an examination of the constituent parts of the body, external and internal, and a breakdown of the body into its primary physical elements. These practices break up any tendency to identify with the body.

Mindfulness is then applied to the sensations that are discerned as pleasant, unpleasant, or neutral. In a continuing progression, from the gross to the more subtle, mindfulness is then applied to the mind, or thought itself, and its objects. Attention is paid to each thought as it occurs, whether it is with or without such factors as passion, hatred, delusion, or freedom. The objective is detachment and a loosening of the tendency to identify with any factors of experience. With the achievement of detachment, the monk has an increased ability to respond actively to the actual circumstances of his life.

Through concentrative attention, a monk sees the momentary quality of his life, and sees that a moment of experience arises based on temporary causes and conditions. He thus can see the real nature of experience, which had previously been obscured by incorrect mental fabrications and the false projection of permanent identity on a transient stream of moments.

The Buddhist *śamatha* practices are associated with *dhyāna,* or the achievement of meditative absorption. *Dhyāna* practice continues the work of mindfulness into an even greater experience of detachment, one in which contact with the normal content of worldly experience is gradually attenuated and almost altogether eliminated. The *dhyāna*s (absorptions) are as follows: four absorptions with form, four absorptions without form, and finally the cessation of conception and feeling. These stages represent a gradual elimination of the verbal, discursive, and affective contents of the mind. They lead a monk gradually out of the world of sense-based experience to a new, detached interior dimension. These stages are increasingly independent of the external world and signify a developing autonomy on the part of the monk. He is no longer bound by the accidental and chaotic sensory stimuli of the world of ordinary experience or by intellectual concerns. He begins to acquire the power of turning away from the "given world" and toward the ability to "create" his own interior world of attenuated, simplified, and peaceful content. This is the meaning of *śamatha,* the calming of the contents of consciousness, and the attainment of release from subjection to external circumstances.

Calming, transic absorption and insight are important features of Buddhist ascesis; they continue to be fundamental in both Hīnayāna and Mahāyāna schools. The Vajrayāna, or Tantric form of Buddhism, also developed elaborate visualization meditations in which carefully delineated images of deities, or *maṇḍala*s, were reproduced with great exactitude within the mind of the meditator. The Tantric forms of Buddhist meditation became firmly established in Tibet.

China. Contemplation and meditation have held a position of high importance in Chinese religious traditions. This is particularly true of the indigenous Taoist tradition and the various schools of Buddhism imported from India.

Taoism. Taoism in its early literary form (here referred to as "classical Taoism") and its later offshoot, which is usually termed "Neo-Taoism," are usually thought of as the primary province of contemplation in the Chinese indigenous tradition.

Lao-tzu (seventh century BCE?) and Chuang-tzu (365–290 BCE?) are the two main figures of classical Taoism. Since their existence as historical figures is questioned, here we shall refer to them only by their works, now known as the *Lao-tzu* (or *Tao-te ching*) and the *Chuang-tzu.* These two books contain the early formulation of the Taoist worldview and ethos. In Taoism there is a contrast between the superficialities of conventional reality and the insight achieved by the Taoist sage. The task of Taoist contemplation is to move from a partial and self-centered view of things to a holistic view of the cosmos and its spontaneously functioning dynamism.

The Tao is the primary object of contemplation and meditation in the Taoist tradition. It is the ultimate principle beyond phenomenal manifestations and yet within which all phenomenal manifestations are brought forth and undergo change. The first chapter of the *Tao-te ching* emphasizes the ineffability of the true Tao:

> The Tao (Way) that can be told of is not the Eternal Tao;
> The name that can be named is not the eternal name.
> The Nameless is the origin of Heaven and Earth;
> The Named is the mother of all things.
> (Chan, 1963, p. 139)

The Tao is the substratum that remains when all verbal and physical phenomena are discarded. Awareness of the Tao can be reached through apophatic contemplation and meditation, that is, only through direct meditative experience. In order to attain inner illumination, the Taoist sage has to follow a way of unknowing, of abandoning learning in favor of looking directly into himself. Real education for the Taoist, in the phrase of Chuang-tzu, is "sitting and forgetting."

Buddhism. From the time when Buddhism entered China from India and Central Asia around the first century BCE, the Chinese were exposed to a bewildering variety of Buddhist teachings. The major Indian schools were represented, including the Mādhyamika (San-lun) and the Yogācāra (Fa-hsiang). Another school that developed in China, the T'ien-t'ai, promulgated an elaborate meditative regime based on a variety of scriptural sources. The Hua-yen school developed a teaching and meditative discipline that led to a vision of the harmony of totality and the mutual interpenetration of all things.

Two schools of Chinese Buddhism, the Ch'an and the Ching-t'u (Pure Land school), developed different understandings of meditation practice, a difference often referred to as that between "self-power" and "other-power." "Other-power" refers to a reliance on the grace of a deity for the achievement of salvation, an idea characteristic of the Pure Land school. The idea behind this emphasis is that human beings are not strong enough to bring themselves to *nirvāṇa* through their own meditative practices. Paradoxically, an adherent of this school is advised to call on the name of the saving deity (Amitābha; Chin., O-mi-t'o-fo; Jpn., Amida) with an undivided mind, thus constituting a mantralike form of apophthegmatic practice. [*See also* Nien-fo.] Meditation in the "other-power" schools tends toward the affective and cataphatic.

"Self-power" schools, like Ch'an (Jpn., Zen) Buddhism, are more austere and apophatic. The word *ch'an* is a transliteration of the Sanskrit term *dhyāna,* which means "meditation" or "contemplation." The Ch'an school emphasized "self-power" and sitting in formless meditation. Because of its exclusive emphasis on meditation, Ch'an developed an iconoclastic attitude toward other forms of religious observance. In Ch'an, personal enlightenment through intense meditation was the goal, and nothing was allowed to stand in the way of this pursuit, not even the religious and doctrinal trappings of Buddhism itself.

In Ch'an monasteries, meditation occupied a major part of the daily routine. Formal meditation usually took place in a separate building erected for the purpose and was supervised by a senior monk. Attention was paid to details of technique, including posture in the lotus position, with an erect spine, and the achievement of comfort and relaxation therein. Ch'an meditation focuses on the process of breathing, leading to a gradual withdrawal from external stimuli. A monk is instructed simply to observe the thoughts, feelings, and visions that may come into consciousness, and let them pass away of their own accord. When a monk is successful in detaching himself from both external and internal stimuli, he enters into an experience of stillness and emptiness. This breaks up the tendency to identify with the body and mind and provides a new perspective on ordinary experience, marked by detachment, equanimity, and freedom from a sense of the ego as a reference point for experience. Thus Ch'an meditation reaches for an experience of formlessness or emptiness that goes beyond one's ordinary ego-centered orientation to experience. This is a realization beyond doctrine and beyond words themselves. The semilegendary founder of Ch'an in China, Bodhidharma, is said to have described Ch'an as "a special transmission outside the scriptures; no dependence on words and letters; direct pointing at the mind of man; seeing into one's own nature and the attainment of Buddhahood."

[*See also* Attention; Mystical Union; Mysticism; *and* Prayer.]

BIBLIOGRAPHY

Chan, Wing-tsit, trans. and ed. *Instructions for Practical Living, and Other Neo-Confucian Writings by Wang Wang-ming.* New York, 1963.

Chan, Wing-tsit, trans. and comp. *A Source Book in Chinese Philosophy.* Princeton, 1963.

Chang Chung-yüan, trans. and ed. *Original Teachings of Ch'an Buddhism.* New York, 1969.

Conze, Edward. *Buddhist Meditation.* London, 1956.

de Bary, Wm. Theodore, Wing-tsit Chan, and Burton Watson, comps. *Sources of Chinese Tradition.* New York, 1960.

Ernest, John, J. E. L. Oulton, and Henry Chadwick, eds. *Alexandrian Christianity: Selected Translations of Clement and Origen.* London, 1954.

Francis of Sales. *Introduction to the Devout Life.* Rev. ed. Translated and edited by John K. Ryan. New York, 1972.

Kadloubovsky, Eugènie, and G. E. H. Palmer, trans. *Writings from the Philokalia on Prayer of the Heart.* London, 1951.

Naranjo, Claudio, and Robert E. Ornstein. *On the Psychology of Meditation.* New York, 1971.

Needleman, Jacob. *Lost Christianity.* New York, 1980.

Radhakrishnan, Sarvepalli, and Charles A. Moore, eds. *A Source Book in Indian Philosophy.* Princeton, 1957.

Schimmel, Annemarie. *Mystical Dimensions of Islam.* Chapel Hill, N.C., 1975.

Scholem, Gershom. *Major Trends in Jewish Mysticism* (1941). New York, 1961.

Suzuki, D. T. *Zen and Japanese Culture.* 2d ed., rev. & enl. Princeton, 1959.

Tart, Charles T. *States of Consciousness.* New York, 1975.

Tsunoda, Ryūsaku, Wm. Theodore de Bary, and Donald Keene, comps. *Sources of Japanese Tradition.* 2 vols. New York, 1958.

FREDERIC B. UNDERWOOD

Buddhist Meditation

Meditation as a means of religious discipline and spiritual attainment is not unique to Buddhism, but in its character and in its irreplaceable centrality to the gaining of ultimate salvation Buddhist meditation has a distinctive nature all its own. Basically, meditation is here conceived as a regimen of carefully structured steps of concentration on chosen objects, which concentration is designed to lead in the end to a "going out" *(nirvāṇa)* from the eternally recurring cycle of birth and death *(saṃsāra)* in which every sentient creature is enmeshed.

The meditative quest of Gautama (Pali, Gotama) under the Bodhi Tree, by which he became an enlightened one, or a Buddha (from *bodhi,* "enlightening knowledge"), remains the classic archetype of the discipline and experience. In the Theravāda (Pali canon) account, Gotama thereby discovered that attachment to individualized existence *(taṇhā)* was the cause of rebirth; in the Mahāyāna account, he discerned that the Buddha nature is inherent in all sentient beings.

Origins. The precise historical origins and components of the Buddhist meditative techniques are difficult to pin down. The Pali canon portrays Gotama as having vainly sought deliverance from *saṃsāra* by means of then-current Indian ascetic and meditative methods. These he ultimately rejected as wrong and insufficient in their extreme asceticism and in their goal of distinctionless union with the absolute *(brahman).* But although Buddhism denied the reality of the Upaniṣadic Self *(ātman),* and although the stated purpose of the new Buddhist meditation was to gain an existential realization of the *un*reality of the self *(anattā)* and to transcend an existence characterized by impermanence *(anicca)* and suffering, or innate unsatisfactoriness *(dukkha),* the aim of Buddhist practice remained spiritually kin to the Upaniṣadic quest of the Self: "The Self, which is free from evil, ageless, deathless, sorrowless, hungerless, thirstless, whose desire is the Real. . . . He should be searched out." [*See* Upaniṣads.]

Substitute *nirvāṇa*—the going out of, or from, selfness and thirst for continued being—for the Upaniṣadic Self, and one has a good description of the thrust toward the Buddhist goal, as well as an intimation of its methodology. So too, though the Yoga system developed independently of Buddhism and remained within the Brahmanic-Hindu fold, the yogic methodology that was developing during the early Buddhist period certainly contributed techniques, and probably followers, to the spreading Buddhist movement. [*See* Yoga.]

Theravāda Structure. Theravāda Buddhism has sought to fashion its meditational theory and practice in faithful adherence to the model provided by Gotama in his attainment of Buddhahood. This model is set forth most extensively in the *Majjhima Nikāya* (Middle-length Sayings), but owing to their analytic depth and rigor, the anonymous *Vimuttimagga* (The Path of Freedom) and Buddhaghosa's massive *Visuddhimagga* (The Path of Purification; both c. 500 CE) became the orthodox manuals of Theravāda meditation. [*See the biography of Buddhaghosa.*]

In these sources, meditation is presented as the only successful means to attain full and final release from the endless round of birth and death. The essence of the method is to so existentialize and internalize an awareness of the inherent nature (impermanent, unsatisfactory, lacking a permanent self) of all existence that the meditator becomes both intellectually and emotionally free from attachment to existence, thereby destroying the desire-driven karmic propulsion into ever new forms of space-time being.

Meditation is envisaged as a progression through three organically interdependent stages. *Sīla*, or morality, is the foundation and thus is intrinsic to the whole process. Only the morally earnest person can meditate properly. As spiritual development takes place, the central ethical values become progressively refined, strengthened, and internalized until they become fully dispositional. The five moral precepts (avoiding killing, stealing, lying, illicit sex, and intoxicants) and five further abstemious, but not ascetic, regulations are the core of *sīla*. The monk's life, originally geared almost exclusively to meditation, gradually acquired an elaborate superstructure of regulations built on this base. [*See* Vinaya.]

The second level or factor is the development of the power of attention *(samādhi)* until it can attain to one-pointed concentration on a single subject *(cittasya ekāgratā)* for long periods of time. The third and highest level of attainment is the fruit of the proper use of this one-pointed concentration of mind, called *paññā* (wisdom). In this state, the fully developed understanding of the true nature of *saṃsāra* results in enlightenment, the attainment of *nirvāṇa*. [*See* Samādhi *and* Prajñā.]

Basic Theravāda Techniques. Solitude—that is, freedom from disturbance by distracting sounds and sights—is essential for the beginner. The classic "lotus" posture is standard: legs folded beneath the torso, with each foot, sole upward, resting on the inner thigh of the opposite leg. The hands rest in the lap, palms upward, left hand underneath. The spine and neck are to be kept in a straight, but not strained, almost erect position. This mode of sitting provides a solid position that can be maintained without undue fatigue for extended periods. The lower centers of sensation, sphincteral and sexual, are thereby quieted and neutralized. The eyes are either half or totally closed.

There are some forty traditional subjects for meditation. They are classified in two ways: in terms of the types of persons for whom they are suitable, and in terms of the kind and level of meditative attainment their use can produce. Five types of personal character are recognized: devotional, intellectual, sensual, choleric, and dull. Meditation on the Buddha, the *sangha* (the Buddhist order), peace, and benevolence fit the devotional type; repulsiveness-of-food themes fit the intellectual type; cemetery meditations fit the sensual type; attention to breathing is recommended for the angry (choleric) type; and the dull type should meditate on the four "illimitables": loving kindness *(mettā)*, compassion *(karuṇā)*, joy in others' joy *(muditā)*, and equanimity *(upekkhā)*. Meditation on specified shapes and colors (*kasiṇas*) suits all types.

In terms of level of attainment, there are two types of results: jhanic and vipassanic. The jhanic (trance) states, representing the Yogic-Upaniṣadic inheritance of Buddhism, are eight in number (or by some counts nine): the four *jhānas* (Skt., *dhyānas*), through which the Buddha is portrayed as passing to gain enlightenment; and four successive states based on contemplation of formless subjects—infinity of space, infinity of consciousness, nothingness, and neither perception nor nonperception. All of these, according to the Pali canon, Gotama rejected in his search for the right method. Typically, these are to be produced on a *kasiṇa*-type base that is progressively refined and dematerialized in its perception until the meditator reaches the attenuated eighth stage, in which "subject" and "object" are barely distinguishable. Theravāda holds that such attainments per se do not constitute nirvanic experience however; that is reserved for the vipassanic type of technique. [*See also* Cosmology, *article on* Buddhist Cosmology.]

Vipassanā (insight) meditation is the quintessentially Buddhist element in the meditational structure. It is devoted exclusively to the intensification of the awareness of all visible-tangible realities, including the totality of the meditator himself, as intrinsically impermanent *(anicca)*, unreal *(anattā)*, and painful *(dukkha)*, the essence of *saṃsāra*. Certain of the forty subjects of meditation seem especially suited to vipassanic concentration. Meditation on the repulsiveness of food (the digestive process), the decaying states of a dead body, the analysis of the body into its thirty-two components, and on the sensations, emotions, and thought process of one's own body-mind lend themselves naturally to the *anicca, anattā, dukkha* analysis. All these component elements and processes are perceived to be atomistic aggregates dependent on each other for achieving existent form, a prime example of dependent origination *(paṭicca samuppāda)*, with no real or permanently self-identical "self" or "soul" present in any part or in the whole. [*See* Pratītya-samutpāda *and* Soul, *article on* Buddhist Concepts.]

The *vipassanā* level of concentration scarcely rises above the jhanic preliminary access concentration. (Access concentration is an "approach road" to the truly jhanic [trance] depths; it is a lightly concentrated state in which ordinary sounds can still be heard but are no longer at the center of attention or distractive to it.) But by its nature, *vipassanā* insight is the *sine qua non* of deliverance from *saṃsāra*, whether formalized as a method or not—although in the end *vipassanā* did become an independent method. Classically, it was used in conjunction with the jhanic type, whose *jhānas*—"peaceful abidings," Buddhaghosa calls them—must be subjected to vipassanic scrutiny lest the meditator become attached to them and consider them nirvanic attainment. But they too are still within the samsaric domain.

The experiential quality of *vipassanā* is not, however, purely negative or neutral; at its higher levels it too produces a jhanic-like result: path awareness, or the direct awareness of the unconditioned *nirvāṇa*. When this path awareness is first experienced it comes as a fleeting, flashing moment of sensing the nirvanic essence directly, brief but unmistakable. The meditator then knows he has reached the level of "stream enterer" *(sotāpanna)*, with only seven more rebirths awaiting him. Then in succession come the stages of "once returner to rebirth" *(sakadāgāmin)*, "nonreturner to human birth" *(anāgāmin)*, and "*nirvāṇa* attainer" *(arahant)*. The mere flashes of path awareness have now been developed until they come more frequently and sustainedly. [*See* Arhat.]

There is a crowning experience that Buddhaghosa says is possible only for *arahant*s and *anāgāmin*s who have also perfected the mastery of the eight jhanic trances. It is called *nirodha-samāpatti* ("complete cessation of thought and perception") and is the fullest, most intense, and longest (up to seven days) maintainable experience of nirvanic bliss that can be attained in this life. It is not, however, essential to after-death *nirvāṇa*, which may be achieved by *vipassanā* alone.

Mahāyāna Developments. That vast and varied development of Buddhist doctrine and institutions known as Mahāyāna, beginning late in the pre-Christian era, inevitably resulted in significant changes in the goals and methods of meditation. The basic techniques of posture and of breath, body, and thought control were retained, as were many of the meditational terms. But the inner meaning of the latter was radically changed, and the whole discipline was restructured in the light of new Mahāyāna doctrines. [*See* Buddhism, Schools of, *article on* Mahāyāna Buddhism.]

Relevant doctrinal changes. Four overlapping and interacting developments of doctrine and practice in Mahāyāna tended to modify the meditational pattern as well. First was the transformation and extension of the Buddha ideal from that of an exalted human who sought and gained immortality in the fifth century BCE to a transcendent being, exemplified variously by the Eternal Buddha of the *Saddharmapuṇḍarīka Sūtra* (Lotus Sutra), the eternally saving Buddha of Limitless Life (Amitāyus) of the Pure Land scriptures, the absolute Buddha essence *(dharmakāya)*, or the impersonal "emptiness" *(śūnyatā)* of the *Prajñāpāramitā* and other Mahāyāna scriptures. [*See* Śūnyam and Śūnyatā.] Second, the Lotus Sutra also taught that the ultimate goal of all human beings was to become Buddhas—implying the later doctrine of the Buddha nature implicit in all beings. Thus the ideal of bodhisattvahood, the selfless serving of others by repeated voluntary rebirths in order to serve and save them, replaced that of the *arahant* seeking release in *nirvāṇa*. The great *bodhisattva*s of compassion and power, absorbing the characteristics of indigenous deities along the way, became prime objects of popular devotion in many Mahāyāna cultures. [*See* Celestial Buddhas and Bodhisattvas.]

Third, the consequence of all this was the laicizing of Buddhist values. Thus the *Vimalakīrti Sūtra* relates how a pious layman of that name, fully involved in secular activity, surpasses all the heavenly *bodhisattva*s in spiritual attainments. But though these doctrines and ideals would seem to guarantee the genuine and effective opening up of the heights of spiritual realization (Buddhahood) to all people, this democratizing tendency was almost completely undercut by the simultaneous multiplication and complication of ritual and meditative techniques in some traditions. Ch'an (Jpn., Zen), with its demeaning of scripturalism and tradition, was one attempt to break through to greater simplicity; Chinese and Japanese Pure Land, with its repetition of the name of the Buddha Amitāyus (Jpn., Amida), was another.

Fourth, the Confucian-Taoist influence fundamentally altered East Asian Mahāyāna. The concept of Heaven, which embraced man in an organic relation, and the notion of the Tao as that infinite primordial formlessness out of which flows all the forms of the universe, both fused in many instances with such central Buddhist concepts as the *dharmakāya* (absolute Buddha essence) and *śūnyatā* (emptiness). Functionally, these became the Buddhist forms of the Tao.

Variant forms of Mahāyāna meditation. These Taoist characteristics were especially influential in the formation of Ch'an/Zen meditational patterns. The Taoist language of intuitive as opposed to rationalistic awareness, its viscerally sensed oneness with reality, its assertion of vacuity as true fullness, of silence as eloquence, of deepest truth as verbally unstatable, and of conceptual absurdities as revelatory of highest wisdom, were all adopted by Ch'an/Zen and made the basis of its meditational method and philosophy. The silent sitting and formless, objectless meditation (Jpn., *shikantaza*) of Japanese Sōtō, and Rinzai's use of the absurd, nonsensical, paradoxical *kōan* are thoroughly Taoist in nature.

Zen. The styles and methods of meditation in Sōtō and Rinzai monasteries vary considerably despite their common heritage. The *kōan* plays only a limited role in Sōtō, even though it has not been totally absent from its tradition. Dōgen, the great thirteenth-century master and founder of the Sōtō sect in Japan, allowed that some persons had gained enlightenment while using *kōan*, but that the true agent of that enlightenment had been their silent sitting in meditation *(zazen)*. [*See the biography of Dōgen*.] He asserted that this was indeed the teaching of the Buddha himself. Hence, the role of the meditation master *(rōshi)* in Sōtō is minimal. Sudden, flashing enlightenment experiences are not deliberately sought; in their place, a quieter and more natural inner-outer harmony of thought, feeling, and action is observed. To sit is to be a Buddha; continued and faithful sitting gradually transforms one's life, enabling one to find and develop one's innate Buddhahood and to encounter one's true *kōan* in life situations.

For Rinzai, the *kōan* replaces the Theravāda *kasiṇa*, so to speak. Rinzai meditation does not seek to create either an attenuated luminous form before the eyes or the state of cessation. Rather, it has as its goal a state of full, visceral oneness with the *dharmakāya*, an awareness that one's own mind is the Buddha mind and a sense of unity, although not blank undifferentiated oneness, with the universe and others, which Rinzai calls enlightenment (Jpn., *satori*). In this sense of "unity-with," one lives and does all one's work. This transition is seen as the great death of the concept-bound, self-bound, habit-bound individual and the transformation of that individual into a full, spontaneously free self in which the inner-outer, conscious-subconscious, self-other, holy-profane dichotomies are organically unified.

To achieve this transformation, Rinzai utilizes the *kōan*. Originally stemming from informal repartee, the interchanges between famous masters and their disciples were called *kōan* (public records or cases), and finally were collected into the Rinzai texts. There are some 1,700 in one famous collection. Jōshū's *mu* ("No!"—that is, there is no Buddha nature in a dog) and Hakuin's "the sound of one hand clapping" are famous ones, often used for beginners in meditation. Each student-monk is given a *kōan* by his master after some preliminary training. Once or twice a day he must present himself to his *rōshi* with his *kōan* and his "answer." The answer may be a word or phrase, a look, a gesture, an action. On the basis of that, the master judges the meditator's progress toward true understanding of the Buddha mind. When the answer shows such intuitive insight that the master is convinced of its authenticity, he pronounces the *kōan* solved. (The meditator's own subjective sense that he has had a *satori* experience will not suffice; the master may judge it to be delusive.) The meditator is then encouraged to expand and deepen this awareness through other *kōans*, which still further break down the person's sense of dualistic separation from his world or division within himself, and to apply this new "Buddha-mindedness" to wider areas of his life. [*See also* Ch'an.]

T'ien-t'ai. Of course, other forms of meditation, basing themselves on various *sūtras* and adopted by various sects, developed in the Chinese and Japanese contexts. The *Śūraṃgama Sūtra*, for example, sets forth a method of concentrating on the various basic sense data and their related sense organs in turn, several types of consciousness, and the component elements of existence.

The sect known as T'ien-t'ai (Jpn., Tendai), being highly inclusive in its doctrinal and practice structures, also developed various meditative techniques. Its basic scriptural warrant was the twenty-fourth chapter of the *Lotus Sutra*, the sect's main scripture, in which sixteen types of *samādhi* (meditation-induced mental concentration) are mentioned.

In T'ien-t'ai, four ways of attaining *samādhi* were recognized: (1) a ninety-day period of exclusive meditation on any proper subject; (2) exclusive invocation of Amitābha's name for ninety days; (3) a seated and walking meditation directed against bad *karman;* (4) a concentration on seeing ultimate reality as (a) empty of substantive actuality *(chi-k'ung),* (b) having immediate but provisional existence for thought and action *(chi-chia),* (c) climactically being *both* empty and existent *(chi-ch'ung)*—again a Taoist-influenced awareness.

Especially important for T'ien-t'ai was the direction given to it by Chih-i (538–597), the school's third patriarch. [*See the biography of Chih-i.*] He emphasized the necessity for balance in meditation and taught the fourth of the methods described above. Chih-i spoke constantly of the necessary presence of two factors at all times: *chih* (Skt., *śamatha*) and *kuan* (Skt., *vipaśyanā*). *Chih* is the stopping and calming of thought. This meditative mode produces an awareness of sheer emptiness *(śūnyatā),* the realization of the great void in an inner stillness, but by itself too nirvanic-passive and withdrawn. *Kuan,* or introspective attention to the workings of one's own mind (not unlike Theravāda *vipassanā),* leads to the awareness of the illusory quality of mind, a sense of its relativistic dependence on exterior objects, and embodied *bodhisattva* compassion. The proper combination of the two at all stages of meditation gives rise to a compassionate wisdom in which all things and situations are seen as neither totally real nor unreal. Japanese Tendai, introduced to Japan by Saichō in the ninth century, soon adopted Esoteric techniques in competition with Shingon, and was also modified by Zen. [*See* T'ien-t'ai.]

Pure Land. The Pure Land schools also had their forms of meditation, and for some devotees, a system of visualization based on the *Kuan wu-liang-shou ching* (Amitāyus Meditation Sutra). Beginning with the attention focused on the setting sun (in the direction of the Western Paradise), the meditator successively visualized sun (with both open and shut eyes), water, ice, lapis lazuli (fundament of the Pure Land), and the Pure Land glories as described in the *sūtra,* climaxing in a vision of Amitābha himself and his two flanking *bodhisattvas*. In Japan, success in this was sometimes linked with the number of invocations of Amida's name. No doubt T'ien-t'ai's second method was influenced by these Pure Land practices.

Still another type of meditative visualization is set forth in the *Pratyutpanna-buddha-saṃmukhāvasthita-samādhi Sūtra,* an early Mahāyāna work possibly intended for the laity. The meditator who would achieve this *samādhi* must prepare for it by scrupulous adherence to the precepts, the study of scripture, and a continual effort to see the Buddhas everywhere and in everything. This is to be capped by a period of intensive meditation. The *sūtra* promises that if one meditates continuously for seven days and nights he will assuredly see the Pure Land and Amitābha. Other possible objects of concentration are also mentioned. One meditates on some particular Buddha, or perhaps on the Buddhas as a whole, and in the ensuing *samādhi* all the Buddhas and their attendants will present themselves before him. One interpretation of this language is that the meditator travels, by visualization, to the lands of the Buddhas and hears them expound the Dharma directly. The *sūtra* promises that these visualizations will be "as in a dream." In the *samādhi* that ensues, the meditator will not be sensible of day or night, inner or outer, or of any distinction of any sort, "not seeing anything." Some see this as an effort to bridge the gap between the burgeoning Pure Land cult of seeing the Buddha Amitāyus and the Prajñāpāramitā "emptiness" *(śūnyatā)* philosophy. [*See* Amitābha; Pure and Impure Lands; *and* Nien-fo.]

Esoteric Buddhism. The so-called Mantrayāna and Vajrayāna methods that developed in Tibet and that have taken a somewhat similar form in Japanese Shingon are considered to be generally Mahāyāna, yet they have distinctive features. Tibetan practice, which includes Tantric and pre-Buddhist Bon elements, strongly emphasizes visualizations and *mantra* repetition. Although these induced visualizations—in which *maṇḍalas* are used as a base and *mantras* as a ritual aid—are ostensibly visual representations of various demons, gods, Buddhas, and *bodhisattvas,* they are in fact only visualized forms of the basic psychic forces, good and bad, within the meditator himself. These the meditator must project into full consciousness, in part by the use of those *mantras* containing divine-name power, and then overcome or appropriate them. Considerable attention and effort are expended on the control of the flow of vital energy into the various *cakras* (psychosomatic centers) in the body, and on the transmutation of the lower forms of energy into the higher. A very important part of the various Tibetan methods, often combined with other visualizations, is the strengthening of the meditator's Buddha awareness by consciously visualizing the inclusion of the Buddha's characteristics into himself, so that in the end he himself is in some measure a Buddha, and of visualizing the whole world as Buddha-filled and offering it to the Buddha in its *maṇḍala* form. But again, the crowning realization is that of the ultimate emptiness. [*See also* Buddhism, Schools of, *article on* Esoteric Buddhism; Maṇḍalas, *article on* Buddhist Maṇḍalas; Mantra; *and* Cakras.]

Japanese Shingon has an elaborate, esoteric ritual structure for its adepts in which various deities are invoked and their power solicited. Visualization here begins at least with the visualization of a luminous disk (reminding one of the luminous circular *kasiṇa* form of Theravāda meditation) into which, one by one, are projected various sacred Devanāgarī (Hindu script) characters, whose power the meditator thus gains. The final goal is to become Buddha in this very body and this very life. [*See* Chen-yen *and* Shingonshū.]

In few of these forms did Mahāyāna fulfill the apparent potential of its *bodhisattva* ideal of "every being a Buddha," and of a meditative discipline within the range of the ordinary person's capacities, permeating everyday life and work. Zen has offered meditation to the laity, but real progress toward enlightenment has usually been understood to necessitate a monastic life. The popular recitation of the Nembutsu ("Namu Amida Butsu," "Reverence to Amida Buddha") of the Japanese Pure Land sects was the nearest approach to a daily lay meditative technique. Sometimes among the Japanese *myōkōnin* (Nembutsu pietists), Amida-consciousness reached a nearly mystical sense of oneness with Amida. And perhaps the Nichiren repetition "Namu Myōhōrengekyō" ("Adoration to the Lotus Sutra") as a mantric chant has become something of a popular meditative practice.

Modern Tendencies. In general, and especially in Zen and Theravāda, the trend in modern meditational teaching has been one of simplification and adaptation of techniques to contemporary conditions and to wider lay practice. In Theravāda, this has taken the form of an almost exclusive emphasis on the less technically demanding *vipassanā* technique. In particular, attention is given to breath and to body-mind processes, as well as to *vipassanā*'s practicality for daily life in the world. Efforts are being made to bring Zen out of the monastery and into lay life by modifying the strictness of its regimen and relating its orientation to the "ordinary mind," which after all is the Buddha mind. And in both traditions there has been a notable missionary penetration of Europe and America in the form of meditation centers and temporary short-term meditation sessions. Some have also incorporated Zen elements into various psychosomatically oriented self-development and self-realization techniques.

[*See also* Soteriology, *article on* Buddhist Soteriology; Nirvāṇa; *and* Buddhism, *article on* Buddhism in India.]

BIBLIOGRAPHY

Buddhaghosa, Badantācariya. *The Path of Purification.* 2d ed. Translated by Bhikkhu Ñyāṇamoli. Colombo, 1964. The comprehensive manual of Theravāda meditation, considered authoritative by Theravādins.

Chang, Garma C. C. *The Practice of Tibetan Meditation.* New York, 1963. One of the few reliable and specific treatments, including text and methodological sections.

Chang, Garma C. C., trans. and ed. *The Teachings of Tibetan Yoga.* New Hyde Park, N.Y., 1963.

Chang, Garma C. C. *The Practice of Zen.* New York, 1970. A clear and knowledgeable exposition of Zen practice for Western readers.

Conze, Edward. *Buddhist Meditation* (1956). Reprint, New York, 1969. A collection of Buddhist meditation texts from *The Path of Purification* and various Sanskrit and Tibetan sources, with a brief introduction.

King, Winston L. *Theravāda Meditation: The Buddhist Transformation of Yoga.* University Park, Pa., 1980. A systematic analysis of *The Path of Purification* pattern, the Indian-Yogic origins, and the dynamic structure of Theravāda meditation, with a chapter on contemporary Burmese forms.

Kornfield, Jack. *Living Buddhist Masters.* Santa Cruz, Calif., 1977. The best overall exposition of a wide variety of contemporary forms of Theravāda meditation in Southeast Asia.

Luk, Charles (K'uan Yü Lu). *The Secrets of Chinese Meditation.* London, 1964. Detailed description of several lesser-known meditational techniques, based in part on the author's own experiences.

Nyanaponika Thera, trans. *The Heart of Buddhist Meditation.* New York, 1975. A clear, authentic discussion and exposition of contemporary Theravāda Buddhist meditation theory and practice. Centered on the vipassanic "bare-attention" type.

Suzuki, D. T., Erich Fromm, and Richard De Martino. *Zen Buddhism and Psychoanalysis.* New York, 1960. An interesting and penetrating discussion of the Zen and psychological interpretations of Zen meditation.

Tucci, Giuseppe. *The Theory and Practice of the Maṇḍala.* Translated by Alan Houghton Broderick. London, 1969. Illuminating discussion of the Indo-Tibetan *maṇḍala* as a "psychocosmogram."

Vajirañāṇa Mahāthera, Parahavahera. *Buddhism Meditation in Theory and Practice.* Colombo, 1962. Clear, systematic exposition of the classic orthodox Theravāda system and theory of meditation in the traditional terminology of the Pali canon.

WINSTON L. KING

MEGALITHIC RELIGION.

[*This entry consists of two articles. The first is a discussion of the religious artifacts that inform our knowledge of the presence of megaliths in prehistoric cultures; the second is an essay on the role of megaliths in historical cultures, especially in Southeast Asia and Oceania.*]

Prehistoric Evidence

In Neolithic western Europe, large stones, or megaliths (from the Greek *megas*, "great," and *lithos*, "stone"), were used for construction of tombs, temples, rings, alignments, and stelae. The largest number of some fifty thousand megalithic monuments are in Spain and Portugal, France, Britain, southern Sweden, and northern Germany. The terms *megalithic culture* and *megalithic religion* have been applied to the massive stone monuments. However, neither a separate megalithic culture nor isolated megalithic religion existed. The culture that produced megalithic monuments was a part of the western European Neolithic and Aeneolithic (a transitional period between the Neolithic and Bronze ages). It consisted of a number of regional culture groups whose religion can be understood in the context of the gynecocentric Old European (i.e., pre-Indo-European) religion inherited from Upper Paleolithic times. [*See* Prehistoric Religions, *article on* Old Europe.] Huge stones were used wherever they were readily available. Monumental architecture, motivated by religious ideas, emerged synchronically with the rise of a sedentary way of life.

Carbon-14 dating has established that western European megaliths were built over a span of at least three thousand years, from the fifth to the second millennium BCE. They were constructed earlier than the Egyptian pyramids and do not descend from forms in the Near East; the majority of archaeologists now believe that their development was indigenous. If there was any diffusion of ideas, it occurred along the seaboard and from the Atlantic coast toward the interior.

Megalithic structures fall into four main categories. The first is the temple, found in the Mediterranean islands of Malta and Gozo. Maltese temples have solid walls of very large stone slabs, and their floor plan has apses that recall the shape of a seated or standing goddess. The second and largest category of megalithic structures is the burial chamber, which is subdivided into dolmens (monuments of two or more upright stones supporting a horizontal slab), passage graves, court tombs, and gallery graves. Some passage graves are monumental buildings whose chambers have corbeled vaults; for example, Newgrange in the Boyne River valley, Ireland, which dates from 3200 to 3000 BCE, rises twenty feet above the ground. (See figure 1.) The third category is the single upright stone, or menhir (the word comes from the Welsh *maen,* "a stone," and *hir,* "long"). Some of the menhirs found in Brittany are as high as six meters. A special kind of menhir, called a statue menhir, is sculpted to represent a divinity. (See figure 2.) The fourth category consists of grouped standing stones, placed either in rows or in elliptical rings.

Archaeologists once assumed that these megalithic monuments had evolved from simple to more complex forms, but the new chronology shows that some very elaborate buildings predate the simple gallery graves.

Temples and tombs were built in the likeness of the Mother of the Dead or Mother Earth's pregnant belly or womb; this is the key to understanding megalithic structures and their floor plans. The idea that caves and caverns are natural manifestations of the primordial womb of the goddess is not Neolithic in origin; it goes back to the Paleolithic, when a cave's narrow passages, oval-shaped areas, clefts, and small cavities were marked or painted entirely in red, a color that must have symbolized the color of the mother's generative organs. The rock-cut tombs and hypogea of Malta, Sicily, and Sardinia are usually uterine, egg-shaped, or roughly anthropomorphic. Red soil is found under each temple of Malta.

In western Europe, the body of the goddess is magnificently realized as the megalithic tomb. The so-called cruciform and double-oval tombs, as well as Maltese temples, are unmistakably human in shape. (See figure 3.) Some monuments replicate the ample contours of figurines of the pregnant goddess.

The earliest form of the grandiose chamber tombs is the passage grave, which consists of a corridor and principal chamber. The natural cave, with its connotations of the goddess's womb (vagina and uterus), was probably the inspiration for the aboveground monumental structures that were erected later. The basic form of the passage grave—a shorter or longer passage and a round, corbel-roofed chamber—dates from the fifth millennium BCE in Portugal, Spain, and Brittany.

The interior structures of many Neolithic court tombs found in Ireland are outlined in a clearly anthropomorphic form. In addition to a large abdomen and head, some structures have legs and even eyes. The term *court cairns* or *court tombs* comes from the semicircular entrance, built with large stones, that characterize these structures. In many instances, the court and one or more chambers attached to the middle of the edifice are all that remain of the cairn (De Valera, 1960, pls. ii–xxx). However, better-preserved examples show that the court marks the inner contour of the anthropomorphic figure's open legs; the chambers or a corridorlike structure next to it, which leads into the very center of the mound, represents the vagina and uterus. The same symbolism is manifested in different areas and periods. The Sardinian *tombe di giganti* of the third and second millennia BCE, consisting of a long chamber entered through the center of a semicircular facade, do not differ in symbolism from the Irish court tombs.

The other type of grave is a long barrow whose shape resembles that of a bone, a symbol of death. Like the court tombs, this type of grave has an entrance at the front that leads into an anthropomorphic or uterus-shaped chamber. (See figure 4.)

Megalithic monuments were built to be seen. Careful excavations and reconstructions have shown that much attention was paid to their outer walls and facades. For example, a reconstruction of a monument at Barnenez, Brittany, dating from the fifth millennium BCE (Giot,

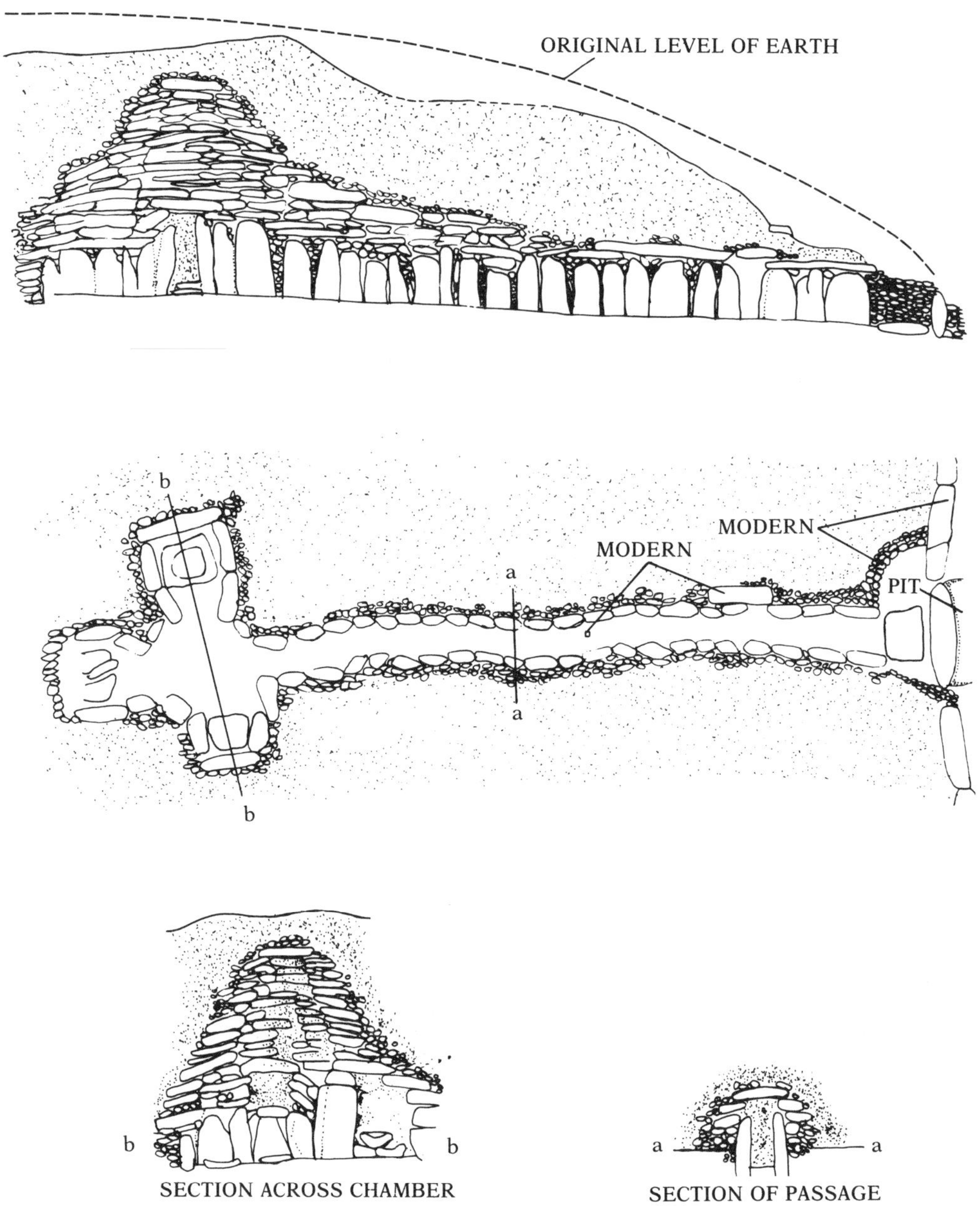

FIGURE 1. *Passage Grave.* The greatest passage grave of the megalithic tradition—Newgrange (built c. 3000 BCE), County Meath, Ireland—is shown here in elevation (top), plan (middle), and sections (bottom). The narrow passage that leads to the burial chamber in the center is some twenty meters long; the corbeled vault of the chamber is nearly seven meters high.

1980), revealed a concentric series of walls with the upper parts of the internal walls visible. Another great structure, dating from the first half of the third millennium BCE, was reconstructed at Silbury, Wiltshire, in southwestern England (Dames, 1976). Later excavations revealed that there were once wooden structures on top and beside the megalithic monuments that were just as important as the monuments. Postholes (indicating the presence of structures) have been observed in low barrows in Brittany, Britain, and Denmark. Traces of a timber facade, a porch at the front end of the barrow, and palisade enclosures have also been discovered (Madsen, 1979). The exquisite decoration in bas-relief on stones at entrances (as at Newgrange) implies that ceremonies took place in front of the cairns. Settlement debris in Irish court cairns has led some scholars to believe that chambered tombs and long barrows should be considered not burial places but shrines. However, excavations of megalithic chambers over the past two centuries have revealed skeletons, suggesting that the monuments served as repositories and were used collectively by the community. Some tombs have yielded as many as 350 disarticulated skeletons; others contain only 5 to 20 skeletons, discovered in compartments where they were placed after the flesh had decayed. In a few instances, skulls were found stacked carefully in corners.

Long cairns in Britain have yielded so-called mortuary houses, which were constructed of timber or stone and had plank floors. The rectangular mortuary houses found at Lochhill and Slewcairn contained three pits; the central one had two posts while the end pits held large split tree trunks (Masters, in Renfrew, 1981, p. 103). Mortuary houses are also known from Denmark (Becker, in Daniel and Kjaerum, 1973, pp. 75–80; Madsen, 1979). These mortuary buildings yielded deposits of charcoal, dark soil, cremated bone, an occasional child's skull, and flint tools, indicative of rituals including sacrifices. It seems that megalithic structures and long barrows, not unlike Christian cathedrals and churches, served as shrines and ossuaries. No doubt the large monuments, exquisitely built and engraved with symbols on curbstones and on inner walls, such as those at Knowth and Newgrange (O'Kelly, 1983), Ireland, and Gavrinis, Brittany, were sacred places where funeral, calendrical, and initiation rites took place. These monuments should be called not "tombs" but rather "tomb-shrines." The egg-shaped mound that covers the tomb-shrine of Newgrange is sprinkled with white quartz and looks like a huge egg-shaped dome. Probably it was meant to represent a gigantic cosmic egg, the womb of the world.

FIGURE 2. *Statue Menhir.* On this stela, the goddess's face is surrounded by a squared-off border of opposed chevrons. Late Neolithic of Provence (Lauris-Puyvert, Bouches-du-Rhône, southern France), final Chassean culture; end of the fourth millennium BCE. SOURCE: After Gragnière, *Gallia Préhistoire* 4 (1961).

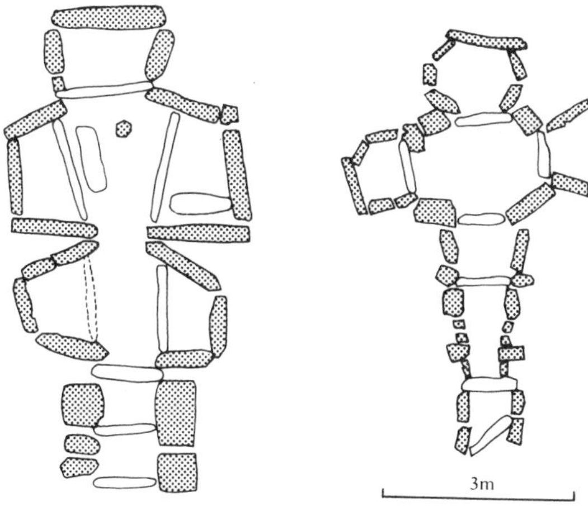

FIGURE 3. *Human-shaped Tombs.* The entire body of the Mother of the Dead is represented in two western European megalithic tombs whose shape sheds an interesting light on the cruciform cathedrals of Europe. Plans are of tombs inside cairns. Neolithic culture of Ireland (County Sligo, northwestern Ireland); second half of fourth millennium BCE.

SOURCE: After Herity (1974).

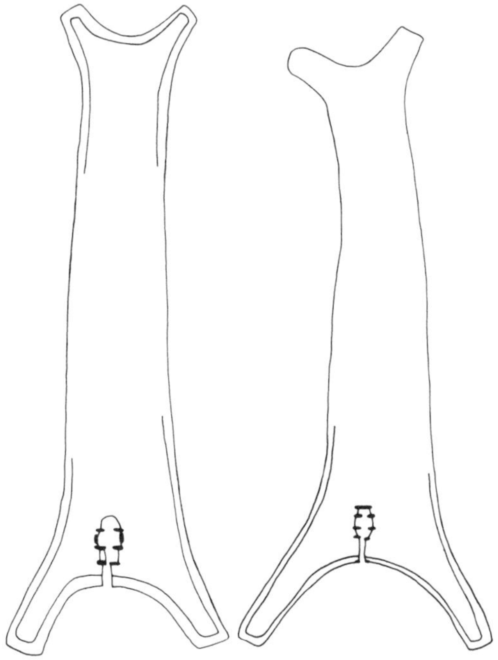

FIGURE 4. *Bone-shaped Barrows.* Some long barrows, such as these at South Yarrows, Orkney (end of fourth millennium BCE), are precisely in the shape of the Old Hag's bone of death.

SOURCE: After Henshall (1963).

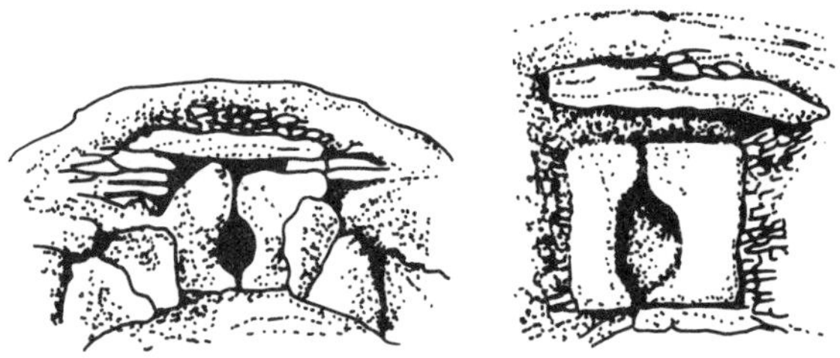

FIGURE 5. *Tomb Entrances.* Narrow entrances to the tombs at (1) Norn's Tump and (2) Windmill Tump are vulvul symbols.
SOURCE: Müller-Karpe (1974).

It is very likely that not all rituals were connected with death of humans and of all nature; some may have been initiation rites. Typically, the entrances to the tombs are narrow, resembling vulvas. (See figure 5.) One enters the mortuary house by either crawling or crouching along a narrow passage of stone. A wall of large curbstones, forming a forecourt, supports the mouth of the passage entrance on both sides. The structure may be a replica of the narrow and difficult entry into the mother goddess's womb.

In megalithic gallery graves of France, Switzerland, and the Funnel-necked Beaker culture in Germany, partition walls sometimes have round holes. Their meaning is apparent if the still-extant veneration of stones with holes is considered; belief in the miraculous power of holed stones is still found in Ireland, Scotland, England, France, and in many other European countries. Trees with holes play a related role. By crawling through the aperture of a stone or tree, a person is symbolically crawling into Mother Earth's womb and giving oneself to her. Strengthened by the goddess's powers, he or she is reborn. The crawling constitutes an initiation rite and is similar to sleeping in a cave, that is, "sleeping with the mother," which means to die and to be resurrected. Well-known sculptures of sleeping women from the Hal Saflieni hypogeum in Malta, dating from approximately 3000 BCE, most likely represent such an initiation rite.

The pregnant mother's (or earth mother's) generative potential is emphasized by the symbol of a mound and omphalos (navel), which is found engraved or in bas-relief on stone slabs. For example, relief engravings completely cover the surface of twenty-three erect slabs within the passage grave of Gavrinis, rendering an overall impression of symbolic unity. This sanctuary, one of the richest megalithic monuments in Brittany, is situated on a small island in the Gulf of Morbihan. The extensive use of wavy and concentric arc motifs is in harmony with the monument's aqueous environment. The dominant symbol found in this sanctuary is the concentric semicircle, interconnected with or surrounded by multiple wavy lines and serpentine forms. Several slabs are decorated with concentric arcs, piled one on top of the other in vertical columns. The arcs in the center are larger than the rest and have an omphalos-like protrusion. (See figure 6.) In my opinion, this image is a glyph of the goddess's rising generative force. Emphasis is on the anthropomorphic vulva or cervix sign in the center. (For other illustrations, see Twohig, 1981, pp. 172–175.)

Symbolically related to the passage grave of Gavrinis is the roughly triangular backstone of a passage grave from La Table des Marchands in Brittany. It has a vulva at its center, flanked by energy signs—four rows of hooks—meant to stimulate the life source. This symbolism is similar to that found on ancient Greek vases, in which the young goddess (Semele, Gaia) is depicted within an artificial mound surrounded by satyrs, goatmen, and Dionysos, who stimulate her generative powers. On other passage-grave slabs, the symbol of an artificial mound surmounted by a knob is surrounded by axes, another energy symbol, or in association with serpentine lines or snakes and footprints. Still other engravings of the same image (called a "buckler" in the archaeological literature, where it has been seriously misunderstood) show wavy lines emanating from the upper part, which may signify the resurgence of plant

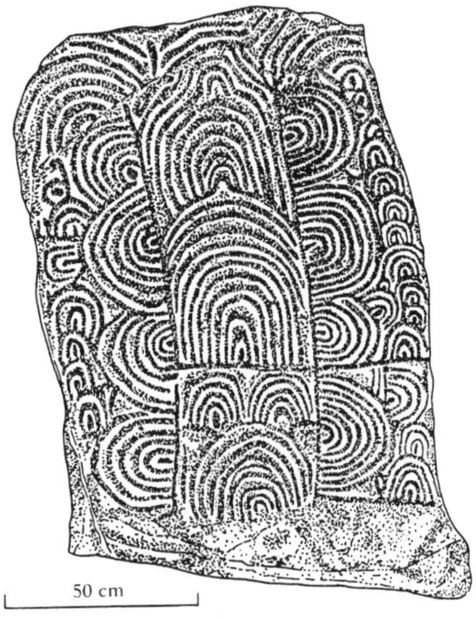

FIGURE 6. *Mound and Omphalos Motif.* The single slabs in the passage grave of Gavrinis are covered with columns of concentric arcs that radiate from a central vulvate opening; the protrusions at the top (in central column) represent omphali. This glyph probably symbolizes the rising generative force of the goddess. Gulf of Morbihan, Brittany; end of fourth millennium BCE.
SOURCE: After Twohig (1981).

life. The beehive-shaped chamber, topped with a flat stone, found in passage graves appears to be a pregnant belly and an omphalos. The so-called buckler sign replicates the same idea in an engraving.

In his analysis of the Silbury Hill monument, Michael Dames shows that in Neolithic Britain the hill functioned as a metaphor for the goddess's pregnant belly (Dames, 1976). The entire structure forms an image of the goddess: the hill is her belly, the ditch forms the rest of her body in a seated or squatting position. The circular summit of Silbury Hill is the goddess's navel, or omphalos, in which her life-producing power is concentrated. Veneration of sacred hills was found in Europe until the twentieth century. Worship of the earth mother was celebrated on mountain summits crowned with large stones.

The second deity associated with the symbolism of the megalithic monuments is the goddess of death and regeneration in the guise of a bird of prey, usually an owl. Her image is engraved or modeled on statue menhirs, slabs of passage and gallery graves, and on walls of subterranean tombs. She herself, her eyes, or her signs appear also on schist plaques, phalanges (bones of toes or fingers), and stone cylinders laid in graves.

The characteristic features of the owl—round eyes and hooked beak—can be seen on the statue menhirs of southern France and Iberia, as well as in reliefs and charcoal drawings in the hypogea of the Paris Basin. (See figure 7.) The face is frequently schematized as a T shape or depicted with only eyes and brows or with a square head, surrounded by chevrons, in the center of the forehead. (See figure 2.) On the slabs of gallery graves of Brittany, only breasts and necklaces are shown in relief as *pars pro toto* of the owl goddess. The images of the owl goddess on schist plaques in the passage graves of Portugal have a prominent nose or beak, schematized arms, three horizontal lines or bands across the cheeks, occasional indications of a vulva, and a chevron design on the back. The goddess's owl face appears on a very fine sculpture discovered at Knowth West, Ireland. Her visage is immersed in a labyrinthine design probably symbolic of the life source or life-giving waters; a vulva is in the center. Images of the owl goddess on vases from Almería in Spain are at times associated with a honeycomb design—a maze of Vs, triangles, and lozenges.

The symbols associated with the owl goddess—wavy lines, hatched or zigzag band, net, labyrinth, meander, honeycomb, tri-line, hook, ax—all seem to be life-source, energy, or life-stimulating signs. Their association with the owl goddess emphasizes regeneration as an essential component of her personality. The agony of death is nowhere perceptible in this symbolism.

The round eyes of the owl goddess stare from bone phalanges and stone cylinders deposited in megalithic tombs in Spain and Portugal. The eyes and brows are incised in the upper part of the bone or stone cylinder and are surrounded by chevrons, triangles, zigzags, and nets. (See figure 8.) Again, the symbols of death (bones, light-colored stone) are combined with aquatic, life-source symbolism.

The goddess's impressive, divine eyes gave rise to one of her names, which came into use after the publication of *The Eye Goddess* by O. G. S. Crawford in 1957. The goddess of the title was said to have originated in the Near East, her cult then diffusing across the Mediterranean to western Europe. Indeed, the resemblance of figurines from the temple of Tell Brak, eastern Syria (c. 3500 BCE), with their staring eyes and brows joined over the beak, to the stone idols of Spain and Portugal with their oculi motif is astonishing. The similarity, however, most probably resulted from a universally held symbolic concept of divine eyes, from which western variants developed. The western European eye goddess dates from the fifth and fourth millennia BCE (in Crawford's day considered to be the third and second millennia BCE). She has close parallels in southeastern Europe and certainly cannot be an imported goddess.

Small stone hourglass figurines, sometimes with triangular heads, are frequently found in Iberian megalithic tombs of the Los Millares type, dating from the end of the fourth or early third millennium BCE. Hourglass figures also are painted on Neolithic cave walls in

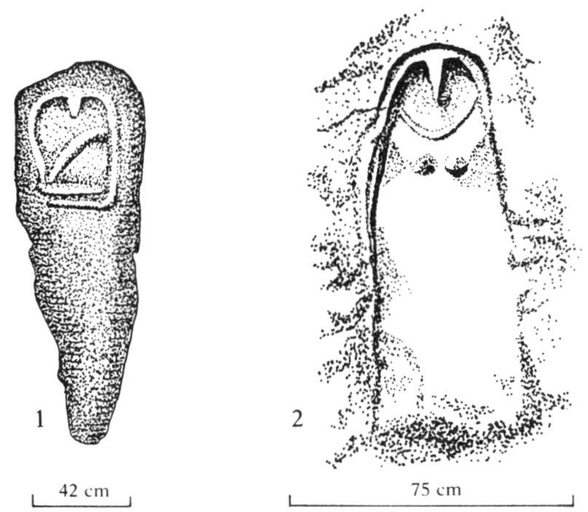

FIGURE 7. *The Owl Goddess.* (1) In this stela, the owl goddess is shown with folded arms; the crosier lies across the upper part of her body (Aven Meunier Island, southern Franch). (2) The owl goddess wears a necklace (a common convention in such representations) in this charcoal drawing from the wall of an antechamber of a Paris Basin hypogeum (c. 3000–2500 BCE).
SOURCE: After d'Anna (1977).

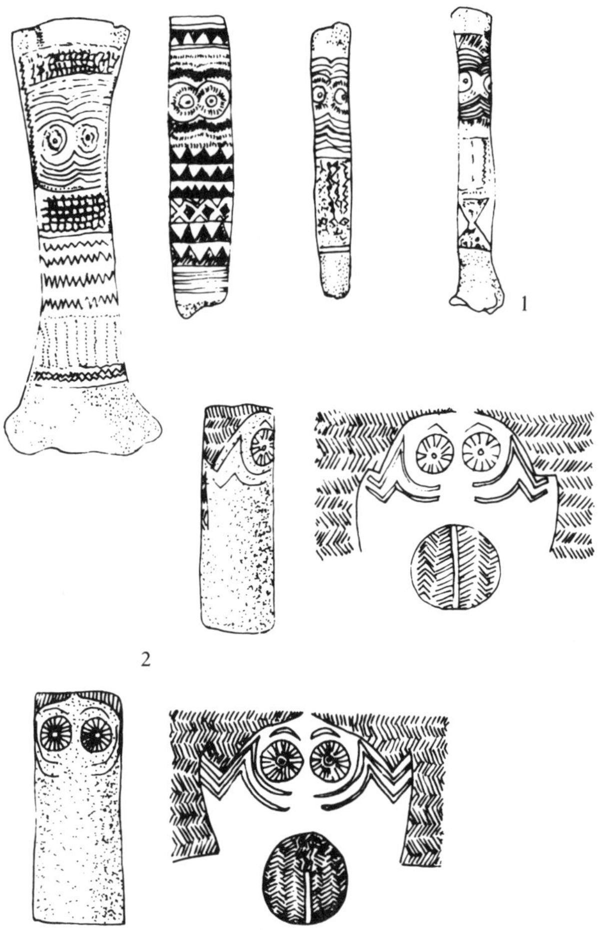

FIGURE 8. *The Eye Goddess.* (1) The eyes on these bone phalanges are surrounded by chevrons, triangles, nets, and other familiar symbols (Almizaraque settlement, Almería, Spain, first half of third millennium BCE). (2) These stone "eye idols" from megalith graves all show two or three lines curving under the goddess's eyes and ending as chevrons on her temples; the zigzag pattern on the top and back may represent hair (Morón de la Frontera, Spain; probably early third millennium BCE). SOURCE: Both, after Leisner and Leisner (1943).

Spain and are engraved on stones of Irish passage graves. The shape may have originated as a doubling of the pubic triangle (vulva) sign, connected at the tip. In Sardinian hypogea, vulva and hourglass signs are interchanged. Engraved triangles and hourglass shapes also appear to be associated on Irish megaliths. Not infrequently, hourglass symbols are engraved in triunes or next to three encircled round holes, as on Curbstone 52 from Newgrange. (See figure 9.) The number three may reflect the triple nature of the goddess. In vase painting, the hourglass sign appears in association with nets, serpentiforms, and snake meanders, which link this symbol with the life source and water of life symbolism. Bird feet or claws that appear attached to some hourglass figures on vases of the Cucuteni culture (northeastern Romania and western Ukraine) and of the Sardinian Ozieri culture speak for the association with the bird-of-prey goddess. The hourglass shape itself may symbolize an incipient form of life in which the goddess of death and regeneration emerges from graves or caves. This sign is related to the butterfly, a horizontal hourglass and symbol of new life. The origins of the goddess's image as a bird of prey are rooted in the Paleolithic, as is documented by portrayals of owls in Upper Paleolithic caves and by the large birds and wing bones of large fowl found in Paleolithic graves.

Disarticulated skeletons and skulls in megalithic tombs are proof that excarnation was practiced. Corpses were offered to the goddess, who was embodied in birds of prey. This practice is illustrated in frescoes of vulture shrines of Çatal Hüyük, central Anatolia. Large birds were also buried in megalithic tombs, probably as sacrifices to the goddess. Excavations have uncovered a large deposit in a chambered tomb at Isbister in Orkney, Scotland. The greatest number of bones came from the white-tailed eagle. Others were from short-eared owls, great black-backed gulls, rooks or crows, and ravens (Hedges, 1983). All these birds feed on carrion.

Geometric engravings on Irish megaliths—crescents, circles, and concentric circles; serpentiforms or zigzags with thirteen to seventeen turnings (the number of the moon's waxing days); subdivisions into four, six, or eight and twelve—suggest a preoccupation with the cycles of time. The involvement of the goddess in configurations of cycles of nature and human life is certain. She must have been the overseer and controller of life and moon cycles.

Many western European tomb-shrines have been constructed so that the entrances align with the winter sol-

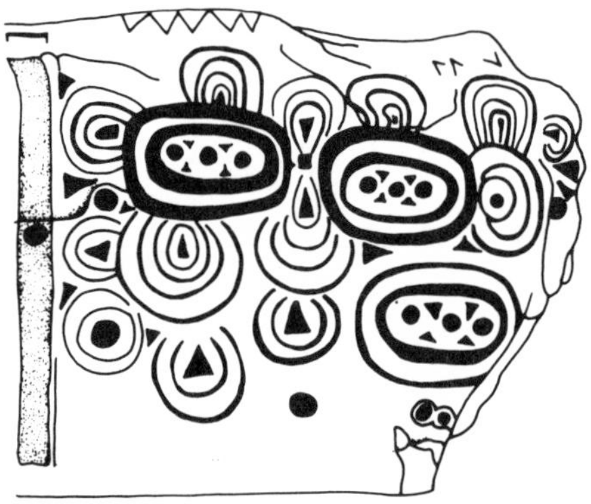

FIGURE 9. *Hourglass Symbol.* Triangles, an hourglass symbol, and triunes (in cartouches) appear on Curbstone 52 from Newgrange, County Meath, Ireland. SOURCE: After Brennan (1983).

stice. The alignment of tomb entrances according to the moon's position at the winter solstice suggests the importance of lunar influences on burial customs and suggests the association with the lunar goddess, who was a cosmic regenerator. These monuments were not built to serve as lunar or solar observatories, as claimed by A. Thom (1979) and other scientists writing on the importance of megalithic astronomy. Rather, their orientation according to lunar and solar phases served essentially for the regeneration of life. Rebirth was in the power of the goddess. In megalithic symbolic art we see the link between the time-measuring symbols and the symbols of her regenerative power, between sundials and divine eyes, and between the gnomon and the cupmark, symbols of the life source and rebirth. Other associated symbols are expressions of regenerative aquatic or plant forces.

Ceremonial ships are engraved on inner tomb walls in megalithic tombs in Brittany and Ireland. All depictions of ships are highly abstracted; some are just a row of vertical lines connected by a bar at the bottom. However, frequently there is a zoomorphic or spiral head, probably that of a serpent, on the keel. Sometimes an abstracted image of the goddess is shown being pulled by what may be a snake or ship. If the ship and serpent are interchangeable symbols (as they are on Egyptian artifacts and on Scandinavian rocks from the Bronze Age), then many winding serpents engraved on tomb walls are life-renewal symbols. Perhaps it is not accidental that some of the winding snakes and zigzags in Knowth and Newgrange are joined to a triangle or lozenge (two triangles joined at their bases), the special signs of the goddess of death and regeneration, just as the feet of the birds of prey are attached to the prow of the ship on Cycladic platters dating from the middle of the third millennium BCE.

Folk stories associate megalithic tombs with fearsome goddesses, such as the goddess Gráinne, the Old Hag of Celtic myths (Burl, 1981, p. 66). The original meaning of *Gráinne* is "ugliness." Some cairns are said to be composed of stones dropped from the apron of the Old Hag. At least forty chambered tombs in Ireland are nicknamed "Diarmaid and Gráinne's Bed." The passage grave at Knockmany, County Tyrone, is called "Annia's Cave," a reference to the home of the hag Anu, guardian of the dead. Breast-shaped hills in County Kerry, Ireland, are still called the "Paps of Anu." Anu is related to the Breton goddess Ankou ("death") and to other death goddesses with similar names (such as the Slavic *Yaga*, from **Enga;* the Proto-Samoyed **Nga;* the Near Eastern *Anat*, etc.). Thus the lunar goddess represented in figurines as the White Lady, or Death, is still alive in folk memories.

In sum, the art of the megalithic monuments reveals the association with the two aspects of the prehistoric Great Goddess, the chthonic and the lunar. The underlying idea of the ground plan and shape of the monuments was the belief in the self-creating Mother Earth who was also the Mother of the Dead. The sculptures (figurines and stelae), bas-reliefs, and engravings represent the lunar goddess in an anthropomorphic shape as White Lady (Old Hag) and in the guise of a bird of prey, usually the owl. This second aspect is the other side (the side associated with necrosis, night, and winter) of the life giver in anthropomorphic or water-bird shape.

[*See also* Goddess Worship; Feminine Sacrality; Prehistoric Religions, *article on* Old Europe; *and* Stones.]

BIBLIOGRAPHY

Almagro Basch, Martín, and Antonio Arribas. *El poblado y la necrópolis megalíticos de Los Millares.* Madrid, 1963.

d'Anna, A. *Les statues-menhirs et stèles anthropomorphes du midi méditerranéen.* Paris, 1977.

Arnal, Jean. *Les statues-menhirs: Hommes et dieux.* Paris, 1976.

Brennan, Martin. *The Stars and the Stones: Ancient Art and Astronomy in Ireland.* London, 1983.

Burl, Aubrey. *Rites of the Gods.* London, 1981.

Crawford, O. G. S. *The Eye Goddess.* London, 1957.

Dames, Michael. *The Silbury Treasure: The Great Goddess Rediscovered.* London, 1976.

Dames, Michael. *The Avebury Cycle.* London, 1977.

Daniel, Glyn E. *The Megalith Builders of Western Europe.* London, 1958.

Daniel, Glyn E. *The Prehistoric Chamber Tombs of France.* London, 1960.

Daniel, Glyn E., and Poul Kjaerum, eds. *Megalithic Graves and Ritual.* Copenhagen, 1973. A collection of essays, including "Problems of the Megalithic 'Mortuary Houses' in Denmark" by C. J. Becker and "The Relations between Kujavian Barrows in Poland and Megalithic Tombs in Northern Germany, Denmark and Western European Countries" by Konrad Jażdżewski.

De Valera, Ruaidhrí. "The Court Cairns of Ireland." *Proceedings of the Royal Irish Academy* 60, sec. C, 2 (1960): 9–140.

De Valera, Ruaidhrí, and Seán Ó Nualláin. *Survey of the Megalithic Tombs of Ireland*, vol. 3, *Counties.* Dublin, 1972.

Eogan, George. *Excavations at Knowth.* Dublin, 1984.

Giot, P. R. *Barnenez, Carn, Guennoc.* Rennes, 1980.

Giot, P. R., Jean L'Helgouac'h, and Jean-Laurent Monnier. *Préhistoire de la Bretagne.* Rennes, 1979.

Hedges, John W. *Isbister: A Chambered Tomb in Orkney.* Oxford, 1983.

Henshall, Audrey S. *The Chambered Tombs of Scotland.* 2 vols. Edinburgh, 1963–1972.

Herity, Michael. *Irish Passage Graves: Neolithic Tomb-Builders in Ireland and Britain, 2500 B.C.* New York, 1974.

Leisner, Georg, and Vera Leisner. *Die Megalithgräber der iberischen Halbinsel: Der Süden.* Berlin, 1943.

L'Helgouac'h, Jean. *Les sépultures mégalithiques en Armorique: Dolmens à couloir et allées couvertes.* Alençon, 1965.

MacKie, Evan. *The Megalith Builders.* Oxford, 1977.

Madsen, Torsten. "Earthen Long Barrows and Timber Structures: Aspects of the Early Neolithic Mortuary Practice in Denmark." *Proceedings of the Prehistoric Society* 45 (December 1979): 301–320.

Masters, Lionel J. "The Lochhill Long Cairn." *Antiquity* 47 (1973): 96–100.

Müller-Karpe, Hermann. *Handbuch der Vorgeschichte,* vol. 3, *Kupferzeit.* Munich, 1974.

O'Kelly, Michael J. *Newgrange: Archaeology, Art and Legend.* London, 1983.

Renfrew, Colin, ed. *The Megalithic Monuments of Western Europe.* London, 1981. A collection of essays, including "The Megalithic Tombs of Iberia" by Robert W. Chapman, "The Megaliths of France" by P. R. Giot, "Megaliths of the Funnel Beaker Culture in Germany and Scandinavia" by Lili Kaelas, "Chambered Tombs and Non-Megalithic Barrows in Britain" by Lionel J. Masters, "The Megalithic Tombs of Ireland" by Michael J. O'Kelly, and "Megalithic Architecture in Malta" by David Trump.

Thom, A. *Megalithic Remains in Britain and Brittany.* Oxford, 1979.

Twohig, Elizabeth Shee. *The Megalithic Art of Western Europe.* Oxford, 1981.

MARIJA GIMBUTAS

Historical Cultures

Megaliths are simply monuments built of large stones. In Southeast Asia and Oceania, a variety of megaliths are found, some thousands of years old, others brand new. Early studies of these structures viewed them primarily in the context of theories suggesting prehistoric migrations of megalith builders. In 1928 the eminent Austrian archaeologist Robert Heine-Geldern wrote the first of a series of influential articles, in which he argued that megaliths were created during two great waves of prehistoric migrations into Southeast Asia. The first group, the "Older Megalithic Culture," was thought to have ushered in the Neolithic age, while the second, the "Younger Megalithic Culture," was credited with the introduction of metal.

Heine-Geldern's view of megaliths as steppingstones by which archaeologists could trace prehistoric migrations dominated Southeast Asian archaeology for many years, giving rise to extensive debates on the "problem of megaliths." In the past few decades, however, fresh waves of archaeologists, equipped with superior tool kits for prehistoric research, have passed over the territory first explored by Heine-Geldern. As the picture of prehistoric Southeast Asia became clearer, Heine-Geldern's theory of migratory megalith builders had to be abandoned. Several prominent archaeologists subsequently issued a joint statement, for the benefit of those who might not have kept up with the current state of archaeological research, that "the label 'megalithic culture' cannot reasonably be applied to any of the phases or levels of social integration recognizable in the recent or prehistoric past of South East Asia" (Smith and Watson, 1979, p. 253). In the wake of the reaction against comprehensive theories linking megaliths to prehistoric migrations, little effort has been made to sort out the historical relationships among the various builders of megaliths in Southeast Asia and the Pacific. But, as we shall see, megaliths play an important role among many societies in the region, particularly those which share a common Austronesian cultural heritage. As Peter Bellwood, a leading authority on Pacific prehistory, observed recently, "The wide occurrence of megalithic monuments and statues in Oceania suggests that their origins may go very deep into the Austronesian past, possibly at least into the first millennium B.C." (Bellwood, 1978, p. 226).

Many types of megaliths are found in the Indo-Pacific region, including menhirs (erect stones), dolmens (flat stones resting on two stone pillars), stone seats, stepped stone pyramids, and various types of stone tombs and sarcophagi. Active megalithic traditions exist today on several Indonesian islands, possibly related to megalithic customs still found among hill tribes of Northeast India such as the Nagas. In Southeast Asia, the most elaborate and well-documented megalithic traditions are found on the island of Nias, which lies about seventy miles off the northwest coast of Sumatra. In Nias, stones were put to many uses, foremost among them being the large menhirs and dolmens erected as monuments to chiefs.

In 1907 a Dutch colonial administrator, E. E. W. G. Schröder, photographed the erection of a dolmen as a monument for a chieftain who had died the previous year. A rectangular stone forty centimeters thick, three and one-half meters long, and two meters wide was dragged by means of logrollers from a quarry to the summit of a hilltop village, a distance of about two kilometers. There it was set on two stone pillars outside the former chief's house as a monument to his glory and as a home for his spirit, whenever the chief might choose to visit the village. The project was organized by his son and successor, who mobilized 525 kinsmen and allies to transport the stone. Schröder's dramatic photographs show the chief's son atop the stone as it is being dragged uphill; he is wearing a warrior's costume and waving his sword.

Such megaliths, called *darodaro,* were personal monuments erected about a year after the death of a chief by his kinsmen and allies. Often the chief's skull was placed in a niche in the *darodaro,* along with his sword and other regalia. The larger the *darodaro,* and the more people who participated in dragging the stone and celebrating the funeral feast, the greater the chief. The same logic also applied to a second type of megalith erected in honor of chiefs, the *batu nitaru'o,* which was an upright stone or menhir placed in front of a living chief's house. The erection of such monuments were important political events, with roots in the fundamental structure of Niasian chiefdoms. Niasian society was divided into patrilineal descent groups, and rank order within each lineage was determined by a cycle of feasts. Every adult male had to give the first six feasts in the cycle. But the "heads" *(ulu)* of lineage branches had to give up to six additional feasts, each more elaborate than the last. Each man would invite to his feasts his personal *öri* ("circle")—a circle of kinsmen, friends, and allies linked by marriage ties or reciprocal feasting. The supreme feast, given only by lineage heads, drew together an *öri* of several lineages and villages, and established the boundaries of a chiefdom: a chiefdom was nothing more than the *öri* of a chief. This supreme feast was called the *batu nitaru'o ba wa'ulu* ("chief's feast of the *nitaru'o* stone"). The larger the stone, the more people belonging to the chief's *öri* who participated, the greater the chief. Political authority was not vested automatically in a man born as a lineage head; it had to be demonstrated through the feast cycle. The *öri* of the chief whose funeral Schröder photographed included sixteen villages.

In addition to the chief's monuments, Niasians also erected smaller megaliths for a variety of purposes related to their belief that stones provided temporary shrines for various spirits. Each village had its *batu banuwa* (village stone) celebrating the origin of the village. Childless women, especially those of high rank, were considered likely to become dangerous ghosts. So they were often provided after their deaths with small *darodaro* in case they should visit the village. Schröder, who spent several years exploring the island in the first decade of this century, recorded a wide variety of megaliths in different villages. In one village, stones had been placed near a bathing place "for the spirits to dry their clothes." In another, he found stone seats with footprints below for childless women, because "she who dies without children leaves no footprints on the earth."

The advent of Christianity brought an end to most of the megalithic customs of Nias in the past few decades, but on the island of Sumba three thousand kilometers to the southeast, megaliths even larger than those of Nias continue to be erected in honor of important chiefs. On Sumba, there is no parallel to the Niasian *batu nitaru'o* (the stones erected by living chiefs), but the death of a chief calls for the erection of a stone sarcophagus reminiscent of the *darodaro.* Like the Niasians, the Sumbanese usually build their villages on hilltops, and the center of the village is dominated by an array of these megaliths, which may weigh as much as thirty tons. Stones *(ondi)* are cut from native limestone, and placed atop a wooden platform *(tena)* which the Sumbanese liken to a ship, complete with a figurehead in the shape of a horse's head. Dragging the stone to the village may take weeks and call for the efforts of several hundred men. As in Nias, a chief *(rato)* stands on the stone and gives directions. Stone dragging is dangerous, and responsibility for managing things so that the stone does not slip and kill or injure someone rests with the chief. Every day, numbers of water buffalo and pigs must be slaughtered to feed the whole party.

As in Nias, Sumbanese social organization is based on alliances between clans, and the strength of an alliance is demonstrated by the number of allies who arrive to participate in the megalithic funeral, bringing gifts of water buffalo and pigs. As many as a hundred buffalo and pigs may be slaughtered for a major funeral, their horns and jawbones later tied to the chief's house as mementos of the feast. The more such trophies, and the larger the stone slab, the greater the chief. At the conclusion of the funeral, the chief's body is placed in the tomb and his favorite horse is killed so that the horse's spirit may lead him to the spirit world.

A different sort of megalithic tradition is found on the island of Bali, a tradition nicely exemplified by a chance discovery made in 1935 by the first archaeologist to work in Bali, William F. Stutterheim. Near a spring sacred to the early Hindu kings of Bali, he found a stone with a weatherworn inscription.

> None of the Balinese could decipher the old engraved letters, nor were the contents of the inscription known to anyone. The stone stood there, as every villager of Manukaya knew it from childhood, wrapped in a white cloth and provided with regular offerings. I was told, however, that on the fourth moon of every year, at full moon, this stone (which is also said to have fallen from the sky) is carried to the holy waters of Tirta Mpul and bathed therein—much to the detriment of the stone, by the way, which is a big slab of soft grey tufa covered as usual with a thin layer of cement. Deciphering the inscription, I found that it was none other than the charter of Tirta Mpul's foundation, made in the fourth month, at full-moon day, in the year 962 A.D. Thus the people have kept alive the connection between the stone and the watering place for a thousand years, and have always celebrated its anniversary on the correct day, but of the true meaning of this connection every recollection was lost.
>
> (Stutterheim, 1935, p. 7)

Bali is now famous as the last surviving Hindu-Buddhist civilization of Indonesia. But the stone of Manukaya draws our attention to deeper, pre-Hindu roots of Balinese religion. Although the Balinese worship Hindu gods, they do so in temples that resemble ancient Polynesian *marae* much more than traditional Indian temples. Balinese temples, like Polynesian *marae,* are basically rectangular walled courtyards open to the sky, with a row of menhirlike shrines at one end. While the Balinese shrines may be much more elaborate than those typical of Polynesia, occasionally replacing stone with wood, the two types of shrines perform the same function of providing a temporary resting-place for visiting spirits of gods or ancestors. Both Balinese and Polynesians believe that the gods are not continuously present, but temporary, invisible visitors who like to alight in menhirs or similar objects for brief visits. Even the details of worship are often quite similar—both Balinese and ancient Polynesians wrapped cloths around the stones for important festivals. Unlike the Balinese, but very much in the spirit of the Niasians and Sumbanese, the ancient Polynesians buried important chiefs within their temples, and sometimes consecrated them with human sacrifices.

The largest Polynesian *marae* were stepped stone pyramids, of which the greatest was the *marae* of Mahaiatea in Tahiti (now destroyed). Mahaiatea was a rectangular pyramid of eleven steps, with a base measuring eighty-one meters by twenty-two meters. Similar structures were once common in Bali, such as the village temple (Pura Desa) of the village of Sembiran, although in Bali such pyramids may be interpreted in a Hindu idiom as *prasada* ("cosmic mountain").

We have noted several common uses for megaliths in the Indo-Pacific region—as tombs and monuments to the power of chiefs, and as temporary shrines or resting-places for ancestral spirits and gods. In Polynesia, we encounter also a different type of megalith, the importance of which is only beginning to be recognized—navigational "sighting stones." These stones, which are found on several islands, appear to have served three related purposes: as markers to align beacons (watch fires?) for ships sailing to neighboring islands; as the centers of navigational schools where students could learn the movements of useful stars by watching star after star appear at a particular point on the horizon marked by a stone, according to the seasons; and as timekeeping devices, predicting the position of sunrise and sunset at the solstices. For example, on the island of Arorae, in the Kiribati (Gilbert Islands), nine stones at the northernmost tip of the island point accurately toward three neighboring islands. Each stone points about five degrees out, perhaps to allow for the drift caused by the equatorial current in different seasons. Although no longer in active use, these megalithic "sighting stones" may have played an important role in prehistoric Pacific voyaging. Much remains to be learned about the functions of these stones and the other megaliths of the Indo-Pacific.

BIBLIOGRAPHY

There are two useful references for locating sources on particular megalithic customs. For Southeast Asia, see H. H. E. Loofs's *Elements of the Megalithic Complex in Southeast Asia: An Annotated Bibliography* (Canberra, 1967), which reflects, however, an outdated theoretical perspective. For Oceania, the literature on megaliths is surveyed in Peter Bellwood's comprehensive *Man's Conquest of the Pacific* (Oxford, 1978). More recent information on megaliths in Southeast Asia is contained in R. B. Smith and William Watson's *Early South East Asia* (Oxford, 1979), in which Glover, Bronson, and Bayard comment on Christie's presentation of the "Megalithic Problem." The megalithic traditions of Nias are described and illustrated in exemplary detail in E. E. W. G. Schröder's *Nias: Ethnographische, Geographische, en Historische Aantekeningen* (Leiden, 1917). A brief summary in English based on Schröder may be found in Edwin M. Loeb's *Sumatra: Its History and People* (1935; Oxford, 1972), which also contains an appendix by Robert Heine-Geldern on "The Archaeology and Art of Sumatra," summarizing his views on megaliths. On navigational stones in the Pacific, see Brett Hilder's article in *Polynesian Navigation,* edited by Jack Golson (Wellington, 1963), and Thomas Gladwin's *East Is a Big Bird: Navigation and Logic on Puluwat Atoll* (Cambridge, Mass., 1970). Sumbanese megalithic customs are outlined in Christiaan Nooteboom's *Oost-Soemba, Een Volkenkundige Studie,* Proceedings of the Royal Anthropological and Linguistic Institute, no. 3 (The Hague, 1940), and in Janet Alison Hoskins's "So My Name Shall Live: Stone-Dragging and Grave-Building in Kodi, West Sumba," *Bijdragen tot de Taal-, Land- en Volkenkunde* 145 (1986): 1–16. William F. Stutterheim's *Indian Influences in Old-Balinese Art* (London, 1935) sketches the major monuments of ancient Bali.

J. Stephen Lansing

MEHER BABA (1894–1969), born Merwan Sheriar Irani; spiritual master who declared himself the avatar (descent of God into human form) of this age. Beginning in 1925, he observed silence for the rest of his life, communicating at first by pointing at letters on an alphabet board and later through gestures. Meher Baba stated that his silence and the breaking of his silence would bring about a universal transformation of consciousness through a release of divine love in the world.

Meher Baba was born in Poona, India, into a family of Persian descent. In 1913, while attending Deccan College, he met the first of five "perfect masters" (fully enlightened or God-realized individuals) who made him aware of his identity as avatar. Stating that he had come "not to teach but to awaken," Meher Baba demonstrated the essential oneness of all life through acts of love and service. Throughout his life he served the poor, the physically and mentally ill, the "God-intoxicated" aspirants whom he called *masts*, and others in need. He indicated that his outer activities were symbolic of the inner awakening that constituted his real work. Giving no importance to the divisions of caste or creed, he drew followers from many faiths and social classes.

Since his death (the "dropping of his body") in 1969, Meher Baba's following has grown considerably, especially in India, the United States, Australia, and Europe. His followers feel themselves to be in a lover-beloved relationship with Meher Baba, believing that he inwardly guides them in their spiritual journey to eliminate the ego (false self) and to realize God as the "true Self." While attempting to heed his wish to found no new religion or sect, his followers in many places do gather informally to share experiences of his love and guidance. Meher Baba's tomb at Meherabad, near Ahmednagar, India, has become a place of pilgrimage for his followers throughout the world.

BIBLIOGRAPHY

Works by Meher Baba. The most comprehensive book containing Meher Baba's guidance concerning spiritual life is *God to Man and Man to God: The Discourses of Meher Baba* (North Myrtle Beach, S.C., 1975). For a detailed description of his cosmology, see *God Speaks: The Theme of Creation and Its Purpose,* 2d ed. (New York, 1973). Both these books were dictated by Meher Baba on an alphabet board. Many later discourses given through hand gestures are collected in *The Everything and the Nothing* (Berkeley, 1971, and Bombay, 1976).

Works about Meher Baba. The fullest biography is C. B. Purdom's *The God-Man* (Crescent Beach, S.C., 1971), which also contains an interpretation of Meher Baba's life and message. For an extensive account of Meher Baba's work with the God-intoxicated, advanced aspirants, *sadhus*, and the poor, consult William Donkin's *The Wayfarers* (San Francisco, 1969). An intimate look at life with Meher Baba can be found in Kitty L. Davy's *Love Alone Prevails* (North Myrtle Beach, S.C., 1981).

CHARLES C. HAYNES

ME'IR

ME'IR (second century CE), Palestinian tanna. According to legend, Me'ir was descended from a family of proselytes that traced its line back to the Roman emperor Nero. He allegedly studied with both ʿAqiva' ben Yosef and Yishma ʿe'l. Me'ir was one of the five rabbis secretly ordained by Yehudah ben Bava' during the Hadrianic persecutions that followed the collapse of the Bar Kokhba Revolt (c. 132–135 CE), and he was one of the seven disciples of ʿAqiva' who issued a famous edict concerning the intercalation of the year that was crucial to the maintenance of the Jewish festivals.

Me'ir is associated with Elishaʿ ben Avuyah, a heretic also known as Aḥer, "the Other." Some rabbinic sources depict Me'ir as a sometime student of Elishaʿ (B.T., *Ḥag.* 15a).

The tomb of the legendary Me'ir Baʿal ha-Nes in Tiberias, a famous place of pilgrimage, is identified in some accounts as the burial place of Me'ir. Other Talmudic traditions suggest that Me'ir died in self-imposed exile in Asia Minor, where, at his request, he was buried beside the sea so that he could be near the waters that wash up on the shores of the Land of Israel (J.T., *Kil.* 9.4, 32c).

Me'ir is prominently linked to the major rabbinic legislative and political activities of his generation. He served as the *ḥakham* ("sage") of the revived Sanhedrin that met at Usha in the Galilee. His ability to defend both sides of opposing legal viewpoints was greatly extolled. Ultimately, his opposition to the authority of the *nasi'* Shimʿon ben Gamli'el was the basis for his exile from Israel.

Legal rulings ascribed to Me'ir make up an important part of the earliest rabbinic compilations, the Mishnah and the Tosefta. The Talmud states that all anonymous rulings in the Mishnah are to be attributed to Me'ir. Epstein (1957) believes that the corpus of his teachings was one of the primary documents used in the redaction of the Mishnah. Since the laws in the Mishnah form the basis for much of Talmudic and later rabbinic thought and practice, it is fair to say that Me'ir is one of the most influential classical rabbinic figures.

Me'ir's dicta deal with most of the central values of rabbinic Judaism; he placed extreme emphasis on the study of Torah and strongly castigated the unlettered. One tradition attributed to him indicates his understanding of rabbinic ritual as a coherent system of practice that demanded punctilious observance: "Rabbi Me'ir used to say, 'There is no man in Israel who does not perform one hundred commandments each day [and recite over them one hundred blessings] . . . And there is no man in Israel who is not surrounded by [reminders of the] commandments: [Every person wears] phylacteries on his head, phylacteries on his arm, has a *mezuzah* on his doorpost and four fringes on his garment around him'" (Tosefta, *Ber.* 6.24–25). Many Midrashic teachings and several fables are also attributed to Me'ir.

[*For discussion of the group of sages to which Me'ir belonged, see* Tannaim.]

BIBLIOGRAPHY

No systematic critical analysis has been made of the rich and extensive corpus of traditions associated with Me'ir. Two biographical treatments of Me'ir are Adolf Blumenthal's *Rabbi Meir: Leben und Wirken eines jüdischen Weisen* (Frankfurt, 1888), which is a classical treatment of rabbinic biography, and Naomi G. Cohen's "Rabbi Meir: A Descendant of Anatolian Proselytes," *Journal of Jewish Studies* 23 (Spring 1972): 51–59, which critically examines the sources pertaining to Me'ir's lineage. Jacob N. Epstein in his *Prolegomena ad Litteras Tannaiticus* (Jerusalem, 1957) discusses, in Hebrew, the role of Me'ir's materials in the formation of the Mishnah. Robert Goldenberg's analysis in *The Sabbath-Law of Rabbi Meir* (Missoula, Mont., 1978) is confined to the examination of Me'ir's contribution to the laws of a single tractate. *Rabbi Meir: Collected Sayings* (Jerusalem, 1967) is a compendium, in Hebrew, of all the references to Me'ir in rabbinic literature, edited by Israel Konovitz. Avigdor Shinan in his "The Brother of Rabbi Meir," *Jerusalem Studies in Hebrew Literature* 2 (1983): 7–20, analyzes a Midrashic story about Me'ir.

TZVEE ZAHAVY

ME'IR BEN BARUKH OF ROTHENBURG (c. 1220–1293), known by the acronym MaHaRaM (Morenu ha-Rav Me'ir ["our teacher, Rabbi Me'ir"]); German Talmudist, authority on rabbinic law, and communal leader. Me'ir's early years were spent studying under Yitsḥaq ben Mosheh of Vienna and Yeḥi'el of Paris; he witnessed the famous Paris disputation of 1240 and saw the Talmud burned publicly in 1242. Eventually he settled in Rothenburg and with the passing years was universally recognized by contemporaries as the greatest of Ashkenazic rabbis. With the increasingly precarious situation of German Jewry in the latter decades of the thirteenth century, culminating in Rudolph I's imposition of the status of *servi camerae* ("servants of the chamber") on all Jews and, in 1286, his confiscation of the properties of Jews who left his domain, many fled. Me'ir himself was apprehended in Lombardy in an attempt to flee Germany and was imprisoned—possibly because of his role as a leader of the mass exodus. He remained in prison for the rest of his life, mostly in Ensisheim Castle in Alsace. Communal efforts to ransom the master never succeeded and, indeed, it was not until 1307 that his body was released for burial in exchange for a huge sum. In the sixteenth century Shelomoh Luria cited a tradition that Me'ir himself forbade payment of the exorbitant price, and Irving Agus has further claimed that the crux of the matter was its nature—was it to be ransom or tax? In these interpretations, Me'ir becomes a martyr for Jewish law and the integrity of the community. Sources contemporary with events more soberly indicate that Me'ir died in the course of protracted negotiations for his release.

Me'ir's preeminence is indicated by the express statements of his contemporaries, the scope and quantity of his *responsa*, and his impact on subsequent halakhic history. Though it is unlikely that Me'ir was ever officially appointed chief rabbi of Germany, he undoubtedly fulfilled that function. Close to one thousand of his *responsa* have been preserved, a number far exceeding the combined mass of all other tosafist *responsa*. On the whole, Me'ir avoids prolix discussions, combining care and decisiveness in his writing. Acknowledging fully the authority of the Talmud, he maintains an independent stance in relation to his contemporaries, even when their rabbinical posture is allied with communal and economic power. About one hundred of his *responsa* deal with community governance and organization. These texts are of great significance; they provide invaluable data on the social history of the period and offer substantial insight into Me'ir's political ideology. In general, Me'ir walks a thin line between the protection of individual rights and the need to give the community the legal weapons necessary for its survival and well-being.

In addition to his *responsa*, Me'ir wrote and edited *tosafot* ("additions") to many tractates of the Talmud; during his latter years in prison he was allowed access to some books and could be visited by students. His habits were noted and recorded by his students, who became the rabbinic leaders of the next generation. Me'ir's magisterial figure is prominent in subsequent Ashkenazic rabbinic development, and many of the decisions and customs recorded in Mosheh Isserles's glosses to the *Shulḥan 'arukh*, authoritative for Ashkenazic Jews, derive from his work.

[*For further discussion, see* Judaism, *article on* Judaism in Northern and Eastern Europe to 1500; *see also* Tosafot.]

BIBLIOGRAPHY

Irving A. Agus's stimulating *Rabbi Meir of Rothenburg*, 2 vols. (Philadelphia, 1947), is the most detailed analysis of Me'ir's life and achievement; Agus also provides translations of a large number of Me'ir's *responsa*. A more sober treatment is E. E. Urbach's *Ba'alei ha-tosafot*, vol. 2, 4th ed. (Jerusalem, 1980), pp. 521–570. Salo W. Baron's *A Social and Religious History of the Jews*, vol. 9, 2d ed. (New York, 1965), pp. 135–193, gives historical background.

GERALD J. BLIDSTEIN

MEISTER ECKHART. *See* Eckhart, Johannes.

MELANCHTHON, PHILIPP (1497–1560), born Philipp Schwartzerd; German theologian and major sixteenth-century reformer, writer of Protestantism's first systematic theology, organizer of the Protestant public school system, and author of two statements of Lutheran belief: the Augsburg Confession and its apology. Although he was a close friend of Martin Luther for twenty-eight years, his humanism and stance on nonessentials brought charges of corrupting Lutheranism.

Born in Bretten, Germany, and orphaned at ten, Melanchthon received tutoring from his grandfather John Reuter and the linguist John Unger. He attended the Pforzheim Latin School where his granduncle John Reuchlin, the Hebraic scholar and humanist, supervised him for two years. For achievement in Latin and Greek, Reuchlin named his nephew Melanchthon—Greek for Schwartzerd, meaning "black earth." He entered Heidelberg University in 1509, at the age of twelve, and was awarded the B.A. in 1511 but was rejected as too young to pursue the M.A. At Tübingen University he received the M.A. in 1514, edited for Thomas Anshelm's press, and published translations of Plutarch, Pythagoras, and Lycidas, comedies of Terence in verse, and his popular *Rudiments of the Greek Language* (1518). Called in 1518 to teach Greek at Wittenberg University, Melanchthon became Luther's lifelong colleague. While teaching, he studied theology and earned a bachelor's degree in 1519, his only theological degree. Thenceforth, Melanchthon taught classics and theology. In 1530 he married Katherine Krapp, who bore him four children.

In 1521 Melanchthon's *Loci communes rerum theologicarum* appeared, Protestantism's first systematic theology, which was highly lauded by Luther. It dealt with basic Reformation tenets on sin, law, and grace, and went through many enlarged editions. Besides maintaining an extensive correspondence, Melanchthon produced classical treatises, translations, commentaries, theological works, and numerous textbooks. He was called Germany's preceptor for reorganizing numerous schools and universities. The Augsburg Confession (1530), Lutheranism's basic statement of faith, was conciliatory toward Roman Catholicism without sacrificing evangelical views; the *Apology for the Augsburg Confession* (1531) was boldly assertive. Melanchthon encountered criticism when in the *Variata* of 1540 he changed the Augsburg Confession to allow a Calvinistic interpretation of the Eucharist. His ecumenical efforts brought temporary unity between Martin Bucer and Luther in 1536 on the real eucharistic presence of Christ. However, his irenic agreement with Cardinal Contarini on justification was rejected by Luther and the papacy. Fearful of antinomianism, Melanchthon, with Luther's support, insisted that good works follow faith, but this view seemed too Roman Catholic for some critics. Melanchthon's contention that the Word, the Holy Spirit, and the consenting human will have a part in conversion evoked charges of synergism—cooperation between God and man. Melanchthon was accused by many of being too humanistic, though not by Luther.

Following Luther's death in 1546 and the Lutheran military defeat at Mühlenberg in 1547, Melanchthon accepted some Catholic views as nonessentials, or *adiaphora,* in the Augsburg-Leipzig Interim of 1548–1549, in order to avoid civil war and the destruction of Wittenberg. Although Melanchthon boldly rejected the Augsburg Interim as too contrary to Protestant views, he later reluctantly accepted the Leipzig Interim after securing justification by faith, clerical marriage, and confession without enumeration of all sins, though scriptural authority was left vague. Other provisions—episcopal rule, baptism as in ancient times, confirmation, extreme unction, repentance, pictures, clerical dress, and numerous Catholic ceremonies—he agreed to as nonessentials. Strict Lutherans strongly objected. The Formula of Concord later asserted that nothing during persecution should be deemed nonessential. Melanchthon died in Wittenberg on 19 April 1560.

BIBLIOGRAPHY

Manschreck, Clyde L. *Melanchthon: The Quiet Reformer.* New York, 1958. Good, full, biographical study of Melanchthon.

Manschreck, Clyde L., trans. and ed. *Melanchthon on Christian Doctrine* (1965). Grand Rapids, Mich., 1982. Translation of Melanchthon's late *Loci communes* (1555).

Maxcey, Carl E. *Bona Opera: A Study in the Development of the Doctrine in Philip Melanchthon.* Neieuwkoop, Netherlands, 1980. Good study of Melanchthon's controversial views on good works.

Pauck, Wilhelm, ed. *Melanchthon and Bucer.* Philadelphia, 1969. Library of Christian Classics, vol. 19. Translation of *Loci communes* (1521).

Rogness, Michael. *Philip Melanchthon: Reformer without Honor.* Minneapolis, 1969. Short, good appraisal of Melanchthon's views.

CLYDE L. MANSCHRECK

MELANESIAN RELIGIONS. [*This entry consists of two articles. The first provides an overview of the general features of Melanesian religious belief and practice. The second discusses themes common in the mythic lore of Melanesian peoples. For detailed treatment of the reli-*

gious systems of specific Melanesian cultures, see New Caledonia Religions; New Guinea Religions; Solomon Islands Religions; *and* Vanuatu Religions.]

An Overview

Anthropologists have disagreed about the exact geographical boundaries of Melanesia, some using the term to designate only the islands east of New Guinea, though without arguing that New Guinea is culturally distinct. Others have suggested that Fiji, because of its links with Tonga, should be considered part of Polynesia. Here, following the most common usage, Melanesia will be understood to extend from New Guinea in the west to Fiji in the east, encompassing the islands of the Torres Straits, the Bismarck archipelago, the Solomons, Vanuatu (formerly the New Hebrides), New Caledonia, and many smaller islands.

Within the northeastern part of this region, a few islands are inhabited by people whose languages and cultures are classified as Polynesian, such as the inhabitants of Tikopia and Bellona. Although these peoples' homes now belong to the same political units as the Melanesian islands, scholars consider them part of Polynesia. Nevertheless, it is difficult to draw a line between the cultures of Melanesia and of Polynesia to the east, Indonesia to the west, and Micronesia to the north, and many continuities exist with these neighboring regions. Furthermore, given its small total land area, Melanesia contains a much larger number of distinct languages and cultures than any other part of the world. This diversity greatly hampers generalization about Melanesia; it is only possible to mention features that recur with some regularity, while acknowledging that a single culture might fail to exhibit any of them.

As has happened elsewhere, an additional complication was introduced by foreign missionaries bringing their own religions and seeking to replace the indigenous ones. The westernmost portion of the island of New Guinea was somewhat influenced by Islam, coming via Indonesia, but in the rest of Melanesia various Christian denominations have greatly altered most traditional religious practices and beliefs. These were further affected by encounters with other foreigners, whose very existence and whose technology changed traditional worldviews; colonial governments also forbade a range of practices, such as ways of dealing with corpses, that often were closely tied to religion. Both missionaries and government officers arrived in some parts of coastal Melanesia in the nineteenth century, but did not enter the Highlands (mountainous interior) of New Guinea until the 1930s. Fifty years later there are still a few parts of this island not yet exposed to missionary influence. Inevitably, our ideas about Melanesian religion derive mainly from a small sample of societies that were either contacted late or that, unlike most, resisted conversion to Christianity. Most of these are found in the interior of New Guinea and of some large islands in the Solomons and Vanuatu, but the group includes a few small islands, such as Manus (Great Admiralty Island) and Wogeo, both north of New Guinea, whose societies were described by anthropologists before the missionaries arrived.

As regards the rest of Melanesia, because conversion has often been recent and not so thorough as to eradicate all traditional beliefs, it is still possible in most cases to learn much about certain aspects of indigenous religion. Theories about the magical causes of disease, sexual attraction, and bad weather often persist long after orthodox Christian ideas about the destiny of the soul have been accepted. Rarely, however, is any religious belief or practice of Melanesians living in the twentieth century precisely like that of their ancestors. The accelerated spread of ideas from other societies as the result of pacification and wage labor, the introduction of modern technology, new conditions such as foreign diseases, and an altered worldview produce changes even in such practices as garden magic and birth ritual. In the vast majority of cases, contemporary Melanesian religions are highly syncretic, and only in a handful of scattered societies is it possible to appreciate the full complexity and emotional impact of the original systems. Given the persistence of many ideas, however, it is still possible to use the present tense to describe selected aspects of the religions, as will be done here.

The Spirit World. One of the few valid generalizations about Melanesian religions is that they all include a belief in a variety of spirits, some of human origin and some not, who interact with living human beings.

Souls. All people are assumed to have a spiritual component or soul (and sometimes more than one). Depending on the culture, it may derive from the descent group of one parent, in which case the child is usually born with it, or it may be inserted into the child by another supernatural being, often well after birth. Belief in reincarnation is found only sporadically. In line with a widespread Melanesian tendency not to speculate about origins, many societies have no theory about the source of the human soul. It is usually thought to be only lightly attached to the body, and to wander in dreams; often it is considered dangerous to awaken a sleeper suddenly, lest he suffer soul loss that can lead to madness or death. The souls of babies are particularly vulnerable to attack or capture by other spirits, whereas the souls of adults are more likely to be captured by human sorcerers performing magic over personal leavings, such as food crumbs, that are thought to contain part of the victim's soul-stuff. Specialist curers may undertake soul rescue in dreams, or sometimes a suspected sorcerer can be persuaded to perform countermagic that releases the soul-stuff.

Ghosts. At death the human soul is transformed into a ghost that usually retains its identity but not necessarily its antemortem personality. In some societies ghosts are expected to be malevolent, resentful of the living, and likely to attack or kill them; in others, they are thought generally to be benevolent, especially toward their close kin; and in others it is assumed that their new condition makes them capricious or unpredictable. Sometimes the ghosts of those who die in particular ways, as in battle or childbirth, are feared even when other ghosts are considered benevolent; so may be the ghosts of former sorcerers.

There is usually a traditional abode of the dead, or a series of abodes, often a different one for each clan. Occasionally these are underground or in the sky, but usually they are on the earth and physically close to human habitations. Although it may be difficult for the ghost to reach the land of the dead, especially if the correct funeral rites have not been performed, very rarely is there any idea of punishment after death for those who have misbehaved in life. The land of the dead is usually much like that of the living, though perhaps somewhat more pleasant; in most societies all of the dead share the same sort of afterlife, gardening, marrying, and behaving much like the living. Ghosts of the newly deceased are thought most likely to stay around their old villages for some time before really severing ties with their kin, but often people have contradictory ideas about the behavior of ghosts, simultaneously believing that they proceed immediately to the land of the dead and that they continue to haunt the village and its environs. In Manus the skull of a particular dead kinsman, in which his ghost resided, would be kept to serve as guardian for each adult man but was banished into a sort of limbo when it failed to confer benefits or when its "ward" died. In many other societies men summon the ghosts of dead kin to help with specific enterprises such as hunting or weather control; they may be aided in this endeavor by keeping some relic of the corpse such as fingernails, but the Manus practice of harboring ghosts within the dwelling house seems to be shared only with the people of Sarera Bay in Irian Jaya. Much more often ghosts are thought to reside either in bones or in special paraphernalia kept in men's houses or cult houses, far from the women and children. In a few societies, however, ghosts are summoned to join the living on special occasions, as at the famous harvest festival of the Trobriand Islands.

Spirits of the dead always have abilities both to aid and to harm that transcend those of living human beings; but they may be thought to take little interest in those left behind, who in turn are primarily concerned to avoid meeting ghosts. As those who remember them die, the names of specific ghosts are forgotten, and conceptually they may be assimilated to spirits of the bush or sea that were never human. In some societies, however, the long deceased are more important and influential than the recently dead, especially if they were the founding ancestors of large descent groups such as clans. Judging from myths, such founding ancestors may have had supernatural attributes even when alive, but in other cases they have been raised near to the status of deities by the period of time that separates them from the living or by the ceremonies carried out on their behalf. Where ancestors are accorded great powers and are regularly appealed to, it is possible to talk of ancestor cults or ancestor worship. The beliefs that ancestors are greatly concerned with the health, fertility, and morality of their descendants and that they can be induced by ritual means such as sacrifice (usually of domestic or wild animals) to grant benefits to the living are found much less often in Melanesia than in surrounding areas, but these beliefs form a prominent part of the religion in many parts of eastern Melanesia and also in the Highlands of New Guinea.

Masalai. Spirits that have never been human play some part in all Melanesian religions, but their nature and importance vary greatly from one society to another. In western Melanesia, including New Guinea and the nearby islands, one of the most important is a type known in Pidgin English as *masalai. Masalai* live in wild places and, although they may assume human form, are typically animals of abnormal appearance—gigantic, brightly colored, sometimes wearing human ornaments such as earrings. Often they are associated with descent groups whose members they aid in distress—if, for instance, they are lost in the bush or drowning—but they do so only if the person has observed relevant rules concerning marriage and food taboos. Offenders may be punished by the *masalai,* who also attack outsiders who stray into their territory. Monstrous births may be attributed to the child's having been conceived in a *masalai* place (and possibly actually being its child); getting lost in the bush can result from being led astray by them; and sudden illness after eating wild animals or plants may be ascribed to either having ingested the *masalai* itself, in one of its transformations, or having "stolen" a food that actually belonged to the *masalai.* (The spirit may later visit the victim in a dream to explain its action.) Melanesia has few dangerous wild animals, but the uninhabited bush and the deep sea teem with dangerous spirits, and many people are uneasy about moving far outside the area of human settlement and cultivation. In some societies, men—as hunters, fishermen, traders, and warriors—think of the bush as peculiarly their own, free of the threat of sexual contamination by women, while in others women are banished from the village when they are in a dangerous condition (e.g., menstruation and childbirth). Usually the village is regarded as uniquely safe from supernatural threat, at least during the day; after dark, spirits more easily invade the human domain. Belief in menacing beings that assume a harmless form at daybreak is widespread in Melanesia.

Deities and culture heroes. Many spirit beings appear only in mythology and play no part in contemporary society apart from being remembered when origins and migrations are discussed. Some societies even lack such mythological figures. In a relatively small number of Melanesian cultures, however, people believe in uniquely powerful spirits who maintain an interest in the whole society rather than in specific descent groups. They are sometimes referred to in the scholarly literature as "deities," especially if they seem well disposed toward mankind; otherwise they may be called "demons" by outside observers. The large majority of Melanesian religions cannot be described as ethical; spiritual beings and forces rarely support the rules of society except in very limited spheres. Exceptions exist, especially in the east (where influence from Polynesia may be involved in some cases) but also in the New Guinea Highlands. In these societies, deities may punish misbehavior with crop failure, human infertility, sickness in the pig herds, or volcanic eruption. If procedures exist for ascertaining the will of the deity, it may be possible to placate him or her, usually with offerings. Otherwise people simply try to avoid or prevent behavior likely to evoke the wrath of the gods, and sometimes explain that they must do everything just as they were told to in the remote past lest disaster befall them.

Interestingly, several Melanesian societies in which the status of women is low have male cults devoted to the worship of female goddesses who promote male interests alone. Much more common are deities who are concerned with only one activity or one aspect of life, such as fishing for bonito, or warfare. Less powerful spirits may be invoked to aid with other activities such as gardening.

Whether or not deities remain near, or accessible to, human settlements after performing initial acts of creation, they may be mentioned in magical spells as a sign that the magic too derives from them. In a number of societies along the north coast of New Guinea, it is reported that meticulous maintenance and performance of ritual secrets imparted by these deities and culture heroes ensures success in a wide range of activities. Other societies are not so conservative, and their members try out any new rituals that seem promising. To the extent that deviations from morality are punished in these, the actual penalties are usually carried out by men wearing masks and manipulating ritual noisemakers such as flutes and bull-roarers to represent the voice of the spirits. The men may not believe that the spirits are present, but women and children are said to be deluded.

In a few areas there exist religious cults that are dedicated to a particular deity or other powerful being, or to the semideified collection of ancestors. In historical times such cults, typically involving secret rituals held in special structures, have spread widely in the New Guinea Highlands, honoring beings who promote health, strength, and fertility. Elsewhere, cults center on dispelling disease and other ills, so that cult performances tend to be triggered by disasters. Whatever their nature, cults, like most major religious activities in Melanesia, tend to involve only mature males.

Religious Specialists. Officiants who intervene between deities and ancestors and the ordinary people have often been called priests, even though they are never full-time specialists. Throughout Melanesia the most esteemed religious expert is a man of mature age who possesses detailed knowledge of ritual, either through training by another expert or by attaining the higher grades of a secret society. Where he is expected to communicate with the ancestors, he is ideally their senior male descendant, but ability to learn and perform rituals may outweigh pure seniority. By contrast with some other parts of the world, ritual specialists are rarely set apart psychologically or sexually, although they may report many direct encounters with spirits in dreams or, while purportedly fully conscious, in waking life. They are taught what they know rather than being inspired. In a number of Melanesian societies mediums are possessed by spirits, like the Manus women who communicate with ghosts through their own deceased young sons, and the curing shamans of the Baktaman of New Guinea, who must be possessed by a particular spirit before assuming their roles. Such people are rarely the most esteemed experts; the mediums of the Kaluli of New Guinea described by Edward L. Schieffelin (1976) are exceptional in this respect.

That for most of Melanesia religious experts have

been described as magicians rather than as priests or shamans reflects the most widely reported attitude toward the supernatural. Power lies in the hands of human adepts rather than with gods or other spirits. Given sufficient knowledge, men can control rain, sun, and wind; they can bring success to themselves and their kin and misfortune to others—making gardens flourish or blighting them, luring a pig into a trap or a rival's garden, sending a snake or crocodile to kill an enemy or causing him to fall from a tree, or enticing a woman from her husband. In some societies they accomplish their ends by manipulation of spirit beings, while in others the results follow automatically if ritual is performed correctly. Particularly as regards eastern Melanesia, much has been written about the concept of an invisible supernatural power, called *mana* (or some cognate term), which can be manipulated by the magician. As originally described by R. H. Codrington in *The Melanesians* (1891), *mana* was thought to be a power derived from "spiritual beings," but the term came to be understood by some other anthropologists as designating power that is impersonal and independent of spirits. Certainly the term exists in both eastern Melanesia and Polynesia, but there have been many debates about its exact significance, as Roger M. Keesing points out in *Kwaio Religion* (1982). [*For discussion of this controversy, see* Solomon Islands Religion.]

It is generally agreed that even when terms like *mana* are used, the speakers tend to have no clearly defined and expressed concept of just what this supernatural power is and how it operates. What interests them are results that can be duplicated. If an act seems to be effective, it does not matter just how the effect is produced. Typically, Melanesian magic involves the recitation of spells that must be carefully memorized; the use of substances thought to be potent in themselves, such as ginger; ritual acts that may involve imitation of the results desired; and maintenance of a state of potency by the observation of taboos, as on washing and sexual intercourse. Failure to achieve the desired results is usually attributed to countermagic performed by someone else, but it may also be blamed on failure to learn or perform correctly. All magic is not this complicated; sometimes only the spell or the act is needed. With the simpler forms, it may be difficult to distinguish magic from technology, and often distinctions are made by an outsider that would seem artificial to the local people. Trying to make a woman conceive by simply putting spider eggs into her food is an example of such a borderline case.

In Melanesia, intent is always involved in magic; there is no equivalent of the African witch or European possessor of the evil eye who harms others involuntarily. In most cases, too, evaluation of the act depends on the relation between the performer and those affected. In a few societies, such as that of the Tangu on the northern coast of New Guinea, there exists a belief in wholly malicious sorcerers all of whose attacks are condemned, but in many other societies a sorcerer is admired so long as he does not attack members of his own group. Usually all men know a little magic—for gardening, hunting, fishing, and sexual attraction—but only a few specialists know the major types such as those dealing with weather control, warfare, sorcery, and the curing of serious diseases. In most Melanesian societies all deaths except those of the very young and the very old tend to be attributed to supernatural causes—sorcery, spirits, or the breach of a taboo—and so do all major accidents and serious illnesses. Diviners and curers seek to ascertain the cause of sickness or death, to help cure the sickness (possibly by identifying the person responsible), and to direct vengeance in the case of death. Magicians are often paid fees when they perform outside their kinship group, unless their work benefits themselves along with others, as is the case with garden magicians. Usually each community contains a number of different specialist magicians, but political leaders are likely to control more than one major form of ritual, either through their own knowledge or by being wealthy enough to hire others. Political leadership is reinforced by religious knowledge, but only in a few coastal societies are there official magicians at the service of the leaders.

Taboos and Totems. The English word *taboo* is derived from a Polynesian word (Tongan, *tabu*), and its cognates appear in many of those Melanesian languages that are related to Polynesian languages. Similar concepts, called by different terms, are found among speakers of unrelated languages. There is debate about the range of meaning of these terms, but they normally include the concept of "forbidden," and often "sacred" as well. The words meaning "taboo" may be nouns, adjectives, or active verbs. The source of taboos varies from one society to another, and so does the kind of thing encompassed by them. Sometimes they can be traced to edicts by deities in mythological times, as is usually the case with incest taboos. So too can special attitudes toward totemic animals or plants. These are species associated with particular descent groups, perhaps because people are thought to be descended from similar but supernatural beings; perhaps because they emerged from the underworld together with these species, as is believed in the Trobriand Islands; or perhaps because of aid given by a member of the species to a human ancestor. Whatever the reason for the connection, members of the descent group are usually forbidden to kill or eat members of their totemic species; if they break the taboo, they may sicken or die. Those who punish such breaches of taboo may be the creatures themselves, their ghosts (which may be possessed by animals and plants as well as people), the ghostly founders of the descent groups, or some impersonal force that acts automatically. All associations between people and natural species are not totemic; sometimes members of a particular descent group simply claim to have first discovered a food plant, or to have particular success in hunting certain animals. Where totems do occur, however, they are a significant part of the religion, but in a different category from spirits.

Many other taboos are tied in with aspects of the local worldview. For example, if the soul is called by the same term as the reflection and shadow, as is often the case, it may be taboo to stare at one's own reflection or to step on someone's shadow, for fear of soul loss. Traditional systems of belief typically involve the observation of many taboos, some of which result from revelation by spirits and some from simple deduction. An unexpected event such as an earthquake may be ascribed to the breach of a previously unknown taboo, the nature of which may be revealed by a supernatural being in a dream. Equally often, however, it is simply decided that any action out of the ordinary that immediately preceded the event actually caused it, especially if the action took place in the wild. To avoid further trouble, it may be decided and announced, for instance, that never again should anyone put a stick down a rat hole. Since taboos acquired in this way rarely form a coherent system, they can seem arbitrary and almost meaningless once their origin has been forgotten, but it may be strongly believed that the maintenance of society and of human life depends on meticulous observation of them.

Women and Religion. Melanesia is famous in the anthropological literature for what has been called sexual antagonism, most often expressed in male fears of contact, which can be dangerous and weakening, with women. At their mildest, such fears and avoidance are no greater than those found in many societies outside Melanesia. Men's reluctance to sleep with menstruating women, and their belief that sexual intercourse saps the strength of a warrior and is antithetical to the practice of religion, can be found almost everywhere. More characteristically Melanesian is the frequently encountered belief that fertile women in themselves are polluting to men, particularly, but not exclusively, when menstruating and during and immediately after childbirth. While menstruating, they may be forbidden to cook for men or to enter gardens, and in many societies have to retire to menstrual huts in the bush. If menstrual blood is feared, so too is the blood shed in childbirth. Not only does a man avoid the scene of childbirth, which also may be relegated to the bush, but he may consider both mother and baby to be polluted for months after the birth. It may be considered dangerous for a man to touch a young baby, surrounded as it is by the dangerous aura acquired from its mother. Later little boys may need to be ritually cleansed of female influences before they will be able to become mature men or to participate in male ceremonies. Where fears of female pollution are high, men usually spend much of their time in men's houses separate from the family dwellings. Such structures may be taboo to women and even to little boys, who will have to undergo special rituals before they can begin to sleep there. In a number of Melanesian societies, fertile women are thought to pollute anything that they step over, such as food, firewood, or human beings. Men must take care never to be physically below women, nor to drink downstream from where women bathe. In extreme cases, as among the Kwaio of Malaita in the Solomons, the whole village is built on ridges so that everything pertaining to men, including ancestral shrines, is uphill from the area assigned to women.

The situation is not always so simple as it seems at first glance. In some societies, such as Wogeo, women too are thought to be endangered by the sexual secretions of men, and menstrual blood may also be considered polluting to a woman (who then has to take great care while eating or chewing betel nut during menstruation) as well as to a man. Furthermore, it has been argued that women actually enjoy and profit from the periods of seclusion associated with menstruation and childbirth, rather than feeling that they are suffering because they are unclean. Certainly women's labors may be lightened if it is thought that crops planted by them will not grow well and that men will sicken if they eat food cooked by women. Furthermore, the possibility that an angry wife might put menstrual blood into the food of a husband who beats her, and so "poison" him, gives her some control over his behavior. If, however, women are thought to be innately malevolent, or to become malevolent because they are subject to discrimination in such matters as diet, their ability to harm men may count against them in that they are likely to be accused of causing deaths, and to be killed in revenge.

In most of Melanesia, however, the low status accorded women also keeps them from being considered powerful magicians. An exception is the so-called Massim region off the eastern tip of New Guinea (including the Trobriand Islands), where female status is relatively high, and where cannibalistic female witches who fly abroad seeking victims are blamed for many deaths. In most other parts of Melanesia, those deaths not attributed to spirits are more likely to be blamed on male sorcerers. If women know magic at all, it typically deals with female fertility and childbirth, and with the growth and health of small children. Nevertheless, women may play a role in religious life insofar as their dreams may be taken as seriously as those of men, so that they too may have meaningful encounters with spirits and can act as soul rescuers, as well as sources of information about the world of spirits. The most respected female adepts are likely to be women past menopause, who are exempt from many of the restrictions of their juniors, and who may even be identified with men.

Where women are considered unfit for the most esteemed activities, the reason may simply be that they are thought to be physically and mentally weaker than men. Often, however, it is held that femininity in itself, or because of its association with female blood and milk, is repulsive to spirits and to wild animals, who flee hunting and fishing equipment if women touch it. Sometimes it is the odor of sexual intercourse rather than of women specifically that is thought to repel other beings; nevertheless, even in those societies that do not practice the sorts of discrimination just described, women are usually forbidden to touch certain male tools and weapons, and warriors must avoid too much contact with women or risk death in battle. Usually these effects are automatic. If women are really feared and avoided in other contexts, boys are likely to need formal rites of separation from their mothers before they can join the men in their exclusive domain.

Rites of Passage. Whether changes of status during life are marked ritually depends on the society and on the individual's position within it. If there is a class system, as in many coastal areas, members of the upper class receive much more ceremonial attention than do ordinary people. Elsewhere ritual may be focused on the firstborn child, regardless of sex, in the belief that some benefits will extend to younger siblings. Often ceremonies mark the first time that the child engages in any new activity, such as going to the gardens or having his first haircut. Although rites of passage always mark a change of status, they need not contain a religious element. Ceremonies revolving around children or grandchildren are often sponsored by older men to enhance their own prestige, and the complexity and amount of display has little to do with the significance of the event except as a marker of wealth and social status. Of all the rites of passage commonly held in Melanesia, weddings are least likely to be religious ceremonies, whereas funerals almost invariably are.

Birth. A first pregnancy, and the birth of a first child, may be celebrated for the mother as marking her final shift of responsibility from her parents to her new status as a parent herself. Unless she experiences difficulties in childbirth, religious rituals are not usually involved except for the observation of many taboos on acts that might affect her or her child. The husband may need to observe these as well. After birth, however, the baby is vulnerable to many inimical forces, and is normally kept in seclusion until his survival seems likely, when his skin has darkened and the umbilical cord has dropped off. He may then be given a name and formally introduced to the community. Both parents continue to observe taboos on behavior that might affect him, staying away from spirit places and wild foods that might be associated with spirits. Spells are recited to promote his health and growth, and rituals may be performed in connection with such events as the appearance of teeth. Among the Siuai of Bougainville, the young child is the object of an elaborate ritual that summons spirits to help him, after which he is a full member of society; usually, though, the most complex rites are reserved for puberty.

Puberty and initiation. In many parts of Melanesia it is taken for granted that once the perils of early childhood are past, a child will mature naturally; supernatural aid is invoked only for illness. In others, boys especially are thought to need the aid of both society and the supernatural if they are to reach healthy adulthood. Puberty rites for boys are likely to be communal events occupying long periods of time. A girl very often undergoes a ceremony at menarche that may involve a period of seclusion, both because of attitudes about menstrual blood and because her emergence afterward is likely to mark her transition to the new status of marriageability. Sometimes elaborate rituals surround the whole period of isolation.

In a very few societies, such as the Orokaiva of New Guinea, boys and girls go through puberty ceremonies together. But much more often boys are separated from all females. In many parts of New Guinea they are subjected to rituals involving vomiting and bloodletting designed to rid their bodies of the pernicious effects of their former contact with women. In some societies, such as the Wogeo, male bloodletting is equated with female menstruation: designed to rid the body of "bad" blood, it is practiced throughout life. By contrast, in a group of societies in south central New Guinea, it is held that boys will mature only if they are "fed" with semen, and highly secret ceremonies involving ritual homosexuality form the center of the puberty rites. [*See* Homosexuality.] Where much secret knowledge is imparted at this time, puberty rites are indistinguishable from initiation into men's societies or cults; but usually the religious content of the rites is limited to the use of spells and practices to promote health, growth, and beauty. Various taboos are connected not only with separation from women but with the healing of any operations on the penis, nose, ears, or skin that also signal the change of status. At the end of the rituals, the boys emerge fully decorated in a new social persona, but may still avoid marriage for some years.

Men's societies forbidden to women extend from New Guinea to Vanuatu; only in this last island group are women reported to have similar societies of their own. Often the male societies are basically political rather than religious, a way for older men to dominate women and boys; but in some areas much secret knowledge of rituals essential to the maintenance of society is in the hands of the few individuals who have passed through various grades of initiation, typically with severe associated ordeals. Passing through all the grades may take a lifetime, and, in parts of Vanuatu, a fortune. Sometimes the actual secrets are minor, apart from the frequent revelation that purported spirits are simply human impersonations; the initiates may only learn how masks are made or how the "voices" of the spirits are produced. In these cases it could be argued that belief in the existence and nonhuman nature of these beings is part of the religion of the uninitiated but not of the initiates. A measure of deception need not, however, indicate the absence of other levels of belief among the initiates. Several recent studies of rites still being carried on in the interior of New Guinea reveal that often the older adepts really believe that they alone are able to keep society functioning; their activities are serious behind the facade of deception and frequent revelations of trivia. Overall, however, there is no necessary connection between the elaborateness of the ceremonies, the degree of hazing involved, and the care with which the secrets are guarded from noninitiates, and the actual religious content. Perhaps because of the way they spread from one society to another, rites that look very similar on the surface may differ greatly in function.

Mortuary rites. Death triggers the ceremonies most characteristic of Melanesia, particularly of the coastal and lowland regions. Beginning with the funeral, these may culminate years later in great festivals involving dances and masked performances and the dispersing of vast amounts of pork and other food to the participants. In most societies formal funerals are held for everyone, though they may be abbreviated when the corpse is that of a baby or an old woman who lacks close kin. At the wake that enables mourners to view the body, diviners often attempt to ascertain the cause of death from the ghost, which then may be ritually dispatched to the land of the dead. Although cremation is practiced in a few places, in many others initial disposal of the body is temporary. It may be exposed on a platform or buried for a few months until decay is complete, but thereafter some or all of the bones may be subject to special treatment. This varies according to local ideas about the relations between body and soul, and about the symbolic significance of bones and of specific parts of the body such as the head.

The period following initial disposal of the body is typically one of intense mourning for the surviving kin, who abstain from work, keep a restricted diet, make themselves as physically unattractive as possible, sometimes lop off a finger joint, and often go into complete seclusion. The heaviest restrictions fall on the widow, whose willingness to submit to them may be taken as evidence that she did not help to kill her husband by magical means. Only in Dobu, a matrilineal society in the D'Entrecasteaux Islands, east of New Guinea, is mourning for the widower more arduous than for the widow. In a number of lowland societies extending as far as Fiji, the wife or wives of prominent men or chiefs were formerly killed to join them in the afterlife, and in southwest New Britain all widows were killed and buried with their husbands, whose ghosts would linger around the settlements until their wives joined them. A widow cannot resume normal life in other parts of Melanesia until she has been formally released from mourning, in ceremonies that mark her reintegration into the community.

Personal possessions of the dead may be broken, trees cut down, and pigs killed either as signs of grief or so that their spiritual essence can be released to accompany the deceased into the afterlife. It may also be considered supernaturally dangerous for survivors to remain in close contact with the personal possessions, which are imbued with soul-stuff. Much of the remaining property, especially pigs and garden crops, is likely to be used in feasts celebrating the lifting of taboos from the mourners. When this is done, relics of the dead, such as the house in which the person died, may be destroyed. But if further ceremonies are planned, some relic will be preserved for use in these.

Major mortuary ceremonies are not held for everyone. Men of high status are usually honored in this way by their kin; but equally often, a leader or a man who aspires to that status sponsors such a ceremony primarily for the personal glory that he will gain. The dead person may be any type of kin, such as a young child or a mother-in-law; their importance as individuals in life or after death may be wholly subordinate to that of the sponsor. Throughout Melanesia leaders attain or ratify their positions by sponsoring ceremonies in which they try to outdo each other in display and generosity. Some of the food dispensed at mortuary ceremonies may derive from that left by the deceased, and so be taboo to some of those who attend. Furthermore, the specific parts played by those attending may reflect their relation to the dead as well as to the sponsor, and if relics are displayed, those holding them are likely to be close kin, who weep as they remember the dead. Unless the ghost is thought to attend, however, the religious content of such ceremonies may be confined to magic designed to produce a successful occasion, as by preventing rain and ensuring that the food supply is adequate. The deceased may be present only in memory. It is, however, common for a few final mortuary taboos to be lifted on these occasions, such as those prohibiting use of the fruit trees and the house site of the deceased.

In some societies apparently similar ceremonies have the deepest religious significance. Ghosts of the dead, sometimes including those of distant ancestors, may be summoned to attend, and rites are directed at them in an attempt to win their favor and avert their wrath. When pigs are killed, their blood soaking into the ground or burnt portions of their bodies are specifically intended as offerings to the ghosts. The fate of the bones of the dead varies with the sorts of continuing relations desired between their former owners and the living, but often they are deposited in sanctuaries such as caves, or in structures that serve as temples in which the bones will be a focus for future rituals. If bones are reburied or deposited in village or garden sites, their presence may create continuing prosperity, fertility, and safety for the descendants who use the land.

Art and Religion. The spectacular art of most of lowland Melanesia is usually, but not invariably, connected with religion. In some societies, such as those of the area around Lake Sentani in Irian Jaya and of the Massim Islands east of New Guinea, almost all utilitarian objects are decorated, and in most cases the decorations have no religious significance. The most dramatic Melanesian sculptures, paintings, and constructions are, however, produced either specifically for religious ceremonies or to honor and commemorate particular spirits. Some of the most colorful constructions, made of painted barkcloth or woven fiber decorated with colored leaves and feathers, may be quite ephemeral; perhaps inhabited by spirits during a ceremony, they are destroyed or dismantled with the departure of the spirits for their own realm. The sculptures and painting that represent spirits may also be kept permanently hidden inside men's houses or ceremonial structures forbidden to noninitiates; viewing of these pieces, and explanation of their meaning, often forms a major part of initiation ceremonies. Women may never see them. The manufacture of ceremonial art, including even the gathering of leaves to conceal the bodies of maskers, is usually carried out in great secrecy, with women and children threatened with death if they approach the area or voice any suspicion that the supposed spirits are actually human creations. Spirits may indeed be summoned into the art objects after they are complete, and sometimes the actual process of manufacture introduces the spirit, as when eyes are painted on the masks of the Tolai of New Britain. In many societies, however, simple impersonation is involved, but magic is usually employed to ensure that the impersonations are successful, and sorcery is used to punish those who speak disrespectfully of the ceremonies.

When carvings are made for rituals—such as those connected with puberty and death—that honor specific individuals, they often include motifs associated with that person's descent group, such as totems and *masalai.* True portrait sculpture is rare but is found in a few areas, as in memorial carvings in parts of the Solomons and most notably in the modeling of features over the dead person's skull in parts of Vanuatu, New Britain, and the Sepik River region of New Guinea. Often memorials are destroyed when the mortuary ceremonies end, and anthropomorphic sculptures that remain permanently in place usually represent more distant ancestors or deities. Such sculptures are prominently displayed in many regions, forming the doorjambs and finials of houses in New Caledonia, and standing outside men's houses and clubhouses in parts of the Solomons, Vanuatu, and Sepik River region.

The ritual art of other areas focuses not on ancestors but on supernatural beings who are only partly human in form, like the shark god of parts of the Solomons or the culture hero with the body of a snake of western New Britain. Still other beings, such as those painted on the facades of Sepik ceremonial houses or constructed elsewhere for ceremonies to bring fertility or drive away sickness, have little or no trace of humanity in their appearance. Particularly in the New Guinea Highlands, divine power may reside in objects such as stones or boards that are painted with abstract designs of uncertain meaning.

Art objects collected for museums have often been arbitrarily identified as representing gods, ancestors, or totems, without any real evidence that they were so regarded by their creators. Detailed studies of Melanesian art in its context are few, and have demonstrated in some cases that people may be uncertain about the precise significance of designs that may still be thought to form an essential part of a ritual. Some anthropologists argue that art and ritual express and communicate messages that cannot be conveyed verbally, so that it is useless to expect native exegesis. The field is then open for the outsider to proffer his own explanations, and many have taken advantage of the opportunity. Some experts, especially those trained in a German tradition of reconstructing culture history in terms of postulated waves of migration, tend to see evidence in art of the previous existence of earlier religious attitudes such as sun worship. Anthropologists have more often relied upon psychoanalytic theory or a structuralism modeled on that of Claude Lévi-Strauss to explain what is being represented at a subconscious level. The same types of interpretation have been applied to myth and ritual.

In some societies, however, the local experts are willing and able to discuss art objects and their relation to religious concepts. As with other aspects of religion, many details remain inexplicable, simply a traditional way of doing things that is not questioned. It may also, of course, be improper to discuss esoteric matters with noninitiates; but outsiders have often been admitted to discussions that are closed to female or junior members of the society itself.

Sacred and Profane. In describing Melanesian societies, many observers have hesitated both to use the word *sacred* and to contrast it with the *profane*. The reasons are several. First, the discovery that often masked men impersonate supernatural beings without feeling any religious awe emphasizes the secular character of many ceremonies. Second, the widespread tendency to rely on magic in which impersonal forces are manipulated by individuals, and the rarity of communal rites dealing with supernatural beings, makes it difficult to apply labels derived from other religious systems. Third, the frequent observation that Melanesian religions tend to be highly pragmatic, concerned with securing benefits in this life rather than rewards in another world, and not concerned with problems of good and evil, has led some to deny that they are really religions at all. The fact that supernatural beings are rarely all-powerful, awesome in appearance, wholly incorporeal in nature, or far removed from human habitations, and in fact that ordinary people so often encounter them in the bush or in their dreams, makes them seem part of everyday life rather than being set apart, natural rather than supernatural.

The rituals of some societies do, however, strike some observers as embodying concepts that can be labeled sacred. Communion with ancestral spirits by priests and other specialists in Fiji, Vanuatu, the Solomons, and Highlands New Guinea; first-fruits rites in New Caledonia; the invocation of powerful nonhuman spirits along the Sepik: all these seem on emotional and cognitive grounds to indicate that the term is applicable. *Sacred* has also been applied to the state of religious practitioners while carrying out ritual, and of those who are temporarily removed from normal society during rites of passage. In these instances it is suggested that women, children, and noninitiates belong to the realm of the profane, and doubly so as regards women if they are regarded as intrinsically polluting to men and antithetical to religious enterprises. Several investigators have, however, argued that such labels and dichotomies are misleading. If men are taboo when sacrificing to the ancestors and women are taboo when menstruating, they are seen as similar rather than separate (see Keesing, 1982, p. 66). Furthermore, the fact that women usually do interact with the spirit world and control some magical techniques of their own invalidates the assumption that they are excluded from the realm of the sacred.

When *sacred* is used today, it tends to be in two contexts. Places consecrated to spirits, such as burial caves, ancestral shrines and groves, and cult houses, may be permanently sacred, as are places inhabited by important supernatural beings such as *masalai.* By contrast, people may be only temporarily sacred during a religious performance; eventually they return to their normal state and to the everyday world. In this, the usual processes of life continue to involve them in contact with supernatural beings and forces, so frequently that it seems meaningless to characterize what is not sacred as profane.

[*See also* Christianity, *article on* Christianity in the Pacific Islands; Taboo; *and* Totemism.]

BIBLIOGRAPHY

Most of the earlier descriptions of Melanesian societies written by anthropologists and missionaries contain lengthy and relatively straightforward accounts of religious beliefs and activities. On the theoretical side they may devote much time to out-of-date controversies about such matters as the nature of totemism or the possible connections between Melanesian religions and those of other parts of the world. Only a few of the better-known examples are mentioned here, but many others exist. Later investigators more often begin with varying theories about the nature of religion and ways to study it, producing works that differ greatly from each other, in which the author's role as interpreter is usually made explicit, and in which the study tends to focus on a particular problem rather than attempt to cover the entire field. Many recent books are consequently both narrower and deeper than earlier ones. The earlier works are particularly useful for an overview and for descriptions of long-vanished ceremonies, while the later works may be considerably more difficult to read but may expose the student to a wide range of theoretical problems and current controversies in the field of religion both in Melanesia and in other parts of the world where small-scale societies still exist.

Allen, Michael. *Male Cults and Secret Initiations in Melanesia.* Melbourne, 1967. An out-of-date but useful survey of the nature and distribution of these institutions, which also examines various theories attempting to account for them and settles for one in which social structure is the important variable.

Barth, Fredrik. *Ritual and Knowledge among the Baktaman of New Guinea.* New Haven, 1975. An interesting attempt to use the author's investigation of an elaborate initiation system as a basis for generalizing about the nature of ritual and the communication of knowledge in other societies.

Bateson, Gregory. *Naven* (1938). 2d ed. Stanford, Calif., 1958. A classic attempt to analyze certain rituals of a Sepik River society with approaches this writer later made famous in such fields as communications theory.

Codrington, R. H. *The Melanesians: Studies in Their Anthropology and Folklore* (1891). Reprint, New Haven, 1957. Based mostly on interviews with Melanesian mission students, supplemented by some visits to the islands of eastern Melanesia, this work is often incorrect in ethnographic detail but contains the classic discussions of *mana* and taboo, and useful descriptions of now-vanished rituals.

Deacon, A. Bernard. *Malekula.* Edited by Camilla H. Wedgwood. London, 1934. Incomplete, having been edited from field notes after the author's death, but the most accessible account of the elaborate New Hebrides (now Vanuatu) graded societies, with much information on religions.

Fortune, Reo F. *Sorcerers of Dobu* (1932). Rev. ed. New York, 1963. Includes a general account of ritual in small islands east of New Guinea, with particular attention to the importance of sorcery beliefs and practices.

Fortune, Reo F. *Manus Religion: An Ethnological Study of the Manus Natives of the Admiralty Islands* (1935). Reprint, Lincoln, Nebr., 1965. A famous account of a religious system uncommon in Melanesia for its ethical content and for the role of ancestral ghosts.

Gell, Alfred. *Metamorphosis of the Cassowaries: Umeda Society, Language, and Ritual.* London, 1975. An innovative attempt to interpret a fertility ritual in a New Guinea society by analyzing the associated language and symbols. The arguments are complex.

Herdt, Gilbert H., ed. *Rituals of Manhood: Male Initiation in Papua New Guinea.* Berkeley, 1982. A collection noteworthy for the attention paid to psychological as well as social and religious aspects of initiation. Contains several detailed descriptions of ceremonies in their wider context.

Hogbin, Ian. *The Island of Menstruating Men: Religion in Wogeo, New Guinea.* Scranton, Pa., 1970. Based on fieldwork carried out in 1934, this general account, written for the nonspecialist, pays particular attention to concepts of pollution and taboo, and contains some discussion of theories about magical ritual.

Keesing, Roger M. *Kwaio Religion: The Living and the Dead in a Solomon Island Society.* New York, 1982. Includes not only description of belief and rites among pagans on Malaita, but discussion of many theoretical issues concerning concepts of pollution, *mana* and taboo, symbolism and meaning, and the social consequences of religious beliefs and practices. Addressed to a general audience.

Lawrence, Peter, and M. J. Meggitt, eds. *Gods Ghosts and Men in Melanesia.* Melbourne, 1965. A series of descriptive essays, all but one dealing with the religions of Australian New Guinea (now Papua New Guinea), with an introduction in which the authors attempt to generalize about Melanesian religions as a whole. A very useful survey, though authors of the essays have not all dealt with the same topics. But it has been rendered somewhat out of date by more recent studies.

Lewis, Gilbert. *Day of Shining Red.* Cambridge, 1980. An interesting and readable critical examination of the usefulness of various theories of ritual in helping to understand the nature and meaning of puberty rites in a New Guinea village.

Malinowski, Bronislaw. *Magic, Science and Religion.* New York, 1948. Contains three famous essays setting forth Malinowski's theories about the differences between magic and religion and the functions of these practices and of mythology, as well as a description of Trobriand beliefs and rituals concerning the dead. Malinowski's theories continue to influence a number of scholars, and are clearly explained here.

Rappaport, Roy A. *Pigs for the Ancestors: Ritual in the Ecology of a New Guinea People* (1968). Rev. ed. New Haven, 1984. A well-known and widely quoted attempt to explain ritual in adaptive terms. In the revised edition, the author answers his critics and presents the results of further thinking on such topics as the importance of sanctity ("sanctified understandings") in human societies.

Schieffelin, Edward L. *The Sorrow of the Lonely and the Burning of the Dancers.* New York, 1976. A short and readable account and analysis of a set of ceremonies in a New Guinea society, with particular attention to their emotional content.

Tuzin, Donald. *The Voice of the Tambaran: Truth and Illusion in Ilahita Arapesh Religion.* Berkeley, 1980. A complex and detailed examination of the meaning of the numerous rituals associated with male initiation, which are characterized by spectacular religious art in a New Guinea society. Questions of belief and psychological reactions to the rituals are discussed as well.

Williams, Francis E. *Drama of Orokolo: The Social and Ceremonial Life of the Elema.* Oxford, 1940. A detailed description of one of the most elaborate and spectacular ceremonial cycles ever recorded for Melanesia, and the implications of its decline and neglect in the colonial period.

ANN CHOWNING

Mythic Themes

The myths of all known Melanesian peoples are subtly, intricately, and often tacitly bound to fundamental matters of worldview, ethos, and personhood in religious systems of meaning. Yet the study of myth in Melanesia has a long, largely unvaried tradition of being descriptively rich but analytically impoverished. Indeed, this fascinating field of study remains a vast *terra incognita* in important respects and lags significantly behind the study of Melanesian ritual, in which significant theoretical and comparative advances have been made. Relatively few ethnographies of Melanesian cultures and societies have focused exclusively or even primarily on making theoretical or comparative sense of the marked diversity and remarkable intricacy of the mythology of this area. Most ethnographic studies contain some references to myth, but in general, myth tends to be merely a secondary feature of the central analytic endeavor and is explored—if at all—largely to enhance the primary interests of analysis. Only recently has Melanesian mythology begun to attract focal analytic attention on its own.

Studies of Melanesian Myth. The legacy of earlier studies of Melanesian myth still burdens present endeavors to summarize and to synthesize what is archivally available. In the late nineteenth and early twentieth centuries, scholars working among the myriad indigenous peoples of the Dutch, French, English, and German Melanesian colonies compiled extensive collections of mythic narratives in many forms. These often simplistic assemblages of myths, however, were ethnographically sterile and left ample room for varied academic fancies and fantasies to supplant Melanesian mythic realities. The collections were sometimes linguistically suspect and often unidentified by genre of oral literature and by sociocultural group. Thus, various kinds of myths, legends, folk tales, and other conventional classes of oral literature, sometimes from different regions, would often be merged in one collection regardless of local or analytic senses of genre. Compilations tended to include an emphasis on origin myths, mythic charters of institutional forms, and myths and legends of culture heroes and migrations. These early collections revealed little about other important aspects of Melanesian myth—of its role in or as a sacred performance and as an assertion of ideology or belief, a map of supernatural landscapes, a model of personhood, a mode of ethnohistorical discourse, a social or ritual charter, and a shared but also contestable collective representation (in the Durkheimian sense). They usually ignored the significance of myth as a vital, flexible, and changing but also enduring aspect of a lived, remembered, and imagined sociocultural reality among those islands of the southwest Pacific that constitute Melanesia.

The boundaries of mythology in Melanesia are sometimes obscure, for the analysis of myth as sacred narrative has been simplistic, uncritical, imprecise, and inconsistent and has not encompassed the many diverse kinds of regional oral traditions. Moreover, scant attention has been given to local genres of narrative, such as the Daribi *namu po* or *po page*, Kalauna *neineya*, Kamano *kinihera*, Keraki *ninyi-ji*, Kewa *lidi* or *ramani*, and Trobriand *kukwanebu*, *libogwo*, or *liliu*. Indeed, there are few ethnographic portraits of the classificatory complexity exhibited in the seventeen genres of Bimin-Kuskusmin oral tradition, or analytic frameworks that could accommodate such complexity. Nonetheless, the sacred qualities of myth often do seem to be marked in a more or less distinctive manner throughout Melanesia. Thus, myths may be distinguished by certain modes of discourse or language (as among Bimin-Kuskusmin, Daribi, or Kwaio); embedded formulas or linked songs or chants (as among Gende, Kamano, or Trobriand Islanders); tacit contextual associations and symbolic allusions (as among Baktaman, Bimin-Kuskusmin, Fore, Gende, Gimi, Gnau, Hua, Huli, Iatmül, Jate, Kai, Kamano, Keraki, Siane, Telefolmin, Umeda, or Usurufa); entitlements to know, to explicate, and to narrate bound to a complex sociology of sacred knowledge and related rules of secrecy, taboo, and revelation (as among Baktaman, Bimin-Kuskusmin, Elema, Keraki, or Marind-Anim); and intricate linkages with forms of art, magic, music, and ritual (as among Abelam, 'Aré'aré, Elema, Ilahita Arapesh, Kwaio, or Sambia). Most myths are cast in the form of narratives and are sometimes interconnected in complex cycles; examples of these mythic cycles are the delicate mosaics of origin myths among the Nalum of the Star Mountains of Irian Jaya, the narratives of the founding ancestress Afek in the Mountain-Ok region of Papua New Guinea, the key Massim myths of canoe voyages and *kula* exchange transactions, and the mythic culture-hero cycles that pervade the whole of Melanesia. Other myths, however, may also be both danced and sung (Waropen), embedded in linked cycles of songs (Kiwai), or enacted in magical or ritual dramas (Elema, Marind-Anim) to enhance their performative efficacy or elocutionary force in creating a sacred cognitive-affective experience.

Despite their occasional entertainment value, the casual way in which they are often told, and their abstract literary qualities, the myths of Melanesia are profoundly anchored to the local foundations of sociocultural existence. They are portraits of various phenomena of sacred significance, "charters" (in Bronislaw Malinowski's sense) that both elucidate and legitimate fundamental institutional forms and practices, and narrated performances that are believed to affect the course of events of concern to human communities. The performance aspects of myth in Melanesia are less well understood than similar features of ritual, although there have been numerous studies of the place of myth vis-à-vis male initiation ritual (as among Awa, Baktaman, Bimin-Kuskusmin, Chambri, Gnau, Ilahita Arapesh, Mianmin, Ndumba, Sambia, or Telefolmin) and noteworthy analyses of myth by Jan van Baal (1966) on Marind-Anim, Catherine H. Berndt (1955) on the Kainantu area (Fore, Jate, Kamano, Usurufa), Kenelm O. L. Burridge (1969) on Tangu, S. Hylkema (1974) on Nalum, John LeRoy (1985) on Kewa, Roy Wagner (1978) on Daribi, and Michael W. Young (1983) on Kalauna. A linguistically and symbolically sophisticated approach to the ethnography of mythological discourse in Melanesia, however, is evident only in incipient and rudimentary form. Attention has been directed primarily toward more descriptive, functional, or structural characteristics of portrayals of mythic personae, landscapes, origins, migrations, and other sacred phenomena. Analysis of these mythical portraits has focused on varied aspects of their subjects' cultural, existential, psychological, social, or even theological significance in times of both stability and change.

Personae of Melanesian Myth. Characters in Melanesian myth are variously and loosely identified as deities or primordial creator spirits, culture heroes, remote or recent ancestors, totemic figures, local spirits, demons or ogres, forest spirits, and tricksters. The notion of a supreme deity or creator is found rarely, or remains doubtful as an interpretation of local belief, in most areas of Melanesia, with the possible exceptions of the hierarchical societies of eastern Melanesia (notably Fiji) and the northwest and northeast coasts of Papua New Guinea. Certain renowned and omnipotent figures sometimes also appear in Melanesian myths, such as Enda Semangko (Kyaka Enga); Honabe (Huli); Marunogere (Kiwai); Oma Rumufa (Siane); Ora Rove Marai (Roro); Parambik (Ngaing); Sinatu, Mubu, and Obomwe (Garia); and Ye (Rossel). Although creative or regulative beings are known in most of the area's mythologies (except among the Tangu), such spirits rarely have the elaborate Polynesian features of the Kalou-Vu and other deities of the Fijian pantheon. Indeed, in eastern Melanesia at the Polynesian frontier cosmogonic myths and their portraits of the generative powers and acts of mythic creators are generally more intricate and are interwoven with representations of social hierarchy. In this subregion, myths tend to place greater emphasis on ideas of duality; totemic concepts; complex culture-hero or trickster cycles (at times almost as elaborate as those of the Polynesian Māui myths); images of regeneration, reproduction, or reincarnation (often in serpentine form and less bound to ideas of garden fertility than in western Melanesia); regional integration; and autochthonous origins—all in support of fundamental creation in and of the cosmos. In other parts of Melanesia, however, mythic creators are usually assigned less than cosmogonic tasks.

Myths of Cosmogony. Myths of origin, found in almost every cultural repertoire of Melanesian myth, generally assume the preexistence of the fundamental characteristics of the cosmos. When described at all, the primeval era is often portrayed either as a mosaic of basic elements, structures, and processes—earth, water, sky, astronomical bodies, the underworld, and the forces of wind, rain, tide, and temperature (Huli, Iatmül, Mae Enga, Marind-Anim, Mbowamb, Rossel)—or as a period of chaos, marked by cataclysms, storms, fires, floods, volcanic eruptions, eclipses, comets, and earthquakes, to be eventually put in order (Bimin-Kuskusmin, Orokaiva, Tangu, Trans-Fly, Waropen). Indeed, this primordial chaos is often paralleled by the mythical moral disorder attributed by many Melanesian peoples to the fringes of their known world (Bimin-Kuskusmin, Marind-Anim, Trans-Fly).

More often, however, such myths largely ignore cosmogony, focusing instead on subsequent modifications or transformations of terrain or seascape, flora, fauna, humankind, and culture or society brought about by important creators, culture heroes, totemic figures, or ancestors. Some of these mythic characters are both creative and regulative. Responsible for particular facets of cosmic order, they dwell in or near human settlements and supplicants, taking an interest in human affairs and often intervening in them. Other mythological beings are primarily or only regulative, possessing few if any creative powers but monitoring and intervening in human affairs after the establishment of the essential cosmic, moral, and social orders.

Culture heroes, on the other hand, are usually only creative. Soon after completing their acts of creation, they abandon human society, taking no further interest in its continuing affairs. But ancestral and totemic figures—through genealogical or ethnohistorical links with social groups founded on principles of descent or locality—tend to be significantly associated with the ongoing sociocultural life of particular communities. They model, validate, and also regulate aspects of the social, economic, moral, political, and ritual orders.

Origins of Humanity. In most Melanesian origin myths, primordial transformations reveal little sense of an original paradise and are attributed to various forms of hostility, to breaches of morality, and to conflict—often incest (Bimin-Kuskusmin, Huli, Marind-Anim, Waropen) but also adultery, desecration, homicide, rape, rebellion, sibling rivalry, suicide, treachery, and theft. The first humans are sometimes created through primeval acts of incest, although myths of ancestral parthenogenesis or virgin birth are also known (Bimin-

Kuskusmin, Sambia, Trobriand Islanders). The original humans are depicted as emerging not only from the bodies of primordial humanoid forebears, but also from various sacred or mysterious cassowaries (Bimin-Kuskusmin), earthworms (Ndika), eggs (Rossel), stems (Kiwai), pigs (Tangu), palms (Keraki), and ground holes (Trobriand Islanders). Sometimes they emerge from other sources and sites—land, sea, sky, or perhaps some unknown, unmapped netherworld. Although they are occasionally completely formed, the first humans most often are molded or hardened by hand or by fire or sun into fully human form. They are then endowed with sensory, sexual, reproductive, and judgmental capacities, as well as other attributes of personhood (Bimin-Kuskusmin, Ilahita Arapesh, Marind-Anim, Trans-Fly). Once they are minimally human, these early beings are usually further endowed not only with the essential cultural artifacts—of gardening, fishing, hunting, and other productive activities—but also with such institutions as marriage, childrearing, ritual, magic, exchange, warfare, sorcery or witchcraft, and other foundations of Melanesian ideas of ethics, morality, and social order.

If the mythic bestowal of life, humanity, and sociality is complex and profound, the advent of death is usually associated with an apparently trivial incident that could well have had a different outcome—often involving some kind of acquisition or display of improper knowledge, emotion, or behavior and sometimes cast in the image of the shedding of skins and the apparent immortality of various lizards and snakes (Bimin-Kuskusmin, Kiwai, Trobriand Islanders). Yet Melanesian ideas of immortality tend to be ambiguous, and mythic beings are often given corporeal forms and mortal fragilities despite their recognized invisibility and supernatural powers. In turn, the complex symbolic relationships of birth, death, rebirth, and regeneration are commonly articulated in myths focused on and perhaps embedded in fertility, initiation, funerary, cannibalistic, and headhunting rituals (Bimin-Kuskusmin, Gimi, Hua, Keraki, Marind-Anim, Trobriand Islanders).

Contours of the Cosmological Landscape. Myths of origin in Melanesia are often concerned with the primordial roles of sun, moon, stars, and other celestial phenomena and with the fundamental separations of water and land, earth and sky, valley and mountain, plain and river, night and day, and other key contours of a cosmological landscape (Bimin-Kuskusmin, Kyaka Enga, Tolai). The distinctions of forest, garden, and hamlet, or of sea, shore, and inland village, however, are often relegated to a later time when the sense of domesticated space and human community became apparent. Separations of the realms of natural and supernatural or living and dead are more problematic in both conception and representation, for many mythic spirits are imagined to live near human settlements and to be involved with their affairs. Indeed, these spiritual abodes are sometimes described as mirror images of, or as significantly overlapping with, the social world of the living.

The acquisition of fire commonly marks the inception of humanity and community. According to many Melanesian myths, the original fire, which is denied to beings other than the morally human, is usually brought by spirits, created by sacred lightning, or hidden in the body of an ancestral being—perhaps an old woman or a totemic animal (Bimin-Kuskusmin, Marind-Anim, Nalum, Trans-Fly). Sometimes the advent of fire is linked to the origin of a major food or of ritual plants and animals—especially taro, sweet potatoes, yams, sago, and valued wild flora, as well as cassowaries, dogs, pigs, marsupials, pythons, fruit bats, crocodiles, dugongs, and sharks. Such foods and the taboos applied to them are mythically portrayed as key sociocultural markers of self and person (Bimin-Kuskusmin, Hua, Manga, Ndumba). The common mythic theme of interwoven animal, plant, and human fertility is often bound to ideas of the generative powers of male and female substances, anthropophagic symbols, and images of human heads and acts of headhunting (Bimin-Kuskusmin, Marind-Anim, Rossel, Trans-Fly).

Origins of Society and Culture. Throughout Melanesia, the beginnings of particular societies are attributed to both autochthonous origins and primordial migrations, which are often revealed in different contexts and serve distinct functions in the domains of ritual and ethnohistory (Bimin-Kuskusmin, Kwermin, Lagaip Enga, Umeda). It is in the context of these migrations that the culture heroes of Melanesia are often found. These culture heroes—including figures known over wide regions, such as Qat (Banks), Sido (Kiwai), Sosom (Marind-Anim), Souw (Daribi), Tagaro (Vanuatu), and Warohunuga (Solomons)—establish key aspects of sociocultural order, test the limits of morality, institute basic productive practices, introduce significant flora and fauna, and otherwise determine or shape the foundations of community. Often coming from a nearby land, the culture hero journeys across the known world, explores new frontiers, discovers new horizons, encounters strangers, enemies, or unknown women, travels to the realm of the dead, and shapes the world of the living. His exploits transform him profoundly and lend significance to the present condition of humankind. As he embarks on his odyssey of discovery, intrusion, indiscretion, insight, and creation, he is often cast as one member of an elder-younger sibling or cross-cousin set, and he marks the cultural boundaries of both cross-generational and male-female relationships. In exploring the moral boundaries of a community, the culture heroes exhibit some affinity with various local spirits, demons, ogres, fools, and tricksters, such as Gabruurian and Kamdaak Waneng (Bimin-Kuskusmin), Kakamora (San Cristoval), Masi (Ulawa), Muu-muu (Mala), Pakasa Uru and Tulagola (Lakalai), Tukis (Buka), and Yevale (Yéi-nan), but these figures never have the creative capacities of Melanesian culture heroes.

The myths of culture heroes introduce the sociological themes that are the foci of so many Melanesian narratives. Matters of egalitarian and hierarchical ethos and social order pervade the mythologies of western and eastern Melanesia, respectively. Ancestor spirits are genealogically and mythically marked in the descent ideologies of patrilineal, matrilineal, and cognatic Melanesian societies in different ways, but most of these societies—except in the patrilineal Highlands of New Guinea and hierarchical eastern Melanesia—emphasize the recently dead and largely ignore more remote ancestors. Although the myths of the classic New Guinea Highlands are substantially lacking in totemic figures or emblems, many fringe Highland and other Melanesian myths do associate totems with clans or moieties (Abelam, Bimin-Kuskusmin, Dobuans, Iatmül, Lakalai, Mountain Arapesh, Ngaing, Orokaiva, South Pentecost). Such mythic totemic figures may have few ritual implications (Keraki, Kiwai, Yéi-nan) or be associated with elaborate ancestor cults (Bimin-Kuskusmin, Marind-Anim).

Although Melanesian myths concerning ancestors and totems serve significantly as a community's corporate property, as charters of local or descent groups, and as the basis of claims on various social resources, many myths subtly depict a range of relations—between siblings, men and women, and generations—as a model extending from the family to the widest contours of social structure. Sibling relations are significant in almost all Melanesian myths. Emphasis is placed on either elder-younger (brother-brother, sister-sister) or male-female (brother-sister) configurations, with implications for matters of either generation or gender in transformations of the mythic sibling model (Bimin-Kuskusmin, Ilahita Arapesh, Mae Enga, Murik). Mythic portraits of generational relations tend to explore themes of authority and sexuality between parent and child and of amity in grandparent-grandchild relationships (Bimin-Kuskusmin, Mae Enga, Mountain Arapesh, Sambia). In turn, myths depicting gender relations tend to focus on substance, power, purity, and pollution; on the sexual division of labor; and on cultural images of virgins, wantons, witches, and female elders. These myths develop local ideas of primordial matriarchy and their ritual and political consequences (Asaro, Awa, Benabena, Bimin-Kuskusmin, Fore, Gadsup, Gahuku-Gama, Gimi, Hua, Jate, Kamano, Sambia, Siane, Tairora, Usurufa, Yagaria).

New Fields of Study. Although the themes noted above have significantly shaped the described or analyzed character of Melanesian myths as they have been portrayed in more than a half century of anthropological study, several other foci are also worthy of special note. First, there is now a quite considerable tradition of concern with syncretic myths, which are subtly linked to mission Christianity or to various millenarian or messianic cargo cults. These analyses, which introduce the critical element of sociocultural change into the study of Melanesian mythology, extend to all major areas of the cultural region. Second, studies conducted in the second half of the twentieth century on Daribi and Kewa myths stress the flexibility, metaphoric character, and creative potential of Melanesian myths, which are seen as complex forms of communication that play on ambiguity, trope, and innovation. Third, analyses of Kalauna and Tangu mythology emphasize the ways in which mythic understandings become variously embedded in both personal and public senses of self, person, experience, and symbol. In these studies, the analysis of Melanesian mythology has finally come to the forefront of anthropological interest, field research, and theoretical concern and promises to enrich this field of inquiry beyond traditional measure.

BIBLIOGRAPHY

The literature on Melanesian myths is immense and enormously varied, although it has remained primarily descriptive until quite recently. In the earlier periods of scholarly interest in Melanesia, the journals *Anthropos* (Salzburg, 1906–), *Baessler-Archiv* (Berlin, 1959–), *Folk-Lore* (London, 1890–), *Journal de la Société des Océanistes* (Paris, 1945–), *Journal of the Polynesian Society* (Wellington, New Zealand, 1892–), *Journal of the Royal Anthropological Institute of Great Britain and Ireland* (London, 1871–), *Man* (London, 1901–), *Oceania* (Sydney, 1930–), *Zeitschrift für Morphologie und Anthropologie* (Leipzig, 1899–), *Deutsche Gesellschaft für Anthropologie, Ethnologie und Urgeschichte* (Braunschweig, Germany, 1870–1920), and other publications printed myriad unannotated texts of Melanesian myths. Despite the sterility of this early practice, the tradition of presenting such textual materials on mythology is being continued not only in some of the periodical literature listed above, but also in the exemplary anthologies of the Summer Institute of Linguistics, the Société d'Études Linguistiques et Anthropologiques de France, and the Institute of Papua New Guinea Studies, as well as in the journals *Bikmaus* (Boroko, Papua New Guinea, 1980–) and *Oral History* (Boroko, Papua New Guinea, 1973–). The vital importance of providing appropriate ethnographic context, however, is now recognized in these endeavors to establish an archive of Melanesian oral traditions.

There are many early but altogether excellent ethnographic studies of Melanesian cultures and societies based on the tradition of field research that give detailed and significant—if not focal—attention to mythology. A fine, sensitive, but highly descriptive presentation of numerous mythic and other texts that provides a rich sense of their ethnographic contexts is to be found in Gunnar Landtmann's *The Folk-Tales of the Kiwai Papuans* (Helsinki, 1917). A somewhat similar study is well represented in G. Camden Wheeler's *Mono-Alu Folklore (Bougainville Strait, Western Solomon Islands)* (London, 1926), which provides extensive annotations of many texts and thoughtful comparisons with diverse Melanesian myths, but which portrays a somewhat superficial sense of relevant ethnographic context.

The problem-centered, theoretical analysis of Melanesian myth, however, becomes more prominent in the era of functionalist concerns, which emphasize the intricate embeddedness of mythology in the cultural fabric of social institutions. Thus, the place of myth in a system of morality enforced and sanctioned through oracles is splendidly illustrated in Reo F. Fortune's *Manus Religion* (Philadelphia, 1935). The intertwined cultural, social, and psychological characteristics of myth and its key functions as a charter of magical, ritual, and social institutions is remarkably portrayed for Trobriand gardening beliefs and practices in Bronislaw Malinowski's *Coral Gardens and Their Magic*, 2 vols. (London, 1935), and for the theoretical and comparative study of myth in Malinowski's *Magic, Science and Religion and Other Essays* (New York, 1948), which draws heavily on a range of Trobriand myths. A sensitivity to the psychocultural nuances of Melanesian mythology, however, is not generally a hallmark of the functionalist tradition and, beyond Malinowski's work, is perhaps best carried forward in John Layard's *Stone Men of Malekula* (London, 1942), which marvelously explores the cultural, psychological, and ritual character and context of myth on the islands of Malekula and Vao in the New Hebrides (now Vanuatu).

The analysis of Melanesian myth moves well beyond a simplistic concern with both function and charter in the seminal but little-recognized studies of the Keraki and other Trans-Fly groups and of the Elema, documented in Francis Edgar Williams's *Papuans of the Trans-Fly* (Oxford, 1936) and *Drama of Orokolo* (Oxford, 1940). A master of ethnography and no slavish adherent of functionalist dogma, Williams challenges the foundations of Malinowski's faith in mythic charters and opens new ground by raising significant questions about the cultural embeddedness, semiotic construction, and psychological importance of myths in Melanesia and elsewhere. In these several regards, Williams's central concern is to address the subtle relationships between mythic and ritual forms—an issue that is also richly explored in the magnificent studies of the Marind-Anim portrayed in Paul Wirz's *Die Marind-Anim von Holländisch-Süd-Neu-Guinea*, 2 vols. (Hamburg, 1922–1925), and in Jan van Baal's *Dema* (The Hague, 1966).

The classic study of the mythology of New Caledonia is beautifully represented in Maurice Leenhardt's *Do Kamo: Person and Myth in the Melanesian World* (1947; reprint, Chicago, 1979). In his exploration of matters of experience, epistemology, and personhood through myth and the nuances of the anthropological study of myth, Leenhardt provokes a depth of insight into Canaque myth that provides inspiration from Lucien Lévy-Bruhl to Claude Lévi-Strauss in the unraveling of Melanesian *mythologiques*. Yet the contemporary study of New Caledonian mythology, as admirably exemplified in Alban Bensa and Jean-Claude Rivièrre's *Les chemins de l'alliance* (Paris, 1982), is far less philosophical in its theoretical foundations and reflective in its methodological moorings and attempts to promote a more "scientific" emphasis on ethnosemantic classificatory schemas and sociopolitical patterns implicated in mythic narratives.

The state of the art in the anthropological study of Melanesian mythology is well examined and summarized for the period ending in the early 1960s in *Gods, Ghosts and Men in Melanesia*, edited by Peter Lawrence and M. J. Meggitt (Melbourne, 1965). This overview suggests how little progress had been made in the study of the myths and religions of Melanesia before the 1960s, which represented what might be called a renaissance of academic interest in Melanesian religions. Prior to this time, there is particularly little exploration of mythology in the New Guinea Highlands, with the notable exception of the monumental study of Fore, Jate, Kamano, and Usurufa origin, *kinihera*, and other genres of myth in Catherine H. Berndt's "Myth in Action" (Ph.D. diss., London School of Economics, 1955).

The modern era in the study of Melanesian mythology exhibits two particularly significant trends: (1) a comparative examination of mythological and other aspects of millenarian, nativistic, or cargo cult movements; and (2) a new emphasis on mythology as the focus of ethnographic interest and theoretical analysis. In the first instance, mythological portraits of the significance of sociocultural change, of altered conceptions of personhood, self, society, and cosmos, and of revitalized traditional or newly syncretic images are compared throughout much of Melanesia in Peter Worsley's *The Trumpet Shall Sound* (London, 1957) and in Kenelm Burridge's *New Heaven, New Earth* (New York, 1969).

In the second instance, however, the study of Melanesian myth comes fully into the mainstream of the best academic explorations of myth. These new and exciting analytic undertakings are perhaps best represented in a limited set of exemplary articles and in the monographic work of five scholars. The mythic exploration of moral ambiguities and dilemmas is insightfully examined in a Kamano text in Catherine H. Berndt's "The Ghost Husband: Society and the Individual in New Guinea Myth," *Journal of American Folklore* 79 (1966): 244–277. Subtleties of the conceptual images and internal paradoxes of Kaliai culture and society as represented in a single myth are unraveled in Dorothy Ayers Counts's "*Akro* and *Gagandewa:* A Melanesian Myth," *Journal of the Polynesian Society* 89 (1980): 33–64. These analyses show the power of exploring the nuances of a single mythic narrative in elaborate sociocultural context. In contrast, a comparative examination of the dialectical relationship between sociocultural experience, moral order, and mythic representation in the Eastern Highlands region of Papua New Guinea is admirably constructed in John Finch's "Structure and Meaning in Papua New Guinea Highland Mythology," *Oceania* 55 (1985): 197–213.

Whether focusing within or beyond a particular sociocultural community, the monographic endeavors variously attend to problems of the comparative analysis of myth. The complex and subtle relations between mythology and matters of personhood, self, morality, and experience in Tangu society are elegantly dissected in Kenelm Burridge's *Tangu Traditions* (Oxford, 1969), which delicately probes the intricate way in which myth is variously embedded in diverse ethnographic contexts and which forcefully demonstrates how myths become crystallizations of cultural themes and of both social and personal experiences. Exploring a tension between the disclosure of immoral realities and the revelation of existential truths, enigmatic and oracular Tangu myths unveil dilemmas of the local human condition. How such mythic crystallizations are constructed and manipulated creatively and through complex understandings of cultural tropes is analyzed admirably for Daribi mythology in Roy Wagner's *Habu* (Chicago, 1972) and *Lethal Speech* (Ithaca, N.Y., 1978), which also attend to broader comparative issues in assessing the commonalities and peculiarities of Daribi myth in New Guinea and in Melanesia. The significance of variations among versions of myths with respect to the cultural discrimination of social differences and to the transformational characteristics of a corpus of myths within a particular society is illustrated in exemplary fashion for Nalum mythology in S. Hylkema's *Mannen in het Draagnet* (The Hague, 1974). The subtle interplay between narrative compositions and pragmatic experiences, between intertextual resonances and textual references, between the surfaces and the depths of constructed layers of meaning, and between the fanciful and the factual of cultural contradictions and social conflicts, is marvelously explored in the "fabricated worlds" of Kewa *lidi* myths in John LeRoy's *Fabricated World* (Vancouver, 1985), which is usefully complemented by a fine collection of the analyzed myths in *Kewa Tales,* edited by LeRoy (Vancouver, 1985). Finally, the problem of how myths—usually conceived as particular forms of collective representations (in the Durkheimian sense)—become articulated with personal symbols and subjective experience and embedded in autobiographical narratives is superbly examined in Michael W. Young's *Magicians of Manumanua* (Berkeley, 1983). These new studies reach well beyond the descriptive and analytic limits of their predecessors and hold much promise for the future of academic understandings of the subtleties of mythological constructions in the Melanesian cultural region.

FITZ JOHN PORTER POOLE

MELQART, whose name means "king of the city," was the patron deity of the Phoenician city of Tyre. He was also known as Baal Sur ("lord of Tyre"). Most scholars agree that the Baal cult that Ahab and Jezebel introduced into Israel (*1 Kgs.* 16) and against which the prophet Elijah fought (*1 Kgs.* 17) was a cult of Melqart.

The earliest known epigraphic reference to this god is on a statue of him found near Aleppo, Syria, dating from about 860 BCE: "The statue that Har-Hadad, king of Aram, raised for his lord Melqart." Because of close commercial ties among major cities, it would not have been unusual for the god of one city to be cultivated in another. Thus, when Esarhaddon of Assyria (680–669 BCE) made a treaty with Tyre governing shipping and overland trade routes, curses were prescribed for breaking the treaty that invoked not only Assyrian gods but Tyrian deities as well: "May Melqart and Eshmun deliver your land to destruction, your people to deportation."

As Tyrian influence expanded throughout the Mediterranean by way of trade and colonization, so did the cult of Melqart, and inscriptions mentioning him have been found at Carthage, on Malta and Sardinia, in Spain, and especially on Cyprus, where there were shrines at Idalion and Lapethos. The Greeks and Romans identified Melqart with Herakles (Hercules), and figures of Melqart-Herakles, often in association with lions or eagles, were popular themes for the reverse types of many Roman colonial coins.

At Tyre itself Melqart was predominantly a god of the sea, reflecting Tyre's role as a maritime power. On the silver coinage of Tyre from the late fifth century BCE onward, Melqart is frequently depicted riding over the waves on a hippocampus. But other sources, particularly Philo Byblius, suggest that he was also a chthonic vegetation god, perhaps of the dying-and-rising type. This would be compatible with the several inscriptions that link Melqart with either Reshef or Eshmun.

BIBLIOGRAPHY

For comparative Semitic material, the best source is René Dussaud's "Melqart," in *Syria: Revue d'art oriental et d'archéologie* 25 (1946–1948): 205–230; for the Hellenistic period and for ties with Greek mythology (e.g., was Melqart the same figure as the Greek Melicertes?), see Michael C. Astour's *Hellenosemitica: An Ethnic and Cultural Study of West Semitic Impact on Mycenaean Greece* (Leiden, 1967). To be consulted more for the questions it raises than the answers it provides is William F. Albright's *Archaeology and the Religion of Israel,* 5th ed. (Baltimore, 1968).

WILLIAM J. FULCO, S.J.

MEMORIZATION, as the act of storing information in the memory, is distinguished by the fact that it can be either mechanical or deliberate. It is through practice and imitation, through the mechanical repetition of the traditional gestures and speech of his social group, that the individual, without actually realizing it, memorizes most of the information necessary for proper social and religious behavior. Taken in this sense, memorization culminates in the acquisition of the innumerable actions, of behavior, thought, and sensibility, that define a social and cultural identity. From the classic texts of Maurice Halbwachs on social memory and Marcel Mauss on bodily techniques to the more recent studies of André Leroi-Gourhan on mechanical operatory chains and Erwin Goffman on interaction rites, this type of memory acquisition has been the object of numerous investigations that need not detain us here. It is sufficient to emphasize that, in contrast to this kind of memorization, there exists another, deliberate form, the techniques of which become especially prominent when certain individuals are momentarily separated from their usual social group in order to take part in an initiatory ritual or to become part of an educational institution. These extreme cases do not apply to all members of a community, however, and those to whom they do apply are never required to memorize everything, but only those gestures, techniques, and special narratives that are of particular importance, as for example certain ritual formulas, declarations of faith, religious chants, prayers, and rules of religious behavior. Deliberate memorization thus appears to be a specialization of the more natural process of acquiring knowledge and techniques, religious or otherwise, that unconsciously determine a person's membership in a particular tradition.

To this initial distinction, between mechanical and deliberate memorization, can be added another, which does not coincide with it, but applies to each term independently: the techniques and practices of memorization, be they mechanical or deliberate, vary according to whether they are associated with orality or writing. Studies by Laura Bohannan, E. A. Havelock, and Jack Goody have established that memory is organized differently when written records and models are available. without writing, memory does not function as exact reproduction, but rather as generative recollection that ties repetition to variation. It would be wrong to think that this second distinction is historical. Oral memory and memory determined by writing can easily coexist in the same culture, as the Greek, Jewish, Celtic, and Hindu examples to be mentioned below will show. This is also still the case in our contemporary cultures. In the exposition that follows, which must be limited to only a few examples, we shall be able to trace a line that leads from the oral to the written. At each stage we shall have to respect the double contribution of mechanical memorization and deliberate memorization.

In societies without writing, riddles, proverbs, myths, fables, and stories depend upon a memory that is more or less shared by the entire community. [*See* Oral Tradition.] In this sense, one can speak of "social memory" or "shared knowledge." However, memorization is often an activity left to the free choice of individuals, to their tastes, affinities, and personal gifts. Henri Junod (1936) recalls a woman among the Tsonga who could tell riddle after riddle until late into the night. He met storytellers of every age and of both sexes: "Such a narrator might know only one story, and repeat it on every occasion, as did Jim Tandane, who told the story of an ogre, Nwatlakoulalambibi, with such enthusiasm that he was nicknamed after his hero! But others can tell six, ten, or twenty stories" (p. 159).

In certain societies, in particular among the Indians of North America, the knowledge and the possession of a myth or chant may be the privilege of an individual, who alone may pronounce it. It is for this reason that a Navajo of New Mexico may give as a sign of his poverty the fact that he does not own a single chant. A chant thus becomes a piece of "property" that concerns his own social and spiritual identity.

Most often, however, it is because certain stories are of an important collective interest that they are entrusted to the vigilant memory of one or more persons. The task of memorization is then taken up by a specific institution, often religious. These institutions are generally controled by an elite close to power. In Rwanda, the oral tradition of the Ubwiiru, in which the rites to be performed by the king were described, was divided into eighteen rituals that were kept strictly secret. In an essay on this oral tradition Pierre Smith (1970) notes that "the individuals in charge of remembering and repeating it word for word—errors could be punished with death—were the most important dignitaries in the kingdom, and the most important three among them, the only ones who knew the text as a whole, partook of the sacred character of royalty" (p. 1385). Such "memory specialists" can be found wherever a community expresses in narrative its needs to preserve its identity. In Oceania, the experts in oral tradition, the "holders of memory," were assembled in colleges analogous to religious confraternities. The most famous among them, portrayed by Victor Ségalen in *Les immémoriaux,* were the *harepo* of Tahiti, who were the keepers of the genealogies, myths, and epics.

> These orators were given true responsibility only after a serious examination, composed of difficult tests. The least mistake in memory was enough to eliminate a candidate, whose preparation was the responsibility of the priests. It is said that the *harepo* practiced in complete isolation, during long nocturnal walks. The transmission of ancestral knowledge

> rested with them. These story tellers were surrounded by a whole set of religious rituals.
>
> (O'Reilly and Poirier, 1956, pp. 1469–1470)

On Easter Island, the *rongorongo*, from noble families often attached to the king, used to teach chants and oral traditions in special huts. Alfred Métraux (1941) describes how this oral tradition is learned: "The student's memory was perfectly trained. During their first years of schooling, they had to learn certain psalms by heart, which they recited while playing cat's cradle: each figure . . . would correspond to a chant to be recited (p. 168).

Among the Inca, the education of the nobility was the responsibility of the *amautas*, who were of aristocratic descent. Their instruction lasted four years. The first year was devoted to the learning of the Quechua language; the second year to learning the religious traditions; and the third and fourth years to the handling of the famous knotted strings, the *quipu*.

Memorization, as it is practiced by such specialists, becomes a technique that can be taught, and that has its appropriate equipment. The Peruvian *quipu*, the *kou-hau* made by the *rongorongo* on Easter Island, the skeins of coconut fiber adorned with knots made in the Marquesas Islands, the wooden tablets of the Cuna Indians in Panama, and the pieces of bark of the Ojibwa Indians of North America do not, strictly speaking, constitute writing systems, but they do represent mnemotechnical means pertaining to oral memory. The same is true of certain systems of pictographic notation, such as the Aztec ideograms. Fernandon de Alva Ixtlilxóchitl recalls that the Aztec used to have writers for each type of history:

> Some would work with the *Annals* [Xiuhamatl], putting in order the things which took place each year, giving the day, the month, and the hour. Others were charged with the genealogies and ancestries of the kings and lords and persons of lineage. . . . Others took care of the paintings of the boundaries, the limits, and the landmarks of the cities, provinces, and towns, and [recorded] to whom they belonged.
>
> (quoted in Léon-Portilla, 1963, p. 157)

These "writers" used pictographs to construct a mnemonic system that later historians could refer to, provided that they also referred to the purely oral tradition of the chants (ibid., p. 156), since as a system of notation it was not sufficient in itself for the total preservation of information. It was necessary in addition to have recourse to the memory that was transmitted by word of mouth through the traditional chants. We find a similar situation, *mutatis mutandis*, in the early days of Islam, when to read the Qur'ān it was necessary that one already know it, since writing was still too rudimentary to be the sole means of transmission.

In oral cultures, memorization remains closely tied to the conditions of performance, despite the use of mnemonic techniques. Between listening and repeating, the absence of a fixed model does not allow for exact word-for-word repetition. Variability is essential, even though the transformations from one speaker to another often go unnoticed. There is no original version that others could reproduce, or from which they could depart. Claude Lévi-Strauss suggests that there is nevertheless a logical model, which follows certain laws of transformation. Although reproduction is not determined by the ideal of fidelity to an original (a "text"), this does not mean that it thereby becomes prey to arbitrariness. Its flexibility, its adaptability, respects certain formal conditions. "Understood in this way," notes Dan Sperber,

> the facts presented by Lévi-Strauss, these peculiar correspondances and regularities, represent the intellectual capital available for primitive thought, and more particularly . . . for storing and retrieving information in the absence of the external memory which writing provides. Thus the study of myths can clarify the nature of human thought itself, in some of its least known aspects.
>
> (*Le savoir des anthropologues*, Paris, 1982, p. 115)

As logical as these rules of transformation can be, and as apt to enlighten us on the workings of the human mind, they are not incompatible with trivial motives. Take, for instance, what Edmund Leach (1954) reports of the Kachin of Burma:

> Kachins recount their traditions on set occasions, to justify a quarrel, to validate a social custom, to accompany a religious performance. The story-telling therefore has a purpose; it serves to validate the status of the individual who tells the story, or rather of the individual who hires a bard to tell the story, for among Kachins the telling of traditional tales is a professional occupation carried out by priests and bards of various grades *(jaiwa, dumsa, laika)*. But if the status of one individual is validated, that almost always means that the status of someone else is denigrated. One might then infer almost from first principles that every traditional tale will occur in several different versions, each tending to uphold the claims of a different vested interest.
>
> (Leach, 1954, pp. 265–266)

This amounts to saying that the priestly bard adjusts his stories to the requirements of the audience who hired him. The horizon of expectation, the "reception," appears to be a constitutive component of oral memory, a component that conditions the very notions of fidelity and truth.

Oral memory does not like writing; we have numerous examples of this. This is not simply because it knows that writing can place it in contradiction with itself. It is primarily because the standard of truth is different for each. To understand this phenomenon better, let us turn to cultures where the two types of memory coexist. First the Celts, where the specialists of the sacred, the druids, ran their own schools, in which the main subject was memorization. According to an Irish judicial treatise, the *ollam* (the highest ranking scholar) was considered the equal of a king; he could recite 350 stories, 250 long ones, and 100 short ones. "As for the tenth-ranked *oblaire,* who makes do with left-overs at a feast, and whose escort is small, only seven stories suffices." The druids, who were the only Celts who knew how to write, refused to use their skill for religious purposes. "They say," wrote Caesar,

> that they learn a great number of verses by heart: some spend twenty years at their school. They believe that religion forbids the use of writing for this purpose, unlike any other purpose such as recording public or private stories, for which they use the Greek alphabet. It seems to me that they established this usage for two reasons. On the one hand, they did not want their doctrine to spread among the people; on the other hand, they did not want those who study to rely on writing and neglect their memory, since it often happens that the use of texts has the effect of reducing efforts to memorize by heart and weakens the memory.
>
> (*Gallic Wars* 6.13)

Georges Dumézil (1940) comments on this testimony as follows: "knowledge is re-incarnated in each generation, in each student; it is not received as a deposit; it assumes a form which, even while retaining its meaning and its essential traits, rejuvenates it and in a certain measure actualizes it." It is this dynamic, flexible, and adaptable character of oral memory that is threatened by writing. This is apparent from recent testimonies as well, such as that of a native of New Guinea (Humboldt Bay), who told an ethnologist, "in putting down our myths and legislative rules in writing you just kill them." According to Freeck C. Kamma (1975) "he meant to say: to fix or stabilize a progressing living reality means to cut it off from accompanying the living community."

In India, the brahmans who teach the Vedas are specialists in the techniques of memory, even though the Vedas have for a long time been fixed in writing. Louis Renou has noted that

> there is something fascinating in the process of memorizing the verses. The master stares at the student while feeding him the verses, so to speak, with an implacable regularity, while the student rocks back and forth in a squatting position. After looking on for a few moments in such a recitation class, one better understands the hymn of the *Ṛgveda* (7.103)
> class, one better understands the hymn of the *Ṛgveda* (7.103)
> in which this monotonous delivery has been likened to the croaking of frogs.
>
> (Renou, 1950, p. 36)

A precise description of the techniques of memorization in the Vedic schools can be found in the fifteenth chapter of the *Ṛk Pratiśakhya,* an old phonetic and grammatical treatise.

E. A. Havelock and Marcel Detienne have insisted on the coexistence of two types of memory in ancient Greece up until the time of Plato: (1) written memory and (2) social memory that is still dependent on oral tradition. Thus it is noteworthy that, although archives were available from the end of the fifth century BCE, it never occured to Greek historians to refer to them as historical sources more reliable than the tradition transmitted by the works of their predecessors (appraised according to their degree of verisimilitude) or transmitted by the experience of sight *(autopsía)* or hearing (testimony). And yet, already from about 470 BCE, Pindar and Aeschylus employ the metaphor that represents memory as an inscription, on the tablets of the soul, of what is fit to be remembered. Shortly before, the poet Simonides is said to have invented the art of memory, a technique built upon the metaphor of writing, which will undergo an important development, passing by way of Roman rhetoric (Quintillian) to the Renaissance. At the beginning of the fourth century BCE, Plato is obviously preoccupied with the negative effects of the invention of writing on memory. And Antisthenes of Athens recommends according more trust to personal memory than to the external memory of written annotations.

Although Homer appears to have been a necessary reference point in ancient Greece, since his written text was learned by heart in the schools and was recited by specialists at religious festivals, there was no religious text that had authority over others. Nor was there a class of religious specialists, comparable to the *pontifices, flamines,* and other Roman colleges, or to the Celtic druids or Vedic brahmans. Essentially pluralist and political, Greek religion was a religion without dogmas. It obeyed customs, which varied from region to region, and from one sanctuary to the next. As a result, correct practice depended on diverse forms of information derived from a variety of sources: the family, the tribe, the town, and so on. Certain religious practices, such as those connected with the mysteries or with divination, were sometimes reserved for certain families or circles of initiates (for example, the Eumolpides and the Ceryces, the Iamides, the Trophoniades), but every Greek, regardless of social status, was capable of addressing a prayer to the gods or performing the actions indispensable to a sacrifice. Deliberate memorization, and for that matter writing as well, appeared as religious practices only in the context of such marginal devotions as Orphism and Pythagoreanism.

In the Judaic tradition, memorization plays a different role in the study of the written Torah than it does in the study of the oral Torah. The written Torah is taught through reading. The transmission of the text, teaching of the scriptures, and public readings, must all be done from a book. Even if these activities eventually result in the memorization of the text, and in fact many rabbis do know the text by heart, it is specified that the written Torah must never be copied from memory. On the other hand, the oral Torah is taught through repetition from memory, even though written notes may be used as a mnemotechnic device, and even though, at an early date, the Mishnah, and then the Talmud, was committed to writing. The masters of the oral Torah, the tannaim ("teachers"), were like living memories, capable of reproducing an impressive number of traditions. Their knowledge, often mechanical and lacking in reflection, was used as a reference source by the rabbis and colleges. A famous example is Naṭronai ben Ḥavivai (eighth century), who wrote down the entire Talmud from memory after immigrating to Spain.

In the Christian tradition, the role of memorization seems to be much less important, although from the fourth century there are references to religious schools where the Psalms, the words of the apostles, prayers, and passages from the Old Testament, were learned by heart. In the Divine Office, for instance, the use of a breviary, even though required to be recited aloud, served as a substitute for memorization. Thus blindness could relieve a monk of the obligation of reciting the hours, save for what he knew from memory.

In Islam, which is a religion of the word as much as a religion of the book, memorization was essential from the very beginning. [*See* Tilāwah *and* Dhikr.] The words of the Prophet, which repeated the Archangel Gabriel's reading of the archetypal book, were transmitted orally by a group of the companions of the Prophet and by specialists in memorization before the Qur'ān was finally written down. From the time of the third caliph, writing made possible the fixation of the tradition, but it never did away with recourse to memory. In effect, to read the Qur'ān in its primitive form, it was necessary to know its contents. Later, writing and memorization continued to be closely related practices. The Qur'anic schools (*madrasahs*) were tied to a mosque. Children came to learn the Qur'ān by heart, even before they could read. These schools also taught the *ḥadīths*, the tradition that was guaranteed by a chain of authorities, or *isnād*. Before being written down in such texts, such as that of al-Bukhārī, this tradition was transmitted orally. The information it gives about the acts and words of the Prophet are used to regulate daily life down to the smallest details, in profane as well as in religious matters. The tradition represents the Prophet himself, sitting in the mosque and teaching the *ḥadīths*. His words are repeated three times by all present, until they are known by heart.

[*See also* Anamnesis.]

BIBLIOGRAPHY

General Works. For a general discussion of memorization and of method, see Maurice Halbwachs's *La mémoire collective* (Paris, 1950); Marcel Mauss's "Les techniques du corps," *Journal de psychologie* 32 (March–April 1935): 271–293, reprinted in Mauss's *Sociologie et anthropologie* (Paris, pp. 365–383; André Leroi-Gourhan's *Le geste et la parole*, vol. 2, *La mémoire et les rythmes* (Paris, 1965); Laura Bohannan's "A Genealogical Charter," *Africa* 22 (October 1952): 301–315; and Jack Goody's *The Domestication of the Savage Mind* (Cambridge, 1977). On specialists in memorization and the typology of things memorized, see Jan Vansina's *Oral Tradition: A Study in Historical Methodology*, translated by H. M. Wright (Chicago, 1965), and Ruth Finnegan's *Oral Poetry: Its Nature, Significance and Social Context* (Cambridge, 1977).

Specific Cultures. The following works discuss the role and nature of memorization in specific regions and religious traditions.

Africa. Henri A. Junod, *Mœurs et coutumes des Bantous*, vol. 2, *Vie mentale* (Paris, 1936). Pierre Smith, "La lance d'une jeune fille: Mythe et poésie au Rwanda," in *Échanges et communications: Mélanges offerts à Claude Lévi-Strauss a l'occasion de son soixantième anniversaire*, edited by Pierre Maranda and Jean Pouillon, vol. 2 (The Hague, 1970), pp. 1381–1408.

North America. Marcelle Bouteiller, "Littérature indienne d'Amérique du Nord," in *Histoire des littératures*, edited by Raymond Queneau, vol. 1 (Paris, 1956), pp. 1513–1523. Robert H. Lowie, *Primitive Society* (New York, 1961), pp. 224–232.

Oceania. Patrick O'Reilly and Jean Poirer, "Littératures océaniennes," in *Histoire des littératures*, edited by Raymond Queneau, vol. 1 (Paris, 1956), pp. 1461–1492. Alfred Métraux, *L'Ile de Pâques* (Paris, 1941), pp. 165–179.

The Inca. M. L. Locke, *The Ancient Quipu or Peruvian Knot-Record* (New York, 1923). Rafael Karsten, *A Totalitarian State of the Past: The Civilization of Inca Empire in Ancient Peru* (1949; reprint, Port Washington, N.Y., 1969).

The Aztec. Miguel León-Portilla, *Aztec Thought and Culture: A Study of the Ancient Nahuatl Mind*, translated by Jack Emory (Norman, Okla., 1963).

Burma. Edmund Leach, *Political Systems of Highland Burma: A Study of Kachin Social Structure.* (Cambridge, Mass., 1954).

New Guinea. Freerk C. Kamma, trans. and comp. *Religious Texts of the Oral Tradition from Western New-Guinea (Irian Jaya)*, pt. A (Leiden, 1975).

The Celts. Georges Dumézil, "La tradition druidique et l'écriture: Le Vivant et le Mort," *Revue de l'histoire des religions* 121 (March–June 1940): 125–133. Françoise Le Roux and Christian-J. Guyonvarc'h, *Les druides*, 3d ed. (Rennes, 1982).

India. Louis Renou, *Sanskrit et culture* (Paris, 1950). Louis Renou, *Les écoles védiques et la formation du Véda* (Paris, 1957).

Ancient Greece. E. A. Havelock, *Preface to Plato* (Cambridge, Mass., 1963). Marcel Detienne, *L'invention de la mythologie* (Paris, 1981). M. Simondon, *La mémoire et l'oubli dans la pensée grecque jusqu'à la fin du cinquième siècle avant J.-C.: Psychologie archaïque, mythes et doctrines* (Paris, 1982).

Judaism. Birger Gerhardsson, *Memory and Manuscript: Oral Tradition and Written Transmission in Rabbinic Judaism and Early Christianity,* translated by Eric J. Sharpe (Uppsala, 1961).

Christianity. Theodor Klauser, "Auswendiglernen," in *Reallexikon für Antike und Christentum,* vol. 1 (Stuttgart, 1950).

Islam. Dale F. Eickelman, "The Art of Memory: Islamic Education and Its Social Reproduction," *Comparative Studies in Society and History* 20 (October 1978): 485–516. Pierre Crapon de Caprona, *Le Coran: Aux sources de la parole oraculaire* (Paris, 1981), pp. 147–162.

PHILIPPE BORGEAUD

Translated from French by Marie-Claude Hays-Merlaud

MEMORY. *See* Anamnesis *and* Memorization.

MENCIUS. *See* Meng-tzu.

MENDELSSOHN, MOSES (1729–1786), German-Jewish philosopher and public figure of the Englightenment period. Born in Dessau, the son of a poor Torah scribe, Mendelssohn received a traditional education that, rather exceptionally, included the study of the philosophy of Moses Maimonides. In 1743 Mendelssohn followed his teacher to Berlin to continue his Jewish studies. There he was able to acquire considerable knowledge of contemporary mathematics, philosophy, poetry, and classical and modern languages. The German dramatist and critic G. E. Lessing encouraged Mendelssohn to publish his first German essays and used him as the model for the tolerant and modest Jew in his play *Nathan the Wise.* In 1763 Mendelssohn received first prize from the Prussian Royal Academy of Sciences for a treatise on evidence in metaphysics; in the same year he was granted the status of "protected Jew" with rights of residence in Berlin. Mendelssohn supported himself successively as family tutor, bookkeeper, manager, and partner of a Berlin Jewish silk manufacturer; his home became a gathering place for Berlin intellectuals. In the nineteenth century members of the Mendelssohn family (most of whom converted to Christianity after Moses' death) achieved considerable financial, academic, and artistic prominence.

General Metaphysical and Religious Writings. Mendelssohn's philosophical position was derived from the English philosophers John Locke (1632–1704) and Shaftesbury (1671–1713) and especially from the German rationalists Gottfried Wilhelm Leibnitz (1646–1716) and Christian Wolff (1679–1754). The publication of Mendelssohn's *Phädon* (1767), a work on the immortality of the soul and named after Plato's dialogue, established his reputation among the enlightened public. Drawing on Leibnitz's theory of monads, Mendelssohn argues that souls are primary, imperishable elements that impose unity on the changing features of the body. Continued personal consciousness of the soul after death is guaranteed by God, inasmuch as divine wisdom and goodness would not allow the soul to relapse into nothingness without fulfilling its natural impulse to self-perfection. *Morgenstunden, oder Über das Dasein Gottes* (Morning Hours, or Lectures on the Existence of God, 1785), the most methodical of Mendelssohn's major works, moves from a discussion of epistemological issues to the importance of a belief in God, providence, and immortality for man's happiness, to a formal ontological proof of God's existence.

Jewish Writings and Activities. In the mid-1750s Mendelssohn collaborated in a short-lived Hebrew weekly and published a commentary to Maimonides' treatise on logic. He was forced to speak out as a Jew, however, after 1769, when he was publicly challenged to explain why he, an enlightened man, did not convert to Christianity. In a reply to the Swiss pastor, Johann Kasper Lavater, Mendelssohn rejected the implication that his loyalty to Judaism was inconsistent with his innermost enlightened religious convictions and devotion to rational inquiry. In the 1770s Mendelssohn used his influence with liberal Christians to deflect threatened anti-Jewish measures in Switzerland and Germany. In connection with efforts to protect the Jews of Alsace, Mendelssohn encouraged Christian Wilhelm von Dohm to write his classic defense of the civic betterment of the Jews but demurred from Dohm's support of limited judicial autonomy for Jews and the right of Jewry to excommunicate recalcitrant Jews.

Mendelssohn's translation of the Pentateuch into German was published in 1780. It was accompanied by a commentary (the *Bi'ur*) that draws on both traditional exegesis and modern literary aesthetics. Often reprinted, the translation draw the ire of some traditionalist rabbis but served as an important bridge to modern culture for many young Jews in the nineteenth century.

Jerusalem, or On Religious Power and Judaism. Mendelssohn's principal contribution to Jewish thought was the result of yet another challenge by a Christian, this time concerning an alleged inconsistency in his supporting the abolition of excommunication while remaining loyal to biblical law, which condones coercion. Mendelssohn's reply, *Jerusalem, oder Über religiöse Macht und Judenthum* (1783), was one of the first works in German to plead for freedom of conscience in religious matters, separation of church and state, and (indirectly) civil rights for the Jews. According to Mendelssohn both states and church have as their final goals the promotion of human happiness. The state is permitted to enforce specific actions, whereas the church's task is to convince its followers of their religious and ethical duties through persuasion alone. To the question of the continued authority of Jewish law, which was adumbrated by Spinoza in the *Tractatus Theologico-Politicus*, Mendelssohn replied that the ceremonial law stemming from the Hebrew Bible is binding solely on the Jewish people; Judaism is a religion of revealed legislation, not of revealed beliefs. The existence and unity of God, the reality of divine providence, and the immortality of the soul are to be affirmed on the grounds of natural reason, not miracles or supernatural revelation. Mendelssohn acknowledges the importance of Spinoza in the history of philsophy but vigorously rejects Spinoza's pantheism. Spinoza's primary concern was the noninterference by the state or religious authorities in the intellectual freedom of the philosopher and scientist. Mendelssohn, while still affirming the continued authority of Jewish law, was concerned with freedom inside one religion as well as freedom of religion for minority communities.

Mendelssohn argued that the identification of church and state in biblical Israel ceased with the destruction of the ancient commonwealth; laws remaining in force are personal religious duties that preserve the universal principles of Jewish faith against lapses into idolatry and polytheism. These laws will not lose their force until God arranges another indubitable supernatural revelation to the Jewish people to supersede that of Mount Sinai. Loyalty to the Jewish law, however, does not prevent Jews from assuming the legitimate duties of citizenship in an enlightened society.

The Place of Mendelssohn in the History of Jewish Thought. Although Mendelssohn's synthesis of philosophical theism and traditional religious observance was viewed as outdated by the next generation of Jewish thinkers influenced by Kant and Hegel, Mendelssohn could be seen as forebear of the conflicting trends of nineteenth-century German Jewry: Reform, for his openness to change; and Neo-Orthodoxy, for his insistence on the binding nature of Jewish ceremonial law. Mendelssohn's disciples among the writers who collaborated with him in the *Bi'ur* were prominent in the Jewish Enlightenment (the Haskalah) that emerged in Prussia in the 1770s and later spread to eastern Europe. Mendelssohn was revered by the Enlighteners *(maskilim)* for having moved from the ghetto to modern society without abandoning the Jewish tradition or the Jewish people. In the 1880s, however, at the end of the Haskalah period, Mendelssohn was assailed for having paved the way to the loss of Jewish distinctiveness and, therefore, to assimilation. In retrospect, his thought and life can be seen to have posed some of the fundamental issues of Jewish religious survival in secular, liberal society.

BIBLIOGRAPHY

The standard edition of Mendelssohn's writings is *Gesammelte Schriften Jubiläumsausgabe*, 7 vols., edited by Fritz Bamberger and others and incompletely published between 1929 and 1938; a completed edition in 20 volumes is being prepared under the editorship of Alexander Altmann (Stuttgart, 1971–). The most recent English translation of *Jerusalem* is by Allan Arkush, with an introduction and commentary by Alexander Altmann (Hanover, N.H., 1983). Useful is *Moses Mendelssohn: Selections from His Writings*, edited and translated by Eva Jospe (New York, 1975). The magisterial biography of Mendelssohn is Alexander Altmann's *Moses Mendelssohn: A Biographical Study* (University, Ala., 1973). On Mendelssohn's role in the intellectual history of Judaism, see Michael A. Meyer's *The Origins of the Modern Jew: Jewish Identity and European Culture in Germany, 1749–1824* (Detroit, 1967), chap. 1; Julius Guttmann's *Philosophies of Judaism*, translated by David W. Silverman (New York, 1964), pp. 291–303; and H. I. Bach's *The German Jew: A Synthesis of Judaism and Western Civilization, 1730–1930* (Oxford, 1984), pp. 44–72).

ROBERT M. SELTZER

MENDICANCY. As a religious term, *mendicancy* (from the Latin *mendicare,* "to beg") denotes renunciation of all worldly possessions and the practice of begging alms from door to door. The custom is of ancient origin and, although its observance has varied in character from place to place, the general impetus for the phenomenon seems to have derived from an idea that the discipline of living solely on alms is conducive to the attainment of spiritual goals. Early in the Vedic period, brahman mendicants had precise rules for soliciting alms, and among the ancient Greeks, mendicant priests went from place to place in quest of alms on behalf of their favorite deities (e.g., Isis and Artemis Opis). Among the Romans, certain priests who were bound by vows of temperance received support from public almsgiving. (According to some critics, these mendicants had occasionally to be reminded to restrain their extravagant demands; see Cicero, *On the Laws* 50.) Although religious mendicancy is a phenomenon that still finds acceptance in varying degrees in a number of cultures, it is chiefly within the Hindu, Buddhist, Christian, and Islamic traditions that it has won sanction as a religious practice.

In the Hindu tradition, pious men with sons to carry on the family line have long had open to them a renunciant ideal by which they may give away their possessions to brahmans and go forth into homelessness, first as a hermit *(vanaprastha)* and later as a mendicant *(saṃnyāsin)* who begs from door to door. [*See* Saṃnyāsa.] Individuals from different ranks of society have sometimes chosen to devote themselves to a life of poverty and meditation, dependent for support upon others. The Hindu mystic's quest for illumination, for union with ultimate reality, generally promotes such an attitude of indifference to worldly concerns, and, since liberation *(mokṣa)* from them is one of the recognized aims of a Hindu's life, the asceticism of the mendicant is perceived as a positive means for achieving that goal.

In Buddhism, the monastic enterprise instituted by Gautama Buddha was probably derived from even more ancient Vedic ascetic movements. For the Buddhist, renunciation of the world is considered meritorious in that it allows the devotee to dedicate his or her energies to the task of delivering people from suffering. Both laypersons and monastics subscribe to mendicancy as a practice leading to the lessening of attachment and, hence, ultimately to *nirvāṇa*. The daily life of the monastic mendicants usually includes regular rounds from house to house for the purpose of gathering alms; whatever food is placed in their bowls is to be accepted gratefully. Monks and nuns are exhorted to follow specific rules (e.g., not discriminating between houses when begging, eating solely from an alms bowl, eating only one meal per day, etc.). They are instructed that no real value obtains in external performances; only if alms-gathering is attended by the desire for *nirvāṇa* can this discipline be meritorious. Although the practice of begging food and alms still prevails in most countries where Buddhist monasticism exists, meals are also often brought to the monasteries so that the lay people may acquire extra merit.

In early Christian history, pious mendicants (Lat., *solitarii, gyrovagi*) wandered through city and countryside, preaching and begging alms, but they usually did not meet with popular acceptance. [*See* Eremitism.] Jerome, for example, complained that some of these *solitarii* were accustomed to wandering from house to house, often leading people astray and living a life of luxury at the expense of other Christians. Monastic or semimonastic communities were in existence by the beginning of the fourth century and, although their inhabitants may have had to resort to begging during hard times, they generally sustained themselves by their own labors. It was not until the time of Francis of Assisi and Dominic (twelfth and thirteenth centuries) that mendicant orders as such arose and eventually became sanctioned by the church hierarchy. [*See* Religious Communities, *article on* Christian Religious Orders.] The appearance of these mendicant orders ensued as a protest against the corruption within certain established monastic communities (a problem with which the mendicant orders themselves had to deal at a later time, when abuses crept into their own communities).

Four mendicant orders were approved by the Council of Lyons (1274): Franciscans, Dominicans, Carmelites, and Augustinians. Francis insisted that his followers own nothing whatever, for they were to be "pilgrims and strangers in this world," living with confidence in God's care and subsisting on alms received from those among whom they preached and worked. After the deaths of Francis and Dominic, however, church authorities mitigated the orders' rules to allow for possession of worldly goods. From time to time, members of the Roman Catholic and Greek Orthodox churches have, in an attempt to return to the simplicity of the message of the Gospel, initiated reform movements that included mendicancy. Their belief was that through ascetic practices such as begging, Christians might rid themselves of the imperfections and sins that kept them from union with God—especially by placing one's daily life in God's hands *(divina providentia)*—by complete reliance on God for subsistence one might more quickly achieve that union with the divine. Toward the end of the Middle Ages, mendicancy as a religious practice was prohibited by the Roman Catholic church because of various abuses that had crept into the system.

Within Islamic tradition, there has generally been disagreement as to the value of mendicancy. Some have argued that, since the Qur'ān contains injunctions against begging, it is debatable whether dependence upon others for one's sustenance is more virtuous than having independent means. Mendicancy on a broad scale came into vogue with the ninth-century Ṣūfīs; these were Muslim ascetics who interpreted *zuhd* ("renunciation") in a strictly spiritual sense, viewing it as the abandonment of all that diverts one from God.

Many of the early Ṣūfīs carried the Islamic theory of *tawakkul* ("trust [in God]") to an extreme, defining it as renunciation of all personal initiative and volition. Since everything is in God's hands, Ṣūfīs were neither to beg nor work for pay but to depend on what God has sent as a gift, either directly or through the generous alms of others. This system often proved ineffective, and some Ṣūfīs wandered from place to place, trusting in God to provide their livelihood. At times, the result was starvation and, gradually, Ṣūfīs concluded that trust in

God and seeking a livelihood were not mutually exclusive. The words *faqīr* and *darwīsh* (Arabic and Persian for "poor") are terms for religious mendicants who ask for food or money in the name of God. They profess a life of poverty and withdrawal from worldly pursuits for the purpose of deepening their spiritual insights and communing more intimately with God. Some mendicants follow their careers independently, and others (like their Christian counterparts) live communally. The doctrines of these mendicants and their orders are derived from Ṣūfī principles and beliefs, particularly those that stress dependence upon God.

Within these four religious traditions, mendicancy has generally connoted withdrawal from worldly possessions and worldly pursuits for the purpose of demonstrating and experiencing a sense of dependency upon God and/or a supreme life principle. Wherever mendicancy has become accepted as a religious practice, almsgiving also has been elevated to an act of merit whose efficacy is rarely surpassed by other virtues. It, too, is considered in positive terms as a way of distancing oneself from society in order to transcend the material world.

[*See also* Almsgiving.]

BIBLIOGRAPHY

Although there are no specific monographs on mendicancy, the following encyclopedias, dictionaries, and texts provide relevant material on the topic.

Boyle, L. E. "Mendicant Orders." In *New Catholic Encyclopedia,* vol. 9. New York, 1967.

Brandon, S. G. F., ed. *A Dictionary of Comparative Religion.* London, 1970.

Hastings, James, ed. *Encyclopaedia of Religion and Ethics.* 13 vols. Edinburgh, 1908–1926. See the index, s.v. *Mendicant orders.*

Hughes, Thomas P. *A Dictionary of Islam.* London, 1885.

Macdonald, D. B. *Religious Attitude and Life in Islam.*

Parrinder, Geoffrey. *Dictionary of Non-Christian Religions.* Philadelphia, 1971.

Spiro, Melford E. *Buddhism and Society.* New York, 1970.

Stutley, Margaret, and James Stutley. *A Dictionary of Hinduism.* London, 1977.

ROSEMARY RADER

MENG-TZU, respectful epithet of Meng K'o, known in the West as Mencius; moral philosopher of the fourth century BCE, whose interpretation and development of Confucius's thought was of paramount importance. Meng-tzu was a native of Tsou, a small state next to Lu (the native state of Confucius) at the base of the Shantung Peninsula. His traditional dates are 372–289 BCE, but recent scholarship indicates that this dating is about 20 years too late. (If the traditional dates are in error by one 19-year *chang,* his dates would be 391–308.) He is sometimes said to have been a student of K'ung Chi (Tzu-ssu), grandson of Confucius, but it is more likely that he studied under one of K'ung Chi's disciples. In any case, his moral philosophy is somewhat similar to ideas in the *Li chi* that tradition has ascribed to Tzu-ssu.

Brief accounts of Meng-tzu's life appear two or three centuries after his death, but nothing is known except what can be inferred from the book *Meng-tzu* (Mencius). This consists of seven parts (sometimes referred to as "books"), each divided in two and subdivided into sections that are usually unconnected, ranging in length from dicta of a short sentence or two to over two thousand words of dialogue between Meng-tzu and disciples, friends, rivals, or royal patrons. Some accounts say that the philosopher himself wrote the *Meng-tzu;* according to others, it was compiled by his disciples, perhaps with his help. It was edited (and parts discarded) by Chao Ch'i in the second century CE, who also added a commentary. The *Meng-tzu* became highly esteemed by Han Yü in the eighth century and by many philosophers of the Sung and later dynasties. Chu Hsi (1130–1200) wrote the most widely read philosophical commentary on the book and included the *Meng-tzu* among his Four Books intended as basic texts for moral education. In the civil service examinations of 1315, the *Meng-tzu* was recognized as one of the Confucian Classics by the Mongol court. Thereafter, Meng-tzu's impact on moral philosophy continued to increase, especially in the teachings of Wang Yang-ming (Wang Shou-jen, 1472–1529). The last and fullest philosophical statement of Tai Chen (1724–1777) is his *Meng-tzu tzu-i su-cheng* (Explication of the Meanings of Terms in *Meng-tzu),* which actually develops Tai's own moral-metaphysical system and criticizes Chu Hsi. By this time, the criterion of good philosophy had become the accuracy of its conformity to Meng-tzu.

Events in Meng-tzu's life that can be dated are derived from the *Meng-tzu,* are limited to the decade beginning 320 BCE, and consist chiefly of his visits to various states. The first two books, containing Meng-tzu's interviews with King Hui-ch'eng of Wei (d. 319) and King Hsüan of Ch'i (319–301), are believed to report actual conversations in chronological order. The same may be more or less true of book 3, which contains Meng-tzu's conversations in the states of T'eng and Sung. Books 4 and 7 assemble many short sayings and may be later additions. Book 5 is largely taken up with Meng-tzu's answers to questions from his disciple Wan Chang about ancient rulers and institutions. Book 6 contains the fullest statements by Meng-tzu on the theme of the innate goodness of man, and opens with his famous argument with Kao-tzu on this subject. (Kao-tzu may have been a disciple of Mo-tzu in youth, and this encounter, although undatable, probably occurred when Meng-tzu was a younger man.)

In his political and social thought, Meng-tzu was both conservative and daringly radical. Institutions of the past, such as rites of mourning, are to be observed strictly, he holds, not just because they are historically given, but because they are psychologically and morally sound (3A5). Government is the responsibility of educated (that is, morally developed) men and should provide for the welfare and moral education for the common people (1A7). The privileges given to those who rule are not a form of exploitation but are a sensible form of the division of labor (3A4). A gentleman must avoid accepting compromising gifts or preferment from a ruler who is not benevolent; if the prince is deaf to suasion, the gentleman may leave the state, and the prince's relatives may depose him (5B9); an incorrigible ruler may lose the right to be called "ruler" and may justifiably be killed (1B8). Living in a time of ever-increasing warfare, Meng-tzu was an insistent pacifist. Fifteen years before the datable events in the *Meng-tzu*, the Chou king, who had long lacked real power, lost his unique claim to the title of king when the rulers of nine leading states each declared himself a "king." Meng-tzu's conversations with the kings of Wei and of Ch'i naturally turn to the desire of each to unify the world under himself; Meng-tzu insists that this cannot be achieved by military force, but only by a ruler so "benevolent" *(jen)* that all people will wish to be his subjects (1A, passim).

The book reveals Meng-tzu as a humorless man who insisted on his dignity, but as an outspoken critic of current political practices he became an evocative model for conscientious and courageous officials in later times. His more daring utterances led to his being vigorously censured by conservative philosophers like Ssu-ma Kuang (1019–89) and autocrats like Emperor T'ai-tsu of the Ming dynasty. But it was one particular aspect of his philosophy that accounts chiefly for his appeal to thinkers from Sung times on. The Neo-Confucian philosophy in the Sung, Yüan, and Ming dynasties had to compete for the attention of intellectuals tempted to a Taoist or Buddhist life of religious contemplation and self-purification. As an alternative, Confucian teachers sought to offer a life that was in effect just as religious, one of continual moral study and self-cultivation with a goal of a Confucian ideal of moral sagehood *(sheng)* consistent with family duties and with political service. Searching for ancient validation for this ideal, they found it in the *Meng-tzu* and in slightly later Confucian moral texts, notably the *Ta-hsüeh* and the *Chung-yung* (the latter ascribed to Tzu-ssu), that discuss the analysis and cultivation of the moral personality.

Meng-tzu was the earliest ancient author (whose words survive) to discuss at length the cultivation of one's *hsin* ("heart-mind") and to give this idea a theoretical base. To Meng-tzu, *hsin* was at the base of morality; we all have a *hsin* that distinguishes right from wrong. It was the careful nurturing of this innate discriminating capacity that Meng-tzu urged upon his listeners. [*See* Hsin.] But the later Confucian advocates of self-cultivation such as Chu Hsi and Wang Yang-ming, addressing the philosophical needs of their respective ages, naturally did not use Meng-tzu's terms in the way he had. In the background of the Neo-Confucians' approach was an already existing concept of the religious life. Thus they could think of self-cultivation as a search for a liberating "enlightenment," in which the true omniscient mind (perhaps here a reflection of the idea of "Buddha mind") would be cleansed of its "defilements" and shine in glory. The Confucian sage, they argued, must have reached a state resembling this by "overcoming himself" (a misinterpretation of *Lun-yü* 12.1) and by ridding his (Mencian) naturally moral mind-heart of every acquired trace of "selfish thought," thoughts that (for Wang Yang-ming) blocked the manifestation of the mind's omniscient "basic essence." All of this would have been strange to Meng-tzu. His concern, as he said repeatedly (3B9), was to preserve the vision of Confucius on the one hand against the intellectual confusions preached by egoist advocates of withdrawal from social responsibility, such as Yang Chu, Tzu Hua, and other Taoistic thinkers, and on the other hand, against the equally serious confusions of the followers of Mo Ti (Mo-tzu). The latter sought to realize the commendable ends of universal peace and good government by a doctrinaire program that was blind to the very concept of moral goodness, defining goodness in materialist and utilitarian terms and denying the natural obligations that, Meng-tzu thought, one had to one's parents and relatives.

Meng-tzu's philosophy of an inner source of morality can be interpreted as his defense of the ideals of Confucius against challenges from these two directions. At the same time, he also drew ideas from his opponents and seems to have sensed and to have tried to remedy a weakness in Confucian thinking. Like Confucius, he assumed that a good human community is one in which educated, that is, morally cultivated, persons are in power, one in which rulers do not treat the common people harshly but provide for their material needs and for their moral education. And like Confucius, he assumed that an essential aspect of the moral education of a gentleman is to learn and accept the *li* (rites), psychologically and morally sound customs inherited from the past, especially those that govern one's relations with parents and superiors. But Confucius had never solved the problem of the student who resists instruction. For the egoist, this was not a problem: he could with consistency take the view that the student's education is the student's concern; furthermore, since he (the egoist) recommended that one withdraw from society's obligations, regarding them as harmful to the self and as unnatural, in the extreme case even hedonism was acceptable. For the Moist, the unwilling student was not a problem either, although for a different reason. The egoist at least advocated self-cultivation; the Moist did not.

Mo-tzu ridiculed "rites and music," thereby revealing that he simply did not comprehend the Confucian ideal of the cultivation of the moral personality. For Mo-tzu, a good society results when what is materially useful (for example, production) is carried out, and what is harmful (for example, war) is not. In effect, Mo-tzu assumes that when attitudes are needed for the right action they can be adopted at will: if I am shown the reasons for the utility of having an impartial concern for others ("universal love") and for a belief in spirits, then I can direct myself to have these beliefs and attitudes. Occasionally Meng-tzu too betrays this extreme voluntarism, as when he counsels King Hsüan to take the "concern" *(en)* he had revealed in his spontaneous sympathy for an ox about to be sacrificed, and simply apply it to his people (1A7). But in criticizing recognizable Moist thinking he rejects this principle. His rival Kao-tzu, probably a Moist in youth, took as his first principle of self-cultivation the idea that "what you do not get from doctrine [*yen*, 'words'] you should not seek in the heart" (2A2). Meng-tzu rejects this out of hand, without even an explanation. "Kao," he said, "never understood *i* ['rightness'] because he thinks of it as something external." For Mencius the *hsin* is the innate seat of moral sensibility, and one cannot simply impose an attitudinal shape on it to satisfy some desideratum.

Thus Confucius's problem is transformed: the teacher's role is to call the student's attention to moral dispositions he already has in his heart. Meng-tzu (2A6, 6A6) identifies four such dispositions: tendencies to kindness *(jen)*, dutifulness *(i)*, propriety *(li)*, and knowledge of right and wrong *(chih)*. These moral "sprouts" *(tuan)* are to be cultivated like plants, that is, gradually, by moral actions that feel right in the doing (2A2, 4A27). All of us have similar tastes in food and beauty; the same is true in questions of morality (6A7). The honored sages of the past were merely moral connoisseurs who anticipated the developed morality that we could have thought out for ourselves: thus Meng-tzu answers the egoist challenge. His formulation is drawn from them, but he takes *i* not as "honor," the esteem of others that it is pleasant to have, but as one's own sense of what is right. For Meng-tzu, Confucian morality is completely in accord with our natures. Again and again, Meng-tzu uses agricultural metaphors: we become good if we are planted in good soil (6A7), and callous if our sprouting sensibilities are stunted by an abusive world (6A8). Still, it is the duty of each of us to appraise himself, to recognize and give priority to the best in himself (6A15), seeing his innate virtues as "titles of nobility" given him by Heaven (6A16–17; 7A1): "seek and you will find it" (6A6, 8, 11; 7A3). Meng-tzu asks us to pay attention to the "sprout" of sensibility and to develop and "extend" the deep-structural and as yet unarticulated capacities in the self (1A7, 2A6, 7A15, 7A17, 7A45, 7B31). His is not the program of the Neo-Confucian moralist, engaged in the perpetual moral "task" *(kung-fu)* of a self-watchful scotching of all "selfish thoughts" so that an already fully knowing "moral mind" can be "unobstructed."

Meng-tzu recognizes that physical desires and needs are part of our constitution, but counsels that we should think of these as governed by our (and Heaven's) "command," while our virtues are to be thought of as our "nature," to be enjoyed (7B24). The Neo-Confucian term "selfish thought" *(ssu i)* is not even part of his vocabulary. Here one must remember that Meng-tzu does not have a concept of a soul implanted in a body with which it is likely to be in conflict, whereas the dualistic tradition in Neo-Confucian thought (represented chiefly by Ch'eng I and Chu Hsi) does see us as *li* ("principle"), the source of good, implanted in *ch'i* ("matter"), the source of selfishness and evil. It was just this dualistic tendency in the dominant thinking of his time that the Ch'ing moral philosopher Tai Chen objected to, drawing on Meng-tzu for his support.

[*See also* Jen and I; Li; Chinese Religion, *article on* Religious and Philosophical Texts; *and the biographies of Wang Yang-ming, Tai Chen, and Mo-tzu.*]

BIBLIOGRAPHY

Graham, Angus C. "The Background of the Mencian Theory of Human Nature." *Tsing Hua Journal of Chinese Studies*, n.s. 6 (December 1967): 215–274.

Lau, D. C. "Theories of Human Nature in Mencius and Shyuntzyy." *Bulletin of the School of Oriental and African Studies* 15 (1953): 541–565.

Lau, D. C. "On Mencius' Use of the Method of Analogy in Argument." *Asia Major*, n.s. 10 (1963): 173–194. This article is reprinted in Lau's translation of Mencius.

Lau, D. C., trans. *Mencius*. Harmondsworth, 1970.

Legge, James, trans. *The Works of Mencius*, vol. 2 of *The Chinese Classics*. 2d rev. ed. (1895). Reprint, New York, 1970.

Nivison, David S. "Mencius and Motivation." *Journal of the American Academy of Religion* 47 (September, supp., 1979): 417–432.

Nivison, David S. "On Translating Mencius." *Philosophy East and West* 30 (1980): 93–122. A critical review of translations of Mencius in English and other languages.

Riegel, Jeffrey K. "Reflections on an Unmoved Mind: An Analysis of Mencius 2A2." *Journal of the American Academy of Religion* 47 (September, supp., 1979): 434–457.

David S. Nivison

MENNONITES. The Mennonites, a Christian denomination, were first called Menists, or Mennonites, in 1541 by Countess Anna of Friesland after the group's primary leader, Menno Simons (1496–1561). She used this name in order to distinguish the Mennonites, as peaceful settlers whom she welcomed in her lands, from other, revolutionary, groups. Historically and theologically, Mennonites are the direct descendants of sixteenth-century Anabaptists, a radical reform group in Europe. [*See* Anabaptism.]

Early History and Doctrine. One of the most significant influences upon Mennonite history and identity has been the experience of decades of persecution during the sixteenth and seventeenth centuries. Numerous martyrologies, including the classic *Martyrs' Mirror* (1660), testify to this experience. The Mennonites lived in an age that was not ready for religious or social pluralism. In their insistence upon a church constituted of believers only, and in their embodiment of the principles of voluntary church membership and the separation of church and state, they represented a counterculture that society could not tolerate. In their reading of the Bible, however, they found these principles to be self-evident, particularly in the teaching and example of Jesus Christ. In keeping with the vision of their Anabaptist forebears, the Mennonites also shared the vision of a New Testament church restored both in essence and in form.

A church-world dualism was implicit in the Mennonites' theology and social view. It had been given early expression in the "Brotherly Union" of 1527, sometimes called the Schleitheim Confession of Faith, article 4 of which states:

> Now there is nothing else in the world and all creation than good or evil, believing and unbelieving, darkness and light, the world and those who are [come] out of the world, God's temple and idols, Christ and Belial, and none will have part with the other.

Toleration came to the Mennonites first in the Netherlands in the 1570s and somewhat later in other parts of Europe, except in Switzerland, where severe restrictions against them remained until the eighteenth century. Increasing freedom in the north led to rapid growth in membership, until by 1700 the Dutch congregations included 160,000 members. The sectarian virtues of frugality and hard work led to considerable affluence and to urbanization. Soon Mennonites became prominent patrons of the arts in the Netherlands. Numerous artists, poets, and writers from among their ranks achieved lasting fame. But the Enlightenment spirit of rationalism and secularism was also a part of these developments, and by 1837 there were only 15,300 members left in the Netherlands. Late-nineteenth- and twentieth-century developments resulted in another increase in membership.

The early pattern of survival through withdrawal from society led to numerous migrations. Records indicate that emigration from the Netherlands eastward to Hamburg and along the coast to Danzig (present-day Gdańsk) began as early as 1534. Eventually large settlements developed in the Vistula delta. In 1788, migrations began from there to the Ukraine. By 1835 some 1,600 families had settled on Russian lands. By 1920 this population had grown to 120,000. But migration began again, this time from Russia beginning in the 1870s, primarily to North America.

A similar pattern prevailed among the Swiss and South German Mennonites. Many escaped Swiss persecution by migrating to the Palatinate or to central Germany. Others immigrated to the United States and Canada, beginning in 1663. The first permanent Mennonite settlement in the United States was established at Germantown, six miles north of Philadelphia, in 1683. Yet the total number of western European Mennonites coming to North America did not exceed 8,000, which, along with the approximately 55,000 immigrants from Prussian, Polish, and Russian lands, contributed to a core immigration to North America of no more than 70,000 up to the mid-1980s. There have also been migrations from North America, primarily from Canada to Mexico, Paraguay, Bolivia, and other Latin American locations. Thus pilgrimage has been central to Mennonite identity.

While Mennonites are noncreedal and affirm the Bible as their final authority for faith and life, they have written numerous confessions throughout their history. Chief among these are the Brotherly Union (1527) and the Dordrecht Confession of Faith (1632). In these the nature of the church as a believing, covenanting, caring, and obedient fellowship is central, as would be in keeping with the vision of restoring the New Testament church. The importance of the new birth and the authority of the Bible are stressed. Peace, including absolute pacifism, is considered an integral part of the gospel and, therefore, part of the discipleship of the believer. This discipleship is possible within the context of an Arminian theology, which acknowledges free will rather than Augustinian determinism. The second Adam, Christ, has undone the damage of the first Adam, making possible a gradual transformation of the disciple's life into the image of Christ himself. Ethics is a part of the Good News. Grace is necessary for discipleship rather than being antithetical to it. The believer who has experienced this grace is ready to receive baptism as a covenanting member of the "Believers' Church," a term commonly used since the 1950s to refer to noninfant baptizers.

Later Developments. Partly through migration and natural increase, but particularly through twentieth-century missionary activities, Mennonites were scattered across the globe by the late twentieth century. In 1984 their total membership was approximately 700,000. The Mennonite World Conference, begun in 1925, meets every five or six years for fellowship and the sharing of ideas, as well as for worship and celebration. It is not a delegate conference, and no decisions binding upon world membership are made.

The extent to which contemporary Mennonites hold to the doctrines of early Anabaptism varies from nation to nation, from group to group, and even from congregation to congregation. Mennonites do form regional and national conferences, but they are basically congregational in polity. The Amish, who split off from Swiss and Alsatian Mennonites in 1693–1697, as well as the Hutterites and some conservative Mennonites, do not form conferences. Historically, pietism, more than other socioreligious movements, has influenced Mennonite theology; fundamentalism has also had an impact in North America. Both movements strengthen the inner, personal, and experiential aspect of faith but weaken social concern, pacifism, and the inherent church-world dualism of the sixteenth century. An enthusiastic recovery of the "Anabaptist vision," led by Harold S. Bender (1897–1962), has modified these influences since the 1940s.

Anabaptists Four Centuries Later (Kauffman and Harder, 1975) provides a profile of late-twentieth-century North American Mennonite religious attitudes and practices. In relation to two doctrinal orthodoxy scales established in the study, 90 percent of the respondents chose the most orthodox response on a liberal-orthodox continuum. About 80 percent of the members could identify a specific conversion experience. The practice of daily personal prayer ranged from a low of 73 percent in one conference to a high of 82 percent in another. More than 80 percent reported regular Sunday school participation, with teenagers having the highest rating. Fewer than 2 percent of the membership had experienced divorce or separation. Some 85 percent considered sexual intercourse before marriage as always wrong. The early emphasis on church-world dualism, pacifism, not taking oaths, and church discipline was affirmed by a range of from 60 to 80 percent, depending upon the conference.

This religious stance is nurtured through worship, attendance at denominational schools, devotional practices, small-group Bible study, and involvement in mission and service projects. Church buildings are generally functional and relatively austere. Worship services are usually sermon-centered. Most congregations enjoy singing, often *a cappella*. The Lord's Supper is celebrated two to four times annually. Some congregations practice the rite of foot washing.

Numerous liberal arts colleges are maintained in North America; they were established originally to train workers for church vocations. Seminaries, Bible schools, secondary schools, and other church institutions are maintained by Mennonites around the world as political and economic conditions permit. Retirement centers, community mental health centers, and medical and disaster aid services are maintained particularly in North America and Europe. The concern for united help for needy people around the world led to organization of the Mennonite Central Committee (MCC) in North America in 1920. A Dutch Mennonite relief agency had been organized two hundred years earlier. In 1983, the MCC had a cash and material aid budget in excess of $25 million, of which over $20 million was spent abroad and the balance on projects in North America. In the same year, a total of 944 workers were involved in fifty-five countries. Approximately one-third of these workers were non-Mennonite.

These activities are a direct extension of the Mennonite conviction that word and deed must be one and that love must be visible. It may, however, also be that these and related activities serve the less altruistic function of legitimizing the social significance and usefulness of a traditionally pacifist and persecuted people. Nevertheless, most Mennonites are deeply concerned about the futility of war and nuclear weapons, as well as about global poverty and the need for peaceful steps toward economic and social justice. These concerns are part of the total global mission to which Mennonites continue to feel committed.

BIBLIOGRAPHY

The standard reference work in English is *The Mennonite Encyclopedia*, 4 vols. plus index, edited by Harold S. Bender and C. Henry Smith (Scottdale, Pa., 1955–1959). Nelson P. Springer and A. J. Klassen have compiled a helpful bibliography, the *Mennonite Bibliography, 1631–1961,* 2 vols. (Scottdale, Pa., 1977). A revised edition of *An Introduction to Mennonite History,* edited by me (Scottdale, Pa., 1981), provides a basic account of the entire Anabaptist and Mennonite movement worldwide from the sixteenth century to the present. J. Howard Kauffman and Leland Harder's *Anabaptists Four Centuries Later* (Scottdale, Pa., 1975) is a statistically rich and well-interpreted study of Mennonite religious attitudes and practices at the time of its publication. A particularly useful volume for a country-by-country study of world Mennonitism is the *Mennonite World Handbook,* edited by Paul N. Kraybill (Lombard, Ill., 1978).

CORNELIUS J. DYCK

MERCIER, DÉSIRÉ JOSEPH (1851–1926), a leading figure in Roman Catholic neoscholastic philosophy at the end of the nineteenth century and Cardinal Primate of Belgium (1906–1926). Born 21 November 1851 in Braine-l'Alleud, near Waterloo, Mercier studied philosophy and theology at Malines and earned a licentiate in theology at Louvain University (1877). Subsequently, he studied psychiatry in Paris.

Ordained a Roman Catholic priest in 1874, Mercier became a staunch supporter of Pope Leo XIII's call for a revival of Thomistic thought in the encyclical *Aeterni patris* (1879). Initially a professor of philosophy at the Malines seminary in 1877, Mercier then became the first holder of a new chair for Thomist philosophy at Louvain University in 1882. He soon sought papal approbation for a new institute at Louvain, and in 1889 Leo XIII approved the Institut Supérieur de Philosophie with Mercier at its head. Calling former students together from around the globe, he assembled an international group of disciples.

Working in opposition to Mill's positivism, and above all to neo-Kantian idealism, Mercier became a major figure in the development of Roman Catholic neoscholastic thought, which sought to mediate between modern natural science and traditional Thomistic metaphysics. While neoscholastic thought of the nineteenth century was concerned mainly with questions of epistemology and the soul-body relationship and locked its responses to these problems into a rigid anti-Kantian tradition, Mercier strove to make Thomistic philosophy dependent upon the thought of his time: to see the "new" in the "old." His main area of concentration was psychology, and in 1892 he founded the first experimental laboratory at his institute in that discipline; later laboratories, emphasizing his regard for experimental methods, followed in cosmology, chemistry, and physics.

In contrast to most Roman Catholic thinkers of his time, Mercier saw philosophy as distinct from theology, and above all as an enterprise that should be free of all apologetics. Without abandoning all tradition, he sought to imbue philosophy with the same ethic of investigation that marked other university disciplines; philosophy must address the people, their times, and their problems. Even when dealing with such questions as truth and certitude, Mercier appealed to human experience. This led to his system of "illationism," which admitted that truth and certitude came from intellectual reflection, but that the content of such abstract thought always had its origins in concrete experience. Though this direction produced much controversy in neoscholastic circles, it was unable to sustain itself as a "school" at Louvain University. Mercier gave expression to his thought in a series of textbooks (his *Course in Philosophy*) that dealt with logic, psychology, metaphysics, and the criteria for truth and certitude (1892–1899). In addition, he founded the influential *Revue néo-scolastique de philosophie* (1894), in which many of the movement's most important debates were carried out.

Appointed archbishop of Malines in 1906, Mercier was created a cardinal by Pius X in 1907. Though never a leading figure in the controversy of modernism that rocked the Roman Catholic church at the beginning of the twentieth century, he did issue a famous Lenten pastoral letter in 1908 against the work of George Tyrrell (1861–1909), a prominent Irish modernist thinker; his letter prompted a vitriolic but brilliant rejoinder by Tyrrell in his *Medievalism* (1908). As a pastorally concerned leader of his diocese, Mercier was deeply involved in the spiritual life and development of both his clergy and the laity; indeed, he sought greater cooperation between both groups as well as advances in social justice. Though Mercier never became a strong political figure in Belgium—his attachment to French culture hindered his understanding of the Flemish and their problems—he did become a figurehead for the Belgian people during the German occupation of World War I (1914–1918), strengthening their morale through sermons and pastoral letters. This proved so effective that the Germans placed him under house arrest, which earned him great prestige among the Belgian people and much praise from the Allies after the war.

Mercier's final years after World War I were dedicated to more universal problems, particularly those of church reunion. He founded the Institute of the Monks of Union at Chevetogne in Belgium in order to further reunion and reconciliation with the Eastern churches and made perhaps his most influential and lasting effort in hosting and participating in the famous "Malines Conversations" (1921–1925). Suggested by Lord Halifax (Charles Lindley Wood, 1839–1934), these meetings were concerned with aiding the mutual understanding and relations between the Roman Catholic and Anglican churches. Mercier's most famous moment came in the fourth session when he presented his paper on "The English Church United Not Absorbed," in which he proposed that the archbishopric of Canterbury be made a patriarchate, that the Roman code of canon law not be imposed in England, that England be allowed its own liturgy, and that all of the historical English sees be left in place while the newly erected Roman Catholic sees (1850) be suppressed. These suggestions generated much controversy and opposition in Rome, and Mercier's death on 26 January 1926 in Brussels effectively meant the end of the "Conversations."

BIBLIOGRAPHY

Works by Mercier. Mercier's main work, the *Cours de philosophie*, 4 vols. (Louvain, 1894–1899): vol. 1, *Logique* (1894); vol. 2, *Métaphysique générale, ou Ontologie* (1894); vol. 3, *La psychologie* (1899); and vol. 4, *Critériologie générale, ou Théorie générale de la certitude* (1899), represented his sequence of philosophy courses given at the Higher Institute for Philosophy at the University of Louvain. Many of Mercier's writings and public utterances were collected in the *Œeuvres pastorales* (Brussels and Louvain, 1911–1929), in seven volumes. Finally, his famous exchange of letters with the commandant of the German occupation forces during World War I appeared as *La correspondance de S.E. cardinal Mercier avec le gouvernement général allemand pendant l'occupation, 1914–1918*, edited by Fernand Mayence (Brussels, 1919); in English translation as *Cardinal Mercier's Own Story* (New York, 1920). The most complete bibliography of Mercier's published writings should be consulted in the commemorative volume *Le cardinal Mercier, 1851–1926* (Brussels, 1927), pp. 341–372.

Works about Mercier. Of the several biographies of Mercier, one may profitably consult John A. Gade's *The Life of Cardinal Mercier* (New York, 1934). A full-scale and scholarly biography of Mercier, taking advantage of the many particular studies that have appeared since his death, and which would place him more accurately in the troubled and multifaceted context of his time, still must be written. Among the most important of these investigations are Alois Simon's major studies, particularly *Le cardinal Mercier* (Brussels, 1960), which provide an assessment of Mercier's contributions both to renewed scholasticism and the general philosophical conversation at the turn of the century in Europe. For new information concerning Mercier's ecumenical activities, one should consult Roger Aubert's "Les conversations de Malines: Le cardinal Mercier et le Saint-Siège," *Bulletin de l'Academie Royale de Belgique* 53 (1967): 87–159; and R. J. Lahey's "The Origins and Approval of the Malines Conversations," *Church History* 43 (September 1974): 366–384.

GARY LEASE

MEREZHKOVSKII, DMITRII (1865–1941), chief proselytizer of the religious renaissance in Russia in the early twentieth century. Scion of an eminent Saint Petersburg aristocratic family, Merezhkovskii was educated at the Third Classical Gymnasium and at the Historical-Philological Faculty of the University of Saint Petersburg (1884–1888). Interested in metaphysical and existential issues, he dissented from the positivism and materialism of his contemporaries and searched, all his life, for a new and all-encompassing higher ideal.

In the 1890s, he championed mystical idealism as the bridge between the atheistic intelligentsia and the believing peasantry, campaigned against mandatory social didacticism in literature, introduced Russians to French symbolism and the philosophy of Nietzsche, and reintroduced them to classical antiquity and the Renaissance. Versatile and erudite, he expressed his ideas in poetry, literary criticism, essays, novels, and plays. Major works of this period are *Symbols* (1892), a book of poems; "On the Causes of the Decline of Russian Literature and on the New Trends in Poetry" (1893), an influential essay sometimes considered the manifesto of Russian symbolism; *New Verse* (1896); and *The Outcaste* (1895), later retitled *Death of the Gods*, a historical novel about Julian the Apostate. Attracted by pagan values of earthly happiness and Christian ideals of personal immortality, and unable to choose between them, by 1896 Merezhkovskii had concluded that Christianity and paganism were two halves of a yet unknown higher truth.

Around 1900, Merezhkovskii advanced a new interpretation of Christianity, designed to synthesize the "truth of heaven" and the "truth of the earth," and based on the second coming of Christ and on a forthcoming third testament. Proclaiming a new religious consciousness that stressed the human need for faith and religious quest, he dismissed historical Christianity as obsolete and rejected the asceticism, altruism, and self-denial preached by Russian Orthodox Christianity. Major works of this period include *Tolstoy as Man and Artist with an Essay on Dostoevsky* (1901–1902), which treats these writers as exemplars of the religious principles of the flesh and the spirit respectively; *Birth of the Gods: Leonardo da Vinci* (1901); and *Antichrist: Peter and Alexis* (1905). Together with *Julian the Apostate*, the last two comprise his historical trilogy, *Christ and Antichrist*.

To disseminate their views (sometimes called God-seeking views), Merezhkovskii, his wife Zinaida Gippius, and Dmitrii Filosofov founded the Religious Philosophical Society of Saint Petersburg (November 1901–April 1903). The society, which featured debates between intellectuals and clergymen on burning issues of the day, became a focal point of the religious renaissance. The minutes of the meetings were published in the Merezhkovskiis' review, *Novyi put'* (New Path, 1902–1904), founded as a showcase for the new trends in art and thought. Permitted to reopen in 1907, after the Revolution of 1905, branches of the society were later founded in Moscow and in Kiev. Through these public activities and through his writings, Merezhkovskii's ideas reached a wide audience, challenged traditional verities, inspired other reinterpretations of Christianity, and even stimulated the Bolshevik secular religion of "God-building," which featured worship of the collective spirit of humanity instead of God.

The Revolution of 1905 led Merezhkovskii to consider social and political questions. He interpreted it as the first stage of a great religious revolution that would usher in the kingdom of God on earth. He denounced autocracy as a tool of the Antichrist, and advocated religious community, viewed as a kind of Christian anarchism, as the solution to social conflict. Hostile to Marxist materialism and collectivism, he claimed that socialism stifles creativity and argued that Jesus Christ is the supreme affirmation of the individual. Major works of this period are *Dostoevsky: Prophet of the Russian Revolution* (1906), *The Coming Ham* (1906), and *Not Peace but a Sword* (1908). He opposed Russia's entry into World War I, welcomed the February Revolution, but regarded the Bolshevik regime as the reign of the Antichrist. He cooperated with attempts to overthrow it, both before and after his emigration in 1919, until his death in Paris, in 1941.

BIBLIOGRAPHY

Most of Merezhkovskii's important works can be found in *Polnoe sobranie sochinenii*, 24 vols. (Saint Petersburg, 1911–1914). Works in English translation include *Death of the Gods* (London, 1901), *The Romance of Leonardo da Vinci* (London, 1902), *Peter and Alexis* (London, 1905), *The Menace of the Mob* (New York, 1921), and an abridged version of *Tolstoi as Man and Artist* (Westminster, England, 1902). Useful secondary literature includes my own *D. S. Merezhkovsky and the Silver Age* (The Hague, 1975) and Charles H. Bedford's *The Seeker: D. S. Merezhkovskiy* (Lawrence, Kans., 1975).

BERNICE GLATZER ROSENTHAL

MERIT.

[*This entry comprises three articles, an overview and two separate discussions of the role of merit in Buddhist and Christian soteriology.*]

An Overview

The terms *merit* and *merit making* are used in connection with religious practices that have the calculated aim of improving the future spiritual welfare of oneself or others. However, the number of contexts in which a specific terminology such as *merit* (Lat., *meritum*) or its older analogue, the Buddhist *puṇya* (Pali, *puñña*) has developed are surprisingly few. It is probably for this reason that most well-known systematic or phenomenological studies of religion have little or nothing to say on the subject. Elsewhere, the use of these terms in writing on religion is widespread but extremely sporadic, occurring mainly in discussions of generally related subjects such as judgment, reward and punishment, grace, and salvation.

In religion west of India, the earliest specific teaching on merit, or merits, is found in rabbinic Judaism, although merit was not the subject of formal definitions. From the third century CE, the concept played an increasingly significant role in Western Christianity; it reached a high point in the Middle Ages, only to be drawn into the vortex of Reformation debate on grace and the relation between works, faith, and man's justification in the sight of God.

Recent years have seen a smooth and indeed justifiable transfer of the English term *merit* (as well as of European equivalents such as the German *Verdienst*) to that area of Buddhist practice and interpretation covered by the Sanskrit term *puṇya* and its equivalents. The term *merit making* implies an observational, analytic stance not usually found in studies of merit in Christianity, which have been more doctrinal or theological in tone. Nevertheless, interesting parallels can be drawn between Buddhism and Christianity as regards merit. Elsewhere, the relationships are much less clear, and comparative questions have to be suggested much more loosely insofar as they are relevant at all. The following observations should be understood as indicating the general context in which specific teachings on merit have arisen in rabbinic Judaism, Buddhism, and Christianity.

India and China. That religious action has practical effects in this existence and others has been widely assumed in the religious systems of Asia, though with many variations. In the Indian context, the common assumption of post-Vedic religion is that of a series of existences, each conditioned by the *karman*, or accrued causal momentum, of the previous existence. Since *karman* can be either bad or good, there is room for improvement through religious practice or moral effort. Thus, loose analogies exist with other religious teachings on reward and punishment, religious works, and spiritual development. The main characteristic of Indian assumptions on the subject, whether Hindu, Jain, or Buddhist, is that karmic cause and effect are in principle self-regulating, not subject to divine decision, arbitration, or satisfaction.

In Jainism, seven "fields of merit" *(puṇyakṣetra)* are

recognized as conducive to a pleasantly advanced rebirth. These have been presented by Padmanabh S. Jaini in *The Jaina Path of Purification* (Berkeley, 1979) as seven categories of meritorious activity: donating an image, donating a building to house an image, having the scriptures copied, giving alms to monks, giving alms to nuns, assisting laymen in their religious or practical needs, assisting laywomen similarly. The concept of *karman* should not in itself, however, be regarded as amounting to a doctrine of merit. This would push the analogy beyond its limits.

In Chinese religion, two relevant strands are discernible. First, there is the tradition of self-discipline and cultivation, in Confucian form oriented socially and pragmatically, in Taoist form linked to the achievement of supernormal powers, longevity, and even immortality. The idea of achieving supernormal physical and psychical powers through strenuous self-discipline is also present in Indian religions, including Buddhism, and hence in all cultural areas influenced by China and India. At the same time, this motivation for religious practice and achievement is not directly related to any concept analogous to merit.

Second, Chinese religion also knows the theme of postmortal judgment, presided over by Yen-lo (counterpart of the Indian god Yama) as god of death and ruler of the hells. Aided by his assistants, Yen-lo brings out the inexorable law of *karman*, and many illustrated works depict this as a warning to the living. (See, for example, the illustrated volumes *Religiöse Malerei aus Taiwan: Katalog and Die Höllentexte,* publications 1 and 2 of the Religionskundliche Sammlung der Philipps-Universität Marburg, 1980, 1981.) Religious imagery of this kind, though clearly related, does not entail a distinct doctrine of merit except insofar as it is influenced by Buddhism.

Egypt and Ancient Near East. In ancient Egypt, the diffusion of the cult of Osiris as lord of the underworld who had died, been judged, and risen again, provided the first common focus for postmortal expectation and concern. Elaborate funerary rites were accompanied by preparations for judgment before Osiris assisted by assessors. The candidate for new life asserted his innocence of numerous moral transgressions and saw his own heart weighed on scales against a feather representing truth in the sense of divine order *(maat).* Gradually, efforts were made to organise the outcome of the judgment in advance by preparing in advance lists of good deeds and declarations of innocence. This process was ritualized and commercialized through the sale of appropriate rolls of text to be filled in with names before death, modern scholars have named these texts collectively *The Book of Going Forth by Day.* On the other hand, these phenomena may be regarded as the earliest indication of attempts to establish an individual's worth—in effect to "make merit" for him, in order to achieve a desired effect after death.

The idea of merit apparently did not develop in Mesopotamia, where notions of existence after death remained shadowy and pessimistic. Nor did Canaanite or early Hebrew views of death include a postmortal goal toward which the individual could work. The Hebrew concept of She'ol as a silent, forgotten abode beneath the earth was related at least in type to the Babylonian.

The clearly delineated cosmological dualism of Iranian religion gave prominence to the alternatives awaiting the individual after death. The spiritual position of the soul was determined in accordance with its behavior before departure from the body. In principle, the thinking is analogous to the Egyptian conceptions mentioned above, for there is evidence of attempts to influence the judgment. Eschatologically, Iranian ideas strongly influenced developing Judaism, so that She'ol became the place of postmortal punishment, while up to seven heavens were enumerated as abodes of pleasure and bliss.

Theistic Religions. A theistic worldview in the Abrahamic tradition does not necessarily entail a detailed doctrine of merit, as may be seen in the cases of the Qumran community, very early Christianity and, later, Islam. In both the teachings of Qumran and of the New Testament, the concept of calculable merit is entirely lacking. What is required is total, inward obedience to the law, or will, of God. The subsequent development of Christian teachings on merit has been variously described and interpreted. Historical priority must be ascribed to the rabbinic teachings on merit, or merits, which, in a transposed form, underlay Paul's interpretation of the death of Jesus. (This relationship has been skillfully delineated by W. D. Davies in *Paul and Rabbinic Judaism,* 2d ed., London, 1955, pp. 227–284.)

The rabbinic doctrine of merit, though articulated in detail in the first four centuries of the common era, is based on two fundamental ideas which reach much further back in Jewish tradition. These are, first, that keeping the Mosaic covenant with God (i.e., observing the Torah), will lead to blessing and welfare and, second, that the responsibility and benefit of this covenant are essentially corporate and pass from generation to generation. Stated negatively, disobedience leads to punishment in the form of social or political suffering, but this punishment can be moderated by credit accumulated by previous generations. Looking forward, the idea of caring for one's children spiritually as well as physically was a motivating force for assiduousness in religious duty and charitable works. The justifiableness of a man, his standing before God in these respects, is summed up in the term *zakkut.*

As Davies points out, this line of thought is not without variations: some rabbis taught that the dividing of the waters at the Exodus took place on account of the merits of Abraham, or the combined merits of Abraham, Isaac, and Jacob, while others stressed the meritorious faith of the Israelites at the time. The underlying spirit of the teaching is neatly expressed in Arthur Marmorstein's summary of the ideas of Rabbi Yanna'i: "A man who kindles light in daytime for his friend when it is light, what benefit has he derived? When does he obtain any advantage from light? In case he kindles it in the night-time, in darkness. The affection Israel has shown in the wilderness was kept for them from that time, from the days of Moses" (Marmorstein, 1920, p. 17). From regarding the keeping of the Torah as meritorious, and beneficial for future generations, it was not far to the idea that God gave the Torah so that merit could be achieved or even the idea that the whole of creation was designed to this end.

As to life beyond death, reference to this was by no means lacking, and it was considered possible that some individuals, through lack of merit, might fail to be rewarded. Nevertheless, the calculation of one's credits and debits was always regarded as ultimately in the hands of God, so that while relatively good men might tremble, even the wicked might hope. In practical terms, merit was typically considered to accrue through "faith, charity, hospitality, the circumcision, Sabbath and festivals, the study of the Torah, repentance, the Holy Land, the Tabernacle, Jerusalem, the tithe, and the observances in general" (ibid., p. 65).

With Islam, it was, and is, expected that realizable duties will be fulfilled. However, God, and only God, knows what is actually possible for each individual; moreover, he is patient of human weakness. Thus, insofar as it is possible, the pilgrimage to Mecca is required of Muslims. This may be regarded as a negative doctrine of merit in that every Muslim has to assess whether or not he or she is able to make the pilgrimage. While Islam has always recognized that some acts are not strictly required but are nevertheless praiseworthy, any assessment of human behavior for the purpose of achieving salvation was quickly ruled out by the strong emphasis on the preeminent knowledge and grace of God, which amounted to predestination. A broadly similar doctrinal structure was to appear, in the Christian world, in Reformation theology, and in Jansenism.

Comparative Reflections. A simple typology of religions with respect to concepts of merit and broadly related aspects of religiosity may be delineated in four parts.

First, it should be noted that much religion simply has not included the concept of merit, especially when notions of the future are shadowy, when a future existence is prepared for by elaborate funerals for royalty only, or when life after death is understood in any case to be the same for everybody. Thus, primal religions—even, for example, the highly developed Japanese Shintō—presuppose neither a radical dividing of the ways based on merit nor any elaborate path of cumulative spiritual development for the individual. Such religions naturally bear powerful religious values, such as a sense of cosmological orientation and belonging. Transactional religiosity, however, is directed in this context towards proximate, this-worldly, goals such as social and economic well-being, the avoidance of disaster and sickness or, in a modern differentiated economy, personal welfare and success.

Second, when clear-cut conceptions of future existence have developed, we see an extension of transactional religiosity into the future, as in Egyptian and Iranian religions, or, in a very different way, in Indian religion. The same holds for Chinese religion, though not without influence from Indian Buddhism. Such transactionalism may or may not be morally differentiated. The key feature here is that an element of future-directed management and even calculation is introduced to cope with an assumed judgment to come or with implications of the present for future existences. In principle, responsibility lies with the individual, although he may seek the assistance of priests, or, in the interesting variation of rabbinic Judaism, draw on the worthy performance of previous generations. Islam also belongs to this type, although in this case there is little interest in calculation and a great reliance on God's compassionate appraisal of what could realistically be expected from each individual in the circumstances of life.

The third type is represented above all by Buddhism and Christianity, although these emerged from quite different assumptions. Here we see that specific doctrines of merit arose at the point of intersection between transactional religiosity and soteriological concern. The natural, or primal, community is left on one side, and the possibility of the transfer of merit from transcendental or intermediate beings is envisaged. Interestingly, this latter idea did not go unopposed in Theravāda Buddhism, where it was criticized on ethical grounds. At the same time, the recommendation of merit-creating activities by the priesthood becomes normal.

Fourth, Buddhism and Christianity are similar not only in having produced an individualized soteriology based, at times, on a doctrine of merit. They have also both seen movements within the tradition which radically internalized the reception of spiritual assistance or grace. For Christianity, this is connected with the Reformation; for Buddhism, such movements are associated with the teachings of the Japanese patriarchs Hōnen (1133–1212) and, above all, Shinran (1173–1262). The latter argued, for example, that there was no value in reciting the Nembutsu (calling on the name of Amida Buddha) on behalf of the deceased because as a human work it could not benefit them in any way. All that was possible was reliance on the grace of Amida Buddha to effect rebirth in the Pure Land in the western heavens. Thus, the soteriological focus was internalized and the idea of merit was transformed from within. These subjectivizing trends within the Buddhist and Christian traditions, though influential, have not become dominant, and, broadly speaking, the vocabulary of merit continues to play a distinctive role in both.

[*See also* Judgment of the Dead.]

BIBLIOGRAPHY

Davies, W. D. *Paul and Rabbinic Judaism,* 2d ed. London, 1955.

Jaini, Padmanabh S. *The Jaina Path of Purification.* Berkeley, 1979.

Marmorstein, Arthur. *The Doctrine of Merits in Old Rabbinical Literature.* London, 1920.

Religiöse Malerei aus Taiwan: Katalog and *Die Höllentexte,* Publications 1 and 2 of the Religionskundliche Sammlung der Philipps-Universität Marburg, 1980, 1981.

MICHAEL PYE

Buddhist Concepts

The notion of merit (Skt., *puṇya* or *kuśala;* Pali, *puñña* or *kusala*) is one of the central concepts of Buddhism, and the practice of merit making is one of the fundamental activities of Buddhists everywhere.

The idea of merit is intimately bound up with the theory of *karman,* the Indian law of cause and effect. According to this theory, every situation in which an individual finds himself is the result of his own deeds in this or a previous lifetime, and every intentional act he now performs will eventually bear its own fruit—good or bad—in this or a future lifetime. Thus present felicity, wealth, physical beauty, or social prestige may be explained as the karmic reward of past deeds of merit, and present suffering, poverty, ugliness, or lack of prestige may be attributed to past acts of demerit. In the same manner, present meritorious deeds may be expected to bring about rebirth in a happier station as a human being or as a deity in one of the heavens, and present demeritorious deeds may result in more suffering and in rebirth as an animal, a hungry ghost (Skt., *preta*), or a being in one of the Buddhist hells. A mixture of meritorious and demeritorious acts will bear mixed karmic results.

This basic understanding of the workings of merit and demerit can be traced back to the time of the Buddha, or the sixth to fifth centuries BCE. It received its fullest elaboration later, however, in the vast collections of *jātaka*s (stories of the Buddha's previous lives), *avadāna*s (legends), and *ānisaṃsa*s (tales of karmic reward), which were and continue to be very popular in both Hīnayāna and Mahāyāna Buddhism.

Merit-making Activities. There are, according to the Buddhists themselves, many ways of making merit. One of the most comprehensive listings of these is the noncanonical catalog of "ten meritorious deeds" (Pali, *dasakusalakamma*), which has been widely influential in South Asia. It comprises the following practices:

1. Giving *(dāna)*
2. Observing the moral precepts *(sīla)*
3. Meditation *(bhāvanā)*
4. Showing respect to one's superiors *(apacāyana)*
5. Attending to their needs *(veyyāvacca)*
6. Transferring merit *(pattidāna)*
7. Rejoicing at the merit of others *(pattānumodana)*
8. Listening to the Dharma, that is, the Buddha's teachings *(dhammasavaṇa)*
9. Preaching the Dharma *(dhammadesanā)*
10. Having right beliefs *(diṭṭhijjukamma)*

It is noteworthy that most of the deeds on this list (with the possible exception of the ninth, which is more traditionally a monastic function) can be and are practiced both by Buddhist laypersons and by monks. It is clear, then, that merit making in general is a preoccupation not only of the Buddhist laity (as is sometimes claimed) but also of members of the monastic community, the *saṃgha.* In this regard, it is interesting too that meditation—a practice that is sometimes said to be an enterprise not concerned with attaining a better rebirth but aimed solely at enlightenment—is also seen as a merit-making activity and is engaged in as such by both monks and laypersons.

Another noteworthy item on this list is *sīla,* the observance of the moral precepts. For the laity, this consists of following the injunctions against killing, stealing, lying, sexual misconduct, and intoxication. On certain occasions, however, *sīla* may also involve the voluntary acceptance of three additional precepts, sometimes counted as four, against eating after noon, attending worldly amusements, using ornaments or perfumes, and sleeping on a high bed. Monks, who by their very status are thought to be more filled with merit than the laity, are expected to observe all the above precepts at all times; in addition, there is a tenth injunction for monks against the handling of money.

The most meritorious practice on this list, however, is giving, or *dāna.* In many ways, this is the Buddhist act of merit *par excellence.* Monks engage in it by giving the Dharma to laypersons in the form of sermons or advice, or by the example of their own lives. Laypersons practice it by giving to the monks support of a more material kind, especially food, robes, and shelter. The ideology of merit thus cements a symbiotic relationship between the *saṁgha* and the laity that has long been one of the prominent features of Buddhism.

Not all lay acts of *dāna* make equal amounts of merit. The specific karmic efficacy of any gift may depend on what is given (quantity and quality can be significant), how it is given (i.e., whether the gift is offered with proper respect, faith, and intention), when it is given (food offerings, for example, should be made before noon), and, especially, to whom it is given. Although *dāna* may sometimes be thought to include gifts to the poor and the needy, offerings made to the *saṃgha* are seen as karmically much more effective. Thus, making regular food offerings to the monks, giving them new robes and supplies, funding special ceremonies and festivals, building a new monastery, or having a son join the *saṃgha* are all typical lay acts of *dāna.* These activities share a common focus on the monks and are consistently ranked as more highly meritorious than other types of social service; they are even more highly valued than observation of the moral precepts.

Metaphorically, acts of merit are seen as seeds that bear most fruit when they are planted in good fields of merit (Skt., *puṇyakṣetra*), and the most fertile field of merit today is the *saṃgha.* This obviously has had tremendous sociological and economic implications. In Buddhist societies, the *saṃgha* often became the recipient of the excess (and sometimes not so excessive) wealth of the laity, and thus from its roots it quickly grew into a rather richly endowed institution.

Traditionally, however, the best "field of merit" was the Buddha himself. The model acts of *dāna* that are recounted in Buddhist popular literature often depict gifts that are made to him. Today, in addition to donations to the monks, offerings are made to images and other symbolic representations of the Buddha and are still thought of as highly meritorious. The roots of *dāna,* therefore, lie not only in a desire to do one's duty to the *saṃgha* but also to express one's devotion to the faith in the Buddha. This experiential cultic side of merit making has often been overlooked, yet it is frequently emphasized in popular Buddhist literature.

Aims of the Merit Maker. In addition to expressing individual faith and devotion, the merit maker may be said to be interested in three things. First, an individual wants to obtain karmic rewards for himself in this or the next lifetime. Thus, for example, he might wish, by virtue of his acts of merit, to enjoy long life, good health, and enormous wealth, and never to fall into one of the lower realms of rebirth where suffering runs rampant, but to be reborn as a well-to-do person or a great god in heaven. Many such statements, in fact, may be found in the inscriptions left by pious Buddhists throughout the centuries to record their meritorious deeds, and in anthropologists' descriptions of present-day merit-making practices.

Second, the merit maker may also be interested in enlightenment. It is sometimes claimed that this is not the case, that beyond receiving karmic rewards the merit maker has no real ambition for *nirvāṇa.* To be sure, in the oldest strata of the Buddhist canon *nirvāṇa* is not thought to be attainable by merit making alone, but Buddhist popular literature soon tended to take a different view. In the Avadānas, for example, even the most trivial acts of merit are accompanied by a vow (Skt., *praṇidhāna*) made by the merit maker to obtain some form of enlightenment in the future. This enlightenment may be a long time in coming, but when it does it is portrayed as the fruit of the merit maker's vow and act of merit, and not as the result of any meditative endeavor.

In present-day Theravāda practice, these same vows take the form of ritual resolves to be reborn at the time of the future Buddha Maitreya and to attain enlightenment at that time. Far from rejecting the possibility of *nirvāṇa,* then, the merit maker, by means of a *praṇidhāna,* can link an act of merit to that very soteriological goal.

The Transfer of Merit. Third, the merit maker may also wish to share his or her merit with others, especially with members of the family. By clearly indicating whom the merit maker intends to benefit by a good deed, an individual can transfer the merit accrued to that other person. This does not mean that one thereby loses some of one's own merit; on the contrary, one makes even more, since the transfer of merit is in itself a meritorious act.

Such sharing of merit is sometimes thought to be in contradiction to one of the basic principles of *karman,* according to which merit making is an entirely individual process whereby one reaps only what one has sown oneself. While this may be correct theoretically, and while it is true that the transfer of merit is not mentioned explicitly in the earliest canonical sources, the practice quickly became very common. It had always been the case, of course, that an individual could undertake an act of merit on behalf of a larger social group.

Thus, the housewife who gives food to a monk on his begging round makes merit not only for herself but for her whole family. Buddhist inscriptions and popular literature, however, testify also to the wishes of donors to have their merit benefit somewhat more remote recipients, such as a deceased parent or teacher, the suffering spirits of the dead, or, more generally, all sentient beings.

Probably one of the motivations for such sharing of merit was the desire to continue, in a Buddhist context, the Brahmanical practice of ancestor worship. The transfer of merit by offerings to the *saṃgha* simply replaced the more direct sacrifice of food to the spirits of the dead.

The literalness with which this transfer was sometimes understood is well illustrated by the story of the ghosts of King Bimbisāra's dead relatives. They made horrible noises in his palace at night because they were hungry, for the king had neglected to dedicate to them the merit of a meal he had served to the *saṃgha*. Therefore he had to make a new offering of food to the monks and properly transfer the merit. Once fed, the ghosts no longer complained.

It is worth noting in this story the crucial role played by the field of merit—in this case the *saṃgha*—in successfully transmitting the benefits of meritorious deeds to beings in the other world: the monks act as effective intermediaries between two worlds. They continued to enjoy this role in China and Japan, where their efficacy in transferring merit to the ancestors was much emphasized.

Merit Making and the Bodhisattva Ideal. Although the doctrine of the transfer of merit has its roots in the Hīnayāna, it was most fully developed in the Mahāyāna. There it became one of the basic practices of the *bodhisattva* (Buddha-to-be), who was thought to be able freely to bestow upon others the merit accrued during a greatly extended spiritual career.

Actually, there are two stages to a *bodhisattva*'s meritorious career. In the first, while seeking enlightenment, he amasses merit by good deeds toward others. In this, his actions are not much different from those described in the Jātakas and attributed to the Buddha in his former lives. In the second stage, the *bodhisattva* (or, in Pure Land Buddhism, the Buddha Amitābha), infinitely meritorious, dispenses merit to all beings.

After initially awakening in himself the mind intent on enlightenment (Skt., *bodhicitta*), the *bodhisattva* begins his career with the path of accumulation of merit *(saṃbhāramārga)*, during which he performs great acts of self-sacrifice over many lifetimes and begins the practice of the perfections of giving, morality, patience, energy, meditation, and wisdom. In all of this, his actions are governed by his vow for enlightenment *(praṇidhāna)*. Unlike the vows of the Hinayanists, however, those of a *bodhisattva* can be quite elaborate (especially in Pure Land Buddhism), and generally involve his willingness to postpone individual attainment of final *nirvāṇa* in order to be able to lead all sentient beings to enlightenment.

As a result of such altruism, certain great *bodhisattvas*, such as Avalokiteśvara, Mañjuśrī, Kṣitigarbha, or Samantabhadra, came to be seen as having stored up virtually inexhaustible supplies of merit, which they can now dispense to sentient beings in order to allay their sufferings. The mechanism by which this is done is that of the transfer of merit, but this is now seen as a more total and compassionate act than in the Hīnayāna. Not only does the *bodhisattva* confer on others the benefit of specific deeds, but he also seeks to share with them his entire store of merit, or, to use a different simile, his own actual roots of merit *(kuśalamūla)*. In this, all desire for a better rebirth for himself has disappeared; the only sentiment remaining is his great compassion *(mahākaruṇā)* for all sentient beings in their many states of suffering.

[*See also* Bodhisattva Path *and* Karman, *article on* Buddhist Concepts.]

BIBLIOGRAPHY

Four kinds of sources are most useful in considering the practice of merit making in Buddhism.

First, there are anthologies of popular Buddhist stories illustrating the workings of merit and demerit. These are too vast and numerous to be described here, but they include the Jātakas (tales of Buddha's former lives), the Avadānas (legends about the lives of individual Buddhists), and innumerable stories of karmic rewards either included in commentaries on canonical works or gathered in separate collections. For translations of examples of each of these three types, see *The Jātaka*, 6 vols. (1895–1905; London, 1973), edited by E. B. Cowell; *Avadāna-çataka: Cent légendes bouddhiques*, translated by Léon Feer (Paris, 1891); and *Elucidation of the Intrinsic Meaning: The Commentary on the Peta Stories*, translated by U Ba Kyaw, edited by Peter Masefield (London, 1980).

Second, there are the descriptions and discussions of merit-making practices in present-day Buddhist societies by anthropologists and other observers in the field. For a variety of these works, which also present significant interpretations of merit making, see, for Sri Lanka, Richard F. Gombrich's *Precept and Practice* (Oxford, 1971), chapters 4–7; for Thailand, Stanley J. Tambiah's "The Ideology of Merit and the Social Correlates of Buddhism in a Thai Village," in *Dialectic in Practical Religion* (Cambridge, 1968), edited by Edmund Leach; and, for Burma, Melford E. Spiro's *Buddhism and Society* (New York, 1970).

Third, there are the inscriptions left by merit makers in India and elsewhere to record their acts of merit. Various examples of these invaluable and fascinating documents may be found in Dines Chandra Sircar's *Select Inscriptions Bearing on Indian History and Civilization*, vol. 1, *From the Sixth Century B.C. to the Sixth Century A.D.*, 2d ed. (Calcutta, 1965).

Finally, there are the more specialized scholarly studies of specific aspects of merit making. Only a few of these can be mentioned here. For a fine discussion of the various connotations of the word for "merit," see Jean Filliozat's "Sur le domaine sémantique de puṇya," in *Indianisme et bouddhisme: Mélanges offerts à Mgr. Étienne Lamotte* (Louvain, 1980). For two very helpful studies of the transfer of merit in Hīnayāna Buddhism, see G. P. Malalasekera's "'Transference of Merit' in Ceylonese Buddhism," *Philosophy East and West* 17 (1967): 85–90, and Jean-Michel Agasse's "Le transfert de mérite dans le bouddhisme pāli classique," *Journal asiatique* 226 (1978): 311–332. The latter is an especially suggestive article and has an English summary. For a social scientist's view of the way in which merit making combines with other forces in defining social roles and hierarchies, see L. M. Hank's "Merit and Power in the Thai Social Order," *American Anthropologist* 64 (1962): 1247–1261. Finally, for a clear discussion of the place of merit in the development of the *bodhisattva* ideal, see A. L. Basham's "The Evolution of the Concept of the Bodhisattva," in *The Bodhisattva Doctrine in Buddhism* (Waterloo, Ontario, 1981), edited by Leslie S. Kawamura.

JOHN S. STRONG

Christian Concepts

The term *merit* derives directly from the Latin *meritum* as used by theologians in Western Christianity beginning with Tertullian (160?–225?). Earlier Christian apologists had stressed the importance of postbaptismal works as a preparation for eternal life, and indeed this line of thought can be traced back in a general way to various New Testament writings. The important question as to whether the third-century teaching on merit emerged naturally out of early Christianity or whether it was a distortion, or at best a countertheme, is variously assessed by Catholic and Protestant theologians. Thus, in an article on merit (1962), Günther Bornkamm emphasized the absence of any concept of merit in the New Testament, while his co-writer Erdmann Schott roundly declared that "only the Roman Catholic church developed a doctrine of merit." However, both of these writers recognize the presence of those elements in early Christian writings, including the New Testament, which writers with a Catholic viewpoint see as the basis for the development of the doctrine. These elements are none other than judgment, reward, and punishment. Thus according to Anselm Forster (1965) references to such themes are so numerous that the apostolic fathers and the apologists simply brought the idea of merit into their proclamation of salvation as circumstances required, without any need for systematic reflection at that time.

The New Testament writers certainly made much use of this complex of ideas, as seen for example in the vision of judgment in *Matthew* 25. However, such ideas do not in themselves amount to or necessarily require the development of a doctrine of merit, as may be observed in parallel situations in the history of religions. Historically, there certainly was no general belief in the New Testament writings that some sufficient degree of merit either should or even could be accumulated for any purpose. The main thrust of early Christian teaching was rather to overcome any calculating religiosity in favor of a trusting reliance on the promises of God and spontaneous, uncircumscribed works of love. This holds good both for the teaching of Jesus himself, as far as this can be precisely ascertained, and also for the teaching of the major theological exponents, John and Paul. A doctrine of merit as such did not clearly arise until the third century.

Patristic View of Merit. With Tertullian, well known for his legal metaphors, the doctrine of merit came into semiformal existence. He distinguished between good works as a source of merit and nonobligatory good works as a source of extra merit, thus introducing an element of calculation. He also taught that human sinners are required to render satisfaction to God, a satisfaction that could be fulfilled by the offering of merits. Other church fathers accepted Tertullian's teaching, above all with a view to the care of postbaptismal life within the church.

Thus Cyprian (c. 205–258), bishop of Carthage, taught that sins could be purged by charitable works and by faith. This did not refer to those sins contracted before baptism, for they were purged by the blood and sanctification of Christ. But, Cyprian says in *On Works and Charity*, "sic eleemosyne extinguet peccatum" ("as water extinguishes fire, so charitable work extinguishes sin") and "eleemosynis atque operationibus iustis" ("as the fire of Gehenna is extinguished by the water of salvation, so the flame of transgressions is assuaged by almsgiving and just works"). He goes on to say that God is satisfied by just works and that sins are purged by the merits of mercifulness *(misericordiae meritis)*. Indeed, by charitable works our prayers are made effective, our lives saved from danger, and our souls liberated from death.

Of importance for later understanding of the doctrine was the debate between Pelagius, Augustine, and others in the first part of the fifth century. Pelagius, whose teaching was current in Rome and North Africa, stressed the power of man through free will to choose and practice the good, and he viewed grace conveyed by the example and stimulus of Christ as a welcome but theoretically not absolutely essential extra. Augustine considered Pelagius's teaching to present a faulty doctrine of man and to render Christian salvation all but superfluous. For the present subject the debate is of importance in that it had the effect of subordinating teaching on merit to the doctrine of grace. Since Pelagianism was condemned as heretical at the councils of Milevum and Carthage (in 416 and 418), Augustine's treatment of the subject set the framework for later Western definitions and ultimately for the divergence that broke out at the Reformation.

It may be noted in passing that the concept of merit was never worked out in detail and did not become a matter of controversy in the Eastern (Orthodox) churches because the operation of divine grace and human free will were and are seen in terms of synergy. By this is meant a cooperation of powers that are unequal but both essential. Although human response and action are necessary within the event of salvation, the preeminent role of grace means that calculations are of no relevance. The perfect example of synergy is provided by Mary, honored as the mother of God *(theotokos)*.

Medieval and Reformation Views of Merit. In medieval Latin Christendom an increasingly carefully defined doctrine of merit was current. This doctrine was, with minor variations, consistent from Peter Abelard up until the Reformation. Both obligatory and nonobligatory (supererogatory) works were regarded as meritorious in the sense that they contributed, within the overall economy of divine grace, to the ensuring of salvation. Grace itself can be understood at various levels: all-important was *gratia praeveniens,* but Peter Lombard distinguished between the self-effective *gratia operans* and the *gratia cooperans* that assists in the creation of merit. Widespread in the Middle Ages was the distinction between acts that ensure divine recognition and acts that merely qualify for it at divine discretion. These two types of merit are referred to as condign merit *(meritum de condigno)* and congruent merit *(meritum de congruo)* respectively. However, the sovereignty of God was maintained by the teaching, for example of Thomas Aquinas, that while merit arises equally from free will and from grace, the effective status assigned to condign merit was itself still dependent ultimately on grace. The underlying idea here, not usually made explicit, is that the church in its teaching function can reliably assert the positive availability of grace in such circumstances. Some discussion centered on the possibility of regaining a state of grace through merit after committing deadly sin, which Bonaventure considered possible and Thomas impossible. Another aspect arose with John Duns Scotus, who emphasized the crucial role of the divine acceptance of merit over against the value inherent in the work itself. This permitted the assertion that God recognizes the merits of supernaturally assisted works within the economy of salvation rather than of those performed by man in his natural state simply because he so wishes. (For more details on these and other aspects of the medieval doctrine of merit, see Schott, 1962.)

The doctrinal subtlety of many medieval theologians was clearly directed toward safeguarding the principle of the prior, determinative grace of God over against any idea that salvation could be ensured by calculated acts on man's part. However, not all medieval Christians had the ability, or, in their often short and hard lives, the leisure, to appreciate these points. Since theology had a place for individual acts that might be meritorious, that is, of assistance in securing salvation rather than damnation, the common assumption was that some of these acts had better be performed. It was plainly believed that bad things had to be compensated for by good things if lengthy or eternal punishment was to be avoided, and this meant in daily religious life: penance, good works, and the sacraments. Thus salvation became for many a transaction, albeit a mysterious one. The sale of indulgences in respect of a plenary remission of sins may be regarded as an extreme example of this and was understandably criticized at the Reformation as an abuse. That the element of weighing, or paying, had become a standard feature of Western Catholic tradition, was evident also, however, in the large numbers of chantries endowed for masses to be said for the patron's benefit, via a transfer of merit, after his death.

The Reformation saw a massive reassertion of grace and a straightforward rejection of reliance on works of any kind. With Martin Luther the language of justification was central but was used paradoxically, as in Pauline literature, to refer to God's gracious justification of man through Christ, even though man himself is not able to stand before God in judgment. With this fundamental shift of emphasis, which became increasingly critical of current religious practice, the doctrine of merit related to works was swept away. Yet the vocabulary of merit did not immediately disappear. Indeed the traditional terminology of condign and congruent merit occurs in Luther's *Dictata super Psalterium* (Lectures on the Psalms) and serves as the basis for a gradual transposition of the concept of merited salvation into that of unmerited salvation (cf. Rupp, 1953, esp. pp. 138f.). Thus the idea of the insufficiency of merit or of works provided Luther at one and the same time with a polemical differentiation from the existing tradition of Western Christianity and an invitation to faith in the saving and transforming power of grace leading to good works as the fruit of Christian life. As far as these matters were concerned, the position of other reformers, including John Calvin with his formula *sola gratia* (by grace alone), was essentially similar. As a result, wholesale changes occurred in the practical forms of religion. At the same time the transactional aspect was concentrated in the doctrine of atonement through the merits of the death of Christ.

Merit in Catholicism. The positive significance of merit in the context of the religious life was reaffirmed for Western Catholicism at the Council of Trent (1545–1563), the relevant definitions and thirty-three anathemas being contained in the sixteenth chapter of the text for the sixth session: "De fructu justificationis, hoc est, de merito bonorum operum, deque ipsius meriti ratione" (Denzinger, 1965). The argument is tightly linked to the concept of justification, which is viewed as a process within the believer that leads to meritorious good works. Since the merit of good works was considered to bring about specific results contributing to the increase of grace in the present life, to eternal life itself, and to the increase of glory, room was left for the continued pastoral management of religious life in terms of relative achievement, within the overall context of divine grace. This has essentially been the basis of Catholic religiosity ever since.

Thus the marketing of indulgences was abandoned, but the attainment of an indulgence through devotional practice (e.g., on "the first nine Fridays") or through special sets of prayers (Our Fathers, Ave Marias, etc.), leading to a reduction of the number of days required to be spent in purgatory (by 500, 1,000, etc.), has continued down to the present. Moreover such remissions can, via the communion of saints and the work of Christ himself, be applied to the suffering of souls already in purgatory, through prayer, fasting, alms, and the saying of Mass. As one popular nineteenth-century work put it: "She [the church] appears before the tribunal of the judge, not only as a suppliant, but also as the stewardess of the treasure of the merits of Christ and his saints, and from it offers to him the ransom for the souls in purgatory, with full confidence that he will accept her offer and release her children from the tortures of the debtor's prison" (F. J. Shadler, *The Beauties of the Catholic Church*, New York, 1881, p. 404). One could hardly hope to find a clearer statement both of the idea of the transfer of merit and of the transactional manner in which merit is, or can be, understood. Other presentations content themselves with a loose statement of the need for both grace and works, thereby allowing elaboration at the pastoral level. Thus a modern catechism declares: "We can do no good work of ourselves toward our salvation; we need the help of God's grace," but also: "Faith alone will not save us without good works; we must also have hope and charity" (Catholic Truth Society, *A Catechism of Christian Doctrine*, London, 1971, pp. 22f.). The consciousness of ordinary Catholic believers may be summed up in the view that while one cannot ensure one's own salvation one is certainly expected to make a contribution.

In recent years theological controversy about merit in the context of Christianity has lost much of its sharpness for three reasons. First, the theme is subsumed, for Protestants, into the greater theme of faith and grace over against works. From this point of view relying on merits or merit is simply a variant form of relying on works and therefore hardly requires separate consideration. Second, although the concept of merit is retained by Catholics, it is usually made clear, at least in formal accounts, that the prior grace of God is an essential condition. Although, admittedly, this does not meet Protestant objections to all and every form of reliance on works, it does mean that from the Catholic side, too, attention is directed fundamentally toward man's position in the overall economy of divine grace. Third, and this applies to Protestant and Catholic theologians alike, interest is directed toward other issues such as the historical and social responsibilities of Christianity, questions arising through the encounter with non-Christian traditions, and philosophical reflections about the very nature of religious language. In such a perspective, while theological viewpoints regarding merit remain distinct, it is not currently considered to be a matter requiring intense or urgent debate.

[*See also* Atonement, *article on* Christian Concepts; Free Will and Predestination, *article on* Christian Concepts; Grace; *and* Justification.]

BIBLIOGRAPHY

Bornkamm, Günther, Erdmann Schott, et al. "Verdienst." In *Die Religion in Geschichte und Gegenwart*, 3d ed., vol. 6, pp. 1261–1271. Tübingen, 1962.

Cyprian. *Quellen zur Geschichte des Papsttums und des römischen Katholizismus*. Edited by Carl Mirbt. Tübingen, 1911. Includes the Latin text of Cyprian's *On Works and Charity*.

Denzinger, Heinrich, ed. *Enchiridion Symbolorum*. Freiburg, 1965. Includes definitions formulated by the Council of Trent. See especially pages 376ff.

Forster, Anselm. "Verdienst (Systematisch)." In *Lexikon für Theologie und Kirche*, vol. 10, cols. 677–680. Freiburg, 1965.

Jedin, Hubert. *A History of the Council of Trent*, vol. 2. Translated by Ernest Graf. London, 1960.

Raemers, W. *Indulgenced Prayers to Help the Holy Souls*. London, 1956.

Rupp, E. G. *The Righteousness of God: Luther Studies*. London, 1953.

Ware, Timothy. *The Orthodox Church*. Harmondsworth, 1963.

Michael Pye

MERLIN. The origins of Merlin, the magician, prophet, and guardian of the legendary British king Arthur and a central figure in medieval Arthurian romance in both French and English, are to be found in a number of early Welsh poems and related material in Latin. The name *Merlin* was created by the twelfth-century pseudohistorian Geoffrey of Monmouth, who described the conception of "a fatherless boy" by a nun who had been impregnated by an incubus in the South Wales town of Caerfyrddin (modern-day Carmarthen). The omniscient boy's advice to King Vortigern suggests that Geoffrey modeled his Merlin on an earlier Welsh story of the wonder-child Ambrosius. Although two later exploits, the removal of Stonehenge from Ireland to England and the disguising of Uter Pendragon as Gorlois so that he might sleep with the latter's wife (a ruse that results in the conception of Arthur), are not found in the earlier sources, Merlin's major role as a political prophet in Geoffrey's *Historia regum Britanniae* is traditional.

The prophet's birth at Caerfyrddin is a sure sign that he is in fact the Welsh Myrddin, whose name is variously spelled *Merddin, Merdin,* and *Myrtin,* which Geoffrey changed to *Merlin* to avoid unfortunate associations with the French *merde.* There are extant a large number of medieval Welsh poems claimed to have been composed by a fictional Myrddin. The majority of these are *post hoc* vaticinations and contemporary comments on political events attributed to the famed prophet, who had acquired this role by the tenth century, as the poem *Armes Prydein* (c. 935) shows, a role he was to retain throughout the Middle Ages. There may also be discerned, however, a substratum of story to which other pre-twelfth-century poems allude and which can be reconstituted from these and other sources. Myrddin, a member of the court of King Gwenddoleu, became insane at the Battle of Arfderydd (fought in 573 in modern-day Cumbria). He fled in terror from King Rhydderch of Strathclyde to the Caledonian Forest (in the Scottish Lowlands), and lived there the life of a wild man (his Welsh epithet is *Wyllt,* "wild"). He was befriended by his sister, or lover, Gwenddydd, to whom he prophesied events at court. These traditions were used by Geoffrey of Monmouth in his poem *Vita Merlini,* which is designed to correct the nontraditional elements and to supplement the picture he had earlier given in his *Historia.* His two Merlins appeared to contemporaries as distinct characters named Merlinus Ambrosius (in the *Historia*) and Merlinus Silvestris (in the *Vita*), but it is better to regard the distinction as being due to Geoffrey's imprecise knowledge of the genuine tradition at the time of his writing of the *Historia.*

The northern Myrddin is found under the name *Lailoken* in the twelfth-century *Vita Kentigerni* of Joceline of Furness, and he has an analogue in the ninth-century Irish character Suibhne Geilt. Lailoken's tale was relocated in South Wales, and, according to the claims of A. O. H. Jarman, the madman was given a new name derived from *Caerfyrddin.* Rachel Bromwich, stressing Myrddin's status as a poet in Welsh bardic tradition, suggests that he was a sixth-century historical poet, none of whose work is extant but who developed legendary features, as happened to Taliesin. There is little doubt that the sagas of two characters have influenced one another, and they are linked in a pre-twelfth-century dialogue poem which may have been known to Geoffrey of Monmouth, who used the device of dialogue in the *Vita.* Although Welsh literature does not show the influence of later Arthurian romance in the character of Myrddin, late medieval Welsh poetry does contain allusions to his imprisonment and death and to erotic elements in the legend.

BIBLIOGRAPHY

A good and concise account of the development of the theme of Myrddin/Merlin is presented in *The Legend of Merlin* (Cardiff, 1960) by A. O. H. Jarman. Consult, also, Jarman's article entitled "A oedd Myrddin yn fardd hanesyddol," *Studia Celtica* 10/11 (1975–1976): 182–197. This article is written in response to Rachel Bromwich's piece, "Y Cynfeirdd a'r Traddodiad Cymraeg," *Bulletin of the Board of Celtic Studies* 22 (1966): 30–37. A thorough review of the important issues is found in *Trioedd Ynys Prydein: The Welsh Triads,* 2d ed. (Cardiff, 1978), which was edited and translated by Bromwich.

BRYNLEY F. ROBERTS

MERTON, THOMAS (1915–1968), Roman Catholic monk, author, and poet. Merton pursued a career that may be divided into three distinct phases: secular, monastic, and public. The secular career encompasses the first twenty-six years of his life and culminates with his entrance into the abbey of Gethsemani, Kentucky, in 1941. The basic elements that influenced his later life were set in place during this period. Merton was born on 31 January 1915 in Prades, France, the first child of artist Ruth Jenkins Merton of Zanesville, Ohio, and artist Owen Merton of Christchurch, New Zealand. The family moved to New York City the next year to escape World War I. The loss of his mother while still a child, his father at age sixteen, and a younger brother in World War II, contributed to Merton's sense of the tragic contingency of human life and, possibly, to his decision to enter monastic life. The influence from two parents who were artists and instinctive pacifists bore fruit in their son's pursuits as writer, poet, and prophet of nonviolence.

Merton attended school in the United States, Bermuda, France, and England before commencing higher education. He entered Clare College of Cambridge University on scholarship and completed his undergraduate education at Columbia University in New York. His friendships with Professor Mark Van Doren, the Pulitzer Prize poet, and fellow student Robert Lax, the future poet, helped to develop his already existing interests in mysticism, poetry, and monasticism. He converted to Roman Catholicism in 1938, completed an M.A. in literature from Columbia in 1939, and entered the abbey of Gethsemani in 1941 while working on a never-completed Ph.D. thesis on Gerard Manley Hopkins and teaching English at Saint Bonaventure University in New York State.

The second phase of Merton's career is his life as a monk of the Cistercian Order of the Strict Observance. The rigor of this life is characterized by perpetual silence, a lifelong vegetarian diet, and many hours of daily prayer starting at 2:00 AM. The purpose of this regimen is the development of a contemplative life. Many of those who knew Merton well believe he became a mystic during these years. The last three years of his life were also lived as a hermit, removed from the communal life of the monastery.

The third phase of Merton's life, the public career, is somewhat coincident with the second and is marked by an intense involvement in writing, social protest, and Asian spirituality. The most famous of his sixty books is *Seven Storey Mountain*, an autobiography about a personal search that brings him from unfocused activism to contemplation and from a life of self-indulgence to self-discipline. The writings of Merton include eight volumes of poetry and some six hundred articles.

If a career in writing was unconventional, Merton's involvement in social protest was even less part of the monastic model. He objected vehemently to the United States' involvement in the Vietnam War, the nuclear arms race, violations of the rights of black Americans, and the dehumanizing effects of technology. This protest caused him difficulty at times with readers who favored a pietistic style of writing, with church superiors, and with members of his monastic community. He persevered in putting his views forward, however, believing that mystics owed their contemporaries the value of their own unique witness.

In the final years of his life, Merton was committed to Hindu and Buddhist spiritual wisdom without diminishing his attachment to Catholic Christianity. Zen Buddhism, most especially, appealed to Merton because of its emphasis on experience rather than doctrine. Merton searched for God through participation in the ancient spiritualities of Asia on a long journey to the East that was his personal pilgrimage and a metaphor of his life. He died of accidental electrocution in Bangkok, Thailand, on 10 December 1968.

BIBLIOGRAPHY

The authorized biography of Thomas Merton, Michael Mott's *The Seven Mountains of Thomas Merton* (Boston, 1984), is an exhaustively researched and yet readable study. It may suffer from lack of a central interpretive theme but sets a standard for subsequent work on Merton. *Merton: A Biography* by Monica Furlong (New York, 1980) is a reliable account, although little attention is given to Merton's monastic vocation or his involvement with Asian spirituality. *Thomas Merton: Monk and Poet*, by George Woodcock (New York, 1978), is a perceptive analysis of the creative dynamics in Merton's literary work. The author, himself a poet and novelist, is sensitive to the religious dimension of Merton's life. My own book, *The Human Journey: Thomas Merton, Symbol of a Century* (New York, 1982), draws out the correlations between Merton's personal life and the tensions and aspirations of the twentieth century. It traces the appeal of Merton to his capacity to assimilate the problems and promise of his own time.

ANTHONY PADOVANO

MESOAMERICAN RELIGIONS. [*This entry consists of seven articles:*

Pre-Columbian Religions
Preclassic Cultures
Classic Cultures
Postclassic Cultures
Contemporary Cultures
Mythic Themes
History of Study

The first article presents a survey of the broad sweep of the cultural and religious history of Mesoamerica before the coming of the Europeans in the early sixteenth century. The next three articles treat in a more detailed manner the religious systems prevalent during the three main periods into which indigenous Mesoamerican civilization has been divided by historians. The fifth article discusses contemporary Mesoamerican religious systems, in which traditional patterns of belief and practice perdure within the region's many varieties of syncretic folk Catholicism. The sixth article examines motifs common throughout the region's mythic traditions. The final article discusses the historical development of the study of religion within the larger field of Mesoamerican studies. For discussion of religious themes in the artistic traditions of Mesoamerica, see Iconography, *article on* Mesoamerican Iconography.]

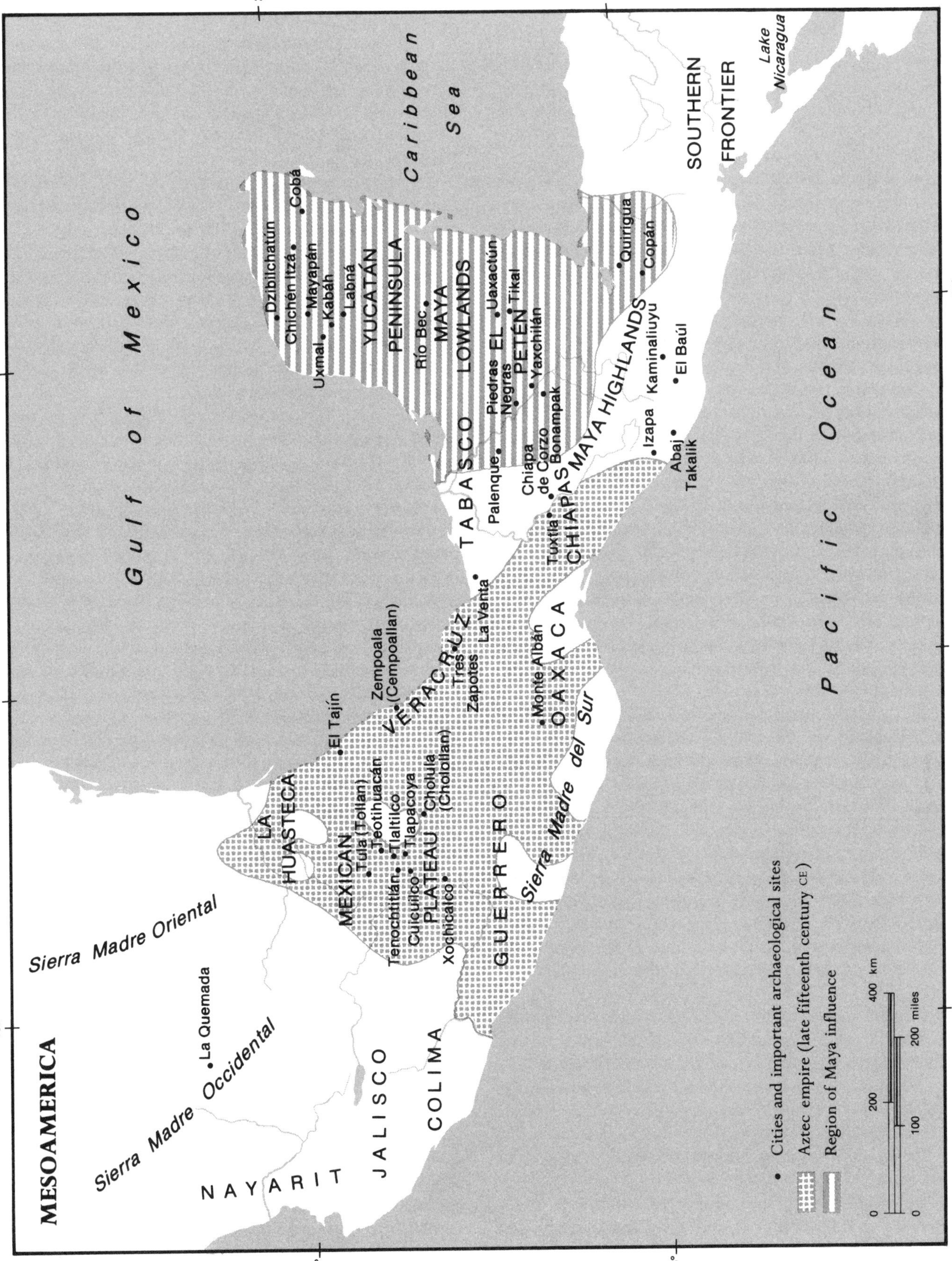
MESOAMERICA
Gulf of Mexico
Caribbean Sea
Pacific Ocean
Lake Nicaragua
SOUTHERN FRONTIER
Dzibilchatún
Chichén Itzá
Cobá
Mayapán
Uxmal
Kabáh
Labná
YUCATÁN PENINSULA
Río Bec
MAYA LOWLANDS
Uaxactún
Tikal
EL PETÉN
Piedras Negras
Yaxchilán
Bonampak
Palenque
Quiriguá
Copán
MAYA HIGHLANDS
Kaminaliuyu
El Baúl
Izapa
Abaj Takalik
TABASCO
Chiapa de Corzo
Tuxtla
CHIAPAS
La Venta
Tres Zapotes
VERACRUZ
Zempoala (Cempoallan)
El Tajín
Monte Albán
OAXACA
Sierra Madre del Sur
LA HUASTECA
MEXICAN PLATEAU
Tula (Tollan)
Teotihuacán
Tlatilco
Tlapacoya
Cholula (Chollollan)
Tenochtitlán
Cuicuilco
Xochicalco
GUERRERO
Sierra Madre Oriental
Sierra Madre Occidental
La Quemada
NAYARIT
JALISCO
COLIMA
21°
15°
90°
96°
102°
Cities and important archaeological sites
Aztec empire (late fifteenth century CE)
Region of Maya influence
0 200 400 km
0 100 200 miles

Pre-Columbian Religions

Through several millennia and up to the present, complex forms of indigenous belief and ritual have developed in Mesoamerica, the area between North America proper and the southern portion of isthmic Central America. The term *Mesoamerica*, whose connotation is at once geographical and cultural, is used to designate the area where these distinctive forms of high culture existed. There, through a long process of cultural transformation, periods of rise, fall, and recovery occurred. On the eve of the Spanish invasion (1519), Mesoamerica embraced what are now the central and southern parts of Mexico, as well as the nations of Guatemala, Belize, El Salvador, and some portions of Honduras, Nicaragua, and Costa Rica.

Distinctive forms of social organization began to develop in this area from, at the latest, the end of the second millennium BCE. Parallel to these social and economic structures, various forms of religion also flourished. Most contemporary researchers agree that Mesoamerican religion, and the Mesoamerican high cultures in general, developed without any significant influence from the civilizations of Asia, Europe, and Africa. But while it is generally accepted that the various forms of high culture that appeared in Mesoamerica shared the same indigenous origin, a divergence of opinions exists regarding the question of how the various religious manifestations are ultimately interrelated.

According to some scholars (e.g., Bernal, 1969; Caso, 1971; Joralemon, 1971, 1976; Léon-Portilla, 1968; Nicholson, 1972, 1976), there was only one religious substratum, which came to realize itself in what are the distinct varieties of beliefs and cults of peoples such as the Maya, the builders of Teotihuacán, the Zapotec, the Mixtec, the Toltec, the Aztec, and others. A different opinion (maintained by, among others, Kubler, 1967, 1970) postulates the existence of various religious traditions in ancient Mesoamerica. Those adhering to this view nonetheless admit to reciprocal forms of influence and even to various kinds of indigenous religious syncretism.

In the following presentation I shall postulate the existence of what is essentially a single religious tradition in Mesoamerica, without, however, minimizing the regional differences or any changes that have altered the continuity of various elements of what can be labeled "Mesoamerican religion."

Earliest Religious Manifestations. Because of lack of evidence, our knowledge cannot extend back to the religious concerns of the earliest inhabitants of Mesoamerica (c. 25,000 BCE). Nevertheless, some archaeological findings show that the early hunter-gatherers had at least some metaphysical or religious preoccupations. Reference can be made to their rock art: paintings and petroglyphs, some of which date to about 10,000 BCE and several of which suggest religious or magical forms of propitiation through hunting, fishing, and gathering (Bosch Gimpera, 1964).

Objects that are more obviously religious in function date only to 2500–1500 BCE, when the earliest village-type settlements appeared in Mesoamerica. By that time, after a slow process of plant domestication that probably began around 6000 BCE, new forms of society had begun to develop. It had taken several millennia for the hunter-gatherers to become settled in the first small Mesoamerican villages. In the evolution of Mesoamerican culture, what has come to be known as the Early Formative period had commenced.

Those living during this period employed an ensemble of objects indicative of their beliefs about afterlife and of their need to make offerings to their deities. At different sites throughout Mesoamerica (especially in the Central Highlands, the Oaxaca area, and the Yucatán Peninsula), many female clay figurines have been found in what were the agricultural fields. Scholars hypothesize that they were placed there to propitiate the gods and ensure the fertility of crops. Burials in places close to the villages (as in Asia, Africa, and Europe) also appear, accompanied by offerings such as vestiges of food and pieces of ceramics. A large proportion of the human remains are those of children or young people.

Olmec High Culture. Villages of agriculturists and potters, who evidently were already concerned with the afterlife and with "sacred" fertility, became gradually more numerous in Mesoamerica. Villages established in hospitable environments experienced significant population growth. Among these, the communities in the area near the Gulf of Mexico in the southern part of the Mexican state of Veracruz and neighboring Tabasco underwent extraordinary changes around 1200 BCE. Archaeological findings in the centers now called Tres Zapotes, La Venta, and San Lorenzo reveal that a high culture was already developing and, with it, a strong religious tradition.

Olman ("land of rubber"), the abode of the Olmec, stands out as the first high culture in Mesoamerica. Its large buildings mainly served religious purposes. The center of La Venta, with its mud-plastered pyramids, its semicylindrical and circular mounds, carved stone altars, tombs, stelae, and many sculptures, anticipates the more complex ensembles of religious structures that proliferated centuries later in Mesoamerica. The central part of La Venta, built on a small island in a swampy area sixteen kilometers from the point where the Tonala

River empties into the Gulf of Mexico, was no doubt sacred space to the Olmec. The agriculturist villagers who had settled in the vicinity of La Venta were already developing new economic, social, political, and religious institutions. If many continued their subsistence activities, especially agriculture and fishing, others specialized in various crafts and arts, commercial endeavors, the defense of the group, and—of particular significance—the cult of the gods. Government was probably in the hands of those who knew how to worship the gods.

Olmec religious iconography. Olmec religious representations have been described as "biologically impossible" (Joralemon, 1976, p. 33). Human and animal features are combined in these representations in a great variety of forms. Early researchers pointed out the omnipresence of a jaguarlike god, who seemingly had the highest rank in the Olmec pantheon. One early hypothesis stated that the main traits of what later became the prominent Mesoamerican rain god derived from these jaguarlike representations.

A more ample and precise approach to Olmec iconography has led P. David Joralemon (1971, 1976) and Michael D. Coe (1972, 1973) to express the opinion that the variety of presentations of the jaguarlike god portray distinct though closely associated divine beings. A number of divine identities integrate various animal and human attributes. The animal features most frequently used in combination with the basically human-shaped face are a jaguar's nose, spots, and mighty forearms, a bird's wings, a serpent's body, and a caiman's teeth. Thus one finds beings that might be described as a human-jaguar, a jaguar-bird, a bird-jaguar-caiman, a bird-jaguar-serpent, a jaguar-caiman-fish, a human-bird-serpent, a bird-caiman-serpent, and a bird-mammal-caiman (Joralemon, 1976, pp. 33–37).

Iconographic comparisons between representations of these kinds and other religious Mesoamerican effigies from the Classic (c. 0–900 CE) and the Postclassic periods (900–1519 CE) reveal that the nucleus of the Mesoamerican pantheon was already developing in the Olmec epoch. One god is sometimes represented as a kind of dragon, frequently featuring a jaguar's face, a pug nose, a caiman's teeth, a snarling, open, cavernous mouth with fangs projecting from the upper jaw, a flaming eyebrow, various serpentine attributes, and at times a hand/paw/wing linked to the occipital region. Other, more abstract, motifs include crossed-band designs in the eyes, crossed bands and a dotted bracket, four dots and a bar, and the symbols for raindrops and maize.

This god, probably the supreme Olmec deity, was worshiped in his many guises, as the power related to fertility, rain, lightning, earth, fire, and water. In him various forms of duality—an essential feature in the Classic and Postclassic Mesoamerican universe in both its divine and human aspects—can be anticipated. Prototypes of other gods that were later worshiped among the Maya, the peoples of the central highlands, and those of Oaxaca, can also be identified in the Olmec pantheon. Among these are the Maize God, the One Who Rules in the Heavens, the Old Lord (protector of the sacred domestic hearth), and the Serpent, who has birdlike attributes and is a prototype of the Feathered Serpent.

The Olmec thought of their gods as endowed with interchangeable traits and attributes. Thus a kind of continuum existed in the sphere of the divine, as if the ensemble of all the godlike forms were, essentially, mere manifestations of the same supreme reality. This distinctive character of the divine—represented through ensembles of symbols, often shifting from one godlike countenance to another—perdured, as will be seen, in the religious tradition of Mesoamerica. That continuity, subject to variations of time and space, did however undergo innovations and other kinds of change. One important change derived from the relationship that was to develop between the perception of the universe of the divine and the art and science of measuring periods of time.

Origins of the calendar. The earliest evidence of calendrical computations—inscriptions discovered in places influenced by Olmec culture—also conveys other related information. Of prime importance is the indication that the political and social order not only was closely linked to the universe of the divine but was also conceived in terms of the measurement of time, all of whose moments are bearers of destiny. In the Stelae of the Dancers at Monte Albán I (epoch I) in Oaxaca (c. 600 BCE), where Olmec influence is present, the human figures, described "as an expression of political and ritual power" (Marcus, 1976, p. 127), are accompanied by hieroglyphs denoting names of persons (probably both human and divine), place names, and dates.

The calendar was doubtless the result of assiduous astronomical observation. Its early diffusion throughout various parts of Mesoamerica implies an old origin (probably 1000–900 BCE); it later came to determine all divine and human activities. Man is represented in several Olmec monuments, such as the Basalt Altar 4 in La Venta, as emerging from the mouth or cave of the supreme "dragon" deity, signifying man's birth into a universe where time moves in sacred rhythms. The recurring Olmec symbols—quadruple and quintuple patternings (indicative of the four corners and the center of the earth), stylized maize plants, and other motifs—seem to reveal that a prototype of what became the classic Mesoamerican image of sacred space had been developed as far back as Olmec times. [*See also* Calendars, *article on* Mesoamerican Calendars, *and* Olmec Religion.]

Maya Religion. Olmec civilization acted as a ferment of many cultural transformations. Archaeological research (Piña Chan, 1982) has identified the traces of its ample diffusion. Besides numerous sites excavated in the Olmec heartland of Veracruz-Tabasco, many villages of the Early Formative type in the Central Plateau, in the western region along the Pacific coast in Oaxaca, and in the land of the Maya show evidence of having undergone processes of rapid change. (The Maya territories include the Yucatán Peninsula and parts of the present-day Mexican states of Tabasco and Chiapas, as well as Guatemala, Belize, and parts of Honduras and El Salvador.)

Antecedents of cultural grandeur. Some notable findings have highlighted the processes that culminated in the grandeur of Maya high culture. They reveal that preoccupation with the sacred cycles of time resulted in extraordinary achievements as early as several decades BCE. One of the findings is Stela 2 of Chiapa de Corzo, Mexico, where a date corresponding to 9 December 36 BCE is expressed in what modern researchers describe as the calendar's Long Count (see below). Two other inscriptions, registered in the same Long Count, have been found in places closer to the ancient Olmec heartland, one on Stela C at Tres Zapotes, Veracruz (31 BCE), and the other on the Tuxtla (Veracruz) Statuette (162 CE). The deeply rooted Mesoamerican tradition of measuring the flow of time, a tradition whose oldest vestiges appear in Monte Albán I, Oaxaca (c. 600 BCE), became more sophisticated around 200–100 BCE with the complexities and extreme precision of the Long Count. To understand its functioning and multiple religious connotations, one needs to be familiar with two basic systems—the 365-day solar calendar and the 260-day count—described later in this article.

Other vestiges that have been unearthed point to cultural changes that were taking place during this period, called the Late Formative. In the Pacific plain of the southernmost Mexican state of Chiapas and in adjacent parts of Guatemala, several centers boasted impressive religious buildings, temples, altars, stelae with bas-reliefs, and a few calendrical inscriptions. Archaeologists rightly consider them to be immediate antecedents of Maya culture. The centers of Izapa, Abaj Takalik, and El Baúl are outstanding for their monuments. Stela 2 at Abaj Takalik contains a carved image of a celestial god and an inscription of a date, which, though partly illegible, is expressed in the system of the Long Count. In El Baúl, other calendrical instriptions correspond to the year 36 CE. Maya culture—one of the variants of Mesoamerican civilization—was about to be born.

Chronology and sources. A Classic period (c. 250–900 CE) and a Postclassic period (900–1519 CE) have been distinguished in the cultural development of the Maya. The most magnificent of their religious and urban centers flourished during the Classic period: Tikal, Uaxactún, and Piedras Negras in Guatemala; Copán and Quiriquá in Honduras; Nakum in Belize; Yaxchilán, Palenque, and Bonampak in what is now the Mexican state of Chiapas; Dzibililchaltún, and Cobá, Kabáh, Labná, Chichén Itzá, Uxmal, Río Bec, and others in the Yucatán Peninsula. At these sites, sophisticated forms of spiritual development emerged. Even Diego de Landa, the Spanish friar who in the sixteenth century set fire to many of the written records of the Maya, could not refrain from remarking on "the number, the grandeur, and the beauty of their buildings" (Landa, trans. Tozzer, 1941, p. 170), especially those devoted to the cult of their gods. Besides their architecture, which included among its techniques the corbel vault, Maya sculpture, mural painting, bas-relief carving on stone stelae, stairways, lintels, panels, and plaques of jade deserve special mention. On them thousands of hieroglyphic inscriptions have been found, some related to the universe of the gods and others having more mundane historical content. These inscriptions at times accompany carved images of gods as well as of rulers and other dignitaries.

To compensate for the obscurities that still surround the spiritual achievements of the Classic period, one has to look for whatever is indicative of a cultural continuity in the Postclassic. From the latter period three pre-Columbian books, or codices, survive and, even more significantly, a considerable number of indigenous testimonies, in Yucatec-Maya, Quiché-Maya, and other linguistic variants, have come down to us in early transcriptions done by Maya priests or sages who survived the Spanish conquest and learned to use the Roman alphabet. Among these testimonies, the *Popol Vuh* (The Book of Counsel) of the Quiché-Maya, the several *Chilam Balam* books of the Yucatec-Maya, and the *Book of Songs of Dzitbalche* (from the Yucatán) stand out as conveyers of the religious wisdom of this remarkable people.

Maya image of the world. To approach the core of the religious worldview of the Classic Maya one has to analyze an ensemble of elements, some with antecedents in the Olmec culture, but enriched and often transformed. The most significant of these elements include the Maya's image of the earth and universe, their calendrical concerns and ideas about time, and the ultimate meaning of the divine and of man within their spatial and temporal universe.

In several Classic monuments, as well as in Postclassic books and other representations, the surface of the earth is conceived as being the back of a huge caiman with saurian, ophidian, and feline attributes that sometimes resemble those of the so-called Olmec Dragon. The monstrous creature appears surrounded by vast waters. In Palenque, in the Tablet of the Cross and the Tablet of the Foliated Cross, cosmic trees rise from the earth monster. In some representations, one sees a double-headed serpent in the sky. The creature also appears with other attributes of the Olmec Dragon such as crossed bands and various celestial symbols. The double-headed serpent covers and embraces the earth. It was this celestial serpent that, dividing the terrestrial monster into two parts, activated this universe and introduced life on earth. Thus a primeval duality presides over and gives rise to the universe.

The surface of the earth, as in the case of the Olmec prototype, is distributed into four quadrants that converge at a central point, the navel of the world. One finds in Classic inscriptions and Postclassic codices hieroglyphs for each of the world quadrants and their associated colors. Cosmic trees and deities reside in the "red east," "white north," "black west," "yellow south," and "green central point." Above and below the surface of the earth are thirteen heavens and nine underworld levels, where thirteen celestial gods and nine "lords of the night" have their respective abodes.

Maya deities. The comparative study of religious iconography, the contents of the three extant Pre-Columbian Maya codices, and the relatively numerous texts of diverse origin within this culture allow us to surmise that the idea of a divine duality was deeply rooted in Mesoamerican thought since at least the Classic period, if not since the Olmec. The Dual God resides in the uppermost of the celestial levels. In the *Popol Vuh* of the Quiché-Maya he-she is addressed both as E Quahalom ("begetter of children") and as E Alom ("conceiver of children"). In the first of the *Songs of Dzitbalche* appears the following reference to the father-mother god:

> The little yellowbird,
> and also the cuckoo,
> and there is the mockingbird,
> they all delight the heart,
> the creatures of the Father, god,
> so likewise the Mother,
> such as the little turtle dove . . .
> (Edmonson, 1982, p. 176)

Our Father/Our Mother has other names as well. There is evidence to identify him-her with the Postclassic Itzamná ("lizard house") the name probably referring to the primeval celestial and terrestrial, being of monstrous countenance, whose house is the universe. This supreme, creator god is invoked at times with the feminine prefix *Ix-*, as in Ix Hun Itzam Na. To him-her, that is, to the "begetter-conceiver of children," is ultimately attributed the creation of the earth, heavens, sun, moon, plants, animals, and, of course, man. As in the case of the Olmec nuclear deity, traits of caiman, bird, serpent, and jaguar can be perceived at times in the god's iconography.

The quadruple patterning expressed in certain Olmec monuments proliferated in Maya religious representations. The divine duality, "begetting and conceiving" children, develops a quadruple being—the various ensembles of gods that have to do with the four quadrants of the universe. The Red Itzamná appears in the east, the White in the north, the Black in the west, and the Yellow in the south. Other quadruple sets are the four Bacabs, supporters of the sky at the four corners of the world; the four Chacs, gods of rain; the four Pahuatuns, deities of wind; the four Chicchans ("owners of thunder"), godlike giant snakes; and the four Balams ("tigers") protectors of the cultivated fields.

Divine reality also permeates the upperworld and underworld levels. Itzamná is at once a celestial, a terrestrial, and an underworld god. The Oxlahum-ti-ku ("thirteen gods") rule in the thirteen heavens, and the Bolom-ti-ku ("nine gods") preside over the nine inferior levels.

Prominent in the Maya pantheon is Kin, the sun god, who, wandering above, creates the day and the cycles of time. When he reaches his home in the west, he enters the fangs of the earth monster and journeys through the obscure regions of the underworld to reappear in the east, from the same monster's fangs. Although the sun god himself cannot be considered the supreme deity of the Maya, his frequent association with the worlds above and below, with the four quadrants of the world, and with all the calendar's periods make him a multifaceted god with innumerable religious connotations. He is often related to Itzamná as a celestial deity and also to Yum Kimil ("lord of death") who abides in the netherworld, the region visited at night by the sun god disguised as a jaguar. The abode of Yum Kimil is also the place to which most of the dead go. Only a few—chosen by the Chacs, the gods of rain—attain a sort of paradise, a place of pleasure situated in one of the heavens. It is not clear whether those who go to the abode of the lord of death are to remain there forever, or whether they are eventually reduced to nothing, or if, on the contrary, after a period of purification, they are transferred to the celestial paradise.

Other gods worshiped by the Maya include the moon

goddess Ixchel (another title of the mother goddess, often described as wife of the sun god). The "great star" (Venus), whose heliacal risings and conjunctions were of such interest to Maya skywatchers, received at times the calendrical name *1 Ahau,* or *1 Lord,* but it was also associated with five other celestial gods, whose identification implies the assimilation of cultural elements in the Postclassic from the Central Plateau of Mexico. There also appear to have been patron gods of specific occupational groups, such as merchants, hunters, fishermen, cacao growers, medicine men, ball players, poets, and musicians.

With regard to the "feathered serpent god," a distinction has to be made. On the one hand, serpent representations in association with bird's elements such as plumage, or with traits belonging to other animals such as the caiman or jaguar, had been extremely frequent since the early Classic period. As we have seen, these complex figures, sometimes described as celestial dragons, earth monsters, cosmic lizards, and so forth, are representations of gods like the Chicchan serpents, deities of rain, or of the multifaceted Itzamná. On the other hand, the idea of a particular god and culture hero, Kukulcan, corresponding to central Mexico's Quetzalcoatl ("quetzal-feathered serpent"), was borrowed from that subarea in the Postclassic. [*See* Quetzalcoatl.]

Priests and forms of worship. The existence of a priesthood and of the many sacred sites and monuments reserved for the various kinds of cult imposed a canon to be observed in the communication with the universe of the divine. The chiefs, *halach uinicoob* ("true men"), could perform some religious ceremonies, but for the most part the cult of the gods was the duty of the priests. Above them was a class of high priests, in Postclassic texts named "rattlesnake-tobacco lords" and "rattlesnake-deer lords." They were in custody of the ancient religious wisdom, the books and the calendrical computations. They were considered prophets and acted in the most important ceremonies. Of a lower rank were the *ah kinoob,* the priests whose title can be translated as "those of the sun." Their duty was to interpret the calendrical signs, to direct the feast-day celebrations, and to "read" the destinies of men. To some of them fell the performance of offerings and sacrifices, including human sacrifices.

Bearers of the rain god's name were the *chac* priests, assistants in the sacrifices and other ceremonies. The lowest rank was occupied by the *ah men* (performers, prayer makers), who were concerned mostly with the local forms of cult. Women who lived close to the sacred buildings, assisted the priests in their duties.

Obviously, great differences existed between the ceremonies performed in the important religious centers and those, more modest, done in a village or at home. Most of the ceremonies were preceded by different forms of fasting and continence. Thus the gods would be propitiated by their acceptance of what people were expected to offer as payment for what they had received. A recurrent belief—not only among the Maya but also in other Mesoamerican subareas—is that, in a primeval time, "when there was still night," the gods entered into a kind of agreement with humans. The latter could not subsist without the constant support of the gods. But the divine beings themselves needed to be worshiped and to receive offerings.

Autosacrifice was practiced in various forms, as can be observed in multiple representations of both Classic and Postclassic monuments. Most often blood was offered by passing a cord or a blade of grass through the tongue, the penis, or some other part of the body. Offerings of animals (quail, parrots, iguanas, opossums, turtles) and of all sorts of plants or plant products (copal, flowers, cacao, rubber, honey) were also frequent.

Human sacrifice was performed following various rituals. The most frequent form was by opening the breast of the victim to offer his or her heart to the god. Other kinds of human sacrifice included shooting arrows at a victim tied to a frame of wood, beheading, and throwing the victim—usually a young girl or child—into a cenote (Maya, *dz'onot,* a natural deposit of water in places where the limestone surface has caved in) or into a lake, as in certain sites in Guatemala. Human sacrifices—never so numerous among the Maya as they became among the Aztec—were performed during the sacred feasts to repay the gods with the most precious offering, the life-giving blood.

A considerable number of prayers in the Maya languages have been preserved. Among them one can distinguish sacred hymns (hymns of intercession, praise, or thanks) those accompanying a sacrifice, and those to be chanted in a domestic ceremony.

Religion and the calendar. The calendar provided the Maya with a frame of mathematical precision, a basis for understanding and predicting events in the universe. Thus all the sacred duties of the priests—the ceremonies, sacrifices, and invocations—were not performed at random but followed established cycles. Observation of the celestial bodies and of whatever is born and grows on the earth, demonstrated that beings undergo cyclical change. The Maya believed that if man succeeded in discovering and measuring the cyclical rhythms of the universe, he would adapt himself to favorable situations and escape adverse ones. The belief that the gods and their sacred forces are essentially related to the cyclical appearances and intervals of the celestial bodies, which are their manifestations, led the sages to conclude that the realm of the divine was ruled by a complex variety of cycles. The Maya saw the manifestations or arrivals of the gods in these cycles; all the deities were thought of as being endowed with calendrical presences, and so the gods were given their respective calendrical names. As for man, the divine presences along the counts of time could not be meaningless: they brought fate, favorable or adverse, and all dates had therefore to be scrutinized to discover the destinies they carried. This probably explains why calendrical and religious concerns became so inseparable for the Maya.

The calendar systems employed by the Maya were not their invention, although they added new forms of precision to them. Two forms of count were at the base of the complexities of all Mesoamerican calendars. One count is that of the solar year, computed for practical purposes as having 365 days and subject to various forms of adjustment or correction. The other count, specifically Mesoamerican, is the cycle of 260 days. In it a sequence of numbers from 1 to 13 is employed. A series of twenty day names, each expressed by its respective hieroglyph, is the other essential element of the calendar.

The solar-year count and the 260-day count meshed to make it possible to give a date not only within a year but also within a fifty-two year cycle, as well as in the so-called Long Count. To represent the calendar's internal structures and forms of correlation is to represent the precise mechanism that provided the norm for the order of feasts, rites, and sacrifices; astrological wisdom; economic, agricultural, and commercial enterprises; and social and political obligations. This mechanism was also the key to understanding a universe in which divine forces—the gods themselves and the destinies they wrought—became manifest cycle after cycle.

The 260-day count places the numbers 1 to 13 on a series of twenty day names whose meanings in the Maya languages are related to various deities and other sacred realities. The twenty days have the following names and associations: *Imix* (the earth monster); *Ik* ("wind" or "life"; associated with the rain god); *Akbal* ("darkness"; associated with the jaguar-faced nocturnal sun god); *Kan* ("ripeness"; the sign of the god of young maize); *Chicchan* (the celestial serpent); *Cimi* ("death"; associated with the god of the underworld); *Manik* ("hand"; the day name of the god of hunting); *Lamat* (day name of the lord of the "great star," Venus); *Muluc* (symbolized by jade and water; evokes the Chacs, gods of rain); *Oc* (represented by a dog's head, which guides the sun through the underworld); *Chuen* (the monkey god, the patron of knowledge and the arts); *Eb* (represented by a face with a prominent jaw; related to the god who sends drizzles and mists); *Ben* ("descending"; the day name of the god who fosters the growth of the maize stalk); *Ix* (a variant of the jaguarlike sun god); *Men* (associated with the aged moon goddess); *Cib* (related to the four Bacabs, supporters of the sky); *Caban* ("earthquake"; associated with the god/goddess of the earth); *Etz'nab* ("obsidian blade"; linked to human sacrifice); *Cauac* (day name of the celestial dragon deities); and *Ahau* ("lord"; the radiant presence of the sun god).

During the first thirteen-day "week" of the 260-day cycle, the numbers 1 through 13 are prefixed to the first thirteen day names. At this point, the series of numbers begins again at 1, so that, for example, *Ik*, whose number is 2 during the first week, has the number 9 prefixed to it during the second week, 3 during the third week, and so on. The cycle begins to repeat itself after 260 (20 × 13) days. [*For an illustration of the same interaction of the series of twenty day names and the thirteen-day week in the Aztec calendar, see table 1 in* Calendars, *article on* Mesoamerican Calendars.] In this 260-day count one also distinguishes four groups of sixty-five days, each of which is broken into five "weeks" of thirteen days (each presided over by a particular god).

The solar count of the *haab*, or year, is divided into eighteen groups, *uinal*s or "months" of twenty days each (18 × 20 = 360), to which five *uayeb*s ("ominous days") are added at the end of the cycle. These eighteen "months" of twenty days and the five final days are the span of time along which the 260-day count develops. The intermeshing of the two counts implies that in each solar year there will be a repetition in the 260-day combination of numbers and day names in 105 instances (365 − 260 = 105). As the number and the day name together form the basic element to express a date, the way to distinguish between such repetitions is by specifying the position of the days in the different eighteen months of twenty days of the solar count.

Thus, if the day 13 Ahau (13 Lord) is repeated within a 365-day solar count, one can distinguish two different dates by noting the day to which it corresponds in the series of the eighteen months. For example, 13 Ahau, 18 Tzec (the day 13 Ahau related to the eighteenth day of the month of Tzec) is different from 13 Ahau, 18 Cumhu (the day 13 Ahau related to the eighteenth day of the month of Cumhu).

The number of possible different interlockings of the two counts comprises 18,980 expressions of the day name, number, and position within the month. Such a number of differently named days integrates a Calendar Round, a cycle of fifty-two years. Each of these 18,890 calendric combinations was designated as the bearer of a distinct divine presence and destiny, obviously not of that many different gods but of a complex diversification of their influences, favorable or adverse, successively oriented toward one of the four quadrants of the world.

But the Maya, like some of their predecessors who were exposed to Olmec influence, could also compute any date in terms of the Long Count, in which a fixed date, corresponding to a day in the year 3133 BCE (probably representing the beginning of the present cosmic age), was taken as the point of departure. The end of the Long Count's cycle will occur on a date equivalent to 24 December 2011. The Long Count was conceived to express dates in terms of elapsed time, or *kin* (a word that has cognates throughout the Maya family of languages and that means "sun, sun god, day, time, cosmic age"). Periods within the Long Count were reckoned in accordance with Mesoamerican counting systems, which employed base 20. These periods, each of which had its presiding deity, were registered in columns of hieroglyphs, beginning with the largest cycle, as follows:

Baktun	(7,200 days × 20 = 144,000 days)
Katun	(360 days × 20 = 7,200 days)
Tun	(20 days × 18 = 360 days)
Uinal	(20 days)
Kin	(1 day)

By means of their dot, bar, and shell numerical signs for 1, 5, and 0, respectively, the Maya indicated how many *baktuns, katuns, tuns, uinals,* and *kins* had, at a given moment, elapsed since the beginning of the present cosmic age. The date was finally correlated with the meshed system of the 365-day solar calendar and the 260-day count, which thus became adjusted to the astronomical year.

Besides these precise forms of calendar, the Maya developed other systems devised to measure different celestial cycles, such as those of the "great star" and the moon. The inscriptions on their stelae allow us to understand some of the main reasons for their astronomical and calendrical endeavors. To the Maya, dates conveyed not only the presence of one god on any given day but also the sum total of the divine forces "becoming" and acting in the universe. The deities of the numbers, of the day names, of the periods within the 260-day count, of the *uinal*s, or months of the year, and of the divisions within a 52-year cycle, as well as of the many other cycles within the Long Count system, converged at any given moment and exerted their influences, intrinsically coloring and affecting human and earthly realities.

Through color symbolism and indications like those of the "directional hieroglyphs of the years," one can identify the cosmic regions (quadrants of horizontal space and also celestial and inferior levels) to which specific cycles and gods address their influence. For the Maya, space separated from the cycles of time would have been meaningless. When the cycles are finally completed, the consequence will be the end of life on earth, the death of the sun, the absence of the gods, and an ominous return to primeval darkness.

The priests known as *ah kinoob* ("those of the sun and of the destinies") whose duty was to recognize and anticipate the divine presences as well as their beneficial or dangerous influences, were consulted by rich and poor alike. Thanks to special rites and sacrifices, favorable destinies could be discovered that would neutralize the influence of adverse fates. In this way one escaped fatalism, and a door was opened to reflection and righteous behavior. The wisdom of the calendar was indeed the key to penetrating the mysterious rhythms of what exists and becomes. This probably explains why the priests were also interested in the computation of dates in the distant past. On Stela F of Quirigua is inscribed a date, 1 Ahau, 18 Yaxkin, that corresponds to a day 91,683,930 years in the past!

In the Postclassic period, the Long Count fell into oblivion and the simplified system of the Count of the *Katun*s (thirteen periods of twenty years) was introduced. The destinies of the *katun*s remained an object of concern and a source of prophetic announcements. In spite of the Spanish conquest, the burning of the ancient books, and the efforts of Christian missionaries, elements of the ancient worldview and religion have survived among the contemporary Maya, as has been documented by the ethnographer Alfonso Villa Rojas (in León-Portilla, 1973, pp. 113–159).

Zapotec and Mixtec Religious Variants. Mountain ranges that encompass several valleys, as well as the slopes that lead to the Pacific plains in the Mexican state of Oaxaca, have been the ancestral abode of the Zapotec, Mixtec, and other indigenous peoples. The Zapotec reached their cultural zenith in the Classic period while the Mixtec achieved hegemony during the Postclassic. Although linguistically different, the Zapotec and the Mixtec were culturally akin. Olmec culture had influenced the Zapotec since the Middle Formative period.

Zapotec religion. From 200 to 800 CE, the Zapotec developed forms of urban life and built magnificent religious buildings in their towns (Monte Albán, Yagul, Zaachila). Their sacred spaces included large plazas around which the temple-pyramids, altars, ball courts, and other religious monuments were raised.

Mainly through what has been discovered in subterranean tombs near the temples, reliable information can be offered about their gods and other beliefs. In paintings preserved on the walls of the tombs, prominent members of the Zapotec pantheon appear, accompanied at times by inscriptions. Pottery—urns in particular—also tell about the attributes of the Zapotec gods and their ideas of the afterlife.

As in the case of the Maya, a supreme dual god, Pitao Cozaana–Pitao Cochaana, presided over all realities, divine and human. Addressed as a single god, he-she was Pije-Tao ("lord of time"), principle of all that exists. Godly beings often appear with the symbolic attributes of the serpent, bird, caiman, and jaguar—motifs also familiar to the Olmec and Maya. Cocijo, the rain god, also had a quadruple form of presence in the world. Pitao Cozobi was the god of maize.

Zapotec writing (since its early beginnings in Monte Albán 1, c. 600 BCE) appears to be the source of the forms of script later developed by the Mixtec and transmitted to the groups of central Mexico. The study of Zapotec writing reveals their calendrical concern.

Zapotec pottery urns, used mostly as containers of water, were placed near the dead in the tombs. Most of them include the molded representation of a god, often the rain god Cocijo. The headdress of the god conveys his emblem, in which the combined traits of serpent, jaguar, and bird are often visible.

In essence we know that the Zapotec of the Classic period believed in a supreme dual god. They also worshiped several deities revered in other Mesoamerican areas. They were so much concerned with death that they placed their dignitaries' remains in sumptuous tombs close to their temples. The Zapotec also knew about time computations.

Mixtec religion. The Mixtec founded new towns, and they conquered and rebuilt places (c. 1000 CE) in which the Zapotec had ruled. The Mixtec were great artists. Among other things, they excelled in the production of metal objects, many of which bear religious connotations. Several Mixtec books of religious and historical content have come down to us. They constitute one of the most precious sources of the cultural history of a Mesoamerican subarea.

In the Mixtec books known as Codex Selden and Codex Gómez de Orozco, an image of their worldview is offered; it closely corresponds to that of the Maya. The earth is represented by the monstrous animal with traits of caiman, serpent, and jaguar. Below it is the underworld. Above the earth, nine levels of the upperworld (not thirteen as in the Maya worldview) are represented. The sun and the moon and the stars are there. The dual god, with the symbols of time and of his-her day names, resides on the uppermost level.

According to other traditions, this god caused the earth to rise out of the waters. Later he-she built a beautiful place on the top of a large rock. The children he-she engendered and conceived are the gods of the various quadrants of the world, gods of rain and wind, gods of maize, and so on. According to Mixtec belief, the earth and the sun had been destroyed several times. The gods waged combat in a celestial ball court. (This is represented in a gold pectoral found with other religious objects in Tomb 7 within the sacred district of Monte Albán, the site that had been built by the Zapotec but that was later conquered by the Mixtec.)

Another extraordinary Mixtec book, known as Codex Vindobonensis, conveys the beliefs of this people about their origins in the present cosmic age. They had come from a place called Yuta Tnoho ("river of the lineages"). There they were born from a cosmic tree. The Mixtec calendar systems corresponded to the 260-day count and the 365-day solar year computed by the Zapotec and the Maya. (Caso 1965, pp. 948–961).

Teotihuacán. As in the Maya and Oaxaca areas, some Early Formative type villages in the Central Plateau experienced important changes. Places like El Arbolillo, Zacatenco, Tlaltilco, Cuicuilco, and others received the ferment of Olmec influence. Special areas began to be reserved for religious purposes; temple pyramids and round platforms were built. Clay images of the fire god Huehueteotl ("old lord"), who much later was also worshiped by the Aztec, have been dated to the Late Formative period (c. 500 BCE).

In Tlapacoya, not far from where Teotihuacán was to be established, another important Late Formative center flourished (c. 300–100 BCE). Here, temple pyramids, tombs, and mural paintings anticipate in many respects what was to be the grandeur of Teotihuacán.

Teotihuacán ("the place where one becomes deified") marks the Classic period's climax in the Central Plateau. Archaeological research has revealed that, here, whatever is implied by the idea of a city became a reality. It took several centuries (100–500 CE) for generations of priests and sages to conceive, realize, modify, enlarge, and enrich the city, which probably was planned to last forever. Beside the two great pyramids of the Sun and the Moon, the Temple of the Feathered Serpent, and the Palace of the Quetzalpapalotl ("quetzal butterflies"), many other enclosures, palaces, schools, markets, and other buildings have been unearthed. Large suburbs, where members of the community had their homes, surrounded the religious and administrative center. The pyramids and palaces were decorated with murals. Gods in the forms of human beings, fantastic serpents, birds, caimans, lizards, and jaguars, as well as flowers, plants, priests, and even complex scenes—such as a depiction of Tlalocan, the paradise of the rain god—were represented in the paintings.

Teotihuacán was the capital of a large state, perhaps an empire, vestiges of whose cultural influence have been found in Oaxaca, Chiapas, and the Guatemalan highlands. According to annals preserved by the Aztec, "In Teotihuacán orders were given, and the chiefdom was established. Those who were the chiefs were the sages, the ones who knew secret things, who preserved old traditions" (from the Codex Matritense, folio 192r, my trans.).

The inhabitants of Teotihuacán worshiped several deities whose iconography is similar to that of gods later revered by other groups in central Mexico: the Toltec (900–1050 CE), and the Acolhua and the Aztec (1200–1519 CE). The Aztec called these gods by the following names: Tlaloc and Chalchiuhticue, god and goddess of the waters, who together constitute one aspect of divine duality; Quetzalcoatl ("quetzal-feathered serpent"); Xiuhtecuhtli, the fire god; Xochipilli ("the one of the flowery lineage"); Xipe Totec ("our lord the flayed one"); Itztlacoliuhqui ("stone knife"), whose traits resemble those of the Toltec and Aztec god Tezcatlipoca ("smoking mirror"); Tlahuizcalpantecuhtli, god of the morning star, and Xolotl, god of the evening star, who were also aspects of the divine duality; and Yacatecuhtli, god of merchants (Caso, 1966; Séjourné, 1966). (For a listing of principal Aztec deities, see table 1.)

In addition to these gods, a large number of other symbols and a few hieroglyphs identified in the mural paintings, sculptures, and ceramics persisted in the corresponding Toltec and Aztec ensemble of religious expressions.

Although some researchers have dismissed the validity of comparing iconographic symbols of one culture with those of another culture from a subsequent epoch, the evidence supporting a common Mesoamerican religious tradition and the fact that one is not dealing with isolated cases of iconographic similarity but rather with ensembles of symbols, seem valid reasons for rejecting the skepticism of those who deny this cultural interrelation. Archaeological finds have shown that Teotihuacán actually influenced Toltec and Aztec cultures, in both of which the religious iconographic similarities are obvious.

It is reasonable to assert that the arrangement of sacred space at Teotihuacán and the gods worshiped there were prototypical for the future religious development of central Mexico. Through them we can better understand the symbols of Teotihuacán, among other reasons because of the relative abundance of the Postclassic historical testimonies.

Aztec consciousness of Teotihuacán as the ultimate source of their own culture led them to see the sacred space of the Place Where One Becomes Deified as a kind of primordial site, where, *in illo tempore,* the Fifth Sun (the present cosmic age) had its beginning. An Aztec text that describes the four previous Suns, or cosmic ages, and their successive violent destructions says about the fifth and new age, "This Sun, its day name is 4 Movement. This is our Sun, the one in which we now live. And here is its sign, how the Sun fell into the fire, into the divine hearth, there at Teotihuacán" (from *Annals of Cuauhtitlan,* folio 77, my trans.).

The Aztec myth about the beginning of the Fifth Sun at Teotihuacán tells how the gods met there to discuss the remaking of the sun and moon and of human beings and their sustenance. "When there was still night," the text relates, the gods gathered for four days around the divine hearth at Teotihuacán to determine who would be the god who would cast himself into the fire and thus become transformed into the sun. There were two candidates, the arrogant Tecuciztecatl ("lord of the conch shells") and the modest Nanahuatzin ("the pimply one"). Tecuciztecatl made four attempts to throw himself into the flames, but each time he backed away in fear. Then it was Nanahuatzin's turn to try. Closing his eyes, he courageously hurled himself into the fire, was consumed, and finally appeared transformed as the sun. Tecuciztecatl, fearful and too late, was only able to achieve transformation into the lesser celestial body, the moon.

To the surprise of the other gods, the sun and moon did not move. The answer to this problem was sacrifice. To give the sun energy, the gods sacrificed themselves, offering their blood. This sacrifice of the gods was the primeval act that had to be reenacted by men. Only through the bloody sacrifice could the sun and life exist; only through the sacrifice of men's blood could existence be prolonged. With their own blood, human beings had to repay the divine sacrifice that had prevented the cataclysms that had put an end to previous Suns. Here was the seed that later flowered as the Aztec rituals of human sacrifice.

Quetzalcoatl and Toltec Religion. It appears that Teotihuacán came to a sudden, and still unexplained, end around 650 CE. Its collapse, however, did not mean the death of high culture in Mesoamerica. From among those cultures that inherited numerous cultural elements from the Classic glory of Teotihuacán, the city of Tula stands out. Tula is about eighty kilometers north of Mexico City. Its name, Tula, means "large town, metropolis," and that is what the Toltec, following the advice of their high priest Quetzalcoatl, actually built.

Quetzalcoatl, a legendary figure, was believed to have been a king who derived his name from that of the

TABLE 1. *Aspects and Associations of Principal Aztec Deities*

Deity	Aspect and Associations
Ometecuhtli/Omecihuatl, also known as Tonacatecuhtli/ Tonacacihuatl	"Lord Two/Lady Two" or "Lord of Sustenance/Lady of Sustenance." The dual divine principle; creator pair.
Coatlicue	"She of the Serpent Skirt." Mother goddess.
Huitzilopochtli	"Hummingbird of the Left," or "Hummingbird of the South." Méxica-Aztec tutelary god; associated with war and the sun.
Quetzalcoatl-Ehécatl	"Feathered Serpent" or "Precious Twin." God of knowledge; associated with vegetation, the Morning Star, and—as Ehécatl—the wind.
Tezcatlipoca	"Mirror That Smokes." Major god of Nahuatl groups; god of fate, both beneficial and destructive; associated with rulership and the night.
Tlaloc	"Earth Lord." God of rain and of the earth's fertility.
Centeotl-Itzlacoliuhqui	"Deified Maize" or "Curved Obsidian." As Centeotl, god of maize. As Itzlacoliuhqui, god of frost and late-ripening corn.
Chalchiuhtlicue	"She of the Skirt of Jade." Goddess of ground waters.
Chicomecoatl-Xilonen	"7 Serpent" or "Young Ear of Maize." Corn goddess; deity of vegetation in general.
Cihuacoatl	"Serpent Woman." Mother goddess; prominent in war and sacrifice; associated with rulership.
cihuateteo	"Deified Women." Young mothers who died in childbirth; helped to carry the sun across the sky.
Huehueteotl	"Old God." Ancient Mesoamerican deity; associated with fire.
Itzpapalotl	"Obsidian Butterfly." Associated with sacrifice.
Mayahuel	Personified maguey plant; goddess of *pulque* (maguey wine).
Mictlantecuhtli/ Mictecacihuatl	"Lord of Mictlan/Lady of Mictlan (land of the dead)." God and goddess of death, darkness, and the netherworld.
Mixcoatl	"Cloud Serpent." God of the hunt.
Ome Tochtli	"2 Rabbit." God of *pulque.*
Teteoinnan-Toci-Tonantzin	"Mother of the Gods," "Our Grandmother," or "Our Little Mother." Earth mother; patron of healers.
Tlazolteotl	"Eater of Filth." Received confessions (filth); patron goddess of midwives.
Tonatiuh	"He Who Makes the Day." The sun.
Xipe Totec	"Our Lord the Flayed One." Vegetation god; patron of goldsmiths and silversmiths.
Xiuhtecuhtli-Ixcozauhqui	"Turquoise Lord" or "Yellow Face." Fire god; patron of rulers.
Xochipilli-Macuiloxochitl-Piltzintecuhtli	"Flower Prince," "5 Flower," or "Young Prince." God of flowers and plants; patron of song, dance, and games.
Xochiquetzal	"Precious Flower." Goddess of flowers and grains; patron of weavers, embroiderers, and painters; patron of harlots.

"feathered serpent god," in whose representations two of the pan-Mesoamerican iconographic elements, the serpent and the plumage of the quetzal, became integrated. It is said that Quetzalcoatl, while still young, retired to Huapalcalco, formerly a village not far from Teotihuacán, to devote himself to meditation. There he was taken by the Toltec to serve as their ruler and high priest.

Native books attribute to him whatever is good and great. He induced his people to worship a benevolent supreme dual god, Ometeotl. This same god was also invoked as the Precious Feathered Serpent or Precious Feathered Twins. Both meanings are actually implied by the term *Quetzalcoatl,* at once the name of the god and that of his priest. The original Toltec text says,

> And it is told, it is said
> That Quetzalcoatl invoked, took as his God,
> The One in the uppermost heaven:
> She of the starry skirt,
> He whose radiance envelops things;

Lady of Our Flesh,
Lord of Our Flesh;
She who is clothed in black,
He who is clothed in red;
She who endows the earth with solidity,
He who covers it with cotton.
And thus it was known
That toward the heavens was his plea directed,
Toward the place of duality,
Above the nine levels of Heaven.
(from *Annals of Cuauhtitlan*, folio 4, my trans.)

The dual god Ometeotl—who in the night covers his-her feminine aspect with a skirt of stars, but who during the day reveals himself as the sun, the greatest of the light-giving stars—appears also as the Lord and Lady of Our Flesh, as he-she who vests himself-herself in black and red (colors symbolizing wisdom), and, at the same time, as the one who gives stability to the earth. Thus the priest taught the Toltec how to draw near to Ometeotl-Quetzalcoatl, the god who dwells in the uppermost heaven:

> The Toltec were solicitous of the things of God; they had but one God; they held him to be their only God; they invoked him; they made supplications to him; his name was Quetzalcoatl. The guardian of their God, their priest, his name was also Quetzalcoatl. And they were so respectful of the things of God that everything that the priest Quetzalcoatl told them they did, and they did not depart from it. He persuaded them; he taught them: This one God, Quetzalcoatl is his name. He demands nothing except serpents, except butterflies, which you must offer to him, which you must sacrifice to him. (from Codex Matritense, folio 179r, my trans.)

The Toltec understood the doctrine of Quetzalcoatl. Under his guidance they were able to relate the idea of the dual god with the ancient image of the world and the destiny of man on earth. Codex Matritense is clear on this point:

> The Toltec knew that the heavens are many; they said that there are thirteen divisions, one upon the other. There abides, there lives the True God and his Consort. The Heavenly God is called the Lord of Duality, and his Consort is called Lady of Duality, Heavenly Lady. Which means: He is king, he is lord over the thirteen heavens. Thence we receive our life, we men. Thence falls our destiny when the child is conceived, when he is placed in the womb. His fate comes to him there. It is sent by the God of Duality.
> (from Codex Matritense, folio 175v, my trans.)

The golden age of the Toltec produced all sorts of achievements: palaces and temples were built; many towns and peoples accepted the rule of Quetzalcoatl. Only some enemies, probably religious adversaries, attempted to bring about the downfall of that age. Some texts speak of the appearance of one named Tezcatlipoca, the Smoking Mirror, a god who came to Tula to force Quetzalcoatl to abandon his city and his followers. According to these accounts, the departure of the wise priest precipitated the ruin of Tula. Other texts speak of two different critical moments. The first was that of the flight of Quetzalcoatl. Although tragic, it did not bring about the complete downfall of Tula. The second crisis took place several decades later. Huemac was the king ruling at that time. His forced departure and death, around 1150, marked the total collapse of Tula. The ruin of the Toltec also meant a diffusion of their culture and religious ideas among various peoples, some distant from Tula. The existence of the Toltec is recorded in annals such as those of the Mixtec of Oaxaca and the Maya of Yucatán and Guatemala.

The Aztec Religious Variant. By the end of the thirteenth century CE, new chiefdoms existed in central Mexico. Some were the result of a renaissance in towns of Toltec or even Teotihuacano origin. Others were new entities made up of the cultures of semibarbarian groups from the north (the so-called Chichimec) and the remnants of Toltec civilization.

At the same time other peoples made themselves present in the Central Plateau. Their language was Nahuatl, the same which the Toltec had spoken. The various Nahuatlan groups—among them the Aztec, or Méxica—had been living in northern outposts, on the frontier of Mesoamerica. In the texts they repeat, "Now we are coming back from the north. . . ." The Aztec return, or, as it is often described, their "pilgrimage," was a difficult enterprise. They had to overcome many hardships until finally they were settled (c. 1325) on the island of Tenochtitlán, in the lake that then covered a large part of the Valley of Mexico. It took the Aztec a century to initiate the period of their greatness in Mesoamerica.

Cultural and religious heritages. The Aztec's worldview, beliefs, and cultic forms, which by the time of Aztec hegemony were already fully integrated as elements of their own culture, had diverse origins. The Aztec preserved ancient traditions that were the common inheritance of many peoples of Mesoamerica, such as the worship of the "old god," Huehueteotl, who had been revered since several hundred years before the beginning of the common era. Other beliefs and practices were probably derived from the cultures that had flourished along the coast of the Gulf of Mexico, such as the veneration of Xipe Totec ("our lord the flayed one"), a god of fertility.

Some deities, such as Tlaloc, Chac, or Cocijo (different names of the rain god, whose presence in Mesoamerica since the Classic period is amply manifested in the archaeological evidence), also became members of the Aztec pantheon. So did the two Toltec gods Quetzalcoatl and Tezcatlipoca. Besides individual gods and ensembles of gods, Aztec culture incorporated the old Mesoamerican spatial image of the world, with its four quadrants, central point, and upperworld and underworld levels (as well as the symbolic meanings attached to these divisions), and it integrated the solar calendar, the 260-day count, and the Mesoamerican system of writing.

To this heritage, the Aztec's own beliefs must be added. Among these are the Aztec's own patron gods: Huitzilopochtli ("hummingbird of the south" or "hummingbird of the left") and Coatlicue ("she of the skirt of serpents").

Consciousness of divine destiny. Aztec accounts speak of the place in the north from which they had come, Aztlán Chicomoztoc ("the place of the herons," "the place of the seven caves"). There they had been oppressed by a dominant people. One day, the "portentous god," Tezcatlipoca, spoke to the Aztec high priest, Huitzilopochtli. Tezcatlipoca offered to liberate the Aztec from their rulers. He would lead them to a place where they could enjoy freedom and from which they would extend themselves as conquerors into the four quadrants of the world. This he would do if the Aztec promised to be his vassals and to have him as their tutelary god.

The Aztec began their march to their promised land. On the way, Huitzilopochtli died. The spirit and power of Tezcatlipoca entered into Huitzilopochtli's bones, and, from that moment on, the god and the priest were one person. When the Aztec, in their search for their predestined land, arrived at Coatepec ("mountain of the serpent"), they learned that the mother goddess Coatlicue was present there and that their own god Huitzilopochtli was to be miraculously reborn as Coatlicue's son. Huitzilopochtli's birth occurred at the precise moment when another goddess, Coyolxauhqui ("she of the face painted with rattles"), was about to kill Coatlicue because of the offense Coatlicue had caused her and her four hundred brothers, the Warriors of the South, when it became known that Coatlicue was inexplicably pregnant.

As Coyolxauhqui and her four hundred brothers were climbing Coatepec, Huitzilopochtli was born to Coatlicue, and he immediately used his weapon, the Fire Snake, to hurt Coyolxauqui and to cut off her head. He then pursued the Warriors of the South, driving them off the top of the mountain and destroying them. Huitzilopochtli stripped the four hundred brothers of their belongings and made them part of his own destiny.

Later, when the Aztec had established themselves on the island of México-Tenochtitlán, they constructed their main temple (the so-called Templo Mayor) to Huitzilopochtli in the form of the mountain Coatepec, and there they ritually reenacted Huitzilopochtli's portentous birth. A representation of the goddess Coatlicue stood near Huitzilopochtli's shrine on top of this "pyramid mountain," as did representations of the beheaded goddess Coyolxauhqui, the Fire Snake, and the four hundred Warriors of the South. The gods' primeval confrontation was reenacted on the feast of Panquetzaliztli ("when the flags are raised"). Objects found during the excavations of the Templo Mayor performed from 1979 through 1982 have corroborated the native texts: all of the symbols of the Mountain of the Serpent and the story of Huitzilopochtli's birth have been recovered from the temple site.

Tributary wars and the reenactment of the sacrifice at Teotihuacán. The Aztec knew the story of the sacrifice at Teotihuacán, where the gods gave their blood and lives to strengthen the "Giver of Life," the sun, whose movement was enabled by the sacrifice. The Aztec, believing they had to imitate the gods, took on the mission of continuing to provide the sun with vital energy. They deemed themselves called to offer the sun that same precious liquid that the gods had shed, and they obtained it from human sacrifice.

As if hypnotized by the mystery of blood, they proclaimed themselves the chosen People of the Sun. Ceremonial warfare, the principal manner of obtaining victims for the sacrifice, became the dominant activity in the Aztec's social, religious, and national life. Thus the Aztec developed what can be described as a mystical imperialism: they devoted themselves to conquest in their effort to maintain the life of the sun and to keep the age of 4 Movement alive. The theme of war in Aztec visual art and in Aztec literature is everywhere linked to that of national greatness. In the primeval myth of Teotihuacán, mention is also made of the eagle and the ocelot (or jaguar), who were present at the divine hearth into which the gods had hurled themselves. Eagles and ocelots therefore became the symbols of warriors.

Fire, which had blazed in the hearth at Teotihuacán, and water, without which nothing green grows on earth, were strangely linked in the minds of the priests. Jointly, they conveyed the idea of the mystical warfare that makes the life of the universe possible. *Atl/tlachinolli* ("water/fire"), *quauhtli/ocelotl* ("eagle/ocelot"), *mitl/chimalli* ("arrow/shield"), *yaoxochitl/xochiaoctli* ("flowery wars/flowery liquor"), *quauhtli/nochtli* ("eagle/prickly pear"—which opposition also has the connotation "the Sun/the red heart"): these are some of the binary forms of symbolic expression that recur in Aztec hymns, chants, and discourses and the echo the Aztec's official worldview:

From where the eagles rest,
From where the ocelots are exalted,
The Sun is invoked.
Like a shield that descends,
So does the Sun set.
In Mexico night is falling,
War rages on all sides.
O Giver of Life!
War draws near . . .
Proud of ifself
Is the city of México-Tenochtitlán.
Here no one fears to die in war.
This is our glory.
This your command,
O Giver of Life!
(from Cantares Mexicanos,
folio 19v, my trans.)

Divine duality. Paintings and ideograms in some of the native books corroborate what is proclaimed in the songs of the Aztec warriors. Again, binary forms of expression—captains' headdresses in the forms of eagles and ocelots, the hieroglyphs for fire and water coupled, and so on—appear consistently related to the universe of the gods, who are esentially dual entities.

Below, in the abode of the dead, reign Mictlantecuhtli and Mictlancihuatl, the god and goddess of that region. Here on the surface of the earth is Our Mother–Our Father, who is at once the Old Lord, He-She of the Yellow Face, and Creator of Fire. And above, in the various celestial levels, other dual divine manifestations exist: Tlaloc and Chalchiuhtlicue (god and goddess of rain and of the terrestrial waters); the precious twins Quetzalcoatl and Cihuacoatl (the feathered serpent and the female serpent); Tezcatlipoca and Tezcatlanextia (the mirror that obscures things and the mirror that makes them brilliant); and, above all other deities, the dual god Ometeotl, a supreme being endowed with both male and female countenances.

In Aztec as in Maya religion, the Dual God, in an unfolding of his-her own being, gave birth to four sons, who are primordial divine forces. In Aztec thought these are known as the four Tezcatlipocas—White, Black, Red, and Blue—who presided over the successive cosmic ages. Their actions connoted confrontations between opposing forces as well as diverse kinds of alteration and becoming. Tezcatlipoca appears sometimes as the adversary of Tlaloc, at other times of Quetzalcoatl. Tezcatlipoca also often becomes identified with other deities, as is the case in the story, related above, of Huitzilopochtli's transformation.

An iconographic analysis of the Aztec gods confirms that they shared the attribute of "divine becoming," that is, of procession through a series of transformations. There are representations in which this "divine becoming" is evident—where, for example, Tlaloc, the rain god, is portrayed as if he were Tlahuizcalpantecuhtli, the god of the morning star, or Mictlantecuhtli, the god of death, or Xochipilli, the god of dance and song. This "becoming" of the gods was linked to the Aztec canon of religious celebrations. Abundant information about the feasts along the 365-day calendar can be found in several of the pre-Columbian texts (the Borbonicus, Matritense, Florentine, Magliabecchianus, Tudela, Ixtlilxochitl, Telleriano-Remensis, and Vaticanus A codices).

Sacrifice and other rites. Penance, abstinence, and the offering of a variety of animals and vegetables were frequent in Aztec celebrations. Intonation of sacred hymns was accompanied by music and dances. More than any other Mesoamerican people, the Aztec practiced human sacrifice during their celebrations. A sort of perpetual drama developed in which the primeval events were reenacted, with the victims playing the roles of the gods who *in illo tempore* offered their blood to make life on earth possible. The forms of human sacrifice were similar to those that had been practiced by the Maya. The largest number of sacrifices took place at the Templo Mayor at the center of México-Tenochtitlán. [*See also* Human Sacrifice, *article on* Aztec Rites.]

Afterlife. Some manners of dying promised glorious destinies: death in battle, death while trying to take captives, the death of a sacrificial victim, and the death of a woman in childbirth (while bearing a future warrior). To die in any of these ways meant that one would travel, after death, to the House of the Sun, to be his companion in the heavens. Persons chosen by the rain god for a special kind of death (by drowning, being struck by lightning, or through a serous disease such as dropsy) were destined to enjoy Tlalocan, the rain god's paradise. Others of the dead were said to go to Mictlan ("the place of the dead"), which was also known as Ximoayan ("the place of the fleshless") and Tocempopolihuiyan ("our common destination, where we lose ourselves").

Doubt and skepticism. In contrast to the officially accepted beliefs, there are some indigenous texts from the Aztec epochs in which doubts are expressed. A conviction that the mystery that surrounds human existence will never be completely unveiled appears again and again in these compositions. These beautiful poems, written by the sages (*tlamatinime,* "those who know something"), at times convey pessimism and even a sort of natural skepticism. Their core question seems to be whether or not it is possible to say true words about the beyond, the universe of the gods, or one's survival of death. The following example is eloquent:

Even if we offer the Giver of Life
Jade and precious ointments,
If with offering of necklaces
You are invoked,
With the strength of the eagle and the jaguar,
With the force of the warriors,
It may be that on earth
No one speaks of truth.
(from Cantares Mexicanos, folio 13r, my trans.)

The contrast between the official religious militarism of the Aztec and the questionings of these sages seems to reflect the vitality of the spiritual world of Mesoamerica.

After the Conquest. The Spanish conquest, which, in the case of the Aztec, was completed in 1521, brought with it the burning of native libraries, the demolition of temples, and the annihilation of whatever appeared to the conquistadors to be "idolatrous." Nevertheless, neither the Conquest nor the zealous activity of the Christian missionaries who followed in its wake succeeded in completely erasing all of the ancient traditions. It is extraordinary to discover that contemporary Maya, Mixtec, Zapotec, Nahuatl, and other groups keep remembrances of the old mythic traditions as part of their lore.

Study of contemporary Mesoamericans' worldviews and religious attitudes reveals that Christianity and indigenous Mesoamerican traditions have combined to form several kinds of syncretistic systems. While in some cases a christianized paganism has developed, in others new forms of Christianity—embedded in an indigenous Mesoamerican world of symbols—have been born.

BIBLIOGRAPHY

Annals of Cuauhtitlan. In *Codice Chimalpopoca,* edited by Rimo Feliciano Velázquez. Mexico City, 1945. Nahuatl text and Spanish translation. A basic source of Mesoamerican indigenous tradition; includes important references to religious beliefs and practices.

Bernal, Ignacio. *The Olmec World.* Berkeley, 1969. A readable account of the archaeological findings in the Olmec area.

Bosch-Gimpera, Pedro. "El arte rupestre de América." *Anales de antropología* 1 (1964); 29–45. A comprehensive survey of rock art in the New World, with an emphasis on Mexico.

Cantares Mexicanos (Collection of Mexican Songs). A sixteenth-century manuscript that includes a large number of compositions, in Nahuatl, of pre-Columbian origin. It is preserved at the Biblioteca Nacional de México in Mexico City. Translations of some of these songs appear in my *Pre-Columbian Literatures of Mexico* (Norman, Okla., 1969).

Carrasco, Pedro. "Pagan Rituals and Beliefs among the Chontal Indians of Oaxaca, Mexico." *Anthropological Records* 20 (1960): 87–117. Discusses Christian and pagan elements in contemporary religious ceremonies of this indigenous group.

Caso, Alfonso. "Zapotec Writing and Calendar." In *Handbook of Middle American Indians,* edited by Robert Wauchope et al., vol. 3. Austin, 1965. A concise presentation, well documented, with which to approach the religious insciptions of the Zapotec.

Caso, Alfonso. "Mixtec Writing and Calendar." In *Handbook of Middle American Indians,* edited by Robert Wauchope et al., vol. 3. Austin, 1965. A valuable complement to the previously listed article.

Caso, Alfonso. "Dioses y signos Teotihuacanos." In *Teotihuacan onceava mesa redonda,* vol. 1. Mexico City, 1966. Well-founded study on the gods worshiped at Teotihuacán.

Caso, Alfonso. "Religión o religiones mesoamericanos?" In *Verhandlungen des XXXVIII Amerikanistenkongresses,* vol. 3. Excellent synthesis of the evidences that support the existence of one religious tradition common to the various Mesoamerican groups.

Codex Maggliabecchianus, XIII: Manuscrit mexicain post-Colombien de la Bibilothèque Nationale de Florence (1904). Graz, 1970. Contains summaries in English and Spanish.

Codex Matritense. 3 vols. Madrid, 1905–1907. Nahuatl texts of the Indian informants of Fray Bernardo de Sahagún (sixteenth century). A classic collection of texts of the indigenous tradition, extremely rich in religious materials, including sacred hymns, speeches, and descriptions of feasts and sacrifices.

Coe, Michael D. *America's First Civilization.* New York, 1968. Excellent introduction to the study of Olmec culture.

Coe, Michael D. "Olmec Jaguars and Olmec Kings." In *The Cult of the Feline: A Conference in Pre-Columbian Iconography,* edited by Elizabeth P. Benson. Washington, D.C., 1972. Discusses the implications of the cult of the "Olmec Jaguar."

Coe, Michael D. "The Iconology of Olmec Art." In *The Iconography of Middle American Sculpture* (an anthology of conference papers, Metropolitan Museum, New York). New York, 1973. Summary and lucid discussion of the meaning of Olmec religious art.

Edmunson, Munro S., ed. and trans. *The Book of Counsel: The Popol Vuh of the Quiche Maya of Guatemala.* New Orleans, 1971. An excellent introduction and a direct English version of this classic of sacred Mesoamerican literature.

Edmunson, Munro S. "The Songs of Dzitbalche: A Literary Commentary." In *Tlalocan: A Journal of Source Materials on the Native Cultures of Mexico* (Mexico City) 9 (1982): 173–208. A new translation of and commentary on these sacred Maya compositions.

Glass, John B. "A Survey of Native American Pictorial Manuscripts." In *Handbook of Middle American Indians,* edited by Robert Wauchope et al., vol. 14. Austin, 1975. A comprehensive guide to these primary sources for the study of Mesoamerican cultures.

Joralemon, P. David. *A Study of Olmec Iconography.* Washington, D.C., 1971. A pioneer interpretation of the religious iconography of the Olmec.

Joralemon, P. David. "The Olmec Dragon: A Study in pre-Columbian Iconography." In *Origins of Religious Art and Iconography in Preclassic Mesoamerica,* edited by H. B. Nicholson. Los Angeles, 1976.

Kubler, George. *The Iconography of the Art of Teotihuacan.* Washington, D.C., 1967. Objects to the idea of a single Mesoamerican "cotradition."

Kubler, George. "Period, Style and Meaning in Ancient American Art." *New Literary History* 1 (1970): 127–144. Adds arguments to support the point of view expressed in the previously listed paper.

Landa, Diego de. *Landa's Relacion de las Cosas de Yucatan.* Translated and edited with notes by A. M. Tozzer. Cambridge, Mass., 1941. The best critical edition of this sixteenth-century classic for the study of Maya culture and religion.

Léon-Portilla, Miguel. *Aztec Thought and Culture: A Study of the Ancient Nahuatl Mind.* Norman, Okla., 1963. A study of Aztec worldview and ideas about ultimate reality; includes numerous Nahuatl texts from the indigenous pre-Columbian tradition.

Léon-Portilla, Miguel. *Pre-Columbian Literatures of Mexico.* Norman, Okla., 1969. An introduction to the extant texts of the Aztec, Maya, Mixtec, Otomí, and other Mesoamerican groups.

Léon-Portilla, Miguel. *Time and Reality in the Thought of the Maya.* Boston, 1973. An ethnohistorical approach to Maya religion and worldview with an emphasis on the Maya's concern for time.

Léon-Portilla, Miguel, ed. *Native Mesoamerican Spirituality: Ancient Myths, Discourses, Stories, Doctrines, Hymns, Poems from the Aztec, Yucatec Quiche-Maya, and Other Sacred Traditions.* New York, 1980. An annotated anthology, with commentary, of texts from the pre-Columbian traditions.

Madsen, William. *Christo-paganism: A Study of Mexican Religious Syncretism.* New Orleans, 1957. A case study in a Nahuatl community in Mexico where religious syncretism has apparently developed.

Marcus, Joyce. *Emblem and State in the Classic Maya Lowlands: An Epigraphic Approach to Territorial Organization.* Washington, D.C., 1976.

Nicholson, Henry B. "Religion in Pre-Hispanic Central Mexico." In *Handbook of Middle American Indians,* edited by Robert Wauchope et al., vol. 10. Austin, 1971. A classification of the principal cult themes and deity complexes.

Piña Chán, Román. *Los Olmecas antiguos.* Mexico City, 1982.

Sahagún, (Fray) Bernardino de. *Historia de los cosas de la Nueva España* (compiled 1569–1582; first published 1820). Translated by Arthur J. O. Anderson and Charles E. Dibble as *Florentine Codex: General History of the Things of New Spain,* 13 vols. in 12 (Santa Fe, N.Mex., 1950–1982). Vivid descriptions of temples, rituals, paraphernalia, and mythology can be found in several of this work's volumes, especially volumes 2 and 3.

Séjourné, Laurette. *El lenguaje de las formas en Teotihuacán.* Mexico City, 1966. Describes religious symbols that appear frequently in Teotihuacán and identifies some of the gods worshiped there.

Thompson, J. Eric S. *Maya Hieroglyphic Writing: An Introduction.* Norman, Okla., 1960. A basic work for the study of Maya symbols and inscriptions.

Thompson, J. Eric S. *Maya History and Religion.* Norman, Okla., 1970. An ethnohistorical approach in which a large number of sources are analyzed by a great scholar who devoted his life to research on the Maya.

Valliant, George C., ed. *A Sacred Almanac of the Aztecs.* New York, 1940. Translation of *Codex Borbonicus: Manuscrit mexicaine de la bibilothèque du Palais Bourbon,* edited by Jules Theodore Ernest Hamy (Paris, 1899).

MIGUEL LÉON-PORTILLA

Preclassic Cultures

Religious practices during Mesoamerica's Preclassic, or Formative, period (1500 BCE–250 CE) can only be inferred from the archaeological remains. One of the most thoroughly investigated regions is the lacustrine Basin of Mexico in the central highlands, where remains of pottery and figurines provide a yardstick for determining the cultural sequence within the Basin and adjacent regions. Throughout the Preclassic this region witnessed a steady population increase and a locally diverse progression from small farming communities with developing social stratification to large towns with complex political hierarchies. The period is divided in four major phases. Different time spans for the major phases, as well as local subphases, have been proposed by various researchers. These are consolidated in the following chronology: Early Preclassic, 1500–800 BCE; Middle Preclassic, 800–500 BCE; Late Preclassic, 500–150 BCE; Terminal Preclassic, 150 BCE–250 CE. (Piña Chan, 1972; Sanders et al., 1979).

Basin of Mexico. During the Early Preclassic, the Ixtapaluca subphase (1400–800 BCE) in the southern part of the Basin of Mexico contains pottery strongly related to the Olmec style of San Lorenzo on the Gulf Coast. The Olmec tradition is also evident in figurines of great refinement, found in large numbers in the Tlatilco cemeteries, which have since been engulfed by present-day Mexico City. Most of these figurines are female. Some indicate advanced pregnancy, suggestive of a concern with human as well as agricultural fertility. Other figurines show two heads on one body or heads with three eyes and two noses, believed to perhaps represent diviner-healers. In general the Tlatilco figurines, which include both Olmec and local styles, are thought to be merely grave offerings without explicit religious function. Olmec influence in the Basin was only marginal; its impact was stronger in the states of Morelos, Puebla, and Guerrero. [*For detailed treatment of the Olmec, see* Olmec Religion.]

In the Middle Preclassic new hamlets appeared around the system of lakes in the Basin of Mexico (which have now virtually disappeared). At Zacatenco and Ticomán, figurines abound but are cruder. As they were no longer placed in graves but appeared in refuse middens, it is assumed that they served as fetishes in household cults. There are no representations of gods or goddesses that can be recognized as such with reference to the iconographic system prevalent in the Classic and Postclassic periods (250–1521 CE). Nor is there definite evidence of civic-ceremonial architecture. It has been argued that a society capable of supporting potters not engaged in full-time food production should also be able to maintain religious practitioners, such as shamans. Certain figurines depicting masked dancers in peculiar costumes have been identified as magicians (shamans) and ballplayers but they are part of the Olmec component, as are the pottery masks (Coe, 1965). Concrete evidence of shamanism, amply demonstrated for North and South America, is lacking for Preclassic Mesoamerica.

In the Late Preclassic, pyramidal mounds of modest proportions occur at some sites in the southern part of the Basin of Mexico and indicate the beginning of ceremonial activities outside the immediate household clusters. This period is notable for a veritable population explosion. Cuicuilco became the dominant political center, with five to ten thousand inhabitants, while Ticomán remained only a minor village. At Cuicuilco several small pyramids were located in the residential zone and may have served the local populace. By 400 BCE a large, oval, truncated pyramid of adobe bricks with rough stone facing was built in tiers or stages, each of which contains an altarlike structure. Access was by a ramp facing east, toward the sunrise. The town and the lower parts of the pyramid were covered by a lava flow that, according to latest estimates, occurred around 400 CE, when Cuicuilco had long ceased to be a dominant center (Heizer and Bennyhoff, 1972). However, earlier eruptions from the nearby Xitle volcano, with spectacular displays of fire, smoke, and molten lava, led to the creation of the first deity in Mesoamerica, the "old fire god." He is portrayed in clay and later exclusively in stone sculpture as an old, toothless male with a wrinkled face who bears on his head a large basin for the burning of incense. Known by his Nahuatl (Aztec) name Huehueteotl ("old god"), he became one of the major deities of the Teotihuacán pantheon and, after the Toltec interlude, reappeared in the Aztec pantheon in different guise as Xiuhtecutli ("turquoise lord" or "lord of the year"). The burning of incense as an offering for petitioning the gods became general practice throughout Mesoamerica, both in household and in elaborate temple rituals. This is indicated by the great variety and number of ceramic incense burners that have been excavated.

Before internal conflicts brought about its decline (200–100 BCE), Cuicuilco had contributed much to the rise of Teotihuacán, a fast-growing settlement in the northern part of the Basin, which during the Terminal Preclassic was to become the dominant political and ceremonial center, with wide ramifications throughout much of Mesoamerica until its final collapse in 750 CE.

Between 150 and 1 BCE, Teotihuacán occupied an area of about six square kilometers and was a highly stratified agrarian community. It developed into an urban center of twenty-five to thirty thousand people in the Tzacualli phase (1–150 CE), when the grid system of the town was laid out with a main north-south axis, known as the Street of the Dead (so named by the Spanish, who thought the place a necropolis). On either side of the axis were erected numerous complexes, each with three temple-pyramid and a central courtyard. The monumental Pyramid of the Sun (sixty-three meters high) and the substructure of the Pyramid of the Moon were completed in this phase during a single fifty-year construction episode. (Again, these names were given by the Spanish.) The ceremonial precinct, over four kilometers in length, served civic and religious functions and became a pilgrimage center. Dependence on seasonal rainfall for agriculture gave rise to a cult of a god of rain and lightning, Tlaloc, who became the supreme deity and continued to be one of the major gods in later cultures up to the Spanish conquest (1521). The establishment of a hierarchical priesthood can be inferred from the art and architecture of this period. In the Classic period (250–750 CE) the pantheon expanded, and Teotihuacán became the largest city of the New World.

Western Mexico. In Guanajuato, to the northwest of the Basin of Mexico, elaborate pottery and finely modeled figurines of the Chupícuaro tradition (500–1 BCE) were lavishly used for tomb offerings, and ceramic flutes, whistles, and rattles were interred in children's graves. Ceremonies included the practice of decapitation, related to warfare. This custom, however, did not become widespread until the Middle and Late Classic.

The Preclassic cultures of western Mexico (in the present-day states of Michoacán, Colima, Jalisco, and Nayarit) remained outside the Mesoamerican cotradition until about 350 CE when the Teotihuacán and Gulf Coast cultures began to penetrate the area and introduced their culture and ideology.

Most noteworthy among these loosely united chiefdoms was their concern for the dead, as evidenced by the Shaft Tomb Complex (c. 200 BCE–400/500 CE). Unparalleled in other parts of Mesoamerica, it extends in a great arc from south-central Nayarit through central Jalisco to Colima. The tombs consist of vertical entrance shafts 1.5 to 8 meters deep, with narrow, short tunnels at the end leading to one or more vaults carved in the hard volcanic soil *(tepetate)*. After interment the shafts were completely filled with rubble and hand-packed dirt; stone slabs prevented the fill from entering the burial chambers. Grave offerings comprise large, hollow ceramic figures in varied local styles, representing men (some of them tomb guards with armor and weapons) and women in different poses and attitudes. The human figures have stylized features and disproportionate bodies but they are very expressive, approaching portraitlike countenances. They reflect the customs, dress, and ornaments of the ancient inhabitants (von Winning, 1974).

Funeral processions and mourning scenes modeled in clay depict rites preceding interment. They show the mourners in orderly arrangement following a catafalque being carried to a house, or groups of mourners surrounding a corpse. Other kinds of grave offerings include complex scenes of villagers and their huts, family gatherings, ball-court scenes, bloodletting and cheek-perforation rituals, and dancers with musicians, all consisting of small, crudely modeled figurines attached to clay slabs. The variety of ceramic house models of one or two stories, some of them multichambered, is interesting inasmuch as no masonry architecture existed in this area. They replicate constructions of wattle daubed with mud, covered with a thatched roof. These were tomb offerings intended as shelters in the afterlife.

Among the smaller, solid figurines are those showing a female strapped to a slab. They appear to represent corpses on biers laid out for funeral rites, ready to be lowered through the shaft into the burial chamber. Similar ceramic "bed figures" occur in coeval contexts in Ecuador, and sporadically in the Old World (von Winning and Hammer, 1972).

A variety of large, hollow animal effigies occur also in the shaft tombs. In Colima dog effigies abound, their well-fed appearance indicates that they had been deliberately fattened to provide food for the departed. (In Aztec times fattened dogs were sold in the market for human consumption.) Skeletons of carefully buried dogs have been found in graves at Tlatilco and Chupícuaro, and it is generally believed that the dogs were supposed to help the souls of the deceased on their paths through the perils of the underworld.

The generally held view that the ceramic sculptures of the Shaft Tomb Complex portray secular subjects indicative of everyday village life has been rejected by Peter T. Furst (1975). Based on ethnographic comparisons—mainly with the beliefs and shamanistic practices among the modern Huichol Indians whose remote ancestors occupied part of the Shaft Tomb zone—he concludes that the art of western Mexico was no less religious than that of the rest of Mesoamerica. However, none of the figures display attributes that clearly identify them as deities or deity impersonators in the manner of other Mesoamerican religion and iconography. Tlaloc and Huehueteotl effigies occur only after the end of the Shaft Tomb period. Lacking temple pyramids and relevant documentary sources, the ceramic sculptures provide the only evidence for a ceremonialism that emphasized a cult of the dead.

Guerrero and the Puebla-Tlaxcala Area. Preclassic ceremonialism was introduced into this area by Olmec intruders. For the period after the decline of Olmec influence (after 800 BCE), information on social, political, and religious aspects is lacking. The Mezcala region of Guerrero produced a remarkable number of highly stylized anthropomorphic figures and masks, ranging from the Preclassic Olmecoid to Teotihuacanoid types, but the stylistic sequence is not datable. Among the small stone sculptures are flat models of temple facades with doorways in which a human figure occasionally stands on top of the stairway. However, masonry temples of this type have not been reported from the Mezcala region, and the date of these artifacts is unknown. These temple sculptures probably were made in the Classic period. In the Tehuacán Valley, developments from early village life to urban communities paralleled those in other parts of Mesoamerica. The archaeological remains give no indication of religious activities.

In sum, the Preclassic figurines that appear all over Mexico north of the eighteenth parallel are similar insofar as their features were incised and clay fillets added. Neither these nor the Shaft Tomb figures represent well-defined deities with determinative attributes such as occur in later periods. With the exception of the Olmec intrusive layer and the emergence of the old fire god at Cuicuilco, and the rain god Tlaloc in Teotihuacán, in all other regions the gods, as Ignacio Bernal once said, had not yet been born.

BIBLIOGRAPHY

Coe, Michael D. *The Jaguar's Children: Pre-Classic Central Mexico.* New York, 1965. An explicit exposition of the Olmec art style and its distribution. Numerous good illustrations of pottery vessels, figurines, masks, and other artifacts from the Mexican highlands.

Furst, Peter T. "House of Darkness and House of Light: Sacred Functions of West Mexican Funeral Art." In *Death and the Afterlife in Pre-Columbian America: A Conference at Dumbarton Oaks, October 27th, 1973,* edited by Elizabeth P. Benson, pp. 33–68. Washington, 1975. Elaborating his earlier published views that western Mexican funerary art objects have a religious rather than a secular or anecdotal significance, Furst considers the Nayarit house models as houses of the dead, the *locus mundi* of the soul.

Heizer, Robert F., and James A. Bennyhoff. "Archaeological Excavations at Cuicuilco, Mexico, 1957." In *Research Reports, 1955–1960 Projects, National Geographic Society*, edited by Paul H. Oelsen, pp. 93–104. Washington, 1972. A revision of the cultural sequence of the Late and Terminal Preclassic periods in the Valley of Mexico. A preliminary summary of the authors' work appears in their article "Archaeological Investigation of Cuicuilco, Valley of Mexico, 1957," *Science* 127 (January 1958): 232–233.

Piña Chan, Román. *Historia, arqueología y arte prehispánico.* Mexico City, 1972. Includes the only comprehensive chronological chart of all the pre-Columbian cultures of Mexico published so far by a Mexican archaeologist.

Sanders, William T., Jeffrey R. Parsons, and Robert S. Santley. *The Basin of Mexico; Ecological Processes in the Evolution of a Civilization.* New York, 1979. An up-to-date synthesis of the sociocultural evolution based primarily on settlement pattern surveys.

von Winning, Hasso. *The Shaft Tomb Figures of West Mexico.* Los Angeles, 1974. A classification according to thematic significance of the ceramic figures of Colima, Jalisco, and Nayarit.

von Winning, Hasso, and Olga Hammer. *Anecdotal Sculpture of Ancient West Mexico.* Los Angeles, 1972. A copiously illustrated and annotated exhibition catalog of ceramic house models and figurine groups from Colima, Jalisco, and Nayarit, with two essays on related topics.

HASSO VON WINNING

Classic Cultures

The Classic period in the Valley of Mexico and its environs (150 BCE–750 CE) was one of florescence and of great achievement and intellectual advancement in the fields of art, government, and ideology. These centuries saw urbanism defined. Intense trade developed along established routes, diffusing ideas and material goods from one corner of Mesoamerica to another and consolidating religious thought and ceremonial.

Data for Classic period religion is based on archaeology; while no written documents from that period have come down to us, we can rightly regard mural painting, architecture, and other works of art as valid documents. Sixteenth-century chronicles describing Aztec religious belief and custom—about eight centuries after the decline of Teotihuacán—nevertheless can help us interpret earlier cultures, if used with caution. Ethnographic evidence can also shed light on ancient cultures, since in many cases there seems to be a continuity of tradition. It is significant, too, that Mesoamerica constituted a unified culture area, unlike the Mediterranean civilization that had interaction with totally different cultures from very early times on. In addition to the shared urbanism of its cultures, pre-Columbian Mesoamerica was in many ways unified by a common ideological system, with regional and temporal variation. This apparent underlying tradition of many basic beliefs allows us to compare one culture with another, but only to a certain extent and allowing for changes over time.

During the Classic period the characteristics of Mesoamerican religion were formalized. Patterns in belief, ritual, and iconography, some of them derived from earlier cultures, were set, and they formed the basis of later societies, especially those of the Toltec and the Aztec. The belief that natural forces were animate, the measurement of time as coordinated with sacred space, and the observation of heavenly bodies were some of the main characteristics. There was an intense ceremonialism supported by iconography and by oral mythic tradition. The gods were numerous, often human in form and often conceived as animals that were the gods' doubles. Religion was integrated with social organization, politics, economy, art, music, and poetry. There was a patron deity for virtually every activity, and all objects received homage and offerings, from certain flowers reserved for sovereigns to humble implements for planting and harvesting. The world was considered a sacred structure, an image of the cosmos.

Sites and structures (and probably human activities such as processions and ritual dancing) were oriented to the sun, moon, stars, and to sacred geographical places. Architectural splendor was manifested in pyramid platforms surmounted by temples; many were painted in symbolic colors, their exteriors and interiors covered with murals. The temple in each city was the *axis mundi,* the center of the universe. Sculpture depicted religious themes, and much pottery was decorated with images of the gods. The worldview of Classic Mesoamerica was peopled with deities who intervened in every phase of life. Men who governed were deeply enmeshed in ritual. Every ruler had his priestly duties, and the priests themselves controlled the ritual calendar and thus the agricultural cycle, which was a basic part of the economy.

Teotihuacán. During the Classic period, Teotihuacán, which means "place where the gods are made," became the center of the Mesoamerican world. A vast settlement occupying more than eight square miles in the valley of the same name, a subvalley of the Basin of Mexico, the city of Teotihuacán was the leading Classic center and the most highly urbanized center in the New World. Although Teotihuacán at its height ruled the trade routes and set religious patterns for many other cultures, in its early period it barely set the stage for its later grandeur.

Founding and early history. Around the beginning of the common era, a small settlement was established in the northern part of what we now call the Teotihuacán Valley. After the eruption of the Xitle volcano in the southern part of the Basin of Mexico (c. 1000 BCE), some residents of Cuicuilco, which had been covered by lava in the eruption, probably moved to the east, into the Teotihuacán area. The refugees would have brought their own deities, especially the fire god. We see him in the Teotihuacán braziers of Huehueteotl ("old god"), who may have originated in Cuicuilco. At an early period Teotihuacán also was strongly influenced by the Puebla-Tlaxcala peoples. During the Patlachique (150–1 BCE) and the Tzacualli (1–150 CE) phases, Teotihuacán experienced explosive growth. People from the eastern and southern parts of the Basin of Mexico concentrated around this center, raising the population of Teotihuacán to eighty thousand or more (Sanders et al., 1979, pp. 184ff.; Millon, 1981, p. 221). This population concentration was reflected in the city's direct control of agricultural production and of the obsidian industry, as well as in its importance as a regional economic center, which at the same time stimulated religious manifestation.

Toward the end of the Tzacualli phase the great Pyramid of the Sun was erected, standing more than 63 meters high and measuring 225 meters on each of its four sides. Shortly after this the Pyramid of the Moon was built with the Avenue of the Dead leading up to it. (These structures were named by the Aztec; we do not know what the Teotihuacanos called them.) The orientation of the Avenue of the Dead is 15°25′ east of north and the major structures were aligned with this axis, slightly "skewed" from the cardinal directions. From the Tzacualli phase on, an exuberance of construction filled Teotihuacán with splendid structures, all carefully planned on a grid pattern (see figure 1 for topographical relations among structures at Teotihuacán).

Caves and cults. The most sacred place in the Teotihuacán complex was the spot where the Sun pyramid stood, underneath which lies a sacred cave. Caves were considered sacred throughout Mesoamerica, and this one designated the site for the construction of the great pyramid. Teotihuacán was a powerful religious magnet and attracted pilgrims from all over. The influx of large groups of pilgrims undoubtedly created the need for more spectacular structures and probably provided the economic means and hands for the work. According to Mircea Eliade in *The Sacred and the Profane* (New York, 1959), sacred time is relived in a sacred space by means of a pilgrimage, and divine space is repeated by building one holy place over another. In Teotihuacán this repetition took place when the great pyramid was erected over a primitive shrine, itself built over a subterranean cave. A cult of long standing existed in this cavern and was one reason that Teotihuacán became a religious center. The presence of drainage channels

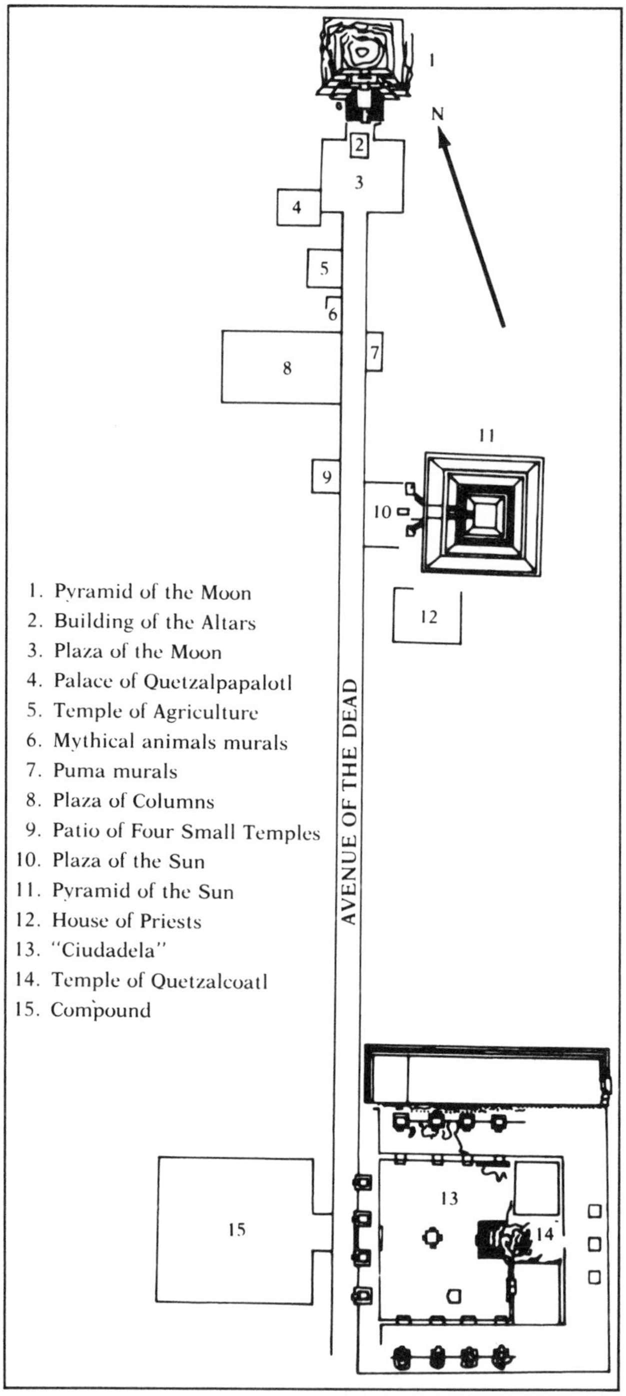

FIGURE 1. *Simplified Scheme of Avenue of the Dead Complex, Teotihuacán*

through which water was brought into the cave (Millon, 1981, p. 234) indicates the performance there of rituals associated with water, and the remains of ritual fires suggest a symbolic juxtaposition of fire and water, which juxtaposition was basic in Mesoamerican religion. It is likely, René Millon suggests, that the guardians of beliefs and cults in the sacred cave had awesome prestige and that this prestige and the importance of religion and ritual in general played a major part in the shaping of Teotihuacán's hierarchical society and in the legitimation of the authority of the state. [*See* Caves.]

Orientation, symbolic planning, and architecture. Urban planning, architecture, myth, and ritual were interrelated in ancient Mexico. The blending of religious-cosmological conceptions with an acute awareness of nature constituted much of the Classic worldview. The orientation of Teotihuacán's major axis, the Avenue of the Dead, was astronomically and calendrically determined. The star group Pleiades was also influential since some structures were oriented to its rising position. The main facades of most of the pyramids, except the Pyramid of the Moon, faced west (that is, in the direction of the setting sun), as did monuments in later Mesoamerican cultures. An astronomical symbol found in strategic positions all over the city was also one of the determinants of the orientation of streets and structures. This symbol is the "pecked cross," actually a quartered circle consisting of dots whose number probably referred to a calendrical-ritual count. It was carved on the floors of ceremonial buildings and also on rocks on the periphery of the city, which were aligned with the monuments (Aveni, 1980, p 223).

There are more than seventy-five temples in the city. Some, found on the Avenue of the Dead, are grouped into complexes of three, perhaps a symbolic number. More than two thousand residential compounds are located in Teotihuacán, and every residential compound had one or more local temples within it. Even within smaller units a miniature temple is often found in the center of a courtyard. That the natural environment and nearby topographical features were part of the worldview of Teotihuacán and that they figured in the planning of the city is evident from the relation of Teotihuacán to the mountains, caves, and bodies of water in its environs. On the mountaintops, rites to the rain gods were held, for here the clouds gathered and formed the precious liquid. Chronicles referring to the Aztec, whose practices can perhaps give us an insight into the earlier period, tell us that mountains were seen as female; water was thought to be held inside them as if in the womb. The mountain north of the Avenue of the Dead, whose form was mirrored by the Pyramid of the Moon, was called Tenan, "the mother" (i.e., of people) by the Aztec. Hills and waterholes were considered sacred, as were trees, for they protected people and provided sustenance in the form of leaves, fruit, and roots.

Teotihuacán, like most of Mesoamerica, was basically an agricultural society. Observance of the seasons was controlled by a ritual calendar and the invocation of rain through propitiation of the gods was an important ceremony. Lake Tezcoco, the great body of water that covered a large part of the Basin of Mexico, came almost to the borders of Teotihuacán and provided aquatic foods and a waterway for transportation. So for the Teotihuacanos, the gods of water were associated with "Our Mother" (as the lake was called in Aztec times) as well as with rain and mountaintops. This setting of natural abundance was enhanced in Teotihuacán by local deposits of obsidian, which was considered divine.

As shown in figure 1, the Avenue of the Dead extends almost two thousand meters from the Sun and Moon pyramids to the Ciudadela (Span., "citadel"), Teotihuacán's religious and political center during much of the metropolis's existence. The vast quadrangle (4.4 hectares) is surrounded on each of its four sides by wide platforms topped by four low pyramids on three sides, and by three at the east or rear (Millon, 1981, p. 203). Entrance to the complex is only from the Avenue of the Dead on the west and from the north, suggesting that entrance to and exit from the area were strictly controlled. Living quarters in the northeast and southeast of the Ciudadela could have housed about 250 persons, probably high cult officials. George L. Cowgill states that while the head of state must have resided in the Ciudadela, his presence here was largely ceremonial and the real governing activity was carried out elsewhere (Cowgill, 1983). A square platform with a staircase on each of its four sides in the middle of the quadrangle suggests large-scale rites; theatrical performances of a religious character evidently were held here.

At the eastern end of the Ciudadela stands the majestic pyramid known as the Temple of Quetzalcoatl, so called because of the feathered serpents that decorate its facade—although the temple was not necessarily dedicated to Quetzalcoatl, who in the Postclassic period was a god of civilization, creation, and the arts. Also on the facade are heads of fire serpents that have been identified erroneously as representations of the rain god Tlaloc. The spectacular Temple of Quetzalcoatl was erected in the second construction period of the Ciudadela (probably 150–200 CE), coeval in part with the Sun and Moon pyramids, and was used (and at times rebuilt) up until the end of Teotihuacán, around 750 CE. But at one period in the city's history (c. 300 CE), another smaller pyramid, the Adosada (Span., "affixed") was attached to its facade, partly blocking the earlier building. The Adosada seems to have enhanced rather than eclipsed the Temple of Quetzalcoatl's religious importance. Perhaps this was an architectural rather than an ideological renovation. According to Cowgill (1983), the religious and political significance combined in the Ciudadela and the Quetzalcoatl pyramid cult was intimately associated with Teotihuacán's rulership. He also suggests that increased activity associated with the Quetzalcoatl temple may have necessitated the building of this extra structure.

A pyramid platform in the southern part of the Ciudadela is decorated with red X designs and with green circles, symbols of water, "that which is precious." The X is clearly an *ollin,* symbol of motion (or of the movement of the sun, according to later Aztec tradition). The joining of water and fire (in this case, the sun) are thus represented during this early period. Although the combination symbolized war in the Postclassic period, here in Teotihuacán it may have had astronomical significance.

Another enormous area of dwellings, pyramids, platforms, temples, and courtyards occupying many hectares along the major avenue, and known as the Avenue of the Dead Complex, has been tentatively identified as the center of governmental functions. The *talud* ("sloping panel") combined with the *tablero* ("vertical panel") is the characteristic Teotihuacán facade for religious structures and has long been recognized as the sign that a building faced in such a way is a temple (Millon, 1981, p. 229). This convention was also applied to public buildings and residential compounds, thus consecrating the entire avenue, as well as giving a sacred character to buildings in other zones that incorporate the *talud-tablero* mode of facing. Juan Vidarte de Linares (cited in Cowgill, 1983) has interpreted the Avenue of the Dead, lined with temple platforms thus built, as a great open-air cathedral.

Art. The art of Teotihuacán is intensely religious. Mural painting (one of the major art forms) on buildings, temples, and shrines, leads Clara Millon (cited in Millon, 1981, p. 213) to consider it the "official graphic medium for transmitting ideas and beliefs . . . ideologically acceptable and desirable." Murals were an ideal medium for communication because they were out in the open for all to see. In the interior of palaces, where the paintings usually had a religious context, their messages, perhaps understood only by priests, must also have constituted a type of didactic "book" on the walls. Sculpture in Teotihuacán was usually architectural: roof merlons with year-sign motifs, serpentine balustrades on stairways (later seen at Tenayuca, Chichén Itzá, and other sites), zoomorphic stone heads on the facades of buildings (on, for example, the Temple of Quetzalcoatl and at one time on the Pyramid of the Sun), and stone figures perhaps representing gods, such as the old fire god. A relief panel recently discovered in the West Plaza of the Avenue of the Dead Complex represents a personage with rain god characteristics holding a rattle in either hand. According to Noel Morelos, the archaeologist who discovered it, the image is somewhat similar to Tlaloc figures in the Tetitla and Tepantitla murals at Teotihuacán. Another rich source of information is pottery, painted or decorated with other techniques, that depicts rituals and either deities or priests.

The large braziers found at Teotihuacán are sometimes called "theaters" because the masks surrounded by symbolic elements that are attached to them are reminiscent of the stage. *Candeleros* (Span., "candlesticks") must have been used for copal incense; the Teotihuacanos had no candles. The use of clay figurines can only be guessed at. Some may have been used on household altars or kept by pilgrims as souvenirs from sacred places. "Portrait figurines," sometimes called "dancers," are small, nude, sexless people in animated positions. Other clay figures are "puppets," with movable arms and legs, nude bodies, and carefully made and adorned heads. Lack of body adornment on the portrait figurines and puppets suggests that they were dressed in bark paper, a ritual material, for ceremonial use. Clay dogs may, as among the Aztec, have represented the animal that accompanied the deceased to the afterworld.

A possible warrior cult, involving relations with other regions of Mesoamerica, is indicated by representations of military figures in the murals, on decorated pottery, and in figurines. Some of the figurines wear warrior vestments, including animal helmets. Painted representations of people holding excised hearts on knives, as in a mural in the Atetelco (another architectural complex, or palace), may indicate the existence of a warrior cult, although they might represent human sacrifice practiced for ritual reasons. Citing the work of Hasso von Winning and George Kubler, Esther Pasztory (1978, p. 133) notes that war-related iconographic themes in Teotihuacán include the sun god as a raptorial bird and as a feline, warriors in animal disguise, and an owl-and-weapon symbol.

Burials. Funerary customs also shed light on the religion of Teotihuacán. Cremation was practiced and was possibly related to the later Aztec belief that a person's possessions must be burned in order to travel to the afterworld, where they would be turned over to the lord of the dead. Interment was also practiced; burials were accompanied by grave goods—vessels whose contents may have been food or other necessities for the other world and miniature objects that were symbolic offerings. Mica decorated some of the large braziers and urns and has been found under floors. Its meaning is obscure, but it is mirrorlike and mirrors were used for divining.

Deities. Names of Teotihuacán gods are unknown to us; therefore we refer to them by their characteristics or symbols, sometimes comparing them to Aztec deities whose iconography and function are similar. Esther Pasztory (1973, p. 147) has noted that the structure of Teotihuacán iconography is in many ways similar to that of the Aztec, for which we have written data, and image clusters have been identified in Teotihuacán that have elements similar to representations of Aztec deities. The presence of water-agricultural deities is indicated by aquatic symbols such as streams, water dripping from shells, fish, frogs, and water lilies. The god associated with rain and the earth is distinguished by traits found on the Aztec deity Tlaloc—goggle eyes and fangs, for example—but also by a water lily in his mouth, a lightning staff, a vessel with water, a year-sign headdress, and crocodilian traits. Pasztory calls him "Tlaloc A." "Tlaloc B" appeared later on the scene when there was a trend toward militarism in Teotihuacán. Some of Tlaloc B's diagnostic traits are a bifurcated tongue, a *bigotera* (Span., "mustache"), and jaguar features. Both "Tlalocs" are associated with water, although the latter, because his image is found in foreign centers and is related to persons who may be representatives of the Teotihuacán state, seems to be connected with military and foreign relations as well. Pasztory (1978, p. 134) sees Tlaloc B, or the "Jaguar Tlaloc," as possibly being the patron deity of Teotihuacán, and claims that the "patron deity cult," later practiced among the Toltec and Aztec (which was different from a cult to deified ancestors) originated in Teotihuacán. She also notes that Teotihuacán was the first culture in Mesoamerica to develop a state cult from the earlier agricultural fertility cult. To this must be added the importance of aquatic sustenance from the nearby lake, to which many of the water symbols may refer.

Evidence of other deities is scanty, but among those believed to have existed in Teotihuacán are Huehueteotl, whose brazier, which was designed to be carried on the head, suggests he is a fire god, and an earth mother figure who may have been associated with water and vegetation. She is represented in the Tepantitla murals surrounded by fertility symbols such as plants, drops of water, seeds, and birds. Formerly she was thought to be a male water god, and in Aztec times she had a number of names, including Xochiquetzal ("precious flower"). A precursor of this goddess may be represented in some figurines whose headdresses bear flowers, usually the characteristic mark of Xochiquetzal. A majestic stone statue discovered near the Pyramid of the Moon may have water association, due to the "meanders" (water symbols) on her garments. The agricultural fertility cult was associated with gods of earth, water, rain, crops, sun, and moon. A large stone disk, with rays surrounding a skull head, seems to represent the sun. It was painted red, the color applied to bodies of the deceased; thus it may represent the setting sun that dies in the west. Deformed figures represented on the walls of the Atetelco suggest Nanahuatzin, the sick god of the Aztec tradition who became the sun, although these may not actually portray him. Another god portrayed is the feathered serpent, but there is no way of knowing if he is the same god the Aztec worshiped under the name Quetzalcoatl. There is also a "flayed god," represented in clay figurines and on pottery vessels. One statue depicts a flayed god (or his surrogate) wearing a human skin. This deity may be related to the later Xipe Totec, Aztec god of vegetation, although this large clay figure dates from the beginning of the Postclassic era.

There may also have been a "dual complex," a male-female creative force, such as existed later in Aztec cosmology. This could be inferred from the two major pyramids. Innumerable figurines with hollow interiors that in turn contain one or more miniature figures fully dressed may represent a creator deity. But the most convincing evidence indicates that the pantheon was built around forces of water and fertility.

Creation of the sun in Teotihuacán. Animals portrayed in a mural painting called the Mural of the Mythological Animals may be an early version of the myth of the four Suns, or eras, that form part of Aztec mythology (Millon, 1972, p. 7). Jaguars devouring fish, a type of *cipactli* (crocodilian) earth creature, and evidence of a cataclysm are seen in the Teotihuacán mural. The creation of the Fifth Sun in Teotihuacán (the Aztec mythical celestial plain), in which the poor deformed god Nanahuatzin threw himself into the fire to become the sun, constitutes one of the great Mesoamerican myths. This myth may have been invented *a posteriori* by the Aztec in order to explain the creation of their own era, the Fifth Sun, associated with the "place where the gods are made" (i.e., Teotihuacán) and with their sacred ancestors, the Teotihuacanos. The impact of Teotihuacán religion and myth on the Aztec is evident from the orientation of the sacred precinct in Tenochtitlán, the Aztec capital. This was based on the fact that, in the myth of the Fifth Sun, the gods in Teotihuacán, after the birth of the sun, faced the four directions to see where it would rise. Four gateways facing these directions were made in Tenochtitlán in memory of the myth. The desire of the Aztec to view Teotihuacán as the sacred ancestral place can be seen here and also in the fact that the Aztec sovereign worshiped there every twenty days.

Ritual. Ritual, as represented in many paintings, was clearly an important aspect of Teotihuacán religion. One example of such a representation is that of the priests, depicted in profile, who face the great central figure in the Tepantitla mural, and who evidently are carrying out a ceremony involving this earth-god figure. Men (as gods' surrogates) in ritual attitudes are also depicted on decorated pottery. The very layout of the major avenues and structures of the city brings to mind the probability of dramatic processions led by religious leaders, involving a large part of the population and possibly pilgrims. Processions would probably have stopped at the small altar-platforms in the center of the avenues, where rites would have been performed. Fray Diego Durán (1971, p. 296) writes about didactic yet amusing skits involving deities that were performed during the later Aztec religious festivals, which may provide us with parallels of earlier ritual celebrations. Colonial chronicles describe Aztec processions in which the costumes of the participants, the materials of which they were made, and their colors were all significant: yellow face paint symbolized maize; "popcorn" garlands represented the dry season. People walked, danced, and sang in the processions; the beat of the drum, the shrill sound of a native flute, and the rhythmic tone of chanted poetry set the pace for their steps. Large braziers may have been carried at the head of the procession, smoke from resin incense floating upward as a medium for communication with the gods. A ritual liquid such as *pulque* may have been poured on the ground. Hands pouring precious symbols in streams are depicted in Teotihuacán murals, representing this type of libation. Processions like these would have been public rituals to celebrate seasonal, calendrical, religious, political, and agricultural events. The changing of the seasons and their effect upon the crops, for example, called for constant celebration and/or propitiation of the gods.

Parallel with the public rituals would have been rites performed at small temples in residential compounds. Household worship probably occurred at times when major events took place but also in relation to the more private cycles of the household. People close to the soil practice innumerable ceremonies important to their well-being. In Postclassic times rites were performed annually (as they still are today) to honor agricultural implements; permission is still ritually requested of the earth to break the surface in order to plant; clay figurines are buried in the fields as offerings; terra-cotta frogs or water-deity figures are thrown into waterholes; food and clay images are placed in caves for the "owners of maize" and plants. Evidence of some concern in Teotihuacán culture for human fertility is provided by figurines of pregnant women, which were most likely used in rites of fecundity.

The end of Teotihuacán and its heritage. The eclipse of Teotihuacán took place around 750 CE, when much of the city was burned, the destruction centering on religious and public buildings. Statues of the gods were broken and their faces mutilated (Jarquin and Martínez, 1982, p. 36). (In the pictorial manuscripts from Postclassic Mexico the conquest of a city is generally depicted by the burning of its temples.) Burning occurred mainly in the heart of Teotihuacán—four hundred instances of burning are evident in the Avenue of the Dead zone alone (Millon, 1981, pp. 236–237)—but to date there is no evidence of foreign invaders, such as non-Teotihuacán weapons or the like. The burning of temples and smashing of images implies ritual destruction, and René Millon points out that many religious structures in Mesoamerica were ritually burned and then reconstructed. The destruction of Teotihuacán's temples was so complete, however, that in spite of later building at the site, the city never again rose to even a portion of its former grandeur.

Meanwhile, other peoples had filtered into the valley, including the Toltec and the Chichimec. As Teotihuacán fell other centers rose. Sites in Tlaxcala expanded. Cacaxtla adopted many Teotihuacán motifs and possibly its cultural ideas as well. Xochicalco, a critical point on a trade route from the south, became powerful. El Tajín acquired more importance in the Gulf Coast region. Teotihuacán as a live metropolis disappeared, but its fame and influence lived on. South to the Maya region, east to the Gulf, west to the Pacific, and north to Altavista (near what would become the United States border), Teotihuacán religion, art, myth, and tradition spread and were adapted to other cultures. This great civilization and religious center took its place as the revered ancestor of many later cultures.

Cholula. About two hundred kilometers to the southeast, Cholula was a sister city to Teotihuacán during the Classic period; Quetzalcoatl was its principal god. According to archaeologist Eduardo Merlo, the earliest pyramid at Cholula (c. 150 BCE), was constructed over a sacred spring, paralleling the Teotihuacán tradition of building over a consecrated spot. The Mural of the Bebedores (Span., "drinkers"; c. 200 CE) in Cholula, at the west side of the great pyramid, portrays elaborate scenes of ritual drinking of *pulque*. This mural is dedicated to agricultural fertility and to *pulque* gods. The main Classic period deity here was the water goddess, and it is interesting that the patron saint of present-day

Cholula, whose sanctuary is built on top of the great pyramid, is the Virgin of Los Remedios, whose special province is the control of the water supply (Olivera, 1970, pp. 212–213).

Cantona, in the Puebla-Tlaxcala Valley, was contemporary with early Cholula and Teotihuacán but was evidently eclipsed by the dramatic rise of the latter. Cantona must have been an important religious pilgrimage center and was possibly a Gulf Coast link with the central highlands. More than sixteen square kilometers in area, this site dates from the Late Preclassic into the Middle Classic and exhibits strong Veracruz influence, as seen in the ball-game cult, represented by sixteen courts. There are thousands of unexplored mounds, many dwellings, one excavated igloo-type sweat bath, and the unexplored remains of about twenty more of these structures. According to archaeologist Diana Lopez, these were used for ritual bathing.

Monte Albán and Oaxaca. The Valley of Oaxaca is an archaeologically rich area in the central part of the present state of Oaxaca in south-central Mexico. Ecological advantages, effectively exploited, contributed to the rise of urbanism here centuries earlier than in other nearby regions north and west of the valley (Paddock, 1966, p. 242). In this setting the splendid Zapotec civilization of Monte Albán arose. This city was built on five artificially leveled hills just east of today's city of Oaxaca and covered a total area of six and a half square kilometers. Monte Albán's main plaza, 150 by 300 meters, dominates the central hill, producing a whole that can be seen as the center and four corners of the universe. This central hill contains both religious and residential buildings: pyramid platforms, a main plaza and smaller ones, a ball court, the royal residence, and subterranean tombs whose entrances are protected by gods and whose interiors were filled with funerary urns in the form of gods. Richard Blanton (in Flannery and Marcus, 1983, p. 84) suggests that Monte Albán, constructed on a hilltop not easily accessible, yet near a rich alluvial plain, was the principal center of the region. Its hilltop location probably was in part a defensive measure against possible incursions, although many other important centers in Oaxaca also were built on mountaintops: for example, Monte Negro, Quiotepec, and Guiengola. There could also have been a religious motivation in this, in that the summits of mountains were often held to be sacred in ancient Mesoamerica and are dedicated to gods of rain.

Although Monte Albán has traditionally been seen as indebted to Teotihuacán for much of its religion, art, and ideas, Kent V. Flannery, Joyce Marcus, and John Paddock (Flannery and Marcus, 1983, p. 161) point out that the Zapotec autonomous tradition was thousands of years old when Monte Albán was built (c. 100 BCE) and that hieroglyphic writing was developed there before Teotihuacán was founded. Strong influence and exchange between the two centers did exist, however. There was an enclave of Oaxaca people in Teotihuacán, whose residents lived in their own zone, produced Oaxaca-style pottery, constructed a stone-lined Oaxaca tomb and stela, or tomb jamb, and who worshiped their own gods, if one may judge from two funerary urns representing a god with serpent buccal mask found in the tomb (Millon, 1973, I, pp. 141–142). Although no comparable Teotihuacano enclave has been found at Monte Albán, Teotihuacán personages are represented on some of the city's monuments. They carry copal incense bags (characteristic of priests) and wear identifying deity, animal, or "tassel" Teotihuacán headdresses. A Teotihuacán-style temple is also depicted. Marcus (Flannery and Marcus, 1983, p. 179) interprets these scenes as visual proof that Teotihuacán and Monte Albán had emissaries who consolidated agreements through rituals, thus placing these treaties in a sacred context.

Early history. Monte Albán has a long history, beginning about 500 BCE. Between 200 BCE and 100 CE (Monte Albán I–II) this center of ten thousand inhabitants constructed large defensive walls and masonry tombs. Three hundred carved stone monuments with calendrical and military themes have been found dating from this period, along with hieroglyphic writing and effigy vessels possibly representing gods (Marcus, in Flannery and Marcus, 1983, pp. 52–53, 95). The nude figures in distorted poses known as *danzantes* (Span., "dancers") were carved on stone slabs along with symbols of sacrifice. They represented captives and as such may refer to ritual death. They also may represent a symbolic display of power. Fear-inspiring propaganda of this type was repeated—in ritual, not sculpture—many centuries later by the Aztec, who invited their enemies to witness mass sacrifices of war captives. Toward the end of this early period there were highly developed traits such as a complex pantheon of deities, ceremonial architecture, a stratified society, increased population, and political, economic, and military influence outside the Valley of Oaxaca (Paddock, 1966, pp. 111–119). The plan of the Zapotec temple at this time, with an inner chamber reserved for members of the cult, points to the existence of full-time priests and an incipient state religion (Flannery, in Flannery and Marcus, 1983, p. 82).

Florescence of Monte Albán. Classic Monte Albán (Monte Albán III) covers the period from 100 to 600 CE. This was a period of florescence during which the population reached its maximum size and both the main plaza and neighboring hills became covered with monumental structures. Restricted entrance to the main plaza suggests that its use may have been mainly for religious and civil leaders, yet its size would indicate that on some occasions rites were celebrated involving the general populace, which Blanton (in Flannery and Marcus, 1983, pp. 131–133) estimates at approximately thirty thousand. The temples had full-time priests plus a high priest (Flannery, in Flannery and Marcus, 1983, pp. 132, 134). As in other Mesoamerican societies, the Zapotec ruler was given a year of religious training, and the priesthood was drawn from noble families. The ruler worshiped at a special shrine.

Tombs, funerary urns, and Zapotec gods. Typical of Monte Albán is the subterranean cruciform tomb, probably constructed during its future occupant's life and over which a temple or residential structure was built. Living quarters over these tombs indicate that the descendants of the deceased (probably usually rulers) practiced ancestor worship (Flannery and Marcus, 1983, pp. 135, 345). Personages represented in the murals of Tomb 104 and Tomb 105, described by Alfonso Caso as gods, evidently depict royal couples dressed in the garb of deities. As in Asia, the dead ruler or forefather had to be propitiated in order to protect the living. The people portrayed in these tombs, then, are the royal, deified ancestors of those buried here. The four rooms of the building over Tomb 105 are oriented to the four cardinal directions, indicating a cosmic plan in the building of Monte Albán. In a niche above the entrance to each tomb is a funerary urn. Within the tomb more urns appear. Urns have been found, too, as offerings in temples and caches. Most of the urns are anthropomorphic in form; many wear zoomorphic masks and headdresses and they are adorned with numerals and glyphs.

One type of urn, the *acompañante* (Span., "companion" or "attendant"), has been found either with the deceased or with the major urns themselves. There are two schools of thought regarding the funeral urns. Alfonso Caso and Ignacio Bernal (1952) define them as gods, while Joyce Marcus (in Flannery and Marcus, 1983, pp. 144–148) interprets them as deceased ancestors. Sixteenth-century chronicles associate calendric names with personages but not with gods. The Spanish at that time did not understand this reference to ancestors because they were unfamiliar with the system of naming forefathers with dates; therefore they often mistook figures of dead rulers for deities, and this confusion has persisted. Because they had no knowledge of Zapotec, Europeans often mistook titles of nobility or references to natural forces (such as *cocijo,* which means "lightning") for names of deities.

Caso and Bernal (1952), who believe them to be gods, identify the figures depicted on the funerary urns as follows: Cocijo, the rain god (who also has maize aspects, judging from the corn cobs in his headdress on some urns); Pitào Cozobi, god of maize and grains; other maize-sustenance deities such as 5 Flower Quiepelagayo and a god referred to as "with bow in the Headdress"; a Zapotec version of Quetzalcoatl; a flayed god (Xipe?), represented carrying a disembodied head; an old god associated with caves and the underworld; 13 Serpent, an earth mother; and animal deities such as the parrot (associated with the sun), the jaguar (associated with rain), and the bat and the *tlacuache* (opossum), both associated with maize.

Natural forces. Joyce Marcus (in Flannery and Marcus, 1983, pp. 345–351) stresses the importance in Zapotec religion of animism—the animate character of things such as trees, stars, hills, but especially powerful natural and supernatural forces. A vital force was *pèe* ("wind, breath, spirit") and this existed in man, animals, the 260-day ritual calendar, light, the sun, the moon, clouds, lightning, rain, fire, and earthquakes. *Pitào,* the augmentative form of *pèe,* means "great breath" or "great spirit," and refers to a sacred quality. Lightning, *(cocijo)* was a highly revered element among the Zapotec because it brought rain. According to Fray Juan de Córdova's *Arte del idioma zapoteca* (1578), the thirteen-day period in the pre-Hispanic calendar (13 numbers × 20 day names = 260 days constituting the ritual-divinatory calendar) was called *cocijo* or *pitào.* Thus the gods were identified with time periods and with phenomena associated with the calendar.

Clouds were held as sacred by the Zapotec. In fact, they considered themselves descended from clouds, just as the Mixtec regarded trees as their primordial ancestors. After death, the Zapotec believed, they once again became clouds. The Zapotec not only had an organized priesthood, temples, and elaborate ritual, but they also considered places such as caves, mountains, certain trees, springs, and other natural sites to be sacred shrines.

Other Oaxaca sites. Monte Albán was the major Zapotec civil and religious center, yet it was not the only sacred place in Oaxaca. Dainzú, a place distinguished by stone reliefs of masked ball players, was coeval with early Monte Albán. The ball players, some in jaguar disguise, are evidently engaged in a ritual game. A number of these carved slabs are set into the lowest level of a pyramid-temple structure. They are similar to Monte Albán's *danzantes.* Stones of the same type have turned up in many sites in the Oaxaca Valley, among them Macuilxochitl and Tlacochauaya. Other sites in the valley, of which there are many (Yagul, Caballito Blanco, Mitla, Loma Larga, Lambityeco) were contemporary in part with Monte Albán and shared the same religious beliefs and practices. Many of these were not occupied until after the Classic period and thus fall outside this discussion. But Oaxaca is rich in archeological zones, many dating from the Classic. In the Ñuiñe culture in the lower Mixtec region (northern Oaxaca and southern Puebla), the pantheon was similar to that of Monte Albán, containing gods of earth, rain, wind, death, fire, jaguar, and perhaps vegetation represented by flayed figures (Moser, in Flannery and Marcus, 1983, p. 212). San José Mogote was largely a Preclassic settlement, but in the Classic period (corresponding to Monte Alban II), there were numerous temples there and, as at Monte Albán, a court for the ritual ball game.

El Tajín and the Gulf Coast Region. About three hundred kilometers east of Teotihuacán lies the lush, humid Gulf of Mexico region, home of numerous archaeological sites. The most important of these is El Tajín, dating from around 100 BCE and continuing through the Classic period and into the early Postclassic. El Tajín continued to be occupied, by the Totonac, on a small scale for a few centuries after this. Although this rich region is called Totonacapan, the Totonac, for whom it was named, were a late group; the modern inhabitants are still Totonac. El Tajín was built by the Maya-related Huastec people. It may be that the baroque flavor in El Tajín art derives from a Maya heritage, but probably this reflects the natural environment with its lush vegetation. *Tajín* means "lightning," "hurricane," "thunder" and names these forces. Like the Zapotec, the Totonac believed that lightning brings rain, but near the Gulf of Mexico the rain often comes in the form of hurricanes, for this is a region of violent winds and precipitation. Thus, Tajín and the god Huracán are often seen as one, the god of tropical storms, who, like the Aztec god Tezcatlipoca, can be both beneficial and destructive.

Religion at El Tajín followed the typical Mesoamerican pattern of temple-pyramids, formal priesthood, a pantheon of gods, ritual calendar, pilgrimages to its center district, periodic festivities, sacrifice and bloodletting, and other traits already mentioned. But El Tajín and the Gulf Coast region exemplify certain distinct characteristics not found elsewhere. For example, the main pyramid at El Tajín is lavishly decorated with niches, which is typical of this site and of nearby Yohualichan ("house of night") in southern Puebla. The ball court, although common in Mesoamerica, occupies a primary importance in El Tajín, where there are ten (Wilkerson, 1980, p. 219). Their wall panels are decorated with spectacular scenes of ritual and sacrifice.

El Tajín became the major religious and administrative center of the region in the first few centuries of the current era. El Tajín's peak, in size, population, wealth, and religious importance, was between 600 and 900 CE, toward the end of the Classic period. This great city has been partially excavated by Mexico's Instituto Nacional de Antropologia e Historia. Its most spectacular building is the Pyramid of the Niches, dedicated to rain and wind gods, whose 365 niches are thought to be related to the solar calendar. Originally the pyramid's facade was painted in various colors, mainly red, the color of life and also of death. A *xicalcoliuhqui*, a fret in stone mosaic, decorates the balustrades on either side of the pyramid's stairway. The *xicalcoliuhqui*, popular in ancient Mexican sites, especially Mitla, but probably of Maya origin, may be symbolic of serpents of rain and wind. Originally, grotesque wind-rain serpents framed the panels of ritual scenes at the top of the temple.

The ball-game cult. Typical of the Gulf area is the *yugo-hacha-palma-candado* (Span., "yoke-ax-palm-padlock") complex, consisting of objects sculptured similar to these forms. The elements of this complex seem to form part of the ritual ball game. In the Maya zone, players are depicted wearing padded waist protectors formed like yokes, and figures are often seen wearing *palmas* in their belts. S. Jeffrey K. Wilkerson (1980, p. 219) states that at El Tajín the paraphernalia of the ball game became cult objects when carved in stone, and that stone copies of the wooden waist protectors, or yokes, were symbols of the jaws of the earth, into which the wearer descended after death. In El Tajín and probably all over Mesoamerica the ball game was a ritual act and concluded with one of the players, usually impersonating a god, being decapitated. Burials in the Veracruz region were frequently accompanied by elaborately carved stone yokes and other ball-game symbols. The ball-game cult started in the Preclassic, probably among the Olmec. The Gulf area was the home of rubber and the cult most likely originated here and then spread out to other regions, diffused by traders who took cacao and rubber (as well as their ideology) from the lowlands to the highlands. Both the cacao tree and ballplayers are represented in murals at Teotihuacán. In the Maya region, some Classic period ball-court markers were associated with symbols of the sun, water, and vegetation. The purpose of the sacrifice of a player at the end of the game, as seen on El Tajín reliefs, was the rejuvenation of agricultural and solar fertility, the cycle of death and rebirth in nature (Pasztory, 1978, p. 139). The stone reliefs at El Tajín portray ballplayers, rites to the rain god and to a deity of pulque, autosacrifice from genitals, decapitation of a ballplayer and his descent into the underworld, and sacrifice by extraction of the heart (Kampen, 1972).

Smiling figures and divine women. Among the ritual manifestations of the Classic period of the Gulf area are the "smiling figures" from Remojadas and El Zapotal, murals from Higueras, and life-size terra-cotta sculptures of *cihuateteo* ("divine women"). El Zapotal, located in southern Veracruz near the Olmec site of Cerro de las Mesas, had its florescent period from 500 to 800 CE. Unlike the Zapotec and Mixtec, who had a cult to the dead, this Totonac culture apparently maintained a cult to death itself. In a major temple at El Zapotal there is an altar 1.6 meters high with a seated terracotta figure of the death god. His skeletal form is surrounded by skulls. Equally dramatic are the monumental clay figures called by the Postclassic term *cihuateteo*. Colonial chronicles identify the *cihuateteo* as women who died in childbirth and who then were deified, joining dead warriors in the task of helping the sun cross the sky. They were considered warriors because they lost their lives while taking a "prisoner," that is, the child. These striking figures wear skirts fastened by large serpent belts and carry trophy-head staffs in one hand. Each woman seems to be covered with a flayed skin, which might indicate a cult to a female vegetation deity (Gutiérrez Solana and Hamilton, 1977, p. 146). The presence of the serpent around the waist may refer, however, to a Serpent Woman who was, in Postclassic times, a goddess (the Aztec goddess Cihuacoatl) associated with war, sacrifice, and political power. Among the other deities represented in the monumental El Zapotal sculptures are male gods of rain, an old fire god—whose presence shows Teotihuacán influence—and a flayed god. Skeletal remains at this site, found in burials where offerings of terra-cotta sculptures were placed, reveal decapitation and dismemberment on a vast scale, probably as a result of sacrifice. Next to one rich offering of sculpture was an ossarium containing eighty-two skulls, many of them women's. The female skulls may indicate a death-fertility cult because, in a later period, sacrifice by decapitation represented the harvesting of first fruits, especially the cutting of an ear of corn. At El Zapotal, yokes, axes, and smiling figures have also been found, although the latter are more typical of Remojadas, a site north of El Zapotal noted for its splendid clay sculpture. The smiling figures are just that: their mouths are open in broad smiles, their legs are apart in an attitude of dancing, their arms flung wide. These have been interpreted as representations of a cognate of Xochipilli, the Aztec god of song and dance, but it is possible that they portray surrogates of the gods, drugged as they go to their sacrifice. The colonial chronicler Durán described the pre-Hispanic custom of giving these god-representatives drinks containing hallucinogens so they would laugh, dance, and fling out their arms on the way to the sacrificial knife. If they were not "happy" this was considered a bad omen.

Las Higueras is a late Classic Totonac site (600–800 CE), with outstanding mural paintings. Represented here are the ever-present Huracán, shown supine at the bottom of the sea, surrounded by sharks; water or "flood" gods, pouring liquid over the land; a female moon; the sun; and a crocodilian earth god. Priests with incense bags, a temple, and ball courts are also represented (Arellanos et al., 1975, pp. 309–312).

[*For coverage of the religion of the Maya during the Classic period, see* Maya Religion.]

BIBLIOGRAPHY

Alcina French, José. "Los dioses del pantéon zapoteca." *Anales de Antropología* (Mexico City) 9 (1972): 9–40.

Arellanos, Ramon, et al. "El proyecto de investigacion 'Higueras'." In *Sociedad Mexicana de Antropologia XIII mesa redonda*. Mexico City, 1975.

Aveni, Anthony F. *Skywatchers of Ancient Mexico*. Austin, Texas, 1980.

Caso, Alfonso, and Ignacio Bernal. *Urnas de Oaxaca*. Mexico City, 1952.

Cowgill, George L. "Rulership and the Ciudadela: Political Inferences from Teotihuacan Architecture." In *Civilization in the Ancient Americas: Essays in Honor of Gordon R. Willey*, edited by Richard M. Leventhal and Alan L. Kolata, pp. 313–344. Cambridge, Mass., 1983.

Durán, (Fray) Diego. *Los dioses y ritos* and *El calendario* (c. 1581). Translated as *Book of the Gods and Rites and The Ancient Calendar* by Fernando Horcasitas and Doris Heyden. Norman, Okla., 1971.

Flannery, Kent V., and Joyce Marcus, eds. *The Cloud People: Divergent Evolution of the Zapotec and Mixtec Civilizations*. New York, 1983.

Gutiérrez Solana, Nelly, and Susan K. Hamilton. *Las esculturas en terracotta de El Zapotel, Veracruz*. Mexico City, 1977.

Jarquín Pacheco, Ana María, and Enrique Martínez Vargas. "Exploración en el lado este de la Ciudadela." In *Memoria del proyecto arqueologico Teotihuacan 80–82*, edited by Rubén Cabrera Castro, Ignacio Rodríguez, and Noel Morelos, pp. 19–47. Mexico City, 1982.

Kampen, Michael Edwin. *The Sculptures of El Tajín, Veracruz, Mexico*. Gainesville, Fla., 1972.

Millon, Clara. "The History of Mural Art at Teotihuacan." In *Sociedad Mexicana de Antropologia XI mesa redonda: Teotihuacan*, pp. 1–16. Mexico City, 1972.

Millon, Clara. "Painting, Writing, and Polity in Teotihuacan, Mexico." *American Antiquity* 38 (1973): 294–314.

Millon, René, ed. *Urbanization at Teotihuacan, Mexico*, vol. 1, *The Teotihuacan Map*. Austin, Texas, 1973.

Millon, René. "Teotihuacan: City, State, and Civilization." In *Supplement to the Handbook of Middle American Indians*, vol. 1, *Archaeology*, edited by Jeremy A. Sabloff, pp. 198–243. Austin, Texas, 1981.

Olivera de Vazquez, Mercedes. "La importancia religiosa en Cholula." In *Proyecto Cholula*, edited by Ignacio Marquina, pp. 211–242. Mexico City, 1970.

Paddock, John. "Oaxaca in Ancient Mesoamerica." In *Ancient Oaxaca*, edited by John Paddock, pp. 83–242. Stanford, Calif., 1966.

Pasztory, Esther. "The Gods of Teotihuacan: A Synthetic Approach in Teotihuacan Iconography." In *Atti del XL Congresso Internazionale degli Americanisti*, vol. 1, pp. 108–142. Genoa, 1973.

Pasztory, Esther. "Artistic Traditions of the Middle Classic Period." In *Middle Classic Mesoamerica: A.D. 400–700*, edited by Esther Pasztory, pp. 108–142. New York, 1978.

Sanders, William T., Jeffrey R. Parsons, and Robert S. Santley. *The Basin of Mexico: The Ecological Processes in the Evolution of a Civilization.* New York, 1979.

Séjourné, Laurette. *Arquitectura y pintura en Teotihuacán.* Mexico City, 1966.

Wilkerson, S. Jeffrey K. "Man's Eighty Centuries in Veracruz." *National Geographic* 158 (1980): 203–231.

DORIS HEYDEN

Postclassic Cultures

This article is devoted to a summary of the religious patterns of the leading peoples of that portion of the Mesoamerican area cotradition located west of the Isthmus of Tehuantepec in the Postclassic period (c. 900–1521 CE). Western Mesoamerica was a complex mosaic of linguistic-ethnic groups organized into various polities, but certain ones stand out most prominently: the Aztec, Tarascan, Otomí, Huastec, Totonac, Mixtec, and Zapotec. Although those who spoke the same language normally shared most cultural characteristics, including religious-ritual patterns, rarely were they unified politically. The more advanced groups were organized into what can be called city-states. Occasionally an especially powerful one of these, usually confederated with others, embarked on an imperialistic course, extending its military and political control over a wide area. The earliest well-documented empire of this type, one that may have dominated much of central Mexico, was that of the Toltec, so named from their capital, Tollan (or Tula), north of the Basin of Mexico. The flowering of the Toltec empire appears to have been essentially coterminous with the Early Postclassic period (c. 900–1200 CE). My coverage will begin with a concise review of what is known concerning Toltec religion.

Toltec Religion. At the time of the Conquest, many traditions were extant concerning the Toltec, the prestigious political and cultural predecessors of the Aztec. Whereas they emphasized dynastic themes primarily, they occasionally included some references to religious-ritual aspects. Together with the archaeological evidence, they provide a picture, however incomplete, of a rich religious tradition directly ancestral to that which prevailed in central Mexico at the time of the Conquest. [*For discussion of the several possible meanings of the term* "Toltec," *see* Toltec Religion.]

Many Aztec deities were anticipated in the Toltec pantheon. The most prominent was Quetzalcoatl, symbolized by a rattlesnake covered with feathers. In Aztec religious ideology this deity particularly expressed creativity and fertility, with emphasis on the vivifying and fructifying role of the wind (or breath), Ehécatl, which Quetzalcoatl bore as an additional appellation. The fusion of snake and bird in his icon can be interpreted as the creative coupling of earth and sky. The Toltec concept of Quetzalcoatl was probably similar, but the situation is complicated by the merging of the supernatural personage with a Toltec ruler, Topiltzin, apparently a particular devotee of the god, whose name he also carried as a title. A rich corpus of traditional narratives surrounded this remarkable figure, Topiltzin Quetzalcoatl, who was the archetype of the Toltec and Aztec priesthood and credited with introducing autosacrificial rituals into the cult. Topiltzin Quetzalcoatl was forced to abandon Tollan, persecuted by the omnipotent, capricious god of gods, Tezcatlipoca. Moving down to the Gulf Coast with a band of followers, Topiltzin Quetzalcoatl died and was cremated, and his soul ascended into heaven and became the Morning Star. He was considered to have been the founder of all "legitimate" political power in central Mexico, and the rulers of Mexico-Tenochtitlán, the Aztec capital, claimed direct dynastic descent from him—with the expectation that he would some day return to reclaim his royal dignity.

Other Toltec deities mentioned in the traditions include the androgynous creative deity with various names, among them Ometecuhtli/Omecihuatl; Xipe Totec, who expressed the concept of fertility in a macabre fashion as his devotees ritually donned the skins of sacrificed human victims; Tlazolteotl-Ixcuina, a major earth and fertility goddess whose cult was reputedly introduced from the Huastec; and Tlaloc, the ancient, preeminent rain and fertility deity. Archaeological evidence confirms the importance of these supernaturals in the Toltec pantheon and indicates the presence of various others: the *pulque (octli)* gods, as well as Mayahuel, the female personification of the maguey plant, the source of the intoxicating beverage *pulque;* the Venus deity, Tlahuizcalpantecuhtli, closely related to Quetzalcoatl; the hunting and war deity, Mixcoatl; Itzpapalotl, another earth and fertility goddess allied to Mixcoatl; and, possibly, the old fire god, Xiuhtecuhtli-Huehueteotl. The Toltec pantheon probably included many other deities not mentioned in the traditions or evidenced by archaeological remains, and it is likely that at the time of the Conquest most were still propitiated in some form in central Mexico.

Toltec ceremonialism was probably similar to the overall system prevailing in the Late Postclassic, especially as regards the calendrically regulated ritual. It is virtually certain that the two basic Mesoamerican calendric cycles, the 260-day (13 × 20) divinatory cycle, called the *tonalpohualli* by the Aztec, and the 365-day (18 × 20 + 5) day vague solar year *(xihuitl)*, were well established by Toltec times and possibly much earlier. Most of the names employed for the twenty day-signs and apparently at least ten of the eighteen twenty-day periods, the "months," were the same as those used in the Aztec system. The major Toltec public ceremonies were undoubtedly geared to the eighteen months and followed the same basic ritual patterns as those current at the time of the invasion of Spanish forces under Hernán Cortés.

Archaeological evidence at Tula (ancient Tollan) and other Toltec-influenced sites, such as Chichén Itzá in Yucatán, demonstrates that Toltec religious architecture was essentially similar to that of the Late Postclassic. Basic continuities are manifest, especially in the forms of the temples and other sacred structures such as skull-racks (Nah., *tzompantli*) and small platform altars (Nah., *momoztli*). Certain specific Toltec traits, exemplified by *chacmools,* the reclining anthropomorphic images positioned in the vestibules of shrines, and reliefs of files of warriors decorating the faces of stone benches (banquettes) along the walls of rooms in structures adjoining the temples, were closely replicated in Aztec sacred architecture, most notably in the Templo Mayor precinct of the imperial capital, Mexico-Tenochtitlán.

After a series of disasters, the Toltec hegemony collapsed, probably in the late twelfth or during the thirteenth century, and barbarous newcomers, collectively known as the Chichimec, flowed in from the north. In the mid-fourteenth century a powerful new Basin of Mexico city-state, Azcapotzalco, arose. Under a remarkably vigorous ruler, Tezozomoc, the Tepanec, as the people of Azcapotzalco were called, established a central Mexican imperial system on the Toltec model. However, it did not long survive the death of Tezozomoc in 1426, and by 1434 the final pre-Hispanic political order emerged in central Mexico. This was headed by two former tributaries of Azcapotzalco, Mexico-Tenochtitlán and Texcoco, joined, as a junior partner, by Tlacopan, an erstwhile ally of, and of the same Tepanec affiliation as, Azcapotzalco. This so-called Triple Alliance generated great military power and by the time of the Conquest dominated much of western Mesoamerica. Most of the leading ethnic-linguistic groups within this area had fallen completely or partially under its sway. The Tarascan of Michoacán, however, successfully maintained their independence and ruled a sizable empire of their own in western Mexico. Most of the Huastec-speaking communities, in the northeastern sector of Mesoamerica, also remained beyond Triple Alliance control.

Aztec Religion. The following summary applies primarily to the Nahuatl-speaking communities of the Basin of Mexico and adjoining territory, whose culture is traditionally labeled "Aztec," although fundamentally similar religious systems prevailed over a much more extensive area. Following this overview of the Aztec religious-ritual system, what is known concerning the religions of the major non-Nahuatl-speaking groups will be summarized, emphasizing aspects that appear to have been especially distinctive to each particular group.

Cosmogony and cosmology. Four great cosmic eras, or "suns," were believed to have preceded the present age. The inhabitants of each era were destroyed at that era's end—with the exception of single pairs that survived to perpetuate the species—by different kinds of cataclysmic destructions: respectively, swarms of ferocious jaguars, hurricanes, rains of fire, and a devastating deluge. The first era was assigned to the earth, the second to the air or wind, the third to fire, and the fourth to water. Different deities presided over each, and each age was also ascribed to one of the four cardinal directions and to its symbolic color. The last era, the Fifth Sun, was to be terminated, with the annihilation of mankind, by shattering earthquakes.

At the commencement of this final period, two major creative deities, Tezcatlipoca and Quetzalcoatl, dispersed the waters of the great flood and raised the sky, thus creating a new earth. Fire was next produced, followed by a fresh human generation. Quetzalcoatl traveled to the underworld, Mictlan, to obtain from its ruler, Mictlantecuhtli, the bones and ashes of previous human beings. With them the assembled gods created the primeval human pair, for whom they also provided sustenance (above all, maize). A new sun and moon were next created by the cremation in a great hearth at Teotihuacán of two gods, one a diseased but courageous pauper and the other wealthy but cowardly, who were thereby transformed into, respectively, the orbs of day and night. The gods then sacrificed themselves to provide food and drink (hearts and blood) for the rising sun. But the sun's terrible sustenance had to be supplied constantly to satisfy his insatiable appetite and unquenchable thirst. War, for the purpose of obtaining victims for sacrifice, was therefore instituted—and this perpetual obligation was laid on mankind.

The earth was conceived by the Aztec in a schematized geographic fashion and mystically and metaphorically as well. In the first conception the earth was visualized as a quadrilateral landmass surrounded by ocean. From its center four quadrants extended out to the varicolored cardinal directions, which, with the center, played a very important cosmological role as a basic principle of organization of numerous supernaturalistic concepts. At each direction stood a sacred tree upon which perched a sacred bird. In the fashion of Atlanteans, four deities supported the lowest heaven at each cardinal point. In the second terrestrial image, the earth was conceived both as a huge crocodilian monster, the *cipactli,* and as a gigantic, crouching, toadlike creature with snapping "mouths" at its elbows and knees and a gaping, teeth-studded mouth, called Tlaltecuhtli, which devoured the hearts and blood of sacrificed victims and the souls of the dead in general. Both creatures were apparently conceived as floating on the all-encompassing universal sea.

There was also a comparable vertical organization of the universe. The heavens were conceived as a series of superposed varicolored tiers to which various deities and certain natural phenomena were assigned. The commonest scheme featured thirteen celestial layers and nine subterrestrial levels.

Gods. A crowded pantheon of individualized, essentially anthropomorphic deities was believed to control the various spheres of the universe. Almost every major natural and human activity was embodied in at least one supernatural personality. This plethora of deities was organized around a few fundamental cult themes. Within each theme can be discerned "deity complexes," clusters of deities expressing various aspects of what amount to subthemes. Three major themes stand out: (1) celestial creativity and divine paternalism; (2) rain-moisture-agricultural fertility; (3) war, sacrifice, and the sanguinary nourishment of the sun and earth. Included within the first theme were such important deities as Ometeotl (Ometecuhtli/Omecihuatl or Tonacatecuhtli/Tonacacihuatl), the androgynous creative deity; Tezcatlipoca, the omnipotent "supreme god"; and Xiuhtecuhtli-Huehueteotl, the old god of fire. Prominent within the second theme were Tlaloc, the paramount fertility deity and producer of rain; Ehécatl-Quetzalcoatl, the wind god; Centeotl-Chicomecoatl, the maize deity (with both male and female aspects); the *octli (pulque)* deity, Ometochtli, who had many individualized avatars, each with its own name; Teteoinnan-Tlazolteotl, the earth mother, with many aspects; and Xipe Totec, the gruesome "flayed god." The third theme featured Tonatiuh, the solar deity; Huitzilopochtli, the special patron of Mexico-Tenochtitlán, who had strong martial associations; Mixcoatl-Camaxtli, the Chichimec hunting and war god; Tlahuizcalpantecuhtli, the god of the planet Venus; and Mictlantecuhtli, the death god. Many minor deities presided over various crafts and occupations, the most important of which was Yacatecuhtli, the merchant deity. A major, protean god who defies neat categorization was Quetzalcoatl, whose creative function especially stands out and, as indicated, with whom a semilegendary Toltec ruler was inextricably entwined.

Ritual. The ritual system was intricate, variegated, and often highly theatrical. Some of the Spanish missionary ethnographers, influenced by Christian ceremonialism, divided the public, calendrically regulated rituals into those that were "fixed" (geared to the *xihuitl,* the 365-day vague solar year) and those that were "movable" (geared to the *tonalpohualli,* the 260-day divinatory cycle). The eighteen "fixed" ceremonies, which were normally celebrated at the end of each "month," or twenty-day period, together constituted the most important series of rituals in the whole system, closely linked to the annual agricultural cycle. Many were primarily concerned with fertility promotion and involved the propitiation of deities that most explicitly expressed this theme. The "movable" *tonalpohualli*-geared ceremonies were generally more modest in scope, but some were quite impressive, especially that which occurred on the day 4 Ollin dedicated to the Sun, which featured a strict fast and ritual bloodletting by the whole community. The sacrifice of war captives and condemned slaves and ritual cannibalism often, but not invariably, accompanied these major ceremonies. There were numerous other significant ritual occasions: key events in the life cycle of the individual, dedications of new structures and monuments, before and after battles, triumphs, investitures (especially royal coronations), and the like. There was also considerable daily domestic ritualism, centered on the hearth fire and the household oratory. Many ceremonies were also conducted in the fields by the cultivators.

The profession of the full-time, specialized priest, *teopixqui* ("keeper of the god"), was highly important. Practitioners were numerous and well-organized, with formal, hierarchic ranking. Much sacerdotal duty also devolved on "rotational priests" who served successive shifts for particular periods of time. Priests usually lived together, practicing sexual abstinence, in a monastic establishment *(calmecac)* in the temple compound. They were obligated to perform a rigorous daily round of offertory, sacrificial, and penitential exercises. Religious activities were focused on the temple *(teocalli)* and the sacred precinct, usually walled, within which it was situated. These precincts also contained the priestly dormitories and schools, sacred pools for purificatory bathing, skull racks, platform altars, courts for the ritual ball game, giant braziers for perpetual fires, gardens and artificial forests, arsenals, and so on. The typical *teocalli* consisted of a solid, staged substructure with a balustraded stairway on one side. At the top was the shrine containing the image—of stone, wood, or clay—of the deity to whom the temple was dedicated. The space between the door of the shrine and the head of the stairs was the usual position for the sacrificial stone.

As indicated, the calendric cycles were intimately interconnected with the ritual system. The most basic cycle, the *tonalpohualli*, a permutation cycle of twenty days and thirteen numbers (totaling 260 days), was employed largely for divinatory purposes. Each day, which possessed an inherent favorable or unfavorable augury, was patronized by deities in two series, one of thirteen ("lords of the day") and one of nine ("lords of the night"), plus the thirteen "sacred birds." The days were also grouped into various divisions; the most common arrangement consisted of twenty periods of thirteen-day "weeks," each of which was patronized, as a unit, by a deity or deity pair. These complex batteries of influences, for good or evil, were carefully taken into account by the diviners *(tonalpouhque)*, particularly when "casting the horoscope" of the newborn child on the basis of the day of his or her birth.

No sharp division existed between the religious-ritual system that served the community as a whole and that was administered by the formally organized, professional priesthood and the more private system dominated by procedures usually defined as magical and practiced by "magicians" and diviners or, as anthropologists usually prefer to call them, shamans. Aztec shamanism was richly developed. Often neglected in general treatments of Aztec religion, its importance deserves special emphasis.

The most generic term for shaman was *nahualli*, also applied to his "disguise," usually a kind of animal familiar into which he could transform himself. The power of the *nahualli* could be used for beneficial or harmful ends. The malevolent practitioner employed a variety of techniques to inflict harm on his victim, including the application of sympathetic magic to destroy the victim by burning his effigy. One of the most important activities of the benevolent shaman was divination. Aside from calendric divination, mentioned above, various techniques were employed: scattering maize kernels and beans, knotting and unknotting cords, scrying by peering into a liquid or an obsidian mirror, and so on. Divining by ingesting various hallucinogens was also practiced. Divination to ascertain the cause of disease was important in curing, which usually involved magical procedures, although many genuinely efficacious empirical therapeutic techniques were also employed. Both the intrusive-harmful-object and soul-loss concepts of illness were recognized.

Various illusionistic tricks were performed on occasion, such as animating wood images, burning structures without actually damaging them, and the shaman's dismembering himself, also without inflicting real harm. Interpreting omens, auguries, and dreams was another important function of the *nanahualtin*, who were frequently consulted at times of crisis. A famous example occurred after the arrival of Cortés, when a bewildered Motecuhzoma Xocoyotzin (Moctezuma II), the ruler of Mexico-Tenochtitlán, turned to the diviners in desperation in an unsuccessful attempt to understand the implications of the sudden appearance of these strange newcomers on the shore of his empire.

The Spanish missionaries were generally successful in eliminating the established native priesthoods, but the individualistic practitioners of magic managed to carry on their activities with little interference. Their repertoire was actually enriched by their adoption of various congenial European magical practices. In the less-acculturated Mexican Indian communities of today, the basically indigenous shamanistic tradition still thrives. [*See also* Aztec Religion *and* Human Sacrifice, *article on* Aztec Rites.]

Tarascan Religion. The Tarascan-speakers, the Purepecha, centered in the modern state of Michoacán in the area around Lake Pátzcuaro, were a numerous and vigorous people who, contemporaneously with the rise of the Triple Alliance empire in central Mexico, built up a smaller but still sizable dominion in western Mexico that effectively blocked Aztec expansion in that direction. Pre-Hispanic western Mexico shared most fundamental Mesoamerican culture patterns but often expressed them in a distinctive fashion. The Tarascan religious-ritual system, which is only incompletely known, was typical in this respect. Compared to that of the Aztec, it appears to have been somewhat less elaborated, with a smaller pantheon and a simpler ceremonialism.

The most important deity seems to have been Curicaueri, the special patron of the Tarascan royal house. Curicaueri was connected with fire, the sun, and warfare, and he was symbolized by the eagle and a flint sacrificial knife. The Tarascan ruler was apparently considered to be his incarnation. Urendecuaucara, the god of the planet Venus, was also of some importance. Other significant members of the pantheon included a deity of *pulque*, a god related to the Aztec Xipe Totec, and a death god, in addition to numerous lesser deities, among them various local patrons. Two goddesses stand out: Xaratanga, an important fertility deity linked with Curicaueri, and Cuerauaperi, the old earth-mother goddess, seemingly cognate with the Aztec Teteoinnan-Tlazolteotl (flaying and skin-wearing rituals were common to both cults).

The Tarascan priesthood was well organized, with a hierarchy of various specialists headed by an influential high priest. Like Aztec priests, the Tarascan priests wore badges of office and carried gourd vessels for tobacco pellets, but unlike Aztec priests they were not celibate. Shamanism was also well developed, and divination by scrying (peering into a liquid surface or a mirror) was of special importance. Tarascan temples *(yacatas)*, consisting of straw-roofed shrines atop massive, partly circular, staged substructures, were sometimes large and elaborate (e.g., the five major temples at Tzintzuntzan, the imperial capital). Sacred images of both wood and stone (and often portable) represented the major deities.

The ceremonial system featured fire rituals. In each temple was a perpetual fire, and even the ruler was obligated to cut and collect wood for these sacred fires. The principal ceremonies, during which the most prominent deities were propitiated, were geared to the standard Mesoamerican annual calendar ($18 \times 20 + 5 = 365$). The basic ritual patterns appear to have been quite similar to those of other Mesoamerican groups, featuring abundant offerings, human and animal sacrifices, and dancing.

Otomí Religion. After the dominant Nahuatl-speakers, the Otomí constituted the most important group in central Mexico. Their center of gravity lay northwest of the Basin of Mexico, but they were also numerous, interdigitated with the Nahuatl-speakers, in the Basin itself. While Otomí were much deprecated, and considered backward rustics by Nahuatl-speakers, there actually seems to have been no sharp cultural division between the two groups. Their religious-ritual systems were quite similar, although that of the Otomí did exhibit some distinctive features. They clearly shared most of the leading deities of the pantheons of their Nahuatl-speaking neighbors.

A particularly important Otomí cult revolved around a fire-death god who bore various names—Otontecuhtli ("lord of the Otomí"), Xocotl, and Cuecuex—and who was merged with Xiuhtecuhtli-Huehueteotl, the standard fire god of the Nahuatl-speakers. He was especially important in the cult of the Tepanec, who from their capital at Azcapotzalco had dominated a large area of central Mexico before the rise of the Triple Alliance. Indeed, Otontecuhtli was considered to have been the divine ancestor of the Tepanec, among whom the Otomian ethnic element was very strong. His particular annual ceremony featured various rituals surrounding the erection of a tall pine pole at the top of which was affixed a special, mortuary version of the god's image formed of amaranth seed dough. Boys scrambled up this pole on ropes, competing to be first in grabbing the image. Both the Otomí- and Nahuatl-speakers called this ceremony the Great Feast of the Dead. It was also designated Xocotlhuetzi ("Xocotl falls") by the Nahuatl-speakers, who had widely adopted it. An integral part of this ceremony was the sacrifice of a victim who was first roasted on glowing coals, then dispatched by the usual heart extraction method.

One source ascribes even greater importance among the Otomí to another deity named Yocippa. He can apparently be identified with Mixcoatl-Camaxtli of the Nahuatl-speakers, who was especially associated with the more nomadic, hunting lifestyle of the Chichimec, with whom some of the less sedentary Otomí were connected. His special annual feast probably can be equated with Quecholli, dedicated by the Aztec to Mixcoatl-Camaxtli, which involved camping out in the fields and hunting and sacrificing deer and other game animals Chichimec-style. In the cult of the major Otomí center of Xaltocan in the northern Basin of Mexico, during the fourteenth century a significant imperial capital in its own right before its conquest by Azcapotzalco, a lunar goddess was preeminent. Lunar deities also appear to have been important in the northeast Otomí-speaking region.

The overall Otomí ritual system was essentially similar to that of the Nahuatl-speakers. It also featured human and animal sacrifice, autosacrifice, incensing with copal and rubber, vigils, fasts, dancing, processions, chanting, and so on. Their calendric systems, including both the 260- and 365-day cycles, were also basically the same.

Huastec Religion. The Huastec occupied the northeast corner of Mesoamerica, mainly in northern Veracruz, southern Tamaulipas, and eastern San Luis Potosí. They spoke a language of the Mayan family, although their territory was separated from that of the other Mayan-speakers by a considerable distance. The Huastec were regarded by the Aztec as possessing numerous exotic traits: head deformation, filed teeth, tattooing, exaggerated nasal septum perforation for insertion of ornaments, yellow and red hair dying, no loincloths worn by males, tendency to drunkenness and general lewdness, and a reputation as great sorcerers, especially illusionists. Nahuatl-speakers had encroached on their territory, and some of their southernmost communities had been subjected to Triple Alliance imperial control. Most, however, were still independent—and often in conflict with each other—at the time of the Conquest.

Huastec religion is not well documented, but it appears to have been as richly developed as most Mesoamerican systems. The pantheon must be largely reconstructed from Aztec sources that refer to various deities associated with the Huasteca and that were represented wearing Huastec costume and ornamentation. The clearest example is Tlazolteotl-Ixcuina, a licentious earth-fertility goddess, who was regularly portrayed with costume elements and insignia of Huastec type. It has been suggested that her alternate name, *Ixcuina,* may actually be a Huastec word meaning "lady of the cotton," a substance with which Tlazolteotl was intimately associated and that flourished in the hot, humid lowlands of the Huasteca. Flaying rituals were important in her cult, and these also seem to have been an element in the Huastec ceremonial complex (possibly also reflecting the presence of a version of Xipe Totec).

Another important deity with strong Huasteca connections, both iconographically and in tradition, was the wind and fertility deity, Ehécatl-Quetzalcoatl. The numerous *pulque* deities, with the common calendric name *Ome Tochtli (2 Rabbit),* were more connected in Aztec sources with the area south of the Basin of Mexico, centered on Morelos. But in the Codex Borgia group of ritual-divinatory pictorials, which probably originated in southern Puebla, western Oaxaca, or Veracruz, these deities typically display Huastec insignia. The alcoholic tendency attributed to the Huastec would support this connection. It is further evidenced by the survival in modern Huastec communities of the ancient deity of earth and thunder, Mam, also considered to be the god of drunkenness. Another Aztec deity, Mixcoatl, usually ascribed to the Chichimec, the barbaric hunting peoples of the north, was also frequently depicted with patently Huastec features. Some version of this god, therefore, probably also figured in the Huastec pantheon.

Archaeological remains from the Huasteca, including engraved shell ornaments, stone images and reliefs, and wall paintings, evidence the presence of other deities, including a death god, whose identifications often remain obscure. Archaeological evidence also indicates that Huastec temples were often circular in form, both the staged substructures and the shrines on top of them. These have sometimes been connected with round temples dedicated to Ehécatl-Quetzalcoatl, whose Huastec iconographic affiliations I have mentioned above.

The Huastec ritual system is barely known, but human sacrifice and autosacrifice are well attested both ethnohistorically and archaeologically. The modern survival of the Volador, or Flying Pole ceremony, indicates its ancient importance. There is also archaeological evidence for the existence of the 260-day divinatory cycle, while one colonial source lists a few apparent Huastec names for the eighteen twenty-day periods of the 365-day annual cycle. It seems likely, therefore, that, as elsewhere in Mesoamerica, the major Huastec ceremonies were geared to these cycles, but no further data are available.

Totonac Religion. The speakers of Totonac, a language unrelated to Nahuatl but perhaps remotely related to the Mixe-Zoquean and Mayan linguistic families centered farther to the east, occupied the lowland tropical area of central Veracruz, extending into the high mountains edging the Mesa Central to the west. At the time of the Conquest their principal community was Zempoala (Cempoallan) near the coast, the first large Mesoamerican urban center visited by the Europeans, a few days after Cortés's landing farther south near the present city of Veracruz. Zempoala and most of the other Totonac-speaking towns had been conquered by the Triple Alliance some years earlier. Totonac culture patterns were basically Mesoamerican, reflecting strong influence from their Nahuatl-speaking neighbors and conquerors, but the Totonac also exhibited various distinctive features, some of which they shared with their northern Gulf Coast neighbors, the Huastec.

Our rather thin knowledge of pre-Hispanic Totonac religion derives from the incompletely known archaeology of the area and, especially, from a lost account, apparently written by the young page reportedly left at Zempoala by Cortés in August 1519 to learn Totonac. Preserved in part in three later missionary chronicles, this source describes a Totonac trinity of deities: the Sun, Chichini; his wife, the great mother-fertility goddess; and their son, who was expected to return at some future time as a kind of redeemer. The goddess might have been a version of Tlazolteotl-Ixcuina, known to have been important in the cults of the Gulf Coast groups, perhaps merged with the maize goddess. The son might be identified with the youthful male maize deity called Centeotl by the Nahuatl-speakers. Some Christian influence here seems obvious, but the basic nature of these deities might have been accurately reported with the possible exception of the redeemer aspect of the son. From archaeological evidence, principally at Zempoala, the cults of other deities are discernible, including those of Ehécatl-Quetzalcoatl and Xochipilli-Macuilxochitl. The latter, the Aztec young god of flowers, dancing, music, and sensuality in general, also had solar associations and overlapped with Centeotl. Undoubtedly the Totonac pantheon was much more extensive than this, but more specific information is lacking.

The early Spanish account mentioned provides some interesting information on the Totonac priesthood. A hierarchy of six major priests is described whose attire and functions were essentially similar to those of Aztec priests. Lesser religious functionaries assisted them, particularly in tending the sacred fires. The priests also instructed children between the ages of six and nine in the tenets of the religious-ritual system. The importance of two elderly penitent "monks," dedicated to the cult of the "great goddess," is stressed. Consulted regularly by the other priests as oracles, they lived in a retreat on a mountaintop, spending most of their time painting ritual books.

The same source describes various aspects of Totonac ritual, including incensing, fasting, circumcision, human sacrifice, autosacrifice involving the passing of straws through a perforation in the tongue, ritual cannibalism, confession of sins to a priest, and child sacrifice followed by the ingestion, "like the sacrament of communion," of a concoction of rubber and seeds mixed with the young victims' blood. The Totonac calendar appears to have been typically Mesoamerican. Although the key early account speaks of only three major ceremonies annually, all of which featured human sacrifice on a limited scale and ritual cannibalism, there is evidence that the usual round of eighteen principal ceremonies was celebrated at twenty-day intervals. The importance of the Volador ceremony is known from modern survivals. Archaeological evidence, especially at the site of Zempoala, demonstrates that Totonac temples were basically similar to those of the Aztec. The sacred images they contained seem to have usually been carved of wood. No specimens survive.

Mixtec Religion. The speakers of Mixtec, a language remotely related to Otomí and closely allied to Zapotec, occupied an extensive region centered in western Oaxaca. Generally characterized by a very broken topography, the Mixteca featured numerous small city-states, politically autonomous but closely linked by an intricate network of dynastic marital alliances, a basically common language, and a shared religious ideology. Although it has recently been claimed by some scholars that the Mixtec religious-ritual system might have been quite different from that which prevailed in central Mexico, it appears to have been similar in most fundamental features. The influence of the adjacent Nahuatl-speakers to the north was very strong in late pre-Hispanic times, and most of the Mixtec city-states were tributary to the Triple Alliance at the time of the Conquest.

No systematic account of pre-Hispanic Mixtec religion is available, but its basic outlines can be reconstructed from a variety of sources. Among these are an unusual wealth of pictorial histories that include much material relevant to the Mixtec pantheon, ritual system, cosmogony, and cosmology. What is known of Mixtec versions of their beginnings indicates that cosmogonical concepts were intertwined with dynastic origins and ritualized community foundations throughout the four quarters of the Mixteca. A "celestial prologue" to Mixtec royal history involved the creation by a primordial demiurge male-female pair (probably corresponding to the Aztec Ometecuhtli/Omecihuatl) of a culture hero, apparently also conceived in twin form, who iconographically and functionally closely resembles Ehécatl-Quetzalcoatl of the Nahuatl-speakers. Descending from the celestial realm, he presided over dynastic and community initiations and consecrations and was apparently considered to have been the divine ancestor of Mixtec royalty. Other dynastic ancestors were believed to have emerged from a cosmic tree near the northern Mixtec community of Yutatnoho/Apohuallan (Apoala).

These semidivine ancestral heroes, as in the Nahuatl-speaking world, interacted closely with various deities, and no sharp line can be drawn between gods and men at this stage. Although it has been suggested that the central Mexican concept of deity, *teotl,* does not conform to its putative Mixtec equivalent, *ñuhu,* the two concepts were probably not dissimilar. In any case, the pictorial iconography of Mixtec supernaturalism was quite close to that of central Mexico. Costume elements and insignia of personages often bear striking resemblance to those of recognized Aztec deities. Each major Mixtec community appears to have had a special patron deity or deities, and the names (mostly calendric) of many of these are known. More than in any other Mesoamerican pantheonic system, the Mixtec supernaturals were designated, both in the texts and pictorially, by their calendric names. Only in part do they agree with their central Mexican counterparts. A number of their verbal names are also known, such as *Dzahui,* name of the basic rain and fertility deity, cognate with the Aztec Tlaloc.

Mixtec ceremonialism was richly developed, particularly that revolving around "sacred bundles." Human sacrifice and autosacrifice were a regular part of propitiatory ritual. Here too the Volador ceremony was important, as was the ceremonial ball game played in formal I-shaped courts. The widespread cult of Xipe Totec, featuring flaying rituals, was well established in the Mixteca, including its attendant ceremony, the "gladiatorial sacrifice," wherein the victim perished in ceremonial combat. As elsewhere, much of the ritual was calendrically regulated. Mixtec temples were often represented in the pictorials and were very similar to those of central Mexico. The holiest shrine of all was called the Mixteca; it was the seat of a far-famed oracle and was located on a mountain top near Ñuudeco/Achiotlan in the heart of the Mixteca Alta—with a subsidiary shrine in a cave in the valley of Yodzocahi/Yanhuitlan to the north.

The Mixtec priesthood was well organized and influential. Candidates were ordinarily recruited when quite young from the ranks of the nobility and underwent a rigorous training for at least a full year as novices. All future rulers received this same sacerdotal education, also being required to serve their year-long novitiate. Following their training, most future priests apparently returned to secular life and married until called to their term of office, during which they usually served a particular deity and were required to be strictly celibate. Maintained by the rulers and constantly consulted by them, in control of all "higher education," they exerted great power in their communities. Shamanism was also well developed. Mixtec practitioners of magic and sorcery particularly specialized in calendric divination but also employed many other techniques, sometimes aided by ingestion of hallucinogens.

Zapotec Religion. The Zapotec-speakers occupied an area of considerable ecological diversity in the eastern portion of Oaxaca. Like the Mixtec, who were close cultural and linguistic relatives, the Zapotec were not politically unified. In the Valley of Oaxaca, Zaachila/Teozapotlan dominated a wide area, and its political offshoot, Daniguibedji/Tehuantepec controlled much of the southern Isthmus of Tehuantepec. At the time of the Conquest most of the major Zapotec communities were tributary to the Triple Alliance.

The Zapotec heritage was an ancient one. Most students believe that the great Classic period (c. 100–700 CE) civilization of Monte Albán was mainly the creation of Zapotec-speakers. By the time of the Conquest, Zapotec supernaturalism was typically Mesoamerican in its richness and complexity. As in the case of the Mixtec, it has recently been suggested that the Zapotec lacked the concept of individualized anthropomorphic deities. It seems likely, however, that Zapotec religious concepts were not that different from those of other advanced Mesoamerican cultures. A large number of Zapotec names for what the Spaniards, at least, regarded as *dioses* (Span., "gods") were recorded in various colonial textual sources. Some appear to have been appellations and general designations of godhead rather than proper names in the usual sense.

A typically Mesoamerican abstract, creative godhead was of considerable importance, known by various appellations: Coquixee, or Coquixilla ("lord of the beginning"), Piyetao ("great spirit"), and others, described in 1578 by Fray Juan de Córdova as the "god without end and without beginning, so they called him without knowing whom," and "god of whom they said that he was the creator of all things and was himself uncreated." Overlapping this deity was Pitao Cozaana (procreator) with an apparent female counterpart, Pitao Huichana (procreatrix). This Zapotec creative power was obviously cognate with a similar concept among the Nahuatl-speakers, known, among other titles and appellations, as Tloque Nahuaque ("master of the near and the adjacent"), Ipalnemoani ("he through whom one lives"), and Ometeotl ("dual deity").

The fertility theme, as usual, received special emphasis and was expressed by various supernatural personalities. Standing out was Cocijo ("lightning"), the fundamental male fertility and rain deity, cognate with the Aztec Tlaloc and the Mixtec Dzahui, along with Pitao Cozobi, a deity of maize and foodstuffs in general, cognate with the Aztec Centeotl. Pitao Xicala (Pecala), "god of desire and dreams," would also seem to fit in this category; he has been equated with the Aztec Xochipilli-Macuilxochitl.

Apparently a widely venerated deity, sometimes even stated to have been the principal Zapotec god, was Pitao Pezelao, lord of death and the underworld. This deity was especially connected with the greatest of the Zapotec oracular shrines, Liobaa/Mictlan (Mitla), which provided a ritual focal point for the Zapotec communities in and adjacent to the Valley of Oaxaca. This god was also closely connected with the veneration of royal ancestors, whose tombs were prominently featured at Liobaa. The macabre Aztec "flayed god," Xipe Totec, whose cult was virtually pan-Mesoamerican but was especially connected with the Oaxaca-Guerrero area, clearly played a role of some importance in Zapotec religion, although the local sources provide scant information. Many more names of ostensible Zapotec deities are extant, but their importance and precise functions are obscure. As was common throughout Mesoamerica, each community featured a special supernatural patron or patrons, including, at times, deified ancestors. These were sometimes important, widely venerated deities; in other cases their cults were apparently only local. As in the Mixteca, they were often designated by calendric names.

Zapotec ceremonialism seems to have displayed virtually all known major Mesoamerican ritual patterns, including human sacrifice and its attendant ritual cannibalism. Oracular sanctuaries, often in caves, were important. In addition to that at Liobaa, one famous cave was situated on an island called in colonial times Laguna de San Dionisio, east of Daniguibedji/Tehuantepec, the capital of the Isthmus Zapotec. Here the deity venerated as "the soul and heart of the kingdom" appears to have been an earth god, perhaps known as Pitao Xoo, and related to Tepeyollotl of the Nahuatl-speakers. The professional priesthood played an influential role in Zapotec society; it was headed by a high priest, *uijatao* ("great seer"), assisted by lesser functionaries: *copa pitao* ("guardians of the deities"), *ueza eche* ("sacrificers"), and *pizana* (or *vigaña*, "young or student priests"). Shamanistic diviners called *colanij* were also important, particularly in calendric divination. As elsewhere, much of Zapotec ritual was calendrically regulated, particularly the vital pancommunity fertility-promoting ceremonies geared to the annual agricultural cycle.

Concluding Remarks. This capsule survey of the religious-ritual systems of the major western Mesoamerican groups in the Postclassic period reveals that they all displayed numerous fundamental ideological and ceremonial similarities in spite of expectable regional differences in gods' names and ritual emphasis. The importance throughout western Mesoamerica of the two basic calendric mechanisms, the 260- and 365-day cycles, in ceremonial regulation and in divination, deserves special emphasis as a common ideological structure linking the various subregions. The question arises, therefore, as to whether we are dealing here with a single fundamental religious-ritual system with numerous regional variants or with various essentially independent systems that happened to share, due largely to historical contacts, most basic features. One way of addressing this question is to ask whether Aztec, Tarascan, Otomí, Huastec, Totonac, Mixtec, and Zapotec priests, if brought together (assuming an effective method of linguistic communication) to compare notes could adequately understand each others' cultic systems. The evidence appears to indicate that the similarities would have far outweighed the differences and that they might well have had no difficulty in basic comprehension. If this view is valid, the religions of these groups could be likened to an essentially common language divided into a number of mutually intelligible dialects—all of which would underscore the fundamental cultural unity of the Mesoamerican area co-tradition.

BIBLIOGRAPHY

Alcalá, Jerónimo de. *La relación de Michoacán*, edited by Francisco Miranda. Morelia, Mexico, 1980. The best edition of the prime sixteenth-century ethnohistorical source on Tarascan history and culture, with a scholarly introduction by the editor and color photoreproductions of all of the illustrations in the manuscript (Escorial, Madrid, c.IV.5). It contains virtually all that is known about pre-Hispanic Tarascan religion.

Alcina Franch, José. "Los dioses del panteón Zapoteco." *Anales de antropología* 9 (1972): 9–43. A useful summary and discussion of the principal deities of the Zapotec-speaking peoples of eastern Oaxaca derived from sixteenth- and seventeenth-century ethnohistorical sources.

Beyer, Hermann. "Shell Ornament Sets from the Huasteca, Mexico." In Tulane University, Middle American Research Institute, publication no. 5, pp. 155–216. New Orleans, 1934. A scholarly study of a series of shell ornaments from the Huasteca that feature what appear to be representations of deities, which are perceptively discussed in relation to their iconography in the ritual-divinatory pictorial manuscripts of central Mexico and in the Codex Borgia group.

Carrasco Pizana, Pedro. *Los Otomíes: Cultura e historia prehispánica de los pueblos mesoamericanos de habla otomiana* (1950). Reprint, Mexico City, 1979. A thorough, well-documented survey of the late pre-Hispanic and Conquest period culture of the Otomí speakers of central Mexico that includes an excellent section on the religious-ritual system.

Caso, Alfonso. *The Aztecs: People of the Sun.* Norman, Okla., 1958. A very useful, well-illustrated, popular summary of Aztec religion.

Caso, Alfonso. "Religión o religiones Mesoamericanas?" In *Verhandlungen des XXXVIII. Internationalen Amerikanistenkongresses, Stuttgart-München, 12. bis 18. August 1968*, vol. 3, pp. 189–200. Stuttgart, 1971. After a broad comparative survey of the religious-ritual systems of the major peoples of pre-Hispanic Mesoamerica, the author concludes that one fundamental religion (rather than various religions) prevailed in this area cotradition.

Dahlgren de Jordán, Barbro. *La Mixteca: Su cultura e historia prehispánicas.* Mexico City, 1954. The most comprehensive treatment of late pre-Hispanic and Conquest period Mixtec culture, based on ethnohistorical sources, both textual and pictorial. It includes an extensive section on religion.

Jansen, Maarten. *Huisi Tacu: Estudio interpretativo de un libro Mixteco antiguo, Codex Vindobonensis Mexicanus 1.* 2 vols. Amsterdam, 1982. A significant study of Mixtec cosmogony, cosmology, and ritual patterns, focusing on the obverse of one of the most important of the pre-Hispanic Mixtec pictorial screenfold histories. It includes pertinent observations on Mixtec religion in general.

Krickeberg, Walter. *Los Totonaca: Contribución a la etnografía histórica de la América Central.* Translated from German by Porfirio Aguirre. Mexico City, 1933. A comprehensive account of the culture of the late pre-Hispanic and Conquest period Totonac, derived largely from ethnohistorical sources. A major section of the book is devoted to the religious-ritual system.

Léon-Portilla, Miguel. *Aztec Thought and Culture: A Study of the Ancient Nahuatl Mind.* Norman, Okla., 1963. A broad survey of Aztec religious ideology, based on relevant primary textual and pictorial sources and stressing the more philosophical aspects.

Marcus, Joyce. "Zapotec Religion." In *The Cloud People: Divergent Evolution of the Zapotec and Mixtec Civilizations*, edited by Kent V. Flannery and Joyce Marcus, pp. 345–351. New York, 1983. A concise summary of Zapotec religion. Marcus suggests that individualized anthropomorphic deities were lacking in the Zapotec pantheon.

Meade, Joaquín. *La Huasteca: Época antigua.* Mexico City, 1942. The most comprehensive available treatment of the archaeology and ethnohistory of the Huastec. It includes considerable material on the religious aspect.

Nicholson, H. B. "Religion in Pre-Hispanic Central Mexico." In *Handbook of Middle American Indians*, vol. 10, edited by Robert Wauchope, Gordon F. Ekholm, and Ignacio Bernal, pp. 395–441. Austin, 1971. A concise overview of the Conquest period Aztec and Otomí religious-ritual systems, based on primary textual and pictorial sources. It includes a proposed typology of the complex Aztec pantheon.

Sahagún, Bernardino de. *Historia general de las cosas de la Nueva España* (compiled 1569–1582; first published 1820). Translated by Arthur J. O. Anderson and Charles E. Dibble as *Florentine Codex: General History of the Things of New Spain, Fray Bernardino de Sahagún*, "Monographs of the School of American Research," no. 14, parts 1–13 (Santa Fe, N.Mex., 1950–1982).

Seler, Eduard. "The Wall Paintings of Mitla." *Smithsonian Institution, Washington, D.C., Bureau of American Ethnology Bulletin* 28 (1904): 242–324. The first adequate reproduction and interpretation of the wall paintings of the great Zapotec sanctuary in the valley of Oaxaca. It includes the pioneer scholarly account of Zapotec deities and religious conceptions.

Seler, Eduard. "Die alten Bewohner der Landschaft Michoacan." In *Gesammelte Abhandlungen zur amerikanischen Sprach- und Altertumskunde*, edited by Eduard Seler, vol. 3, pp. 33–156. Berlin, 1908. A comprehensive account of Conquest period Tarascan culture, based mainly on the *Relación de Michoacan* and containing one of the earliest attempts—by the greatest Mesoamerican scholar of his time—to analyze the religion in a scholarly fashion.

Spores, Ronald. "Mixtec Religion." In *The Cloud People: Divergent Evolution of the Zapotec and Mixtec Civilizations*, edited by Kent V. Flannery and Joyce Marcus, pp. 342–345. New York, 1983. A concise summary of Conquest period Mixtec religion by a leading Mesoamerican ethnohistorian-archaeologist specializing in this area.

Stresser-Péan, Guy. "Ancient Sources on the Huasteca." In *Handbook of Middle American Indians*, vol. 11, edited by Robert Wauchope, Gordon F. Ekholm, and Ignacio Bernal, pp. 582–602. Austin, 1971. A well-documented account of what is known concerning Conquest period Huastec culture, including a brief but informative treatment of the religious-ritual system.

H. B. Nicholson

Contemporary Cultures

Traditionally, Mesoamerican religions have in general regarded the world as sacred and ordered, that is, as a cosmos. A god or gods had established this order at the beginning of time, and the powers that sustain it are magical. Creation myths tell of this ordering, which embraces all facets and institutions of the present world. Mesoamericans have traditionally believed that numinous powers dwell in the phenomena of nature, and they have sought a harmonious relationship with these powers.

Contact with Christianity has produced syncretic tendencies. At present religious and social life shows various degrees of a syncretism between the old traditions, Spanish administrative forms, and sixteenth-century Spanish Catholicism. The rational and mechanistic way of thinking of the modern age is increasingly taking hold of the Mesoamerican tribes. As a result the entirety of the world has been broken down into a sacral world and a secular world. The breakdown affects the different tribes in varying degrees: for example, among the Huichol, the Tarahumara, and the Seri, native tradition is largely intact, whereas the Tarascan tradition has been almost completely eradicated. Missionaries from Protestant sects have been trying since the beginning of the twentieth century to eliminate the community obligations of *cargo* (see below), membership in *cofradías* ("brotherhoods"), and belief in the saints and the Virgin, which are widespread among these peoples. Within various communities converts to Protestant Christianity form a group apart and to a great extent refuse traditional obligations.

Today, younger Indians seek to become *Ladinos*, that is, hispanicized, to a greater degree than did their parents. On the other hand, many Indian communities still think of themselves as living at the center (or the "navel") of the world (as do the Chamula and the Tzo'ontohal, both of Chiapas state) or as being the "true people" (as do the Lacandon Maya). Each settlement can be considered the center of the cosmos. However, the myths of the past have survived only in more or less fragmentary form in popular religion, and even then Christian ideas have mingled with them to some extent.

Cosmogony and Cosmology. Various tribes such as the Chinantec, the Tzotzil, and the Totonac have preserved only scattered memories of the stories of the several (variously one, three, or four) previous world-eras that were destroyed by catastrophes involving elements such as water and fire. According to the Huichol there existed before time and the genesis of the world a land named Wirikuta in which ancestors, human beings, animals, and plants lived, indistinguishable from one another, in perfect harmony. Among the Tarahumara, the creator of human beings, Onorúame, seems to have been fused with the Christian God, Tata Dioshi (from Span., *Tata Dios*, "God the Father"), who created the world. The creator god of the Lacandon Maya, Hachakyum, was conceived of in a similar way.

The Pokomam have retained from their pre-Christian traditions the idea that in the beginning the world lay in darkness, but according to the Totonac it was always illumined by stars. According to the Tarahumara the sun was originally too close to earth and had to be moved away, and the Huichol tell a similar story.

The Zapotec, the Tzotzil, and the Totonac believe that the world is an island surrounded by water. According to the Quiché and other tribes, the world's four corners point in the four cardinal directions and are distinguished by four trees. Among the Yucatec these trees are ceibas, and are symbolized by crosses, while among the Huichol they are brazil-nut trees. According to the Yucatec the *balamob* sit as watchers at the four cardinal points, while according to the Totonac there are four bearers beneath the earth, who with the help of four hills support the world. The center is marked by a cenote, or sinkhole, according to the Yucatec, or a tree according to the Huichol, while for other tribes the village church is at the center. The idea of an *axis mundi,* visualized as a "world pole" or "world tree" that keeps heaven separate from the earth, lives on among the Huichol. The four cardinal directions are assigned four colors, which vary in different traditions. Among the Yucatec east is still clearly the principal cardinal direction.

Above the earth are a number of heavens (seven according to the Yucatec). For the Tzotzil, the pyramid of heaven, which is supported by a ceiba, can be either six-stepped or three-stepped. The Totonac maintain that heaven is divided into several horizontal layers. Heaven is supported by four bearers called the *bacabob,* and the rain gods called the *chaacob* dwell in it, according to the Yucatec. The Lacandon Maya speak of three heavens, the uppermost called Chembeku, and the middle one called Kakoch.

The cosmic world-structure is considered by many tribes to be threatened. The Zapotec await a destruction of the world by fire and a day of judgment, beliefs which manifest Christian influence; the Totonac expect the collapse of the world in the year 2000. According to the Lacandon Maya the world will be annihilated by a jaguar or by Kisin, the god of the underworld, who attempts each night to destroy the cosmos.

All tribes are familiar with the idea of an underworld (known as Metnal among the Yucatec) which is located beneath the earth and in which the dead dwell. The Tzotzil's image of the underworld is a nine-stepped pyramid; according to the Huichol the underworld has five levels. According to the Chinantec the sun traverses it at night. In Yaralun, the underworld of the Lacandon Maya, evildoers are burned or changed into animals. The Tarahumara have an idea of hell that derives from Christian influence, but they also retain an aboriginal notion of a land of the dead.

Creation of Human Beings. According to the Pokomam and to some extent the Quiché and Cakchiquel, the primordial night was inhabited by savage human beings who knew no religion or government (i.e., their cosmos had no order at all) and who were destroyed by God; the Totonac tell of a primordial dwarfish people of hunters and gatherers. Ideas regarding the origin of the present human race differ widely. The human beings of previous worlds were changed into apes according to the Tzotzil and the Chinantec; the reason, say the latter, is that they could not acknowledge the coming of the Sun-Christ, a hybrid figure from Christian and native traditions. The Tzotzil believe that Christ created Adam and Eve. Because of a human lapse, or mistake, the ancestors of the Huichol had to leave Wirikuta, their paradise, and the original unity gave way to the distinction of plants, animals, and human beings, and people spontaneously divided into men and women. According to the Pokomam, a boy and a girl survived from the original people of the night. After a life in paradise these two were led astray by the Evil One; they were driven from paradise and came to Chinautla, the place of origin of all human beings of the present age.

The first human race was created out of clay according to the Lacandon Maya (as were the animals, according to the Tarahumara). The second human race descended from the ceiba that was the world tree. Both of these races died out, but, before that happened, a union of the two produced present-day humankind. A later variant assigns the creation of the Lacandon Maya and the plants to Hachakyum, and the creation of the white race, mules, cows, sugar, and wheat to Yantho (perhaps derived from the Spanish word *santo,* thus referring to the Christian God). The Zapotec had their origin from rocks, caves, and trees. Father Maize and Mother Maize were the first ancestors of the Chinantec. The Trique, Quiché, and Cakchiquel have a mythologem of human dispersion and, connected with it, a story concerning the division of languages.

Divinities. In the supreme position of the pantheons of many contemporary Mesoamerican cultures is God the Father, who possesses more or less Christian attributes; he is known among the Tzotzil as San Salvador and among the Yucatec as Halal Dios ("great god"), who does not have any direct dealings with humankind. Among the Tarascan and Yaqui, Christ is in the supreme position. God the Father has been syncretistically identified with the Sun among the Quiché and Tepehua; he is honored as Santissimo Sacramento by the Totonac. Christ is the Sun among the Tzotzil, the Chamula, and the Otomí, and a culture hero and the god of maize among the Chortí. A fusion of God the Father and Christ as Dios Tatik Jesucristo is to be found among the Tzeltal; there is a fusion of God the Father with Onorúame (the supreme divinity) among the Tarahumara.

Among the Cora, Tayá'u ("father"), God, Jesus Christ, Sun, and Fire form a single entity that dwells beneath the earth. Among the Zapotec, God and the several Christs in the pantheon are ambivalent toward humanity. These beings are the cause of sorrow, suffering, and death. Christ is not victor over death nor does he ascend into heaven. In like manner, according to the Nahuatl, God does not love human beings and is not loved in return; he is instead a destroyer. The Nahuatl, too, have a plurality of Christs.

In harmony with the Indian vision of the world, biblical events such as the birth, passion, and crucifixion of Christ are seen as having occurred at particular spots in the individual settlements during the mythical period of origins.

Mary. Especially as the Virgin of Guadalupe, Mary occupies a central position in the religions of most tribes. She is often identified with the moon goddess (as among the Chortí, the Otomí, and to some extent the Tarahumara) or with the earth mother (as among the Chortí and the Tzeltal). She is the goddess of fertility and the patron of pregnant women among the Chortí and the Tzotzil, and she is the mother of God the Father and of Christ among the Tzotzil and the Nahuatl. Among the Nahuatl she has replaced the ancient goddess Tonantzin ("mother") and is called by that name. She is mother of all divinities and the provider for all the peoples of Mexico, and she is more powerful than God. Among the Totonac she appears in the guises of various figures; the Tepehua identify her with the Morning Star.

Veneration of the Virgin of Guadalupe calls for special remark. In December 1531, Mary is said to have appeared in the form of an Indian virgin (and speaker of Nahuatl) on the hill of Tepeyac that was sacred to the Aztec goddess Tonantzin, one of the three manifestations of the earth goddess and virginal mother of Huitzilopochtli. There is some continuity with the aboriginal tradition in that the Indians have kept the name *Tonantzin* for Mary, but Tonantzin's personality—in being identified with Mary—has changed completely. Mary of Guadalupe is beautiful, dark-haired, kind, and gracious, and looks like an Indian woman; she protects her children from suffering, heals their illnesses, and helps them with their everyday problems. Payment for this aid takes the form of promises of pilgrimage, offerings of flowers and candles, and votive offerings. If the promise is broken or other religious transgressions are committed, the original Aztec character of the gracious goddess reasserts itself, and she punishes with misfortune, sickness, and death. The new Catholicism with its Indian coloration (Guadalupinism) became, during the early days of New Spain, a symbol of differentiation from the Catholicism of the conquerors; it also became the focal point for the religious self-understanding of the Indians.

The saints. Except among the Yucatec and the Lacandon Maya, the saints play an important role. They have replaced the old local divinities who watched over particular places; they stand guard over the order of the world, the harvest, the game, and human life. Over a large area, and specifically in central Mexico, they not only function as local divinities but are also linked to the forces of nature. Among the Chortí, Saint Francis is the god of the center of the earth, husband of Mary, and father of Christ in the latter's role as god of maize; all this is a christianized reflection of pre-Columbian relationships. This trinity of Christ, Saint Francis, and Mary is symbolized by three crosses. The Tzeltal have identified the saints with the thirteen divinities of heaven of the native tradition, who now function as aides to Dios Tatik Jesucristo; the Huichol have incorporated the saints into their pantheon, which contains over a hundred divinities. The saints act no differently than their human charges: they lie, lose their composure, take revenge, have love affairs, and so on. The saints of the Indians are distinguishable from those of the *Ladinos* even by their clothing.

Sun, moon, and star gods. Of the pre-Columbian divinities, the Sun continues to play the paramount role (except among the Cuicatec) as organizer of the world. At his side stands the Moon as goddess of fertility, water, and earth, and as mother (among, e.g., the Quiché and the Yaqui). Her place among the Cuicatec and the Huichol, however, is an insignificant one. The southern Tepehua identify the Moon with Jesus Nazareno. Except among the Cuicatec the stars seem to have lost little of their importance; this is true especially of the Pleiades and the Morning Star, notably among the Chortí in connection with their ritual calendar, among the Yucatec of Quintana Roo, among the Cora, and among the Tarahumara. As previously mentioned, the Tepehua equate the Morning Star with Mary.

Agricultural deities. Likewise, few divinities already prominent among the farming peoples of pre-Columbian Central America have lost their importance. These divinities are associated with vegetation; they include the lightning god, the thunder god, the deity of the earth, the rain gods, the maize god, and the god of the wind. According to the Chortí the rain gods sit with the wind gods as *chicchan* (snakelike monsters) at the four corners of the world and bear the names of saints. The Yucatec pray to the cross as a representation of the rain god. Among the Tzotzil the rain god is also the lord of the mountains and of the animals of the forest. Gusi, the ancient Cocijo, was venerated up until the early twentieth century by the Zapotec, who sometimes associated him with Saint Peter. The Amuzgo offer animal sacrifices in caves in order to placate the rain god; the Mixtec do the same for Sabi, especially before the onset of the rainy season. Among the Totonac, Old Thunder is older than the Sun and tries to prevent the latter's rise. Among the Quiché destructive winds are equated with Santiago (Saint James), among the Chortí they are associated with the Devil; the Tarahumara regard them as wicked. Among the Nahuatl, rain dwarfs known as *yeyecatl* have taken the place of Ehécatl, the Aztec wind god.

The Earth, often worshiped by maize growers as the goddess of fertility (the Mixtec even have a secret cult to her), is the mother of maize. In the north her influence decreases. For the Quiché she possesses both good and evil powers. The cross is her symbol. The Tzeltal ascribe the fertility of the fields to Uch, the god of growth. The Mixtec offer animal sacrifices and drink offerings to the earth spirit.

Where maize is the basic food it is also the central, independent, usually male divinity, who often has guardians of his own (the Chortí, who identify maize with Christ, call these guardians the *mer-tcor,* while the Yucatec call them the *balamob*). The Tzotzil regard the water god as the giver of maize; he has a daughter named Čob ("increaser of maize"). The Huichol recognize maize both as a goddess in serpent form, one of the *tateima* ("our mothers"), and as Tatei 'Utuanke, the mother of maize.

Ancestors and spirits. In some tribes (e.g., the Yucatec) the ancestors are greatly revered. Among the Quiché the essence of the ancestors is their great moral power at work in the cosmos. They discuss the living with Juyup Tak'aj, the divinity of the earth. According to the Tzotzil they watch over their descendants and reward and punish them.

Other deities and symbols. Alive everywhere is a belief in malevolent spirits of the dead, demons (especially those that cause illnesses), ghosts of both sexes, and goblins. Especially among the Yucatec (and to an extreme degree among those of Quintana Roo), the Chortí, the Tzotzil, and other tribes the cross is very important; it combines the pre-Columbian symbol for the cosmic tree with the symbol of Christianity. There has been an almost complete loss of the numinous aspect of fire (except among the Huichol) or the hearthstone (except among the Totonac).

A god who survived almost without exception is the lord of the mountains, valleys, animals, caves, and waters, though in some cases his influence is minimal, as among the Totonac and the Yaqui. Among the Mixtec, this god, called Tabayaku, also issues warnings of impending danger to the social cosmos.

The Devil plays an important role in all tribes, even among the quite secularized Tarascan, for whom he is the most important supernatural force. Among the Tarahumara the Devil has merged with Chamúku, an indigenous spirit of villainy.

The Lacandon Maya have forgotten many of their spiritual traditions. Their chief gods are located at Yaxchilán, where the holy stone is also kept. This stone ensures that the Lacandon Maya will survive the next destruction of the world. Their most important god, Hachakyum, who is omnipotent and multilocal, came from a seed that Kakoch, the second heaven, inserted in the earth. The stars in the sky are the seeds of plants which belong to Hachakyum. The Lacandon Maya believe that the Sun wages a daily battle with Kisin, the ruler of the underworld and the lord of death and chaos, that it may once again bring the light, and thereby order, to human beings. Metzabok is lord of lightning, thunder, rain, and illnesses. K'ak, the god of fire, sends fevers. Okna is the name of the ancient but ever-young moon goddess, who is also the goddess of fertility. Kayum is the god of music and dance, and Bor is the divinity of sugarcane liquor.

In speaking of the Huichol it must be added that Tatewarí, or Grandfather Fire, who placed the four trees at the corners of the world, and Tayaupá, or Grandfather (or Father) Sun, both live beneath the earth and are regarded as protectors of humankind. Watákame ("the clearer of the fields") has charge over the entire organization of agriculture. The Huichol venerate (under the title "Elder Brothers") the god of maize, the god of the deer, the god of peyote *(híi-kúri),* and Káuyúumaari. The first three form a symbolic unity. Káuyúumaari is the trickster, the culture hero who brought peyote to human beings, and the messenger of the gods to the shamans; he protects against enemies and harmful magic. He is considered to be the Devil and the god of death. Female divinities are regarded as grandmothers, mothers, and aunts, and have charge of such areas as the earth, fertility, growth, and so on.

Community Offices. In Mesoamerican ethnology, *cargo* is commonly understood as the exercise of a sacral or profane office in a community. The forms of community government arose after the Conquest under the influence of the Spaniards, but in these forms ancient pre-Columbian structures lived on. Indian communities understood themselves and to some extent still understand and experience themselves today as cosmic wholes. The earthly order is an image of the divine order. A hierarchy of offices forms the backbone of this order; there is no distinction between civil and religious offices because a separation of sacred and profane in this sense is unknown.

The offices usually form a pyramid with four steps (with several variants), with authority concentrated at the top. The *alcalde,* the highest authority, represents the community before the outside world; in internal matters this official primarily supervises the accomplishment of religious duties. The *regidor* is responsible for administrative tasks. The *mayordomo* is the master of religious ceremonies, the protector of the village saints, and the sponsor of religious festivals. The *topil* is the announcer of news and the policeman of the community. The idea is that every male member of the community should accept the burden *(cargo)* of office at least once. Because of the expenses involved only wealthier men can fill the higher offices.

This official hierarchy sees to administrative and public order, the administration of justice, care of the church, attention to the saints, the satisfaction of the obligations of a community toward the supraterrestrial powers, the links between the community and the nation and between the local worldview and the official church. It demonstrates the integrity and strength of the community to the individual members.

Under the influence of the modern world the official hierarchy began to divide into a religious and a secular hierarchy; this led in turn to some rivalry between the two. Communities have been affected by this development in varying degrees; some manifest a conservative tendency, with the old structures still almost intact (as in Guatemala and the Yucatán), while others have modernized, with the old structures almost totally dismantled (e.g., the Otomí in the highlands of Mexico). A continuing process of acculturation is clearly at work.

Acculturation has an unfavorable effect on the shamans and the most important persons in the religious hierarchy, who represent the ancient traditions to the greatest degree. The changing worldview is forcing the shamans in particular into the position of outsiders. As seen from the new point of view their powers, which were originally magical and cosmic, are judged to be sorcerous and acosmic. The giver of health and salvation is transformed into a feared and threatening enchanter or else is no longer taken seriously. Yet even in communities claiming to be modern it is not possible to do without the shamans because the ancient powers of the native spirits are still believed to influence families and individuals, sending illnesses or allowing themselves to be used by sorcerers for evil purposes. Mistrust and anxiety arouse suspicion that the shamans themselves may be practicing black magic. In addition, the shamans, along with those in the highest office, possess nagualist powers. Therefore they know the behavior of each of the inhabitants of the community, and punish those who are found to be culpable.

Except among the Huichol, shamans are the only ones allowed to use psychotropic drugs, which include *híi-kúri* (among the Huichol, the Cora, the Tarahumara, the Tepecano, and the Ichcatec), fungi, and seeds (in the central and southern highlands of Mexico). These are used for ceremonial purposes such as initiation into offices, healing of the sick, divination, and so on.

A further element in the religio-political structure of a community is the *cofradía* (roughly, "brotherhood"). These organizations have been inherited from the Spanish Catholic Middle Ages. The functions of each include cultivation of its special saint and the organization of festivals according to a ceremonial calendar. When urgent tasks (e.g., in the fields) prevent the members of a community from taking part in a festival, the *cofradías* often represent the community as a whole, as is done among the Mixtec. When there are several *cofradías* in a community, the one connected with the local saint is most highly regarded. Within a *cofradía* there is a hierarchy of rank among the members.

Rituals and Feasts. Feasts break the everyday routine that is imposed by agricultural pursuits. They give this work deeper meaning, make it worth doing, and create a reciprocal relationship between divinities and humankind. Though by and large the same as in the pre-Columbian period, the festivals today are organized according to the Christian calendar; some tribes, however, have preserved memories of the pre-Columbian ritual calendar (this is true of the Maya in the Guatemalan highlands and in Chiapas, and of the Totonac, the Amuzgo, the Chinantec, the Mazatec, and the Mixe).

Feasts unite the individuals in each village, and unite each village as a whole with the divinities. They are meant to gladden the saints, the gods, the lord of the mountains, those who sustain the heavens, and Jesus Christ; as a result they ensure the protection and well-being of the community. These divinities are present in, for example, the images of saints and the cross. A failure to observe calendar feasts or a negligent celebration of them can have catastrophic consequences, since the numinous powers have a right to these feasts. Office-holders and the *cofradías* are responsible for their proper celebration. The office-holders whose duty it is to finance the festivals consider it an honor to spend immense sums for the purpose. Not the least important effect of this generosity is to demonstrate to visitors from neighboring settlements the capabilities and unity of the celebrating community. Many Indians who have left their native places regard the village's feasts—for example, that of the village saint—as a reason to visit home. If several villages conduct a joint celebration, the various communities bring their own saints to the place where the feast is held.

Feasts include masses, prayers, sacrifices, bullfights, and processions with the images of the saints, the Virgin, Christ, and the cross. Depending on the geographical area, the Catholic church may play a formal part or, on the contrary, play almost no part at all. Performances of danced dramas (e.g., passion plays) from the period of the Conquest and of others from pre-Columbian times, as well as pilgrimages, music, dancing, eating, and the drinking of alcoholic beverages to the point of complete drunkenness, are all components of feasts.

Festive celebrations occupy approximately a third of the year and comprise the year's principal divisions, thus giving the participants a sense of the structure of time. Feasts celebrated throughout Mesoamerica are the Feast of the Holy Cross, All Souls' Day, All Saints' Day, the Feast of Saints Peter and Paul, the Feasts of Saint Francis Xavier and of Saint John, Christmas (which receives little attention, however, from the Chortí), and Holy Week. In addition, there are feasts for other saints, for the Virgin (especially the Virgin of Guadalupe on 12 December), and so on. The most important of these additional feasts are connected with the local saint, the harvest, the time of sowing, and the period in between these last two, when agricultural activity is minimal. Thus celebrations are conducted between December and February in the midwest and the eastern highlands of Guatemala and in southern Mexico; between December and March, and occasionally in the period between ripening and harvest, in Chiapas and the Yucatán; in June and July in the highlands of Guatemala and in Mexico; and in January, June, August, and December among the Nahuatl. The Yucatec have a new fire ceremony on Holy Saturday. Among the Tarascan there are no festivities at all during April, June, and July. The Tarahumara begin their agricultural cycle in March with appropriate feasts, while the harvest comes in November. The Papago, Pima, and Yaqui plant during August and September and harvest in November and December, with possibly a second harvest between February and June. The Huichol's celebrated peyote hunt takes place between October and February.

In addition to the feasts there are rituals that have to do exclusively with the agricultural cycle. The church has, for practical purposes, no part in these. The shaman is the principal figure here: he organizes the rituals when the crop has reached a critical stage or when catastrophe threatens. The rituals include prayers for rain (which are common to all tribes); sacrifices to the lightning or the wind (especially in the Maya lowlands, the Guatemalan highlands, and southern Mexico); sacrifices to the *milpa*, or cornfields (among the Maya); blessing of the seed (in the Mexican highlands and among the Lacandon Maya, the Tzotzil, and the Tzeltal); and the offering of the first fruits, or the Feast of the Green Maize (in the Maya lowlands and among the Papago, the Pima, the Yaqui, the Tepehua, and the Tarahumara). The Cora have round dances during the maize cycle. The gifts offered in sacrifice include flowers, copal, turkeys, sheep, goats, and prayers. Sexual abstinence is frequently required in connection with such festivities, especially of those who perform the rite. The people of San José in Petén, Guatemala, no longer perform the "old secrets" (i.e., the old rites) on the grounds that they are too powerful for the present day.

The festivals of the Indians are distinguished from those of the *Ladinos* by a closer connection with the agricultural cycle. Gradual acculturation, technologization, industrialization, and so on are bringing changes in the economic structure, such as a flight from the land, and thus the abandonment of agriculture. These changes do not threaten the existence of the feasts but do lead to a loss of their meaning. The result is psychic rootlessness and disorientation.

Illness as Cosmic Disturbance. Since the pre-Columbian period the house has been regarded as an image of the cosmos. The Zapotec distinguish between the house (a holy place) and the *campo*, or field in the countryside (an evil place). The house surrounds its own sacred place, the domestic altar, and this is true of all tribes except for some of the Otomí and some northern tribes. Hearthstones *(tenemastes)* are still regarded as numinous in the Guatemalan highlands and among the Totonac.

Sickness is conceived as a disturbance of the cosmos, a disharmony between the sick person and the divine; that is, the sick person is "acosmic." A return to health depends on a restoration of harmony, and this restoration is the task of the shaman. The methods used to reestablish order are both magical (prayers, the accomplishment of certain rituals, the recitation of magical formulas, oracles) and medicinal (extracts or decoctions of herbs and roots, salves, doses of healing substances, etc.).

Sickness is thought to be more psychic than physical. In addition, it often is believed to have its origin in transgressions of religious customs; broken promises; neglect of the gods, saints, or deceased ancestors; disruption of social relations; and so on.

Across broad areas of Mesoamerica the principal causes of sickness are considered to be the "winds" *(aires)* that originate in accidents, contact with ritually unclean persons or objects, harmful magic, or defective ritual behavior. Causes of various kinds are given for *susto* or *espanto* ("anxiety, fear"), which leads to loss of one's soul. Loss of the soul is also caused by spirits, demons, fiends, goblins, the evil eye, harmful magic, the spirits of the dead, or the *nagual* of a shaman or office-holder. In order to cure the sickness caused by these agencies, the healer must succeed in bringing the soul back by magic.

Life Cycle. Some of the pre-Columbian legacy in the area of the life cycle has been lost. In general, the ritual kinship *(compadrazgo)* system has remained, especially in connection with baptism but also in connection with marriage; it is very rare in connection with death.

Lunar eclipses are generally regarded as having a negative influence, and are thought to produce deformed offspring. At the moment of his birth a human being is assigned a destiny that he cannot escape. Beside the crib of a Nahuatl infant, God and the Devil struggle for the child's soul. If God wins, the newborn child is given a good shadow, is successful in life, and goes to heaven; if the Devil wins, the child is given a dark shadow, fails in life, and goes to hell.

If twins are born the second of them is killed among the Mosquito, the Sumo, and the northern Tepehua. The Zapotec gather from signs whether a child has special powers that fit him to be a shaman or diviner. Tribes generally have prescriptions for the purification of mothers. The Sumo, the Paya, and the Mosquito have the practice of paternal confinement. Children are generally regarded as susceptible to harm from the evil eye. Among the Tarahumara, on the third day after the birth of a boy or the fourth after the birth of a girl the shaman performs a special ceremony for the health of parents and child.

Some tribes (e.g., the Huastec and the Tequistlatec) put a typically masculine tool in the hands of a newborn male and a typically feminine one in the hands of a newborn girl. A magical connection will see to it that the child carries out properly the task assigned to him or her in life. The Totonac offer numerous sacrifices for the welfare of a newborn child. The Mixtec offer sacrifices to springs or to the idols of the hills in order to win a long life for the child.

In all tribes the child receives a baptism that goes back to pre-Columbian rituals. The Chortí bathe the child in copal incense in order to protect it. The Tequistlatec maintain silence about the birth until the baptism is performed in order to keep evil spirits from learning of the newborn infant and doing it harm. Baptism protects the child. The Huichol sprinkle the newborn child with holy water and then formally present it to the gods.

Most tribes use the umbilical cord and the afterbirth for a number of magical practices, the meaning of which can no longer be determined in all cases. One purpose is to bestow special qualities on the child. If the purpose is to ensure the fertility of the fields, the umbilical cord is buried in the *milpa.*

A custom that seems on the verge of complete disappearance is that of giving a person, along with a public name, another that is kept secret; the second is his real name and is identical with his being. Anyone who learns this name has power over him and can inflict harm; therefore only his closest relatives are allowed to know it, or else it is never or rarely mentioned. The Maya in the Guatemalan highlands and Chiapas give a newborn child a Spanish name and an Indian name; the Indian name is probably a carryover from the old custom of a secret name.

Every human being is believed to have at least two souls. The "shadow soul" leaves the body after death and takes up permanent residence in the afterworld. In special instances the possibility of reincarnation is envisaged. At birth every human being receives an alter ego *(nagual* or *tonal)* in the form of an animal, or, rarely, of a plant or a mineral, that accompanies him or her to the end of life. Usually a person has only one alter ego; the Huave and Totonac, however, allow for several. *Nagual* and *tonal* are usually used as synonyms, but the following distinction may be made: *tonal* refers to an alter ego over which the person has no power; *nagual* refers to the alter ego of strong personalities (such as office-holders, shamans, witches, and sorcerers) who are able to control it and use it to change their shapes at will. In regions of high acculturation, belief in both is rapidly disappearing.

The practice of marking the passage from childhood to adulthood has almost completely disappeared. Marriage is more a secular than a religious matter. A church ceremony is hardly to be found outside of acculturated regions.

The Dead. Every dead person is a "living" dead person; the dead have rights, and the living have duties toward them. Fear of the dead has caused the ancient customs connected with the cult of the dead to be preserved longest. These ancient rituals and the belief that the dead return annually have been supplemented by Catholic prayers for the salvation of the soul and by the celebration of All Souls' Day. With regard to the dead the Zapotec distinguish between people and "nonpeople." There is no ritual for nonpeople (i.e., the unbaptized, the murdered, those killed in accidents, and suicides), since these are regarded as outside the proper order of things. They are buried in a different cemetery.

Initially, everything possible is done to distance the dead from the world of the living. The procedure may include even the complete destruction of the dead person's possessions and house (as is done among the Jicaque of Honduras and the Tipai of Baja California) but is usually limited to the correct carrying out of the burial rite and the solemnities connected with it: a farewell feast, commemorations, and so on. Weeping, wailing, and keening are generally practiced; the original purpose of these was to send away the demons who were lying in wait for the soul of the dead person. The Amuzgo avoid lamentation because it keeps the dead here on earth, so that they cannot find rest.

The corpse is washed and clothed in the best, or at least clean, garments. A night vigil is held by candlelight; the vigil is not infrequently a merry one (as among the Tucatec and the Mazatec) and is often accompanied by music (as among the Tzotzil, the Nahuatl, the Ichcatec, and the Cocho).

Burial gifts among all tribes include food and personal possessions; toll payments for the journey in the form of money (among the Mixe, the Popoloca, the Mazatec, the Otomí, and the Totonac) or foodstuffs; grass for the animals that wait on the road into the other world (among the Huastec, the Mixtec, and the Trique); and the sacrifice of an animal, for example, a dog (e.g., in Nicaragua and among the Lacandon Maya). The position in which the person is buried often differs according to sex or social status. The Tzotzil, the Tzeltal, and some Chinantec groups bury the dead with their heads to the west, while the Amuzgo bury the married in that position. The Chontal and some Chinantec communities bury the dead with their heads to the north, while the Amuzgo bury the unmarried in that way.

Well-nigh universal among Mesoamerican tribes is a ritual purification of those possessions of the dead person that are to be used again. Participants in the funeral likewise have themselves purified. The procedure washes away anything of the dead person that may still cling to them. Mourning activities continue for nine days (among the Lena, the Yucatec, the Huastec, the Tzotzil, and the tribes of the highlands of Mexico). The assumption is evidently made that after nine nights have passed the soul of the dead person has definitely departed. Important among ceremonies for the dead is that of the lifting of the cross. Under the table or bed on which the dead person lies is placed a cross of mud or ashes (as among the Mazatec and the Popoluca), or of marigolds (as among some Nahuatl), or a cross made of colored sand (as among the Cuicatec). The cross is believed by the Nahuatl who practice this rite to absorb the *aires* of the dead person. After the nine days the cross is "lifted up" and brought to the grave of the deceased.

Ideas of the different existence that awaits human beings beyond death are vague. The Catholic description of the otherworld, which includes heaven, purgatory, limbo, and hell, is widespread (e.g., among the Yucatec and the Nahuatl). All the tribes believe in the idea of a journey into the afterworld. A *trique* is thought of as dwelling in purgatory for twenty-nine days before entering the land of God. A murdered person becomes a wandering soul (among the Nahuatl), or dwells with Old Thunder and the souls of women who died in childbirth (according to the Totonac). The Lacandon Maya, the Tzotzil, the Mazatec, and the Nahuatl believe that the dead are led across a river into the underworld by a black dog. Punishments await the Tzotzil and the Totonac before they abide in a joy that lasts as long as their lives had lasted on earth; then they are reborn. Deceased children experience an immediate rebirth, according to the Totonac, or enter heaven, according to the Yucatec and the Nahuatl. The Mixtec believe that the dead live in the cemetery, which is far from the community, or somewhere in the west. Some Totonac communities believe that the dead accompany the sun. Deceased Cora dwell in the northwest in the caves of a hill and spend their time dancing. According to the Quiché, the hearts of the dead become insects (e.g., flies) and return to the interior of the church and to the homes of their families. Married Zapotec (*angelitos*, lit., "little angels") go straight to heaven, the unmarried (*difuntos*, lit., "defunct ones") to a joyless other world.

According to some Totonac the underworld is a negative image of the present world, since day and night are reversed. According to the Tarahumara, night is day in the land of the dead, and the moon is the source of heat and light. Heaven, for the Tarahumara, resembles the present world or is full of flower gardens in which God, the saints, the angels, and the souls of good human beings dwell. Unbaptized children go to limbo. Echoes of pre-Columbian ideas are discernible: fallen women and women who die in childbirth enter heaven without delay; the drowned go to the earthly paradise of the rain dwarfs, according to the Nahuatl. The souls of the Huichol first go to the dance floor of the dead in the west. Then they return to the world. On their way back they are purified in five increasingly hotter pools; for their sins they must eat rotten fruit and drink stagnant water. Then they have the choice of going back to the dance floor or accompanying the sun. Criminals are banished forever to the underworld (according to the

Lacandon Maya, the Yucatec, and the Nahuatl) or to hell (among the Cora).

[*See also* Christianity, *article on* Christianity in Latin America. *For detailed treatment of the religious systems of contemporary Mesoamerican peoples, see* Huichol Religion; Nahuatl Religion; Otomí Religion; Tarascan Religion; Tlaxcalan Religion; *and* Totonac Religion.]

BIBLIOGRAPHY

Anders, Ferdinand. *Das Pantheon der Maya.* Graz, 1963.

Bruce, Robert D. *Lacandon Dream Symbolism,* vol. 1, *Dream Symbolism and Interpretation among the Lacandon Mayas of Chiapos, Mexico.* Mexico City, 1975.

Bruce, Robert D., Carlos Robles Uribe, and E. Ramos Chao. *Los Lacadones,* vol. 2, *Cosmovisión Maya.* Mexico City, 1971.

Christensen, Bodil, and Samuel Martí. *Brujerías y papel precolombino.* Mexico City, 1971.

Eliade, Mircea. *The Sacred and the Profane.* New York, 1959.

Fontana, Bernard L. *Tarahumara: Where Night Is the Day of the Moon.* Flagstaff, Ariz., 1979.

Frazer, James G. *The Golden Bough: A Study in Magic and Religion.* 12 vols. 3d ed., rev. & enl. London, 1911–1915.

Girard, Rafael. *Die ewigen Mayas: Zivilisation und Geschichte.* Zurich, 1969.

Gossen, Gary H. *Chamulas in the World of the Sun: Time and Space in a Maya Oral Tradition.* Cambridge, Mass., 1974.

Kearney, Michael. *The Winds of Ixtepeji: World View and Society in a Zapotec Town.* New York, 1972.

Lewis, Oscar. *Tepoztlán, a Village in Mexico.* New York, 1960.

Myerhoff, Barbara G. *Peyote Hunt: The Sacred Journey of the Huichol Indians.* Ithaca, N.Y., 1974.

Nash, June C. *In the Eyes of the Ancestors: Belief and Behavior in a Mayan Community.* New Haven, 1970.

Redfield, Robert. *Tepoztlán, a Mexican Village: A Study of Folk Life* (1930). Reprint, Chicago, 1964.

Redfield, Robert. *The Folk Culture of Yucatan.* Chicago, 1941.

Roys, Ralph L. *The Indian Background of Colonial Yucatan.* Norman, Okla., 1972.

Scholes, France V., and Ralph L. Roys. *The Maya Chontal Indians of Acalan-Tixchel.* Norman, Okla., 1968.

Steward, Julian H., ed. *Handbook of South American Indians* (1957). 7 vols. Reprint, New York, 1963.

Tedlock, Barbara. *Time and the Highland Maya.* Albuquerque, N.Mex., 1982.

Vogt, Evon Z. *Zinacantan: A Maya Community in the Highlands of Chiapas.* Cambridge, Mass., 1969.

Vogt, Evon Z. *The Zinacantecos of Mexico: A Modern Maya Way of Life.* New York, 1970.

Wauchope, Robert, ed. *Handbook of Middle American Indians.* 16 vols. Austin, 1964–1976.

Wipf, Karl A. "Mythos, Mythologie und Religion." In *Imagination, Kreativität, und Transzendenz,* edited by Gion Condrau, pp. 119ff. Munich, 1979.

Wipf, Karl A. *Wanderer in der Nacht: Religionsgeschichtliche Interpretationen zu altamerikanischen Chroniken.* Hallein, Austria, 1980.

Wipf, Karl A. "Zur Theorie des Mythos." In *75 Jahre Mannus und deutsche Vorgeschichte,* pp. 389ff. Bonn, 1984.

KARL A. WIPF
Translated from German by Matthew J. O'Connell

Mythic Themes

In Mesoamerican cultures, as elsewhere, myths explain man and his universe. They clarify the origins and meanings of things, legitimize control exercised by certain groups or individuals, justify historical facts, and serve as a unifier of the people who create or transmit the myths. The creation of the universe is one of myth's major themes, followed by the origins of human beings and of everything important to them.

Creation Myths. In the mythology of the Aztec, for which we have sources that are more complete than for any other pre-Conquest Mesoamerican people, the original androgynous creator deity, Ometecuhtli/Omecihuatl ("lord and lady two"; also known as Tonacatecuhtli/Tonacacihuatl, "lord and lady sustenance"), lived in the thirteenth heaven, Omeyocan ("place of duality"). Here he-she gave birth to four sons; each one was a different color and assigned to a different world-quadrant. According to the sixteenth-century source called *Historia de los Mexicanos por sus pinturas* (in Garibay Kintana, 1973), these were Red Tezcatlipoca, also called Camaxtli, Mixcoatl, or Xipe; Black Tezcatlipoca, who was always called by the name Tezcatlipoca; White Tezcatlipoca, known primarily as Quetzalcoatl or Yohualli Ehecatl ("night wind"); and Blue Tezcatlipoca, who was Huitzilopochtli or Omitecuhtli ("lord of bones"). These four gods created fire, the calendar, the lord of the land of the dead, a great sea, aquatic gods, a spiney earth-monster, and twelve more heavens. Then they made the first man and woman, Cipactonal and Oxomoco, a pair of sorcerers and the parents of mankind. The other twelve heavens were occupied by gods of sky, earth, and fire. Among the Yucatec Maya, Itzamná (god of the firmament, the sun, Venus, and the Pleiades) together with Ixchel, goddess of the moon, formed the creator pair. For the Zapotec, the creator of all gods was Coquixee, who was also god of dawn.

The universe. Each region of Mesoamerica had its particular creation myths, but common to most was the idea of successive creations of the universe, called Suns. Each of these eras was ruled by a god who embodied or personified the sun during that period. In central highland Mexico there were held to have been four such previous Suns, or eras, each of which ended in a cataclysm, then a fifth, which is the present world. The number of years theoretically covered by each era is a multiple of fifty-two, usually by thirteen, for fifty-two years was a complete cycle (comparable in the reckoning of time to our century) and thirteen was an important calendrical number.

Both *Historia de los Mexicanos por sus pinturas* and another sixteenth-century document, *Leyenda de los soles* (also in Garibay Kintana, 1973), describe the creation and destruction of the Suns as these events had figured in Aztec mythology. But before the beginning of the first era there was no sun (that is, the heavenly body) in the sky, so the primary gods decided to create a source of light. They formed only half a sun, but since it shed little light they made the other half.

The first age was called 4 Ocelotl (4 Jaguar) and Tezcatlipoca became its sun. Giants lived during this time but were devoured by jaguars when the Sun ended. The second era was 4 Ehécatl (4 Wind), when Quetzalcoatl-Ehécatl was the sun. This epoch was destroyed by great winds; the survivors turned into monkeys. The third creation was 4 Quiauitl (4 Rain), the Sun of the rain god Tlaloc. This world ended in a rain of fire and the few survivors became butterflies, birds, and dogs. In the fourth age, 4 Atl (4 Water), Chalchiuhtlicue, the water goddess, was the sun. The world disappeared in a great deluge and any survivors turned into fish. The force of the flood caused the sky to fall down, so Tezcatlipoca and Quetzalcoatl made themselves into great trees and raised it back into place. For this feat Quetzalcoatl and Tezcatlipoca became stars. The name of the Fifth Sun, 4 Ollin (4 Movement), refers to the movement of the earth caused by solar phenomena; this era was presided over by Tlaltecuhtli, the earth god. It was to be destroyed by earthquake. The number 4 assigned to each cosmogonic age refers to the day of the ritual 260-day calendar on which it began (Nicholson, 1971).

Sun, moon, and stars. The myth of the Fifth Sun (the present era) is one of the best known in Mesoamerica. Fray Bernardino de Sahagún, in his *Historia de las cosas de la Nueva España* (also known as the Florentine Codex; see Sahagún, 1950–1982), tells how, when all was in darkness, the gods gathered at Teotihuacán (identified in Aztec tradition with the historical city of Teotihuacán) to create a new sun. Two gods offered to sacrifice themselves: rich Tecuciztecatl, who did penance with costly objects, and Nanahuatzin, poor and diseased, whose offerings were only reeds, grass balls, maguey spines, and paper. After four nights of penance, both gods were led to a sacred fire. Tecuciztecatl was terrified by the strength of the fire and withdrew, whereupon Nanahuatzin threw himself into the flames, which purified him and turned him into the sun. Inspired by this metamorphosis, Tecuciztecatl also leaped into the fire. But it had died down and no longer burned brightly, so he turned into a lesser light, the moon. After Nanahuatzin, an eagle flew into the flames and thus was associated with the sun and its followers, the warriors. A jaguar went into the fire after Tecuciztecatl but was only singed; he therefore came out spotted and was associated with the night. After this, the rest of the gods sacrificed themselves so the sun could have their blood and strength in order to be able to move across the sky. Even then, Ehécatl, the Wind, had to blow fiercely to help him on his way. Sahagún gives an alternate explanation of the dimmer light of the moon: when both celestial bodies had the same brilliance one of the gods hit the moon in the face with a rabbit, which dulled it. The mark can still be seen if one looks closely.

According to some sources, the sun and the moon were created in a sacred cave. Mendieta (1945) says that after Nanahuatzin became the sun "the other" god went into a cave and came out transformed into the Moon. In some Mesoamerican cultures the Sun was esteemed above all gods, as among the Mixtec and the Aztec, who associated the Sun with war and human sacrifice (Spores, 1983).

A Maya version of the sun creation myth, found in the *Popol Vuh* (Tedlock, 1985, pp. 134–160), relates the adventures of the twin heroes Hunahpu and Xbalanque in their victorious struggles against the underworld; eventually they became the sun and the moon. In this chronicle the universe was first made by a dual creative force, Tepeu ("lord") and Gucumatz ("plumed serpent"). The sun, moon, and stars were made later. Everything had been in suspense—calm, silent, motionless, and empty. There were as yet no people, animals, birds, fish, trees, rocks, or caves, nor was there vegetation of any type. Only a great sea and sky existed. Tepeu and Gucumatz, with the aid of Huracán ("lightning, heart of the sky"), made the waters recede and the earth and mountains rise up. Then followed fauna and flora, the creation of mankind, and finally the sun and moon (the hero brothers) and their many helpers, the stars. But in most Maya myths, especially in the Yucatán region, the sun is male and the moon is his consort. According to Thompson (1970), the moon goddess was also an earth and creation deity, patron of medicine, childbirth, divination, and weaving. She was called Ixchel ("our mother"). The young Sun wooed and won the Moon,-but, like the young Aztec mother goddess Xochiquetzal, she proved unfaithful. (She had an affair with her brother-in-law, the planet Venus, although eventually she returned to her husband.) When the Sun and the Moon quarrel this friction causes an eclipse.

The earth. The *Historia de los Mexicanos por sus pinturas* describes a primordial sea in which floated a great crocodilian monster, which was the earth. According to another sixteenth-century chronicle, *Historia de México*

(Garibay Kentana, 1973), Quetzalcoatl and Tezcatlipoca, seeing that there was only water, descended from the sky with Tlaltecuhtli ("earth lord"), a monster whose joints were covered with eyes and fangs. Transformed into great serpents, the two gods grasped the monster, one on each side, and squeezed until the monster split in half. One half became the earth, the other the sky. The other gods, seeing the poor creature ripped apart and wishing to console it, then created valleys and mountains from its nose; rivers and caverns from its mouth; springs, wells, and small caves from its eyes; trees, flowers, and herbs from its hair; and grass and small flowers from its skin. Tlaltecuhtli, the Earth, is said to cry out at night, demanding human hearts and blood to fertilize him-her, in order to produce fruits. In the Totonac region, the earth is conceived of as being flat and like a litter that is carried by four earth bearers at the four corners of the world. When one of the bearers shifts the weight an earthquake occurs (Kelly, 1966).

Mankind. The first four gods created by the primeval couple made a man and a woman, Oxomoco and Cipactonal, who were ordered to till the soil and to spin and weave. Then they were given maize kernels for divination. Their children formed early mankind. The *Historia de los Mexicanos por sus pinturas* relates that when the sky fell and Quetzalcoatl and Tezcatlipoca raised it again, they had to create four men to help. In yet another myth, when the first four gods made a sun to light the world and this was fed hearts and blood to help it move, war was invented and men were created in order to wage that war. In the Tlaxcala tradition, Camaxtli, the hunting and war god, hit a great rock with his staff and four hundred Chichimecs came out to settle the land. The Chichimec, who later changed their name to Otomí, regarded both Camaxtli and the rock as their mythical ancestors. According to accounts from Tezcoco related in *Historia de México*, an arrow shot from the sky landed near Tezcoco and formed a great hole in which appeared a man and a woman. But they were in the form of busts, with half bodies. They copulated with their tongues and had children who settled Tezcoco. Another account states that Citlalicue ("skirt of stars," i.e., the Milky Way) sent sixteen hundred sons and daughters to Teotihuacán, but they perished there. According to Mendieta (1945), Citlalicue gave birth to a flint knife. This frightened her other children so that they threw it out of the sky and it landed in Chicomoztoc ("seven caves") near Acolman in the vicinity of Teotihuacán. (*Acolli* means "shoulder" and *maitl*, "hand," therefore this place refers to the busts mentioned above.) But the sixteen hundred sons and daughters sent by Citlalicue (or who miraculously came from the flint knife) were more divine than human and demanded that their mother provide people to serve them. She replied that they should make this request of Mictlantecuhtli ("lord of the dead"). Quetzalcoatl (or his twin, Xolotl) then went in search of bones and ashes of the deceased with which to re-create people. He went to Mictlan (the land of the dead), but Mictlantecuhtli refused to give up the bones. So Quetzalcoatl stole them and fled. He tripped making his escape, however, breaking the bones (which is why some people are tall, some short). Quetzalcoatl carried the bones to the western paradise, Tamoanchan, where the gods performed autosacrifice on themselves and Quetzalcoatl bled his penis. From the mixture of these gods' blood a male and a female were created, and mankind descended from them.

According to the *Popol Vuh*, man was created three times. During the first age, animals were made, but they could not talk or worship the gods, so it was decided to create creatures who could. Man was first made of mud, but disintegrated when wet. During the second creation, therefore, people were made of the wood of the *tzité* tree, whose red beans were used in divination. These figures acted like people and multiplied, but they had no souls or minds so the gods destroyed them. The wooden children of these wooden people were also destroyed by dogs, who resented being beaten with wooden sticks, and by their household utensils, who rebelled against being put into the fire. In the third creation, the people were formed of maize. Since their bodies were made of the basic Mesoamerican food, they not only survived and became the ancestors of present-day mankind, but they recognized their divine creators and worshiped them. In fact, they were so intelligent that the gods had to blow mist into their eyes to dim them; otherwise they might have rivaled the deities.

Maize. Once humans were created, food had to be found for them. When Quetzalcoatl saw a red ant carrying a maize kernel he turned himself into a black ant and followed her to see where the food was hidden. When she entered the Tonacatepetl ("hill of sustenance"), Quetzalcoatl followed and stole some maize. He took it to Tamoanchan, where the gods accepted the grain as human sustenance. But when Quetzalcoatl tried to carry the whole hill back, he failed. Oxomoco and Cipactonal, the first humans, then divined with maize and stated that only Nanahuatl (Nanahuatzin) could successfully steal the corn, which he did. The Tlaloques, rain gods who were white, blue, yellow, and red—the colors of different varieties of maize and also of the world directions—were advised of this and took the grains from Nanahuatl, together with beans, amaranth, *chia*, and other foods. In the care of the Tlaloques maize became available to people.

The *Historia de México* relates that Centeotl ("divine

maize") was the son of the vegetation deities Piltzintecuhtli and Xochiquetzal. In order to obtain sustenance, all the gods had to go into the cavern where these three lived. Centeotl went under the earth, and from his body grew many plants, among them maize, amaranth, sweet potato, and cotton. Because of this Centeotl was called Tlazopilli ("beloved lord").

In the Veracruz region the god of maize is called Homshuk ("he who germinates, he who flowers, he who is eaten"). At the beginning of time, when Homshuk was tiny, his father died and his mother threw the boy into the river, whence he was rescued by a witch and her husband, who adopted him. He grew up as a friend of all the animals, so that when his adoptive parents thought he had become appetizing enough to be eaten and tried to kill him, the animals saved him. The couple died because of their deceit, and Homshuk then went to look for his real parents. He found his father in the land of the dead and after many trials freed him. A lizard took the good news to the mother but got it backwards, which so saddened Homshuk that he went to the river to meditate. Here he met Huracán ("lightning"), who tried to eliminate him with harsh rains and winds. Homshuk cleverly trapped Huracán inside the earth, however, but eventually freed him on the condition that each year when Homshuk was beginning to sprout, Huracán would bathe him with gentle rains (Münch, 1983; Williams-García, 1954).

Among the Aztec of central Mexico, maize was represented by a complex of deities. Young maize was Xilonen, whose name derives from *xilotl,* the tender ear of corn that is just ripening. Ripe maize was Chicomecoatl (7 Serpent), the calendrical name of the goddess. Atlatonan ("our mother of Atlan"), the patron of lepers, was also a maize goddess. It may be, therefore, that she represented diseased maize, or *huitlacoche,* which is, nevertheless, highly edible. Centeotl was the masculine form, representing dried maize. In some chronicles Chicomecoatl and Chalchiuhtlicue, water goddess, are synonymous. The interaction of vegetation with water is obvious.

During one of the Aztec festivals in honor of maize, an "impersonator" of Xilonen was sacrificed. She wore a green feather in her headdress, symbolizing the maize tassel, and her hair represented maize silk. At the time of the sacrifice the feather and hair were first cut off, then the victim was decapitated, the head representing the ear of corn. The girl's body was flayed and the skin worn for a time by a priest. This ritual, carried out in a setting of seeds, plants, and maize, honored the first fruits of an early harvest and the renewal of vegetation.

The *Popol Vuh* provides another example of decapitation associated with plant and human fertility. Hun-Hunahpu had his head cut off in Xibalba, the underworld. His head was placed in a tree, which then flowered as it never had before, and the head turned into the tree's fruit. When a young maiden admired it, the "skull-fruit" spit in her hand, making her pregnant. From this magic union the mythical twins Hunahpu and Xbalanque were born (Tedlock, 1985).

The mythology of the Huichol of western Mexico relates that long ago they needed a basic food. A Huichol boy heard that beyond the mountains there was something called maize, so he went in search of it. Seeing a bird in a tree, the boy decided to shoot it, but the bird revealed that it was really the Mother of Maize, who can adopt many forms. She took the Huichol boy home, fed him tortillas, and introduced him to her five daughters. They were white, red, yellow, blue, and spotted (with kernels of five colors). He took Blue Maize for his wife, but his mother refused to accept her, thinking only that here was another mouth to feed. So Blue Maize in all sadness ground herself and turned into *atole,* maize gruel.

Maguey and pulque. Maize was the basic cereal, but the maguey agave, or century plant, also played an important part in ancient Mesoamerican life. The maguey provides a juice that is fermented into *pulque,* a ritual liquor in pre-Hispanic times and still made today. In addition, maguey fibers produced a strong thread, sometimes woven into cloth; paper was made from the pulp; spines made daggers for autosacrifice; the strong leaves were used for roofing; and dried maguey was burned for fuel.

The *Historia de México* relates how Quetzalcoatl-Ehécatl stole a young maiden goddess, Mayahuel, and took her down to earth. Pursued by the girl's monster guardians, she and Quetzalcoatl-Ehécatl became transformed into two branches of a tree. The monsters, finding her, split the tree in half, then pounced upon Mayahuel's branch and tore it apart. Quetzalcoatl-Ehécatl buried her remains and from these grew the maguey.

Primal Ancestors. Clouds, rocks, and trees are mythical ancestors in some ancient Mesoamerican cultures. From the Mixtec region of Oaxaca comes a myth that relates that long ago a man went into the mountains where he made a hole in a sacred *madroño* tree and had sexual intercourse with it. A number of months later the tree gave birth to a little man called Fourteen Strengths, who then went home with his father. Fourteen Strengths grew and worshiped his mother, the tree that would never die. Eventually the Sun killed both the tree-child and some great rocks, but the Mixtec people considered both to be their ancestors. A sixteenth-century friar, Antonio de los Reyes, recorded an oral tradition stating that Mixtec gods and noble lineages descended from trees in Apoala, in Oaxaca. The tree birth of the Mixtec people is shown in the pictorial manuscript known as the Codex Vienna. This tradition is also shown on a carved bone from Monte Albán, where the founder of a ruling family is depicted being born from a tree (Furst, 1977).

Another of the major birth traditions in Mesoamerica is associated with caves. Chicomoztoc ("seven caves") was the place of emergence for seven ethnic groups who migrated in search of their promised land. One group was the Méxica-Aztec. Chicomoztoc is equivalent to Teocolhuacán in the Aztec migration; Teocolhuacán means "place of sacred grandfathers, or ancestors."

The dog is also considered a primal ancestor in some cultures. Chichimec, the name of an ethnic group in ancient Mexico, means "dog lineage" in the Nahuatl (Aztec) language. Chichimec also signifies "nomad," and many people, including the Aztec, claimed a Chichimec background early in their history. The theme of a dog as mythical ancestor is also found in the Sierra de Puebla and among the Huichol. The Huichol myth states that after a great flood only a farmer, Watákame, and his little black dog survived, having been magically placed inside a box made of wild fig tree, by Great Grandmother Nakawé. When the waters receded, Watákame, who had saved five maize ears from the flood, planted the kernels and harvested the maize but had no wife to make tortillas from the corn. Yet each night when he returned to his cave he discovered fresh tortillas and corn gruel. "Who can be preparing the food?" he asked, and one day he hid where he could observe the entrance to his cave home. To his amazement the black dog shed its skin and a lovely young woman emerged, who ground the maize to make *nixtamal,* a mixture of maize, lime, and water, for tortilla dough. Nakawé advised the man to burn the dog's skin so his companion would retain her human form. This he did, while the woman screamed that she was burning. Watákame cured her burns with the *nixtamal,* and from this union with the former dog a new race emerged (Anguiano and Furst, 1978).

The Great Gods. The Mesoamerican pantheon, especially that of the Aztec, was crowded with deities. This was due in part to the custom of the adoption of the gods of conquered people by their conquerors. Each deity, furthermore, was represented in different ways with different names, giving the impression of many divine beings. Each had some calendrical association. The pantheon is so vast that only a few gods or deity-clusters (in their Aztec forms) will be mentioned here, and only in brief synthesis.

Tezcatlipoca was the supreme god among the Nahuatl-speaking peoples. He was in all places at all times, invisible and impalpable, as was Hunab Ku in the Maya region. Tezcatlipoca was the god of fortune, or fate, and the sorcerer *par excellence.* His double was Tepeyollotl, associated with caves and the night sky. Tezcatlipoca's name means "mirror that smokes," and he is normally depicted with a mirror in the place of one of his feet. His complex character is indicated by a few of his appellations: Tloque Nahuaque ("he whose slaves we are"), Monenequi ("the arbitrary one"), and Yaotl ("the enemy"). Tezcatlipoca gave people riches, fame, and power, but he took these away arbitrarily if he felt like it. He provoked wars and sent disease and drought. But he was also the youth, Telpochtli, patron of the *telpochcalli,* the school for boys. [*See* Tezcatlipoca.]

Huitzilopochtli, part man, part legend, was the tutelary god of the Méxica-Aztec. In the form of a "sacred bundle" he guided his people during their migration from Aztlán, their homeland, to the Basin of Mexico, where they founded their capital, Tenochtitlán. One myth tells of Huitzilopochtli's miraculous birth on Coatepec ("serpent mountain") near Tula. His mother, Coatlicue, became pregnant by a feather and this enraged her four hundred sons and their sister, Coyolxauhqui. When they attempted to kill Coatlicue, Huitzilopochtli was born from her womb, armed with his magic weapon, the "fire serpent." With this he routed the attackers and decapitated and dismembered Coyolxauhqui. This victory is commemorated by the carving of the defeated Coyolxauhqui at the Templo Mayor at Tenochtitlán (the Aztec capital, now Mexico City). Huitzilopochtli was also the god of war and was associated with the sun. His symbol was the eagle, king of the birds. In his human aspect he was the leader of the Aztec, who viewed themselves as the "chosen people." [*See* Huitzilopochtli.]

Quetzalcoatl ("quetzal-feathered serpent") has been called the god of civilization. He was patron of the *calmecac,* the school for priestly learning, as well as a teacher of the arts. As Ehécatl (one of his forms), he was the wind that swept the roads before the rain. He was the main god of the Toltec, whose high priest took his name. In Aztec legend about their Toltec antecedents, Quetzalcoatl was forced to leave Tollan when Tezcatlipoca made him drunk on *pulque,* whereupon he had sexual intercourse with his sister. On his departure from Tollan, Quetzalcoatl went east, where he turned into the Morning Star. Among the Maya, Kukulkan, which means "feathered serpent," is sometimes considered to have been identical with Quetzalcoatl, who journeyed to the Yucatán Peninsula instead of becoming a star. Gucumatz, the creator god of the *Popol Vuh*, was the "serpent with green feathers." A god with similar attributes in the Tarascan pantheon was Tariacuri. [*Seec also* Quetzalcoatl.]

Deified Natural Forces. Two vital forces of nature that played an important role in Mesoamerican mythology and symbolism were fire and water. Together they form the *atl tlachinolli* ("flaming water"), depicted as a flame intertwined with a stream of water. In Aztec times this symbolized war, but earlier it may have referred to the heat and moisture necessary for the growth of vegetation. The extreme contrast between wet and dry seasons in Mesoamerica caused the people to propitiate water in all its aspects. Tlaloc was the Aztec rain and earth god. He was called Chac by the Maya, Huracán by the Veracruz Totonac, and Chupithiripeme by the Tarascan; in Oaxaca he was called Cocijo. Tlaloc's assistant, the Tlaloques, were little images of himself; they broke jars at the four world-corners to let different types of water (gentle rain, excess rain, etc.) flow. Among the highland Totonac the little water gods changed costumes to produce different kinds of weather: rain, fog, wind, and so on. Water in rivers, lakes, and streams was called Chalchiuhtlicue, Tlaloc's wife. [*See also* Tlaloc.]

Fire was Xiuhtecuhtli ("turquoise lord"), also called Ixcozauhqui ("yellow face," the color of the flame). Among the Aztec, the New Fire ceremony was held every fifty-two years to ensure the continued existence of the universe for another such time period. Fire in female form was Chantico, goddess of the hearth. The Tarascan fire god, Curicaveri, was the messenger of the Sun, and, like Xiuhtecuhtli, he was also the patron of rulers. In a Popoloca myth from the Mixtec region, a Popoloca man asked the sun to stop and give him some fire, but since the sun was in a hurry to cross the sky, he gave the man part of his flowing yellow beard. This became fire on the earth.

The Great Mother had many names among the Aztec. A few of these names and some of the goddess's associations follow: Toci ("our grandmother"); Tonantzin ("our mother"); Teteoinnan ("mother of the gods"); Cihuacoatl ("serpent woman"), who was associated with war and power; Tlazolteotl ("filth goddess"), who heard confession; and Xochiquetzal ("precious flower"), a young mother goddess related to vegetation who was patron of childbirth, harlots, and sexual pleasure and also of weavers. Water, maize, and fire goddesses also fit into this all-enveloping earth-sky-fertility complex. Among the Maya the great goddess was the moon, Ixchel, who was also the patron of midwives and weavers. The Tarascan mother goddess, who was the mother of the gods and who was associated with birth and death, was Cuerauaperi, while Xaratanga was the young goddess of plant germination, the moon, and love.

Death and the Afterworld. According to Sahagún's *Historia general*, a deceased person went to one of several places. Those who died by drowning, by leprosy, or by venereal disease, or who were struck by lightning, were buried and then went to Tlalocan, a paradise rich in vegetation, which was ruled by Tlaloc. Women who died in childbirth (*cihuateteo*, "divine women") went to Cihuatlampa. Men slain in war and warriors sacrificed to the gods went to Tonatiuh Ichan, the home of the sun. They and the *cihuateteo* helped the sun cross the sky. After four years the warriors changed into birds or butterflies and spent their time among the flowers. Tiny nursing children who died went to a place where there was a "milk tree." Those destined to go to Mictlan (the land of the dead) were cremated together with ritual paper vestments and prized possessions that would protect them on their long journey to the nine underworlds. Rulers and nobles were accompanied by slaves to attend them; the slaves were slain and buried but not cremated. The body of a ruler was dressed in the garb of four gods and a jade bead was placed in his mouth, as a substitute for the heart. The soul had to pass through crushing mountains that clashed together, to cross across eight deserts, to climb eight steep hills, to travel through a place swept by obsidian-bladed winds, to ford a wide river by being carried on the back of a yellow dog, and to make it past a fierce jaguar who accepted the jade bead instead of devouring the heart. Mictlantecuhtli, the Aztec lord of the dead, was known as Ah Puch to the Maya. The Maya rulers, warriors, and priests went to a pleasant afterworld where grew a giant ceiba (silk-cotton tree) that held earth and sky together and under whose branches there was always food and drink.

BIBLIOGRAPHY

Anguiano, Marino, and Peter T. Furst. *La endoculturación entre los huicholes.* Mexico City, 1978.

Craine, Eugene R., and Reginald C. Reindrop, trans. and eds. *The Chronicles of Michoacán.* Norman, Okla., 1970.

Durán, Diego. *Los dioses y ritos* and *El calendario* (c. 1581). Translated as *Book of the Gods and Rites, and the Ancient Calendar* by Fernando Horcasitas and Doris Heyden. Norman, Okla., 1971.

Furst, Jill Leslie. "The Tree Birth Tradition in the Mixteca, Mexico." *Journal of Latin American Lore* 3 (1977): 183–226.

Garibay Kentana, Angel Maria, ed. *Teogonía e historia de los Mexicanos: Tres opúsculos del siglo XVI.* 2d ed. Mexico City, 1973. Contains the following documents: *Historia de los Me-*

xicanos por sus pinturas (pp. 23–90), *Historia de México* (pp. 91–120), and *Crónica de Pedro Ponce de Léon* (pp. 121–153).

Kelly, Isabel. "World View of a Highland Totonac People." In *Summa Antropológica en homenaje a Roberto J. Weitlaner*, pp. 395–411. Mexico City, 1966.

Mendieta, Geronimo de. *Historia Ecclesiástica Indiana* (1596). 4 Vols. Mexico City, 1945.

Münch, Guido. *Etnología del Istmo Veracruzano*. Mexico City, 1983.

Nicholson, H. B. "Religion in Pre-Hispanic Central Mexico." In *Handbook of Middle American Indians*, vol. 10, *Archaeology of Northern Mesoamerica*, part 1, volume edited by Gordon F. Ekholm and Ignacio Bernal, pp. 395–446. Austin, 1971.

Sahagún, Bernardino de. *Historia de los cosas de la Nueva España* (compiled 1569–1582; first published 1820). Translated by Arthur J. O. Anderson and Charles E. Dibble as *Florentine Codex: General History of the Things of New Spain*. 13 vols. in 12. Sante Fe, N. Mex, 1950–1982.

Spores, Ronald. "Mixtec Religion." In *Cloud People: Divergent Evolution of the Zapotec and Mixtec Civilizations*, edited by Kent V. Flannery and Joyce Marcus, pp. 342–345. New York, 1983.

Tedlock, Dennis, trans. and ed. *Popul Vuh: A Highland Maya Book of the Dawn of Life*. New York, 1985.

Thompson, J. Eric S. *Maya History and Religion*. Norman, Okla., 1970.

Williams-García, Roberto. "Trueno Viejo = Huracán = Chac Mool." *Tlatoani* (Mexico City) 8–9 (1954): 77.

DORIS HEYDEN

History of Study

A number of different kinds of primary sources exist for the study of the religious systems of ancient Mesoamerica. Foremost among them are archaeological remains, the investigation of which provides the only means of obtaining information about Mesoamerican cultures from the Preclassic period (beginning c. 1500 BCE) to the period shortly before the early sixteenth century CE, when the Aztec empire was destroyed by the Spanish. Most of the archaeological remains are structures that were devoted to religious purposes.

Early Texts. Few pre-Hispanic pictorial documents were saved from the religious zeal of the Spanish conquerors. A number of these are *tonalamatl*s, or "books of destiny," which deal with the ritual divinatory calendar of 260 days. [*See* Calendars, *article on* Mesoamerican Calendars.] They are of special importance for the study of pre-Hispanic religion because they contain in their screenfold pages illustrations of the religious aspects of the calendar as well as other esoteric paintings that deal with Mesoamerican astronomical conceptions. Some of these books have not been completely deciphered or interpreted.

The most important *tonalamatl*s are those of the Borgia group (originally from the Mixteca-Puebla region), the Dresden Codex (from the Maya area), and the Codex Borbonicus from the Mexican Plateau. Besides these pre-Hispanic manuscripts are others that the Spanish priests and rulers commissioned for their own purposes; these were usually executed in a Spanish pictorial style. Among these commissioned works, the Codex Magliabecchiano and the Florentine Codex, both of which contain important religious data, deserve special mention.

During the century following the Conquest a number of manuscripts were written by priests whose special interest in the religious beliefs and practices of the Indians was dictated by their desire to suppress the indigenous religious systems. Fray Toribio Motolinía was one of the first twelve Franciscan friars to travel, in 1524, to the recently conquered "New Spain" to evangelize the Indians. His work is one of the earliest testimonies on native Mesoamerican culture; unfortunately, only a portion of his writing survives. A reconstruction by Edmundo O'Gorman of the original work has been published under the title *Memoriales, o Libro de las cosas de la Nueva España y de los naturales de ella* (1971).

Without any doubt, the most important work about the customs of the ancient Mexicans is that compiled by Fray Bernardino de Sahagún. His informants were old Indians who dictated in Nahuatl to young Indians who had been trained by Sahagún; they produced two manuscripts that have been named after the places where they are now kept: the Florentine Codex and the Matritense Codex. The former is the more celebrated; it is also known under the title given it by Sahagún, *Historia general de las cosas de la Nueva España*. Produced in twelve volumes between 1569 and 1582, it was first published in 1820. It has been translated into English by Arthur J. O. Anderson and Charles E. Dibble and published as *Florentine Codex: General History of the Things of New Spain* (13 vols., 1950–1982). The first five books of Sahagún's work, which deal with the gods, myths, calendar, temples, and priests of the Aztec capital, Tenochtitlán, constitute the most important source for the study of the religion of the ancient Mexicans.

Fray Diego Durán, a Dominican, arrived in New Spain as a child and learned Nahuatl and some of the old traditions from the native people of the Valley of Mexico. He also had access to old manuscripts. He devoted the second volume of his *Historia de las Indias de Nueva España e Islas de Tierra Firme* (concluded 1581) to descriptions of the gods, rites, and calendar of ancient Mexico. Fray Diego de Landa, who was responsible for the burning of massive numbers of precious ancient Maya manuscripts (and of Indians!) in the city of Mani in 1562, was also the author of the most important early book about Maya culture and religion, *Rela-*

ción de las cosas de Yucutan (first published in 1864). Fray Juan de Torquemada, a Franciscan, was the first person to write a "comparative" history of the peoples of New Spain. He was deeply interested in historiography, and many of the long digressions in his book *Monarquia indiana* (1615), which utilize biblical and classical references, were designed to show that the aboriginal Indian cultures followed universal laws of history. Four chapters of his book contrast native religion with the "true" religion, Christianity.

The Eighteenth Century. The Jesuit priest Francisco Javier Clavigero was fluent in Nahuatl and had some knowledge of other Indian languages. He had received excellent training in the humanities and, furthermore, had a deep, experiential understanding of the native Mexicans. He was the first to write a work devoted solely to the history of Mexico, his *Storia antica del Messico* (1780–1781), which was written and published in Italy during his exile there. The work contains an excellent chapter on religion. Although in his writings Clavigero tends, as might be expected given the time during which he wrote, to use Christian scripture and theology as norms of judgment, this tendency hardly colors his description of native religion. Indeed, it surfaces only in one passage within which he characterizes the ancestral religion of the Indians as a jumble of mistaken, cruel, and childish practices—the knowledge of which might help the ancient Indians' descendants to see the great advantages of Christianity. Clavigero shared the belief, widespread among his contemporaries, that the ancient Mexicans displayed a knowledge of biblically recorded events, and he iterates the belief, then common, that Quetzalcoatl was none other than Thomas, the disciple of Jesus, who had traveled to America to evangelize its inhabitants. Clavigero's book was widely read, and it helped to further a growing interest in the history and culture of ancient Mexico. It also fostered the spirit of nationalism among New Spain's mestizo population.

Mexico after Independence. Shortly after Mexican independence in 1821, the Museo Nacional was established to house pre-Conquest antiquities. In conjunction with the museum's founding, a number of studies of Mexico's ancient culture were carried out. Influenced by current liberal, positivistic ideas, a group of Mexican scholars began to study the ancient Mexican civilizations. Manuel Orozco y Berra, Francisco del Paso y Troncoso, Cecilio A. Robelo, and Alfredo Chavero were the first to investigate Mesoamerican religions in this new manner. The first volume of Orozco y Berra's *Historia antigua y de la conquista de México* (4 vols., 1880–1881; reprint, 1960), is devoted to a study of native myths and thought, which he compares to Pythagorean and Hindu philosophies, doubtless with the purpose of demonstrating the universal value of Nahuatl ideas. Among other works of scholarship produced were Paso y Troncoso's erudite and well-documented commentary, *Codex Borbonicus: Descripción historia y exposición del códice pictório de los antiguos náuas* (1898). Robelo compiled a *Diccinario de mitología nahuatl* (2d ed., 1911), which contains source material and scholarly interpretation about ancient Mexican religion in general. Chavero wrote several works on ancient Mexican religion, including *Historia antigua y de la conquista* (1888), the first volume of an ambitious publication project directed by D. V. Riva Palacio and entitled *México a través de los siglos* (Mexico through the Ages). In this volume, Chavero espouses the belief that religious ideas provide a means of measuring the degree of advancement of the Mexican people and of determining their social tendencies. He maintains the thesis that native Mexican religion was materialistic inasmuch as it did not include a belief in a spirit or a soul. Later scholars have dismissed Chavero's interpretations as sheer fantasy.

The commencement of the publication of the periodical *Anales del Museo Nacional de México* in 1877 marked the transformation of research from a private endeavor into an academic pursuit in Mexico. During the second half of the nineteenth century, the Mexican contribution to the reconstruction of the Indian past was greater than that of any other national group.

Other National Schools of Thought. The German traveler, naturalist, and man of letters Alexander von Humboldt visited New Spain in 1803–1804 and brought back to Europe a vision of the New World that had up until then eluded the attention of European scholars. Humboldt was so impressed by the vestiges he saw of the ancient pre-Columbian cultures that he proclaimed these civilizations comparable to that of ancient Egypt. He published his most important books on the Americas in French. In one of them, *Vue des Cordillères, et monuments des peuples indigènes de l'Amérique* (1810), he deals extensively with the pre-Hispanic calendars, myths, and rituals. By the second half of the nineteenth century, waves of European travelers were visiting Mexico. They made drawings and took photographs of the pre-Hispanic ruins and carried off ancient manuscripts and objects, thus broadening interest in the ancient Mesoamerican cultures.

France. In 1858, a group in France founded the Société des Américainistes de France and started a specialized journal. As an outgrowth of this, the first Americanist congress was held in Nancy in 1874. Some of the first French scholars to write about Mesoamerican religion were Albert Réville (*Les religions du Mexique de* *l'Amérique Centrale et du Pérou,* 1855), Hyacinthe de Charency (*Le mythe du Votan,* 1871), and Léon de Rosny (*L'interprétation des anciens textes Mayas,* 1875, among dozens of other works). Much later, the ethnologist Jacques Soustelle, of the French sociological school, worked in the field of Mesoamerican religion. In his book *La pensée cosmologique des anciens Mexicaines* (1940), Soustelle claimed that the Mexican image of the universe reflected the people who created it, and he asserted that the gods Huitzilopochtli and Quetzalcoatl corresponded to the ideals of a distinct faction of the dominant class of Aztec society.

Germany. From Humboldt's time up to the present, German scholars have been producing studies on the subject of Mesoamerican religion, either as parts of works about religion in general (e.g., Friedrich Majer's *Mythologische Taschebuch oder Darstellung und Schilderung der Mythen: Religiösen Ideen und Gebrauche aller Völker,* 2 vols., 1811–1813) or in the form of monographs specifically focusing on Mesoamerica (e.g., J. G. Müller's *Geschichte der amerikanischen Urreligionen,* 2d ed., 1867; and Konrad Haebler's *Die Religionen mittleren Amerika,* 1899). Perhaps the most eminent scholar of Mesoamerican religion that Germany produced was Eduard Seler. He was influenced in his interpretations of the origin of myths by his contemporary F. Max Müller, and even more by Ernst Siecke's ideas concerning lunar mythology. Seler's most important work was his commentary, *Codex Borgia: Eine altamerikanische Bilderschrift der Bibliothek der Congregatio de Propaganda Fide* (3 vols., 1904–1909). The first part of volume 4 of Seler's collected works (*Gessamelte Abhandlung zur amerikanischen Sprach- und Altertumskunde,* 5 vols., 1902–1915; reprint, 1960–1961) is devoted to the mythology and religion of the ancient Mexicans. Hermann Beyer, one of Seler's followers, published more than forty articles (1908–1924) relating to pre-Hispanic religion and symbolism. Beyer tried to prove that the Aztec's vision of the cosmos was monistic and pantheistic.

Another of Seler's disciples, Konrad T. Preuss, was the first to use pre-Hispanic Mesoamerican religion as the basis for ethnographic studies. His most important work was *Die Nayarit-Expedition,* volume 1, *Die Religion der Cora-Indianer* (1912). Walter Krickeberg in 1928 published a compilation of American myths, *Märchen der Azteken und Inkaperuaner, Maya und Muisca;* in 1956 he brought out *Altmexikanische Kulturen,* in which he emphasized the strong connection between religion and art in Mexican thought.

England. The interest in American antiquities was stimulated in England by E. K. Kingsborough's project, *Antiquities of Mexico,* which eventually produced nine huge volumes (1830–1848). For the most part, British scholars specialized in Maya archaeology. Among them was J. Eric S. Thompson, who from 1927 to 1972 published a number of books and articles and contributed to the deciphering of Maya hieroglyphic writing. In *Maya History and Religion* (1970), Thompson summarized all his research. In his last years, he expressed doubts about the possibility that Maya religion will ever be thoroughly understood, especially given the kind of data that are available to scholars.

Lewis T. Spence, the British historian and mythologist, took quite a different approach; he was one of the few students of Mesoamerica who were primarily specialists in religion. Besides his books on the Americas (e.g., *The Mythologies of Ancient Mexico and Peru,* 1907; *The Civilization of Ancient Mexico,* 1912; *The Myths of Mexico and Peru,* 1913; *The Gods of Mexico,* 1923; and *The Magic and Mysteries of Mexico,* 1930), he wrote about the legendary continents of Atlantis and Lemuria and about the mysteries of ancient Britain and Spain and those of Egypt, Rome, Babylonia, and Assyria. Although some of Spence's interpretations are rather subjective and prejudiced, he is noted for introducing some ideas that retain importance for contemporary scholars. For instance, he claims that Quetzalcoatl's cult was a "wisdom"-type religion that taught a highly developed form of mysticism and that was similar to the mystery religions that flourished in ancient times in Britain, Greece, and Egypt. The differences between Old and New World systems were superficial, he said, and they arose from a variance in magical practices. The Mesoamerican mystery religion was basically a complex rain cult upon which the solar cult and, later, the Quetzalcoatl rain cult had been superimposed.

United States. Another important researcher in the field of Mesoamerican mythology was the American Daniel Garrison Brinton, who was active from 1854 to 1897. His two most important works were *The Myths of the New World: A Treatise on the Symbolism and Mythology of the Red Race of America* (1868) and *Nagualism: A Study in Native American Folklore and History* (1894). Brinton claimed to be using modern methods of scholarship and, in contrast to prevailing scholarly consensus, maintained that the gods of the American tribes had their origins in the observation of natural phenomena rather than in historical chiefs or heroes. He tried to prove that the gods of Mesoamerica were human and benign, that they were loved rather than feared, and that their worship carried within it the seeds of benevolent emotion and sound ethical principles.

Contemporary Perspectives. During the 1950s several important books on the subject of Mesoamerican religions appeared. One of these, *El pueblo del Sol* (1953; Eng. trans., *The Aztecs: People of the Sun,* 1958), by the

Mexican archaeologist Alfonso Caso, was the first book written on a popular level to give a complete overview of Aztec religion. Caso distinguished three levels of religiosity in Aztec culture: the popular and polytheistic, the priestly, and the philosophical, which, according to Caso, almost attained to monotheism. He stressed the point that the Aztec's actions and, indeed, their very sense of life were derived from the belief that they were a people with a mission. The Aztec conceived of themselves as a people favored by the Sun, allied to the forces of goodness and engaged in a moral struggle against the forces of evil.

Miguel Léon-Portilla has written several books and articles on Mesoamerican religion. His first, *La filosofía náhuatl* (2d ed., 1959; Eng. trans., *Aztec Thought and Culture: A Study of the Ancient Nahuatl Mind,* 1963), attempted to demonstrate that among the ancient Mexicans there was a group of genuine philosophers distinct from the class of priests. He argued that there existed among the ancient Mesoamericans two opposite points of view regarding life and the universe. One was mystic-militaristic, oriented toward war and bloody sacrifice (the main purpose of which was to preserve the life of the sun, which was menaced by the threat of final cataclysm). The other worldview, represented by the Nahuatl symbol for knowledge, Quetzalcoatl, was philosophical and attempted to find the meaning of life through intellectual means. Léon-Portilla, in his book *Tiempo y realidad en el pensamiento Maya* (1968; Eng. trans., *Time and Reality in the Thought of the Maya,* 1973), also wrote on the interworkings of conceptions of time and reality in Maya religion; this work is complemented by Alfonso Villa Rojas's important essay "Los conceptos de espacio y tiempo entre los grupos mayances contemporaneos," which is appended to Léon-Portilla's *Tiempo y realidad* (pp. 119–167 of the 1968 ed.).

The French archaeologist Laurette Séjourné, whose theories about Mexican religion have had more influence outside Mexico than have those of any other scholar, began writing on Mexican religion in 1950. Her book *Pensamiento y religión en el México antiguo* (1957; Eng. trans., *Burning Water: Thought and Religion in Ancient Mexico,* 1957) synthesizes her interpretations of Mexican religion. According to Séjourné, those peoples who have not reached a stage in which the concept of the human soul—closely linked with the cosmic soul—has been revealed are in a prereligious or magical stage. She believes that the myth of Quetzalcoatl represents the main revelation of Aztec religion and that the cult of Quetzalcoatl constitutes a religion similar to others that have flourished in other parts of the world. Séjourné sees the Quetzalcoatl cult as differing from these other religions only in its symbolic language; like other religious stories, however, the myth of Quetzalcoatl describes the experience of the soul, which passes through different stages until it reaches that of liberating consciousness.

The main exponent of a Marxist approach to the study of Mesoamerican religions is Alfred López Austin. A master of the Nahuatl language, López Austin has tried to prove that religion is part of the larger phenomenon he calls "worldview," and that religion can be studied only in the context of global society. In his latest book, *Cuerpo humano e ideología: Las concepciones de los antiguos nahuas* (1980), López Austin stresses the need for an ideological system to explain the constitution and development of human processes. The book examines Nahuatl concepts concerning the human body (of which the soul was considered a part) from within a frame constructed through an understanding of the society within which these concepts arose. López Austin's interpretations of what he calls "soul entities" represent a very new kind of reading of ancient Mesoamerican religious thought.

In her book *The Transformation of the Hummingbird: Cultural Roots of a Zinacantecan Mythical Poem* (1977), Eva Hunt employs the social-scientific theories of Comte, Marx, Durkheim, Freud, Lévi-Strauss, and Turner—among others—as tools of interpretation. She attempts to interpret a modern Maya-Zinacantecan poem in light of its antecedents in Mesoamerican mythology. She concludes that Mesoamerican religion is of a type characteristic of agrarian states, and that it is based upon an agrarian paradigm of space and time. This kind of historical-evolutionary perspective has been used since Preuss's time in different ways and under different names. William R. Holland ("Highland Maya Folk Medicine," Ph.D. diss., University of Arizona, 1962), Evon Z. Vogt (*Tortillas for the Gods: A Symbolic Analysis of Zinacantecan Rituals,* 1976), and Gary H. Gossen (*Chamulas in the World of the Sun: Time and Space in a Maya Oral Tradition,* 1974) are three contemporary scholars who have used this approach in their studies of Maya culture; in my own work, I have been attempting to apply the method to Mesoamerica as a whole.

Other recent studies explore the relations between energy, man, and the cosmos in ancient Mesoamerican thought. These concepts have been associated with the Oceanic concept of *mana* in my own works and in those of Arid Hvidtfeldt (*Teotl and Ixiptlatli: Some Central Conceptions in Ancient Mexican Religion,* 1958). Several authors have linked these concepts with hot-positive and cold-negative energy, and with the acute consciousness of entropy—which, according to Christian Duverger in his *La fleur létale: Économie du sacrifice aztèque* (1979), characterized the thought of the Aztec.

The twelfth "round table" of the Sociedad Mexicana de Antropologia was held in Cholula, Mexico, in 1972. During the conference, which was entitled "Religion in Mesoamerica," ninety-six scholars presented papers, most of which were later published in a volume entitled *Religion en Mesoamerica,* edited by J. Litvak King and N. Castillo Tejero (1972). Discussion at the conference centered on a perennial question in Mesoamerican studies: is "Mesoamerican religion" one religious system or many?

During the last few decades, new discoveries in the fields of Mesoamerican ethnography and Maya epigraphy, along with the continued adherence of scholars to diverse modes of thought, have led to an increasing amount of research dealing specifically with the religious systems of Mesoamerica.

Types of Study. The study of Mesoamerican religions has been, for the most part, the domain of archaeologists, ethnologists, and a few historians. Most of the literature has been published in anthropological journals such as *American Anthropologist* (Washington, D.C., 1899–), *Anthropos* (Salzburg, 1906–1979), *Zeitschrift für Ethnologie* (Berlin, 1869–), and the *Anales del Museo Nacional* (Mexico City, 1877–1945). Up until now, the main task for all scholars studying Mesoamerican traditions has been to gather all available ethnohistorical and ethnographic material and to attempt, on the basis of this evidence, to reconstruct the different aspects of Mesoamerican cultures, including their religious systems. This reconstruction continues, as new archaeological discoveries are constantly providing new data. Besides the data collected to date, present-day researchers have at their disposal the various interpretive theories proposed by earlier scholars. In the late nineteenth and early twentieth centuries these interpretations tended to be naturalistic, astronomical interpretations being especially popular. Ethnological studies have shown that it may be possible to use knowledge of modern Indian religions to help interpret data concerning pre-Conquest religion, and vice versa. Comparative studies of religious traditions within the Mesoamerican region have been popular, but studies comparing Mesoamerican religions with those of other parts of the globe have lately fallen out of favor. Most of these latter sorts of studies have taken a diffusionist approach. There are, however, still a few scholars working along these lines, favoring either the idea of a trans-Pacific contact or arguing against it. Among the former are Paul Kirchoff (e.g., "The Diffusion of a Great Religious System from India to Mexico," in *XXXV Congreso Internacional de Americanistas, México, 1962,* vol. 1, 1964, pp. 73–100) and David H. Kelley (e.g., Hugh A. Moran and David H. Kelley's *The Alphabet and the Ancient Calendar Signs,* 2d ed., 1969).

Iconographic studies have played an important role in the study of Mesoamerican religion (see, especially, the work of George Kubler, Doris Heyden, Henry B. Nicholson, Esther Pasztory, and Richard Townsend). Too, the by-now generally accepted principle that religion should be studied within its social and economic context has led to the study of ritual as an important part of the economic system by, for example, Johanna Broda (e.g., "El tributo en trajes guerreros y la estructura del sistema tributario mexicano," in *Economía, política e ideología en el México Prehispanico,* edited by Pedro Carrasco and Johanna Broda, 1978).

Historical, rather than structural, interpretations of myths have been favored by most writers on Mesoamerican mythology. There is also a school of thought that explains Mexican religion as a blend of two tendencies, one with a magico-ritualistic base, and another (similar to the mystery religions) that looks for the liberating consciousness. Some researchers are studying the techniques used by Mesoamericans to attain direct approach to the supernatural through altered states of consciousness. One might also mention the emphasis placed by almost all scholars on astronomical explanations of Mesoamerican religion. This trend has been reinforced in recent years by the new fields of archaeoastronomy and ethnoastronomy. Other themes of recent scholarship include the division of the universe into quarters, the association of animals and colors, the symbolism of animals and plants, the dual forces of the universe, and the taxonomy of the universe. The concepts of the soul, of cosmic energy, and of time and space are also topics currently being investigated.

One may add in closing that the study of Mesoamerican religion—with the exception of a few scholars' work—has lacked a strong theoretical foundation.

BIBLIOGRAPHY

There are no published works that thoroughly examine the history of study of Mesoamerican religions. The following titles give important, though partial, overviews. Ignacio Bernal's *Bibliografía de arqueología y etnografía: Mesoamerica y Norte de México, 1514–1960* (Mexico City, 1962) provides a comprehensive listing of titles dealing with Mesoamerica from the time of the European discovery up to 1960. The reader is also referred to *Guide to Ethnohistorical Sources,* vol. 13 of the *Handbook of Middle American Indians,* 16 vols., edited by Robert Wauchope (Austin, 1973).

YOLOTL GONZÁLEZ TORRES

MESOPOTAMIAN RELIGIONS. [*This entry consists of two articles,* An Overview *and* History of Study. *The first focuses on the distinctive features of Mesopotamian religions, the deities, and the cultic institutions and forms; the second surveys the modern scholarly study of these religions.*]

An Overview

Ancient Mesopotamia is the country now called Iraq. Its northern part, down to an imaginary line running east-west slightly north of modern Baghdad, constituted ancient Assyria, with the cities of Ashur (modern Qal'at Shergat), which was the old capital; Calah (Nimrud); and Nineveh (Kouyundjik), which took its place later, at the time of the Assyrian empire in the first millennium BCE. The country consists of rolling plains resting on a bed of rocks. Rainfall over most of the area is sufficient to sustain a cereal crop. The main river is the Tigris, which traverses the country from northwest to southeast. The language spoken in historical times was Assyrian, a dialect of Akkadian, a Semitic language related to Hebrew and Arabic.

The southern part of Mesopotamia, south of the imaginary line mentioned, was ancient Babylonia, with Babylon (Babil) as its capital. The country here is flat, alluvial plain, and the average rainfall is too scant to allow a cereal crop. The country thus depends on artificial irrigation for its agriculture. It was in antiquity crisscrossed by a formidable net of rivers and canals. Such rains as fall are, though, sufficient to bring up pasture of grasses and herbs in the desert for a short grazing season in the spring. The language spoken was the Babylonian dialect of Akkadian.

The designations *Assyria* and *Babylonia* are appropriate only for the second and first millennia BCE, or, more exactly, from about 1700 BCE on, when Ashur and Babylon rose to political prominence. Before that time the later Assyria was known as Subartu, while what was to become Babylonia consisted of two main parts. Dwellers of the region north of an imaginary line running east-west slightly above Nippur (Nuffar) in historical times spoke Akkadian, while those of the region south of it spoke Sumerian, a language unrelated to any other known language or language family. The northern region was known as Akkad in Akkadian and as Uri in Sumerian, while the southern one was called Sumer or, more correctly, Shumer in Akkadian, Kiengir in Sumerian.

The capital of Akkad was in early times the city of Kish (Uheimir); later on, the city Akkad (not yet located) took its place. The country was traversed by two rivers, the Tigris flowing along the eastern border areas and the Euphrates farther to the west. The course of the Euphrates was, however, not the same then as it is today. Its main branch flowed by Nippur and east to Shuruppak (Fara), then south to Uruk (Warka), and on to Ararma (in Akkadian, Larsa; now Senkereh) and Ur (Muqayyir). Above Nippur an arching branch, the Arahtu, took off in a westerly direction, flowing by Babylon before rejoining the main course; another branch flowed south to Isin (Ishan Bahriyāt). In an easterly direction a major arching branch, the Iturungal, took off, flowing by Adab (Bismāya) to Zabalam (Bzeikh), Umma (Joha), and Patibira (Medina) before rejoining the main course at Ararma. At Zabalam the Iturungal sent a branch east, then south, to serve Girsu (Tello), Lagash (Tel al Hiba), and Nina (Zurghul). The main course of the Euphrates south of Uruk sent a branch south to Eridu (Abu Shahrein).

Economically, as mentioned, both Akkad and Sumer depended mainly on irrigation agriculture. There were, however, also other important economies. The region around Uruk and south along the Euphrates was, then as now, famous for its date groves; herding of sheep and oxen provided wool and dairy products as well as meat; fishing and hunting were important along the rivers and in the southern marshlands.

Capital cities in Sumer were Uruk and Ur; later on, Isin and Ararma. Of central religious and political importance was Nippur, seat of the god Enlil.

History

The earliest settlement of Mesopotamia of which we have evidence took place in the north, in the plains of the later Assyria. Here small agricultural villages, dependent essentially on rain agriculture and herding, occurred as early as the seventh millennium BCE. In the south, the later Babylonia, settlement began in the sixth millennium only, with what is known as the Ubaid period. The people who settled were most likely the forebears of the later Sumerian-speaking people of the region. Their settlement form seems originally to have been one of campsites and seminomadic small villages located along natural watercourses. They depended partly on irrigation hoe agriculture, partly on herding and fishing. Each tribe had a fixed center, a "treasury" in which it kept stores and religious objects that would have been inconvenient to take along on wanderings. Such tribal centers appear to have formed the nuclei of many of the later cities and central sanctuaries, to judge from their names.

The period of the earliest occupation, the Ubaid pe-

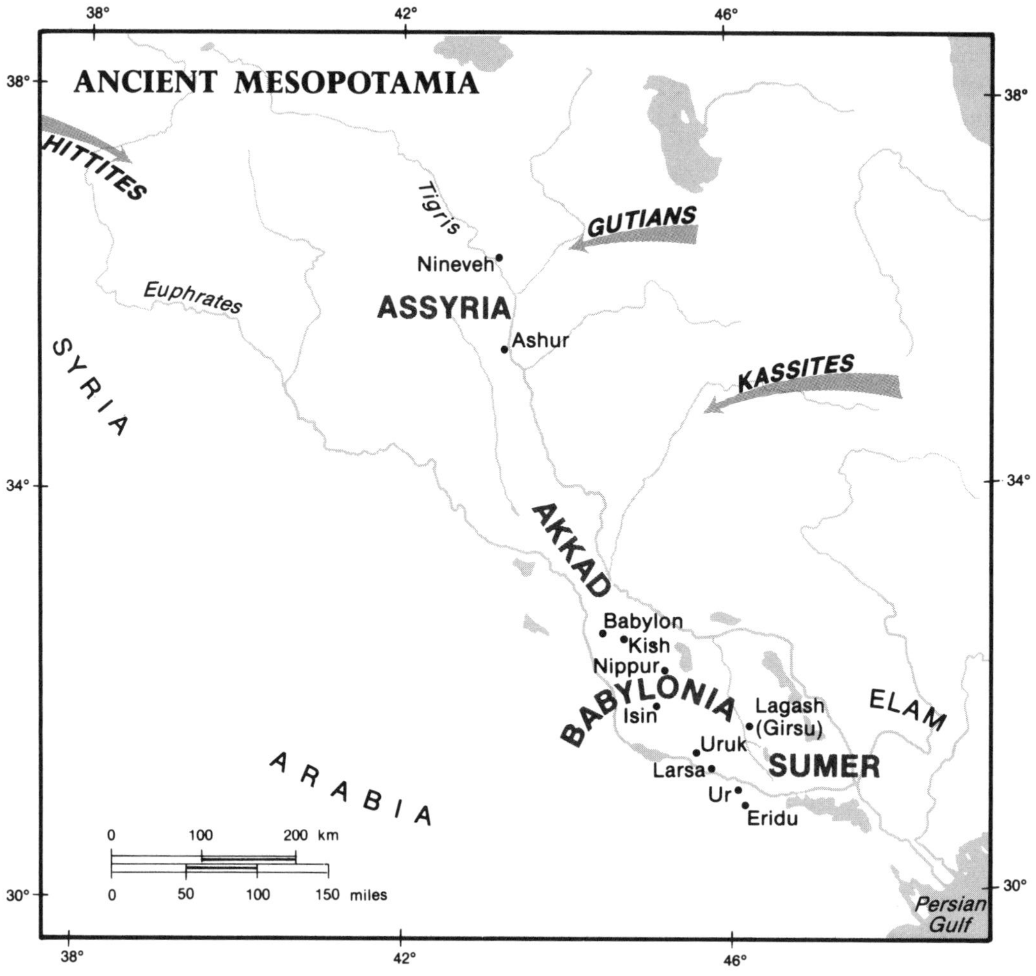

riod, was a long one, and it saw, toward its end, the rise of the first cities. They lined the edge of the southern marshes and may well have owed their existence to a combination of the varied economies of the region: irrigation farming, herding, fishing and hunting; the key requirement for the rise of a city is the availability of economies able to sustain a massing of population on a small space.

Among these first cities were Eridu, Ur, and Uruk, and with the Uruk period, which followed in the late fifth millennium, the cities and the lifestyle they fostered had grown to a point where, as the period was coming to an end around 3500 BCE, we can speak for the first time of true civilization, characterized by magnificent sculpture, monumental architecture, and—most important of all—the invention and development of writing.

As to political forms then in vogue, the occurrence of the term for general assembly *(unkin)* in the early inscriptions is of interest. It belongs in a political pattern called "primitive democracy." Supreme power was vested in a general assembly, which served as a court, as a legislative assembly, and as the authority for electing officers, such as the religio-economic manager, the *en,* and in times of crisis, a war leader, the *lugal,* who served for the time of the emergency only. This pattern made its imprint on early myths and survived as a feature of local government down into the second millennium. In the following Jemdet Nasr and Early Dynastic periods there are suggestions that the pattern of primitive democracy was extended from a local to a national scale with the formation of a league of the city-states along the Euphrates, which met for assembly in Nippur. What specific circumstances could have induced these city-states to forget their local rivalries and join in a common effort is not known for certain, but a plausible guess would be that pressure from invading Akkadian-speaking nomads from the west, which should date to about this time, would have constituted a danger clear and present enough to impose unity, at least for a while.

Whatever unity may have been imposed by the common need to stem the Akkadian advance can have been of short duration only. The Early Dynastic period quickly became one of wars between city-states, which vied with one another for hegemony over the country. The first city to achieve such status was Kish in the north, and its rulers maintained that status long enough to make the title "king of Kish" a term for overlordship over all of Sumer and Akkad. After Kish, various other cities, prominent among them Uruk and Ur, held the hegemony for shorter periods, always precariously and open to successful challenge.

The warlike conditions of life made their mark on the kind of political leadership that had evolved, that of the *en* and the *lugal*. The *en* was basically a person who produced abundance. He or she participated as spouse of the city deity in the yearly fertility drama of the Sacred Marriage, and generally, through personal charisma, managed city affairs productively. One might speak of a "priest-king" or "priest-queen." The *lugal* was quite different. The term means "great householder," not "great man," as it is generally translated, and the *lugal* was originally the son of a major landowner, chosen in the assembly for his military prowess and for the house servants of his paternal house, who would form the core of the army and its high command. As times grew more warlike—and evidence for war appears already with the late Uruk period—the *en*, if he wished to retain his leadership, was forced to turn his abilities to military leadership also, while the *lugal*, who originally had been chosen for the term of an emergency, tended to become permanent as the threat of war became so. This imposed on him responsibility also for the religious, administrative, and economic tasks that belonged originally to the *en*, so that the functions of the two offices tended to merge. The old title of *en* was continued in Uruk. Almost everywhere else that of *lugal* was preferred. A new title of rather more restricted claim, which made its appearance in the Early Dynastic period, was that of *ensi*, "productive manager of the arable lands." It designated the official in charge of plowing, and thus of the city's draft animals, which in war would serve the chariotry of its army. The *ensi*, therefore, tended to become the political head of the community, its ruler. [*See* Kingship, *article on* Kingship in the Ancient Mediterranean World.]

At the very end of the Early Dynastic period a ruler of the city of Umma succeeded in extending his domain to include all of Sumer and Akkad. After an unsuccessful campaign in the north he was defeated and his realm taken over by Sargon of Akkad (c. 2334–2279). Sargon's successors kept a precarious hold on the south until, at the accession of Naram-Sin (c. 2254–2218), that region made itself independent. Akkad continued to flourish, however, deriving its wealth from its position on the major overland route from the Mediterranean to Iran and India, a route the Akkad rulers carefully policed. The city's wealth may have been the cause of an attack on it by a coalition of neighboring countries. Naram-Sin met their armies one by one and defeated them, thus regaining control of all of Mesopotamia. This feat so awed his fellow citizens that they deified him and chose him city god of Akkad. Under Naram-Sin's successors Akkad went into decline, and the Gutians, invaders from the eastern mountains, for a while took control. They were defeated, and the country liberated, by Utuhegal of Uruk, who in turn was succeeded by the famous third dynasty of Ur. Under that dynasty a well-integrated administrative system was developed. The formerly independent city rulers now became governors appointed by, and responsible to, the king and his corps of central officials.

The third dynasty of Ur ended in disaster. A breakthrough of Mardu tribes, nomads of the western desert, disrupted communications and isolated the former city-states from the capital, Ur, which lost control of all but the immediately adjacent territory. Eventually the city fell to an invading force from Elam and was mercilessly looted. Its fall spelled the end of Sumerian civilization even though the language, as the vehicle of culture and learning, continued to be taught in the schools.

The third dynasty of Ur was followed by two long-lived dynasties, one of Isin and one of Larsa, which divided the country between them. They in turn gave way to the short-lived rule of all of Babylonia by Hammurabi of Babylon (fl. 1792–1750), famous for his law code, and his son Samsu-iluna. Late in the latter's reign the south and middle of Babylonia again made itself independent, now under the name of the Sea Land. It covered much the same territory as had Sumer, and its kings consciously stressed their role as heirs to Sumer's ancient language and culture. The dynasty of Babylon fell to a raid by the faraway Hittites around 1600 BCE. When the Hittites had withdrawn, invaders from the mountains, the Kassites, took control and ruled Babylonia for a substantial length of time. One of these Kassite kings, Ulamburiash, conquered the Sea Land and thus unified Babylonia once more. The major rivals of the Kassite kings were the rulers of Assyria, which since the time of Hammurabi had grown in power and influence.

The Kassite dynasty fell before an attack by Shutruk-Nahunte of Elam, who controlled the country for a while. Then a move to regain independence developed in Isin, and the energetic ruler Nebuchadrezzar I (1124–1103) completely liberated the country, defeated Elam, and brought back the statue of Marduk, the city god of Babylon, which the Elamites had earlier taken as booty. From this time on begins the rise of that god to a position of supreme power in, and creator of, the cosmos. Before then the traditional view with Enlil as supreme god had held sway as the officially accepted one.

The following centuries saw a steady rivalry between Babylonia and Assyria, with the latter eventually victorious. After a gradual extension of their authority over Syria by the Assyrians, Tiglath-pileser III (745–727) conquered Babylonia, and under his successors, Sargon II, Sennacherib, Esarhaddon, and Ashurbanipal, it remained an Assyrian dependency even though at times it had its own Assyrian-appointed king and a semblance of independence. Throughout this time, however, Babylonia remained a thorn in the side of its Assyrian overlords. It even drove Sennacherib to the extreme of obliterating the city, only to have it restored by his son Esarhaddon.

Assyria fell in 609 BCE, after the capital, Nineveh, had been captured in 612 in a combined attack by the Medes and the army of Babylonia. Here an Aramean, Nabapolassar, had achieved freedom from the Assyrian yoke and founded a dynasty. After participating with the Medes in the destruction of Nineveh and Assyria, he turned to the conquest of Syria, which was accomplished by the crown prince Nebuchadrezzar, who followed his father to the throne in 605.

In 539 BCE Babylon opened its gates to the Persian king Cyrus. The last indigenous ruler, Nabonidus, had incurred the hatred of the Marduk priesthood through his championship of the moon god Sin of Harran and his attempts at religious reform. For part of his reign he left rule in Babylon to his son Belshazzar and withdrew himself to the Tema Oasis in Arabia. With him ended Babylonian independence.

Divine Forms: The Numinous

Basic to all religion, and so also to ancient Mesopotamian religion, is, I believe, a unique experience of confrontation with power not of this world. The German theologian and philosopher Rudolf Otto called it the numinous experience and characterized it as experience of a *mysterium tremendum et fascinans*, a confrontation with a "wholly other" outside of normal experience and indescribable in its terms. It is the human response to it in thought (myth and theology) and action (cult and worship) that constitutes religion.

Since what is met with in the numinous experience is not of this world, it cannot be described, for all descriptive terms necessarily reflect this-worldly experience and so fall short. At most, therefore, it will be possible to seek to recall and suggest the human response to the numinous experience as closely as possible by way of analogy and evocative metaphor. Every religion, accordingly, has evolved standardized versions of such metaphors. They form the link from firsthand to secondhand experience, become the vehicle of religious instruction, and form the body of collective belief. They will differ, naturally, with the different civilizations in which they are grounded and from which their imagery is taken. Study of any given religion must thus begin with the study of its favorite and central metaphors, taking due care not to forget that they are but metaphors and so are no end in themselves but are meant to point beyond. [*See* Iconography, *article on* Mesopotamian Iconography.]

Physiomorphism. Turning, then, to the world of ancient Mesopotamian religion, its most striking characteristic seems to be an innate bend toward immanence. The numinous was here experienced as the inwardness of some striking feature or phenomenon of the situation in which it was encountered, as a will and power for that phenomenon to be in its particular form and manner and to thrive. It was therefore natural that it should be considered to have the form and name of the phenomenon whose inwardness it constituted. It was also natural that the early settlers should have been drawn particularly to those numinous forces that informed phenomena vital to their survival, the early economies, and that they should have wished to hold onto them and maintain them through cult and worship.

The original identity of numinous powers with the phenomena they were thought to inform is indicated by divine names such as *An* ("heaven") for the god of heaven, *Hursag* ("foothills") for the goddess of the near ranges, *Nanna* ("moon") for the moon god, *Utu* ("sun") for the sun god, *Ezen* ("grain") for the grain goddess, and so forth. Occasionally an honorific epithet, such as *en* ("productive manager, lord") or *nin* ("mistress"), was added, as in *Enlil* ("lord wind") and *Nintur* ("mistress birth-hut"). In some cases the mythopoeic imagination elaborated on a phenomenon to bring out its character more vividly, as when the numinous thundercloud Imdugud ("rain cloud") takes form as an enormous bird floating on outstretched wings and emitting its thunderous roar through a lion's head, or when Gishzida ("well-grown tree") is given form as the stock of a tree entangled in roots having the form of snakes, thus visualizing the belief of the ancients that tree roots could come alive as snakes.

The early selectivity of powers experienced in phenomena of vital economic importance to the settlers shows in the distribution of city gods, who must be considered coeval with their cities, over the various regional economies of the country. The extreme south is marshland with characteristic economies such as fishing, fowling, and hunting. Here was Eridu, the city of Enki, whose other names were *Daradim* ("wild goat fashioner") and *Enuru* ("lord reed-bundle"), signifying power in the marsh vegetation and in the reed bundles with which reed huts were constructed. Farther east, in Nina, resided Enki's daughter Nanshe, goddess of fish, the numinous force producing the teeming schools of fish that gave the fisherman his livelihood. South of Nina, in Kinirsha, was the home of Dumuzi-Abzu ("producer of healthy young ones of the marsh"), the mysterious numinous will and power for the young of marsh fauna to be born healthy and unimpaired. Through the marshlands along the Euphrates runs also the country of the ox herdsman and the orchardman. To the ox herdsman's pantheon belonged the bull god Ningublaga and his consort Nineiagara ("lady of the creamery"). In Ur resided Nanna, the moon god envisaged by the herdsman as a frisky young bull with gleaming horns—the new moon—grazing in the pasture of heaven. In Ararma, farther up river, resided the sun god Utu, whose round face was seen as the round face of a bison. At Uruk, finally, was the cow goddess Ninsuna ("mistress of the wild cows"), who was herself visualized as cow-shaped, and her bull-god husband, Lugalbanda. The ox herdsmen grazed their herds on the young shoots of reed and rushes in the marshes along the Euphrates. Closer to the river itself was the country of the orchardmen, who depended on the river for the irrigation of their plantations. To them belonged Ninazu of Enegir, seemingly a god of waters, and his son Ningishzida ("master of the good tree") of Gishbanda, a deity of tree roots and serpents. His wife was Ninazimua ("mistress of the well-grown branch"). Damu, city god of Girsu on the Euphrates, was a vegetation god, especially, it would seem, the power for the sap to rise in plants and trees in the spring. Farther up still, at Uruk—in antiquity as today a center of date culture—there was Amaushumgalana, the power for animal growth and new life of the date palm, and his consort Inanna, earlier Ninana ("mistress of the date clusters"), a personification of the date storehouse.

At Uruk the country of the orchardmen and the oxherds joins that of the shepherds; called the *edin,* it is a wide, grassy steppe in the heart of Sumer, ringed around by the Euphrates and the Iturungal. Here on the western edge is Uruk with Inanna of the shepherds, goddess of the rains that call up verdure and grazing in the desert, and her young husband, Dumuzi ("producer of healthy young ones"). This pair was also worshiped in Patibira on the southern edge, and in Umma and Zabalam on the eastern edge. On the southern edge lies also Ararma with the sun god Utu and his son Shakan, god of all four-legged beasts of the desert, and to the north is the domain of Ishkur, god of the thundershowers that turn the desert green like a garden in the spring.

North and east of the *edin,* finally, lay the plowlands with cities dedicated to cereal and chthonic deities, or deities of the chief agricultural implements, the hoe and plow. Shuruppak on the Euphrates was the home of Ansud, goddess of the ear of grain and daughter of Ninshebargunu ("mistress mottled barley"). Farther up the river was Nippur with Ansud's divine husband, Enlil; and since Enlil's winds were the moist winds of spring that made the soil workable, he also was god of the oldest and most versatile agricultural implement, the hoe. Nippur—the city rather than its sacred quarter around Enlil's temple, Ekur—was also the home of Enlil's son Ninurta ("master plow"), god of the younger implement, the plow, and charged in Nippur with the office of plowman *(ensi)* on his father's estate. Identified by the ancients with Ninurta were the gods Pabilsag ("first new shoot"), who in Isin was husband of the city goddess Nininsina ("mistress of Isin"); and Ningirsu ("master of [the city] Girsu"), who in Girsu, southeast of the *edin,* was essentially a god of the thundershowers and the floods of spring. Farther north, in Cutha, resided the netherworld gods Meslamtaea ("the one issuing from the luxuriant *mesu* tree")—presumably originally a tree deity—and Nergal. In Kish resided Sabbaba ("ever spreading the wings"), a god of war and originally, perhaps, of the thundercloud. In Babylon Merodakh, or Marduk ("calf of the storm"), was the city god. He was a god of the thunderstorm envisaged as a roaring young bull.

Anthropomorphism. It seems reasonable to consider the physiomorphic forms the original and oldest forms under which the gods were envisaged, yet one should probably not altogether exclude the possibility that the human form may be almost equally early. The two forms were not mutually exclusive, and a deity might well choose to appear now under one, now under another. Seal impressions from the late Uruk period show the ritual scene of the sacred marriage with the goddess Inanna in her physiomorphic form of storehouse gateposts on some, in her human form on others. A later example is a statement about Gudea, ruler of Lagash (fl. c. 2144–c. 2124 BCE), who lived shortly before the third dynasty of Ur and whose goddess mother was the cow goddess Ninsuna. He is said to have been "born of a good cow in its woman aspect." As late as the early first millennium, a hymn to the moon god revels in attributing to the god physiomorphic and anthropomorphic forms alike: he is a prince, a young bull, a fruit self-grown, a womb giving birth to all, and a merciful, forgiving father.

Although human and nonhuman forms thus could coexist peacefully, there are indications that they were not always equally favored. The human form was clearly seen as more dignified and appropriate than the nonhuman one and tended to eclipse it. [*See* Anthropomorphism.]

One outcome of this attitude was representations in which the two different kinds of form were blended but with the human features dominant. In Girsu, for instance, at the end of the Third Early Dynastic period a mace head dedicated to Ningirsu, god of thundershowers and floods, shows the donor in a pose of adoration before the god in his old form of a thunderbird. Somewhat later, when Gudea saw the god in his dream, Ningirsu was essentially human in form although he retained the thunderbird wings and merged the lower part of his body with a flood. From the time of Gudea stems also a vase dedicated to Ningishzida that shows the god in his cella with the door open and flanked by two gatekeepers in dragon form. The god appears in his original form of the stock of a tree entwined by serpent-shaped roots. To this same period belongs a relief that shows Ningishzida introducing Gudea to Ningirsu. Here he is in completely human form except for two heads of serpents peeping out from his body at the shoulders. In much similar fashion, vegetation deities on seals are shown with branches and greens protruding from their bodies as if—in the words of the archaeologist Henri Frankfort—their inner being was seeking to burst asunder the imposed human form.

Composite forms such as the above still recognize the relevance of the nonhuman forms and preserve their essential characteristics even if the human form clearly dominates; but more radical trends away from the physiomorphic representation deliberately separated the deity from the phenomenon which he or she informed. The deity became a power in human shape; the phenomenon subsided into a mere thing owned or managed by the deity, and the form derived from it into a mere emblem.

Thus, for instance, the goddess Hursag ("foothills") ceased being the deified foothills themselves and became instead Ninhursaga ("mistress of the foothills"). Similarly, the deified wild cow became Ninsuna ("mistress of wild cows"). Gishzida ("good tree") turned into Ningishzida ("master of the good tree"). Ningirsu's form of thunderbird was referred to by Gudea as his emblem, and it adorns—and perhaps protects—Ninurta's war chariot on the famous Stela of the Vultures. Inanna, as goddess of the morning and evening star, had the physiomorphic form of the small, round disk which that star looks like in the Near East. That too became an emblem carried as a standard by the contingent from her clan when Gudea called it up for work on the temple he was building.

As so often with religious beliefs, so also here: no change is ever a clean break. Although demoted to emblems, the old forms did not altogether lose their potency. It is in these forms, as standards, that the gods followed the army in war and gave victory, and it is in these forms that the gods sanctioned oaths. Oaths were taken by touching them.

At times the aversion felt for the older, nonhuman forms must have been intense enough to engender open enmity. This seems to have been the case with the thunderbird, which from being Ningirsu's early shape became first a mere emblem of his and then was listed by editors of the myth about him, called *Angim,* among the god's captured enemies pulling his triumphal chariot. In still later time the bird—often shown as a winged lion rather than as a lion-headed bird—even became the god's chief antagonist. Thus in the Akkadian myth of Anzu (the Akkadian name of the bird) the god victoriously routs and subdues his own former self. A pictorial representation of the battle graced his temple in Nimrud. In these later materials Ningirsu is called by the name of Ninurta, the god of Nippur with whom he was early identified.

Sociomorphism. Man is a social being: he exists in a context of family and society generally, so in attributing to the gods human form the ancients almost unavoidably attributed to them also social role and status. One such basic context implied in the human form was that of family and household. In the case of major deities the household could be sizable, resembling that of a manorial lord.

The factors that determined the grouping of deities into a given divine family are not always obvious and may have been of various kinds—similarity of nature, complementarity, spatial proximity, and so forth. Similar character probably dictated the grouping of seven minor cloud goddesses as daughters of the god of thundershowers, Ningirsu. The nature of their mother, Ningirsu's wife, Baba, is less clear; she may have been a goddess of pasture. Ningirsu's son Igalima ("door leaf of the honored one") appears to be a deification of the door to Ningirsu's court of justice. Since clouds were seen to rise as mist from the marshes, the positing of the rain-cloud god Asalluhe as son of the god of the marshes, Enki, seems understandable. So too does the marriage of Amaushumgalana, the power producing the date harvest, to Inanna, the goddess of the storehouse. A logical connection seems observable also between the aspect of Enlil in which he is god of the older agricultural implement, the hoe, and that of his son Ninurta, god of the younger implement, the plow; but only too often no explanation readily suggests itself.

Our most complete picture of a major divine household is given by Gudea in the hymn known as Cylinder B. It lists the minor gods who served as functionaries in

Ningirsu's house, that is, his temple, lending divine guidance to the human staff. Thus Ningirsu's oldest son Shulshagana served as majordomo, the traditional role of the eldest son. His brother Igalima functioned as chief gendarme responsible for the maintenance of law and order on the estate. Ningirsu's septuplet daughters served as his handmaidens and also presented petitions to him. He had two harpists—one for hymns, one for elegies—and a chambermaid, who bathed him at night and saw to it that his bed was provided with fresh straw. For the task of administering his estate and sitting in judgment in disputes that might arise, the god had a divine counselor and a secretary *(sukal)*. There were two generals, and an assherd to look after the draft animals. Goats and deer on the estate were cared for by a divine herder of deer; a divine farmer looked after the extensive agricultural holdings; a tax gatherer supervised the fisheries; and a ranger protected the wildlife of the estate against poachers. A high constable and a night watchman kept the estate safe.

In addition to their local functions of looking after their estates, most of the major deities had also wider, national responsibilities as officers of the divine polity into which the sociomorphic view was gradually transforming the cosmos. Highest authority in this divine state was a general assembly of the gods, which met in Nippur in a corner of the forecourt of Enlil's temple, Ekur, called Ubshuukkinna. An and Enlil presided; the gods took an oath to abide by the decision of the assembly, and voted by saying "Heam" ("May it be!"). The assembly served as a court—it once even banned Enlil himself—and it elected cities and their rulers to hold sway over all of Sumer and Akkad. The election was for a term only, and when the assembly decided a term was ended, it voted to overthrow the reigning city and transfer its kingship to another city and ruler.

Besides the office of king, the divine state knew also more permanent offices. For the most part these offices, which were called *me* ("office, function"), were reinterpretations of functions already innate in the gods in question, the phenomena and processes of which they were the indwelling will and power; they were now envisaged as the official duties of members of a divine bureaucracy. A comprehensive statement of this view of the cosmos is found in the myth *Enki and the World Order*, which tells how Enki, acting on behalf of Enlil, institutes the proper course of natural phenomena and the manner of engaging in human industries, appointing in each case a divine official to be responsible for them. The regime of the Tigris and the Euphrates thus comes under the administration of the "inspector of canals," the god Enbilulu. Other officials are appointed for the marshes and the sea; the storm god Ishkur is made the official in charge of the yearly rains. For agriculture the farmer god Enkimdu and the grain goddess Ezinu are appointed; for the wildlife, the god of beasts, Shakan; for the flocks, Dumuzi, the shepherd; for just boundaries, the god of justice, Utu; for weaving, the spider goddess, Uttu; and so forth.

The Pantheon

A pantheon seeking to interrelate and to rank the innumerable deities the ancient Mesopotamians worshiped, or merely recognized, in cities and villages throughout the land evolved gradually through the diligent work of scribes, who produced lists of divine names as part of their general lexical endeavors. The resulting scheme as it is known to us from old Babylonian copies was based primarily on the prominence in the cosmos of the cosmic feature with which the deity in question was associated, secondarily on his or her family and household ties. It is thus anthropomorphic and sociomorphic in character. First came the deities of heaven, the winds, the eastern foothills, and the underground fresh waters, each with his or her family and household. Then followed deities of smaller entities such as the moon, the sun, and the morning and evening star. A following section dealing with deities of the Lagash region was probably not part of the original list, since that region was considered enemy territory down to the time of the third dynasty of Ur. Last came the deities of the netherworld. In its main lines, and necessarily highly selectively, the pantheon may be presented as follows (Akkadian names, when different from the Sumerian ones, are given in parentheses).

An. An (Anum) was god of the sky and father of the gods. The main center of An's cult seems to have been in Uruk. An was given form mythopoeically as a mighty bull whose bellowing was heard in the thunder. The rain was seen as his semen impregnating the earth *(ki)* and producing vegetation. As the cloudy skies vanished with the spring, An as Gugalanna ("great bull of heaven") was thought to have been killed and gone to the netherworld. A different tradition saw An (Anum) as the sky in its male aspect married to An (Antum), the sky in its female aspect. She, like her husband, was given bovine form and seen as a cow, whose udders, the clouds, produced the rain. An important aspect of An was his relation to the calendar, the months having their characteristic constellations that announced them. To this aspect belonged monthly and yearly festival rites dedicated to An. [*See also* An.]

Enlil. God of wind and storms, Enlil was the most prominent member of the divine assembly and executor of its decrees. The city of Enlil was Nippur (Nuffar), with his temple, Ekur. He was married to the goddess

Ninlil ("lady wind"), who was also known as Ansud ("long ear of grain"). Her mother was Ninshebargunu, the barley goddess, and her father, Haya, was keeper of the seal with which the doors of Enlil's granaries were secured. Originally in keeping with the agricultural ambience of his wife, Enlil would seem to have been the power in and for the moist winds of spring that soften the hard crust on the soil and make it tillable. Thus he was also god of the oldest tool of tillage, the hoe. With the hoe, after he had invented it, he broke—according to one myth—the hard crust on the earth at Uzumua ("flesh-grower"), in Nippur, so that mankind could shoot up like plants from the earth. [*See also* Enlil.]

Two quite different myths deal with the wooing of Ninlil or Ansud by Enlil. In one he follows successfully established procedures for winning her. In the other, more primitive one, Ninlil, disregarding her mother's instructions, deliberately tempts Enlil to take her by force by bathing in the canal of the town. Enlil is then banished from the city by the assembly of gods for his misdeed and leaves for the netherworld. Ninlil, pregnant with the moon god Suen (Sin), follows him. On the road Enlil, posing successively as gatekeeper of Nippur, man of the river of the netherworld, and ferryman, persuades her to lie with him that she may conceive a further child, who may take Suen's place in the netherworld. Thus Suen's netherworld brothers, Meslamtaea, Ninazu, and Ennugi, are engendered. The myth ends—oddly to a modern reader—with a paean to Enlil as a source of fertility: "A lord of great consequence, a lord of the storehouse are you! A lord making the barley grow up, lord making the vines grow up are you! Lord of heaven, lord of abundance, lord of earth are you!"

The aspect of Enlil in which he was the benevolent provider of abundance is clearly an old one, and it was never lost sight of. With time, however, his character took on also more grim features. As leader of the divine assembly and executor of its decrees, he became the power for destruction of temples and cities, the all-obliterating storm with which the assembly overthrew dynasties and their capitals as it shaped history. This later aspect of Enlil is prominent in laments, where more and more the will of the assembly becomes subsumed in his will, and it is for him alone to relent and to restore what he had destroyed. In the first millennium, as Marduk of Babylon rose to preeminence, Enlil, as representative of the often-rebellious south, even came to be treated as enemy and evil in northern Babylonia, as is clear from his role in ritual texts; or he was totally ignored, as in the late creation epic *Enuma elish,* which celebrates Marduk as the creator and ruler of the cosmos.

Besides the tradition which had Ninlil or Ansud as consort of Enlil, there existed a variant one in which he was paired with the goddess Ninhursaga, the older Hursag ("foothills"). Here probably also belongs an aspect of Enlil in which he was seen as a mountain deity, his name in that capacity being Kurgal ("great mountain") and that of his main temple, Ekur ("mountain house"). The connection between this mountain aspect and his aspect as god of the wind appears to correlate with the fact that the ancients believed the home of the winds to be in the mountains. Enlil would thus originally have been specifically the east wind, *imkura* ("wind of the mountains").

On Ninhursaga, Enlil begat the seasons of the year, Winter and Summer, and he also fathered the god of the yearly flood of the Tigris, Ningirsu. In the form the myth of the latter takes in Gudea's references to it, Ningirsu is the semen of Enlil reddened in the deflowering. This may be taken to refer to the waters of the melting snow in the high mountains in Iran (Enlil as Kurgal) in the spring. The waters make their way through the foothills *(hursag),* where the clay they absorb gives them a reddish hue, to pour into the Tigris, swelling it to flood, Ningirsu.

Ninurta. In Nippur, the town itself—as distinct from the sacred area around Ekur—had as city god a son of Enlil called Ninurta, whose wife was the goddess Nin-Nibru ("queen of Nippur"). Ninurta's name may be interpreted as containing a cultural loanword, *urta* ("plow"), thus identifying him as god of that implement, much as his father, Enlil, in one aspect was god of the older agricultural tool, the hoe. Ninurta held in Nippur the office of plowman *(ensi)* for Ekur, and at his yearly festival the king opened the plowing season behind a ceremonial plow. Ninurta was early identified with Ningirsu of Girsu, and myths pertaining to the latter were freely attributed to him, so that it often is difficult to determine which traits are original to whom.

A clear case is that of the myth *Lugale,* which can be shown to belong originally to Ningirsu. It depicts the god as a young warrior king who learns that a rival has arisen in the mountains and plots to kill him. He sets out with his army for a preemptive strike, attacks impetuously, and faces disaster, but is saved by advice from his father to send out a heavy rain, which lays the dust that his adversary, one Azag, had raised against him, nearly suffocating him. He then succeeds in killing Azag and goes on to organize the regime of the Tigris, bringing its waters down for irrigation. Before that they had flowed into the mountains, where they froze. To hold the waters on their new course, Ningirsu constructs a barrier of stone, the foothills *(hursag),* and when his mother comes to visit he presents it to her as a gift, renaming her Ninhursaga ("mistress of the foothills"). Last he sits in judgment over Azag's warriors, various kinds of stones that he had captured, and imposes rewards or punishment according to their conduct in the war. His judgments determine the nature and the distinguishing traits of the stones in question for all time. He finally returns victoriously home.

To Ningirsu probably also belongs the myth *Angim* (mentioned above), which describes the god's victorious return from war and how he has to tone down his boisterous behavior lest he upset his father, Enlil. The basis for the tale would seem to be a spell for averting thunderstorms—Ningirsu was god of the thunderstorm—from Nippur. Conceivably a hymn praising Ninurta in his relation to various stones could be in origin Ningirsu material.

So perhaps also is a myth telling how the thunderbird stole the tablets of destiny from Enki in Eridu, how Ninurta set out to recover them, intending to keep them for himself, and how, when his weapon stunned the bird, it let go its hold of the tablets, and they of themselves returned to Enki. Frustrated in his ambition, Ninurta then raised a flood against Eridu, but Enki craftily had a turtle dig a pit, and he lured Ninurta into it. Underlying the myth is apparently a concept of the rain cloud rising as mist from the swamps, Enki's underground waters *(apsu)*, and, moving in over the mountains, the flight of the thunderbird. The return of the waters in the flood is seen as the god's jealous attack on Enki, and his imprisonment in the turtle's pit must stand for the eventual dwindling of the flood to a trickle between towering banks, the pit. [*See also* Ninurta.]

Nusku. To Enlil's houshold belonged Nusku, in origin a god of lamps. He served as Enlil's trusted vizier and confidant.

Ninhursaga. Ninhursaga ("mistress of the foothills"), earlier simply Hursag ("foothills"), was the power in the fertile near slopes of the eastern mountains, the favorite grazing grounds in the spring. Her cities were Kesh, not yet identified, and Adab, the modern mound Bismaya. In addition to the name *Ninhursaga,* the goddess was also known as *Ninmah* ("august mistress"), *Dingirmah* ("august deity"), and *Nintur* ("mistress birth-hut"), her name as goddess of birth. Her Akkadian name was *Beletili* ("mistress of the gods"). She, An, and Enlil formed in the third millennium the ruling triad of cosmic powers. [*See also* Ninhursaga.]

Enki. Enki (Ea) was god of the underground fresh waters that come to the surface in rivers, pools, and marshes. The Sumerians imagined them as a vast subterranean freshwater sea, which they called Abzu or Engur. Enki's city was Eridu (Abu Shahrein), where he resided in the temple called Eengura ("house of the deep"). A myth tells how he built it and celebrated its completion with a feast for his father, Enlil, in Nippur. Enki's mother was the goddess Namma, whom the scribes listed as Enlil's housekeeper. Other evidence suggests that she was the deified riverbed that gave birth to the god of the river, Enki. Her name seems to mean "mistress vulva," and it may be that the mythopoeic imagination of the ancients saw the chasm of the empty riverbed as the vulva of the earth. Enki's spouse was called Damgalnunna ("great spouse of the prince"), a name that tells us little about her. Enki's vizier was a Janus-faced god, Sha (Usmu).

The name *Enki* means "productive manager [lord] of the soil," which must seem highly appropriate for the god of river waters in a society dependent on irrigation agriculture. In a hymn he describes himself in this aspect, saying: "When I draw near unto heaven, the rains of abundance rain down; when I draw near unto the earth, the early flood at its height comes into being; when I draw near unto the yellowing fields, grain piles are heaped at my command." Water not only slakes the thirst of men, animals, and plants, it also serves to cleanse. In that aspect, as power to cleanse, Enki appears in rituals of purification from all that defiles, including evil spirits attacking man, causing disease and uncleanness. One such elaborate ritual, meant to purify the king of possible evil caused by an eclipse, has the form of a trial before the sun god in which Enki sends a messenger, the exorcist, to speak for the claimant, the polluted king, and undertakes to enforce the verdict. This he does by washing all evil away with his water. The ritual is called Bitrimki ("bathhouse"). In other rituals Enki provided the effective incantation and prescribed the needed cleaning and healing acts, and it is not too much to say that he occupied a central position in all white magic for combating demons of illness. [*See also* Enki.]

Since Enki always knew what to do to drive away demons, he generally rated as the most resourceful and ingenious of the gods. He was skilled in every craft, and under different names he served as patron deity for most of them. His practical ingenuity also made him a born organizer. He was the one who organized the cosmos for Enlil in the myth *Enki and the World Order,* discussed above. Enki in the myths told about him never uses force; instead he gains his point by cunning deftly exercised. An example is the story of Adapa, the steward of Enki, or rather of Ea, for the text uses his Akkadian name. When Adapa once was summoned to appear before Anu in heaven for having broken the wing of the south wind, Ea told him how to gain the goodwill of the two gods who guarded the gate so that they would intercede for him. Ea also warned him not to eat and not to drink, for he would be offered the bread of death and the water of death. All went as planned, and Anu was appeased by the intercession of the doormen. When Adapa refused food and drink, however, Anu was surprised and asked why. Adapa told him, and Anu burst into laughter. The food and drink would actually have made Adapa immortal, which Ea knew and did not want to happen.

A rather more momentous occasion on which Enki showed his cunning was when he saved the human race from destruction at the hand of Enlil. We are told about it in the Sumerian story of the flood, which forms part of the myth called the *Eridu Genesis.* Mankind, having been created and provided with leadership—in the form of kings—by the gods, prospered and proliferated, to the extent that the noise they made became so irksome to Enlil that he persuaded the assembly of the gods to wipe out man with a universal flood. Enki, who was present, was able to warn the pious King Ziusudra to build an ark. Ziusudra followed the advice and was eventually accepted among the gods and granted eternal life as reward for saving all living things.

A far more detailed—and conceivably more original—version of this story is found in the Akkadian tale of Atrahasis ("the surpassingly wise"), who here takes the place of Ziusudra. The story falls into two halves, each clearly originally a separate tale. The first half tells how in the beginning the gods themselves had to work for their food, digging the needed irrigation canals. They eventually rebelled, and Ea thought of the solution, creating man to do the hard work. To that end a god was killed and his blood mixed into the clay from which man was to take form. The mother goddess gave birth to him, and there was general rejoicing. The second half tells how mankind proliferated on earth and with their noise kept Enlil from going to sleep. Enlil therefore tried to cut down on man's numbers by a succession of diseases and famines, but each time Ea found ways of stopping the evils before it was too late, and soon man again proliferated as before. Finally Enlil decided on a desperate means: wiping out mankind with a flood. Again Ea frustrated the plan, by having Atrahasis build an ark in which he survived with his family and the animals. As he emerged from the ark he offered a sacrifice, and the gods were delighted, for all through the flood, with no humans to offer sacrifice, they had suffered severely from hunger. Only Enlil was wroth, but him Ea appeased by instituting plans for population control: barrenness, child disease, and so forth. Thus harmony in the universe was reestablished. As given in the tale of Atrahasis, the story of the flood is the most detailed we have. A shorter version—shorn of any motivation for the flood—was added to the *Epic of Gilgamesh* by the later editor Sinliqiunnini. In the story of Adapa, Enki used his ingenuity against Anu; in the flood story, against Enlil. [*See also* Atrahasis.]

A third myth, *Enki and Ninmah,* pits Enki against the third in the triad of highest deities, Ninhursaga, whom the myth calls Ninmah. Like the Atrahasis story, this composition consists of two separate myths only very loosely connected. The first of these is a Sumerian counterpart to the first part of the Atrahasis story, where the refusal of the gods to work had Enki propose the creation of man. Here he is fathered by "the engendering clay of Abzu," which once also fathered Enki, and he is given form and is borne by Enki's mother, Namma. The second myth begins with a party given by Enki to celebrate the birth of man. As he and Ninmah, who had assisted Namma as birth helper, drink deeply, Ninmah begins to boast that she controls men's fortunes, determining whether they will be good or bad. (That makes little sense if she was, as here, a mere midwife. Apparently, in the original myth underlying this part of the composition she was, as in the Atrahasis story, the one who gave shape to the embryo of man and bore it as an infant.) Enki accepts her challenge, waging that he can counter anything she can think up. She then creates a series of misshapen or otherwise defective human beings, but for each one Enki is able to think of a place in society where it can function and support itself. When Ninmah finally gives up, Enki proposes that he try his hand and that she find a place for his creature. He then fashions an embryo and has it given premature birth by a woman provided by Ninmah. There is nothing Ninmah can do for it, and she breaks out in lament. Enki, however, calms her with a conciliatory speech, pointing out that it is precisely her contribution, the maturing of the embryo in the womb, that it lacked. The man's contribution to the engendering of a child is not enough by itself; the woman's is needed too. And so he praises her powers.

The question thus raised, of the respective share of the male and the female partner in procreation, seems to have been variously answered at different times. The first part of *Enki and Ninmah* gives the woman all the credit. Man was engendered from clay, formed, and given birth—as it specifically states—without a male being involved. Somewhat similarly, the tale of Atrahasis has man created from clay and divine blood and formed and given birth by Nintur, that is, by Ninmah. Enki's contribution in both cases was chiefly the idea of making man. In the second part of *Enki and Ninmah,* however, this changes. Enki's power to create an embryo, although not to mature it and give it birth, is stressed; and finally, in the account of the creation of man in *Enuma elish* at the turn of the first millennium, the birth goddess has vanished, and Enki does the creation all by himself.

One final odd composition with Enki as its hero remains to be mentioned, *Enki and Ninhursaga.* It begins with praise of the island of Dilmun (modern Bahrain) and its pristine purity at the beginning of time. It then tells how Enki provided it with fresh water and made it a port and an emporium. Next we hear how Enki attempts to seduce Ninhursaga but is rejected until he proposes marriage, making her his wife. She gives birth to a daughter, whom Enki seduces as soon as she becomes nubile, fathering a second daughter, whom in turn he seduces and makes pregnant. Her daughter, Enki's granddaughter, is Uttu, the spider goddess, and Ninhursaga warns her against Enki. Uttu therefore refuses to let him into the house unless he brings wedding gifts of fruits. He does so, and when Uttu lets him in, he takes her by force. Uttu's screams bring Ninhursaga, who removes Enki's semen and sows it. From it eight plants grow up. Later, passing by, Enki notes the plants, and as his vizier gives them names, Enki eats them. Ninhursaga, discovering what has happened, vows never to look upon him with her life-giving eye. The plants, Enki's semen, which he swallowed, then begin to develop as embryos in his body. Being male, he is unable to give birth to them, and so falls critically ill. The gods are greatly distressed, but the Fox offers to bring Ninhursaga. It does so; she is released from her vow, places Enki in her vulva, and successfully gives birth to eight deities, who are named and given status, their names serving as grotesque puns on the words for the part of Enki's body from which they come. The last is the goddess of Dilmun.

The stress on Dilmun, and on Enki's amorous success with his daughter, granddaughter, and, in one version, great-granddaughter, the "comely spider goddess Uttu," is hardly meant to be taken seriously. Presumably, the earthy humor of the composition was intended to amuse visiting sailors from Dilmun when they were entertained at the court of Ur.

Asalluhe. Asalluhe ("man-drenching Asar"), city god of Kuar, near Eridu, and god of rain clouds, was Enki's son. He appears predominantly in incantations against all kinds of evil doings. Floating as a cloud above the earth, he was in a position to observe what was going on below and duly reported it to his father, Enki, who was not in a similar, favorable position to observe. On hearing Asalluhe's account, however, out of his profound knowledge he was able in each case to tell how the evil was to be countered. Identified with Asalluhe in later times was Marduk.

Marduk. Marduk, or preferably Merodakh, city god of Babylon, was an old Sumerian deity who, like Ninazu in Eshnunna (discussed below) and Meslamtaea in Cutha, was taken over by the Akkadian invaders. His name, abbreviated from *(A)marudak* ("calf of the storm"), characterizes him as a god of thunderstorms visualized as a bellowing young bull. The thundershowers of spring mark the appearance of verdure in the desert and of plowing and sowing; thus Marduk's chief festival, the Akiti (Akitu), or "time of the earth reviving," was further described as "of the seed plowing." His city was Kadingira ("gate of the god"), translated into Akkadian as Babilim. The name indicates a settlement grown up at the entrance to a sanctuary, presumably Marduk's temple Esagila ("house with head held high"). Throughout the third and second millennia, it would seem, Marduk's status was little more than that of a local city god. With the advent of the first millennium, however, began his rise to supreme god of the universe and his rivalry for that honor with Ashur of Assyria. [*See also* Marduk.]

Marduk's claim to supremacy was celebrated in the creation epic *Enuma elish,* in which he is presented as savior of the gods and creator and organizer of the cosmos. The myth begins by tracing world origins from a watery chaos of fresh waters, Apsu, and salt waters, Tiamat, the sea. From them stemmed various generations of gods: Lahmu and Lahamu; Anshar and Kishar, the horizon; Anu, heaven; and Nudimmud or Ea. The younger gods, getting together to dance, proved disturbing to the older generations, who prized peace and quiet. Tiamat, as a long-suffering mother, bore with it, but Apsu decided to get rid of the troublemakers. However, before he could carry out his evil design he was overcome and slain by Ea, who then built for himself a house on top of Apsu's body. There Ea engendered his son Marduk. Anu, inordinately fond of his grandchild, fashioned the four winds for little Marduk to play with. The winds disturbed the still surface of the sea, creating billows. This greatly vexed the older gods, and they were able to rouse Tiamat to action. An army was assembled to destroy the younger gods and was placed under the command of Tiamat's paramour Kingu. The threat to the gods was serious and caused consternation among them. Both Ea and Anu, who were sent to cope with the crisis one after the other, failed and turned back. Finally, since the gods were in deepest despair, Ea suggested to the leader of the gods, Anshar, that Marduk be summoned to champion the gods. Marduk came and was willing to undertake the task, but he demanded full authority. The gods agreed, gave him the power for his word to come true, and made sure by a test that his word now had that effect. Marduk then rode to battle on his storm chariot. The sight of him overwhelmed the enemy; only Tiamat dared face him, but after an angry exchange of words, as she opened her maw to swallow him, he drove in the winds and then killed her with an arrow. Her army he took captive, enclosing it in a net held by the four winds. Out of the carcass of Tiamat Marduk then created the extant universe. He split her in two, and made out of one part heaven; out of the other, earth. To prevent her waters from escaping he provided bolts and guards. In heaven, directly opposite Ea's Apsu, he built his own house, Esharra, which the text says was the sky. He then fashioned the constellations, organized the calendar, fixed the polestar, and gave the moon and sun orders about their motion.

When Marduk returned home, he was hailed by the gods, who reaffirmed their allegiance to him. His first demand of them, then, was that they build him a city, to be called Babylon. He then pardoned the captive gods, who gratefully hailed him as king and savior and promised to build his city for him. Their willingness moved Marduk to think of a means of lightening their labors, and he decided to create man. An assembly was called. Kingu was denounced as the instigator of the rebellion and was slain, and out of his body Ea fashioned man. Marduk then divided the gods into two groups, one celestial and one terrestrial. The gods for the last time took spade in hand and built the city Marduk wanted, Babylon. At a great housewarming party to celebrate the completion of Babylon, Marduk was appointed permanent king of the gods. The myth ends with the gods naming Marduk's fifty names, each of which expressed a power that he held. Marduk's consort was the goddess Sarpanitum; his son, the god of Borsippa near Babylon, was Nabu, god of the scribal art. [*See also* Nabu.]

Nanna. Nanna (also Suen or Sin) was the god of the moon. His city was Ur (Muqayyir); his temple there, Egishnugal. His wife was Ningal. His own name, *Nanna*, would seem to designate him as the full moon, while *Suen* would be the name of the sickle moon. He was regularly envisioned in a bull shape, an image that the hornlike shape of the sickle moon may have encouraged. He was also visualized as a herder driving his herd—the stars—across the pastures of heaven, or as riding in the heavens in a boat, the sickle moon. A late myth—actually an incantation to ward off the evils of an eclipse of the moon—tells how he was attacked by storm demons after they had lured the storm god, Ishkur, and Inanna, who aspired to queenship of heaven, to their side. The attack was noted, however, by Enlil, who alerted Enki and had him send Marduk to the rescue. [*See also* Nanna.]

Utu. The god of the sun and of justice and fair dealings was Utu (Shamash). His cities were Ararma (Larsa) in the south and Sippar in the north. His temple in both cities was called Ebabbar; his wife was Ninkarra (Aya). As judge, Utu presided each day in various temples at specific places called "the place of Utu." He was greeted in the morning as he rose on the horizon, heard cases all day, and was sped on his way in the evening, at sundown. During the night he sat in judgment in the netherworld. The cases he heard, whether by day or by night, were apparently normally such as were brought by the living against ghosts and demons that plagued them. [*See also* Utu.]

Ishkur. Ishkur (Adad) was the god of rains and thunderstorms. A text, basically a spell to avert a threatening thunderstorm from Nippur, tells him to go away so as not to disturb his father, Enlil, with his clamor. His original form seems to have been that of a bull. In many ways he resembles Ningirsu, but he seems to be more specifically a herder's god, the power in the spring rains that bring up pasture in the desert. [*See also* Adad.]

Inanna. Inanna (Ishtar) was earlier called *Ninana*, which can be understood as either "mistress of the date clusters" or "mistress of heaven." The center of her worship was, in the south, at Uruk, in the temple called Eana, and in the north at Hursagkalamma, near Kish. Characteristic of her is her great complexity and many-sidedness. It is apparent that a variety of originally different deities were syncretized in her and also that the ancients had been able to blend these differences into a fascinating, many-faceted, and convincing character. Normally she was envisioned as a rather willful, high-handed, young aristocratic girl of marriageable age or else as a young bride. Her lover or husband is a form of the god Dumuzi (Tammuz). In the complex image the goddess presents it seems possible to distinguish the following aspects, presumably once independent figures.

1. As goddess of the storehouse of dates, Inanna was at home in Uruk, situated in a famous date-growing region. Her name *Ninana* here stands for "mistress of the date clusters"; the name of her temple, *Eana*, for "house of the date clusters." Here, at the gate of the storeroom *(egida)*, she received her bridegroom, Amaushumgalana ("the one great source of the date clusters"), that is, the one great bud that the date palm sprouts annually. He was the power that made the date palm produce; their wedding and his entering Inanna's house constitute a mythopoeic view of the bringing in of the date harvest. As the rite of this marriage was performed later, the ruling king not only took the role of, but actually became, Amaushumgalana, while the goddess would have been incarnate in the queen, Ninegala ("mistress of the palace"). In the literature relating to

Inanna's wedding she is therefore often called by that epithet, and in love songs written for that occasion it is often difficult to tell whether they celebrate Inanna's love for Amaushumgalana or perhaps rather that of the human queen for her husband. The cult of Inanna in her aspect of goddess of the date storehouse was a happy one. There was no sense of loss, no "death" of the god. The dates, eminently storable, were always with the community, and so was the power they represented.

2. Rather different was another aspect, also at home in Uruk, but in the Uruk of sheepfolds rather than of date groves. In this aspect Inanna was the power of the thundershowers of spring, on which the shepherds depended for pasturage in the desert. In this aspect she was paired with Dumuzi, the shepherd. Her early form was apparently that of the lion-headed thunderbird, which remained with her as an attribute. Besides it, and more or less replacing it, was also the form of the lion alone.

3. Closely related to Inanna's aspect as goddess of the thunderstorm was her aspect as goddess of war. The thunderous rumble of the primitive war chariot made it easy to see and hear thunder as the chariot's counterpart in the sky. The ferocious nature of other forms such as lions and bulls fitted easily into the image. As goddess of war, Inanna led the Dance of Inanna, the moving of the battle lines toward each other as if they were lines of dancers. In the myths about her she subdues the insubmissive Ebeh mountain range in southern Assyria.

4. An astral aspect of both Inanna and the Akkadian Ishtar is that of goddess of the morning and evening star, with which she forms a triad with her father, the moon god, and her brother, the sun god. Her precise function in this role is not clear except insofar as her appearance marked the beginning and the end of the working day. As goddess of the morning and evening star her name was understood to mean "mistress of heaven," and her celestial affinities conceivably also encouraged an interpretation of the name of her temple, *Eana,* as "house of heaven" and a belief that it had originally descended from heaven. There is even evidence that in later times she managed to supplant the goddess of heaven, An (Antum), as spouse of the god of heaven, An (Anum), and became queen of heaven. In the *Eclipse Myth* she unsuccessfully conspires with the storm demons to obtain that position, but in a later myth, the *Elevation of Inanna,* the august assembly of the gods itself petitions An to marry her, and she is invested with supreme powers among the gods.

5. Finally, as protector of harlots, Inanna was herself envisaged as a harlot. Her original form in this aspect was that of the owl, which, like the harlot, comes out at dusk. Correspondingly her name as harlot was *Ninnina* ("mistress owl"). In Akkadian her name was *Kilili.* [*See also* Hierodouleia.]

In the myths dealing with Inanna a frequently occurring motif is her insatiable desire for power. In the *Eclipse Myth,* as noted, it leads her to conspire with the evil storm demons; in *Enki and the World Order* she complains bitterly that all other goddesses have offices and only she has none, so Enki tries to assuage her. In the myth *Inanna and the Parse,* that is, Inanna and the divine offices called in Sumerian *me,* we are told how she visited Enki in Eridu, how he drank deeply at the party welcoming her, and how in an expansive mood he conferred upon her one office after another. Wisely, she decided to leave immediately for home with her newly won offices, so that when Enki woke up sober and wanted the offices back it was too late. The myth lists the offices one by one; they constitute a formidable list. Owing, probably, in large part to the syncretistic background of the image of Inanna, the offices attributed to her show little unity or coherent pattern; rather, they form a motley collection of variorums. That did not trouble the ancients though; instead, they gloried in Inanna's versatility, and a major hymn to her even makes a point of praising her as goddess of opposites, of insult and veneration, downheartedness and good cheer, and so on. [*See also* Inanna.]

Inanna's lust for power is also an important motif in the best known of the myths about her, *Inanna's Descent to the Netherworld.* It prompts her to descend to the realm of death to wrest queenship over it from its rightful queen, Ereshkigal. The attempt fails, and Inanna is killed and turned into a cut of meat gone bad and hung on a peg. When she fails to return, her loyal handmaiden Ninshubura seeks help, first from Enlil in Nippur, then from Nanna in Ur, and finally from Enki in Eridu. Only Enki can think of a means to help. He creates two creatures from the dirt under his fingernails and sends them to the netherworld with instructions to condole with Ereshkigal, who, as is her custom, laments children who have died before their time. Then, when moved by the creatures' concern she grants them a wish, they are to ask for the tainted meat hanging on a peg and to throw on it the grass and water of life which Enki has given them. They follow the instructions, and Inanna rises alive. As she is about to leave the netherworld, however, its ruling gods stop her and decree that she must provide a substitute to take her place. So she is accompanied by a detachment of netherworld police to ensure that she will designate a substitute to go back with them.

On the journey back to Uruk she is met by one loyal servant after another, all clad in mourning for her, and she refuses to hand any of them over to the demons.

When they reach Uruk, however, they come upon her young husband, Dumuzi, sitting in fine clothes and enjoying himself listening to the music of reed pipes. This flagrant lack of concern infuriates Inanna, and in a flash of jealous rage she hands him over to the demons, who carry him off. In his distress he calls upon his brother-in-law, Utu, god of justice and fairness, and asks Utu to change him into a gazelle—in another version into a snake—so that he can escape his captors. Utu does so, and Dumuzi escapes, only to be again caught; again he escapes, until finally he is caught for good in his sheepfold. The story ends with Dumuzi's sister Geshtinanna, the goddess of the grapevine, seeking him. Eventually, advised by the Fly, she finds him and joins him in the netherworld. In distress at the undeserved misfortune of both Dumuzi and his sister, Inanna decrees that they may share the obligation to serve in the netherworld as her substitute: Dumuzi will serve half a year below; then he will return to the world above while his sister takes over. She in turn will return after half a year as he goes below.

This ends the tale, and a closer look at it will suggest that *tale* rather than *myth* is the proper designation, for it is most easily understood as a composite of dead myths put together for dramatic effect by the storyteller and haphazardly embellished. The myth of Inanna's death and transformation into a cut of spoiled meat is best understood as an original myth in which she represents the underground storehouse for meat; she becomes like a grave when the meat rots in summer, but she is revived—as the storehouse is restocked with fresh meat from the flocks fed on the grass and water of life, the pastures of spring. The myth has nothing to do with Inanna's aspect as the morning star, in which the storyteller has her present herself when she seeks entry into the netherworld. The second part of the tale was originally a separate myth dealing with Dumuzi rather than with Inanna, and it has also come down, in slightly variant forms, as a separate, self-contained myth.

Dumuzi. Like Inanna, and perhaps even more so, does her lover and bridegroom, Dumuzi (Tammuz), present a highly complex, syncretized image, one in which it is not always easy to sort out cleanly the various strands woven into it. [*See also* Dumuzi.] Some fairly distinct aspects do, however, stand out and may reasonably be assumed to represent originally separate, independent deities. They are the following.

1. *Dumuzi as Amaushumgalana,* the power for productivity in the date palm. His marriage to Inanna as numen of the storehouse celebrates the bringing in of the date harvest. His cult was based in Uruk.

2. *Dumuzi the shepherd,* the power causing ewes to produce normal, well-shaped lambs. His bride was Inanna as goddess of the spring rain showers that call up verdure for pasture in the desert. The vanishing of the power he represented when the lambing season came to an end was seen as the death of the god, to be observed with wailing and lament.

3. *Dumuzi of the beer.* No separate distinctive name sets apart this aspect of the god. The texts dealing with it sometimes use the name *Dumuzi,* sometimes *Damu.* They involve the search for him after his death by his sister and mother.

4. *Damu the child,* the power for the sap to rise in plants and trees in the spring. Considered lost during the dry summer, he was sought by his mother and found coming down the river, presumably with the beginning of the early flood in spring. His cult was based in Uruk.

5. *Damu the conscript,* an aspect of the god under which he was seen as a young boy liable for military service. He has been taken forcibly from his mother by brutal recruiters, and she seeks him, gradually realizing that he is dead. What precise power he represented is not clear; most likely it was one connected with the welfare of cattle herds. His cult was based in Girsu (Tello) on the Euphrates.

The myths about these various aspects of Dumuzi naturally fall into two groups, those dealing with wooing and wedding and those dealing with his death and the search for him. To the first group belongs a dialogue between Inanna and Dumuzi in which he has found a house for them near her parents. She does not know that they have chosen him as her future husband, and he teases her, stating that his family is like her family, as it were. Eventually he enlightens her, and she is well pleased. The Inanna of this tale seems very young. Slightly older, she appears in a tale in which Dumuzi's sister Geshtinanna tells him that Inanna invited her in and told her how she, Inanna, suffered from love for her brother. Dumuzi is quick to ask leave to go, and is off to ease the damsel's suffering. At about the same age, Inanna appears in a different story, awaiting Dumuzi toward evening. They had met and fallen in love the day before, and when Dumuzi appears he impetuously propositions her. She promptly turns him down and apparently—the text is broken here—makes him propose properly. When the text resumes they are on their way to her mother's house to announce the engagement.

Another story tells how Inanna's brother Utu has arranged a marriage for her but is unsure about how she will receive the news. He therefore speaks obliquely, proposing to bring her fresh flax for a linen sheet. He does not say that it is to be her bridal sheet, but she immediately understands. Afraid to hear her brother's choice in case it turns out to be a wrong one, she postpones the crucial question, pretending that she has nobody to ret the flax, spin it, double the thread, weave it, dye it, and bleach it, but each time Utu offers to bring the flax already prepared. So at last she has to come to the point: who is to lie down with her on it? When Utu tells her it is Amaushumgalana, she is overjoyed. The wedding itself is recounted in a tale which begins with Inanna sending for her bridegroom and attendants, specifying what gifts they are to bring. They appear before the house, but Inanna is in no hurry. She bathes and dresses in all her finery and listens to instructions from her mother about the obedience due to her parents-in-law. Eventually she opens the door to Dumuzi—the formal act that concludes a Sumerian marriage—and presumably (the text is broken here) leads him to the bridal chamber for the consummation of the marriage. A wedding feast probably follows the next morning. When the text resumes, Dumuzi is leading his young bride to his house and wants first to take her to his personal god that he may bless the marriage. But Inanna is thoroughly frightened, so Dumuzi tries to hearten her by telling her what an honored position she will occupy in the household and how no domestic work whatever will be demanded of her.

The other group of myths, centering on the death of the young god, is perhaps best represented by the myth called the *Dream of Dumuzi*. In it, Dumuzi has an ominous dream that Geshtinanna interprets as boding death for them both. Dumuzi sends her up on a mound as lookout, and she reports the arrival of a boat with evil recruiters. Dumuzi decides to hide in the desert, but first he tells his sister and colleague where he will be. When the recruiters land and offer bribes for information, Geshtinanna is steadfast; however, the colleague betrays his friend. Dumuzi is captured but appeals to Utu to help him escape by turning him into a gazelle. Utu does so, and Dumuzi does escape, only to be again caught. This repeats itself until he flees to his fold. The pursuers break in, wrecking everything on their way, and Dumuzi is killed. A similar myth, the *Most Bitter Cry*, also describes the attack on the fold and the rude awakening of Dumuzi, naked and a prisoner. He manages to escape and flees toward Uruk. As he tries to cross the Euphrates, however, he is swept off by the flood and drowns before the eyes of his horrified mother, Duttur, and wife, Inanna.

Lugalbanda and Ninsuna. Lugalbanda ("fierce king") and Ninsuna ("mistress of the wild cows") were apparently city god and goddess of Kullab, a city that was early absorbed into Uruk. Both were deities of cattle, but with the absorption of his city Lugalbanda seems to have lost definition, and even his divine status. He appears in historical times predominantly as an ancient king of the first dynasty of Ur, and his achievement in the extant epic about him, that of a supernaturally gifted messenger, was probably tacked on precisely because nothing else was known about him. Ninsuna for her part managed to keep her divine status. She was the tutelary goddess of Gudea of Lagash and, curiously enough, in that role was the consort of Ningishzida, not of Lugalbanda.

Ningirsu. Ningirsu ("master of Girsu") was the city god of Girsu, with the temple Eninnu. His wife was the goddess Baba. Ningirsu was god of the thunderstorms in spring and of the spring flood of the Tigris. His early form was that of the thunderbird, an enormous eagle or vulture with a lion's head out of which thunder roared. Ningirsu was early identified with Ninurta of Nippur, and a great deal of his mythology was therefore transferred to the latter (it has been discussed above). *Ninurta* was also the name under which the god was borrowed by the Assyrians when he became prominent as god of war.

Gatumdug. Gatumdug was goddess of the city of Lagash (Al Hiba), south of Girsu. The meaning of her name is not clear, but other evidence suggests that she was also a goddess of birth giving.

Nanshe. The goddess of fowl and fish was Nanshe. She was city goddess of Nina (Zurghul), with the temple Siratr. She was, according to Gudea, the interpreter of dreams for the gods.

Ninmar. City goddess of Guabba and seemingly a goddess of birds was Ninmar.

Dumuzi-Abzu. Dumuzi-Abzu was city goddess of Kinirsha, and the power for fertility and healthy new life in the marshes.

Nininsina. Nininsina ("mistress of Isin") was city goddess of Isin (Ishan Bahriyat), south of Nippur, which served as capital of Sumer for most of the time after the third dynasty of Ur until the advent of the Old Babylonian period. She seems to have been envisaged in the shape of a dog and was presumably the goddess of dogs. Her special powers were those of the physician. Her daughter Damu—different from the boy of Girsu on the Euphrates—followed in her mother's footsteps as goddess of healing.

Ereshkigal. The name of the goddess Ereshkigal (Allatum) meant "queen [of the] greater earth." The ancients believed that there was a "larger heaven" above the visible sky that connected with a "larger earth" below the observable earth. In the larger earth was the realm of the dead, of which Ereshkigal was queen, although a variant—and conflicting—belief located the realm of the dead in the eastern mountains. The ancients imagined it as a walled city. As with cities on earth, the wall served not only to keep out enemies but also to keep in people—as, for instance, the slaves—who were not free to leave the city. It had its own police and a court where the sun god presided during the night. Existence there was dreary. If one had no son to make funerary offerings, one lived like a beggar, but with many sons one could enjoy a degree of comfort. Reasonably well off were also young men killed in battle—they had their parents take care of them—and small children, who played with golden toys. In the second and first millennia ideas about existence below seem to have become even darker: dust was said to cover all; the dead were clad in feathers like birds; and when an Assyrian prince visited the netherworld in a vision, he found it full of horrifying monsters. Ereshkigal herself was cast in the image of a mourning woman, pulling her hair and raking her body with her nails for grief as she lamented the children dead before their time. In the late myth of Nergal and Ereshkigal she plaintively tells of her joyless life: even when young she never played as other young girls did. Ereshkigal's husband seems to have been originally Gugalanna ("great bull of heaven"). A variant, perhaps later, tradition has Ninazu as her spouse, and finally Nergal became king of the netherworld with Ereshkigal as his queen.

Ninazu. The meaning of the name *Ninazu* is not clear, but it apparently has to do with water. Most likely, since he was a netherworld god, his name refers to the waters underground. His wife was Ningirda ("mistress [well-]rope"), a daughter of Enki. In the north, in Eshnunna (Tel Asmar) in the Diyala region, where his Akkadian name was *Tishpak* ("outpouring"), he was a god of rain storms. His city in the south was Enegir on the lower Euphrates.

Ningishzida. Ningishzida ("master of the well-grown tree") was the god of trees, especially the powers in the root that nourish and sustain the tree. As god of tree roots he was naturally seen as an underground, netherworld power. His office there was that of throne bearer, an old title for the head of the constabulary. Ningishzida's wife was Azimua ("well-grown branch"). His city was Gishbanda on the lower Euphrates. The ancients thought that there was a common identity between tree roots and snakes, the latter being roots moving freely. Accordingly, Ningishzida was also the god of serpents, and his older form, as noted above, was that of the stock of a tree around which serpent roots wind, the whole resembling the Greek caduceus.

Nergal. The other names of Nergal ("lord great city"), originally probably designating different gods, were *Meslamtaea* ("the one issuing from the luxuriant *mesu* tree") and *Irra. Meslam* or *Emeslam* ("house Meslam") was the name of Nergal's temple at Cutha, in Akkad. [*See also* Nergal.]

A myth preserved in a copy found at Tell al-ʿAmarna in Egypt and dating from the thirteenth century BCE tells how Nergal came to be king of the netherworld. Once when the gods were feasting they sent a message down to Ereshkigal inviting her to send up her vizier, Namtar, to fetch her a portion of the delicacies. She did so, and when he arrived all the gods rose respectfully except one, Nergal, who rudely remained seated. When Namtar reported this, Ereshkigal furiously demanded that the offending god be delivered up to her so that she could kill him. But when Namtar came for Nergal, Ea had changed his appearance so that Namtar did not recognize him. Later, however, Ea told Nergal to take a throne down to Ereshkigal to placate her. Nergal was understandably reluctant, but Ea insisted and gave him demons to hold open the gates of the netherworld so that he could get out fast if needed. However, he met with no resistance, pulled Ereshkigal down from her throne by the hair, and threatened to kill her. When she pleaded for her life, offering marriage and rule over the netherworld, Nergal accepted, kissed her, and wiped away her tears, saying wonderingly, "It was but love you wanted of me from months long ago to now." A later version greatly enlarges on the tale. It has Nergal visit the netherworld twice, the first time to bed Ereshkigal against Ea's advice and to escape, the second time to stay after Ereshkigal has passionately pleaded with the gods for his return.

Another myth, the *Irra Epic,* celebrates Nergal under the name *Irra* (an Akkadian name meaning "scorched earth"), which most likely originally designated a separate god. The epic tells how Irra was roused to action by his weapon, Sibittu (the name means "heptad"), and how he persuaded Marduk to leave him in charge of the world while Marduk went to have his jewels cleaned. Irra's first act was to foment rebellion in Babylon and have it ruthlessly put down by the commandant of the Assyrian garrison in that city. Next Irra had riots, rebellions, and wars spread all over the country, and might have destroyed it completely had not his vizier, Ishum, reasoned with him and persuaded him to leave a remnant. The epic ends with self-praise by Irra, who nowise regrets his deeds of violence—rather, he suggests that he may cut loose again at any time.

Ashur. Ashur was city god of Ashur (Qal'at Shergat) and chief god of Assyria. No recognizable features characterize him other than those that belong to his role as embodiment of the political aspirations of his city and nation. Even his wife and the name of his temple are not truly his own; they were borrowed from Enlil as part of Ashur's aspiration to the universal dominion for which Enlil stood. Basically, thus, he may in origin simply have been a *numen loci*—a spirit inhabiting a place and imbuing it with its character—named from the place where his presence was sensed. [*See also* Ashur.]

The Temple

The earliest Mesopotamian temples may have been in origin storehouses in which nomadic or seminomadic tribes kept their sacred objects and provisions, which were too cumbersome to carry along on their wanderings. Very soon, though, these structures would have been considered, as always later, dwellings of the gods to whom they belonged. The earliest recognizable form was that of a dwelling house with a large, rectangular middle room from which two smaller rooms projected at the end, creating a T-shaped effect. With time the projecting rooms disappeared and left a rectangular room that was entered from a door in one of the side-walls near its end. At the short end-wall farthest from the door was a dais that kept the seat of the owner, in this case the god, out of the floor-level draft. In later times a niche in this end-wall steadied a baldachin, or tentlike aedicula, further protecting the god. Before the dais a curtain shielded him from profane eyes. On low benches along the side-walls stood statues of worshipers to remind the god of the people they represented and their needs. The god himself was, to judge by depictions dating from as early as the late Uruk period, represented by a statue in physiomorphic or anthropomorphic form. Facing it—conceivably inside the hanging—stood a large vase with greenery of various kinds, sometimes placed over a drain, into which petitioners received in audience by the god would pour libations before presenting their petitions.

Temples were by preference built on existing high ground; in addition, frequent rebuildings, during which stumps of the old walls were left while their upper parts were dumped in the space between them as fill to make a new building site, tended to create a small mound under the new rebuilding. In fact, this development, by which a temple came to stand on the walls of earlier ones, became in later time so much a part of the concept of a temple that builders created underground artificially filled-in walls for the actual walls to rest on. Such a filling was known as a temple terrace *(temen)*. At the time of the third dynasty of Ur, possibly already in the time of the dynasty of Akkad, these mounds were built high, with stairs leading up to the temple on top, and were squared off to form a stage tower, the so-called ziggurat. [*See* Pyramids, *overview article*.] With larger temples it became customary in early dynastic times to surround them with a protective oval wall, called an *ibgal*. The pattern for this may conceivably have been the long curved pile of camel-thorn gathered for fuel with which bedouins—then as now—ringed their camps in the desert. It served the double purpose of protection and a handy fuel supply. Inside the oval, along its sides, were the various storerooms, kitchens, and workshops for the temple personnel, while the house on top of the terraced tower constituted the god's living quarters: bedroom, bath, and so on. Often a few side rooms were added to the central structure.

In time—as can be seen by comparisons of temple plans from Khafaje with those for the later one at Ishchali—a tendency toward squaring off the oval and greatly enlarging the plan of the temple on the high terrace led to a new concept of the older design. The central room was enlarged so that its lower parts with the door became the size of a court. At its end the hanging or hangings were replaced with walls having doors in the middle, thus creating a rectangular cella with the niche and dais at the middle of the far side-wall, a so-called broad-room cella, which became standard for Sumero-Akkadian and Babylonian temples from the third dynasty of Ur on. The remainder of the original central room developed into a court with surrounding rooms. A gate and covered landing midway up the stairs leading to the temple above often served as court of justice in which the god sat in judgment. In Assyria the development from the bent-axis approach took a different course. There the door was relocated around the corner nearest to it to the middle of the end-wall facing the wall with the niche and dais, thus creating the long-room type of temple. [*See also* Temple, *article on* Ancient Near Eastern and Mediterranean Temples.]

The temple, rising over the houses of the community, was visible and tangible proof of the god's presence and, more, that he was himself a member of the community and had a stake in it, with his house, his servants, his oxen and sheep, and his fields in grain. To have the temple was a privilege. To build it or rebuild it needed divine approval, which was not always granted. The story of the *Cursing of Akkad* told of the dire consequences of King Naram-sin's willful decision to rebuild Ekur in Nippur without Enlil's permission. Even rebuilding after enemy attack and demolition needed divine cooperation. The god had to be roused from his state of shock after the catastrophe to make him able to act, so laments to soothe him and to recall past happiness were part of the ritual. Originally these laments had clear reference to a specific historical situation; later they were generalized for wider use. In later times they became obligatory for any rebuilding, since that implied demolition of the existing structure, and some even became part of the daily program of temple music and were used to awaken the temple personnel in the morning. Older than the laments for the destruction of a temple are, it would seem, hymns to temples. They celebrate the specific powers inherent in the temple to uphold the welfare of the country. The *Cursing of Akkad* tells how the peace of the country, its harvest of grain, and so on vanish when corresponding parts of Ekur are demolished. In fact, the temples shared in inordinate measure in the particular kind of holiness that characterizes the gods inhabiting them, and it is often difficult to distinguish between god and temple. The temple shares name and function with its god as if it were his embodiment.

The Cult

The communal cult of the gods was of two kinds, celebrating the appropriate festivals of the various gods at appropriate times and providing daily services such as would be required by any high human dignitary. The earlier of these are undoubtedly the festivals, most of which are best understood as communal magic rites for prosperity developed into cult dramas performed by community representatives. There is evidence for various types of such dramas: the Sacred Marriage, the Death Drama, the Journey Drama, and the Plowing Drama. Others may have existed. [*See* Drama, *article on* Ancient Near Eastern Ritual Drama.]

The Sacred Marriage is attested in Uruk as early as the late Uruk period. The ruler *(en)* "became" the god of the date palm, Amaushumgalana, and brought the harvest as wedding gift to the date storeroom of the temple. His wife—one presumes—similarly "became" the goddess of the storehouse, Inanna, and opened the door for him, thereby concluding the marriage and lasting union of the powers for producing and storing the dates. Their meeting at the gate is depicted on the famous Uruk Vase and on contemporary cylinder seals. In this early form the source of abundance clearly was the god. In later times—as shown by materials from Isin and Larsa—emphasis oddly changed, and the goddess came to be seen as the conveyor of bounty. The high point was now a blessing by the goddess of the marital couch after the king had proved his prowess as bridegroom. By Isin-Larsa times, too, focus was no longer narrowly on dates but on prosperity generally. A special form of the rite—perhaps at home among herders—saw it still quite directly as sympathetic magic for fertility. Here the rising of the king's member in the sexual congress of the rite immediately made plants and greenery shoot up. [*See* Hieros Gamos.]

The Death Drama had the function of performing for the dying god of fertility—characteristically Dumuzi—the rites of lament due to the dead. Such data as we have suggest that processions of mourners went into the desert in early summer lamenting the god in dirges sung by representatives of his mother, sister, and young widow. The rite was a magic strengthening of the emotional bonds with the god, a seeking to have him back. [*See* Dying and Rising Gods.]

In the Journey Drama, the god, perhaps represented by his image or an emblem, traveled to visit a god in some other city. There are references to a yearly visit to Eridu by Ningirsu traveling from the Lagash region, and similarly there are texts connected with such a journey by Ninurta of Nippur. Whether in so traveling these gods conferred a boon on Enki and Eridu, or conversely were themselves the beneficiaries, is not always clear. In a myth about Enmerkar, founder of Uruk, a ritual journey he made to Eridu is mentioned in terms suggesting that he was reconfirmed or enhanced in his office of lord *(en)*, that is, of provider. Most likely also the myth of Inanna and the offices she obtained from a not-too-sober Enki preserves memories of a rite in which Inanna's various offices were authenticated from Eridu. A rather full statement of a ritual journey is given in a text describing how Nanna of Ur travels up by boat to visit his father, Enlil, in Nippur, bringing first fruits from the products of the south. He is warmly received and leaves to go back to Ur with matching gifts from the agricultural lands around Nippur. The Plowing Drama of Ninurta's festival that opened the plowing season in Nippur is thus far unique. The king himself guided the plow, and a report was made to Enlil.

Last there is the Battle Drama. It seems to be at home with gods of the thunderstorms of spring, Ninurta and Marduk, and it is conceivable that it was once performed to activate these powers, to rouse the thunderstorms that were seen—as in the relevant myths—as the divine warrior attacking the mountains. There is, however, no evidence so far to indicate performance in such terms. The name of Marduk's main festival, Akitu ("time of the earth reviving"), does, as mentioned earlier, refer to an early aspect of him as the power causing natural abundance, but there is no indication of any battle drama. Such ritual evidence as we have for this type of drama all shows a later, completely politicized form behind which little if any trace of earlier implications survives. The materials for the Battle Drama are contained largely in cultic commentaries from Ashur, which, however, are clearly Babylonian in origin and reflect the bitter political rivalry between Babylon and the Sea Land to the south. Braziers and torches are lighted to signify the burning of Kingu, Anu, and Enlil. A chariot arriving with great show of martial prowess is Nabu, who was sent against Enlil and now returns victorious. A loaf of bread is bounced by the king and a bishop, who represent Marduk and Nabu. The loaf is the heart of Anu, whom Marduk bound and whose heart he tore out.

The Babylonian epic of creation, *Enuma elish,* which tells how Marduk "vanquished Tiamat and assumed kingship," reflects the same political conflict, with Marduk representing Babylon and Tiamat representing the sea and the Sea Land. It is generally—and perhaps rightly—assumed to be a cult myth corresponding to a dramatic ritual reenactment of this primordial battle each new year. [*See* Enuma Elish.] However, our knowledge about the actual ritual of the Akitu festival in later times is scant in the extreme. We know that *Enuma elish* was read on one occasion and that Sennacherib, when he tried to transfer the festival to Assyria with Ashur as its hero, decorated the gates to his Akitu house with a relief showing the battle with Tiamat, but that is all. Otherwise such information as we have indicates that on the tenth of the month of Nisan, Marduk traveled by boat to the Akitu house, where a feast was celebrated on the eleventh, and that he then returned to Babylon. That is all. Not usable, unfortunately, for reconstructing the festival is a lengthy commentary called—not too happily—*Death and Resurrection of Marduk.* It has been shown to be an Assyrian, anti-Babylonian propaganda pamphlet, and it does not mention any death of Marduk. [*See also* Akitu.]

The trend toward sociomorphism imposed on the gods the patterns of the human family and household, and this in turn implied service such as was rendered to a human magnate in providing for his bodily comfort and assisting in the running of his estate. All of this became the daily temple cult, as described earlier. A further implication of anthropomorphism and sociomorphism was that since the god had become ruler of the community, it was essential to know what he wanted done. Thus a variety of methods of communication was developed. Some of these left the initiative to the god: he might show signs in the stars or on earth that the initiated could interpret. Others were available when man needed to know the divine will. The earliest of these methods of communication of which we have evidence are dreams sought by incubation in the temple, and inspection of the liver of a sacrificed kid for propitious or nonpropitious shape. This latter method was used by Gudea as a check on the message obtained when he was dreaming. An extensive and highly detailed literature serving as textbook for these and many other manners of prognostication developed during the second and first millennia. Originally meant as guides for rulers and war leaders, this literature soon broadened its scope to take in the fortunes of ordinary citizens. [*See* Divination.]

For conveying human wishes and needs to the gods and asking for help, a ritual of seeking audience to present petition and prayers was developed. The petitioner was led in before the deity with his greeting gift, usually a lamb or a kid. Here he libated water or wine in a huge vase with greenery that stood before the deity, and he spoke a formal greeting prayer. He then presented his petition. As the ritual for seeking an audience with the god was an occasional one, dependent on special circumstances, so the cult comprised other rituals for use in exceptional situations. I have mentioned the elaborate one called Bitrimki ("bathhouse"), which aimed at lustration of the king when he was threatened by the defiling evil of an eclipse of the moon; others were available for the rebuilding of a temple or for making or replacing a cult statue. In this last ritual great pains were taken to nullify by powerful incantations the fact that the statue was a work of human hands, and to make of it instead a god born in heaven.

The cult so far described was the communal, public cult. There was, however, a private cult as well. City life and its ever-greater differentiation between the fortunes of families and individuals and those of other families and individuals encouraged feelings that special success was due to a god's personal interest in a man and his family, while, conversely, misfortune would seem to be due to the god's abandonment of his ward for some reason or other. Thus the term for having luck became "to acquire a god." Since no achievement could be had without divine help, that of engendering a child necessarily implied such intervention. A god and goddess entered the body of the human father and mother and made the mother conceive. Thus the god and goddess who were assumed to have helped became family deities and were visualized in the image of a father and mother. As such they also took on the protective roles of parents, chief among which was to defend their wards against demons of disease and inspire successful thought and action. They had their altars and received daily offerings in the house of their wards, and prayers and petitions were addressed to them there.

The close connection between the personal god and success could not but raise problems, for experience showed that virtue was not always rewarded; rather, a virtuous man might fall ill or suffer other miseries such as should have happened to evildoers only. The obvious solution, that the virtuous man unwittingly must have offended his god, was accepted in a measure, and prayers often asked for enlightenment as to how a sufferer had sinned, so that he could do penance and mend his ways; but as a general explanation it did not carry full conviction, and the vexing problem of the righteous sufferer arose. It is dealt with in two major compositions datable to Middle Babylonian times. One is called *Ludlul* ("let me praise"), after its beginning, "Let me praise the possessor of wisdom." It tells of a pious and just man who suffers one misfortune after the other but does not lose his trust in Marduk. Eventually Marduk takes pity on him and restores him to health and prosperity. No real answer to the problem of why he had to suffer is attempted; the text merely holds out the conviction that the gods can have a change of heart and take pity. The other composition is known as the *Theodicy.* It is in the form of a dialogue between two friends about the fact that evil men appear to prosper, whereas good men fall on evil days. Here, too, there is no real answer, only a conviction that eventually retribution will come to evildoers.

The question of the innate justice—or, rather, injustice—of existence is also dealt with in a famous work known as the *Epic of Gilgamesh.* It tells how Gilgamesh, an ancient ruler of the city of Uruk endowed with exceptional vigor, drives his people too hard. They complain to the gods, who create Enkidu, a wild man who becomes a friend and brother of Gilgamesh. Together they set out to kill a famous warrior, Huwawa, who lives far away in the cedar mountains. They succeed. After their return to Uruk, Gilgamesh scornfully turns down a marriage proposal from the city goddess Ishtar. In her anger at being rejected she borrows the bull of heaven in order to kill Gilgamesh, but he and Enkidu overcome it. Then, however, things catch up with the two friends: the gods decide that Enkidu must die for having killed Huwawa. Gilgamesh is inconsolable at the loss of his friend and at the thought that he, too, must die. He therefore sets out on an arduous journey to an ancestor of his, Utanapishtim, who had gained eternal life. Eventually Gilgamesh reaches him, but Utanapishtim has no solace to offer. He invites Gilgamesh to try fighting Sleep—Death's younger brother, so to speak—but Gilgamesh fails miserably to keep awake. So Utanapishtim gives him clean clothes and sets him on his way home. There is no escape from death, however unjust it seems that man may not live forever.

It seems likely that the original epic ended here. At a later date, probably in the Middle Babylonian period, a certain Sinliqiunnini reworked the epic from a radically different point of view. Where the outlook of the earlier epic was tragic—a tale of a quest for eternal life that failed—the reworking saw Gilgamesh as a heroic traveler to romantic foreign parts who recovered hidden knowledge of the ancient times. A long story about the flood was added, as well as a further tale about a plant with the power to rejuvenate, which Gilgamesh obtained only to lose it again by carelessness. An introduction and conclusion stressed Gilgamesh's achievements, including lasting fame as builder of the city walls of Uruk. Finally, part of a Sumerian tale in which Enkidu describes conditions in the netherworld was tacked on, perhaps by some copyist. Passionate protest against existential evil thus became pleasure in romantic quest for hidden knowledge in faraway lands. [*See also* Gilgamesh.]

BIBLIOGRAPHY

Bottéro, Jean. *La religion babylonienne.* Paris, 1952.

Dhorme, Édouard. *Les religions de Babylonie et d'Assyrie.* Paris, 1945.

Dijk, V. van. "Sumerische Religion." In *Handbuch der Religionsgeschichte,* vol. 1, edited by Jes Peter Asmussen, Jørgen Laessøe, and Carsten Colpe, pp. 431–496. Göttingen, 1971.

Frankfort, Henri, et al. *Before Philosophy.* Harmondsworth, 1949. First published as *The Intellectual Adventure of Ancient Man* (Chicago, 1946).

Hooke, S. H. *Babylonian and Assyrian Religion.* New York, 1953.

Jacobsen, Thorkild. *The Treasures of Darkness: A History of Mesopotamian Religion.* New Haven, 1976.

Laessøe, Jørgen. "Babylonische und assyrische Religion." In *Handbuch der Religionsgeschichte,* vol. 1, edited by Jes Peter Asmussen, Jørgen Laessøe, and Carsten Colpe, pp. 497–525. Göttingen, 1971.

Meissner, Bruno. *Babylonien und Assyrien,* vol. 2. Heidelberg, 1925.

Pritchard, J. B., ed. *Ancient Near Eastern Texts relating to the Old Testament.* 3d ed. Princeton, 1969.

Ringgren, Helmer. *Religions of the Ancient Near East.* Translated by John Sturdy. Philadelphia, 1973.

THORKILD JACOBSEN

History of Study

The study of ancient Mesopotamian religions, like studies of ancient Mesopotamia in general, was in its early phases severely hampered by an as yet imperfect understanding of the script and languages—Sumerian and Akkadian—of its source materials, as well as by the relatively limited and fragmentary nature of the materials then available. To some extent, similar difficulties still exist, and new finds, as well as new insights, may challenge even seemingly assured results.

General Presentations. The earliest attempt at a comprehensive presentation of ancient Mesopotamian religions is François Lenormant's *La magie chez les Chaldéens et les origines accadiennes* (1874). Lenormant posited an early Sumerian (then called Akkadian) animistic stage of belief in spirits that were controlled by magicians. Contrasting with this was the religion of the Semitic inhabitants (now called Akkadians), a debased form of monotheism in which hypostases of the supreme god, called Ilu, had become separate powers in natural phenomena, especially astral phenomena. These two competing kinds of beliefs were eventually unified into a single system under Sargon of Akkad, whom Lenormant dated at about 2000 BCE. Part of this systematization was also the ordering of local deities into the later pantheon.

The next major contribution to the study of Mesopotamian religions, and one of a wider scope, was A. H. Sayce's *Lectures on the Origin and Growth of Religions as Illustrated by the Religion of the Ancient Babylonians* (1887). Sayce's book deals with various Babylonian deities, such as Bel-Merodakh (Marduk), Tammuz, and Istar (Ishtar), among others. He also discusses what he called "the sacred books of Chaldea," as well as cosmogonies and astro-theology. Sayce saw evidence of totemism in the animal forms that many of the gods could assume. Because Prometheus brought fire to man, Sayce saw him as a parallel to the deity Lugalbanda ("fierce king"). In his overall view of religious development, Sayce essentially followed Lenormant.

The Sumerian beliefs in spirits that were controlled by a body of "medicine men" was termed by Sayce "organized animism." The Sumerian word for "spirit" was thought to be *zi*, and "the *zi* was simply that which manifested life, and the test of the manifestation of life was movement" (p. 327). The spirits in those major cosmic elements that were considered good gradually developed into gods. The level of power of motion possessed by an object, or in a force of nature, was the test of its supernaturalism (that is, of the existence of a spirit within it). Sayce writes,

> The spirit of the moon, for example, developed into a god, but the god was abstracted from the visible moon itself, and identified with the creative force of the lunar orb which manifested itself in motion. The new god might in turn be abstracted from the creative force, more especially if he was assimilated to the sacred steer; in this case the creative force would become his spirit, in no way differing, it will be seen, from the spirit that was believed to reside in man. (p. 334)

Sayce attributed to the Semitic-speaking Akkadians a change from the gods as creators to the gods as fathers, a change encouraged by anthropomorphism and the creation of a family-based pantheon.

In his later *The Religions of Ancient Egypt and Babylonia* (1902), Sayce modified his position and rejected the idea that the gods might have developed out of older spirits. He assumed instead that the idea was brought in by immigrants from the south, who founded a tradition centered on the god Ea of the ancient city of Eridu.

Much more comprehensive than any previous treatment was Morris Jastrow's *The Religion of Babylonia and Assyria* (1898). Jastrow discusses the land and peoples of Babylon and Syria, the general traits of the Old Babylonian pantheon, the gods and their consorts prior to the days of Hammurabi, the pantheon of Hammurabi, Gudea's pantheon, and the minor gods in the period of Hammurabi. The book also deals with the gods appearing in temple lists and in legal and commercial documents of the area. Other topics that Jastrow investigates rather extensively are the animism that survived in Babylonian religions, the Assyrian pantheon, the triad and the combined invocation of the deities, the Neo-Babylonian period, and the Babylonian cosmology. Jastrow's work also examines the religious literature—magical texts, prayers and hymns, penitential psalms, oracles, omens, the *Epic of Gilgamesh*, and other myths and legends. Finally, there is a discussion of the Babylonian view of life after death, and the temple and cult in Babylonia and Syria.

Because Jastrow avoided theorizing as much as possible, his treatment is sober and descriptive. He also deliberately avoided distinguishing Sumerian from Akkadian contributions. Jastrow argued that animism was still basic to the religion of Babylonia and Assyria, and he observed that the gods had evolved from their role as spirits of the settlement plots. As these settlements grew into cities, the spirits grew correspondingly in stature and importance. The detailed bibliography of the field up to 1898 that Jastrow included in his book is particularly valuable. A later work by Jastrow, *Die Religion Babyloniens und Assyriens* (1905–1912), although never completed, is essentially a lengthy study of divination texts.

To the third edition of *Die Keilinschriften und das Alte Testament* (1903), which was edited by Eberhard Schrader, the German Assyriologist Heinrich Zimmern contributed his study *Religion und Sprache*, on the religious system of the Babylonians; the formation of the pantheon; local cults; the Semitic and Sumerian elements still evident in Babylonian religion; the Babylonians' reliance on the heavens in the formation of beliefs, practices, and myths; and the Babylonian view of life. Zimmern's presentation was strongly influenced by the school of *Astralmythologie* that flourished in Germany at the time. Therefore, an overly great number of gods were seen as solar in character. For example, Marduk was said to represent the sun of morning and spring; Ninurta, whose name was then read as *Ninib*, represented the eastern or western sun; the destructive glowing south-, noon-, and summer-sun were represented by Nergal; and so on. The purview of the book called for comparisons with biblical materials (twenty-one pages were devoted to a comparison of Marduk and Christ), but the methods used have since been discounted.

In 1910 Édouard Dhorme's *La religion assyro-babylonienne* was published; the materials are organized with such clarity and relevance that the book remains one of the most notable early treatments of Mesopotamian religions. Dhorme's work focused on the sources of the Assyrian and Babylonian religions and their conception of the divine, including the gods, gods of the cities and of kings, gods and men, moral laws, prayers, sacrifice, and the priesthood. A new, enlarged edition was published in 1945 under the title *Les religions de Babylonie et d'Assyrie.* Although it achieved a far greater coverage of detail, it lost the enlightening clarity that characterizes the earlier work.

A most useful, purely factual, and well-documented presentation was given by Bruno Meissner in the second volume of his *Babylonien und Assyrien* (1925). For ready access to the main data of pantheons, cults, divination, and magic, it remains unrivaled.

Jean Bottéro, in his *La religion babylonienne* (1952), sought to present the development of Babylonian religion among the Semitic-speaking inhabitants of Mesopotamia during the last two millennia before the common era. The work is marked by a great sensitivity and respect for the ancient achievement. A few of the subjects Bottéro discusses are deserving of special mention: religious sentiment, the theology of the divine, and cults of adoration and sacrament. His method of treatment is reminiscent of what is known as the phenomenology of religion.

A different approach, one that belongs to the Myth and Ritual school, is represented by S. H. Hooke's *Babylonian and Assyrian Religion* (1953), a well-written and very readable account of essentials of its subject that is free of any extreme positions. Other general presentations that may be mentioned are L. W. King's *Babylonian Religion and Mythology* (1899), Giuseppe Fulani's *La religione babilonese e assira* (1928–1929), Charles F. Jean's *La religion sumérienne* (1931), Hans Hirsch's *Untersuchungen zur altassyrischen Religion* (1961), and W. H. P. Römer's article "Religion of Ancient Mesopotamia" (in *Historia Religionum,* vol. 1, *Religions of the Past,* edited by C. Jouco Bleeker and Geo Widengren, 1969). Also important are J. van Dijk's "Sumerische Religion" and Jørgen Laessøe's "Babylonische und assyrische Religion," in volume 1 of *Handbuch der Religionsgeschichte,* edited by Jes P. Asmussen, Jørgen Laessøe, and Carsten Colpe (1976). Finally, there is my own book *The Treasures of Darkness: A History of Mesopotamian Religion* (1976).

Special Studies. As important as the general presentations of ancient Mesopotamian religions are, a wealth of special studies are in many cases even more essential for advancing our understanding of these religions' major aspects. Unfortunately, considerations of space do not allow any comprehensive and systematic treatment of these contributions; it is only possible to comment on a somewhat random and necessarily subjective selection.

The nature of the concept of divinity in Mesopotamia is treated in Johannes Hehn's *Die biblische und die babylonische Gottesidee* (1913) and in Elena Cassin's *La splendeur divine: Introduction à l'étude de la mentalité mesopotamienne* (1968). Rich in materials is Knut Tallquist's *Akkadische Götterepitheta* (1938). For discussion of the pantheon, one must consult Anton Deimel's *Pantheon Babylonicum* (1914) and part one of the fourth volume (1950) of his *Sumerisches Lexikon* (which part is also entitled *Pantheon Babylonicum*). Both of these works by Deimel are still standard references. [*For information regarding monographs on individual Mesopotamian deities, see the bibliographies of* An; Enlil; Nanna; Utu; Inanna; Dumuzi; Marduk; Nabu; Nergal; Dagan; *and* Ashur.]

The origins and development of the pantheon were dealt with by Tharsicius Paffrath in his book *Zur Götterlehre in den altbabylonischen Königsinschriften* (1913) and by W. G. Lambert in his article "The Historical Development of the Mesopotamian Pantheon: A Study in Sophisticated Polytheism," in *Unity and Diversity,* edited by Hans Goedicke and J. J. M. Roberts (1975). A representative collection of myths and epics in translation may be found in *Ancient Near Eastern Texts relating to the Old Testament* (3d ed., 1969), edited by J. B. Pritchard. Available treatments of mythology include Samuel Noah Kramer's *Sumerian Mythology* (1944; rev. ed., 1972); D. O. Edzard's article "Mesopotamien," in the first volume of *Wörterbuch der Mythologie,* edited by H. W. Haussig (1965); Giorgio R. Castellino's *Mitologia Sumerico-Accadica* (1967); and Alexander Heidel's *The Babylonian Genesis* (1942; 2d ed., 1963) and *The Gilgamesh Epic and Old Testament Parallels* (1949; 2d ed., 1963).

Aspects of the daily cult are the focus of Agnès Spycket's book *Les statues de culte dans les textes mesopotamiens* (1968). Other books of interest include Friedrich Blome's *Die Opfermaterie in Babylonien und Israel* (1934) and Yvonne Rosengarten's *Le concept sumérien de consommation* (1960). For the times of the annual festivals there is Benno Landsberger's magisterial (and still standard) work, *Der kultische Kalender der Babylonier und Assyrer* (1915). The *raison d'être* of the festivals was first clarified by Svend Aage Pallis in his book *The Babylonian Akîtu Festival* (1926). Of crucial importance because it dismissed once and for all some serious misunderstandings of the Akitu, was Wolfram von Soden's article "Gibt es ein Zeugnis dafür das die Babylonier an die Wiederauferstehung Marduks geglaubt haben?" (Is There Any Proof that the Babylonians Believed in the Resurrection of Marduk?), which appeared in *Zeitschrift für Assyriologie* 51 (1955). Rites of divine journeys are treated in *Nanna-Suen's Journey to Nippur* (1973), edited by A. J. Ferrara, and in Daniel David Reisman's Ph.D. dissertation, "Two Neo-Sumerian Royal Hymns" (University of Pennsylvania, 1969). Royal inauguration rituals are discussed in Karl Friedrich Müller's *Texte zum assyrischen Königsritual* (1937), which is the first volume of his *Das assyrische Ritual.* Ritual meals are treated in Rintje Frankena's *Tākultu: De sacrale maaltijd in het Assyrische ritueel* (1954).

In my article "Religious Drama in Ancient Mesopotamia," in *Unity and Diversity* (1975), I give a general treatment of festival rites. The religious aspects of kingship are the subject of René Labat's *Le caractère religieux de la royauté assyro-babylonienne* (1939) and of Henri Frankfort's *Kingship and the Gods* (1948). An interesting strand in the fabric of kingship is treated in Ilse Siebert's *Hirt, Herde, König* (1969). Communal laments are covered in Raphael Kutscher's book *Oh Angry Sea (a-ab-ba-hu-luh-ha): The History of a Sumerian Congregational Lament* (1975). Penitential psalms are the focus of Julian Morgenstern's *The Doctrine of Sin in the Babylonian Religion* (1905), Walter Schrank's *Babylonische Sühnrites* (1908), Walter G. Kunstmann's *Die babylonische Gebetsbeschwörung* (1932), and Geo Widengren's *The Accadian and Hebrew Psalms of Lamentation as Religious Documents* (1936) and *Hymnes et prières aux dieux de Babylonie et d'Assyrie* (1976). Excellent translations may be found in Adam Falkenstein's *Die Haupptypen der Sumerischen Beschwörung literarisch untersucht* (1931). Divination is treated in Georges Conteneau's *La divination chez les Assyriens et les Babyloniens* (1940) and C. J. Gadd's *Ideas of Divine Rule in the Ancient Near East* (1948). On magic, there are L. W. King's *Babylonian Magic and Sorcery* (1896) and B. A. van Proosdij's *L. W. King's Babylonian Magic and Sorcery* (1952). Wisdom, finally, has been comprehensively and very competently treated in W. G. Lambert's *Babylonian Wisdom Literature* (1960).

Uncertainties. The script and languages of ancient Mesopotamia continue to present great difficulties to the modern student. These are so serious that almost no translations of Akkadian texts made prior to the twentieth century can safely be taken at face value; they need to be checked by a competent Assyriologist. As for Sumerian, it is doubtful that scholars will be able to claim certainty for their translations before the year 2000. At present no consensus about basic features of writing and grammar exists, and translations of one and the same text may differ radically. Extreme caution is thus indicated.

THORKILD JACOBSEN

MESROB. *See* Mashtots', Mesrop.

MESSIANISM. [*This entry consists of three articles:*

An Overview
Jewish Messianism
Islamic Messianism

The first article presents a cross-cultural overview of the concept of a messiah and the notion of messianism in various religions, especially Christianity. The following two articles discuss messianism in the Jewish and Islamic traditions.]

An Overview

The term *messianism* is derived from *messiah,* a transliteration of the Hebrew *mashiaḥ* ("anointed"), which originally denoted a king whose reign was consecrated by a rite of anointment with oil. In the Hebrew scriptures (Old Testament), *mashiaḥ* is always used in reference to the actual king of Israel: Saul (*1 Sm.* 12:3–5, 24:7–11), David (*2 Sm.* 19:21–22), Solomon (*2 Chr.* 6:42), or the king in general (*Ps.* 2:2, 18:50, 20:6, 28:8, 84:9, 89:38, 89:51, 132:17). In the intertestamental period, however, the term was applied to the future king, who was expected to restore the kingdom of Israel and save the people from all evil.

At the same time, prophetic oracles referring to an ideal future king, though not using the word *messiah,* were interpreted as prophecies of this same eschatological figure. These passages include *Isaiah* 9:1–6 and 11:1–9, *Micah* 5:2–6, and *Zechariah* 9:9, and certain of the "royal" psalms, such as Psalms 2, 72, and 110. Precedence for this later conception lies in the royal ideologies of the ancient Near East, where the king played the role of the savior of his people: every new king was expected to bring fertility, wealth, freedom, peace, and happiness to his land. Examples are found both in Egypt and in Mesopotamia. The French scholar Édouard Dhorme, in his book *La religion assyro-babylonienne* (1910), quoted some texts indicating such expectations under the heading "The Messiah King." [*See also*

Kingship, *article on* Kingship in the Ancient Mediterranean World.]

Judaism. In the Judaism of the intertestamental period, messianic expectations developed in two directions. One was national and political and is most clearly set out in the pseudepigraphic *Psalms of Solomon* (17 and 18). Here the national Messiah is a descendant of David. He shall rule in wisdom and righteousness; he shall defeat the great powers of the world, liberate his people from foreign rule, and establish a universal kingdom in which the people will live in peace and happiness. The same kingly ideal is expressed in the description of the rule of Simon in *1 Maccabees* 14:4, which echoes the messianic prophecies of the Old Testament.

Some apocryphal documents, especially the *Testament of Levi,* speak also of a priestly messiah, one who is to bring peace and knowledge of God to his people and to the world. The Qumran community even expected two anointed ones, a priest and a king, but very little is known about their functions.

The other line of development is found above all in the Ethiopic *Apocalypse of Enoch (1 Enoch)* and in *2 Esdras* (also called *4 Ezra*). It centers around the term *son of man.* This term is used in the Old Testament to refer generally to a human being (*Psalms* 8:5, 80:18 [English version 80:17] and several times, addressing the prophet, in *Ezekiel*). In the vision recorded in *Daniel* 7, the term is used in verse 13 with reference to a "manlike being," which, in contrast to the usual four animals representing the four great powers of the ancient world, stands for Israel in its prominent role at the last judgment.

In the apocalyptic books mentioned, the son of man is a transcendental figure, more or less divine, preexistent, and at present hidden in heaven. At the end of time he will appear to judge the world in connection with the resurrection of the dead. The pious will be freed from the dominion of the wicked, and he will rule the world forever in peace and righteousness. He is often referred to as "the chosen One" but only occasionally as "the anointed One," that is, the Messiah. Obviously, this interpretation of *Daniel* 7:13 takes "son of man" to refer to a person and not to an object of comparison. The problem is the extent to which these passages are pre-Christian. *2 Esdras* was definitely written after the fall of Jerusalem in 70 CE, and those parts of *1 Enoch* in which references to the son of man occur do not appear among the Aramaic fragments of the same work found at Qumran. On the other hand, the New Testament seems to presuppose this same interpretation of *Daniel* 7:13.

Christianity. Early Christianity took many of the Jewish ideas about the Messiah and applied them to Jesus. *Messiah* was translated into Greek as *Christos,* that is, Christ, thereby identifying Jesus with Jewish messianic expectations. Matthew interpreted *Isaiah* 9:1 (EV 9:2), "The people who walk in darkness shall see a great light," as fulfilled in Jesus (*Mt.* 4:14–18). *Micah* 5:1 (EV 5:2) is quoted to prove that the Messiah should be born in Bethlehem (*Mt.* 2:6). *Zechariah* 9:9 is read as a prediction of Jesus' entry into Jerusalem (*Mt.* 21:5), and if the story related by Matthew is authentic, it must mean that Jesus wanted to proclaim himself as the Messiah. *Psalms* 2:7 ("You are my son") is quoted or at least alluded to in connection with the baptism of Jesus (*Mt.* 3:17, *Mk.* 1:11, *Lk.* 3:22). (The Jewish Messiah, however, was not regarded as God's son.) *Psalms* 110:1 is used to prove that the Messiah cannot be the son of David (*Mt.* 22:44); other parts of Psalm 110 are behind the exposition in *Hebrews* 5, 6, and 7. However, the New Testament rejects the political messiahship described in the *Psalms of Solomon.* Jesus refused to be made king (*Jn.* 6:15); he proclaimed before Pilate: "My kingdom is not of this world" (*Jn.* 18:26). Despite this, he was accused of pretending to be "the king of the Jews" (*Jn.* 19:19).

The New Testament, however, although maintaining that the Messiah is the Son of God, also uses the epithet "Son of man." According to the Gospels, Jesus uses it of himself. In a few cases it could possibly mean simply "a human being" or "this man" (*Mk.* 2:10, *Mt.* 11:8, and parallels; *Mt.* 8:20 and parallels). A number of passages refer to the coming of the Son of man at the end of time (*Mt.* 24:27, 24:37; *Lk.* 18:18, 18:22, 18:69; *Mt.* 10:23; *Mk.* 13:26); these imply the same interpretation of *Daniel* 7:13 as that implied by *1 Enoch* and *2 Esdras* but add a new element in that it is Christ who is to come a second time, returning as the judge of the world. A third group of "Son of man" references allude to the suffering and death of Jesus, sometimes also mentioning his resurrection (*Mk.* 8:31, 9:9, 9:31, 10:33, 14:21, 14:41; *Lk.* 22:48 and others). These introduce the idea of a suffering messiah, which is not entirely unknown in Jewish messianism but is never linked with the Son of man. (If the latter is sometimes described in terms of the "servant of the Lord," the chapter on the suffering servant, *Isaiah* 53, is never applied to him.) In the *Gospel of John* the Son of man is almost always the glorified Lord as king and judge; he is also described as preexistent in heaven (*Jn.* 1:51, 3:13, 8:28). *Hebrews* 2:6–8 applies Psalm 8, in which "son of man" was originally meant as "human being," to Jesus, thus giving the expression an eschatological meaning.

A new feature was introduced in New Testament messianism by the identification of Jesus with the suffering servant of *Isaiah* 53. *Mark* 9:12 says that it "was written of the Son of man that he should suffer many things and be treated with contempt" (cf. *Is.* 53:3). *Acts of the Apostles* 8:32 explicitly quotes *Isaiah* 53:7–8 as fulfilled in Jesus, and *1 Peter* 2:22–24 quotes or alludes to parts of *Isaiah* 53 as referring to him. It would seem that this identification is an original creation of Jesus (or, possibly, of the early church).

Thus, New Testament Christology utilizes a great many traits drawn from Jewish messianism. At the same time, it adds a new dimension: the idea that Jesus, though he has already in person fulfilled the messianic expectations, is to return in order to bring them to their final fulfillment.

Islamic Messianism. Ideas comparable to that of the second coming of Christ are found in Islam, probably owing to Christian influence. While the Qur'ān envisages God as the judge on the Day of Judgment, later Muslim tradition introduces certain preparatory events before that day. Muḥammad is reported to have said that the last day of the world will be prolonged in order that a ruler of the Prophet's family may defeat all enemies of Islam. This ruler is called the Mahdi, "the rightly guided one." Other traditions say that he will fill the world with justice as it is now filled with wrong, an apparent echo of ancient kingship ideology. Some identify the Mahdi with Jesus (Arab., ʿIsā), who is supposed to appear before the end of the world to defeat al-Dajjāl ("the deceiver"), the false messiah, or Antichrist. Such traditions were utilized by founders of new dynasties and other political or religious leaders, especially among the Shīʿah. The last such example was the rebel leader Muḥammad Aḥmad of Sudan, who from 1883 temporarily held back the British influence in this area.

"Nativistic" Movements. With some justification the concept of messianism is used to describe a number of "nativistic" cults in different parts of the world that have emerged as the result of a clash between colonialist Christianity and native religions. Following Vittorio Lanternari (1965), however, a distinction should be made between messianic and prophetic movements. "The 'messiah,'" he says, "is the awaited savior, the 'prophet' is he who announces the arrival of one who is to come. The prophet himself can be the 'messiah' after he has died and his return is expected as a redeemer, or when the prophet himself, leaning upon an earlier messianic myth, declares himself to be the prophet-messiah" (p. 242n.).

Examples of such movements are known from all parts of the aboriginal world. As early as the sixteenth century, successive waves of Tupi tribes in Brazil moved to the Bahia coast, impelled by a messianic quest for the "land without evil." Another such migration to find the "land of immortality and perpetual rest" is reported to have inspired the Spaniards' idea of El Dorado. Similar migrations took place in later centuries, led by a kind of prophet described as "Man-God" or "Demi-God," that is, local shamans who came to the natives as religious leaders and reincarnations of the great mythical heroes of native tradition and announcing an era of renewal.

The Ghost Dance movement in the western United States was initiated in 1869 by a certain Wodziwob, who had visions through which the Great Spirit announced that a major cataclysm would soon shake the entire world and wipe out the white man. The Indians would come back to life, and the Great Spirit would dwell among them in the heavenly era. Wodziwob's son, Wovoka (John Wilson), established contacts with the Mormons in 1892 and was considered by them to be the Messiah of the Indians and the Son of God.

In the Kongo region in Africa, Simon Kimbangu, who had been raised in the British Baptist Mission, appeared in 1921 as a prophet to his people. His preaching was a combination of Christian and indigenous elements. He prophesied the imminent ousting of the foreign rulers, a new way of life for the Africans, and the coming of a Golden Age. Both he and his successor, Andre Matswa, expected to return after death as the liberators of their people. Several movements of a similar kind are known from other parts of Africa.

In the early twentieth century, Melanesia and New Guinea saw the emergence of the so-called cargo cults. Common to them all is the belief that a Western ship (or even airplane), manned by whites, will come to bring riches to the natives, while at the same time the dead will return to life and an era of happiness will follow. Some prophets of these cults were regarded as incarnations of spirits. [*See also* Cargo Cults.]

It would seem that all these movements originated among people under oppression and gave expression to their longing for freedom and better conditions. Obviously, the conditions under which Christianity arose are somewhat comparable.

[*See also* Millenarianism *and* Revival and Renewal.]

BIBLIOGRAPHY

The standard work for early Jewish messianism is Sigmund Mowinckel's *He That Cometh* (Oxford, 1956). Briefer, but including the Egyptian and Mesopotamian texts referred to in the article, is my book *The Messiah in the Old Testament* (London, 1956). A good introduction to the Son of man question is Carsten Colpe's article "Huios Tou Anthrōpou," in the *Theolog-*

ical Dictionary of the New Testment, edited by Gerhard Kittel (Grand Rapids, Mich., 1972). See also Rollin Kearns's *Vorfragen zur Christologie,* 3 vols. (Tübingen, 1978–1982), and Maurice Casey's *Son of Man: The Interpretation and Influence of Daniel 7* (London, 1979). Islamic messianism has been dealt with most recently by Hava Lazarus-Yafeh in her book *Some Religious Aspects of Islam* (Leiden, 1981), pp. 48–57, and by Jan-Olaf Blichfeldt in *Early Mahdism* (Leiden, 1985). On Islam see also my article "Some Religious Aspects of the Caliphate," in *The Sacral Kingship* (Leiden, 1959). Edgar Blochet provides some early observations in *Le messianisme dans l'hétérodoxie musulmane* (Paris, 1903). A comprehensive survey of the millenarian movements is found in Vittorio Lanternari's *The Religions of the Oppressed* (New York, 1965). Lanternari's book includes a good bibliography.

HELMER RINGGREN

Jewish Messianism

The term *messianism* denotes a movement, or a system of beliefs and ideas, centered on the expectation of the advent of a messiah (derived from the Hebrew *mashiaḥ,* "the anointed one"). The Hebrew verb *mashaḥ* means to anoint objects or persons with oil for ordinary secular purposes as well as for sacral purposes. In due course the nominative form came to mean anyone with a specific mission from God (i.e., not only kings or high priests), even if the anointing was purely metaphorical (prophets, patriarchs), and ultimately it acquired the connotation of a savior or redeemer who would appear at the end of days and usher in the kingdom of God, the restoration of Israel, or whatever dispensation was considered to be the ideal state of the world. [*See* Eschatology.]

This specific semantic development was due to the Jewish belief that the ultimate salvation of Israel, though wrought by God, would be presided over or realized by a descendant of the royal house of David. He, the "son of David," would be the Lord's anointed *par excellence.* From its original Jewish context the word *mashiaḥ* then passed into general use, denoting movements or expectations of a utopian character or otherwise concerned with the salvation of society and the world. The messianic complex appears at times as restorative in character (the *Paradise Lost–Paradise Regained* syndrome), in the sense that it envisages the restoration of the past and lost golden age. At other times it appears as more utopian, in the sense that it envisages a state of perfection the like of which has never existed before ("a new heaven and a new earth"); the Messiah will not merely renew the days of yore but will usher in a "new age."

The term *mashiaḥ* in this specific eschatological sense does not occur in the Hebrew scriptures. *Isaiah* 45:1 calls the Persian king Cyrus II the Lord's "anointed" because it was evidently as the chosen instrument of God that he permitted the Israelite exiles to return from Babylonia to Jerusalem. Using later terminology one may, perhaps, commit a technical anachronism and describe as "messianic" those scriptural passages that prophesy a future golden age, the ingathering of the exiles, the restoration of the Davidic dynasty, the rebuilding of Jerusalem and the Temple, the era of peace when the wolf will lie down with the lamb, and so on.

Such is the nature of messianism that it develops and flourishes in periods of suffering and frustration. When the present is satisfactory it need not be redeemed but should be perpetuated or renewed (e.g., by periodic or cyclical renewal rites). When the present is profoundly unsatisfactory, messianism emerges as one of the possible answers: the certainty of a satisfactory natural, social, and historical order (and this certainty was particularly strong in Israel, based as it was on God's promise enshrined in his eternal covenant) is projected on the horizon of an ideal future. As the biblical account amply shows, already in biblical times the present was generally perceived as far from satisfactory (wicked and sinful kings, enemy incursions, defeats), and hence ideas concerning an ideal order under an ideal Davidic king began to crystallize.

The tendency to look toward future fulfillment was reinforced by the destruction of the First Temple (587/6 BCE), the Babylonian exile, and the subsequent return to Zion under Cyrus, hailed by "Second Isaiah" as an event of a messianic order. But this "messianic" salvation proved a sad disappointment. The severe persecution under the Syrian Seleucid ruler Antiochus IV (r. 175–163 BCE) similarly led to messianic-eschatological hopes, as evidenced by the *Book of Daniel,* the composition of which is generally dated in that period. But the great salvation wrought by the victory of the Maccabees similarly proved, in the long run, a sad disappointment. The revolts against the oppressive "kingdom of wickedness," Rome, in 65–70 CE (which ended with the destruction of Jerusalem and the Second Temple) and again in 132–135 CE (the Bar Kokhba Revolt, which ended in the practical destruction of Palestinian Jewry) no doubt had messianic elements. Thereafter messianism was a mixture of firm and unshakable hope in ultimate redemption, on the one hand, and, on the other hand, fear of the dangers and disastrous consequences of messianic explosions—"messianic activism," as the historian would call it, or "premature messianism," as the theologian would call it.

The messianic doctrines that developed during the second half of the Second Temple period from approximately 220 BCE to 70 CE (also called the "intertestamentary" period) were of diverse kinds, reflecting the mentality and spiritual preoccupations of different circles. They ranged from this-worldly, political expectations—the breaking of the yoke of foreign rule, the restoration of the Davidic dynasty (the messianic king), and, after 70 CE, also the ingathering of the exiles and the rebuilding of the Temple—to more apocalyptic conceptions, such as the spectacular and catastrophic end of "this age" (including a Day of Judgment), the ushering in of a new age, the advent of the kingdom of heaven, the resurrection of the dead, a new heaven and a new earth. The main protagonist might be a military leader, a kingly "son of David," a supernatural figure such as the somewhat mysterious "son of man" mentioned in some books of the Hebrew scriptures as well as in apocryphal apocalyptic texts. [*See* Apocalypse.] Many scholars think that Jesus deliberately avoided the use of the term *messiah* because of its political overtones (especially as he was announcing a kingdom that was not of this world) and preferred the unpolitical term "son of man." On the other hand, those responsible for the final redaction of the *Gospel of Matthew* thought it necessary to provide Jesus with a lineage proving his descent from David in order to legitimate his messianic status, since the *mashiaḥ* (Gr., *christos*) had to be identified as the "son of David."

These examples, incidentally, also show that the origins of Christianity have to be seen in the context of the messianic ferment of contemporaneous Jewish Palestine. Messianic ideas developed not only by way of interpretation of biblical texts (e.g., the *pesher* of the Qumran community and the later *midrash* of rabbinic Judaism) but also by "revelations" granted to apocalyptic visionaries. The latter tradition is well illustrated by the last book of the New Testament, the *Book of Revelation*.

But messianic ideas and expectations could also be based on "rational" (i.e., nonvisionary) insights, especially when the interpretation of scriptural prophecies took the form of calculations and computations of the dates allegedly hinted at in the obscure symbolism of the texts. Jewish messianic enthusiasts would often base their calculations on the *Book of Daniel* (much as Christian millenarians would compute the end time from the "number of the beast" mentioned in *Revelation* 13:18). Since the high-pitched hopes generated by these calculations would often lead to disaster (or at best to severe disappointment), the Talmudic rabbis had very harsh words about "those who compute the [messianic] end."

One tradition, probably influenced by *Zechariah* 3–4, appears to have held a doctrine of two messianic figures, the one a high-priestly "anointed one" of the house of Aaron, the other a royal messiah of the house of David. This belief, which was held by the Qumran community (also known as the Dead Sea Sect), obviously implies that these complementary messianic figures are not so much saviors and redeemers as symbolic types presiding over the redeemed and ideal social order. Echoes of this doctrine seem to be present in the (apparently polemical) insistence of the New Testament *Letter to the Hebrews* that Jesus was both king and high priest. The doctrine seems to have survived into the Middle Ages (by what channels is not quite clear), for it is found also among the Karaites.

Another version of the "double messiah" developed in the second century CE, possibly as a reaction to the catastrophic failure of the Bar Kokhba Revolt. The messiah of the house of Joseph (or Ephraim)—a possible echo of the motif of the ten lost tribes—falls in battle against the forces of Gog and Magog (the Jewish counterpart to the Battle of Armageddon). He is thus not a suffering messiah but a warrior messiah who dies a hero's death, to be followed by the victorious messiah of the house of David. This view of a double messiah also expresses an essential duality in Jewish (but not only in Jewish) messianism: messianic fulfillment is preceded by cosmic, natural, and social upheavals and catastrophes. (The Christian transformation of the Jewish motif is the idea of the Antichrist let loose to rule the world before being finally vanquished at the Second Coming.) Hence, whenever severe sufferings and tribulations were visited on the Jewish people, these could be, and often were, interpreted as the predicted premessianic catastrophe (the "birth pangs" of the messianic age, in the language of the Talmud) heralding an imminent messianic consummation.

Messianism in the wider sense of an ideal future need not imply the belief in a particular, individual savior or redeemer figure. While *Isaiah* 11 and 2:2–4 envisage a peaceful and utopian world under a Davidic king, the parallel text *Micah* 4:4 has even fewer miraculous elements and speaks of an earthly happiness, with every man dwelling under his vine and under his fig tree. For Jeremiah too, though his vision of the future also emphasizes the moral dimensions—compare *Jeremiah* 31:30ff. and 32:36–44 with Ezekiel's "new heart" and "heart of flesh" instead of the previous heart of stone (*Ez.* 2:4, 11:19, 18:31, 32:9, 36:26)—the promised boon is that "there shall enter into the gates of this city [Jerusalem] kings and princes sitting upon the throne of David, riding in chariots and on horses" (*Jer.* 17:25). Noteworthy in this text is not only its this-worldly ideal, with Jerusalem as a bustling royal city, but also the reference to kings, in the plural. The idea of the *one* messianic savior-king had not yet developed.

In later, especially modern and secularized, versions of messianism, the idea of a personal messiah increasingly gave way to the notion of a "messianic age" of peace, social justice, and universal love—conceptions that could easily function as progressive, liberal, socialist, utopian, and even revolutionary transformations of traditional messianism. Thus the Philadelphia program of American Reform Judaism (1869) substituted for the belief in a personal messiah the optimistic faith in the advent of a messianic era characterized by "the unity of all men as children of God in the confession of the One and Sole God," and the Pittsburgh Platform (1885) spoke of the establishment "of the kingdom of truth, justice and peace." Twentieth-century disillusionment with the idea of progress seems to have given a new lease on life to more radical and utopian forms of messianism.

In the intertestamentary period, messianic beliefs and doctrines developed, as we have seen, in a variety of forms. Messianism became increasingly eschatological, and eschatology was decisively influenced by apocalypticism. At the same time, messianic expectations became increasingly focused on the figure of an individual savior. In times of stress and crisis messianic pretenders (or forerunners and heralds announcing their advent) would appear, often as leaders of revolts. Josephus Flavius as well as the author of *Acts* 5 mentions several such figures. Moreover, the Messiah no longer symbolized the coming of the new age, but he was somehow supposed to bring it about. The "Lord's anointed" thus became the "savior and redeemer" and the focus of more intense expectations and doctrines, even of a "messianic theology." Compare, for example, the implications of Paul's reading of *Isaiah* 52:20, "and the Redeemer [i.e., God] cometh to Zion," as "the Redeemer [i.e., Christ] cometh *from* Zion" (*Rom.* 11:26).

Since many Jews of the Diaspora lived under Christian domination, which meant also Christian persecution and missionary pressure, theological polemics inevitably centered on christological—that is, messianic—themes. (Is Jesus the promised messiah? Why do the Jews refuse to acknowledge him? Because of carnal blindness or diabolic wickedness?) Since both religions recognized the Hebrew Bible as holy scripture, polemic often assumed an exegetical character (i.e., it claimed a correct interpretation of the "messianic" prophecies in the Bible). [*See* Polemics, *article on* Jewish-Christian Polemics.] As a rule, Jewish messianism never relinquished its concrete, historical, national, and social expectations and was little impressed by the "spiritual" character of Christian doctrine.

Christian polemics, from the early church fathers to the Middle Ages and later, accused the Jews of an inferior and crude materialism that made them read the scriptures *kata sarka,* with eyes of flesh rather than with eyes of the spirit. Paradoxically, the Jews considered this reproach as a compliment, since for them the claim that the Messiah had come was, in an unredeemed world plagued by wars, injustice, oppression, sickness, sin, and violence, utterly meaningless. In the famous disputation of Barcelona (1263), forced upon the Jews by Dominican missionaries and held in the presence of King James I of Aragon, the Jewish spokesman, the great Talmudist and qabbalist Moses Nahmanides (Mosheh ben Naḥman, c. 1194–c. 1270), simply quoted *Isaiah* 2:4 and observed that His Most Christian Majesty, in spite of his belief that the Messiah had come, would probably find it difficult to disband his army and send home all his knights so that they might beat their swords into plowshares and their spears into pruning hooks.

Throughout Jewish history there has existed a tension between two types of messianism, already briefly mentioned before: the apocalyptic one, with its miraculous and supernatural elements, and a more "rationalist" one. Throughout the Middle Ages old, and usually pseudepigraphic, apocalypses and messianic *midrashim* were copied and new ones were produced by messianic enthusiasts and visionaries. The rabbinic attitude, at least the official one, was more sober and prudent: too many messianic outbursts had ended in disaster, namely, cruel suppression by the gentile rulers. A burned child dreads the fire, and the rabbinic hesitations (probably a result of the traumatic experience of the Bar Kokhba Revolt) found eloquent expression in the homiletic interpretation of *Song of Songs* 2:7: "'I charge you, you daughters of Jerusalem, that you stir not up nor awake my love till he please'—this verse contains six charges to Israel: not to rebel against the kingdoms of this world, not to force the end of the days . . . and not to use force to return to the Land of Israel" (B.T., *Ket.* 111a). On a more theoretical level, already one Talmudic master had given the opinion that "there is no difference between this age and the messianic age but the oppression of Israel by the heathen kingdoms [which will cease after Israel regains its freedom under a messianic king]."

The great medieval authority, the philosopher-theologian Moses Maimonides (Mosheh ben Maimon, 1135/8–1204), although he enumerated belief in the advent of the Messiah among the basic articles of faith, was careful to rule in his legal code as follows:

> Let no one think that the messianic king would have to perform signs or miracles . . . and let no one think that in the messianic era the normal course of things would be changed

> or the order of nature altered. . . . What scripture says on the subject is very obscure, and our sages [too] have no clear and explicit traditions in these matters. Most [of the prophecies and traditions] are parables, the real meaning of which will become clear only after the event. These details are therefore not articles of religion, and one should not waste time on their interpretation or on the computation of the date of the messianic advent, since these things are conducive neither to the love of God nor to the fear of God.
>
> (*Mishneh Torah,* Kings 11, 12)

In Maimonides' own lifetime, messianic movements occurred in parts of the Diaspora, and as the acknowledged leader of his generation he had to do his best, without offending the messianic enthusiasm of the pious folk, to prevent disasters and backlashes by carefully preaching his more sober approach (e.g., in his *Epistle to Yemen* and *Epistle on the Resurrection of the Dead*). Nevertheless, messianic longing and apocalyptic imagination, fired by persecutions and suffering, continued to flourish and to ignite messianic outbursts. There was no dearth of messianic pretenders ("pseudomessiahs") or precursors announcing the advent of the Redeemer, provided the people would prepare themselves by appropriate means (e.g., penitential austerities).

But no matter whether messianic hopes and beliefs were apocalyptic or more sober, a matter of feverish agitation or of theological dogma, they had become an essential part of the Jewish faith and of the Jewish experience of life and of history. The apocalyptic texts might be rejected by some as too fantastic, but the heritage of messianic prophecy was accepted by all—not only in its biblical form but even more decisively in its subsequent rabbinic development. The most influential factor was, perhaps, the constant emphasis of messianic beliefs (the ingathering of the exiles, the restoration of the Davidic kingdom, the rebuilding of Jerusalem and the Temple) in the daily liturgy, in the grace recited after every meal, and especially in the prayers on Sabbath and holy days. This is not the only instance in the history of religions that illustrates how the prayer book and the liturgy can exert a more pervasive influence than theological tracts.

Messianic movements accompanied Jewish history throughout the Middle Ages, and there were probably many more than have come to our knowledge through chronicles, rabbinic *responsa,* and other incidental references. Most of them were local phenomena of short duration. The movement usually petered out after its suppression by the authorities or the disappearance (or execution) of the leader. In this respect the movement inspired by the seventeenth-century messianic pretender Shabbetai Tsevi is an exceptional case. Messianic movements are attested in Persia from the eighth century (Abu Issa al-Isfahani and his disciple Yudghan) to David Alroy (Menaḥem al-Dūjī) in the twelfth century. Abu Issa, who proclaimed himself the messiah of the house of Joseph, duly fell in battle against the Abbasid forces against which he had marched with ten thousand followers, while David Alroy (known best from Disraeli's fanciful novel) staged a revolt against the sultan. Several messianic pretenders appeared in the eleventh and twelfth centuries in western Europe, particularly in Spain. Later, under the influence of Qabbalah, messianic activism became more mystical and even magical. Spiritual activism, when all realistic and practical outlets are closed, easily becomes magical activism, and Jewish legend tells of masters who undertook to force the messianic advent by means of extreme mortifications, special meditations, and qabbalistic incantations. These legends, the most popular of which was that concerning Yosef della Reyna, usually end with the qabbalist adept falling prey to the demonic powers that he had sought to vanquish.

To understand the various messianic movements properly, one would have to examine carefully, individually, and in detail the specific historical circumstances and external pressures as well as internal tensions that precipitated them. The common fate of Jews everywhere as a despised and persecuted minority, existing in a hostile environment yet sharing the same religious culture and messianic hope, provides a general framework; nevertheless it is clearly inadequate as an explanation of specific messianic movements. The permanent presence of messianic dynamisms is also attested by the phenomenon of smaller or larger groups of Jews leaving their countries of origin in the Diaspora in order to settle in the Holy Land. While less blatantly millenarian than the acute messianic outbursts, these movements often had messianic motivations. Although the Messiah had not yet appeared or called the faithful to the Promised Land, the motivation was often "preeschatological" in the sense that a life of prayer and ascetic sanctification in the Holy Land was thought to prepare or even hasten the advent of the Redeemer.

With the emergence of Qabbalah after the thirteenth century, and especially its development after the expulsion of Jews from Spain and Portugal, qabbalistic mysticism became a major element and driving social force in Jewish messianism. This process requires a brief elucidation. As a rule mystical systems have little or no relationship to time or to the process of time, history, and hence to messianism. After all, the mystic aspires to a supratemporal sphere, the anticipation of timeless eternity and the "everlasting now" rather than to the crowning consummation of history. It is therefore not surprising to find messianic tension decreasing in inverse proportion to the mystical tension. This principle seems to hold true also regarding classical Spanish Qabbalah. The new Qabbalah, Lurianic Qabbalah, that developed after the Spanish expulsion in the great centers of the Ottoman empire, but especially in Safad in the Holy Land, was remarkable for its high, one would almost say explosive, messianic charge, especially in the form that it received at the hand of the most original, charismatic, and outstanding qabbalist in that group, Isaac Luria (1534–1572).

Lurianic Qabbalah interpreted the history of the world in general, and Israel's exile, suffering, and redemption in particular, in an idiom of a type that might be called gnostic, that is, in terms of a cosmic, or rather divine, drama in which God himself was involved. One might also describe the system as a theosophical *Heilsgeschichte.* According to this strangely "gnostic" myth, a primordial catastrophe or "fall" occurred—long before Adam's original sin—at the moment when the divine light-essence externalized itself with a view to creating the world. The vessels that were to carry and transmit the divine light collapsed (the "breaking of the vessels") and the divine light-sparks fell into chaos and have since been imprisoned and "exiled" there, where—and this is part of their tragedy—they sustain the life of the demonic realm. [*See* Qabbalah.]

Israel's exile and suffering thus merely reflect on the historical, material, and external level the more fundamental mystery of the exile and suffering of the divine fallen sparks. Redemption thus means the liberation of the divine sparks from the defiling embrace of the demonic powers and their return to their divine source, no less than the liberation of Israel from subjugation to the gentiles and its return to the Holy Land. Indeed, the latter process would follow as natural consequence from the former, which it was Israel's true and mystical vocation to bring about by a life of piety and holiness. This is spiritual activism at its most extreme, for here God has become a *salvator salvandus.* To the harassed and hounded Jew, exile became meaningful because it was seen as a reflection of, and participation in, the profounder exile of God, and God himself required Israel's cooperation in the redemption of himself, his people, and his creation. It is not surprising that, at least at first, the personality of the Messiah played a relatively minor role in this system. He was not so much a redeemer as a sign and symbol that the mystical messianic process had been consummated. In fact, the messianic doctrine of Lurianism comes close, at least structurally, to an evolutionist scheme.

This qabbalistic system provided the background of one of the most remarkable messianic episodes in the course of Jewish history—the movement centered on the person of Shabbetai Tsevi. The ignominious debacle of Shabbateanism, with its aftermath of heresy, antinomianism, and apostasy, left a trail of spiritual confusion and disarray as a result of which both Qabbalah and messianism declined, at least in their public and social role. [*See the biography of Shabbetai Tsevi.*] Apart from a few minor messianic convulsions, "automessianism" (as Martin Buber called it) declined steadily. The messianic idea remained alive in Judaism, influencing no doubt also non-Jewish ideologies of utopia and hope (see the influential work of the Marxist thinker Ernst Bloch, *Das Prinzip Hoffnung*), but no more messianic pretenders appeared. Orthodox Judaism continued to believe in the traditional doctrine of a personal messiah but *de facto* retreated into a shell of strict halakhic observance. The myth had lost its power to trigger messianic movements.

Hasidism, the great spiritual revival launched in eighteenth-century eastern Europe by the Besht (Yisra'el ben Eli'ezer, 1700–1760), certainly did not relinquish traditional messianic beliefs, but its main emphasis was on closeness to God through spiritual inwardness or (at times) ecstasy. Gershom Scholem has described this process (though the subject is still a matter of scholarly debate) as a "neutralization of the messianic element." But while Hasidism attempted to provide an answer, in a traditional idiom, for the spiritual seekers as well as for the pauperized masses in the ghettos of eastern Europe, the Jewry of western and central Europe entered the modern age (civil emancipation, assimilation, Reform Judaism).

The implications of these developments for Jewish messianism are still a matter for research. Many of the modern ideologies undoubtedly preserved some of the traditional messianic overtones. At times they made deliberate use of messianic terminology. Of course the progressive liberals and later socialists, and needless to say the national revival known as Zionism, did not think in terms of Armageddon, or a heavenly Jerusalem descending from above, or the "son of David" riding on an ass, but rather of civil liberties, equality before the law, universal peace, all-around ethical and human progress, the national emancipation of the Jewish people within the family of nations, and so on. But all these aspirations were somehow surrounded with a messianic halo. Jews rarely asked the literalist questions so congenial to Christian fundamentalism. They do not, as a rule, inquire whether a particular historical event is the "fulfillment" of a particular biblical prophecy. But it is impossible, for most of them, to pass through apocalyptic events such as the Holocaust, or to experience the end of exile and the reestablishment of Israel as a sovereign commonwealth, without the stirring of messianic chords in their souls.

In fact, since the Yom Kippur War—that is, since the seventies of the twentieth century—a trend toward a "messianization" of politics has become noticeable in Israel, especially among groups advocating settlements on the West Bank or Jewish rights on the Temple Mount. Some of this messianized Zionism goes back to the teaching of Avraham Yitsḥaq Kook, chief rabbi of Palestine from 1921 to 1935. In the Prayer for the State of Israel the chief rabbinate refers to the state—in an incredibly primitive dispensationalist fashion—as "the beginning of the sprouting of our Redemption." Others, however, feel that messianism as an eschatological concept should be kept out of the pragmatics and ambiguities of current politics, since it tends to demoralize and mythologize them instead of moralizing them (in the prophetic sense). It is still too early for a definitive historical and sociological evaluation of these conflicting tendencies, and of the nature and role of messianism in contemporary Judaism.

[*See also* Apocalypse, *articles on* Jewish Apocalypticism to the Rabbinic Period *and* Medieval Jewish Apocalyptic Literature; *and* Zionism.]

BIBLIOGRAPHY

Cohen, Gerson D. "Messianic Postures of Ashkenazim and Sephardim." In *Studies of the Leo Baeck Institute*, edited by Max Kreutzberger, pp. 115–156. New York, 1967.

Friedmann, H. G. "Pseudo-Messiahs." In *Jewish Encyclopaedia*. New York, 1925. A history of messianic pretenders throughout Jewish history.

Klausner, Joseph. *The Messianic Idea in Israel, from Its Beginning to the Completion of the Mishnah*. New York, 1955.

Mowinckel, Sigmund. *He That Cometh: The Messianic Concept in the Old Testament and Later Judaism*. Translated by G. W. Anderson. Oxford, 1956.

Scholem, Gershom. *The Messianic Idea in Judaism and Other Essays on Jewish Spirituality*. New York, 1971.

Silver, A. H. *A History of Messianic Speculation in Israel*. Rev. ed. Boston, 1959.

Werblowsky, R. J. Zwi. "Messianism in Jewish History." In *Jewish Society through the Ages*, edited by H. H. Ben-Sasson and Samuel Ettinger, pp. 30–45. New York, 1971. A short survey and analysis.

R. J. Zwi Werblowsky

Islamic Messianism

The Muslim figure of the Mahdi, the "rightly guided" or "God-guided" one (the term is derived from Arabic as passive participle of the verb *hadā*, to "guide"), shares much with preceding Judeo-Christian messianic experience. The expectation of a divinely sent eschatological prophet at the end time has played as great a role in the history of Islam as in its brother faiths. Yet as a general Muslim phenomenon, notions of the Mahdi cannot be fully understood as solely eschatological, and comparison with Jewish messianism or with the Christian conception of the second coming of Christ does not resolve its complexity in the Muslim context. Nor should it be considered exotic and sectarian, reflecting merely extreme views. Messianic expectations were part of the self-formation of the original Muslim community and contributed to dividing Muslims into two great competing branches, Sunnī and Shīʿī. Islamic appropriation of the messianic complex of myths has played an important role in various cultural and ideological settings and has served as an essential factor in reformist and revivalist movements, religious schools, and metaphysical teachings.

Earliest Expression of the Mahdi Myth. The definite messianic orientation of nascent Islam can be gauged by the intense mood of eschatological expectancy pervading the Near East during the fifth and sixth centuries CE and amplified in the eschatological tension of the Qur'anic orientation toward an idealized hereafter. The overwhelming stress in the Qur'ān on the theme of the Day of Judgment, the Signs of the Hour *(ashrāt al-sā'ah)*, and the rewards of the righteous and torments of the wicked evokes the literary and psychological mood of apocalypticism. During the period immediately preceding the Last Day ominous signs of cosmic disorder will occur: chaotic smoke or formless darkness, the manifestation of the beast *(al-dābbah)* from the earth, a sunrise in the west, and various stellar abnormalities. All these will drive men to the final gathering place, and summoned there will also be al-Dajjāl (the Antichrist) and the nations of Gog and Magog, heralding an exceptional period of terror and fear. The term *al-mahdī* nowhere occurs in the Qur'ān, even though the notion of God's guidance forms one of the fundamental axioms of the text, tied to its teaching on divine guidance for the faithful paralleled by God's leading the unfaithful astray. Thus surah 18:17 states: "He whom God guides, he alone is the rightly guided [*al-muhtadī*, participle from the eighth form of *hadā*], but he whom [God] leads astray, for him you will find no patron as a guide to the right way." While the Qur'ān does not embrace a strong rhetoric of salvation, it is deeply concerned with the human predicament and how we may be delivered from it, or to use characteristic Islamic expressions, how we may triumph over it and be among the successful, receiving saving guidance *(hudan, hidāyah)* and thereby avoiding loss.

Allied with these notions is the vision of the holy community in its intimate relation with God and his prophet. Given that some Christians and Jews in Arabia foretold that an eschatological prophet (surah 2:89) who would vindicate their particular community would soon appear, and that throughout the Near East messianic typology had been exploited as a prop for imperial or kingly legitimation (notably the Byzantine emperor, the Abyssinian negus, and the Jewish king Dhū Nuwās in Yemen), the Muslim claim that Muḥammad is the final link in the chain of prophecy, the "seal" of the prophets, may originally have been understood in a messianic sense. More to the point is the position and function that Muḥammad filled as the divinely led guide of his newly forged community, instilling it with a sense of universal historical mission and dynamic urgency of cosmic import. After his death, the expanding Muslim state had to resolve the dilemma of the nature of authoritative guidance under the impact of successive determining events. Two basic tendencies were to emerge over the course of the first two centuries (the seventh and eighth centuries CE): that of the Shīʿah, who maintained the necessity for the continuation of prophetic charisma in the line of Muḥammad's descendants through the office of the imamate, and that of the Sunnī majority, who adhered to the office of the caliphate as legitimate successor to the prophet's leadership yet generally divested the caliph of spiritual and religious charisma and preferred to derive authority and guidance from the Qur'ān itself as the basis for juridical and religious decisions.

The figure of the Mahdi emerged out of religio-political developments that took place between the assassination of ʿUthmān, the third caliph, in AH 35/655 CE, and the martyrdom of al-Ḥusayn, Muḥammad's grandson and the son of ʿAlī ibn Abī Ṭālib, the cousin and son-in-law of Muḥammad, a quarter-century later. The notion of the Mahdi as the expected deliverer must have emerged out of the ambitious and turbulent groups of Arabs supporting ʿAlid claims to legitimate leadership of the community, and from a particular set of socio-political conditions allied with a distinct interpretation of Islamic revelation. The kind of super-spirituality associated with the earliest beliefs in the coming of the Mahdi could not have been suddenly implanted into Muslim thought, but the term itself, in its meaning of "the God-guided one," first appeared in 686 CE with the Shīʿī revolt in Kufa of al-Mukhtār, who spread propaganda in the name of the third surviving son of ʿAlī, Muḥammad ibn al-Ḥanafīyah. The movement founded by al-Mukhtār known as the Kaysānīyah was responsible for popularizing a number of religious aspects of the Shīʿī theory of the imam, such as the explicit designation of the imam *(naṣṣ)* and the concealment and expected return of the imam or Mahdi (the doctrines of *ghaybah* and *rajʿah*). [*See* Imamate *and* Ghaybah.]

Shīʿī Development of the Mahdi Myth. The peculiar apocalyptic ideology of the Kaysānīyah and its cognate groupings was marked by its revolutionary orientation and a tendency toward a type of radical utopianism enveloped within its Mahdi doctrine, embracing the motif of revenge and concrete political expectations. The Mahdi was understood as a prophetic eschatological figure who had disappeared from mortal sight and subsisted miraculously in a semiparadisial state until the time of his awaited reappearance; according to the prophetic tradition, at that time he would lead the army of the righteous and initiate the terrible drama of the eschaton, "filling the earth with justice and equity as it is now filled with injustice and oppression." He functions both as the avenger for the wrongs suffered by the Shīʿah and the herald of the ultimate theocracy on earth, when punishment for wickedness and tyranny will be administered, followed by the inauguration of a blissful reign of social and religious perfection preceding Resurrection Day. The Mahdi was connected with those events held to be divinely established and foretold as preceding the Day of Judgment and described in the Qur'ān as the Signs of the Last Hour.

Significantly, the Kaysānīyah made an explicit comparison between the person of their imam or Mahdi and the role of Jesus as portrayed in the Qur'ān. Despite the fact that the Qur'ān cannot be said to treat Jesus as the Christ or Messiah, his second coming as a sign of the Hour of Resurrection is generally admitted in Muslim tradition (see surahs 4:159 and 43:61), and his bodily ascension in docetic fashion followed by his ultimate death after his return were widely accepted in early Muslim exegesis. There is an apparent merging or conflation of the Mahdi figure and the apocalyptic drama he initiates with the drama of restoration already connected with the second coming of Jesus. The various Jewish or Christian precedents for the Mahdi figure proposed by some scholars are all uncertain (e.g., Elijah returned, the Ephraimite messiah, a Nestorian christological term *mahdoya* perhaps applied to Muḥammad), yet there remains an undeniable impact of religious ideas connected with earlier prophetic eschatological figures. This legacy was integrated with the real events that shaped the self-awareness of the early Shīʿah in their development of these notions.

Within the wider Shīʿī movements of the first three Islamic centuries, the title of Mahdi was repeatedly employed by various ʿAlid pretenders, such as the Hasanid

Muḥammad al-Nafs al-Zakīyah, who led a failed revolt against the Abbasid caliph al-Manṣūr in 758, or ʿUbayd Allāh, the founder of the Fatimid Ismāʿīlī dynasty in North Africa in 909; it was even adopted as a regnal title by the Abbasid caliph al-Mahdī (r. 775–785). Although it was the revolutionary circles spawned by the Kaysānīyah who exploited the term at first, another no less significant wing of the Shīʿah represented by the Husaynid ʿAlids (the line of the twelve imams) made the expectation of the future deliverer central in their teaching. However, the line of Husaynid imams did not participate in any overtly chiliastic or millenarian political movement and they appear to have avoided the use of the term Mahdi as a self-designation, referring instead to the imam, or the Qā'im ("standing one," the one who will arise), or Hādī al-Muhtadīn ("the guide of those who are rightly guided"). In this early period it is probable that the notion of the imam and the Mahdi overlapped to some extent, given the fact that every imam-claimant whose followers upheld the belief of his concealment and return could be considered a potential or actual Mahdi. The radical Shīʿī circles in Iraq experienced a surge of speculative religious activity by the early eighth century CE; their connections with older gnostic, monastic, and mystical traditions are obscure but had important consequences for their understanding of the imam, and thus for the Mahdi figure. Beliefs touching on the sinlessness of the imam/Mahdi, his supernatural knowledge, the mode of his ascensional being, his power of intercession and remission of sin, and his future glory and vindication were developed and in time admitted as integral to the Mahdi figure among the largest body of the Shīʿah, the Twelvers. This continuous line of imams had withstood the tendency of rival groups to "stop" at a particular imam and await his reappearance as the Mahdi, as well as the offshoots of a number of messianic pretenders characteristic of radical Shīʿī prophetism, until the death of the eleventh imam, al-Ḥasan al-ʿAskarī, in 874. The son of this imam was then declared to be alive but in concealment, and until his near-return, communication with him was possible through a succession of agents (the four *safīrs* during the time of the minor *ghaybah*). After 941, the leading scholar-jurists of the Twelver Shīʿah accepted the total concealment of the twelfth or hidden imam as Mahdi until his return in the fullness of time; thus was initiated the era of the major *ghaybah* still in effect. This decision represented the adoption of the radical Shīʿī position on the Mahdi that the Husaynid line had previously rejected, but it was now focused on the elaboration of a more spiritual image of the Mahdi in terms of a personal, redemptive faith. This faith was buttressed by specific ritual and cultic practices specific to Twelvers and permeated by their particular theology of disinheritance, martyrdom, and righteous suffering. [*See* Shiism.]

The Mahdi Figure in History. The basic features of the Mahdi myth have not altered appreciably since its early appearance. The Mahdi will appear during the period of anarchy and chaos preceding the end time, a time marked by upheavals and dissension (Arab., *fitnah,* lit., "trial," "discord") marking the final trial of mortals by God, and by the revolts or seditions *(malāhim)* breeding schism. This long period of social and political disintegration will lead to the domination of evil, falsehood, and injustice in both the social and natural realms. Such chaos will serve as a test of the purity of the faithful who remain. In the final stage of this process, the Mahdi will reappear to usher in a new era of restoration and to reconfirm the validity of God's revelation. This will be achieved by restoring the justice of the past through the reestablishment of the protean Muslim faith and community (i.e., form of government) in a brief intervening golden age. Some accounts have him making his return in Mecca on 10 Muḥarram, the day of ʿĀshūrā', and proceeding from there to Kufa to execute divine wrath and retribution, accompanied by the army of the faithful; he will reign for seven or seventy years before his death, with the aid of angelic armies and assisted by the returned Jesus.

Within the Shīʿī cult of the charismatic leader, the identity of the Mahdi is known (though he is in concealment), and it is the time of his return that is not known, for the belief in the Mahdi is identified with the return of the Hidden Imam or Ṣāhib al-Zamān, "master of the end time." Some Sunnī Muslims, however, say that no one can know the identity of the Mahdi until he actually appears and makes his claim, while others limit the function of the Mahdi to Jesus alone. He is to appear like an ordinary man whose career is that of a reformer or conqueror, although some Sunnīs accept that the Mahdi is in hiding with no suggestion of supernatural concealment. The whole Mahdi notion was sometimes viewed by Sunnī theologians with such caution and suspicion that his title or role was omitted, and this trend has received renewed currency today. Two of the four fundamental collections of Sunnī traditions, those of Bukhārī and Muslim, make no mention of the Mahdi, and the preeminent theologian al-Ghazālī (d. 1111) omits any discussion of him in his classic *Iḥyā' 'ulūm al-dīn* (Revivification of the Religious Sciences), alluding only to the Qur'anic Signs of the Hour. Yet Sunnīs accept the general Muslim belief in a Renewer or Reformer *(mujaddid),* who appears every century in some part of the Islamic world and whose function as the reviver of the faith and the strength of the community partly parallels the role awarded the Mahdi. It was in the hearts of the Muslim masses that the belief in the Mahdi was kept alive, so that in times of particular strain, caused by alien domination or social instability, this belief could be readily activated and his imminent arrival expected to accomplish the correction of history. The established tendency to view prophecy as history foretold and history as prophecy fulfilled, and the accumulated mass of myth surrounding the Mahdi, combined with the idealization of the community's early history as the archetype for the sacred drama of the end time built into the Muslim consciousness, enabled the ill-defined Sunnī conception of the Mahdi to be adjusted to the situation at hand, or so formulated that an appropriate candidate could declare himself to be the Expected One.

There are many instances in Muslim history of Mahdi claimants who sought to challenge and overthrow the existing political order by force of arms. Mahdi movements seldom achieved genuine political success unless they succeeded in laying a foundation based on existing tribal loyalties, on a rural or marginally urban sense of dispossession or alienation, or on patterns of sociopolitical opposition. Several elements have contributed to the manifestations of messianically inspired figures. The tradition of millenarianism as the fitting vehicle for social protest and religious dissent was established early on in Muslim history. Another, still actively contributing factor is the dynamic and spiritually combative posture of Islamic consciousness and ideology, wedded to its own self-definition as a universal and ultimate salvational order. Generally, successful movements pass through three progressive phases: (1) initially, an intensive propagandizing for a form of Islamic revivalism aimed at winning support among the discontented and deprived; (2) with increasing adherents, the formation of a military organization undertaking the propagation of its claims and military ventures; and (3) the emergence of a territorial state whose theocratic aspirations gradually become obsolete.

Ibn Tūmart (d. 1130), who began his career as a moral reformer, founded the Almohad empire, which at its height extended across North Africa from what is now Marrakesh and Fez in Morocco to Tunisia and Tripolitania. His claim to be the Mahdi was combined with a strictly Sunnī theological creed and an extreme asceticism, as well as a pretended ʿAlid lineage and possession of the symbols of ʿAlid legitimacy such as the sword of the Prophet. His conception of the Mahdi *cum* caliph stressed the infallibility of the ruler, a trait usually absent from Sunnī views of the caliphate, but essential to the Shīʿī imamate.

With the beginning of the century preceding the first millennium in Islam, a special importance was attached to predictions of a Mahdi. Among various figures reflected in its glow may be mentioned the Ṣūfī teacher Sayyid Muḥammad Nūrbakhsh, who led a Mahdist movement arising in Badakhshān (Iran) and then Iraq, as well as several important preacher-reformers in Muslim India, including Mīr Sayyid Muḥammad of Jaunpūr (d. 1505 in Baluchistan), and the Mahdāwīyah of Hindustan, originally a strongly puritanical Sunnī peasant commune of militant ascetics at odds with the official religious leaders of the courts. Their leader, Shaykh ʿAlāʾī, was tortured to death for refusing to give up his Mahdist claim. In the Turko-Persian sphere this era witnessed major convulsions that led to the successful appropriation of the Mahdi ideology at the hands of tribal leaders, notably the emergence of the Safavid dynasty in Iran at the turn of the sixteenth century, led by Shah Ismāʿīl, himself a self-proclaimed Mahdi.

The vitality and power of the Mahdi legacy in Islam found particularly dramatic expression with the Mahdi of the Sudan, Muḥammad Aḥmad ibn ʿAbd Allāh. His movement, the Mahdīyah, swept the Nilotic Sudan in the last two decades of the nineteenth century, contributing substantially to the emergence of the Sudan as a nation-state in the twentieth century. In June 1881 this prominent Sudanese holy man made his public manifestation as the Mahdi on the island of Aba, and in the course of a relatively short time, his movement transformed the Sudan into an Islamic theocracy and then into an Islamic kingdom that, from the Mahdi's death in 1885 until its overthrow in 1898–1899, was ruled by his senior lieutenant and temporal successor, Khalīfah ʿAbd Allāh. The Mahdīyah was the last outburst in a series of great spiritual movements of a Sunnī revivalist nature that developed into dynastic, theocratic states: the Wahhābīyah in Arabia, the Fulbe movement of Shehu Usuman dan Fodio in Sokoto, and the Sanūsīyah in Cyrenaica. The Sanūsī Ṣūfī brotherhood exploited the associations of the Mahdi legacy, and its head was given the title of Mahdi; it was the Sudanese Mahdi, however, who wholeheartedly embraced the Mahdist figure and consciously tried to reproduce the supposed conditions of the original "Muhammadan" community and attempted to reproduce the career of the Prophet. The partly ascetic, partly communistic character of his movement was buttressed by allusions to the body of millenarian myths, such as his claim to possess the sword of the Prophet, a theme originally developed by the early Shīʿah as a messianic emblem of legitimacy and authority. [*See* Wahhābīyah; Jihād; *and the biographies of Dan Fodio and Muḥammad Aḥmad.*]

In Iran, the important movement of the Bāb, the "precursor" of the Mahdi, Sayyid ʿAlī Muḥammad Shīrāzī (executed 1850), shook the complacency of the Twelver Shīʿah by demonstrating that the Mahdi legacy continued to be a valid alternative for some Shīʿīs, despite the prevailing political quiescence of their religious hierarchy. The Bābī movement resulted in the formation of the Bahāʾī faith as a separate religion by the early twentieth century. [*See* Bābīs *and* Bahāʾīs.] Further east in the Punjab, Mirzā Ghulām Aḥmad of Qādīān (d. 1908), who founded the Aḥmadīyah movement, claimed the role of the Mahdi for himself, and his followers in Pakistan and Western Europe continued to proselytize on his behalf even in the late twentieth century. Aḥmadī doctrines agree in the main with those of Sunnī Islam but renounce violent means or any political claims. The Mahdi himself is considered an incarnation both of Jesus and Muḥammad, and at the same time an avatar of Kṛṣṇa, being the second, or promised, messiah. [*See also* Aḥmadīyah.]

The Mahdi Legacy. Much that is said about the Mahdi falls into categories other than that of abstract ideas. The legends about his role, his person, tasks, and powers are concrete, often narrative discourse, and must be understood in the context of the religious and spiritual life of Muslims. At the same time, the social and political realms of the community are inseparable from the complex of myths surrounding the Mahdi. The restorative and the radical utopian trends in Muslim messianism feed off each other, and the tension between these two directions that the Mahdi myth evokes explains how it can generate either the catastrophic apocalyptic eruption into history or the speculative, even mystical, "neutralization" of chiliastic longings.

The Mahdi figure has served a mythic function in revitalizing a dogmatic or anachronistic leadership, in mobilizing the masses who were suffocating from dispossession or social marginality or were hard pressed by alien domination, or in providing an ideological and religious backbone for aiding believers to deal creatively with their historical realities. The more apocalyptic and combative forms of this myth tended toward revolutionary historical change and are more historically significant. The congruence of heresy and messianism is no accident in Islam, and ostensibly "heretical" ideas actually played a legitimate role in its history as indigenous elements. The vital forces contained in the Mahdi figure are potentially chaotic and destructive even while maintaining the creative tension inherent in contradictory interpretations of revelation. Today this legacy continues to be drawn upon; it still feeds the hopes and fears of Muslims, whether in the great Shīʿī revival now underway in Iran and Lebanon or among Arab fundamentalist leaders pushing for reform and islamization of government and society.

[*See also* Eschatology, *article on* Islamic Eschatology; Nubūwah; *and* Modernism, *article on* Islamic Modernism.]

BIBLIOGRAPHY

No comprehensive study of the whole range of Mahdi themes and historical movements exists. A general orientation is provided in Christiaan Snouck Hurgronje's "Der Mahdī," in his *Verspreide Geschriften* (Bonn, 1923), vol. 1, pp. 147–181, and an informed medieval Muslim view is given in Ibn Khaldūn's *The Muqaddimah: An Introduction to History*, translated by Franz Rosenthal (London, 1958), vol. 2, pp. 156–232. Important studies of the early appearance, background, and development of the Mahdi in the Shīʿī movements are Jan-Olaf Blichfeldt's *Early Mahdism* (Leiden, 1985) and A. A. Sachedina's *Islamic Messianism: The Idea of Mahdi in Twelver Shīʿism* (Albany, N.Y., 1981). For the early Abbasid revolution, one can consult Moshe Sharon's *Black Banners from the East: Incubation of a Revolt* (Jerusalem, 1983). Edgard Blochet's survey *Le messianisme dans l'heterodoxie musulmane* (Paris, 1903) is still useful for the radical Shīʿī movements, although it should be read with caution.

The mainstream Twelver tradition about the Mahdi and its mystical overtones can be glimpsed in Shaykh al-Mufīd's *Kitāb al-irshād: The Book of Guidance into the Lives of the Twelve Imāms*, translated by I. K. A. Howard (London, 1981), pp. 524–554; in Henry Corbin's *En Islam iranien: Aspects spirituels et philosophiques*, vol. 1, *Le shīʿisme duodécimain* (Paris, 1971), chaps. 2, 6, and 7; and in Corbin's contributions to the *Eranos-Jahrbuch* 28 (1959) and 32 (1968). Ismāʿīlī Shīʿī messianic experience is treated by P. J. Vatikiotis in *The Fatimid Theory of State* (Lahore, 1957); by David Bryer in "The Origins of the Druze Religion," *Der Islam* 52 (1975): 47–85, 239–262, and 53 (1976): 5–27; and by Marshall G. S. Hodgson in *The Order of the Assassins: The Struggle of the Early Nizārī Ismāʿīlīs against the Islamic World* (1955; reprint, New York, 1980). For the Indian Mahdis of the sixteenth and seventeenth centuries, a brief survey is provided by S. A. A. Rizvi in *Muslim Revivalist Movements in Northern India* (Agra, 1965); for the Aḥmadīyah, see Spencer Lavan's *The Ahmadiyyah Movement: A History and Perspective* (New Delhi, 1974).

A good study of the diverse aspects of Mahdism and post-Mongol Ṣūfī-Shīʿī combinations is Michel M. Mazzaoui's *The Origins of the Safawids: Shīʿism, Ṣūfism, and the Gulāt* (Wiesbaden, 1972). On the Bāb and nineteenth-century Iran, see Edward G. Browne's *Materials for the Study of the Bābī Religion* (Cambridge, 1918) and A. L. M. Nicolas's *Seyyèd Ali Mohammed dit Le Bāb* (Paris, 1905).

DOUGLAS S. CROW

METALS AND METALLURGY. Archaic, nonliterate peoples, as well as prehistoric populations, worked meteoric iron long before they learned to use the ferrous ores occurring on the earth's surface. They treated certain ores like stones, that is, they regarded them as raw material for the manufacture of lithic tools. A similar technique was applied until recently by certain peoples having no knowledge of metallurgy: they worked meteorites with silex (flint) hammers and fashioned objects whose shapes resembled their stone models in all respects. This was how the Greenland Inuit (Eskimo) made their knives out of meteoric iron (Andrée, 1984, pp. 121ff.). When Cortés asked the Aztec chieftains where they had gotten their knives, they pointed to the sky. Like the Maya of Yucatan and the Inca of Peru, the Aztec used only meteoric iron, which they valued more highly than gold. In fact, excavations have revealed no trace of terrestrial iron in the prehistoric deposits of the New World (Forbes, 1950, pp. 401ff.).

Paleo-Oriental peoples presumably held similar ideas. The Sumerian word *an-bar,* the earliest vocable designating iron, is written with the signs for "sky" and "fire." Campbell Thompson renders it "celestial lightning (or meteorite)," but it is usually translated "celestial metal" or "star-metal" (Eliade, 1978, p. 22; Bjorkman, 1973, pp. 114ff.). For a long period the Egyptians too knew only meteoric iron, and the same is true of the Hittites: a text of the fourteenth century BCE states that the Hittite kings used "the black iron of the sky" (Rickard, 1932, vol. 1, p. 149). Iron, therefore, was scarce, and its use was principally ritual.

The Discovery of Smelting. It required the discovery of the smelting of ores to inaugurate a new stage in the history of mankind. Unlike the production of copper or bronze, the metallurgy of iron very soon became industrial. Once the secret of smelting magnetite and hematite was discovered, there was no longer any difficulty in obtaining large quantities of iron, for deposits were very rich and easy to exploit. But the handling of telluric ores differed from that of meteoric iron, as it did also from the smelting of copper and bronze. It was not until after the discovery of furnaces, and particularly after perfecting the technique for "hardening" metal brought to the point of white heat, that iron achieved its preeminent position. It was the metallurgy of terrestrial iron that made this metal fit for everyday use. The beginnings of iron metallurgy on an industrial scale can be fixed at a period between 1200 and 1000 BCE, in the mountains of Armenia. From there the secret of smelting spread across the Near East, the Mediterranean, and central Europe, although, as I have noted, iron, whether of meteoric origin or from superficial deposits, was known in the third millennium in Mesopotamia, in Asia Minor, and probably also in Egypt (Forbes, 1950, p. 417; Eliade, 1978, pp. 23ff., 201ff.).

Mines: The Womb of Mother Earth. The discovery of furnaces had important religious consequences. Besides the celestial sacredness of the sky, immanent in meteorites, there was now the telluric sacredness of the earth, in which mines and ore share. Metals "grow" in the bosom of the earth. Caves and mines are assimilated to the womb of Mother Earth. The ores extracted from mines are in some sense "embryos." They grow slowly, as if obeying a temporal rhythm different from that of vegetable and animal organisms; nevertheless, they do grow, they "ripen" in the telluric darkness. Hence, their extraction from Mother Earth is an operation performed prematurely. If they had been given the time to develop (that is, if they were to come to term in geological time), ores would become ripe, "perfect" metals. Belief in the natural growth, and thus in the metamorphosis, of metals is of very ancient origin in China and is also found in Vietnamese Annam, in India, and in the Malay archipelago. The peasants of Vietnamese Tonkin, for example, have a saying: "Black bronze is the mother of gold." They believe that gold is engendered naturally by bronze, but only if the bronze has lain a sufficiently long period in the bosom of the earth. "Thus the Annamites are convinced that the gold found in the mines is formed slowly *in situ* over the centuries and that if one had probed the earth originally, one would have discovered bronze in the places where gold is found today" (Przyluski, 1914, p. 3). Similar beliefs survived even into eighteenth-century Europe (Eliade, 1978, pp. 46ff.).

The Egyptians, who, according to Plutarch and Diodorus, hated iron—which they called "the bones of Seth"—considered that the flesh of gods was made of gold; in other words, that the gods were immortal. That is why, after the model of the gods, Pharaoh was also assigned flesh of gold. Indeed, as repeatedly proclaimed in the Hindu Brāhmaṇas, "Gold is immortality." Consequently, in many cultures, to obtain the elixir that transmutes metals into alchemical gold is tantamount to obtaining immortality. [*See* Gold and Silver.]

In Eastern as in Western alchemy, the transmutation of metals into gold is equated with a miraculously rapid maturation. The elixir (or the philosopher's stone) completes and consummates the work of nature. One of the characters in Ben Jonson's play *The Alchemist* (1610) asserts that "lead and other metals . . . would be gold if they had time," and another character adds, "And that our Art doth further." That is to say, the alchemist prolongs the dream and the ideology of miners and metalworkers: to perfect nature by accelerating the temporal rhythm, with the difference that the *aurum alchemicum*—the elixir—confers health, perennial youth, and even immortality. [*See* Elixir.] As is well known, by the end of the eighteenth century alchemy was supplanted by the new science of chemistry. But the alchemist's ideals survived, camouflaged and radically secularized, in nineteenth-century ideology.

In many parts of the world miners practice rites involving a state of purity, fasting, meditation, prayers, and cultic acts. The rites are governed by the nature of the intended operation, for the performance of them is meant to introduce the worker into a sacred zone, supposedly inviolable: he enters into contact with a sacrality that does not participate in the familiar religious universe, for it is a deeper and also a more dangerous sacrality. The miner feels that he risks entering a domain that does not rightfully belong to man: the underground world with its mysteries concerning the slow mineralogical gestation taking place in the womb of Mother Earth. All the mythologies of mines and mountains, their countless fairies, genii, elves, phantoms, and spirits, are the multiple epiphanies of the sacred presence that the individual confronts when he penetrates the geological levels of life (Eliade, 1978, pp. 53ff.).

Thus, the Melanesians opened a new mine only after long rituals and ceremonials. The Malay *pawang* (medicine man) derived a very fair revenue from propitiating and scaring those spirits who had to do with mines and mining (W. W. Skeat, quoted in Eliade, 1938, p. 92). Among many African peoples, the chief, surrounded by a shaman and the workers, recites a special prayer to his ancestral spirits, who preside over the mine, and only then does he determine where the digging shall be done (Cline, 1937, p. 119). In Europe, until the end of the Middle Ages, miners opened a mine only after the celebration of a religious ceremony (Sébillot, 1894, p. 421).

Furnaces and the "Growth" of the Ore. Laden with this dark sacrality, the ores are taken from the mine to the furnaces. Then begins the most difficult and riskiest operation. The artisan takes the place of Mother Earth in order to hasten and perfect the "growth" of the ores. The furnaces are in some sense a new, artificial womb in which the ore completes its gestation. Hence the countless precautions, taboos, and rituals that accompany smelting.

In Africa, camps are set up in the vicinity of the mines, and there the workers live, in a state of purity, throughout the mining season, which sometimes lasts for several months (Cline, 1937, p. 119). The Kitara believe that if the bellows-maker has had sexual relations during the course of his work, the bellows will constantly fill up with water and refuse to function (ibid., p. 121). The belief that the sexual act can in some way compromise the success of the work is general throughout sub-Saharan Africa. This prohibition is even stated in the ritual songs sung during the work. Indeed, smelting represents a sacred marriage—the mixture of "male" and "female" ores—and consequently all the sexual energies of the workmen must be kept in reserve, to ensure the magical success of the union that is taking place in the furnaces. The nuptial symbolism is present in many metallurgical ceremonies. The Kitara smith treats the anvil like a bride. When men bring it into the house they sing as though for a nuptial procession. In accepting it, the smith sprinkles it with water so that it "may bear many children" and tells his wife that he has brought a second wife home to help her (ibid., p. 118).

The Magico-Religious Powers of the Smith. The metallurgist, like the blacksmith and before him the potter, is a "master of fire." It is by means of fire that he brings about the passage of a material from one state to another. Smelting proves to be not only the means of "acting faster" but also of acting to make a different thing from what already existed in nature. This is why, in archaic societies, smelters and smiths are held to be masters of fire, along with shamans, medicine men, and magicians. But the ambivalent character of metal—laden with powers at once sacred and demonic—is transferred to metallurgists and smiths: they are highly esteemed but are also feared, segregated, or even scorned. Thus, in West Africa, smiths play important roles in secret societies, enjoy the prestige normally accorded magicians, and form separate clans. In the Kongo and surrounding regions, they have a close association with priests and chiefs (and sometimes are one and the same); elsewhere (e.g., among the Chagga, Hamitic Bantu-speaking agricultural workers) the smith is both feared and respected. By contrast, in pastoral Hamitic cultures and among steppe hunters, smiths are despised and form a caste set apart (Eliade, 1978, pp. 90ff.; see also Dieterlen, 1965, pp. 10ff.). In Indonesia and elsewhere in South Asia, the smith and the smelter are much respected for their secret powers (O'Connor, 1975, pp. 177ff.).

The tools of the African smith share this sacred quality. The hammer, the bellows, and the anvil are considered animate and miraculous; they are regarded as capable of operating by their own magico-religious force, unassisted by the smith. The art of creating tools is essentially superhuman—either divine or demonic (for the smith also forges murderous weapons). Remnants of ancient mythologies belonging to the Stone Age have probably been added to, or woven into, the mythology of metals. The stone tool and the hand ax were charged with a mysterious power; they struck, inflicted injury, caused explosions, and produced sparks, as did the thunderbolt. The ambivalent magic of stone weapons, both lethal and beneficial, like the thunderbolt itself, was transmitted and magnified in the new instruments forged of metal. The hammer, successor to the ax of the Stone Age, becomes the emblem of the powerful storm gods. Indeed, storm gods and the gods of agricultural fecundity are sometimes conceived as smith-gods (for examples, see Eliade, 1978, pp. 92ff.; Dieterlen, 1965, passim).

In many mythologies divine smiths forge the weapons of the gods, thus insuring them victory over dragons or other monstrous beings. [*See* Blades.] In the Canaanite myth, Koshar-wa-Hasis (literally, "adroit-and-clever") forges for Baal two clubs with which he will kill Yamm, lord of the seas and underground waters. In the Egyptian version of the myth, Ptah (the potter god) forges the weapons that enable Horus to conquor Seth. Similarly, in the Vedas, the divine smith Tvaṣṭṛ makes Indra's weapons for his battle with Vṛtra; Hephaistos forges the thunderbolt that will enable Zeus to triumph over Typhon. But the cooperation between the divine smith and the gods is not confined to his help in the final combat for sovereignty of the world.

The smith is also the architect and artisan of the gods, supervises the construction of Baal's palace, and equips the sanctuaries of the other divinities. In addition, this god-smith has connections with music and song, just as in a number of societies the smiths and braziers are also musicians, poets, healers, and magicians. Thus, the mythic African smith is a culture hero. He has been enjoined by God to complete creation, to organize the world, to educate men, that is, to reveal to them the arts and the religious mysteries. For this reason, in many African cultures, smiths play the central role in puberty initiations and in male secret societies. Similarly, in early Greece, certain groups of mythical personages—Telchines, Cabiri, Curetes, Dactyls—were both secret guild associations performing initiations of young boys and corporations of metalworkers (Eliade, 1978, pp. 101ff.). Blacksmiths were equally important in the initiatory rituals of the ancient Germans and in the Japanese male societies. In old Scandinavia there was a close connection between the profession of the smith and the art of the poet and musician. The same associations are to be found among the Turco-Tatars and Mongols, where the smith is linked with horses, singers, and poets. Tzigane nomads are, even today, a combination of smith, tinker, musician, healer, and fortuneteller (ibid., pp. 98ff.). It seems, then, that on many different levels of culture (an indication of great antiquity) there is an intimate connection between the art of the smith, occult techniques (shamanism, magic, healing, etc.), and the arts of song, of the dance, and of poetry.

All these ideas and beliefs articulated around the trades of miners, metallurgists, and smiths have markedly enriched the mythology of *homo faber* inherited from the Stone Age. But the wish to collaborate in the perfecting of matter also had other important consequences. In assuming the responsibility for changing nature, man took the place of time; what would have required eons to ripen in the subterranean depths, as the artisan believed, he could obtain in a few weeks, for the furnace replaced the telluric womb. Millennia later, the alchemist did not think differently. [*See* Alchemy, *overview article.*]

BIBLIOGRAPHY

Aitchison, Leslie. *A History of Metals.* 2 vols. London, 1960. A classic work.

Andrée, Richard. *Die Metalle bei den Naturvölkern mit Berücksichtigung prähistorischer Verhältnisse.* Leipzig, 1884. Outdated but still useful.

Bjorkman, Judith Kingston. *Meteors and Meteorites in the Ancient Near East.* Center for Meteorite Studies, Publication no. 12. Tempe, Ariz., 1973.

Cline, Walter. *Mining and Metallurgy in Negro Africa.* Menasha, Wis., 1937. Indispensable; should be completed and corrected by the most recent publications of French Africanists.

Dieterlen, Germaine. "Contribution à l'étude des forgerons en Afrique occidentale." In *Annuaire, 1965–1966, École Pratique des Hautes Études, cinquième section, Sciences religieuses,* vol. 73, pp. 3–28. Paris, 1966. An important study.

Eliade, Mircea. "Metallurgy, Magic and Alchemy." *Zalmoxis: Revue des études religieuses* 1 (1938): 197–203.

Eliade, Mircea. *The Forge and the Crucible.* 2d ed. Chicago, 1978. Originally published under the title *Forgerons et alchimistes* (Paris, 1956).

Forbes, R. J. *Metallurgy in Antiquity.* Leiden, 1950. A valuable synthesis with an excellent bibliography.

Lechtman, Heather. "Andean Value Systems and the Development of Prehistoric Metallurgy." *Technology and Culture* 25 (January 1984): 1–36. Important.

O'Connor, Stanley J. "Iron Working as Spiritual Inquiry in the Indonesian Archipelago." *History of Religions* 14 (1975): 173–190.

Przyluski, Jean. "L'or, son origine et ses pouvoirs magiques." *Bulletin de l'École Française d'Extreme Orient* 14 (1914): 1–16.

Rickard, T. A. *Man and Metals: A History of Mining in Relation to the Development of Civilizations.* 2 vols. New York, 1932.

Sébillot, Paul. *Les travaux publics et les mines dans les traditions et les superstitions de tous les pays.* Paris, 1894. Old but still useful.

Singer, Charles, Eric J. Holmyard, and A. R. Hall. *A History of Technology,* vol. 1, *From Early Times to the Fall of Ancient Empires.* Oxford, 1954. Indispensable.

MIRCEA ELIADE

METAMORPHOSIS. *See* Shape Shifting.

METAPHYSICS is generally understood as a philosophical inquiry into the fundamental nature of reality. The word *metaphysics* derives from the Greek *meta ta phusica* ("after the things of nature"), a classificatory rubric used by commentators on and editors of Aristotle's corpus to refer to an untitled group of texts concerned with "first philosophy." Western medieval and modern philosophers often have construed metaphysics as the most basic and most comprehensive of philosophical inquiries, one that is primarily focused on the ontological status of objects, the existence of entities that transcend nature, and the generic features exhibited in experience. African and Eastern philosophers usually have conceived of metaphysics (in the sense implied by the word's etymology) as more closely interwoven with the axiological (or value-laden) character of the cosmos and the moral quality of human community.

A distinctive feature of Western metaphysics is the attempt to understand the universe by means of a logical investigation of concepts rather than an empirical inquiry based on sensory evidence. Such metaphysical sentiments rest upon a relative distrust of the variable, visible, and sensible world and involve a quest for the invariable, invisible, and intelligible world. They also assume a basic unity of thought and being, of logic and the world. Rationally coherent and logically consistent systems of thought are believed to reveal the way the world really is.

The origins of Western metaphysics go back to Parmenides of Elea (c. 515–475 BCE). In the poem usually titled *On Nature,* Parmenides provides the first exemplary philosophical argument of Western metaphysics. In the form of a journey to the heavens to receive wisdom from "the goddess," Parmenides attacks the reality of the physical world, condemns difference as illusory, and proposes that fundamental reality is invariable, invisible, and intelligible, as well as single, indivisible, and homogeneous. This metaphysical viewpoint rests upon the deployment of the basic binary opposition of reality and appearance, in which the realm of the former is qualitatively different from and superior to the realm of the latter.

Parmenides' metaphysical conception of being, grounded in his logical reasoning and monistic conclusions, has been a major influence in Western metaphysics. This Parmenidean legacy can be seen in Plotinus's One, Spinoza's God, and Hegel's Absolute. The most immediate influence of Parmenides is found in Plato's *Phaedo,* in which, despite subtle gradations, the reality/appearance distinction is appropriated to undergird the existence of a separate order of Forms accessible only to the mind and more real than the senses. In his heroic efforts to refute the skepticism of the Sophists, Plato (427–347 BCE) extends the ontological binary opposition of reality/appearance to epistemology, morality, and politics, thus including distinctions such as knowledge/opinion, nature/convention, and philosopher/sophist. In this way, Plato's metaphysics, like that of some African and Eastern thinkers, is inseparable from ethics and political philosophy.

The religious significance of Plato's metaphysics is his doctrine of recollection, which defends the immortality of the soul. In *Meno,* Plato portrays Socrates interrogating a slave boy, an interrogation that results in the boy arriving at a geometric truth. Socrates then argues that since this truth was not told to the boy but rather elicited from him, the truth must reside in the boy at birth and in a previous existence: his questions merely prompted the boy to remember what he had forgotten from an earlier life. Similar arguments, related to the existence of a separate order of Forms, are found in the *Phaedo,* while a more speculative account of the transmigration of souls, life after death, and the soul fleeing the bondage of the body is put forward in the tenth book of the *Republic.*

Aristotle (384–322 BCE) set forth the first Western metaphysical system, including a new vocabulary, an articulation of the central issues, and a thorough treatment of these issues. He conceives of metaphysics as a "first philosophy" that investigates the fundamental principles presupposed by the other sciences. Aristotle's metaphysics can be viewed as a profound and persistent polemic against the notions of indeterminacy and infinity. Its aim is to establish a fixed beginning point, the limits of inquiry, the determinateness of concrete individual objects, and the termination of epistemic chains of justification. Aristotelian notions of causality (material, formal, efficient, and final), substance, being, essence, form, and actuality set the terms for Western metaphysical discourse through the twentieth century. The legacy of Aristotle's metaphysics in religious thought is found most clearly in the Christian systematic theology of Thomas Aquinas and the Neo-Thomist tradition of the Catholic church exemplified in thinkers such as Étienne Gilson (1884–1978) and Jacques Maritain (1882–1973).

The last great metaphysical system of classical antiquity was the Neoplatonism best represented by the hellenized Egyptian philosopher Plotinus (205–270 CE), his pupil Porphyry (232–306?), the Syrian school of Iamblichus (250–330?), the Athenian school of Proclus (c. 410–485), and the Latin Christian school of Boethius (480–524). This system (and its various versions) is rooted in

Plato's devaluation of the sensible world and elevation of the intelligible world. Yet, as in certain themes in Plato's second and seventh letters, Neoplatonism promotes a kind of mysticism and asceticism that deeply influenced the Christian theology of the African thinker Augustine (354–430). This mysticism is based on an intuition of the unity and wholeness of being, the One, which differentiates itself downward into lesser degrees in spirits, souls, and, lastly, physical objects. This process of emanation from undifferentiated unity to modes of differentiated disunity results in a return (or epistrophe) to unity and wholeness.

The Syrian philosopher Porphyry not only made Plotinus's lectures available but also wrote a short introduction to Aristotle's *Categories,* entitled *Isagoge,* that directed attention to the relation between the essential and accidental attributes of things and the status of universals. This influential text, translated into Latin by Boethius, provided the framework and language for metaphysical reflection in the early Middle Ages by Christian theologians such as John Scottus Eriugena (fl. 847–877), Anselm (c. 1033–1109), and Bonaventure (c. 1221–1274).

The thirteenth-century translations of Aristotle and his Arabian commentators into Greek and Latin by Robert Grosseteste and William of Moerbeke facilitated the crowning achievement of Western metaphysics in the late Middle Ages: the magisterial system of Thomas Aquinas (c. 1224–1274) and the critical nominalism of William of Ockham (c. 1280/1285–1349?). Thomas creatively appropriated Aristotelian metaphysics into a Christian philosophy, whereas William paved the road for the new "modern way" *(via moderna)* by separating metaphysics from Christian faith and thereby emphasizing religious faith and church tradition. William influenced major figures of the Reformation.

The modern conception of metaphysics in the West begins with René Descartes (1596–1650), who tried to apply the rigor and standards of mathematics and geometry to metaphysical claims. Descartes's quest for indubitability within the immediate awareness of a thinking self and his call for clarity and distinctness in truth-claims reflect an ingenious and influential philosophical response to the rise of modern science, especially the wedding of quantitative models with physics and chemistry. Barukh Spinoza (1632–1677) and Gottfried Wilhelm Leibniz (1646–1716) followed the Cartesian project of scientific rigor and philosophical boldness by setting forth deductive metaphysical systems. Spinoza's mechanical and deterministic view of the universe, in which the only two known attributes of substance are thought and extension, yielded a pantheistic conception of God as identical with nature. This conception would inspire later forms of German idealism. Leibniz's rationalist commitments to *a priori* reasoning, the analysis of concepts according to logical necessity and rational intelligibility, produced refined versions of ontological arguments for the existence of God that sharpened modal logical tools for subsequent efforts by Christian theists.

The crisis of modern Western metaphysics begins with the major empiricists: John Locke (1632–1704), George Berkeley (1685–1753), and, especially, David Hume (1711–1776). All three assumed the Cartesian starting point for philosophical reflection as within the arena of immediate awareness of a thinking self. But in contrast to Descartes, Locke argues that sense impressions are the primary data for knowledge of the world, self, and God. This restriction requires that we cannot have "clear and distinct ideas" of substance and essence, only empirical access to their properties and powers. Therefore, the most privileged notions in traditional Western metaphysics, such as substance and essence, were rendered problematic. Berkeley further questioned the distinction between ideas of objects and properties of objects that cause ideas, thereby radically calling into question material substance. Hume changed the course of Western metaphysics by dissolving philosophical conceptions of the self, subject, and mind into mere bundles of sensations and perceptions. By replacing philosophical notions of necessity and causality with psychological accounts of imagination and sociological notions of habit and custom, Hume defended an inescapable skepticism regarding the possibility of metaphysics. This position presented religious thinkers with the options of a rational agnosticism or a nonrational religious faith.

The significance of Immanuel Kant (1724–1804) lies in his rescue of Western metaphysics by specifying the limits of human knowledge. This rescue took the form of rejecting the dogmatism of Cartesian metaphysical projects and circumscribing the skepticism of Hume's empiricism. The result was a critical idealist metaphysics that preserved the objectivity of knowledge-claims yet prevented human access to ultimate reality. The aim of Kant's metaphysics was to disclose the universal conceptual scheme that people employ in theoretically ordering the world and practically acting within it. For Kant, religious faith became a mere appendage to ethics, a practical postulate for moral behavior.

The last great metaphysical system in the modern West—a response, in part, to Kant—was that of Georg Wilhelm Friedrich Hegel (1770–1831). Like Plato, Aristotle, and the Neoplatonists, Hegel attempted to penetrate to the fundamental nature of reality by means of rational deliberation. Yet he conceived of this reality as a historical and dialectical process intelligible only to the discerning and retrospective philosopher. Hegel's metaphysics emphasized the radical dependence of God upon the world and promoted a divine immanent presence in human history.

Western metaphysics has been under severe attack since Hegel. Apart from the ambitious project of Alfred North Whitehead (1861–1947), the vitalistic program of Henri Bergson (1859–1941), the versions of logical atomism of Bertrand Russell (1872–1970) and the early Ludwig Wittgenstein (1889–1951), and Paul Ricoeur's (b. 1913) recent metaphysics of narrativity, post-Hegelian philosophy has been strongly antimetaphysical. The Christian existentialism of Søren Kierkegaard (1813–1855) and the transcendental phenomenology of Edmund Husserl (1859–1938) inspired the ontological hermeneutics of Martin Heidegger (1889–1976), which claims to have "destroyed" the Western metaphysical tradition. The logical positivism of the Vienna Circle (Otto Neurath, Moritz Schlick, Rudolf Carnap, and others) and ordinary-language philosophy served as stepping-stones for the later Ludwig Wittgenstein's linguistic conventionalism, which claims to have "dodged" the bewitching traps of Western metaphysics. The perspectivism of Friedrich Nietzsche (1844–1900) and the structuralist vocabulary of Ferdinand de Saussure (1857–1913) provided resources for the present-day poststructuralist skepticism of Jacques Derrida (b. 1930), which claims to have "deconstructed" the Western metaphysical tradition. Lastly, the pragmatism of William James (1842–1910) and John Dewey (1859–1952) and the epistemological holism of W. V. Quine (b. 1908) and Nelson Goodman (b. 1906) are employed by Richard Rorty (b. 1931) in his contemporary attempt to "demythologize" the Western metaphysical tradition. Whether the influential attacks of Heidegger, Wittgenstein, Derrida, and Rorty on Western metaphysics are skeptical moments in the history of Western philosophy (like those of Pyrrho and Montaigne in times past) or proleptic precursors of a new stage remains an open question. The religious significance and implications of these attacks—within and outside the West—remain relatively unexplored.

BIBLIOGRAPHY

Ayer, A. J. *Philosophy in the Twentieth Century.* New York, 1982. A noteworthy and well-written sequel to Bertrand Russell's *A History of Western Philosophy* (1945) by a major figure active on the contemporary scene since the 1930s.

Hancock, Roger. "Metaphysics, History of." In *The Encyclopedia of Philosophy,* edited by Paul Edwards, vol. 5. New York, 1967. The best short and concise article-length treatment of major historical developments in Western metaphysics. An extensive bibliography on central figures and periods is included.

Passmore, John. *A Hundred Years of Philosophy.* 2d ed. Middlesex, England, 1970. The most comprehensive and detailed history of academic Western philosophy dealing with post-Hegelian developments. Reliable reportage and exposition, but lacks an overarching interpretive framework.

Rorty, Richard. *Philosophy and the Mirror of Nature.* Princeton, 1979. A highly provocative, imaginative, and learned interpretation of Western philosophy that puts forward devastating critiques of metaphysics.

Russell, Bertrand. *A History of Western Philosophy.* New York, 1945. The most informative, stimulating, and engaging history of Western philosophy available in one volume in English, by one of the most brilliant thinkers of the twentieth century.

CORNEL WEST

METEMPSYCHOSIS. *See* Transmigration.

METEOROLOGICAL BEINGS. Religious people of very different times and cultures have tended to "humanize" meteorological phenomena by telling stories about the displays of celestial power and fruitfulness they witnessed, converting those events into elements of a sacred narrative intended to explain how the world and humankind have come to be the way they are. The experience of life in a properly religious world differs radically from our experience of life today. For one thing, it makes no distinction between the natural and human realms. Whereas for us a storm is invariably an "it," the storm has been much more a "thou" for the better part of human history. It is not the storm that religious people have worshiped but the sacred power, will, and qualities that are somehow revealed there, although it would be quite incorrect to speak of the "personification" of inanimate nature or, for that matter, to invoke some sort of animistic theory to explain why meteorological phenomena play the important roles in religious life that they do. For religious people, storms are everywhere manifestations of the sacred. [*See* Hierophany.] As such they engage the whole human person—meaning his or her emotional, imaginative, and intellectual faculties taken together—in a vital relationship.

Moreover, the various qualities of storm and rain have suggested, both to our religious forebears and to our contemporaries living in the so-called traditional societies, countless analogies that have enabled them to express—perhaps even to discover—certain important truths about their experience of life and their religious aspirations. For example, by analogy with atmospheric lightning, Iglulik Inuit shamans refer to a mystical experience called *qaumaneq* ("lightning" or "illumination") that confers clairvoyance. Indeed, lightning, or dreams about it, typically figures in shamanic initiations or callings; and by the same token the rapidity or suddenness of spiritual "illumination" has been compared to lightning in many of the religions of history.

Storms have both a benign, life-sustaining aspect, because they bring rain, and a dark, chaotic one, owing to their potential for destruction. The high winds and distant roll of thunder that in one instance may announce an imminent end to prolonged drought may in another have inspired an apocalyptic vision, or a collective memory preserved in myth, of the world's complete destruction by flood. The storm gods, for their part, often garner trust as senders of the moisture upon which living things depend, but just as often they are feared as agents of divine punishment, retribution, or simply inexplicable malevolence. Symbols derived from the phenomena of storm thus express quite effectively humankind's deeply rooted ambivalence toward the sacred. Or, put another way, they express the profound anxiety that men and women have felt about the sacred powers that sustain the world, powers over which human beings have little if any control.

Finally, and what is most important, storm symbols function the way other religious symbols do in making it possible for the human situation to be translated into cosmological terms and vice versa. They reveal a fundamental oneness between human life and the structure of the world and so have led people out of their isolation in subjectivity, beyond the human condition as it were, toward a stance vis-à-vis their own experience of life that one could easily describe as a kind of transcendence. That much, at least, accounts for the essentially religious character of these symbols.

In this article I propose to continue the morphological description of sky symbols begun elsewhere, concentrating now on the divine figures connected with dramatic meteorological events, chiefly thunder, lightning, and rain. [*See also* Sky.] No single explanation can account for the uniformity and variety of the storm gods in history. Some are also supreme beings, some appear in animal guise. All of them display in varying proportions what I have chosen to call "two kinds of sovereignty," the one more "spiritual" and derived from the ideas and values associated with the sky and sky gods, the other more "physical" and connected with the earth and its fertility.

Storm Deities and Their Forms. If all the sky gods were arranged on a line according to their dominant powers and attributes, the result would be a broad array with, at one end, deities who display most fully the characteristics that make them creators, sovereigns, lords of the universe, law givers, and moral overseers. To the second half of the array would belong a collection of progressively more varied and colorful deities whose chief traits describe a generative, vitalizing mission in the world. These latter are typically male deities, often spouses of the Great Mother, and givers of rain, hence prone to develop into more specialized storm gods and fecundators. All are epiphanies of force and violence, those necessary sources of energy on which biological life and civil order in the world depend; and, over a broad geographical expanse throughout Africa, Europe, and Asia, many have a connection with the bull. (The bull and the thunderbolt appear historically very early in connection with the storm gods. The Kannada word *ko,* which means "ox, sky, or lightning, ray of light, water, horn, mountain," preserves intact the full semantic range of this complex of symbols.)

The so-called specialization of the sky gods either in the direction of *dei otiosi* or into the gods of storm and rain derives from the ambivalent structure of the sky symbols generally and has led scholars to speak of the "passive," transcendent nature of the sky gods and, conversely, of their tendency to give way to more active, vital divine forms. Of course nowhere in history does one find either specialized type, the far-off ruler whose celestial attributes predominate, or the storm god-fecundator, in isolation; invariably there are mixtures of the two. Sometimes both functions belong to a single deity's sphere of activity; elsewhere a rather clear division of labor prevails, with the storm god usually subordinate to a celestial ruler who is often the storm god's father. In certain cases the storm deity represents the exercise of legitimate force on behalf of some higher authority; in other cases his link with agriculture is more important.

Specialization usually brings with it a radical change of form: that is, the storm gods can be said to have abandoned absolute transcendence in favor of powers and attributes that did not belong to their original celestial make-up. For that reason they are apt to betray foreign influences too. For example, Parjanya, the Indian god of hurricanes and son of Dyaus, the ancient Indo-Aryan sky god, was said to rule the waters and all living things. He made the whole universe tremble with his storms. His specialization, though, rendered him no longer omniscient like his father (with whom the authors of the *Ṛgveda* sometimes confused him) nor a sovereign like Varuṇa. As a result, in Vedic times he yielded his place to Indra, a warrior king, also god of rain and easily the chief god of the *Ṛgveda.* Indra, for his part, is always compared to a bull or a ram, two animals associated with Rudra, a non-Aryan divinity, many of whose attributes Indra would absorb over the course of time. In fact Indra's connection with bulls, *soma,* and the Maruts (to the degree they personified the wandering souls of the dead) would suggest that he also acquired certain lunar prerogatives: that is, Indra *qua* symbol expanded in the direction of a larger integrated expression of life's power and sacrality, one that included even elements belonging to the symbolism of the moon.

The point is that storm gods, no matter how early in time they appear and no matter what type of culture they belong to, always show evidence of long and complicated histories. Thus, in using the term *specialization* here to account for the forms the storm gods take, I do not mean to imply that storm, rain, and fertility gods are necessarily late developments, for we have no reason to doubt the antiquity of dramatic, stormy elements in the sky god's make-up. There is a unity of structure to the sky symbolism that we can only assume has been present from the very beginning, and that unified structure includes both distant supreme soverignty and active, even violent, involvement with life processes in the human world.

Meteorological Phenomena as Attributes of a Supreme Being. Some religious people have seen none other than the supreme sky diety behind the stormy atmospheric displays that, for them, attest to his all-knowing presence, will, and power. The Andaman Islanders know such a deity in Puluga, whose breath is the wind and whose voice is thunder. Hurricanes signal his anger, and lightning bolts are the punishment he executes against those who violate his laws.

The tribes of Southeast Australia report that Baiame created all things out of nothing, but Baiame is creative in another sense, for in causing the rain to fall he makes the whole earth new and green. Natives can discern his voice in thunder. On the east coast of Australia other tribes worship Daramulun, who also speaks in thunder and sends them rain. Daramulun is said to have created the first ancestor during his stay on earth, giving him the laws and customs that have passed from one generation to the next ever since. Most importantly, Daramulun left behind the initation ceremony, which entails, among other things, a solemn display of the bull-roarer, said to make a noise like thunder and to represent the supreme being's continued presence among his people. Indeed, almost all the Australian sky gods communicate their presence in thunder, lightning, the wind and the rainbow, which is to say that meteorological traits belong inseparably to their supreme, celestial modes of being.

The Ambivalence of the Storm Deities: Creativity and Chaos. Stormy attributes help to express the dual nature of supreme beings, who on account of their power over life and death are apt to inspire both trust and fear in equal measure. For example, the Maasai of Kenya pray to a supreme being named Ngai ("sky" or "rain") who lives high above our world where the winds circulate through his nostrils. Lightning is the dreadful glance of his eye, thunder a cry of joy at something he has seen, and raindrops are the joyful tears he sheds at the sight of fat beehives during the rainy season when cattle grow sleek. By analogy with the sky's polychrome appearance, the Maasai refer to a black, red, gray, and white Ngai, but they ultimately reduce those four to the black and red Ngai alone, two opposed and complementary forms of deity. The black Ngai is good because, like the black, cloudy sky, he brings rain; whereas the red Ngai, like the red, hot sky, withholds it. (In Babylonian mythology it is the gigantic bird Imdugud that rescued human beings from drought. It covered the sky with the black storm clouds of its wings and consumed the Bull of Heaven, whose hot breath had scorched the crops down below.)

The Inca of pre-Columbian times worshiped Illapa (whom the Aymara knew as Thunupa). Both dreaded as a storm god and adored as a bringer of rain, Illapa was pictured as a man with club and sling who draws water from a heavenly stream (the Milky Way) using pitchers that he leaves in the safekeeping of his sister until he breaks them with his thunder club.

By some early accounts the Aztec rain god Tlaloc has four pitchers, and according to the one he uses, the result will be a good maize crop or a harvest spoiled by vermin and frost. No Aztec deity enjoyed a more active or widespread cult than he. Tlaloc, the giver of rain, but also the wrathful deity of lightning, was conceived in multiple form as *tlaloques* (lesser, sometimes dwarflike, storm deities) assigned to the four directions, or as the leader of a group of *tlaloques,* who were said to dwell on mountaintops in caves, where storm clouds brew. Descriptions of Tlaloc's heavenly paradise supply further clues about his ambiguous nature. It is a place of infinite abundance and perpetual verdure where those who had died by drowning or had been struck by lightning or were suffering from such afflictions as leprosy, venereal disease, skin ailments, gout, and dropsy enjoyed eternal happiness. They were the only dead whom the Aztec did not bury; all others were cremated.

According to Juan Ignacio Molina and other writers of the second half of the eighteenth century, the Mapuche knew a supreme being with many forms of address. One of his epithets, "two faces" (black and white), apparently referred to the rain and sunshine prayed for in public rites but also to the deity's ambivalent attitude—both indulgent and severe—toward his worshipers. Older sources dating back to the seventeenth century call this deity Pillán; he was said to produce thunder and lightning and all manner of violent and destructive weather phenomena such as volcanic eruptions, river floods, tidal waves, and epidemics. On the other hand, Pillán was considered a protector of the crops and hence a beneficent weather god as well.

Two Kinds of Sovereignty. It is not uncommon for storm gods to display this dual character, especially in parts of the world where sudden, unpredictable shows of meteorological force dominate the landscape and must surely have compelled people to theological reflection. For example, by contrast with the reassuring periodicity of the Egyptian cosmos, the environment in which Mesopotamian civilization grew and flourished could only have led men and women to conclude that order was not a given but rather something to be achieved through the continual integration of many different competing wills, each one powerful and frightening. As a result, the Mesopotamians envisioned a huge cosmic state that included human beings, animals, inanimate objects, natural phenomena, and even such abstractions as justice, righteousness, and the form of a circle. An assembly of gods presided over this "state," led by Anu (An), the god of heaven, and next to him in rank, Enlil his son, the god of storm. So far as the Mesopotamians were concerned, Enlil had revealed himself both in nature and in history. The violence that fills a storm and is expressed there *was* Enlil.

But a meteorological analogy also made it possible to interpret such catastrophic events as the destruction of Ur by the Elamite hordes sweeping down from the eastern highlands as Enlil's handiwork too: that is, in some deeper, truer sense those barbarians were also a storm, Enlil's storm, in and through which the god himself had executed a verdict passed on Ur and its people by the divine assembly. In keeping with the Mesopotamian vision of a cosmic bureaucracy, Enlil's specialized juridical role was distinguished from that of another diety, Enki, known as "lord of the earth," who administered the waters, specifically, rivers, canals, irrigation, and the organization of all productive forces. Enki's ministerial role derived from the sovereignty exercised by Anu and Enlil. Anu and, later, Marduk represent the magical or "spiritual" component of that sovereignty, whereas Enlil's sovereignty is of a more physical kind; and the latter's stormy attributes, though in this case they have little to do directly with fertility, have everything to do with the problem of legitimate force, especially the legitimate force that must have been an important concern—and a deep source of anxiety—for the citizens of such a highly regulated cosmos.

While it is true that in many cases the sky god withdrew in favor of storm gods and other divinities with more specific and concrete functions, in other instances the sky god assumed a new role. That is certainly what happened in the Greek and Roman traditions, where Zeus and Jupiter stood for both kinds of sovereignty, being at once divine guarantors of cosmic order, supreme rulers, moral arbiters, even personifications of law, as well as gods of rain and fertility. Zeus preserves in his name the Sankrit root *div* ("shine" or "day"), leaving no doubt as to his celestial nature and shared heritage with the ancient Indo-European sky god Dyaus. However, scholars in the past were so quick to seize upon the etymology of Zeus's name as the key to his religious significance that they usually inquired no further into Zeus's unique and complicated mode of being, much of it vividly expressed in his meteorological attributes.

The many epithets for Zeus in Homer explain why he came to be equated with weather deities elsewhere in Asia Minor: he is called at various times Ombrios and Hyetios ("the rainy one"), Ourios ("he who sends favorable winds"), Astrapios ("sender of lightning"), and Bronton ("thunderer"). Other epithets tell of an affinity with crops and the dark earth: Georgos ("the farmer"), Chthonios ("earth-dweller"), and even Zeus Katachthonios ("the underground Zeus"). Zeus's theriomorphic aspect—he is sometimes a bull, as in the myth of Europa, or a wolf to whom sacrifice was performed in time of drought or storm—is further evidence of his link to agriculture and rain.

The transforming quality of lightning that accounts for its role in shamanic initiations may help to explain yet another of Zeus's prerogatives, for whatever was used to purify from sin and much of what pertained to rites of initiation fell directly or indirectly under his control. Lightning marked his direct epiphany, and wherever it struck, a sanctuary was raised to Zeus Descending.

The whole complex of ideas, powers, and attributes belonging to Zeus's stormy aspect reappears on a different level of symbolic expression in the divine twins. The Dioscuri, or "Zeus's sons," like many other pairs of mythic twins, issued from the union of a god and a human mother and thus represented in a peculiar way the sacrality of the sky god on earth. In the Indo-European tradition, the twins are usually sons of the sky god, warriors, magic healers, saviors, and fertility gods; as gods of light, they are often associated with the dawn, the morning and evening stars, and the pair, thunder and lightning. The Dioscuri, for example, became popular as rescuers from personal distress, especially from danger at sea. Saint Elmo's fire, the electric discharge from the ship's mast during a thunderstorm, was widely regarded as their corporeal epiphany. Also, like Herakles, they were said to have been initiated at Eleusis. The various pairs of divine twins in the Indo-European tradition—the Germanic Freyr and Njǫrð, the Vedic Aśvins, and the Dioscuri, to name three—were invoked to witness the swearing of oaths. Likewise, at Olympia a statue of Zeus Horkios ("Zeus of the oath"), before which competitors took their oaths, had in either hand thunderbolts with which to punish false swearers; and according to the Homeric formulas of oaths, Zeus was always the first deity called upon to guarantee an oath and punish any violation that might occur.

In ancient Rome when a building was struck by lightning, fulgural ritual prescribed that an opening be made in the roof over the spot so that the god could always have free access to the place he had chosen for his sanctuary. The most solemn oath was that sworn in the name of Iuppiter Lapis ("Jupiter present in the thunderstone"). The sacred stone was used when the *fetiales* took an oath and made sacrifices upon allying themselves with a foreign power. We know from Vergil that such an alliance received its highest sanction from the storm god himself. The priest, pronouncing a curse on the contractor who should first violate the sacred compact, hurled the stone at the sacrificial swine saying, "Jupiter, strike down the Romans as I now strike this pig, and strike them more heavily, for your power is greater than mine." This action represented in ritual form the stroke of lighting, and it has survived into the twentieth century in the practice of Masurian (East Prussian) peasants who hurl a stone ax in a ritually designated manner against the door to protect their homes from lightning. Comparable practices are documented for other traditions.

Yahveh developed along lines that in some ways parallel the development of Zeus and Jupiter. Throughout the history of Israel, he shows himself a god of sky and storm, omnipotent creator, absolute sovereign, author of the norms and laws that make human life possible and good. By contrast Indra's exaggeratedly "physical" sovereignty develops into a personification of cosmic and biological energy. Indra is not a creator; instead the creative function is specialized in Indra's case into a generative, vitalizing one. Of course the *Ṛgveda* does feature a sky father called Dyaus Pitṛ, a cognate form of *Zeus Pater* and *Jupiter,* but by Vedic times Indra had already assumed the role of celestial sovereign in India, and storms are the supreme manifestations of his creative force. He wields the thunderbolt, frees the waters, absorbs fabulous amounts of *soma,* fertilizes the fields and bestows fertility on human women, displays fantastic sexual powers himself, and leads an army of lesser storm gods, the Maruts, to victory for the Indo-Aryan invaders.

The Germanic deities Óðinn (Odin) and Þórr (Thor) offer a clear example of a storm god's specialized function and the two kinds of sovereignty implicit in this cosmic division of labor. Óðinn belongs primarily to a category of divine sovereigns that includes the Chinese T'ien, the Indian Varuṇa, and Ahura Mazdā of Zoroastrian belief, although in the course of his development, he took on certain attributes of agricultural and fertility gods as well, becoming in the process a chthonian master of the souls of dead heroes. Óðinn typifies what the great Indo-Europeanist Georges Dumézil has called "the magical sovereign" because, like Varuṇa, he employs the power to bind and discerns the future. Þórr, on the other hand, god of tempests and combat, represents a second, more physical and less spiritual, kind of sovereignty, and his "physicality" takes in more than his martial qualities. Modern Scandinavian folklore studies, the remnants of old agrarian cults, and archaeological findings have all tended to prove that Þórr was originally much more than a warrior. Through rain, the happy side-effect of his atmospheric battles and the exploits of his hammer, he assisted the growth of crops; and Swedish peasant names for him recall the Saami (Lapp) cult dedicated to a fertility god who gives rain or sun according to the needs of the soil and sees to it that growing things mature and bear fruit.

Storm Animals. The world's mythology and folklore describe a whole host of animals associated with thunder, lightning, and rain. The goat, the ram, or horses, for example, frequently accompany the storm god or pull his thundering vehicle across the sky. But the most common and widespread of the storm animals are probably the thunderbird or woodpecker, the dragon, and the bull.

North American Indians worship various supernatural beings in avian guise who produce thunder by the whir of their wings and lightning with flashes—a winking or twinkling—of their eyes (Cree, Hare, Tlingit, and other tribes). The distribution of this thunderbird belief is very wide, but the kind of bird in question ranges from a crane (Pawnee), jackpine partridge (Beaver), or humming bird (Lilloet) to a gigantic eagle (Sauk, Hare, and others). In eastern North America, the thunderbirds are typically four in number, one for each of the cardinal directions; and over the same region, they are considered to be locked in a cosmic struggle with evil water spirits, panthers, or horned serpents. This antagonism on the level of myth finds cultic expression in the division into sacred moieties characteristic of the eastern tribes who rely on agriculture for their subsistence. However, it may also reflect a dualism known elsewhere in world mythology that usually pits the thunder god against a reptilian water monster (the way Indra opposes Vṛtra or the way Marduk battles Tiamat). The same sort of struggle recurs, for example, in northern Siberia and among the Buriats around Lake Baikal, this time between the ruler of birds (a great eagle) and a many-headed water snake. The thunderbird motif also appears in the Gran Chaco, in Ecuador, and among the Carib-speaking peoples on the northern coast of South America. In fact the thunderbird's range would seem to indicate it was a much more vital presence in the minds and hearts of religious people in earlier times than now.

Across Europe, around the Mediterranean, and in parts of Inner Asia, at least, the woodpecker was believed to have supernatural powers because of its association with thunder, rain, and fertility. There is much evidence to suggest that the belief arose in Neolithic times with the spread of cultivation by means of the hoe and, later, the plow. In many places the woodpecker also has a connection with divine twins and, like the storm gods, with war and agriculture. For example, according to Roman legend Romulus and Remus were cared for not only by the she-wolf but also by the woodpecker; and Mars, god of war and at one time a god of agriculture, was said to have fathered the two by the vestal virgin Rhea Silvia. In other words the woodpecker has a dual nature corresponding to the storm's ambivalent values: destructive power and fertility.

Among the classes of dragons in China, there is first the dragon *(chiao)*, originally an evil, snakelike creature that lived and always stayed in water. Then there is a river-god dragon, the *lung-wang*, a form strongly influenced by the Indian *nāga*, originally a snake and, in fact, a version of the *chiao* that spread to India along with other elements of coastal culture. Under Indian influence the *chiao* dragon became a *lung-wang*, or river god, with cults in many places along major waterways in China.

The *lung* dragon associated with storms is neither the dragon *chiao* nor the *lung-wang*. It too lives in water but has the unique ability to ascend to Heaven in the springtime and to summer there as the rain dragon. The *lung* can frequently be seen in the sky during thunderstorms and is basically a benevolent animal that produces rain and ensures fertility. In the Chinese classics it sometimes corresponds to Heaven itself and therefore also to the emperor. (Later Chinese myths describe a thunder god whose characteristics derive from the wild boar, the promoter of wet-field agriculture.)

The mythologies of India, Africa, Europe, and Asia regularly associate a divine bull with the gods of the atmosphere and fertility, Indra and Rudra being two such examples. In pre-Aryan India the cults of Mohenjo-Daro and Baluchistan included important bull cults, and temples dedicated to Śiva are full of his bovine images. At Ur in the third millennium, the god of the atmosphere was a bull; in ancient Assyria men swore by a god in the form of a bull; and the supremacy achieved by such storm gods as Teshub, Hadad, and Baal in the religions of the Near East is notable for their connections with bulls. What is venerated in these and other bull gods of lightning who are married to the great earth goddess is both their transcendence, expressed in violent weather phenomena, and their physical potential as fecundators. In other words the interdependence of the "celestial" and "generative" functions in the figure of the bull seems abundantly clear. The same could be said of storm gods and of every storm hierophany.

[*See also* Rain; Clouds; and *entries on specific deities mentioned herein.*]

BIBLIOGRAPHY

I do not know of a monograph devoted to the storm gods or to the symbolism of meteorological phenomena. One general source, however, is Mircea Eliade's "The Sky and Sky Gods," chapter 2 of his *Patterns in Comparative Religion* (New York, 1958), pp. 38–123. A bibliography devoted specifically to storm gods in the Near East and their relation to the bull can be found on page 120. Other general sources are James G. Frazer's *The Worship of Nature*, vol. 1 (New York, 1926), Raffaele Pettazzoni's *The All Knowing God*, translated by H. J. Rose (London, 1956), and C. Blinkenberg's *The Thunderweapon in Religion and Folklore* (1911; New York, 1977).

Literature on the divine twins is quite extensive. Two old but still fascinating studies are Rendel Harris's *The Cult of the Heavenly Twins* (Cambridge, 1906) and *Boanerges* (Cambridge, 1913). For excellent bibliographies on the subject, see Donald J. Ward's *The Divine Twins: An Indo-European Myth in Germanic Tradition* (Berkeley, 1968) and Raymond Kuntzmann's *Le symbolisme des jumeaux au Proche-Orient ancien: Naissance, fonction, et évolution d'un symbole* (Paris, 1983).

On the range of the thunderbird belief, see Trumen Michelson's *Contributions to Fox Ethnology II*, United States Bureau of American Ethnology (Washington, D.C., 1930), pp. 51–56. For its religious meanings, a reliable source is Åke Hultkrantz's *Religions of the American Indians*, translated by Monica Setterwall (Berkeley, 1979).

On the woodpecker as a thunderbird, see "The Thunderbird," chapter 6 of Edward A. Armstrong's *The Folklore of Birds: An Enquiry into the Origin and Distribution of Some Magico-Religious Traditions*, 2d ed., rev. & enl. (New York, 1970), pp. 94–112. See also Rendel Harris's *Picus Who Is Also Zeus* (Cambridge, 1916).

The standard work on the dragon in China and Japan is still M. W. de Visser's *The Dragon in China and Japan* (Amsterdam, 1913). A more recent and probably more useful source is Wolfram Eberhard's *The Local Cultures of South and East China*, translated by Alide Eberhard (Leiden, 1968), pp. 238–250.

PETER C. CHEMERY

METHODIST CHURCHES. Methodism arose from the search of John Wesley and his brother Charles for a deepened religious life within the ordered ways of the Church of England, which John described as "the best constituted national church in the world." He sought no drastic reform in doctrines but rather a greater emphasis upon a personal experience of God's saving and perfecting grace and more opportunity for a spiritual quest within Christian groups, undeterred by denominational barriers. He downplayed the divisive element of his movement, publishing in 1742 an elaboration of Clement of Alexandria's description of a perfect Christian as *The Character of a Methodist* and offering this simple definition in his *Complete English Dictionary* (1753): "A Methodist, one that lives according to the method laid down in the Bible."

John Wesley, both as the living leader and later as the almost legendary "Mr. Wesley" of "the people called Methodists," so greatly influenced the developing thought and churchmanship of Methodism that he demands a far greater proportion of attention than if he had been the mere titular founder of a new denomination.

After his heart was "strangely warmed" on 24 May 1738, Wesley began to preach salvation by faith with the conviction of personal experience, and he gathered around him an organized society in London, the first of many that spread throughout the British Isles. These societies were intended to supplement, not supplant, the worship of the church. In his *Rules* (1743) he argued that a society was simply "a company of men 'having the form, and seeking the power of godliness,' united in order to pray together, to receive the word of exhortation, and to watch over one another in love, that they may help each other to work out their salvation." There was only one condition for membership, "a desire . . . to be saved from [their] sins." To test and reinforce his followers' sincerity, however, the *Rules* insisted that members should avoid evil, do good, and seek holiness, for which illustrative examples were given in all three categories.

In order to proclaim his message and administer his societies Wesley enrolled a steadily increasing number of lay preachers to join the handful of sympathetic clergy who engaged in an itinerant evangelical ministry under his supervision. In 1744 he called these together in London to confer about doctrine and organization. This was the first annual conference of Wesley's Methodism, although the Welsh Calvinistic wing of the movement, who looked to George Whitefield as their chief inspirer, had been holding their "Associations" for several years.

The primary purpose of the Conferences of 1744–1747 was to formulate the major doctrinal emphases of Methodist preaching: salvation by grace through faith, confirmed and exemplified by good works; the witness of the Holy Spirit to a person's salvation from the penalties of past sin and to his power over present temptations to sin; and the theoretical possibility of personal triumph over temptation, under the title of Christian perfection, which Wesley defined as perfect love to God and man, though consistent with human error and with no guarantee of permanence. These doctrines, as taught and illustrated in Wesley's first four volumes of *Sermons* (1744–1760) and his *Explanatory Notes upon the New Testament* (1755), formed the basis of all Methodist preaching.

The early Conferences also consolidated the organization of Methodism into a "connexion," a network of societies served by lay preachers itinerating regularly on a circuit, or round, covering a district such as a county in tours lasting from four to six weeks, but also itinerating between circuits periodically—at first every three months, then every six, and eventually every year. Each year Wesley's own preaching and administrative journeys took him over most of England. In 1747 Ireland was added to his tour, and in 1751, Scotland. Wesley and his itinerant preachers developed a strong family identity among the societies.

This connexional unity became so strong that in 1749 Wesley published two sets of extracts from the minutes of his conferences, each with the same title—*Minutes of Some Late Conversations between the Revd. Mr. Wesleys and Others*—one summarizing Methodist teaching, the other Methodist organization. In effect they constituted a declaration that Methodism had become an established ecclesiastical body. Inevitably this process of consolidation aroused much criticism of Methodism: the preachers' teaching, so unfamiliar to non-Methodists, was incorrectly described as unorthodox; their vigor, warmth, and ebullience were pejoratively labeled "enthusiasm"; and Wesley's unconventional preaching in the open air and in other men's parishes, and, worse still, his authorizing laymen to preach, were regarded by even sympathetic clergy as a grave breach of ecclesiastical order. Preachers and people were occasionally mobbed, but the somewhat quiescent church authorities took no concerted action.

The chief threat, indeed, came from within the movement. The people's desire to receive the sacraments from their preachers fed the preachers' natural ambitions to improve their status and to transform the society into a church. John Wesley was inclined to let things run their course, but the vehement opposition of his brother Charles led him to tighten the rein on his preachers, most of whom from 1752 onward signed agreements "never to leave the communion of the Church of England without the consent of all whose names are subjoined." Avowed separation from the church was narrowly averted at the Conference of 1755, when all agreed "that (whether it was *lawful* or not) it was no ways *expedient*." This deferred any open separation for almost thirty years.

Meanwhile British immigrants, especially from Ireland, brought Methodism to America, where it became so firmly rooted that Wesley responded to their plea for help by sending out matched pairs of itinerant preachers in 1769, 1771, 1773, and 1774, of whom by far the best known and most influential was Francis Asbury, who remained throughout the Revolutionary War (1775–1783). With some difficulty Asbury persuaded the American Methodists not to sever their ties with Wesley in their eagerness for religious independence, and thus Wesley himself was able to assist Americans in the birth of the first independent church within Methodism.

The year 1784 was "that grand climacteric year of Methodism." Aided by Dr. Thomas Coke, Wesley prepared a deed poll that legally defined the term *Conference*, and made that body heir to British Methodism after Wesley's death. Wesley also entrusted to Coke a major part in publishing a revision of *The Book of Common Prayer* for the use of American Methodists, and discussed with him a complementary plan for securing a threefold ministry in American Methodism. Already convinced that in any ecclesiastical emergency the power of ordination resided in presbyters, Wesley ordained two of his preachers, first as deacons and then as elders. With their assistance he then commissioned Coke as "superintendent" of the American flock, with instructions to share his new authority with Asbury upon his arrival in America.

At the "Christmas Conference" in Baltimore (1784–1785) with Wesley's blessing, a new denomination was launched, the Methodist Episcopal Church. In England Methodism still remained a society, governed by a presbyter of the Church of England and at least theoretically within the fold of that church. After Wesley's death in 1791, however, under the terms of his deed poll, the Conference of preachers became the ruling body, with a modified presbyterian system of government rather than the modified episcopalian polity that was being developed in America. Although some of Wesley's Anglican friends had occasionally referred to "the Methodist church" during his lifetime, not until 1893 did the class tickets indicating membership in the Wesleyan Methodist Society carry the word *church.*

When in 1739 Wesley had written, "I look upon *all the world* as *my parish*," he was defending his disregard of ecclesiastical boundaries in Britain, but in fact he did also cherish a vision of a world renewed in the image of Christ, and was convinced that his liberal, pragmatic approach to theology and to churchmanship should make good missionaries of his people—as indeed it did. He heartily supported Coke's missionary plans, and a month before his death wrote to a native American preacher, "Lose no opportunity of declaring to all men that the Methodists are one people in all the world." Within a century after Wesley's death immigrants and missionaries from both sides of the Atlantic had planted Methodism on each continent and in almost every country.

Methodist missionary expansion during the nineteenth century varied little whether it came from the British or the American type of church polity, because polity was overshadowed by ethos, and the ethos sprang from Wesley. Methodists everywhere remained within a tightly knit "connexion" governed by a conference. They followed Wesley in assigning major responsibilities to laymen, and were progressive in enrolling women as leaders, and even as preachers. They emphasized evangelical preaching and continued to experiment with an adventurous and flexible organization. While making good use of their rich heritage of Charles Wesley's hymns they observed those almost uniquely Methodist forms of worship, the watch-night, the covenant service, and the love-feast, as well as the close fellowship of the class-meeting and the bands, with their cherished tickets of membership. They constantly remembered their early rules, by "avoiding evil of every kind—especially that which is most generally practised," and by "doing good of every possible sort, and as far as is possible to all men."

It is true that the full appreciation of some of these features fell off even during the nineteenth century, and a few were almost forgotten in the twentieth, such as Wesley's constant charge, "Press on to perfection." Human frailty brought about fragmentation into many independent denominations, a process furthered during the twentieth century by the hiving off of national churches from the parent bodies.

The first major division in England, the Methodist New Connexion (1797), was a revolt against the autocracy of the leading Wesleyan preachers, but the Primitive Methodists (1811) and Bible Christians (1819), though also favoring more lay leadership, left because they wished to restore evangelism. The Wesleyan Methodist hierarchy came under increasing attack from 1849 onward in a disruptive pamphlet warfare that led to eventual democratic reforms at the cost of losing many thousands of members. Happily, some of these breaches were progressively healed through the formation of the United Methodist Free Churches in 1857, the United

Methodist Church in 1907, and the Methodist Church in 1932.

In America, where membership had almost drawn level with that in the British Isles by Wesley's death, Methodism expanded and divided far more rapidly than in Britain during the nineteenth and twentieth centuries. The controversy over the institution of slavery and other disruptive forces similar to those in England were at work in America. Coke and Asbury had unsuccessfully sought to eradicate slavery from the Methodist Episcopal Church, but even in the abolitionist strongholds of New York and Philadelphia race remained an issue among Methodists. There, blacks forsook their second-class membership to form their own congregations, which eventually became the African Methodist Episcopal Church (1816) and the African Methodist Episcopal Zion Church (1820), each with a community of over a million in the 1980s. In 1844 the whole Methodist Episcopal Church split into north and south over the issue, though other factors also were at work, including varying views of the episcopacy. In 1870 the Methodist Episcopal Church South blessed the incorporation of their own black members into the Colored (now "Christian") Methodist Episcopal Church. Slavery was also a factor in the formation of the Wesleyan Methodist Connection (1843), which did not name itself a "church" until 1947, and which also sought a return to earlier Wesleyan evangelism and the abolition of the episcopacy. The Free Methodist Church (1860) arose after lengthy preliminaries from a widespread desire to recover Wesley's teaching upon Christian perfection. A similar emphasis within American Methodism upon the need to recover scriptural holiness led to the piecemeal formation of the Church of the Nazarene.

In American Methodism and its missions, as well as in the British Commonwealth, a measure of consolidation took place during the nineteenth and twentieth centuries, notably in the union of the northern and southern churches with the Protestant Methodists in 1939 to form the Methodist Church, which in 1968 united with the Evangelical United Brethren (itself a union of churches with a German-speaking background) to form the United Methodist Church, with a membership of eleven million out of a total world Methodist community of something like fifty million.

These and other unions were consummated largely because of the coming together in Christian fellowship of representatives from dozens of autonomous Methodist churches and missions from all over the world, first decennially from 1881 in the Ecumenical Methodist Conference, then quinquennially from 1951 in the World Methodist Council. Welcome guests at these gatherings are representatives from churches where Methodism has subsumed its identity in an interdenominational union, such as the United Church of Canada (1925), the Churches of North and South India, the Uniting Church in Australia, or other such unions in Belgium, China, Ecuador, Japan, Pakistan, the Philippines, and Zambia. As an important element in the World Council of Churches, Methodism remains true to the spirit of its founder, who gloried in the catholicity of his early societies, open to persons of all creeds, and who firmly maintained, in spite of attacks by his critics, that "orthodoxy, or right opinions, is at best but a very slender part of religion."

[*See also the biographies of the Wesleys, Asbury, Coke, and Whitefield.*]

BIBLIOGRAPHY

A valuable summary of the history, doctrines, spread, activities, and leaders of Methodism in its many branches through more than two centuries can be found in *The Encyclopedia of World Methodism*, 2 vols., edited by Nolan B. Harmon (Nashville, 1974). The unplanned development of Methodism from a movement into a denomination is described by Frank Baker in *John Wesley and the Church of England* (Nashville, 1970). Fuller details of some British aspects of Methodism, especially in their later stages, are given in *A History of the Methodist Church in Great Britain*, 3 vols. to date, edited by Rupert Davies and Gordon Rupp (London, 1965–1984), and the rise and development of the main stream in the United States is portrayed in *The History of American Methodism*, 3 vols., edited by Emory Stevens Bucke (Nashville, 1964). The latter work should be supplemented by Frank Baker's *From Wesley to Asbury* (Durham, 1976), which traces the transition of British Methodism to the American scene, and by Frederick A. Norwood's *The Story of American Methodism* (Nashville, 1974), which traces later developments in the history of the United Methodists. For the latest statistics about world Methodism, see the World Methodist Council's *Handbook of Information* (Lake Junaluska, N.C., 1982).

FRANK BAKER

METHODIUS. *See* Cyril and Methodius.

MEYKAṆṬĀR (thirteenth century CE), Tamil Śaiva Siddhānta author and theologian. Meykaṇṭār ("he who saw the truth") was the first of the four *santāna ācāryas* ("hereditary teachers," here referring to four successive theologians) of the Tamil Śaiva Siddhānta school of philosophy-theology. Originally called Svētaraṇam, Meykaṇṭār, who lived in Tiruveṇṇainallūr, received the name by which posterity recognizes him from his guru Parañcōti Muṉivar. Meykaṇṭār's prominence rests almost entirely on his composition of a single work, the

Civañāṉapōtam (Skt., *Śivajñānabodha,* The Understanding of the Knowledge of Śiva). The *Civañāṉapōtam,* written in the early thirteen century, is held to be the *mutaṉūl* ("primary treatise") of the fourteen theological texts that have canonical status in Tamil Śaivism. These fourteen texts are collectively called the *Meykaṇṭaśāstra,* although Meykaṇṭār is the author of only one of the fourteen, but the fundamental one, the *Civañāṉapōtam.*

The *Civañāṉapōtam* consists of twelve Tamil *sūtras* along with two sets of glosses, the *cūttirakkaṉṉaḻivu* (the words of the *sūtra* divided into sentences) and the *cūrṇikai* (a brief gloss on the sentences setting forth their meaning in simple prose), as well as a commentary composed of articles *(atikaraṇam),* each consisting of a thesis *(mēṟkōḷ),* reason *(ētu),* and illustrative verses *(utāraṇam).* The twelve *sūtras* of the *Civañāṉapōtam* are also found in the *Rauravāgama,* one of the Sanskrit Āgamas also held sacred by Tamil Śaivas. Whether Meykaṇṭār translated the *sūtras* from Sanskrit into Tamil or the author of the *Rauravāgama* borrowed from the *Civañāṉapōtam* is difficult, if not impossible, to ascertain and is a subject about which there is no scholarly consensus. Suffice it to note here that possession of a Sanskrit Agamic prototype for the authoritative text is hardly surprising when one considers the concern of medieval Hindu sectarian schools to establish their legitimacy.

The *Civañāṉapōtam* is a highly systematic and logical presentation of basic Śaiva Siddhānta ideology. The first six *sūtras* establish the existence, attributes, and interrelations of the three fundamental components of Śaiva Siddhānta ontology: *pati* (the Lord, i.e., God, Śiva), *pacu* (the soul), and *pācam* (the bondage that enslaves souls and separates them from knowledge of God). Meykaṇṭār cites the fact that the world evidences intelligible processes of creation, maintenance, and dissolution to establish God's existence. God is claimed to be both immanent in souls and yet different from them. The soul's knowledge of reality, however, is clouded by its being conjoined with an innate impurity *(cakajamalam,* i.e., *āṇavamalam,* the basic component of *pācam).* But the soul can be illuminated by the Lord's grace and overcome its bondage. The soul is thus an entity that is defined by its relations—either to "bondage" *(pācam),* "impurity" (*malam,* i.e., the structure of finite, phenomenal existence), or to the Lord *(pati),* who bestows divine knowledge and bliss. Specific aspects of the soul's realization of its *advaita* relation with *pati* are the subject of the final six *sūtras* of the *Civañāṉapōtam.* Here in germ are the basics of a Śaiva Siddhānta path of spiritual realization: the necessity of a guru who is free of bondage and hence manifests the Lord, the use of the five-syllabled mantra ("nama śivāya"), and above all the centrality of devotional love (*bhakti;* Tam., *aṉpu*) for God, and the value of associating with other *bhaktas* (devotees).

[*See also the biographies of Māṇikkavacakar and Umāpati Śivācārya.*]

BIBLIOGRAPHY

The *Civañāṉapōtam* has been translated into English several times. Of these, the most complete, accurate, and accessible is *Śiva-ñāna-bōdham: A Manual of Śaiva Religious Doctrine,* translated and interpreted by Gordon Matthews (Oxford, 1948). Closely following the *Civañāṉapōtam* in its summary of the Śaiva Siddhānta is John H. Piet's *A Logical Presentation of the Śaiva Siddhānta Philosophy* (Madras, 1952). A valuable study of the entire canonical corpus of Śaiva Siddhānta theological texts, which also contains in appendices both the Tamil and Sanskrit *sūtras* of the *Civañāṉapōtam* and the *Rauravāgama* along with English translations, is Mariasusai Dhavamony's *Love of God according to Śaiva Siddhānta* (Oxford, 1971). A large volume on Śaiva Siddhānta thought, occasionally marred by a Protestant Christian bias but nonetheless still useful for its thoroughness and occasional insight, is H. W. Schomerus's *Der Çaiva-Siddhānta: Eine Mystik Indiens* (Leipzig, 1912).

GLENN E. YOCUM

MIAO RELIGION. *See* Southeast Asian Religions, *article on* Mainland Cultures.

MICAH (fl. eighth century BCE), or, in Hebrew, Mikhah; Hebrew prophet whose prophecy is recorded in the biblical *Book of Micah.* Although the *Book of Micah* employs a personal approach in which the prophet occasionally speaks directly in the first person to reveal his deep feelings (e.g., 1:8, 3:8 [citations herein follow the English version]), the prophet reveals neither his personal life nor his background, in contrast to many other prophets, including his contemporary, Isaiah. He does not even provide an account of his call. We know only his general period of time as stated in the superscription (1:1), which is derived from a later hand. There is also a reference to Micah's hometown, Moresheth (cf. Moresheth-gath, 1:14), which is located southwest of Jerusalem. Interestingly, this information is repeated later, in *Jeremiah* 26:18, demonstrating the strong impact of Micah's prophecy.

According to the superscription, the period of Micah's activity was during the time of Jotham, Ahaz, and Hezekiah, kings of Judah in the second half of the eighth century BCE. It was a politically stormy time dominated by the Syro-Ephraimite war and Assyrian military threats against Judah. Yet these major military events, which underlie Isaiah's prophecy, are not specifically addressed in Micah's speeches, for he was mainly concerned with the internal situation—the social and moral injustices of the rulers of Judah. Micah's attack on the false prophets (3:5–12) is noteworthy in that he was the first to devote an entire speech to the problem.

A large part of *Micah* concerns prophecies of salvation and the "new age." Many scholars consider the relationship between oracles of doom and prophecies of salvation to be mutually exclusive, and tend to distinguish between the oracles of doom, that is, the authentic Micah, and prophecies of salvation, which they consider later additions. As a rule, these scholars consider the major parts of chapters 1–3 (except, perhaps, 2:12–13) the core of Micah's own prophecy, with the remainder reflecting thinkers of later periods who were influenced by Micah (as in *Jer.* 26:18) and sought to update the outcome of the old prophecies.

This distinction between Micah and his later editors is based upon a particular modern scholarly understanding of the nature of the authentic prophecies. Stylistic and linguistic criteria, however, are not the decisive factors in determining the original text as opposed to additions. This distinction is based upon theme rather than stylistic literary analysis. We should, however, take into consideration the possibility that prophecies of judgment may mingle with oracles of salvation, that the prophet did not merely record his surroundings but also developed a specific perspective on the new age, which he sought to share with his audience. Micah's criticism of his present world leads to his prophecy of the new age, the period of peace and justice. A distinction between original prophecies of doom and supplementary prophecies of salvation would therefore be misleading.

Much has been written about the relationship between the two contemporaries, Micah and Isaiah, because of the similarity between the visions of the "new age" in *Micah* 4:1–5 and *Isaiah* 2:1–4 (or 5). Since Micah's vision is not in chapters 1–3 of *Micah*, which contain oracles of doom (considered to be the words of Micah himself), scholars tend to regard this vision as inauthentic. Isaiah's vision is likewise regarded as an addition, since it is a prophecy of salvation. It has been stated above, however, that the distinction between oracles of doom and prophecies of salvation may be an artificial one. Notice should be taken of Micah's conclusion: "For all the people walk each in the name of its god, but we will walk in the name of the Lord our God for ever and ever" (4:5, RSV). Insofar as this differs from Isaiah's emphasis on the universality and centrality of the mountain of God, the house of the God of Jacob, Micah's national approach here conveys a message that contrasts with Isaiah's universalism. Furthermore, Micah speaks specifically about the total destruction of Jerusalem (3:2; cf. *Jer.* 26:18), while Isaiah avoids such a description of the holy city. In this context we may also question Micah's criticism of the other prophets. For instance, when he condemns them for calling for peace (3:5), is he referring to Isaiah's call for peace during the Syro-Ephraimite war (*Is.* 7:4–9)?

There are no definite criteria for determining where Micah's various speeches begin and end in the text. He starts with the subject of Judah's military troubles, and then in chapter 2 presents a sharp social criticism of those who oppress the poor and take their houses and property. In chapter 3 this attack is addressed more directly to rulers who tyrannize their citizens. In 3:5–12, Micah admonishes the prophets for misleading the people concerning the political situation. The style of discourse of chapters 1–3 maintains the characteristic prophetic conception of cause and effect: that the political and military situation reflects social and moral misbehavior. Wars and political disasters do not occur in a vacuum: political events are initiated by God as a punishment; they are God's response to the moral misconduct of the rulers of Judah.

Micah 4:1–5 describes the new age, the period of peace, while 5:1–5 concentrates on the new ruler of Israel, a descendant of the house of David, who will come from the town of Bethlehem. At 5:9 a prophecy begins concerning the destruction of the state's symbols of power—the military horses, chariots, and fortresses—as well as the destruction of foreign religious idols. It prophesies a conflict between God and Israel in which God condemns Israel for its betrayal. The speech ends with a moral-religious revelation (6:6–8). The lament of 7:17 is followed by a prophetic liturgy (7:8–20), which concludes with God's praise and the assurance that God will continue to protect his people as he has done in the past.

Despite numerous textual difficulties, Micah's message is clear and precise, and he clarifies the role of the prophet:

> But as for me, I am filled with power,
> with the Spirit of the Lord,
> and with justice and might,
> to declare to Jacob his transgression
> and to Israel his sin. (3:8)

Above all, the book lucidly states the meaning of Yahvistic religion in terms of God's demands upon the worshipers. Micah stresses the elements of justice, love, and kindness as God's preference in worship (6:6–8).

BIBLIOGRAPHY

Hillers, Delbert R. *Micah.* Philadelphia, 1984.

Mays, James Luther. *Micah: A Commentary.* Philadelphia, 1976.

Wolff, Hans Walter. *Mit Micha Reden.* Neukirchen, 1978.

Wolff, Hans Walter. *Micah the Prophet.* Philadelphia, 1981.

YEHOSHUA GITAY

MICHAEL CERULARIOS. *See* Cerularios, Michael.

MICHAEL PSELLUS. *See* Psellus, Michael.

MICRONESIAN RELIGIONS. [*This entry consists of two articles. The first,* An Overview, *surveys the autochthonous religious traditions of the area of Oceania known as Micronesia. The companion article,* Mythic Themes, *examines the major mythological motifs of these island traditions.*]

An Overview

The western Pacific islands of Micronesia are scattered over an equatorial area exceeding in size that of the contiguous forty-eight states of the United States, but their combined land surface is little more than one thousand square miles. Today, there are about only 140,000 inhabitants, although in the past the population was appreciably greater. Of the four island groups constituting the culture area, the Marianas are high islands of volcanic origin; the Carolines are mixed, consisting of atolls and high islands of volcanic origin; and the Marshalls and Gilberts are all low islands. The time period in which their traditional religions is here discussed is a contrived point of time that anthropologists call the ethnological present—after the people had been discovered and observed by Europeans but before their culture had been seriously upset. It would be impossible to discuss the religion in any other terms, and so the present tense will be used throughout except for the Marianas, whose Chamorros were wiped out centuries ago and replaced by outsiders. The people are horticulturalists, with a strong reliance on fishing. Their basic settlement pattern is the farmstead, rather than the nuclear village, which is post-European. They speak Malayo-Polynesian languages. In physical characteristics they have admixtures of Polynesian, Indonesian, and Melanesian elements, and this background is reflected in various aspects of the culture. Matrilineages and matriclans are the backbone of the social structure, except in the Gilberts, where ambilineal kin groups are found. Social stratification is moderate, except in Yap, where two castes, each with a number of ranked classes, exist. Chieftainship is hereditary.

Traits of the Religion. Because of the regional differences fostered by geographic distances as well as varying degrees of influence from adjacent culture areas, a holistic character cannot be assigned to Micronesian religion. Moreover, the religion is a mélange of many elements: celestial and terrestrial deities, nature spirits, demons, and ancestral ghosts, with a strong infusion of magic, taboo, and divination. No one trait dominates the system. It is as if Micronesians were tolerant, willing recipients of anything that might have a prospect of satisfying their need for symbols appropriate for organizing and interpreting experience.

Death, the Soul, and the Afterworld. There is little speculation about the origin of death, but there are abundant explanations for its causes. Aside from natural causes, which are given some recognition, other causes include sorcery, hostile demons, angry ancestors, vindictive gods, and taboo violations. Palliatives, revolving mostly around the concept of the soul and the prospect of an afterlife, have been devised to make the harshness of death easier on both the deceased and the living.

Although concepts of the soul vary, there is a universal belief in a single soul for each person. It is located in the head and, though invisible, has the same size and appearance as the living body. At death it escapes through the top of the head, the nose, or the mouth, at which time it may assume the appearance of a bird. The soul is free to wander about or even to fly to distant places during dreams. If the departure is temporary there are no aftereffects. If the soul does not return before the dream is terminated, death ensues.

The career of the soul after death is generally believed to begin with a temporary lingering near the place of death. This is a time of tension, and steps are taken to encourage the soul, which can be dangerous, to leave the vicinity of the body and move on to its ultimate destination in the afterworld. For instance, for three nights following a death, the Gilbertese perform a ritual during which the people gather together in the darkness holding sticks of pandanus leaves and the butt ends of coconut leaves and, while advancing from south to north, beat the ground and trees before them with their staves. Not a word is uttered. On the third night, at the conclusion of the slow march, female relatives come to utter the final spells, which they say "straighten the path of the soul to the land of ghosts."

The journey to the realm of the dead is never direct

or uneventful. Before reaching it the soul stops at some place, usually spoken of as in the west, but many Carolinians specify it as a spot on the island of Angaur (the southernmost of the Palan Islands), where it bathes and continues on. Sometimes the soul must avoid clashing rocks. The tarrying point may vary according to the final destination, which in turn may depend on the status and mode of death of the deceased.

The ultimate destination of the soul is most often thought to be the sky world, often referred to as Lang (cf. Polynesian *lani*), where the celestial gods live. This world greatly resembles the one left behind by the deceased, except that it is more beautiful and tranquil. The souls of the dead may leave it occasionally to visit their loved ones on earth, where under proper circumstances they are warmly welcomed.

There are alternative afterworlds to which special categories of souls may go. Thus, distinctive endings may await warriors, chiefs, serfs, victims of murder, women who have died in childbirth, infants, and so on. According to the ancient Chamorros of the Marianas, the souls of those who died violently went to a sort of hell called Sasalaguan, where a demon cooked them in a caldron that he stirred constantly, whereas those who died a natural death went to live in an underworld paradise. Carolinians conceive of a place of punishment that might be a garbage well or a snake pit. Throughout Micronesia there is frequent mention of places of reward or punishment after death, suggesting the possibility of Christian influence, but this is by no means certain.

Mourning and Funerals. The emphasis placed on mortuary practices is in large part designed to placate the souls of the recently deceased and speed them on their journey to the afterworld lest they endanger the living. It functions, too, to assuage the grief of those left behind by providing an outlet for emotions.

The corpse is handled with great care and reverence. It is bathed, anointed with fragrant oils, and powdered with turmeric, and the urethra, vagina, and rectum are plugged. In some isolated instances, surviving spouses perform necrophilic acts (intercourse, fellatio, cunnilingus) on the dead person. The corpse is then wrapped in special large pandanus mats. Disposal of the body ordinarily takes place within a day, but chiefs may lie in state for longer periods of time.

In the grave, the head of the corpse is usually oriented to the east, but in some places the west or north is customary. On the island of Yap, the position in which the body is buried has much to do with the manner of death: older people or those who die a natural death are buried with their knees bent and the head oriented toward the west; warriors are buried with their legs stretched out, the head toward the north; and those who have died of bronchial diseases are buried in a sitting position, the knees pressed against the chest, the face turned sideways.

Inhumation is the favored way to dispose of the dead. Cremation is not practiced. Burials are often beneath the floor of the house or close by, although cemeteries are used in some places. Palauans prefer interment under the broad stone platforms in front of the house, whereas Yapese think the corpses pollute the ground and bury the dead in cemeteries. The ancient Chamorros most often buried their deceased under stone-pile houses and less often in caves or earthenware urns. However, they preserved the skulls in their houses and brought them out when beseeching the ancestors for help. In the Gilbert Islands, too, the skull is very often preserved in a box and anointed frequently by the widow or child of the deceased. The teeth that fall out are saved and the canines used to make necklaces worn while dancing.

Grave goods, consisting of bracelets, tortoise shells, "money," and other valuables, are not uncommon. When a chief in the Marshalls dies, an adult may be killed and buried close to him as a companion, but usually the living relatives are content instead to have a large canoe cut up and placed in the grave.

Howling, lamentation, tearing of the hair, and beating of the breasts are all exaggerated, especially on the part of women, who are the most conspicuous mourners. Formal dirges, always in chorus, are lengthy, slow, and conventionalized, with adaptations to fit the deceased's characteristics and life history.

Ancestor Worship. A strong ancestral cult pervades the daily religious life. All the criteria of true ancestor worship are present: the historicity of the ancestors of the familial ghosts, the transference to them of reverence and religious acts usually associated with gods, and the use of ritualistic practices designed to effect interaction between the living and the dead.

Although knowledge of the ancient religion of the Chamorros is fragmentary, old Spanish accounts show the existence of a flourishing cult of the spirits of the dead, who were called the *anite*. They were believed to be the sacred and powerful guardians of their living descendants, who both feared and venerated them. Their skulls were kept in baskets. The skull cult is responsible for the large number of isolated skulls and skull-less burials that are found near the capped uprights, called *latte*, that are arranged in straight parallel rows and were presumably the foundations of large pile houses and canoe sheds. The *anite* were sometimes invoked directly, but their help was often sought through professional mediums called *makana*.

An elaborate manifestation of ancestor worship appears throughout the Carolines, where each lineage has a pool of ancestral ghosts whose membership in it comes by virtue of matrilineal descent. Most recent ghosts, as well as those possessing special aptitudes, are the ones who are best remembered, whereas the rest become innominate and forgotten with the passage of time. Each matrilineage has a "number one" ghost who attains his or her position by virtue of superior ability in aiding the members of the lineage, thus displacing the previous leading ghost. Ancestral ghosts are highly concerned with the moral behavior of their unilineal relatives, but while they may be protective and called upon for aid, they are capable of inflicting punishment on relatives for antisocial or unethical behavior. The ones most revered are those who, speaking through mediums of their choice, most consistently show their ability to describe events in distant places, prognosticate epidemics, reveal the fate of voyagers at sea, predict an abundance of fish, and advise on means of treating illness. Sometimes these especially successful ghosts, who may come from any station in life, become apotheosized, as happened with the great Yapese divinity, Yongolap, and later the widely dispersed Ulithian infant, Marespa. Instances of apotheosis have been found not only in the Carolines but in the Gilberts and Marshalls as well.

Shrines to the ancestral dead are maintained in homes. Offerings form an important part of the ancestral cult and are brought to the shrines on appropriate occasions, as when a lineage feels the need to communicate with a dead ancestor about an illness or problem caused by the displeasure of the ghost. The most common offerings may be betel nuts, coconut oil, turmeric, loincloths, girdles, necklaces, and wreaths, all of which find their way into the hands of the custodian of the shrine.

Mediums provide the most direct communication with the dead. Usually they are selected at random by the ghosts themselves as their mouthpieces. In Palau the mediums may be the heads of subclans. If there is some urgency about hearing from the spirits, possession may not be left to chance but induced by self-suggestion, aided by some drink made from herbs or the chewing of an excessive amount of betel. While possessed, the medium, who is usually a male, quivers and becomes limp. He speaks in a voice resembling that of the ancestor when he or she was alive and dispenses advice on such matters as illness, deep-sea voyages, impending lineage decisions, and the accumulation or disposal of property.

Demons. Contrasting with ancestral ghosts and gods, who though they may punish mortals are basically paternal toward them, are terrestrial spirits who by nature are generally hostile. For lack of a better word, they may be called demons. The majority are lowly and anonymous; the rest are more elevated and named. Both kinds live in close intimacy with human beings. What they have in common is that they are the source of many of the trials and tribulations endured by people in their daily lives: crop failures, bad luck in fishing, spoilage of palm toddy, illness, blindness, insanity, and so on. Although they are touchy and demand respect, terrestrial spirits are never the object of a cult, even though offerings and incantations may be used to placate them.

The belief in demons is seen in every subarea of Micronesia. It is a matter of record that the Chamorros of the Marianas dreaded nature spirits of the kind under discussion. Demons appeared, usually at night, in the form of old men, terrible monsters, or horses. They also manifested themselves as the shadows cast by trees, lightning flashes, pale moonlight, and the electrical discharges of savanna grass. Elsewhere in Micronesia they are variously described as anthropomorphic; male, female, or sexless; clothed or nude; transparent or nontransparent; white, black, brown, or blue. Some say that they look like balls of fire. Their haunts may be houses, graves, trees, beaches, or the sea. They may be seen either in daytime or at night.

Important positive functions are served by malevolent demons. They are blamed for many woes that cannot be accounted for empirically. By serving as scapegoats they displace potentially disruptive human emotions onto themselves rather than the afflicted person's neighbors. Furthermore, they provide relief from anxiety and the paralyzing inaction that comes from not knowing the source of one's misfortunes, for by labeling and classifying the demons people are given means for controlling them, such as avoidance, bribery, coaxing, and flattery. Finally, through attention to the demons the community is led to feel proper concern toward many aspects of daily living.

Magic. Micronesians have more to rely upon than spirit beings in relating to supernatural power. Available to them is an essentially technological approach that we may broadly call "magic," in which ideally the very performance of a rite effects a successful result. In practice, magic among the Micronesians is overwhelmingly imbued with religious characteristics, especially seen in the incantations that accompany most such rites. Although they are sometimes used for the public good, magical techniques are ordinarily employed in the service of the individual. They are intended to achieve an immediate objective rather than to support the ethical system or the moral order.

Properties of the rites. Magic is privately owned and individually performed, although a practitioner may occasionally use helpers who do not have a hand in carrying out the techniques of the ritual proper. The principal technique is the use of words, these being purposely fashioned into unintelligible phrases and sentences of great esoteric symbolism. The magician simply learns the words by rote from a magician who has "sold" them to him.

Objects constitute the next most important ingredient in magical techniques. Most commonly they consist of various kinds of coral, sea urchins, spider lilies, turmeric leaves and roots, papaya leaves, young coconut leaflets, and twigs of a "magical" tree, *Premna gaudichaudii* (of the verbena family). Also employed are various body gestures, such as clapping, tapping the body, crossing the hands over the breast, and rubbing the belly; these are always accompanied by spells. Direction, space, weapons, food gathering, fire, and symbols of transportation have some but not much place in magic.

Clear-cut distinctions between imitative and contagious magic cannot always be made, but of the two, imitative magic in its purer form is the more common. Contact magic is occasionally seen in the use of sorcery, where rope, clothing, combs, or other objects belonging to the intended victim are worked over. There is little use of nail parings, hair, exuviae, or other things belonging to the body.

Practitioners. Magicians work only part time and usually are men. Women may be general practitioners, but they are excluded from almost all the major specialized fields, with the notable exception of medicine. An ordinary person knows some magic that he uses for himself or his family, but he can scarcely be called a magician. He has none of the sacredness of the professional.

One who aspires to become a major magician receives his training from an expert, who sells his knowledge in exchange for gift payments. The arrangement is not an impersonal, commercial one, however, for the teacher is a close friend or a relative who takes a personal interest in his pupil. In turn, the pupil honors him by beginning his ritual with an appeal to the ghost of the teacher if he has since died. During the student's apprenticeship both parties must observe many taboos.

Spheres of anxiety. The areas in which magic flourishes are those where Micronesians feel helpless in the face of inadequate empirical solutions. One of these, of course, is illness, with its discomforts, pains, and threat to life itself. While natural causes are given due recognition, disease is more often believed to be the result of sorcery, demons, ghosts, taboo violations, and other supernatural factors. The native doctor uses empirical treatments, such as massage, poultices, bonesetting, emetics, and cathartics, but he resorts basically to magical aid in diagnosis, etiology, and therapy.

Not surprisingly for people surrounded by water, Micronesians constantly worry over the ocean's inconstancies and dangers, and they have developed abundant techniques to cope with its harmful aspects. In the Marianas and Carolines, the threat of tropical storms and typhoons is always present. Specialists exist to drive them away. Everywhere, heavy surf and tidal waves menace the shoreline, so magicians endeavor to calm the waves, thus alleviating the threat to crops of salt spray and inundation. Great loss of life results when navigators, aside from having to deal with the sea itself, fail to maintain a proper course because they lack scientific devices. They fortify themselves as best they can, not only with appeals to spirits and the ancestral dead, but also with rituals, amulets, and talismans.

While it is a source of food, the sea also promotes anxiety by withholding marine fauna from fishermen, and so there exist both private and communal specialists whose job it is to release the reluctant creatures. The most complex forms of fish magic are those carried out for the benefit of the whole community. On Ulithi, for example, such magic is performed once a year by a major magician and his assistants, who have been commissioned by the chief of the atoll. It takes place intermittently over two lunar months, during which time the small band of men goes from island to island, reenacting parts of a myth that explains how in a dream a spirit reveals to a woman the secret of fishing as a reward for letting him have her yellow wraparound skirt.

Paradoxically, little or no magic at all is applied to food plants, probably because these grow well with little assistance other than such practical steps as working the soil, weeding, and fertilizing. Yet the swamp gardens in which the *Araceae*—true taro, giant taro, and elephant ears—and certain other plants are raised by women are surrounded with an inordinate number of taboos, which function to accentuate a sacred attitude toward plant foods rather than foster their growth. The magic that protects food plants is indirect; it is concerned with wind, salt spray, and, especially in the Gilberts, drought. What horticultural magic there is applies principally to something in the men's domain—the raising of coconut palms and the protection of palm toddy from ruinous beetles. This sphere of anxiety is attenuated by magicians commissioned by either the community or private individuals.

Islanders have a deep sentiment toward their swift but vulnerable canoes, which are indispensable for fishing, travel, and communication. As the canoe is being built it has the benefit of protective magic by the carpenter, who through prayer may also invoke the aid of the patron god of canoe builders. These things do not necessarily guarantee success, for they may be imperfectly executed, foiled by sorcery, or spoiled by taboo violation. Once the boat is completed, further magical protection continues to be applied indefinitely.

Of all interpersonal relations, love between a man and a woman in any society can be among the most frustrating and unpredictable because it does not follow the rules of reason. So it is that in the islands of Micronesia, where erotic activity is highly permissive, there are numerous magical approaches to the resolution of affairs of the heart. For example, in Truk a man may go to an old woman who knows how to make the object of his ardor respond favorably. She makes him a "medicine bag" over which she chants a spell, and he carries it with him until success is achieved. The old woman also gives the lovesick man a bent coconut leaf, which he must frequently work, like an accordion, while murmuring a verse.

There is other magic for almost anything else that worries the people: to produce courage, conjure up rain, exorcise trees ready to be cut down, coax a demon to leave a proposed burial site, and so on.

Sorcery. Those who for one reason or another wish to harm others but lack the personal power to do so openly resort to sorcery, or harmful magic. It is a technique for retaliating against real or imagined wrongs. Since by definition evil magic is an antisocial, criminal act, it is kept secret, so what we know about it is ascertained with some difficulty. What little is known, however, shows that in principle there is no real difference from beneficial magic except intent. Incantations are sometimes uttered over selected objects, such as live lizards, starfish, and dragonflies, and these are placed in or near the intended victim's house. Contagious magic, too, may be used, this being the most popular of all in Palau. There the sorcerer effects his purpose by using some object that has been in intimate association with the victim, especially his cast-off betel quid.

People are not defenseless against sorcery. If they know it is being used, or simply have a suspicion of it, they can take appropriate steps, chiefly through the use of amulets, which are profuse and variegated throughout the culture area. They are of many different materials and shapes. However, they are useless without an accompanying incantation, the words of which are privately owned and characterized by strangeness, alliteration, and much symbolism. Appropriate gestures complete the counter spell.

Witchcraft, including the evil eye, is apparently unknown, but in any event it should not be confused with sorcery, for its power lies in some inner evil force rather than a learned technique.

Divination. Not surprising for a Stone Age people without reliance on scientific technologies, the Micronesians have a strong urge to have revealed to them, through means having supernatural overtones, information about the unknown past, present, and future. The most obvious way of divining is through mediums who serve as mouthpieces for the dead, but there are alternative methods for ascertaining the unknown. Fortuitous signs, such as heavy sheet lightning, cloud formations, the sounds of a lizard, the flight of birds, a crab creeping over the sleeping mat, or the wriggling of snakes, are passive and relatively unimportant. They lack the force of deliberately induced signs.

The single most prestigious and popular method of deliberate divination consists of the interpretation of knots in palm pinnae, or leaflets. Such a method varies throughout the Carolines, Gilberts, and Marshalls, but in its classic, complex form it appears in the general Yapese and Trukese spheres of influence, where it is known as *pwe* (*bwe, bei*, etc.). The charter for knot divination may be found in various mythological accounts, where certain celestial spirits descend in a spirit canoe and teach *pwe* to mankind. A German ethnographer, Laurentius Bollig, commenting on its role early in the twentieth century, wrote that nothing can be done without *pwe*—no fishing, house building, traveling, medicine—and that lovesick and seriously sick people resort to it. There is good reason to believe that *pwe* is related to the *I ching* trigrams of ancient China.

Rites of Passage. Rites that make the transition of the individual from one social status to another in the course of a lifetime are principally those that sacralize birth, the attainment of adult status, marriage, and death. All of them have marked magico-religious overtones, but birth and marriage rites are relatively weak in Micronesia; the most important of all are mortuary rites (see above). This leaves those rites of passage that come into play upon the attainment of puberty.

Male initiation rites are fairly prosaic, and except for the Gilberts, where the youth's scalp is lacerated with the point of a shark's tooth, there are no traumas such as tooth evulsion, circumcision, or starvation. At the first sign of pubic hair in a boy, his family arranges for the ritual. In the central Carolines it usually has three elements: the adoption of adult clothing, the performance of magic, and the giving of a feast. The youth's sisters are forbidden to witness the ritual or share the food. The whole matter is treated as essentially a domestic, rather than a communal, affair.

The transitional rites for a girl are much more complex than for a boy. At the first sign of menstrual blood, the parents take the prescribed steps. In the central Carolines, the girl is sent to the communal menstrual lodge, where she abandons her grass skirt for a woven wraparound. At that time a magico-religious formula is recited by the mother over her daughter, during which strips of sacred coconut leaves are snapped together before her eyes. The feast that honors the onset of the menarche takes place eight days after the girl's period has begun. This ritual is discussed further in the section below.

The Sacred and Taboo. Many things in the world of Micronesians may be considered sacred. Much is holy, sacrosanct, or consecrated by religion to an extent approaching that of the Polynesians. Innumerable taboos exist to keep the profane from violating the sanctity of that which is set apart by a religious attitude and thereby rendering it ordinary and unholy. At the same time taboos function to preserve the moral order and show everyone "the correct path to walk."

The kinds of places that are often sacred and subject to taboo are burial sites, ancestral shrines, certain spots in reefs, and taro gardens. Of these, taro gardens are especially saturated with sacred restrictions. In Ulithi, for instance, it is taboo to enter them under eight conditions: if one has eaten or defecated during the day; if one is in mourning or has recently washed a corpse or dug a grave; if one is a menstruating woman; if one is a barren woman; if one has had sexual relations during the previous six days; if one is a fish magician and has used a certain kind of hook during the previous five lunar months; and if one is a healer who is treating a patient. A specific malevolent female deity who lives in sacred gardens, rather than a vague supernatural force, punishes violators of the restrictions by inflicting on them such diseases as elephantiasis and yaws or causing small boils to develop on their bodies. She may vent her wrath more widely by sending insects to attack the plants growing in the gardens and making them die.

Things, too, may be sacred and thus taboo: totemic plants and animals, effigies of spirits (rare), talismans, amulets, love charms, and the paraphernalia of magicians (e.g., conch shells, spears, young coconut leaves).

Persons who are sacred and surrounded with taboos include chiefs, priests, high-ranking magicians, warriors, new mothers, and newly menstruating girls. Their sanctity is acquired rather than immanent, but it is protected against profanement with unusual rigorousness. For instance, no one may touch the head, face, or back of a magician of major rank or walk erect while he is seated. Cooking, eating, sexual, and other taboos may remain in force for a lifetime.

Females who experience a highly sacred state of taboo are those undergoing the puberty rite described previously. A girl who has just begun her new physiological life goes immediately to the community menstrual house, accompanied by another girl who will remain her companion and aide for a matter of months. She may not leave the house or do her own cooking, nor may she eat with other people, touch their food, or allow them to partake of her own food or drinking water. She may not trespass on the quarters of other women living in the house. She is especially enjoined not to enter the village. On her first day she places on her head a woven fiber skirt of the kind worn by adults. This gesture has a special meaning, for if she should fail to observe it the sun will become hot and scorch everything. Special lewd dances are performed separately by men and women of the community of the first day of the girl's isolation. They are said to "belong" to the great spirit, Yongolap, and are intended to prevent the coming of a typhoon.

Often in Micronesia a taboo seems to have no connection with the sacred. It may appear to be merely a secular edict decreed by a chief. For instance, in Palau a taboo is used to withdraw from general use objects that are reserved for a general purpose. If there is a shortage of betel pepper or if pigs, coconuts, and so on are to be saved for an important feast, a sacred prohibition is imposed on these things. In Ulithi a high chief may declare a whole island taboo against fishing, sailing, and bathing in the sea because the inhabitants have failed to present to him all the giant green turtles that they have captured.

What makes such seemingly secular restrictions true taboos is that their origin, as well as the authority by which they are imposed, always have some foundation in the sacred. Although anthropologists customarily say that the punishments that follow the violation of a taboo are automatic and impersonal, involving no deliberation by a deity or other spirit entity sitting in judgment, this narrow view does not apply to Micronesia, where native words for "taboo" (Ifalukan, *tabw*; Ulithian, *etap*; Yapese, *machmach;* Trukese, *rin;* Palauan, *blul;* et al.) are freely associated with these apparently secular edicts. Somewhere or other a sacred factor will be found behind such prohibitions. That they may be rationalizations is besides the point.

Purificatory rites for the removal of taboos or states of taboo are performed by part-time specialists in such matters. Subjects for purification are, for example, corpse handlers, grave diggers, new mothers, and newly pubescent girls.

The Role of Women. Women play a clearly subordinate part in Micronesian systems of supernaturalism. This is due, in part, to the ambivalent attitude held by men toward menstrual blood and reproduction. It is also due to the division of labor, for many magico-religious roles are adjuncts to activities that are sex-limited and exclude women: navigation (except for some aspects), fishing in deep water, canoe building, house construction, the martial arts, and the like. In addition there are some kinds of magic—such as typhoon control, wave control, and divination—that are not direct aspects of any professional activities and yet belong exclusively to men, possibly because of a widespread concept of the social inferiority of women, especially common in Yap.

Because agricultural activities are carried out mostly by women, it is not surprising that most of the little rituals to insure good crops are in their hands. Even here, however, men have an indirect part by exercising magic to thwart typhoons and abnormally high wave action, which threaten plants and trees through overturning, inundation, and salt spray, each of which can be disastrous to the food supply.

Women are not shut out of one of the major kinds of magical activity, the healing of the sick. They also play a prominent part in love rituals. They serve occasionally as mediums between the dead and the living, yet here again this is primarily the sphere of men. For instance, of the forty-four "number one" lineage ghosts on a certain atoll, only six were female, the sex of five others not being ascertained.

Women find vicarious prestige as creators in cosmogonic myths. One of the most famous females is the Carolinian goddess Ligoupup (Ligopup), who is said to have always existed and to have created the world. She lives directly under the surface of the earth, where she lies on her stomach in continuous slumber. When she stirs in her sleep the world trembles and earthquakes result. In some places she is thought to be the ancestor of all the gods, even though she had no mate. She gave birth to a son, Solal (Saulal), who is the lord of the nether regions and the sea and the creator of all fish. She also gave birth to a daughter, who went to the sky world and married a god, giving birth to Aluelap (Analap), the ruler of heaven, inventor of all knowledge, and dispenser of glory. Aluelap fathered Lugeilang, who is the guardian of heaven and the father of the renowned trickster and demigod Olofat. The preceding account shows Ligoupup at her best, but other Carolinian myths detract from her importance either by attributing most of her accomplishments to male gods or by providing alternative explanations for the origin of the main celestial and terrestrial deities.

A common explanation in the Carolines and Marshalls for the creation of the islands of the earth is that sand or some other material was strewn on the surface of the primeval sea by a female. Excepting for Ligoupup, the numerous women mentioned are relatively obscure. Moreover, the sand strewers are sometimes males. Nevertheless, females predominate as the most frequent strewers.

Women fare worse in the awesome creation myths of the Gilberts and Marshalls. The primal beings of the Gilberts are males—Sir Spider (Na Areau the Elder and the Younger), Turtle (Tabakea), and Eel (Riiki). They account for the First Spell, the splitting asunder of the Cleaving Together of sky and earth, the dispelling of darkness and the creation of light by casting the eyes of the first man upward to form the sun and moon and parts of his body to form the stars, and many more formidable accomplishments, none of which was brought about by females.

The cosmogonic myths of the Marshalls, which like those of the Gilberts seem to be connected historically with Polynesia, are likewise dominated by males, especially the creator, Loa (cf. Polynesian Tangaroa, Tangaloa), and the great magician and shapeshifter Edao.

If women have an exclusive place in Micronesian religion it is as founders of totemic clans in a type of organization based on matrilineal descent. Although totemism was apparently stronger in the past, it undeniably exists, especially in the area from Palau to Truk to Ponape. The animals and plants that founded the clans are eponymous, meaning that the totemites bear their name. The female ancestors were porpoises, turtles, sharks, sea bass, freshwater eels, sea cucumbers, owls, bananas, and a kind of yam, among other things. Strong taboos exist against eating one's totemic animal or plant. On Ponape, one who violates one's totem is killed, or at least expelled, and cannot shut his eyes and mouth in death.

BIBLIOGRAPHY

There is no adequate overview of Micronesian religion. A composite picture has to be constructed from ethnographic and ethnohistorical sources, supplemented by certain broad studies of Micronesian folklore. Most materials are in German, the most extensive publications being those appearing in the monumental assemblage of monographic reports edited by Georg Thilenius, *Ergebnisse der Südsee-Expedition, 1908–1910* (Hamburg, 1927–). They deal mainly with the Caroline Islands and are highly factual rather than analytic. Other German sources are, for the Palaus, J. S. Kubary's "Die Religion der Pelauer," in volume 1 of *Allerei aus Volks- und Menschenkunde*, edited by Adolf Bastian (Berlin, 1888); for Yap, Sixtus Walleser's "Religiöse Anschauungen und Gebräuche der Bewohner von Jap," *Anthropos* 8 (1913): 607–629, 1044–1068; and for the Marshalls, August Erdland's *Die Marshall-Insulaner* (Münster, 1914). Of publications in English there are two useful, wide-ranging folkloristic works. The first is the excellent article by Katharine Luomala, "Micronesian Mythology," in volume 2 of *Funk and*

Wagnall's Standard Dictionary of Folklore, Mythology, and Legend, 2 vols., edited by Maria Leach (New York, 1949–1950). The other is my survey *Tales from Ulithi Atoll: A Comparative Study in Oceanic Folklore* (Berkeley, 1961). For the Marianas, Laura Thompson has salvaged material from old Spanish sources in her two publications, *Guam and Its People* (San Francisco, 1941) and *The Native Culture of the Marianas Islands* (Honolulu, 1945). For the Gilberts, there is the collection of Arthur Grimble's early writings, *Migration, Myth and Magic from the Gilbert Islands* (London, 1972), as well as his better-known *A Pattern of Islands* (London, 1954), both of which lack the sophistication of a trained anthropologist but are nevertheless invaluable for their firsthand observations. Finally, for a study of a single atoll that has applicability for the whole area of the Carolines that is known as the Woleai, there is my *Ulithi: A Micronesian Design for Living* (New York, 1966), which condenses a great amount of magico-religious information contained originally in a less readily accessible report to the Coordinated Investigation of Micronesian Anthropology, *The Ethnography of Ulithi Atoll* (Los Angeles, 1950).

WILLIAM A. LESSA

Mythic Themes

Micronesian myths (as distinguished from folk tales) are the domain of clan elders and sometimes of trained specialists, who cite them in regard not only to community land claims, rights, values, authority, and prestige but also to functions of deities, sequences of rulers, and origins of place names. On Truk in the Caroline Islands the specialists *(idan)* narrate myths according to the practice of the school that has trained them; they observe taboos, and they speak a secret jargon consisting of standard words with altered meanings, archaic expressions, and words spoken backward. On Ponape, also in the Carolines, the sacred narratives, called "establishing the foundation," tend to be organized into a cultural and historical developmental sequence about the origins of physical objects and of society, and about migrations, wars, and religion; the narratives also include songs that are based on myths. The Kiribati of the Gilbert Islands and Ocean Island systematize their sacred narratives so that they begin with creation, continue with traditions about the migrations of clan ancestors from Samoa and about their settlement and experiences in the Gilberts, and usually end with the narrating clan elder's genealogy.

Creation and Cosmogonic Deities. Even within the same archipelago or on the same island, diversity and contradiction characterize the myths about the origin of the world, the pantheon, the islands, living beings, and customs. In the Carolines, for example, the functions of named gods often shift from island to island. However, a persistent Micronesian theme is that a preexistent god or goddess created and generated everything or delegated all or part of the work to newly created subordinates.

According to the Jesuit missionary Diego Luis de Sanvitores, who wrote between 1668 and 1672, the Chamorros of Guam believed that parentless Puntan and his unnamed sister lived before the earth and sky existed. Concerned for the welfare of mankind, which was as yet uncreated, Puntan at his death gave all his powers to his sister, enabling her to fashion the earth and sky from his breast and back, the sun and moon from his eyes, and the rainbow from his eyebrows.

On Truk, Ligoupup, the Carolinian earth mother, is replaced as the primal deity by Anulap ("great spirit"). Anulap either creates the world himself or has Ligoupup—his wife, whom he made from his blood—do it. Their children commit incest and, along with a girl who is born from a boil that afflicts Anulap, found the clans, for which Ligoupup establishes social rules and to whom she gives healing medicines. Faraulep islanders state that Solal, a god who was half man and half fish, planted his staff in the primeval sea; it grew mightily, after which his brother Aluelap, who was also half man and half fish, climbed it to sprinkle down earth and so make land. Aluelap now rules the sky while Solal rules the sea and the district under it.

In the Marshall Islands, parentless Loa (or Lowa) is said to have glanced down and murmured until a reef, islands, plants, and a white tern rose from the primeval sea. The tern then created the sky by flying back and forth as if weaving a spiderweb. Loa's commands produced deities, each with specific duties. A couple born from a blood tumor on his leg had two children who tattooed nearly every living being. Because the sky rested on people's heads, two maternal nephews of Irojerilik (god of the west and of reproduction), netted it and raised it by flying about in the same way as had the tern.

The myths of the Kiribati show much Polynesian influence; they poetically and metaphorically elaborate the themes of creation from a person's body, of the planted staff, of divine incest, and of sky-raising. Their primordial deity, Na Areau, may be not only the creator but also a world-transformer, shape-shifter, and trickster or there may be two Na Areaus, an elder who creates the world and a younger who puts the world in order. Although Na Areau's name means "Sir Spider," the Kiribati rarely think of him as such. Na Areau brooded alone on the rock-hard carapace of the undifferentiated universe, called "the darkness and the cleaving together." With his potent staff he penetrated its hollow interior, where, some say, the last child of Rock and Nothingness (who were the offspring of Sand and

Water) was Na Areau the Younger. The elder Na Areau then vanished to leave the work to the younger, who, after naming and activating the preexistent, recumbent Fools and Deaf Mutes, had them free and raise the carapace of the universe, which became the sky. In one version, he took the eyes of the elder Na Areau to form the sun and the moon, his brains to make the stars, and his spine for the Ancestral Tree on Samoa, a land that Octopus and Wave had formed. Humanlike and nonhumanlike deities, male and female, grew happily on and under the tree, each in his place, until Red-tailed Tropic Bird, who lived at the crest of the tree, defecated on those below. Na Areau then burned the tree, forcing the ancestors to seek new homes in the Gilbert Islands, which had been created by Na Areau's commands (or other means). Red-tailed Tropic Bird then settled in Makin, where it ate people until ever-benevolent Tituābine, whose pet it was, ordered it killed. Red-skinned men grew on what had been its pandanus perch, and women grew on the coconut tree that had been planted by the goddess on her pet's grave. These newcomers became kings in the local assembly house. Other Kiribati also have local ancestral trees that have sprung from an ancestor's grave.

Some Kiribati and Ocean islanders replace Na Areau in his role as the transformer with Auriaria, son of Tituābine and Tabakea ("hawksbill turtle"), who are sister and brother born as a result of Earth and Sky rubbing together. According to this alternative version, Na Areau sprang from Tabakea's head. When Auriaria, having directed the separation of Earth and Sky, struck Heaven with the staff given him by Tabakea, the islands on top of Heaven tumbled upside down into the sea with Tabakea under Ocean Island. Then Auriaria planted his staff on Samoa, which he had raised from the sea, so that the staff could grow into the Ancestral Tree. Later he married Na Areau's daughter, whose descendants now live in the Gilbert Islands.

The high god who had been described in most detail, Anulap of the Truk area, lives in a mansion, one part for himself, the other for his ten siblings. Flounder, who has both eyes on the same side, guards Anulap, and Sandpiper on the clashing rocks at Anulap's door shrieks as souls of the dead try to enter, allowing only the worthy to pass safely between the rocks. The now aged, white-haired, long-breasted, weak, and virtually inactive god has two men to raise his eyelids so that he can see; they also open his mouth and raise his upper lip so that he can eat. Like Puntan, Anulap does not receive worship. Nonetheless, he is omniscient, the creator, the ruler of the pantheon, and, with his brother Semenkoror, he is the god of wisdom, the greatest *idan*. Among the high gods there are others of similar inactivity. The Ifaluk high god Aluelap's only activity is to advise his son Lugeilang ("middle of heaven"), who raises Aluelap's eyelids to get his attention. Yet there are also high gods who actively help people. Yalafath of Yap, a most helpful deity, had Dessra, the thunder god, bring people fire; Yalafath also sent his wife as a frigate bird to scout a flooded island's needs, and once, after resuscitating a dead boy, he gave the boy and his mother sand to form islands and seedlings to plant.

Human Ancestors. Except in those Micronesian mythic traditions in which the primal deity and his or her spouse have children, it is usually unclear how the first people originated. Rather, attention is paid to particular individual mythic figures, male or female, and the role of the opposite sex is often denied. Husbandless females, human or animal, bear human beings and animals, and so establish clans. Children also emerge from parts of the body or from maggots on the body of a deity who is more often male than female. Even trees bear people, as in the Gilberts, and in some traditions a tree growing from a person's head splits open to release children. In one story, the earthly parentage of a clan's female ancestor is denied when she, a fingertip-size baby, falls from heaven.

A female animal ancestor often becomes her clan's totem. In one of several variations on the "swan maiden" theme a Yap man, by hiding the fins of a dolphin girl who came ashore to dance, captures and marries her. Years later, on finding her fins, she leaves her human family to return to the sea, and her daughters establish the Dolphin totemic clan. Occasionally a totem animal is helpful, as in the Ponapean story in which stingrays blanket the sea, tossing a disrespectful minor chief from one to another until they finally kill him for sending their totem descendant, the king, a pregnant woman's corpse instead of the bananas he had requested.

Many traditions include the tale of an animal mother's beautiful daughter who marries a king who has never seen his mother-in-law. For example, in one version Good Lizard makes channels on Ponape Island as she crawls to visit her daughter, who was married to the king, holder of the dynastic title Lord of Teleur. When the husband brings his mother-in-law her food, she tells him not to look at her. He disobeys, panics, and sets fire to the enormous guest house he had prepared for his wife's mother. His wife runs into the flames; he, for love of her, follows, and the three perish.

There are numerous myths about marriages between sky gods and mortal women. Olofat, the Caroline Islands trickster, is the son of Lugeilang and an earthly woman, from whose head he emerges. Like many culture heroes, he grows precociously. Later, he flies to his sky father on a column of smoke. A Kiribati semidivine clan ancestor, Bue ("burn"), snares his father the Sun in order to demand knowledge and magic; Bue is not, like the Polynesian Māui who performed a similar feat, trying to regulate the sun's speed. On both Ponape and Kusaie it is said that Ijokelekel (or Isokalakal, meaning "shining noble" or "wonderful king") is the son of the Ponapean thunder god Nan Djapue and the latter's aged clan sister from Kusaie Island. The tart lime given to her by Nan Djapue makes her pregnant, and in her womb Ijokelekel learns that he is to take revenge on the irreverent Lord of Teleur, the ruler, who had once imprisoned Nan Djapue for seducing his wife. When he is a young adult, Ijokelekel sails against this Lord of Teleur with 333 warriors and their families. Ijokelekel defeats his enemy, seizes power, and puts an end to a long line of increasingly oppressive rulers who had set their subjects impossible tasks. For instance, a certain Lord of Teleur had demanded a rare shell; a boy, aided by fish, went under the sea to get the shell, but on his return he and his family committed suicide to escape having to perform any further such tasks.

Tricksters and Death. Cycles of myths tell of divine and semidivine tricksters who are magicians, shape-shifters, transformers, and gross adulterers. When the demigod Olofat, who is known throughout the Carolines, was insulted by boys in the sky world, he gave their pet sharks teeth and their stingrays barbs such as they have now. Pretending ignorance of his relationship to him, Olofat jealously kills his half brother. When Half-Beak kills Olofat for stealing his wife, Lugeilang resuscitates him. Na Areau also enrages gods and men. When carpenters jam a housepost down on him he, like Olofat in a similar story, has a side passage ready. With red earth and coconut he simulates blood and flesh and deceives his enemies into thinking he is dead; then he appears and mocks them. In the myths of the Marshall Islands, Edao and Djelemut are either the sons of Irojerilik and Libage ("Lady Turtle") or spring from the thunder god Uelip's head. Edao constantly outwits his elder brother and others, and, like Na Areau, he plays the oven trick: telling his host of an easy way to get food, he lies down in a hot earth oven, is covered over, and later strolls up from the beach to uncover an oven full of fish and taro. His foolish host, imitating him, perishes, and the trickster takes his wife.

In these Micronesian myths there is little interest in the origin of permanent death. Olofat's sister adds to his decree that all must die and stay dead that Olofat too, but not the gods, must die when the world ended. Forgetfulness leads to permanent death when children forget to dig up their mother's corpse as directed or when those who, having learned a man's god-given secret of eternal life, forget a part of the secret and fail to revive him. Stories of temporary death and resuscitation are frequent. When the Palauan semidivine Milad dies in a flood, the gods whom she had once sheltered restore her to life, and send Mud Hen, a personified mythic bird (progenitor of *Rallus pectoralis*), to fetch the "water of immortality" in a leaf. However, selfish Mud Hen has a hibiscus bush pierce the leaf. While the spilled "water" makes the hibiscus immune to harsh conditions, Milad loses the chance of immortality. The angry gods, striking Mud Hen's head, give it a red stripe to make it a symbol of wickedness and ugliness. All mud hens now have that stripe.

The Land and Its Fruits. According to the myths of the area numerous islands and islets developed not only from sand but also from taro, flowers, branches, and the like that were cast on the sea, often by disgruntled women leaving home. Dead bodies could also be the bases of islands. Palau developed from a giant's corpse, and the people of Palau from its maggots; Lelu developed from a whale-mother's corpse. Except on Fais and Mille, island-fishing is less important in the myths of Micronesia than in those of Polynesia. When Motikitik (a cognate of Mauitikitiki, or Māui) fishes up Fais, his dead mother's signal confirms that he, not his brothers, owns it and can divide it into its present three parts. Because it acquired the magical hook, a Yap district dominates Fais politically; were the hook lost, Fais would sink. Edao capsized Mille to test some diviners' skill in coconut-leaf divination; they located the island, fished it up, and made a drain hole that is now a taro pit. Stories of building an island, usually with rocks flying magically into place, are common. Aided by an octopus, explorers found an exposed reef on which to build Ponape and shelter it with mangroves and a barrier reef. Later Oljipa and Oljopa (Sipa and Sopa) constructed eighty or ninety artificial islets, Nan Matol (the "Micronesian Venice"), as sites for a ceremonial center, now in ruins. Oljopa was perhaps the first to bear the royal title Lord of Teleur. According to folk belief, actual bands of "little people," also known in other islands, did the actual work of construction.

The principal cultivated plants or certain varieties of these came directly or indirectly from celestial beings, usually women. Even today Micronesian gardeners think any new variety of plants has fallen from heaven. When three swamp taros *(Cyrtosperma)* fell into the sea from the Kiribati sky they became porpoises, swam to Arorae, turned back into taros, and were planted by a man whom Tituābine instructed. Two sky men gave taro to Majuro Island after Namu had rejected it. Milad taught Palauans to cultivate *Colocasia* taro; each island learned differently.

More than one mythical woman who bore both human beings and food plants had a coconut son. Limokare, Irojerilik's sister, planted her coconut son Tepoler after he told her of benefits that would grow from him and therefore prove his value to his hostile, older, human brother. Like other Pacific islanders, Micronesians tell of coconut trees growing from the head or grave of an eel or a person. Ligoupup saw her first child's eyes and mouth in the nuts from the coconut tree growing on his grave. When a female eel, which Yalafath sent to Yap to populate the island with people, was killed generations later, a coconut tree grew from her buried head, a banana plant from her middle, and a swamp taro from her tail.

Ponapean kava grew from a bit of the god Luk's flesh that he gave a kind woman to plant, and sugarcane grew on the grave of a man he had ordered buried. Observing that rats stupefied themselves on kava and then chewed sugarcane as a chaser, people imitated them, as did the sky dwellers.

According to the myths, easy ways to get food eventually fail through envy or carelessness. Jealous neighbors who chopped down Milad's god-given tree, which produced breadfruit and fish, thereby caused a life-destroying flood; Palauan carved wooden storyboards portray the scene. Travelers bring home new foods or carry them elsewhere. Yalafath, on sending his guest Galuai flying home on a chicken-festooned pole, said that if he took proper care of the chickens they would excrete yams. Soon Galuai became careless and the hungry chickens, by eating the yams, lost their magic (as, in another tale, did another man's mistreated money-excreting bird). Travelers, including gods, who eat from an inexhaustible taro plant, coconut tree, or fishpond in an alien land, or from a tree growing in midocean, must watch out for supernatural hazards.

Origin of Fire and Technology. People ate only sun-baked food until male spirits, usually from the sky and consigned to earth against their will, rewarded helpful women or boys with the knowledge of fire and cooking. Edao taught a generous boy; a disoriented spirit (only a head) instructed a Mortlock boy who escorted him home (and also restored the life of the boy's brother). When a Yap woman extricated the thunder god from a prickly pandanus he put two sticks under his arm to imbue them with fire and then demonstrated how to make fire with them and cook; he also taught her pottery-making. Fire from a god's body is a recurrent motif in Oceanic mythology. On Truk, Rat, a personified mythic being, taught a sympathetic woman to make fire and cook after Lugeilang had set Rat's muzzle on fire and driven him from heaven for thievery. On Mortlock and Namoluk, Olofat, after escaping from being burned alive for his tricks, became the god of fire and the condemned, and sent fire to earth in a starling's beak.

In the myths of the Kiribati, fire came from the ocean. Because the sunbeam that was caught by the boy Te-ika ("the fish") set numerous fires in the ocean world, his father Bakoa ("shark"), Lord of the Ocean, exiled him. On earth Tabakea, Lord of the Land, beat Te-ika and his sunbeam to death with sticks that absorbed the fire. Subsequently he revived Te-ika with the same sticks because of Bakoa's grief, but the fiery boy died at the water's edge. Like Māui in Polynesia, Na Areau in the Gilberts repeatedly demanded fire from its keeper (here, Lightning); but unlike Māui, he does not want in order to learn the secret of making fire. He wished only to provoke the thunder god Tabuariki to a wrestling match and to weaken him by breaking his arm.

Spirits keep secret their fishing techniques, gear, and magic except from generous and deserving individuals. A woman to whom a sea spirit has divulged family secrets in exchange for her new yellow skirt has to flee from the sea spirit's angry father to another island where, however, she sells her secrets. In exchange for secretly borrowing his canoe, spirits later show a Ulithi man how to make fishtraps. According to a complex myth, the people of Truk did not know how to fish until the god Solal taught a neglected, one-legged boy, whose success then led villagers to make him chief.

Because of the enormous hazards of seafaring, experts in the practice, lore, and magic of canoe-building and navigation are highly prized by the islanders. Experts from the Marshall Islands fear that they may, at sea, forget their mnemonic, informational, magical, and courage-inspiring chants; others fear watchful Rainbow's punishment for mistakes at sea. In Ulithi when Palulop ("great navigator"), a sky man residing on earth, teaches his sons navigation, the as-yet-unborn Ialuluwe (Aluluei) listens; on Ulithi as elsewhere in the Caroline Islands, he subsequently became the supreme sea god. Like the Polynesian Tinirau he has two faces, one looking ahead and the other looking back at dangers men cannot see. Of his sons, Rongerik studies diligently under his father, as a future navigator should, and later has to rescue his brother Rongolap, who had thought only of women and had neglected his studies.

Three women who transmitted navigational lore to men are the Yap goddess Legerem, who taught canoe-building, navigation, and star lore; the Kiribati ancestress Branch of Buka, whose grandfather taught navigation and bonito-fishing to her rather than to her selfish brothers; and, in the Carolines, Aluluei's daughter, who, having given three navigation gods an inexhaustible drinking nut, received from them knowledge that was as yet unknown to her father.

Certain mythical canoes made of rock, sand, taro tubers, or pandanus drupes obey verbal commands even if the owner is not aboard. Others skim through the air, reflecting Micronesian interest in flying by magic over their vast island area; in one myth a man's hollow wooden bird carries him to his abducted wife. More pragmatically, two Bikini men are said to have invented the Tridacna adze and the paddling canoe. Subsequently the Marshall Islanders learned about a celestial woman's invention of masts and sails with which she had enabled Djebro, youngest of her five sons, to win a race to become king. Like other Pacific islanders, a canoe-maker may find his felled tree restored by an offended spirit. When this happened to Rongerik, Aluluei told him to first greet a trilling bird named Seilangi, god of carpenters. This done, happy Seilangi made Rongerik's canoe in one night to start him on his great career as a navigator.

BIBLIOGRAPHY

The following publications, which are supplementary to those cited by William A. Lessa in the foregoing overview article, are organized according to three eras of collection of mythological materials.

The Belief among the Micronesians, the third volume of James G. Frazer's *The Belief in Immortality and the Worship of the Dead* (London, 1924), gives English translations from the first era of Spanish and German collections of myths, tales, and legends that despite Frazer's title relate to more than simply death and immortality. These collections date up to and include 1914, and, beyond this, the volume also contains many examples from *Yap,* by Wilhelm Müller, in *Ergebnisse der Südsee-expedition, 1908–1910* (ESSE), edited by Georg Thilenius (Hamburg, 1917–1918), a work that is conventionally identified as ESSE II.B.II.1–2. Frazer's *Myths of the Origin of Fire* (London, 1930) includes Micronesian examples from English sources such as *The Caroline Islands,* by Frederick William Christian (1899; reprint, London, 1967), and English translations of Spanish and German sources, including examples from several ESSE volumes.

As almost every ESSE volume includes myths (some are devoted entirely to narratives and chants), the series is an indispensable primary source. Also during the first era, the series "Anthropos Bibliothek" published August Erdland's *Die Marshall-Insulaner* (Münster, 1914) and *Die Bewohner der Truk-inseln,* by Laurentius Bollig (Münster, 1927), both of which take into account the islanders' own classification of genres. *Südseemärchen aus Australien, Neu-Guinea, Fidji, Karolinen, Samoa, Tonga, Hawaii, Neu-Seeland,* by Paul Hambruch (Jena, 1921), has valuable notes on the distribution of certain myths.

As the first era was that of Spanish, then German political control of the Marianas, Carolines, and Marshalls (the Gilberts remained British), the second era of collection was that of the Japanese between the two World Wars. Lack of translation from the Japanese has made largely inaccessible such publications as those by Masamichi Miyatake and Masaachi Noguchi for Palau and especially by Hisataka Hijakata for Palau and Satawal. Until Hijakata taught Palauans to carve portable storyboards, they had carved mythic scenes only on men's clubhouses.

The third collecting era in the three archipelagoes began after World War II with the Coordinated Investigation of Micronesian Anthropology (CIMA) and led many Americans to do fieldwork in the area. In mythology there is, besides Lessa's two valuable monographs, a work of special note: Edwin Grant Burrows's *Flower in my Ear: Arts and Ethos of Ifaluk Atoll* (Seattle, 1963), which discusses myths and chants in terms of style and social values. A collection by Roger E. Mitchell, *Micronesian Folktales* (Nagoya, Japan, 1973), includes notes on distribution. Seventeen pages of annotated listings of Micronesian, including Kiribati, mythology appear in *A Select Bibliography of the Oral Tradition of Oceania* by Margaret Orbell (Paris, 1974).

Collections by Micronesians themselves appear in increasing numbers. Most remarkable is *The Book of Luelen: Luelen Bernart,* translated and edited by John L. Fischer, Saul H. Riesenberg, and Marjorie G. Whiting (Honolulu, 1977). Luelen (1866–1946?), a Ponapean man, wrote and dictated between 1934 and 1946 what he considered significant for his family to know about Ponape, including its myths, oral history, and song texts. *Annotations to the Book of Luelen* by the same translators and editors (Honolulu, 1977), adds explanations, variants, and comparative data.

Yale University's Human Relations Area Files (HRAF) has produced English translations of parts of the German ESSE and other works. An example is the complete translation into English of the German work by Augustin Krämer and Hans Nevermann, *Ralik-Ratak (Marshall-Inseln)* (ESSE II.B.XI; Hamburg, 1938), as HRAF no. 1003. Most Micronesian school readers retell the traditions, but *Pohnpei ni Mwehin Kawa: Old Ponape,* edited by Pensile Lawrence and others (Saipan, 1973), uses Paul Hambruch's *Ponape* (ESSE II.B.VII.3; Hamburg, 1936), quoting his Ponapean texts and translating into English Hambruch's free German translations.

KATHARINE LUOMALA

MIDRASH AND AGGADAH. Regardless of what specifically the Hebrew word *midrash* stands for in its two occurrences in a postexilic book of the Hebrew scriptures (*2 Chr.* 13:22, 24:27), where the reference is clearly to something written or written in (Heb., *ketuvim;* Gr., *gegramménoi*), by the last century BCE it stands for oral interpretation, that is, interpretation of the Torah, the Law of Moses; and one who interprets the Law is referred to as *doresh ha-torah.* This we learn from the literature of the Dead Sea sectarians (*Damascus Covenant* 6.7, 7.18f., 8.29; *Manual of Discipline* 6.6, 8.15; see also *Ecclesiastes* 1:13). Indeed, it is possible that already at the beginning of the second century BCE there were in existence schools where Torah interpretation was going on. In the Hebrew of *Ben Sira* (c. 200–180 BCE), the author, Simeon ben Joshua ben Sira, or Sirach, by whose time "wisdom" is already equated with the Torah, speaks as follows: "Turn to me, you who are untaught, and lodge in my school [*beit midrash;* literally, 'house, or place, of *midrash*'; *en oikō paideias*]." *Midrash* is therefore a school activity. In the *beit ha-midrash,* the school, learning is to be found, wisdom is to be acquired, there is a master, and there are disciples; through interpretation, understanding of the Torah is attained: "The book of the covenant of the Most High God, the Law (Torah) which Moses commanded us . . . fills men with wisdom, like the Pishon, and like the Tigris at the time of the first fruits. It makes them full of understanding like the Euphrates, and like the Jordan at harvest time" (*Sir.* 24:23–26)—and there is more to this effect.

Origins of the Midrash. A question that may never be answered satisfactorily is that of when, precisely, the interpretation of the Torah began. For from the moment any text is adopted as a rule or guide of life, some interpretation—added explanation, commentary—inevitably becomes necessary. In scripture itself, though most commandments are lucidly drawn up, there are four occasions when even Moses was in need of further instruction regarding procedures for laws already established (*Lv.* 24:10–23; *Nm.* 9:4–14, 15:32–36, 27:1–11). The Midrash also calls attention to Moses facing difficulty in understanding specifically what God has ordered (*Mekhilta'*, ed. Jacob Lauterbach, 1.15; cf. *Sifrei Zuṭa'*, ed. Saul Lieberman, 6.16; but see also Harry Fox in *Tarbiz* 49, 1980, 278ff.). In scripture such cases are reported probably to underscore that no human legislator, not even Moses, is the originator of biblical laws, that Moses only transmits what the Lord ordains; the Law of Moses is God's law which he communicates through Moses. But these cases at the same time illustrate that no written code can be operative without supplementary instruction. And supplementary instruction is what *midrash* provides.

There is therefore a measure of justice to the traditional view that the written Torah had to be accompanied from the outset by expository teachings of some kind, transmitted and inherited orally (the oral Torah). But we are in no position to fix the time when precisely such very ancient supplementary teaching began. In legendary lore there are views that, for example, statutory prayer services were first established by the patriarchs (B.T., *Ber.* 26b); that benedictions of the grace after meals were added by Moses, Joshua, David, and Solomon (ibid., 48b); and that already at Sinai at the giving of the Ten Commandments interpretation was taking place (*Mekhilta'* 2.267). But such statements have no historical value and perhaps are not meant to be taken as history in the strict sense. They represent a tendency to project later institutions farther and farther back in time in order to suggest high antiquity and that these are not recent unauthorized inventions.

Whatever very ancient interpretation may have been like (reflected also in glosses, popular etymologies, and parables within the Hebrew scriptures themselves; cf. I. L. Seeligmann in *Supplement to Vetus Testamentum,* vol. 1, 1953, pp. 150–181), it is unquestionable that from roughly 250 BCE, when the Pentateuch was translated into Greek (as the Septuagint), and continuing for seven hundred years and beyond, when major collections of Midrashic literature continued to be redacted, *midrash* flourished in the Jewish academies of Palestine. From the end of approximately the second century CE, *midrash* flourished to a lesser extent in the Babylonian Jewish academies as well, though it was principally a Palestinian creation.

Hellenistic-Roman influence on intellectual and cultural life in Jewish Palestine affected Midrashic activity, as can be seen in the penetration of Greek (and other foreign) terms, the terminology for some rules of interpretation, the circulation of tales and epigrams, the parables drawn from royal and imperial establishments, a few cultic details, and the significance given to the numerical value of Hebrew words *(gimaṭriyyah).* In short, while it would be inexcusably uncritical to assume that wherever there is influence there is simultaneously direct dependence and borrowing, the rich and constant intellectual preoccupation with explanation of the language and content of scripture by teachers to students in the schools, and to the public at large by means of sermons in the synagogues, is an echo of the stimulation provided wherever—not only in Palestine—the spirit of Greek learning and letters came to the attention of the learned classes. Native traditions were not necessarily abandoned; indeed, they might now be held onto more tightly, but they would also be interpreted in ways comprehensible to those who lived in an age when Greek models of thinking and expression dominated the overall intellectual climate.

Aggadic Midrash. *Midrash* (i.e., interpretation, commentary, exegesis, amplification) was applied to all of scripture, and in tannaitic times (approximately the first two centuries CE), especially to four books of the Pentateuch, *Exodus* through *Deuteronomy,* because these contained the bulk of biblical *halakhah,* the regulations governing the conduct of society as well as individual practice. However, even in these books there is considerable nonhalakhic material, what is called *aggadah,* and the first book of the Pentateuch, *Genesis,* is almost entirely *aggadah.* Aggadic subject matter was therefore also commented on in the tannaitic *mid-*

rashim, and some of the leading masters of *halakhah* were also leading masters of *aggadah*. Thus we have aggadic *midrashim* not only on *Genesis* but also in the midrashic compilations on the other Pentateuch books as well, and aggadic discussion is thus included not only in the tannaitic *midrashim* but in subsequent works devoted to all the books of the Hebrew Bible.

The word *aggadah* may be rendered as "narrative, recitation, account based on scripture," but the term, the concept, implies and refers to very much more in the Midrashic and Talmudic corpora. By *aggadah* is meant that which strictly speaking is not classified as *halakhah*, as required, normative practice. *Aggadah* includes narratives, historical composition, poetry, speculation, genealogical records, fanciful interpretation, moral exhortation—in short, the exposition of the whole variety of scriptural contents beyond the codified, legislative, and juristic, prescribed courses of action which constitute *halakhah*.

There are instances where a sharp line between aggadic comment and halakhic cannot be drawn easily; see, for example, *Keritot* 6.3 (and cf. Eliʿezer in *Keritot* 6.1). On the whole, however, a halakhic discussion is easily distinguished from an aggadic one. In the former, legalistic concern is uppermost, norms of practice are sought, there is close attachment to what the sages regard as literal meaning, argument by authorities is erudite and acute, there is constant resort to tradition, rules of interpretation are followed with due regard for their function (those of Hillel in the first century, those of ʿAqiva' and Yishmaʿe'l in the second century), and casuistry is employed as in all legal and scholastic disciplines. On the other hand, *aggadah* is unrestrained contemplation and interpretation associated with the vocabulary and themes of all parts of the Bible. There is free application of the subject of one verse in scripture to another verse far removed from it, so that, for example, in undertaking to comment on *Leviticus* 1:1, the teacher or preacher introduces *Psalms* 103:20 and by skillful adaptation can demonstrate that the *Psalms* verse explains the intention of the *Leviticus* verse. *Aggadah* is very often sermonic, interpretation for the benefit of the folk in the synagogue, and therefore, though there are, so to speak, rules of interpretation for *aggadah* as well, they do not really confine the *aggadot* within strictly drawn hermeneutical perimeters.

Considerable liberty of interpretation was permitted to and practiced by the authors of *midrash aggadah*, who employed all the rhetorical devices common among textual scholars of their time, used, for instance, in the interpretation of Homer. Thus much is made of punning, of homophones, of methods of dream interpretation, of figures of speech, and of acronyms. A frequent form of interpretation is the parable of kings and their subjects. Verses receive not just one but many interpretations, which indictes not the rejection of previous explanation but the simultaneous legitimacy of a number of meanings which the biblical, divinely revealed text contains and hence, also, beneath-the-surface lessons. *Midrash aggadah* is employed for polemic purposes, against internal challengers as well as antagonists from the outside. For example, when Pappos interprets *Job* 23:13 as a statement of God's omnipotent and arbitrary power, ʿAqiva' hushes him up by means of an alternative interpretation that every decision of God is just, (*Mekhilta'* 1.248). Or when Israel is mocked because the Temple was destroyed (presumably, a sign of God's rejection of Israel), one sage declares that this was, on the contrary, a sign of God's love for Israel, in that he let out his wrath on the sticks and stones of the structure (his own habitation) rather than on the people themselves (*Lam. Rab. on Lam.* 4:11 ed. Buber, 74b). Comments like these were obviously made as a consolation after profound tragedy. And they reveal too the ready resort to paradox: even misfortune may be for the good (see also *Genesis* 45:5–8; for paradox in *halakhah*, see *Tanḥuma'* on *Numbers*, ed. Buber, 52a–b).

Along with polemics, *midrash aggadah* does not hesitate to indulge in varieties of apologetics. Thus examples of questionable behavior of the patriarchs and Israel's heroes (the twelve sons of Jacob, David, and Solomon) are frequently excused and presented in a positive light, while their enemies' characters are in almost all respects regarded as wicked—typical folkloristic treatment. Events in scripture are identified as foreshadowings of experiences later in the sages' own times and of the age to come. By means of *midrash* the protests and resentments of later generations find eloquent outlet, and this in turn leads to attempts at theodicy. In the retelling of biblical narratives legendary lore is drawn upon in order to emphasize particular values and ideals; so, too, to contrast the ways of the nations of the world with Israel's ways. And in virtually all interpretation, especially where more than immediate, literal meaning is sought, the aim of aggadic *midrash* is moral and didactic. This is particularly noteworthy in the stories told about famous sages: in these, fancy and fact are so closely intertwined it is rare that the one can be separated from the other.

Aggadic *midrash* also preserves evidence of gnostic speculation by certain rabbis on the theme of creation, on the chariot spoken of by Ezekiel, on the overpowering reality of the godhead and his celestial retinue, on major historic experiences of Israel (at the sea after the redemption from Egyptian bondage and at the Sinai revelation), on the contrast between the fate of man after the Fall and before it and what might have been otherwise.

With such latitude available to aggadic *midrash*, all aspects of life come under review—the relations of man to God and of man to fellow man. Piety of conduct (in the light of the law and in action surpassing legal prescription) and piety of thought are exemplified. Public virtue and private virtue are discussed in the light of moral expectation, related to biblical verses, which are quoted and given novel interpretation, and interrelated with the particular theme in the mind of the teacher or preacher.

For example, scripture (*Ex.* 19:1–2) reports that "On the third new moon after the Israelites had gone forth from the land of Egypt, on that very day, they entered the wilderness of Sinai. Having journeyed from Rephidim, they entered the wilderness of Sinai and encamped [here the verb is plural: *va-yaḥanu*] in the wilderness. Israel encamped [here the verb is singular: *va-yiḥan*] there in front of the mountain."

To draw the moral of these verses the homilist first invokes a verse from *Proverbs* in which the subject is the excellence of wisdom, which for the homilist and his audience is already understood as the Torah. Then *Proverbs* 3:17—"Its [wisdom's] ways are ways of pleasantness, and all its paths are peace"—is made to shed light on the *Exodus* report. Thus the Holy One, blessed be he, actually wished to give the Torah to Israel at the time they left Egypt, but the Israelites kept quarreling with each other, saying all the time, "Let us head back to Egypt" (*Nm.* 14:4). Note what is written (*Ex.* 13:20): "They set out from Succoth and encamped at Ethan"—both verbs are in the plural, for as the Israelites moved on ("set out"), they quarreled, and as they halted ("encamped"), they quarreled; but when they reached Rephidim, they all made peace and became a united assembly (a single band). (And when is the Almighty exalted? When Israel forms a single band, as it is said [*Am.* 9:6], "His band he founded on the earth" [*Lv. Rab.* 30.12, 710]—possibly an appeal not to break up into conflicting sects.) How do we know that they all became a united assembly? For the verse (*Ex.* 19:2) says, "Israel encamped there in front of the mountain," and this time the verb is in the singular: *va-yiḥan*; it is not written, "they encamped," with the verb in the plural, *va-yaḥanu*. Said the Holy One, blessed be he, the Torah, all of it, is peace (-loving); to whom shall I give it? To the nation that loves peace. Hence (*Prv.* 3:17), "and all its paths are peace" (*Mekhilta'* 2.200; *Lv. Rab.* 9.9, 188; *Tanḥuma'* on *Ex.*, ed. Buber, 37b, 9).

A number of elements, typical of *midrash* as a whole, appear in this passage. To begin with, there is the association of a verse "far removed" (in *Proverbs*) with the particular verse (in *Exodus*) to be interpreted—which is meant to demonstrate that all parts of scripture endorse each other and that it can be shown, when necessary, that they are not in conflict. Second, there is meticulous attention to minutiae—the significance even of shifts from plural to singular (by dropping one consonant)—from which an important lesson can be derived. Third, verses are cited at every opportunity to serve as proof text; in many *midrashim* this feature is even more lavishly exhibited than in our passage, and there is no trace of their authors' possessing concordances to help them in their search for apt quotations. Finally, of course, there is the chief theme with which the *midrash* may be concerned, in our case, the theme of peace (which may be a warning against sectarianism or even an exhortation not to contemplate rebellion against the ruling powers). That study of the Torah thrives on peace and leads to peace is what the Midrashic and Talmudic sages frequently tried to stress.

Goals and Themes of the Midrash. There are very many *midrashim* even more complex in their structure and content, but basically it may be said that all Midrashic teaching undertakes two things: (1) to explain opaque or ambiguous texts and their difficult vocabulary and syntax thus supplying us with what we would call literal or close-to-literal explanation or, for lack of that, purely homiletical guess; (2) to contemporize, that is, so to describe or treat biblical personalities and events as to make recognizable the immediate relevance of what might otherwise be regarded as only archaic. As we have seen, a scene from the account of the revelation of the Ten Commandments becomes a homily on Torah and peace. Patriarchs will be described as mourning for the destruction of the Temple. Esau comes to represent the Roman empire. The twelve sons of Jacob become extraordinary military heroes. And so it goes for the rest of scripture: the past addresses the present, directly or indirectly, and drops hints of the future. There are Midrashic interpretations that grow out of both a lexical problem in the verse and the desire to apply the explanation to the thinking and need of the later age. For example, for *ve-anvehu* ("and I will glorify him" [*Ex.* 15:2]) Abba' Sha'ul says, "Take after him [*ani ve-hu'*; lit., "I and he"], even as he is gracious and compassionate, so should you be gracious and compassionate"; thus a meaning of the problematic *anvehu* is provided and along with that the moral lesson of *imitatio dei* (*Mekhilta'* 2.25).

Although, as I have said earlier, the Midrash takes into account whatever scripture refers to, there are at least three themes to which much reflection and commentary are devoted. The first is the absolute unity and incomparability of God. The cue for this is of course in scripture (*Dt.* 6:4 and elsewhere), but the kind of emphasis given is essentially postbiblical—that is, that no dualism or plurality of gods is to be tolerated; no worship of God is to be modeled after pagan worship; that regardless of what overtakes Israel, God's justice is not to be denied; that unlike frequent frivolous treatment of their gods by the pagan world, Israel must love God absolutely, with no reservations, come what may. In the Midrash God may be spoken of anthropomorphically; this does not embarrass the sages; they know that such speech is metaphorical and inevitable (therefore its presence in scripture itself); what they fear is blasphemy and anything that can lead to the desecration of God's name.

A second recurring theme is Israel—that is, Israel of the biblical past, Israel of the present, and the ideal Israel of the age to come. To the patriarchs of Israel there had already been the promise that God would maintain a unique relationship with their descendants. And though God may grow angry at them and visit them with punishments and disasters, the bond between God and their people is a permanent one (see also *Ezekiel* 20:30–44). Israel is under obligation to carry out his commands, and in Midrashic and Talmudic centuries this meant not merely the commands as formulated "briefly" in the scriptures but as interpreted at length by the sages: "'If you do not hearken unto me' (*Lv.* 26:14), that is, if you do not hearken to the interpretation, the instruction [*midrash*] of the sages" (*Sifra'* 111b; see also *Sifrei, Dt.* 49, ed. Finkelstein, 114f.). Along with this fundamental view come all sorts of promises of ultimate reward for adherence to the terms of the covenantal relationship and all sorts of regulations concerning how Israel is to remain distinct from the nations of the world in whose midst Israel of the present must live. The self-consciousness demanded by the original covenant and its subsequent reaffirmations is not merely taken for granted or left implicit; it is repeatedly articulated.

No less pervasive is the third theme, that of Torah, which has two meanings, often simultaneous but often also distinct, and it is not always easy to decide which is intended. The word *torah* can stand both for the study of the Torah and for putting into practice the teachings of the Torah. While obedience to the commands of the Torah is already a frequent biblical injunction, what especially characterizes the demands of the sages in the Midrash is their tireless exhortation that all must study Torah, that neglect of study is not just a sign of a poor education but a deficiency in one's role in life. The sages do not deny that one may merit a share in the life of the world to come even if he is not a scholar or student. But this hardly satisfies them, and ever and again they return to the duty and privilege of Torah study. It is a person's required curriculum from the time he begins scripture study at the age of five—from the time he begins to speak, he should be taught selected verses on the theme of Torah—until the day of his death. Many hyperbolic sayings occur in this connection, and these are indicative of the lengths to which the sages were prepared to go in order to impress on all classes in society, rich and poor, the supreme obligation and value of Torah study. It is the emphasis on Torah study, indeed, that gradually transformed the originally prophetically oriented religion of Judaism into an intellectually directed religious experience in which scholars are the elite. [*See also* Torah.]

The Process of Composition. The bulk of aggadic *midrash* commentary which we possess very likely came into being as homilies in connection with the Torah reading as part of synagogue worship. Unfortunately, it is still impossible to fix the time when public Torah reading was first institutionalized. It was certainly in existence by the end of the last century BCE and the first century CE, for Philo Judaeus, Josephus Flavius, and the New Testament all refer to the study and exegesis of Torah (and prophetic selections) as a weekly Sabbath program. The weekly reading (in Palestine, according to a three-and-a-half-year cycle) served as the principle of organization, the scheme of arrangement for the Midrashic homilies.

The different Midrashic compilations display a certain variety of composition—there are *midrashim* that comment on the biblical text verse by verse (exegetical *midrashim;* e.g., *Genesis Rabbah*) and those that comment only on the opening verse or verses of the pericope and then move on to the next biblical unit (homiletical *midrashim;* e.g., *Leviticus Rabbah*) In these exegetical and homiletic *midrashim,* before the principal Midrashic interpretation there may be an introductory homily or homilies, *petiḥta', petiḥata',* or proems, as a kind of overture to the principal interpretation; perhaps (as suggested by Joseph Heinemann in *Scripta Hierosolymitana,* 1971) these served as brief sermons before the Torah reading. Tanḥuma' Yelammdenu *midrashim* tend to introduce the aggadic discourse by citation of a halakhic question and answer, doubtless not only to convey a rule of practice but to underscore that *halakhah* and *aggadah* are one in aim. There are Midrashic texts drawn up for the round of special days in the year, feasts and fast days and other appointed occasions (e.g., *Pesiqta' de-Rav Kahana'*). There are still other compilations, but what is significant is that in all these texts, regardless of stylization, there is created an intellectual, didactic, hortatory tone which all the *midrashim* share, and thus all the *midrashim* sound as though they all were in manner or approach alike. At a later time (from about the seventh century on), Midrashic views are combined to create a literary composition—for example, on the sacrifice of Isaac or Abraham, on the rabbinic martyrs of the Hadrianic period, on Abraham's discovery of and commitment to the one God, on the death of Moses, and so forth.

There seem occasionally to have existed books of *aggadah* even in rabbinic times, but the rabbis disapproved of them. Like all other branches of study, except for scripture, aggadic *midrash* was delivered and attended to as part of the oral law, that branch of the total tradition that was not to be put in writing: Midrash, Mishnah, Targum, Talmud, the *halakhot* and the *aggadot*—in other words, what the rabbis taught.

The creators of the aggadic *midrashim* were the rabbis, but this does not mean that they drew only on scholarly sources or had only scholarly exposition in mind. The rabbis did draw on these, especially when biblical terms were difficult; but they also drew on folklore, on popular legends, on anecdotes, on deliberately imaginative identifications which would make the passage they were interpreting intelligible and also surprising to their audience. They might use current Greek words and epigrams to add special vividness to their interpretation. They might adopt allegorical methods of explanation. Everyone, including women and children, attended the synagogue to hear the preacher. Midrashic method became so popular that even nonscholarly men could express themselves in the form, or so the Midrash relates. For example, a rabbi's ass driver undertakes to refute a Samaritan when the rabbi himself is at a loss for a proper retort (*Gn. Rab.* 32.10, 296f.); an unlearned man offers an interpretation of a verse the rabbi had not thought of, and the rabbi promises the man that he will use that interpretation in a sermon in the man's name (ibid., 78.12, 932f.). When a homily is admired, one might praise it as "a precious gem."

Exposure and attention to aggadic *midrash* were certainly widespread, especially when the hearts of the people craved comforting. But aggadic *midrash*, as I have mentioned, was also part of the oral law and was also a subject of the *beit ha-midrash*, the academy. There is no lack of comments emphasizing the value of this study, but the very repetitions in favor of *aggadah* create the impression that scholars had to be encouraged again and again not to neglect it. Early allegorists said, "If you wish to recognize him who spake and the world came to be [i.e., if you wish to have correct thoughts about the creator of the universe], study *aggadah*, for it is thus that you will recognize him who spake and the world came to be and cleave to his ways (*Sifrei Dt.* 49, ed. Finkelstein, p. 115). The superlative estimate of *aggadah* is here evident: what leads one to a proper knowledge of God and to attachment to his ways is to be found not in pursuit of halakhic studies (alone?) but in reflection on the acts of God as described in many places of the *aggadah*. But the feeling is inescapable that such sentiments imply a criticism of those scholars who, because they are chiefly masters of the law, experts in the complex disciplines of dialectic and halakhic subtleties, tend to regard *aggadah* condescendingly. The very freedom of speculation it permits and its very lack of fixed rules of mandatory conduct probably make the sages uncomfortable. Moreover, the exacting analytic exercises demanded by *halakhah* may have made single-minded halakhists feel superior to that which appealed to popular taste. On the other hand, for the folk as a whole the *aggadah* was a perennial refreshment of spirit and of the courage to endure. This the scholars did not deny, and that experience of refreshment remained true for centuries to come.

Principal Compilations. The following is a list of the principal Midrashic compilations and treatises; critical editions are listed briefly within parentheses. Particular but noncritical editions are listed without parentheses.

First are the tannaitic *midrashim;* these are essentially halakhic, but they contain a good deal of aggadic material as well:

1. *Exodus: Mekhilta' de-Rabbi Yishma'e'l* (edited by Jacob Lauterbach; a second edition was edited by Hayyim Horovitz and Israel Rabin) and *Mekhilta' de Rabbi Shim'on bar Yoḥ'ai* (edited by Jacob Epstein and Ezra Melamed).
2. *Leviticus: Sifra'*, edited by I. H. Weiss. There is also an edition by Meir Ish Shalom [Friedmann] that is critical but only a beginning; Louis Finkelstein has published Vatican Manuscript Codex Assemani LXVI of the treatise with a long and instructive introduction. Finkelstein's critical edition of *Sifra'* has begun to appear.
3. *Numbers: Sifrei de-vei Rav*, and *Sifrei zuṭa'* (both edited by Horovitz).
4. *Deuteronomy: Sifrei* (edited by Finkelstein) and *Midrash Tanna'im*, edited by David Hoffmann.

The following are aggadic *midrashim* from the amoraic period (c. third through fifth or sixth century) to the thirteenth century:

1. The collection known as Midrash Rabbah on the Pentateuch and the Five Scrolls *(Song of Songs, Ruth, Lamentations, Ecclesiastes,* and *Esther).* The individual works were drawn up in different times: *Genesis Rabbah* (edited by Julius Theodor and Chanoch Albeck), from the late fourth to early fifth century, is

the earliest, and just a little later is *Leviticus Rabbah* (edited by Mordecai Margulies). For *Deuteronomy Rabbah*, see also the edition by Saul Lieberman. On this collection as a whole, see Zunz (1892).

2. *Tanḥuma'* on the Pentateuch and *Tanḥuma'*, edited by Solomon Buber.
3. *Pesiqta' de-Rav Kahana'* (edited by Bernard Mandelbaum).
4. *Midrash Tehillim* (Midrash of the Psalms), edited by Buber.
5. The Yemenite *Midrash ha-gadol* on the Pentateuch, by David ben Amram Adani (thirteenth century), which draws on earlier Midrashic compilations (some no longer extant) and even Maimonides to form a collection of its own:
   - *Genesis* and *Exodus* (edited by Margulies)
   - *Leviticus* (edited by Nahum Rabinowitz and Adin Steinsalz)
   - *Numbers* (edited by Solomon Fisch; a second edition was edited by Tsevi Rabinowitz)
   - *Deuteronomy* (edited by Fisch)
6. *Yalquṭ Shim'oni*, also of the thirteenth century, by a rabbi Shim'on, which gathers its material from many earlier *midrashim* and covers the whole of Hebrew scriptures.

[*See also* Biblical Exegesis, *article on* Jewish Views.]

BIBLIOGRAPHY

On all this literature see the classic presentation by Leopold Zunz, *Die gottesdienstlichen Vorträge der Juden* (1832; 2d ed., Hildesheim, 1966) but even better the Hebrew translation thereof, *Ha-derashot be-Yisra'el* (Jerusalem, 1947), which is brought up to date and corrected by Chanoch Albeck in the light of later research. Other Midrashic collections not listed here, albeit of considerable importance, are also described and discussed in this work.

The best presentation of the sages as aggadic teachers is Wilhelm Bacher's *Die Agada der Tannaiten*, 2 vols. (1884–1890; reprint, Berlin, 1965–1966); *Die Agada der palästinischen Amoräer*, 3 vols. (Strasbourg, 1892–1899); and *Die Agada der babylonischen Amoräer* (Strasbourg, 1878). Bacher introduces each of the principal teachers separately, organizes the teachings around major categories as embodied in many scattered sayings, and comments on them. This work is also available in Hebrew translation by A. Z. Rabinowitz). See also E. E. Epstein-Halevi's *Ha-aggadah ha-historit biyyogerafit le-or meqorot Yevaniyim ve-Laṭiniyim* (Jerusalem, 1973).

The nature of Judaism as a religion as it emerges from aggadic Midrash especially (but not exclusively) is best represented by Solomon Schechter's *Some Aspects of Rabbinic Theology* (London, 1909), reprinted as *Aspects of Rabbinic Theology* (New York, 1961); George Foot Moore's *Judaism in the First Three Centuries of the Christian Era, the Age of Tannaim*, 3 vols. (1927–1940; reprint, Cambridge, Mass., 1970); Joseph Bonsirven's *Palestinian Judaism in the Time of Jesus Christ*, translated by William Wolf (New York, 1964); and E. E. Urbach's *The Sages: Their Concepts and Beliefs*, 2 vols., translated from the second Hebrew edition by Israel Abrahams (Jerusalem, 1975). For additional reading one may consult the selected titles listed below.

Albeck, Chanoch. "Introduction." In *Genesis Rabbah*. Edited by Chanoch Albeck and Julius Theodor. Berlin, 1931. Reprinted under the title *Midrash; Rabbath Genesis*. Jerusalem, 1965.

Bickerman, Elias J. "La chaîne de la tradition pharisienne." *Revue biblique* 59 (1952): 44–54.

Fischel, Henry A. *Rabbinic Literature and Greco-Roman Philosophy: A Study of Epicurea and Rhetorica in Early Midrashic Writings*. Leiden, 1973.

Ginzberg, Louis. *Legends of the Jews*. 7 vols. Translated by Henrietta Szold et al. 1909–1938. Reprint, Philadelphia, 1946–1955.

Goldin, Judah. *The Song at the Sea*. New Haven, 1971.

Halperin, David J. *The Merkabah in Rabbinic Literature*, American Oriental Series, no. 62. New Haven, 1980.

Heinemann, Isaak. *Darkhei ha-agadah*. Jerusalem, 1970.

Heinemann, Joseph, ed. *Derashot ba-tsibbur bi-tequfat ha-Talmud*. Jerusalem, 1970.

Heinemann, Joseph, "The Proem in the Aggadic Midrashim: A Form-Critical Study." In *Studies in Aggadah and Folk Literature*. Edited by Joseph Heinemann and Dov Noy, pp. 100–122. *Scripta Hierosolymitana*, vol. 22. Jerusalem, 1971.

Kasher, M. M. *Torah sheleimah*. 37 vols. New York, 1927–1982.

Lieberman, Saul. *Hellenism in Jewish Palestine*. New York, 1962.

Marrou, Henri I. *A History of Education in Antiquity*. Translated by George Lamb. New York, 1956.

Scholem, Gershom G. *Jewish Gnosticism, Merkabah Mysticism, and Talmudic Tradition*. 2d ed. New York, 1965.

Spiegel, Shalom. "Introduction". In *Legends of the Bible* by Louis Ginzberg. New York, 1956.

Spiegel, Shalom. *The Last Trial*. Translated by Judah Goldin. New York, 1964.

Stern, David M. "Rhetoric and Midrash: The Case of the Mashal." *Prooftexts* 1 (1981): 261–291.

Strack, Hermann L. *Introduction to the Talmud and Midrash*. 5th ed., rev. Philadelphia, 1931.

JUDAH GOLDIN

MIGRATION AND RELIGION. Migration almost always affects religion. This is so because when people migrate to a new place they alter routines of daily life, and new experience inevitably acts upon even the most tenaciously held religious tradition. Conversely, religion often inspires migration.

Religious Motives. Organized religious groups may decide to move to a place where their pursuit of holiness will face fewer obstacles. Some successful colonies of this kind played important historic roles by defining patterns of conduct for larger, less religiously incandescent communities that succeeded them.

Among Christians and Muslims, though rarely for other religions, armed migration also played an important part in spreading and defending the faith. Crusade and *jihād,* between them, defined the frontier between *dār al-Islām* and Christendom for more than a millennium, from the first Muslim conquests of the seventh century until the secularized statecraft of the eighteenth pushed religious antipathy to the margins of military enterprise. [*See* Crusades *and* Jihād.] The Muslim conquest of India (eleventh to seventeenth century) was likewise sustained by a flow of fighting men who came to Hindustan in order to combat infidelity, and, perchance, to acquire fame and wealth in the process.

Personal and private pursuit of holiness has also inspired innumerable pilgrims to visit shrines that are usually located where their religion originated or had its earliest efflorescence. A contrary flow of holy men beyond the frontiers of the society of their birth has often led to the conversion of strangers, even across linguistic and cultural barriers. Overall and in general we may therefore say that religiously inspired migration, whether peaceable or warlike, had a great deal to do with the definition of civilizational and cultural frontiers in historic times.

Pilgrimage affirmed and helped to homogenize religious and secular culture within each civilization. [*See* Pilgrimage.] It became especially important for Islam. Long after the caliphate collapsed, the thousands of pilgrims who traveled to Mecca each year from all over the Muslim world maintained a loose but effective unity among the community of the faithful. Holy war and peaceable conversion on the other hand, enhanced heterogeneity by bringing new populations within the circle of one or another religion from time to time. Diversity did not bother Hindus and Buddhists very much, but new frictions arose among Jews, Christians, and Muslims with every missionary success, since converts inevitably retained some remnants of older "pagan" outlooks and habits. For these faiths, therefore, local and sectarian diversity remained in perpetual conflict with the ideal of uniform and punctilious obedience to God's will as authoritatively defined by religious experts and administrators.

Second only to crusade and counter-crusade, religiously inspired collective migrations offer the most dramatic manifestations of how human motility and religiosity interact. [*See* Zionism.] The migrants' goal, of course, is to find a place where the will of God can be more perfectly obeyed. Undoubtedly, most sectarian enterprises of this sort do not last very long. The mass suicide of Jim Jones's followers in the jungles of Guyana in 1978 was a reminder of how such ventures may collapse in grisly failure. At the other extreme, the Puritans of Massachusetts and the Mormons of Utah dominated their chosen localities for generations and still influence the mainstream of American life. In Russia, communities of Old Believers played almost as prominent a part, for they, too, throve on the frontiers and influenced the wider community around them by pioneering privately managed trade and industry in the eighteenth and nineteenth centuries.

In the deeper past, monastic communities offered the most important examples of collective migration undertaken for religious reasons. Buddhist, Taoist, Shinto, and Christian monasteries were often set up in remote rural localities where the monks' devotion and learning propagated and sustained the faith among surrounding populations while also providing a focus for economic exchange and (at least sometimes) for political activity as well. Such monastic centers were especially important in times and places where towns were absent or poorly developed, and tended to become marginal in proportion to the rise of secular urban centers. [*See* Monasticism.]

The initial establishment of such monasteries was achieved by deliberate, collective migration of bodies of monks or nuns. Subsequent recruitment came from far and wide, since the inhabitants did not reproduce themselves. Monastic establishments thus depended on and could only thrive by retaining connection with the currents of personal migration in search of holiness that flowed within (and sometimes between) each of the Eurasian civilizations.

Private, personal migration for religious reasons is difficult to document since itinerant holy men, living on alms, seldom recorded their experience in writing. The forest retreats of ancient India where the Upaniṣads were generated constitute the oldest attested examples of personal, private migration away from the toils of ordinary society in order to pursue religious enlightenment and truth. They were, perhaps, archetypical. At any rate, India's warm climate was propitious since it allowed seekers after holiness to survive on little food and with little clothing. The ascetic way of life, in turn, encouraged and sustained mystic visions of transcendental reality—visions that validated the holy way of life and confirmed the aspiration of escaping from the ills of this world by entering into contact with suprasensory reality.

Transient and personal master-disciple relationships among Indian holy men took a new and enduring form among the followers of Gautama, the Buddha. For, on the occasion of his death (484 BCE), the Buddha's followers defined a holy way of life that combined itinerant mendicancy with periods of rest and recuperation in specially constructed monasteries. Following this regimen, Buddhist monks soon penetrated far beyond the borders of India, traveling along the caravan routes of Asia to the Far East and boarding merchant vessels bound for Southeast Asia as well. In ensuing centuries, holy men of other faiths (Manichaeans and Nestorian Christians especially) adopted similar modes of life. Later still, Taoists and adherents of Shintō established monastic communities modeled more or less closely on the Buddhist prototype.

Wandering holy men, whether of the Buddhist or some other persuasion, had much in common with the merchant-peddlers who frequented the same trade routes. Indeed, these itinerant holy men *were* a kind of merchant whose stock-in-trade consisted of esoteric knowledge and personal experience of the transcendental world. They lived, in effect, by exchanging their special access to the supernatural for the alms that sustained their bodily wants. [*See* Mendicancy.]

Mainstream Christianity and Islam went in opposite directions in developing the Buddhist pattern of religiously motivated migration. Early in the history of Christian asceticism, monastic rules inhibited the private pursuit of holiness by itinerant almstakers. Yet this did not prevent the systematic establishment of new monasteries at distant frontier locations. Rather, monasteries played a leading role in spreading Christian civilization beyond the borders of the Roman empire, both in the west among Germanic peoples and in the east among the Slavs. Then, after the voyages of discovery by Europeans during the sixteenth century, missionary orders met with enormous success in converting Amerindians to Roman Catholicism, but failed to win many Asians or Africans to their faith. Protestant missions flourished mainly in the nineteenth century, and probably converted more Asians and Africans to the secular aspects of Western civilization than to their various versions of Christianity. [*See* Missions.]

Within the realm of Islam, on the other hand, the initial effort to make the entire community perfectly obedient to God left no room for monks or any other kind of specially holy personages. The Qur'ān accordingly forbade monastic vows. As a result, when the first burst of conquest came to a halt, pious Muslim merchants took over the missionary role that had been exercised for other faiths by monks and other religious specialists. Thus with the advent of Islam the convergence between missionary and merchant, already apparent in Buddhist practice, became complete.

To be sure, from the twelfth century onward, dervish communities, somewhat analogous to the monastic orders of other religions, arose within Islam. They flourished most in the frontier lands where the expanding Turkish power encountered the Christian populations of Asia Minor and the Balkans. Dervish forms of piety had an important role in converting Christians to Islam along that frontier, but the dervishes never escaped the taint of heterodoxy.

There is profound irony in the upshot of all these various religiously motivated patterns of migration. Puritans of New England as much as Old Believers in Russia, along with all the variegated company of monks and holy men who propagated Hinduism, Buddhism, Christianity, and other faiths along remote frontiers, all sought to escape from the corruptions of civilized society as exemplified in their initial homelands. Yet the net effect of their efforts at withdrawal and pursuit of a more perfect obedience to the precepts of their religion was to spread civilized skills and knowledge among previously simpler societies. Institutional success in the form of flourishing monastic or civil communities, dedicated to holiness though they might be, perversely propagated the very corruptions of civilization which the founders had so earnestly wished to escape from. Of course, discrepancy between intentions and accomplishments is normal in human affairs, but the gap is seldom so patent as in these instances.

Secular Motives. Migration undertaken for other than religious reasons also had the overall effect of spreading civilized complexity. Its immediate impact on religion was usually to provoke some sort of blending of old and new traditions as immigrants encountered new peoples and new conditions of life along with alien faiths and religious practices. But religious interactions exhibited many variations, depending on conditions of the encounters and on choices individual leaders and teachers made in coping with unprecedented novelties.

If one seeks to make sense of such diversity it is useful to distinguish between migrations that carry a particular population up a cultural gradient and migrations that carry people in an opposite direction toward frontiers where civilized institutions weaken or disappear.

A people that moves up a cultural gradient may do so as conqueror or captive. Peaceable infiltration of individuals or small family groups is also theoretically possible but remained statistically unimportant until the nineteenth century, when the advent of superior public peace, efficient communications, and mechanically powered transport made that kind of migration feasible on a mass scale for the first time. It follows that the Israelites' conquest of Canaan on the one hand and the African slave trade on the other are the appropriate models for most historical migration, unlike the sort of individual and family migration that did so much to populate the United States between the 1840s and 1920s.

In matters of religion, conquerors and captives alike

have three options when arriving in lands whose skills are superior to their own. The newcomers may accept the established religion of the land to which they have come, retaining only a few telltale traces of their own older practices. The Akkadian invaders of ancient Sumer seem to have accepted this option at the very beginning of civilized history; Turks coming into the realm of Islam either as slaves or as conquerors did the same. So did the African slaves imported to North America to work on plantations.

Slaves had little choice as a rule. Forcibly separated from the social context that had nurtured them, they could not, as more or less isolated individuals, carry very much of their native religion with them. Conquerors, however, were in a position to choose. Nevertheless, simple maintenance of accustomed rites and ideas was seldom possible. New experiences, ideas, and circumstances crowded in on successful conquerors. To resist their subjects' religions took a special effort, all the more difficult in view of the fact that the established rituals of the land were already adapted to the circumstances of civilized and agricultural life.

The Bible record shows how hard it was for the Israelites to maintain their desert faith in the land of Canaan after settling down to an agricultural existence. Energetic, violent means were needed to repress Baal worship. This was the work of kings and prophets, who in reaffirming the old religion in fact transformed it. That transformation is what made Judaism so enormously influential in the world at large, but its influence also attests the exceptional character of the prophetic response to the conditions of agricultural civilization.

Other invaders who rejected the religion of the land they had conquered were nonetheless affected by contact with people of a different faith. This happened even when the subjected population accepted the faith of their conquerors en masse. The contamination of Turkish Islam with Christian elements was a pronounced feature of Ottoman life, for example, while the Mughals in India alternated between a policy of permitting and resisting the parallel contamination of their faith with Hindu practices and ideas. A similar situation prevailed in the crusading states of the Levant, and when the Mongol empire was at its height, Khubilai Khan's policy of patronizing all available religions, so as not to foreclose any avenue of access to the supernatural, shocked and puzzled Christians and Muslims alike.

A third policy that attracted many "barbarian" conquerors was to try for the best of both worlds by espousing a heretical form of civilized religion. This marked the conquerors off from their subjects and helped to maintain a collective *esprit de corps* among the invaders, while also allowing the new rulers to benefit from advantages of civilized religion—for example, literacy, an authoritative scripture, and a hierarchical priesthood. The German tribesmen who adhered to Arian Christianity when invading the Roman empire in the fourth and fifth centuries followed such a policy. The Uighurs, who became Manichaeans, and the Khazars, who became Jews, illustrate a variation on the same theme, for the religions of their choice served to mark them off from neighbors and subjects while at the same time offering rulers the support of a fully civilized faith.

Nevertheless, such barbarian polities were transitory and so were the heresies they found attractive. The reactions that mattered were assimilation to civilized forms of religion on the one hand and inventive rejection on the other that has been so central in the history of Judaism, of Shintō, and, since the mid-nineteenth century, to the evolution of Hinduism and Islam as well.

Migrations undertaken for economic or political reasons that carry a people to lands less developed than those they leave behind ordinarily have less impact on traditional religious practices. The Chinese migration from north to south that created the imposing mass of contemporary China, for example, had no very obvious effect on Chinese religion. The same may be said of Japanese expansion northward through their islands and of the German *Drang nach Osten*.

Only in modern times did it become possible for family groups and isolated individuals to migrate safely toward an open frontier. In such circumstances, of course, pioneers left organized religion behind. This prepared the ground for itinerant revivalists. Emotionally vibrant forms of established religion fared best in such circumstances, with conspicuous individual conversion the goal.

Proletarian migrants into cities faced circumstances similar in some important respects to the deculturation and individual isolation of the rural frontier. It is not really surprising therefore that the Methodists who first addressed themselves to unchurched urban populations of Great Britain were also among the most successful on the American frontier.

Other varieties of religious revivalism are currently flourishing among urban immigrants, both in the United States and beyond its borders. Islamic revivalism is the most politically prominent of such movements, but sectarian forms of Christianity also have a vigorous life in American cities and in many developing nations, while offshoots of Buddhism can also be observed making headway in urban contexts, both Eastern and Western. Marxism, too, is no more than a secular heresy competing in this environment for human commitment to its materialist doctrines.

Concluding Remark. In the world at large, as populations increase and migratory flows swell to unexampled proportions, religious interminglings and interactions—both hostile and pacific—are sure to intensify. The future history of humankind will in all likelihood be written around the clash of religions and cultures that is taking place around us, for secular thought and abstract reasoning are weak reeds by comparison with the tidal flows of faith and feeling that govern human conduct today as much as at any time in the past.

BIBLIOGRAPHY

Curtin, Philip D. *Cross-Cultural Trade in World History.* Cambridge and New York, 1984. An in-depth discussion of trade between people of different cultures and of the complex cultural exchanges between diverse human societies that were brought about by trade.

Diesner, Hans-Joachim. *The Great Migration: The Movement of Peoples across Europe, AD 300–700.* London, 1978. A splendidly illustrated, thoroughly researched study on the main groups of migratory (barbarian) peoples that crisscrossed Europe during the Middle Ages and on the emergence of new societies and civilizations as a result of this diaspora.

Folz, Robert, et al. *De l'antiquité au monde médiéval.* Paris, 1972. A minute and erudite discussion of the period of the most spectacular migrations, invasions, and conquests in both western European and Islamic worlds.

French, Allen. *Charles I and the Puritan Upheaval.* London, 1955. A background of the Puritan exodus, the "Great Migration."

Goblet d'Alviella, Eugène. *The Migration of Symbols.* London, 1894. Groundbreaking work on the circulation of religious symbols as a result of movements of peoples.

Kirsten, Ernst, et al., eds. *Raum und Bevölkerung in der Weltgeschichte: Bevölkerungs-Ploetz.* 3d ed. 4 vols. Würzburg, 1965–1966. A collection of demographical data from the beginnings of recorded history until late 1950s, from every part of the inhabited world.

Knowles, David. *Christian Monasticism.* New York, 1969. A learned and concise history of monasticism. Monks' religious fervor, mobility, and political influence made them ideal for the spread of religion in the remotest corners of the world.

Mayer, Hans Eberhard. *The Crusades.* Oxford, 1972. Succinct work on the history of the Crusades and on all the territorial and population changes connected with these holy wars.

McNeill, William H., and Ruth S. Adams, eds. *Human Migration: Patterns and Policies.* Bloomington, Ind., 1978. A collection of essays by scholars in the field that stands as a standard reference source for the complex topic of population movements.

Noth, Albrecht. *Heiliger Krieg und Heiliger Kampf im Islam und Christentum.* Bonn, 1966. A comparative study on the ideology and practice of holy war in Islam and Christianity, reviewing aspects of population displacements and territorial changes in the western Mediteranean region.

Parry, J. H. *The Age of Reconnaissance.* London, 1963. Probably the best study on the history of European colonization between the fifteenth and seventeenth centuries.

Price, A. Grenfell. *The Western Invasions of the Pacific and Its Continents: A Study of Moving Frontiers and Changing Landscapes, 1513–1958.* Oxford, 1963. An investigation into the physical and cultural changes suffered by the Pacific territories as a result of the white peoples' invasions.

Rawley, James A. *The Transatlantic Slave Trade: A History.* New York, 1981. A comprehensive analysis of the African diaspora as a result of the slave trade during European and American colonial history.

Simon, Marcel, et al., eds. *Les pèlerinages de l'antiquité biblique et classique à l'occident médiéval.* Paris, 1973. This volume focuses on the pilgrimage traditions of the Jews, Christians, and Muslims of the Mediteranean basin and of ancient Greece. It also provides an important theoretical treatment of the notion of pilgrimage.

Strobel, August. *Der spätbronzezeitliche Seevölkerstum: Ein Forschungsüberblick mit Folgerungen zur biblischen Exodusthematic.* Berlin, 1976. A remarkable contribution to the controversial study of the "sea people" and the great migration that turned around the history of the ancient Near East.

Yeivin, Samuel. *The Israelite Conquest of Canaan.* Istanbul, 1971. An exemplary investigation, based on literary and archaeological evidence, of the Israelite invasion.

WILLIAM H. MCNEILL

MI-LA-RAS-PA (Milarepa; 1040–1123), the best-known and most highly venerated anchorite of Tibetan Buddhist tradition. His name derives from the words *Mila,* his family name, and *repa,* "cotton cloth," a reference to the yogic garb of white cotton that he wore during his many years of solitary meditation in mountain retreats. Mi-la-ras-pa is the author of a large collection of Tantric songs of high literary value that mark a historical watershed in the development of Tibetan literature. Through his disciples, Mi-la-ras-pa is also a key figure in the inception of the Tibetan Bka'-brgyud-pa school, which finds its origins in the Indian *siddha* Ti-lo-pa (988–1069). At the same time, each of the Tibetan schools looks back to Mi-la-ras-pa as a spiritual forebear, and he is considered one of the major fathers of Tibetan Buddhism as a whole, particularly in its eremetical dimensions.

Mi-la-ras-pa's significance for Tibetan Buddhism derives above all from the way his life provides an example and model for all Tibetan Buddhists, whether monk, hermit, or layperson, and regardless of social origin or condition of life. This model is articulated in many places in Tibetan lore, both written and oral, but especially in two well-loved and influential works, a biography of Mi-la-ras-pa by the "Mad Yogin of Tsang" and a collection of Mi-la-ras-pa's Tantric songs, *The Hundred Thousand Songs.* As with other Vajrayāna hagiography, the extent to which the image of Mi-la-ras-pa presented in these texts is the imprint of a single historical person or an assimilation to an original figure of stories, teachings, and songs of disparate origin is unclear and relatively unimportant. The model that Mi-la-ras-pa's life provides, with its humanity and universality, can be summarized by his emergence from low beginnings, his search for a teacher and the relationship between them, the importance of solitary meditation to his spiritual growth, and his success as a Tantric master.

Can one aspire to spiritual awakening no matter what one's condition of life or previous history? Mi-la-ras-pa's biography answers this universal question in an encouraging way. Mi-la-ras-pa was born to a wealthy family in south central Tibet, near the Nepalese border. After his father's early death, however, a rapacious uncle appropriated the estate that he was supposed to manage during Mi-la-ras-pa's minority, reducing Mi-la-ras-pa and his mother and sister to virtual serfdom. Out of a desire for revenge, Mi-la-ras-pa's mother sold some small property she owned through her family, using the proceeds to send her son to study with a sorcerer in order to learn magic that would bring ruin on the uncle. Armed with this mother's hatred and her desire for the fullest possible revenge, the young Mi-la-ras-pa pursued his studies of black magic with great determination.

Mi-la-ras-pa learned his art well, and his biography states that in time he succeeded in killing thirty-five of his relatives and destroying the crops of others, to his mother's great satisfaction. Relatives of those killed conspired to kill Mi-la-ras-pa and his mother; threats passed between the feuding families. These difficulties had great impact on Mi-la-ras-pa, and he soon came to realize the enormity of what he had done and the bankruptcy of his situation. After a period of agitation and sleeplessness, he determined that he must make a new beginning and follow a spiritual path. Eventually, his sorcerer master having released him from service, Mi-la-ras-pa was able to set out on his search. It was from these dark beginnings that Mi-la-ras-pa emerged to become one of Tibet's most loved and respected spiritual teachers.

In all branches of Buddhism, especially in the Tibetan Vajrayāna tradition, in order to follow the spiritual path one needs a personal teacher who has himself attained a measure of realization. As one text puts it, without a teacher the Buddhas have no voice. Knowing this, Mi-la-ras-pa set out in search of a master who would accept him and train him. He first applied to a Rñiṅ-ma ("old school") master, who soon told Mi-la-ras-pa that he could not help him. However, this master mentioned the name of another nearby teacher, one Mar-pa, and it is said that at the sound of his name, Mi-la-ras-pa felt a shock of happiness and found himself irresistably drawn to this person. Mi-la-ras-pa later saw in this reaction an indication of a strong karmic connection to Mar-pa, a connection that is held in Vajrayāna Buddhism to be a necessary binding factor in the master-disciple relationship. In order to search for Mar-pa, Mi-la-ras-pa continued his travels. At the same time, both Mar-pa and his wife Bdag-med-ma dreamed that Mar-pa's chief student, in need of only a little purification, was about to arrive.

Mi-la-ras-pa met Mar-pa on the road by one of the latter's fields, where Mar-pa immediately set Mi-la-ras-pa to plowing. Told that he must work for his bread, Mi-la-ras-pa spent his daylight hours performing various tasks of heavy labor for Mar-pa, whose demeanor was austere, majestic, and demanding. In spite of Mi-la-ras-pa's entreaties and pleadings, Mar-pa would not permit Mi-la-ras-pa to join the other students, commenting that Mi-la-ras-pa could work for bread or for teachings, but not for both. Sinking into black despondency, Mi-la-ras-pa tried to run away to another teacher, but quickly realized that his real relationship was with Mar-pa, and so returned. According to Mi-la-ras-pa's biography, although Mar-pa pretended to be angry with Mi-la-ras-pa, he repeatedly conveyed his concern and love for him to Bdag-med-ma. Only much later, when Mar-pa finally initiated him and accepted him as his main spiritual son, did the genius of Mar-pa's training begin to become clear to Mi-la-ras-pa.

Within Tibetan Buddhism, the relationship between Mar-pa and Mi-la-ras-pa exemplifies the master-disciple relationship at its best. Historically, Mar-pa's hard training of Mi-la-ras-pa hearkens back to Mar-pa's own study under the Indian *siddha* Nā-ro-pa and to the difficult and demanding master-disciple relationships characteristic of the Indian Buddhist *siddhas* in general. At the same time, Mi-la-ras-pa's biography particularly emphasizes the humanity of the chief protagonists, which has inspired Tibetans with a sense of the reality and possibility of the spiritual path. [*See the biography of Mar-pa.*]

After many years of testing and purification, Mar-pa finally acceeded to Mi-la-ras-pa's request for initiation. Mar-pa then sent Mi-la-ras-pa into retreat to meditate, marking the beginning of another major phase of Mi-la-ras-pa's training. The next twenty years of Mi-la-ras-pa's life were characterized by long periods of solitude broken by periodic visits to Mar-pa for further instructions. During this period, Mi-la-ras-pa lived in various caves underneath the Everest Range, sustaining himself with offerings from nearby villages and subsisting on broth made from nettles when these were not forthcoming. Much of Mi-la-ras-pa's biography and most of his hundred thousand songs focus on this period of his life. Indeed, one of the primary functions of Mi-la-ras-pa's biography in Tibet has been its clear statement of the primacy of meditation.

Eventually, disciples began to gather around Mi-la-ras-pa in his mountain solitude. The final portion of Mi-la-ras-pa's biography presents this accomplished dimension of his life. The image it portrays of the realized Tantric teacher has been a well-known and influential one in subsequent Tibetan Buddhist history. The main themes of Mi-la-ras-pa as a realized teacher hearken back to the eighty-four Indian *mahāsiddhas*: like them, his insight and compassion were profound, and he understood his disciples thoroughly and guided them skillfully according to their needs; he was an eccentric yogin who referred to himself as "mad" *(smyon pa)* and delighted in mocking established religion, showing up its foibles and deceits; he was a great magician, whose unpredictable and awesome powers were exercised in the compassionate service of others; he was the composer of mystic songs that expressed his realization; and further like the *siddhas*, Mi-la-ras-pa was close to the people, fond of laughing and joking, and taking their part.

But for all that, Mi-la-ras-pa is also thoroughly Tibetan. He never left Tibet, did not know Sanskrit, and was relatively unlearned in the vast Indian Buddhist academic traditions that so preoccupied many of his Tibetan contemporaries. His songs reflect the amalgamation of indigenous bardic forms with the Indian *dohā* tradition. His love of the Tibetan mountain wilds and his mountain renunciant life are thoroughly Tibetan and established a new, major contemplative option in Tibetan Buddhism. Most important, through his pupil Sgam-po-pa (1079–1153), and his other major disciples, Mi-la-ras-pa left as legacy a lineage that has played a central role in the religious life of Tibet.

As in the case of earlier Vajrayāna hagiography, Mi-la-ras-pa's biography is a vehicle for illuminating the history of the Vajrayāna, for conveying Tantric ideals, perspectives and ideas, and for eliciting devotion toward particular Vajrayāna forebears. But beyond this, again like earlier Tantric hagiography, the biography becomes an important part of the ongoing attempt to invoke in a tangible and living form Mi-la-ras-pa's enlightened presence as an inspiration and a help in present times. Thus the biography and hundred thousand songs provide the content, while various Mi-la-ras-pa liturgies (*pūjas* and *sādhanas*) provide the liturgical means, for that invocation. In light of these latter Mi-la-ras-pa texts, the themes and songs of Mi-la-ras-pa's life are not just past history, and not simply indirect in their ability to inform the present.

[*See also* Buddhism, *article on* Buddhism in Tibet; Buddhism, Schools of, *article on* Tibetan Buddhism; *and* Mahāsiddhas.]

BIBLIOGRAPHY

The Life of Milarepa, translated by Lobsang P. Lhalungpa (New York, 1977), is a translation of the well-loved Tibetan biography by the "Mad Yogin of Tsang" (Tsang Nyon Heruka; 1452–1507), which replaces the earlier translation of the same text by W. Y. Evans-Wentz, *Tibet's Great Yogi Milarepa,* 2d ed. (Oxford, 1928). For all its merits, the Evans-Wentz translation reflects an outdated ambiance in its use of biblical-style English and in its relative ignorance of Vajrayāna matters. Mi-la-ras-pa's songs are translated by Garma C. C. Chang in *The Hundred Thousand Songs of Milarepa,* 2 vols. (New Hyde Park, N.Y., 1962).

REGINALD RAY

MILLENARIANISM. [*This entry consists of two articles treating notions associated with millenarian and apocalyptic movements and ideologies. The first,* An Overview, *is a broad discussion of millenarianism in a cross-cultural context. The second,* Chinese Millenarian Movements, *focuses on the perennial significance of millenarian movements and rebel eschatologies in the religious history of China.*]

An Overview

Millenarianism, known also as millennialism, is the belief that the end of this world is at hand and that in its wake will appear a New World, inexhaustibly fertile, harmonious, sanctified, and just. The more exclusive the concern with the End itself, the more such belief shades off toward the catastrophic; the more exclusive the concern with the New World, the nearer it approaches the utopian.

Millenarian Thought. Complexity in millenarian thought derives from questions of sign, sequence, duration, and human agency. What are the marks of the End? At what stage are we now? Exactly how much time do we have? What should we do? Although warranted by cosmology, prophecy, or ancestral myth, the End usually stands in sudden proximity to the immediate era. The trail of events may at last have been tracked to the cliff's edge, or recent insight may have cleared the brier from some ancient oracle.

The root term, *millennium,* refers to a first-century eastern Mediterranean text, the *Apocalypse of John* or *Book of Revelation,* itself a rich source of disputes about the End. John of Patmos here describes in highly figured language a penultimate battle between forces of good and evil, succeeded by a thousand-year reign of saintly martyrs with Jesus, and then the defeat of Satan, the Last Judgment, a new heaven, and a new earth. This interim, earthly reign is literally the millennium (from Lat. *mille,* "thousand"; Gr., *chil,* whence "chiliasm," sometimes applied pejoratively to belief in an indulgent, carnal millennium, or "chiliad"). Not all millenarians expect an interim paradise before an ultimate heavenly assumption; not all anticipate precisely one thousand years of peace; not all stipulate a messianic presence or a saintly elite. Like John, however, they have constant recourse to images, for millenarians are essentially metaphorical thinkers.

In theory, as a speculative poetic enterprise, millenarianism is properly an adjunct of eschatology, the study of last things. In practice, millenarianism is distinguished by close scrutiny of the present, from which arise urgent issues of human agency. Once the fateful coincidence between history and prophecy has been confirmed, must good people sit tight, or must they gather together, withdraw to a refuge? Should they enter the wilderness to construct a holy city, or should they directly engage the chaos of the End, confront the regiments of evil? Millenarians answer with many voices, rephrasing their positions as they come to terms with an End less imminent or less cataclysmic. Where their image of the New World is that of a golden age, they begin with a restorative ethos, seeking a return to a lost purity. Where their image is that of the land of the happy dead or a distant galaxy of glory, their ethos is initially retributive, seeking to balance an unfortunate past against a fortunate future. Few millenarians remain entirely passive, quietly awaiting a supernatural transformation of the world; those who go about their lives without allusion to the looming End customarily escape notice. Most millenarians conflate the restorative and retributive. They act in some way to assure themselves that the New World will not be unfamiliar. Images of a fortunate future are primed with nostalgia.

A millenarian's sense of time, consequently, is neither strictly cyclical nor linear. However much the millennium is to be the capstone to time, as in Christian and Islamic traditions, it is also in character and affect the return of that carefree era posited for the start of things. However much the millennium is to be an impost between two of the infinite arches of time, as in Aztec and Mahāyāna Buddhist traditions, it is for all mortal purposes a release from pain and chaos for many generations.

To the uninitiated, the millenarian mathematics of time may seem mysteriously scaled: how can one account for that arbitrary algebra that assigns the value 3,500 years to the location "a time, and times, and half a time" (*Rv.* 12:14)? Millenarian thought is figurative in both senses of that word—metaphorical and numerological. Intricate play with numbers of years is founded upon a faith in the impending aesthetic wholeness of the world-historical process. Millenarian searches for laws of historical correspondence between the individually human and the universally human bear a formal similarity to one another, whether the searchers are nineteenth-century social visionaries (the Saint-Simonian Gustave d'Eichthal, the young Hegelian August von Cieszkowski, the Confucian reformer K'ang Yu-wei), seventeenth-century theologians (the Puritan chronologist Joseph Mede, the natural philosopher Isaac Newton, the Shī'ī Neoplatonist Muḥammad Sadr al-Dīn), or twelfth-century monastics (the abbess Hildegard of Bingen, the abbot Joachim of Fiore, the White Lotus monk Mao Tzu-yüan). Each discerns a pattern of historical ages that promises both completion and recapitulation.

World religions have known two deep reservoirs of millenarian thought, one noumenal and gnostic, the other phenomenal and nomothetic. When the reservoirs empty into each other—when mathematicians allude to secret knowledge or contemplatives allude to laws of physics (as in fifth-century southern China, seventeenth-century Western Europe, twentieth-century North America)—millenarianism waxes strong. Alchemy and astrology, nuclear physics and molecular genetics share with qabbalistic magic and Tantric yoga an appreciation for techniques of prediction and mutation. Popularly set in sharp contrast to millenarian "fanatics," scientists and mystics have in fact been crucial to the cultural continuity of millenarian thought; they have preserved an intense concern with processes of transformation and the pulsing of time.

Among the world religions we can locate two constellations of millenarian thought about an epochal pulsing of time, one Zoroastrian-Jewish-Greek-Christian, the other Hindu-Buddhist-Taoist-Confucian. In the Mediterranean littoral, an epochal aesthetic was elaborated by scribal elites who were resistant first to Greek rule (thus producing the Jewish *Book of Daniel* and the lost sources for the Mazdean *Apocalypse of Hystaspe*), then to Roman rule (producing the Egyptian *Potter's Prophecy* and Judeo-Christian apocalypses such as *Enoch* and the *Epistle of Barnabas*), and finally to Muslim rule (producing the Syrian-Christian *Revelations* of Pseudo-Methodius). Feasting upon a cosmopolitan diet of Zoroastrian cosmology, Jewish notions of Sabbath, and Greco-Roman ideas of historical recurrence, these literati stamped the disturbing flux of empires with the template of the divine creative week, which they saw being played out again at length in human history through a reassuringly predictable series of world kingdoms over a period of six or seven thousand years. At the end lay a millennial sabbath, transposed from a time of perpetual rest to a time of truce and earthly reward prior to the final onslaughts of the dragon, tyrant, or false messiah.

This demonic figure of imperium acquired a righteous cousin, the Last World Emperor, whose inexplicable abdication would open the way to his black kin. The dialectic between devious shape-changing evil and prematurely vanishing good, played out against a Christian backdrop that placed a redemptive event close to the center of Roman history, gradually reversed epochal theory, which had begun with a fourfold schema of decadence from golden antiquity. The upshot by the fourteenth century was a progressive tripartite schema bounded on one side by Fall and Flood, on the other by fire and judgment, and aesthetically framed: here a primordial earthly paradise spoiled by a fork-tongued beast; there a climactic earthly paradise spiked by a horned beast, the Antichrist. Between these ran three broad historical ages, each with its bright dawn and horrid nightfall. These ages were identified with other trinities (Father-Law-Justice, Son-Faith-Grace, Spirit-Love-Freedom). Over the next centuries, the millennium itself was annexed to the third age and enshrined in historical rhetoric (classical, medieval, renaissance; feudal, capitalist, socialist). Nineteenth-century exponents of infinite progress had only to remove the limiting aesthetic frame.

Across East Asia, a millenarian aesthetic developed within contexts far less adversarial, and we find no figure antiphonal to the universal perfect ruler (the Hindu *cakravartin*, the Buddhist Rudra Cakin, the Javanese hybrid *Ratu Adil*) or to the future incarnate savior (the Hindu Kalkin, the Maitreya Buddha, a reborn Lao-tzu). Furthermore, the epochal scheme was overwhelmingly degenerative: it fixed all recorded history within the last of the four increasingly chaotic eras (*yuga*s) of the aeon *(kalpa)*. The problem here was not to expand the prophetic horizon but to foreshorten the 4.3 million-year Indian *kalpa* cycle so that hundreds of thousands of distressing years of the fourth era, the *kaliyuga*, did not still lie ahead.

Each *kalpa* was to end in a cosmic disaster that would, after some blank time, initiate a new cycle whose first *yuga* was always a golden age. Strategic foreshortening brought present catastrophe stern to snout with a renewed world. The foreshortening began in northern India with early Mahāyāna Buddhist images of *bodhisattva*s, compassionate enlightened beings who chose to work in this world for the benefit of others rather than withdraw into final *nirvāṇa*. Almost simultaneously, Chinese commentators during the Later Han period (25–220 CE) alloyed the Confucian golden age of antiquity, the Ta-t'ung, to the T'ai-p'ing golden age, which according to Taoist sexagenary cycles could be both ancient and imminent, as the Yellow Turban rebels in 184 sincerely hoped. By the sixth century, the colossal four-cycle Indian cosmology had collapsed under the weight of Taoist alchemy, pietist Pure Land Buddhism, and popular Chinese worship of the Eternal Mother (Wu-sheng Lao-mu) and the *bodhisattva* Prince Moonlight (Yüeh-kuang T'ung-tzu).

There were then three accessible ages, associated cosmologically with the Taoist Former, Middle, and Latter Heavens, typologically with the three Buddhas (Lamplighter, Śākyamuni, and Maitreya), and synecdochically with the Buddhas' lotus thrones of azure, red, and white. Each age begins with a new Buddha and then declines, again in triplets: True Doctrine, or Dharma; Counterfeit Doctrine; and Last Days of Doctrine. Since the days of the historical Buddha, Śākyamuni (and, traditionally, of Confucius and Lao-tzu), we have squatted uncomfortably in the dissolute Last Days, awaiting Maitreya or his predecessor, Prince Moonlight, who is due to sweep in at the height of catastrophes one thousand years after Śākyamuni's *parinirvāṇa*. Profitably vague as it was, such a schedule made it clear that Venerable Mother, responsible for sending each of the Buddhas, intended our imminent return to the Pure Land, the Western Paradise.

The upshot of this foreshortening was an epochal aesthetic which, by the fourteenth century, called for rounded contours to a humanly proportioned history, and a millenarian White Lotus rebellion, which in 1351 drew the curtain on the Yüan dynasty and set the stage for the Ming (from Ming Wang, the Chinese name for the Manichaean "perfect ruler," the Prince of Radiance). This aesthetic survived to inform the White Lotus uprisings of the eighteenth century, the Taiping Rebellion of 1851 to 1864, the Dao Lanh sect founded in 1849 by the Vietnamese Buddha Master of Western Peace, Doan Minh Huyen, the Ōmotokyō, founded in 1892, by the Japanese farmer Deguchi Nao, and the Saya San rebellion in Burma from 1930 to 1932.

Stretched between the Mediterranean and East Asian constellations, Manichaeism and Islam transected both. Mani's lithe dualism darkened the Antichrist and highlighted the Amitābha (Pure Land) Buddha and the Ming Prince of Radiance. Islam shared with the Mediterranean a demonic end-time imposter, al-Dajjāl, and with East Asia a degenerative epochal theory, but more important was its caravan of redeemers. By 1300, Shī'ī Muslims had at least four candidates for the job of world-renewer: the twelfth spiritual guide, or imam, who had disappeared in the ninth century and was in hiding or occultation; a twelfth caliph, under whose reign would appear the restorer of the faith, the Mahdi, to usher in a short golden age before the End; and ʿĪsā (Jesus) who would do military honors at the End. Ismāʿīlī and Ṣūfī emphasis on the hiddenness of the imam may have colored later Christian visions of a Last World Emperor dying (or vanishing) prematurely, and Shīʿī Mahdism certainly splashed across North India and Indonesia. Eventually, imam, caliph, and Mahdi merged; in Africa even ʿĪsā had joined ranks by the mid-1800s. Two epochal motifs also merged then, a punctual one, according to which a renewer of the faith would appear at the end of each Islamic century, and a symmetrical one, according to which the twelfth imam would reappear in the thirteenth century AH (1785/6 to 1881/2 CE), which was a century of worldwide Mahdist movements—northern Nigeria (1804), India (1810, 1828, and 1880), Java (1825), Iran (1844), Algeria (1849, 1860, and 1879), Senegal (1854), and the Sudan (1881).

Common to millenarian aesthetics in all the world religions is this epochal scenario: a calm inaugural and a riotous finale to each act; the circling of two protagonists near the End, one imperial, the other sacramental; and a time at the End that is at once encore, intermezzo, and the throwing open of the doors.

Millenarianism stands therefore in contrast to the modern pessimism that paints miniatures of global devastation yet mounts no panorama of a future marvelous world. Though flood, plague, famine, or war may summon visions of collective death, millenarians promise more than an accurate prediction of catastrophe. They promise an earth lifted beyond safety to grace. Even at their most catastrophic, millenarians insist that a classical tragedy must be fought through only to reach a genuinely good time. From this conviction of drama derive those socially uncompromising rituals of breaking—obscenity, nudity, fasting, celibacy, rebellion—so coincident with millenarian movements. At their most utopian, millenarians tone down the nightmare of the final act: the earth will be transformed by sheer unanimity. Through evangelism, prophecy, and technologies of translation (speaking in tongues, polyglot scriptures, computer mailing), people will, in the face of local despair, embrace the same faith. A single faith, warmly bespoken, must entail a universal community whose very existence will effect the harmony, sanctity, and security long sought. A time of crisis thus becomes a time of redemption.

Characteristically, millenarians are least specific concerning the millennium itself, a time of instant and perfect communication whose seamlessness makes anatomical detail unnecessary. Millenarians are, rather, diagnosticians of bodies in metastasis. It is hardly coincidental that millenarianism in such diverse contexts as central Africa, western Europe, and northeastern Brazil has been chartered by homeopathic healers, who best appreciate the dramatic working-through of crisis. Not all healers become prophets, but most millenarian prophets claim therapeutic powers that extend from the ailing human body to the ailing body politic. Themselves usually colporteurs of regional symbolic systems, the prophet-healers take millenarianism from diagnosis to prescription, from philosophy to jubilee.

Millenarian Movements. If millenarian thought is curled inside calendar scrolls, millenarian movements are engraved on maps. Their rhetoric has to do less with time than with place. Just as millenarian thought focuses upon golden ages, so millenarian movements have golden places: Heaven on Earth, the Pure Land, the Blessed Isle, the Land Without Evil, California (this last from a sixteenth-century Spanish romance read by Hernán Cortés). And since in most iconographies what is closest to perfect is closest to the eye of the storm, millenarians are sure that any migration they make is no retreat but a step toward the New World. Millenarian crying of doom and recruitment of the elect must be understood as the epochal duty of taking into the calm center the kernel of humanity.

Prime metaphor of millenarian movements, migration can also become the prime experience, palpable or vicarious. Millenarians encourage those sensations of the migrant that observers may mistake for motives: exile and wandering, put in scriptural tandem with the peripatetic Buddha, the Wandering Jew, the itinerant Jesus, and Muḥammad's Hijrah; nostalgia for lost lands; contrary moods of excited expectation and deep remorse; inflation of the spiritual benefits of transit, sustained by epics of a terrifying, miraculous crossing; ambivalence toward the New World as both brave and strange. [*See* Exile.]

Whether a millenarian group solicits new gods or extorts aid from the old, it will confuse old home with new. Imagery of migration brings into view earlier mythical dislocations (deluge, expulsion) even as it makes evident the need to accommodate to a new land. The more intransigent the notion of home, the more people must provide themselves with apologies for imagined or actual movements away from it, and the more they will tend toward migration as a commanding metaphor.

We know that the English Puritan settlement of "New" England, like the Spanish Franciscan conquest of "New" Spain, had such millenarian resonance that neither Puritans nor Franciscans were able to acknowledge the historical integrity of the so-called Indians. We know also that for many societies, visitors of a different complexion already had a millenarian role in myths of migration and ancestry (the pink-skinned Europeans for the Fuyughe of the New Guinea highlands, the white-skinned Europeans for the MuKongo of the region of the Kongo, the dark-skinned Mongols, or "Tartars," for western Europeans). For victor as for vanquished, millenarian vertigo has conditioned initial contacts, later misunderstandings, violence, and oppression.

If millenarianism is the religion of the oppressed, it is no less the religion of the oppressor. What prompts the oppressed to envision a new moral order is likely to be the same as what, some decades earlier, prompted the oppressor to move on or over or through. So millenarianism may be both cause and result of migration. This is seen most vividly in the conjunction of Sudanese Mahdism with long-term migration south from an expanding Saharan desert, accelerated pilgrimage across the Sudan to Mecca during the thirteenth century AH, and Egyptian disruption of slave trade from 1850 to 1880.

There is, to many millenarian movements, a primary ecology dependent upon this experience of migration, whether lived or fantasized. Millenarians commonly foresee an End in which the elements of the world are used up, consumed by fire, lava, or flood. As the faithful migrate, the world does too, its elements recombining. How else could that ultimate harmony between the human and the natural be established? Although the elemental reshuffling may be divinely operated, millenarians have typically excited notice by their own human, mimetic acts of violence, their putative disregard for the wealth of the world and the bonds of social life. Cattle killing or pig killing, bonfires of earthly possessions, neglect of crops—these are more than public commitments to prophets or prophecies; they are attempts to act in concert with what seems to be a driving rhythm of history—humanity and nature cracking apart in war and earthquake or crumbling more silently through immorality and faithlessness.

The New World implied by most millenarian movements presumes not only a new natural physiognomy but also a new human physiognomy, one that is messianic in import. We can make no easy distinctions between messianic and millenarian movements. Few messianic leaders appear without heralding an instantaneous New World. Obversely, where there are no focal messianic leaders, as in the Chinese Eight Trigrams Rebellion in 1813, millenarians usually take upon themselves a collective messianic mantle, with cloth enough to re-dress themselves and the world.

For those who follow prophets toward a New World already marked out—Jan Beuckelzoon's Münster (Germany, 1534), Jemimah Wilkinson's Jerusalem (New York, 1788–1794), Antonio Conselheiro's Canudos (Brazil, 1893–1897), Julian Baltasar's Cabaruan (the Philippines, 1897–1901), Rua Kenana's Maungapohatu (New Guinea, 1907–1916)—the millennium begins in miniature as a sacred prologue. For civic millenarians—the Japanese of Nichiren's Tokaido region in the 1250s, the Italians of Girolamo Savonarola's Florence in the 1490s, the Americans of the 1860s in Emanuel Leutze's mural *Westward the Course of Empire Takes Its Way* in the Capitol, Washington, D.C.,—the burden of pointing the way toward the millennium lies not upon any prophetic enclave or diasporal elite but upon the entire population. The city, the city-state, the state itself becomes the vehicle for world renovation.

So millenarianism may beat at the heart of aggressive nationalism, as in the French revolutionary anthem "La Marseillaise" (1792) or at independence day extravaganzas everywhere. It has underlain beliefs in a Russian mission to redeem civilization, as promoted by the novelist Johann Heinrich Jung-Stilling, the occultist Baroness Barbara Juliane von Krüdener, and Tsar Alexander I before his Holy Alliance of 1815; a Hungarian mission, as in *The Entry of the Magyars,* (1892–1894), a cyclorama celebrating Hungary's "millennial constitution"; a German mission—the Nazi Third Reich; and a Greek mission—the Zoeist Fraternity of the 1950s. Ancient easterly migrations from the Asian steppes by Huns, Magyars, Aryans, and Dorians have thus been rousted out of annals, written into history, and gilded to serve as a national mandate. Talk of a "Third World" as the last hope for a failing planet is a contemporary extension of the same civic millenarian ideal.

"First World" scholars tend to link civic millenarianism with modern Christian postmillennial theology, which holds that Jesus' second coming will postdate the start of the millennium, and that no great tumult will intervene between this world and the New World. Millenarians of this type may be told only by their rhythms from the gentler rocking of reformers. In contrast, premillennialists, paradoxically considered both more primitive and more revolutionary, actively prepare for the advent. The New World, inaugurated by Jesus, ruptures the historical chain and affirms the supernal nature of deity. ("Amillennialists," such as Augustine of Hippo, run the millennium concurrently with the life of the church, so that there can be no separate future earthly kingdom.)

Millenarian movements do not settle conveniently into a pre- or postmillennial stance; even within Latin Christianity, these categories had little bearing before the nineteenth century. From the time of Lucius Lactantius (c. 240–320) until the Reformation, the issue for millenarians was whether the millennium would occur before or after the advent of the Antichrist. When early Protestants convinced themselves that the Roman papacy was the Antichrist, their heirs had to rephrase the advent debate in terms of the reappearance of Jesus. In the seventeenth century, another generation built up historical arguments in favor of Protestantism by adducing a theory of dispensations through which God progressively revealed divine law. Their heirs mustered courage to reread the *Book of Daniel* and the *Book of Revelation* as if these books could at last be compassed. Such courage led John Nelson Darby (1800–1882) to lower from the flies a startlingly theatrical machine that inspired many subsequent premillennial scenarios: the "secret rapture," an unannounced ascension of the living elect while Jesus returns to do battle on the earth below (cf. *1 Thes.* 4:17). Certified by the widely distributed Cyrus Scofield Bible commentary (1909; amended 1919), this machine resembles Hellenistic blueprints of the gnostic sage's ascent to the lower heavens during world conflagration. Both tend to cloud the supposedly radical thrust of premillennialism.

In larger perspective, it is less useful to distinguish between conservatives and radical millenarians than to note that millenarian movements go through phases: an expansive phase during which believers move out to a ripening world and an astringent phase during which they pull in toward a holy refuge. These phases are equally political. In the stubbornest withdrawal to the most undesirable, inaccessible places (like Jim Jones's village in the Guyanese jungle from 1972 to 1978), millenarians become *prima facie* political threats, whether or not they speak of loyalty to earthly regents. Total withdrawal so often suggests cabal that the more a millenarian group seeks full disengagement, the more the ruling elite may suspect conspiracy and subversion. Similarly, in their expansive phase, millenarians may be the missionary outriders of empire (Christopher Columbus, for example, his monogram qabbalistic, his "Christ-bearing" mission self-consciously prophetic) or the counterforce to empire (the Plains Indian Ghost Dance of the 1880s, the Contestado of Brazil in the 1910s, the New Mexican La Raza movement in the 1960s); they may be the impetus for nationalism (the Tana Bhagat of India, 1915) or the barrier against it (the Watchtower and Kitawala movements in south-central Africa since 1909, Alice Lenshina's Lumpa Church in Zambia in the 1960s); they may be universalists (the International Workers of the World and their general strikes of 1905 to 1920) or ethnic separatists (Juan Santos presenting himself in 1742 as Apu-Inca, descendant of the last Inca, Atahuallpa, or the Altai Turks in 1904 awaiting the Oirot Khan's return and freedom from the Russians). Expansive or astringent, millenarian movements are inherently political but not inherently reactionary or revolutionary.

Typologies of millenarian movements. Altogether, as a system of thought and social movement, millenarianism spins on two axes: golden age or new era; primitive paradise or promised land. This oscillation leads perplexed observers to depict millenarian movements as volatile, metamorphic, undirected, and ephemeral. Journalistic or academic, administrative or missiological, works on the subject abound with images that have shaped policy. Millenarianism is described in five iconic sets:

1. a contagion to be quarantined (as with Mormonism in Utah in the later 1800s);
2. a quicksand to be fenced off (as in the legal actions against the American Shakers in the early 1800s and the present-day anticult campaigns against the Unification Church);
3. a simmering stew to be watched, on the premise that a watched pot never boils (as in police surveillance of the group surrounding Catherine Théot in Paris in 1793 and 1794);
4. a boil to be lanced (as in the English kidnaping of the prophet Birsa from Munda country in northeastern India in 1895 or the Belgian imprisonment of Simon Kimbangu and his first disciples from 1921 to 1957);
5. an explosion to be contained (the German war against the Maji Maji of German East Africa [modern-day Tanzania] in 1905 and 1906 or the Jamaican government's preemption of Rastafarian music and rhetoric in the last two decades).

Millenarianism appears here as an epiphenomenon, a symptom of or a pretext for something more sinister. These images (and policies) have an august history. Church councils in Latin, Byzantine, and Protestant Christianity, legal scholars of Sunnī Islam and rabbinic Judaism, the presiding monks of Buddhist *saṃghas*—all have long regarded millenarianism as a disguised attack on codes of behavior that are meant to govern faith and cult. Rulers and their bureaucracies—Confucian, Islamic, Hindu—have regarded millenarianism as a ritual mask worn by crafty rebels.

Present-day typologists are somewhat more sympathetic. For them, millenarianism is emblematic, a ceremonial flag waved furiously over swamps of injustice. Such an interpretation was codified by the French and German Enlightenments, then refurbished by liberals in the nineteenth century until positivist denials of a religious instinct made religion itself seem epiphenomenal.

Latter-day social scientists have made millenarianism doubly emblematic, for they describe it as the sign of transition from a religious to a secular society.

Current typologies work along three scales: temporal focus, soteriology, and sociopolitical engagement. On the first scale, typologists range those movements oriented toward (1) the reconstitution of an earlier social structure (called nativist, traditionalist, conservationist, restorative), (2) the imaginative making of peace with change (called acculturative, adjustive, perpetuative, revitalist, reformative), and (3) the creation of an ideal future society (called messianic or utopian). The second scale runs from those movements concerned exclusively with individual salvation (called redemptive, revivalist, thaumaturgic) to those that demand an overhaul of economy and etiquette (called transformative or revolutionary). The third scale starts at total isolation and finishes with collective assault on the state. This scale especially has been plodded and plowed by rhetoric (reactionary/progressive, passive/active, prepolitical/political, mythological/ideological). Like mule teams, these binary terms are hardworking but perpetually sterile, since millenarians delight in the yoking of opposites.

Dynamic typologies, plotted by such scholars as Mary Douglas (1970), James W. Fernandez, (1964), and Wim M. J. van Binsbergen (1981), are quadrivalent, balancing social pressures against social structures. Douglas uses two variables, social cohesion and shared symbolic systems. Fernandez takes acculturation as his ordinate, instrumentality as his abscissa. Van Binsbergen considers both the source of disequilibrium (infrastructural, superstructural) and the nature of the threat ("peasantization," "proletarianization"). Such typologies, more appreciative of the complexity of millenarian movements, still hesitate before the phase shifts through which most movements go.

Motives for the fabrication of typologies may themselves be classified as prophylactic or exploitative. Most typologies mean to be prophylactic. Political scientists, for example, may hope to forestall the rise of charismatic tyranny; anthropologists in colonial settings may want to persuade authorities to handle millenarian movements more reasonably and with less show of force; missionaries may wish to avoid spawning highly independent churches or syncretic cults. Other typologies are exploitative. Marxist and capitalist alike place millenarians on a sociohistorical ladder so as to direct their obvious energies upward, toward national liberation and socialism or toward modern industrialism and oligopoly. Occultists and irenic church people place millenarians on one rung of the ladder of spiritual evolution so as to draw them toward higher consciousness, the Aquarian age, or one broad faith.

Explanations for millenarian movements. Despite the many topologies, there are but two current scholarly explanations for the birth of millenarian movements. The first asserts thatr millenarianism arises from feelings of relative deprivation in matters status, wealth, security, or self-esteem. Millenarian movements appear in periods of crisis, when such feelings become most painful. The crisis may be as blatant and acute as the sack of a city or as subtle and prolonged as the passage from isolated agrarian community to industrial megalopolis. Whichever it is, the crisis engenders personal fantasies of invulnerability and escape, which are transformed by charismatic individuals who are often members of displaced elites. These prophets shape public expressions of protest at a time when more straightforward political action seems useless. In the necessarily unsuccessful aftermath, millenarians master the cognitive dissonance between expectation and failure by perpetuating millenarian beliefs within a revised chronology and a new missionary plan. The underlying causes for feelings of deprivation will not have been resolved, so a millenarian tradition, halfway between social banditry and the politics of party, burns on.

The second, complementary explanation says that millenarian movements spring from contact between two cultures when one is technologically far superior to the other. Millenarianism spreads within the settled, inferior culture, whose polity is critically threatened. The newcomers, usuallty white and literate, disrupt traditional systems of kinship, healing, and land rights. Most wrenching are the factorial economics introduced by the newcomers, whose quantitative uses of time and money rasp across the qualitative webs of social reciprocity. The indigenes must redefine their notions of power, status, and law, or they must stave off the well-armed traders, their navies, and their missionaries. Acknowledging the superiority of the newcomers' technology but not that of their ethic of possessive individualim, the indigenes begin to speculate about the true origin of the goods and gods of the stingy, secretive newcomers. The result is the contact cult (also called a "crisis cult" or "cargo cult") devoted to frenzied preparation for the receipt of shiploads of goods (cargo) that will dock unaccompanied by whites or in the company of fair-skinned but unselfish ancestors. Already under intense pressure, the people ceremonially destroy sacred objects and standing crops. They believe that this world is ending and a new one must begin, best with the newcomers gone and themselves masters of the secret of wealth.

Contact is the sociology for which deprivation is the psychology. Contact leads to millenarianism when one group feels unalterably deprived vis-à-vis a new other.

The two explanations, compatible with stock images of eruption and contagion, rely on the premise of a closed system. At the millenarian core lies frustration; out of frustration squirms fantasy, and fantasy breeds violence. Early Freudian analyses of hysteria, psychosis, and schizophrenia have been employed here to wire the circuit between individual fireworks and collective explosion.

Deprivation theories prevail despite decades of criticism for their being slackly predictive. Scholars have noted that relative deprivation does not account specifically for millenarianism; it may as easily induce fracas, sabotage, or personal depression. Conversely, millenarian movements have not "burst out" where relative deprivation has been most apparent: eighteenth-century Ireland, nineteenth-century Ethiopia, the southeastern coast of modern India. Indeed, as critics may add, where across this imperfect world has relative deprivation ever been absent or a crisis lacking?

At this point, theorists invoke a *homo ex machina*, the charismatic prophet who processes the raw stuff of frustration. As a person whose life portends or echoes social crises, the prophet articulates the myth-dream of the people and so becomes invested with the power to direct its expression. Wherever gambols a weak social theory about religious movements, sure to follow is the fleece of charisma. For face-to-face groups, as W. R. Bion showed in his *Experiences in Groups* (New York, 1961), prophetic leaders may embody group fantasies of rebirth. For larger groups—like most millenarian movements—charisma becomes narcotic, a controlled substance rather than a theory of social relations.

Theorists have given particularly short shrift to the remarkable prominence of women as millenarian prophets. In all but Islam and Judaism, women have stridden at the head of millenarian movements, with men as their scribes, publicists, and ideologues. The list is long; a few examples must do: Priscilla and Maximilla of the New Prophecy (the Montanists) in Asia Minor in the late second century; Guglielma of Milan and her women disciples in the late thirteenth century; Donna Beatrice's Antonine movement in the Lower Congo from 1703 to 1706; Joanna Southcott with perhaps twenty thousand followers in England before her death in 1814; Ellen Gould White, chief oracle of the Seventh-day Adventists in the United States, in the late nineteenth century; Jacobina Maurer of the Brazilian Muckers movement from 1872 to 1898; the visionary Gaidaliu in Assam from 1929 to 1930 and 1961 to 1965; Mai Chaza's Guta ra Jehova (City of Jehovah) in Rhodesia from 1954 to 1960; Kitamura Sayō's Dancing Religion (Tenshō Kōtai Jingukyō) founded in Japan in 1945.

Deprivation theories maintain that women, an injured group, use religion as a means to power otherwise denied them by patriarchies. This makes religion a negative (compensatory) vehicle for women and a positive (creative) vehicle for men, and it fails to explain the power that women gain over men through millenarian movements. There is as yet no sufficient discussion of female charisma. Indeed, where prophetic leadership is male, analysis customarily proceeds from the instrumental, socioeconomic background to doctrine and political tactics; where female, it proceeds from affective, sexual background to ritual and spirit possession. Active men, reactive women: a contact theory of the sexes.

Contact theories are tricky. Amazed by discoveries of previously unknown tribes in the Amazon region and in the Philippines, industrial societies exaggerate the isolation of nonindustrial people. Nonetheless, contact is always a matter of degree: from armies with bulldozers abruptly grading runways in Melanesia to pandemics of smallpox hundreds of miles from (European) vectors. Contact is never so much a shock that some prophecy or other has not already accumulated around a piece of strangeness that years before drifted in on a storm tide or fell from the clouds.

In addition, we have sparse evidence that a number of peoples—the Guaraní of South America, the Karen of Burma, the Lakalai of the island of New Britain, and perhaps the Pacific Northwest Indians—had myths, rituals, and cults whose motifs were millenarian and whose origins were prior to contact with an in-pressing "superior" (Eurasian) culture.

Furthermore, not every uneven contact lights a millenarian "fuse." While the same material imbalance between Europeans and natives faced both Polynesians and Melanesians, millenarian movements have been infrequent among the politically stratified societies of Polynesia. More loosely bunched and socially fluid, Melanesians had inadequate etiquette by which to carry out diplomacy between distinctly separate orders. The customary structure of discourse, not contact itself, seems to have been a key variable in the general absence of cargo cults in Polynesia and their flowering in Melanesia, where consistently powerful Europeans could not be dealt with as easily as could another and analogous order.

At best, deprivation predisposes, contact precipitates. There are six other factors whose presence predisposes to millenarian movements:

1. permeable monastic communities and lay sodalities that extend loyalties beyond the family;
2. itinerant homeopathic healers who carry ritual and rumor across regional borders;
3. a mythopoetic tradition in popular drama and folk-

tale, which makes history prophetic and the people the bearers of prophecy;
4. numerology and astrology, which encourage people habitually to search out relationships between number, event, and time;
5. rituals of inversion, such as carnival or exhaustive mourning, in which endings and beginnings are willfully confused;
6. migration myths that call for the return to an ancestral land or for the return of the dead to a renewed land.

There are negatively prejudicial factors as well. Millenarian movements are least likely at the extremes of the economic spectrum—that is, among those who have complete freedom of mobility and among those absolutely constrained. No millenarian movements occur within groups whose positions are secure, comfortable, and protected by mechanisms of caste (classical North Indian, Japanese, and Roman aristocracies). Nor do millenarian movements occur within groups whose mobility has been severely restricted by political oppression (prisoners, inmates of concentration camps), economic oppression (slaves), physical illness (hospital patients, the starving), or mental illness (asylum inmates, the autistic).

This verges on tautology: millenarian movements happen where physical movement is possible. But the near tautology is suggestive. Where cultural ideals of physical movement differ, so, correspondingly, may the nature of social movements. For example, to be harshly schematic, Western Europeans have stressed vertical, direct, outbound motion in their sports, their dancing, their tools, and their manners; the head and shoulders lead, with the mass of the body in tow. Sub-Saharan Africans such as the Dogon have a kinesthetic of orchestral, highly oppositional, polyrhythmic motion in which the body twists at the hips. The northern Chinese have in their martial arts, their medicine and calligraphy a kinesthetic of sustained circular motion, an integrated body linked to the flow of universal energy. These differences may be expressed in the European proclivity for a tight echelon of prophets leading an undifferentiated millenarian body, the African tendency toward coextensive and fissiparous leadership, the Chinese history of generational continuity from one guiding millenarian family to the next. Kinesthetic differences may also determine the relative importance of the precipitants of millenarianism: where a society looks for whole-body motion, the triggering instances must affect the entire society; where a society looks for articulated or isolated motions, the triggering instances may be more local.

The following four factors recur cross-culturally as major precipitants of millenarian movements:

1. the evangelism of foreign missionaries whose success requires the reordering of native patterns of marriage, family, diet, and calendar;
2. displacement by refugees or invaders, or as a result of persecution, economic decline, or natural calamity;
3. confusion about landholdings due to shifting settlement, the superposition of a new legal grid, or the advent of new technologies, as foreshadowed most particularly by census taking, geological surveys, rail laying, and road building;
4. generational distortion, where the traditional transfer of loyalties and moral authority is profoundly disturbed by war deaths, schooling, long-distance migrations, or urbanization.

These are, of course, related. Threaded throughout are anxieties about inheritance, boundaries, and language (its intelligibility, its capacity for truth-telling). Set within a matrix of predisposing factors, granted some rumors and good weather, these anxieties should specifically engage the wheels of millenarianism, with its special freight of ages, places, and figures of speech. Expansive millenarianism occurs when believers are imperiled or impressed by forces within their society; astringent millenarianism occurs when the forces seem foreign.

Patterns of millenarian movements in world history. The world's great religions share a larger historical pattern of millenarian activity (although Vedānta Hinduism may be a partial exception). Founded on the fringes of empire or at the fracture line between competing kingdoms, these religions find themselves several centuries later at the center of an empire. Millenarian thought then appears in canonical form, drawing its impetus from those forces of imperial expansion that compel the recalculation of calendars, histories, distances, and sacred geography. The new arithmetic signals a shift in scales of measurement, mediated as much by mystics as by scientists. When an empire seems to have reached its limits, millenarian movements flourish, usually several generations before the dynastic collapse.

When the millennium does not arrive, or when millenarian movements are co-opted by a new dynasty, as in Ming China or Safavid Iran, millenarianism does not fade away. End-of-the-world images linger in the dreams and speech of the people, and end-time ideas are filtered through monasteries, lay brotherhoods, and scientific communities. As these are gradually attracted to the nodes of political power, millenarian movements reappear either as adjuncts of conquest or as resistance to it. Millenarian activity peaks again when the limits of territorial coherence are felt within the empire and along its colonial periphery.

This sequence may obtain for other than the great world religions (e.g., for the Aztec, Iroquois, and Bakongo), but materials are lacking that would sustain such an argument for the many preliterate cultures. It is tempting, in the same way that millenarianism itself is tempting, to offer a global explanation—such as climatic cycles—for its rhythms. The quest for global explanations, however, like the quest for a fountain of youth, tells more about the explorers than it does about the territory.

Contemporary Fascination with the End. Why does millenarianism presently seem in such need of some kind of covering law? The answers to this question have to do with the characteristics of the North Atlantic ecumene, which is responsible for most of the law making.

A first answer is that millenarians tend not to fall within the bell of the ecumene's emotional curve. Although sternly depressed about current affairs, millenarians are at the same time exultant about the prospects for a New World. European and North American psychologists interpret ambivalence as a symptom of inner discord; the greater the ambivalence, the more serious the illness. But "sensible" middle-class citizens join UFO cults, buy fifteen million copies of Hal Lindsey's *The Late Great Planet Earth* (Grand Rapids, Mich., 1970), and order bulk goods from End Time Foods, Inc., in Virginia. Why?

A second answer is that millenarians threaten the stability of the ecumene, upsetting the development of outlying colonies. Millenarians seem haphazardly amused by industrial investment and international tariffs. Why do they keep popping up to make a hash of foreign policy, and why do they prefer the "magical" to the "practical"?

A third answer is that the wars of this century have burned the mark of the beast on North Atlantic arts, philosophy, and history. The beast roared through the no-man's-lands of World War I and the gas chambers and radioactive cinders of World War II. Apocalypse has lost its reference to millennium; it has become simply a synonym for disaster.

We can also trace the growth of a catastrophic mood in North Atlantic science over a century of work in astronomy, cosmology, ecology, climatology, and, recently, morphogenetics and mathematics (the last two united by catastrophe theory, which accounts topologically for instant changes of state). The mood has prevailed in popular science from Henry Adams's 1909 essay on the second law of thermodynamics ("The Rule of Phase Applied to History") to the syzygy scare of the so-called Jupiter effect (1974–1982).

A fourth, more upbeat answer is that archaeology, theology, politics, and the Gregorian calendar have conspired to regenerate the utopian side of millenarianism. Although no millenarian movements and exceedingly few prophecies were geared to the year 1000 (few then used such a calendar), the historical myth persists because it seems to many that the year 2000 will be truly millennial. The discovery of the Dead Sea Scrolls since 1947 has underscored the contention, popularized by Albert Schweitzer in 1906, that eschatological hope was vital at the time of apostolic Christianity and should therefore be part of all true Christian belief. Israel's statehood in 1948 and its 1967 reunification of Jerusalem have convinced fundamentalist Christians of the nearness of the Second Coming, for which a principal sign is the Jews' return to Zion. So we see in the ecumene a telephone hot line for news of the latest scriptural prophecies fulfilled, an international conference on end-of-world prophecies (in Jerusalem in 1971), and a new perfume called Millenium: "In the life of every woman's skin there comes a turning point, a time when her face begins to look older. Now there is an alternative."

Outside the ecumene, detached from Christian dates, Hindu and Buddhist revivalists (Hare Krishna, Divine Light Mission, Sōka Gakkai) preach the last era, the *kaliyuga* or *mappō*. Shīʿīs awaiting the Mahdi at century's end (AH 1399/1979–1980 CE) experienced instead the Iranian revolution. Mexican intellectuals of the Movement of the Reappearance of Anauak, following the Aztec calendar, find this a time of cataclysm. Marxists, flipping through an economic almanac, tear off the leaves of late capitalism.

The fifth answer, then, is that from within and without the ecumene, notions of change have taken on a prepotently millenarian cast.

The Significance of Millenarianism. Claims for the significance of millenarianism, either as a system of thought or as a tradition of social movements, range from the thoughtfully deprecatory (that it is one more index to the predicament of capitalism) to the modestly dismissive (that it is an expression of a universally human fantasy of returning to the womb and resuming unhindered power in a practically timeless world) to the complimentary (that it is a rich mode of dissent where other modes are either unavailable or unavailing) to the genuinely laudatory (that in the form of the myth of the eternal return and its rituals of cosmic renewal, it is the taproot of religion and revolution). The truth, as usual, lies athwart.

[*For a broad survey of myths dealing with the end of*

time, see Eschatology; *for religious concepts that share the symbolism found in millenarian movements, see* Golden Age *and* Utopia.]

BIBLIOGRAPHY

Millenarian scholarship, chiefly a phenomenon of the North Atlantic ecumene, has followed the same patterns of historical change.

During the sixteenth century, while European merchants redefined time as fortune, millenarians appeared in Roman Catholic histories of heresy and Protestant martyrologies. For Catholics and for the Magisterial Reformers, millenarianism was occasioned by lust (impatience, appetite without love); for radical Protestants, millenarianism came of a desperately loving desire to return to the apostolic model. Then, as today, the bell cows of any overview were the communalistic Taborites in fifteenth-century Bohemia, Thomas Müntzer's rebels in the German Peasants' Revolt of 1524–1525, and the antinomian Anabaptist kingdom at Münster in 1534. In these three episodes the consequences of the millenarian program were so played out that most subsequent commentaries used them to distinguish between legitimate and illegitimate visions of religious and social renewal.

Early seventeenth-century histories, written in a confusing era of religious warfare, tended to describe millenarianism as the confused or gangrenous extension of piety, for which in English was coined the word *enthusiasm,* an outlier of the syndrome of melancholia. Melancholics seemed to resemble the age itself, mixing categories and muddling the practical, the extravagant, and the fantastic.

After the near revolutions of midcentury—the French Fronde with its *illuminés,* the English Civil War with its Levellers and Fifth Monarchists—millenarianism was implicated in political plotting and secret communication. So the medical figure of contagion, used earlier against witchcraft, was resurrected in works about millenarians, who might be possessed or mad or deluded but were likely first to have been infected by conniving knaves. Every one of these explanations was offered for the mass appeal of the great Jewish false messiah, Shabbetai Tsevi, who in 1666, at the height of his career, converted to Islam under penalty of death.

Eighteenth-century accounts, although sometimes pietist and sympathetic to millenarians, moved toward a vaguely biological description: millenarianism was seen as corpuscular, nervous, iatromechanical. In an era of newly accurate clocks and mortality statistics, historical source-criticism and the propaganda of Newtonian science, millenarians seemed to have lost their sense of time and power of memory.

Most modern assumptions about millenarianism were in place soon after the French Revolution. Encyclopedias of religion and dictionaries of sects sank the stakes: millenarianism was a personal reaction to internal chemical imbalance or to feelings of envy or lust; it was a social ploy or a disguise for politicking, money making, or ambition. Later in the century, under the impact of revivalism and labor agitation, millenarianism became part of the sociology of crowds; as a personal disorder it was associated homologically with *dementia praecox* (soon to be called schizophrenia). Anthropologists worked with Europocentric genetic metaphors: if millenarian movements occurred within Western civilization, they were classified as throwbacks to the spiritual childhood of religion; if outside, they were seen as infantile tantrums of primitive societies.

At least three thousand studies of millenarianism have been printed in this century, more and more often with a sympathetic preamble. Even so, because millenarians seem destined to inevitable disappointment, people of all political persuasions have resented the millenarian label, none more so than revolutionaries who want to make it clear that their programs for a New World are neither illusory nor doomed. Since Ernst Bloch's *Thomas Müntzer als Theologe der Revolution* (Munich, 1921), millenarian scholarship has been especially sharpened by political as well as religious polemic.

At midcentury, out tumbled a spate of works insisting on the centrality and continuity of millenarianism: for European culture, Normal R. C. Cohn's *The Pursuit of the Millennium* (1957), 3 ed. (New York, 1970); for peasant culture, Eric J. Hobsbawm's *Primitive Rebels* (New York, 1959); for world culture, *La table ronde*'s full issue on "Apocalypse et idée de fin des temps" (no. 110, February 1957); and the human condition, Mircea Eliade's *Cosmos and History: The Myth of the Eternal Return* (New York, 1954). Simultaneously, in *When Prophecy Fails* (1956; reprint, New York, 1964), Leon Festinger, Henry W. Riecken, and Stanley Schachter developed a theory of cognitive dissonance to explain the endurance of millenarian beliefs from the point of view of social psychology. The capstone was a conference in 1960 sponsored by *Comparative Studies in Society and History,* (The Hague, 1958–), the journal that is still the most active in millenarian studies. The event set the agenda for at least a decade of research, prompting scholars to fashion typologies and to formulate distinctions between varieties of millenarian activity. The conference results were not published in book form until a decade later: *Millennial Dreams in Action: Studies in Revolutionary Religious Movements,* edited by Sylvia L. Thrupp (New York, 1970).

Although the works discussed above remain the most consistently cited sources in millenarian studies, their popularity is largely a measure of the comfort they have afforded a North Atlantic ecumene that is increasingly upset by liberation movements and cold war apocalypse diplomacy. Millenarianism, they assure us, has a history, a tradition, a phenomenology, a philosophy, and a psychology.

Henri Desroche's *Dieux d'hommes: Dictionnaire des messianismes et millénarismes de l'ère chrétienne* (Paris, 1969), although incomplete and outdated, codified much earlier scholarship. That year also saw a general turn away from theories of social pathology and mental illness to explain millenarian movements. Sophisticated analysis has turned toward the creative and polysemous nature of millenarianism. The following are some of the most thoughtful and evocative works published in English since 1969.

The oxymorons of millenarian thought have been deftly handled by Marjorie E. Reeves in *The Influence of Prophecy in the Later Middle Ages: A Study of Joachimism* (Oxford, 1969) and *Joachim of Fiore and the Prophetic Future* (London, 1976), which should be supplemented by a series of articles by Robert

E. Lerner, including "Medieval Prophecy and Religious Dissent," *Past and Present* 72 (1976): 3–24; J. G. A. Pocock's *Politics, Language and Time* (New York, 1971), especially his essay "Time, History and Eschatology in the Thought of Thomas Hobbes," pp. 148–201; and Sacvan Bercovitch's *The Puritan Origins of the American Self* (London, 1975), which is excellently extended in his article "The Typology of America's Mission," *American Quarterly* 30 (Summer 1978): 135–155. Theodore Olson's *Millennialism, Utopianism, and Progress* (Toronto, 1981) moves heroically from the Greeks to the present, slipping and sliding along the way but always serious and sometimes passionate. Joseph Needham's purview is even broader; Needham masterfully draws out the similarities as well as the differences between European and Chinese approaches to time, in "Time and Eastern Man" in his *The Grand Titration: Science and Society in East and West* (Buffalo, N.Y., 1969), pp. 218–298. Like Needham, Charles Webster underlines the philosophical but also the social relations between science and millenarianism in his *The Great Instauration: Science, Medicine and Reform, 1626–1660* (New York, 1976).

Social anthropologists have been at the forefront of theory about millenarian movements. Alluded to in the text were Mary Douglas's *Natural Symbols: Explorations in Cosmology* (New York, 1970); James W. Fernandez's "African Religious Movements," *Annual Review of Anthropology* 7 (1978): 195–234, and "African Religious Movements: Types and Dynamics," *Journal of Modern African Studies* 2 (1964): 531–549; and Wim M. J. van Binsbergen's *Religious Change in Zambia* (Boston, 1981). Highly influential for his sophistication and for his theory of differential access to redemptive media is Kenelm Burridge's *New Heaven, New Earth* (New York, 1969). An interesting and thoroughgoing Marxist approach is presented by Berta I. Sharevskaya in *The Religious Traditions of Tropical Africa in Contemporary Focus* (Budapest, 1973); more accessible may be her article "Toward a Typology of Anticolonial Religious-Political Movements in Tropical Africa," *Soviet Anthropology and Archaeology* 15 (1976): 84–102. Less anthropological but nicely eclectic is Stephen Sharot's *Messianism, Mysticism, and Magic: A Sociological Analysis of Jewish Religious Movements* (Chapel Hill, N.C., 1982).

For particularly well done case studies of millenarian movements, see Mangol Bayat's *Mysticism and Dissent: Socioreligious Thought in Qajar Iran* (Syracuse, N.Y. 1982); Pierre Clastres's *Society against the State*, translated by Robert Harley and Abe Stein (New York, 1977), concerning the Guaraní of South America; Hue-Tam Ho Tai's *Millenarianism and Peasant Politics in Vietnam* (Cambridge, Mass., and London, 1983); Susan Naquin's *Millenarian Rebellion in China: The Eight Trigrams Uprising of 1813* (New Haven and London, 1976) and *Shantung Rebellion: The Wang Lun Uprising of 1774* (New Haven, 1981); my own *The French Prophets: The History of a Millenarian Group in Eighteenth-Century England* (Berkeley, 1980); and Anthony F. C. Wallace's *The Death and Rebirth of the Seneca* (New York, 1972).

Further bibliographies may be found in my "The End of the Beginning: Millenarian Studies, 1969–1975," *Religious Studies Review* 2 (July 1976): 1–15; Harold W. Turner's *Bibliography of New Religious Movements in Primal Societies*, 4 vols. (Boston, 1977–); and Bryan R. Wilson's *Magic and the Millennium* (New York, 1973), pp. 505–531.

HILLEL SCHWARTZ

Chinese Millenarian Movements

The yearning for a utopia where one is free from want and where peace and prosperity reign supreme has been very much an integral part of Chinese religion since pre-Ch'in times (before 221 BCE). Confucius (551–479 BCE) maintained the notion of a golden age when Sage-Kings such as Yao and Shun reigned effortlessly in perfect harmony. Lao-tzu also espoused the idea of small agricultural communities where life was simple and government was noninterfering. The Moist concept of undifferentiated and nondiscriminating love was expressed in the form of *ta-t'ung* ("grand unity" or "great equality"), which had been incorporated into the Confucian text *Li chi* (The Classic of Rites). However, all these utopian states were understood to have existed in the distant past.

As time progressed, the conceptualization of utopia became more concrete and contemporary. During the Ch'in-Han period (221 BCE–206 CE), mysterious lands in the extreme east and west of China were regarded either as paradises inhabited by immortals, or as idealized countries where justice and honesty prevailed. The realm of Hsi Wang Mu, or Queen Mother of the West, on Mount K'un-lun in the west and the three fairy islands of P'eng-lai ("proliferating weeds"), Fang-chang ("square fathom"), and Ying-chou ("ocean continent") in the eastern seas belonged to the first category, while the land of "Great Ch'in" (Ta-Ch'in), an idealized version of the Roman empire, belonged to the second.

In contrast to pre-Ch'in utopias, all these ideal realms were understood to be contemporaneous with those who visited or reported on them. However, they were accessible to only a few privileged members of society. The Queen Mother of the West, for example, entertained only emperors and regaled them by her turquoise pond with her peaches and wine of immortality. The three fairy islands were similarly inaccessible to ordinary mortals; they either sank into the ocean when approached, or caused big storms to drive people off course.

Toward the second half of the Han dynasty, the formerly evasive Queen Mother of the West had apparently undergone a dramatic change. She now became the object of worship among large segments of the population. In 3 BCE, for example, thousands of her followers in twenty-six commanderies of the Han empire, including the capital city of Ch'ang-an (present-day Sian), went into a state of frenzy in anticipation of her arrival, which promised salvation. Barefoot, their hair disheveled, they sang and danced in the streets. [*See* Hsi Wang Mu.]

Early Movements. Two major soteriological movements developed almost two centuries later. The first, centered in western China (present-day Szechwan and Shensi), was headed by Chang Lu, who created a theocratic state between 186 and 216 CE. Tracing his teaching to his grandfather Chang Tao-ling (34?–156? CE), Chang Lu taught that illness was a sign of sin and could be healed by confession. Furthermore, he advocated the establishment of communal facilities to expedite the realization of his utopia on earth. These facilities provided free food for the needy and undertook all kinds of public works for the good of the commonweal. Chang's movement, known as the Five Pecks of Rice (Wu-tou-mi) or Way of Celestial Masters (T'ien-shih Tao), survived the Han-Wei dynastic transition because of his accommodation with political authorities. It became the recognized orthodox Taoist tradition in China, and Chang Tao-ling was revered as the first Taoist patriarch. [*See the biographies of Chang Lu and Chang Tao-ling.*]

There was another religious movement in eastern China which, under the leadership of Chang Chüeh (d. 184 CE), existed contemporaneously with Chang Lu's and in many ways resembled the latter in both belief and organization. It was called the Way of Highest Peace (T'ai-p'ing Tao) because of its alleged subscription to the text *T'ai-p'ing ching* (Classic of Highest Peace). However, it differed from Chang Lu's movement in that it rebelled in 184 and was ruthlessly crushed by the Han imperial forces. This rebellion, known as the Yellow Turban Rebellion because of the color of the headgear worn by the rebels, represented the first large-scale religiously inspired rebellious movement in Chinese history. [*See the biography of Chang Chüeh.*]

Some scholars argue that the impetus for the militancy of the Yellow Turbans came from the *Classic of Highest Peace*, which, despite its Confucian and perhaps even Buddhist borrowings, was obviously a Taoist text concerned with eschatology and changing the course of history. Compiled in the form of a continuing dialogue between the Celestial Master, an emissary of Tao, and his disciples, the *Classic of Highest Peace* offers description of an ideal society and provides expectation of a renewal of the world through heavenly agents. The significance of the text's eschatology lies in the fact that it relativizes the validity of the existing society. It sees drastic change in the course of history as imminent and desirable, for the demarcation between this world and the beyond will be broken down, and the dawning of a mystical new order will be at hand.

Thus, from the original view of an ideal world existing in the remote past, through the transitional view of the utopia existing in distant lands contemporaneously, Chinese religion finally came to the view of the perfect realm existing in the future, the arrival of which would signal the end of the present age.

The Medieval Period. The several centuries after the collapse of the Han dynasty were a time of burning religious zeal, caused in part by the people's desire to seek solace from a rapidly disintegrating society brought about by "barbarian" invasions and incessant warfare. With Confucianism in eclipse, both Taoism and the newly introduced Buddhism made great inroads into the hearts and minds of the Chinese. Especially attractive to the suffering masses was the promise of messianic deliverance offered by both Taoist and Buddhist sectarian groups. It was during this time, specifically from the fourth century on, that a Chinese-style millenarianism developed, complete with the identification of an eschatological crisis, the appearance of a messianic figure, the apocalyptic battle, the guaranteed survival of the elect, and the portrayal of the "New Jerusalem."

In sectarian Taoism, millenarianism was expressed in the cult of Lao-tzu, who now assumed the name of Li Hung the Perfect Lord. Between the fourth and the fifth centuries numerous rebel leaders, claiming to be incarnations of Li Hung, staged uprisings. As described in the *Tung-yüan shen-chou ching* (Classic of Divine Spells from the Deep Cavern), a Taoist text compiled in the early fifth century, the millenarianism of the Li Hung cult contains the following themes:

1. There is an impending crisis of cosmic proportions caused by the accumulation of evil. The time of reckoning will be the year *jen-ch'en* (which occurs once every sixty years in the Chinese calendar, but was generally understood to specify the year 392 CE), when floods surging upwards of several thousand feet and epidemics of every imaginable kind will afflict the world.
2. The savior Li Hung will appear to deliver his believers from this cataclysmic disaster and to eradicate all nonbelievers, who will be discarded as chaff. This apocalyptic battle will result in the total triumph of Li Hung and his chosen ones.
3. An era of unutterable joy and peace will ensue. The ravages of war will be eliminated. The cosmos will be reconstituted. The entire earth will be covered with seven treasures. One sowing will yield nine

> crops and human lifespan will be extended to three thousand years, after which it will be renewed again. All men and women will be sages and evil people will no longer exist.

This Taoist millenarianism was paralleled by a Buddhist version of the same period. Centered around the messianic figure of "Prince Moonlight" (Yüeh-kuang T'ung-tzu), a minor character in the legendary biography of the Buddha, this Buddhist millenarianism has essentially all the features of its Taoist counterpart, with the apocalyptic happenings designated to take place in the two successive years of *shen* and *yu*. In fact, the similarity between the two versions of millenarianism is so striking that one is compelled to assume that Taoism and Buddhism must have overlapped or merged together at the popular level during their parallel development at this time.

"Prince Moonlight" was later superseded by a much more powerful and famous Buddhist savior—the Buddha Maitreya. In Buddhist mythology, Maitreya was the Buddha who "has yet to come." He was believed to dwell in the Tuṣita heaven, waiting to descend to earth to save all believers. There is the further understanding that when he arrives the world will be experiencing the last days of the Buddhist *dharma* (an age known as the *mo-fa*), and that with one bold stroke he will rid the world of all evil elements and usher in a new golden age. The Maitreya Buddha was thus perceived as a savior, as his coming would signal the end of existing misery and injustice. Unlike Amitābha Buddha, who promised salvation in the form of rebirth in his Pure Land and made no attempt to improve this world, the Maitreya Buddha served as a world redeemer who would radically and dramatically change the status quo and transform the world into a realm of bliss and abundance. What made Maitreya worship even more subversive was the belief, pervasive since the fifth century, that his coming was imminent (rather than in the distant future as originally believed). This immediately turned him into a symbol for numerous antidynastic movements, all of which aimed at the speedy toppling of the existing order. [*See* Maitreya.]

In addition to Taoist Li Hung and Buddhist Maitreya, there was yet another millenarian tradition in medieval China—Manichaeism. Originally introduced from Persia during the early T'ang dynasty (618–907), Manichaeism subscribed to a dualistic view of the world wherein the forces of Light, under the leadership of Mani, would engage in a fierce struggle with the forces of Darkness. Followers of this tradition held the belief that cosmic history progressed in three stages: the first stage characterized by a clear division between the realms of Light and Darkness, the second by a blurring of this division that resulted in the struggle between the two, and the third by the ultimate triumph of Light over Darkness and the creation of a realm of everlasting peace. Believing themselves to be living near the end of the second stage, followers of Mani led a pure and puritanical life in order to guarantee victory over the forces of Darkness and evil. They practiced strict vegetarianism, refused to worship spirits, ghosts, and even ancestors, and buried their dead naked. Indeed their vegetarian diet had become such a distinguishing feature that they were pejoratively referred to as "vegetable eaters and devil (Mani) worshipers" *(ch'ih-ts'ai shih-mo)*. Their antinomian values, demonstrated by such practices as naked burial and nonobservance of ancestral rites, earned them further suspicion from the authorities. [*See* Manichaeism, *overview article*.]

The White Lotus Society. All the above-mentioned millenarian traditions interacted with one another as they evolved. By the fourteenth century, such a substantial merger had taken place among them that they were collectively known as the White Lotus, a catch all label used by the government to encompass most of the proscribed millenarian groups. In fact, White Lotus had a very distinguished beginning. It was allegedly the name of a lay Buddhist group organized in 402 by the eminent monk Hui-yüan to worship the Buddha Amitābha. [*See the biography of Hui-yüan.*] Later, the Pure Land master Mao Tzu-yüan (1086–1166) also used this name to designate his pious vegetarian group. In any event, White Lotus had obviously metamorphosed into a millenarian sectarian movement under the leadership of Han Shan-t'ung (d. 1355) toward the end of the Yüan dynasty (1280–1368). Combining Maitreyan with Manichaean elements, Han boldly declared the "incarnation of Maitreya Buddha and the birth of the Manichaean Prince of Light." Although he was captured and executed, Han was the symbol of the religious movement that eventually brought an end to the Yüan regime.

During the ensuing Ming dynasty (1368–1644) (some scholars even argue that the very name *Ming*, which means "light," is indicative of the Manichaean influence on the founder of the dynasty), the White Lotus tradition became even more systematized. Central to this mature White Lotus belief was the notion of Wu-sheng Lao-mu, or the Eternal Mother, who, as progenitor of the human race, had vowed to save all her repentant children from certain demise. She would deliver them to the *chen-k'ung chia-hsiang* ("native land of true emptiness") where they would enjoy peace and affluence forever. This dual concept of the Eternal Mother and her Native Land of True Emptiness became the identifying creed of the White Lotus sectarians. It served as a profession of faith and a powerful bond that drew all the sect members together into one big religious family. This concept also enabled them to relativize their attachment to their earthly parents and their native communities, and allowed them to see that this world was not the best of all possible worlds, that a "new beginning" would arrive in time to replace the existing order, and that this "new beginning" would sit in judgment over the entire past.

Like the Manichaeans before them, White Lotus believers maintained that time progressed in three major epochs: the age of the Lamplighting Buddha of the past, the age of the Śākyamuni Buddha of the present, and the age of the Maitreya Buddha of the future. Crucial to this time scheme was the expectation that the third or future age was imminent, to be ushered in by an apocalyptic conflagration that would scourge the world to remove all evil elements. (Some sects used the epithets Blue Sun, Red Sun, and White Sun to represent the respective ages.) This cataclysmic turning point was known as the kalpic transition *(chieh)*, characterized by floods, epidemics, earthquakes, and all kinds of unspeakable disasters during which the whole cosmic order would be torn asunder and the elect and the doomed would be separated. When the Maitreya Buddha finally appeared as the messenger of the Eternal Mother to deliver the surviving faithful, the world would be reconstructed and the reunion between the Mother and her lost children would take place. The saved would enjoy the new order, which, according to the description of the *pao-chüan* ("precious scrolls")—a special genre of religious tracts compiled by the sectarians in profusion during the sixteenth and seventeenth centuries—would be peaceful, immortal, and egalitarian.

Because of this millenarian and antinomian orientation of the White Lotus sectarians, they were feared and ruthlessly persecuted by successive dynasties. Their very expectation of the advent of the third age was a negation of the present age, thus undermining the authority as well as the legitimacy of the existing regime. As it turned out, this obsession with salvation in the future age did occasionally inspire ambitious individuals within the sects to proclaim the descent of the Maitreya Buddha and to raise the banner of rebellion in an attempt to usher in the third age. To be sure, the correlation between millenarianism and rebellion was never a direct one, yet the government was always suspicious of millenarians, who, it had reason to fear, were not averse to using violence in order to hasten the end of the present age. There was only a fine line separating the anticipation of the *kalpa* from the expedition of its arrival. Given the fact that the leaders of these sectarian groups were often uprooted, restless, and disgruntled elements in society, this official apprehension is understandable.

Suspicion was further reinforced by the vicarious sibling relationship of the sect members, which undermined the Confucian emphasis on blood ties, as well as the relative equality of the sexes within the sectarian group, flouting the orthodox insistence on strict sexual distinctions. Sectarian organization itself, though lacking centralization, was nevertheless capable of forming large-scale regional networks in a short time because of shared beliefs among the majority of the sects. Quite often, different groups in different geographic areas would subscribe to the same precious scrolls, thus espousing the same doctrines. Many of these tracts had been handed down through generations of sect leaders, allowing the creation of a hereditary folk religious elite. Notable groups such as the Ta-ch'eng sect of Wang Sen (d. 1619) maintained an uninterrupted hereditary transmission for at least two centuries. This resilience of the sects was a great source of worry for the government.

The Taiping Rebellion. The most famous and spectacular millenarian movement in traditional China was, of course, the Taiping Rebellion (1850–1864) led by Hung Hsiu-ch'üan (1813–1864). Hung was a frustrated examination candidate who had received Christian literature from a Chinese convert. With that minimal exposure, he wove together a religion that was a mixture of traditional Chinese eschatology and Christian salvationism. He also organized the God-Worshipers Society, which, reacting to ethnic tensions and prompted by Hung's own sense of mission, rebelled in 1850.

Hung Hsiu-ch'üan's religion is best understood through the designation he chose for his movement after 1850. He named it T'ai-p'ing T'ien-kuo ("heavenly kingdom of highest peace"). T'ai-p'ing, it should be recalled, was the ideal of the Yellow Turbans who rebelled in 184, and had inspired various millenarian groups throughout Chinese history. T'ien-kuo was derived from the Judeo-Christian notion of God's kingdom. Together, the two compound terms indicate Hung's unshakable faith that God's kingdom, in the form of Highest Peace, could be realized on earth, and that he himself would be the instrument through which this momentous task would be accomplished. Declaring himself to be the second son of God and the younger brother of Jesus, Hung saw himself as the redeemer of China, if not of the world as well. At once anti-Confucian and anti-Manchu, his brand of messianic salvationism was by far the most radical China ever witnessed.

Hung's Heavenly Kingdom was characterized by the

proclaimed equality of all men and the liberation of all women. To be sure, there was the inevitable discrepancy between theory and practice. Yet this Taiping ideal was unequivocally enunciated and applied to concrete situations in the form of policy promulgations such as the land tenure system. This system provided equitable land redistribution, going so far as to observe no distinction between the sexes in land allotment.

When the Taiping army captured Nanking in 1853, Hung made it his Heavenly Capital. Nanking, scene of the signing of the treaty that concluded the Opium War between China and Great Britain only eleven years earlier, was seen by Hung as the "New Jerusalem" promised in the *Book of Revelation.* But internal strife, coupled with Manchu military reforms and growing Western hostility toward the Taipings, finally resulted in their crushing defeat in 1864.

Chinese millenarianism can thus be seen having a history that goes back to the early medieval period. It exerted its greatest appeal among marginal or peripheral members of society who, though not necessarily economically deprived, were denied access to power and prestige in the orthodox world. Through mutual aid and group solidarity these people were able to gain self-respect and a sense of worth from their affiliation with sectarian organizations. The charismatic and talented among them might even achieve positions of power and influence within the sect. This was particularly true of women, who were otherwise totally barred from meaningful contacts outside of their families. Ethically relativistic because of their orientation toward the future millennium, members of these movements often invited the wrath and oppression of the authorities. They interpreted times of economic distress, social turmoil, and natural disasters as signals of the advent of the third age, an age when they would emerge triumphant in their combat against exploitation and injustice, as well as against death itself. They therefore became agitated and expectant, if not openly rebellious, and always potentially subversive. Their antinomian values and behavior posed a direct challenge to the orthodox tradition, while their millennial yearning to build a better world often implied their rejection of the present one. In a certain sense, twentieth-century Chinese revolutionaries, including the Communists, have operated much in the same mode as the earlier millenarian sectarians in their attempt to change the world.

[*See also* Taoism, *article on* Taoist Religious Community; T'ai-p'ing; *and the biography of Lao-tzu.*]

BIBLIOGRAPHY

Bauer, Wolfgang. *China und die Hoffnung auf Glück.* Munich, 1971. Translated by Michael Shaw as *China and the Search for Happiness: Recurring Themes in Four Thousand Years of Chinese Cultural History.* New York, 1976. A delightful work that details the history of utopian thought in China. Full of insights and lengthy quotes.

Groot, J. J. M. de. *Sectarianism and Religious Persecution in China* (1903–1904). Reprint in 2 volumes, Taipei, 1963. First published around the turn of the twentieth century, this work examines the beliefs and rituals of the Chinese sects through official records and decrees.

Naquin, Susan. *Millenarian Rebellion in China: The Eight Trigrams Uprising of 1813.* New Haven, 1976. An interesting work that traces the unfolding of a millenarian rebellion through the analysis of the confessions of the rebels.

Naquin, Susan. *Shantung Rebellion: The Wang Lun Uprising of 1774.* New Haven, 1981. Another work by Naquin using the same valuable rebel confessions for another rebellion.

Overmyer, Daniel L. *Folk Buddhist Religion: Dissenting Sects in Late Traditional China.* Cambridge, Mass., 1976. A trail-blazing work on Chinese sectarianism, particularly the White Lotus movement. It contains insightful comparisons with European religious movements.

Seidel, Anna. "The Image of the Perfect Ruler in Early Taoist Messianism: Lao-tzu and Li Hung." *History of Religions* 9 (November 1969–February 1970): 216–247. A celebrated work on Taoist messianism in the early medieval period. The Li Hung cult is analyzed.

Shek, Richard Hon-chun. "Religion and Society in Late Ming: Sectarianism and Popular Thought in Sixteenth and Seventeenth Century China." Ph.D. diss., University of California, Berkeley, 1980. This work explores the social and intellectual setting, as well as the history of the development, of White Lotus millenarianism in Ming-Ch'ing China.

Zürcher, Erik. " 'Prince Moonlight': Messianism and Eschatology in Early Medieval Chinese Buddhism." *T'oung pao* 68 (1982): 1–75. A seminal work on Buddhist millenarianism in the fourth and fifth centuries. Contains full translation of the pertinent Buddhist text.

RICHARD SHEK

MĪMĀṂSĀ.

MĪMĀṂSĀ. The word *mīmāṃsā* means "investigation" in ordinary Sanskrit. Since the term is applied to an important South Asian philosophical school, it must originally have meant "the investigation of the proper interpretation of the Vedic texts." The Mīmāṃsā school is thus better known as the Pūrva-mīmāṃsā school, which is sometimes called the Dharma-mīmāṃsā (inquiry into the nature of *dharma* as laid down by the Vedas, the supreme authority). Uttara-mīmāṃsā is the descriptive name for the Vedānta school, which deals with the nature of *brahman* as laid down in the latter part *(uttara)* of the Vedas, and in the Upaniṣads, hence also called Brahma-mīmāṃsā (inquiry into the nature of *brahman*). The word *dharma* is of prime importance in this context. It stands here for one's "duty" *(codanā)* enjoined by the Vedas, which includes both the religious or sacred duties or actions and the moral duties as well. *Dharma* also denotes the "virtue" attainable by performing such duties or following such courses of actions. Thus *dharma* is the main topic for discussion in the Mīmāṃsā school.

The Vedic scriptures were seriously attacked by the Śramaṇas (mendicant Brahmanic philosophers) about 500 BCE, and as a result its authority was apparently being devastated by criticisms. Hence the Mīmāṃsā school originated among the Vedic priests who wanted to reestablish this authority by resolving the apparent contradictions and other textual problems found in the Vedic scriptures. The Mīmāṃsā school in this way developed the science of exegesis. A *Mīmāṃsā Sūtra* was compiled as early as the first century BCE and it was ascribed to an ancient sage, Jaimini. It is regarded as the key text of the school.

Regarding *dharma,* Mīmāṃsā maintains a form of fundamentalism. It claims that the scriptures are the only means of knowing what is *dharma* and what is not. Only by following the injunctions of the scriptures can we attain *dharma,* or the "good," that cannot be attained by any other means. Other means of knowledge (perception, inference, reasoning, etc.) are of no help in the realm of *dharma,* for concerns of *dharma* are with transcendental matters, the imperceptibles and the unverifiables, such as the afterlife, heaven, and the moral order. Hence the Mīmāṃsā school defines the essence of the Vedas *(vedatā)* as that which informs us about such a transcendental realm. And the authority of the Vedas in such matters is self-evident. The truth of the scriptural statements is self-validating. The Vedas are to be regarded as eternal and uncreated. The scriptures are *revealed* texts, there being no author of them. In short, the truths of the Vedas are transempirical, hence no empirical evidence can conceivably bear on them.

The problem of interpretation has led the Mīmāṃsā school to the study and discussion of topics which are of great philosophical interest. The Mīmāṃsā developed itself into a kind of philosophical discipline, incorporating into it a theory of knowledge, epistemology, logic, a theory of meaning and language, and a realistic metaphysic. With its emphasis on the philosophy of language and linguistics, the Mīmāṃsā has sometimes been called the *vākya-śāstra* ("theory of speech"). It also formulated various rules of interpretation in order to resolve and eliminate the apparent inconsistencies of the scriptural texts.

Later on, the Mīmāṃsā school was divided into two subschools (c. 600–700 CE), following the two important exponents of the school, Kumārila Bhaṭṭa and Prabhākara. They are called the Bhāṭṭa school and the Prābhākara school. Of the many minor differences between the two subschools, only a few of the more notable ones have been noted here.

Kumārila speaks of six *pramāṇas* ("legitimate ways of knowing")—perception *(pratyakṣa),* inference *(anumāna),* verbal testimony *(śabda* or *aptāvacana),* comparison *(upamāna),* presumption *(arthāpatti),* and nonapprehension *(anupalabdhi).* Prabhākara accepts the first five only. Since he rejects "absence" *(abhāva)* as a separate reality, as a "knowable" entity *(prameya),* he does not need "nonapprehension" to establish such entities. For the Bhāṭṭas, a cognition is not a perceptible property, but it is inferred from the "cognizedness" *(jñātatā)* of the object cognized: since this pot is cognized by me, a cognition of it must have occurred in me. For the Prābhākaras, a cognition is self-cognized—it perceives itself. But both regard knowledge to be self-validating. Kumārila admits both Vedic and non-Vedic *śabda* (sentences, speech) to be *pramāṇa.* Prabhākara holds that real *śabda-pramāṇa* is the Vedic *śabda.* Both try to establish the Vedic authority not on God but on such transcendental reality as *dharma* and *mokṣa.* The Bhāṭṭas explicitly hold the *jñāna-karma-samuccaya-vāda,* that both knowledge and action lead to liberation. The Prābhākara view does not seem to be very different.

The two subschools differ in their views about the correct incentive for man's action (which includes both moral and religious acts). The Prābhākaras say that it is only the sense of duty while the Bhāṭṭas argue that both sense of duty and the desire for benefit constitute the correct incentive for action. On another rather technical matter, the two disagree. The Bhāṭṭas believe that the sentences get their meanings from their atomistic constituents, the individual word-meanings, while the Prābhākaras believe that the words directly constitute the sentence-meaning as a whole only insofar as they are syntactically connected *(anvita)* with other words in the sentence.

[*See also* Vedānta.]

BIBLIOGRAPHY

Jha, Ganganath. *Prābhākara School of Pūrva-mīmāṃsā.* Allahabad, 1911.

Rāmānujācārya. *Tantra-rahasya* (1923). 2d ed. Edited by Rudrapatha Shamasastry and K. S. Ramaswami Sastri. Gaekwad's Oriental Series, no. 24. Baroda, 1956. Contains an introduction by the editors.

Shastri, Pashupatinath. *Introduction to Pūrva Mīmāṃsā* (1923). 2d ed. Edited and revised by Gaurinath Sastri. Varanasi, 1980.

BIMAL KRISHNA MATILAL

MIND. *See* Artificial Intelligence; Epistemology; Consciousness, States of; *and* Neuroepistemology.

MINERVA, a Roman goddess, was the protector of intellectual and manual skills. The oldest form of her name, *Menerva,* may derive from the Indo-European root **men-*, which is expressive of mental processes. Various Etruscan transcriptions of the name, though earlier attested than any Italic form, probably should be regarded as borrowed from the Latin.

Minerva appears neither in the so-called Numan calendar, which registers the oldest public festivals in Rome, nor in connection with a priesthood. Her first occurrence is with Jupiter and Juno as a member of the divine triad that was worshiped on the Capitoline Hill in Etruscan-ruled Rome at the end of the sixth century BCE. Archaeological findings in Santa Marinella and Veii-Portonaccio bear witness to a contemporaneous cult of Minerva in southern Etruria.

Images of the goddess show many features of the Greek Athena: helmet, shield, spear, and aegis stamped with the likeness of a Gorgon. Recent discoveries in Pratica di Mare (the ancient Lavinium) show that the influence of Greek art did not exert itself exclusively through the Etruscan medium. The mythological episodes that were selected in Italy represent the goddess as a patroness of warlike heroes and gods (especially Herakles and Mars) and as a palladium (a token of invincibility).

Minerva was worshiped throughout Italy and on several Roman hills: with Jupiter and Juno on the Capitoline and the Quirinal and alone on the Aventine. There were also sanctuaries of the "captive Minerva" (brought from Falerii in 241 BCE) on the Caelius and of Minerva as patroness of physicians on the Esquiline. The emperor Domitian (81–96 CE), a prominent votary of the goddess, increased the number of her cult places.

Minerva was the special patroness of craftsmen, and at least from the time of Augustus (27 BCE–14 CE) craftsmen attended the festival of the Quinquatrus (19–23 March). The festival was publicly solemnized by gladiatorial exhibitions and included a *tubilustrium* (a ritual purification of war trumpets), further evidence of a link with Mars and war. Flute players celebrated a festival of their own ("little Quinquatrus") on 13 June.

The cult of Minerva, supported by the municipal institution of capitols (imitations of the Roman temple of the Capitoline triad) and the devotion of craftsmen and soldiers, diffused widely throughout the Roman empire until the beginning of the Christian era.

BIBLIOGRAPHY

Articles in three classical encyclopedias provide detailed and cautiously interpretative views of the subject: Franz Altheim's "Minerva," in *Real-Encyclopädie der klassischen Altertumswissenschaft* (Stuttgart, 1932); Filippo Coarelli's "Minerva," in *Enciclopedia dell'arte antica* (Rome, 1963); and Konrat Ziegler's "Minerva," in *Der kleine Pauly: Lexicon der Antike* (Stuttgart, 1969). The most recent discoveries are commented on by Ambros J. Pfiffig in *Ein Opfergelübde an die etruskische Minerva* (Vienna, 1968), for Santa Marinella, and by F. Castagnoli in *Il culto di Minerva a Lavinium,* "Problemi attuali di scienza e di cultura," no. 246 (Rome, 1979), for Pratica di Mare.

JEAN-LOUIS GIRARD

MINISTRY. The term *ministry* traditionally refers to offices of leadership in the Christian church, but there has been a growing recognition that it also describes the way the mission of the whole church is conducted. Both in terms of specific offices (ministers) and in terms of the work of the church in general, ministry has biblical roots. In Hebrew, *sheret* ("to serve") applies to temple officers and was normally translated *leitourgein* in the Septuagint. This use was carried over into the New Testament, where the various linguistic forms of *leitourgein* are used not only for general acts of service to others (*Rom.* 15:27, *2 Cor.* 9:12, *Phil.* 2:30) but also for worship (*Acts* 13:3) and particularly for priestly and Levitical functions under the Old Covenant (*Lk.* 1:23; *Heb.* 8:2, 8:6, 9:21, 10:11). But the New Testament introduced the words *diakonia* ("service") and *diakonein* ("to serve"), referring to the menial work done by a *diakonos* ("servant") or *doulos* ("slave") to indicate the quality of ministry in the church. These words represent not status but the serving relationship of the minister to the one served: following the example of Christ (and, subsequently, the example of the apostle Paul) is at the heart of the Christian understanding of ministry (*Jn.* 13:1–20; *1 Cor.* 4:16, 11:1; *Phil.* 3:17).

Scholars dispute how far the New Testament reflects a uniform and obligatory pattern of ministerial orders. Roman Catholic scholars generally hold that it does, but most Protestant scholars believe that the New Testament offers several patterns of ministry (*Eph.* 4:11–12; *1 Cor.* 12:27–31; *1 Tm.* 3:1–13, 4:11–16, 5:3–10, 5:17–22). The former view maintains that the orders of ministry are fixed by tradition and that their authority is transmitted by historical succession from the apostles through bishops or the pope as the vicar of Christ (apostolic succession). The latter view regards ministerial orders as essentially functional and focused on faithful transmission of the apostolic testimony.

There is, however, agreement that all ministry traces its authority to Jesus Christ and to the apostles who testified to his saving work and resurrection (*Mt.* 16:13–24, 18:18, 28:18–20; *Jn.* 20:23). Although the apostle Paul could not claim personal connection with the Galilean ministry, he did claim commission from Jesus Christ as the heart of his own call to apostleship (*Gal.* 1:1, 1:11–24, 2:1–21). Churches also generally agree that officers in the church's ministry (i.e., the clergy) have particular responsibility for preaching, for administration of the sacraments (or ordinances), and for the oversight and nurture of their congregations. [*See* Apostles; Discipleship; *and* Church.]

By the beginning of the second century, three principal orders of ministry—bishop or pastor (*episcopos*, "overseer"), presbyter or priest (*presbuteros*, "elder"), and deacon (*diakonos*, "servant")—had become widely accepted, and although various confessional groups may not agree how far or when these orders became dependent on the Roman pontiff, the primacy of the pope seems to have been widely acknowledged by the time of Leo I (d. 461) and continued in the West until the Reformation. In the Eastern church the break with Rome, the Great Schism, is often given the date 1054, but scholars recognize that this was the end of a process of estrangement over centuries. However, the threefold ministry remained unchanged in both halves of Christendom through a millennium of Christian history. [*See* Priesthood, *article on* Christian Priesthood, *and* Papacy.]

Catholic branches of the church claim unbroken succession with this earlier history and believe that these offices are prescribed (i.e., *iure divino*) and guaranteed by apostolic succession. Ordination is a sacrament whereby the Holy Spirit is transmitted through the bishop's imposition of hands, which imparts special grace to administer the sacraments and to exercise authority in the church. In the Roman Catholic church these powers derive ultimately from the pope, while among the Orthodox it is exercised by the bishop within the corporate authority of the Orthodox community. Old Catholics and Anglo-Catholics hold a position on apostolic succession close to that of Rome but do not acknowledge the infallible authority of the papacy.

The sixteenth-century Reformation challenged the absolute authority of ecclesiastical tradition and its priesthood. Protestants turned from papal authority to the authority of the Bible, which led to revisions in their understanding of the church and its ministry. In the main, they claimed to restore the New Testament pattern, and in reaction to ecclesiastical legalism they tended to appeal to the Bible as a divine law book. New Testament "restorationism" appears in the early Luther, based on a primary appeal to scripture and on scripture exegeted by "the priesthood of all believers." Luther may be described as advocating a form of "evangelical pragmatism," since he accepted any pattern consistent with scripture that served the effective preaching of the word and the proper administration of the sacraments. Lutheranism has therefore adopted episcopal, consistorial, and congregational forms of churchmanship. [*See* Reformation.]

Attempts to restore a more biblical pattern of church and ministry are to be found in almost every form of Reformation church, and not least the Reformed church. Differences between Ulrich Zwingli (1484–1531) and the Anabaptists (Swiss Brethren) were not over the primacy of scripture but over its interpretation. John Calvin (1509–1564) systematized the Reformed position, claiming that church and ministry are of divine institution (*Institutes* 4.1, 4.3). Like many in his day, he regarded apostles, prophets, and evangelists as peculiar to the apostolic age, although he recognized that they might be revived "as the need of the times demands." Pastors and teachers, he argued, were indispensable. Pastors exercised general oversight discipline and preached and administered the sacraments; teachers were responsible for doctrine. Calvin also recognized the New Testament office of deacon in care of the poor (within which he included the office of the "widow"). He insisted on both the inward call of a minister and the recognition by the church of that call. In matters of discipline the pastor was to share power with a consistory of elders so that power would not be exclusively in the hands of a single person.

Calvin's fourfold ordering of ministry was taken over by the Reformed church and the Puritans in the British Isles and colonial America in the Presbyterian and Congregational churches. Similar forms of ministry arose out of English Separatism (e.g., Baptist churches) and the Christian Church (Disciples of Christ) movement of the American frontier. Differences between the classic Reformation positions and later restoration movements turned not so much on the appeal to the Bible as on other matters affecting scriptural interpretation: the relationship of the church to civil authorities, insistence on the church's purity, ministerial training, and how far literal appeal to scripture may be modified by the Holy Spirit revealed in scripture. Extreme restorationists reject any deviation from the New Testament pattern; at the other extreme, the Society of Friends (Quakers) claims that the spirit of the scriptures requires no specially ordained ministers.

A different modification of the church's ministry is seen in the Anglican settlement. In the sixteenth century, Henry VIII sought to separate from Rome without changing the shape of the national church, and his daughter, Elizabeth I, followed his lead. She wooed English Catholics by maintaining traditional vestments, liturgy, and forms of church government (episcopal). From the first the Church of England tried to reconcile appeal to scripture and to church tradition. Originally the settlement was based on the authority of the crown (the divine right of kings), but at the turn of the seventeenth century appeals to the divine right of the episcopacy began to appear. Differences concerning the role of the episcopacy are reflected in the so-called high church (Anglo-Catholic), broad church (Latitudinarian), and low church (Evangelical) traditions within Anglicanism. [*See* Anglicanism.]

In the eighteenth century, John Wesley, founder of Methodism, refused to separate from the Church of England. He finally became convinced that priests and bishops were of the same order in the New Testament and that he had the right to ordain ministers for America, but he refused to designate bishops and instead appointed superintendents. The decision to employ the term *bishop* in American Methodism probably arose from the determination to assert independence from Anglicanism. But although Wesley believed that the threefold order of ministry is scriptural, he offered an essentially pragmatic interpretation of these offices. His position was fundamentally the evangelical pragmatism seen in Luther. [*See* Methodist Churches.]

By the mid-1980s there was no acceptance of the ordination of women in the Roman Catholic and Orthodox branches of the church, but a growing acceptance of women into the ordained ministry of Protestant denominations and in some provinces of Anglicanism was evident. Protestant and Anglican practices stem from the theological belief that the call to ministry is open to all God's people. The ecumenical movement has also prompted many churches to reexamine earlier claims and to recognize that they have much to learn from each other. Statements on ministry prepared for the Consultation on Church Union (1984), which reflected the views of ten American Protestant denominations, and by the World Council of Churches (1982) indicate a significant and growing consensus. This consensus reveals an emphasis on the servanthood of ministry as evidenced in the ministry of Jesus; an awareness that the whole church is the proper context in which the ordained ministry should be considered; an awareness that the doctrines of church and ministry cannot be separated; and a recognition that the traditional threefold ordering of ministry should not be lightly discarded. This growing consensus shows that many Christian churches seek to manifest their essential unity and to arrive at a point where their ministries may be mutually recognized.

[*See also* Ecumenical Movement. *For broad discussions of issues related to Christian ministry, see* Ordination *and* Leadership.]

BIBLIOGRAPHY

The tendency today is to consider the doctrines of church and ministry holistically, and in any reading list on ministry, books about the doctrine of the church should find a place. Among the older books considering ministry, *The Apostolic Ministry*, edited by Kenneth E. Kirk (London, 1946), and T. W. Manson's *The Church's Ministry* (Philadelphia, 1948) must be mentioned because they illustrate a classic debate on apostolic succession in relation to episcopacy. For a general account of where the churches stand on the issues, *The Nature of the Unity We Seek*, edited by Paul Minear (Saint Louis, 1958), may be consulted, and also the relevant documents in *The Documents of Vatican II*, edited by Walter M. Abbott (New York, 1966), for the Roman Catholic position.

One of the most thorough historical studies to be conducted in the United States is *The Ministry in Historical Perspectives*, edited by H. Richard Niebuhr and Daniel D. Williams (New York, 1956), and H. Richard Niebuhr's theological interpretation of that evidence, *The Purpose of the Church and Its Ministry* (New York, 1956), underscores the recognition that church and ministry cannot be separated. *The Pioneer Ministry*, by Anthony Tyrrell Hanson (London, 1961), an important biblical study of ministerial leadership in the Pauline churches, responds to assumptions made earlier in Kirk's book, while my own book *Ministry* (Grand Rapids, Mich., 1965) places this Anglo-Saxon debate within its ecumenical context. Ronald E. Osborn's *In Christ's Place: Christian Ministry in Today's World* (Saint Louis, 1967) arrives at similar conclusions on the basis of New Testament evidence.

The most important recent documents on ministry are those coming out of bilateral conversations, such as *The Ministry in the Church* (Geneva, 1982), published by the Roman Catholic/Lutheran Joint Commission; the documents produced by the Consultation on Church Union, such as the *Digest of the Plenary Meetings* (Princeton, 1979–) and *The COCU Consensus: In Quest of a Church of Christ Uniting* (Princeton, 1985); and the documents published by the World Council of Churches, particularly the "Lima Document," in *Baptism, Eucharist and Ministry*, "Faith and Order Paper no. 111" (Geneva, 1982).

ROBERT S. PAUL

MINOAN RELIGION. *See* Aegean Religions.

MĪRĀ BĀĪ (c. 1498–1546), India's most famous medieval woman saint. A devotee of the Kṛṣṇa incarnation of the god Viṣṇu and a poet of great power, she was one of the major poet-saints of North India who contributed to the *bhakti* (devotional) revival of Hinduism. Her *pa-*

das (devotional songs) are especially popular in the areas where Hindi, Rajasthani, and Gujarati are spoken, but they are sung throughout the country. The story of her life and the legends that have grown around her are also known throughout India.

A Rajput princess from the principality of Merta in central Rajasthan, Mīrā lost her mother at a young age and was brought up by her grandfather, who was a devout worshiper of Viṣṇu and encouraged her religious leanings. He also gave her a classical education, including a rigorous training in music that is evident in her songs. In 1516, in order to cement a political alliance, she was married to Prince Bhoj Rāj, the heir apparent of Rāṇā Sāngā, the king of Mewar. According to legend, Mīrā, who considered herself the spiritual bride of Kṛṣṇa, insisted on keeping her idol of Kṛṣṇa with her during the wedding ceremony, and further alienated her in-laws by refusing to perform the rites of the family goddess Durgā-Kālī.

Shortly after the marriage, Bhoj Rāj died, but Mīrā rebelled against custom again by refusing to immolate herself on her husband's funeral pyre. Instead, absorbing herself totally in her devotion to Kṛṣṇa, she began to spend all her time at the temple in town, singing and dancing before the image of Kṛṣṇa, mingling with the male devotees, and receiving religious mendicants. Her family was dismayed at this behavior. When Rāṇā Sāngā died in 1528, the new king, Mīrā's brother-in-law, tried to restrain her; according to legend, there were even attempts to poison her. Tired of the harassment, Mīrā fled Mewar and became a wandering ascetic. Eventually she settled down in the holy city of Dwarka and lived the rest of her life there as a devotee attached to the local Ranachor temple. The popular legend about her death is that when she was at prayer in the temple one day, her body physically melted to merge with the idol of Kṛṣṇa.

It is difficult to determine how many *padas* Mīrā Bāī composed. Dozens of modern printed editions are in existence, ranging in length from less than fifty to several hundred songs. Some are based on older manuscripts, but the majority have been collected from oral tradition. In addition to the printed editions, there are many orally current songs that have not yet been recorded. Furthermore, because of the widespread dissemination of Mīrā's songs, many different versions of each one exist. Which of the songs attributed to Mīrā are authentic and which are later compositions is a scholarly problem that has not yet been satisfactorily solved, but is of no particular concern to the living religious culture.

Unlike other medieval poet-saints, Mīrā Bāī did not sing about a wide range of subject matter. Her central theme is her love for Kṛṣṇa, all the different facets of which are expressed in an intensely emotional first-person voice. The songs in which she gives voice to the agony of separation from her divine Lord are the most poignant and the most beloved. The special appeal of all her songs lies in their lyricism, their rich imagery and, most of all, their quality of spontaneity and total sincerity.

Mīrā Bāī's position in the devotional tradition of Hinduism is a special one. Above and beyond her popular songs, she stands as a model of saintly personality, the embodiment of selfless love and total dedication, her flouting of social conventions in the name of the superior imperatives of the life of devotion all the more powerful because she was a woman and a Rajput princess. But she is also special in that her particular way of devotion defies classification under one or the other of the two divergent schools of North Indian *bhakti:* the *saguṇa* school, which worships the divine incarnations, engages in temple worship, and is based on philosophic dualism, and the *nirguṇa* school, which conceives of the divine as beyond all form, rejects temple worship, and is based on philosophic monism. In Mīrā's devotional practice as well as in her songs, no sharp line of demarcation is drawn between the two orientations: Kṛṣṇa is both the concrete mythological incarnation and the abstract God above all form, and her relationship to him is both a personal one and one of total absorption and identity. It is in this broad transcendence of philosophic categories as well as in the power of her devotional songs that Mīrā Bāī's universal popular appeal lies.

[*For further discussion of* bhakti *in North Indian religious movements, see* Bhakti; Hindi Religious Traditions; *and* Vaiṣṇavism, *article on Bhāgavatas. Hindi devotional poetry is further discussed in* Poetry, *article on* Indian Religious Poetry.]

BIBLIOGRAPHY

The most succinct sketch of Mīrā Bāī and her place in the *bhakti* revival of Hinduism is S. M. Pandey's "Mīrābāī and Her Contributions to the Bhakti Movement," *History of Religions* 5 (Summer 1965): 54–73. Usha S. Nilsson's *Mira Bai* (New Delhi, 1969) contains a discussion of Mīrā's poetry and translations of some of her best known poems. For a critical study of Mīrā's life based on analysis of historical sources, see Hermann Goetz's *Mira Bai: Her Life and Times* (Bombay, 1966). A. J. Alston's *The Devotional Poems of Mīrābāī* (Delhi and Mystic, Conn., 1980) is a complete translation, with introduction and notes, of the most scholarly edition of Mīrā's songs, Paraśurām Chaturvedī's *Mīrāṁbāī kī padāvalī,* 15th ed. (Allahabad, 1973).

KARINE SCHOMER

MIRACLES. [*This entry includes two articles. The first,* An Overview, *surveys the religious function and meaning* *of miracles in a variety of religious traditions. The companion article,* Modern Perspectives, *concerns the problem of belief in miracles in a modern, secular worldview.*]

An Overview

The history of religions has preserved the record of miracles, that is, events, actions, and states taken to be so unusual, extraordinary, and supernatural that the normal level of human consciousness finds them hard to accept rationally. These miracles are usually taken as manifestations of the supernatural power of the divine being fulfilling his purpose in history, but they are also caused to occur "naturally" by charismatic figures who have succeeded in controlling their consciousness through visions, dreams, or the practices of meditation. Although miracles have assumed diverse forms, healing miracles and exorcisms have often attracted most attention.

However diverse the forms may be, miracles are preeminently sociological phenomena. It is, of course, true that no miracles exist without miracle workers who often claim religious authority of one kind or another based on their performance of miracles; but as the etymological meaning of the word *miracle* (Lat., *miraculum*) may suggest, one of the conditions indispensable for the creation of miracles is the presence of those people, spectators, who take the performance of miracle workers to be wonderful, extraordinary, and worthy of admiration. These people are often the followers of miracle workers, witnesses of miracles, or professional priests or laymen of the cults at whose shrines, temples, or caves miracles have occurred, and it is they who are often responsible for the creation and propagation of miracle stories in which the saving power of the divine beings and the extraordinary personality of miracle workers are extolled.

Miracles in the "Primitive" Tradition. In primitive societies religious specialists, such as magicians, medicine men, sorcerers, and shamans, are known for their performance of miracles as well as for their exercise of magico-religious powers. They have acquired such miracle-working powers through the practices of meditation, vision quest, or a series of initiatory sicknesses and dreams.

In some parts of Asia, Australia, and North America, it is believed that illness is caused by the intrusion of a magical object into the patient's body, or through his possession by evil spirits. Healing is effected by magicians, sorcerers, or medicine men through the extraction of the harmful object or the expulsion of demons. Among the Aranda in central Australia, for example, a man is initiated into the profession of medicine man through a series of hardships and rituals: one of the older medicine men pierces the index finger of the novice with a pointed magical wand. By this operation the novice acquires the ability to drive out the objects causing illness in his future patients. The old medicine man also seizes the tongue of the novice and cuts a hole in it with a sharp stone knife. This is done to enable him to suck out the evil magical forces to be found in the bodies of his patients.

The vision quest among the Indians of North America is a means of acquiring supernatural power through personal contact with the divine. In California, the vision is sought by shamans wishing to effect a cure. The shaman occupies a unique place among religious specialists due to his ability, in a trance state, to make the ecstatic journey to the beyond. He is engaged in the spiritual journey most often when he has to cure the sick; when he finds that the illness of a sick person has been caused by the loss of his soul, the shaman searches for the lost soul in heaven, in distant space, and most frequently in the underworld.

The shaman acquires the power of healing as well as other magico-religious powers through his unique psychic experience. In Siberia, as a rule, the future shaman is sick for an indefinite period of time; he stays in his tent or wanders in the wilderness, behaving in such eccentric ways that he could be mistaken for a madman: he becomes suddenly frenzied, loses consciousness, feeds on tree bark, or flings himself into water and fire. These pathological symptoms can properly be interpreted in terms of initiatory trials, which the future shaman is destined to undergo in order to be miraculously transformed into a "new being."

Significantly, in the state of sickness, dreams, and visions, the future shaman has the experience of being dismembered, reduced to bones, and then given entirely new internal organs. For example, a Tunguz shaman (Ivan Cholko) states that before a man becomes shaman he is sick for a long time, his head being in a state of confusion. The spirits of the dead shaman-ancestors come, cut his flesh in pieces, and drink his blood. They also cut off his head and throw it into a caldron. According to a Buriat shaman (Mikhail Stepanov), before a man becomes shaman he is sick for a long time. Then the spirits of dead shamans come and teach him; he becomes absentminded, speaking with the dead shamans as if he were with living persons. He alone is able to "see" the spirits. They torture him, strike him, and cut his flesh in pieces with knives. During this surgical operation the future shaman becomes half dead; the beating of his heart is scarcely heard, his breathing is weak, and his face and hands are dark blue. A Yakut shaman (Petr Ivanov) gives further details concerning the initiatory ordeal of dismemberment, followed by the renewal of the body: his limbs are removed and disjointed with an iron hook by the spirits of ancestral shamans; the bones are cleaned, the flesh scraped, the body fluids thrown away, and the eyes torn out of their sockets. After this operation all the bones are gathered up, joined together with iron, and new eyes are put in place. He is thus transformed into a new being, a shaman.

The experiences described above by no means exhaust the shaman's transforming initiatory trials. The Inuit (Eskimo) shaman, for example, acquires the *qaumaneq* (mystical light). "The first time a young shaman experiences this light," Knud Rasmussen states, "it is as if the house in which he is suddenly rises; he sees far ahead of him, through mountains, exactly as if the earth were one great plain, and his eyes could reach to the end of the earth" (*Intellectual Culture of the Igtulik Eskimos,* Copenhagen, 1930, p. 113). According to Franz Boas: "When a person becomes shaman, a light covers his body. He can see supernatural things. The stronger the light is within him, the deeper and further away he can see, and the greater is his supernatural power. The light makes his whole body feel well. When the intensity of this light increases, he feels a strong pressure, and it seems to him as though a film were being removed from his eyes which prevented him from seeing clearly. The light is always present with him. It guides him, and enables him to see into the future and back into the past" (*The Eskimo of Baffin Land and Hudson Bay,* New York, 1901, p. 133).

Shamans must demonstrate to spectators the new, superhuman condition that they have acquired: they gash themselves with knives, touch red-hot iron, and swallow burning coals. Shamans are masters over fire. They also incarnate the spirit of fire to the point where, during séances, they emit flames from their mouths, noses, and whole bodies. The practice of fire walking is imposed on shamans and medicine men in, for instance, Australia, Indonesia, China, and among the Manchu. Sometimes a shaman must prove his miraculous powers by resisting the most severe cold or by drying a wet sheet on his naked body. Among the Manchu, for example, nine holes are made in the ice during winter; the candidate has to dive into the first hole, come out through the second, and so on to the ninth hole. A young Labrador Inuit obtained the title of *angakkoq* (shaman) after remaining five days and nights in the icy sea and proving that he was not even wet. A shaman sometimes shows his miraculous powers to the public by climbing a ladder of knives. Among the Lolo in southern China, a double ladder made of thirty-six knives is built, and the barefoot shaman climbs it to the top, then comes down on the other side. Similar feats are also attested in other parts of China and among the Chingpaw of Upper Burma. [*See* Shamanism.]

Miracles in the Mediterranean World. In archaic Greece, Abaris, Aristeas, and Epimenides were known for their wonders and miracles. Abaris was a shamanic figure; carrying the golden arrow in his hand, he passed through many lands, dispelling sickness and pestilence, and giving warning of earthquakes and other disasters. He was also known to fly through the air on his arrow, a symbol of magic flight. Aristeas of Proconnesus could appear at the same time in two places far apart, sometimes assuming the form of a crow. Epimenides was a master of the techniques of ecstasy, well known for his miraculous powers; he journeyed through many lands, bringing his health-giving arts with him, prophesying the future, interpreting the hidden meaning of past occurrences, and expelling the demonic evils that arose from misdeeds of the past.

Especially noteworthy is Pythagoras, whose image in the Hellenistic Mediterranean world was quite complex in nature. According to his biographies by Porphyry and Iamblichus dating from the third and fourth centuries CE, Pythagoras was a "divine man" *(theios anēr),* combining the figure of the popular miracle worker, the portrait of the philosopher, and the idealized image of the practical statesman. His image as miracle worker was enhanced by several recurring motifs: (1) Pythagoras was seen in two cities at the same time; (2) he could recall his previous existences; (3) he was endowed with the ability to stop an eagle in flight; and (4) he could predict events in the future. It is highly probable that, as Neo-Pythagoreanism gained popularity among ordinary people, the image of Pythagoras the thaumaturge was promoted by a circle of followers quite distinct from those who wished to cultivate his reputation as a philosopher and scientist.

Apollonius of Tyana, a wandering Pythagorean philosopher of the first century CE, also worked miracles. It is generally accepted that early traditions about his activity as a miracle worker were incorporated into subsequent accounts of his life, which were apologetically intended to present him as a philosopher. Apollonius described exorcisms and instances of healing the blind, the lame, and the paralytic in India (see Philostratus, *The Life of Apollonius of Tyana* 3.38–39); more important than that, he performed similar miracles himself. Apollonius reportedly performed even the miracle of raising the dead while he was in Rome (4.45): a girl had died just before her marriage, and the bridegroom was following her bier lamenting; the whole of Rome lamented with him, for she belonged to a consular family. Apollonius, meeting the funeral procession, said, "Put down the bier, for I will put a stop to your tears for the girl." Then he asked her name. The crowd thought he was going to deliver a funeral oration, but he merely touched her and said something in secret over her, and thus he awoke her from her seeming death. In the magical papyri, his name is attached to a spell, a fact indicating his considerable popularity as a magician. According to Dio Cassius, the Roman emperor Caracalla (r. 211–217) built a temple in honor of Apollonius, who was a "perfect example of the magician."

The figure of Moses was one of the most important propaganda instruments that Jews of the Hellenistic period used in their competition with non-Jewish schools and cults. In *Deuteronomy* 34:10–12, Moses is described as the greatest prophet in Israel, known for his signs and wonders as well as for his mighty powers and great and terrible deeds. This Moses was presented to the Hellenistic world as a miracle-working philosopher, as is exemplified in Philo Judaeus's *On the Life of Moses.*

There are many stories in late Judaism narrating how rabbis worked miracles of healing. The best known, perhaps, is the healing of the son of Yoḥanan ben Zakk'ai by Ḥanina' ben Dosa'. Both rabbis lived in Palestine around 70 CE. Ḥanina' ben Dosa' went to study the Torah with Yoḥanan ben Zakk'ai, whose son was seriously ill. Yoḥanan requested: "Ḥanina', my son, pray for mercy for him that he may live." Ḥanina' ben Dosa' laid his head between his knees and prayed, and then the boy was cured (B.T., *Ber.* 34).

Miracles of healing were performed also by kings, for example, the Roman emperor Vespasian (r. 70–79). While the emperor was in Alexandria, a blind man approached him, acting on the advice of the god Sarapis; he fell at Vespasian's feet, demanding with sobs a cure for his blindness and imploring the emperor to moisten his eyes with the spittle from his mouth. Another man with a maimed hand, also inspired by Sarapis, asked Vespasian to touch it with his heel. "To the great excitement of the bystanders," states Tacitus, Vespasian "did as the men desired him. Immediately the hand recovered its functions and daylight shone once more in the blind man's eyes" (*Histories* 4.81; see also Dio Cassius, *Roman History* 65.8, and Suetonius, *Vespasian* 7.2–3).

Throughout late antiquity, Epidaurus was a holy site especially celebrated for the epiphany of Asklepios, the divine healer. [*See* Asklepios.] According to Strabo, Asklepios was believed to "cure diseases of every kind." His temple was always full of the sick as well as containing the votive tablets on which treatments were recorded (*Geography* 8.6.15). Asklepios would appear to the sick sleeping in his temple—more precisely, in the innermost chamber *(to abaton)* of the sanctuary; he would approach the sick in dreams and visions, or, as Aelius Aristides put it, in a "state of mind intermediate between sleep and waking." [*See* Dreams.] This practice of temple sleep, incubation *(incubatio)*, was of vital importance to the sick; it was in the state of such dreams and visions that one was healed or given instructions by Asklepios. The healing god would touch his patient's body with his hands, apply drugs, or undertake surgical operations. Consequently, the eyesight of the blind would be restored, the lame would walk, the mute would speak, and the man whose fingers had been paralyzed would stretch each of them one by one. Some examples of Asklepios's miracles follow.

Ambrosia of Athens, blind in one eye, came to Epidaurus to seek help from Asklepios. But as she walked around the temple, she mocked at the many records of divine healings: "It is unbelievable and impossible that the lame and the blind can be cured by merely dreaming." In her sleep she had a dream: Asklepios approached and promised to heal her; only in return she must present a gift offering in the temple—a silver pig, in memory of her stupidity. After saying this, Asklepios cut open her defective eye and poured in a drug. Her sight was soon restored. The following miracle story about a man with an abscess inside his abdomen reminds us of the initiatory dreaming of Siberian shamans. While asleep in the temple, the man saw a dream: Asklepios ordered the servants who accompanied him to hold him tightly so that he could cut open his abdomen. The man tried to escape but could not. Then Asklepios cut his belly open, removed the abscess, and stitched him up. Sometimes, the healing power of Asklepios reached the patient far away from his temple. Arata, a woman of Lacedaemon, was dropsical. While she remained in Lacedaemon, her mother slept in the temple on her behalf and saw a dream: Asklepios cut off her daughter's head and hung up her body in such a way that her throat was turned downward. Out of it came a huge quantity of fluid matter. Then he took down the body and put the head back onto the neck. After the mother had seen this dream, she went home and found her daughter in good health; the daughter had seen the same dream.

The Mediterranean world knew Egypt as the home of thaumaturgy, theosophy, and esoteric wisdom. There, the goddess Isis was praised for her miraculous healings; she was credited with bringing the arts of healing to men and, once she had attained immortality, taking pleasure in miraculously healing those who incubated themselves in her temple (Diodorus Siculus, *The Library of History* 1.25.2–5). At her hands the maimed were healed and the blind received their eyesight. According to the inscriptions found on the island of Delos dating from about the first century BCE, Isis worship was attended by a functionary specifically called an *aretalogos,* an interpreter of dreams, who may have functioned as a proclaimer of miraculous events. The temple of the god Sarapis at Canopus, not far from Alexandria, was also famous for its divine healing; Sarapis would visit those who slept in his temple, giving them advice in dreams.

Yogins, Taoist Contemplatives, and Yamabushi. Indian ascetics practicing Yoga are well known for their miraculous powers. [*See* Yoga.] The yogin sits cross-legged and firm on a flat space with his eyes fixed on a certain object beyond him. He has to master, at the same time, the breathing techniques *(prāṇāyāma);* at first, the breath is kept for one minute and then exhaled. This practice goes on for days, weeks, and months until the period of retention of the inhaled breath is gradually increased.

According to the Indo-Tibetan Tantric tradition, the ascetic is able to produce "inner heat" on the basis of rhythmical breathing and various "visualizations." During a winter-night snowstorm, the degree of his progress is tested by his ability to dry a large number of soaked sheets draped directly over his naked body. "Sheets are dipped in the icy water," reports Alexandra David-Neel. "Each man wraps himself in one of them and must dry it on his body. As soon as the sheet has become dry, it is again dipped in the water and placed on the novice's body to be dried as before. The operation goes on until daybreak. Then he who has dried the largest number of sheets is acknowledged the winner of the competition" (*With Mystics and Magicians in Tibet,* London, 1931, pp. 227-228).

The yogin acquires the "miraculous powers" (*siddhi*s) when he has reached a particular stage of his meditational discipline called *saṃyama,* referring, more specifically, to the last stages of yogic technique, that is, concentration *(dhāraṇa),* meditation *(dhyāna),* and *samādhi.* [*See* Magico-Religious Powers.] For example, by practicing *saṃyama* in regard to the subconscious residues (*saṃskāra*s), the yogin knows his previous existences; through the practice of Yoga, he arrives successfully at the state of mind in which he is one with the things meditated, namely, his subconscious residues. This enables him to ideally relive his former existences. Through *saṃyama* exercised in respect to notions *(pratyaya),* the yogin also knows the mental states of other men; he sees, as on a screen, all the states of consciousness that notions are able to arouse in their minds. Some of the yogin's "miraculous powers" are even more extraordinary: he can make himself invisible by practicing *saṃyama* concerning the form of the body. "When the yogin practices *saṃyama* on the form of the body," Vācaspatimiśra comments, "he destroys the perceptibility of the color *(rūpa)* that is the cause of perception of the body" (Eliade, 1958, p. 87).

In India, the yogin has always been considered a *mahāsiddha,* a possessor of miraculous powers, a magician. However, a yogin is still far from attaining his final goal of absolute freedom so long as his miraculous powers serve him as his "possession." As soon as he consents to use the magical forces gained through his ascetic discipline, the possibility of his realizing absolute freedom diminishes; only a new renunciation, a determination not to use the miraculous powers, would lead the ascetic to a higher spiritual horizon.

Taoists in ancient China are convinced that man can become an "immortal" *(hsien-jen, shen-hsien,* or *sheng-jen),* that man is able to transcend his human condition by various means, including the practice of meditation. The *Chuang-tzu* tells of one such extraordinary man living on a remote mountain: "He does not eat the five grains, but sucks the wind, drinks the dew, climbs up on the clouds and mist, rides a flying dragon, and watches beyond the four seas" (chap. 1). Moreover, "by concentrating his spirit, he can protect creatures from sickness and plague and make the harvest plentiful" (ibid.). Abstention from cereals belongs to a basic requirement in Taoism for nourishing life, as is illustrated by Ko Hung's *Pao-p'u-tzu* dating from the early fourth century CE. "Sucking the wind" and "drinking the dew" are technical terms in Taoism for breathing exercises. It is certain that the story speaks about a Taoist contemplative on his ecstatic journey, transcending the universe. Especially interesting in the story is the fact that he is able to "concentrate his spirit," that is, to solidify his spiritual potency. The ability to solidify the spiritual potency or light belongs to the privilege of such religious specialists as shamans, yogins, and Taoist saints. According to Max Kaltenmark, the solidification of the spiritual potency points to an essential feature of the Taoist technique of meditation, which consists in freezing the faculties of the soul, concentrating them in a single point.

The practice of meditation essential for attaining immortality leads inevitably to the possession of miraculous powers. According to the *Pao-p'u-tzu,* the Taoist immortal Ko Hsüan, one of Ko Hung's paternal uncles, would stay at the bottom of a deep pond for almost a whole day in hot summer weather. This "miracle" was possible because of his mastery of "embryonic respiration": he was able to accumulate his breaths and to breathe like a fetus in its mother's womb. Ko Hsüan was a disciple of the famous Taoist immortal Tso Tz'u, of whom it is said that, despite abstinence from eating cereals for almost a whole month, his complexion remained unchanged and his vitality stayed normal (*Pao-p'u–tzu,* chap. 2).

Mountain ascetics in Japan known as *yamabushi* acquired magico-religious powers through a series of disciplines. The *yamabushi* was the master of heat and fire; he walked barefoot on red hot charcoals without injury; he proved his extraordinary power when, with only a white robe on his naked body, he entered a bath of boiling water and came out entirely unscathed; and he surprised his spectators by climbing a ladder of swords, the sharp edge facing upward. Like a shaman, he was a spiritual being. In his inner consciousness he was a bird in control of cosmic space; at the culminating moment of a ceremony, the *yamabushi* in a trance would spread his arms and fly in the sky in imitation of a bird. In view of the extraordinary powers at his disposal, it is not surprising that he cured the sick, exorcised demons, and fought triumphant battles against evil spirits.

Miracles in Founded Religions. The founders of three major religions of the world—Buddhism, Christianity, and Islam—have each taken a different attitude toward miracle; Jesus Christ was utterly positive in working miracles, whereas Muḥammad, as represented in the Qur'ān, categorically rejected them. Significantly, the Buddha took the middle course, so to speak. Despite this remarkable divergence among these founders, the subsequent history of these religions demonstrates unmistakably that miracles and miracle stories have been an integral part of man's religious life.

Buddhism. The Buddha was well aware that the practice of meditation essential for attaining enlightenment leads eventually to the possession of "miraculous power" (Skt., *siddhi;* Pali, *iddhi*). But he did not encourage his disciples to seek *siddhi*s. "O *bhikku*s," the Buddha said, "you must not show the superhuman power of *iddhi* before the laity. Whoever does so shall be guilty of an evil deed" (*Vinaya Texts,* trans. T. W. Rhys Davids and Hermann Oldenberg, vol. 3, Delhi, [1885] 1965, p. 81). The true task was not to acquire miraculous powers but to transcend the world of pain and suffering and to attain the state of enlightenment (see *Dīgha Nikāya* 24.3). Moreover, the possession of one miraculous power or another in no way promoted, in the Buddha's mind, the propagation of the central message of Buddhism; yogins, ecstatics, and other ascetics could perform the same miracles.

"Miraculous powers" are one of the five classes of "superknowledge" (Skt., *abhijñā;* Pali, *abhiññā*), which are (1) *siddhi,* (2) divine eye, (3) divine hearing, (4) knowledge of another's thought, and (5) recollection of previous existences. By virtue of deepening meditation, the Buddhist saint is able to acquire the *siddhi* in its various forms: he becomes invisible at his own will; he goes, without feeling any obstacle, to the far side of a wall or rampart or hill, as if through air; he penetrates up and down through solid ground, as if through water; he walks on water without breaking through, as if on solid ground; and he travels cross-legged in the sky, like the birds on the wing" (*Dīgha Nikāya* 2.87, 11.4).

According to biographical sources, the Buddha himself was sometimes led to work miracles; for example, when he returned to his native city, Kapilavastu, for the first time after attaining enlightenment, he rose in the air, emitted flames of fire and streams of water from his body, and walked in the sky (see *Mahāvastu* 3.115). According to Aśvaghoṣa's *Buddhacarita* (19.12–13), in order to convince his relatives of his spiritual capacities and prepare them for conversion, the Buddha rose in the air, cut his body to pieces, let his head and limbs fall to the ground, and then joined them together again before the amazed eyes of the spectators. Among the eminent disciples of the Buddha, Moggallāna (Skt., Maudgalyāyana) was well known as the "chief of those endowed with miraculous powers."

As Buddhism was transplanted to China, its missionaries often resorted to the display of miraculous powers. Especially in northern China, Buddhist saints performed magical feats for evangelical purposes; Fo-t'u-teng, who came to China at the beginning of the fourth century CE, worked the miracles of producing rain, creating a lotus out of a bowl of water, and drawing water from dried-up wells. The fame of the monk Dharmakṣema was based not only on his scholarly contributions but also on his supernatural powers to produce rain and foretell the outcome of political events or military campaigns. One may not be prepared to accept all of these miracle stories told by pious biographers, but they were undoubtedly created with the good intention of glorifying the Buddha, who was able to endow his ardent followers with such miraculous powers.

Christianity. Jesus Christ performed the miracles of healing and exorcism. In the miracle stories that, together with his sayings and passion narratives, occupy an important place in the synoptic Gospels, Jesus of Nazareth is presented as the supreme thaumaturge, the great miracle worker, the magician. In fact, there was a charge that Jesus was in league with Beelzebul (*Mk.* 3:22, *Mt.* 12:24, 12:27) and, according to a rabbinic tradition (see B.T., *San.* 43a), Jesus was executed for his practice of sorcery, misguiding the people of Israel.

Typically, the miracle stories of healing and exorcism in the synoptic Gospels all emphasize three motifs: (1) the history of the illness, (2) the actual process or techniques of the healing, and (3) a demonstration of the cure to the satisfaction of spectators. There is no doubt that the miracle stories were utilized internally for the strengthening of Christian faith and externally for propaganda purposes in a world in which such stories were commonly told of heroes of faith.

Particularly interesting are the techniques that Jesus employed for healing and exorcism. There is no question that he considered prayer to be essential for working miracles (*Mk.* 9:29). But, as a thaumaturge, he had to work up his emotions; in healing a leper Jesus was moved with "anger" *(orgistheis)*, stretched out his hand, and touched him (*Mk.* 1:40–45). Jesus displayed the emotional frenzy of the thaumaturge (see also *Lk.* 4:39). In the story of the deaf and mute man (*Mk.* 7:32–37), Jesus puts his fingers into his ears, spits and touches his tongue. Looking up to heaven, he sighs and says to him, "Ephphatha" ("Be opened"). In *Mk.* 8:22–26 Jesus heals a blind man by spitting on his eyes and laying his hands on them. Groaning sighs and spittle were often used by the thaumaturges. [*See* Spittle and Spitting.] As to the use of Semitic words for healing purposes, the account in the *Gospel of Mark* (5:41) of Jesus restoring a girl to life by saying, "Talithȧ Koum" ("Little girl, stand up"), retains the original Aramaic words even in otherwise translated versions. According to the German theologian Martin Dibelius, the preservation of such foreign words and phrases may show that the stories were utilized as a kind of handbook to Christian miracles and magic. The image of Jesus as the thaumaturge can still be identified in the *Gospel of John* (see 9:6, 11:33, 11:35, 11:38, 11:43).

Especially interesting is a cycle of miracle stories in the *Gospel of Mark* (4:35–5:43) that includes the stories of the Gerasene demoniac, the woman with an issue of blood, and the daughter of Jairus. Each of these has all the characteristics of the popular miracle story, and each contributes to the impression that Jesus is a "divine man," tempting New Testament scholars to talk about the development of "divine man Christology" in the *Gospel of Mark;* the miraculous power of Jesus is such that the Gerasenes beg him to leave their district, the touch of his clothes effects a cure, and he raises the dead by strange-sounding words. Moreover, Jesus is presented as performing the miracles of stilling the storm (4:35–41), feeding the five thousand people (6:34–44; see also 8:1–9), and walking on water (6:45–52).

Jesus Christ was followed by his apostles in working miracles (*Acts* 2:43, 5:12), and it seems that they worked the miracles of healing and exorcism "in the name of Jesus Christ" (*Acts* 3:6, 16:18; see also 19:13–17). Stephen and Philip demonstrated great wonders and signs among the people (*Acts* 6:8, 8:5–7), while Peter healed the lame and the paralytic, restoring the dead to life (*Acts* 3:1ff., 9:32ff., 9:36ff.). Even his "shadow" was believed to have healing power (*Acts* 5:15). Paul is also presented in *Acts* as a great miracle worker: he healed a cripple at Lystra (14:8ff.), performed an exorcism in the name of Jesus Christ (16:18), and cured Publius's father, who was sick with fever and dysentery, by putting his hands on him (28:8). Even handkerchiefs and aprons that had touched Paul's body were believed to be effective for curing sickness and exorcism (19:11–12). In *Acts* 13:4–12, Paul evokes belief in the proconsul Sergius Paulus by showing his superior thaumaturgy over the Jewish magician Bar-Jesus and another magician, Elymas.

As we can see from the portrayal of these apostles in *Acts*, the Christian community in the Hellenistic Mediterranean world had a tendency to view its heroes as "divine men"; Paul's opponents in Corinth, especially those he argued against in *2 Corinthians*, understood a Christian apostle as one who exhibited the aura and power of a "divine man," and they claimed it of themselves and wanted Paul to demonstrate it of himself. Accordingly, Paul had to write to the Corinthians that he had shown the signs of a true apostle among them, "with signs and wonders and mighty works" (*2 Cor.* 12:12; see also *Rom.* 15:18–19a; *1 Cor.* 12:9–10; *Gal.* 3:5).

Jesus Christ and his apostles in the first century set the examples to be followed by the faithful. In the subsequent history of Christianity, charisma or divine gift of "power" was represented on earth by a limited number of exceptional charismatic figures, such as the martyrs of the second and third centuries, the bishops of the late third century, and, finally, the succession of great Christian saints of ascetic origin, from Anthony onward.

Islam. Muḥammad, the "seal of the prophets," rejected every request to pose as a miracle worker; in contrast to Moses and other Hebrew prophets, as well as Jesus, who all worked miracles *(mu'jizāt)*, Muḥammad made no attempt to advance his religious authority by performing miracles, although people demanded them, saying, "Why does he not bring us a sign from his Lord?" (surah 20:133). To those people who wondered why signs, that is, miracles, had not been sent down on him from God, Muḥammad responded: "The signs are only with God, and I am only a plain warner" (29:49; see also 13:27–30, 17:92ff.).

According to Muḥammad, as presented in the Qur'ān, all the existing things in the universe are the signs *(āyāt;* sg., *āyah)* pointing to the reality of God in action. Natural phenomena, such as rain, wind, the structure of heaven and earth, the rhythmical alternation of day and night, and so forth, are not simply "natural" occurrences; they should be understood as "signs" or "symbols" manifesting God's mercy and compassion for man's well-being on earth. God declares, "We shall show them our signs in the horizons and in themselves" (41:53; see also 51:20–21). The universe is thus miraculously transformed into a forest of symbols; human beings dwell within the forest of divine symbols, and these symbols can be deciphered by anyone if he is spiritually prepared to interpret them as symbols. There should be no miracles except for these "signs."

However, the majority of the Islamic community has never ceased to expect miracles. Muḥammad is presented in the traditions (*ḥadīth*s) as having worked miracles in public on many occasions. It was especially Ṣūfī saints who performed miracles *(karāmāt).* Often called the "friends of God" *(awliyā',* sg. *walī),* they worked miracles by divine grace. On the one hand, it is often said by the Ṣūfīs that saints must not seek after the gift of miracle working, which might become a serious obstacle in the path to the union with God. On the other hand, the biographies of leading Ṣūfīs abound in miracle stories that certainly have been utilized for evangelical purposes: saints traveled a long distance in a short time; walked on water and in the air; talked with such inanimate objects as stones, as well as with animals; miraculously produced food, clothing, and other necessities of life; and made predictions of future events. Even after their death, saints are believed to work miracles at their own graves on behalf of the faithful, and their intercession is piously invoked.

[*For related discussions, see* Magic *and* Healing; *for a look at some theoretical issues involved in belief in miracles, see* Supernatural, The.]

BIBLIOGRAPHY

There is no comprehensive book dealing with the topic of miracles in the general history of religions. On the problem of interpretation concerning miracles and magico-religious powers in "primitive" societies, see Ernesto de Martino's *Il mondo magico* (Turin, 1948), translated by Paul S. White as *The World of Magic* (New York, 1972). On the miracles and miraculous powers of shamans, there is an admirable account in Mircea Eliade's *Shamanism: Archaic Techniques of Ecstasy,* rev. & enl. ed. (New York, 1964). This book contains an excellent bibliography.

Richard Reitzenstein's *Hellenistische Wundererzählungen* (1906; reprint, Darmstadt, 1963) still remains a classic for the study of the miracle stories in the Hellenistic Mediterranean world. Otto Weinreich has offered a detailed analysis of some of the major motifs appearing in the Greco-Roman stories of healing miracles. See his *Antike Heilungswunder: Untersuchungen zum Wunderglauben der Griechen und Römer* (Giessen, 1909). Valuable information on the miracle stories pertaining to the cult of Asklepios is presented in Emma J. Edelstein and Ludwig Edelstein's *Asclepius: A Collection and Interpretation of the Testimonies,* 2 vols. (Baltimore, 1945). See also Károly Kerényi's important study *Die göttliche Arzt: Studien über Asklepios und seine Kultstätten,* rev. ed. (Darmstadt, 1956), translated by Ralph Manheim as *Asklepios: Archetypal Image of the Physician's Existence* (New York, 1959). Miracle stories in rabbinic Judaism have been collected by Paul Fiebig in his *Jüdische Wundergeschichten des neutestamentlichen Zeitalters* (Tübingen, 1911).

On the miraculous powers of yogins, there is a brilliant account in Mircea Eliade's *Yoga: Immortality and Freedom,* 2d ed. (Princeton, 1969), still the standard work on the theory and practice of Yoga. On Taoist immortals and their miraculous powers, there is a brief but excellent account in Max Kaltenmark's *Lao Tseu et le taoïsme* (Paris, 1965), translated by Roger Greaves as *Lao Tzu and Taoism* (Stanford, Calif., 1969).

On miracles in the life of the Buddha, see a valuable account in Edward J. Thomas's *The Life of Buddha as Legend and History,* 3d rev. ed. (London, 1949).

The modern study of the miracle stories in the synoptic Gospels was initiated shortly after the end of World War I by such brilliant form critics as Martin Dibelius and Rudolf Bultmann. See a fascinating study by Dibelius, *Die Formgeschichte des Evangeliums,* 2d rev. ed. (Tübingen, 1933), translated by Bertram Lee Woolf as *From Tradition to Gospel* (New York, 1935). See also Bultmann's admirable analysis of the miracle stories in his *Die Geschichte der synoptischen Tradition,* 3d ed. (Göttingen, 1958), translated by John Marsh as *The History of the Synoptic Tradition* (New York, 1963). More recently, Gerd Theissen has studied the miracle stories from the perspective of the sociology of literature. See his *Urchristliche Wundergeschichten: Ein Beitrag zur formgeschichtlichen Erforschung der synoptischen Evangelien* (Gutersloh, 1974), translated by Francis McDonagh and edited by John Riches as *The Miracle Stories of the Early Christian Tradition* (Philadelphia, 1983). David L. Tiede, in his very useful study *The Charismatic Figure as Miracle Worker* (Missoula, Mont., 1972), distinguishes between the aretalogy of the sage-philosopher and the aretalogy of the miracle worker. On Christian saints and their miracles, there is an excellent study by Peter Brown, *The Cult of the Saints: Its Rise and Function in Latin Christianity* (Chicago, 1981).

On Muḥammad's reinterpretation of the concept *āyah* ("sign"), there is an admirable account by Toshihiko Izutsu, *God and Man in the Koran: Semantics of the Koranic Weltanschauung* (Tokyo, 1964), pp. 133ff. Reynold A. Nicholson has written on Muslim saints and their miracles in his *The Mystics of Islam: An Introduction to Sufism* (1914; reprint, London, 1963), pp. 120–147. See also a fascinating account by Annemarie Schimmel, *Mystical Dimensions of Islam* (Chapel Hill, N.C., 1975), pp. 204ff.

MANABU WAIDA

Modern Perspectives

The attitude toward miracles in the Western world is a strange combination of belief and disbelief. Most of the Mediterranean cultures that laid the groundwork for Western thinking believed that human beings have two modes of coping with animate and inanimate reality. One is the ordinary way, the other the religious or miraculous way. (Most nineteenth-century Western anthropologists called the second way magical.) Humans act in the ordinary way when they use habit, conventional thinking processes, or acquired skills. When these methods fail, when humans cannot adequately deal with the physical world, or when other human beings are hostile or unchanged by threats, war, contracts, or persuasion, another option is available: they can seek the help and intervention of a spiritual or nonphysical dimension of reality, which exists alongside and interpenetrates the ordinary physical dimension. This supplication can be quite conscious or it can be performed unconsciously through actions that imply control over these powers. Help can be invoked through concentration, meditation, ritual, spell, or ecstatic trance. Aid can be sought for knowledge, protection, or deliverance. The spiritual powers called upon can be either beneficent, malignant, or neutral. When a result appears in response to such an action, a miracle is said to occur. The miracle may occur within an individual or in the external world.

Four different attitudes toward miracles are to be found in Western cultures at the present time. (1) Christianity's view, which has remained quite consistent from the teachings and practice of Jesus to the present time, holds that miracles are natural manifestations of God. (2) Rational materialism maintains that material reality accounts for all data of experience and infers therefrom that spiritual reality is an illusion and that miracles do not exist. This view has encouraged liberal Christianity to doubt the reality of the miracles found in the New Testament and to rule out the possibility of their happening at present. This view has influenced conservative Christianity as well, for conservatives believe that miracles did occur within the dispensation of God at the time of Jesus but that they do not occur now. (3) A resurgence of interest in and study of phenomena not accounted for within the framework of materialism constitutes yet another approach to miracles, which has recently engaged the scientific community. (4) A fourth attitude toward miracles prevails in Hinduism, Buddhism, and Western Christian Science. In this view, material reality is seen as illusion. A miracle occurs once an individual realizes this truth. This approach is increasingly popular in the West, for it provides an alternative to rational materialism.

Christianity and Miracle. Christianity is both a historical religion and a living one. The historic Christian faith is one of the few in which miracles are seen as constituent of the orthodox faith. It continues the Old Testament tradition of God acting powerfully in the physical world. As C. S. Lewis (1947) points out, historical Christianity sees the incarnation of God in the world as the greatest miracle that culminates in the crucifixion and resurrection. Through this invasion of God the powers of evil are defeated and the kingdom of heaven begins to manifest itself on earth. Reginald H. Fuller (1963) sees the New Testament miracles as signs of the breakthrough of the kingdom into the ordinary world, though he questions the historicity of most miracles.

I have shown in detail in *The Christian and the Supernatural* (1976) that the miraculous in the ministry of Jesus and the apostles described in the New Testament falls into six categories:

1. The most common miracles are physical and mental healings, from curing ailments like a fever (*Mk.* 1:30) to raising the dead.
2. Another class of miracles involves exorcism, or healing through the expulsion of a spiritual force causing mental or physical illness. Most mental and physical sickness was perceived not as the action of God but as the infiltration of negative spiritual powers at war with God, an infiltration that morally caused sin, physically caused disease, and mentally caused madness or possession.
3. The third category comprises communication with the spiritual world and with God through dreams, visions, revelations, or prayer. Such communication is a basic principle of the teachings and practice of Jesus.
4. Nature miracles comprise a fourth category. Examples include Jesus walking on the water (*Mk.* 6:48), the stilling of the storm (*Mk.* 4:38), physical disappearance (*Lk.* 4:30), and the feeding of the multitudes (*Mk.* 6:35).
5. In another category of miracles Jesus shows telepathic, clairvoyant, and precognitive power (*Mk.* 2:6, *Jn.* 1:47, *Mk.* 11:1). Sometimes his statements are prophetic, as when he foretells his own death and resurrection, relates the destruction of Jerusalem, and speaks of the coming of the Kingdom.
6. In the final category of miracles are the resurrection appearances of Jesus, which combine both the physical and the spiritual in a religious experience that is dynamic and transforming.

Similar miracles are reported among the apostles after the ascension of Jesus in *Acts of the Apostles* and in other books of the New Testament. This tradition of miracles continued without interruption in both Roman Catholicism and Orthodox Christianity; services for healing and exorcism are found in the official service books of both. Writing during the fifth century, Sozomenos reports that miracles began to occur again at the end of the Arian controversy, when churches held by Arians were returned to Orthodox pastors (*Ecclesiastical History* 7.5). Throughout Christian history miracles have been reported to occur around saintly people. To this day several attested miracles are required by the Roman Catholic church before a saint is canonized.

During the Reformation, both Luther and Calvin wrote that the age of miracles was over and that their occurrence should not be expected. At the same time Protestantism was overwhelmed by the rationalism and materialism of the Enlightenment, and discussion of the miraculous nearly disappeared. The Roman Catholic church upheld its practice without trying to defend it intellectually, and shrines like Lourdes drew great crowds. The academic Protestant community came to believe that the practice of Christianity was largely a matter of morality and that neither God nor the spiritual world contacted or influenced practical human life to any great extent. Rudolf Bultmann presented this thesis consistently and thoroughly.

Philosophical Materialism. Materialism as an adequate explanation for all things originated in the thinking of several classical Greek thinkers, was developed by Aristotle, and came to fruition in the eighteenth and nineteenth centuries. My book *Encounter with God* (1972) traces this development from its first beginnings to its full-blown denial of any aspect of reality not perceived by the five senses and not objectively verifiable. This view, diametrically opposed to the view of Hinduism and Buddhism, dominated the intellectual and academic life of the West in the nineteenth and early twentieth centuries and influenced nearly all disciplines from psychology and anthropology to comparative religion and Christian theology. In several books B. F. Skinner dismisses human consciousness as the ghost in the box. Melvin Konner in *The Tangled Wing* (New York, 1982) writes that there is only the blind action of natural selection, sifting material genes. A person is only a gene's way of making another gene. This skeptical materialism has arisen many times in human history—in China, Greece, and Rome—but only recently has it effectively taken over nearly a whole culture.

This worldview considers all miracles and all contact with any dimension of reality other than the concrete physical one absurd, the result of ignorance, superstition, or the refusal to search long enough for the purely physical causes. Supposedly intelligent people will classify miracle with magic and ignore any experience purporting to be miraculous.

Scientific Study of Paranormal Experience. Since the mid-twentieth century, when man succeeded in splitting the atom and the implications of Heisenberg's principle of indeterminacy and Einstein's theory of relativity were fully realized, theoretical physics has become much less certain that it can provide final answers. In *Physics and Philosophy* (New York, 1962) Werner Heisenberg suggests that we live in an open universe and that the conventional words describing God and spirit may have greater correspondence with reality than the highly developed words of physics. The mathematical thinking of Kurt Gödel, the analysis of scientific theory presented by Thomas S. Kuhn in *The Structure of Scientific Revolutions* (Chicago, 1962), the findings of psychosomatic medicine, the work of modern anthropologists, the data in Andrew Greeley's *The Sociology of the Paranormal: A Reconnaissance* (1975), the scientific study of parapsychological phenomena, and the theory underlying the depth psychology of C. G. Jung all cast doubt on Western materialist determinism.

In the heyday of materialism in London a group of serious scientists organized the Society for Psychical Research in 1882. An American society was organized three years later in which William James was active. Sigmund Freud was a member of the original society and contributed to its publications. Jung too studied and published on the subject of paranormal experience; he discussed synchronicity, mediumship, and telepathy and provided models for understanding these events. Joseph Banks Rhine at Duke University did many scientific studies of events that did not fit into the materialistic paradigm.

Finally, the professional organization calling itself the Parapsychological Association was accepted as an affiliate by the American Association for the Advancement of Science in 1969. One of the most comprehensive surveys of scientific parapsychology to date is that of Robert F. Jahn (1982). Jahn describes four categories of psychic phenomena; three of these are divided further. These categories are similar to the Christian ones. In the following outline, I have added explanations of the terms.

- I. Extrasensory Perception (ESP)
  - A. Telepathy: information passing from mind to mind without physical means
  - B. Clairvoyance: perception of events or happenings at a distance in space
  - C. Precognition/Retrocognition: perception of events in future time or past time
  - D. Animal ESP
- II. Psychokinesis (PK): the affect of mind or psyche or spirit on a material environment
  - A. Physical Systems
    - 1. deliberate, actually effected by conscious intent
    - 2. spontaneous, as in poltergeist phenomena
  - B. Biological Systems
    - 1. psychic healing
    - 2. plant PK

III. Survival: experiences of the deceased
  A. Reincarnation: evidence of a former life of the individual
  B. Apparitions: experience of the person deceased or spiritual reality
  C. Mediumship: using others to make contact with this nonphysical domain
IV. Out-of-Body Experiences (OOBE): the experience of having existence as a psyche, but no longer tied to the physical body

Once it is acknowledged that human beings can receive verifiable information through means other than the five senses and that this reception breaks the rules of space and time, the serious scientific study of miracle becomes possible. It becomes possible to examine critically data that are not easily verifiable, such as communication from the deceased and the transformative power of religious experience. A strict materialistic framework considers communication through nonphysical means as absurd as a miracle, because it assumes that some physical signal has to enter the closed system and move the cogs so that the message can get through. An alternate theory of perception is required to avoid such an impasse. [*See* Otherworld.]

Since the first decade of the twentieth century the medical profession has come to realize that a materialist point of view cannot explain or heal all human disease. Both James and Jung point out that the experience of meaninglessness is a disease causing both emotional and physical sickness. In *The Broken Heart* (1977) James J. Lynch describes the medical consequences of loneliness and calls organized religion to task for not providing ways to meet this human need, which is largely ignored in a mechanistic, materialistic society. O. Carl and Stephanie Simonton have described a meditative treatment for cancer in *Getting Well Again* (1978). Herbert Benson describes what he calls the faith factor in *Beyond the Relaxation Response* (1983).

In *The Structure and Dynamics of the Psyche* (1960), Jung presents a theory of synchronicity developed in conjunction with the Nobel Prize–winning atomic physicist Wolfgang Pauli. He offers a hypothesis as to how events can be influenced both by physical causality operating within the material world and by other forces as well. Jung never denied physical causality, but he concluded that it could not explain all happenings, a conclusion also reached by other scientists. Those events not explainable in purely causal terms Jung called acausal or synchronous (see figure 1). In his theory each instant of time contains meaning; there is a coherence in each period of duration, and these coherences have their source in the nonphysical, psychoid, or, in Christian terminology, the spiritual aspect of reality.

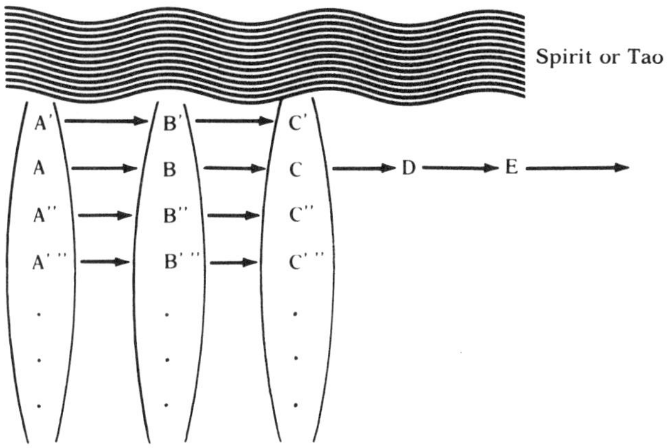

FIGURE 1. *Synchronicity.* In this diagram, A causes B, B causes C, and so forth. In Jung's notion of synchronicity, each event (A, B, C, D, etc.) is related to every other event at any given moment and to the flow of meaning represented by the wavy band at the top.

The Chinese call this the Tao, and the Chinese book of oracles, *I ching,* is based upon this principle. Miracles exemplify synchronous events. In oracular information, dream interpretation, religious experience, healing, and nature miracles the synchronous appears autonomously or through mediation.

The most recent studies seem to suggest that the issue of miracle or paranormal experience remains an open question in the Western world.

[*See also* Philosophy, *articles on* Philosophy and Religion *and* Philosophy of Religion.]

BIBLIOGRAPHY

Benson, Herbert, and William Proctor. *Beyond the Relaxation Response.* New York, 1984.

Eliade, Mircea. *Shamanism: Archaic Techniques of Ecstasy.* Rev. & enl. ed. New York, 1964. The authoritative study of the shaman and the technique of esctasy by which the otherworld is mediated to the physical world.

Frank, Jerome D. *Persuasion and Healing.* Baltimore, 1961. A comparative study of the various schools of modern psychotherapy, healing in primitive society, religious revivalism, and Communist thought reform.

Fuller, Reginald H. *Interpreting the Miracles.* London, 1963. An attempt to study New Testament miracles using the framework of Rudolf Bultmann.

Greeley, Andrew M. *The Sociology of the Paranormal: A Reconnaissance.* Beverly Hills, Calif., 1975. Hard sociological data on the incidence of religious experience and its effect on human beings.

Jahn, Robert F. "The Persistent Paradox of Psychic Phenomena: An Engineering Perspective." *Proceedings of the Institute of Electrical and Electronics Engineers* 70 (February 1982): 136–170. The finest and most up-to-date summary of parapsychological research.

Jung, C. G. *The Structure and Dynamics of the Psyche.* Translated by R. F. C. Hull. New York, 1960. Gives Jung's theory of personality and synchronicity.

Kelsey, Morton. *Dreams: The Dark Speech of the Spirit.* Garden City, N.Y., 1968. An analytical and historical study of dreams as conveyors of information from the space-time world. Republished without appendix as *God, Dreams and Revelation* (Minneapolis, 1974).

Kelsey, Morton. *Encounter with God.* Minneapolis, 1972. Provides a study of the development of Western philosophical materialism and the evidence that points beyond its worldview.

Kelsey, Morton. *Healing and Christianity.* New York, 1973. A study of the miracles of healing and exorcism found in the ministry of Jesus and in the history of the Christian Church, together with a consideration of their psychological, medical, and philosophical base.

Kelsey, Morton. *The Christian and the Supernatural.* Minneapolis, 1976. An analysis of miraculous elements in the New Testament.

Kelsey, Morton. *Companions on the Inner Way: The Art of Spiritual Guidance.* New York, 1983. Contains both a philosophical base for religious experience and miracles and an analysis of the nature of religious experience.

Lewis, C. S. *Miracles* (1947). Rev. ed. New York, 1968. An excellent analysis of the subject from a Christian viewpoint.

Lynch, James J. *The Broken Heart: The Medical Consequences of Loneliness.* New York, 1977. A serious medical study of the effect of human and religious values on health.

Simonton, O. Carl, Stephanie Simonton, et al. *Getting Well Again.* Los Angeles, 1978. The theory and practice of using meditation for the treatment of cancer.

MORTON KELSEY

MI'RĀJ. The belief that Muḥammad ascended to heaven in the course of his life and beheld the secrets of the otherworld as no other person had ever beheld them is shared by all factions of Islam. In Muslim religious literature, the idea of the Mi'rāj, Muḥammad's ascension to heaven, is closely associated with that of the Isrā', his nocturnal journey. Neither term appears as such in the Qur'ān, yet both developed in close connection with crucial, though ambiguous, Qur'anic passages.

Qur'anic Associations. The term *isrā'* is taken from surah 17:1, "Glory be to him who carried his servant by night from the Holy Mosque to the Further Mosque, the precincts of which we have blessed, that we might show him some of our signs." It is reasonably certain that "his servant" refers to Muḥammad, "the Holy Mosque" to Mecca (surahs 2:144, 2:149, 2:150, 2:191, 2:196, 2:217, 5:2, 8:34, 9:7, 9:19, 9:28, 22:25, 48:25, 48:27), and "by night" to a journey begun by night (44:23), without reference to the journey's miraculous nature. Far less certain, however, is the intended meaning of "the Further Mosque" *(al-masjid al-aqṣā).* Since the earliest prophetic traditions *(ḥadīth),* this term has been explained either as a sanctuary on earth ("terrestrial" Jerusalem, the temple precinct) or in heaven ("celestial" Jerusalem, the environs of the divine throne). There is no apparent connection between the *isrā'* verse and a dream *(ru'yā)* shown to Muḥammad by God and mentioned in the same surah (17:60), although the *ḥadīth* would interpret this dream as a vision of Jerusalem that Muḥammad communicated to the unbelieving Meccans.

The association of "the Further Mosque" with the terrestrial Jerusalem, which became the most widely accepted explanation, seems to be supported by the Qur'anic phrase "the precincts of which we have blessed," referring to the Holy Land (21:71, 21:81, 7:137, 34:18), although Palestine in general is referred to as the "nearer part of the land" (30:3). This explanation was favored under the Umayyads, who were intent on glorifying Jerusalem as a holy territory rivaling Mecca, then ruled by their opponent 'Abd Allāh ibn Zubayr. The interpretation of "the Further Mosque" as al-Ji'rānah, a place on the fringes of the holy precinct of Mecca from which Muḥammad set out on his pilgrimage *('umrah)* of Dhū al-Qa'dah 630, has been rejected on decisive evidence (Maurice Plessner, "Muhammad's Clandestine 'Umra in the Ḏū'l-Qa'da 8 H. and Sūra 17,1," *Revista degli studi orientali* 32 [1957]: 525–530; Rudi Paret, "Die 'ferne Gebetsstatte' in Sure 17,1," *Der Islam* 34 [1959]: 150–152).

The association with the celestial Jerusalem was favored in the classical sources of *ḥadīth* and Qur'ān commentary, which tended to use *isrā'* for the ascension to heaven and thus linked Muḥammad's night journey with his ascension. This explanation, which also included the purification of Muḥammad's heart as a preparatory stage, tended to interpret the story as Muḥammad's divine initiation to his prophetic career.

As a term for ascension, the word *mi'rāj,* literally "ladder," appears to conceal a vaguely understood reference to Jacob's ladder (*Gn.* 28:12). The term was probably borrowed from the Ethiopic *ma'āreg* (Ethiopic *Book of Jubilees* 21:37) as a translation of the Hebrew *sullām.* The background for the cryptic references in the Qur'ān may be provided by various motifs: the apocalyptic images of a heavenly ladder that recur in Jewish *heikhalot* literature; symbolic notions of a seven-runged ladder on which the soul ascends through the gates of heaven, found in the liturgy of Mithras; and gnostic ideas of the ladder as a means of ascending to heaven, as in the Mandaean *sumbilta* and the Manichaean pillar of glory.

In fragmentary Qur'anic references, God is called "the

Lord of the Stairways" (*dhū al-maʿārij,* 70:3; see also 43:33, 40:15), to whom the angels, the spirit, and the divine command "mount up" *(taʿruju, yaʿruju)* in a day (70:4, 32:5). God knows what comes down from heaven and what goes up to it (34:2, 57:4). The notion of heavenly ascent appears to be implied when Pharaoh gives orders to build a tower so that he may reach the cords of heaven and climb up to the god of Moses (40:36–37), or when Muḥammad is challenged by his opponents to go up into heaven (17:93). To this he replies, "Let them ascend the cords" (38:10) and "Stretch up a rope to heaven" (22:15), for even if God opened to them "a gate in heaven" (15:14), or if they had "a ladder" into heaven (*sullam,* 52:38, 6:35) and were climbing to it (6:125), they would not believe.

Three Qur'anic passages not explicitly referring to heavenly ascent appear nevertheless to be linked with Muḥammad's visionary experiences of heaven. Surahs 81:19–25 and 53:1–12 give a parallel account of a vision in which Muḥammad saw a divine messenger on the horizon, and surah 53:13–18 gives an account of a vision in which he beheld the greatest signs of God near the lote tree on the edge of Paradise. In both cases the heavenly messenger approaches the Prophet from a distance but does not carry him off.

On the basis of the Qur'anic evidence it appears certain that *miʿrāj* and *isrā'* refer to experiences Muḥammad had prior to his emigration from Mecca to Medina in 622, since the relevant Qur'anic passages can be traced back to that period. It cannot be ascertained, however, whether or not these experiences occurred toward the beginning of Muḥammad's prophetic activity in Mecca, although they seem to have their natural setting in that time.

Narrative Lore. The Qur'anic references became associated with legends that proliferated rapidly during the first two centuries of Islam through the activity of the *quṣṣāṣ,* pious and popular storytellers. Their stories in turn were taken up and recast in the *ḥadīth* methodology of the Prophet's biography *(sīrah)* with the aim of establishing a scholarly consensus *(ijmāʿ)* concerning this legendary and mainly oral tradition. This consensus, reflected in the *Sīrat Muḥammad* by Ibn Isḥāq (d. 767), revised by Ibn Hishām (d. 834), admitted both interpretations of "the Further Mosque" and harmonized the two by assigning *isrā'* the particular meaning of the nocturnal journey to Jerusalem. This harmonization implied the elimination of an earlier tradition that made Mecca the starting point of the ascension and the substitution of Jerusalem, the starting point of Christ's ascension, where, perhaps since ʿAbd al-Malik's caliphate (685–705), the Prophet's footprint was shown to Muslim pilgrims.

Sīrat Muḥammad. Ibn Isḥāq's account of the miraculous events occurring during a single night combines all features in a continuous narrative, yet inverts the events. One night Muḥammad is asleep near the Kaʿbah at Mecca (or in the house of Umm Hāni') when he is awakened by the angel Gabriel, who leads him to a winged animal called Burāq. Gabriel places the Prophet on the back of this steed, and they journey together to Jerusalem. In Jerusalem they meet several prophets, notably Abraham, Moses, and Jesus. By leading a public prayer service *(ṣalāt),* Muḥammad takes precedence over all the other prophets assembled there. When the Prophet finishes all that has to be done in Jerusalem, so the narrative continues, the beautiful ladder *(miʿrāj)* on which the dying fix their eyes, and which the human souls ascend to heaven, is brought. Gabriel makes Muḥammad ascend it and brings him to the gates of the seven heavens, one after the other. At each gate Gabriel is asked to identify Muḥammad and testify that revelation has already been made to him. Then follows a long description of Muḥammad's experiences in the heavens, in each of which he meets one of the prophets. Finally, Muḥammad beholds the garden of Paradise (as, from the first heaven, he has witnessed the tortures of Hell) and appears before God's throne to converse with him. God then reduces the number of obligatory daily prayers incumbent on the Muslim community from the original fifty to five. Muḥammad returns to Mecca and the next morning informs the Meccans that during the night he has gone to Syria and come back again. The public, including his close companion Abū Bakr, is naturally skeptical at first, and many of the Prophet's followers apostatize.

Ḥadīth. Influenced in part by the Jewish and Christian apocalyptic traditions, *ḥadīth* literature embellished the basic narrative of the Prophet's ascent to heaven with a great variety of detail that focused on the preparation for the ascent, the riding animal, and the experiences in heaven. It was also at this point that the story of the purification of Muḥammad's heart was prefixed to the ascension narrative. As Muḥammad is sleeping in the neighborhood of the Kaʿbah, angels appear, lay him on his back, open his body, and, with water from the well of Zamzam, wash his heart and bowels, cleansing them of doubt, idolatry, ignorance, and error. They then bring a golden vessel filled with wisdom and belief and fill his body with faith and wisdom. Purified in his heart and dedicated to be a prophet, Muḥammad is taken up to the lowest heaven.

The animal that carries Muḥammad to Jerusalem, Burāq (etymologically probably Arabic, "little lightning flash"), is depicted as a miraculous beast of exceptional fleetness. It is described as a brilliant steed of either gender, saddled and bridled, in size between a donkey and a mule, with a long back, shaking ears, and "a cheek like that of a man." Wings on its shanks propelled legs that moved in one stride as far as its eyes could reach. It was the riding beast of prophets in the past, Abraham in particular, and more recently Jesus. Upon the arrival in Jerusalem, according to some traditions, Gabriel tied it to a rock or ring, while, according to others, Burāq served as a flying steed for Muḥammad's ascension, taking over the function of the ladder. In its pictorial representations Burāq received a human face, a woman's head, and a peacock's tail. From the earliest extant image in a 1314 manuscript of Rashīd al-Dīn's *Jamīʿ al-tawārīkh* (Universal History) to the most splendid Persian and Turkish miniatures of later centuries, the steed, its rider, and its guide became a highly cherished motif of Islamic painting and poetry. Beautiful miniatures of Muḥammad's *miʿrāj* can be found, for example, in the fifteenth-century *Miʿrāj-nāmah* translated into Eastern Turkish by Mīr Ḥaydar and calligraphed in Uighur script by Mālik Bakhshī of Herat (see Marie-Rose Séguy, *The Miraculous Journey of Mahomet*, New York, 1977).

The meeting of the Prophet with Abraham, Moses, and Jesus at Jerusalem may be modeled on accounts of the transfiguration of Jesus on Mount Tabor (*Mt.* 17:1, *Mk.* 9:1, *Lk.* 9:28). Muḥammad encounters Adam as judge over the souls of the dead in the first heaven, Joseph in the third, and Enoch/Idrīs in the fourth. Jesus and John the Baptist appear together in the second heaven, whereas Aaron and Moses appear separately in the fifth and sixth. Moses weeps, realizing that Muḥammad is higher than himself in God's esteem and that his followers will be more numerous than his own. Muḥammad refuses his advice to ask God to reduce the obligatory daily prayers to fewer than five. Finally, in the seventh heaven, that of Abraham, Muḥammad finds himself in the presence of God's throne, reaches the lote-tree marking the limit of knowledge that creatures possess, and beholds the rivers of Paradise, where he is offered vessels of water, wine, milk, and honey but partakes of the milk alone.

Adaptations and Interpretations. The theme of the Prophet's ascension found its place in the literature of Islamic theology, philosophy, and Sufism. Muslim theologians were preoccupied with the question, already discussed since early times, of whether the night journey and ascension took place in a literal or a spiritual sense. Al-Ṭabarī (d. 923) strongly favored the belief, shared by the majority of Muslims, that the Prophet was transported literally, with his body and while awake. Others, in particular the Muʿtazilah, held that he was carried in spirit to Jerusalem and heaven while his body remained at Mecca; this view was supported by a statement attributed to Muḥammad's favorite wife, ʿĀʾishah. Al-Taftāzānī (d. 1389) states that the event happened in body and spirit but does not rule out its possible occurrence in sleep or in spirit alone. The question of whether or not Muḥammad saw God face to face on the occasion of the ascension constituted another debate within Islamic theology, in particular against the background of the controversy concerning the beatific vision of the believer.

The Neoplatonic philosophers of Islam gave an allegorical meaning to the Prophet's ascension. The *Epistles* of the Ikhwān al-Ṣafāʾ (Brethren of Purity), completed in 969, adopted the pattern of cosmological descent and eschatological ascent and interpreted the latter as the ascent *(miʿrāj)* of the human soul that abandons its bodily existence and returns to its angelic state of pure spirituality. Abū al-ʿAlāʾ al-Maʿarrī (d. 1057) wrote a parody, *Risālat al-ghufrān* (The Epistle of Forgiveness), on the traditional accounts of the *miʿrāj*. Two treatises of al-Ghazālī (d. 1111) are focused on the theme of ascension: his *Miʿrāj al-sālikīn* (The Ladder of Those Who Follow the Path) elucidates the theme from seven different topical angles, while his *Mishkāt al-anwār* (The Niche for Lights) offers a Neoplatonic interpretation in purely psychological terms. Ibn al-Sīd al-Baṭalyawsī (d. 1127), in his *Kitāb al-ḥadāʾiq* (Book of Gardens), describes the ascent of the purified spirits to the supernal world on "the ladder of ascensions" *(sullam al-maʿārij)* that follows a straight line connecting the terrestrial and celestial spheres.

For the Ṣūfīs, the night journey and ascension of the Prophet became the prototype of the soul's itinerary to God as it rises from the bonds of sensuality to the height of mystical knowledge. It is doubtful whether, as is frequently asserted, Abū Yazīd al-Bisṭāmī (d. 875) claimed to have experienced *miʿrāj* himself, leading to mystical union with God. Al-Ḥallāj (d. 922) meditated on the theme in his *Kitāb al-ṭawāsīn*. Al-Qushayrī (d. 1074) collected accounts current among moderate Ṣūfīs in his *Kitāb al-miʿrāj* and included in it a discussion of the ascension attributed to Enoch/Idrīs, Abraham, Elijah, Moses, and Jesus. He reserved ascension in body and spirit for the prophets and conceded to the Ṣūfīs only the dream experience of ascent to heaven. Al-Hujwīrī (d. 1077) makes a clear distinction in his *Kashf al-maḥjūb* (Elucidation of the Secrets) between the ascension of prophets, which occurs outwardly and in the body, and that of the saints, which takes place inwardly and in the spirit only. Ibn al-ʿArabī (d. 1240) expounded the Prophet's night journey and ascension as a symbol of the soul's itinerary toward mystical union in his *Kitāb al-isrāʾ* and also devoted two lengthy sections of his

Futūḥāt (Revelations) to the subject. In one section he has a mystic and a philosopher make the journey together; the philosopher has to stop short at the seventh heaven, while no secrets remain hidden from the mystic. In the other section applies the Prophet's ascension to the mystical experience of Ṣūfī ecstasy, recording his own mystical ascent and his conversations with the prophets about mystic themes.

The Miʿrāj provided an ideal type for the symbolic narratives created by Ṣūfī philosophers and poets intent on explaining the spiritual heights of mystical union. In the fine Persian *Miʿrāj-nāmah,* attributed to Ibn Sīnā (d. 1037) or Yaḥyā Suhrawardī (d. 1191), yet probably written by an anonymous eleventh-century author, the theme of the postmortem ascent of the soul to heaven under conduct of the angel is overshadowed by the ecstatic ascent of the mystic to the divine throne in imitation of the ascension of the Prophet, the archetypal mystic. This symbolic narrative may be understood, topically although not historically, as bridging the gulf between Ibn Sīnā's Arabic allegory, *Ḥayy ibn Yaqẓān,* and ʿAṭṭār's (d. 1220) grandiose mystical Persian epic, *Manṭiq al-ṭayr* (Conversation of the Birds), both of which, in their respective ways and not unlike the Persian *Miʿrāj-nāmah,* move from the level of the symbolic interpretation of the narrative to the plane of the existential exegesis of mystic ascent experienced in the human soul.

The theme of *miʿrāj* appears in many aspects in Persian Ṣūfī poetry from Rūmī (d. 1273) to Iqbal (d. 1938). For Rūmī the Miʿrāj became the symbol of the radical difference between discursive reason and mystical union. Gabriel, the symbol of reason and the guide of the heavenly journey, remains outside the divine presence while the Prophet, the symbol of the true lover of God, enjoys "a time with God" in the chamber of union and mystery. The *Jāvīd-nāmah* of Iqbal describes a contemporary version of the spiritual journey made by the poet from earth through and beyond the spheres to the presence of God.

Later popular accounts of the Prophet's ascension collect and systematize the material scattered in the older sources, largely augmenting the matter without increasing its depth. Al-Suyūṭī (d. 1505) presents a fine disquisition on the traditions of *isrāʾ* and *miʿrāj,* discussing their nature, time, place, and details in *Al-āyah al-kubrā fī sharḥ qiṣṣat al-isrāʾ*. Al-Nuʿmānī, a disciple of Ibn Ḥajar al-ʿAsqalānī (d. 1449), collects a medley of traditions, theological views, and mystical statements concerning the Prophet's night journey and ascension in *Al-sirāj al-wahhāj* (The Glowing Lamp). The most popular *miʿrāj* book down to modern times is the *Kitāb al-isrāʾ wa-al-miʿrāj* of al-Ghaythī (d. 1573), on which Dardīr (d. 1786) wrote a gloss. Al-Barzanjī's (d. 1766) *Qiṣṣat al-miʿrāj* appears to be modeled on al-Ghaythī's work. The Uighur *Miʿraj-nāmah,* composed in 1436/7, documents the spread of the legend in Central Asian languages.

The Christians of the Middle Ages possessed a certain knowledge about the Muslim legends surrounding Muḥammad's miraculous journey to heaven. This is evidenced by the famous Latin version of the legend, apparently prepared by Ibrāhīm al-Ḥakīm, a Jewish physician active at the court of Alfonso X of Castile (1264–1277). This Latin version *(Liber scalae)* and a French translation from Latin *(Eschiele Mahomet)* became the focal point of the discussion surrounding the question of Dante's Muslim sources in his *Commedia* (raised by the Spanish Jesuit Juan Andrès about 1780, again advanced by Ozanam in 1838 and Labitte in 1842, and clearly formulated by Blochet in *Les sources orientales de la divine comédie*, Paris, 1901).

BIBLIOGRAPHY

Historians of religions have long realized the significance of Muḥammad's ascension as a theme in comparative religion. D. W. Bousset's groundbreaking study "Die Himmelsreise der Seele," *Archiv für Religionswissenschaft* 4 (1901): 136–169, 229–273, set the stage for an inquiry into the soul's ascent to heaven in world religions. Following Bousset's line of research and Edgar Blochet's study of the theme in "L'ascension au ciel du prophète Mohammed," *Revue de l'histoire des religions* 40 (1899): 1–25, 203–236, Geo Widengren has traced the Iranian motifs of Muḥammad's Miʿrāj in two works, *The Ascension of the Apostle and the Heavenly Book* (Uppsala, 1950) and *Muhammad, the Apostle of God, and His Ascension* (Uppsala, 1955), which attempt to establish an "ideal" ritual of the Prophet's ascension. Marie-Thérèse d'Alverny documents the theme of the soul's ascent in Latin sources of medieval philosophy in "Les pérégrinations de l'âme dans l'autre monde d'après un anonyme de la fin du douzième siècle," *Archives d'histoire doctrinale et littéraire du Moyen-Âge* 15–17 (1940–1942): 239–299, while Alexander Altmann demonstrates the impact of Muslim sources on the theme of the ascension in Jewish religious philosophy in "The Ladder of Ascension," *Studies in Mysticism and Religion Presented to Gershom G. Scholem,* edited by E. E. Urbach, R. J. Zwi Werblowsky, and Chaim Wirszubski (Jerusalem, 1967), pp. 1–32. The problems of typological similarity between Muḥammad's Miʿrāj and shamanic experiences of ascension are outlined by Mircea Eliade in *Shamanism* (New York, 1964) and taken up by J. R. Porter in "Muhammad's Journey to Heaven," *Numen* 21 (1974): 64–80.

The question of Muslim sources in Dante's *Commedia* has been treated systematically by Miguel Asín Palacios in his important work *La escatologia musulmana en la Divina comedia* (Madrid, 1919), translated and abridged by Harold Sunderland as *Islam and the Divine Comedy* (New York, 1926). The controversy Asín Palacios's book stirred up is recorded in the second Spanish edition (Madrid and Granada, 1943). The basis of the discussion was significantly broadened with the independent publication of the French and Latin versions of the legend: *Il "Libro della scala" e la questione delle fonti arabo-spagnole della Divina commedia,* edited by Enrico Cerulli (Vatican City, 1949), and *La escala de Mahoma,* edited by José Muñoz Sendino (Madrid, 1949). The trends of more recent discussion on the point can be traced in Peter Wunderli's survey "Zur Auseinandersetzung über die muselmanischen Quellen der Divina Commedia," *Romanistisches Jahrbuch* 15 (1964): 19–50, and Enrico Cerulli's *Nuove ricerche sul Libro della scala e la conoscenza dell'Islam in Occidente* (Vatican City, 1972).

GERHARD BÖWERING

MIRIAM, or, in Hebrew, Miryam; Israelite prophetess who flourished, according to tradition, in the thirteenth century BCE. Biblical tradition recalls Miriam as the sister of Moses and Aaron who helped Moses lead the Hebrew slaves out of Egypt (*Mic.* 6:4). *Exodus* 15:20–21 describes how she led the women of Israel in a hymn of victory to YHVH, Lord of Israel, after he had split the Sea of Reeds, enabling the Hebrews to pass through and escape their Egyptian pursuers:

> Miriam the prophetess, sister of Aaron, took the drum in her hand. All the women went out after her with drums and dances. Miriam declared to them: "Sing to the Lord, for he has triumphed; horse and its rider he has hurled into the sea."

Modern scholars now tend to view the sibling relationships between Miriam, Aaron, and Moses as an embellishment on earlier traditions. Miriam was originally identified as an associate of Aaron, Israel's first priest, and later as his sister. When biblical tradition similarly developed a sibling relationship between Aaron and Moses, the great leader, prophet, and lawgiver of Israel, Miriam became known as the sister of Moses too (*Nm.* 26:39). In the story of Moses' birth (*Ex.* 2:2–7), the unnamed older sister who guards him is assumed by Jewish and Christian tradition to have been Miriam. If her name were of Egyptian origin, as some have explained, that would reinforce the conclusion that she was of the priestly tribe of Levi, as several prominent Levites bore Egyptian names.

Miriam figures primarily in one episode in the Pentateuch, *Numbers* 12:1–16, in which she and Aaron reproach Moses for having taken a Cushite wife—who may or may not be identified with his Midianite wife, Zipporah—and in which they challenge the superiority of Moses' prophetic stature to their own. YHVH responds to their challenge by asserting the unique and intimate nature of his revelations to Moses and responds to their reproach by afflicting Miriam with leprosy. Moses intercedes on Miriam's behalf at Aaron's request—thereby demonstrating his intimacy with God—and after a seven-day quarantine, Miriam's health is restored. The legendary quality of the episode is suggested by the fact that Miriam's leprosy became an admonition to any who would fail to heed the priests (*Dt.* 24:8–9). Miriam predeceased Aaron and Moses (*Nm.* 20:1) and, so far as we know, never married.

BIBLIOGRAPHY

On the difficulty of establishing Miriam's historical position, see Martin Noth's *A History of Pentateuchal Traditions,* translated with an introduction by Bernhard W. Anderson (Chico, Calif., 1981), pp. 180–183. Miriam is most extensively discussed in connection with the challenges to Moses, for analysis of which see G. B. Gray's *A Critical and Exegetical Commentary on Numbers* (Edinburgh, 1903), pp. 120–128. The most exhaustive, but a very technical, analysis is Heinrich Valentin's *Aaron: Eine Studie zur vor-priesterschriftlichen Aaron-Überlieferung* (Göttingen, 1978), pp. 306–364; Valentin also discusses (pp. 377–384) *Exodus* 15:20. Martin Buber's *Moses: The Revelation and the Covenant* (New York, 1958), pp. 167–169, attempts to connect the two challenges to Moses. On Miriam's name, see Alan H. Gardiner's "The Egyptian Origin of Some English Personal Names," *Journal of the American Oriental Society* 56 (1936): 189–197, esp. pp. 194–197.

EDWARD L. GREENSTEIN

MIRRORS. It has been surmised, although not proved, that in the Neolithic period polished stone disks were used as mirrors. Actual mirrors have been known since the Bronze Age, and they have been used through all of subsequent history. Ancient sources ascribe a depiction of the mirror to Hephaistos. The first known mirrors were made of metal (bronze, silver-plated bronze, and occasionally silver or gold), but later, beginning with Roman times, glass mirrors appeared, although until modern times they were in widespread use only among Europeans. The preferred shape of prehistoric, ancient, and medieval mirrors was round, although they were also oval, rectangular, polygonal, scalloped, and so on. Together with the looking-glass mirror, the hand mirror with a handle on the side or the back became widespread. There were portable and stationary mirrors; a large handle sometimes served also as a stand. The reverse side of the mirror, the border of the mirror side, and the handle were often ornamented with engraving, relief work, and inscriptions, so that mirrors were sometimes beautiful works of art.

Mirrors and the Soul. The physical basis of beliefs connected with the mirror is its ability to reflect the sun's rays and to depict living and nonliving objects; its shape also contributed to its symbolic value. The optical phenomenon of reflection—the exact duplication in a mirror of objects of the external world—could be interpreted by primitive and ancient man only within the boundaries of religious concepts, and first and foremost within a system of animistic beliefs. For example, the mirror was thought to depict a person's spiritual double—his soul, which existed separately from him. An encounter with this double could have positive, neutral, or negative consequences. Or it was believed that if a person looked into a mirror his soul, which existed within him and was vitally essential to him, would be torn from him and would disappear through the mirror; this would have negative or fatal consequences for the person. Thus, the Andamanese believed that their soul was reflected in the mirror; the same belief was held by the Papuans of New Guinea and the inhabitants of New Caledonia. Among the Melanesians, *atai*, the term for "soul," also means "a reflection."

In Judaism, the image in the mirror was viewed as a symbol of the essence of the original. For the ancient Hindus, a reflection in the water or in a mirror was the soul of a man (*Śaṅkhāyana Āraṇyaka* 6.2, 8.7; *Aitareya Āraṇyaka* 3.2.4). They also thought that in order for the serpent of heaven to see itself, it was necessary to make a serpent on earth look at itself in a mirror.

It was probably Plato who first expressed the idea of an analogy between painting and the reflection in a mirror. The problem of the relation between an object and its reflection was of great importance in Indian religious and philosophical thought. The author of the *Milindapañha* (Questions of King Milinda), written around the turn of the common era, wrote: "Suppose, sire, there were no mirror, no light, and no face—could an image be produced? Oh no, revered sir. But if, sire, there were a mirror, light, and a face—could an image be produced? Yes, revered sir, it could be produced."

Taboos and dangers associated with mirrors. Among many peoples it was forbidden to see one's reflection in certain lakes, rivers, and pools. The ancient Indian *Laws of Manu* contains the following injunction: "Let him not look at his own image in water." Analogous beliefs also existed among the ancient Greeks, who thought that dreaming of one's own reflection foretold death; English folk verses express the same idea. Here too is the basis of the classical myth of Narcissus, the beautiful Greek youth who fell in love with his own reflection in a pool of water and pined away.

Such beliefs are part of a wider class of beliefs connected with man and his shadow, which has the likeness of a man and which in sunlight unfailingly accompanies man, inseparable from him. The loss of a person's shadow-soul led to his death. Corpses, the ancient Greeks thought, had no shadows; for this reason sacrifices to them were made at midday, when shadows were minimal. The recurrent motif of the lost shadow-soul (used in modern times in a tale by E. T. A. Hoffmann) makes it clear why among the Russians, Tajiks, and many other peoples a broken mirror is a clear portent of misfortune, usually of death: the broken reflection of the soul means its disappearance.

Mirrors and death customs. Among many peoples, after a death occurs all the mirrors in the house are turned to the wall or covered with fabric: it is feared that the soul of the deceased, imprinted in the mirrors, will be carried off by evil spirits, who are particularly active when there is a corpse in the house. In some parts of Europe, especially in Germany, traditional belief held that a person who saw himself in a mirror after the death of one close to him would himself die. The Muslims of Bombay are forbidden to look into a mirror if there is a sick person in the house.

Among other peoples a specially broken mirror, or a fragment of a mirror, is placed in a grave during burial rites. To those who broke or destroyed burial objects, such destruction was equivalent to the death of these objects. The "soul" (or, more correctly, the "shade") of a thing was thus able to follow the person's soul to the other world. In this way, according to the beliefs of the Khakass, "the man has died, his body will rot, but his soul will live in the land of the dead. Even things must be killed, so that their souls will emerge from them and follow the man's soul into the land of the dead." In the ancient burial sites of the Sarmatian tribes and the inhabitants of Ferghana and southern Siberia, deliberately broken mirrors have been found where other burial objects have been recovered whole. Broken objects placed in graves were specifically mirrors, and not any other things, for the soul of the dead person was embodied in the mirror, and the breaking of the mirror symbolically reflected the death of the person.

The symbolic value of a broken mirror extends to another group of beliefs concerning the threat a dying person can pose for living souls. Various magical means have been undertaken to dispose the spirits of the dead favorably toward oneself, to make them remain in the grave and not emerge from it, or at least to keep them from appearing among the living. In Inner Asia the numerous rites of this type include the breaking of a mirror (that is, the soul of a person) as a precaution against the soul of the dead person appearing among the living.

Mirrors and the bond between souls. The mirror has not been considered an inseparable incarnation of the soul everywhere, nor has the fragmenting of a mirror always been thought to lead without fail to the death of its possessor. In an ancient Chinese legend, for example, a loving husband and wife once had to part. They broke a mirror and each took a half as a pledge of fidelity. When, after a time, the wife deceived her husband, her part of the mirror turned into a magpie, which flew to the husband and told him of his wife's adultery. But not only husbands and wives broke mirrors; lovers and relatives did so on parting as well. This practice was evidently based on a concept of the fusion of the souls of husband and wife, relatives, and other close persons—an idea of their possessing, together with their individual souls, a common soul, which was embodied in the mirror belonging to them as a pair or as a group.

Positive Powers Associated with Mirrors. Over the course of time, beliefs connected with the mirror multiplied and became complex, and both positive and negative associations with mirrors were formed. The round shape and the gleam of the mirror, and its reflection of the sun's rays, gave rise to a belief in its connection with the sun; at the same time, the mirror was sometimes regarded as a source of water and of the feminine principle. In ancient Japan a bronze mirror was revered as an image of the sun and as an embodiment of Amaterasu Ōmikami, the supreme deity, whose name means "great goddess shining in heaven." In Lettish folklore there is a saying that "when the sun rises it shines like a mirror." In Tajik folklore, the mirror is associated with water: a stream of water originates from it, and whenever a hero casts down a mirror, at that place lakes, rivers, and ponds are formed. In Demeter's sanctuary at Patrae there was a sacred spring. A mirror was tied to a string, dipped in the water, and then examined: it showed whether a sick person would live or would die.

Fertility. The association of the mirror with the feminine principle and with the cult of fertility has been widespread. The Chinese have a belief that the mirror attracts the "water of life," and the mirror is thought to have been associated with the feminine deity. In China women hang mirrors on their beds. Among the Tibetans the mirror has functioned as an antipode to the phallic meaning of the arrow; the mirror has been a symbol of the female sex, and like it has been called *gsang-bai gnas* ("secret place"). In ancient Greece the mirror was an attribute of Dionysos; it was held in the hands of male and female dancers during the Dionysian dances. And in Roman times the mirror became an emblem of Bacchus.

On a golden cup from Khasanlu (in what is now Iran) dating from the beginning of the first millennium BCE, there is a depiction of a female deity riding on a lion; in her uplifted left hand is a mirror. The western Asiatic deity Kubaba, the divine protectress of Karkhemysh (in northern Syria), is also depicted on a lion and with a mirror, in a relief dating from around 900 BCE. The transposition of accents in a woman-mirror opposition, a kind of semantic inversion in which the mirror becomes the dominating member, is found in objects of the ninth and eighth centuries BCE from Khurvin and Luristan. Gold medallions from Scythian burial mounds depict a goddess sitting on a chair and holding a mirror in her raised hand; before her stands a young Scythian drinking from a rhyton. These are evidently images of the wedding of the Scythian goddess Tabiti and the Scythian king. In southern Inner Asia, small sculptures dating from the turn of the common era and its early centuries bear witness to the image of a goddess with a mirror. Among the Sarmatians and the Sakas of the Aral Sea region, mirrors accompanied the burial of priestesses. All these manifestations derive from the female divinity whose attribute was a mirror, and who, while mainly a deity of the earth and of fertility, was also directly associated with the cult of the sun. In particular, the mirror was endowed with a magical ability to increase fertility and sexual powers.

It is therefore natural that the mirror has occupied an important place in wedding ceremonies. In ancient India the bridegroom placed a mirror in the left hand of his betrothed (*Sāṅkāyana Gṛhyasūtra* 1.12.7), and an earthly wedding thus became a reflection of a heavenly one. In modern India, the bridegroom and the bride look at themselves simultaneously in a mirror or a series of mirrors. Other variants of this ritual use of mirrors exist among the Tajiks, the Iranians, and other peoples; the religious ritual of looking in a mirror strengthens the bond between the bridegroom and the bride. In Inner Asia, the newly married pair are required to enter a new house together with a mirror, which is carried by a woman who has many children. The Muslim mystic Aḥmad al-Ghazālī (d. 1126) compared lovers to mirrors.

Luck and happiness. Connected to this is a mythologem: the mirror as an attribute of happiness and a fortunate fate. Having seen his reflection, the ancient Hindu received good fortune (*Bhāradvāja Gṛhyasūtra* 2.22); in another source, "a long life and good fortune." Similar beliefs existed among the ancient Chinese as well. Because it was thought that the mirror protected one from evil and brought happiness, mirrors were worn on the bosom by persons ranging from the warrior to the bride. In the Han period (206 BCE–220 CE) a mirror was placed on the breast of a corpse; it was believed that this would protect the heart and drive the evil spirit away from the corpse. Inscriptions on Chinese mirrors strengthened the mirror's magic power and gave it a single focus. The wishes most commonly expressed in such inscriptions are for wealth, influence, health, longevity, and many descendants.

Cosmogonic and divine nature of mirrors. The mirror has had a cosmogonic meaning in a number of traditions. In Muslim mysticism the created world is a mirror whose face may be compared to heaven and whose back is analogous to the earth. This image, used by the Ṣūfī poet and mystic Jalāl al-Dīn Rūmī (1207–1273), also evokes the divine nature of the mirror or, indeed, of the reflection in it. Rūmī also wrote that divine wisdom is reflected in the mirror, and that he who is devout to the highest degree can attain this wisdom directly from the mirror, bypassing books and preceptors. In Sufism the shaykh (a spiritual leader) is regarded as a mirror reflecting God's spiritual light. The mirror is also linked with the human heart. God looks into the human heart, and he whose heart is righteous is provided with a mirror, which reflects the six sides of the world; therefore God can see this world by looking into a person's heart. The mirror shows each person his own true appearance. But death, like the mirror, shows whether the dead person's deeds during his life were pious or demonic, and in this way death is like a mirror. These complex relations between God, man, and the mirror are reflected in the words of the Muslim mystic Ibn al-ʿArabī (d. 1240): "God becomes the mirror in which the spiritual man contemplates his own reality, and man in turn becomes the mirror in which God contemplates his names and qualities."

Mirrors and shamanism. A vast range of beliefs and rituals connect the mirror with shamanism. The mirror enables the shamans to see and drive away spirits, and to look into the future. Buriat shamans explain that mirrors came down from heaven as gifts from the heavenly beings, and mirrors and their fragments have been used by shamans as a means for healing. The ceremonial garb of the Mongolian shaman includes hanging mirrors, generally nine in number. They have been called "the blue bees of heaven" and "the mount of the shamans," for the white steed of the shamans is said to dwell in a mirror.

One shamanic use of mirrors has been the warding off of evil spirits and evil power. Sculpted human figures with mirrors in their hands were placed near the stone tombs of the Liao dynasty (the northern adversaries of China in the tenth and eleventh centuries), apparently to ward off spirits that might disturb the peace of the dead. Similar figures are depicted in a painting found in one of the tombs. It also seems clear that such beliefs existed among the Kidan' people, who were ruled by this dynasty. Finally, the shamans' mirrors reflected not only what was outer but also what was inner, including people's secret thoughts. The shamans' omniscience stemmed from the power of their mirrors.

Magic mirrors. The concept of magic mirrors has been widespread among the most varied peoples. Tales of clairvoyant mirrors are known in several variants: mirrors foretelling the future, mirrors showing far-off places and objects, mirrors answering questions, mirrors helping to find treasures, and so on. Magic mirrors may also be a cause of blindness, and there are mirrors that make objects invisible, mirrors that kill enemies, mirrors that grant wishes, and even mirrors that restore youth to those looking in them. Some mirrors, functioning as bad omens, turn black and became turbid. Many stories of magic mirrors recount the awakening of love by means of a reflection in a mirror. All these functions of magic mirrors are based on the religious associations discussed above.

Metaphoric Uses of Mirrors. The term *mirror* is widely used in all languages in a metaphoric sense. A Buddhist work speaks of the "way of truth, called the mirror of truth." Shakespeare often uses the word in the sense of a true description: "mirror of all Christian kings." In Russian literature the mirror is the expression of what is within, an idea also reflected in the popular saying "The eyes are the mirror of the soul." This echoes the Latin maxim "Speech is a mirror of the soul: as a man speaks, so he is." In the words of the Persian poet Rūmī, one may "see the face of faith in the mirror of actions."

BIBLIOGRAPHY

There is no scholarly monograph on the religious concepts associated with the mirror. For the most detailed examination of the origin of beliefs concerning the mirror, see James G. Frazer's *Taboo and the Perils of the Soul,* vol. 3 of *The Golden Bough,* 3d ed., rev. & enl. (London, 1911). Much later material, particularly about iconographic elements, can be found in G. F. Hartlaub's *Zauber des Spiegels: Geschichte und Bedeutung des Spiegels in der Kunst* (Munich, 1951). For further information on this topic, see R. W. Swallow's *Ancient Chinese Bronze Mirrors* (Peiping, 1937); Wolfgang Züchner's *Griechische Klappspiegel* (Berlin, 1942); my own work *Orudiia truda i utvar' iz mogil'nikov Zapadnoi Fergany* (Moscow, 1978); Annemarie Schimmel's *The Triumphal Sun: A Study of the Works of Jalāloddin Rumi* (London, 1978); Alex Wayman's "Notes on Mirror Words and Entities in the Area of India," *Ural-Altaische Jahrbücher* 47 (1975): 204–206; and his "The Mirror as a Pan-Buddhist Metaphor-Simile," *History of Religions* 13 (1974): 251–269.

B. A. Litvinskii
Translated from Russian by Sylvia Juran

MISHNAH AND TOSEFTA. The Mishnah is a law code and school book, containing the legal and theological system of Judaism. It was brought to closure about 200 CE under the auspices of the head of the Jewish community of the Holy Land at that time, Yehudah ha-Nasi', and has remained the foundation stone of Judaism from that time to the present. The Tosefta is a collection of supplements to the Mishnah, with approximately three-fourths devoted merely to citation and amplification of the contents of the Mishnah. The other fourth of the whole is constituted by laws essentially autonomous of, but correlative to, the Mishnah's laws. The Tosefta has no independent standing, being organized around the Mishnah. Tosefta was formulated and gathered together some time in the centuries following the closure of the Mishnah, with the fifth century being a safe guess for the time of closure. These two documents together are extensively cited and analyzed in the two Talmuds, one produced in Babylonia about 500 CE, the other in the Land of Israel about 400 CE.

The Mishnah (with the Tosefta) is important in Judaism because it is represented, from the time of its closure onward, as part of "the one whole Torah of Moses, our rabbi," that is, as revealed to Moses at Sinai by God. The Mishnah and all of the documents flowing from it later on, beginning with the Tosefta and the two Talmuds, thus form an integral part of the canon of Torah, that is, of Judaism. The Torah myth distinguishes two Torahs of Sinai. One is in written form, the other, oral. This oral Torah, encompassing the Mishnah and its continuators and successors, was revealed alongside the written Torah. But it was transmitted in a different way. While, as its name indicates, the one was written down, the other was formulated for memorization, and it was then transmitted in this easily memorized form.

Viewed structurally, the two Torahs of Judaism may be compared to the conception of an old and a new testament in Christianity, thus:

$$\frac{\text{Old Testament}}{\text{New Testament}} = \frac{\text{Written Torah (Hebrew scriptures)}}{\text{Oral Torah (Mishnah and its continuators)}}$$

The top line on both sides speaks of the same holy book, but with the words particular to Christianity and Judaism, respectively. That is to say, the biblical books that Christians know as the "Old Testament," Judaism knows as the "written Torah." The Mishnah is the first and principal expression of this other Torah, the oral Torah revealed to Moses at Sinai. It thus is as important to Judaism as the New Testament is to Christianity.

Contents. Six divisions, or orders, comprise the Mishnah's system: Zera'im (Seeds, or Agriculture), Mo'ed (Appointed Times), Nashim (Women), Neziqin (Damages, i.e., civil law), Qodashim (Holy Things, i.e., cultic law), and Ṭohorot (Purities, i.e., cultic taboos). Each division is divided into tractates, and each tractate into chapters and paragraphs. There are, in all, 63 tractates, divided into some 531 chapters.

The critical issue in economic life (i.e., in farming) is treated in the Mishnah's first division, Agriculture, or Seeds. This is in two parts. First, Israel, as tenant on God's holy land, maintains the property in the ways God requires, keeping the rules that mark the land and its crops as holy. Next, the hour at which the sanctification of the land comes to form a critical mass, namely, in the ripened crops, is the moment ponderous with danger and heightened holiness. Israel's will so affects the crops as to mark a part of them as holy, the rest of them as available for common use. The human will is determinative in the process of sanctification.

In the second division, Appointed Times, what happens in the Land of Israel at certain special times, especially in the lunar year, marks off areas of the land as holy in yet another way. The center of the Land of Israel and the focus of its sanctification is the Temple. There the produce of the land is received and given back to God, the one who created and sanctified the Holy Land. At these unusual moments of sanctification, the inhabitants of the Holy Land in their social being in villages enter a state of spatial sanctification. That is to say, the village boundaries mark off holy space, within which one must remain during the holy time. This is expressed in two ways. First, the Temple itself observes and expresses the special, recurring holy time. Second, the villages of the Holy Land are brought into alignment with the Temple, forming a complement and completion to the Temple's sacred being. The advent of the appointed times precipitates a spatial reordering of the land, so that the boundaries of the sacred are matched and mirrored in village and in Temple. At the heightened holiness marked by these appointed times, therefore, the occasion for an affective sanctification is worked out. Like the harvest, the advent of an appointed time, a pilgrim festival, also a sacred season, is made to express that regular, orderly, and predictable sort of sanctification for Israel that the system as a whole seeks.

If for the moment we now leap over the next two divisions, the third and fourth, we come to the counterpart of the divisions of Agriculture and Appointed Times. These are the fifth and sixth divisions, Holy Things and Purities. They deal with the everyday and the ordinary, as against the special moments of harvest, on the one side, and special time or season, on the other.

The fifth division, Holy Things, is about the Temple on ordinary days (i.e., not during appointed times). The Temple, the locus of sanctification, is conducted in a wholly routine and trustworthy, punctilious manner. The one thing that may unsettle matters is the intention and will of the human actor. This actor, the priest, is subjected to carefully prescribed limitations and remedies.

The division of Holy Things generates its companion, the sixth division, Purities, the one on cultic cleanness. In the sixth division, once we speak of the one place of the Temple, we address, too, the cleanness that pertains to every place. A system of cleanness, taking into account what imparts uncleanness and how this is done, what is subject to uncleanness, and how that state is overcome—that system is fully expressed in response to the participation of the human will. Without the wish and act of a human being, the system does not function. It is inert. Sources of uncleanness, which come naturally and not by volition, and modes of purification, which work naturally, and not by human intervention, remain inert until human will has imparted susceptibility to uncleanness, until, that is, human will introduces into the system some object of uncleanness—food and drink, bed, pot, chair, or pan—that becomes subject to contamination. The movement from sanctification to uncleanness takes place when human will and work initiate it.

This now brings us back to the middle divisions, the third and fourth, Women and Damages, respectively. They take their place in the structure of the whole by showing the congruence, within the larger framework of regularity and order, of human concerns of family and farm, politics and workaday transactions among ordinary people. For without attending to these matters, the Mishnah's system does not encompass what, at its foundations, it is meant to comprehend and order: Israel's whole life. So what is at issue is fully cogent with the rest.

In Women, the third division, attention focuses upon the point of disorder marked by the transfer of that disordering anomaly, woman, from the regular status provided by one man to the equally trustworthy status provided by another. That is the point at which the Mishnah's interests are aroused: once more, predictably, the moment of disorder.

In Damages, the fourth division, are two important concerns. First, there is the paramount interest in preventing the disorderly rise of one person and fall of another, in sustaining the status quo of the economy, of the house and household, of Israel, the holy society in eternal stasis. Second, there is the necessary concomitant in the provision of a system of political institutions to carry out the laws that preserve the balance and steady state of persons.

The third and fourth divisions take up topics of concrete and material concern, the formation and dissolution of families and the transfer of property in that connection, the transactions, both through torts and through commerce, that lead to exchanges of property and the potential dislocation of the state of families in society. They deal with the concrete locations in which people make their lives, household and street and field, the sexual and commercial exchanges of a given village.

So the six components of the Mishnah's system insist upon two things: first, stability, second, order. They define as a problem something out of line, therefore dangerous. Laws for a woman must be made, in particular, when she changes hands, moving from father to husband, or, in divorce, from husband to father. Laws for the governance of civil transactions must make certain that all transactions produce equal and opposite results. No one emerges larger than when he entered; none is diminished. Equal value must be exchanged, or a transaction is null. The advent of sacred time, as we shall see, not only imposes the opposite of the Temple's rules upon the village. The holy day also has the effect of linking the Israelite to one place, a particular place, his or her village. So for a moment sacred time establishes a tableau and creates a diorama, a still place of perfection in a silent and perfected moment.

Context. The Mishnah came into being during the first and second centuries of the common era. The document contains ideas likely to have circulated even before the destruction of the Temple in 70 CE, among people whose traditions were carried forward and ultimately written down in the Mishnah itself. But the structure of the system presented by the Mishnah is well attested only after the Bar Kokhba War (c. 132–135). It is attributed principally to authorities who flourished in the middle of the second century. Accordingly, using antecedent ideas and laws, the document came into being at the end of two wars—the first war against Rome (66–73), culminating in the destruction of the Temple, and the second, Bar Kokhba's. Since the Mishnah emerges after a time of wars, the one thing we should expect to find is a message about the meaning of history, an account of events and their meaning. Central to the Mishnah's system might well be a picture of the course of Israel's destiny, in the tradition of the biblical histories—*Samuel, Kings,* or *Chronicles,* for instance—and in the tradition of the prophets of ancient Israel, the several Isaiahs, Jeremiah, and the rest.

The Mishnah's principal point of insistence is the opposite. It speaks of what is permanent and enduring: the flow of time through the solar seasons, marked by lunar festivals and Sabbaths; the procedures of the cult through the regular and enduring sacrifices; the conduct of the civil society through norms of fairness to prevent unjust change; the pursuit of agricultural work in accord with the rules of holiness; the enduring, unchanging, invisible phobias of cultic uncleanness and cleannesss. The Mishnah has no division devoted to the interpretation of history. There is no pretence even at telling what had just happened. There is scarcely a line to address the issue of the meaning of the disasters of the day.

The Mishnah does not address one-time events of history. Its laws express recurrent patterns, eternal patterns as enduring as the movement of the moon and sun around the earth (as people then understood it) and as regular as the lapping of the waves on the beach. These are laws on plowing, planting, harvesting; birth, marriage, procreation, death; home, family, household; work, rest; sunrise, sunset—private lives, not the stuff of history. The laws speak of the here and now, not of state or of tradition, past or future. Since, in the time in which the ideas of the Mishnah took shape, most other Jews expressed a keen interest in history, the contrast cannot be missed. The Mishnah imagines a world of regularity and order in the aftermath of the end of ancient certainties and patterns. It designs laws after the old rules all were broken. It speaks of an eternal present—generally using the continuous present tense and describing how things are—to people beyond all touch with their own past, its life and institutions.

Since, as we know, in the aftermath of the war against Rome in 132–135, the Temple was declared permanently prohibited to Jews, and Jerusalem was closed off to them as well, the Mishnah's laws in part speak of nowhere and not now. Why not? There was no cult, no Temple, no holy city, to which at this time the description of the Mishnaic laws applied. Much of the Mishnah deals with matters to which the sages had no material access. They had no practical knowledge at the time of their work on cultic law. They themselves were not members of the priestly caste. Yet we have seen that the Mishnah contains a division on the conduct of the cult, namely, the fifth, as well as one on the conduct of matters so as to preserve the cultic purity of the sacrificial system along the lines laid out in the *Book of Leviticus*, the sixth division.

There is a further point of unreality. Many of the tractates of the first division, on agriculture, deal with the rations provided for the priests by the Israelite farmers out of the produce of the holy land. The interests of the division overall flow from the Levitical taboos on land use and disposition of crops; the whole is an exercise of most acute interest to the priests.

Furthermore, a fair part of the second division, on appointed times, takes up the conduct of the cult on special days, the sacrifices offered on Yom Kippur, Passover, and the like. Indeed, what the Mishnah wants to know *about* appointed seasons concerns the cult far more than it does the synagogue, which plays a subordinate and trivial role.

The fourth division, on civil law, for its part, presents an elaborate account of a political structure and system of Israelite self-government based on Temple, priesthood, and monarchy, in tractates *Sanhedrin* and *Makkot*, not to mention *Shavu'ot* and *Horayot*. This system speaks of king, priest, Temple, and court. Not the Jews, kings, priests, and judges but the Romans conducted the government of Israel in the Land of Israel in the time in which the second-century authorities did their work.

Well over half of the document—the first division, the second, part of the fourth, all of the fifth, and most of the sixth—speaks of cult, Temple, government, priesthood. But these things did not yet exist. They derived, moreover, from other groups in Israelite society. The Mishnah takes up a profoundly priestly and Levitical conception of sanctification as the principal statement on Israel's condition. Sages had no control of these matters. Furthermore, in the very time the document was written, the Temple lay in ruins, the city of Jerusalem was prohibited to all Israelites, and the Jewish government and administration, which had centered on the Temple and based its authority on the holy life lived there, were in ruins. So the Mishnah's sages could not report any facts they had observed on their own. Much of the Mishnah speaks of matters not current at the time it was created because the Mishnah's sages wished to make a statement on what really matters: the holiness of Israel as they defined it.

Later Developments. From what has been said, we should never be able to account for the persistence of the Mishnah as half of the whole "Torah" of Judaism. The bulk of the document was irrelevant to its own time, all the more so to the ages that would follow. The two Talmuds, indeed, pick and choose what they want from the Mishnah, and, in so doing, revise the system of the whole. The Talmud of the Land of Israel, for example, provides elaboration and commentary for only thirty-nine of the Mishnah's sixty-two tractates, omitting reference to the fifth and nearly the whole of the sixth division. The Babylonian Talmud, for its part, treats the fifth division but ignores nearly all of the first. What both Talmuds do in common is ignore the system and structure of the whole and divide the Mishnah into tiny bits and pieces. These were then subjected to close and thorough analysis. The upshot is that the two Talmuds took up the whole. By continuing what Yehudah ha-Nasi' had treated as concluded, they carried forward the unending process of revelation and canon. That is to say, the heirs of the Mishnah revered the document but also took responsibility for interpreting it. In the very process of their quite accurate and careful reading, they in fact accomplished a considerable reformation of the Mishnah itself.

[*See also* Tannaim *and* Talmud.]

BIBLIOGRAPHY

Tosefta. The best edition is Saul Lieberman's *Tosefta,* 3 vols. (New York, 1955–1967), including *Zera'im* (1955), *Mo'ed* (1962), and *Nashim* (1967), together with a monumental commentary by the same scholar. For the other three divisions, M. S. Zuckermandel's *Tosefta'* (1881) is available. I have made an English translation of the second through the sixth divisions in *The Tosefta, Translated from the Hebrew,* vols. 2–6 (New York, 1977–1981), and an English translation of the first division, under the editorship of Richard S. Sarason, is scheduled to appear. A brief scholarly account is Moshe David Heer's "Tosefta," in *Encyclopaedia Judaica,* vol. 15 (Jerusalem, 1971).

Mishnah. The best available edition, including a commentary, is Chanoch Albeck's *Shishah Sidrei Mishnah* (Tel Aviv, 1952ff.). No critical edition exists. Herbert Danby has made a one-volume translation in *The Mishnah* (London, 1933), and I have made a complete translation and commentary on the second through the sixth divisions of the Mishnah and Tosefta in *A History of the Mishnaic Law* (Leiden, 1974–); included in the latter work are *Appointed Times,* 5 vols. (1981ff.), *Women,* 5 vols. (1980), *Damages,* 5 vols. (1983–1984), *Holy Things,* 6 vols. (1979–1980), and *Purities,* 22 vols. (1974–1977). An account of how the Mishnah has been studied in classical and modern times is given in my edition of *The Modern Study of the Mishnah* (Leiden, 1973), and the religious world view of the Mishnah is described and interpreted in my book *Judaism: The Evidence of the Mishnah* (Chicago, 1981). A brief introduction, presenting a quite different approach, is E. E. Urbach's "Mishnah," in *Encyclopaedia Judaica,* vol. 12 (Jerusalem, 1971).

JACOB NEUSNER

MISSIONS. [*This entry consists of three articles dealing with missions undertaken by religious organizations:*

Missionary Activity
Buddhist Missions
Christian Missions

The first is a general account; the companion pieces focus on two religious traditions in which missionizing has been of particular importance. For discussion of Muslim missionary activity, see Da'wāh. *For a directly related discussion from a cross-cultural view, see* Conversion.]

Missionary Activity

Many records and some suggestive studies of the foundations, motivations, dynamics, techniques, and sociocultural effects of missionary activity in specific locales exist. Most of them are written from the perspective of the missionaries. Certain encounters of major religious orientations in various parts of the world have also been documented, but few systematic, cross-cultural, and comparative studies of missions and missionary activities have yet been produced.

There is no lack of material dealing with the dissemination of and conversion to a specific religion from the standpoint of that religion's advocates, nor of the theological warrants or mandates given by a particular faith for its propagation. Cultural historians and social scientists have also studied the effects of religious change in specific periods, and psychologists have attempted to identify the psychodynamics of conversion. Still, systematic overviews of organized proselytism and the common ideational, social, and institutional foundations on which it rests are sparse. (See Rambo, 1982.)

In the nineteenth century, to be sure, certain evolutionary theories of the development of "high" cultures offered rather triumphalist accounts of the spread of "ethical religions" over territories previously governed by animistic or polytheistic faiths. In the early twentieth century, certain theories of religio-cultural "diffusion" attempted to comprehend world historical development in ways that would also account for the spread of religions by analogy with the spread of artifacts such as the plow or the clock. More recently, theories of political-economic and cultural imperialism have gained considerable prominence as a framework for interpreting missionary activity, a fact that will require comment here. None of these efforts, however, has resulted in a compelling account of the nature, character, and dynamics of missionary activities that bear cross-cultural scrutiny. (See Sharpe, 1975.)

Foundations and Motivations. Nonetheless, it is possible to venture some generalizations about missionary activity that seem relevant for all the great missionizing religions. The first point is that missionizing religions are religions that, impelled by a unique revelation or a great discovery about the nature of being, or a momentous social transformation and revitalization of purpose sparked by spiritual impulses, have generated a salvific metaphysical-moral vision that they believe to be of universal import for humanity. This vision induces a passion for transcendence that intellectually, morally, and emotionally frees its adherents from local deities and cults, from familial, tribal, clan, caste, or ethnic loyalties, from fixed political-economic conditions, and from traditional "paganisms." The missionary impulse is to become "homeless," for it finds its true home in a transcendent realm that relativizes all that is understood to be "natural." It further evokes a desire to bring about the universal acceptance and application of the vision, which it holds to be universally true in principle.

Every missionizing religion, thus, is by definition transcultural; where it is not entirely transmundane, it is cosmopolitan. It endows its advocates with a transcendental, ecumenical, cross-cultural, and global perspective, which understands humanity as trapped in chaotic conditions of spiritual and/or physical oppression from which humanity must be delivered by accepting a new foundation of meaning and a new discipline, one that liberates from evil and falsehood and binds to good and truth.

A missionary is one who seizes or is seized by a universalistic vision and who feels a mandate, a commission, a vocation to bring the vision and its benefits to "all." Thus, missionary activity, both domestic and foreign, is most intense in those moments when the metaphysical-moral vision of a religion is engendered or revitalized and held to be pertinent to new conditions. "Home" missions often take the form of new programs for youth, "purification" of religious and cultural practice, proselytism of marginal groups, protest against lax practices among the social elite (including the established clergy), and, often, moral or spiritual attempts to put domestic social, political, and economic policies on a new foundation. "Foreign" missions attempt to take the vision beyond the land of origin and thereby to lay the foundations for a new spiritual world order by transforming the souls and minds of individuals and the social habits of their society. Missionary activity always to some degree alienates its converts from previous belief and practice, for it introduces a different way of organizing faith and life. Both domestic and foreign missionary activity is marked by intense intellectual activity, for the whole of reality has to be reconsidered from the new perspective.

One or another universalistic vision has provided the foundations and motivations for Buddhism, Christianity, Islam, and that new secular civil religion, communism, to name but four of the most obvious missionizing religions. Certain strands and periods of Judaism, Zoroastrianism, and "syncretistic" religions such as Bahā'ī, Sikhism, and the Unification Church (Moonies) have a similar dynamic. A universalistic metaphysical-moral vision is less pronounced, however, in the beliefs of the tribal religions and Shintō, and less overt in many strands of Confucianism, Judaism, and Zoroastrianism. However great their spiritual, moral, and intellectual achievements, these latter religions are constitutively tied to specific sociopolitical contexts and, often, to ethnic particularities. These religions may also claim to possess a universalistic message; they may welcome converts, and their metaphysical-moral visions may be espoused by other religions; but they are spread more by the migrations of peoples or by the gradual incorporation of immediate neighbors than by organized missionary activities. Hinduism represents a special and exceedingly complex case, for while it is similar to nonmissionizing traditions in many respects, and while it seems to have spread essentially by a process called sanskritization—the gradual adoption of Vedic practices and brahmanic authority by non-Aryan peoples on the Indian subcontinent (see Srinivas, [1952] 1978)—it has had periods of vigorous missionary activity. Indeed, today, active missions are being carried out by "evangelical" forms of Hinduism such as the Ramakrishna Mission, ISKCON (Hare Krishna), and the Transcendental Meditation movement of Maharishi Mahesh Yogi.

This is not to say that when missionizing religions expand they cease to have cultural, political, ethnic, or economic content and become purely transcendental: that is seldom the case. Rather, the missionizing religions believe that they have a message based on a salvific metaphysical-moral vision, which is in some fundamental respects separable from accidental sociohistorical trappings. This is true even if the bearers of the message believe that at its core are implications for social and cultural patterns that ought also to be spread for the salvation of humanity. Those living religions claiming the most universalistic visions and evidencing the most extensive missionary zeal beyond the place of origin—Buddhism, Christianity, Islam, and communism—have never been able to extricate themselves fully from localistic elements.

Some Dynamics of Missionary Activity. As a population is missionized, new patterns of educational, familial, cultural, and political-economic conditions are routinized into a transformed "tradition" on new foundations. The tendency to identify the universalistic message with the newly established local or regional patterns of life within particular groups is widespread. The vision "for all" once again becomes "our" vision, "for us," until such time as a new burst of piety and learning renews the awareness of the universalistic vision and revitalizes missionary efforts, demanding a purging of false tendencies to syncretism. Missionary religions are continually or episodically engaged in religious renewal and reformation from within. The great missionizing religions are in part to be contrasted with the occasionally proselytizing, primal, and localistic religions precisely by the enduring and recurring vitality of their universalizing, in contrast to the particularizing and syncretizing tendencies of the localistic religions. It is not surprising that missionary religions are those with an authoritative scripture and "orthodox" doctrine that serve as the standards for periodic renewal.

The great universalistic teachings of the missionizing

religions are, however, always treasures borne in "earthen vessels," to paraphrase Paul, the model of all Christian missionaries. And the line between the treasure and the vessel is frequently extremely fine. Early Buddhist missionaries, to cite another example, were sent out presumably armed with nothing but the pure and unadulterated message of Gautama's great discovery of the secret of true enlightenment. Wittingly or not, however, they carried with them both the philosophical presuppositions of Indian religious thought, which were the terms in which and through which the Buddha found his truth, and the political, social, and cultural patterns of Indian society. Theravāda Buddhism, as it missionized in Sri Lanka, Burma, and Thailand, brought with it sociopolitical principles that derived from Hindu traditions and which, in part, the Buddha sought to overcome and transcend. (See Smith, 1978.) In Mahāyāna Buddhism as well, careful scholars can speak of the "Indianization of China." (See Hu, 1937.)

Later, when this stream of Buddhism became wedded to motifs from Confucian and Taoist sources, its movement into Korea and Japan carried powerful elements from these traditions with it. And it is well known that both Christianity and Islam carried Greco-Roman patterns of thought, medicine, and political theory—as well as Hebraic understandings of ethical monotheism—with them as they expanded in the medieval periods. Islam has also always borne a certain Arabic cultural stamp wherever it goes, and communism today bears everywhere the marks of Germanic philosophy, Enlightenment social theory, Western technological hopes from the days of the industrial revolution, and often something of Soviet nationalism. Along with the Gospel, modern Christian missions transmit Western definitions of human rights and scientific methods in the fields of education, technology, management, and agriculture. (See Stackhouse, 1984.) These cursory examples serve to illustrate the point that while missionary activity must always be understood first of all in terms of the universal metaphysical-moral vision that calls it into being and gives it its transcultural *raison d'être*, it is also always laden with particular philosophical, social, cultural, and political elements.

Missions and Cultural Imperialism. Two factors differentiate missionary expansion from cultural imperialism. First, the truly religious missionary recognizes a distinction between the message and the accoutrements, the universalistic kernel and the incidental husk. However difficult it is to distinguish the two, the primary concern is with the former. Transformation of the latter is allowed in terms of and for the sake of the former. The imperialist understands the message only in terms of its sociocultural trappings in highly particularist ways. Such imperialism obtains when, for example, Buddhism in Burma becomes identical with the prerogatives of the Burman as opposed to those of the Chin, Kachin, or other Burmese peoples; when Christianity becomes German in the Nazi period or Afrikaner in South Africa; when Islam in, for instance, Iran, is understood to be coterminous with the fate of the country itself; or when communism is thought to be identical with "socialism in one country" and allied with a personality cult. These domestic forms of cultural imperialism have had their vicious international corollaries wherever particular social traditions, political expansions, or opportunities for economic exploitation are confused with a universalistic religious message and spread by coercive means among colonialized peoples abroad in the name of religion.

Second, missionary activity is rooted in the fundamental assumptions that, once people are exposed to "the truth" that has been proclaimed, they will choose this truth and that they ought to be free to encounter and choose even "foreign" truth. Missions presuppose that a truly universalistic vision is convincing to the mind and compelling to the will. Missions thus require, or provoke, a situation in which some degree of freedom of thought, speech, and religious organization is allowed, where the will and the mind can be exercised in accordance with conscience and conviction. However much missionary activity has been carried out hand in hand with military power, economic opportunism, "brainwashing," and forced conversion, there has been and remains in principle a sharp tension between missionary efforts and imperialistic imposition of religion by force, or "mind-control," a fact increasingly documented by missiologists examining the relative validity of the charge that missions are but the ideological instrument of colonial practice. Those incapable of imagining the transformation of values, attitudes, and habits in conversion to a new truth, however, always attribute the change to nefarious forces.

It is certainly true that every missionizing religion has had periods during which something like the classic Islamic pattern could be documented: H. A. R. Gibb writes of Islam that "while the faith itself was not spread by the sword, it was under the wing of Muslim dominance that its missionaries found most favorable conditions for their activities of conversion. This view of Islam . . . was universally held by its adherents; the theologians found justification for it in the Koran, the jurists made it the basis of their expositions of Muslim law, and the mass of the people accepted it as a self-evident fact" (Gibb, 1932, p. 56; cf. Bulliet, 1979). Comparable views could be cited regarding periods of Buddhist expansion at the hands of pious war lords,

Christian missions in Latin America, or communist movements in Eastern Europe. Nevertheless, the Qur'ān and the authoritative teachings of every other missionizing religion agree that forced conversion is false and that truly universal religion must depend on the freely convinced mind and heart of the convert. Thus, wherever missions go and do not immediately preclude other missionary efforts by force, they open up new vistas for heart, mind, and social practice to which people are invited to turn. (See Song, 1982; Macy, 1983.)

Reactions of Missionized People. Every missionary religion must be received as well as proclaimed. Where it is not received, missionary activity dies out, and doubt about the universality of the originating vision sets in. Where it is received under coercion, and not in the heart, mind, or customs of the people, the indigenous religion goes underground, eventually resurfacing as a revitalized indigenous religion and rallying point to overthrow those who hold power or as a heterodox or heretical religion in contention with the one brought by missions. Where the missionary religion is received in the heart and mind, newly converted people soon send out their own missionaries. But it is almost never received as given. It is filtered through the philosophical, sociopolitical, and historical perspectives of the recipients. Thereby, it is inevitably modified by its reception and, over time, at least partially purged of those missionary-borne incidental elements that can be seen as "merely" cultural or sociopolitical.

One of the most fascinating studies of the reception of a religion is the study by Kenneth Ch'en (1973) of the way in which Buddhism was modified, acculturated, and indigenized in China. A message, such as that exported from Indian Buddhism, that called for the breaking of family ties and demanded that kings give honor to monks simply did not make sense in a culture where filial piety and homage to the emperor were absolutely central to both belief and social order. Ch'en demonstrates that, as one speaks of the "indianization of China" with the spread of Buddhism, one must also speak of the "sinicization of Buddhism." In China key Buddhist texts were given fresh interpretation; apologetic literature, new poems, and new laws and regulations were promulgated that modified and, indeed, transformed aspects of the Buddhist message so that it could graft onto, and in some ways revitalize, dimensions of the indigenous folk religions and of the Confucianism and Taoism of that land. Comparable stories can be told of every missionizing religion: the Christianity of Eastern Orthodoxy in Greece is not the same as that of the Kimbanguists of central Africa; the Islam of Tunisia differs from that of Mindanao in significant ways; Communism in Moscow is distinct from that of "Euro-communism" or that of Marxist-inspired movements in Central America. Today, the degree to which this "contextualization" or indigenization is valid is the subject of heated debate within many of the great world religions.

In this connection, it must be noted that some religions engage in missionary activity precisely as a result of being invited, sought, or adopted with great eagerness. Robin Horton (1975) has shown, for example, that in Africa where traditional systems have been displaced by exploitative cultural contact, war, crop failure, or the failure of a social system to survive its own internal strains, missionary groups bearing universalistic messages are readily embraced, for they offer fresh, symbolic, and cognitive models by which life and its perplexities may be interpreted. Often, the appropriation of a new religion is accompanied by a rational quest for new technological, educational, and sociopolitical frameworks for organizing the common life. Missionaries often agree that such a quest is at the core of their metaphysical-moral vision. Certainly a comparable phenomenon has occurred in quite different locales, as Garrett (1982) has shown in regard to the Pacific Islands, and Downs (1983) has demonstrated concerning the christianization of tribal peoples of Assam in the last century. More ancient examples are the historic reception in the sixth and seventh centuries of Chinese Buddhism into Japan at the hands of the imperial court (along with Confucian ideals of a well-organized society); the reception in the ninth to eleventh centuries of Eastern Orthodox Christianity into Russia, bringing with it Byzantine art, literature, and political theory; and the reception in the twelfth to fifteenth centuries of Islam (as mediated through India) in the Malay archipelago, accompanied by aspects of mysticism and caste-related political order.

In almost no instance, however, is a new religion received without some resistance. This resistance is sometimes easily overcome. When the indigenous faith is a highly literate and complex religion, however, the resistance is usually prolonged and powerful. The fact that Buddhism originated in India and at one time had nearly swept the subcontinent, but now can scarcely be found there, is one of the dramatic examples of this resistance. Hinduism reasserted itself by a ten-century-long process involving the adoption of some aspects of Buddhism (especially the revitalization of devotional practice in *bhakti*), by the bloody slaughter of Buddhist monks, by extensive philosophical argumentation, and by out-organizing and out-teaching Buddhism among the people. Similarly, Confucianism reasserted itself in China during the "neo-Confucian" period of renewal in the ninth century by a similar process—one that relegated the Buddhists to a somewhat inferior status. Islam encountered intellectual and military resistance when it threatened expansion into Europe from the time of Charlemagne through the Crusades, and the Christianity that expanded into western Asia is now weak and scattered because of Islamic resistance. And most Western Jews and Christians today resist the Hindu, Islamic, and Buddhist missions, as well as the host of hybrid or syncretistic cults rooted in these, or in some heterodox Christian faith, that are to be found in most of the major cities of the West today. (See Needleman and Baker, 1978; Barker, 1981.)

One notable feature of the phenomenon of "mission" and "resistance" is the fact that missions that do not succeed among the intellectual and political-economic elites of a new country but that do succeed among the people become fatefully drawn into perennial tensions between the rulers and the ruled. If conversion is successful among the masses, but not among leadership, intense resistance results. If conversion occurs only among marginal groups, ethnic conflict is frequent, and minorities are suspected of being agents of foreigners. If missions are successful among some sections of the leadership and among wide segments of the people, the stage is set for revolutionary change.

Types of Missionaries. In surveying mission and missionary activity, however, one must not only note the primacy of the metaphysical-moral vision—its relationship to social and cultural patterns, its patterns of reception, and resistances to it—one must also consider certain similarities of institutional form that are characteristic of missionary activity. What groups or classes of people undertake missionary activity, and how do they organize to do so?

Missionaries, merchants, and soldiers. The earliest, unofficial missionaries are, more often than not, traders. One does not have to accept the Marxist interpretation of the relationship between commercial exploitation and religion to observe that, indeed, the spreading of a new religious insight repeatedly follows commercial traffic lanes and that this insight is frequently borne by merchants. Further, it must be noted that both commercial and missionary activities can only be conducted in conditions of relative peace and political stability. Such conditions often obtain, and when they do not, soldiers are frequently brought in to establish them, accompanied by new waves of missionaries. Since traders and soldiers vary widely in their behavior, from the simply marauding to the relatively benevolent, missionary activity has often been conducted within a network of shifting alliances, both economic and military, on the far end of trade routes. It is not possible to make any single generalization about these relationships, however, for missionaries have resisted exploitative trade as often as they have endorsed it and have fought imperial military "pacification" as often as they have embraced it. (See, e.g., Christensen and Hutchison, 1982; cf. Reed, 1983.)

The cross-cultural frequency of missionary activity by merchants, however, invites speculation as to why this general class has played so significant a role in missionizing. Perhaps it is because merchants are people who seek increased opportunity by taking the risk of leaving the settled and accepted patterns of life at home. The very act of engaging in trade on a cross-cultural basis, however crass the individual motivation might be, requires a somewhat more cosmopolitan perspective on the world than is frequently present in those societies where religion and morality run in channels circumscribed by fixed economic roles and duties for people of each specific ethnic, gender, age and class status. In addition, those societies that send merchants farthest and equip caravans or ships the most extensively for trade are usually the more highly developed economically, politically, militarily, and socially. It would not be strange for them to hold the view that their "superiority" in this respect is due in substantial part at least to the "superior" religious, spiritual, and ethical foundations of their faith.

Professional missionaries. New religions are seldom, if ever, however, fully developed in a new location by the sometimes quite unholy alliance of missionaries, merchants, and soldiers, or by general processes of cultural diffusion that accompany them. The introduction of a religion through commercial channels (the character and quality of which influence reception and/or resistance) has everywhere been succeeded by the arrival of professional missionaries. For most religions throughout most of history, the professional missionary has been monastic, that is, organized into ascetic, trained, and disciplined religious orders intentionally "homeless" for the sake of the metaphysical-moral vision held to be universally true.

Missionary monks and nuns attempt to spread their religious convictions by public proclamation and commentary on sacred texts at both popular and learned levels; by teaching hymns, chants, and prayers; by establishing new centers of worship where the truth they know can be celebrated; and by service—that is, by medical, educational, pastoral, and social relief and social advocacy. Needless to say, all missionary religions have relied on "wondrous," magical, or technological demonstrations of "spiritual" power from time to time. The stories well known in the West about saintly missionary monks such as Patrick, Columba, Boniface, Ramón Lull, and Francis Xavier are paralleled in the lore of Buddhism, in the formation of the *maṭhas* as a Hindu reaction to the challenge posed by Buddhism, and in the roles played by the "schools" of jurists and even more by the Ṣūfī orders of Islam. (In Eastern Europe, accounts of the "dedicated heroes, martyrs, and organizers" of communist proletarian movements are written for children and young people.)

To carry out their tasks, missionaries have four requirements. First, they must have a dedication, a commitment, a piety, if you will, linked to learning. Missionaries must be able to articulate the faith and to interpret it in intellectual and cultural terms that are foreign to them. They must be able to understand and put into perspective whatever they encounter in the course of their work. It is no accident that several sciences, including modern comparative linguistics and anthropology, to a large extent have their roots in missionary activity. Everywhere, professional missionaries are given to literary activity; they have published apologetics, propaganda, tracts, commentaries, and they are responsible for the composition and dissemination of poetry, song, and history. (See Kopf, 1969.)

Second, missionary professionals require a reliable institutional foundation, a polity, to sustain them. Missionary orders and societies are surely among the world's first transnational, nonprofit corporations. These polities, however, are ever subject to incorporation into the existing polities of the host countries. Thus, the Buddhist *saṃgha,* spread under the protectorate of kings, is ever tempted to become simply an instrument of state. Converted Christian communities in India are always in peril of becoming more a subcaste than a church; and the *ṭarīqahs* of Islam tend to become simply trade guilds or sanctified tribal brotherhoods. (See Trimingham, 1971.)

Economic support may derive from state funds, charitable bequests, the establishment of plantations, handicraft manufacturing centers, agricultural communes, and religious taxes. The economic ties of a missionary enterprise with its country of origin or with the elites of the host country are the source of enormous distrust of missionary activity. (See Reed, 1983.)

And fourth, missionaries must have a clear policy, one that coordinates strategies and tactics and prevents divergent teachings from confusing potential converts. These policies must cover such matters as how much of the indigenous culture to allow and what to disallow, how to deal with marriage practices, "pagan" festivals, various "fraternities" that are marginally stamped with traditional religious practices, and the like.

Modern Practices. Modern missionary efforts have been pursued not so much by monastic orders (although these orders continue to missionize around the world) as by nonmonastic missionary "societies." This situation is prompted primarily by the rather unique developments of "free-church" Protestant polities, economic support systems, and policies. While the established churches in Europe had been sending out monastic missionaries for centuries, and the Moravians anticipated later developments, the formation of the London Missionary Society in 1795 inaugurated a new form of paraecclesial organization that continues to this day and is now being emulated by non-Christian missionaries. Missionary societies, of which there are now hundreds, raise funds by free-will contributions and form nonmonastic "voluntary associations" staffed by a combination of nonparochial clergy, lay professionals, and volunteers, not only to save souls from "paganism" but to sweep away superstition and oppression, to offer agricultural, technical, medical, and educational assistance, and to engender a desire for democratic institutions, human dignity, self-sufficiency, and social liberation. Some modern theorists, indeed, suggest that these efforts at social service and social change are the very core of missionizing. (See Dunn, 1980; Yuzon, 1983.)

A notable example of the side effects of this recent pattern can be illustrated by reference to the Young Men's Christian Association. Formed in England in 1844 as a part of a "home mission" voluntary association for youth flocking to the cities to get jobs in factories, and attempting to provide a wholesome place where young men could find physical, mental, social, and spiritual benefit on a biblical foundation, the movement spread to North America and to most of the countries around the world where missions were active. It was often the agent of evangelization and the womb of efforts at social change by young men who came under its influence. Other religions responded by forming counterorganizations on a comparable basis. Today, one can find not only the YMCA but the Young Men's Buddhist Association, the Young Men's Hebrew Association, and the Young Men's Muslim Association, as well as youth hostels for Hindus and for communists, scattered throughout much of Asia; some also are to be found in Africa and South America.

Comparable are the "independent" paramissionary efforts with regard to religiously based women's organizations, hospitals, orphanages, institutions for the handicapped, schools for children, farmers' cooperatives, workers' alliances, peasant "base communities," and urban and industrial missions, phenomena so common and accepted in Protestant-influenced countries that they seem entirely unremarkable. Nevertheless, the proliferation of communities of a "voluntary-associational" type based on religious foundations, as they developed in the wake of the independent missionary societies, and the frequent persecution of these communities by totalitarian governments, is one of the most remarkable and explosive social effects of missionary activity in the last century, one not yet fully documented on a comparative basis. In the dedication and commitment that lie behind these voluntary-associational communities—the dedicated lives, organizational skills, financial and personal sacrifice, concern for others, and devotion to the propagation of the faith—one gains a glimpse of the continued vitality of the missionary spirit.

Today, the great Asian religions are not at their peak in terms of missionary activity, although Buddhist and Islamic groups in Southeast Asia have formed a few missionary centers to repropagate the faith in the People's Republic of China, now that the doors of trade and travel are partially open again. Christianity, Islam, and communism are very active, with the latter two having the closest ties to the spread of political control and Christianity again moving along channels established by international commerce. All continue to make major gains in areas where none of the great missionizing religions has established a sustained foothold, with more modest, but significant, gains among "overseas" peoples of Hindu or Confucian background—the Indians of Malaysia and the Chinese of Indonesia, for example.

Increasingly, the great missionizing religions are confronting not only adherents of primal or folk religions but one another. Thus far, missionary efforts to convert adherents of the other great missionary religions have been only marginally successful. This is in part because severe restrictions on missionary activities by other faiths are frequent in Islamic and communist lands.

Although some theorists have argued that these religions are moving toward a great synthesis of world faiths (an essentially Hindu argument), and while others have attempted to find the common moral and symbolic patterns present in all human religions as the clue to their hidden unity (a humanist argument), the way in which these religions will deal with one another in the future is not at all certain. (See Oxtoby, 1983.) [*See* Religious Pluralism.] None of the great missionary faiths can be satisfied with relativism, the view that what is ultimately true for some is not true for others. The main possibilities are, thus, direct confrontation (with each backed by the political, military, and economic power of the regions where they are predominant), dialogic exchange of perspective in a common quest for transcultural religious truth, and/or openness to redoubled efforts to mutual conversion by allowing free and open debate among the peoples of the world.

Since direct confrontation is perilous in a nuclear age, we can only pray for a social openness to religious freedom and religious missions in all lands. This would, of course, entail not only earnest dialogue but debate and conversion in several directions and the disruption of many closed societies and minds. In that context we might expect a new burst of piety and learning, a fresh perception of the true metaphysical-moral vision to be spread around the world, and a growing awareness of the various cultural accretions not essential to true faith. This choice, however, entails a profound presumption that, in the long run, the truth will prevail, and that a true faith can withstand the test of open competition and examination. Not all are willing to accept the risk of that test and its corollary—that those whose faith fails the test should convert.

BIBLIOGRAPHY

Works on missions and missionary activity within particular traditions are plentiful, but, to my knowledge, no substantive and systematic overview of comparative missiology exists. The works on the following list have been selected to illustrate the range and kinds of materials that would be pertinent to further comparative study in this area.

Barker, Eileen, ed. *Of Gods and Men: New Religious Movements in the West.* Macon, Ga., 1981.

Bulliet, Richard. *Conversion to Islam in the Medieval Period.* Cambridge, Mass., 1979.

Ch'en, Kenneth. *The Chinese Transformation of Buddhism.* Princeton, 1973.

Christensen, Torben, and William R. Hutchison. *Missionary Ideologies in the Imperialist Era.* Århus, Denmark, 1982.

Downs, Frederick S. *Christianity in North East India.* Delhi, 1983.

Dunn, Edmond J. *Missionary Theology: Foundations in Development.* Lanham, Md., 1980.

Forman, Charles W. "A History of Foreign Mission Theory in America." In *American Missions in Bicentennial Perspective,* edited by R. Pierce Beaver, pp. 69–140. Pasadena, Calif., 1977.

Garrett, John. *To Live among the Stars.* Suva, Fiji Islands, 1982.

Gibb, H. A. R. *Whither Islam* (1932). Reprint, London, 1973.

Horton, Robin. "On the Rationality of Conversion." *Africa* 45 (1975): 219–235, 373–399.

Hu Shih. *Independence, Convergence and Borrowing.* Cambridge, Mass., 1937.

Kane, J. Herbert. *A Concise History of the Christian World Mission.* Grand Rapids, Mich., 1978.

Kopf, David. *British Orientalism and the Bengal Renaissance.* Berkeley, 1969.

Latourette, K. S. "Missions." In *Encyclopaedia of the Social Sciences,* edited by E. R. A. Seligman. New York, 1933.

Luzbetak, Louis J. *The Church and Cultures.* Techny, Ill., 1970.

Macy, Joanna. *Dharma and Development.* West Hartford, Conn., 1983.

Needleman, Jacob, and George Baker, eds. *Understanding the New Religions.* New York, 1978.

Oxtoby, Willard G. *The Meaning of Other Faiths.* Philadelphia, 1983.

Rambo, Lewis R. "Current Research on Religious Conversion." *Religious Studies Review* 8 (April 1982): 146–159.

Reed, James. *The Missionary Mind and American East Asia Policy.* Cambridge, Mass., 1983.

Sanneh, Lamin O. *West African Christianity.* Maryknoll, N.Y., 1983.

Sharpe, Eric J. *Comparative Religion: A History.* London, 1975.

Smith, Bardwell, ed. *Religion and Legitimation of Power in Thailand, Laos, and Burma.* Chambersburg, Pa., 1978.

Song, Choan-Seng. *The Compassionate God.* Maryknoll, N.Y., 1982.

Srinivas, M. N. *Religion and Society among the Coorgs of South India* (1952). Reprint, New Delhi, 1978.

Stackhouse, Max L. *Creeds, Societies and Human Rights: A Study in Three Cultures.* Grand Rapids, Mich., 1984.

Trimingham, J. Spencer. *The Sufi Orders in Islam.* London, 1971.

Yuzon, Lourdino A., ed. *Mission in the Context of Endemic Poverty.* Singapore, 1983.

MAX L. STACKHOUSE

Buddhist Missions

According to an ancient tradition, the Buddha himself sent out the first group of disciples to spread the new faith: "Go, monks, preach the noble Doctrine, . . . let not two of you go into the same direction!" This canonical saying illustrates both the missionary ideal that has inspired Buddhism from the earliest times and the way in which it was to be carried out: not by any large-scale planned missionary movement, but rather by the individual efforts of itinerant monks and preachers. And this, in fact, is our general impression of the way in which Buddhism grew from a minor monastic movement in northern India in the fifth century BCE into a world religion covering, at its heyday, a territory that reached from Sri Lanka to Mongolia, and from Iran to Japan. Apart from the missionary ideal and the prescribed inherent mobility of the clergy, its dissemination outside its homeland was no doubt facilitated by three other features of Buddhism. In the first place, the members of the order, "who had gone into the homeless state" and thereby rejected all worldly distinctions, stood outside the caste system. Unlike brahman priests, they were free to associate with people of every description, including foreigners, without fear of ritual pollution. Second, Buddhism, especially Mahāyāna Buddhism, had a liberal attitude toward all religions. Thus it easily accepted non-Buddhist creeds as preliminary and partial revelations of truth, a tendency toward adaptation and syncretism that also appears in its readiness to incorporate non-Buddhist deities into its pantheon. Third, the scriptural tradition of Buddhism—unlike that of Brahmanism—is not associated with any sacred or canonical language, so that its holy texts could freely be translated into any language. In fact, especially in China, the most prominent foreign missionaries were all active as translators, usually with the help of bilingual collaborators.

The Pattern of Diffusion. The general picture of the spread of Buddhism is one of gradual dissemination at grassroots level, inspired by the Buddha's exhortation and carried out by wandering monks who preached "for the benefit of all beings" (an ideal that became even more explicit in Mahāyāna Buddhism) and who established monastic centers in the new territories they entered. As the clergy was wholly dependent on the contributions of lay believers, these monastic settlements (*vihāras*) tended to be established near the larger cities and to branch out along the major highways that connected them. The spread of Buddhism was also closely related to the development of long-distance trade: it was carried all over Asia by monks who attached themselves to trade caravans and merchant vessels. Thus, paradoxically, this eminently missionary religion has never been characterized by large-scale missionary movements comparable to those we find in Christianity or Islam. At times, the devotion and patronage of rulers (the emperor Aśoka in India in the third century BCE, the kings of the Kushan empire in the first and second centuries CE, and several imperial sponsors in medieval China and Japan) no doubt stimulated its propagation, but Buddhism has never been imposed upon large populations by coercion, or spread by force of arms. Rather it was disseminated by countless individuals who carried the message of Buddhism, together with its scriptures, monastic institutions, icons, and rituals, to the most distant parts of Asia. To some extent, it was also carried by the pilgrims and students who came to India to visit the holy places, to collect texts, and to study under Indian masters.

History of Diffusion from India. This pattern of diffusion accounts for the slow pace of the process, for it took Buddhism some twenty centuries to spread over Asia, from its first propagation in the Ganges basin about 400 BCE to its last major conquest, the conversion of the Mongols in the sixteenth century. By the third century BCE it had spread over India and into Sri Lanka. Under the Kushan rulers in the northwest, in the first and second centuries CE, it reached Parthia (modern-day Iran) and the region of Bukhara and Samarkand. About the same time it was propagated via the oasis kingdoms of Central Asia to China, where it is attested for the first time in 65 CE. The earliest known missionaries and translators (Parthians, Kushans, Sogdians,

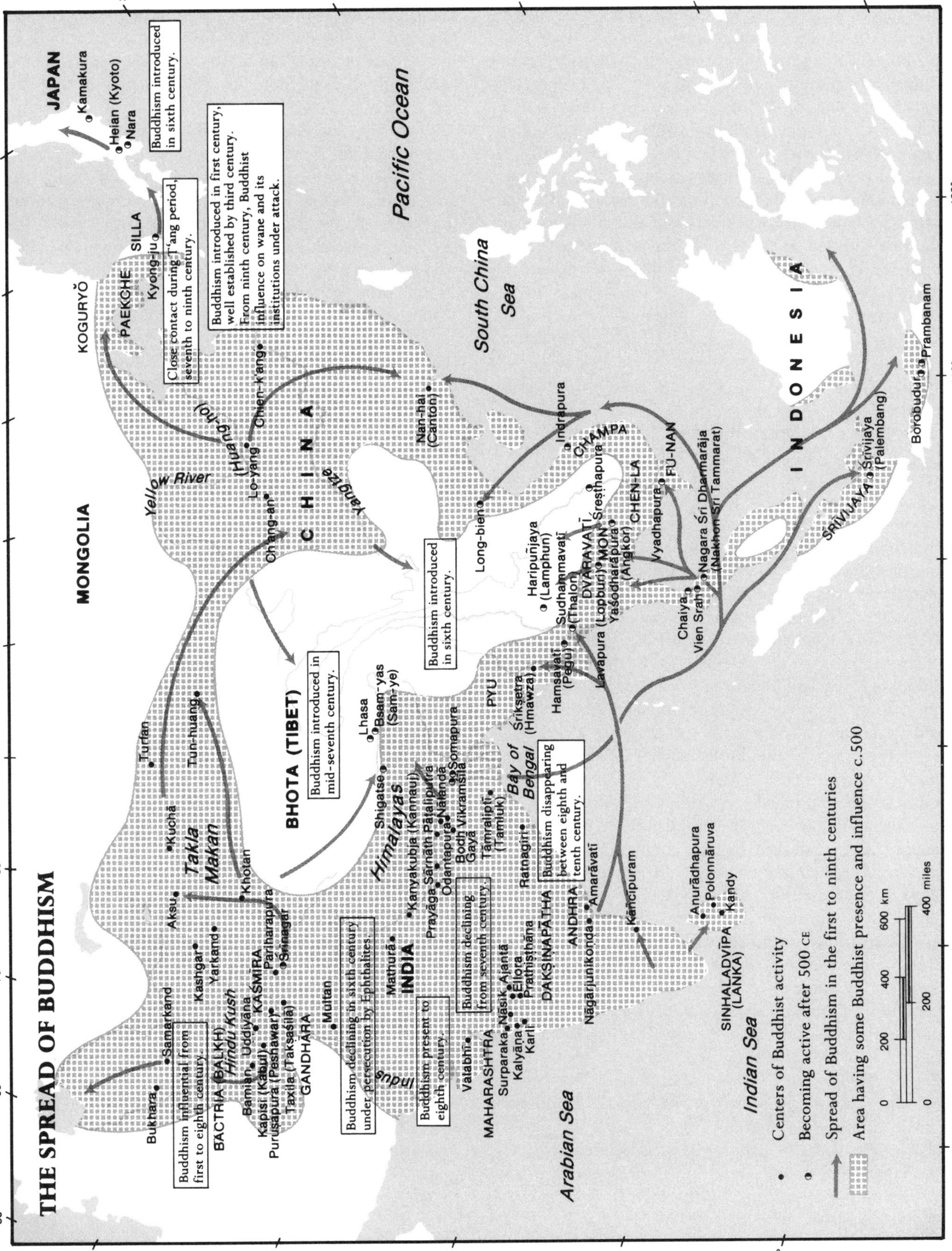
THE SPREAD OF BUDDHISM
MONGOLIA
JAPAN
Kamakura
Heian (Kyoto)
Nara
Buddhism introduced in sixth century.
KOGURYŎ
PAEKCHE
SILLA
Kyong-ju
Close contact during T'ang period, seventh to ninth century.
Buddhism introduced in first century, well established by third century. From ninth century, Buddhist influence on wane and its institutions under attack.
Pacific Ocean
South China Sea
Yellow River
(Huang-ho)
Lo-yang
Chien-k'ang
Ch'ang-an
CHINA
Yangtze
Nan-hai (Canton)
Buddhism introduced in sixth century.
BHOTA (TIBET)
Buddhism introduced in mid-seventh century.
Lhasa
Bsam-yas (Sam-ye)
Shigatse
Himalayas
Turfan
Kucha
Tun-huang
Takla Makan
Khotan
Aksu
Kashgar
Yarkand
Bukhara
Samarkand
Buddhism influential from first to eighth century.
BACTRIA (BALKH)
Hindu Kush
Bamian
Uddiyana
Kapisi (Kabul)
Purusapura (Peshawar)
Taxila (Taksasila)
GANDHARA
KASMIRA
Pariharapura
Srinagar
Multan
Indus
Buddhism declining in sixth century under persecution by Ephthalites.
Buddhism present to eighth century.
Mathura
INDIA
Kanyakubja (Kannauj)
Prayaga
Sarnath
Pataliputra
Nalanda
Odantapura
Somapura
Vikramasila
Bodh Gaya
Buddhism declining from seventh century.
Tamralipti (Tamluk)
Valabhi
MAHARASHTRA
Surparaka
Nasik
Ajanta
Ellora
Kalyana
Karli
Prathisthana
DAKSINAPATHA
ANDHRA
Ratnagiri
Amaravati
Nagarjunikonda
Buddhism disappearing between eighth and tenth century.
Bay of Bengal
Kancipuram
Arabian Sea
Indian Sea
SINHALADVIPA (LANKA)
Anuradhapura
Polonnaruva
Kandy
PYU
Sriksetra (Hmawza)
Hamsavati (Pegu)
Lavapura (Lopburi)
Sudhammavati (Thaton)
Haripuñjaya (Lamphun)
DVARAVATI
MON
Sresthapura
Yasodharapura (Angkor)
CHEN-LA
Vyadhapura
FU-NAN
CHAMPA
Indrapura
Long-bien
Chaiya
Vien Srah
Nagara Sri Dharmaraja (Nakhon Sri Tammarat)
INDONESIA
SRIVIJAYA
Srivijaya (Palembang)
Borobudur
Prambanam
Centers of Buddhist activity
Becoming active after 500 CE
Spread of Buddhism in the first to ninth centuries
Area having some Buddhist presence and influence c.500
0 200 400 600 km
0 200 400 miles

and Indians) arrived at the Chinese capital Lo-yang in the middle of the second century CE by the transcontinental Silk Road, the main artery of trade between the Chinese Han empire and the Roman orient. Just as Buddhism was carried to China by caravan trade, the development of Indian seaborne trade to the coastal regions of Southeast Asia from the second century CE onward provided the channel through which it started to expand in that direction. From the second to the fifth centuries, commercial contacts and the diffusion of Indian culture led to the rise of several more or less Indianized kingdoms in which Buddhism flourished: the Thaton region in southern Burma; the kingdom of Funan with its center on the lower Mekong; that of Champa in southeastern Vietnam; the Malay Peninsula; and the Indonesian archipelago, where Palembang on Sumatra was already an important Buddhist center by 400 CE.

Secondary Centers of Diffusion: China and Tibet. By 600 CE, when China after centuries of disunity had been reunited under the Sui and T'ang dynasties (589–906 CE), Buddhism in many forms had become a major religion in all parts of China and an important element in the cultural life of all social strata. China had thereby become a secondary center of diffusion, from which Buddhism was spread to Korea, Japan, and northern Vietnam. In all these regions, various types of Chinese Buddhism were introduced as part of a general process of the sinicization of these regions. In the fifth century Buddhism reached Korea and became popular among the ruling elite. The transplantation of Chinese Buddhist sects and schools went on throughout Korean history. From Korea, Buddhism reached Japan about the middle of the sixth century, but the real influx of Chinese-type Buddhism into the emerging island empire began in the early seventh century, when the Japanese court embarked on its remarkable program of massive borrowing of Chinese culture and institutions. Between 625 and 847, all early schools of T'ang Buddhism were transplanted to Japan through the deliberate efforts of prominent scholarly monks, most of whom were sent to China as members of "cultural embassies" from the Japanese court. Much later, in the twelfth century, other Chinese schools—notably the devotional cult of the Buddha Amitābha (Ching-t'u, Pure Land Buddhism, known in Japan as Jōdo) and the Ch'an (Jpn., Zen) or Meditation sect—were introduced. To the present day, Japan has remained the stronghold of Buddhism in countless varieties.

The last wave of expansion is associated with the propagation of Buddhism in Tibet and Mongolia, where it eventually developed into the mainly Tantric creed known as Lamaism. Buddhism penetrated the Tibetan kingdom around 650 CE, but became dominant only in the eleventh century. It was from Tibet that Lamaism finally spread to the nomads of the Mongolian steppe in the sixteenth century.

Pilgrimage and Study in India and China. The diffusion of Buddhism from India was for centuries accompanied by a reverse process: the steady flow of pilgrims and scholars to India. Apart from the many inscriptions that they left, the process is documented mainly by the invaluable travelogues of Chinese pilgrims: Fa-hsien, who left China in 399 and spent six years in India; Hui-sheng, who visited northwestern India in 518–522; I-ching, who spent twenty-four years (671–695) in India and Southeast Asia, and above all, the great scholar Hsüan-tsang (c. 596–664), who left a detailed description of his stupendous journey (621–645) in his *Hsi-yü chi* (Record of the Western Regions). India was the holy land of Buddhism, and the desire to make a pilgrimage certainly played a role in the decision of these travelers to undertake their journeys. It should be stressed, however, that the travelers were at least as much motivated by scholastic as by religious considerations: to collect texts, and to study the Doctrine at Indian centers of learning such as Pāṭaliputra (modern Patna) and Nālandā. They knew what they were looking for, and they came back loaded with canonical and scholastic texts that they later translated.

But as we have seen, in T'ang times China itself became a center of diffusion and there the pattern was repeated by countless Korean and Japanese monks who came to China to collect Chinese Buddhist texts and to study Buddhism in its vastly modified Chinese forms. After their return from China, some of these monks became prominent "Masters of the Doctrine" whose names are linked with the most influential trends in Japanese Buddhism. Saichō introduced the Tendai (Chin., T'ien-t'ai) sect in 804; two years later, Kūkai brought Esoteric (Tantric) Buddhism to Japan; and Ennin, apart from his fame as a transmitter of the Doctrine, left an extensive diary of his nine-year stay on the continent (838–849), a diary that presents a fascinating panorama of Buddhist life in T'ang China.

For centuries, India continued to draw pilgrims and students from all over the Buddhist world; the flow came to an end only with the decline of Buddhism in India itself and, finally, with the destruction of the holy places by the Muslim invasions of around 1200. However, Chinese inscriptions found at Bodh Gayā do show that as late as the eleventh century some Chinese pilgrims still followed the examples of Fa-hsien and Hsüan-tsang. For the next seven centuries, Buddhism was nonexistent in its country of origin, to the extent that its holy places became completely forgotten and had to be rediscovered by modern archaeologists. However, as the result of the (still rather modest) revival of Buddhism in India in the twentieth century, pilgrimage has been resumed and is growing steadily.

[*For a fuller account of the dissemination and propagation of Buddhism outside of India, see* Buddhism, *articles on various regional cultures.*]

BIBLIOGRAPHY

Apart from my own book *Buddhism: Its Origin and Spread in Words, Maps and Pictures* (New York, 1962), which presents merely an outline of the diffusion of Buddhism in Asia, there is no monographic study on the subject. Contributions, of very unequal quality, on the introduction and development of Buddhism in various countries can be found in *The Path of the Buddha: Buddhism Interpreted by Buddhists,* edited by Kenneth W. Morgan (New York, 1956). The spread of Buddhism in India and the northwest is extensively treated in Étienne Lamotte's *Histoire du bouddhisme indien: Des origines à l'ère Śaka* (Louvain, 1958). For the rest, the reader must be referred to the relevant parts of monographs dealing with Buddhism in the separate regions. For the diffusion of Indian culture, with Buddhism as one of its essential elements, the best survey is G. Coedès's *Les états hindouïsés d'Indochine et d'Indonésie,* 2d ed. (Paris, 1964); Central Asia is covered in Simone Gaulier, Robert Jera-Bezard, and Monique Maillard's *Buddhism in Afghanistan and Central Asia,* 2 vols. (Leiden, 1976). The introduction and earliest development of Buddhism in China (first to fifth century CE) is extensively treated in my book *The Buddhist Conquest of China,* 2 vols. (1959; reprint, Leiden, 1972); for later periods the best survey is Kenneth Ch'en's *Buddhism in China: A Historical Survey* (1964; reprint, Princeton, 1972). For early Korean Buddhism the reader must still be referred to the somewhat outdated work of Charles A. Clark, *Religions of Old Korea* (New York, 1932). For Japan, the most recent survey is Shinshō Hanayama's *A History of Japanese Buddhism,* translated and edited by Kosho Yamamoto (Tokyo, 1960). For the introduction of Buddhism into Tibet and the formation of Lamaism, see the relevant parts of David L. Snellgrove and Hugh E. Richardson's *A Cultural History of Tibet* (1968; reprint, Boulder, 1980). Apart from one popular work, René Grousset's *Sur les traces du Bouddha* (Paris, 1929), the accounts of the Chinese pilgrims are still accessible only through largely outdated translations. For Fa-hsien, see *The Travels of Fa-hsien 399–414 A.D., or Records of the Buddhist Kingdoms,* rev. ed., translated by Herbert A. Giles (London, 1959); for Hsüan-tsang, *Si-yu-ki, Buddhist Records of the Western World,* 2 vols., translated by Samuel Beal (1884; reprint, Oxford, 1906); additions and corrections in *On Yuan Chwang's Travels in India,* 2 vols., translated by Thomas Watters and edited by T. W. Rhys Davids and S. W. Bushnell (London, 1904–1905); for I-ching, *A Record of the Buddhist Religion as Practiced in India and the Malay Archipelago, A.D. 671–695,* translated by Junjiro Takakusu (1896; reprint, Delhi, 1966). Of Ennin's travelogue there is an excellent translation by Edwin O. Reischauer, *Ennin's Diary: The Record of a Pilgrimage to China in Search of the Law* (New York, 1955), to be used with its companion volume, *Ennin's Travels in T'ang China* (both, New York, 1955).

ERIK ZÜRCHER

Christian Missions

Mission, the extension of the church beyond its existing frontiers, has been characteristic of the Christian fellowship from its earliest beginnings. In its claim to universal relevance, the Christian church resembles the other great missionary religions, Buddhism and Islam, which are also alike in looking back to a single historic founder. "Go forth, therefore, and make all nations my disciples" (*Mt.* 28:19). It is perhaps doubtful whether Jesus of Nazareth expressed himself in precisely these terms; but there is no reason to suppose that his followers gravely misunderstood his intentions. His personal ministry was directed to Jews; but when he found among non-Jews what he recognized as adequate faith, he showed no inclination to exclude them from his fellowship.

The Early Followers of Jesus. The earliest followers of Jesus seem to have understood the universal dimension of their faith as the fulfillment of Old Testament prophecy (Isaiah, Zechariah), according to which all nations would come up to Jerusalem to receive the law of the Lord in the form of the new covenant in Jesus. Two new factors reversed this original Christian understanding. The first was persecution, which led to many Christians being dispersed from Jerusalem. The second was the adventurous spirit of certain Greek-speaking Jews who crossed over a well-marked boundary and in Antioch began to proclaim the gospel to non-Jews, apparently with considerable success. This new Christian perspective was rationalized by Saul of Tarsus, also called Paul, who, believing that he had received a commission as apostle of the gentiles, worked out a master plan for establishing Christian groups in all the main centers of the Greco-Roman world. He looked to Rome, and beyond that even to Spain, the western limit of the Mediterranean world.

So great a project was far beyond the strength of one man, but the impulse given by Paul never died. The Christian proclamation was carried out almost entirely anonymously; indeed, the names of the founders of the great churches of the Roman empire remain for the most part unrecorded. Yet this early work had surprisingly rapid success. Within a century of the death of the founder, churches came into existence in many parts of Asia Minor, in Greece, in Italy, in Egypt, almost certainly in France and Spain, and perhaps even as far away as India. To this day, the Thomas Christians in Kerala claim that their church was founded by the apostle Thomas in person.

Whence this rapid success? By around AD 100, many more Jews lived outside Palestine than within its borders. The strict monotheism of the Jewish faith, and the high moral standards inculcated by their law, had attracted many to at least a partial acceptance of the Jewish faith, and this served for some as a preparation for the Christian gospel. In that hard and often cruel world, a fellowship of people who really loved one another and cared for one another's needs clearly had attractive power. The fervent expectations of the Christians, both for the world and for the individual, must have come as a message of hope to those who had none. Jesus became known as the Savior of the world.

Persecution and Stabilization. The persecutions to which the early Christians were periodically exposed seem to have done little to hinder the advance of their faith. Not all Christians were being persecuted all the time, and the number of martyrs was greatly exaggerated in tradition. To be sure, there were signs of hysteria among the faithful, and some failed to stand fast. But persecution often undermined its own purpose because the courage, dignity, and charity shown by martyrs often won the allegiance and admiration of some who might otherwise have remained indifferent. This has been a recurring phenomenon through the centuries up to the great persecution in Buganda in the 1880s, and in more recent events in Germany and Russia. [*See* Persecution, *article on* Christian Experience.]

The great change in the Christian situation came in 313 when Constantine made Christianity the religion of the empire at a time when its followers cannot have numbered more than about 10 percent of the population. From that time on, the resemblance between Christianity and the other missionary religions has been startlingly close. From the time of Aśoka in India (third century BC) to Sri Lanka and Thailand in 1983, Buddhism has always maintained close relations with the ruling powers. In all Muslim countries, and in all those which have come under Marxist domination, the identification of the state with religion or ideology has been undisguised and taken for granted. But since Christians claim to be followers of the Prince of Peace, close connections between interests of state and interests of religion have proved a burden and an embarrassment rather than a help. Justinian, who reigned from 527 to 565, seems to have been the first Roman emperor to accept coercion as a legitimate instrument of conversion to Christianity. [*See* Church and State *and* Constantinianism.]

By the year 600, the Mediterranean world was almost entirely Christian, with outliers among the Goths, in the approaches to Inner Asia, in Ethiopia, and in what is now Sudan. At the end of the century, Gregory the Great (540–604) saw the importance of the world which lay north of the Alps and which was yet to be converted. Hence the pope's mission to the Angles in Kent. This was the first mission of the church to be officially organized; it paved the way for the central control over the missions which Rome exercised for many centuries.

A Long Period of Uncertainty. In the year 600, it might have seemed that the gospel was destined to carry all before it. Then suddenly everything went into reverse. In 610 an obscure prophet named Muḥammad began to preach a new faith to the tribes of Arabia. By the time of his death he had given to these tribes unity, a simple demanding creed, and a sense of destiny. Only a century later, the Muslim armies were at Tours, in the very heart of France, and were repelled only by the vigor and military skill of Charles Martel (685–741). By that time the Christian churches had almost disappeared in Palestine, Syria, and Egypt, and were gravely threatened in Persia, North Africa, and large parts of Asia Minor. In 1453, the Turks succeeded in capturing Constantinople and destroying the Eastern Empire, which for a thousand years had been the bulwark of the Christian world. Many causes have been adduced for the disappearance of so many churches. Military weakness was no doubt one, but there were others as well: dissensions among Christians, the rise of national feeling in Egypt and elsewhere, and the superficiality of conversion in such areas as North Africa, where the church had failed to express Christian truth in the languages of the local people.

In this period, the wisdom of Gregory was vindicated. During the centuries between 632 and 1232, the Christian faith spread west, north, and east until the conversion of Europe was complete. There was a dark side to this advance. When at the end of the eighth century Charlemagne succeeded in conquering the long-refractory Saxons, he agreed to spare their lives on the condition that they accept baptism. It was only one of many regions in which cross and sword went together. In Scandinavia, conversion proceeded more easily. In many areas the ruler was the first to accept the faith, and this brought about a quiet revolution. Iceland seems to have been unique in accepting the faith (around AD 1000) by genuinely democratic methods. With the conversion of Jagiello (1383), king of the Lithuanians, conversion seems to have reached its natural term.

Monks and nuns played a creative part in the building of churches. In the remote places where they settled they introduced better methods of agriculture and new crops. They laid the foundations of literature in the languages of Europe. They gave to isolated peoples a sense of belonging to one great unity: the catholic church. Out of these beginnings grew the splendid cultures of medieval Europe.

Missionary activity sometimes took on the form of conflict between the old and the new. Such actions as Boniface's felling the oak of Thor at Geismar must not be misinterpreted as mere missionary vandalism. The people of that time believed that the powerful spirit who inhabited the oak would be able to take condign vengeance on any intruder, thus they expected Boniface to fall dead upon the spot. When he survived, they concluded that the god whom he preached was more powerful than their own.

The Eastern church, with its base in Constantinople, beginning with the conversion in 988 of Vladimir, grand duke of Kiev, created the great Slavonic cultures, the Christian origins of which are not disputed even by Marxist opponents of religion. These cultures survived the fall of Constantinople. During the fifteenth century, the faith was received by more remote peoples to the east and north, a process that continued until by the end of the nineteenth century it had reached the shores of the Pacific Ocean.

With the great Franciscan and Dominican movements of the thirteenth century, the missionary enterprise of the Western church looked beyond the limits of Europe; the "friars travelling abroad in the service of Christ" reached strange lands far afield. One of their most remarkable achievements was the creation of an archbishopric in Peking; the first archbishop to fill the post, John of Monte Corvino, lived there from 1294 to 1328, greatly respected by all. But the church's hope of converting the Inner Asian peoples was frustrated by the Muslims' success in winning them to the Islamic faith. The lines of communication with Inner Asia were too tenuous, however, and in the fifteenth century the mission to China faded away. For the moment Christian expansion seemed to be at an end.

The Colonial Period. The last decade of the fifteenth century saw the discovery of America by Columbus in 1492 and the opening up of the sea route to India by Vasco da Gama in 1498. These two events changed the relationships between the nations of the world and in time gravely affected the presentation of the Christian gospel to the non-Christian world.

Roman Catholic monopoly. For two centuries the greater part of the missionary enterprise of the Western church was in the hands of the Portuguese, who, following the precedent of Muslim evangelism in Europe, expected their converts to accept Portuguese names, manners, and customs. There was, however, never total adoption of this principle. By the end of the sixteenth century, the Portuguese had on their hands three considerable blocks of Indian Christianity. In those possessions which they directly controlled, the process of Europeanization was almost complete. The Thomas Christians in Kerala and the Parava converts on the coast of Coromandel, on the other hand, declared and maintained their intention to be and to remain Indian Christians, a stance from which they have not departed in four centuries.

Moreover, in these years two notable attempts were made to adapt Christian thought to the ideas and ways of Asia. The Italian Matteo Ricci in 1601 succeeded in reaching Peking. He and his Jesuit colleagues, by mastering the Chinese language, winning the favor of the emperor and other leaders by their skill in astronomy and other sciences, and by adapting Christian faith to Chinese ideas, were able to maintain their mission, albeit with varying fortunes, through nearly three centuries. In southern India another Italian, Roberto de Nobili, learned Tamil and Sanskrit, and in order to win over the brahmans turned himself into a brahman, and not without success. Unfortunately, in 1744 Rome condemned all such efforts at adaptation, thereby sterilizing the Roman mission for the next two hundred years.

Internationalization of missions. The Lutherans sent their first missionaries to India in 1706. In 1794 the English Baptists, represented by their great pioneer William Carey and his colleagues, set up their work in Bengal. Thus the enormous resources of the English-speaking world, followed by those of the Dutch, the Swiss, and Scandinavians, were let loose throughout the world.

From this time on, relations between the Western governments and Christian missionary forces became unimaginably complicated. On the whole, the British maintained an attitude of lofty neutrality toward missionary activity, modified by the personal interest of a number of Christian government officials. But as government financial aid became available for educational and medical programs and for other forms of service, the Christian missionaries in the forefront of such enterprises profited greatly, perhaps excessively, from the provision of such aid. On the other hand, in British India the Indian rulers prohibited all Christian propaganda in their areas; religious freedom in India was proclaimed not by the British but by the government of independent India after 1947. In northern Nigeria, the British clearly favored Islam at the expense of Christianity.

In German, Dutch, and Belgian colonies, the association of governments with missions was undesirably close. In China, because of Napoleon III's decision that all missionaries, of whatever nationality, must be in possession of French passports, Roman Catholic missions were inevitably stigmatized as dangerous and foreign. By contrast, Hudson Taylor, the director of the largest Protestant mission, instructed his missionaries that in case of trouble they were to turn not to consular authorities but to the local representatives of the Chinese governments.

A new factor emerged when the Japanese government showed itself as the great colonial power in the East. American missionaries in Korea sympathized deeply with Korean national aspirations and were opposed, though quietly and discreetly, to Japanese colonial enterprise.

Varieties of missionary enterprise. Over two centuries there has been significant diversification of missionary enterprise, including the activities of women missionaries, which indeed have been far more numerous and diverse than those of men. Almost every conceivable means of communication has been employed. Education, on the basis of the Christian conviction that all truth and all knowledge are from God, has been emphasized. Together with this priority has gone the widespread distribution of Christian literature in countless languages. Medical and social services were conceived and have been rendered by Christians, not as propaganda but as manifestations of the universal love of Christ, and they were perceived as such by many who were served. Public lectures to interested non-Christians have in many areas left deep impressions on the minds of the hearers, though debates between the adherents of different religious systems have tended more to exacerbation than to conviction. Preaching in the open air in villages and public places has made many hearers aware of the existence of alternative systems of belief. Quiet study groups, under the guidance of sympathetic Christians, have helped to clarify questions about Christian belief. Where no open propaganda has been permitted, the mere presence of loving Christians as neighbors has proved remarkably effective as witness to the faith.

The nature of conversion. No full and scientific study of the process of conversion in the non-Christian world has as yet been written. Undoubtedly in a number of cases the desire for social advancement and a better manner of life has played a powerful part. But is this a blameworthy motive in the case of those who have been subjected for centuries to ruthless oppression reinforced by religious sanction? For many in the twentieth century, as in the first, the gospel comes with promise of deliverance from the power of evil forces which are believed at all times to threaten and beleaguer the well-being of humans. For some, the gospel represents an immense simplification of religion. It has been stated that in India more people have been converted to Christianity by reading the first three chapters of *Genesis* than in any other way, for the majestic simplicity of these chapters appeals deeply to those perplexed by the complexity of Hindu mythology. Other converts, oppressed by the burden of sin, are drawn by the promise of forgiveness in Christ, so different from the inexorable law of *karman* in Hinduism. Others, conscious of moral infirmity, have come to believe that Christ can offer the inner rehabilitation which they feel they need. Yet others have been impressed by the intensity of mutual love manifest in the society of Christian believers. Varied as the process may be, in all there is a central unity. Christ himself stands at the center of everything. Only when the risen Christ is seen as friend, example, savior, and lord can genuine Christian conversion be expected to take place. Conversion to Christ is not necessarily identical with acceptance of the church; but in the vast majority of cases this follows, though this second acceptance may prove to be more difficult than the first.

Missionary motives. For more than four centuries the Western powers have exercised a dominating influence on the destinies of the rest of the world. Since so many people, especially in Muslim countries, have identified the West with the Christian West, there has been a natural tendency to regard Christian missionary enterprise as no more than an expression of Western aggression and imperialism. How far is there any adequate basis for this equation?

Many careful studies of missionary motivation have been made. Clearly no human motives are entirely pure. But only in a minority of cases can it be shown that national and imperialistic motives have played a strong part in missionary devotion. More frequently the glory of Christ has been the central and dominant motive. Some missionaries have gone so far in identifying with those they have come to serve as to renounce their own nation and to accept naturalization in the countries they have made their own. All have accepted some measure of acculturation in new surroundings. All who have served long years in alien lands have accepted with equanimity the destiny of becoming strangers in their own homes. The number of missionary martyrs is legion, their sacrifice equaled only by the devotion of their friends in many nations around the world who have also given their lives in the service of Christ.

The Twentieth Century. When in 1910 the first World Missionary Conference was held at Edinburgh, twelve hundred delegates from all over the world (including, however, no Roman Catholic or Orthodox Christians) could look back on a century of almost unimpeded progress. Converts had been won from every form of religion. In almost every country—a notable exception being Tibet—churches had come into existence, and the process by which the foreign mission was being transformed into the independent self-governing church was well advanced.

The years which followed were marked by a number of major setbacks to Christian missionization, such as the Russian revolution and the fading of religion in many Western communities. Yet the *World Christian Encyclopedia,* edited by David B. Barrett (1982) makes it plain that the achievements of the prior seventy years had been greater than those of the preceding century. For the first time in history the possibility of a universal religion appeared a reality. Roughly one-third of the inhabitants of the world had come to call themselves Christians. The progress of Christian missions continues in almost every area of the world. In India, Christians, already the third largest religious community after Hindus and Muslims, are also the most rapidly increasing in number.

Hostile critics of the Christian enterprise have maintained that the gospel has failed to touch deeply the mind and conscience of peoples outside the West, that the Christian churches in these areas are fragile and exotic blooms that came with the colonial powers, have been dependent exclusively on foreign aid and support, and that with the disappearance of the colonial powers these churches will also disappear. The twentieth century has shown that there is no ground at all for these expectations. After the communist takeover in China (1949), it was held even by a number of Christians that "missionary Christianity" in China had no roots and that there was little if any chance of its survival. When relaxation of government control occurred in 1980, however, it was revealed that several million Chinese had remained faithful to the Christian church. Chinese Christians have made known their determination to be fully independent of every kind of foreign control and to work out for themselves a form of Christian faith which will be genuinely Chinese. Elsewhere, if all foreign support has been compulsorily withdrawn, as in Burma, the churches have simply declared their maturity and have planned for a future of self-support and radical independence. Where this has taken place, accessions to the Christian faith have been more numerous than they were in the flourishing colonial days.

Changing world order. As a world phenomenon, the Christian church has not remained unaffected by the violent changes that have taken place in the troubled twentieth century. During the nineteenth century the dominant nations and the churches which were dependent on them assumed that they could plant Christian missions wherever they pleased, sometimes imposing their will by force on unwilling peoples. In the twentieth century all this has changed. A number of nations (e.g., Burma, Guinea, Saudi Arabia) prohibit all religious activity by foreigners which is directed at native citizens. A number of others make it very difficult for missionaries to obtain visas or residence permits. Yet others (e.g., Nepal) admit missionaries with few restrictions, but only on condition that they engage in what the government regards as nation-building activities (such as educational or medical services). Where all access is made impossible, churches in neighboring areas fall back upon the help that can be rendered by prayer alone.

The churches have gladly accepted the claim of these nations to independence and national dignity. No case is on record of a missionary leaving his or her assignment through unwillingness to accept the changed conditions of service. Christian witnesses have desired to stay on and to become in fact what they always wanted to be—servants of those to whom they came to minister. Even in China missionaries stayed on until it became clear that there was no longer any useful service that they could render. From Burma and other areas, foreigners withdrew because they felt that their work was done, since the local churches could carry on without their aid, and that their continued presence might embarrass—and possibly endanger—their Christian friends. Some have been deported, at very short notice, for political reasons.

Anti-Western sentiments and resentments have been strong in many countries of the world since the end of the nineteenth century. Since 1947, decolonization has taken place with quite unexpected rapidity. Yet wounds remain. Some nations have desired to emancipate themselves from Western influences, but this has proved impossible. The more far-sighted leaders have seen it as their task to retain all that is valuable in the Western inheritance and at the same time to assert or to rediscover the integrity of their own national traditions. [*See* Ecumenical Movement.]

From foreign mission to independent church. The major change in the twentieth century was the process of transfer of power from foreign mission to independent local church, a process almost complete by the end of the century in almost every country in the world. The churches in some emerging nations think that the process has not gone fast enough or far enough; that it is on the way cannot be doubted by any observer of the process of change. Where churches are still wrestling with the problems and the prejudices of the past, they may be unwilling to accept the help of foreigners. Where they have reached maturity, as in India and Korea, and are becoming aware of the immense tasks still before them, they are in many cases glad to accept the help of foreigners, provided that these are prepared to keep their proper place and to accept only such responsibilities for service or leadership as the local church may lay upon them. Nor need it be supposed that all missionaries will be from the Western world; missionary interchange among developing nations is one of the most interesting features of the contemporary situation.

The independence of churches outside Europe and North America is increasingly shown in a number of remarkable ways. One that has attracted considerable attention is the rise of African independent churches, all of which have grown out of the mission-controlled churches of the past. Some of these are unorthodox. But the great majority desire to remain part of the main lines of the Christian tradition and have yet to create for themselves a place in which to feel at home, to think out the gospel for themselves, and to decide for themselves which of the ancient traditions of Africa can be retained within the Christian structure. Many Christians, even in the mainstream churches outside the West, are rethinking their own past in the light of divine providence, expecting to find signs of the working of God no less in their own pre-Christian history than in the special history of which the Old and New Testaments are the record. Some in India, for example, have suggested that the Upaniṣads are the real "old testament" of the Indian Christian and should take rank at least on the same level as the Hebrew scriptures. The nature of this quest is neatly summed up in the title of a book by Raimundo Panikkar, *The Unknown Christ of Hinduism* (New York, 1981). Genuinely indigenous theology is still in its beginnings, and it has to be confessed that the reapings in this field are still rather scanty; but what there is gives promise of a richer harvest in days to come.

One reason for the Christian quest to discover Christ beyond the historical bounds of Christendom is to be found in the remarkable resuscitation in the twentieth century of the ancient non-Christian faiths. Rediscovering the treasures of their own past, non-Christians feel able to approach Christians with renewed confidence and a sense of security. The Buddhist knows himself to be in contact with the great mystery of nothingness, the Hindu to be in contact with the unchangeable mystery of infinite being, the Muslim with the mystery of the infinite exaltation of God. There need be no Christian doubt about the greatness of these religions. Christian and non-Christian alike have much to teach one another in a manner different from that of the past.

The basis of this approach is a conventional rationale of mutual respect. Through centuries millions of men and women have lived by the teachings that they have received in these various religions, and, therefore, these may not be treated as though they did not matter, even though some of their teachings may be displeasing to the adherents of other religions. So one who engages in dialogue with those of faiths other than his own must come to it in the spirit Chaucer described in the words "gladly would he learn and gladly teach." Confident in the value of what he has experienced through his own faith, the Christian is able to delight in everything that he learns from others of what is true and good and beautiful, and at the same time maintain his hope that those who have seen in their own faith what he must judge to be partial may come to find the full-orbed reality of the true, the good, and the beautiful as he himself has seen it in Jesus Christ. If mission is understood in this sense, some of the asperities of the missionary approach in the past may be mitigated.

A New Understanding of Mission. Almost all Christians who are members of churches outside Europe and North America are conscious of belonging to a single great worldwide fellowship, regardless of the denominational label they may bear. Several, though not all, are ardent supporters of contemporary ecumenical movements for the unity and renewal of the church. But they too are almost at one in holding that reconsideration of the meaning of the term *mission* is long overdue. Those who have traveled in the lands of older Christian traditions and sensed the decay in Christian allegiance of many in these countries are inclined to think that mission should be labeled as a product intended for universal and international export. In the past, the gospel traveled across continents and oceans almost exclusively in one direction. Has not the time come to establish two-way traffic, to have the gospel travel across continents and oceans in many directions? If this is true, the word *mission* may be in need of new and contemporary definition.

[*For further discussion of Christian missions in particular geographical and historical contexts, see the regional surveys under* Christianity.]

BIBLIOGRAPHY

The *World Christian Encyclopedia: A Comparative Study of Churches and Religions in the Modern World, A.D. 1900–2000*, edited by David B. Barrett (Oxford, 1982), is an astonishing repertory of information about the Christian faith and all other faiths in all the countries of the world. The *Concise Dictionary of the Christian World Mission*, edited by Stephen C. Neill, Gerald H. Anderson, and John Goodwin (Nashville, 1971), gives in much more condensed form information on almost every aspect of the Christian mission. By far the most extensive survey of the whole field is K. S. Latourette's *A History of the Expansion of Christianity*, 7 vols. (New York, 1937–1945), to be supplemented by the same writer's *Christianity in a Revolutionary*

Age: A History of Christianity in the Nineteenth and Twentieth Centuries, 5 vols. (New York, 1958–1963). My own *Christian Missions* (Baltimore, 1964) has gathered together information from many parts of the world.

No satisfactory history of Roman Catholic missions exists; the best so far is *Histoire universelle des missions catholiques,* 4 vols., edited by Simon Delacroix (Paris, 1956–1958). No English work on Eastern Orthodox missions can be recommended. Two works in German by Josef Glazik, *Die russisch-orthodoxe Heidenmission seit Peter dem Grossen* (Münster, 1954) and *Die Islammission der russisch-orthodoxe Kirche* (Münster, 1959), are classic.

Special studies of many areas are available. For China, K. S. Latourette's *A History of Christian Missions in China* (New York, 1929), is authoritative up to the date of publication. A reliable survey of what has been happening in China since 1948 remains to be written. My *History of Christianity in India,* 2 vols. (Cambridge, 1984–1985), provides substantial coverage. For Africa, C. P. Groves's *The Planting of Christianity in Africa,* 4 vols. (1948–1958; reprint London, 1964), is a work of patient research but is overweighted on the Protestant side.

Countless lives of Christians, Western, Eastern, and African, have been written, but almost all the older works need to be rewritten in the light of modern knowledge. As a notable example of a biography of a twentieth-century saint, mention may be made of Hugh Tinker's *The Ordeal of Love: C. F. Andrews and India* (New York, 1979). Georg Schurhammer's *Francis Xavier: His Life, His Times,* 4 vols. (Rome, 1973–1982) is a superb example of what can be achieved by intense industry continued over almost sixty years.

Peter Beyerhaus's *The Responsible Church and the Foreign Mission* (London, 1964) is a pioneer work on the transformation of a foreign mission into an independent local church. The works of Roland Allen, especially *Missionary Methods: St. Paul's or Ours?,* 6th ed. (London, 1968), let loose questionings and discussions which have continued to the present day.

On the Christian confrontation with the non-Christian religions, the World Council of Churches in Geneva has published a whole series of valuable books, under the editorship of Stanley J. Samartha. On contemporary trends in mission thinking and theology, the interconfessional and international series "Mission Trends," edited by Gerald Anderson and Thomas Stransky (Ramsey, N.J., 1974–), will be found full of up-to-date and relevant information on almost all matters related to the Christian mission.

STEPHEN C. NEILL

MITHRA. After Ahura Mazdā and together with Anāhitā, Mithra is one of the major deities of ancient Iran, one that later crossed the borders of the Iranian world to become the supreme god of a mystery religion popular throughout the Roman empire. In the Avesta and the later Zoroastrian literature Mithra turns up frequently; indeed, an entire Avestan hymn is dedicated to him (*Yashts* 10). He was also the subject of the Mithrakāna, a great festival that took place annually in the seventh month of the Zoroastrian calendar, which was itself dedicated to him. He is known to us from many other sources: in the inscriptions of the Achaemenids, beginning with Artaxerxes II (404–359 BCE), he is mentioned and invoked together with Ahura Mazdā and Anāhitā; on the coins of the Kushan empire he is named as Mioro and is depicted as a solar deity; in Parthian and Sogdian Manichaeism he is the *tertius legatus;* in Persian Manichaeism, he appears as the *spiritus vivens;* and so forth.

Mithra is essentially a deity of light: he draws the sun with rapid horses; he is the first to reach the summit of Mount Harā, at the center of the earth, and from there watches over the entire abode of the Aryans; he shines with his own light and in the morning makes the many forms of the world visible. If his name is synonymous with the word *mithra,* meaning "contract, covenant," as Antoine Meillet (1907) suggests, his functions are not restricted to merely personifying that notion. In the Iranian world, besides being a deity of light with strong solar characteristics (which explains his identification with the Mesopotamian Shamash), Mithra has a clear significance as a warrior god. Thus, in relation to the gods of the Indo-Iranian pantheon, he is closer to Indra than to the Vedic Mitra. He also, however, has the traits of a divinity who ensures rain and prosperity and who protects cattle by providing it ample pasturage.

The cult of Mithra, together with that of Anāhitā, constitutes the principal innovation of Zoroastrianism as it evolved after Zarathushtra (Zoroaster) and represents its major compromise with ancient polytheism. It was probably Mithra's role as defender and guardian of *asha,* truth and order—the fundamental principle of earlier Indo-Iranian religion, as well as of Zoroastrianism—that redeemed him from Zarathushtra's original general condemnation of polytheism.

BIBLIOGRAPHY

Boyce, Mary. "On Mithra's Part in Zoroastrianism." *Bulletin of the School of Oriental and African Studies* 32 (1969): 10–34.

Dumézil, Georges. *Les dieux souverains des Indo-Européens.* Paris, 1977.

Gershevitch, Ilya, trans. and ed. *The Avestan Hymn to Mithra.* Cambridge, 1959.

Gershevitch, Ilya. "Die Sonne das Beste." In *Mithraic Studies,* edited by John R. Hinnells, vol. 1, pp. 68–89. Manchester, 1975.

Gnoli, Gherardo. "Sol Persice Mithra." In *Mysteria Mithrae,* edited by Ugo Bianchi, pp. 725–740. Leiden, 1979.

Lentz, Wolfgang. "The 'Social Functions' of the Old Iranian Mithra." In *W. B. Henning Memorial Volume,* edited by Mary Boyce and Ilya Gershevitch, pp. 245–255. London, 1970.

Meillet, Antoine. "Le dieu indo-iranien Mitra." *Journal asiatique* 10 (1907): 143–159.

Schmidt, Hanns-Peter. "Indo-Iranian Mitra Studies: The State of the Central Problem." In *Études mithriaques,* edited by Jacques Duchesne-Guillemin, pp. 345–393. Tehran and Liège, 1978.

Thieme, Paul. *Mitra and Aryaman.* New Haven, 1957.

Windischmann, Friedrich. *Mithra: Ein Beitrag zur Mythengeschichte des Orients.* Abhandlungen für die Kunde Morgenlandes, vol. 1.1. Leipzig, 1857.

GHERARDO GNOLI
Translated from Italian by Roger DeGaris

MITHRAISM. A "mystical" religion with a structure akin to that of other mystery religions, Mithraism was founded on the notion of a god who remains unconquered throughout a complex series of events. Although it had Iranian roots, as we can see by the fact that Mithra was always known as a Persian god, the religion took shape and developed outside Iran, spreading throughout the Roman empire. The cult appealed to the Roman world because of its mysteriosophic views, which centered on the concept of the life of the soul and its ascension through the seven planetary spheres. The ascension was symbolized by seven grades of initiation, culminating in the transcendent level of the fixed stars, or *aeternitas.*

Sources. The background and sources of Mithraism are most likely to be found in Asia Minor, where Persian communities and their priests, the Magi, were established toward the end of the Achaemenid period (sixth to fourth centuries BCE). These communities favored a syncretic approach to the local religions, and Mithraism may have arisen from some hybrid of the Magi. It cannot, however, be explained without mention of the encounter of the Iranian and Mesopotamian religious worlds. The spread of astrological motifs, today more thoroughly understood, suggests that the astral religion of Babylonia, particularly developed in the first millennium BCE, had an important role in the formation of Mithraism. It is also correct to suppose that at an earlier time the Iranian god Mithra was identified with the Mesopotamian solar deity, Shamash. Many factors indicate that in the second half of the first millennium BCE there was significant diffusion of the cult of Mithra throughout the more westerly regions of the Achaemenid domain, from Asia Minor to Babylonia and Armenia. In this case, however, we cannot speak of Mithraism but only of a cult of Mithra different from that found in Zoroastrian Iran. In any event, the Greek version of the Iranian god during the end of the first century BCE is clear, as shown in the monuments of Mithradates Kallinikos and Anthiochus I, the rulers of Commagene, in which Mithra is identified with Helios, Apollo, and Hermes.

The testimony of Plutarch in his *Life of Pompey* is important in understanding the religion's development in the Roman empire. It concerns a cult of Mithra as practiced among the pirates of Cilicia, the district in southern Asia Minor from which the mysteries celebrated during the lifetime of Plutarch were supposed to have come. Plutarch's source is more ancient (perhaps Posidonius), so we can perhaps trace the Roman cult back to 100 BCE. The incubation period of the new religion was rather long. Statius in the *Thebais* (about 80 CE) describes an image of Mithra Tauroctonus ("bull-slayer") and attests to the arrival of the cult in Rome itself. This was the beginning of the wide diffusion of Mithraism that occurred under the Flavian emperors in the last quarter of the first century CE.

We cannot identify the specific stages of the Iranian god's transformation into the mystery god of the Romans. We can deduce, however, that at the basis of the transformation were two essential characteristics of the Iranian divinity: Mithra is the divinity of light, closely linked to the sun, and he is a divinity of salvation.

The solar characteristics of the Iranian Mithra are documented in the sources, but in Iran Mithra was not a personification of the sun, though his name, *Mihr,* is one of the names of the sun. In the Avesta, the god seems to have a connection with Hvar Khshaēta ("resplendent sun"), analogous to the connection of the Roman Mithra with Sol. The nature of the Iranian god as a god of salvation can be inferred from myriad indications. In the Parthian epoch, for example, there existed a great syncretic myth of the Cosmocrator Redemptor, of which Mithra, born of a rock or out of a cave, was the protagonist. His birth, which would later be celebrated on 25 December, was accompanied by special signs and by luminous epiphanies and taken as a symbol of a kind of royal initiation (Widengren, 1965).

History. The Mithraic mysteries spread between the end of the first century and the fourth century CE, gradually dying out toward the end of that period. Their maximum expansion occurred toward the middle of the third century. They spread throughout a great part of the Roman empire. Rome and Ostia, Latium, southern Etruria, the Campania, and Cisalpine Gaul are, in Italy, the places and provinces that offer the most evidence of this diffusion, but a number of other sites must also be kept in mind: Aquileia and the main ports of Sicily, Syracuse, Catania, and Palermo; Austria and Germany along the Rhine frontier; the Danubian provinces Pannonia, Mesia, Dacia; the Tracia; Dalmatia; the valley of the Rhone and Aquitania in France; Belgium; and England, in the London region and to the north along Hadrian's wall. The mysteries were diffused to a lesser extent in the Iberian Peninsula and Macedonia, while there was almost no trace of them in Greece. Evidence shows that they were present along the Asian and African coasts of the Mediterranean, although their presence was limited (especially in the Asian provinces) to the major maritime ports.

For the most part the evidence is archaeological, iconographic, and epigraphic. The greatest scholar of Mithraism, Franz Cumont, has attempted to reconstruct the religion's mythology, theology, cosmology, eschatology, and rites, basing his work primarily on the numerous sculptural reliefs that have been preserved.

The Mithraeum, a kind of temple, served as a meeting place for followers of the religion. Partly underground, it was a replica of the cave *(spelaeum)* in which Mithra caught the mystic bull and killed it. Built in a long rectangle, it had lateral brick benches on which the participants in the ceremonies could sit and gaze at the image of Mithra Tauroctonus placed in a special niche at the end of the nave. An altar was often placed in front of the image of the Tauroctonus. On the ceiling the starry firmament was generally depicted. Because the grotto was supposed to be a representation of the world, it contained reproductions of the signs of the zodiac and of the planets. Water played a purificatory role in Mithraism, and a natural or artificial spring had to be near every Mithraeum. Very often other rooms surrounded the spelaeum proper, designed, perhaps, for initiation rites or as chapels. As a rule these were entered through a pronaos. These places of worship, so unusual and different from the high temples dedicated to the divinities of the public cults, had the additional characteristic of being of modest size. The worship service, which culminated in a common banquet, was officiated over by a small community, usually consisting of a few dozen people.

Esoteric and initiatory in nature, Mithraism was, in fact, a private cult, intended for only the few. Though it professed universalism, the cult excluded women. It had emerged in a predominantly military environment and was practiced and spread primarily by the Roman army, which elevated loyalty and compliance with agreements and promises to the status of a supreme value. It was not only a soldiers' religion, however; it also appealed to other social and professional groups, including, for example, public officials and persons who worked in commercial enterprises. It has often been pointed out, quite rightly, that Mithraism promoted camaraderie on the battlefield and in the barracks, as well as in offices and enterprises (Will, 1955, pp. 125ff., pp. 356ff), among individuals who rarely had a permanent residence and who were called upon to carry out their work, because of duty or interest, in the most varied parts of the empire.

Doctrines. In the Roman cult, initiates progressed through seven levels: Corax ("raven"), Nymphus ("bride"), Miles ("soldier"), Leo ("lion"), Perses ("Persian"), Heliodromus ("courier of the sun"), and Pater ("father"). Each grade was protected by a particular celestial body: respectively, Mercury, Venus, Mars, Jupiter, the moon, the sun, and Saturn.

The doctrines of the Mithraic mysteries have been much discussed, both in terms of their origin and content and in terms of their uniqueness and orientation. Several views opposed to the Iranian origin of the titulary god of the mysteries notwithstanding (Wikander, 1950), there is a broad consensus on the religion's Iranian background. Some scholars, however, do not believe that Mithraism's Iranian roots have much significance for an accurate understanding of the religion, which they feel should be considered only in terms of what occurred in the empire and in Roman society (Gordon, 1972). This position is no less exaggerated than that which wishes to explain the entire religion, or most of it, by its Iranian heritage.

From the total body of evidence we can infer that Mithra's central act of killing the bull—in Zoroastrianism the work of Ahriman, if it is a question of the primordial bull, and of the Saoshyant if it is a question of the bull of the Frashōkereti—has a regenerative function: death produces a new life, richer and more fecund. Mithra, the god of light who has saved creation from the threat of darkness, clasps the right hand of the Sun, who kneels before the Tauroctonus. Mithraists consecrated the alliance between Mithra and the Sun through a banquet, which prefigured the ritual. Mithra reaches the heavens in the Sun's chariot. It is certainly this image of Mithra that most moved and exalted the initiate, for it renewed hope in the ascension of the soul beyond the planetary spheres all the way to *aeternitas.*

Mithraism is thought to have developed in the Hellenistic period through one of two processes: by a slow and complex evolution of fertility cults or, as seems more likely, through the survival of initiatory models characteristic of archaic societies—specifically, warrior initiations, or *Männerbünde* (Widengren, 1965). In any case, it showed a great ability to adapt and to expand while remaining a religion of initiates. It had to give way, however, to a triumphant Christianity, and the intolerance and politics of such emperors as Constantine and Theodosius did the rest. At the end of the fourth century, the religion was attacked by Christians because of certain liturgical and doctrinal resemblances between Christianity and Mithraism: Christians saw Mithraism's "baptism" as inspired by Satan, and its "eucharist" as a diabolical parody of the Christian sacrament. As a result the religion was in its death throes. Numerous Mithraea were abandoned, destroyed, or transformed and incorporated into Christian churches.

[*For further discussion of Mithraism, see* Mithra; Mystery Religions; Roman Religion, *article on* The Imperial Period; *and* Sun.]

BIBLIOGRAPHY

Bianchi, Ugo, ed. *Mysteria Mithrae: Proceedings of the International Seminar on the Religio-Historical Character of Roman Mithraism, with Particular Reference to Roman and Ostian Sources.* Leiden, 1979.

Colpe, Carsten. "Development of Religious Thought." In *The Cambridge History of Iran,* vol. 3, edited by Ehsan Yarshater, pp. 819–866. Cambridge, 1983.

Cumont, Franz. *Textes et monuments figurés relatifs aux mystères de Mithra.* 2 vols. Brussels, 1896–1899.

Cumont, Franz. *Les mystères de Mithra.* Brussels, 1913. Translated as *The Mysteries of Mithra,* 2d rev. ed. (New York, 1956).

Duchesne-Guillemin, Jacques, ed. *Études mithriaques: Actes du Deuxième Congrès International.* Acta Iranica, no. 17. Tehran and Liège, 1978.

Gordon, R. L. "Mithraism and Roman Society: Social Factors in the Explanation of Religious Change in the Roman Empire." *Religion* 2 (1972): 92–121.

Hinnells, John R., ed. *Mithraic Studies: Proceedings of the First International Congress of Mithraic Studies.* 2 vols. Manchester and Totowa, N.J., 1975.

Nock, Arthur Darby. "The Genius of Mithraism." *Journal of Roman Studies* 27 (1937): 108–113.

Pettazzoni, Raffaele. *I misteri: Saggio di una teoria storico-religiosa.* Bologna, 1924.

Saxl, Fritz. *Mithras: Typengeschichtliche Untersuchungen.* Berlin, 1931.

Turcan, Robert A. *Mithra et le mithriacisme.* Paris, 1981.

Vermaseren, Maarten J. *Corpus inscriptionum et monumentorum religionis Mithriacae.* 2 vols. The Hague, 1956–1960.

Vermaseren, Maarten J. *Mithras, de geheimzinnige God.* Amsterdam, 1959. Translated as *Mithras, the Secret God* (London, 1963).

Widengren, Geo. "The Mithraic Mysteries in the Graeco-Roman World with Special Regard to Their Iranian Background." In *La Persia e il mondo greco-roman,* issued by the Accademia Nazionale dei Lincei, pp. 433–456. Rome, 1965.

Wikander, Stig. *Études sur les mystères de Mithra.* Lund, 1950.

Will, Ernest. *Le relief culturel gréco-romain.* Paris, 1955.

GHERARDO GNOLI
Translated from Italian by Roger DeGaris